Contemporary Mathematicians

Gian-Carlo Rota
Editor

Joseph S. Oliveira
Assistant Editor

Birkhäuser
Boston · Basel · Stuttgart

Garrett Birkhoff

Selected Papers on Algebra and Topology by Garrett Birkhoff

Edited by
Gian-Carlo Rota
Joseph S. Oliveira

Birkhäuser
Boston · Basel · Stuttgart
1987

Garrett Birkhoff
Mathematics Department
Science Center
Harvard University
Cambridge, MA 02138
U.S.A.

Editors
Gian-Carlo Rota
Joseph S. Oliveira
Department of Mathematics
Massachusetts Institute of Technology
Cambridge, MA 02139
U.S.A.

Library of Congress Cataloging in Publication Data
Birkhoff, Garrett, 1911–
Selected papers on algebra and topology.
(Contemporary mathematicians)
"Bibliography of Garrett Birkhoff's papers and books, 1933–1982": p.
1. Algebra, Universal—Collected works. 2. Topology —Collected works. 3. Lattice theory—Collected works.
I. Rota, Gian-Carlo, 1932– . II. Oliveira, Joseph S. III. Title. IV. Series.
QA251.B497 1986 512 86-28420

CIP-Kurztitelaufnahme der Deutschen Bibliothek
Birkhoff, Garrett:
Selected papers on algebra and topology / by Garrett Birkhoff. Gian-Carlo Rota ; Joseph S. Oliveira ed.—Boston ; Basel ; Stuttgart : Birkhäuser, 1986.
(Contemporary mathematicians)
ISBN 3-7643-3114-3 (Basel ...)
ISBN 0-8176-3114-3 (Boston)
NE: Birkhoff, Garrett: [Sammlung]

Printed and bound by Arcata Graphics/Halliday, West Hanover, Massachusetts.
Printed in the United States of America.

ISBN 0-8176-3114-3
ISBN 3-7643-3114-3

Preface

The present volume of reprints are what I consider to be my most interesting and influential papers on algebra and topology. To tie them together, and to place them in context, I have supplemented them by a series of brief essays sketching their historical background (as I see it). In addition to these I have listed some subsequent papers by others which have further developed some of my key ideas.

The papers on universal algebra, lattice theory, and general topology collected in the present volume concern ideas which have become familiar to all working mathematicians. It may be helpful to make them readily accessible in one volume. I have tried in the introduction to each part to state the most significant features of each paper reprinted there, and to indicate later developments.

The background that shaped and stimulated my early work on universal algebra, lattice theory, and topology may be of some interest. As a Harvard undergraduate in 1928–32, I was encouraged to do independent reading and to write an original thesis. My tutorial reading included de la Vallee-Poussin's beautiful *Cours d'Analyse Infinitesimale*, Hausdorff's *Grundzüge der Mengenlehre*, and Frechet's *Espaces Abstraits*. In addition, I discovered Carathéodory's 1912 paper "Uber das lineare Mass von Punktmengen" and Hausdorff's 1919 paper on "Dimension und Ausseres Mass," and derived much inspiration from them. A fragment of my thesis, analyzing axiom systems for separable metrizable spaces, was later published [2].* This background led to the work summarized in Part IV.

My undergraduate courses were intended for the career of a mathematical physicist, for which the reading just mentioned would today seem inappropriate. Functional analysis was at the time becoming an independent subject. Von Neumann, Stone, and Banach were writing their great classics, and the ergodic theorem had just been proved. Central to all these developments was the concept of a function space. First defined in Fréchet's Thesis, this concept made point-set topology relevant to mathematical physics.

My courses at Harvard covered layerings of topics in analysis and mathematical physics. I was essentially a self-taught algebraist. My only training beyond analytic geometry and determinants was in a course on combinatorial topology given by Marston Morse. He explained the canonical form of a matrix of integers under row and column equivalence. I was fascinated by the definition of a group in Miller, Blichfeldt, and Dickson's *Finite Groups*, which I found in Harvard's departmental library. I then conceived the naive project of classifying finite groups.

Working alone in Munich the summer after graduation, I classified commutative groups,

*Numbers in brackets refer to the Bibliography of Garrett Birkhoff's Books and Papers, 1933–1986, on pages ix–xv.

unaware that Kronecker had proved his fundamental theorem on Abelian groups 75 years earlier. There I had the good idea of calling on Carathéodory, whose paper I had perused; I mentioned to him my interest in group theory. He recommended that I read Speiser's *Gruppentheorie* and van der Waerden's *Modern Algebra.* I took his advice, and after a few months had the good fortune of being assigned Philip Hall as adviser at Cambridge University. It became apparent to me that I was more interested in algebra than in mathematical physics, as it was represented in Cambridge at the time by Dirac.

Always modest, Hall did not explain to me his own beautiful results on finite groups. Instead, at my request, he assigned me a problem in group theory whose solution he thought might be publishable. I solved it in a few days, and published the results in the paper "A Theorem on Transitive Groups" [1]. In the same year, I determined the characteristic subgroups of a finite Abelian group [10] having found a mistake in an earlier paper by Miller on the subject.

Although I continued to be fascinated by finite groups, I only published one other paper [19] on group theory, co-authored with Philip Hall. We estimated the least common multiple of the orders of groups of automorphisms for all the groups with given order g.

Through the study of the structure of groups, and especially of six 1930–32 papers by Remak, I was led to formulate the concept of a lattice. My ideas about universal algebra arose from my interest in the structure of lattices. It became obvious to me that Emmy Noether's techniques for treating homomorphisms of rings and groups with operators were inadequate for the study of lattices, and would have to be replaced by equivalence relations having the substitution property, what are now called congruence relations. In turn my background in set theory and general topology proved valuable in developing lattice theory and universal algebra from that time on.

My interest in groups soon led me to read about *Lie groups.* A decade later, my study of Lie groups bore fruit in my book *Hydrodynamics: A Study of Logic, Fact, and Similitude*, and in my solution of the Riemann–Helmholtz problem [67]. Both of these problems fall outside the scope of this volume.

After the Second World War, I became involved in activities far removed from the work in algebra of 1932–40. A conclusion that emerges from my experience of that time is the value of serendipity. Every project of work that I undertook because of my intrinsic interest bore fruit, but often a very different fruit from that which I expected at the start of that project.

Acknowledgment. I wish to thank Gian-Carlo Rota for his initiative in arranging the publication of this volume and for suggesting many improvements in earlier drafts. I am also grateful to Walter Taylor and Kirby Baker for supplying material which I have used freely in my essays.

Garrett Birkhoff

Contents*

*Numbers in brackets refer to the Bibliography of Garrett Birkhoff's Books and Papers, 1933–1986, on pages ix–xv.

Bibliography of Garrett Birkhoff's Books and Papers, 1933–1986

Books

Lattice Theory, Amer. Math. Soc., New York, 1940; revised edition, 1948; third edition, 1967 (translated into Russian and Japanese).

A Survey of Modern Algebra (with Saunders Mac Lane), Macmillan Co., New York 1941; revised edition, 1953; third edition, 1965; fourth edition, 1977 (translated into Spanish, Japanese, Polish, Greek, Slovakian, and Portuguese).

Hydrodynamics: *A Study in Logic, Fact, and Similitude*, Princeton University Press, 1950; second edition, 1960 (translated into French and Russian). Reprinted by Greenleaf Press.

Jets, Wakes, and Cavities (with E. H. Zarantonello), Academic Press, New York, 1957 (translated into Russian).

Ordinary Differential Equations (with Gian-Carlo Rota), Ginn-Blaisdell, Boston, 1959; second edition, 1969; third edition, Wiley, 1978.

Algebra (with Saunders Mac Lane), Macmillan Co., New York, 1967; second edition, 1979 (translated into French, Italian, and Czech).

Modern Applied Algebra (with Thomas C. Bartee), McGraw-Hill, New York, 1970 (translated into Japanese, German, and Hungarian).

The Numerical Solution of Elliptic Equations, Regional Conference Series in Applied Math., SIAM Publications, 1971.

Source Book in Classical Analysis, Harvard University Press, 1973; with the assistance of Uta Merzbach.

Numerical Solution of Elliptic Problems (with Robert E. Lynch), SIAM Publications, 1984.

Papers

[1] "Theorem on Transitive Groups," *Proc. Camb. Phil. Soc.* **29** (1933), 257–9.

[2] "Axiomatic Definitions of Perfectly Separable Metric Spaces," *Bull. Am. Math. Soc.* **39** (1933), 601–7.

*[3] "On the Combination of Subalgebras," *Proc. Camb. Phil. Soc.* **29** (1933), 441–64.

[3a] "On the Combination of Subalgebras," *Proc. Camb. Phil. Soc.* **30** (1934), 200.

*[4] "Applications of Lattice Algebra," *Proc. Camb. Phil. Soc.* **30** (1934), 115–22.

[5] "Hausdorff Groupoids," *Annals of Math.* **35** (1934), 351–60.

*[6] "On the Lattice Theory of Ideals," *Bull. Am. Math. Soc.* **40** (1934), 613–19.

*[7] "Ideals in Algebraic Rings," *Proc. Nat. Acad. Sci.* **20** (1934), 571–3.

*[8] "The Topology of Transformation-Sets," *Annals of Math.* **35** (1934), 861–75.

[9] "Transfinite Subgroup Series," *Bull. Am. Math. Soc.* **40** (1934), 847–50.

---

* Appears in this volume.

[10] "Subgroups of Abelian Groups," *Proc. Lond. Math. Soc.* **38** (1935), 385–401.
[11] "Orthogonality in Metric Linear Spaces," *Duke Math. J.* **1** (1935), 169–72.
*[12] "Combinatorial Relations in Projective Geometries," *Annals of Math.* **36** (1935), 743–8.
[13] "Sur les espaces discrets," *Comptes Rendus* **201** (1935), 19–20.
[14] "Integration of Functions with Values in a Banach Space," *Trans. Am. Math. Soc.* **38** (1935), 357–78.
*[15] "On the Structure of Abstract Algebras," *Proc. Camb. Phil. Soc.* **31** (1935), 433–54.
*[16] "Abstract Linear Dependence and Lattices," *Am. J. Math.* **57** (1935), 800–4.
[17] *Proc. Int. Math. Congress, Oslo*, Vol. 2. (1936) Ref. Pages 37, 50, 152.
[18] "On the Combination of Topologies," *Fund. Math.* **26** (1936), 156–66.
*[19] "On the Order of Groups of Automorphisms" (with Philip Hall), *Trans. Am. Math. Soc.* **39** (1936), 496–9.
*[20] "A Note on Topological Groups," *Compositio Math.* **3** (1936), 427–30.
*[21] "The Logic of Quantum Mechanics" (with John von Neumann), *Annals of Math.* **37** (1936), 823–43.
*[22] "Lie Groups Simply Isomorphic with No Linear Group," *Bull. Am. Math. Soc.* **42** (1936), 883–8.
[23] "On the Integration of Operators," *Proc. Nat. Acad. Sci.* **23** (1937), 11–13.
*[24] "Moore-Smith Convergence in General Topology," *Annals of Math.* **38** (1937), 39–56.
*[25] "The Meaning of Completeness," *Annals of Math.* **38** (1937), 57–60.
*[26] "Continuous Groups and Linear Spaces," *Mat. Sbornik N.S.* **1** (1937), 635–42.
*[27] "Representability of Lie Algebras and Lie Groups by Matrices," *Annals of Math.* **38** (1937), 526–32.
*[28] "An Extended Arithmetic," *Duke Math. J.* **3** (1937), 311–6.
*[29] "Rings of Sets," *Duke Math. J.* **3** (1937), 443–54.
[30] "On Product Integration," *J. Math. and Physics*, MIT, **16** (1937), 104–32.
[31] "Galois and Group Theory," *Osiris* **3** (1937), 260–8.
*[32] "Analytical Groups," *Trans. Am. Math. Soc.* **43** (1938), 61–101.
*[33] "Dependent Probabilities and Spaces (L)," *Proc. Nat. Acad. Sci.* **24** (1938), 154–9.
[34] "Lattices and their Applications," *Bull. Am. Math. Soc.* **44** (1938), 793–800.
[35] "The Mean Ergodic Theorem," *Duke Math. J.* **5** (1939), 19–20.
*[36] "A Characterization of Boolean Algebras" (with Morgan Ward), *Annals of Math.* **40** (1939), 609–10.
[37] "An Ergodic Theorem for General Semi-Groups," *Proc. Nat. Acad. Sci.* **25** (1939), 625–7.
[38] "General Ergodic Theorems" (with L. Alaoglu), *Proc. Nat. Acad. Sci.* **25** (1939), 628–30.
[39] "General Ergodic Theorems" (with L. Alaoglu), *Annals of Math.* **41** (1940), 293–309.
*[40] "Neutral Elements in General Lattices," *Bull. Am. Math. Soc.* **46** (1940), 702–5.
[41] "Metric Foundations of Geometry," *Proc. Nat. Acad. Sci.* **27** (1941), 402–6.
*[42] "Lattice-Ordered Groups," *Annals of Math.* **43** (1942), 298–331.
*[43] "Generalized Arithmetic," *Duke Math. J.* **9** (1942), 283–302.
[44] "What is a Lattice?" *Am. Math. Monthly* **50** (1943), 484–7.
[45] "The Radical of a Group with Operators," *Bull. Am. Math. Soc.* **48** (1943), 751–3.
[46] "Metric Foundations of Geometry I," *Trans. Am. Math. Soc.* **55** (1944), 465–92.
*[47] "Subdirect Unions in Universal Algebra," *Bull. Am. Math. Soc.* **50** (1944), 764–8.
*[48] "Lattice-Ordered Lie Groups," in *Festschrift Speiser*, Orell Fussli Verlag, Zurich, 1945.
*[49] "Universal Algebra," *Proc. First Canadian Math. Cong.* (1945), Toronto Univ. Press, 310–26.
[50] "Reversibility Paradox and Two-Dimensional Airfoil Theory," *Am. J. Math.* **68** (1946), 247–56.
*[51] "Distributive Postulates for Systems Like Boolean Algebras" (with George D. Birkhoff), *Trans. Am. Math. Soc.* **60** (1946), 3–11.
[52] "Sobre los grupos de automorfismos," *Revista de la Unión Mat. Argentina* **11** (1946), 155–7.
[53] "Tres notas sobre el algebra lineal," *Revista Mat. Fis. Tucumán* **5** (1946), 147–51.

*[54] "A Ternary Operation in Distributive Lattices" (with S. A. Kiss), *Bull. Am. Math. Soc.* **53** (1947), 749–52.

[55] "Formulación de una conjetura de G. D. Birkhoff mediante una ecuación integral," *Boletin Soc. Mat. Mexicana* **3** (1946), 57–60.

[56] "Explosives with Lined Cavities" (with D. P. MacDougall, E. Pugh, and Sir Geoffrey Taylor), *J. Appl. Phys.* **19** (1948), 563–82.

[57] "Remarks on Streamlines of Discontinuity," *Revista Acad. Ci. Lima* **50** (1948), 105–16.

*[58] "Representations of Lattices by Sets" (with Orrin Frink, Jr.), *Trans. Am. Math. Soc.* **64** (1948), 299–316.

[59] "Dimensional Analysis of Partial Differential Equations," *Electrical Engineering* (1948), 1185–8.

*[60] "Representation of Jordan and Lie Algebras" (with Philip M. Whitman), *Trans. Am. Math. Soc.* **65** (1949), 116–36.

[61] "Note on Newtonian Force Fields" (with Lindley J. Burton), *Canadian J. Math.* **1** (1949), 199–208.

[62] "Hydrodynamical Paradoxes," *Library, Vol. X. Int. Congress Philosophy*, North Holland, Amsterdam, 1948, pp. 349–50.

[63] "Fluid Flow Patterns" (with Thomas E. Caywood), *J. Appl. Phys.* **20** (1949), 646–59.

[64] "Recent Developments in Free Boundary Theory," *Proc. Int. Congress Appl. Mech.* London **2** (1948), 7–16.

[65] "Théorie et applications des treillis: Groupes réticulés," *Ann. Inst. Henri Poincaré* **11** (1950), 227–50.

[66] "Wall Effects in Cavity Flow" (with Milton Plesset and N. Simmons), *Quar. Appl. Math.* **8** (1950), 151–68.

[67] "Extensions of Lie Groups," *Math. Zeits.* **53** (1950), 226–35.

[68] "Moyennes des fonctions bornées," *Colloque Internationale d'Algebre Vol. 24*, Centre Nationale de Recherche Math., Paris, 1949, pp. 143–54.

[69] "Numerical Quadrature of Analytic and Harmonic Functions" (with David M. Young), *J. Math. and Phys.* MIT **29** (1950), 217–21.

[70] "Effective Conformal Transformation of Smooth, Simply-Connected Domains" (with David M. Young, Jr., and E. Zarantonello), *Proc. Nat. Acad. Sci.* **37** (1951), 411–14.

[71] "Numerical Methods in Conformal Mapping" (with D. M. Young and E. H. Zarantonello), *Proc. Vol. IV Amer. Math. Soc. Symp. Appl. Math.* (1953), 117–40.

[72] "Wall Effects in Cavity Flow. II" (with Milton Plesset and N. Simmons), *Quar. Appl. Math.* **10** (1952), 81–6.

[73] "Induced Mass with Free Boundaries," *Quar. Appl. Math.* **10** (1952), 81–6.

[74] "Some Problems of Lattice Theory," *Proc. Int. Congress Math.* Cambridge **2** (1950), 4–7.

[75] "New Theory of Vortex Streets," *Proc. Nat. Acad. Sci.* **38** (1952), 409–10.

[76] "Formation of Vortex Streets," *J. Appl. Phys.* **24** (1953), 98–103.

[77] "Fourier Analysis of Wave Trains" (with Jack Kotik), in *Gravity Waves* (G. Keulegan, ed.), *Nat. Bu. Standards Circular* (1952), 221–34.

[78] "Induced Mass with Variable Density," *Quar. Appl. Math.* **11** (1953), 109–10.

[79] "Note on Maximum Shock Deflection" (with John M. Walsh), *Quar. Appl. Math.* **12** (1954), 83–6.

[80] "Conical, Axially Symmetric Flows" (with John M. Walsh), *Riabouchinsky Jubilee Volume* (1954), 1–12.

[81] "Note on the Heat Equation" (with Jack Kotik), *Proc. Am. Math. Soc.* **5** (1954), 162–7.

[82] "Fourier Synthesis of Homogeneous Turbulence," *Comm. Pure Appl. Math.* **7** (1954), 19–44.

[83] "Classification of Partial Differential Equations," *J. SIAM* **2** (1954), 57–67.

[84] "Modèle de turbulence homogène" (with J. Kampé de Fériet), *Comptes Rendus* **239** (1954), 16–18.

[85] "Note on Taylor Instability," *Quar. Appl. Math.* **12** (1954), 306–9.

[86] "Wave Resistance of Ships" (with Jack Kotik and B. Korvin-Kroukovsky), *Trans. Soc. Nav. Arch. Marine Eng.* (1954), 359–96.

[87] "Induced Potentials," in *von Mises Anniversary Volume* (G. Birkhoff and G. Szego, eds.), Academic Press, 1954, pp. 88–96.

[88] "Calculations of Plane Cavity Flows" (with Herman H. Goldstine and E. H. Zarantonello), *Rend. Sem. Math. Torino* **13** (1954), 205–24.

[89] "Some Transformations of Michell's Integral" (with Jack Kotik), *Publ. Nat. Tech. Univ. Athens* (1954), No. 10, 26.

[90] "Non-linear Network Theory" (with J. B. Diaz), *Quar. Appl. Math.* **13** (1956), 431–43.

*[91] "Lattice-ordered Rings" (with Richard S. Pierce), *Anais Acad. Bras. Ciencias* **28** (1956), 41–69.

[92] "Stability of Spherical Bubbles," *Quar. Appl. Math.* **13** (1956), 451–3.

[93] "Extensions of Jentzsch's Theorem," *Trans. Am. Math. Soc.* **85** (1957), 219–27.

[94] "Rising Plane Bubbles" (with David Carter), *J. Math. Mech.* **6** (1957), 769–80.

[95] "Regularity of Partial Differential Equations" (with Thomas Mullikin), *Proc. Am. Math. Soc.* **9** (1958), 18–25.

[96] "Von Neumann and Lattice Theory," *Bull. Am. Math. Soc.* **64** (1958), 50–6.

[97] "Spherical Bubble Growth" (with W. Horning and R. Margulies), *Physics of Fluids* **1** (1958), 201–14.

[98] "Kinematics of Homogeneous Turbulence, Parts A–C" (with J. Kampé de Fériet), *J. Math. Mech.* **7** (1958), 663–704.

[99] "Reactor Criticality and Non-Negative Matrices" (with Richard S. Varga), *J. SIAM* **6** (1958), 354–77.

[100] "Reactor Criticality in Transport Theory," *Proc. Nat. Acad. Sci.* **45** (1959), 567–9.

[101] "Implicit Alternating Direction Methods" (with Richard S. Varga), *Trans. Am. Math. Soc.* **92** (1959), 13–24.

[102] "Do Vortex Sheets Roll Up?" (with J. Fisher), *Rend. Circ. Mat. Palermo* **8** (1959), 77–90.

[103] "Albedo Functions for Elliptic Equations," *Proc. Symp. Boundary Value Problems in DE's* (R. E. Langer, ed.), Univ. Wisconsin Press, Madison, 1959, pp. 163–78.

[104] "Mathematical Problems of Nuclear Reactor Theory," in *Frontiers of Numerical Math.* (R. E. Langer, ed.), Univ. Wisconsin Press, Madison, 1960, pp. 23–42.

[105] "Completeness of Sturm–Liouville Expansions" (with Gian-Carlo Rota), *Am. Math. Monthly* **67** (1960), 835–41.

[106] "Positivity and Criticality," *Nuclear Reactor Theory* (G. Birkhoff and E. Wigner, eds.), *Proc. XI Symp. Applied Math.*, Am. Math. Soc., (1959), 116–26.

[107] "Lattices in Applied Mathematics," *Lattice Theory* (R. P. Dilworth, ed.), *Proc. II Symp. Pure Math.*, Am. Math. Soc., (1960), 155–84.

[108] "Jets, Wakes and Cavities," *Proc. Second Symp. Naval Hydrodynamics* (1958), 261–76.

[109] "Smooth Surface Interpolation" (with H. L. Garabedian), *J. Math. and Phys.* **39** (1960), 258–68.

[110] "Calculation of Potential Flows with Free Boundaries," *Proc. Am. Soc. Civ. Eng.* (1961).

[111] "Lagrangian Hydrodynamic Computations and Molecular Models of Matter" (with R. E. Lynch), *Los Alamos Rep. LA-2618*, (1961) (summarized in *Ann. Harvard Comp. Lab.* **31** (1962), 23–31).

[112] "Lattice-ordered Demigroups," *Dubreil Seminar*, (1961).

[113] "Confocal Conics in Space-time" (with R. Morris), *Am. Math. Monthly* **69** (1962), 1–4.

[114] "Kinematics of Homogeneous Turbulence, Part D," *J. Math. Mech.* **11** (1962), 319–40.

[115] "Helmholtz and Taylor Instability," *Hydrodynamic Instability* (G. Birkhoff, Richard Bellman, and C. C. Lin, eds.), *Proc. XIII Appl. Math.*, Am. Math. Soc. (1962), 55–76. [For a fuller account, see G. Birkhoff, "Taylor Instability and Laminar Mixing," *Los Alamos Rep.* LA-1862 (1954), with App. A–H issued as Rep. LA-1927 (1956).]

[116] "Uniformly Semi-primitive Multiplicative Processes," *Trans. Am. Math. Soc.* **104** (1962), 37–51.

[117] "Alternating Direction Implicit Methods" (with R. S. Varga and D. M. Young), *Advances in Computers* **3** (1962), 189–273.

*[118] "A New Interval Topology for Dually Directed Sets," *Revista Tucumán* **14** (1962), 325–31.

[119] "Reactor Criticality in Neutron Transport Theory," *Rend. Mat. Univ. Roma* **22** (1963), 102–26.
[120] "Binary Collision Modeling" (with J. Eckerman), *J. Math. Mech.* **12** (1963), 543–56.
[121] "Free Boundaries in Partial Lubrication" (with D. F. Hays), *J. Math. and Phys.* **12** (1963), 126–38.
[122] "Variational Principles for Nonlinear Networks," *Quar. Appl. Math.* **21** (1963), 159–62.
[123] "Averaged Conservation Laws in Pipes," *J. Math. Anal. Appl.* **8** (1964), 66–77.
[124] "Well-set Cauchy Problems and C_0-semigroups," *J. Math. Anal. Appl.* **9** (1964), 303–24.
[125] "Free Boundary Problems for Viscous Flow in Channels," *Cavitation in Real Liquids* (R. M. Davies, ed.), Elsevier, 1964, pp. 102–21.
[126] "Error Bounds for Spline Interpolation" (with Carl de Boor), *J. Math. Mech.* **13** (1964), 827–36.
[127] "Positive Linear Operators," *Proc. Am. Math. Soc.* **16** (1965), 14–16.
[128] "Discretization Errors for Well-set Cauchy Problems" (with Richard S. Varga), *J. Math. and Phys.* **44** (1965), 1–23.
[129] "History of the Putnam Competition," *Am. Math. Monthly* **72** (1965), 469–83.
[130] "Piecewise Polynomial Surface Fitting" (with Carl de Boor), *Approximation of Functions*, (H. L. Garabedian, ed.), Elsevier, 1965.
[131] "Uniformly Semi-primitive Multiplicative Processes, II," *J. Math. Mech.* **14** (1965), 507–12.
[132] "Essentially Positive ... Linear Differential Equations" (with Leon Kotin), *Bull. Am. Math. Soc.* **71** (1965), 771–2.
[133] "Partial Difference Methods," *Proc. IBM Scientific Computing Symposium*, Int. Bus. Mach. Corp. (1963), 17–36.
[134] "Transition and Turbulence in Hypersonic Wakes," *Phys. of Fluids* **9** (1966), 446–52.
[135] "Asymptotic Behavior ... of Differential-Delay Equations" (with Leon Kotin), *J. Math. Anal. Appl.* **13** (1966), 8–18.
[136] "Numerical Solution of the Telegraph and Related Equations" (with R. E. Lynch), *Num. Solution of Partial Differential Equations* (J. Bramble, ed.), Academic Press, 1966, 289–315.
[137] "Rayleigh–Ritz Approximation with Piecewise Cubic Polynomials" (with C. de Boor, B. Swartz, and B. H. Wendroff), *J. SIAM Numer. Anal.* **3** (1966), 188–203.
[138] "Integro-Differential Delay Equations of Positive Type" (with Leon Kotin), *J. of Diff. Eq.* **2** (1966), 320–7.
[139] "Numerical Solution of the Reactor Kinetics Equations," in *Numerical Solutions of Nonlinear Differential Equations*, (Donald Greenspan, ed.), Univ. of Wisconsin Press, 1966.
[140] "Equilibrium Equations in Thermal Networks" (with Bruce Kellogg), *Generalized Networks*, vol. 16, published for Polyt. Inst. Brooklyn, N.Y. (Wiley), 1966, 443–52.
[141] "Linear Second Order Differential Equations of Positive Type" (with Leon Kotin), *J. d'Analyse* **18** (1967), 43–52.
[142] "Local Spline Approximation by Moments," *J. Math. Mech.* **16** (1967), 987–90.
[143] "Linear Transformation with Invariant Cones," *Am. Math. Monthly* **74** (1967), 274–6.
[144] "A Limitation of Fourier Analysis," *J. Math. Mech.* **17** (1967), 443–8.
[145] "Hermite Interpolation Errors for Derivatives" (with Arthur Priver), *J. Math. Phys.* **46** (1967), 440–7.
[146] "Piecewise Hermite Interpolation..." (with M. H. Schultz and R. S. Varga), *Numerische Math.* **11** (1968), 232–56.
[147] "The Draftsman's and Related Equations" (with Wm. J. Gordon), *J. Approx. Theory* **1** (1968), 199–208.
[148] "Third Order Positive Cyclic Systems" (with Leon Kotin), *J. of Diff. Eqs.* **5** (1969), 182–96.
[149] "Similarity and the Transport Equation," *Sedov Anniversary Volume*, SIAM Publications, (1969), 55–62.
[150] "Harmonic Solutions of Transport Equations" (with I. Abu-Shumays), *J. Math. Anal. Appl.* **28** (1969), 211–21.
[151] "Piecewise Bi-cubic Interpolation and Approximation in Polygons," in *Approximations with Special Emphasis on Spline Functions* (I. Schoenberg, ed.), Academic Press, 1969.

[152] "Rayleigh-Ritz Approximation by Trigonometric Polynomials" (with George Fix), *Indian Math. J.* **9** (1967), 269–77.
[153] "Mathematics and Psychology," *SIAM Rev.* **11** (1969), 429–69.
*[154] "Heterogeneous Algebras" (with John D. Lipson), *J. Combinatorial Theory* **8** (1970), 115–33.
[155] "What can Lattices Do for You?" in *Trends in Lattice Theory* (J. C. Abbott, ed.), van Nostrand, 1970, pp. 1–40.
[156] "Positive Cyclic Systems of Linear Differential Equations" (with Leon Kotin), *J. of Diff. Eq.* **7** (1970), 407–16.
[157] "Accurate Eigenvalue Computations for Elliptic Problems" (with George Fix), in *Numerical Solution of Field Problems of Continuum Physics* (G. Birkhoff and R. S. Varga, eds.), *SIAM-AMS Proc. II*, Am. Math. Soc., (1970), 111–51.
[158] "Exact Analytic Solutions of Transport Equations" (with I. Abu-Shumays), *J. Math. Anal. Appl.* **32** (1970), 468–81.
[159] "Tri-cubic Polynomial Interpolation," *Proc. Nat. Acad. Sci.* **68** (1971), 1162–4.
*[160] "Current Trends in Algebra," *Am. Math. Monthly* **80** (1973), 760–82.
[161] "Optimal Smoothing of Gaussian Periodic Data" (with Arthur Priver), *Indiana Univ. Math. J.* **21** (1971), 103–13.
[162] "Angular Singularities of Elliptic Problems," *J. Approximation Theory* **6** (1972), 215–30.
[163] "The Impact of Computers on Undergraduate Mathematical Education in 1984," *Am. Math. Monthly* **79** (1972), 648–57.
[164] "Piecewise Analytic Interpolation and Approximation in Triangulated Polygons," in *Math. Foundations of the Finite Element Method*... (A. K. Aziz, ed.), Academic, 1972.
[165] "Statistically Well-set Cauchy Problems" (with J. Bona and J. Kampé de Fériet), *Prob. Methods in Applied Math.* **3** (1973), 1–120.
[166] "Interpolation to Boundary Data in Triangles," *J. Math. Anal. Appl.* **42** (1973), 474–84.
[167] "Elimination by Nested Dissection" (with Alan George), in *Complexity of Sequential and Parallel Numerical Algorithms* (J. F. Traub, ed.), Academic Press, 1973.
[168] "Mathematical Analysis of Cavitation," *Proc. IUTAM Symposium on Non-Steady Flow of Water at High Speeds* (L. I. Sedov and G. Yu. Stepanov, eds.), Nauka, Moscow, 1973, pp. 1–38.
*[169] "The Role of Modern Algebra in Computing," in *Computers in Algebra and Number Theory* (G. Birkhoff and Marshall Hall, eds.), Am. Math. Soc., (1971), 1–47.
[170] "Smooth Interpolation in Triangles" (with R. E. Barnhill and W. J. Gordon), *J. Approx. Theory* **8** (1973), 114–28.
[171] "Compatible Triangular Finite Elements" (with Lois Mansfield), *J. Math. Anal. Appl.* **47** (1974), 531–53.
[172] "Multivariate Approximation by Locally Blended Univariate Interpolants" (with J. C. Cavendish and William J. Gordon), *Proc. Nat. Acad. Sci.* **71** (1974), 3423–5.
[173] "Optimal Few-Point Discretizations of Linear Source Problems" (with S. Gulati), *SIAM J. Numer. Anal.* **11** (1974), 700–28.
*[174] "Universal Algebra and Automata" (with John D. Lipson), *Proc. Tarski Symposium* (Leon Henkin *et al.*, eds.), *Proc. XXV Symp. Pure Math.*, Am. Math. Soc., (1974), 41–51.
[175] "Two Hadamard Numbers for Matrices," *Comm. Ass. Comp. Mach.* **18** (1975), 25–29.
[176] "Mathematics and Computer Science," *Am. Scientist* **63** (1975), 83–91.
[177] "Numerical Solution of Hydrodynamic Problems" (with V. A. Dougalis), *Proc. AICA Int. Symp. Computer Methods* (1975), 7–13.
[178] "House Monotone Apportionment Schemes," *Proc. Nat. Acad. Sci.* **73** (1976), 21–23.
*[179] "Note on Universal Topological Algebra," *Algebra Universalis* **6** (1976), 21–23.
[180] "Autonomous Families of Differential Systems" (with Leon Kotin), *J. Math. Anal. Appl.* **55** (1976), 466–75.
[181] "Comparison of Numerical Methods for Solving Wave Equations" (with V. Dougalis), *First Int. Conf. Numer. Ship Hydrodynamics*, David Taylor Model Basin, (1976), 231–52.

*[182a] "The Rise of Modern Algebra to 1936," in *Men and Institutions in America*, Texas Tech. Graduate Studies #13 (1976), 41–63.

*[182b] "The Rise of Modern Algebra, 1936–1950," in *Men and Institutions in America*, Texas Tech. Graduate Studies #13 (1976), 65–85.

[183] "Applied Mathematics and its Future," in *Science and Technology in America* (Robb W. Thomson, ed.), Nat. Bureau Standards Publ. #465, 1977, pp. 82–104.

[184] Review of H. H. Goldstine, *Historia Math* **5** (1978), 479–82.

[185] "Some Leaders in American Mathematics," in *Bicentennial Tribute to American Mathematics* (Dalton Tarwater, ed.), Math. Assn. Am., 1978, pp. 25–78.

[186] "Similarity in two-phase flow," *Proc. IUTAM Cont. on Group-Theoretic Methods in Mechanics* (N. H. Ibragimov and L. V. Ovsjannikov, eds.), 1978, pp. 58–79.

[187] "Isotropic distributions of test matrices" (with S. Gulati), *ZAMP* **30** (1979), 148–56.

[188] "Algebra of multivariate interpolation," in *Constructive Approaches to Math. Models* (Coffman and G. J. Fix, eds.), Academic Press, 1980, pp. 345–63.

[189] "Added mass of cylinders" (with R. E. Lynch), *Computers in Simulation* **22** (1980), 291–7.

[190] *Review* of J. Dieudonné, "Abrégé d'Histoire des Mathématiques: 1700–1900," *Adv. in Math.* **34** (1979), 185–94.

[191a] Review of G. Grätzer, "General Lattice Theory," *Bull. Am. Math. Soc.* **1** (1979), 789–92.

[191b] Review of books on computers by Peter Henrici and others, *Bull. Am. Math. Soc.* **2** (1980), 503–5.

[191c] Review of Roberto Torretti, *Philosophy of Geometry from Riemann to Poincaré*, Reidel, 1978; *Adv. Math.* **34** (1979), 399–400.

[191d] Review of H. Mehrtens, "Die Entstelung der Verbandstheorie," in *Historia Math*, 1980.

[192] "Computer developments 1935–1955, as seen from Cambridge , U.S.A.," in *A History of Computing in the Twentieth Century* (N. Metropolis, J. Howlett and G.-C. Rota eds.), Academic Press, 1980, pp. 21–30.

[193] "Solving Elliptic Problems: 1930–1980," in *Elliptic Problem Solvers* (Martin Schultz, ed.), Academic Press, 1981, pp. 17–38.

[194] "Some Applications of Universal Algebra," *Coll. Math. Soc. Janos Bolyai* **29** (1977), 107–28; appears in a collection of papers by North-Holland (1981).

[195] "George D. Birkhoff's Theory of Gravitation," in *Selected Studies* (T. M. Rassias and G. M. Rassias, eds.), North-Holland, 1982, pp. 57–77.

[196] "Ordered Sets in Geometry," in *Ordered Sets* (Ivan Rival, ed.), Reidel, 1983, pp. 407–436. Appendix by M. K. Bennett on pp. 436–443.

[197] "Numerical Fluid Dynamics," *SIAM Rev.* **25** (1983), 1–34.

[198] "Review of Steve Heims' John von Neumann and Norbert Wiener," *Historia Math.* **10** (1983), 243–8.

[199] "Nonlinear Product Integration," in *Global Analysis-Analysis on Manifolds* (T. M. Rassias, ed.), Teubner, 1983, pp. 43–50.

[200] "Computing added mass coefficients" (with J. F. Brophy and R. E. Lynch), in *Elliptic Problem Solvers II* (G. Birkhoff and A. Schoenstadt, eds.), Academic Press, 1984, pp. 427–37.

[201] "Convexity Lattices" (with M. K. Bennett), *Algebra Universalis* **20** (1985), 1–26.

[202] "The Establishment of Functional Analysis" (with Erwin Kreyszig), *Historia Mathematica* **11** (1984), 285–321.

[203] "A Peano axiom for convexity lattices" (with M. K. Bennett), *Bull. Calcutta Math. Soc.* (1983), 33–43.

[204] "Some mathematical problems of numerical ocean acoustics," *Comput. Math. with Appl.* **11** (1985), 643–54. Reprinted in *Numerical Ocean Acoustics* (Ding Lee and M. H. Schultz, eds.), Pergamon Press, 1986.

Ph.D. Students of Garrett Birkhoff

1936–1963

1936 Joel Brenner (finite groups)
1940 John Dyer-Bennet (free real algebra)
1941 Philip Whitman (free lattices)
1942 Murray Mannos (vector lattices)
1945 Richard Arens (general topology)
1945 Jeremiah Certaine (*l*-groups)
1946 Pesi Masani (product integration)
1947 Thomas Caywood (potential theory)
1947 Frank Stewart (product integration)
1948 George Mostow (Lie groups)
1948 Marion Heineman (kinetic theory—physics)
1950 Bruce Crabtree (derivatives in hypercomplex algebras)
1950 Chandler Davis (*l*-semigroups)
1950 William A. Pierce (free mobility axioms for geometry)
1950 John Sopka (Reynolds operators)
1951 Lawrence J. Markus (ordinary DE's)
1951 David Young (numerical analysis)
1953 Martin Abkowitz (submarine dynamics—physics)
1953 Samuel Kneale (hydrodynamics)
1956 James Howland (potential theory)
1959 Thomas Mullikin (C_0-semigroups)
1960 Martin Leibowitz (neutron slowing down—applied math.)
1961 John Bennett (numerical analysis—applied math.)
1962 Thomas Brown (ordinary DE's)
1962 Tyrrel Rockafellar (convex programming)
1963 Robert E. Lynch (numerical analysis—applied math.)
1963? Uta Merzbach (history of math.)

1965–1978

1965 Jose Canosa (reactor dynamics—physics)
1965 Martin Schultz (num. analysis)
1966 I. Abu-Shumays (neutron theory—physics)
1966 Kirby Baker (free vector lattices)
1966 Henry Wente (Plateau problem)
1967 S. Nagpaul (lubrication theory—applied math.)
1968 George Fix (num. analysis—applied math.)
1968 Walter Taylor (ultraproducts, etc.)
1969 Bernie J. Hulme (num. analysis—biharmonic DE)
1969 Emmett Keeler (math. economics)
1969 John Lipson (flowgraphs—applied math.)
1970 Donald Rose (sparse matrices—applied math.)
1970 Vern Poythress (univ. algebra)
1970 Gary Wakoff (num. analysis—applied math.)
1971 Richard Goodman (num. analysis)
1971 Arthur Priver (computer graphics—applied math.)
1971 Alan G. Waterman (univ. algebra)
1971 Jerry Bona (statistically well-set Cauchy problems)
1973 Gerald Edgar (general topology)
1973 George Markowsky (lattices)
1976 Vassilios A. Dougalis (num. fluid dynamics)
1976 Peter Olver (groups and DE's)
1978 Barbara Epstein (math. model of Tokomak—applied math.)

I

Lattices

General Remark

Lattice theory first became established as a significant branch of mathematics in the 1930s. This establishment resulted from the work of a small number of mathematicians: von Neumann, Ore, Stone, Kantorovich, myself, and about fifteen others (see the bibliography of [LT1])[1]. The story of its establishment has been admirably told by H. Mehrtens in his authoritative *Entstehung der Verbandstheorie.*

The first ten papers reprinted in the present volume vividly reflect the rapid progress of lattice theory in those years. They were motivated by two main ideas: the idea that lattices, like groups, have a fascinating algebraic theory of their own, which needed to be explored, and the idea that lattices provide the best algebraic tool for treating combinatorial and structural problems, much as group theory provides the best algebraic tool for analyzing symmetry. A third idea, that lattices play a central role in universal algebra, is the theme of the papers, mostly written after 1940, that are reproduced in Part II of this volume.

Besides these ten papers, which predate [LT1], two others ([51] and [54]) that predate [LT2] are reprinted in Part I. They develop ideas about distributive lattices that originated with my co-authors, during the closing years of World War II. My role was to incorporate their ideas into the main body of lattice theory, which had become established by the time they were written.

Some readers may wonder why I published so few papers on pure lattice theory after 1940. Apart from the interruption due to World War II, there were three main reasons for this. First, since many able workers had been attracted to the field by the late 1940s, my keenest interest was in finding new *applications* of lattice theory, especially outside of pure mathematics. This was why I wrote [107], for example. A similar interest in broadening the scope of lattice theory also motivated my papers on lattice-ordered groups, lattice-ordered rings, etc. My publications concerned with these topics, mostly written in the decades 1940–1960, are reprinted and discussed in Part V.

Thirdly, after 1940, my periods of activity in the subject occurred while I was preparing [LT2] (in 1945–47) and [LT3] (in 1960–66). It seemed most efficient to published the new results which I obtained during those years in these books, where they could be presented in context without duplication.

Summaries. After these preliminary remarks, I shall now summarize my individual papers and subsequent related developments.[2]

[3], [4]. Papers [3], [3a], [4] constitute a first attempt at identifying lattice theory as a significant branch of algebra. In them I first proposed the name "lattice" for what Fritz Klein

had called a "Verband," boldly asserting [3, p. 441] that lattice theory provides a vantage point "from which to attack combinatorial problems in ... abstract algebra." They were written when my background in university algebra was limited to a year's study of group theory and van der Waerden's *Moderne Algebra*, as has been explained in the Preface. Although Philip Hall had called my attention to Fritz Klein's then recently published papers, neither we nor Klein were aware of Dedekind's overlapping studies of "Dualgruppen" even though they had been reprinted just two years earlier in Volume 2 of his *Ges. Math. Werke*, edited by Emmy Noether, R. Fricke, and Oystein Ore.

I observed in [3] that "the subalgebras of any algebra form a lattice," thus vaguely foreshadowing the ideas to be discussed in Part II. I also showed that the normal subgroups of any group form a modular lattice; that the free modular lattice with three generators contains 28 elements, and proved an abstract Jordan–Hölder theorem. I was soon to find out (see [3a]) that these results had been obtained by Dedekind.

I also proved some new results about lattices, showing that the free modular lattice with four generators is infinite. Every distributive lattice L is isomorphic to some ring of sets (Theorem 25.2), and if L is *finite* of length h, only h points are required (cf. [28], Theorem 17.2). By coincidence, Stone was simultaneously proving the closely related theorem that every Boolean algebra is isomorphic with a field of sets (*Proc. Nat. Sci.* **20** (1934), 197–202); our combined results are sometimes called the Birkhoff–Stone theorem. Stone developed his isomorphism into much deeper topological representation theorems, published in 1936–37.[3]

In connection with the Jordan–Hölder theorem, I further derived some basic properties of *semimodular* lattices, which Fritz Klein called "Birkhoffsche Verbände."[4]

Paper [4] gave "three necessary and sufficient conditions for a finite B-lattice to be a C-lattice," i.e., for a finite modular lattice M to be distributive, in terms of properties of the functionals on M satisfying

$$(*) \qquad \rho[x] + \rho[y] = \rho[x \wedge y] + \rho[x \vee y].$$

Thus it explored the analogy between dimension (in projective geometries) and measure (including probability).

[6], [7]. In 1932–33, I had attended G. H. Hardy's lectures on algebraic and analytic number theory. He had lectured brilliantly on the unique factorization theorem in quadratic number fields, but essentially ignored ideal theory.[5] Thus he never mentioned Dedekind's classic unique factorization theorem for ideals in an arbitrary algebraic number field, nor its abstract generalization by Emmy Noether. Yet from a lattice-theoretic standpoint, the *structure lattice* of all the ideals of the subring of integers in an algebraic number field is obviously of primary importance.

Papers [6] and [7] attempt to relate the abstract theory of lattices (Dedekind's "Dualgruppen") to both Hardy's and Emmy Noether's ideas. In [6], some properties of ideals in general commutative rings were analyzed, in the spirit of van der Waerden's *Moderne Algebra*. In [7], various theorems were proved which relate the structure of the lattice of integers (under divisibility) in an algebraic number field to the unique factorization theorem.

[9]. This early paper on extensions of the Jordan–Hölder Theorem from finite groups to arbitrary groups with operators, and a closely related paper by A. Kurosh (*Math. Annalen* **111** (1935), 13–18), initiated a whole series of further extensions. These had many authors; see the references cited in [LT1, p. 48] and [LT2, pp. 88–9].

[12]. Projective geometry. Already in 1933, I discovered that projective geometries have a simple lattice-theoretic characterization as *irreducible complemented modular lattices* of finite length, and that conversely every complemented modular lattice of finite length has a unique factorization into projective geometries and a Boolean algebra. This was the main result of [12].

Continuous geometries. After learning about this result and its proof, von Neumann was immediately struck by its connections with the spectral theory of Hermitian operators on Hilbert space $\mathfrak{H}$.[6] Namely, the closed subspaces of $\mathfrak{H}$ invariant under the action of any Hermitian operator form an *orthocomplemented* modular lattice, the factors of which are associated with the different eigenspaces.

Intrigued by the then new lattice-theoretic approach, he quickly constructed a novel family of *continuous*-dimensional projective geometries, about which he lectured in 1935–36. Notes for these lectures, written up by L. R. Wilcox, were issued by the Institute for Advanced Study in 1936. The next year, von Neumann lectured on "Continuous geometries with transition probabilities", and then surveyed his new results in AMS Colloquium Lectures given in 1937.

Unfortunately, the preparation of all these lectures for publication was delayed by von Neumann's increasing involvement with defense research, as well as by his other research activities. The final version of his 1935–36 lectures is his posthumous book *Continuous Geometries* (Princeton University Press, 1960). (For later work on 'orthomodular' lattices, see the references mentioned in connection with [21] below.)

The content of his 1936–37 lectures, originally edited in 1937 by Frank Smithies (now of St. John's College, Cambridge University), and then carefully studied and polished by Israel Halperin, was finally published in 1981 as AMS Memoir #252. Halperin's prefaces to this memoir and to *Continuous Geometries* constitute the most authoritative historical references for this work of von Neumann.

Von Neumann algebras. Von Neumann's and my joint paper [21], discussed below, was a related effort; so was his work on the spectral theory of "rings of operators" with F. J. Murray (see [21, ftnt. 13]). This is because the idempotents (or *projections*) in such rings correspond to closed subspaces, and thus forms a lattice. For this connection, see Irving Kaplansky's "Projections in Banach algebras", *Annals of Math.* **55** (1951), 235–49, and Lynn Loomis, "The lattice-theoretic background of the dimension theory", AMS Memoir #18 (1955.). Continuous geometries correspond to to rings of operators of type II_1 in the von Neumann–Murray classification, while those of their type I_N correspond to finite-dimensional projective geometries.

[16]. Geometric lattices. The year 1935 in which [12] was published also saw the birth of the theory of geometric lattices,[9] a theory not foreshadowed in Dedekind's work. First Hassler Whitney developed an axiomatic theory of rank and linear dependence for sets of vectors, and showed that his "matroid" axioms are applicable to graphs. I recognized that matroids are essentially *atomic semimodular lattices* of finite length, and hence that they are complemented modular lattices of finite length if and only if their duals are also "matroid" lattices; these results are the essential content of [16]. In a third paper, Saunders Mac Lane interpreted various famous geometric configurations as matroids.

Two years later (*Duke Math. J.* **4** (1938), 455–68), Mac Lane showed the connection of Whitney's matroid and the Steinitz exchange axiom, giving applications to the theories of transcendence degrees and *p*-bases. In the meantime, Louis Weisner (*Trans. AMS* **38** (1935), 474–92) and Philip Hall (*Quar. J. Math.* **7** (1936), 134–51) had shown that Möbius functions could be defined on locally finite partially ordered sets. In 1938, I saw how to express the chromatic polynomial of a map in terms of the Möbius function of its lattice of submaps. I published an axiomatic study of "matroid lattices" in [LT1, §§74–77], later amplified in my book [LT2, Chap. VII].

The affine subspaces of any vector space also form a matroid lattice, as had been shown (in different language) in a 1937 paper by Menger, Alt, and Schreiber.[7] However, a complete lattice-theoretic characterization of 'affine geometries' was first found 45 years later by M. K. Bennett.[8]

A strong push to the theory of matroid lattices was given in 1953, when they were suggestively renamed "geometric lattices" by Mme. Dubreil-Jacotin and her collaborators. Geometric lattices were made the subject of Part III of their monograph.

Beginning around 1964, Gian-Carlo Rota made basic contributions to the theories of both Möbius functions (*Zeits. f. Wahrscheinlichkeitsrechnung* **2** (1964), 340–68), and geometric lattices. These were followed by the book by H. Crapo and G.-C. Rota, *Combinatorial Geometries* (M.I.T. Press, 1970).

Broadly speaking, combinatorial geometry, as the theory of geometric lattices has come to be called is concerned with those properties of linear dependence over an arbitrary field (or division ring) which can be stated without reference to the field. These properties concern the number of elements in a basis, inequalities between the ranks of minors in a matrix, exchange properties of bases, and matching properties. Such properties have equivalent and far more general formulations in terms of geometric lattices. These arise not only as special cases of linear dependence of vectors, but also in the study of graphs, convex polyhedra, simplicial complexes, and other incidence structures, as well as in algebra, in the theory of algebraic dependence of polynomials and transcendence degrees of fields.

At present, the two most active research problems in geometric lattices are:

(1) *The representation problem.* Under what conditions can a geometric lattice be represented by vectors over a given field F, with closure as the linear span? At present, combinatorial conditions are known for representability over $GF(2)$ (Whitney), $GF(3)$ (Reid) and over all fields (Tutte). It is conjectured that over any finite field $GF(p^n)$, representability depends on the absence in the lattice L of a finite number of *obstructions*, that is, forbidden configurations in the Hasse diagram of the lattice.

(2) *The critical problem.* (Crapo–Rota) This consists in locating the zeros of the characteristic polynomial of a geometric lattice, as defined by the Möbius function. Many extremal combinatorial problems, notably the classical problem of graph-coloring, can be re-stated as critical problems. It is at present conjectured that the location of integer zeros of the characteristic polynomial depends on the absence of certain obstructions in the Hasse diagram of the lattices. (Also see G. D. Birkhoff's *Collected Mathematical Papers*, vol. iii, p. 29ff.).

Geometric lattices arise also in a great variety of combinatorial problems. Some idea of the scope of these applications may be gleaned by perusing *Proc. Symp. Pure Math.*, vols. XIX and XXXIV. Am. Math. Soc., 1969 and 1978; *Studies in Foundations and Combinatories* (G.-C. Rota, ed.), Academic Press, 1978; and *Ordered Sets* (Ivan Rival, ed.), Reidel, 1981.

[21]. Quantum mechanics. The most widely cited of the articles reprinted in Part I is my paper with von Neumann on "The Logic of Quantum Mechanics." This paper explored in depth the implications for the logic of quantum mechanics of the remark that the closed subspaces of Hilbert space $\mathfrak{H}$ form a complemented, *nearly* modular lattice $L(\mathfrak{H})$. Specifically, the finite-dimensional (hence closed) subspaces and their complements form a dense, orthocomplemented

modular sublattice $M(\mathfrak{H})$ of $L(\mathfrak{H})$, and $L(\mathfrak{H})$ is the order completion of $M(\mathfrak{H})$. These properties are common to the closed subspaces of both real and complex Hilbert space; moreover the *algebraic* properties are shared by the analogous subspaces (and their orthocomplements) of vector spaces over arbitrary division rings.

In the physically relevant case of complex Hilbert space, our paper built on von Neumann's book *Mathematische Grundlagen der Quantenmechanik*, which had been published three years earlier. We divided our paper into: A) Physical background, B) Algebraic analysis, C) Conclusions, and D) Appendix. As an explanation of the relevance of lattice theory to the logic of quantum mechanics, the exposition of Parts A and B could hardly be improved today, Part D, the most technical, is a concise characterization of the connection between orthocomplementations of finite dimensional projective geometries over division rings and definite diagonal Hermitian forms with respect to involutory anti-automorphisms.

Part C discussed from a philosophical standpoint the basic question of whether or not the modular identity can be assumed in "quantum logic"; it does not hold for the orthomodular lattice $L(\mathfrak{H})$ of all closed subspaces in infinite-dimensional Hilbert space, although it does hold in $\mathbb{R}^n$ and the hermitian space $\mathbb{C}^n$. In my 1960 paper [107] (not reprinted in this volume), using some technical considerations supplied by Paul Cohen, I showed that this law was not plausible for the position and momentum operators of a free particle.

It is to be hoped that other physical examples will be studied in the future, which special reference to experimental verifications of the orthomodular lattice model of quantum logic.

Many papers and books have pursued the questions raised in [21]. Among these, the following are especially relevant:

(1) J. von Neumann, *Continuous Geometry*, Princeton Univ. Press, 1960.
(2) George W. Mackey, *Foundations of Quantum Mechanics*, Benjamin, 1963, esp. pp. 56–81.
(3) S. H. Holland, "The current interest in orthomodular lattices," in J. C. Abbott (ed.), *Trends in Lattice Theory*, van Nostrand, 1970, pp. 41–126.
(4) E. C. Beltrametti and Gianni Cassinelli, *The Logic of Quantum Mechanics*, Addison-Wesley, 1981.
(5) G. Kalmbach *Orthomodular Lattices*, Academic Press, 1983.

[34]. "Lattices and their applications." Because of the widespread interest in lattices stimulated by the work of Menger, Ore, Stone, von Neumann, a few of their students, and my own publications, an AMS Symposium on Lattice Theory was held in April, 1938. Taken with the other papers presented there (see *Bull. AMS* **34**, pp. 793–827), [34] gives a good picture of the most significant results about lattices that were known at that time. However, since it was purely expository, and is readily accessible, [34] has not been reprinted in this volume.

The absence of the word "theory" in its title, and the presence of the word "applications" (as in [4]), were intentional. They foreshadow the emphasis of [107], written 22 years later, and some comments in my review [191a] of Grätzer's book *General Lattice Theory*, written 18 more years after that.

[36], [40]. Distributivity. The last four papers of Part I treat *distributive* lattices. They were written (from 1939 to 1947) after those discussed above. Paper [36] (with Morgan Ward) proved that an atomistic and dually atomistic lattice is necessarily a Boolean algebra if every element a in it has a unique complement a' such that $a \wedge a' = 0$ and $a \vee a' = I$. We conjectured that the same might be true for lattices in general.[10]

However, in a notable paper which constructed from any poset P the free lattice generated by P as a subset (*TAMS* **57** (1945), 123–54) Dilworth proved the startling contrary result that *every* lattice is isomorphic with a sublattice of a lattice with unique complements. For a contemporary presentation, see pp. 170–5 of Crawley and Dilworth (2).[11] Dilworth's method has been extended to a theory of reduced free products of lattices, due mainly to C. C. Chen and G. Grätzer (see Grätzer (4, pp. 288–95 and p. 304)).

Subsequent articles have proved some new special cases of the Birkhoff–Ward conjecture: L atomic, L an ortholattice, L algebraic. See Grätzer (4) for references, and Adams and Sichler (1) for an up-to-date survey of related ideas.

Paper [40] concerns neutral elements in general lattices. In the first of his two great papers, Ore had defined an element of a modular lattice M to be *neutral* when it acts distributively on all other pairs of elements, showing that the set of all netural elements of M is a (distributive) sublattice. Von Neumann had given a related but different difinition of the *center* of any complemented modular lattice. In [40], I defined as *neutral* in any lattice L, the elements a such that, for all x, $y \in L$, the sublattice generated by $\{a, x, y\}$ is distributive. I showed that these elements form a distributive sublattice N, whose complemented elements constitute the center of L.

The preceding result was sharpened in the early 1960s by G. Grätzer, J. Hashimoto, S. Kinugawa, and Iqbalunnissa (see Grätzer (3, pp. 138–51) for references). These authors observed that an element a of a lattice L is neutral if and only if, for all x, $y \in L$,

$$(a \wedge x) \vee (x \wedge y) \vee (y \wedge a) = (a \vee x) \wedge (x \vee y) \wedge (y \vee a)$$

(cf. [LT3, p. 69]). The displayed condition is easier to verify than the distributivity of the sublattice generated by $\{a, x, y\}$. It is also true that, in the lattice of all subgroups of a finite group, the center consists of those characteristic subgroups whose order and index are relatively prime [LT3, p. 175].

(1) M. E. Adams and J. Sichler, "Lattices with unique complementation," *Pacific J. Math.* **92** (1981), 1–13.
(2) P. Crawley and R. P. Dilworth, *Algebraic Theory of Lattices*, Prentice-Hall, Englewood Cliffs, 1973.
(3) R. P. Dilworth, "Lattices with unique complements," *Trans. AMS* **57** (1945), 123–54.
(4) G. Grätzer, *General Lattice Theory*, Birkhäuser, Basel, 1978.

[51]. Newman algebras. Paper [51] is of special personal interest as being co-authored by George D. Birkhoff. In a remarkable paper (*J. Lond. Math. Soc.* **16** (1941), 250–72), M. H. A. Newman had developed a unified theory of Boolean algebras *and* Boolean rings, based entirely on the distributive laws, the properties of 0 and 1, and the existence of complements. He had *proved* the commutativity and associativity of $\wedge$, $\vee$, and $+$ from these assumptions, and showed that any "Newman algebra" satisfying them is a direct sum of a Boolean algebra and a Boolean ring.

In some summer lectures on Boolean algebra, G. D. Birkhoff independently discovered Newman's decomposition. A careful study of the techniques used led to some substantial simplifications in Newman's proofs.

The G. D. Birkhoff–Newman theorem was the pioneering discovery of a non-trivial product variety, and apart from the essentially trivial example of "rectangular bands," it is the only known naturally occurring one. However, it can be generalized to *products* $V \times W$ of any two varieties of the same similarity type, by adding an operation that satisfies $p(x, y) = x$ on V and $p(x, y) = y$ on W; see pp. 265–8 of Walter Taylor, *Algebra Univ.* **5** (1975), 263–303. For Newman algebras, $p(x, y) = x2 + y2'$, and most of §4 of [51] can be seen as a verification of laws for this polynomial.

[54]. Median operations. Paper [54] introduced the (now classic) self-dual ternary *medium* operation

$$(1) \qquad (x, y, z) = (x \wedge y) \vee (y \wedge z) \vee (z \wedge x) = (x \vee y) \wedge (y \vee z) \wedge (z \vee x)$$

in distributive lattices, preserved by all translations. $x \to x + a$ of a Boolean algebra, and by all order-automorphisms. Similar results were found at about the same time by A. A. Grau (*Bull. AMS* **53** (1947), 567–72); see [LT2, pp. 137–8]. Problems 64 and 65 of [LT2] concerned medians, and were solved in 1950–51 by Ph. Vassiliou, R. Croisot, and M. Sholander (see *Math. Revs.* **12**, p. 472).

Many mathematicians have studied medians axiomatically in the 35 years since [54] appeared, frequently using its equations (3.2)–(3.4) as defining axioms. Thus, J. Hashimoto (*Math. Japan* **2** (1951), 49–52) proved the equivalence of bounded modular lattices with the variety having 0 and 1 and the following "median" operation: $(x, y, z) = [x \wedge (y \vee z)] \vee (y \wedge z)$. On modular lattices this is equal to its dual, and it reduces to the Birkhoff–Kiss median in distributive lattices. Later, Sholander made other studies of median operations in *Proc. AMS* **5** (1954), 801–12. The axioms and basic results have had several independent rediscoveries; the paper of Bendelt and Hedlíková (1) contains a valuable survey section telling the whole story.

Especially general is the recent paper of Isbell (3), which considers nonsymmetric generalizations such as that of Hashimoto mentioned above, but from a more geometrical standpoint. For example, (x, y, z) may be thought of as "the nearest point to x and y and z."

In lattice theory, the median $(x, y, z) = (x \wedge y) \vee (y \wedge z) \vee (z \wedge x)$ has turned out to be very important, even though without distributivity it is not equal to its dual as in equation (1). Most of its important consequences have come from the simple laws:

$$(x, x, y) = (x, y, x) = (y, x, x) = x,$$

which play a central role in B. Jónsson's theory of distributive congruence lattices (4). For some idea of the scope of these developments, including the finite basis theorem of K. Baker, see the survey articles by Jónsson and Quackenbush in (2, Appendices 3 and 5).

Sequels to [54]

(1) H. J. Bendelt and J. Hedlíková, "Median algebras," *Discrete Mathematics* **45** (1983), 1–30.
(2) G. Grätzer, *Universal Algebra*, 2nd Edition, Springer-Verlag, New York, 1979.
(3) J. R. Isbell, "Median algebra," *Trans. AMS* **260** (1980), 319–62.
(4) B. Jónsson, "Algebras whose congruence lattices are distributive," *Math. Scand.* **21** (1967), 110–121.

Since the discussion of [16] was written, two more important books on matroid theory have appeared: Joseph P. S. Kung, *A Source Book in Matroid Theory*, Birkhäuser, 1986, and Neil White (ed.), "Theory of Matroids," *Encyclopedia of Mathematics, Vol. 1*, Cambridge University Press, 1986.

Notes

[1] I have found it convenient to identify the three editions of my book *Lattice Theory* as [LT1], [LT2], and [LT3], respectively.

[2] *Acknowledgement.* Many of the summaries included below, in Parts I and II, are condensations of more thorough discussions kindly prepared by Walter Taylor.

[3] *Trans. Am. Math. Soc.* **40** (1936), 37–111, and **41** (1973), 375–81; Stone had announced his main results in *Proc. Nat. Acad. Sci. USA* **20** (1934), 197–202. For progress stemming from Stone's deeper results, see the book *Stone Spaces*, by P. T. Johnstone (Academic Press, 1981).

[4] See *Trans. Am. Math. Soc.* **49** (1941), 325–353 (for further details as regards Dilworth's reference to Birkhoff's Lattices).

[5] Cf. Sections 15.7 and 15.8 of Hardy and Wright's classic *The Theory of Numbers* (4th ed., 1960). The first (1938) edition had not yet appeared when I audited Hardy's course.

[6] See especially his "Zur Algebra der Funktionaloperatoren ...", *Math. Annales* **102** (1929), 370–427 (*Collected Works*, vol. ii, #2), which made use of other "modern" algebraic ideas.

[7] *Ann. Math.* **37** (1936), 456–82. Their footnote on page 482 reviews their earlier work, of which I had been unaware when I submitted my paper (Feb. 1, 1934).

[8] See M. K. Bennett, in pp. 436–43 of *Symposium on Order* (Ivan Rival, ed.), Reidel, 1982.

[9] See *Am. J. Math.* **57** (1935), 507–33 and 800–4; also ibid. **58** (1936), 236–40.

[10] Similar questions had been asked by E. V. Huntington already in *Trans. Am. Math. Soc.* **5** (1940), 288–309.

[11] Numbers in parantheses refer to the four references listed below. I have appended similar short lists of references to some of my other summaries. (G.B.)

[Extracted from the *Proceedings of the Cambridge Philosophical Society*, Vol. XXIX. Pt. IV.]

On the combination of subalgebras. By GARRETT BIRKHOFF*. (Communicated by Mr P. HALL.)

[*Received* 15 May, *read* 30 October 1933.]

I. *Generalities.*

1. *Introduction.* The purpose of this paper is to provide a point of vantage from which to attack combinatorial problems in what may be termed modern†, synthetic, or abstract algebra. In this spirit, a research has been made into the consequences and applications of seven or eight axioms, only one [V] of which is itself new‡.

The 'lattice theory' evolved from these leads directly to a number of interesting applications, scattered throughout the paper, in general point-set, group and ring theory. Perhaps the most novel are concerned with the completeness with which a small set of formal rules describes the implications of very general processes—as in Theorems 5·1 and 25·2.

2. *Algebras and subalgebras.* Let $\mathfrak{C}$ be any class of 'elements', and let $\mathfrak{D}$ denote the 'space' of the ordered sets σ of elements of $\mathfrak{C}$. Let F be a class of 'operators' $f_1, f_2, f_3, \ldots$. Let further each f_i of F assign, to any 'point' in a certain domain $\mathfrak{D}_i$ of $\mathfrak{D}$, an element $f_i(\sigma)$ of $\mathfrak{C}$. Then the couple $(\mathfrak{C}, F)$ will be defined to be a *generalized algebra,* to be called, for shortness in this paper, *algebra.*

A subclass $\mathfrak{S}$ of $\mathfrak{C}$ is said to be *closed* if and only if the hypothesis that σ lies in $\mathfrak{D}_i$ and its elements lie in $\mathfrak{S}$ implies the conclusion that $f_i(\sigma)$ lies in $\mathfrak{S}$. It is fairly obvious that we have

THEOREM 2·1: *If* $(\mathfrak{C}, F)$ *is an algebra, and* $\mathfrak{S}$ *is a closed subclass of* $\mathfrak{C}$, *then* $(\mathfrak{S}, F)$ *is itself an algebra.*

For this reason $(\mathfrak{S}, F)$ will be called a *subalgebra* of $(\mathfrak{C}, F)$.

Let Π be any collection of subalgebras S_k of $(\mathfrak{C}, F)$. By the *meet* $\Delta\{\Pi\}$ of Π we mean the set of elements in every S_k of Π. If σ lies in $\mathfrak{D}_i$ and its elements in $\Delta\{\Pi\}$, then its elements lie in

* Henry Fellow at Trinity College, Cambridge. I wish to thank Mr Philip Hall of King's College for many helpful suggestions and criticisms.

† In the sense of van der Waerden's *Moderne Algebra*, 2 vols. (Berlin, 1930–1). A technical definition is given in section 2, which includes groups, rings, the synthetic algebras of modern writers, Boolean algebra, and the topology of Frechet (the operation being the limit point of a sequence).

‡ Cf. F. Klein's "Abstrakte Verknüpfungen", *Math. Ann.* 105 (1931), 308, and his "Zerlegungssatz bei abstrakte Verknüpfungen", *Math. Ann.* 106 (1932), 114. These will be cited in later references as K 1 and K 2. The following papers by R. Remak, *Journal für Math.* 162 (1930), 1–16; 163 (1930), 1–44; 164 (1931), 197–242; 165 (1931), 159–79; 166 (1932), 65–100; 167 (1932), 360–78, have been very suggestive to the author.

any S_k; hence so does $f_i(\sigma)$, and $f_i(\sigma)$ is in $\Delta\{\Pi\}$. Therefore $\Delta\{\Pi\}$ is itself a subalgebra. Evidently $\Delta\{\Pi\}$ is contained in every S_k.

By the *join* $\Lambda\{\Pi\}$ of Π we mean the meet of those subalgebras of $(\mathfrak{C}, F)$ which contain every S_k. $\Lambda\{\Pi\}$ is by the preceding paragraph a subalgebra, and evidently contains every S_k.

3. *Lattices.* Let $(\mathfrak{C}, F)$ be any algebra, and let $\mathfrak{A}$ denote any set of subalgebras of $(\mathfrak{C}, F)$, closed with respect to the operations of join and meet. If we regard the subalgebras as elements of $\mathfrak{A}$, then

$\overline{\text{I}}$. Any class Π of elements of $\mathfrak{A}$ has a meet $\Delta\{\Pi\}$ in $\mathfrak{A}$, and a join $\Lambda\{\Pi\}$ in $\mathfrak{A}$. If Π contains just one element A, then $\Delta\{\Pi\} = \Lambda\{\Pi\} = A$.

$\overline{\text{II}}$. If every element of Π_1 is in Π_2, and every element of Π_2 is in Π_1, then $\Delta\{\Pi_1\} = \Delta\{\Pi_2\}$ and $\Lambda\{\Pi_1\} = \Lambda\{\Pi_2\}$.

$\overline{\text{III}}$. Let $\mathfrak{F}$ be any set of classes Π_k of elements of $\mathfrak{A}$, and let $\mathfrak{S}$ be the sum of the Π_k. If $\mathfrak{F}_\delta$ denotes the class of the $\Delta\{\Pi_k\}$, and $\mathfrak{F}_\lambda$ that of the $\Lambda\{\Pi_k\}$, then $\Delta\{\mathfrak{F}_\delta\} = \Delta\{\mathfrak{S}\}$, and $\Lambda\{\mathfrak{F}_\lambda\} = \Lambda\{\mathfrak{S}\}$.

$\overline{\text{IV}}$. If Π contains just two elements A and B, then $\Delta\{\Pi\} = A$ implies $\Lambda\{\Pi\} = B$, and conversely.

If we define a *lattice* to be any set of elements satisfying $\overline{\text{I}}$–$\overline{\text{IV}}$, we can express our results as

THEOREM 3·1: *The subalgebras of any algebra constitute a lattice.*

Since a lattice is an algebra in the sense of § 2, the sublattices of a lattice themselves constitute a lattice.

4. *Finite lattices.* By use of finite induction, we can often prove properties of finite lattices without being able to generalize the proofs. For finite lattices, we shall find it useful to substitute for $\overline{\text{I}}$–$\overline{\text{IV}}$ the following equivalent and more familiar properties*:

I. Any two elements A and B of $\mathfrak{A}$ have a meet† (A, B) in $\mathfrak{A}$ and a join $A \cap B$ in $\mathfrak{A}$.

II. $(A, A) = A \cap A = A$, irrespective of A.

III *a.* $(A, B) = (B, A)$ and $A \cap B = B \cap A$.

III *b.* $(A, (B, C)) = ((A, B), C) \equiv (A, B, C)$ and

$$A \cap (B \cap C) = (A \cap B) \cap C \equiv A \cap B \cap C.$$

IV. If $(A, B) = A$, then $A \cap B = B$, and conversely. In this case we write $A \subset B$ or $B \supset A$, and say 'A is contained in B', or 'B contains A'.

* Klein calls a finite lattice a "Verband" in K 2; a sublattice an "Unterverband". He calls a finite C-lattice (which we shall define later) an "A-Menge" in K 1.

† van der Waerden (*Moderne Algebra*, 1, p. 37) calls $\mathfrak{A}$ a system of double composition. He (*ibid.* p. 60) inverts the symbols (,) and $\cap$. Our usage of (,) for common part is, however, more widely accepted.

From the remarkable symmetry in both sets of axioms, there follows

THEOREM 4·1: *Every lattice or theorem concerning lattices has a symmetric counterpart obtainable by the substitutions* τ:

$$(,) \rightleftarrows \cap,\ \supset \rightleftarrows \subset.$$

Further, since from $A \subset B$ and $A \supset B$ follows $A = (A, B) = B$, we have

THEOREM 4·2: *If* $A \subset B$ *and* $A \supset B$, *then* $A = B$.

5. *Completeness of axioms.* Conversely, suppose that we are given any lattice $\mathfrak{L}$ of elements L_i. Let us define an algebra $(\mathfrak{C}, F)$ whose elements C and operators f_i are alike in (1, 1) correspondence with the elements of $\mathfrak{L}$. Let $\mathfrak{D}_i$ consist of all ordered sets Γ of the C_k, corresponding to each of which will be a Π in $\mathfrak{L}$. Finally, define $f_i(\Gamma)$ to correspond to $(L_i, \Lambda\{\Pi\})$.

Then the elements of any subalgebra of $\mathfrak{C}$ (i) are in (1, 1) correspondence with the elements of some sublattice of $\mathfrak{L}$, (ii) include all elements which correspond to elements contained in the join of the elements of this sublattice. But, conversely, the set of elements of $\mathfrak{C}$ corresponding to the elements contained in any element L_i of $\mathfrak{L}$ is a subalgebra. This establishes a (1, 1) correspondence ϕ between the subalgebras of $(\mathfrak{C}, F)$ and the elements of $\mathfrak{L}$.

Finally, the meet of subalgebras corresponds under ϕ to the meet of the corresponding elements of $\mathfrak{L}$, and the join to their join. That is, the lattice of the subalgebras of $(\mathfrak{C}, F)$ is abstractly identical with the given lattice. Combining with Theorem 3·1, we get

THEOREM 5·1: *The algebras of subalgebras with respect to join and meet are collectively identical with the algebras of lattices.*

6. *Elementary consequences.* The symmetry expressed in Theorem 4·1 combined with that of Postulate III *a* enables us to make two or four symmetric deductions from a single argument. Thus we can infer, from $A \cap B = (A \cap A) \cap B = A \cap (A \cap B)$,

THEOREM 6·1: $A \cap B \supset A$, $A \cap B \supset B$; $(A, B) \subset A$, $(A, B) \subset B$.

And since $A \cap B = A$ and $B \cap C = B$ imply

$$A = A \cap B = A \cap (B \cap C) = (A \cap B) \cap C = A \cap C,$$

we have

THEOREM 6·2: $A \supset B$ *and* $B \supset C$ *imply* $A \supset C$; $A \subset B$ *and* $B \subset C$ *imply* $A \subset C$.

COROLLARY 6·2: $A \cap B \supset (A, B)$.

29-2

We shall find the following general principle very useful:

THEOREM 6·3: *If to every element of* Π *there corresponds an element of* Π' *which contains it, then* $\Lambda\{\Pi\} \subset \Lambda\{\Pi'\}$. *If to every element of* Π *there corresponds an element of* Π' *which is contained in it, then* $\Delta\{\Pi\} \supset \Delta\{\Pi'\}$.

To prove the first assertion, let $\Sigma = \Pi + \Pi'$.

$$\Lambda\{\Sigma\} = \Lambda\{\Pi\} \cap \Lambda\{\Pi'\},$$

by $\overline{\text{III}}$. Let Γ contain every element S_k' of Π' and every join $S_i \cap S_k'$ satisfying $S_i \subset \Pi$ and $S_i \subset S_k'$. $\Lambda\{\Gamma\} = \Lambda\{\Pi'\}$ will follow from $\overline{\text{II}}$. But by hypothesis, $\overline{\text{II}}$ and $\overline{\text{III}}$, $\Lambda\{\Gamma\} = \Lambda\{\Pi\} \cap \Lambda\{\Pi'\}$. The first assertion is then merely the identity

$$\Lambda\{\Pi'\} = \Lambda\{\Gamma\} = \Lambda\{\Sigma\} = \Lambda\{\Pi\} \cap \Lambda\{\Pi'\}.$$

The second assertion is a consequence of the first and Theorem 4·1.

COROLLARY 6·3: *Let* S *be any element of a lattice* $\mathfrak{C}$, *defined by a finite succession of meets and joins from given elements of* $\mathfrak{C}$. *If we substitute containing (contained) elements for the given elements, the resulting element contains (is contained in)* S.

Corollary 6·3 holds for simple meets and joins by Theorem 6·3; as stated it is the direct consequence of this fact and induction.

Triple application of Theorem 6·3 shows us that if we have any class $\mathfrak{B}$ of elements B_k of $\mathfrak{C}$, and let $\mathfrak{B}'$ denote the class of elements (A, B_k), (1) since $(A, B_k) \subset B_k$, then $\Lambda\{\mathfrak{B}'\} \subset \Lambda\{\mathfrak{B}\}$; (2) since $(A, B_k) = A$, then $\Lambda\{\mathfrak{B}'\} \subset A$; (3) therefore $\Lambda\{\mathfrak{B}'\} \subset (A, \Lambda\{\mathfrak{B}\})$. Thus we have

THEOREM 6·4: *Let* $\mathfrak{B}$ *be any class of elements* B_k *of* $\mathfrak{C}$, *and* A *any element of* $\mathfrak{C}$. *If* $\mathfrak{B}'$ *and* $\mathfrak{B}''$ *denote respectively the classes of elements* (A, B_k) *and* $A \cap B_k$, *then*

$$(A, \Lambda\{\mathfrak{B}\}) \supset \Lambda\{\mathfrak{B}'\} \quad \textit{and} \quad A \cap \Delta\{\mathfrak{B}\} \subset \Delta\{\mathfrak{B}''\}.$$

COROLLARY 6·4*: $(A, B \cap C) \supset (A, B) \cap (A, C)$ *and*

$$A \cap (B, C) \subset (A \cap B, A \cap C).$$

Hence if $A \subset C$, $\quad A \cap (B, C) \subset (A \cap B, C)$;

that is, if $C \supset A$, $\quad (C, B \cap A) \supset (C, B) \cap A$.

7. *New definitions.* Let $\mathfrak{C}$ be any finite lattice. Let its order be denoted by ω, and its elements by $A_1, \ldots, A_\omega$. Further, let $M \equiv \Delta\{\mathfrak{C}\}$ and $J \equiv \Lambda\{\mathfrak{C}\}$. Then by Theorem 6·1, $M \subset A_k \subset J$, irrespective of k.

We shall now introduce a refinement of notation. By $A_i > A_j$ or $A_j < A_i$ we mean $A_i \supset A_j$ but $A_i \neq A_j$. In this case we say that

* Theorem 6·1 and Corollary 6·4 are proved in K 2.

A_i is *over* A_j, and A_j *under* A_i. A_i is said to *cover* A_j if and only if it is over A_j and over no element which is itself over A_j. In this case, A_j is said to be *covered by* A_i.

Similarly, let $\mathfrak{C}$ be any sublattice of $\mathfrak{C}$; i.e. a subclass of $\mathfrak{C}$ which contains the meet and join of any pair of its own elements. A_k is said to cover $\mathfrak{C}$ if and only if (i) A_k is not in $\mathfrak{C}$, (ii) $A_k \supset A_{k'}$, for some $A_{k'}$ in $\mathfrak{C}$, (iii) $A_k > A_{k''}$, then $A_{k''}$ does not satisfy (i) and (ii).

A *chain* $\widehat{AB}$ *connecting* A *with* B is defined to be any sequence of elements of which the first is A, the last is B, and each covers the preceding. By starting with $A < B$, and interpolating terms when possible, we see by exhaustion that, since $X_1 < X_2 < \ldots < X_n = X_1$ is impossible by Theorem 6·2, we have

THEOREM 7·1: *If* $A < B$ *are two elements of a finite lattice, then a chain* $\widehat{AB}: A = X_0 < \ldots < X_n = B$ *exists, connecting* A *with* B.

II. *B-lattices.*

8. *Definition.* In the following sections we consider a particular class of lattices, which we shall call *B-lattices*. By a B-lattice is meant any lattice satisfying

V. If $A \subset C$, then $A \cap (B, C) = (A \cap B, C)$.

V, taken in conjunction with I–IV, is invariant under the substitution of Theorem 4·1; hence that as well as all other theorems of §§ 4–7 are true for B-lattices.

THEOREM 8·1: *The following two conditions are consequences of* V:

(ξ) *If* A *and* B *cover* C, *and* $A \neq B$, *then* $A \cap B$ *covers* A *and* B.

(ξ') *If* C *covers* A *and* B, *and* $A \neq B$, *then* A *and* B *cover* (A, B).

On account of symmetry, it will suffice to prove that A covers (A, B) in (ξ'). But $(A, B) \subset A$ by Theorem 6·1. If $(A, B) = A$, then $A \subset B$. But $A \neq B$, hence $A < B < C$ would follow. Consequently $(A, B) \neq A$, and $(A, B) < A$.

Suppose now that $(A, B) < X < A$, for some X. Then

$$B \cap (A, B) \subset B \cap X \subset B \cap A,$$

by Corollary 6·3, whence $B \subset B \cap X \subset C$. Since C covers B, this would imply either $B \cap X = B$ or $B \cap X = C$. But, if $B \cap X = B$, then $X \subset B$ as well as $X \subset A$, and $X \subset (A, B)$, contradicting $(A, B) < X$. If $B \cap X = C$, then $(A, B \cap X) = (A, C) = A$; yet, since $X < A$, by V, $(A, B \cap X) = (A, B) \cap X = X$, contradicting $X < A$.

If $X_0 < X_1 < X_2 < \ldots < X_n$ is a chain $\widehat{X_0 X_n}$ connecting X_0 with X_n, then n is known as the *length* of $X_0 X_n$. We can prove

THEOREM 8·2: *In a finite lattice,* (ξ) *and likewise* (ξ') *implies that, if a chain* $\widehat{AB}$ *of length n exists, then any chain* $\widehat{AB'}$ *connecting A with B is of length n.*

Theorem 8·2 holds for $n = 1$, since in that case B covers A, and there is only one chain $\widehat{AB}$. Suppose that Theorem 8·2 holds for $n = 1, \ldots, N$, and that $\widehat{AB} : A = X_0 < \ldots < X_{N+1} = B$ exists. Let $\widehat{AB'} : A = Y_0 < \ldots < Y_\tau = B$ be any second chain connecting A with B.

Either $X_1 = Y_1$, or $X_1 \neq Y_1$. If $X_1 = Y_1$, then $Y_1 < \ldots < Y_\tau = B$ must be of length N, since $Y_1 = X_1 < \ldots < X_{N+1} = B$ is. If $X_1 \neq Y_1$, then, by Theorem 8·1, $X_1 \cap Y_1$ covers X_1 and Y_1, while, by Theorem 6·3, $X_1 \cap Y_1 \subset B$. Hence by Theorem 7·1 we can form a chain $X_1 < X_1 \cap Y_1 < \ldots < B$ of length N [since $X_1 < X_2 < \ldots < B$ is of length N] connecting X_1 with B. Transposing the part $X_1 \cap Y_1 < \ldots < B$, we can form a chain $Y_1 < X_1 \cap Y_1 < \ldots < B$, of length N. Therefore $Y_1 < Y_2 < \ldots < Y_\tau = B$ is of length N in this case also. Or, in any case, $\widehat{AB'}$ is of length $N + 1$.

9. *Rank.* Let $\mathfrak{L}$ be any finite lattice satisfying (ξ) or (ξ'); let $M \equiv \Delta\{\mathfrak{L}\}$ and $J \equiv \Lambda\{\mathfrak{L}\}$. By Theorem 7·1, $\widehat{MJ}$ exists, and, by Theorem 8·2, any two $\widehat{MJ}$ have the same length $\rho\{\mathfrak{L}\}$. $\rho\{\mathfrak{L}\}$ is known as the *rank* of $\mathfrak{L}$. Similarly $\rho\{A\}$, the length of $\widehat{MA}$, is known as the *rank* of A. We can immediately see that the rank of any element covering A is $\rho\{A\} + 1$, and that of any element covered by A is $\rho\{A\} - 1$.

Suppose that $\mathfrak{L}$ satisfies (ξ). In $\mathfrak{L}$ let, moreover, A cover C, $X > C$, and $X \not\supset A$. Construct $C = C_0 < C_1 < \ldots < C_n = X$ connecting C with X. $C_1 \neq A$, since $A \not\subset X$; hence, by (ξ), $C_1 \cap A$ covers C_1, $X > C_1$, and $X \not\supset C_1 \cap A$ [$n \neq 1$]. But, if $C_k \cap A$ covers C_k, $X > C_k$, and $X \not\supset C_k \cap A$, then $C_{k+1} \neq A \cap C_k$ [since $C_k \cap A \not\subset X$]; hence, by (ξ), $C_{k+1} \cap A \cap C_k = C_{k+1} \cap A$ covers C_{k+1} [$k \neq n$], $X > C_{k+1}$ [$k + 1 \neq n$], and $X \not\supset C_{k+1} \cap A$. By finite induction, we conclude that $C_n \cap A$ covers C_n, whence we have

THEOREM 9·1: *If* (ξ) *holds in a finite lattice* $\mathfrak{L}$, *then in* $\mathfrak{L}$ *the statements that A covers C,* $X > C$, *and* $X \not\supset A$ *imply that* $A \cap X$ *covers X. Similarly, if* (ξ') *holds, the statements that C covers A,* $X < C$, *and* $X \not\subset A$ *imply that X covers* (A, X).

THEOREM 9·2: (ξ) *implies that*

$$\rho\{A \cap B\} - \rho\{B\} \leqq \rho\{A\} - \rho\{(A, B)\}.$$

Similarly (ξ') *implies that* $\rho\{A\} - \rho\{(A, B)\} \leqq \rho\{A \cap B\} - \rho\{B\}$.

To prove the first assertion, form the chain

$$A = A_0 > A_1 > \ldots > A_m = (A, B),$$

and consider A_{k-1} and $A_k \cap B$. Either $A_{k-1} \subset A_k \cap B$, and

$$A_{k-1} \cap B = A_k \cap B,$$

or

$$A_{k-1} \not\subset A_k \cap B, \quad A_k \cap B > A_k,$$

and A_k covers A_{k-1}, whence $A_{k-1} \cap B$ covers $A_k \cap B$. Therefore $\rho\{A_{k-1} \cap B\} - \rho\{A_k \cap B\}$ is 0 or 1, and

$$\rho\{A \cap B\} - \rho\{A\} \leqq m = \rho\{A\} - \rho\{(A, B)\}.$$

The second assertion follows from the first and Theorem 4·1.

COROLLARY 9·2: *If* (ξ) *and* (ξ') *hold, then the rank satisfies*

$$\rho\{A\} + \rho\{B\} = \rho\{A \cap B\} + \rho\{(A, B)\},$$

and $A > B$ *implies that* $\rho\{A\} > \rho\{B\}$.

Consider the lattice corresponding to the (composition) subgroups of the octic group. It satisfies (ξ'), yet it is not a B-lattice. This shows that 1° neither subgroups nor composition subgroups necessarily constitute B-lattices, and 2° (ξ) and (ξ') taken separately do not imply the conclusions of Corollary 9·2.

10. *Conclusion.* Let now $\mathfrak{B}$ be any lattice in which the conclusions of Corollary 9·2 hold. In $\mathfrak{B}$, it will then be true for any three elements A, X, C that:

$$\rho\{(A \cap X) \cap C\} + \rho\{A \cap X, C\} = \rho\{A \cap X\} + \rho\{C\},$$

$$\rho\{(A, (X, C))\} + \rho\{A \cap (X, C)\} = \rho\{A\} + \rho\{(X, C)\}.$$

If also $A \subset C$, then $(A \cap X) \cap C = X \cap C$, and $(A, (X, C)) = (A, X)$, whence after subtraction and transposition we have

$$\begin{aligned}\rho\{(A \cap X, C)\} - \rho\{A \cap (X, C)\} &= [\rho\{A \cap X\} + \rho\{(A, X)\} - \rho\{A\}] \\ &\quad - [\rho\{X \cap C\} + \rho\{(X, C)\} - \rho\{C\}] \\ &= \rho\{X\} - \rho\{X\} = 0.\end{aligned}$$

But, by Corollary 6·4, $A \subset C$ implies $A \cap (X, C) \subset (A \cap X, C)$. Therefore, if $A \cap (X, C) \neq (A \cap X, C)$, by Corollary 9·2

$$\rho\{A \cap (X, C)\} < \rho\{(A \cap X, C)\},$$

and we have just eliminated this possibility. Consequently $A \subset C$ implies $A \cap (X, C) = (A \cap X, C)$, and we have

THEOREM 10·1: *If the conclusions of Corollary* 9·2 *hold in the lattice* $\mathfrak{B}$, *then* $\mathfrak{B}$ *is a* B*-lattice.*

Combining Theorem 8·1, Corollary 9·2 and Theorem 10·1, we obtain

THEOREM 10·2: *In a finite lattice $\mathfrak{L}$, the following three sets of conditions are equivalent:*

(1) *$A \subset C$ implies $A \cap (X, C) = (A \cap X, C)$.*

(2) *If A and B cover C, and $A \neq B$, then $A \cap B$ covers A and B. If C covers A and B, and $A \neq B$, then A and B cover (A, B).*

(3) *To every element L of $\mathfrak{L}$ we can assign a number $\rho\{L\}$, satisfying*

(α) *$L > M$ implies $\rho\{L\} > \rho\{M\}$,*

(β) $\rho\{L\} + \rho\{M\} = \rho\{(L, M)\} + \rho\{L \cap M\}$.

11. *B-lattice property.* Let $\mathfrak{B}$ be any finite B-lattice, and let $M \equiv \Delta\{\mathfrak{B}\}$. We can easily prove

THEOREM 11·1: *If $X_1, \ldots, X_n$ cover M, and*

$$Y \subset X_1 \cap \ldots \cap X_n \equiv \bar{X},$$

then $X_k \not\subset Y \cap X_1 \cap \ldots \cap X_{k-1}$ for just $\rho\{\bar{X}\} - \rho\{Y\}$ integers k.

For, if $X_k \not\subset Y \cap X_1 \cap \ldots \cap X_{k-1}$, then

$$\rho\{Y \cap X_1 \cap \ldots \cap X_k\} - \rho\{Y \cap X_1 \cap \ldots \cap X_{k-1}\} = 1$$

by Theorem 9·1; in the contrary case,

$$\rho\{Y \cap X_1 \cap \ldots \cap X_k\} - \rho\{Y \cap X_1 \cap \ldots \cap X_{k-1}\} = 0.$$

Summing the differences from $k = 1$ to $k = n$, we have the theorem. It follows as a corollary that, if q denotes the number of integers k for which $X_k \subset X_1 \cap \ldots \cap X_{k-1}$, then $X_k \subset Y \cap X_1 \cap \ldots \cap X_{k-1}$ for just $\rho\{Y\} + q$ integers k.

Suppose that X covers M, while Y is an element of greatest rank not containing X. Then, if X_k covers M, either $Y \supset X_k$ or $Y \not\supset X_k$ and $X_k \cap Y \supset X$. But in the latter case

$$\rho\{X \cap (X_k \cap Y)\} = \rho\{X_k \cap Y\} = \rho\{Y\} + 1 = \rho\{X \cap Y\};$$

and $X \cap Y \supset X_k$. Hence in either case $X \cap Y \supset X_k$. That is, we have

THEOREM 11·2: *If X covers M, $Y \not\supset X$, and $\rho\{Y\}$ is as large as is compatible with $Y \not\supset X$, then $Y \cap X$ contains every element covering M.*

And if in $\mathfrak{B}$ we confine our attention to the B-sublattice of elements containing a given element F, and contained in the join G of the elements F_k which cover F, we see that no F_k is contained in *every* element G_k covered by G, for otherwise by Theorem 11·2 an element of rank $\rho\{G\}-1$ would contain every F_k, hence G, which is absurd. Thus we have

THEOREM 11·3: *Let F be any element of $\mathfrak{B}$, let $F_1, \ldots, F_\omega$ denote the elements covering, and $F_1', \ldots, F_{\omega'}'$ those covered by, F. If G denotes $F_1 \cap \ldots \cap F_\omega$, G' denotes $(F_1', \ldots, F_{\omega'}')$, $G_1, \ldots, G_\chi$ the elements covered by G, and $G_1', \ldots, G_{\chi'}'$ those covering G', then*

$$(G_1, \ldots, G_\chi) = F = G_1' \cap \ldots \cap G_{\chi'}'.$$

THEOREM 11·4: *If $X_1, \ldots, X_\omega$ are the elements covering M, and $Y \subset X_1 \cap \ldots \cap X_\omega$, then Y is the join of the X_k which it contains.*

For suppose the contrary to be true, and let $\rho\{Y\}$ be as small as possible. Let $\bar{Y}$ be the join of the X_k contained in Y;

$$\rho\{\bar{Y}\} = \rho\{Y\} - 1.$$

Also, $\bar{Y}$ is the only element covered by Y; if another, say Z, existed we should have $Y = \bar{Y} \cap Z$, and Y would be the join of the X_k which $\bar{Y}$ and Z, hence Y itself, contained.

Moreover, letting $W_1, \ldots, W_\chi$ denote the elements covered by $X_1 \cap \ldots \cap X_\omega$, we get $(W_k, Y) \supset \bar{Y}$ [through study of rank] irrespective of k. Hence $(W_1, \ldots, W_\chi, Y) \supset \bar{Y}$, $M \supset \bar{Y}$ by Theorem 11·3, and Y itself covers M.

III. *B-sublattice generated by three elements.*

12. *Notation.* Let G_1, G_2, G_3 be any three elements of a B-lattice. Let us define from them the following elements:

TABLE I.

$F_k \equiv (G_i, G_j)$	$F \equiv (G_1, G_2, G_3)$	$H \equiv G_1 \cap G_2 \cap G_3$
$H_k \equiv G_i \cap G_j$	$A_k \equiv F_i \cap F_j$	$A \equiv F_1 \cap F_2 \cap F_3$
$B \equiv (H_1, H_2, H_3)$	$B_k \equiv (H_i, H_j)$	$M_k \equiv G_k \cap F_k$
$C_k \equiv F_k \cap (G_k, H_k) = [\text{by V}] = (H_k, G_k \cap F_k)$		$N_k \equiv (G_k, H_k)$

different alphabetical subscripts being understood to imply different numerical subscripts. This notation and understanding will be used throughout this portion of the paper.

13. *Tables of combination.* We observe that $(F, X) = F$, $F \cap X = X$, $(H, X) = X$, and $H \cap X = H$, for any X of Table I. Proper use of Postulates I–V gives us the meet of any other pair of elements of Table I. The results of systematic reduction are stated in Table II.

Theorem 4·1, and the remark that, if we keep the G_k fixed, and interchange the operations of meeting and joining, we merely

TABLE II.

	F_j	F_k	A_j	A_k	A	N_j	N_k	G_j	G_k	C_j	C_k	M_j	M_k	B	B_j	B_k	H_j	H_k
F_k	F	F_k	F_k	F	F_k	F_k	F	F_k	F_k	F_k	F_k	F_k	F_k	F_k	F_k	F_k	F_k	F_k
A_k	F_j	F	F_i	A_k	A_k	F_i	A_k	F_i	A_k	A_k	A_k	A_k	A_k	A_k	A_k	A_k	A_k	A_k
A	F_j	F_k	A_j	A_k	A	A_j	A_k	A_j	A_k	A	A	A	A	A	A	A	A	A
N_k	F_j	F	F_i	A_k	A_k	F_i	N_k	F_i	N_k	A_k	N_k	A_k	N_k	N_k	N_k	N_k	N_k	N_k
G_k	F_j	F	F_i	A_k	A_k	F_i	N_k	F_i	G_k	A_k	N_k	A_k	G_k	N_k	N_k	G_k	G_k	G_k
C_k	F_j	F_k	A_j	A_k	A	A_j	N_k	A_j	N_k	A	C_k	A	C_k	C_k	C_k	C_k	C_k	C_k
M_k	F_j	F_k	A_j	A_k	A	A_j	N_k	A_j	N_k	A	C_k	A	M_k	C_k	C_k	M_k	M_k	C_k
B	F_j	F_k	A_j	A_k	A	N_j	N_k	N_j	N_k	C_j	C_k	C_j	C_k	B	B	B	B	B
B_k	F_j	F_k	A_j	A_k	A	N_j	N_k	N_j	G_k	C_j	C_k	C_j	M_k	B	B	B_k	B_k	B
H_k	F_j	F_k	A_j	A_k	A	N_j	N_k	G_j	N_k	C_j	C_k	M_j	C_k	B	B_j	B	B_i	H_k

TABLE III.

	H_j	H_k	B_j	B_k	B	M_j	M_k	G_j	G_k	C_j	C_k	N_j	N_k	A	A_j	A_k	F_j	F_k
H_k	H	H_k	H_k	H	H_k	H_k	H	H_k	H	H_k	H_k	H_k	H_k	H_k	H_k	H_k	H_k	H_k
B_k	H_j	H	H_i	B_k	B_k	H_i	B_k	H_i	B_k	B_k	B_k	B_k	B_k	B_k	B_k	B_k	B_k	B_k
B	H_j	H_k	B_j	B_k	B	B_j	B_k	B_j	B_k	B	B	B	B	B	B	B	B	B
M_k	H_j	H	H_i	B_k	B_k	H_i	M_k	H_i	M_k	B_k	M_k	B_k	M_k	M_k	M_k	M_k	M_k	M_k
G_k	H_j	H	H_i	B_k	B_k	H_i	M_k	H_i	G_k	B_k	M_k	B_k	G_k	M_k	M_k	G_k	G_k	M_k
C_k	H_j	H_k	B_j	B_k	B	B_j	M_k	B_j	M_k	B	C_k	B	C_k	C_k	C_k	C_k	C_k	C_k
N_k	H_j	H_k	B_j	B_k	B	B_j	M_k	B_j	M_k	B	C_k	B	N_k	C_k	C_k	N_k	N_k	C_k
A	H_j	H_k	B_j	B_k	B	M_j	M_k	M_j	M_k	C_j	C_k	C_j	C_k	A	A	A	A	A
A_k	H_j	H_k	B_j	B_k	B	M_j	M_k	M_j	G_k	C_j	C_k	C_j	N_k	A	A	A_k	A_k	A
F_k	H_j	H_k	B_j	B_k	B	M_j	M_k	G_j	M_k	C_j	C_k	N_j	C_k	A	A_j	A	A_i	F_k

interchange the columns of Table I, enable us to read off the table of joins from the table of meets. Alternatively, reapplication of Postulates I–V gives us Table III.

14. *Consequences.* It follows immediately from Tables II and III that the elements of Table I constitute a sublattice. But, if we regard them as distinct, they still satisfy Postulates I–V. Hence we have

THEOREM 14·1: *The number of distinct elements generated by three elements of a B-lattice has twenty-eight for its maximum value.*

We have also mentioned how, as a consequence of Theorem 4·1, we have

THEOREM 14·2: *Table* III *is identical with Table* II *under the interchange* $H \rightleftarrows F$, $B \rightleftarrows A$, $M \rightleftarrows N$, *subscripts remaining fixed.*

15. *B′-lattices.* By a B'-lattice is meant any B-lattice satisfying

V′. To every pair of elements $X \supset Y$ corresponds an abstract *quotient* X/Y, and the quotient $X \cap Y/X$ is the same as $Y/(X, Y)$ [in symbols $X \cap Y/X \sim Y/(X, Y)$].

Methodical application of V′ to Tables II and III gives us, among others, the following universal relations for B'-lattices:

TABLE IV.

(1) $H/H_k \sim H_j/B_i \sim B_k/B \sim M_k/C_k \sim G_k/N_k$.

(2) $H_i/G_j \sim G_k/F_i \sim B_k/N_j \sim M_k/A_j$, no matter how we choose $i, j \neq i, k \neq j, i$.

(3) $C_k/A \sim B/C_k \sim N_k/A_k \sim B_k/M_k$; *moreover the quotient is invariant under permutations of k.*

(4) $F_k/F \sim A_i/F_j \sim A/A_k \sim C_k/N_k \sim M_k/G_k$.

Since, under τ of Theorem 4·1, $\tau\{X\} \cap \tau\{Y\} = \tau\{(X, Y)\}$ and $(\tau\{X\}, \tau\{Y\}) = \tau\{X \cap Y\}$, it follows that any relation

$$X \cap Y/X \sim Y/(X, Y),$$

which is, expanding through the identity $\tau\{\tau\{X\}\} = X$,

$$\tau\{(\tau\{X\}, \tau\{Y\})\}/\tau\{\tau\{X\}\} \sim \tau\{\tau\{Y\}\}/\tau\{\tau\{X\} \cap \tau\{Y\}\},$$

has a counterpart

$$\tau\{X\}/(\tau\{X\}, \tau\{Y\}) \sim \tau\{X\} \cap \tau\{Y\}/\tau\{Y\}.$$

That is, we have a perfect symmetry between the relations between quotients, and those deducible when we invert and transform by τ.

We then have

THEOREM 15·1: *If $A/B \sim A'/B'$ holds in every B'-lattice, and if τ denotes the substitution join $\rightleftarrows$ meet, then so does*

$$\tau\{B\}/\tau\{A\} \sim \tau\{B'\}/\tau\{A'\}.$$

We observe that, in Theorem 8·1, $C = A \cap B$, whence $C/A \sim B/(A, B)$. It follows that in the proof of Theorem 8·2, the quotients $X_1 \cap Y_1/X_1$ and X_1/A are collectively the same as $X_1 \cap Y_1/Y_1$ and Y_1/A. This gives us, by mere repetition of the inductive reasoning of Theorem 8·2,

THEOREM 15·2 (of Jordan): *Let $A \subset B$ be any two elements of any finite B'-lattice, and let $\widehat{AB}: A = X_0 < \ldots < X_n = B$ and $\widehat{AB}': A = Y_0 < \ldots < Y_n = B$ be any two chains connecting A with B. Then the quotients X_k/X_{k-1} are collectively the same as the quotients Y_k/Y_{k-1}.*

IV. *C-lattices.*

16. *Properties.* By a C-lattice is meant a lattice $\mathfrak{C}$ satisfying*, regardless of the choice of A, B, C in $\mathfrak{C}$,

VI $$(A, B \cap C) = (A, B) \cap (A, C)$$

and $$A \cap (B, C) = (A \cap B, A \cap C).$$

Postulate VI is symmetrical, and implies V. Therefore the theorems of §§ 4–15, except 14·1, are true for C-lattices. In addition, if Roman capitals denote the elements of $\mathfrak{C}$,

$$(\mathrm{A}, \mathrm{B}_1 \cap \ldots \cap \mathrm{B}_n) = (\mathrm{A}, \mathrm{B}_1 \cap \ldots \cap \mathrm{B}_{n-1}) \cap (\mathrm{A}, \mathrm{B}_n)$$

by VI, whence by induction we get

THEOREM 16·1: *If A and $B_1, \ldots, B_n$ are elements of a C-lattice, then $(A, B_1 \cap \ldots \cap B_n) = (A, B_1) \cap \ldots \cap (A, B_n)$, and*

$$A \cap (B_1, \ldots, B_n) = (A \cap B_1, \ldots, A \cap B_n).$$

And from Theorem 16·1 we can proceed to prove†

THEOREM 16·2: $\mathop{\Delta}\limits_{i=1}^{m} \left\{ \mathop{\Lambda}\limits_{j=1}^{n_i} (A_j^i) \right\} = \mathop{\Lambda}\limits_{j_1=1}^{n_1} \ldots \mathop{\Lambda}\limits_{j_m=1}^{n_m} \left\{ \mathop{\Delta}\limits_{i=1}^{m} (A_{j_i}^i) \right\}$, *and similarly* $\mathop{\Lambda}\limits_{i=1}^{m} \left\{ \mathop{\Delta}\limits_{j=1}^{n_i} (A_j^i) \right\} = \mathop{\Delta}\limits_{j_1=1}^{n_1} \ldots \mathop{\Delta}\limits_{j_m=1}^{n_m} \left\{ \mathop{\Lambda}\limits_{i=1}^{m} (A_{j_i}^i) \right\}$, *for arbitrary A_j^i of a C-lattice.*

* By Theorem 4·2 and Corollary 6·4, as has been remarked before [cf. K 2], VI is equivalent to a pair of one-sided inequalities, and V to a single one. But formally, V and VI are simpler, so we use them. Klein calls a C-lattice an "A-menge" in K 1.

† Cf. a similar theorem by W. V. Quine: *Journal London Math. Soc.* 8 (1933), 89.

The theorem is an identity if $m=1$; the general case may be reduced inductively by the chain of equalities

$$\underset{i=1}{\overset{m}{\Delta}}\left\{\underset{j=1}{\overset{n_i}{\Lambda}}(A_j{}^i)\right\}$$

$$=\left(\underset{i=2}{\overset{m}{\Delta}}\left\{\underset{j=1}{\overset{n_i}{\Lambda}}(A_j{}^i)\right\},\ \underset{j_1=1}{\overset{n_1}{\Lambda}}(A_{j_1}{}^1)\right) \qquad [\text{by } \overline{\text{III}}]$$

$$=\underset{j_1=1}{\overset{n_1}{\Lambda}}\left\{\underset{i=2}{\overset{m}{\Delta}}\left\{\underset{j=1}{\overset{n_i}{\Lambda}}(A_j{}^i)\right\},\ A_{j_1}{}^1\right\} \qquad [\text{by Theorem } 16{\cdot}1]$$

$$=\underset{j_1=1}{\overset{n_1}{\Lambda}}\left\{A_{j_1}{}^1,\ \underset{j_2=1}{\overset{n_2}{\Lambda}}\dots\underset{j_m=1}{\overset{n_m}{\Lambda}}\left\{\underset{i=2}{\overset{m}{\Delta}}(A_{j_i}{}^i)\right\}\right\} \ [\text{by induction and } \overline{\text{II}}]$$

$$=\underset{j_1=1}{\overset{n_1}{\Lambda}}\ \underset{j_2=1}{\overset{n_2}{\Lambda}}\dots\underset{j_m=1}{\overset{n_m}{\Lambda}}\left\{\underset{i=1}{\overset{m}{\Delta}}(A_{j_i}{}^i)\right\} \quad [\text{by Theorem } 16{\cdot}1 \text{ and } \overline{\text{III}}].$$

As usual we are using Theorem 4·1 to cut the proof in half.

From Theorem 16·2 we can deduce

THEOREM 16·3: *Any element generated by a finite number of operations upon finite elements A_k of a C-lattice can be expressed as the meet of joins,* and *as the join of meets, of the A_k.*

We can proceed by induction to reduce meets of (joins of meets), through meets of (meets of joins) by Theorem 16·2, to meets of joins by $\overline{\text{III}}$.

17. *Arithmetization.* An important step on the road to the complete arithmetization of finite C-lattices is

THEOREM 17·1: *Let $\mathfrak{C}$ be any finite C-lattice, and $\mathfrak{S}$ any sublattice of $\mathfrak{C}$ which contains every element under $\Lambda\{\mathfrak{S}\}$. Further, let A be any element covering $\mathfrak{S}$* (cf. § 7). *Then*

$$\rho\{(A \cap \Lambda\{\mathfrak{S}\})\} = \rho\{\Lambda\{\mathfrak{S}\}\} + 1,$$

and the sublattice generated by A and $\mathfrak{S}$ contains every element under $(A \cap \Lambda\{\mathfrak{S}\})$.

Let B be any element covered by A. B is in $\mathfrak{S}$, hence $(B \cap \Lambda\{\mathfrak{S}\}) = \Lambda\{\mathfrak{S}\}$. But $A \not\subset \Lambda\{\mathfrak{S}\}$, hence $(A \cap \Lambda\{\mathfrak{S}\}) \neq \Lambda\{\mathfrak{S}\}$. Consequently, by Theorem 9·1, $\rho\{(A \cap \Lambda\{\mathfrak{S}\})\} = \rho\{\Lambda\{\mathfrak{S}\}\} + 1$.

Suppose that $X \subset (A \cap \Lambda\{\mathfrak{S}\})$, so that $X = (X, A \cap \Lambda\{\mathfrak{S}\})$. By Postulate VI, $X = (X, A) \cap (X, \Lambda\{\mathfrak{S}\})$. If $X \not\supset A$, then $(X, A) < A$, and $[A$ covering $\mathfrak{S}]$ $(X, A) \subset \Lambda\{\mathfrak{S}\}$, whence

$$X = (X, A) \cap (X, \Lambda\{\mathfrak{S}\}) \subset \Lambda\{\mathfrak{S}\},$$

and X is generated by $\mathfrak{S}$. If $X \supset A$, then

$$A \cap (X, \Lambda\{\mathfrak{S}\}) = (A \cap X, A \cap \Lambda\{\mathfrak{S}\}) = (X, A \cap \Lambda\{\mathfrak{S}\}) = X,$$

and X is evidently generated by A and $\mathfrak{S}$. Thus the theorem is proved.

Again let $\mathfrak{C}$ be any finite C-lattice, and let ρ denote the rank of $\mathfrak{C}$. We shall reconstruct $\mathfrak{C}$ along simplified lines.

Let P_1 be any element covering $M \equiv \Delta\{\mathfrak{C}\}$. Let

$$P_{k+1} \quad [k = 1, \ldots, \rho - 1]$$

be any element covering the sublattice $\mathfrak{H}_k$ generated by $P_1, \ldots, P_k$. We can argue that

(1) Any element of $\mathfrak{H}_\rho$ is the join* of certain of the P_k, or else M. Hence any element of $\mathfrak{H}_\rho$ is defined by the P_k which it contains.

(2) The rank of $\Lambda\{\mathfrak{H}_\rho\}$ is ρ, by induction and Theorem 17·1, hence $\Lambda\{\mathfrak{H}_\rho\} = J$. For the same reason, $\mathfrak{H}_\rho$ contains every element under J, and $\mathfrak{H}_\rho = \mathfrak{C}$.

(3) If $X \supset P_k$ and $Y \supset P$, $(X, Y) \supset P_k$; conversely, if $(X, Y) \supset P_k$, $X \supset (X, Y) \supset P_k$ and $Y \supset (X, Y) \supset P_k$. Hence (X, Y) contains P_k if and only if X and Y both do.

(4) If $X \supset P_k$ or $Y \supset P_k$, $X \cap Y \supset [X \text{ or } Y] \supset P_k$. Conversely, if neither $X \supset P_k$ nor $Y \supset P_k$, then $(X, P_k) < P_k$ and $(Y, P_k) < P_k$ are in $\mathfrak{H}_{k-1}$; hence $(X \cap Y, P_k) = (X, P_k) \cap (Y, P_k)$ is in $\mathfrak{H}_{k-1}$, and $X \cap Y \not\supset P_k$.

Therefore, taking $X \supset P_k$ in the point-theory sense, we have

THEOREM 17·2: *Let $\mathfrak{C}$ be any finite C-lattice of rank ρ. Then we can identify the elements of $\mathfrak{C}$ with subsets of ρ points, in such a way that the* join *of two elements X and Y of $\mathfrak{C}$ is identified with the* sum *of the subsets identified with X and Y, and the* meet *with their* common part.

If we know which of the P_i contain a given P_{i_0}, by (4) and (1) we know which elements of $\mathfrak{C}$ contain P_{i_0}; hence we know the structure of $\mathfrak{C}$. Moreover, if $i < i_0$, then $P_i \not\supset P_{i_0}$; while if $P_i \supset P_{i'} \supset P_{i_0}$, then $P_i \supset P_{i_0}$. Conversely, to any system of ascribing a selection of $P_{k+1}, \ldots, P_\rho$ to P_k, satisfying the condition that if P_{k+h} is ascribed to P_k, and $P_{k+h+h'}$ to P_{k+h}, then $P_{k+h+h'}$ is ascribed to P_k, there correspond subsets of $P_1, \ldots, P_\rho$ satisfying I, and hence II–VI. That is, we have

THEOREM 17·3: *Any finite C-lattice can be specified by a constant ρ, and a way of assigning* transitively *to each k a selection of the numbers $k+1, \ldots, \rho$. Conversely, each such assignment specifies a C-lattice of rank ρ.*

Moreover, if we consider $\widehat{MJ}$, and observe that each element of a connected chain must be represented by a proper subset of the

* For, by Theorem 16·3, it is the join of certain meets, and any meets are in $\mathfrak{H}_{\rho-1}$, at which point we can use induction and $\overline{\text{III}}$.

next, we see that, in Theorem 17·2, $\mathfrak{C}$ cannot be represented as a class of subsets of fewer than ρ points. Thus we have

THEOREM 17·4: *The rank of any finite C-lattice $\mathfrak{C}$ is the least number ρ such that $\mathfrak{C}$ can be represented as a class of subsets of ρ points.*

18. *Direct join.* Let $\mathfrak{A}$ and $\mathfrak{B}$ be any two algebras of the same kind; i.e. with corresponding f_i and $\mathfrak{D}_i$ [cf. § 2]. Then we can define a *direct join* $\mathfrak{A} \times \mathfrak{B}$ of $\mathfrak{A}$ and $\mathfrak{B}$, by the two conditions*:

(1) The elements of $\mathfrak{A} \times \mathfrak{B}$ consist of all couples $[A, B]$, A being an arbitrary element of $\mathfrak{A}$, and B of $\mathfrak{B}$. A is known as the $\mathfrak{A}$-component, and B as the $\mathfrak{B}$-component, of $[A, B]$.

(2) A given ordered set of elements $[A_k, B_k]$ of $\mathfrak{A} \times \mathfrak{B}$ lies in $\mathfrak{D}_i$ if and only if the components, taken separately, do so; in this case $f_i\{[A_k, B_k]\} \equiv [f_i\{A_k\}, f_i\{B_k\}]$.

We observe that this definition is symmetrical in $\mathfrak{A}$ and $\mathfrak{B}$; i.e. that† $\mathfrak{A} \times \mathfrak{B} \sim \mathfrak{B} \times \mathfrak{A}$, and that the associative law holds; i.e. that $(\mathfrak{A} \times \mathfrak{B}) \times \mathfrak{C} \sim \mathfrak{A} \times (\mathfrak{B} \times \mathfrak{C})$. Also the number $0\{\mathfrak{A} \times \mathfrak{B}\}$ of elements in $\mathfrak{A} \times \mathfrak{B}$ is $0\{\mathfrak{A}\} \times 0\{\mathfrak{B}\}$.

The reader can easily supply the proof of

THEOREM 18·1: *The direct join of two lattices is a lattice; that of two B-lattices is a B-lattice; that of two C-lattices is a C-lattice.*

19. *C-lattices.* In the case of finite C-lattices, we have in addition

THEOREM 19·1: *A necessary and sufficient condition that a finite C-lattice $\mathfrak{C}$ should be the direct join of C-lattices $\mathfrak{C}_1$ and $\mathfrak{C}_2$ of smaller order, is that two elements A and B of $\mathfrak{C}$ other than M and J exist, satisfying $A \cap B = J$ and $(A, B) = M$.*

The condition is necessary. For let J_1 and J_2 be the joins of $\mathfrak{C}_1$ and $\mathfrak{C}_2$ respectively, and M_1 and M_2 their meets. Then certainly $[J_1, M_2] \cap [M_1, J_2] = [J_1, J_2]$, and $([J_1, M_1], [M_2, J_2]) = [M_1, M_2]$. But irrespective of $[C_1, C_2]$, $[J_1, J_2] \cap [C_1, C_2] = [J_1, J_2]$ and $([M_1, M_2], [C_1, C_2]) = [M_1, M_2]$; hence $[M_1, M_2]$ corresponds to the meet M of $\mathfrak{C}$, and $[J_1, J_2]$ to its join J. If $[J_1, M_2]$ corresponded to M, then $J_1 > C_1$ would have no solutions, $\mathfrak{C}_2$ would contain just one element, which contradicts the hypothesis $0\{\mathfrak{C}_2\} = 0\{\mathfrak{C}\}$. Similarly $[J_1, M_2] \neq J$, $[M_1, J_2] \neq M$, and $[M_1, J_2] \neq J$.

* This definition corresponds to the conventional one of direct product for groups, rings, and topological manifolds, and direct sum of linear algebras. The theorems of § 19 are related to the Zerlegungssatz of K 2.

† By $\mathfrak{X} \sim \mathfrak{Y}$ we mean that there exists a (1, 1) correspondence between the elements and operators of $\mathfrak{X}$ and $\mathfrak{Y}$, which preserves $\mathfrak{D}_i$ and the formation of elements by operations. This yields (1, 1) isomorphy in group and ring theory, and homeomorphy in topology.

The condition is sufficient. For let $\mathfrak{C}_1$ consist of those elements C_1 satisfying $C_1 \subset A$, and $\mathfrak{C}_2$ of those elements C_2 satisfying $C_2 \subset B$. Let $[C_1, C_2]$ correspond to $C_1 \cap C_2$. Now since

$$A \cap B = J, \quad X = (X, A \cap B) = (X, A) \cap (X, B);$$

hence every element of $\mathfrak{C}$ corresponds to some element of $\mathfrak{C}_1 \cap \mathfrak{C}_2$. Furthermore, since $(C_1 \cap C_2, A) = (C_1, A) \cap (C_2, A) = C_1 \cap M = C_1$, and (similarly) $(C_1 \cap C_2, B) = C_2$, this correspondence is (1, 1). Finally

$$\begin{aligned}[C_1, C_2] \cap [C_1', C_2'] &= C_1 \cap C \cap C_1' \cap C_2' = [(C_1 \cap C_1') \cap (C_2 \cap C_2')] \\ &= [C_1 \cap C_1', C_2 \cap C_2']\end{aligned}$$

and

$$\begin{aligned}([C_1, C_2], [C_1', C_2']) &= (C_1 \cap C_2, C_1' \cap C_2') \\ &= (C_1, C_1') \cap (C_1, C_2') \cap (C_2, C_1') \cap (C_2, C_2') \\ &= [\text{by } 16\cdot2] = (C_1, C_1') \cap M \cap M \cap (C_2, C_2') \\ &= (C_1, C_1') \cap (C_2, C_2') = [(C_1, C_1'), (C_2, C_2')].\end{aligned}$$

Thus the correspondence preserves joins and meets, and the theorem is proved.

Suppose that $A \cap B = C \cap D = J$, and $(A, B) = (C, D) = M$. Then, by Theorem 16·2, $(A, C) \cap (B, C) \cap (A, D) \cap (B, D) = J$, while obviously $((A, C), (B, C), (A, D), (B, D)) = M$. This, taken in connection* with Theorem 19·1, gives us

THEOREM 19·2: *A finite C-lattice has a unique expression as the direct join of C-lattices not themselves direct joins of C-lattices of lower order. The factors of any expression of the C-lattice as a direct join are direct joins of the factors of this unique decomposition into 'prime' factors.*

20. *Decomposition lemma.* Let $\mathfrak{C}$ be a C-lattice in which Axiom I holds but not Axiom $\bar{\text{I}}$; i.e. in which the operations of join and meet can be applied only to *finite* sets of elements. Further, suppose that the elements of $\mathfrak{C}$ can be well-ordered. We shall show that $\mathfrak{C}$ is isomorphic with a class of sets of points of a suitably chosen manifold, with respect to the operations of join and meet upon finite subclasses of these sets. But first we must demonstrate the truth of a preliminary

LEMMA: *If $\mathfrak{A}$ and $\mathfrak{B}$ are two disjoint sublattices of $\mathfrak{C}$ having the property that $X \cap B \supset A$ [A in $\mathfrak{A}$, B in $\mathfrak{B}$] implies that X is in $\mathfrak{B}$, and $(Y, A) \subset B$ that Y is in $\mathfrak{A}$, and if B' is neither in $\mathfrak{A}$ nor in $\mathfrak{B}$, then by augmenting $\mathfrak{A}$ by all elements X satisfying $X \cap B \cap B' \supset A$, and $\mathfrak{B}$ by all elements Y satisfying $(Y, A) \subset B \cap B'$, we get two disjoint sublattices having the same property.*

* Strictly, we should show in detail that, if $\mathfrak{C}_1 \times \mathfrak{C}_2 = \mathfrak{C}$, then the sublattices (C_1, M) and (M, C_2) correspond to the factors which are discussed in the preceding paragraph.

The distributive axiom shows that we get sublattices. To see that they are disjoint we observe that $(Y, A) \subset B \cap B'$ implies $(Y \cap B \cap B', A \cap B \cap B') = B \cap B'$. But $A \cap B \cap B' \subset \mathfrak{A}$; hence from $Y \cap B \cap B' \subset \mathfrak{A}$ would follow $B \cap B' \subset \mathfrak{A}$, and hence $B' \subset \mathfrak{A}$, which is contrary to hypothesis.

Suppose that U is in $\mathfrak{A}$ augmented, and V in $\mathfrak{B}$ augmented; i.e. that $U \cap B \cap B' \supset A$, and $(V, A) \subset B \cap B'$. If $X \cap V \supset U$, then

$$A = (A, A) \subset (A, U) \cap B \cap B' \subset (A, X \cap V) \cap B \cap B' \subset (A, X) \cap B \cap B' \subset X \cap B \cap B',$$

and X is in $\mathfrak{A}$ augmented. Similarly if $(Y, U) \subset V$, then

$$B \cap B' \supset (B \cap B' \cap V, A) \supset (B \cap B' \cap Y, B \cap B' \cap U, A) \supset (B \cap B' \cap Y, A) \supset (Y, A),$$

and Y is in $\mathfrak{B}$ augmented.

The process of augmentation just described will be referred to as (α).

21. *Decomposition theorem.* Let now $A \not\subset B$ of $\mathfrak{C}$ be given. Taking $\mathfrak{A}$ as the sublattice of elements containing A, and $\mathfrak{B}$ to be vacuous, (α) operating on $\mathfrak{A}$, $\mathfrak{B}$ and B gives us new sublattices $\mathfrak{A}$ and $\mathfrak{B}$, containing A and B respectively, and satisfying the hypotheses of the Lemma.

As we run through the various ordinals well-ordering the elements of $\mathfrak{C}$, we can extend these sublattices so as to include all elements corresponding to previous ordinals:

(1) If the element of $\mathfrak{C}$ corresponding to an ordinal is in a sublattice defined by a preceding ordinal, we leave the sublattices unchanged.

(2) If the element is in no such sublattice, we augment by (α).

Since (α) works whether an ordinal has an immediately preceding ordinal or not (finite combinations alone being admitted, the sum of an ordered set of sublattices, each included in the next, is a sublattice), we must conclude that there can be no first ordinal for which this does not work, and we have

THEOREM 21·1: *If $A \not\subset B$, then we can divide the elements of $\mathfrak{C}$ into two disjoint sublattices $\mathfrak{A}$ and $\mathfrak{B}$, of which the first includes A, the second B, and the pair has the property that if U is in $\mathfrak{A}$, and V in $\mathfrak{B}$, then $U \cap V$ is in $\mathfrak{A}$, and (U, V) in $\mathfrak{B}$.*

22. *$\bar{C}$-lattices.* One obvious transfinite generalization of condition VI is:

$$\overline{\text{VI}}.\quad A \cap \underset{k}{\Delta}\{B_k\} = \underset{k}{\Delta}\{A \cap B_k\} \quad\text{and}\quad (A, \underset{k}{\Lambda}\{B_k\}) = \underset{k}{\Lambda}(A, B_k).$$

Any lattice satisfying $\overline{\text{VI}}$ is known as a $\bar{C}$-lattice.

Suppose that A and B are two elements of the $\bar{C}$-lattice $\mathfrak{C}$ which satisfy $A \not\supset B$. Then the meet $\Delta\{X\}$ of the solutions X of $B \cap X \supset A$ satisfies $B \cap \Delta\{X\} = \Delta\{B \cap A\} \supset A$, and similarly the join $\Lambda\{Y\}$ of the solutions Y of $(A, Y) \subset B$ satisfies

$$(A, \Lambda\{Y\}) = \Lambda\{(A, Y)\} = B.$$

Furthermore

$$\Delta\{X\} \cap \Lambda\{Y\} = \Delta\{X \cap \Lambda\{Y\}\} \supset \Delta\{X \cap B\} \supset A,$$

and likewise $(\Delta\{X\}, \Lambda\{Y\}) \subset B$. Moreover, if $\Lambda\{Y\} \supset A$, then

$$A = (A, \Lambda\{Y\}) = \Lambda\{(A, Y)\} \subset B,$$

which is contrary to hypothesis. Therefore $\Lambda\{Y\} \neq \Delta\{X\} \cap \Lambda\{Y\}$, and $\Lambda\{Y\} \not\supset \Delta\{X\}$.

Finally, suppose that $(V, X) \subset \Lambda\{Y\}$, where $B \cap X \supset A$. Then certainly

$$\begin{aligned}\Lambda\{Y\} &= \Lambda\{Y\} \cap (V, X) \supset \Lambda\{Y\} \cap (V, \Delta\{X\}) \\ &= (\Lambda\{Y\} \cap V, \Lambda\{Y\} \cap \Delta\{X\}) \supset (\Lambda\{Y\} \cap V, A) \supset (A, V).\end{aligned}$$

Similarly if $U \cap Y \supset A$, then $U \cap B \supset A$. Hence we can assert

THEOREM 22·1: *Let $\mathfrak{C}$ be any $\bar{C}$-lattice. We can ascribe to any pair $A \not\subset B$ of elements of $\mathfrak{C}$ a second pair $\bar{A} \not\subset \bar{B}$ satisfying* (1) *$\bar{A} \cap \bar{B} \supset A$ and $(\bar{A}, \bar{B}) \subset B$,* (2) *$\bar{A} \subset A$ and $\bar{B} \supset B$,* (3) if *$(\bar{A}, X) \subset \bar{B}$, then $X \subset \bar{B}$, and if $\bar{B} \cap X \supset \bar{A}$, then $X \supset \bar{A}$.*

23. *Pseudo-complements.* Let A be any element of the $\bar{C}$-lattice $\mathfrak{C}$. A has two *pseudo-complements* in $\mathfrak{C}$; A', the meet of those elements X satisfying $A \cap X = J$, and the join A'' of those elements Y satisfying $(A, Y) = M$. By $\overline{\text{VI}}$, $A \cap A' = J$ and $(A, A'') = M$; hence A' is the least element satisfying $A \cap A' = J$, and A'' the greatest element satisfying $(A, A'') = M$.

$$(1)\quad A' = A' \cap (A, A'') = (A' \cap A, A' \cap A'') = A' \cap A''.$$

Therefore $A' \cap A''$. Also $(A')' \subset A$, $(A'')'' \supset A$, $((A')')' = A'$, and $((A'')'')'' = A''$.

(2) In order that $X \cap (A, B) = J$, it is necessary and sufficient that $X \cap A = X \cap B = J$; i.e. that $X \supset A'$ and $X \supset B'$. It follows that $(A, B)' = A' \cap B'$. Similarly we can prove that

$$(A \cap B)'' = (A'', B'').$$

Let $(B - A)$ be defined as (B, A'). Then we can prove the so-called *de Morgan* formula

$$\begin{aligned}(B - A) \cap (A - B) &\equiv (B, A') \cap (A, B') \\ &= (B \cap A, B \cap B', A' \cap A, A' \cap B') = (A \cap B, (A, B)') \\ &\equiv B \cap A - (B, A).\end{aligned}$$

We then have

THEOREM 23·1: *To every element A of a $\bar{C}$-lattice $\mathfrak{C}$ correspond pseudo-complements A' and A'' satisfying* (i) $A \cap A' = J$, $(A, A'') = M$, *and* $A' \supset A''$, (ii) *if* $A \cap X = J$, *then* $X \supset A'$; *if* $(A, Y) = M$, *then* $Y \subset A''$, (iii) $(A')' \subset A$, *and* $(A'')'' \supset A$, (iv) $(A, B)' = A' \cap B'$, *and* $(A \cap B)'' = (A'', B'')$, (v) *if*

$$(B - A) \equiv (B, A'),$$

then $(B - A) \cap (A - B) = B \cap A - (B, A)$.

24. *Symmetrical $\bar{C}$-lattice.* By a symmetrical $\bar{C}$-lattice, we mean one in which

VII. To every element A corresponds an $\bar{A}$ satisfying $(A, \bar{A}) = M$, and $A \cap \bar{A} = J$.

It follows immediately from Theorem 23·1 that $A' \subset \bar{A} \subset A'' \subset A'$, and consequently $\bar{A} = A' = A''$. Reconsideration of Theorem 23·1 then yields

THEOREM 24·1: *In a symmetrical $\bar{C}$-lattice,*

$$(1)\ \bar{\bar{A}} = A, \qquad (2)\ \overline{(A, B)} = \bar{A} \cap \bar{B} \text{ and } \overline{A \cap B} = (\bar{A} \cap \bar{B}),$$

$$(3)\ (A, \bar{B}) \cap (\bar{A}, B) = (A \cap B, \overline{(A, B)}).$$

Let $\mathfrak{C}$ be any *finite* symmetric $\bar{C}$-lattice. Recurring to the arithmetization process of 17, and forming at each step the meet of $\Lambda\{\mathfrak{H}_k\}$ and $\overline{\Lambda\{\mathfrak{H}_{k-1}\}}$, we see that $\mathfrak{C}$ contains the element corresponding under Theorem 17·2 to the point P_k alone. It follows that $\mathfrak{C}$ contains every subset of the points $P_1, \ldots, P_\rho$, and only these. Thus we have

THEOREM 24·2: *The finite symmetrical $\bar{C}$-lattices are collectively identical with the algebras of all subsets of ρ points.*

V. *Applications.*

25. *Symbolic logic and point-set theory.* If we identify join with logical sum, meet with logical product, and the negation of A with the $\bar{A}$ of VII, the axioms of Boolean algebra* imply I–VII. Moreover, symmetrical $\bar{C}$-lattices obey the axioms of Boolean algebra. Thus we see that we have reproved the known result

THEOREM 25·1: *The class of finite Boolean algebras, or finite algebras satisfying* I–IV *and* VII, *is abstractly identical with the class of finite algebras of point-sets with respect to sum, common part, and complement.*

Let us refer to Theorem 21·1. Ascribe to every $A \not\subset B$ a point $P_{A,B}$ 'contained' in the elements of $\mathfrak{A}$, and not in those of $\mathfrak{B}$. We

* Cf. Whitehead and Russell, *Principia mathematica*, vol. 1, p. 218.

can form the manifold of all such points, and the class of sets, in (1, 1) correspondence with the elements of $\mathfrak{C}$, in which a set contains a given $P_{A,B}$ if and only if the corresponding element of $\mathfrak{C}$ 'contains' $P_{A,B}$.

It follows from Theorem 21·1 that this identifies $\mathfrak{C}$ with an algebra of point-sets with respect to finite joins and meets. But it is known that any such algebra satisfies Axioms I–IV and VI. That is*, we have

THEOREM 25·2: *The algebras satisfying Axioms* I–IV *and* VI *are collectively identical with the algebras of classes of sets of points with respect to finite joins and meets.*

On the other hand we can prove

THEOREM 25·3: *There exists an algebra satisfying Axioms* $\overline{\text{I}}$–$\overline{\text{IV}}$ *and* $\overline{\text{VI}}$ *which is* (1, 1) *isomorphic with no algebra of classes.*

For, if we identify join with least upper bound, and meet with greatest lower bound, the numbers in the closed interval (0, 1) satisfy $\overline{\text{I}}$–$\overline{\text{IV}}$ and $\overline{\text{VI}}$.

Consider now a point P contained in the element $\frac{1}{2}$, and not in $\frac{1}{4}$. Those elements containing P, and those not containing it, would form a Dedekind section, which would determine a third element not exceeding $\frac{1}{2}$, nor inferior to $\frac{1}{4}$. But this element would be at the same time the meet of elements containing P, and the join of elements not containing it; i.e. it would at the same time contain P and not contain it, which is impossible. Therefore $\frac{1}{4}$ cannot represent a proper subset of $\frac{1}{2}$.

This naturally raises the question of what supplementary axioms are necessary to qualify infinite meets and joins.

26. *Group theory.* If we identify *meet* with *common part*, and *join* with *subgroup generated by*, then the subgroups, the normal subgroups, and the characteristic subgroups of any group† constitute lattices. It follows that the results of §§ 4–7 can be incorporated into group theory.

But more than that, suppose that $\mathfrak{A}$, $\mathfrak{X}$ and $\mathfrak{B}$ are three normal subgroups of the group $\mathfrak{G}$, that $\mathfrak{A} \supset \mathfrak{B}$, and that G is an element of the normal subgroup $(\mathfrak{A}, \mathfrak{X} \cap \mathfrak{B})$. Then G is in $\mathfrak{A}$, and a product of the form XB $[X \subset \mathfrak{X}, B \subset \mathfrak{B}]$. $X = GB^{-1}$; hence X is in $\mathfrak{A}$, and G in $(\mathfrak{A}, \mathfrak{X}) \cap \mathfrak{B}$. Adding Corollary 6·4, and the fact that factor-groups have the properties of the abstract quotients of V′, we have

THEOREM 26·1: *The normal subgroups and the characteristic subgroups of any group constitute B'-lattices.*

* We are in the statement of Theorem 25·2 assuming that any class can be well ordered. Cf. van der Waerden, *Moderne Algebra*, 1, p. 194.

† In Theorems 26·1–26·2 there is no restriction on finiteness.

Consequently the results of §§ 8–15 apply to normal and characteristic subgroups. In particular from Table IV, (3), noting in addition that if $i \neq j$, then $C_i \cap C_j = B$, and $(C_i, C_j) = A$, we get the following extension of a theorem of Remak*

THEOREM 26·2: *Let G_1, G_2, G_3 be arbitrary normal subgroups of a given group. Then the factor-groups*

$$\frac{(G_2, G_3) \cap (G_1, G_2 \cap G_3)}{(G_1, G_2) \cap (G_2, G_3) \cap (G_3, G_1)}; \quad \frac{(G_1 \cap G_2, G_2 \cap G_3, G_3 \cap G_1)}{(G_2, G_3) \cap (G_1, G_2 \cap G_3)};$$

$$\frac{(G_1 \cap G_2, G_1 \cap G_3)}{G_1 \cap (G_2, G_3)}; \quad \frac{(G_1, G_2 \cap G_3)}{(G_1, G_2) \cap (G_1, G_3)}$$

are (1, 1) *isomorphic with each other, and abstractly invariant under all permutations of the subscripts. Finally, the factor-group*

$$\frac{(G_1 \cap G_2, G_2 \cap G_3, G_3 \cap G_1)}{(G_1, G_2) \cap (G_2, G_3) \cap (G_3, G_1)}$$

is the direct product of two factors, each (1, 1) *isomorphic with all of the above factor-groups.*

Incidentally, Remak's work on subgroups of a direct product proves

THEOREM 26·3: *If the order of finite group $\mathfrak{G}$ is not divisible by a square, then the normal subgroups of $\mathfrak{G}$ constitute a C-lattice.*

Finally, from Theorems 11·4 and 26·1 we can deduce as a corollary

THEOREM 26·4: *Any normal (characteristic) subgroup which is contained in the join of the least normal (characteristic) subgroups of a given group $\mathfrak{G}$ is the direct product of suitably chosen least normal (characteristic) subgroups of $\mathfrak{G}$. Similarly any normal (characteristic) subgroup containing the meet of the greatest normal (characteristic) subgroups of $\mathfrak{G}$ is the meet of the greatest normal (characteristic) subgroups which contain it.*

27. *Ring theory.* If we identify *meet* with *common part,* and *join* with *subring generated by,* then the subrings, left-sided ideals, right-sided ideals, and two-sided ideals of any ring constitute lattices. It follows that the results of §§ 4–7 are a part of number theory.

More than that, since with ideals, the subring generated by corresponds via the operation of addition to the subgroup of the Abelian group which is generated by corresponding subgroups, we have

THEOREM 27·1: *The left-sided ideals, right-sided ideals, two-sided ideals of any algebraic ring constitute B-lattices.*

* "Über Untergruppen direkter Produkte von drei Faktoren", *Journal für Math.* 166 (1932), 100.

Consequently the results of §§ 8–14 apply to all these. And since the residue class of two two-sided ideals satisfies V′ of § 15, we can also incorporate the results of § 15 into the theory of rings. In fact, the theorems of § 26 can all be rephrased for rings.

Finally, since we can consider the powers of primes dividing a number as points contained in it, we have

THEOREM 27·2: *The numbers of any field in which unique factorization exists constitute a C-lattice with respect to g.c.f. and l.c.m.*

28. *Geometry.* Consider the family of linear manifolds in Cartesian n-space which pass through the origin. They evidently constitute a lattice with respect to intersection and projection*. Furthermore they form a B'-lattice, for reasons like those of § 26; the quotient L/M $[L \supset M]$ is the set of elements of L orthogonal to M. We can therefore incorporate §§ 4–15 into geometry.

In particular, from Theorems 14·1 and 26·2 we can deduce

THEOREM 28·1: *The number of linear manifolds which can be constructed by successive projections and intersections from three given manifolds* G_1, G_2, G_3 *has 28 as its maximum value. The interrelations of these are given by Tables I–IV of §§ 12–15. Finally, the dimension-number of* $(G_1 \cap G_2, G_2 \cap G_3, G_3 \cap G_1)$ *exceeds that of* $(G_1, G_2) \cap (G_2, G_3) \cap (G_3, G_1)$ *either by zero or by an even positive integer.*

Moreover, through representation in function-space we see that the theory of B'-lattices has applications in the theory of the linear dependence of functions.

29. *B-sublattice generated by four elements.* From the geometrical representation of § 27 we can draw a theoretical inference concerning B-sublattices generated by four elements; or, equivalently, the 'free' B-lattice generated by four elements.

The free lattice generated by A and B contains in addition (A, B) and $A \cap B$ only, and is a C-lattice. The free B-lattice generated by three elements contains twenty-eight elements, and is described in Tables I–III; it is not a C-lattice. Further, it follows from Theorem 17·2 that the free C-lattice generated by n elements is finite if n is finite—and therefore that the orders of the C-sublattices generated by n elements are bounded uniformly by n.

A plausible conjecture would be that a similar theorem held for B-lattices. But on the contrary, we can prove

THEOREM 29·1: *The free B-lattice generated by four elements is infinite.*

* By the *projection* of two such linear manifolds, we mean the set of vectors linearly dependent upon them.

Let $A=\left(\frac{12}{13}, \frac{-3}{13}, \frac{-4}{13}\right)$, $B_0=\left(\frac{12}{13}, \frac{-3}{13}, \frac{4}{13}\right)$,

$C_0=\left(\frac{12}{13}, \frac{3}{13}, \frac{4}{13}\right)$, $D=\left(\frac{12}{13}, \frac{3}{13}, \frac{-4}{13}\right)$,

and $O=(0, 0, 0)$, all in Cartesian 3-space. Let $\mathfrak{B}$ denote the B-lattice generated as in § 27 by the straight lines $\overline{OA}$, $\overline{OB_0}$, $\overline{OC_0}$, and $\overline{OD}$. We shall show that $\mathfrak{B}$ is infinite, directly implying Theorem 29·1.

The planes OB_0C_0 and OAD intersect in $(0, 1, 0) \equiv F$; therefore $\overline{OF}$ is in $\mathfrak{B}$. Let now G_{k+1} denote the intersection on the unit sphere σ about O, of the planes OB_kD and OC_kA. If $\overline{OB_k}$ and and $\overline{OC_k}$ are in $\mathfrak{B}$, then so is $\overline{OG_{k+1}}$. Let B_k and C_k denote the intersections on σ of OFG_k with OAB_0 and ODC_0 respectively. If OG_k is in $\mathfrak{B}$, then so are OB_k and OC_k.

It follows by induction from the above that every $\overline{OB_k}$, $\overline{OC_k}$, and $\overline{OG_k}$ is in $\mathfrak{B}$. But it is geometrically evident that these are all distinct [cf. the diagram representing the intersections of lines and planes with σ]. Thus the theorem is proved.

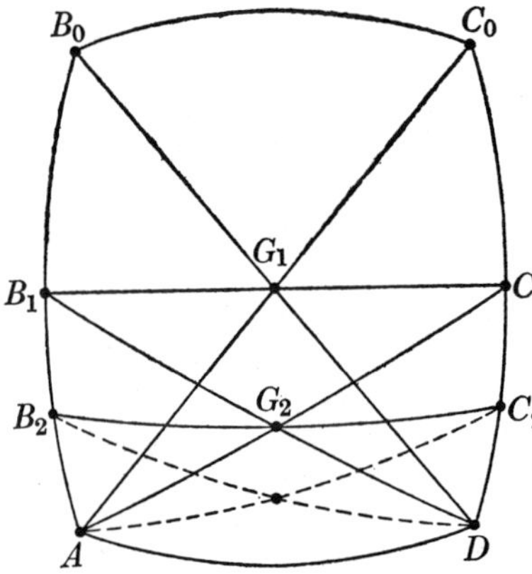

[Extracted from the *Proceedings of the Cambridge Philosophical Society*. Vol. XXX. Pt. II.]

Note on the paper "On the combination of subalgebras."* By GARRETT BIRKHOFF.

Professor Oystein Ore of Yale University has kindly called my attention to the close relation between my paper and some earlier researches of Dedekind†. I should like to correlate, as far as possible, my results with his.

My "lattices" are obviously his "Dualgruppen"; he calls *B*-lattices "von Modultypus", and *C*-lattices "von Idealtypus". My "duality" Theorem 4·1 is also implicit in his work, while the theorems of my § 6 are essentially thorough statements hinted at by his special results.

He gives my Theorems 8·1 (his XIV, p. 261), 8·2 (his XVI, p. 264), and Corollary 9·2 (his formula (55), p. 266). He does not obtain the fundamental equivalence relations of my Theorem 10·2, getting instead (IX, p. 255, and X, p. 259) one which I did not derive.

Part III of my article duplicates his results (pp. 246—48), except that Theorems 15·1—15·2 are important new developments.

There is no further duplication, except that my Theorem 26·1 is foreshadowed in Dedekind's observations (pp. 270—71) concerning the subgroups of Abelian and "Hamiltonian" groups.

* *Proc. Camb. Phil. Soc.* 29 (1933), 441—64.

† Cf. Vol. II of his *Gesammelte Werke*, Braunschweig, 1931, to which all page references are made. The articles bearing on mine are XXVIII (pp. 103—47) and XXX (pp. 236—71).

[Extracted from the *Proceedings of the Cambridge Philosophical Society*, Vol. XXX. Pt. II.]

Applications of lattice algebra. By GARRETT BIRKHOFF. (Communicated by Mr P. HALL.)

[*Received* 8 October, *read* 11 December 1933.]

1. *Introduction.* By a finite lattice† is meant any finite class $\mathfrak{L}$ having the following properties:

I. Any two elements A and B of $\mathfrak{L}$ have a meet (A, B) in $\mathfrak{L}$ and a join $A \cap B$ in $\mathfrak{L}$.

II. $(A, A) = A \cap A = A$, irrespective of A.

III *a*. $(A, B) = (B, A)$ and $A \cap B = B \cap A$.

III *b*. $(A, (B, C)) = ((A, B), C) \equiv (A, B, C)$ and $A \cap (B \cap C) = (A \cap B) \cap C \equiv A \cap B \cap C$.

IV. If $(A, B) = A$, then $A \cap B = B$, and conversely. In this case we write $A \subset B$ or $B \supset A$, and say 'A is contained in B', or 'B contains A'.

By a B-lattice is meant any lattice satisfying

V. If $A \subset C$, then $A \cap (B, C) = (A \cap B, C)$.

By a C-lattice is meant any lattice satisfying

VI *a*. $(A, B \cap C) = (A, B) \cap (A, C)$ and

VI *b*. $A \cap (B, C) = (A \cap B, A \cap C)$.

In this paper we shall determine three necessary and sufficient conditions that a finite B-lattice should be a C-lattice. Two applications of these will then be made. The first leads to a determination of the extent of the correlation between joins and meets of the normal subgroups of a finite group, and sums and common parts of point-sets. The second leads to measure and probability axioms.

2. *Preliminary lemmas.* It is known‡ that, in any finite B-lattice, we can assign to each element A a rank $\rho\{A\}$, satisfying

(α) $A > B$ implies $\rho\{A\} > \rho\{B\}$, and

(β) $\rho\{A\} + \rho\{B\} = \rho\{(A, B)\} + \rho\{A \cap B\}$.

Further, it is known§ that, in any lattice,

VI*. $(A, B \cap C) \supset (A, B) \cap (A, C)$ and $A \cap (B, C) \subset (A \cap B, A \cap C)$.

† The terminology and symbols of this paper are borrowed wholesale from the author's article "On the combination of subalgebras", *Proc. Camb. Phil. Soc.* 29 (1933), 441–464. This will be referred to as "Subalgebras" in later footnotes.

‡ "Subalgebras", Theorem 10·2, condition (2). By $A > B$ is meant $A \supset B$ but $A \neq B$.

§ "Subalgebras", Corollary 6·4.

In finite B-lattices, VI a and VI b are consequently equivalent to

$$\rho\{(A, B \cap C)\} - \rho\{(A, B) \cap (A, C)\} = 0$$

and

$$\rho\{A \cap (B, C)\} - \rho\{(A \cap B, A \cap C)\} = 0.$$

But the relation (β) shows that

$$\begin{aligned}
&\rho\{A \cap (B, C)\} - \rho\{(A \cap B, A \cap C)\} \\
&\quad = \rho\{A\} + \rho\{(B, C)\} - \rho\{(A, B, C)\} - \rho\{A \cap B\} - \rho\{A \cap C\} \\
&\qquad\qquad + \rho\{A \cap B \cap C\} \\
&\quad = \rho\{A\} + \rho\{B\} + \rho\{C\} - \rho\{B \cap C\} + \rho\{A \cap B \cap C\} - \rho\{A\} - \rho\{B\} \\
&\qquad\qquad + \rho\{(A, B)\} - \rho\{A\} - \rho\{C\} + \rho\{(A, C)\} - \rho\{(A, B, C)\} \\
&\quad = \rho\{(A, B)\} + \rho\{(A, C)\} - \rho\{(A, B, C)\} - \rho\{A\} - \rho\{B \cap C\} \\
&\qquad\qquad + \rho\{A \cap B \cap C\} \\
&\quad = \rho\{(A, B) \cap (A, C)\} - \rho\{(A, B \cap C)\}.
\end{aligned}$$

From this chain of equalities we obtain

LEMMA 1†: *Either* VI a *or* VI b *is a sufficient condition that a finite B-lattice should be a C-lattice.*

But

$$\rho\{A\} + \rho\{(B, C)\} - \rho\{(A, B, C)\} - \rho\{A \cap B\} - \rho\{A \cap C\} + \rho\{A \cap B \cap C\}$$

is equal to

$$\rho\{A \cap B \cap C\} - \rho\{(A, B, C)\} - \rho\{A \cap B\} - \rho\{A \cap C\} - \rho\{B \cap C\} + \rho\{A\} + \rho\{B\} + \rho\{C\},$$

which, taken with the symmetry‡ of the situation, gives

LEMMA 2: *Either of the following conditions is necessary and sufficient for a finite B-lattice to be a C-lattice:*

1°. $\rho\{A \cap B \cap C\} - \rho\{(A, B, C)\} = \rho\{A \cap B\} + \rho\{B \cap C\} + \rho\{A \cap C\} - \rho\{A\} - \rho\{B\} - \rho\{C\}$,

1°′. $\rho\{A \cap B \cap C\} - \rho\{(A, B, C)\} = \rho\{A\} + \rho\{B\} + \rho\{C\} - \rho\{(A, B)\} - \rho\{(B, C)\} - \rho\{(C, A)\}$.

3. *Fundamental reduction.* Suppose that a B-lattice is not a C-lattice; it will follow, by Lemma 1 and VI*, that, for suitably chosen A, B, C, $\rho\{(A, B \cap C)\} - \rho\{(A, B) \cap (A, C)\} > 0$. Let

$$X \equiv (B, C) \cap (A, B \cap C),$$

† This result was found by R. Dedekind, *Gesammelte Werke*, Braunschweig, 1931, Vol. II. p. 115.

‡ "Subalgebras", Theorem 4·1.

so that $(B, C) \subset X \subset B \cap C$. We can deduce from ($\beta$) that

$$\begin{aligned}
\rho\{(X, B\cap C)\} - \rho\{(X,B)\cap(X,C)\} \\
&= \rho\{X\} + \rho\{B\cap C\} - \rho\{B\cap C\cap X\} - \rho\{(X,B)\} - \rho\{(X,C)\} \\
&\qquad + \rho\{(B,C,X)\} \\
&= \rho\{X\} + \rho\{B\cap C\} - \rho\{B\cap C\} - [\rho\{X\} + \rho\{B\} - \rho\{X\cap B\}] \\
&\qquad - [\rho\{X\} + \rho\{C\} - \rho\{X\cap C\}] + \rho\{(B,C)\} \\
&= [\rho\{(B,C)\} - \rho\{B\} - \rho\{C\}] + \rho\{X\cap B\} - \rho\{X\} + \rho\{X\cap C\} \\
&= -\rho\{B\cap C\} + [\rho\{B\} + \rho\{(A, B\cap C)\} - \rho\{(A,B)\}] \\
&\qquad - [\rho\{(B,C)\} + \rho\{(A, B\cap C)\} - \rho\{(A,B,C)\}] \\
&\qquad + [\rho\{C\} + \rho\{(A, B\cap C)\} - \rho\{(A,C)\}] \\
&= \rho\{(A, B\cap C)\} - \rho\{(A,B)\} - \rho\{(A,C)\} + \rho\{(A,B,C)\} \\
&= \rho\{(A, B\cap C)\} - \rho\{(A,B)\cap(A,C)\} > 0.
\end{aligned}$$

Therefore $(X, B\cap C) \neq (X,B)\cap(X,C)$, for suitable

$$(B, C) \subset X \subset B \cap C.$$

Now let U denote $B\cap(X,C)$, and V denote $C\cap(X,B)$. We can infer that

$$\begin{aligned}
(U, V) &= (B\cap(X,C),\ C\cap(X,B)) \\
&= \dagger (X,B)\cap(X,C)\cap(B,C) = (X,B)\cap(X,C)
\end{aligned}$$

[since $(B,C)\subset X$ and B]. Moreover,

$$U\cap V = B\cap C\cap(X,B)\cap(X,C) = B\cap C.$$

Consequently $(U,V)\subset X\subset U\cap V$.

But $(X,U) = \dagger (X,B)\cap(X,C) = (U,V)$, and similarly

$$(X, V) = (U, V).$$

Hence $(X, U\cap V) = X \neq (U,V) = (X,U)\cap(X,V)$. Symmetry‡ then yields

LEMMA 3: *Either of the two following conditions is sufficient to ensure that a finite B-lattice is a C-lattice:*

(i) $(U,V)\subset X\subset U\cap V$ and $(X,U)=(X,V)=(U,V)$ imply that $(X, U\cap V) = (X,U)\cap(X,V)$.

(ii) The hypotheses of (i) imply that

$$X\cap(U,V) = (X\cap U, X\cap V).$$

4. *Alternative condition.* If a B-lattice is not a C-lattice, we can assume an exception to Lemma 3, (i). Suppose such an exception, and let L be any element contained in X and covering§ (U, V). Obviously $(L,U)=(L,V)=(U,V)$, yet

$$(U,V)\subset L\subset U\cap V.$$

† "Subalgebras", Tables I—III. ‡ "Subalgebras", Theorem 4·1.

§ By the phrase 'A covers B' is meant $A > B$, while $A > X > B$ has no solution. L evidently exists ("Subalgebras", Theorem 7·1).

Hence

$$\rho(L \cap V, U) = \rho\{L \cap V\} + \rho\{U\} - \rho\{U \cap V\} = \rho\{L\} + \rho\{V\} - \rho\{(U, V)\} - \rho\{V\} + \rho\{(U, V)\} = \rho\{L\},$$

and† $M \equiv (L \cap V, U)$ covers (U, V).

Again, it is obvious that $(L, M) = (M, V) = (U, V)$. In addition, $M \cap V = (L \cap V, U) \cap V = (L \cap V, U \cap V) \supset (L, L) = L$, whence

$$(L, M \cap V) = L \cap (U, V) \neq (L, M) \cap (L, V).$$

Similarly $N \equiv (L \cap M, V)$ covers (L, V), while

$$(L, M) = (M, N) = (L, N), \text{ and } (L, M \cap N) \neq (L, M) \cap (L, N).$$

Inverting the logic of the situation, we see that, if there is no exception of this peculiar type, a given B-lattice is a C-lattice. We then have

LEMMA 4: *A sufficient condition for a B-lattice to be a C-lattice is that, if L, M, and N each cover E, and* $L \neq M \neq N$, *then*

$$(L, M \cap N) = E.$$

5. *Theoretical conclusion.* It is obvious that the condition of Lemma 4 is necessary, since in a C-lattice

$$(L, M \cap N) = (L, M) \cap (L, N) = E.$$

Further, it is equivalent to the condition that $L \cap M \cap N$ covers $M \cap N$ [so that $L \cap M$ and $L \cap N$], since $L \cap M \cap N \supset M \cap N$, and, by ($\beta$),

$$\rho\{L \cap M \cap N\} - \rho\{M \cap N\} = \rho\{L\} - \rho\{(L, M \cap N)\}.$$

Combining this with Lemmas 1 and 2, and known‡ necessary and sufficient conditions for a lattice to be a B-lattice, we obtain the fundamental

THEOREM 1: *The following three§ sets of conditions are each necessary and sufficient for a finite lattice* $\mathfrak{L}$ *to be a C-lattice:*

(1)‖ $A \subset C$ *implies* $A \cap (X, C) = (A \cap X, C)$, *while*

$$(A, B \cap C) = (A, B) \cap (A, C).$$

(2) *If A and B cover C, and* $A \neq B$, *then* $A \cap B$ *covers A.*
If C covers A and B, and $A \neq B$, *then A covers* (A, B).
If A, B, and C each cover D, and $A \neq B \neq C$, *then* $A \cap B \cap C$ *covers* $A \cap B$.

† "Subalgebras", p. 446, § 9. ‡ "Subalgebras", Theorem 10·2.

§ There are really six conditions, because of the symmetry between join and meet, which ascribes to (1)—(3) symmetric counterparts.

‖ Condition (1) can be very considerably weakened. Reference to (2) and VI* permits us to replace '$A \subset C$' by 'A is covered by C', and '$A \cap (X, C) = (A \cap X, C)$' by '$A \cap (X, C) \supset (A \cap X, C)$' in the first half, to qualify the second half by demanding that A, B, and C shall all cover the same element E, and to replace the equality by an inequality.

(3) *To every element L of $\mathfrak{L}$ we can assign a number $\rho\{L\}$, satisfying*

(α) $L > M$ *implies* $\rho\{L\} > \rho\{M\}$,

(β) $\rho\{L\} + \rho\{M\} = \rho\{(L, M)\} + \rho\{L \cap M\}$,

(γ) $\rho\{A \cap B \cap C\} - \rho\{(A, B, C)\} = \rho\{A \cap B\} + \rho\{B \cap C\} + \rho\{C \cap A\} - [\rho\{A\} + \rho\{B\} + \rho\{C\}]$.

6. *Application to group theory.* It is known † that the normal subgroups of any group constitute a B-lattice. Further, to be a C-lattice is ‡ equivalent to being (1, 1) isomorphic with a class of point-sets relative to the operations of sum and common part. Accordingly, we can interpret the conditions of Lemmas 1–4 as conditions that the normal subgroups of a given finite group G should behave like point-sets.

It happens that the work of Remak gives a group-theoretical interpretation to the condition of Lemma 4. In the notation of the lemma, L/E, M/E, and N/E are least normal subgroups of the factor-group G/E. Remak has shown § that the least normal subgroups of a given group satisfy the condition of Lemma 4 if and only if no two are 'coherent'; that is, are related by a (1, 1) isomorphism preserved under all inner automorphisms of G/E. This proves

THEOREM 2: *A necessary and sufficient condition that* (I) *the normal subgroups of a group G should combine into joins and meets just as* ‖ *point-sets combine into sums and common parts is that* (II) *G should be many-1 isomorphic with no group having two coherent least normal subgroups.*

Since any two (1, 1) isomorphic subgroups of the centre of a group are coherent, we have the fairly obvious

COROLLARY 1: *A necessary condition that* (I) *should hold is that G should be many-1 isomorphic only with groups whose centres are cyclic.*

Equally obvious ¶ is

COROLLARY 2: *A sufficient condition that* (I) *should hold is that the principal series of G should contain no two* (1, 1) *isomorphic Abelian factor-groups.*

† "Subalgebras", Theorem 26·1. ‡ "Subalgebras", Theorem 25·2.

§ Cf. R. Remak, "Über minimale invariante Untergruppen, etc.", *Journ. f. Math.* 162 (1930), 1–16.

‖ More precisely, be (1, 1) isomorphic in the sense of van der Waerden, *Moderne Algebra* (Berlin, 1930–31), I, pp. 28–9.

¶ Since coherent normal subgroups are Abelian; see R. Remak, *op. cit.*, Theorem 2.

From a theorem† concerning the number of points required to represent a C-lattice in (1, 1) fashion, we can infer

COROLLARY 3: *If a group G satisfies* (II), *and the number of factor-groups in a principal series of G is n, then the normal subgroups of G are* (1, 1) *isomorphic with subsets of a 'space' of n points.*

Finally, from the fact‡ that a C-lattice is a finite Boolean algebra if and only if it is the join of the elements covering the meet of all its elements, we obtain

COROLLARY 4: *The joins and meets of the normal subgroups of a group G are* (1, 1) *isomorphic with the sums and products of the elements of a Boolean algebra, if and only if G is the direct product of simple groups, no two Abelian ones of which are* (1, 1) *isomorphic.*

7. *Lattice functions.* By a 'lattice function' is meant any triple $(\mathfrak{L}, \Gamma, \mu)$ of the following nature:

I. $\mathfrak{L}$ is a finite class of abstract elements.

II. Γ assigns, to every pair of elements A and B of $\mathfrak{L}$, a *join* $A \cap B$ and a *meet* (A, B), satisfying II–IV of § 1.

III. μ assigns to each element A of $\mathfrak{L}$ a number $\mu\{A\}$.

An interesting question is, when does a lattice function act like a measure function with respect to sum and common part? That is to say, if in II we understand by the 'join $A \cap B$', the 'sum $A + B$', and by the 'meet (A, B)', the 'common part (A, B)', what additional conditions make it possible to find a class of point-sets in (1, 1) correspondence with the elements of $\mathfrak{L}$, such that

II*. the correspondence preserves combination into sums and common parts, and

III*. $\mu\{A\}$ corresponds to the measure of A?

We shall investigate a class of answers to this problem, clearly suggested by condition (3) of Theorem 1. For it is remarkable that qualifications (α)–(β) on the ρ-function closely resemble properties of mass-functions. It is accordingly a plausible conjecture that these qualifications are sufficient to ensure, not only the point-set character of $(\mathfrak{L}, \Gamma)$, but the mass character of ρ as well.

8. *Essential construction.* We shall find that there is a great deal of truth in this conjecture, although it is false when taken in the most literal sense. If we add a sufficiently large constant to the ρ-function, for instance, we do not alter (α)–(γ), yet we

† "Subalgebras", Theorem 17·4.
‡ "Subalgebras", p. 460.

make it possible to construct a correspondence which satisfies II* and III*. This is a direct corollary of

THEOREM 3: *A sufficient condition that a lattice function should be a mass-function is that it should satisfy* (α)–(γ), *and be non-negative.*

Let $\mathfrak{G}_1, \ldots, \mathfrak{G}_\rho$ denote a sequence of sublattices of $\mathfrak{L}$, chosen as follows. $\mathfrak{G}_1$ contains just one element, the meet A_1 of all the elements of $\mathfrak{L}$. Letting A_{k+1} denote an element (1) not in $\mathfrak{G}_k$, and (2) minimizing $\mu\{A_{k+1}\}$ relative to elements satisfying (1), we define $\mathfrak{G}_{k+1}$ as the set of elements F such that

$$F \subset A_1 \cap \ldots \cap A_{k+1} \equiv S_{k+1}.$$

We can continue this process until we reach $\mathfrak{G}_\rho = \mathfrak{L}$.

Let s_1 denote the segment $0 \leqslant x < \mu\{A_1\}$ of the x-axis, and $s_k [k=2, 3, \ldots]$ the segment $\mu\{S_{k-1}\} \leqslant x < \mu\{S_k\}$. To a random element L of $\mathfrak{L}$ make correspond the point-set defined as the sum of those s_k whose k satisfies $L \supset A_k$. We shall show that this correspondence is (1, 1), and satisfies II* and III*.

First observe that $(\mathfrak{L}, \Gamma)$ is a C-lattice, by Theorem 1. Obviously, for any two elements L and M of $\mathfrak{L}$,

$$(L, S_1) = (M, S_1) = A_1.$$

Suppose that $(L, S_{k-1}) = (M, S_{k-1})$, while either (1) both $L \supset A_k$ and $M \supset A_k$, or (2) neither $L \supset A_k$ nor $M \supset A_k$. In case (1),

$$(L, S_k) = (L, S_{k-1}) \cap (L, A_k) = (M, S_{k-1}) \cap (M, A_k) = (M, S_k).$$

In case (2), since [by (α)] $\mu\{(L, A_k)\} < \mu\{A_k\}$, by choice of A_k, $(L, A_k) \subset S_{k-1}$. Hence

$$(L, S_k) = (L, S_{k-1}) \cap (L, A_k) = (L, S_{k-1})$$
$$= (M, S_{k-1}) = (\text{similarly})\ (M, S_k).$$

That is, if L and M correspond to the same point-sets, then $L = M$, thus proving that the correspondence is (1, 1).

To prove II*, note that (a) L is the join of those A_k which it contains, by induction from the fact that either $(L, A_k) = A_k$, or $(L, S_k) = (L, S_{k-1})$; also (b) $(L \cap M, A_k) = (L, A_k) \cap (M, A_k) = A_k$ if and only if $(L, A_k) = A$ *or* $(M, A_k) = A$—otherwise

$$(L, A_k) \subset S_{k-1}, \quad (M, A_k) \subset S_{k-1},$$

and $$(L \cap M, A_k) = (L, A_k) \cap (M, A_k) \subset S_{k-1}$$

—and (b') $((L, M), A_k) = (L, M, A_k) = A_k$ if and only if $L \supset A_k$ *and* $M \supset A_k$.

To prove III*, we use induction again. Obviously, irrespective of L, $\mu\{(L, S_1)\} = \mu\{A_1\}$ is equal to the measure of the set corresponding to $(L, S_1) = A_1$. Suppose that $\mu\{(L, S_{k-1})\}$ is equal to the measure of the set corresponding to (L, S_{k-1}). If $L \not\supset A_k$, since $(L, S_k)=(L, S_{k-1})$, $\mu\{(L, S_k)\}$ is equal to the measure of the set corresponding to (L, S_k). If $L \supset A_k$, then

$$\mu\{(L, S_k)\}=\mu\{(L, S_{k-1}) \cap (L, A_k)\}$$
$$=\mu\{(L, S_{k-1})\}+\mu\{A_k\}-\mu\{(A_k, S_{k-1})\}$$

[by (β)], and again $\mu\{(L, S_k)\}$ is equal to the measure of the set corresponding to (L, S_k). By induction, to $(L, S_\rho)=F$, we get III*.

9. *Application to the theory of probability.* The theory of elementary finite probabilities—as contrasted with the analytic theory of asymptotic probabilities—is identical with the theory of classes. For it is assumed that there are a number of *cases*, each of the same probability, which can be identified with elements of the class of all possible cases. Any hypothesis H classifies the cases as 'favourable to H' or 'unfavourable to H'. The class of cases 'favourable to H and H'' is the meet of the class favourable to H with the class favourable to H'; the class of cases 'favourable to H or to H'' is the sum of the class favourable to H and the class favourable to H'. By the 'probability of H' is meant the fraction of all cases composed by the cases favourable to H. If now we allow, as a probability hypothesis, the probability that a random point of a 'space' of n points should lie in a given set of the space, we have clearly identified the theory of probability with the theory of point-sets, translating 'cases' into 'points'.

But on the basis of Theorem 3 we can easily prove

THEOREM 4: *A system of necessary and sufficient conditions that a given lattice function $(\mathfrak{L}, \Gamma, \mu)$ should be* (1, 1) *isomorphic with a finite class of sets of finite points, in such a way that $\mu\{L\}$ denotes the number of points in the set corresponding to L, is that $\mu\{L\}$ should satisfy* (α)–(γ), *and be a positive integer or zero.*

That the conditions are necessary is a mathematical commonplace. That they are sufficient is shown by repeating the proof of Theorem 3, only defining s_1 as the set of points $1, \ldots, \mu\{A_1\}$, and s_k $[k=2, 3, \ldots]$ as the set of points $\mu\{A_{k-1}\}+1, \ldots, \mu\{A_k\}$ on the x-axis. Theorem 4, translated into probability language, becomes

THEOREM 4′: *Let $H_1, H_2, H_3, \ldots$ be any set of abstract elements called 'hypotheses', to any pair H_i and H_j of which correspond a 'logical sum $H_i \cap H_j$' and a 'logical product (H_i, H_j)' in the set. Further, to each H_i let there be assigned a number $\mu\{H_i\}$. Then necessary and sufficient conditions that the H_i should correspond to a set of real hypotheses concerning a finite number of equally probable eventualities, in such a way that 'logical sum' and 'logical product' have their true import, while $\mu\{H_i\}$ is the probability of H_i, are that II–IV of* §1 *and* (α)–(γ) *of Theorem* 1 *should be satisfied, while in addition* (δ_1) $\mu\{H_i\}$ *is rational, and* (δ_2) $0 \leqq \mu\{H_i\} \leqq 1$.

ON THE LATTICE THEORY OF IDEALS†

BY GARRETT BIRKHOFF

1. *Outline.* The ideals of any ring define, relative to g.c.f. and l.c.m., a combinatorial system having properties which we shall presently define as characterizing *B-lattices*.

In this article we shall first develop some new properties of B-lattices as abstract systems; the main results of this part of the work find expression in Theorems 1–5. Then we shall apply this theory and some older results to the ideals of commutative rings R which possess a principal unit l and satisfy the Basis Theorem. In addition to developing the known theory of *einartig* ideals by combinatory methods, we give a necessary and sufficient condition that the *B-lattice* defined by the ideals of R should be isomorphic with a *ring* of point sets in the sense of Hausdorff.‡

2. *Notation*; *Lattice Algebras.* We shall in general use capital letters to denote systems, and small letters for elements. $a \in A$ will mean "a is an element of the system A"; $B \subset A$ will mean "$b \in B$ implies $b \in A$"; $B < A$ will mean $B \subset A$ but $B \neq A$.

By a *lattice algebra* will be meant any system L which satisfies the following postulates:

(L1). Any $a \in L$ and $b \in L$ determine a unique "*join*" $a \cap b \in L$ and a unique "*meet*" $(a, b) \in L$.
(L2). $a \cap b = b \cap a$ and $(a, b) = (b, a)$ for any $a \in L$ and $b \in L$.
(L3). $a \cap (b \cap c) = (a \cap b) \cap c$ and $(a, (b, c)) = ((a, b), c)$ for any $a \in L$, $b \in L$, and $c \in L$.
(L4). $a \cap (a, b) = a$ and $(a, a \cap b) = a$ for any $a \in L$ and $b \in L$.

From (L1)–(L4) follow $a \cap a = (a, a) = a$. Moreover $a \cap b = b$ is equivalent to $(a, b) = a$; in this case we write $a \subset b$ or $b \supset a$, and $a \subset b$ taken with $b \subset c$ implies $a \subset c$. Moreover, $a < b$ means $a \subset b$ but $a \neq b$, while "b covers a" means $a < b$, but that no $x \in L$ satisfies $a < x < b$.

The reader may find it helpful to regard lattices as distorted

† Presented to the Society, March 30, 1934.
‡ Hausdorff, *Mengenlehre*, 1927, p. 77.

Boolean algebras in which $a \cap b$ is substituted for $a+b$, and (a, b) for $a \cdot b$.

The following additional conditions are optional:

(L5). If $a \subset c$, then $a \cap (b, c) = (a \cap b, c)$.
(L6). $(a, b \cap c) = (a, b) \cap (a, c)$ for any $a \in L$, $b \in L$, and $c \in L$.

If a lattice satisfies (L5), it is called a B-lattice; if it satisfies (L6), it is called a C-lattice. Any C-lattice is a B-lattice, and also satisfies $a \cap (b, c) = (a \cap b, a \cap c)$.

3. *Subdirect Decomposition.* We shall consider in §§3–4 only lattices L which have a "*largest*" element j satisfying $a \cap j = j$ for every $a \in L$; such is always the case in applications.†

We shall say that $a \in L$ and $b \in L$ are *coprime* if and only if $a \cap b = j$. We shall say that two sublattices‡ $A \subset L$ and $B \subset L$ are *coprime* if and only if $a \in A$ and $b \in B$ imply $a \cap b = j$. We shall say that the sublattices of a finite or transfinite§ sequence of sublattices $A_1 \subset L, \cdots, A_n \subset L$ are *strongly coprime* if and only if every A_i is coprime with the sublattice generated by‖ the other sublattices of the sequence.

Let $B_1, \cdots, B_n$ be any (finite or transfinite) sequence of lattices, whose largest elements are $j_1, \cdots, j_n$. By an *f-type* vector $[b_1, \cdots, b_n]$, $(b_i \in B_i)$, we mean one in which $b_i = j_i$ except for a *finite* set of subscripts i. By the *subdirect product* $B_1 \hat{x} \cdots \hat{x} B_n = B^*$ of the B_i is meant the lattice whose elements are the f-type vectors just defined, and such that by definition

$$[b_1, \cdots, b_n] \cap [b_1', \cdots, b_n'] = [b_1 \cap b_1', \cdots, b_n \cap b_n'],$$

$$([b_1, \cdots, b_n], [b_1', \cdots, b_n']) = [(b_1, b_1'), \cdots, (b_n, b_n')].$$

B^* is evidently a lattice with largest element $[j_1, \cdots, j_n]$. Further, if B_i^* denotes the sublattice of elements of the form $[j_1, \cdots, j_{i-1}, b_i, j_{i+1}, \cdots, j_n]$ of B^*, then B_i^* is isomorphic with B_i, the lattices $B_1^*, \cdots, B_n^*$ are strongly coprime, and any element of B^* can be expressed as the meet of a finite num-

† In fact, if the number of elements of L is finite, this follows from (L1)–(L3.)

‡ A sublattice A of L is any subsystem such that $a \in A$ and $a' \in A$ imply $a \cap a' \in A$ and $(a, a') \in A$.

§ That is, in which the subscripts run through transfinite ordinals.

‖ By the "sublattice generated by" is meant the least sublattice containing.

ber of elements in the various B_i^*. Finally, if the B_i are B-lattices, then so† is B^*.

Conversely, let B be any B-lattice, and let $B_1, \cdots, B_n$ be any finite or transfinite sequence of strongly coprime sublattices of B such that any $b \in B$ can be expressed as the meet $(b_{i_1}, \cdots, b_{i_m})$ of a finite number of $b_{i_k} \in B_{i_k}$.

For any $b \in B$ and $b' \in B$ we can evidently so reorder the B_i that $b = (b_1, \cdots, b_m)$, $b' = (b_1', \cdots, b_m')$, and $b \cap b' = b'' = (b_1'', \cdots, b_m'')$, where $b_i \in B_i$, $b_i' \in B_i$, $b_i'' \in B_i$, and m is finite. But by (L2)–(L3), we have

$$(b, b') = ((b_1, \cdots, b_m), (b_1', \cdots, b_m')) = ((b_1, b_1'), \cdots, (b_m, b_m')).$$

Further if we set $a_i = (b_i, b_i', b_i'')$, then

$$a_i \cap b'' = a_i \cap b \cap a_i \cap b' = a_i \cap (b_1, \cdots, b_m) \cap a_i \cap (b_1', \cdots, b_m'),$$

whence by (L5), setting $c_i = (b_1, \cdots, b_{i-1}, b_{i+1}, \cdots, b_m)$, and c_i' and c_i'' equal to the corresponding dashed expressions, we have

$$(a_i \cap c_i'', b_i'') = (a_i \cap c_i, b_i) \cap (a_i \cap c_i', b_i'),$$

whence, by strong coprimeness, after reduction, $b_i'' = b_i \cap b_i'$.

That is, B is a homeomorphic image of the subdirect product $B^* = B_1 \hat{x} \cdots \hat{x} B_n$. But if $b_i = b_i'$, and b^* in B^* is the image of (b_i, b_i') of B_i, then $b^* \cap [b_1, \cdots, b_n] = b_i \neq b_i' = b^* \cap [b_1', \cdots, b_n']$, whence, by (L1), $[b_1, \cdots, b_n] \neq [b_1', \cdots, b_n']$, and the homeomorphism is an isomorphism. In summary, we have proved the following theorem.

THEOREM 1. *A given B-lattice B (with largest element) is isomorphic with the subdirect product $B_1^* \cdots B_n^*$ (B_i^* any B-lattice with largest element) if and only if B contains strongly coprime sublattices $B_1, \cdots, B_n$ respectively isomorphic with $B_1^*, \cdots, B_n^*$ such that any $b \in B$ can be expressed as a meet $(b_{i_1}, \cdots, B_{i_m})$, where m is finite and $b_{i_k} \in B_{i_k}$.*

Notice that if n is finite, then a subdirect product is a direct product; while if $n = 2$, then strong coprimeness is equivalent to coprimeness.

4. *Uniqueness Theory.* Let L be any lattice (with a largest element), and suppose that L is isomorphic with two subdirect products $A_1 \hat{x} \cdots \hat{x} A_m$ and $B_1 \hat{x} \cdots \hat{x} B_n$. We know by the sec-

† The identical relations (L2)–(L5) can be checked seriatim.

ond paragraph of § 3, how to identify the A_i (and B_i) with strongly coprime sublattices of L in such a way that any element of L can be represented as the meet of a finite number of elements of the various A_i (or B_i). The reader can easily check the statement that, since $(a_i, a_j) = b_k$, $(b_k \in B_k)$, if and only if $a_i \in B_k$ and $a_j \in B_k$, each B_i is the subdirect product of its intersections with the various A_i; this proves the following statement.

THEOREM 2. *If* $L = A_1 \hat{\times} \cdots \hat{\times} A_m = B_1 \hat{\times} \cdots \hat{\times} B_n$ *is any lattice,*† *then* $L = F_{1,1} \hat{\times} \cdots \hat{\times} F_{m,n}$, *where* $A_i = F_{i,1} \hat{\times} \cdots \hat{\times} F_{i,n}$ *and* $B_j = F_{1,j} \hat{\times} \cdots \hat{\times} F_{m,j}$.

COROLLARY 1. *A lattice has at most one expression as a subdirect product of factors not themselves subdirect products.*

COROLLARY 2. *A finite lattice has a unique expression as the direct product of lattices not themselves direct products of lattices with fewer elements. The factors of any expression of the lattice as a direct product are direct products of the factors of this special decomposition into prime factors.*

These corollaries are of extremely general application.‡ We now assume in addition that L satisfies the following postulate.

(ϕ) Any sequence $a_1, a_2, a_3, \cdots$ of elements of L, such that $a_k < a_{k+1}$ for every k, is finite.

Well-order the expressions $L = L_1^i \hat{\times} \cdots \hat{\times} L_n^i$ of L as a subdirect product, and apply Theorem 2 iteratedly. If we concentrate our attention on the corresponding well-ordered set of meets $(a_1^i, \cdots, a_{\alpha_i}^i) = a$ representing a fixed $a \in L$ (each a_h^i lying in just one of the L_k^j for each $j \leqq i$, by Theorem 2), we see that the expression $(a_1^i, \cdots, a_{\alpha_i}^i)$ undergoes§ in virtue of (ϕ) at most a finite number of transmutations. Hence we can proceed through limit-numbers, and, by transfinite induction, we have the following result.

---

† By definition of subdirect product, either $m = n = 1$ and the theorem is trivial, or the A_i, B_j, and L have largest elements.

‡ See Theorem 3.1 of the author's paper *On the combination of subalgebras*, Proceedings of the Cambridge Philosophical Society, vol. 29 (1933), pp. 441–464. This article will be cited in future references as "Subalgebras."

§ Each transmutation replaces an a_h^i by the meet of $a_{h'}^{i+1} > a_h^i$ and $a_{h''}^{i+1} > a_h^i$.

THEOREM 3. *A lattice satisfying* (ϕ) *has one and only one expression as a subdirect product of factors not themselves subdirect products.*

Theorem 3 can evidently be applied to the ideals in rings which satisfy the ideal-chain theorem.

5. *Standard Exceptions to* (L6). Let B be any B-lattice, suppose g_1, g_2, and g_3 to be any three elements of B, and refer to Tables I–III of "Subalgebras"—only replacing A_i, B_i, M_i, N_i, C_i, F_i, and H_i by a_i, b_i, m_i, n_i, c_i, f_i, and h_i.

Suppose $c_i = c_j$ for some $i \neq j$. Then $a = (c_i, c_j) = c_i \cap c_j = b$, whence $(g_1, h_1) = (g_1, h_1, h_2, h_3) = (g_1, f_1 \cap f_2 \cap f_3) = (f_2 \cap f_3) \cap (g_1, f_1)$ [by (L5)] $= f_2 \cap f_3 \cap f = f_2 \cap f_3$, which is to say, $(g_1, g_2, \cap g_3) = (g_1, g_2) \cap (g_1, g_3)$. If therefore (L6) is violated at all, we must have some instance where the c_k are all distinct, yet $(c_i, c_j) = a$ and $c_i \cap c_j = b$ for $i \neq j$, whence $(c_1, c_2 \cap c_3) \neq (c_1, c_2) \cap (c_1, c_3)$. This proves the following fact.

THEOREM 4. *If a B-lattice is not a C-lattice, it contains a sublattice of order five and fixed structure not a C-lattice.*

Combining Theorem 4 with the result, due to Dedekind,† that any lattice not a B-lattice contains a sublattice of order five and fixed structure not a B-lattice, we get the following result.

COROLLARY. *If a lattice is not a C-lattice, it contains a sublattice of order five which is not a C-lattice.*

6. *Specialization by Induction.* Suppose B of §5 satisfies condition (ϕ) of §4, and consider the exception referred to in Theorem 4. We can by (ϕ) choose $c_1^* \supset c_1$ *covered* by b (see §2). Theorems 8.1 and 9.1 of "*Subalgebras*" show us successively that c_3 covers (c_1^*, c_3), $b = c_2 \cap c_3$ covers $c_2^* = c_2 \cap (c_1^*, c_3)$, hence c_1^* and c_2^* both cover $a^* = (c_1^*, c_2^*)$. Similarly $b = c_3 \cap c_2^*$ covers $c_3^* = c_3 \cap (c_1^*, c_2^*)$, and, since $c_3^* \supset a^*$, $(c_1^*, c_3^*) = (c_2^*, c_3^*) = a^*$. This proves the following theorem.

THEOREM 5. *If B is any B-lattice satisfying* (ϕ), *then either B is a C-lattice or we can find a sublattice of B consisting of a least element* a^*, $c_1^* \neq c_2^* \neq c_3^* \neq c_1^*$ *covering* a^*, *and* $b = c_1^* \cap c_2^* = c_2^* \cap c_3^* = c_3^* \cap c_1^*$ *covering* c_1^*, c_2^*, *and* c_3^*.

† *Gesammelte Werke*, 1931, vol. II, p. 255.

7. *Facts about Ideals.* Throughout, R will be understood to denote a commutative ring which has a principal unit l and satisfies the Basis Theorem. Our notation will be that of van der Waerden† except that we shall denote by (A, B) the l.c.m., and by $A \cap B$ the g.c.f., of any two given ideals A and B. This is the inverse of van der Waerden's notation.

The following are either known or immediate corollaries of known results:

(1). *The only ideals in R are R and 0 if, and only if, R is a field.*

(2). *If I is a largest ideal in R, then $0:I$ is a least ideal if and only if it is a principal ideal.*

(3). *Any ideal I covered by R is a prime ideal.*

8. *Application of Theorem* 1. On the basis of Theorem 1, it is possible to reconstruct the combinatorial theory of an important class of ideals.

By an ideal *of genus* 1 will be meant any ideal I which contains an appropriate finite product $P_1^{n_1} \cdots P_\omega^{n_\omega}$ (where P_i denotes any ideal covered by R). We shall prove the following result.

THEOREM 6. *The ideals of genus* 1 *in R are a B-lattice, which is the subdirect product of the sublattices $\mathfrak{P}_1, \mathfrak{P}_2, \mathfrak{P}_3, \cdots$ of the primary ideals under the ideals $P_1, P_2, P_3, \cdots$ covered by R.*

That they are a lattice of which the $\mathfrak{P}_i$ are sublattices is obvious, while that they are a B-lattice follows from Theorem 27.1 of "*Subalgebras.*"

But the $\mathfrak{P}_i$ are strongly coprime, since if $Q_1, \cdots, Q_m$ satisfy the relation $Q_k \not\subset P_i$ for every k, and Q is primary under P_i, then $Q \cap (Q_1, \cdots, Q_m) = R$, being contained in no ideal covered by R. And by a theorem of E. Noether, any ideal can be expressed as the meet of a finite number of primary ideals. Theorem 6 is now merely a translation of Theorem 1 in terms of ideals.

9. *Application of Theorem* 5. It is not difficult to show from known results the following theorem.

THEOREM 7. *If R contains a largest ideal I, and another ideal $A \subset I$ for which $(A:I)/A$ is not a principal ideal, then the ideals of R are not a C-lattice.*

† *Moderne Algebra*, 1930–31; especially vol. 2, Chap 12, in which will be found the Basis and Ideal-chain Theorems.

For since l, commutativity, and the Basis Theorem are preserved under homeomorphism, we can assume $A=0$; while by (2) we can assume $(0:I)$ is not a least ideal.

By the Ideal-chain Theorem we can further choose a largest subideal $J>0$ in $0:I$, and then $x \not\in J$, $y \not\in Rx$ satisfying $y \in J$, and $w=x+y$. But a second homeomorphism permits us to assume $(Rx, Ry)=0$, yet $x \neq 0$, $y \neq 0$. This makes it obvious that $(Rx, Ry) \cap Rw \neq (Rx \cap Rw, Ry \cap Rw) \ni x$.

Conversely, suppose the ideals of R are not a C-lattice. By Theorem 5, R has a homeomorphic image R^* which contains three least ideals $A \neq B \neq C$ such that $A \cap B = B \cap C = C \cap A$.

Consider $R^*/(0:A)$; it is a field, whence, by (1), $0:A$, and similarly $0:B$ and $0:C$, are largest ideals† in R. For if $ra \neq 0$ $[a \in A, r \in R^*]$, then $ra \in A$ generates A; consequently r^{-1} exists such that $r^{-1}ra=a$ and $r^{-1}r \equiv l\ (0:A)$.

Again, if $0 \neq b \in B \subset A \cap C$, then $b=a+c$, where (since $a=0$ or $b=0$ would imply $B=C$ or $B=A$) $a \neq 0$, $c \neq 0$. And since $(A, C)=0$, $0=rb=r(a+c)=ra+rc$ implies $ra=rc=0$. Consequently $0:B \subset (0:A, 0:C)$, and $0:A=0:B=0:C=I$, where I is a largest ideal in R^*, yet, by (2), $0:I$ is not a principal ideal in R^*. Referring back to the corresponding ideals in R, we see that R does not satisfy the conclusions of Theorem 7.

We can combine Theorem 7, its converse, and Theorem 25.2 of "*Subalgebras*" in the following theorem.

THEOREM 8. *For the ideals of R to be isomorphic (with respect to l.c.m. and g.c.f.) with a system of point sets (with respect to sum and product), it is necessary and sufficient that if I is any largest ideal in R, and* $A \subset I$ *another ideal, then* $(A:I)/A$ *is a principal ideal in* R/A.

It is a corollary that the identity $A:(A:Q)=(Q \cap A)$ upon ideals is a sufficient condition for distributive combination.

HARVARD UNIVERSITY

† $R=0:A$ is of course excluded since $l \not\subset 0:A$.

Reprinted from *Bull. Am. Math. Soc.* **40** (1934), 613–619

Reprinted from the Proceedings of the NATIONAL ACADEMY OF SCIENCES,
Vol. 20, No. 11, pp. 571–573. November, 1934.

IDEALS IN ALGEBRAIC RINGS

BY GARRETT BIRKHOFF*

HARVARD UNIVERSITY

Communicated October 15, 1934

1. *Reduction by Ordinary Primes.*—This paper is a study of factorization in algebraic rings, and outlines a very direct attack which goes deep into the problem. Among other things, it shows that the divisibility (or "ideal") structure of an algebraic ring is either entirely canonical or very irregular. It further gives an arithmetic criterion for determining which algebraic integers give rise to canonical ideal structure.

For brevity, detailed proofs are omitted; of course they have been constructed. For brevity also, the nomenclature and notation of footnote 1 will be used without explanation.

Now let x be any algebraic integer, and let

$$f(x) = x^n + a_1x^{n-1} + a_2x^{n-2} + \ldots + a_n = 0 \qquad (1)$$

be the irreducible equation for x. The rational integers and x generate a ring R, and we shall denote by $L(R)$ the system whose elements are the non-zero ideals $A, B, C, \ldots$ of R, and whose operations are g.c.f., l.c.m., product and ideal quotient. R and $L(R)$ are thoroughly familiar concepts to algebraists, and will be fixed throughout the paper.

By the "index" of an ideal $A \epsilon L(R)$ we mean the order of the residue ring R/A. Any A must contain a rational integer $a \neq 0$, and so must have a finite index dividing a^n. To every prime p consequently corresponds the system $L_p(R)$ of ideas whose index is a power of p.

Moreover it is true, although the proof is not easy, that $L(R)$ is essentially** the direct product of the $L_p(R)$. We can summarize this symbolically by writing

$$L(R) = L_2(R) \times L_3(R) \times L_5(R) \times \ldots \qquad (2)$$

and confine our attention to the various individual $L_p(R)$.

2. *Strong Isomorphism and Strong Semi-Isomorphism.*—Let $I \supset J$ and $K \supset L$ be any four ideals of R. A (1, 1) correspondence between the elements of the residue rings I/J and K/L will be called a "strong isomorphism" if and only if it preserves addition and multiplication, and is preserved under multiplication by an arbitrary $z \epsilon R$; it will be called a strong semi-isomorphism if and only if it preserves addition and is preserved under multiplication by an arbitrary $z \epsilon R$. In the first case we write $I/J \cong K/L$; in the second, $I/J \simeq K/L$.

THEOREM 1: If I, $J < I$ and $K < I$ are distinct ideals satisfying $(J, K) = I$, and if $I/J \simeq I/K$, then L exists, an ideal satisfying $(L, J) = (L, K) = I$ and $[L, J] = [L, K] = [J, K]$.

We form L from those residue classes $[J, K] + j + k$ of $[J, K]$ for which $j \epsilon J$ and $k \epsilon K$ correspond under the given strong semi-isomorphism.

3. *Irregular Case.*—The situation concerning the ideal of R/pR is totally clarified by the remark that we can apply Euclid's algorithm to polynomials modulo p, so that the ideals of R/pR correspond (1, 1) with the divisors of $f(x)$ modulo p which generate them. We now prove

THEOREM 2: Suppose that $g^2(x)$ divides $f(x)$ modulo p, that $g(x)$ is irreducible modulo p, and yet that the ideal $g(x)R \not\supseteq pR\ (p^2)$. Then the ideals of R do not satisfy

$$[(J, K), (J, L)] = (J, [K, L]). \qquad (3)$$

Set $I = (g(x)R, pR)$, $J = (g(x)R, p^2R)$, and $K = (g^2(x)R\ pR)$. We obtain ideals satisfying the hypotheses of Theorem 1, and therefore satisfying $[(J, K), (J, L)] = (J, K) < J = (J, [K, L])$, contrary to (3).

4. *Canonical Case.*—It can be proved that if $g^2(x)$ does not divide $f(x)$ modulo p while $g(x)$ is an irreducible factor of $f(x)$ modulo p, then $(g(x)R, pR)$ is a principal ideal generated by some $g(x) + kp\ (p)$. But if $g(x)R \supset pR(p^2)$, then $(g(x)R, pR)$ is a principal ideal, modulo any p^n. Finally, it is true that every largest ideal of $L_p(R)$ contains pR. Consequently, applying paragraph one of §3, we see that unless the hypotheses of Theorem 2 are satisfied for some $g(x)$, every largest ideal of $L_p(R)$ is a principal ideal, modulo any p^n.

But it can be proved that if T is a principal ideal in $L_p(R)$, then the transformation $I \longrightarrow TI$ carries $L_p(R)$ into the subsystem of ideals contained in T, isomorphically relative to g.c.f. and l.c.m. Using induction on index, we obtain

THEOREM 3: If no $g(x)$ satisfies the hypotheses of Theorem 2, then $L_p(R)$ is "canonical"—that is, isomorphic with the system of the products of a set of ordinary primes, relative to g.c.f., l.c.m., product and quotient.

5. *Consequences.*—Now we use our relation (2) to pass from $L_p(R)$ to $L(R)$. But we first note that any canonical system of ideals is "regular" in the sense of Grobner[3]—that is, that if $A \subset B$, then $A : (A : B) = B$—and that by Theorem 8 of footnote 2 any "regular" system of ideals satisfies (3). Therefore

THEOREM 4: The properties of satisfying (3), of being regular and of being canonical, are effectively equivalent in R, and all are equivalent to the property that if $g(x)$ is any irreducible factor of $f(x)$ modulo p, then either $g^2(x)$ does not divide $f(x)$ modulo p, or else $(g(x)R, p^2R) \supset pR$.

The author intends to publish elsewhere complete proofs of the assertions made above, together with related theorems and applications to the arithmetics of specific algebras. As an example of the results proved, we shall cite

THEOREM 5: The number of different simple factors J/K in $L_p(R)$ relative to strong isomorphism, is twice the number of irreducible factors of $f(x)$ modulo p.

* Society of Fellows, Harvard University.

** Technically, the "subdirect product" in the sense of footnote 2, §3.

1 O. Ore, "Abstract Ideal Theory," *Bull. Am. Math. Soc.*, **39**, 728–45 (1933).

2 G. Birkhoff, "On the Lattice Theory of Ideals," *Ibid.*, **40**, 613–19 (1934).

3 W. Grobner, "Uber irreduziblen Ideale in kommutativen Ringe," *Math. Ann.*, **110**, 161–94 (1934).

Annals of Mathematics
Vol. 36, No. 3, July, 1935

COMBINATORIAL RELATIONS IN PROJECTIVE GEOMETRIES

By Garrett Birkhoff

(Received February 1, 1934, Revised December 27, 1934)

1. **Introduction.** The following note can be interpreted in various ways. The obvious interpretation is that projective geometries have an alternative characterization in terms of elementary combinatorial operations and a finiteness condition.

More remote from current notions is the conclusion that projective geometries can be correlated in a perfectly definite scheme[1] with (1) Boolean algebras (2) "fields" of point-sets (3) "rings" of point-sets (4) systems of normal subgroups (5) systems of ideals (6) modules of a "modular" space[2] (7) systems of subalgebras of abstract algebras.

Of theoretical interest also is the correlation sketched in §§7–8 between the systems which we define and the theory of the reduction of group representations, of compact Lie groups, and of semi-simple hypercomplex algebras.

2. **Projective geometries as complemented modular lattices.** Let V be any n-dimensional vector space with coördinates in a number-field F. A set L of vectors $\xi, \eta, \zeta, \cdots$ of V is called a "vector subspace" if and only if (1) $\xi \in L$ and $\eta \in L$ imply $(\xi + \eta) \in L$ (2) $\zeta \in L$ and $x \in F$ imply $(x \cdot \zeta) \in L$.

Let L and M be any two vector subspaces of V. The set $L \frown M$ of vectors common to L and to M is a vector subspace of V, and so is the set $L \smile M$ of all sums $\xi + \eta$ of a vector $\xi \in L$ and a vector $\eta \in M$. It is easy to prove—and this will be done under more general hypotheses in proving Theorem 1—that

L2: $L \frown M = M \frown L$ and $L \smile M = M \smile L$.
L3: $L \frown (M \frown N) = (L \frown M) \frown N$ and $L \smile (M \smile N) = (L \smile M) \smile N$.
L4: $L \frown (M \smile L) = L \smile (M \frown L) = L$.
L5: If L is contained in N [in symbols, if $L \subset N$], then $L \smile (M \frown N) = (L \smile M) \frown N$.
L7:[3] To any L corresponds a "complement" L' satisfying $L \frown L' \frown M = L \frown L'$ and $L \smile L' \smile M = L \smile L'$ irrespective of M.

---

[1] Each of the seven families listed is closely tied up with the set of all combinatorial systems satisfying L2–L4 and appropriate auxiliary conditions such as L5, L7, and the distributive law (L6).

[2] I.e., subspaces of a modified vector space whose coefficients are merely the numbers of a ring of integrity. Cf. H. Grell, "*Beziehungen zwischen den Idealen verschiedener Ringe*," Math. Ann. 97 (1926), 490–523.

[3] A less concise but more understandable equivalent for L7 is: "The system contains a least element (=subspace) O such that $O \frown L = O$ for any L, and a greatest element Q such that $Q \smile M = Q$ for any M. And to any L corresponds at least one L' such that $L \frown L' = O$ and $L \smile L' = Q$."

The vector subspaces of V may also be regarded as elements of a "projective geometry" $P(V)$, and as such have a number of familiar geometrical properties. For instance, if we call the one-dimensional subspaces of V "points," the two-dimensional subspaces "lines," etc., then

P1: Two distinct points are contained in one and only one line.
P2: If A, B, C are points not all on the same line, and D and E ($D \neq E$) are points such that B, C, D are on a line and C, A, E are on a line, then there is a point F such that A, B, F are on a line and also D, E, F are on a line.
P3: Every line contains at least three points.[4]
P4: The points on lines through any k-dimensional[5] element and a fixed point not on the element are a $(k + 1)$-dimensional element, and every $(k + 1)$-dimensional element can be defined in this way.

By a "projective geometry" is meant[6] any abstract system which shares with $P(V)$ properties P1–P4, and in which there is a finite upper bound to the dimensions of the elements.

Moreover any projective geometry satisfies L2–L7—after intersection and conjunction ("meet" and "join") have been defined in the obvious manner. In fact, L5 and L7 are the only properties whose truth is not evident.

To prove L5, observe that (1) since $L \smile M$ and N each contain both L and $M \frown N$, $L \smile (M \frown N) \subset (L \smile M) \frown N$, and (2) counting dimensions[7]

$$\begin{aligned} \dim L \smile (M \frown N) &= \dim L + \dim M \frown N - \dim L \frown M \frown N \\ &= \dim L + \dim M + \dim N - \dim M \smile N - \dim L \frown M \\ &= \dim L \smile M + \dim N - \dim L \smile M \smile N \\ &= \dim (L \smile M) \frown N \end{aligned}$$

To prove L7, let L be any k-dimensional element of a projective geometry. By P4 we can find plonts $B_1, \cdots, B_{n-k}$ such that $B_{i+1} \not\subset L \smile B_1 \smile \cdots \smile B_i$. Set $L' = B_1 \smile \cdots \smile B_{n-k}$. By P4, $L \smile L'$ is the whole space; hence

$$\dim L \frown L' = \dim L + \dim L' - \dim L \smile L' = k + (n - k) - n = 0$$

and $L \frown L'$ is empty. L7 is now obvious.

Hence if we define any system with two binary operations satisfying L2–L5 and L7 as a "complemented modular lattice," then

Theorem 1: *Any projective geometry P determines a complemented modular*

[4] Unless F contains only the numbers 0 and 1.

[5] To preserve the correspondence with dimensionality in the primitive vector space, and for other reasons, we shall term what is usually called a "k-space" a "$(k + 1)$-dimensional element."

[6] O. Veblen and J. W. Young, "*Projective geometry,*" Boston, 1910.

[7] We use Theorems S_n2 and S_n3 of Veblen and Young, Vol. I, pp. 32–3, which show that $\dim L + \dim M = \dim L \frown M + \dim L \smile M$.

lattice $C(P)$ *by a transformation under which* (1) *distinct elements (points, lines, planes, etc.) of* P *go over into distinct elements of* $C(P)$ (2) *intersections go over into "meets," and conjunctions into "joins."*

3. **Covering and dimensions in modular lattices.** This section and the next three will be devoted to proving a converse of Theorem 1.

First, let C be any modular lattice—i.e., any system with two binary operations satisfying L2–L5. An element a of C is said to "properly contain" an element b of C [in symbols, $a > b$] if and only if $a \supset b$—i.e., $a \smile b = a$—and $a \neq b$. The element a is said to "cover" b if and only if $a > b$, and $a > c > b$ has no solution—i.e., if and only if a is a minimal element properly containing b.

If there is a finite number n such that every sequence $a_1 > a_2 > a_3 > \cdots$ of decreasing elements of C contains at most n terms, then C is said to be of "finite dimensions," and it has been proved by Dedekind[8] that under these circumstances

(3.1) C has a "least" element o_C contained in every other element, and a "greatest" element q_C containing every other element. One can assign a "dimension integer" $d(a)$ to each $a \in C$ such that (i) $d(o_C) = 0$, (ii) a covers b if and only if $a \supset b$ and $d(a) = d(b) + 1$, (iii) $d(a) + d(b) = d(a \frown b) + d(a \smile b)$.

By the "dimensions" of C is naturally meant $d(q_C)$. To express the analogy with projective geometries, let us further call the one-dimensional elements of C "points," and the two-dimensional elements, "lines."

Any modular lattice C satisfies P1, since if a and b are any two points of C, then

$$\dim a \smile b = \dim a + \dim b - \dim a \frown b = 1 + 1 - 0 = 2$$

C also satisfies P2, since under the hypotheses of the latter (replacing the capitals by small letters),

$$\begin{aligned} \dim (a \smile b) \frown (d \smile e) &= \dim a \smile b + \dim d \smile e - \dim a \smile b \smile d \smile e \\ &= 2 + 2 - \dim a \smile b \smile c = 4 - 3 = 1 \end{aligned}$$

and $f = (a \smile b) \frown (d \smile e)$ satisfies the conclusions of P2. Finally, C satisfies the first half of P4, by a repetition of the argument proving P1.

4. **Reducibility in complemented modular lattices.** Suppose C is a *complemented* modular lattice. We can easily show

Lemma 1: *Any element* a *of* C *such that* $d(a) > 0$ *is the join of* $d(a)$ *suitably chosen points of* C.

---

[8] Ges. Werke, Braunschweig, 1932, Vol. II, p. 264. Cf. also the author's "*On the combination of subalgebras*," Proc. Camb. Phil. Soc. 29 (1933), 441–64. (3.1) shows incidentally that the usual theory of linear dependence can be obtained purely abstractly.

Suppose a is not itself a point. Then there exists a point $c < a$, and if c' denotes the complement of c, then

$$c \cup (c' \cap a) = (c \cup c') \cap a = a \qquad \text{[by L5 and L7]}.$$

Moreover $c \cap (c' \cap a) = (c \cap c') \cap a = o_C$; hence $d(c) + d(c' \cap a) = d(a)$. Lemma 1 now follows by finite induction on dimensions, and application of the same principle to $c' \cap a$.

5. **Conjoint points.** As matters now stand, P3 is the only property of projective geometries not established in complemented modular lattices.[9] The work of §§5–6 will be devoted to settling the status of P3.

To do this, we first define a relation of "conjointness" among the points of C, by stating (1) any point of C is conjoint with itself (2) a point p_i of C is conjoint with a different point p_j of C if and only if a third point p_k exists contained in $p_i \cup p_j$.

Lemma 2: *The relation of conjointness has the properties of equivalence—it is reflexive, symmetric, and transitive.*

It is reflexive by (1); further, since $p_i \cup p_j = p_j \cup p_i$, it is symmetric. Finally, if a is conjoint with c, and c with b, then there exist new points e and d on $a \cup c$ and $c \cup b$; consequently either c is a third point on $a \cup b$ or else the hypotheses of P2 are satisfied, and a new point f exists on $a \cup b$.

Lemma 3 *If the join $p_1 \cup \cdots \cup p_r$ of any set of points of C contains a point q, then q is conjoint with at least one of the points $p_1, \cdots, p_r$.*

For we can clearly so choose k that $q \subset p_1 \cup \cdots \cup p_k$, yet $q \not\subset p_1 \cup \cdots \cup p_{k-1}$. Then $p_k \cup q$ must intersect $p_1 \cup \cdots \cup p_{k-1}$ on a third point (considering the dimensional arithmetic), whence by definition p_k and q are conjoint.

6. **Direct decomposition.** By Lemma 2, the points of C can be divided into a number of non-overlapping sets $\alpha_1, \cdots, \alpha_r$ such that two points are conjoint if and only if they are in the same set.[10] Let a_k denote the join of the points of α_k $[k = 1, \cdots, r]$, and let c be any element of C.

By Lemma 1, c is the join of those points which it contains, and so $c = (c \cap a_1) \cup \cdots \cup (c \cap a_r)$. This orders to each element of C a set of r elements $c_1 = c \cap a_1 \subset a_1, \cdots, c_r = c \cap a_r \subset a_r$. The ordering is a (1,1) correspondence if (and only if) for every choice of $c_1 \subset a_1, \cdots, c_r \subset a_r$ and $k = 1, \cdots, r$ it is true, writing c for $c_1 \cup \cdots \cup c_r$ and b_k for $c_1 \cup \cdots \cup c_{k-1} \cup c_{k+1} \cup \cdots \cup c_r$, that $c \cap a_k = c_k$. But by L5 $c \cap a_k = (c_k \cup b_k) \cap a_k = c_k \cup (b_k \cap a_k)$, and since no point can lie in both b_k and a_k (by Lemma 3), $b_k \cap a_k = o_C$; hence $c \cap a_k = c_k$.

Moreover the ordering preserves *inclusion*, and therefore is isomorphic

[9] In fact, I suspect that conversely P1 + P2 + P4 and finite dimensionality imply L2–L7, but I have not checked this.

[10] O. Ore has since shown that a similar partition into disjoint classes exists between the "prime factors" of any modular lattice; these are "points" in the case we consider.

with respect to meet and join—and consequently carries complements into complements. Therefore

THEOREM 2: *Any complemented modular lattice C of finite dimensions is isomorphic with the direct product of the sublattices $A_1, \cdots, A_r$ of elements contained in the joins $a_1, \cdots, a_r$ of its complete sets of conjoint points.*

Those α_k containing more than one point define sublattices in which by Lemma 2 P3 is satisfied; the other α_k define Boolean algebras of two elements. Consequently, uniting the different Boolean algebras so defined, we get

THEOREM 3: *Any complemented modular lattice of finite dimensions is isomorphic with the direct product of a finite Boolean algebra and a finite number of projective geometries.*

Conversely, since L2–L5 and L7 are preserved under combination into direct products, any direct product of a finite Boolean algebra and a finite number of projective geometries is a complemented modular lattice of finite dimensions.

7. Application to group representations.[11] Let Γ be any group of orthogonal (or unitary) transformations of a space S. Any linear manifold A invariant under Γ is said to "half-reduce" Γ; the group of linear transformations induced by Γ on A is denoted by Γ_A. Clearly if A is invariant under Γ then so is the orthogonal complement A' of A, while Γ is determined by Γ_A and $\Gamma_{A'}$. For this reason Γ is said to be "fully reduced," and we write $\Gamma = \Gamma_A + \Gamma_{A'}$.

The linear manifolds of S invariant under Γ are evidently a sublattice of the projective geometry of all linear manifolds of S—and hence constitute a modular lattice M_Γ of finite dimensions. But we have seen that each element of M_Γ has a complement in M_Γ; that is, M_Γ is *complemented.*

Therefore by Lemma 1 S has a representation as the join of dim M_Γ "irreducible" invariant manifolds (i.e., manifolds which contain no proper invariant submanifolds). Moreover by Theorem 2 these are unique to within conjointness.

But if A, B, and C are on a "line" of M_Γ, then the factor-space S/A formed by projecting A into the origin defines a (1,1) linear transformation of B onto C carrying Γ_B into Γ_C. That is, by definition, Γ_B and Γ_C are "equivalent" if[12] B and C are conjoint in M_Γ. Taken with the above, this shows

(7.1) Any group of orthogonal (or unitary) transformations can be reduced in one and (apart from equivalence) only one way into the sum of irreducible components.

8. Other applications. Similarly, since the adjoint of any compact Lie group can be orthogonalized, since invariant linear manifolds of the space of the adjoint correspond to normal subgroups of the nucleus of the group, and since

[11] §§ 7–8 were added in revision.

[12] The converse is also true—associate with equivalent representations on A and on B the manifold $C_{x,y}$ of points $x.\alpha + y.\beta$ [x and y fixed numbers; $\alpha \in A$ and $\beta \in B$ corresponding under the given "equivalence"]; then C will be invariant.

"conjoint" irreducible manifolds correspond (as Remak has shown by a simple analysis)[13] to "centrally isomorphic" least normal subgroups, which can only be one-parameter normal subgroups, we obtain

(8.1)[14] The nucleus of any compact Lie group is the direct product of simple group nuclei and one-parameter group nuclei. The representation as a direct product is unique except as to one-parameter group nuclei, and the number of these is fixed.

And finally, once it has been proved that in any "semi-simple"[15] hypercomplex algebra A, to any invariant subalgebra S there corresponds a "complementary" invariant subalgebra S' of elements $(a - 1_S \cdot a - a \cdot 1_S + 1_S \cdot a \cdot 1_S)$ of A [1_S the principal unit of S], satisfying $S \smile S' = A$, $S \frown S' = 0$, it follows directly that

(8.2) Any semi-simple hypercomplex algebra is the direct sum of simple hypercomplex algebras.

9. **Open questions.** It was seen at the end of §6 that the converse of Theorem 3 held; therefore in one sense conditions L2–L5 and L7 are complete. But there are two directions in which work remains to be done.

For instance,[16] can all the laws of combination of projective manifolds be obtained from L2–L5 and L7 by the ordinary rules of inference? That this cannot be assumed is illustrated by the fact that every finite field obeys the law $ab = ba$, although this is no longer true without the restriction of finiteness.

Again, it would be desirable to characterize combinatorially those projective geometries which are associated with actual vector spaces—or equivalently,[17] which satisfy the Theorems of Desargues and Pascal.

Other questions are: (1) Can the (non-desarguesian) finite plane projective geometries be constructively enumerated? (2) What are the dimensions of the "free" modular lattice generated by n symbols? of the "free" complemented modular lattice so generated? If they are finite, then the answer to the question of paragraph two is yes. (3) Characterize in geometrical terms those projective geometries in which

L7*: $(L \frown M)' = L' \smile M'$, $(L \smile M)' = L' \frown M'$, and $(L')' = L$.

Society of Fellows, Harvard University.

---

[13] "*Über minimale invariante Untergruppen*," Jour. f. Math. 162 (1930), 1–16.

[14] E. Cartan, "*Groupes simples clos*," Jour. de Math. pures et appliquées 8 (1929), p. 11.

[15] I.e., algebra without nilpotent invariant subalgebra.

[16] This question was kindly suggested to me by K. Gödel.

[17] O. Veblen and J. H. Maclagan Wedderburn, "*Non-Desarguesian* and *non-Bascalian geometries*," Trans. Am. Math. Soc. 8 (1907), 379–88.

ABSTRACT LINEAR DEPENDENCE AND LATTICES.

By Garrett Birkhoff.

1. *Introduction.* In a preceding paper,[1] Hassler Whitney has shown that it is difficult to distinguish theoretically between the properties of linear dependence of ordinary vectors, and those of elements of a considerably wider class of systems, which he has called "matroids."

Now it is obviously impossible to incorporate all of the heterogeneous abstract systems which are constantly being invented, into a body of systematic theory, until they have been classified into two or three main species. The purpose of this note is to correlate matroids with abstract systems of a very common type,[2] which I have called "lattices."

As this correlation is purely formal, the discussion will be descriptive rather than detailed.

2. *The fundamental construction.* Let us refer to Whitney's definition of a matroid as a set M whose subsets have a numerical rank function with certain properties (R_1)-(R_3). It is easy to define mutual dependence by abstraction from the theory of vectors, and to see that if we suppress elements of rank zero, and regard mutually dependent elements as merely repeated occurrences of the same element, then we get a matroid M^* with the same structural properties as M. Moreover M^* has the additional property that no element is dependent on any other element.[3]

Now let us call a subset of M^* "linearly complete" if and only if it contains all elements dependent on it. By what we have just shown, distinct elements of M^* are distinct linearly complete subsets. Moreover

Lemma 1. *The product $N \cdot N'$ of any two linearly complete subsets N and N' of M^*, is linearly complete.*

For suppose e any element of M^* not in $N \cdot N'$; by symmetry, we can suppose e not in N. Therefore

[1] H. Whitney, "On the abstract properties of linear dependence," *American Journal of Mathematics*, vol. 57 (1935), pp. 509-533. His main definition is in his section two.

[2] Cf. the author's "On the combination of subalgebras," *Proceedings of the Cambridge Philological Society*, vol. 39 (1933), pp. 441-464. This article will be referred to subsequently as "Subalgebras."

[3] This assertion corresponds to S. MacLane's assumption "without loss of generality" of his conditions (R_4)-(R_5) in his note on "Some interpretations of abstract linear dependence, etc.," *supra*.

$$1 = r(N + e) - r(N) \qquad \text{[by definition of } N\text{]}$$
$$\leqq r(N \cdot N' + e) - r(N \cdot N') \qquad \text{[by Whitney's Lemma 4].}$$

Hence $r(N \cdot N' + e) \geqq r(N \cdot N') + 1$, and e is not dependent on $N \cdot N'$, proving the lemma.

Observe now that M^* is itself linearly complete, and has the property $M^* \cdot N = N$ for any subset N. Finally, the operation of intersection is idempotent, commutative, and associative. Consequently

THEOREM 1. *The linearly complete subsets of M^* can be regarded as the elements of a new system $L(M^*)$, satisfying*

(L_1) *Any a of $L(M^*)$ and b of $L(M^*)$ determine a unique "product" $a \cap b$ in $L(M^*)$.*

(L_2) $a \cap a = a$, $a \cap b = b \cap a$, *and* $a \cap (b \cap c) = (a \cap b) \cap c$.

(L_3) *There exists a "unit" i [namely, M^*] such that $a \cap i = a$ irrespective of a.*

(L_4) *In any sequence of products $a_1, a_1 \cap a_2, a_1 \cap a_2 \cap a_3, \cdots$ some two terms are equal. [Remark: This is a simple corollary of the fact that $L(M^*)$ is finite].*

Moreover distinct single elements of M^* appear as distinct single elements of $L(M^*)$.

3. *An incidental theorem.* We shall now prove a result which is obvious in the case in hand—provided we define the "join" $N \cup N'$ of N and N' directly as the product of all linearly complete subsets containing N and N'. (This definition is equivalent to defining $N \cup N'$ as the set of all elements linearly dependent on $N + N'$). The formal proof *in abstracto* has however been included, to give a neat new approach to the theory of abstract lattices.[4]

THEOREM 2. *It is an abstract consequence of Theorem 1 that any elements a and b of $L(M^*)$ determine a unique "join" $a \cup b$ with the properties*

[4] It is extremely useful in applications. For instance, it shows that if we adjoin a purely formal "unity" i, we can subsume the theory of "effective implication" as defined by E. V. Huntington in his note "Effective equality and effective implication in formal logic," *Proceedings of the USA Academy of Sciences*, May, 1935, under the theory of lattices in the finite [but not the infinite!] case. Viewed in this light, his propositions 32, 33, 34, 36, 37 appear as extensions to the infinite case of Theorems 4. 2, 6. 1, 6. 2, 6. 3 of "Subalgebras."

With regard to precedence, it was Professor Huntington's paper which suggested Theorem 2 to me originally.

(L_5) $a \cap (a \cup b) = a \cup (a \cap b) = a$.

(L_6) $a \cup a = a$, $a \cup b = b \cup a$, *and* $a \cup (b \cup c) = (a \cup b) \cup c$.

The main thing is to define $a \cup b$. To do this, note first that $i \cap a = a$ and $i \cap b = b$. Second, not that if $c \cap a = a$ and $c' \cap a = a$, *then*

$$(c \cap c') \cap a = c \cap (c' \cap a) = c \cap a = a.$$

Therefore if we set $c_0 = i$, and try to find successive elements $c_1, c_2, c_3, \cdots$ such that $c_k \cap a = a$, $c_k \cap b = b$, and yet $c_0 \cap \cdots \cap c_k$ differs from every $c_0 \cap \cdots \cap c_j$ $[j < k]$, then by (L_4) we obtain after a finite number of attempts, an element $d = c_0 \cap \cdots \cap c_n$ such that (1) $d \cap a = a$ and $d \cap b = b$ (2) if $c^* \cap a = a$ and $c^* \cap b = b$, then $c^* \cap d = c_1 \cap \cdots \cap c_k$ for some $k < n$—which, since

$$c^* \cap d = c^* \cap (d \cap d) = (c^* \cap d) \cap d = c_1 \cap \cdots \cap c_k \cap d = d$$

[by iterated use of (L_2)], means $c^* \cap d = d$.

Conditions (1)-(2) and (L_2) show that d is determined uniquely by a and b; we shall *define* $a \cup b$ as d. To prove that $a \cup b$ satisfies (L_5)-(L_6) is now merely a question of substituting from (1)-(2), and using condition (L_2).

This completes the proof, the details of which the reader should be able to fill in without difficulty.

4. *Principal results.* But by definition, an "abstract lattice" is any system which satisfies (L_1)-(L_2) and (L_5)-(L_6). Consequently, we have

THEOREM 3. *$L(M^*)$ is an abstract lattice.*

Not all lattices correspond to matroids; in particular, every lattice corresponding to a matroid contains only a finite number of elements. The facts as to which lattices correspond to matroids can however be summarized as follows.

A finite lattice corresponds to a matroid if and only if (1) if b and c are smallest distinct elements larger than a, then $b \cup c$ is a smallest element larger than b. (This is the "dual" [under the inversion of inclusion [5]] of the abstract property of composition subgroups used in the classic proof of the Theorem of Jordan-Hölder) (2) every element can be expressed as the "join" of elements of rank one.

---

[5] It being observed that the definition of a lattice is invariant under inversion of meet and join. Property (1) amounts in the case in hand to the property that if two linearly complete subsets of M^* of rank $(n+1)$ intersect in a subset of rank n, then the rank of their join is $(n+2)$.

Moreover the "rank" $r(N)$ of any subset N of elements $e_1, \cdots, e_k$ of M^* is equal to the length of any chain [in the sense of the Theorem of Jordan-Hölder] in $L(M^*)$, between the lattice-element corresponding to the null subset, and the "join" of the lattice-elements corresponding (under Theorem 1) to the e_i. That is,

THEOREM 4. *The structure of $L(M^*)$ determines that of M^*—and hence that of M.*

5. *Theoretical consequences.* The results of the last sections suggest trying to interpret theorems on matroids as theorems on lattices, and conversely. This can be done in at least two cases.

The less interesting of these is Whitney's Theorem 3, which may be regarded as a reappearance [6] of the first formula of Theorem 9.2 of "Subalgebras."

A more interesting correspondence concerns Whitney's Theorem 15 on separability, which is a generalization of a well-known theorem on graphs. This theorem may, in the light of the above results, be regarded as a specialization of a theorem [7] on the "strong" uniqueness of the representation of *any* lattice as the direct product of irreducible (= non-separable) components.

6. *Geometrical correspondence.* In another paper,[8] S. MacLane has shown that M^* also corresponds to a schematic configuration of dimensions $r(M^*) - 1$, and has pointed out a relationship with projective geometries. This defines an obvious correspondence *via* matroids between "matroid lattices" (or lattices satisfying conditions (1)-(2) of § 4) and schematic configurations.

In terms of this correspondence, results proved elsewhere [9] by the author directly imply

THEOREM 5. *A schematic configuration is the direct product of a finite number of projective geometries and single points, if and only if the dual [under the inversion of join and meet] of the corresponding matroid lattice, is again a matroid lattice.*

---

[6] This formula very likely has a long previous history.

[7] Proved in the author's "On the lattice theory of ideals," *Bulletin of the American Mathematical Society*, vol. 40 (1934), p. 616, Theorem 2.

[8] Cf. footnote 3, above. A much weaker result of the same sort was obtained by the author, in Theorem 5 of "On the structure of abstract algebras," to appear shortly in the *Proceedings of the Cambridge Philological Society.*

[9] "Subalgebras," Theorem 10.2, and "Combinatorial relations in projective geometries," *Annals of Mathematics*, vol. 36 (1935), pp. 743-748.

(By the "direct product" of two projective geometries P and P^* is meant the system whose elements are the couples (A, A^*) [A any m-plane of P and A^* any m^*-plane of P^*], and in which (A, A^*) lies in (B, B^*) if and only if A lies in B and A^* in B^*. This is the inverse of the notion of separation into non-separable components mentioned above).

Theorem 5 and well-known results [10] show that such schematic configurations can in general be realized by vectors in spaces whose coördinates lie in suitable finite fields.

Society of Fellows,
Harvard University.

Reprinted from *Am. J. Math.* **57** (1935), 800–804

[10] O. Veblen and W. H. Bussey, "Finite projective geometries," *American Transactions*, vol. 7 (1906), pp. 241-259.

Annals of Mathematics
Vol. 37, No. 4, October, 1936

THE LOGIC OF QUANTUM MECHANICS

By Garrett Birkhoff and John von Neumann

(Received April 4, 1936)

1. **Introduction.** One of the aspects of quantum theory which has attracted the most general attention, is the novelty of the logical notions which it presupposes. It asserts that even a complete mathematical description of a physical system $\mathfrak{S}$ does not in general enable one to predict with certainty the result of an experiment on $\mathfrak{S}$, and that in particular one can never predict with certainty both the position and the momentum of $\mathfrak{S}$ (Heisenberg's Uncertainty Principle). It further asserts that most pairs of observations are incompatible, and cannot be made on $\mathfrak{S}$ simultaneously (Principle of Non-commutativity of Observations).

The object of the present paper is to discover what logical structure one may hope to find in physical theories which, like quantum mechanics, do not conform to classical logic. Our main conclusion, based on admittedly heuristic arguments, is that one can reasonably expect to find a calculus of propositions which is formally indistinguishable from the calculus of linear subspaces with respect to *set products*, *linear sums*, and *orthogonal complements*—and resembles the usual calculus of propositions with respect to *and*, *or*, and *not*.

In order to avoid being committed to quantum theory in its present form, we have first (in §§2–6) stated the heuristic arguments which suggest that such a calculus is the proper one in quantum mechanics, and then (in §§7–14) reconstructed this calculus from the axiomatic standpoint. In both parts an attempt has been made to clarify the discussion by continual comparison with classical mechanics and its propositional calculi. The paper ends with a few tentative conclusions which may be drawn from the material just summarized.

I. Physical Background

2. **Observations on physical systems.** The concept of a physically observable "physical system" is present in all branches of physics, and we shall assume it.

It is clear that an "observation" of a physical system $\mathfrak{S}$ can be described generally as a writing down of the readings from various[1] compatible measurements. Thus if the measurements are denoted by the symbols $\mu_1, \cdots, \mu_n$, then

[1] If one prefers, one may regard a set of compatible measurements as a single composite "measurement"—and also admit non-numerical readings—without interfering with subsequent arguments.

Among conspicuous observables in quantum theory are position, momentum, energy, and (non-numerical) symmetry.

an observation of $\mathfrak{S}$ amounts to specifying numbers $x_1, \cdots, x_n$ corresponding to the different μ_k.

It follows that the most general form of a prediction concerning $\mathfrak{S}$ is that the point $(x_1, \cdots, x_n)$ determined by actually measuring $\mu_1, \cdots, \mu_n$, will lie in a subset S of $(x_1, \cdots, x_n)$-space. Hence if we call the $(x_1, \cdots, x_n)$-spaces associated with $\mathfrak{S}$, its "observation-spaces," we may call the subsets of the observation-spaces associated with any physical system $\mathfrak{S}$, the "experimental propositions" concerning $\mathfrak{S}$.

3. **Phase-spaces.** There is one concept which quantum theory shares alike with classical mechanics and classical electrodynamics. This is the concept of a mathematical "phase-space."

According to this concept, any physical system $\mathfrak{S}$ is at each instantly hypothetically associated with a "point" p in a fixed phase-space Σ; this point is supposed to represent mathematically the "state" of $\mathfrak{S}$, and the "state" of $\mathfrak{S}$ is supposed to be ascertainable by "maximal"[2] observations.

Furthermore, the point p_0 associated with $\mathfrak{S}$ at a time t_0, together with a prescribed mathematical "law of propagation," fix the point p_t associated with $\mathfrak{S}$ at any later time t; this assumption evidently embodies the principle of *mathematical causation.*[3]

Thus in classical mechanics, each point of Σ corresponds to a choice of n position and n conjugate momentum coördinates—and the law of propagation may be Newton's inverse-square law of attraction. Hence in this case Σ is a region of ordinary $2n$-dimensional space. In electrodynamics, the points of Σ can only be specified after certain *functions*—such as the electromagnetic and electrostatic potential—are known; hence Σ is a function-space of infinitely many dimensions. Similarly, in quantum theory the points of Σ correspond to so-called "wave-functions," and hence Σ is again a function-space—usually[4] assumed to be Hilbert space.

In electrodynamics, the law of propagation is contained in Maxwell's equations, and in quantum theory, in equations due to Schrödinger. In any case, the law of propagation may be imagined as inducing a steady fluid motion in the phase-space.

It has proved to be a fruitful observation that in many important cases of classical dynamics, this flow conserves volumes. It may be noted that in quantum mechanics, the flow conserves distances (i.e., the equations are "unitary").

---

[2] L. Pauling and E. B. Wilson, "*An introduction to quantum mechanics*," McGraw-Hill, 1935, p. 422. Dirac, "*Quantum mechanics*," Oxford, 1930, §4.

[3] For the existence of mathematical causation, cf. also p. 65 of Heisenberg's "*The physical principles of the quantum theory*," Chicago, 1929.

[4] Cf. J. von Neumann, "*Mathematische Grundlagen der Quanten-mechanik*," Berlin, 1931. p. 18.

4. **Propositions as subsets of phase-space.** Now before a phase-space can become imbued with reality, its elements and subsets must be correlated in some way with "experimental propositions" (which are subsets of different observation-spaces). Moreover, this must be so done that set-theoretical inclusion (which is the analogue of logical implication) is preserved.

There is an obvious way to do this in dynamical systems of the classical type.[5] One can measure position and its first time-derivative velocity—and hence momentum—explicitly, and so establish a one-one correspondence which preserves inclusion between subsets of phase-space and subsets of a suitable observation-space.

In the cases of the kinetic theory of gases and of electromagnetic waves no such simple procedure is possible, but it was imagined for a long time that "demons" of small enough size could by tracing the motion of each particle, or by a dynamometer and infinitesimal point-charges and magnets, measure quantities corresponding to every coördinate of the phase-space involved.

In quantum theory not even this is imagined, and the possibility of predicting in general the readings from measurements on a physical system $\mathfrak{S}$ from a knowledge of its "state" is denied; only statistical predictions are always possible.

This has been interpreted as a renunciation of the doctrine of pre-determination; a thoughtful analysis shows that another and more subtle idea is involved. The central idea is that physical quantities are *related*, but are not all computable from a number of *independent basic* quantities (such as position and velocity).[6]

We shall show in §12 that this situation has an exact algebraic analogue in the calculus of propositions.

5. **Propositional calculi in classical dynamics.** Thus we see that an uncritical acceptance of the ideas of classical dynamics (particularly as they involve n-body problems) leads one to identify each subset of phase-space with an experimental proposition (the proposition that the system considered has position and momentum coördinates satisfying certain conditions) and conversely.

This is easily seen to be unrealistic; for example, how absurd it would be to call an "experimental proposition," the assertion that the angular momentum (in radians per second) of the earth around the sun was at a particular instant a rational number!

Actually, at least in statistics, it seems best to assume that it is the *Lebesgue-measurable* subsets of a phase-space which correspond to experimental propositions, two subsets being identified, if their difference has *Lebesgue-measure* 0.[7]

[5] Like systems idealizing the solar system or projectile motion.

[6] A similar situation arises when one tries to correlate polarizations in different planes of electromagnetic waves.

[7] Cf. J. von Neumann, "*Operatorenmethoden in der klassischen Mechanik*," Annals of Math. 33 (1932), 595–8. The difference of two sets S_1, S_2 is the set $(S_1 + S_2) - S_1 \cdot S_2$ of those points, which belong to one of them, but not to both.

But in either case, the set-theoretical sum and product of any two subsets, and the complement of any one subset of phase-space corresponding to experimental propositions, has the same property. That is, by definition[8]

The experimental propositions concerning any system in classical mechanics, correspond to a "field" of subsets of its phase-space. More precisely: To the "quotient" of such a field by an ideal in it. At any rate they form a "Boolean Algebra."[9]

In the axiomatic discussion of propositional calculi which follows, it will be shown that this is inevitable when one is dealing with exclusively compatible measurements, and also that it is logically immaterial which particular field of sets is used.

6. **A propositional calculus for quantum mechanics.** The question of the connection in quantum mechanics between subsets of observation-spaces (or "experimental propositions") and subsets of the phase-space of a system $\mathfrak{S}$, has not been touched. The present section will be devoted to defining such a connection, proving some facts about it, and obtaining from it heuristically by introducing a plausible postulate, a propositional calculus for quantum mechanics.

Accordingly, let us observe that if $\alpha_1, \cdots, \alpha_n$ are any compatible observations on a quantum-mechanical system $\mathfrak{S}$ with phase-space Σ, then[10] there exists a set of mutually orthogonal closed linear subspaces Ω_i of Σ (which correspond to the families of proper functions satisfying $\alpha_1 f = \lambda_{i,1} f, \cdots, \alpha_n f = \lambda_{i,n} f$) such that *every* point (or function) $f \in \Sigma$ can be uniquely written in the form

$$f = c_1 f_1 + c_2 f_2 + c_3 f_3 + \cdots \quad [f_i \in \Omega_i]$$

Hence if we state the

Definition: By the "mathematical representative" of a subset S of any observation-space (determined by compatible observations $\alpha_1, \cdots, \alpha_n$) for a quantum-mechanical system $\mathfrak{S}$, will be meant the set of all points f of the phase-space of $\mathfrak{S}$, which are linearly determined by proper functions f_k satisfying $\alpha_1 f_k = \lambda_1 f_k, \cdots, \alpha_n f_k = \lambda_n f_k$, where $(\lambda_1, \cdots, \lambda_n) \in S$.

Then it follows immediately: (1) that the mathematical representative of any experimental proposition is a closed linear subspace of Hilbert space (2) since all operators of quantum mechanics are Hermitian, that the mathematical representative of the *negative*[11] of any experimental proposition is the *orthogonal*

[8] F. Hausdorff, "*Mengenlehre,*" Berlin, 1927, p. 78.

[9] M. H. Stone, "*Boolean Algebras and their application to topology,*" Proc. Nat. Acad. 20 (1934), p. 197.

[10] Cf. von Neumann, op. cit., pp. 121, 90, or Dirac, op. cit., 17. We disregard complications due to the possibility of a continuous spectrum. They are inessential in the present case.

[11] By the "negative" of an experimental proposition (or subset S of an observation-space) is meant the experimental proposition corresponding to the set-complement of S in the same observation-space.

complement of the mathematical representative of the proposition itself (3) the following three conditions on two experimental propositions P and Q concerning a given type of physical system are equivalent:

(3a) The mathematical representative of P is a subset of the mathematical representative of Q.

(3b) P implies Q—that is, whenever one can predict P with certainty, one can predict Q with certainty.

(3c) For any statistical ensemble of systems, the probability of P is at most the probability of Q.

The equivalence of (3a)–(3c) leads one to regard the aggregate of the mathematical representatives of the experimental propositions concerning any physical system $\mathfrak{S}$, as representing mathematically the propositional calculus for $\mathfrak{S}$.

We now introduce the

POSTULATE: *The set-theoretical product of any two mathematical representatives of experimental propositions concerning a quantum-mechanical system, is itself the mathematical representative of an experimental proposition.*

REMARKS: This postulate would clearly be implied by the not unnatural conjecture that all Hermitian-symmetric operators in Hilbert space (phase-space) correspond to observables;[12] it would even be implied by the conjecture that those operators which correspond to observables coincide with the Hermitian-symmetric elements of a suitable operator-ring M.[13]

Now the closed linear sum $\Omega_1 + \Omega_2$ of any two closed linear subspaces Ω_i of Hilbert space, is the orthogonal complement of the set-product $\Omega_1' \cdot \Omega_2'$ of the orthogonal complements Ω_i' of the Ω_i; hence if one adds the above postulate to the usual postulates of quantum theory, then one can deduce that

The set-product and closed linear sum of any two, and the orthogonal complement of any one closed linear subspace of Hilbert space representing mathematically an experimental proposition concerning a quantum-mechanical system $\mathfrak{S}$, itself represents an experimental proposition concerning $\mathfrak{S}$.

This defines the calculus of experimental propositions concerning $\mathfrak{S}$, as a calculus with three operations and a relation of implication, which closely resembles the systems defined in §5. We shall now turn to the analysis and comparison of all three calculi from an axiomatic-algebraic standpoint.

II. ALGEBRAIC ANALYSIS

7. Implication as partial ordering. It was suggested above that in any physical theory involving a phase-space, the experimental propositions concern-

[12] I.e., that given such an operator α, one "could" find an observable for which the proper states were the proper functions of α.

[13] F. J. Murray and J. v. Neumann, "*On rings of operators*," Annals of Math., 37 (1936), p. 120. It is shown on p. 141, loc. cit. (Definition 4.2.1 and Lemma 4.2.1), that the closed linear sets of a ring M—that is those, the "projection operators" of which belong to M—coincide with the closed linear sets which are invariant under a certain group of rotations of Hilbert space. And the latter property is obviously conserved when a set-theoretical intersection is formed.

ing a system $\mathfrak{S}$ correspond to a family of subsets of its phase-space Σ, in such a way that "x implies y" (x and y being any two experimental propositions) means that the subset of Σ corresponding to x is contained set-theoretically in the subset corresponding to y. This hypothesis clearly is important in proportion as relationships of implication exist between experimental propositions corresponding to subsets of different observation-spaces.

The present section will be devoted to corroborating this hypothesis by identifying the algebraic-axiomatic properties of logical implication with those of set-inclusion.

It is customary to admit as relations of "implication," only relations satisfying

S1: x implies x.
S2: If x implies y and y implies z, then x implies z.
S3: If x implies y and y implies x, then x and y are logically equivalent.

In fact, S3 need not be stated as a postulate at all, but can be regarded as a definition of logical equivalence. Pursuing this line of thought, one can interpret as a "physical quality," the set of all experimental propositions logically equivalent to a given experimental proposition.[14]

Now if one regards the set S_x of propositions implying a given proposition x as a "mathematical representative" of x, then by $S3$ the correspondence between the x and the S_x is one-one, and x implies y if and only if $S_x \subset S_y$. While conversely, if L is any system of subsets X of a fixed class Γ, then there is an isomorphism which carries inclusion into logical implication between L and the system L^* of propositions "x is a point of X," $X \in L$.

Thus we see that the properties of logical implication are indistinguishable from those of set-inclusion, and that therefore it is *algebraically* reasonable to try to correlate physical qualities with subsets of phase-space.

A system satisfying S1-S3, and in which the relation "x implies y" is written $x \subset y$, is usually[15] called a "partially ordered system," and thus our first postulate concerning propositional calculi is that *the physical qualities attributable to any physical system form a partially ordered system.*

It does not seem excessive to require that in addition any such calculus contain two special propositions: the proposition $\square$ that the system considered *exists*, and the proposition $\circledcirc$ that it does *not exist.* Clearly

S4: $\circledcirc \subset x \subset \square$ for any x.

$\circledcirc$ is, from a logical standpoint, the "identically false" or "absurd" proposition; $\square$ is the "identically true" or "self-evident" proposition.

8. Lattices. In any calculus of propositions, it is natural to imagine that there is a weakest proposition implying, and a strongest proposition implied by,

[14] Thus in §6, closed linear subspaces of Hilbert space correspond one-many to experimental propositions, but one-one to physical qualities in this sense.

[15] F. Hausdorff, "*Grundzüge der Mengenlehre,*" Leipzig, 1914, Chap. VI, §1.

a given pair of propositions. In fact, investigations of partially ordered systems from different angles all indicate that the first property which they are likely to possess, is the existence of greatest lower bounds and least upper bounds to subsets of their elements. Accordingly, we state

DEFINITION: A partially ordered system L will be called a "lattice" if and only if to any pair x and y of its elements there correspond

S5: A "meet" or "greatest lower bound" $x \cap y$ such that (5a) $x \cap y \subset x$, (5b) $x \cap y \subset y$, (5c) $z \subset x$ and $z \subset y$ imply $z \subset x \cap y$.

S6: A "join" or "least upper bound" $x \cap y$ satisfying (6a) $x \cup y \supset x$, (6b) $x \cup y \supset y$, (6c) $w \supset x$ and $w \supset y$ imply $w \supset x \cup y$.

The relation between meets and joins and abstract inclusion can be summarized as follows,[16]

(8.1) In any lattice L, the following formal identities are true,

L1: $a \cap a = a$ and $a \cup a = a$.
L2: $a \cap b = b \cap a$ and $a \cup b = b \cup a$.
L3: $a \cap (b \cap c) = (a \cap b) \cap c$ and $a \cup (b \cup c) = (a \cup b) \cup c$.
L4: $a \cup (a \cap b) = a \cap (a \cup b) = a$.

Moreover, the relations $a \supset b$, $a \cap b = b$, and $a \cup b = a$ are equivalent—each implies both of the others.

(8.2) Conversely, in any set of elements satisfying L2–L4 (L1 is redundant), $a \cap b = b$ and $a \cup b = a$ are equivalent. And if one defines them to mean $a \supset b$, then one reveals L as a lattice.

Clearly L1–L4 are well-known formal properties of *and* and *or* in ordinary logic. This gives an algebraic reason for admitting as a *postulate* (if necessary) the statement that a given calculus of propositions is a lattice. There are other reasons[17] which impel one to admit as a postulate the stronger statement that the set-product of any two subsets of a phase-space which correspond to physical qualities, itself represents a physical quality—this is, of course, the Postulate of §6.

It is worth remarking that in classical mechanics, one can easily define the meet or join of any two experimental propositions as an *experimental proposition*—simply by having independent observers read off the measurements which either proposition involves, and combining the results logically. This is true in quantum mechanics only exceptionally—only when all the measurements involved commute (are compatible); in general, one can only express the join or

[16] The final result was found independently by O. Öre, "*The foundations of abstract algebra.* I.," Annals of Math. 36 (1935), 406–37, and by H. MacNeille in his Harvard Doctoral Thesis, 1935.

[17] The first reason is that this implies no restriction on the abstract nature of a lattice—any lattice can be realized as a system of its own subsets, in such a way that $a \cap b$ is the set-product of a and b. The second reason is that if one regards a subset S of the phase-space of a system $\mathfrak{S}$ as corresponding to the *certainty* of observing $\mathfrak{S}$ in S, then it is natural to assume that the combined certainty of observing $\mathfrak{S}$ in S and T is the certainty of observing $\mathfrak{S}$ in $S \cdot T = S \cap T$,—and assumes quantum theory.

meet of two given experimental propositions as a class of logically equivalent experimental propositions—i.e., as a *physical quality*.[18]

9. Complemented lattices. Besides the (binary) operations of meet- and join-formation, there is a third (unary) operation which may be defined in partially ordered systems. This is the operation of *complementation*.

In the case of lattices isomorphic with "fields" of sets, complementation corresponds to passage to the set-complement. In the case of closed linear subspaces of Hilbert space (or of Cartesian n-space), it corresponds to passage to the orthogonal complement. In either case, denoting the "complement" of an element a by a', one has the formal identities,

L71: $(a')' = a$.
L72: $a \cap a' = \circledcirc$ and $a \cup a' = \square$.
L73: $a \subset b$ implies $a' \supset b'$.

By definition, L71 and L73 amount to asserting that complementation is a "dual automorphism" of period two. It is an immediate corollary of this and the duality between the definitions (in terms of inclusion) of meet and join, that

L74: $(a \cap b)' = a' \cup b'$ and $(a \cup b)' = a' \cap b'$

and another corollary that the second half of L72 is redundant. [*Proof*: by L71 and the first half of L74, $(a \cup a') = (a'' \cup a') = (a' \cap a)' = \circledcirc'$, while under inversion of inclusion $\circledcirc$ evidently becomes $\square$.] This permits one to deduce L72 from the even weaker assumption that $a \subset a'$ implies $a = \circledcirc$. *Proof*: for any x, $(x \cap x')' = (x' \cup x'') = x' \cup x \supset x \cap x'$.

Hence if one admits as a postulate the assertion that *passage from an experimental proposition a to its complement a′ is a dual automorphism of period two, and a implies a′ is absurd*, one has in effect admitted L71–L74.

This postulate is independently suggested (and L71 proved) by the fact the "complement" of the proposition that the readings $x_1, \cdots, x_n$ from a series of compatible observations $\mu_1, \cdots, \mu_n$ lie in a subset S of $(x_1, \cdots, x_n)$-space, is by definition the proposition that the readings lie in the set-complement of S.

10. The distributive identity. Up to now, we have only discussed formal features of logical structure which seem to be common to classical dynamics and the quantum theory. We now turn to the central difference between them—the *distributive identity* of the propositional calculus:

L6: $a \cup (b \cap c) = (a \cup b) \cap (a \cup c)$ and $a \cap (b \cup c) = (a \cap b) \cup (a \cap c)$

which is a law in classical, but not in quantum mechanics.

[18] The following point should be mentioned in order to avoid misunderstanding: If a, b are two physical qualities, then $a \cup b$, $a \cap b$ and a' (cf. below) are physical qualities too (and so are $\circledcirc$ and $\square$+)). But $a \subset b$ is not a physical quality; it is a relation between physical qualities.

From an axiomatic viewpoint, each half of L6 implies the other.[19] Further, either half of L6, taken with L72, implies L71 and L73, and to assume L6 and L72 amounts to assuming the usual definition of a Boolean algebra.[20]

From a deeper mathematical viewpoint, L6 is the characteristic property of set-combination. More precisely, every "field" of sets is isomorphic with a Boolean algebra, and conversely.[21] This throws new light on the well-known fact that the propositional calculi of classical mechanics are Boolean algebras.

It is interesting that L6 is also a logical consequence of the compatibility of the observables occurring in a, b, and c. That is, if observations are made by independent observers, and combined according to the usual rules of logic, one can *prove* L1–L4, L6, and L71–74.

These facts suggest that the distributive law *may* break down in quantum mechanics. That it *does* break down is shown by the fact that if a denotes the experimental observation of a wave-packet ψ on one side of a plane in ordinary space, a' correspondingly the observation of ψ on the other side, and b the observation of ψ in a state symmetric about the plane, then (as one can readily check):

$$b \cap (a \cup a') = b \cap \square = b > \circledcirc = (b \cap a) = (b \cap a')$$
$$= (b \cap a) \cup (b \cap a')$$

REMARK: In connection with this, it is a salient fact that the *generalized* distributive law of logic:

$$\text{L6*:} \quad \prod_{i=1}^{m} \left(\sum_{j=1}^{n} a_{i,j} \right) = \sum_{j(i)} \left(\prod_{i=1}^{m} a_{i,j(i)} \right)$$

breaks down in the quotient algebra of the field of Lebesgue measurable sets by the ideal of sets of Lebesgue measure 0, which is so fundamental in statistics and the formulation of the ergodic principle.[22]

11. **The modular identity.** Although closed linear subspaces of Hilbert space and Cartesian n-space need not satisfy L6 relative to set-products and closed linear sums, the formal properties of these operations are not confined to L1–L4 and L71–L73.

In particular, set-products and straight linear sums are known[23] to satisfy the so-called "modular identity."

---

[19] R. Dedekind, "*Werke*," Braunschweig, 1931, vol. 2, p. 110.

[20] G. Birkhoff, "*On the combination of subalgebras*," Proc. Camb. Phil. Soc. 29 (1933), 441–64, §§23–4. Also, in any lattice satisfying L6, isomorphism with respect to inclusion implies isomorphism with respect to complementation; this need not be true if L6 is not assumed, as the lattice of linear subspaces through the origin of Cartesian n-space shows.

[21] M. H. Stone, "*Boolean algebras and their application to topology*," Proc. Nat. Acad. 20 (1934), 197–202.

[22] A detailed explanation will be omitted, for brevity; one could refer to work of G. D. Birkhoff, J. von Neumann, and A. Tarski.

[23] G. Birkhoff, op. cit., §28. The proof is easy. One first notes that since $a \subset (a \cup b) \cap c$ if $a \subset c$, and $b \cap c \subset (a \cup b) \cap c$ in any case, $a \cup (b \cap c) \subset (a \cup b) \cap c$. Then one notes

L5: If $a \subset c$, then $a \cup (b \cap c) = (a \cup b) \cap c$.

Therefore (since the linear sum of any two finite-dimensional linear subspaces of Hilbert space is itself finite-dimensional and consequently closed) set-products and *closed* linear sums of the *finite dimensional* subspaces of any topological linear space such as Cartesian n-space or Hilbert space satisfy L5, too.

One can interpret L5 directly in various ways. First, it is evidently a restricted associative law on mixed joins and meets. It can equally well be regarded as a weakened distributive law, since if $a \subset c$, then $a \cup (b \cap c) = (a \cap c) \cup (b \cap c)$ and $(a \cup b) \cap c = (a \cup b) \cap (a \cup c)$. And it is self-dual: replacing $\subset, \cap, \cup$ by $\supset, \cup, \cap$ merely replaces a, b, c, by c, b, a.

Also, speaking graphically, the assumption that a lattice L is "modular" (i.e., satisfies L5) is equivalent to[24] saying that L contains no sublattice isomorphic with the lattice graphed in fig. 1:

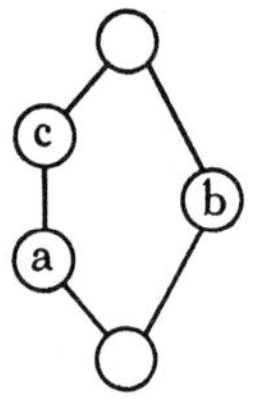

FIG. 1

Thus in Hilbert space, one can find a counterexample to L5 of this type. Denote by $\xi_1, \xi_2, \xi_3, \cdots$ a basis of orthonormal vectors of the space, and by a, b, and c respectively the closed linear subspaces generated by the vectors $(\xi_{2n} + 10^{-n}\xi_1 + 10^{-2n}\xi_{2n+1})$, by the vectors ξ_{2n}, and by a and the vector ξ_1. Then a, b, and c generate the lattice of Fig. 1.

Finally, the modular identity can be proved to be a consequence of the assumption that there exists a numerical dimension-function $d(a)$, with the properties

D1: If $a > b$, then $d(a) > d(b)$.
D2: $d(a) + d(b) = d(a \cap b) + d(a \cup b)$.

This theorem has a converse under the restriction to lattices in which there is a finite upper bound to the length n of chains[25] $\circledcirc < a_1 < a_2 < \cdots < a_n < \square$ of elements.

Since conditions D1–D2 partially describe the formal properties of probability, the presence of condition L5 is closely related to the existence of an

that any vector in $(a \cup b) \cap c$ can be written $\xi = \alpha + \beta$ $[\alpha \in a, \beta \in b, \xi \in c]$. But $\beta = \xi - \alpha$ is in c (since $\xi \in c$ and $\alpha \in a \subset c$); hence $\xi = \alpha + \beta \in a \cup (b \cap c)$, and $a \cup (b \cap c) \supset (a \cup b) \cap c$, completing the proof.

[24] R. Dedekind, "*Werke*," vol. 2, p. 255.

[25] The statements of this paragraph are corollaries of Theorem 10.2 of G. Birkhoff, op. cit.

"a priori thermo-dynamic weight of states." But it would be desirable to interpret L5 by simpler phenomenological properties of quantum physics.

12. **Relation to abstract projective geometries.** We shall next investigate how the assumption of postulates asserting that the physical qualities attributable to any quantum-mechanical system $\mathfrak{S}$ are a lattice satisfying L5 and L71–L73 characterizes the resulting propositional calculus. This question is evidently purely algebraic.

We believe that the best way to find this out is to introduce an assumption limiting the length of chains of elements (assumption of finite dimensions) of the lattice, admitting frankly that the assumption is purely heuristic.

It is known[26] that any lattice of finite dimensions satisfying L5 and L72 is the direct product of a finite number of abstract projective geometries (in the sense of Veblen and Young), and a finite Boolean algebra, and conversely.

REMARK: It is a corollary that a lattice satisfying L5 and L71–L73 possesses independent basic elements of which any element is a union, if and only if it is a Boolean algebra.

Again, such a lattice is a single projective geometry if and only if it is *irreducible*—that is, if and only if it contains no "neutral" elements.[27] $x \neq ◎, □$ such that $a = (a \cap x) \cup (a \cap x')$ for all a. In actual quantum mechanics such an element would have a projection-operator, which commutes with all projection-operators of observables, and so with all operators of observables in general. This would violate the requirement of "irreducibility" in quantum mechanics.[28] Hence we conclude that the *propositional calculus of quantum mechanics has the same structure as an abstract projective geometry.*

Moreover, this conclusion has been obtained purely by analyzing internal properties of the calculus, in a way which involves Hilbert space only indirectly.

13. **Abstract projective geometries and skew-fields.** We shall now try to get a fresh picture of the propositional calculus of quantum mechanics, by recalling the well-known two-way correspondence between abstract projective geometries and (not necessarily commutative) fields.

Namely, let F be any such field, and consider the following definitions and constructions: n elements $x_1, \cdots, x_n$ of F, not all $= 0$, form a right-ratio $[x_1 : \cdots : x_n]_r$, two right-ratios $[x_1 : \cdots : x_n]_r$, and $[\xi_1 : \cdots : \xi_n]_r$ being called "equal," if and only if a $z \in F$ with $\xi_i = x_i z$, $i = 1, \cdots, n$, exists. Similarly, n elements $y_1, \cdots, y_n$ of F, not all $= 0$, form a left-ratio $[y_1 : \cdots : y_n]_l$, two left-ratios $[y_1 : \cdots : y_n]_l$ and $[\eta_1 : \cdots : \eta_n]_l$ being called "equal," if and only if a z in F with $\eta_i = z y_i$, $i = 1, \cdots, n$, exists.

[26] G. Birkhoff "*Combinatorial relations in projective geometries,*" Annals of Math. 36 (1935), 743–8.

[27] O. Öre, op. cit., p. 419.

[28] Using the terminology of footnote,[13] and of loc. cit. there: The ring MM' should contain no other projection-operators than 0, 1, or: the ring M must be a "factor." Cf. loc. cit.[13], p. 120.

Now define an $n-1$-dimensional projective geometry $P_{n-1}(F)$ as follows: The "points" of $P_{n-1}(F)$ are all right-ratios $[x_1: \cdots :x_n]_r$. The "linear subspaces" of $P_{m-1}(F)$ are those sets of points, which are defined by systems of equations

$$\alpha_{k1}x_1 + \cdots + \alpha_{kn}x_n = 0, \qquad k = 1, \cdots, m.$$

($m = 1, 2, \cdots$, the α_{ki} are fixed, but arbitrary elements of F). The proof, that this *is* an abstract projective geometry, amounts simply to restating the basic properties of linear dependence.[29]

The same considerations show, that the ($n-2$-dimensional) hyperplanes in $P_{m-1}(F)$ correspond to $m = 1$, not all $\alpha_i = 0$. Put $\alpha_{1i} = y_i$, then we have

$$(*) \qquad y_1x_1 + \cdots + y_nx_n = 0, \qquad \text{not all } y_i = 0.$$

This proves, that the ($n-2$-dimensional) hyperplanes in $P_{m-1}(F)$ are in a one-to-one correspondence with the left-ratios $[y_r: \cdots :y_n]_l$.

So we can identify them with the left-ratios, as points are already identical with the right-ratios, and (*) becomes the definition of "incidence" (point $\subset$ hyperplane).

Reciprocally, any abstract $n-1$-dimensional projective geometry Q_{n-1} with $n = 4, 5, \cdots$ belongs in this way to some (not necessarily commutative field $F(Q_{n-1})$, and Q_{n-1} is isomorphic with $P_{n-1}(F(Q_{n-1}))$.[30]

14. **Relation of abstract complementarity to involutory anti-isomorphisms in skew-fields.** We have seen that the family of irreducible lattices satisfying L5 and L72 is precisely the family of projective geometries, provided we exclude the two-dimensional case. But what about L71 and L73? In other words, for which $P_{n-1}(F)$ can one define complements possessing all the known formal properties of orthogonal complements? The present section will be spent in answering this question:[30a]

---

[29] Cf. §§103–105 of B. L. Van der Waerden's "*Moderne Algebra,*" Berlin, 1931, Vol. 2.

[30] $n = 4, 5, \cdots$ means of course $n - 1 \geqq 3$, that is, that Q_{n-1} is necessarily a "Desarguesian" geometry. (Cf. O. Veblen and J. W. Young, "*Projective Geometry,*" New York, 1910, Vol. 1, page 41). Then $F = F(Q_{n-1})$ can be constructed in the classical way. (Cf. Veblen and Young, Vol. 1, pages 141–150). The proof of the isomorphism between Q_{n-1} and the $P_{n-1}(F)$ as constructed above, amounts to this: Introducing (not necessarily commutative) homogeneous coördinates $x_1, \cdots, x_n$ from F in Q_{n-1}, and expressing the equations of hyperplanes with their help. This can be done in the manner which is familiar in projective geometry, although most books consider the commutative ("Pascalian") case only. D. Hilbert, "*Grundlagen der Geometrie,*" 7th edition, 1930, pages 96–103, considers the non-commutative case, but for affine geometry, and $n - 1 = 2, 3$ only.

Considering the lengthy although elementary character of the complete proof, we propose to publish it elsewhere.

[30a] R. Brauer, "*A characterization of null systems in projective space,*" Bull. Am. Math. Soc. 42 (1936), 247–54, treats the analogous question in the opposite case that $X \cap X' \neq \circledcirc$ is postulated.

First, we shall show that it is *sufficient* that F admit an *involutory antisomorphism* $W: \bar{x} = W(x)$, that is:

Q1. $w(w(u)) = u,$
Q2. $w(u + v) = w(u) + w(v),$
Q3. $w(uv) = w(v)\, w(u),$

with a *definite diagonal Hermitian form* $w(x_1)\gamma_1 \xi_1 + \cdots + w(x_n)\gamma_n \xi_n$, where

Q4. $w(x_1)\gamma_1 x_1 + \cdots + w(x_n)\gamma_n x_n = 0$ implies $x_1 = \cdots = x_n = 0,$

the γ_i being fixed elements of F, satisfying $w(\gamma_i) = \gamma_i$.

Proof: Consider ennuples (not right- or left-ratios!) $x: (x_1, \cdots, x_n)$, $\xi: (\xi_1, \cdots, \xi_n)$ of elements of F. Define for them the vector-operations

$$xz: (x_1 z, \cdots, x_n z) \qquad (z \text{ in } F),$$

$$x + \xi: (x_1 + \xi_1, \cdots, x_n + \xi_n),$$

and an "inner product"

$$(\xi_1 x) = w(\xi_1)\gamma_1 x_1 + \cdots + w(\xi_n)\gamma_n x_n .$$

Then the following formulas are corollaries of Q1–Q4.

IP1 $(x, \xi) = w((\xi, x)),$
IP2 $(\xi, xu) = (\xi, x)u,\ (\xi u, x) = w(u)(\xi, x),$
IP3 $(\xi, x' + x'') = (\xi, x') + (\xi, x''),\ (\xi' + \xi'', x) = (\xi', x) + (\xi'', x),$
IP4 $(x, x) = w((x, x)) = [x]$ is $\neq 0$ if $x \neq 0$ (that is, if any $x_i \neq 0$).

We can define $x \perp \xi$ (in words: "x is orthogonal to ξ") to mean that $(\xi, x) = 0$. This is evidently symmetric in x, ξ, and depends on the right-ratios $[x_1: \cdots :x_n]_r$, $[\xi_1: \cdots : \xi_n]_r$ only so it establishes the relation of "polarity," $a \perp b$, between the points

$$a: [x_1: \cdots :x_n]_r, \qquad b: [\xi_1: \cdots : \xi_n]_r \text{ of } P_{n-1}(F).$$

The polars to any point b: $[\xi_1: \cdots : \xi_n]_r$ of $P_{n-1}(F)$ constitute a linear subspace of points of $P_{n-1}(F)$, which by Q4 does not contain b itself, and yet with b generates whole projective space $P_{n-1}(F)$, since for any ennuple $x: (x_1, \cdots, x_n)$

$$x = x' + \xi \cdot [\xi]^{-1}(\xi, x)$$

where by Q4, $[\xi] \neq 0$, and by IP $(\xi, x') = 0$. This linear subspace is, therefore, an n-2-dimensional hyperplane.

Hence if c is any k-dimensional element of $P_{n-1}(F)_1$ one can set up inductively k mutually polar points $b^{(1)}, \cdots, b^{(k)}$ in c. Then it is easy to show that the set c' of points polar to every $b^{(1)}, \cdots, b^{(k)}$—or equivalently to every point in c—constitute an n-k-1-dimensional element, satisfying $c \cap c' = ◎$ and $c \cup c' = ▯$. Moreover, by symmetry $(c')' \supset c$, whence by dimensional considerations $c'' = c$. Finally, $c \supset d$ implies $c' \subset d'$, and so the correspondence $c \to c'$ defines an involutory dual automorphism of $P_{n-1}(F)$ completing the proof.

In the Appendix it will be shown that this condition is also necessary. Thus the above class of systems is exactly the class of irreducible lattices of finite dimensions > 3 satisfying L5 and L71–L73.

III. Conclusions

15. **Mathematical models for propositional calculi.** One conclusion which can be drawn from the preceding algebraic considerations, is that one can construct many different models for a propositional calculus in quantum mechanics, which cannot be differentiated by known criteria. More precisely, one can take any field F having an involutory anti-isomorphism satisfying Q4 (such fields include the real, complex, and quaternion number systems[31]), introduce suitable notions of linear dependence and complementarity, and then construct for every dimension-number n a model $P_n(F)$, having all of the properties of the propositional calculus suggested by quantum-mechanics.

One can also construct infinite-dimensional models $P_\infty(F)$ whose elements consist of all closed linear subspaces of normed infinite-dimensional spaces. But philosophically, Hankel's principle of the "perseverance of formal laws" (which leads one to try to preserve L5)[32] and mathematically, technical analysis of spectral theory in Hilbert space, lead one to prefer a continuous-dimensional model $P_c(F)$, which will be described by one of us in another paper.[33]

$P_c(F)$ is very analogous with the model furnished by the measurable subsets of phase-space in classical dynamics.[34]

16. **The logical coherence of quantum mechanics.** The above heuristic considerations suggest in particular that the physically significant statements in quantum mechanics actually constitute a sort of projective geometry, while the physically significant statements concerning a given system in classical dynamics constitute a Boolean algebra.

They suggest even more strongly that whereas in classical mechanics any propositional calculus involving more than two propositions can be decomposed into independent constituents (direct sums in the sense of modern algebra), quantum theory involves irreducible propositional calculi of unbounded complexity. This indicates that quantum mechanics has a *greater logical coherence*

[31] In the real case, $w(x) = x$; in the complex case, $w(x + iy) = x - iy$; in the quaternionic case, $w(u + ix + jy + kz) = u - ix - jy - kz$; in all cases, the λ_i are 1. Conversely, A. Kolmogoroff, "*Zur Begründung der projektiven Geometrie*," Annals of Math. 33 (1932), 175–6 has shown that any projective geometry whose k-dimensional elements have a *locally compact topology* relative to which the lattice operations are continuous, must be over the real, the complex, or the quaternion field.

[32] L5 can also be preserved by the artifice of considering in $P_\infty(F)$ only elements which either are or have complements which are of finite dimensions.

[33] J. von Neumann, "*Continuous geometries*," Proc. Nat. Acad., 22 (1936), 92–100 and 101–109. These may be a more suitable frame for quantum theory, than Hilbert space.

[34] In quantum mechanics, dimensions but not complements are uniquely determined by the inclusion relation; in classical mechanics, the reverse is true!

than classical mechanics—a conclusion corroborated by the impossibility in general of measuring different quantities independently.

17. **Relation to pure logic.** The models for propositional calculi which have been considered in the preceding sections are also interesting from the standpoint of pure logic. Their nature is determined by quasi-physical and technical reasoning, different from the introspective and philosophical considerations which have had to guide logicians hitherto. Hence it is interesting to compare the modifications which they introduce into Boolean algebra, with those which logicians on "intuitionist" and related grounds have tried introducing.

The main difference seems to be that whereas logicians have usually assumed that properties L71–L73 of negation were the ones least able to withstand a critical analysis, the study of mechanics points to the *distributive identities* L6 as the weakest link in the algebra of logic. Cf. the last two paragraphs of §10.

Our conclusion agrees perhaps more with those critiques of logic, which find most objectionable the assumption that $a' \cup b = \square$ implies $a \subset b$ (or dually, the assumption that $a \cap b' = \circledcirc$ implies $b \supset a$—the assumption that to deduce an absurdity from the conjunction of a and not b, justifies one in inferring that a implies b).[35]

18. **Suggested questions.** The same heuristic reasoning suggests the following as fruitful questions.

What experimental meaning can one attach to the meet and join of two given experimental propositions?

What simple and plausible physical motivation is there for condition L5?

Appendix

1. Consider a projective geometry Q_{n-1} as described in §13. F is a (not necessarily commutative, but associative) field, $n = 4, 5, \cdots, Q_{n-1} = P_{n-1}(F)$ the projective geometry of all right-ratios $[x_1 : \cdots : x_n]_r$, which are the *points* of Q_{n-1}. The (n − 2-dimensional) *hyperplanes* are represented by the left-ratios $[y_1 : \cdots y_n]_l$, incidence of a point $[x_1 : \cdots x_n]_r$ and of a hyperplane $[y_1 : \cdots : y_n]_l$ being defined by

$$\sum_{i=1}^{n} y_i x_i = 0 \tag{1}$$

All linear subspaces of Q_{n-1} form the lattice L, with the elements $a, b, c, \cdots$. Assume now that an operation a' with the properties L71–L73 in §9 exists:

L71 $(a')' = a$

L72 $a \cap a' = \circledcirc$ and $a \cup a' = \square$,

L73 $a \subset b$ implies $a' \supset b'$.

[35] It is not difficult to show, that assuming our axioms L1–5 and 7, the distributive law L6 is equivalent to this postulate: $a' \cup b = \square$ implies $a \subset b$.

They imply (cf. §9)

L74 $(a \cap b)' = a' \cup b'$ and $(a \cup b)' = a' \cap b'$.

Observe, that the relation $a \subset b'$ is symmetric in a, b, owing to L73 and L71.

2. If a: $[x_1: \cdots :x_n]_r$ is a point, then a' is an $[y_1: \cdots y_n]_l$. So we may write:

(2) $$[x_1: \cdots :x_n]_r' = [y_1: \cdots :\eta_n]_l,$$

and define an operation which connects right- and left-ratios. We know from §14, that a general characterization of a' (a any element of L) is obtained, as soon as we derive an algebraic characterization of the above $[x_1: \cdots :x_n]_r'$. We will now find such a characterization of $[x_1: \cdots :x_n]_r'$, and show, that it justifies the description given in §14.

In order to do this, we will have to make a rather free use of *collineations* in Q_{n-1}. A collineation is, by definition, a coördinate-transformation, which replaces $[x_1: \cdots :x_n]_r$ by $[\bar{x}_1: \cdots :\bar{x}_n]_r$,

(3) $$\bar{x}_j = \sum_{i=2}^{n} \omega_{ij} x_i \qquad \text{for } j = 1, \cdots, n.$$

Here the ω_{ij} are fixed elements of F, and such, that (3) has an inverse.

(4) $$x_i = \sum_{j=1}^{n} \theta_{ij} \bar{x}_j, \qquad \text{for } i = 1, \cdots, n,$$

the θ_{ij} being fixed elements of F, too. (3), (4) clearly mean

$$\delta_{kl} = \left\{ \begin{matrix} 1 \text{ if } k = 1 \\ 0 \text{ if } k \neq 1 \end{matrix} \right\|:$$

(5) $$\sum_{j=1}^{n} \theta_{ij} \omega_{kj} = \delta_{ik}, \qquad \sum_{i=1}^{n} \omega_{ij} \theta_{ik} = \delta_{jk}.$$

Considering (1) and (5) they imply the contravariant coördinate-transformation for hyperplanes: $[y_1: \cdots :y_n]_l$ becomes $[\bar{y}_1: \cdots :\bar{y}_n]_l$, where

(6) $$\bar{y}_i = \sum_{i=1}^{n} y_i \theta_{ij}, \qquad \text{for } j = 1, \cdots, n,$$

(7) $$y_i = \sum_{j=1}^{n} \bar{y}_j \omega_{ij}, \qquad \text{for } i = 1, \cdots, n.$$

(Observe, that the position of the coefficients on the left side of the variables in (4), (5), and on their right side in (6), (7), is essential!)

3. We will bring about

(8) $$[\delta_{i1}: \cdots :\delta_{in}]_r' = [\delta_{i1}: \cdots :\delta_{in}]_l \qquad \text{for } i = 1, \cdots, n,$$

by choosing a suitable system of coördinates, that is, by applying suitable collineations. We proceed by induction: Assume that (8) holds for $i = 1, \cdots,$ $m - 1 (m = 1, \cdots, n)$, then we shall find a collineation which makes (8) true for $i = 1, \cdots, m$.

Denote the point $[\delta_{i1}: \cdots :\delta_{in}]_r$ by p_i^*, and the hyperplane $[\delta_{i1}: \cdots :\delta_{in}]_l'$ by h_i^* our assumption on (8) is: $p_i^{*\prime} = h_i^*$ for $i = 1, \cdots, m-1$. Consider now a point a: $[x_1: \cdots :x_n]_r$, and the hyperplane a': $[y_1: \cdots :y_n]_l$. Now $a \leqq p_i^{*\prime} = h_i^*$ means (use (1)) $x_i = 0$, and $p_i^* \leqq a'$ means (use (8)) $y_i = 0$. But these two statements are equivalent. So we see: If $i = 1, \cdots, m-1$, then $x_i = 0$ and $y_i = 0$ are equivalent.

Consider now p_m^*: $[\delta_{m1}: \cdots :\delta_{mn}]_r$. Put p_m': $[y_1^*: \cdots :y_n^*]_l$. As $\delta_{mi} = 0$ for $i = 1, \cdots, m-1$, so we have $y_i^* = 0$ for $i = 1, \cdots, m-1$. Furthermore, $p_m^* \cap p_m^{*\prime} = 0$, $p_m^* \neq 0$, so p_m^* not $\leqq p_m^{*\prime}$. By (1) this means $y_m^* \neq 0$.

Form the collineation (3), (4), (6), (7), with

$$\theta_{ii} = \omega_{ii} = 1, \qquad \theta_{mi} = \omega_{im} = y_m^{*-1} y_i^* \quad \text{for } i = m+1, \cdots, n,$$

all other $\theta_{ij}, \omega_{ij} = 0$.

One verifies immediately, that this collineation leaves the coördinates of the p_1^*: $[\delta_{i1}: \cdots :\delta_{in}]_r$, $i = 1, \cdots, n$, invariant, and similarly those of the $p_i^{*\prime}$: $[\delta_{i1}: \cdots :\delta_{im}]_l$, $i = 1, \cdots m - 1$, while it transforms those of

$$p_m^{*\prime}: \; [y_1^*: \cdots :y_n^*]_l$$

into $[\delta_{m1}: \cdots :\delta_{mn}]_l$.

So after this collineation (8) holds for $i = 1, \cdots, m$.

Thus we may assume, by induction over $m = 1, \cdots, n$, that (8) holds for all $i = 1, \cdots, n$. This we will do.

The above argument now shows, that for a: $[x_1: \cdots :x_n]_r$, a': $[y_1: \cdots :y_n]_l$,

(9) $$x_i = 0 \text{ is equivalent to } y_i = 0, \qquad \text{for } i = 1, \cdots, n.$$

4. Put a: $[x_1: \cdots :x_n]_r$, a': $[y_1: \cdots :y_n]_l$, and b: $[\xi_1: \cdots :\xi_n]_r$, b': $[\eta_1: \cdots :\eta_n]_l$.

Assume first $\eta_1 = 1$, $\eta_2 = \eta$, $\eta_3 = \cdots = \eta_n = 0$. Then (9) gives $\xi_1 \neq 0$, so we can normalize $\xi_1 = 1$, and $\xi_3 = \cdots = \xi_n = 0$. ξ_2 can depend on $\eta_2 = \eta$ only, so $\xi_2 = f_2(\eta)$.

Assume further $x_1 = 1$. Then (9) gives $y_1 \neq 0$, so we can normalize $y_1 = 1$. Now $a \leqq b'$ means by (*i*) $1 + \eta x_2 = 0$, and $b \leqq a'$ means $1 + y_2 f_2(\eta) = 0$. These two statements must, therefore, be equivalent. So if $x_2 \neq 0$, we may put $\eta = -x_2^{-1}$, and obtain $y_2 = -(f_2(\eta))^{-1} = -(f_2(-x_2^{-1}))^{-1}$. If $x_2 = 0$, then $y_2 = 0$ by (9). Thus, x_2 determines at any rate y_2 (independently of $x_3, \cdots, x_n$): $y_2 = \varphi_2(x_2)$. Permuting the $i = 2, \cdots, n$ gives, therefore:

There exists for each $i = 2, \cdots, n$ a function $\varphi_i(x)$, such that $y_i = \varphi_i(x_i)$. Or:

(10) $$\text{If } a: [1:x_2: \cdots :x_n]_r, \qquad \text{then } a': [1:\varphi_2(x_2): \cdots :\varphi_n(x_n)]_l.$$

Applying this to a: $[1{:}x_2{:}\cdots{:}x_n]_r$ and c: $[1{:}u_1{:}\cdots{:}u_n]_r$ shows: As $a \leqq c'$ and $c \leqq a'$ are equivalent, so

$$(11)\qquad \sum_{i=2}^{n} \varphi_i(u_i)\, x_i = -1 \text{ is equivalent to } \sum_{i=2}^{n} \varphi(x_i)\, u_i = -1.$$

Observe, that (9) becomes:

$$(12)\qquad \varphi_i(x) = 0 \text{ if and only if } x = 0.$$

5. (11) with $x_3 = \cdots = x_n = u_3 = \cdots = u_n = 0$ shows: $\varphi_2(u_2)x_2 = -1$ is equivalent to $\varphi_2(x_2)u_2 = -1$. If $x_2 \neq 0$, $u_2 = (-\varphi_2(x_2))^{-1}$, then the second equation holds, and so both do.

Choose x_2, u_2 in this way, but leave $x_3, \cdots, x_n, u_3, \cdots u_n$ arbitrary. Then (11) becomes:

$$(13)\qquad \sum_{i=3}^{n} \varphi_i(u_i)\, x_i = 0 \text{ is equivalent to } \sum_{i=3}^{n} \varphi_i\,(x_i)\, u_i = 0.$$

Now put $x_5 = \cdots = x_n = u_5 = \cdots = u_n = 0$. Then (13) becomes:

$$\varphi_3(u_3)x_3 + \varphi_4(u_4)x_4 = 0 \text{ is equivalent to } \varphi_3(x_3)u_3 + \varphi_4(x_4)u_4 = 0,$$

that is (for $x_4, u_4 \neq 0$):

$$\text{(a)}\quad x_3x_4^{-1} = \varphi_4(u_4)^{-1}\,\varphi_3(u_3)$$

(14) is equivalent to

$$\text{(b)}\quad u_3u_4^{-1} = \varphi_4(x_4)^{-1}\,\varphi_3(x_3).$$

Let x_4, x_3 be given. Choose u_3, u_4 so as to satisfy (b). Then (a) is true, too. Now (a) remains true, if we leave u_3, u_4 unchanged, but change x_3, x_4 without changing $x_3x_4^{-1}$. So (b) remains too true under these conditions, that is, the value of $\varphi_4(x_4)^{-1}\,\varphi_3(x_3)$ does not change. In other words: $\varphi_4(x_4)^{-1}\,\varphi_3(x_3)$ depends on $x_3x_4^{-1}$ only. That is: $\varphi_4(x_4)^{-1}\,\varphi_3(x_3) = \varphi_{34}(x_3x_4^{-1})$. Put $x_3 = xz$, $x_4 = x$, then we obtain:

$$(15)\qquad \varphi_3(xz) = \varphi_4(x)\,\psi_{34}(z).$$

This was derived for $x, z \neq 0$, but it will hold for x or $z = 0$, too, if we define $\psi_{34}(0) = 0$. (Use (12).)

(15), with $z = 1$ gives $\varphi_3(x) = \varphi_4(x)\alpha_{34}$, where $\alpha_{34} = \psi_{34}(1) \neq 0$, owing to (12) for $x \neq 0$. Permuting the $i = 2, \cdots, n$ gives, therefore:

$$(16)\qquad \varphi_i(x) = \varphi_j(x)\alpha_{ij}, \qquad \text{where } \alpha_{ij} \neq 0.$$

(For $i = j$ put $\alpha_{ii} = 1$.)

Now (15) becomes

$$(17)\qquad \begin{aligned} \varphi_2(zx) &= \varphi_2(x)w(z) \\ w(z) &= \alpha_{42}\psi_{34}(z)\alpha_{23}. \end{aligned}$$

Put $x = 1$ in (17), write x for z, and use (16) with $j = 2$:

$$\varphi_i(x) = \beta w(z)\gamma_i, \qquad \text{where } \beta,\ \gamma_i \neq 0. \tag{18}$$
$$(\beta = \varphi_2(1),\ \gamma_i = \alpha_{i2}).$$

6. Compare (17) for $x = 1, z = u; x = u, z = v$; and $x = 1, z = vu$. Then

$$w(vu) = w(u)w(v) \tag{19}$$

results (12) and (18) give

$$w(u) = 0 \text{ if and only if } u = 0. \tag{20}$$

Now write $w(z)$, γ_i for $\beta w(z)\beta^{-1}$, $\beta\gamma_i$. Then (18), (19), (20) remain true, (18) is simplified in so far, as we have $\beta = 1$ there. So (11) becomes

$$\sum_{i=2}^{n} w(u_i)\ \gamma_i\ x = -1 \tag{21}$$

(21) is equivalent to

$$\sum_{i=2}^{n} w(x_i)\ \gamma_i\ u_i = -1$$

$x_2 = x$, $u_2 = u$ and all other $x_i = u_i = 0$ give: $w(u)\gamma_2 x = -1$ is equivalent to $w(x)\gamma_2 u = -1$. If $x \neq 0$, $u = -\gamma_2^{-1}\ w(x)^{-1}$, then the second equation holds, and so the first one gives: $x = -\gamma_2^{-1}\ w(u)^{-1} = -\gamma_2^{-1}(w(-\gamma_2^{-1}w(x)^{-1}))^{-1}$. But (19), (20) imply $w(1) = 1$, $w(w^{-1}) = w(w)^{-1}$, so the above relation becomes:

$$x = -\gamma_2^{-1}(w(-\gamma_2^{-1}w(x_1^{-1}))^{-1} = -\gamma_2^{-1}w((-\gamma_2^{-1}w(x)^{-1})^{-1})$$
$$= -\gamma_2^{-1}w(w(x)(-\gamma_2)) = -\gamma_2^{-1}w(-\gamma_2)w(w(x)).$$

Put herein $x = 1$, as $w(w(1)) = w(1) = 1$, so $-\gamma_2^{-1}w(-\gamma_2) = 1$, $w(-\gamma_2) = -\gamma_2$ results. Thus the above equation becomes

$$w(w(x)) = x, \tag{22}$$

and $w(-\gamma_2) = -\gamma_2$ gives, if we permute the $i = 2, \cdots, n$,

$$w(-\gamma_i) = -\gamma_i. \tag{23}$$

Put $u_i = -\gamma_i^{-1}$ in (21). Then considering (22) and (19)

$$\sum_{i=2}^{n} x_i = 1 \text{ is equivalent to } \sum_{i=2}^{n} w(x_i) = 1 \tag{24}$$

obtains. Put $x_2 = x$, $x_3 = y$, $x_4 = 1 - x - y$, $x_5 = \cdots = x_n = 0$. Then (24) gives $w(x) + w(y) = 1 - w(1 - x - y)$. So $w(x) + w(y)$ depends on $x + y$ only. Replacing x, y by $x + y$, 0 shows, that it is equal to $w(x + y) + w(0) = w(x + y)$ (use 20). So we have:

$$w(x) + w(y) = w(x + y) \tag{25}$$

(25), (19) and (22) give together:

$w(x)$ is an involutory antisomorphism of F.

Observe, that (25) implies $w(-1) = -w(1) = -1$, and so (23) becomes

$$w(\gamma_i) = \gamma_i. \tag{26}$$

7. Consider a: $[x_1:\cdots:x_n]_r$, a': $[y_1:\cdots:y_n]_l$. If $x_1 \neq 0$, we may write a: $[1:x_2x_1^{-1}:\cdots:x_nx_1^{-1}]_r$, and so a': $[1:w(x_2x_1^{-1})\gamma_2:\cdots:w(x_nx_1^{-1})\gamma_n]_l$. But

$$w(x_ix_1^{-1})\gamma_i = w(x_1^{-1})w(x_i)\gamma_i = w(x_1)^{-1}w(x_i)\gamma_i,$$

and so we can write

$$a':[w(x_1):w(x_2)\gamma_2:\cdots:w(x_n)\gamma_n]_l$$

too. So we have

$$y_i = w(x_i)\gamma_i \qquad \text{for } i = 1, \cdots, n, \tag{27}$$

where the γ_i for $i = 2, \cdots, n$ are those from **6.**, and $\gamma_1 = 1$. And $w(1) = 1$, so (26) holds for all $i = 1, \cdots, n$. So we have the representation (27) with γ_i obeying (26), if $x_i \neq 0$.

Permutation of the $i = 1, \cdots, n$ shows, that a similar relation holds if $x_2 \neq 0$:

$$y_i = w^+(x_i)\gamma_i^+, \tag{27$^+$}$$

$$w^+(\gamma_i^+) = \gamma_i^+, \tag{26$^+$}$$

$w^+(x)$ being an involutory antisomorphism of F. ($w^+(x)$, γ_i^+ may differ from $w(x)$, γ_i!) Instead of $\gamma_1 = 1$ we have now $\gamma_2^+ = 1$, but we will not use this.

Put all $x_i = 1$. Then a': $[y_1:\cdots:y_n]_l$ can be expressed by both formulae (27) and (27$^+$). As $w(x)_1w^+(x)$ are both antisomorphism, so $w(1) = w^+(1) = 1$, and therefore $[y_1:\cdots:y_n]_l = [\gamma_1:\cdots:\gamma_n]_l = [\gamma_1^+:\cdots:\gamma_n^+]_l$ obtains. Thus $(\gamma_1^+)^{-1}\gamma_i^+ = (\gamma_1)^{-1}\gamma_i = \gamma_i$, $\gamma_i^+ = \gamma_1^+\gamma_i$ for $i = 1, \cdots, n$.

Assume now $x_2 \neq 0$ only. Then (27$^+$) gives $y_i = w^+(x_i)\gamma_i^+$, but as we are dealing with left ratios, we may as well put

$$y_i = (\gamma_1^+)^{-1}w^+(x_i)\gamma_i^+ = (\gamma_1{}^+)^{-1}w^+(x)\gamma_1^+\gamma_i.$$

Put $\beta^+ = \gamma_1^+ \neq 0$, then we have:

$$y_i = \beta^{+-1}w^+(x_i)\beta^+\gamma_i. \tag{27^{++}}$$

Put now $x_1 = x_2 = 1$, $x_3 = x$, all other $x_i = 0$. Again a': $[y_1:\cdots:y_n]_l$ can be expressed by both formulae (27) and (27^{++}), again $w(1) = w^+(1)$. Therefore

$$[y_1:y_2:y_3:y_4:\cdots:y_n]_l = [\gamma_1:\gamma_2:w(x)\gamma_3:0:\cdots:0]_l$$
$$= [\gamma_1:\gamma_2:\beta^{+-1}w^+(x)\beta^+\gamma_3:0:\cdots:0]_l$$

obtains. This implies $w(x) = \beta^{+-1}w(x)\beta^+$ for all x, and so (27^{++}) coincides with (27).

In other words: (27) holds for $x_2 \neq 0$ too.

Permuting $i = 2, \cdots, n$ (only $i = 1$ has an exceptional rôle in (27)), we see: (27) holds if $x_i \neq 0$ for $i = 2, \cdots, n$. For $x_1 \neq 0$ (27) held anyhow, and for some $i = 1, \cdots, n$ we must have $x_i \neq 0$. Therefore:

(27) *holds for all points* a: $[x_1 : \cdots : x_n]_r$.

8. Consider now two points a: $[x_1 : \cdots : x_n]_r$ and b: $[\xi_1 : \cdots : \xi_n]_r$. Put a': $[y_1 : \cdots : y_n]_l$, then $b \leqq a'$ means, considering (1) and (27) (cf. the end of **7.**):

$$\sum_{i=1}^{n} w(x_i)\gamma_i \xi_i = 0. \tag{28}$$

$a \leqq a'$ can never hold ($a \cap a' = 0$, $a \neq 0$), so (28) can only hold for $x_i = \xi_i$, if all $x_i = 0$. Thus,

$$\sum_{i=1}^{n} w(x_i)\gamma_i x_i = 0 \text{ implies } x_1 = \cdots = x_n = 0. \tag{29}$$

Summing up the last result of **6.**, and formulae (26), (29) and (28), we obtain:

There exists an involutory antisomorphism $w(x)$ *of* F (*cf.* (22), (25), (19)) *and a definite diagonal Hermitian form* $\sum_{i=1}^{n} w(x_i)\gamma_i \xi_i$ *in* F (*cf.* (26), (29)), *such that for* a: $[x_1 : \cdots : x_n]_r$, b: $[\xi_1 : \cdots : \xi_n]_r$ $b \leqq a'$ *is defined by polarity with respect to it:*

$$\sum_{i=1}^{n} w(x_i)\gamma_i \xi_i = 0. \tag{28}$$

This is exactly the result of §14, which is thus justified.

THE SOCIETY OF FELLOWS, HARVARD UNIVERSITY.
THE INSTITUTE FOR ADVANCED STUDY.

ANNALS OF MATHEMATICS
Vol. 40, No. 3, July, 1939

A CHARACTERIZATION OF BOOLEAN ALGEBRAS

BY GARRETT BIRKHOFF AND MORGAN WARD

(Received January 9, 1939)

Introduction

When is a lattice a Boolean algebra—that is, isomorphic with a field of sets? The classical conditions are:[1] (1) The distributive law holds, (2) every element has a complement. Now it is well known[2] that (1) and (2) imply (3) no element has more than one complement. We are thus led to conjecture that (2) *and* (3) *imply* (1); in other words, that a necessary and sufficient condition that a lattice be a Boolean algebra is that each of its elements have a unique complement.

The only published result bearing on this question is G. Bergmann's[3] theorem that the distributive law holds if and only if *relative* complements are unique; that is, if and only if given $a \leqq x \leqq b$, there exists one and only one y with $x \cap y = a, x \cup y = b$.

We prove here the truth of our conjecture for all complete atomistic lattices.[4] These include lattices of finite length and of finite order. We do not know whether or not our conjecture is unrestrictedly true.

Exact statement of theorem

Let L be a complete lattice which is "atomistic" in the sense that if $O < a < I$, then $p_\alpha \leqq a \leqq q_\beta$ where p_α covers O and q_β is covered by I. Let us further define a "point" as an element p covering O.

THEOREM 1: *If each element of L has one and only one complement, then L is isomorphic with the Boolean algebra of all subsets of its points.*

THEOREM 2: *In order for L to be a Boolean algebra, it is necessary and sufficient that each element have one and only one complement.*

The second theorem follows from the first, and the known results stated in the introduction.

PROOF OF FIRST THEOREM. To each set S of points p_α, make correspond the join $x(S)$ of the p_α in S. Dually, associate with each set S of elements q_β covered by I, the meet $y(S)$ of the q_β in S. It will follow from generalized

---

[1] E. V. Huntington "Postulates for the algebra of logic," Trans. Am. Math. Soc. 5 (1904), pp. 288-309. His hypotheses (1) — (7) define lattices.

[2] See for example, A. N. Whitehead's "Universal Algebra" Cambridge (1898) p. 36. The result is due to R. Grassmann.

[3] "Zur Axiomatik der Elementargeometrie" Monatschr. f. Math. u. Phys. 36 (1929), pp. 269-84.

[4] The terminology of the present paper is that of G. Birkhoff's "Lattice theory and its applications" Bull. Am. Math. Soc. 44 (1938), pp. 793-800. By "a covers b," we mean that $a > b$ while $a > x > b$ has no solution.

associativity, that $x(S \cup T) = x(S) \cup x(T)$ and $y(S \cup T) = y(S) \cap y(T)$. Again, the complement of $x(I)$ can contain no point, since $x(I)$ contains every point;[5] hence it is O, and $x(I) = I$. Dually, $y(I) = O$.[5]

Again, given α, β, either $p_\alpha \leqq q_\beta$, or $p_\alpha \cap q_\beta = O$ and $p_\alpha \cup q_\beta = I$—that is, p_α and q_β are complementary. But not every q_β contains p_α, since $y(I) = O < p_\alpha$. Hence (by the existence of unique complements) a suitable subscript notation will make $p'_\alpha = q_\alpha$ and $p_\alpha \leqq q_\beta$ if $\alpha \neq \beta$.

This notation will further identify subsets of p_α with subsets of q_α, and, since every p_α $[\alpha \in S]$ is less than or equal to every q_β $[\beta \in S']$, it will make $x(S) \leqq y(S')$. (Here S' denotes the set complementary to S.) From this important inequality we infer that

$$x(S) \cup y(S) \geqq x(S) \cup x(S') = x(S \cup S') = I,$$

$$x(S) \cap y(S) \leqq y(S') \cap y(S) = y(S \cup S') = O.$$

Consequently $x(S)$ and $y(S)$ are complementary.

Also, $x(S) \cap x(S') \leqq y(S') \cap y(S) = y(S \cup S') = O$ and $x(S) \cup x(S') = x(S \cup S') = I$; hence $x(S)$ and $x(S')$ are complementary. But since $x(S)$ and $x(S')$ are complementary, $x(S)$ contains no p_α not in S, distinct sets S determine distinct $x(S)$, and the partially ordered system of the $x(S)$ is isomorphic with the algebra of all subsets of the p_α.

It remains to show that every member a of L is an $x(S)$. But denote by S the set of $p_\alpha \leqq a$. Evidently $x(S) \leqq a$; moreover $a \cap x(S')$ will by the last paragraph contain no points; hence $a \cap x(S') = O$. On the other hand, $a \cup x(S') \geqq x(S) \cup x(S') = I$; hence a is the unique complement $x(S)$ of $x(S')$, completing the proof.

HARVARD UNIVERSITY AND
CALIFORNIA INSTITUTE OF TECHNOLOGY.

---

[5] We are letting I denote simultaneously: the biggest element in L, the set of all p_α, and the set of all q_β.

NEUTRAL ELEMENTS IN GENERAL LATTICES[1]

GARRETT BIRKHOFF

1. **Introduction.** O. Ore has defined "neutral" elements in modular lattices as elements a satisfying $a \cap (x \cup y) = (a \cap x) \cup (a \cap y)$ for all x, y and dually.[2] In the case of complemented modular lattices, the neutral elements compose the "center" in J. von Neumann's theories of continuous geometries and regular rings—that is, the set of elements having unique complements.[3]

The purpose of the present note is to extend the notion of neutral elements to general lattices. More precisely, call an element a of a lattice "neutral" if and only if every triple $\{a, x, y\}$ generates a distributive sublattice. It is proved that the neutral elements of any lattice L form a distributive sublattice, consisting of the elements carried into $[I, O]$ under isomorphisms of L with sublattices of direct products. Actually, this sublattice is the intersection of the maximal distributive sublattices of L.

Further, complements of neutral elements, when they exist, are unique and neutral. The sublattice of complemented neutral elements may be called the "center" of a lattice: it consists of those elements carried into $[I, O]$ under isomorphisms of L with direct products.

2. **Fundamental definition.** We define an element a of a lattice L to be "neutral" if and only if every triple $\{a, x, y\}$ generates a distributive sublattice of L.

LEMMA 1. *If a is "neutral," then the dual correspondences $x \rightarrow x \cap a$ and $x \rightarrow x \cup a$ are endomorphisms[4] of L.*

PROOF. By definition, $(x \cup y) \cap a = (x \cup a) \cap (y \cup a)$ and $(x \cap y) \cap a = (x \cap a) \cap (y \cap a)$, and dually. We note that this condition, which is sufficient to guarantee neutrality in the case of modular lattices, does not guarantee neutrality in general—see the graph below.

---

[1] Presented to the Society, September 8, 1939.

[2] O. Ore, *On the foundations of abstract algebra* I, Annals of Mathematics, (2), vol. 36 (1935), pp. 406–437. For the definitions of lattices and modular lattices (called by Ore structures and Dedekind structures), as well as of sublattice, distributive lattice, O, I, and so on, compare the author's *Lattices and their applications*, this Bulletin, vol. 44 (1938), pp. 793–800—or the author's *Lattice Theory*, American Mathematical Society Colloquium Publications, vol. 25, 1940.

[3] J. von Neumann, *Lectures on Continuous Geometries*, Princeton, 1935–1936. Cf. also R. P. Dilworth, *Note on complemented modular lattices*, this Bulletin, vol. 45 (1939), pp. 74–76.

[4] We define an endomorphism as a homomorphism of L with itself.

LEMMA 2. *If a is neutral, then $x \cap a = y \cap a$ and $x \cup a = y \cup a$ imply $x = y$.*

PROOF. By direct computation, using the distributive law twice,

$$x = x \cap (x \cup a) = x \cap (y \cup a) = (x \cap y) \cup (x \cap a)$$
$$= (x \cap y) \cup (y \cap a) = y \cap (x \cup a) = y \cap (y \cup a) = y.$$

Using x in the graph, we see that this condition by itself is also not sufficient. However, Lemmas 1–2 together are sufficient to guarantee neutrality.

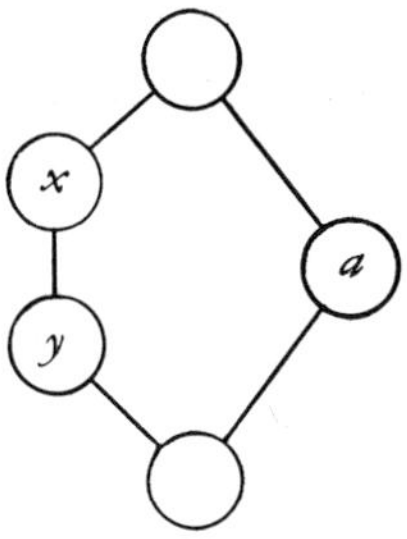

FIG. 1

Indeed, consider the correspondence $x \rightarrow [x \cap a, x \cup a]$ from L to the product[5] ST of the sublattice S of elements $s \leqq a$, with the sublattice T of elements $t \geqq a$. By Lemma 1, it is homomorphic onto a sublattice of ST; by Lemma 2, it is one-one; hence it is isomorphic. Moreover $x \rightarrow [a, a] = [I, O]$, since a is the I of S and the O of T.

But conversely, $[I, O]$ is obviously "neutral" in ST, since each component is. Hence it is neutral in every sublattice of ST, including L, and we conclude[6] that the following holds:

THEOREM 1. *An element of a lattice is neutral if and only if it is carried into $[I, O]$ under an isomorphism of the lattice with a sublattice of a direct product.*

3. **Neutral elements a sublattice.** Just as in the case of modular lattices, we have the following theorem:

THEOREM 2. *The neutral elements of any lattice form a distributive sublattice.*

PROOF. Let a and b be neutral. Then since the product of two

[5] By the "product" ST, is meant the system of couples $[s, t]$, $s \in S$, $t \in T$, where $[s, t] \cap [s', t'] = [s \cap s', t \cap t']$ and dually.

[6] N.B., we do *not* assume that L itself has an O or an I.

endomorphisms of L is an endomorphism, it follows that the correspondence

$$x \to [x \cap a \cap b, (x \cup a) \cap b, (x \cap a) \cup b, x \cup a \cup b]$$

defines a homomorphism of L onto a sublattice of a product $STUV$ of four sublattices of itself. Moreover by Lemma 2, $(x \cap a)$ and $(x \cup a)$ and therefore x, are determined uniquely by their images under the homomorphism. Hence the homomorphism is an isomorphism. But $a \cup b$ goes into $[I, I, I, O]$ under this—and hence into $[I, O]$ of $(STU)V$. Thus $a \cup b$ is neutral; dually, $a \cap b$ is neutral, which was to be proved.

4. **Intersection of maximal distributive sublattices.** The set of neutral elements of a lattice is also characterized in another way by the next theorem:

THEOREM 3. *The set of neutral elements of a lattice L is the intersection of its maximal distributive sublattices.*

PROOF. First, if a is not neutral, then some triple $\{a, x, y\}$ is not distributive. Hence *no* maximal distributive sublattice obtained by enlarging the distributive sublattice generated by $\{x, y\}$ can contain a. Consequently, the intersection of the maximal distributive sublattices of L contains no non-neutral elements.

Conversely, if a is neutral, and S is a distributive sublattice of L, consider the sublattice generated by $\{a, S\}$. The endomorphisms $x \to x \cap a$ and $x \to x \cup a$ carry it into sublattices generated by a distributive sublattice and I or O. But such sublattices are always distributive—hence so is the sublattice generated by $\{a, S\}$, since it is a sublattice of a product of distributive lattices. Thus every *maximal* distributive sublattice contains a, and the intersection of the maximal distributive sublattices contains every neutral element (as well as no non-neutral elements).

5. **Center of a lattice.** When one comes to complements of neutral elements, one finds that the following statement holds:

THEOREM 4. *Complements of neutral elements, when they exist, are unique and neutral.*

PROOF. Using Theorem 1, we see that $[I, O] \cap [x, y]$ is $[O, O]$ if and only if $x = O$, while $[I, O] \cup [x, y]$ is $[I, I]$ if and only if $y = I$. Hence $[I, O]$ has no complement except $[O, I]$ in the sublattice of ST isomorphic with L, proving uniqueness. Moreover $[O, I]$ is itself neutral, completing the proof.

COROLLARY 1. *The neutral elements of a complemented lattice form a Boolean algebra.*

We define the "center" of a lattice as the set of its complemented neutral elements.

THEOREM 5. *The center of any lattice L is a complemented distributive sublattice—and hence a Boolean algebra.*

PROOF. If a and b are neutral elements of L, with (neutral) complements a' and b', then

$$(a \cap b) \cap (a' \cup b') = (a \cap b \cap a') \cup (a \cap b \cap b') = O \cup O = O,$$

$$(a \cap b) \cup (a' \cup b') = (a \cup a' \cup b') \cap (b \cup a' \cup b') = I \cap I = I,$$

and so $a \cap b$ is complemented. Dually, $a \cup b$ is complemented, completing the proof.

We can now specialize Theorem 1 by proving the following:

THEOREM 6. *An element is in the center of a lattice L if and only if it is carried into $[I, O]$ under an isomorphism of L with a direct product.*

PROOF. By Theorem 1, such an element is neutral, and it has the complement $[O, I]$. Conversely, suppose a and a' are complementary neutral elements of L. Then for all x,

$$x = x \cap I = x \cap (a \cup a') = (x \cap a) \cup (x \cap a').$$

Hence the correspondence $x \rightarrow [x \cap a, x \cap a']$ is one-one between L and the couples $[u, v]$ with $u \leqq a$, $v \leqq a'$; the inverse correspondence is $[u, v] \rightarrow u \cup v$. But it obviously preserves inclusion; hence it is an *isomorphism*. Finally, it carries L into the product ST of the lattice S of elements $s \leqq a$, with the lattice T of elements $t \leqq a'$, while it carries a into $[a \cap a, a \cap a'] = [I, O]$ in ST.

HARVARD UNIVERSITY

Reprinted from *Bull. Am. Math. Soc.* **46** (1940), 702–705

Reprinted from the
TRANSACTIONS OF THE AMERICAN MATHEMATICAL SOCIETY
Vol. 60, No. 1, pp. 3-11
July, 1946

DISTRIBUTIVE POSTULATES FOR SYSTEMS LIKE BOOLEAN ALGEBRAS

BY
GEORGE D. BIRKHOFF AND GARRETT BIRKHOFF

1. **Introduction.** Boole [2, p. 41](1) pointed out a close analogy between ordinary algebra and the "algebra of logic," now called Boolean algebra. Both have operations of addition and multiplication which are commutative and associative; both have a 0 for addition and multiplication and a 1 for multiplication; in both, multiplication is distributive on sums.

The connection was first made precise by Stone [5]. Stone defined a "Boolean ring" as a ring in which $aa=a$, and showed that this implies $a+a=0$ and $ab=ba$. He showed that by simple constructions, one could transform Boolean algebras into Boolean rings and vice versa.

Stone and most earlier authors (see Huntington [3]) used commutative and associative laws. In a remarkable paper [4], Newman based his developments entirely on distributivity, the existence of complements, and the properties of 0 and 1. Every such distributive, complemented algebra is the direct sum of the *Boolean subalgebra* of elements satisfying $a+a=a$, and the (not necessarily associative) *Boolean subring* of elements satisfying(2) $a+a=0$.

During lectures on Boolean algebra, but using stronger postulates, G. D. Birkhoff independently discovered Newman's decomposition theorem. Our discussion of this in the summer of 1944 led to the results presented below.

As Newman's postulates are independent (cf. J. London Math. Soc. vol. 17 (1942) pp. 34–47 and vol. 14 (1944) pp. 28–30), we have been unable to weaken them. However, we have been able to make large parts of his argument much shorter and simpler, at the cost of a weak additional postulate (P3′ below), added to those of his Theorem 1b. We show that one need only apply Boole's method of expansion [2, p. 151], systematically.

We first show (§2) that the postulates are left-right symmetric by a new and simple argument. We then show (§3) that the existence and properties of "even" elements follow from more general considerations than those of Newman, and give (§4) a simplified proof of his decomposition theorem. In §5, we give a new set of postulates for distributive lattices; in §6, we give an

Presented to the Society, February 23, 1946; received by the editors December 5, 1945.

(1) Numbers in brackets refer to the Bibliography at the end of the paper.

(2) It is easily shown that any "idempotent" ring (in which $aa=a$ for all a) satisfies $a+a=0$ and $ab=ba$; the proof of [5] applies to the nonassociative case. Conversely, in any such ring, $a+1$ is a complement of a. Finally, any idempotent and commutative multiplication table for basis-elements defines an idempotent ring (cf. L. E. Dickson, *Algebras and their arithmetics*, Chicago, 1922, p. 22); the idempotence follows from the binomial theorem and commutativity.

entirely novel approach to postulates for Boolean algebras and (associative) Boolean rings. Finally, in §7, we show that in addition to the "metamathematical" principles of duality and left-right symmetry, only three postulates are needed for Boolean algebras and three for distributive lattices—but that two are not quite enough.

2. **Postulates; first deductions.** Consider any system with two binary operations which satisfies the following postulates:

P1. $a(b+c)=ab+ac$. P1′. $(a+b)c=ac+bc$.

P2. $\exists 1$, such that $a1=a$ for all a.

P3. $\exists 0$, with $a+0=a$. P3′. $0+a=a$.

P4. To each a corresponds at least one a', such that $aa'=0$ and $a+a'=1$.

That is, multiplication is *distributive* on sums, we have a *multiplicative right-unit*, an *additive zero*, and *right-complements*. We shall now show that multiplication is idempotent, that complementation is involutory and unique, that right-complements are left-complements, that the multiplicative right-unit is also a left-unit, and that the additive zero is also a multiplicative zero. The postulates which are superfluous in each proof are listed to the right of the statement of the result.

T1. $aa=a$. (Cf. [4, p. 1].) (*without* P1′, P3′).

Proof. $a=a1=a(a+a')=aa+aa'=aa+0=aa$.

T2. $(a')'=a$ *for all a and* $(a')'$. (Cf. [4, p. 3].)

Proof.

$$\begin{aligned}(a')' &= 0 + (a')'(a')' && \text{by P3}', \text{T1}\\ &= a'(a')' + (a')'(a')' = (a' + (a')')(a')' \\ &= 1(a')' = (a + a')(a')' = a(a')' + 0 && \text{by P4}\\ &= 0 + a(a')' = aa' + a(a')' = a(a' + (a')') \\ &= a\cdot 1 = a.\end{aligned}$$

Remark. Without using P2, we have shown that $(a')'=a\cdot(a')'=a\cdot 1$.

COROLLARY 1. $a'a=0$ *and* $a'a=1$.

COROLLARY 2. *If* $ab=ac=0$ *and* $a+b=a+c=1$, *then* $b=c$; *complements are unique.*

For if a' is any complement of a, $b=((a')')'=c$.

COROLLARY 3. $1\cdot a=a$, for all a.

Proof. $1\cdot a=(a+a')a=aa+a'a=a+0=a$.

T3. $a\cdot 0=0\cdot a=0$, *for all a.*

Proof. $0=aa'=a(a'+0)=aa'+a0=0+a0=a0$, and $0=aa'=(0+a)a'$

$=0a'+aa'=0a'+0=0a'$, all without using P2. But by T2 every element is a complement; hence $0a'=0$ for all a implies $0a=0$ for all a.

COROLLARY. *If* $0=1$, *then* $0=0+0=0+a\cdot 0=0+a\cdot 1=a\cdot 1=a$; *hence all elements are equal.*

Remark. By T2, Corollary 1, which is symmetric to P4, and T2, Corollary 3, which is symmetric to P2, we now have *complete left-right symmetry* in the properties of addition and multiplication.

An easier way to guarantee this would of course be to substitute the commutative laws $ab=ba$ and $a+b=b+a$ for P1′ and P3′.

3. **Even elements.** We now define $1+1=2$, $2+2=4$, and call the left-multiples $y2$ of 2 *even* elements. This is the opposite of Newman's usage. We note that by P1, P2 and T1 alone, $4=2+2=2\cdot 1+2\cdot 1=2(1+1)=2\cdot 2=2$; also, by definition, $4=(1+1)+(1+1)$.

T4. *An element x is even if and only if it is additively idempotent:* $x+x=x$ (*without* P1′, P3′).

Proof. Clearly $y2+y2=y(2+2)=y2$; conversely, if $x=x+x$, then $x=x\cdot 1+x\cdot 1=x(1+1)=x2$.

T5. *Any multiple xt or ux of an even element x is even.*

Proof. If $x=x+x$, then $xt=(x+x)t=xt+xt$ and $ux=u(x+x)=ux+ux$ for all t, u.

T6. *The correspondence $x\to x+x=x2$ is an idempotent endomorphism; that is,* $(x+y)2=x2+y2$, $(xy)2=(x2)(y2)$, *and* $(x2)2=x2$ (*without* P3′).

Proof. By P1′, $(x+y)2=x2+y2$. Again, $(x2)2=x2+x2=x(2+2)=x2$ by P1, P2, T1. Finally, by P1, P1′, P2, T1

$$\begin{aligned}(x2)(y2) &= (x+x)(y+y) = (x+x)y+(x+x)y = (xy+xy)+(xy+xy)\\ &= ((xy)2)2 = (xy)2.\end{aligned}$$

It is a corollary of T6 that the *even elements form a subalgebra*, in which addition is idempotent.

We remark that T4–T6 not only do not require P3′, but only require P3–P4 insofar as they are needed to prove T1. That is, T4–T6 are valid in any system with idempotent multiplication and a right-unit, in which the distributive laws P1–P1′ are valid. These considerations are developed further in §7.

4. **Direct decomposition theorem.** Now let $2'$ denote the right-complement of 2, so that $2\cdot 2'=0$, $2+2'=1$; we shall call the left-multiples of $2'$, *odd* elements. Using the results of §2, it is easy to obtain a direct decomposition theorem.

T7. *The odd elements are the additively nilpotent elements. More precisely, the conditions* $x=y2'$, $x=x2'$, $x+x=x2=0$ *are equivalent.*

Proof. If $x+x=0$, then $x=x(2+2')=x2+x2'=0+x2'=x2'$. If $x=x2'$, then $x=y2'$ trivially, all without P3. Finally, $y2'+y2'=y(2'+2')=y(2'\cdot 2)$ $=y0=0$ by T2, Corollary 1, and T3. We remark that T7 follows if we have a right unit 1, a right-additive and right multiplicative zero, right distributivity, and left-complements.

T7′. *Any multiple of an odd element is odd.*

Proof. If $x+x=0$, then $xt+xt=(x+x)t=0t=0$, and $ux+ux=u(x+x)$ $=u\cdot 0=0$ for all t, u, by P1, P1′, T3.

T8. *Any system satisfying* P1, P1′, P2, P3, P3′, P4 *is the direct union of the subalgebras of even and odd elements.*

Proof. Consider the correspondences $z\rightarrow(z2, z2')=(x, y)$ and $(x, y)\rightarrow x+y$. If x is even and y is odd, then

$$(x + y)2 = x2 + y2 = (x + x) + 0 = x \qquad \text{by P1, T7, P3,}$$

$$(x + y)2' = x2' + y2' = (x + x)2' + y = y \qquad \text{by P1, P3}',$$

since $(x+x)2'=x2'+x2'=x(2'+2')=x0=0$. Conversely, for any z, $z2$ is even and $z2'$ odd, and $z=z\cdot 1=z(2+2')=z\cdot 2+z2'$. Hence the correspondences are one-one and reciprocal. Further, $(z+z_1)2=z2+z_12$ and $(z+z_1)2'=z2'+z_12'$; hence addition is component-by-component. Finally,

$$\begin{aligned}(x + y)(x_1 + y_1) &= (xx_1 + xy_1) + (yx_1 + yy_1) && \text{by P1–P1}'\\ &= (xx_1 + 0) + (0 + yy_1) && \text{as shown below}\\ &= xx_1 + yy_1 && \text{by P3–P3}'.\end{aligned}$$

(To show that $xy_1=yx_1=0$, note that xy_1 and yx_1 are both even and odd by T5, T7′; while if u is both even and odd, then $u=u+u=0$ by definition and T7.) Hence multiplication is also component-by-component, xx_1 being even and yy_1 odd by T5, T7′.

We can now prove that *the even elements form a Boolean algebra*, while *the odd elements form a (not necessarily associative) ring, in which multiplication is commutative and idempotent.* But as we have nothing to add to Newman's proof, we shall not repeat his argument(3).

5. **Postulates for distributive lattices.** Instead, we shall give a new proof that the even elements form a Boolean algebra, which will yield as a by-product a new set of postulates for distributive lattices. By confining ourselves to even elements, we have the additional postulate

(3) One can show successively $a+1=1+a$, $a+b=b+a$, $1+(1+c)=(1+1)+c$, $1+(b+c)$ $=(1+b)+c$, $a+(b+c)=(a+b)+c$; the trick is to right-multiply respectively by $a+a'$, $b+b'$, $c+c'$, $b+b'$, $a+a'$ and expand. Cf. [4, p. 260].

P5. $a+a=a$.
Using this, we can show

T9. $a+1=1+a=1$.

Proof. By P2–T2, P1–P1′, T1, T4=P5, and P3′, we have

$$a + 1 = (a + 1)(a + a') = (aa + 1a) + (aa' + 1a')$$
$$= (a + a) + (0 + a') = a + a' = 1.$$

By symmetry (§2), we get $1+a=1$.

We shall now show that *any system which satisfies* P1–P1′, P2–P2′, T1, *and* T9 *is a distributive lattice with* 1. It is a corollary that the even elements in any system satisfying P1–P1′, P2, P3–P3′ and P4 form a Boolean algebra (complemented distributive lattice). We shall prove the usual postulates for a distributive lattice as a chain of identities.

T10. $a+a=a$.

Proof. By P2, T9, P1, T1, and with P5, we have $a=a1=a(a+1)=aa+a\cdot 1 =a+a$.

T11. $ab+a=a+ab=a+ba=ba+a=a$.

Proof. $a+a\cdot 1=a(b+1)=ab+a1=ab+a$. The other proofs are entirely similar.

T12. $a(a+b)=a(b+a)=(a+b)a=(b+a)a=a$.

Proof. $a(a+b)=aa+ab=a+ab=a$, by P1, T1, T11. The other proofs are entirely similar.

T13. $a+b=b+a$.

Proof. By T12, P1, P1′, T12, we have

$$a + b = a(b + a) + b(b + a) = (a + b)(b + a)$$
$$= (a + b)b + (a + b)a = b + a.$$

T14. $a[(a+b)+c]=a$, $b[(a+b)+c]=b$, $c[(a+b)+c]=c$.

Proof. By P1, T12, and T1, we have

$$a[(a + b) + c] = a(a + b) + ac = a + ac = a,$$
$$b[(a + b) + c] = b(a + b) + bc = b + bc = b,$$
$$c[(a + b) + c] = c(a + b) + cc = c(a + b) + c = c.$$

T15. $a+(b+c)=(a+b)+c$.

Proof. $a+(b+c)=a[(a+b)+c]+(b[(a+b)+c]+c[(a+b)+c])$ by T14.

By P1′, this is $[a+(b+c)][(a+b)+c]$. By left-right symmetry, this can be shown to be $(a+b)+c$.

T16. *$a+bc=(a+b)(a+c)$ and $ab+c=(a+c)(b+c)$.*

Proof. By P1–P1′, T1, T12, T15, and T11, we have

$$(a+b)(a+c) = a(a+c) + b(a+c) = a + (ba + bc)$$
$$= (a + ba) + bc = a + bc.$$

The other identity follows by symmetry.

We now define the *dual* of an identity to be the equality obtained from it by interchanging addition and multiplication. Thus P1–P1′ and T16 are dual; T1 and T10 are dual; T11 and T12 are dual. Since the proofs of T13 and T15 involve only these laws, it follows that *dual proofs can be made to show*

T17. $ab=ba$.

T18. $a(bc)=(ab)c$.

But T1, T10, T17, T13, T18, T15, T12, T13, and P1–P1′ are the usual postulates for a distributive lattice; this completes our demonstration.

Remark. 1. Since the postulates for a distributive lattice are self-dual, it follows that T16, P3–P3′, $a0=0a=0$, and T10 are postulates for a distributive lattice with zero.

Remark 2. Just after T12, we can easily show that the conditions $a+b=a$, $b+a=a$, $ab=b$, and $ba=b$ are all equivalent to each other—and hence define $a \geqq b$ in a self-dual manner. We can show $a \geqq a$, that $a \geqq b$ and $b \geqq a$ imply $a=b$. But we need T15 or T18 to prove transitivity.

6. **Subdirect decomposition theorem.** We shall now use an entirely different and shorter argument to characterize the most general direct union of a Boolean algebra and an associative Boolean ring.

THEOREM. *The most general algebra satisfying* P1–P1′, P2–P2′, P3, P4, *and* P6, $(ab)c=(ac)(bc)$, *is a direct union of a Boolean algebra and an associative Boolean ring.*

Proof. Each identity is valid in every homomorphic image of an algebra A, if it is valid in A. It is also valid in the direct union $A \oplus B$, if it is valid in A and B individually. Hence it is valid in any *subdirect union* (in the sense of [1]) of algebras in which it holds. It follows, by the principal conclusion of [1], that all consequences of these identities which hold in every *subdirectly irreducible* algebra satisfying them, hold in *every* algebra satisfying them.

But now observe that (by definition) every correspondence $x \rightarrow xa$ of an algebra A is an *endomorphism*, if and only if P1′, P6 hold.

LEMMA 1. *Any algebra which satisfies* P1–P1′, P2–P2′, P3, P4, P6, *and contains an element a not* 0 *or* 1, *is subdirectly reducible.*

Proof. Since the correspondences $x\to xa$, $x\to xa'$ are endomorphisms (P1′, P6), the correspondence $x\to(xa, xa')$ is a homomorphism of A onto a subdirect union. Since $xa=ya$ and $xa'=ya'$ imply (P2, P4, P1)

$$x = x1 = x(a+a') = xa + xa' = ya + ya' = y(a+a') = y1 = y,$$

this homomorphism is an isomorphism. Again, by T1, $aa=a$ and by P2′, $1a=a$ $(a\neq 1)$, while $a'a'=a'$ and $1a'=a'$ similarly, where $a'=1$ would imply $0=aa'=a1=a$, contrary to hypothesis. Hence both endomorphisms determine proper congruence relations, and A is subdirectly reducible.

LEMMA 2. *The only algebras consisting of* 0 *and* 1 *which satisfy* P1–P1′, P2–P2′, P3, P4, P6 *are the Boolean algebra of two elements and the Boolean ring of two elements.*

Proof. By P2, P2′, P3, we have

$$0\cdot 1 = 1\cdot 0 = 0,\quad 1\cdot 1 = 1,\quad 0+0 = 0,\quad 1+0 = 1. \tag{1}$$

Since $0+0=0$, $0'$ cannot be 0 and must be 1. This gives, by P4,

$$0+1 = 1. \tag{2}$$

Again, $0\cdot 0=1$ would imply the contradiction

$$1 = 0\cdot 0 = (1\cdot 0)\cdot 0 = (1\cdot 0)\cdot(0\cdot 0)\ (\text{by P6}) = 0\cdot 1 = 0;$$

hence $0\cdot 0=0$. The only sum or product not determined is $1+1$; the possibilities $1+1=1$ and $1+1=0$ give the two cases mentioned in Lemma 2.

COROLLARY. *Any algebra satisfying* P1–P1′, P2–P2′, P3, P4, *and* P6 *is a subdirect union of Boolean algebras and Boolean rings of two elements.*

It is a further corollary that addition and multiplication are commutative and associative, and indeed that all the results of §§2–4 hold.

Remark 1. We can replace P2′ by $0a=0$ in the preceding argument: in the proof of Lemma 1, $0a'=aa'=0$, where $0\neq a$, and $(a')(a')'=0=0(a')'$, where $a'=0$ would imply $a=a+a'=a+0=1$, hence $x\to(xa', x(a')')$ subdirectly reduces A. In Lemma 2, $1\cdot 0=0$ is lost in (1); but since $1\cdot 1=1$, $1'\neq 1$, hence $1'=0$ and $1\cdot 0=1\cdot 1'=0$ still holds.

Remark 2. Thus replacing P3′ in §2 by P6 and P2′ or $0a=a$ effectively guarantees that the odd elements form an *associative* ring; otherwise it has no effect.

Remark 3. We can prove analogous results for systems satisfying P1, P2, P3′, T9, P6, $ab+c=(a+c)(b+c)$, $(a+c)+(b+c)=(a+b)+c$ and the commutative law of multiplication. By assumption, the correspondences $x\to xa$ and $x\to x+a$ are endomorphisms, for all a. Again, $a=(1\cdot 1)a=(1a)(1a)=aa$. It follows that if $xa=ya$ and if $x+a=y+a$, then

$$x = x1 = x(1 + a) = x + xa = xx + xa = x(x + a) = x(y + a)$$
$$= xy + xa = yx + ya = y(x + a) = y(y + a) = y.$$

Thus the correspondence $x \rightarrow (xa, x+a)$ is a *isomorphism*. Again $1a = aa$ and $0+a = a = a(1+1) = a+a$; hence any system containing an $a \neq 0$, 1 is subdirectly reducible. And the only system of 0 and 1 satisfying our postulates is a distributive lattice.

7. **Self-dual and symmetric postulates; counterexamples.** We have already observed that the laws of Boolean algebra are left-right symmetric for addition and multiplication (§2, Remark), and self-dual under interchange of addition and multiplication (§5, Remark 1). Thus they are invariant under an *octic group* of symmetries(4). The same remark applies to distributive lattices.

This suggests introducing the group of symmetries on the postulates as a "metamathematical" postulate, and seeing how few other postulates are required. It is evident that the following *three* are sufficient for Boolean algebra:

P1. $a(b+c) = ab+ac$. P2. $a1 = a$. P4. $a+a' = 1$.

For we get P1, P1′, P2, P3, P3′, P4 immediately, and from T1, by dualization, we get $a+a = a$.

This easy success suggests trying to see whether P1, P2, and their transforms under the octic group of left-right symmetries and duality do not constitute a sufficient set of postulates for a distributive lattice. In fact, one can prove directly that

$$1 = 0 + 1 = (0 \cdot 1) + 1 = (0 + 1)(1 + 1) = 1 \cdot (1 + 1)$$
$$= 1 \cdot 1 + 1 \cdot 1 = 1 + 1,$$

by the dual-symmetric P3′ of P2, P2, the dual-symmetric of P1, P3′ again, P1, and P2 respectively. Multiplying through by a (using P2), and dualizing, we get *idempotence*:

(1) $$a + a = a, \qquad aa = a.$$

Furthermore, consider the "free algebra" generated by 0, 1, a. Let $s, s_1, s_2, \cdots$ denote generically *sums* of terms 1 and a, and $p, p_1, p_2, \cdots$ denote dually *products* of terms 0 and a. We can prove by induction that all elements other than 0, 1, a are such sums or products.

Indeed, from the cases $s = 1$ and $s = a$, it follows by induction since $a(s+s_1) = as+as_1$ and $a+a = a$ that

(2) $$as = sa = a, \quad \text{whence} \quad a + p = p + a = a,$$

(4) This is in accordance with the philosophic principle that "The final form of any scientific theory T is (1) based on a few simple postulates, and (2) contains an extensive ambiguity, associated symmetry, and underlying group G, in such wise that . . . T appears nearly self-evident in view of the Principle of Sufficient Reason." (G. D. Birkhoff)

by duality. We shall now prove that

$$sp = ap = p_1 \qquad (s \neq 0, 1). \tag{3}$$

Indeed, $ap=ap$, $(s+1)p=sp+p=ap+pp$ (by induction and (1)) $=(a+p)p$ $=ap$ by (2), and $(s+s')p=sp+s'p=ap+ap$ (by induction) $=ap$ by (1). This completes the proof of (3). By duality, we get

$$s + p = s + a = s_1 \qquad (s \neq 0, 1). \tag{4}$$

Since $s+s=ss=s$ and $p+p=pp=p$, we have a homomorphism of the "free algebra" onto the system with five elements 0, 1, a, s, p and the rules of operation described by P1, P2, (1)–(4) and their left-right symmetric and dual transforms. This self-dual and symmetric image algebra however satisfies P1, P2; hence P1, P2 *and their transforms do not constitute a set of postulates for distributive lattices.* (Though by §5, P1, P2, and T9 and their transforms do.)

An even more simple counterexample consists of two elements: $0=1$ and a, with identical addition and multiplication tables given by:

$$00 = 0 + 0 = 0,$$
$$0a = a0 = 0 + a = a + 0 = aa = a + a = a.$$

In this system, addition and multiplication are idempotent, commutative, and associative; all distributive laws hold; 0 is an additive and 1 a multiplicative unit; a is a multiplicative zero and additive unity. Moreover by forming the direct product of it and the Boolean algebra of two elements, we can make $0 \neq 1$.

It would be interesting to determine what were the different elements of the form s and p in the "free" self-dual and symmetric algebra generated by a (with 0 and 1) subject to P1 and P2.

It would also be interesting to determine the independent subsets of the postulates (for distributive lattices) generated by P1, P2, T9 and their transforms under the octic group of left-right symmetries and duality.

BIBLIOGRAPHY

1. G. Birkhoff, *Subdirect unions in universal algebra*, Bull. Amer. Math. Soc. vol. 50 (1944) pp. 764–768.

2. George Boole, *The laws of thought*, 1854, republished by the Open Court Publishing Co.

3. E. V. Huntington, *New sets of independent postulates for the algebra of logic*, Trans. Amer. Math. Soc. vol. 35 (1933) pp. 274–304; corrections on pp. 557, 971.

4. M. H. A. Newman, *A characterization of Boolean algebras and rings*, J. London Math. Soc. vol. 16 (1941) pp. 256–272.

5. M. H. Stone, *Representations of Boolean algebras*, Trans. Amer. Math. Soc. vol. 40 (1936) pp. 37–111.

HARVARD UNIVERSITY,
CAMBRIDGE, MASS.

A TERNARY OPERATION IN DISTRIBUTIVE LATTICES

GARRETT BIRKHOFF AND S. A. KISS

It can be easily seen that the *graph* [1, p. 9],[1] of the Boolean algebra B^n of 2^n elements (consisting of the vertices and edges of an n-cube) has $2^n(n!)$ "link-automorphisms," whereas B^n has only $(n!)$ lattice-automorphisms. In an unpublished book,[2] one of us has developed new operations in B^n and other distributive lattices, which admit such a wider group of invariance. The purpose of this note is to show the role of the symmetric and self-dual ternary operation [1, p. 74]

$$(1) \qquad \begin{aligned}(a, b, c) &= (a \cap b) \cup (b \cap c) \cup (c \cap a)\\ &= (a \cup b) \cap (b \cup c) \cap (c \cup a)\end{aligned}$$

in a general distributive lattice L, with reference to the wider group of symmetries which it admits.

THEOREM 1. *In any metric distributive lattice* [1, p. 41], *the following conditions are equivalent*: (i) $a\cap b \leqq x \leqq a \cup b$, (ii) $|a-x|+|x-b| = |a-b|$, (iii) $(a, x, b) = x$.

PROOF. V. Glivenko [3, p. 819, Theorem V] has shown the equivalence of (i) and (ii); condition (i) says that x is metrically "between" a and b in the sense of Menger. But now if $a\cap b \leqq x \leqq a\cup b$, then $(a, x, b) = (a\cap b)\cup(b\cap x)\cup(x\cap a) = (a\cap b)\cup[x\cap(a\cup b)] = x$. Conversely, if $(a, x, b) = x$, then

$$x = (a \cap b) \cup (b \cap x) \cup (x \cap a) \geqq a \cap b,$$

and dually, $x \leqq a \cup b$. Hence (i) and (iii) are equivalent.

DEFINITION. The segment joining a and b is the set of x satisfying any (hence all) of the conditions of Theorem 1 (cf. Duthie [4]); we denote it $[a, b]$.

THEOREM 2. *The element* (a, b, c) *is the intersection of the sets* $[a, b]$ $[b, c]$ $[c, a]$.

PROOF. This is obvious from condition (i) and formula (1).

COROLLARY 1. *The element* (a, b, c) *minimizes*

Received by the editors October 21, 1946, and, in revised form, January 16, 1947.

[1] Numbers in brackets refer to the bibliography at the end of the paper.

[2] S. A. Kiss, *Transformations on lattices and structures of logic*, Bull. Amer. Math. Soc. Abstract 52-1-4.

$$|x-a|+|x-b|+|x-c|.$$

PROOF. In fact, $|x-a|+|x-b| \geqq |a-b|$ and symmetrically. Adding, we get for all x

$$2\{|x-a|+|x-b|+|x-c|\} \geqq |a-b|+|b-c|+|c-a| \tag{2}$$

By Theorems 1 and 2, equality holds if and only if $x=(a, b, c)$.

Since (a, b, c) can be defined in terms of distance and a, b, c, we get, further, the following corollary.

COROLLARY 2. *Any isometry of a metric distributive lattice preserves the operation* (a, b, c).

In neither nondistributive lattice of five elements, does every triple of elements a, b, c, determine a unique x minimizing $|x-a|+|x-b|+|x-c|$; it would be interesting to know what the lattices are in which this "midpoint" is uniquely determined.

By using a weighted dimension function [1, Theorem 3.9] on B^2, we can find easily lattice-automorphisms which are not isometries. However, in the finite-dimensional case, we can obtain a converse to the preceding corollary.

We define *distance* in the graph of a finite-dimensional lattice in the usual way, by making all segments have length one. Thus if $d[x]$ is the number of "links" in the longest chain joining O and x, $|x-y|=d[x\cup y]-d[x\cap y]$. This makes L a metric lattice [1, Theorem 3.9].

THEOREM 3. *The isometries of the graph of a finite-dimensional distributive lattice L are precisely the automorphisms with respect to the ternary operation* (a, b, c).

PROOF. Corollary 2 above proves one half. To prove the converse, since any isometry carries "linked" elements into "linked" elements, it suffices to note the following lemma.

LEMMA. *In L, a and b are "linked" (that is, a covers b or b covers a) if and only if* $(a, x, b)=a$ *or* b *for all* x.

PROOF. By Theorem 1, $(a, x, b)=a$ or b for all x if and only if $[a, b]$ consists only of a and b—that is, if and only if a and b are equal or linked.

DEFINITION. We shall call elements a, a' of a distributive lattice *complementary* if and only if $(a, x, a')=x$ for all x.

It is easily seen that a given a can have only one complement.

For if it has two, say a' and a'', then $a''=(a, a'', a')=(a, a', a'')=a'$, for any symmetric ternary operation. It is also easily seen that if a and a' are complementary, then we have a "double algebra" with an "extreme pair";[3] we denote $x\cap y=(x, a, y)$ and $x\cup y=(x, a', y)$, and get a distributive lattice.

More generally, the 2^n mutually distributive operations introduced by one of us[2] in B^n are the operations (x, a, y), one for each of the 2^n different elements a of B^n.

Added January 15, 1947. It may be shown that distributive lattices can be defined in terms of the ternary operation (a, b, c), by postulating

(3.1) $\qquad (0, a, I) = a \qquad$ for a fixed pair O, I,

(3.2) $\qquad (a, b, a) = a,$

(3.3) $\qquad (a, b, c) = (b, a, c) = (b, c, a) \qquad$ (symmetry),

(3.4) $\qquad ((a, b, c), d, e) = ((a, d, e), b, (c, d, e)).$

The proof is straightforward, if we try to prove the right known set of postulates.[4] The greatest trouble comes in proving that (a, b, c) is actually defined by (1) in the distributive lattice defined by the binary operations $a\cap b\equiv(a, 0, b)$ and $a\cup b\equiv(a, I, b)$. This trouble is resolved by using Theorem 2 above. Law (3.4), which contains both ordinary distributive laws as special cases, may be proved by direct substitution.

The structure of the group of automorphisms of B^n with respect to the ternary operation (a, b, c) is of interest for its own sake, and because it is the structure of the group of symmetries of the n-cube.

For any fixed a, the correspondence

(4) $\qquad x \to (x\cap a')\cup(x'\cap a) = x + a$

(here $+$ denotes addition in the additive group of the corresponding Boolean ring) is an automorphism for (a, b, c); this defines a *simply transitive, elementary Abelian* subgroup of order 2^n, of symmetries of the n-cube; the case $a=I$, $x\to x'$ gives the "antipodal reflection" generating the center of the group. We also have the subgroup "of

[3] Cf. M. H. A. Newman, *A characterization of Boolean lattices and rings*, J. London Math. Soc. vol. 16 (1941) p. 257.

[4] Namely, those of p. 7 of *Distributive postulates for systems like Boolean algebras*, by G. D. Birkhoff and G. Birkhoff, Trans. Amer. Math. Soc. vol. 60 (1946) pp. 3–11. It might be possible to base postulates on the conditions of §§8–10 of E. Pitcher and M. F. Smiley, *Transitivities of betweenness*, Trans. Amer. Math. Soc. vol. 52 (1942) pp. 95–114.

stability" leaving the vertex O fixed, and consisting of the lattice-automorphisms of B^n. The entire group is the product of these two subgroups.

There is an obvious analogy between the ternary operation (1) and the ternary operation $ab^{-1}c$ of a group G; in the latter case, the group of automorphisms for $ab^{-1}c$ is the holomorph[5] of G. This similarly is the product of the subgroup of group-automorphisms and a simply transitive subgroup of right-translations $x \to xa$. It would be interesting to extend our ternary operation to Newman's "double systems" (reference of footnote 2).

However, it should be noted that in doing this, we should not use the ternary operation $a+b+c$ of Baer-Certaine. For with respect to this, B^n has $2^n(2^n-1)\cdots(2^n-2^{n-1})$ automorphisms; hence we cannot even *define* (a, b, c) in terms of it.

Bibliography

1. Garrett Birkhoff, *Lattice theory*, Amer. Math. Soc. Colloquium Publications, vol. 25, New York, 1940.

2. W. D. Duthie, *Segments of ordered sets*, Trans. Amer. Math. Soc. vol. 51 (1942) pp. 1–14.

3. V. Glivenko, *Géometrie des systèmes de choses normées*, Amer. J. Math. vol. 58 (1936) pp. 799–828.

4. ———, *Contribution à l'études des systèmes de choses normées*, ibid. vol. 59 (1937) pp. 941–956.

Harvard University and
Standard Oil Development Company

[5] J. Certaine, *The ternary operation* $(abc)=ab^{-1}c$ *of a group*, Bull. Amer. Math. Soc. vol. 49 (1943) pp. 869–877; this operation had previously been discussed by R. Baer. It satisfies $(aab)=b$, instead of $(aab)=a$.

Reprinted from *Bull. Am. Math. Soc.* **53** (1947), 749–752

II

Universal Algebra

Philosophically, the idea of a general "logic of algebra" goes back to Peacock, Babbage, and Boole,[1] and before that to Leibniz. Their idea was that the *symbolic method* of algebra has its own logic. This idea permeated Whitehead's 1897 book *Universal Algebra*,[2] but was not developed there as a systematic theory. Instead, his book was a *survey* of some of the new branches of algebra (Boolean algebra, Grassmann's exterior algebra, etc.) that had originated in the nineteenth century, thus enormously enlarging the scope of algebra. Its character is described by the following (translated) excerpts from its review in the *Jahresb. über die Fortschritte der Math.* **29** (1898), pp. 66–7:

> "By 'universal algebra' is meant different systems of symbolic demonstration ["Schlussbildung"] which are related to ordinary algebra. The most important examples are Hamilton's quaternions, Grassmann's calculus of extension, and Boole's symbolic logic. The book under review contains an exposition of the general principles of universal algebra.... A second volume will comprise a thorough study of quaternions and matrices, together with a unification of the symbolic expressions of different algebraic structures ["Gebäude"].
>
> The main idea of the treatise is *not* the unification of different branches of algebra, ... but a comparative study of special structures."

What was to have been the second volume of *Universal Algebra* became amalgamated with an intended continuation of Bertrand Russell's *Principles of Mathematics*, emerging as the famous three-volume treatise *Principia Mathematica* (1910, 1912, 1913).[3]

The ostensible aim of this treatise was to develop Peano's "pasigraphy" into a symbolic logic capable of treating all of mathematics. But in fact, nearly half of it was a very original digression on the "arithmetic of relations" (see Part III).

A technical unification of many branches of algebra was achieved by the Emmy Noether school in the 1920s, and brilliantly expounded in van der Waerden's *Moderne Algebra* (first ed., 1930–31). This unification was based on "the fundamental group-theoretic concepts of group, subgroup, isomorphism, homomorphism, normal subgroup, quotient-group" (op. cit., p. 17). Its Chapter VI derived two "isomorphism theorems" and a "Jordan–Hölder theorem" valid in any "*group with operators*." This class of "algebras" included groups, rings, vector spaces, and linear algebras, but excluded lattices.

Today, an *algebra* $\mathfrak{A} = [S; F]$ is usually defined as a set S of *elements* combined by a set F of finitary *operations* f_i: $S^{\nu(i)} \to S$. These operations are most commonly unary ($\nu = 1$) or binary ($\nu = 2$), but they can be "nullary" ($\nu = 0$) (i.e., specify distinguished elements with special properties), or ternary ($\nu = 3$), etc. Universal algebra is concerned with general properties of large classes of such "algebras."

The first substantial explicit study of "algebras" in this generality was my paper [15] of 1935, entitled "On the structure of abstract algebras." It included a general construction of "free" algebras having any number of "generators", given any set of "operations" and "identities." Deepest and most original was the so-called HSP-Theorem. This asserts that any "family" (now usually called a "variety") of algebras having specified operations that satisfy specified identities is closed under the formation of direct products, subalgebras, and epimorphic images—*and conversely.*

In [15] was also proved the result that the congruence relations on any algebra form a sublattice of the "symmetric partition lattice" of all equivalence relations on its elements. This theorem made evident the central role played by lattices in the study of the structure of algebras.

An even more convincing demonstration of this role was provided by Oystein Ore's two masterful papers of 1935–6.[4] There Ore demonstrated the power of Dedekind's lattice-theoretic approach, by deriving the unique factorization theorem and other basic results about the structure of groups with operators from the fact that their invariant subgroups form a *modular lattice.*

"Universal algebra" was not mentioned in any of these papers. It was not until 1940 that, in [LT1, p. 2], I proposed this as an appropriate name for the study of general properties of "algebras." The title of Whitehead's 1897 book seemed to me appropriate because of the book's concern with the logic of the symbolic method, and because symbol manipulation is the essence of algebra.

The subject of universal algebra is elusive; thus [15] was ambiguous as to which theorems depend on the "finitary" nature of the f_i. Partly for this reason, and partly because of the paucity of substantial theorems valid for all "algebras," it was not until 1944–46 that I wrote again on the subject.

I then wrote three more papers ([47], [49], [52]). The first of these reduced the 1933–34 "Birkhoff–Stone representation theorems" for distributive lattices and Boolean algebras (cf. [3]) to corollaries of a *subdirect decomposition theorem* of "universal algebra," and easy proofs of the "subdirect reducibility" of any distributive lattice or Boolean algebra with more than two elements.

My second paper of this period ([49]) was expository, and intended to call attention to the scope and promise of the subject, as a "new field of research." It cited results in Philip Whitman's Harvard Ph.D. Thesis on free lattices, and unpublished results of Bruce Crabtree, a Harvard graduate student, as well as the unique factorization theorem of Jónsson and Tarski.

The third paper ([52]) showed that every group of α elements is isomorphic with the group Aut(L) of a distributive lattice L having at most $2^{\alpha^2+\alpha}$ elements.

Shortly after this, I showed that Ore's main structure theorems hold in any algebra having a one-element subalgebra and permutable congruence relations. I announced the results at the 1946 Princeton Bicentennial, and published them in [LT2, Chap. VI].

During the mid-1940s, Philip Hall and Saunders Mac Lane were also thinking about universal algebra. Hall talked about "clones" with Bernard and Hanna Neumann and his students. The British school of universal algebra evolved from these discussions. Among the many publications on universal algebra by British researchers, P. M. Cohn's *Universal Algebra* (1965) and Hanna Neumann's *Varieties of Groups* (1967) are the most comprehensive; their references provide authoritative guides to much related work.

A flood of papers on category theory in the 1950s and 1960s was initiated by the famous Eilenberg–Mac Lane 1945 paper "General theory of natural equivalences" (*Trans. AMS* **58** (1945), 231–94). These adopt a very different approach to universal algebra, in which the concept of morphism is taken as basic. Unlike lattices, categories are only *partial* "algebras" because morphisms can only be composed exceptionally. Thus "universal algebra" as defined above does not apply to them, although every variety of algebras determines the category whose objects are its algebras, and whose arrows are the morphisms between them.

From 1947 on, to identify the concern of papers such as those mentioned above, but perhaps also to include Bourbaki's philosophical remarks about mathematical "structures," the Subject Index of Math. Reviews included Universal Algebra as one of its 10 subheadings under ALGEBRA: ABSTRACT. Hence universal algebra may be considered to have become "established" about a decade after lattice theory.

Paper [58], written in 1948 with Orrin Frink and reviewed in Part IV, initiated a new direction in universal algebra, by giving necessary and sufficient conditions for a (complete) lattice to be isomorphic with Sub($\mathfrak{A}$) for some algebra with *finitary* operations. (Every complete lattice $[L; \wedge, \vee]$ is isomorphic with the lattice of all subalgebras of the infinitary algebra $\mathscr{L} = [L; \bigvee, M]$ of L, with respect to joins of arbitrary "arity" and the set M of all unary operations $f_a\colon x \mapsto x \wedge a$, $a \in L$ [3, Thm. 5.1].) The analogy with compactness was pointed out by Dilworth, and from these ideas evolved the concept of an *algebraic lattice.*

After 1950, universal algebra underwent an explosive development. I tried to survey the most interesting pre-1965 developments in [LT3, Chaps. VI–VIII]. To include *automata* within the scope of "universal algebra," as well as the usual definition of a vector space, I also wrote papers [154] and [175] with John Lipson around 1970. An important event of those years was the founding of the journal *Algebra Universalis* by George Grätzer (published by Birkhäuser) in 1971.

For more thorough and up-to-date expositions of universal algebras, the following books should be consulted:

(1) P. M. Cohn, *Universal Algebra.* First ed., Harper and Row, 1965; 2d ed., D. Reidel, Dordrecht, 1981.
(2) George Grätzer, *Universal Algebra.* First ed., van Nostrand, 1968; 2d ed., Springer-Verlag, 1979.
(3) Bjarni Jónsson, *Topics in Universal Algebra.* Springer Lecture Notes in Math., #250, 1972.
(4) S. Burris and H. P. Sankappanavar, *A Course in Universal Algebra.* Springer-Verlag, 1981.

[15]. On the structure of abstract algebras (1935). This paper is complementary to Ore's papers of 1935–36 on the same theme. For the special case of groups (with or without operators), Ore exploited in depth Dedekind's observation that their congruence relations form a modular lattice, to obtain strong structure theorems. In contrast, [15] was notable for its extreme generality. It begins by introducing the *congruence lattice* Con($\mathfrak{A}$), the *subalgebra lattice* Sub($\mathfrak{A}$), and the *automorphism group* Aut($\mathfrak{A}$), which are defined even for infinitary and partial algebras $\mathfrak{A}$, and so apply also to topological algebras (see the comments on [179]).

Indeed, its statement (Thm. 2) that any complete lattice is isomorphic to some Sub($\mathfrak{A}$) is only true if infinitary algebras are included. Theorem 24, on the other hand, which states that Con($\mathfrak{A}$) is a *sublattice* of the lattice $\Pi(S)$ of all partitions of $\mathfrak{A} = [S; F]$, is not true unless infinitary operations are *excluded.*

This pioneering paper is hard reading, not only because of its ambiguity about the inclusion of infinitary operations, but also because its words "homomorphic equivalence relation," "structure lattice," "index," "family," and "species" are usually replaced today by "congruence relation," "congruence lattice," "arity," "variety," and "species."[5] Some readers may be disturbed because only *L*2–*L*4 are assumed in defining "lattices" (§4), forgetting that Dedekind had shown that these imply L1.

Some results of [15] concern lattices. Thus it was shown there that the free modular lattice M_{28} with three generators is a subdirect ("meromorphic") product of copies of *2* and M_5. Also, every finite partition lattice $\Pi(S)$ is simple. Its identities *L*51–*L*52 have a curious history. It was stated in [15] that they had been proved to characterize M_5 "by a difficult argument ... submitted to the referee." The proof having been lost, the assertion was republished as Problem 45 in [LT3, p. 157]. Two years later, Jónsson proved the stronger result that either *L*51 *or* *L*52 (which imply each other) characterize M_5.[6]

The main result of [15] is the Galois correspondence established between varieties ("families") of *algebras* of a given species (closed under direct products, taking subalgebras and homomorphic images) and families of *laws* (identities) closed under two rules of inference (Thms. 6–10). This is often called the HSP–Theorem today. The proof includes a sketchy construction of the free algebra with *n* generators associated with any variety *V* of algebras. The result that the free lattice with 3 generators is infinite is proved in §25.

The paper ends by formulating several questions about lattices of partitions, and also by asking whether every finite modular lattice is a subdirect product of finite projective geometries and copies of *2*.

The most interesting question about partition lattices is: is every lattice isomorphic to a sublattice of the "partition lattice" $\Pi(S)$ of all partitions of some set *S*? A decade later, Whitman showed that this was indeed true, after previously solving the word problem for lattices in his Harvard Ph.D. Thesis.[7] In 1953, Jónsson (3) proved that every lattice *L* can be embedded as a sublattice in a partition lattice with all joins of "Type 3," and that every *modular* lattice can be so embedded with all joins of Type 2. The problem remained for many years whether a finite *L* can always be embedded in $\Pi(S)$ with *S* finite. This was proved in 1980 by P. Pudlák and J. Tůma (4); their proof requires a *S* of astronomical size. Thus, for instance, returning to the questions of [15, §31], the *dual* of $\Pi(4)$ is embeddable in a finite partition lattice $\Pi(S)$, but the known methods require $|S| > 2^{1000}$. For a general review of partition lattices which is up to date except, of course, for the Pudlák–Tůma Theorem consult §IV.4 of Gratzer (1).

As regards the second question, Hall and Dilworth (2) proved in 1944 that there exists a modular lattice not embeddable in any complemented modular lattice. In fact, the class of complemented modular lattices lies in a proper subvariety of the variety of all modular lattices, as was proved by Grätzer and Lakser in 1973; see (1, p. 213). Moreover it now looks as if there is no natural external description of all modular lattices, such as a certain family of congruence lattices (see §61 of B. Jónsson's survey article in (1, Appendix 3). There is in fact no known direct description of any modular lattice *M* which does not obey some extra law; for instance we cannot consider the free modular lattice with *n* generators to be such an *M*, since its word problem is recursively unsolvable if $n > 4$, as R. Freese proved in 1980 (5).

(1) G. Grätzer, *General Lattice Theory*, Birkhäuser, 1978.
(2) M. Hall and R. P. Dilworth, *Annals of Math.* **45** (1944), 450–6.
(3) B. Jónsson, *Math. Scand.* **1** (1953), 193–206.
(4) P. Pudlák and J. Tůma, *Algebra Univ.* **10** (1980), 74–95.
(5) Ralph Freese, *Trans. AMS* **261** (1980), 81–91.
(6) G. Grätzer, *Universal Algebra*, Van Nostrand, 1968; second edition, Springer-Verlag, 1979.

[47]. "Subdirect unions in universal algebra." Until 1940, most general structure theorems of algebra assumed the Hilbert–E. Noether Teilerkettensatz, brilliantly formulated in van der Waerden's *Moderne Algebra.* Paper [47] makes instead the more general hypothesis that all operations are *finitary* (see [47 ftnt. 2]). Its eight corollaries, which apply to various classes of

algebras, illustrate the scope of its main theorem. Two of these have already been discussed above.

The name "subdirect product" was avoided in [47] because in 1944, the word "algebra" was still often used (as suggested by Sylvester) to mean "linear associative algebra." To avoid conflict with the established meaning of "direct products" (today usually called "tensor" or "Kronecker" products) of linear algebras, the phrase "subdirect *unions*" was adopted.

[49]. "Universal algebra." Paper [49] was probably the first systematic exposition of universal algebra. It was presented to a general mathematical audience at the First Canadian Mathematical Congress in 1945, by which time my ideas about the subject had begun to crystallize. I reconsidered the terminology of [15], and most of the terminology of [49] has become standard.

This paper was intended to suggest problems rather than to solve them. Thus, after defining the semigroup End($\mathfrak{A}$), it asks whether every semigroup can be realized as some End($\mathfrak{A}$). (The 1972 Grätzer–Lampe Theorem gives, of course, a much sharper result.) Moreover, [49§11] suggests that Peano algebras should be studied.

It points out (§5) that the main concepts of a 1944 paper by Baer on characteristic subgroups of groups have analogs in any algebra $\mathfrak{A}$. The HSP-Theorem was omitted, but the discussion of "free algebras" in §§9–10 provides a satisfactory SP-Theorem, lacking in [15]. These remarks were borne out in B. H. Neumann's 1962 theorem correlating free algebras with the "fully characteristic" congruence relations on word algebras [LT3, p. 152].

Notes

[1] See pp. 164–6 of E. T. Bell's *Development of Mathematics*, McGraw-Hill, 1940; also H. W. Becher in *Historia Math.* **7** (1980), 389–400.

[2] Whitehead took the title from that of an article by Sylvester on matrices, in *Am. J. Math.* **6** (1883), 270–86.

[3] See J. van Heijenoort, *From Frege to Gödel*, Harvard Univ. Press, 1967, p. 216.

[4] *Annals of Math.* **36** (1935), 406–39, and 37 (1936), 265–92.

[5] Actually, [LT2] already introduced some of these changes, while [LT3] distinguished the $\cap$, $\cup$, $\subseteq$ of set theory from the corresponding (and more general) $\wedge$, $\vee$, $\leq$ of abstract lattice theory. From 1944–45 on, partly because of the results of [47] and [52], all "algebras" not labelled "infinitary" have been assumed to have only finitary operations.

[6] B. Jónsson, *Math. Scand.* **22** (1968), 187–96.

[7] See P. M. Whitman, *Annals of Math.* **42** (1951), 325–30, and **42** (1942), 104–150; *Bull. AMS* **52** (1946), 507–22.

[Extracted from the *Proceedings of the Cambridge Philosophical Society*, Vol. XXXI. Pt. IV.]

ON THE STRUCTURE OF ABSTRACT ALGEBRAS

By GARRETT BIRKHOFF, Trinity College

[Communicated by MR P. HALL]

[*Received* 26 April, *read* 3 June 1935]

1. *Introduction.* The following paper is a study of abstract algebras *qua* abstract algebras. As no vocabulary suitable for this purpose is current, I have been forced to use a number of new terms, and extend the meaning of some accepted ones.

An outline of the material will perhaps tell the reader what to expect. In §§ 2–7, the notion of abstract algebra is defined, and relations between abstract algebras of two kinds (groups and "lattices") derived from a fixed abstract algebra are indicated.

In § 8, abstract algebras are divided by a very simple scheme into self-contained "species". Within each species, a perfect duality is found between families of formal laws and the families of algebras satisfying them; this occupies §§ 9–10. After a digression in § 11, some illustrations are discussed in §§ 12–15.

In §§ 16–18, the "lattice" $E(C)$ of the equivalence relations between the objects of a fixed aggregate C is defined; in §§ 20–21 such lattices are shown to be interchangeable with lattices of Boolean subalgebras and lattices of subgroups. Other miscellaneous facts are proved in § 19, § 22, and § 23. In § 24, the interesting truth is established that, if C is an algebra, then the equivalence relations which are homomorphic are a "sublattice" of $E(C)$.

In § 25 an open question is settled, and the paper concludes in §§ 26–31 with some observations on topology. Many incidental results have of course not been mentioned.

The reader will find it easier to follow the exposition if he remembers that operations are considered as fundamental throughout, while algebras and to an even greater extent elements within the same algebra are juggled freely.

2. *Abstract algebras defined.* By an "abstract algebra" is meant, loosely speaking, any system of elements and operations such as a ring, a field, a group, or a Boolean algebra. A tentative formal definition is the following.

Let $\mathfrak{C}$ be any class of "elements", and let F be a class of "operators" f_1, f_2,

f_3, ... Further, let there be assigned to each f_i of F a set $\mathfrak{D}_i$ of sequences† of elements of $\mathfrak{C}$, to be called the "proper domain" of f_i. And, finally, let each f_i be a single-valued function of its proper domain to $\mathfrak{C}$—in other words, let f_i assign to each sequence σ of $\mathfrak{D}_i$ a unique "f_i-value" $f_i(\sigma)$ in $\mathfrak{C}$.

Then the couple $(\mathfrak{C}, F)$ will be called an "abstract algebra" A, or for brevity in this paper, an "algebra". The number of different elements of $\mathfrak{C}$ will be called the "order" of A.

3. *The group of automorphisms of an algebra.* It would be pointless to prove in detail what is already known, that every algebra has a group. It is enough to restate in explicit language the outlines of the usual doctrine.

By an "automorphism" of an algebra $(\mathfrak{C}, F)$ is meant a (1, 1) transformation α of $\mathfrak{C}$ into itself such that

(*a*) $\sigma\epsilon\mathfrak{D}_i$ implies $\alpha(\sigma)\epsilon\mathfrak{D}_i$ and conversely.

(*b*) $f_i(\alpha(\sigma))=\alpha(f_i(\sigma))$ for any $\sigma\epsilon\mathfrak{D}_i$.

And by a "group" is meant any algebra $(\mathfrak{A}, G)$ satisfying

G 1: To each element α of $\mathfrak{A}$ corresponds a unique "inverse" $\alpha^{-1}=g_1(\alpha)$ in $\mathfrak{A}$.

G 2: To each sequence (α, β) of two elements of $\mathfrak{A}$ there corresponds a unique "product" $\alpha\beta=g_2(\alpha,\beta)$ in $\mathfrak{A}$.

G 3: $(\alpha\alpha^{-1})\beta=\beta$ and $\beta(\alpha\alpha^{-1})=\beta$ for any α and β in $\mathfrak{A}$.

G 4: $(\alpha\beta)\gamma=\alpha(\beta\gamma)$ for any α, β, and γ in $\mathfrak{A}$.

THEOREM 1‡: *The automorphisms of any algebra form a group, and any group can be realized as the group of the automorphisms of a suitable algebra.*

4. *The lattice of subalgebras of an algebra.* Only recently the object of special research has been what I consider to be a dual notion, that of the "lattice" of the subalgebras of an algebra.

Let $\mathfrak{S}$ be any subclass of $\mathfrak{C}$ (in the notation of § 2) with the property that if σ lies in $\mathfrak{D}_i$ and its elements in $\mathfrak{S}$, then $f_i(\sigma)$ also is in $\mathfrak{S}$. Then the couple $(\mathfrak{S}, F)$ will be called a "subalgebra" of the algebra $(\mathfrak{C}, F)$.

By a "lattice" is meant any system of double composition satisfying the commutative, associative and absorption laws. That is, in the notation of § 2, a lattice is an algebra $(\mathfrak{L}, H)$ satisfying

L 1: Any two elements A and B of $\mathfrak{L}$ have a unique "meet" $A\cap B=h_1(A,B)$ and a unique "join" $A\cup B=h_2(A,B)$ in $\mathfrak{L}$.

L 2: $A\cap B=B\cap A$ and $A\cup B=B\cup A$ for any A and B of $\mathfrak{L}$.

L 3: $A\cap(B\cap C)=(A\cap B)\cap C$ and $A\cup(B\cup C)=(A\cup B)\cup C$ for any A, B, and C of $\mathfrak{L}$.

L 4: $A\cap(A\cup B)=A\cup(A\cap B)=A$ for any A and B of $\mathfrak{L}$.

† By a "sequence" we mean a "well-ordered set". We can use the locutions "finite sequence" and "enumerated sequence" to express that the ordinal number of the set is finite, or that of the ordered positive integers.

‡ The first statement is known; the second will be proved in § 15.

THEOREM 2†: *The subalgebras of any algebra form a lattice, and any lattice can be realized as the lattice of the subalgebras of a suitable algebra.*

5. *Some general isomorphisms.* Let A be any abstract algebra. We shall adopt the notation $G(A)$ for the group of the automorphisms of A, $L(A)$ for the lattice of the subalgebras of A. Expressions such as $G(L(A))$ and $L(L(G(A)))$ are then self-explanatory.

We shall also adopt the usual definitions‡ of isomorphism and homomorphism. We shall supplement these by saying that a (1, 1) correspondence between a lattice L and a lattice $\bar{L}$ is "dually isomorphic" if and only if it inverts the operations of meet and join—i.e. if and only if the hypothesis that a and b of L correspond respectively to $\bar{a}$ and $\bar{b}$ of $\bar{L}$ implies that $a \frown b$ and $a \smile b$ correspond respectively to $\bar{a} \smile \bar{b}$ and $\bar{a} \frown \bar{b}$.

We shall now state some perfectly general operation-preserving correspondences which occur repeatedly in algebra.

(1) Every automorphism α of A induces an automorphism on $G(A)$, $L(A)$, $G(G(A))$, $L(G(A))$, and so on down the line. Moreover, products and inverses are preserved under this correspondence. Therefore a homomorphic correspondence exists between $G(A)$ and a subgroup of any $G^* = G(\ldots(A)\ldots)$.

The special case $G^* = G(G(A))$ gives the important homomorphism between $G(A)$ and the group of the "inner" automorphisms of $G(A)$; this defines an isomorphism between $G(A)$ and $G(G(A))$ if and only if $G(A)$ is complete.

Again, if A is a lattice, and $G^* = G(L(A))$, the homomorphism is an isomorphism, since each element of A is a sublattice.

(2) An automorphism α of A is said to "centralize" a complex C of elements of A if and only if it leaves every element of C fixed—i.e. carries it into itself.

This assigns to every subalgebra S of A the subgroup $\mathfrak{S}(S)$ of $G(A)$ centralizing it, and to every subgroup $\mathfrak{S}$ of $G(A)$ the subalgebra $S(\mathfrak{S})$ of elements of A centralized by $\mathfrak{S}$. And since $S \supset T$ implies $\mathfrak{S}(S) \subset \mathfrak{S}(T)$, while $\mathfrak{S} \supset \mathfrak{T}$ implies $S(\mathfrak{S}) \subset S(\mathfrak{T})$, the correspondence inverts inclusion relations§.

In any case $S(\mathfrak{S}(S)) \supset S$ and $\mathfrak{S}(S(\mathfrak{S})) \supset \mathfrak{S}$. If for any S (or $\mathfrak{S}$) the correspondence is *reciprocal*—that is, $S(\mathfrak{S}(S)) = S$ (or $\mathfrak{S}(S(\mathfrak{S})) = \mathfrak{S}$)—we shall say that S or ($\mathfrak{S}$) is "replete". Since inclusion is inverted, we can assert

THEOREM 3: *If the replete elements of $L(A)$ and $L(G(A))$ are sublattices L_1 of $L(A)$ and L_2 of $L(G(A))$ respectively, then L_1 and L_2 are dually isomorphic.*

† These facts were proved by the author in "On the combination of subalgebras", *Proc. Cambridge Phil. Soc.* 29 (1933), 441–64: $A \frown B$ is the set of elements common to the subalgebras A and B, $A \smile B$ is the meet of the subalgebras containing both A and B. In later citations, the above paper will be referred to for short as "Subalgebras".

‡ Cf. B. L. van der Waerden's *Moderne Algebra*, 1 (Berlin, 1930–1), 28–32.

§ The notion of inclusion in an abstract lattice is naturally defined by writing $a \subset b$ if and only if $a \smile b = b$.

29-2

It is by proving the hypotheses of Theorem 3, in the case where A is the field of algebraic numbers, that it has been† shown that the lattice of finite extensions of the rational domain is dually isomorphic with the lattice of the subgroups of finite index in the group $G(A)$ (relative to the four rational operations).

A similar correspondence exists‡ between any discrete Abelian group and the group of its characters; consequently

(5·1) If G is any enumerable Abelian group, and X is the group of the characters of G, then $L(G)$ and $L(X)$ are dually isomorphic. Hence if G is any finite Abelian group, then $L(G)$ is dually isomorphic with itself.

(3) We can easily combine the above relations. By (1) each automorphism of A induces an automorphism on $A_1 = L(A)$, $A_2 = G(A)$, etc. Taking the subgroups of $G(A)$ centralizing the various subalgebras of the A_i, and proceeding as in (2), one obtains blurred dual isomorphisms between $L(G(A))$ and the $L(A_i)$.

The special case of A_2 yields an interesting blurred dual isomorphism of $L(G(A))$ with itself.

6. *Lattice graphs*. Lattices lend themselves to graphical representation much more readily than groups. In fact we have

THEOREM 4: *Any finite lattice can be represented by one or more graphs in space, but not every graph represents a lattice.*

In constructing representations, we shall need the notion of "covering". An element a of a lattice L is said to "cover" an element b of L if and only if $a \supset b$ (i.e. $a \cup b = a$), $a \neq b$, and $a \supset c \supset b$ implies either $c = a$ or $c = b$.

Now we can associate with any finite lattice L a graph $\Gamma(L)$ composed of (i) small circles in (1, 1) correspondence with the elements of L, and (ii) non-horizontal line segments drawn between circle-pairs if and only if the element of L which corresponds to the upper circle "covers" the element corresponding to the lower one.

Such a diagram§ represents inclusion relations, and hence the operations of taking joins and meets. The best way to make this plain is probably to give examples. Accordingly, the reader will find graphed in Fig. 1, (1*a*) the lattice of the Boolean algebra of eight elements, (1*b*) the lattice of *its* Boolean subalgebras (isomorphic with the lattice of the subgroups of the four-group), (1*c*) the lattice of the subrings of the ring of integers modulo p^3, and (1*d*) the symmetrical equivalence lattice of degree four (cf. § 18).

† E. Steinitz, *Algebraische Theorie der Körper* (Berlin, 1930), p. 143.

‡ L. Pontrjagin, "Theory of topological commutative groups", *Ann. of Math.* 35 (1934), 361–88, Theorems 2 and 4. If X is continuous, we admit only closed subgroups. (5·1) was added in revision; the surprising thing is that it has not been explicitly stated before.

§ This representation dates back at least to H. Vogt, *Résolution algébrique des équations* (Paris, 1895), p. 91.

Incidentally, by the "class of conjugate elements" including any element a of an algebra A is meant the set of a and its images under the group $G(A)$ of the automorphisms of A. Two different classes of conjugate elements are evidently disjoint.

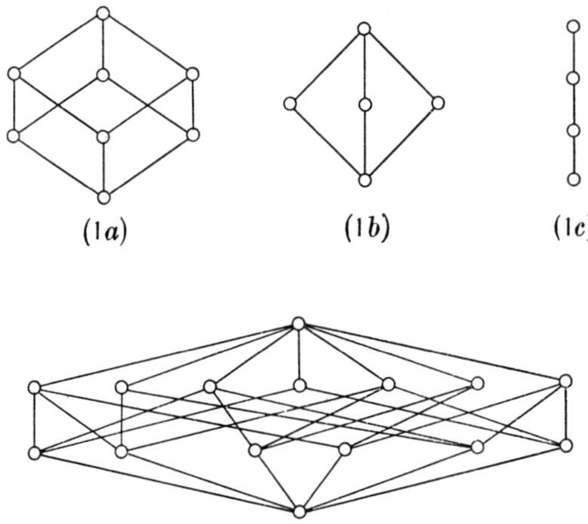

(1*a*) (1*b*) (1*c*)

(1*d*)

Fig. 1.

THEOREM 5: *Any finite lattice L specifies and is specified by a "geometrico-tactical configuration" Ta(L) in the sense of E. H. Moore*†. *The "rank" of Ta(L) is equal to the number of different classes of conjugate elements of L.*

We shall merely give the construction, and leave the proof, which has many details but is not difficult, to the reader.

The elements of $Ta(L)$ are to be the elements of L; the "sets" of $Ta(L)$ are to be the classes of conjugate elements of L; $a \in L$ is to be called "incident" with $b \in L$ if and only if $a \neq b$ and either $a \supset b$ or $a \subset b$; the "sets" are to be ordered in such a way that if the set of a comes before the set of b, and a is incident with b, then $a \subset b$.

7. *Algebraic synthesis.* In this section we shall define three simple ways of building up algebras synthetically from smaller algebras having the same operators.

Let $A_1, \ldots, A_n$ be any well-ordered set of algebras having the same operators f_k. By the "direct product" $A_1 \times \ldots \times A_n$ is meant‡ the algebra A (1) whose elements are the different ennuples $a = [a_1, \ldots, a_n]$ of elements $a_1 \in A_1, \ldots, a_n \in A_n$, (2) whose operators are the f_k, (3) in which the proper domain $\mathfrak{D}_k$ of f_k consists of

† E. H. Moore, "Tactical memoranda I–III", *Am. Jour. Math.* 18 (1896), 264. The definition is too long to repeat.

‡ This definition includes the standard definitions of direct products of groups and topological manifolds, and of the direct sum of linear algebras (of hypercomplex numbers).

those and only those sequences σ of elements $a^j = [a_1^j, \ldots, a_n^j]$ of A $(j = 1, \ldots, r)$ each of whose "component" sequences σ_i of elements $a_i', \ldots, a_i^r$ is in the proper domain of f_k in A_i, and (4) whose f_k-values over $\mathfrak{D}_k$ are given by

$$f_k(\sigma) = [f_k(\sigma_1), \ldots, f_k(\sigma_n)]. \qquad (7\cdot1)$$

In the special case $A_1 = \ldots = A_n = B$, we write $A = B^n$.

It is important to observe that $A_1 \times \ldots \times A_n$ is determined to within isomorphism by the *aggregate* of the A_i, and that†

$$(A_1 \times \ldots \times A_m) \times (B_1 \times \ldots \times B_n) \sim A_1 \times \ldots \times A_m \times B_1 \times \ldots \times B_n. \qquad (7\cdot2)$$

It is a corollary that the commutative and associative laws hold.

It is often useful to represent an algebra as a subalgebra or a homomorphic image of a direct product. We shall see in § 11 that one can usually put such representations into "canonical" forms having additional properties, which we shall state next.

A subalgebra S of $A \times B$ is called a "meromorphic" product‡ of A and B (in symbols, $S = A :\cdot B$) if and only if (1) to each $a \epsilon A$ corresponds a $b \epsilon B$ such that $[a, b] \epsilon S$, (2) to some $a \epsilon A$ correspond distinct elements b_1 and b_2 of B such that $[a, b_1] \epsilon S$ and $[a, b_2] \epsilon S$, and (3) the counterparts of (1)–(2) under the inversion $A \rightleftharpoons B$ also hold.

Similarly the image H of $A \times B$ under a homomorphism θ is called a "central" product of A and B (in symbols, $H = A :. B$) if and only if (1) to any two distinct elements a_1 and a_2 of A corresponds an element $b \epsilon B$ such that $[a_1, b]$ and $[a_2, b]$ have distinct images under θ, and (2) the counterpart of (1) under the inversion $A \rightleftharpoons B$ also holds.

The reader should be cautioned that $A :\cdot B$ and $A :. B$ (unlike $A \times B$) are not determined to within isomorphism by A and B. With this in mind, we can assert

(7·3) $S = A :\cdot B$ implies $S = B :\cdot A$ and $H = A :. B$ implies $H = B :. A$.

(7·4) $S = (A :\cdot B) :\cdot C$ implies $S = A :\cdot (B :\cdot C)$. But $H = (A :. B) :. C$ need not§ imply $H = A :. (B :. C)$.

(7·5) Any $A :\cdot B$ is homomorphic to A and to B.

The proofs, which are uninteresting, are omitted.

A CLASSIFICATION OF UNIFORM ALGEBRAS

8. *Uniform operators and species of algebras.* General classifications of abstract systems are usually characterized by a wealth of terminology and illustration, and a scarcity of consequential deduction. Whatever value is in the following plan

† By $A \sim B$ (A and B any algebras), we denote "A and B are isomorphic".

‡ This definition generalizes a usage in group theory started by R. Remak, *Journal für Math.* 163 (1930), 6.

§ For a counter-example, cf. 6 of the author's paper "Group synthesis", now in the hands of the editors of the *Trans. Amer. Math. Soc.*

therefore is derived from Theorems 8–10, their corollaries, and the perspective it gives to the results stated in §§ 12–13. But first we shall need several definitions.

Let A be any algebra, k_i any ordinal number, and f_i any operator of A. The operator f_i is called "k_i-ary", or a "uniform" operator of "index" k_i, if and only if (using the terminology of § 2) the proper domain of f_i is the set of all sequences of length k_i. That is, if and only if f_i assigns to each sequence $(x_1, \ldots, x_{ki})$ of elements of A, a single value $y = f_i(x_1, \ldots, x_{ki})$ in A.

In the remainder of the paper, every operator will be understood to be uniform.

Definition 1: *Let ρ be any aggregate of ordinal numbers $k_1, \ldots, k_s$. An algebra A will be called "of species Σ_ρ", if and only if its operators $f_1, \ldots, f_s$ are of indices $k_1, \ldots, k_s$.*

Thus groups are (uniform) algebras of species (2, 1), lattices of species (2, 2), and Boolean algebras of species (2, 2, 1).

9. *Functions and laws within a species.* The explicit nature of several implicitly accepted fundamental processes of abstract algebra becomes clear when we take as their proper domain a particular species of (uniform) algebra. The main difficulties are with regard to definition. Therefore we state

Definition 2: *By a "function of rank 0" associated with the species Σ_ρ is meant a primitive symbol (which is usually a Latin letter with or without subscripts). By a "function of rank n" is meant any symbolic formula*

$$f_i(\phi_1, \ldots, \phi_{ki}) \tag{9·1}$$

in which the ϕ_j are functions of ranks $< n$, and n is the least ordinal exceeding the ranks of all the ϕ_j.

Thus in a Boolean algebra, the expressions a, $a+b$, and $a+bc$ are functions of rank 0, 1, and 2 respectively, on the primitive symbols a, b, and c.

By simple induction on rank, we can show that any substitution ξ of one element of an algebra $A \in \Sigma_\rho$ for all occurrences of each primitive symbol of a function ϕ of Σ_ρ determines a "value" $\xi(\phi) \in A$ which results when the operations are performed in order of rank.

Definition 3: *By a "law" of an algebra A is meant any equation between two functions ϕ and ϕ' of the species of A such that $\xi(\phi) = \xi(\phi')$ no matter what substitution ξ of elements of A for the primitive symbols (which will usually be the same for ϕ as for ϕ') is made.*

Thus equations G 2–G 4 of § 3 are laws of groups, and equations L 2–L 4 of § 4 are laws of lattices.

By a "law" of a set of algebras (of a given species) is meant of course a law of every algebra of the set. We can assert, as a direct consequence of the definitions,

THEOREM 6: *If a law is true of a set* $\mathfrak{A}$ *of algebras, then it is true of any subalgebra or homomorphic image of any one, and of any direct product of any number of the algebras of* $\mathfrak{A}$.

COROLLARY 1: *If* A *and* B *both satisfy a given set of laws, then so do any* $A :\cdot B$ *and* $A :. B$.

COROLLARY 2: *The set of laws of any aggregate of algebras* A_i *is the same as that of the direct product* A^* *of all the* A_i.

For by Theorem 6 all the laws of the set hold for A^*, and by studying separate components we obtain the converse.

THEOREM 7: *Let* A *be any algebra.* (1) *If, for* $h = 1, \ldots, k_i$, $\phi_h = \phi'_h$ *is a law of* A, *and* f_i *is any operator of* A *of index* k_i, *then* $f_i(\phi_1, \ldots, \phi_{ki}) = f_i(\phi'_1, \ldots, \phi'_{ki})$ *is a law of* A. (2) *If* $\phi = \phi'$ *is a law of* A, *then any substitution* η *of one function* $\eta(x_j)$ *for all occurrences of each primitive symbol* x_j *in* $\phi = \phi'$ *yields a law* $\eta(\phi) = \eta(\phi')$ *of* A.

Conclusion (1) is true since f_i is single-valued. That $\eta(\phi)$ and $\eta(\phi')$ are functions of the species of A follows by induction on type; $\eta(\phi) = \eta(\phi')$ then follows *a fortiori* since each $\eta(x_j) \in A$.

In Theorem 7, A can obviously be replaced by any set of algebras of the same species.

10. *Families of algebras and the dual families of laws.* Theorems 6 and 7 suggest the following definitions:

DEFINITION 4: *Let* $\mathfrak{B}$ *be any set of algebras of a species* Σ. *Then the set* $\mathfrak{F}(\mathfrak{B})$ *of all algebras which can be constructed from algebras of* $\mathfrak{B}$ *by the taking of subalgebras, homomorphic images, and direct products is called the "family" of algebras generated by* $\mathfrak{B}$. *Reciprocally* $\mathfrak{B}$ *is called a "basis" of* $\mathfrak{F}(\mathfrak{B})$.

DEFINITION 5: *Let* B *be any set of equations between functions of a species* Σ. *Then the set* $\Phi(B)$ *of all equations between functions of* Σ *which can be inferred from* B *by rules* (1) *and* (2) *of Theorem* 7 *is called the "family" of equations generated by* B, *and* B *is called a "basis" of* $\Phi(B)$.

It is evident that $\mathfrak{F}(\mathfrak{F}(\mathfrak{B})) = \mathfrak{F}(\mathfrak{B})$, and $\Phi(\Phi(B)) = \Phi(B)$; therefore a family of algebras (or equations between functions) of a species Σ is a set which generates itself. From this we see that the set of algebras (or equations between functions) common to any two families of algebras (or equations between functions) of Σ is itself a family of algebras (or equations between functions). So that if we duplicate the definitions of "join" and "meet" of the footnote of § 4, we get

THEOREM 8: *The families of algebras of a species* Σ *are a lattice* $L(\Sigma)$, *and the families of equations between functions of* Σ *are a second lattice* $L^*(\Sigma)$.

Let B be any set of equations between functions of a species Σ. Form the "free"† algebras $F(B, m)$, whose elements are the classes of functions on m

primitive symbols equated under $\Phi(B)$. By rule (1) of Definition 5, $F(B,m)$ is an algebra of Σ, and by (2), $F(B,m)$ satisfies all the laws of B. Moreover, by Theorem 7 every algebra of species Σ generated by m elements and of which B is a set of laws is a homomorphic image of $F(B,m)$. Conversely, every law of $F(B,m)$ involving m primitive symbols is by definition an equation of $\Phi(B)$. Hence if we define $\mathfrak{F}(B)$ as the family of algebras generated by the $F(B,m)$, we see

THEOREM 9: *To every set B of equations between functions of a species Σ corresponds a family $\mathfrak{F}(B)$ of algebras such that $\Phi(B)$ is the set of laws of $\mathfrak{F}(B)$. $\mathfrak{F}(B)$ is the family of the homomorphic images of the "free" algebras $F(B,m)$.*

Reciprocally, let $\mathfrak{A}$ be any set of algebras $A_1, \ldots, A_s$ of orders $a_1, \ldots, a_s$ of a species Σ. Let $x_1, \ldots, x_n$ be any set of n primitive symbols, and let $\xi_{i,j}$ denote any of the a_i^n single-valued transformations of the x_k into A_i. The transforms will generate in A_i a subalgebra $S_{i,j}$. Form the direct product S^* of all such $S_{i,j}$, and associate with each x_k that element of S^* each of whose (i,j)th components is the transform of x_k under $\xi_{i,j}$. These elements will generate a subalgebra of S^*, which will be denoted by $F(\mathfrak{A},n)$. By Definition 4, $F(\mathfrak{A},n)\in\mathfrak{F}(\mathfrak{A})$, and so by Theorem 6 every law of $\mathfrak{A}$ is a law of $F(\mathfrak{A},n)$.

But if $\Phi(\mathfrak{A})$ denotes the family of equations between functions of species Σ true of $\mathfrak{A}$, then by Definition 3 the equations in $F(\mathfrak{A},n)$ between the values of functions of the elements corresponding to the x_k constitute precisely the subset of $\Phi(\mathfrak{A})$ involving n primitive symbols. That is,

$$F(\mathfrak{A},n) \sim F(\Phi(\mathfrak{A}),n). \qquad (10\cdot1)$$

It is a corollary that $\mathfrak{F}(\Phi(\mathfrak{A}))$ is contained in $\mathfrak{F}(\mathfrak{A})$. But by Theorem 6, $\mathfrak{F}(\mathfrak{A})$ is contained in $\mathfrak{F}(\Phi(\mathfrak{A}))$, proving

THEOREM 10: *The correspondence of each family $\mathfrak{F}$ of algebras of a species Σ to the family $\Phi(\mathfrak{F})$ of equations between functions of Σ which are laws of $\mathfrak{F}$, and of each family Φ of equations between functions of Σ to the family $\mathfrak{F}(\Phi)$ of algebras of Σ for which the equations of Φ are laws, is reciprocal—that is, $\mathfrak{F}(\Phi(\mathfrak{F}))=\mathfrak{F}$ and $\Phi(\mathfrak{F}(\Phi))=\Phi$.*

This theorem shows that the laws of formal inference and of algebraic synthesis are both logically complete.

Since this (1, 1) correspondence inverts inclusion, we have

COROLLARY 1: *In Theorem 8, $L(\Sigma)$ and $L^*(\Sigma)$ are dually isomorphic.*

COROLLARY 2: *Let $\mathfrak{A}$ be any set of algebras $A_1, \ldots, A_s$ of orders $a_1, \ldots, a_s$. The order of any algebra generated by m elements and obeying the laws of $\mathfrak{A}$ is at most*

$$\prod_1^s a_i^{a_i^m}.$$

† In case B is the set of equations G 2–G 4 of § 3 on algebras of species (2, 1), we have the so-called "free" groups. Another connection with standard usage is made by calling $F(B,m)$ the "calculus" on m symbols defined by the laws of B.

THEOREM 11: *Let $\mathfrak{A}$ be any finite set of algebras of finite order of a species Σ containing a finite number of operators of finite index. Then the laws of $\mathfrak{A}$ involving a finite number m or fewer primitive symbols have a finite basis.*

Each function on m primitive symbols determines an element of

$$F^* = F(\Phi(\mathfrak{A}), m),$$

and since the order of F^* is finite (by Corollary 2 above), there exists a finite number M such that each element of F^* is determined by a single "representative" function of rank not greater than M. But the (finite) set of equations equating each function on m primitive symbols of rank not greater than $M+1$ to the representative of the corresponding element of F^* defines F^*, and is consequently the basis desired.

11. *Meromorphic and central products.* In § 7 it was stated that meromorphic products and central products were canonical representations of subalgebras and of homomorphic images of direct products, respectively. To this effect we prove

THEOREM 12: *Let A and B be any algebras (of the same species). If S is a subalgebra of $A \times B$, then we can find subalgebras A_S of A and B_S of B, such that either $S \sim A_S$, $S \sim B_S$, or $S \sim A_S :\cdot B_S$.*

Let A_S be the range of the A-components, and B_S that of the B-components of the elements of S. A_S and B_S are clearly subalgebras. Moreover $S \subset A_S \times B_S$, while (1) and its inverse are satisfied. Hence either $S = A_S :\cdot B_S$, or (2) is not satisfied and $S \sim A_S$, or the inverse of (2) is not satisfied and $S \sim B_S$.

THEOREM 13: *If C is a homomorphic image of $A \times B$, and to every element x of A or B corresponds an operation having x for its value, then we can find homomorphic images $\bar{A}$ of A and $\bar{B}$ of B such that either $C \sim \bar{A}$, $C \sim \bar{B}$, or $C = \bar{A} :. \bar{B}$.*

The construction consists in identifying elements a and a' of A if and only if $[a, b]$ and $[a', b]$ have the same homomorphic image for every $b \in B$—and doing the same thing for B. The details are uninteresting.

12. *The family of modular lattices.* Lattices by definition constitute a family within the species of algebras "of double composition"—i.e. of type (2, 2). We have already seen that they are of very general occurrence.

In this section we shall consider the subfamily of "modular" lattices—that is, of the lattices satisfying the following "modular" identity discovered by Dedekind†,

L 5: $(A \cap B) \cup (C \cap (A \cup B)) = ((A \cap B) \cup C) \cap (A \cup B)$, which is to say, $A \subset B$ implies $A \cup (C \cap B) = (A \cup C) \cap B$ irrespective of C.

† *Gesammelte Werke*, 1, p. 121. Cf. also a paper by O. Ore on modular lattices, for which he prefers the term Dedekind structures, *Annals of Math.* 36 (1935), 406–37.

The normal subgroups of any group†, the ideals of any ring†, subspaces in abstract vector space†, and linear sets in projective geometries‡ constitute modular lattices. Further, so do the modules of any ring, and Galois extensions§ of the rational domain. Whether all modular lattices can be realized in these ways is an open question.

Closely allied with lattices are those algebras (of species (2, 2, 1)) which satisfy, besides L 1–L 4,

L 7: To any A corresponds a "complement" $\bar{A}$ satisfying $A \cap \bar{A} \cap B = A \cap \bar{A}$ and $A \cup \bar{A} \cup B = A \cup \bar{A}$ irrespective of B.

(12·1)‡ The algebras A of finite order in the family of algebras satisfying L 1–L 5 and L 7 have the Boolean algebra of order two and the finite projective geometries for a basis, and any such A is the direct product of algebras of the basis.

Theorem 14: *The free modular lattice generated by three elements is a meromorphic product of modular lattices of orders two and five.*

To prove Theorem 14, we must refer to Tables I–III of "Subalgebras". The 28-lattice described there has (in the notation of Table I) the following homomorphic images:

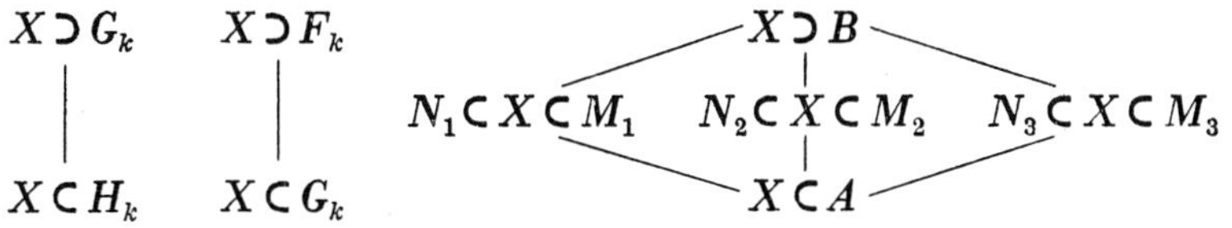

Moreover, its elements have unique expressions, no two alike, as 7-vectors with components in these images. Hence the 28-lattice is isomorphic with a sublattice of their direct product. Theorem 12 completes the proof.

Since the only homomorphic image of the 5-lattice graphed above is the trivial 1-lattice satisfying, with 2-lattices,

L 6: $A \cap (B \cup C) = (A \cap B) \cup (A \cap C)$,

we obtain the

Corollary: *Any lattice equation on three primitive symbols is either a consequence of L 5, or else, taken with L 5, it gives L 6.*

† "Subalgebras", Theorems 26·1, 27·1, and (essentially) § 28. On the other hand, the closed (normal) subgroups of the translations of the line do not satisfy L 5. To show this, let r and s be any two incommensurables, and take the subgroups generated by the translations $x \to x + r$, $x \to x + s$, and $x \to x + 2r$.

‡ G. Birkhoff, "Combinatorial relations in projective geometries", *Annals of Math.* 36 (1935), 743–8.

§ "Hausdorff groupoids", *Annals of Math.* 35 (1934), 360.

As a matter of practical curiosity, the author studied the 5-lattice graphed above. By a difficult argument which was submitted to the referee, he proved that the algebras of finite order in the family of algebras satisfying

L 51: $A \cup (X \cap B) \cup (Y \cap B) \supset B \cap (A \cup X) \cap (A \cup Y) \cap (X \cup Y)$

L 52: $A \cup (X \cap B) \cup (Y \cap B) \cup (X \cap Y) \supset B \cap (A \cup X) \cap (A \cup Y)$

coincided with the set of the meromorphic products of the 5-lattice and its subalgebras.

13. *The family of distributive lattices.* At present the most satisfactory illustration of the theory of §§ 8–10 is furnished by the family of "distributive" lattices—that is, the subfamily of modular lattices for which L 6 is a law. But first let us repeat some simple definitions.

By a "ring" of point-sets is meant† any system of point-sets containing the sum and the product of any two of its members. By a "σ-ring" is meant one which contains the sum and the product of any enumerable collection of its members. A ring (σ-ring) is called a "field" ("σ-field") if and only if it contains the complement of any one of its members.

(13·1)‡ Any ring of point-sets is a distributive lattice, and any distributive lattice can be realized as a ring of point-sets.

(13·2)§ Any field of point-sets is a Boolean algebra, and any Boolean algebra can be realized as a field of point-sets.

(13·3) L 2–L 4 and L 6 are a basis for the laws of the lattice of two elements, and L 2–L 4 and L 6–L 7 are a basis for the laws of the Boolean algebra of two elements.

Thus we see that the algebras defined by rings (or fields) of point-sets are *families* of algebras. Now any subalgebra or direct product of σ-rings (or σ-fields) is itself a σ-ring (σ-field), as can be shown by easy constructions. But

THEOREM 15‖: *The σ-rings of point-sets are not a family of algebras, and neither are the σ-fields.*

† F. Hausdorff, *Mengenlehre* (Berlin, 1927), Chapter v.

‡ "Subalgebras", Theorem 25·2. Other instances of distributive lattices are listed in F. Klein's "Einige distributive Systeme in Mathematik und Logik", *Jahr. d. D.M.V.* 38 (1929), 35–40.

§ Proved by M. H. Stone, "Boolean algebras and their application to topology", *Proc. U.S.A. Acad.* 20 (1934), 197–202. The family of Boolean algebras is hence generated by any Boolean algebra containing more than one element. It is a corollary that any family of equations between functions of species (2, 2, 1) which contains an equation not derivable from L 2–L 7 contains the equation $x = y$. Cf. J. Lukasiewicz, "Ein Vollständigkeitsbeweis des zweiwertigen Aussagenkalkuls", *Comptes Rendus de Varsovie*, 24 (1932), 153.

‖ Added in revision.

For we can exhibit homomorphic images of a σ-ring and a σ-field not themselves σ-rings (σ-fields). Take all Borel-measurable sets on the line interval [0, 1]; they define a σ-field, and hence a σ-ring. But the homomorphic image M^* formed by neglecting sets of measure zero is not realizable even as a σ-ring, let alone a σ-field, of point-sets.

For this was shown in Theorem 25·3 of "Subalgebras" for the σ-subring of intervals $[0, x]$.

Considering the algebra of intervals $[0, x]$ and $[0, x)$ alone, we see that there exists an algebra of point-sets containing the sum and the product of any sequence of its elements, having a homomorphic image—obtained by setting $[0, x]=[0, x)$—not realizable as a similar ring of point-sets.

On the other hand, A. Tarski† has recently shown that the algebras of point-sets containing the complement of any one, and the sum and product of any sequence of its elements, do constitute a family of algebras.

14. *Application to hypercentral groups.* Much of the value of the definition of lattices lies in the theorems which it permits us to state. We shall illustrate by this restating two known facts about "hypercentral" groups—that is, groups all of whose factor-groups have a proper central‡.

(14·1) If H is a hypercentral group of finite order, and $L_p(H)$ denotes the subset of $L(H)$ formed by the subgroups of H whose orders are powers of the prime p, then

$$L(H)=L_2(H)\times L_3(H)\times L_5(H)\ldots.$$

(14·2) The subgroups of any hypercentral group satisfy the condition (1) if C covers A and B, and $A \neq B$, then A and B cover $A \cap B$ (cf. § 6, ¶ 2).

There are innumerable other ways in which groups illustrate the above theory.

15. *Any abstract group is a group of automorphisms.* We shall now prove the result announced in § 3, namely

THEOREM 1: *Let S be any abstract group. Then there exists an algebra A_G, the group of whose automorphisms is isomorphic with S.*

Let the elements of A_G be identified with the single elements a and the couples (a, b) of elements a and b of S. And let the operators of A_G be unary operators f_c associated with the elements c of S, plus one binary operator g, defined by

$$f_c(a)=c, \quad f_c(a,b)=a, \quad g[(a,b),(a',b')]=bb',$$
$$g[a,(a',b')]=g[(a,b),b']=g[a,a']=1.$$

Now let α be any automorphism of A_G. Since $\alpha(f_a)=f_a$ for each $a \in S$, clearly

† *Fund. Math.* 24 (1935), 177–98.

‡ Or equivalently satisfying one of the chain of equations between functions of species (2, 1):

$$ab=ba, \quad (a^{-1}b^{-1}ab)\,c=c\,(a^{-1}b^{-1}ab), \ldots.$$

(14·1) is a consequence of a result in Burnside's *Theory of groups of finite order*, 2nd ed. (Cambridge, 1911), p. 166; (14·2) follows from Speiser's *Gruppentheorie*, 2nd ed., Theorem 80.

$\alpha(a)=a$ for each $a\epsilon A_G$; hence $\alpha(a,b)=(a,b')$ for each $(a,b)\,\epsilon A_G$. But if we denote $\alpha(1,1)$ by $(1,c)$, $(c\epsilon S)$, then

$$b=\alpha(b)=\alpha(g[(a,b),(1,1)])=g[\alpha(a,b),\alpha(1,1)]$$
$$=g[(a,b'),(1,c)]=b'c,$$

whence $\alpha(a,b)=\alpha(a,bc)$ for any $(a,b)\,\epsilon A_G$.

But for fixed c, each transformation $\alpha(a,b)=(a,bc)$ and $\alpha(a)=a$ is an automorphism of A_G. Since the group of such transformations is isomorphic with S, the theorem is proved.

A more complicated construction was found by the author which permitted A_G to be a distributive lattice.

EQUIVALENCE LATTICES

16. *Equivalence relations defined.* Let C be any class of objects, which for convenience we shall suppose to be letters of the alphabet. The number of objects in C will be noted by $n(C)$.

DEFINITION 6: *By an "equivalence relation" on C is meant any reflexive and "circular" relation—that is, any rule x assigning to each pair* (a, b) *of objects of C one of the two expressions axb or* $a\bar{x}b$, *in such a way that* (1) *axa for any object a of C, while* (2) *axb and bxc imply cxa for any objects a, b, and c of C.*

The expression axb is read "a is equivalent to b under x", and $a\bar{x}b$ is read "a is not equivalent to b under x".

The reader should encounter no difficulty in proving that any reflexive and circular relation is reflexive, symmetric, and transitive—and conversely. That is, Definition 6 amounts in effect to the more conventional one of Hasse†.

A well-known argument now yields

THEOREM 16: *There is a* (1, 1) *correspondence between equivalence relations x on C and partitions of the objects of C into non-overlapping "x-categories"‡, under which axb if and only if a and b are in the same x-category.*

The number $H^*(n+1)$ of different equivalence relations on $n+1$ objects can easily be calculated.

For by the usual theory of permutations and combinations, to any fixed object a and any number h $(0\leqslant h\leqslant n)$ correspond just $\binom{n}{h}$ choices of a category S_a of h

† Hasse, *Höhere Algebra*, 1 (1927), 17. What Hasse (and I) call an "equivalence relation", Carnap calls an "equality relation", and P. A. Macmahon would call a "distribution of $n(C)$ objects of type $(1^{n(C)})$ into classes of type (m)".

‡ "Abstraction class" according to Carnap (*Logische Aufbau der Welt* (Berlin, 1928), p. 102).

objects besides a and equivalent to a. And the remaining $n-h$ objects can be divided into categories in just $H^*(n-h)$ ways. Therefore, by Theorem 16

$$H^*(n+1)=\sum_{h=0}^{n}\binom{n}{h}H^*(n-h). \tag{16·1}$$

This recurrence relation has been studied†.

17. *Symbols for equivalence relations.* The handling of equivalence relations is greatly simplified by assigning to each equivalence relation x on C a "special symbol" and a "generic symbol".

To obtain the special symbol for x, first imagine the objects of C written in a certain order, and for this purpose identify them with the numbers $1, 2, 3, \ldots, n(C)$.

Then arrange the objects of each x-category in order, suppress the x-categories containing just one object, and arrange the others in the order of their first objects. The symbol is completed by inserting commas between the different x-categories, and enclosing the entire expression in parentheses.

Thus the special symbols involving the first four integers are (), (12), (13), (14), (23), (24), (34), (12, 34), (13, 24), (14, 23), (123), (124), (134), (234), and (1234).

To obtain the generic symbol for x, count the number of objects in each category, arrange the resulting integers in order of decreasing magnitude, separate them by plus signs, and enclose the whole in parentheses.

Thus the generic symbols for equivalence relations involving four objects are $(1+1+1+1)$, $(2+1+1)$, $(2+2)$, $(3+1)$, (4).

The following proposition is obvious,

Theorem 17: *The number of generic symbols for equivalence relations on C is equal to the number of partitions of the integer $n(C)$.*

18. *The lattice $E(C)$.* In this section we shall show how one is naturally led to consider the equivalence relations on a class C as the elements of a lattice $E(C)$.

Definition 7: *Let C be any class of objects, and let x and y be equivalence relations on C. By the "meet" $x \cap y$ of x and y is meant the relation u on C defined by the rule*‡ (1) *aub if and only if axb and ayb; by the "join" $x \cup y$ of x and y is meant the meet v of all equivalence relations z on C such that* (2) *axb or ayb implies azb.*

It is easy to show that $x \cap y$ is an equivalence relation (i.e. reflexive and circular), and that therefore so is $x \cup y$. It is also easy to verify L 2–L 4 of § 4, whence we have

Theorem 18: *Under Definition 7, the equivalence relations on C are the elements of a lattice $E(C)$.*

† A. C. Aitken, *Edin. Math. Notes*, 28 (1933), xviii-xxiii.

‡ $x \cap y$ is merely the conventional "logical product" of the relations x and y. The operation of join is, however, new.

$E(C)$ is evidently determined to within isomorphism by $n(C)$; the corresponding abstract lattice may therefore be called "the symmetrical equivalence lattice of degree $n(C)$", and any sublattice of $E(C)$ an "equivalence lattice".

The symmetrical equivalence lattices are the analogues in lattice theory of the symmetrical permutation groups.

19. *Covering and rank conditions.* It is clear that an equivalence relation x *contains* an equivalence relation y—i.e. that $x \frown y = y$—if and only if the x-categories are unions of suitable entire y-categories. Consequently (recurring to the definition of covering made in § 6) x covers y if and only if one x-category is the union of two y-categories, and the other x-categories are the same as the other y-categories. This makes it easy to deduce

THEOREM 19: *If x and y cover z, and $x \neq y$, then $x \smile y$ covers x and y. Again, x covers y if and only if $x \not\subset y$ of type* $(2+1+1+\ldots+1)$ *exists, satisfying* $x = y \smile z$.

Hence if we define (1) a "chain" connecting $y \epsilon E(C)$ with $x \supset y$ as any sequence of elements $x_0 = y, \ldots, x_n = x$ of $E(C)$ such that x_k covers x_{k-1} for $k = 1, \ldots, n$, and (2) the "rank" $\rho(x)$ of $x \epsilon E(C)$ as the excess of $n(C)$ over the number of x-categories, we obtain

THEOREM 20: *x covers y if and only if $x \supset y$ while $\rho(x) = \rho(y) + 1$. Consequently any two chains connecting the same two elements have the same length. Moreover any element of rank m can (by induction and Theorem 19) be represented as the join of m, but not of $m-1$, elements of rank one. Finally*†

$$\rho(x \smile y) \leqq \rho(x) + \rho(y) = \rho(x \smile y) + \rho(x \frown y). \qquad (19{\cdot}1)$$

20. *Equivalence lattices and Boolean algebras.* It is well known that any finite Boolean algebra B_n of order 2^n can be identified with the field of all sets of n points.

Let S be any subalgebra of B_n; S is finite and contains the empty set. Therefore the elements of B_n corresponding to the "points" of S will be disjoint subsets whose sum is the complement of the empty set. Conversely, any such choice of disjoint sets of points of B determines a reciprocal subalgebra S of B. And finally, this (1, 1) correspondence inverts inclusion, so that we have

THEOREM 21: *If $n(C)$ is finite, then $E(C)$ is dually isomorphic with the lattice of the subalgebras of the Boolean algebra of order* $2^{n(C)}$.

21. *Equivalence lattices and groups.* Let G be any group, and S any subgroup of G. If a and b are any elements of G, we shall write aSb if $ab^{-1} \epsilon S$; $a\bar{S}b$ unless $ab^{-1} \epsilon S$. This is known‡ to define an equivalence relation on the elements of G.

† The first inequality is a consequence of the previous statement; the second requires Theorems 19 and 9·2 of "Subalgebras".

‡ H. Hasse, *op. cit.* p. 60; the proof is, from the standpoint of group theory, elementary.

Let T be any second subgroup of G. To say that ab^{-1} is in $S \frown T$ is to say that ab^{-1} is in S and in T; hence the ordering of equivalence relations to subgroups preserves meets.

Suppose that ab^{-1} is in $S \smile T$. Then $a = s_1 t_1 \dots s_n t_n b$, where the s_i are in S and the t_i are in T. So that if U is any equivalence relation including S and T, then

$$bU(t_n b), (t_n b)\, U\, (s_n t_n b), \dots, (t_1 s_2 \dots b)\, Ua,$$

whence aUb, and U includes the equivalence relation ordered to $S \smile T$. But the equivalence relation ordered to $S \smile T$ clearly includes those ordered to S and to T; hence by Definition 7 the ordering preserves joins.

It follows that every subgroup lattice is isomorphic with a suitable equivalence lattice. But conversely, if we order to each equivalence relation x on n letters the group G_x of all permutations intransitive on the x-categories, then clearly $G_x \frown G_y = G_{x \frown y}$, while it can be shown* that $G_x \smile G_y = G_{x \smile y}$, whence we have

THEOREM 22: *Every subgroup lattice is isomorphic with an equivalence lattice, and conversely.*

COROLLARY: *Every lattice of subgroups of a finite group is dually isomorphic with a lattice of subalgebras of a finite Boolean algebra, and conversely.*

22. *Automorphisms of* $E(C)$. We now prove a not altogether surprising but by no means trivial result.

THEOREM 23: *The automorphisms of* $E(C)$ *are induced by the permutations of the objects of* C. *If* $n \equiv n(C) > 2$, *they constitute the symmetric group of degree* $n(C)$.

For if $n > 2$, then each element of rank $n-2$ having the generic symbol $([n-k]+k)$ covers exactly $2^{k-1} + 2^{n-k-1} - 2$ elements, $(k \leqslant \frac{1}{2}n)$. Therefore (since rank and covering are invariant under automorphisms) the totality of elements having the generic symbol $([n-1]+1)$ is invariant under any automorphism of $E(C)$. Further, any element of rank one is specified by the elements of genus $([n-1]+1)$ which contain it, and any element at all is specified by the elements of rank one which it contains. Hence any automorphism is completely specified by the permutation it performs on the elements of genus $([n-1]+1)$—corresponding to a permutation of the objects of C. Inspection shows that this is still true if $n \leqslant 2$.

If $n > 2$, the permutations of the objects of C induce precisely the symmetric group on the n elements of $E(C)$ of genus $([n-1]+1)$, completing the proof.

COROLLARY: *Two elements* x *and* y *of* $E(C)$ *are conjugate under the group of the automorphisms of* $E(C)$ *if and only if they have the same generic symbol. Hence*

* The technique consists in passing from G_x to $G_{x \smile y}$ through a finite or transfinite sequence of such intransitive groups, and showing that $G_x \smile G_y$ cannot fail to contain any first one of them.

under the definition of Theorem 5, the geometrico-tactical configuration corresponding to $E(C)$ has a "rank" equal to the number of partitions of the integer $n(C)$.

For the generic symbols describe precisely the conditions under which the x-categories can be transformed into the y-categories by a suitable permutation of the objects of C.

23. *Homomorphic equivalence relations*†. Consider the equivalence relations on the elements of an *algebra* A. Of especial importance are naturally those which are preserved under the operations of A. These are characterized by

DEFINITION 8: *An equivalence relation x on an algebra A is called "homomorphic" if and only if the x-category of the value of any sequence σ is a single-valued function of the x-categories of the elements of σ—that is, if and only if $a_j x b_j$ ($a_j \epsilon A$; $j = 1, \ldots, k_i$; $b_j \epsilon A$) implies*

$$f_i(a_1, \ldots, a_{ki})\, x f_i(b_1, \ldots, b_{ki}). \tag{23·1}$$

It is obvious that the x-categories of any homomorphic equivalence relation on A are the elements of a homomorphic image of A.

THEOREM 24: *Let A be any algebra whose operators are of finite index. Then the homomorphic equivalence relations on A are a sublattice $H(A)$ of the symmetrical lattice $E(A)$ of all equivalence relations on A.*

That is, the meet u and the join v (under Definition 7) of any two homomorphic equivalence relations x and y are homomorphic equivalence relations.

If $a_j u b_j$ ($j = 1, \ldots, k_i$), then $a_j x b_j$ and $a_j y b_j$; whence, denoting $f_i(a_1, \ldots, a_{ki})$ by a and $f_i(b_1, \ldots, b_{ki})$ by b, by hypothesis axb and ayb, and consequently aub.

Similarly, if $a_j v b_j$ ($j = 1, \ldots, k_i$), then we can form chains‡ $c_1^j = a_j, \ldots, c_{2n+1}^j = b_j$ such that $c_{2h-1}^j x c_{2h}^j$ and $c_{2h}^j y c_{2h+1}^j$. Hence, writing $c_h = f_i(c_h', \ldots, c_h^{ki})$, we obtain $c_{2h-1} x c_{2h}$ and $c_{2h} y c_{2h+1}$, and consequently $c_1 v c_{2n+1}$, which is to say avb. This completes the proof.

The following special results are known:

(23·2) The lattice of the homomorphic equivalence relations on any group or ring is a modular lattice§.

(23·3) The lattice of the homomorphic equivalence relations on any finite modular lattice is a Boolean algebra‖.

† This section was added in revision.

‡ We need k_i to be finite to ensure that n should be finite.

§ "Subalgebras", Theorems 26·1 and 27·1, and Speiser, *op. cit.* Theorem 23. By an abstraction of the same method, we can show that if an algebra A is such that to any homomorphic equivalence $a(x \cup y)b$ corresponds an element c such that axc and cyb, then the lattice of the homomorphisms of A is a modular lattice. It is the lattice $H(A)$ which describes the "structure" of A; hence we may call it the "structure lattice" of A.

‖ This result was implicitly announced by Ore in a lecture at Harvard University, and will presumably appear in his paper already cited.

24. *Simple algebras.* Any algebra A has two homomorphic images—itself and the trivial algebra of one element. These correspond respectively to the equivalence relation o under which aob if and only if $a = b$, and the equivalence relation p under which apb for any a and b of A.

If the lattice of the homomorphic equivalence relations on A contains only these two elements, then A is called "simple"†; otherwise A is called "composite".

LEMMA 1: *The 5-lattice* (1*b*) *graphed in* § 6 *is simple.*

The proof is left to the reader.

THEOREM 25: *Any finite symmetrical equivalence lattice* $E(C)$ *is simple.*

Let x be any homomorphic equivalence relation on $E(C)$ other than o, so that axb $(a \neq b)$. Then $c \in E(C)$ with the special symbol (ij) exists such that $c \cap (a \cup b) = c$, but $c \cap (a \cap b) = o_E$ is the element of $E(C)$ with the special symbol (). Naturally cxo_E.

If $d \in E(C)$ has the special symbol (kj), or (jk), $(k \neq j)$, then $e \in E(C)$ with the special symbol (kj), or (jk), generates with c and d a sublattice satisfying Lemma 1; whence $o_E xd$. Repeating this process, we can show that dxf for $f \in E(C)$ with the special symbol (hk), irrespective of h. Hence $o_E xf$ for any f with generic symbol $(2+1+1+\ldots+1)$—and so, by Theorem 20, $o_E xz$ for any $z \in E(C)$ whatever, proving $x = p$. This completes the proof.

A "projective geometry" is a system P of elements called points, lines, planes, etc., having incidence relations of a certain type. Every pair of elements a and b of P intersect in a "meet" element $a \cap b$, and generate a least containing element or "join" $a \cup b$. From the known facts (1) every element is the join of those points which it contains, (2) the join of any two distinct points is a line, (3) every line contains at least three points, and (4) L 2–L 4 are satisfied, it can be proved that

THEOREM 26: *Any projective geometry is simple.*

Let x be any homomorphism of P other than o, so that axb for $a \neq b$; whence $(a \cup b)x(a \cap b)$. By (1), P contains a point q such that $q \cap (a \cup b) = q$, but $q \cap (a \cap b) = o_P$, the empty set. If r is any other point, by (2) and (3) the line $q \cup r$ contains a third point s. But o_E, q, r, s, and $q \cup r$ are a sublattice of P satisfying the hypotheses of Lemma 1, and so $o_E xr$.

That is, $o_E xr$ for any point r, and so by (1) $o_E xt$ for any element t of P, and $x = p$, proving the theorem.

25. *The free lattice generated by three elements.* An open question‡ of some interest is settled by

THEOREM 27: *The free lattice generated by three elements is of infinite order.*

† This is the accepted usage for both groups and linear algebras.
‡ F. Klein, "Beiträge zur Theorie der Verbände", *Math. Zeitschrift*, 39 (1934), 227–239.

It is sufficient to exhibit an equivalence lattice of infinite order generated by three elements. But let C be the class of the points of 3-space with integral coordinates $(m, 1, m)$, $(1, m+1, m)$, and $(m, m, 1)$. And let e_i be the equivalence relation such that ae_ib ($a, b\epsilon C$; $i=1, 2, 3$) if and only if a and b have the same x_i-coordinate.

The e_i generate a sequence $t_k \epsilon E(C)$, in which

$$t_1=e_1,\ t_{6n+2}=t_{6n+1}\cup e_2,\ t_{6n+3}=t_{6n+2}\cap e_3,\ t_{6n+4}=t_{6n+3}\cup e_1,\ t_{6n+5}=t_{6n+4}\cap e_2,$$
$$t_{6(n+1)}=t_{6n+5}\cup e_3, \quad \text{and} \quad t_{6(n+1)+1}=t_{6(n+1)}\cap e_1.$$

Those points which are in the same t_k-category as the point $(1, 1, 1)$ are listed in the following table:

$$t_{6n}: \ \sum_{k=1}^{n} (k, 1, k)$$

$$t_{6n+1}: \ \sum_{k=1}^{n} (1, k+1, k) + \sum_{k=1}^{n} (k, 1, k) + \sum_{i=1}^{\infty} (i, i, 1)$$

$$t_{6n+2}: \ (1, 1, 1) + \sum_{k=1}^{n} (1, k+1, k)$$

$$t_{6n+3}: \ \sum_{k=1}^{n} (1, k+1, k) + \sum_{k=1}^{n+1} (k, k, 1) + \sum_{i=1}^{\infty} (i, 1, i)$$

$$t_{6n+4}: \ \sum_{k=1}^{n+1} (k, k, 1)$$

$$t_{6n+5}: \ \sum_{k=1}^{n+1} (k, k, 1) + \sum_{k=1}^{n+1} (k, 1, k) + \sum_{i=1}^{\infty} (1, i+1, i).$$

Hence the t_k are all different, proving the theorem.

COROLLARY: *Any finite lattice satisfies a law on functions of three symbols which cannot be inferred from* L 2–L 4.

TOPOLOGICAL LATTICES

26. *Topological algebras.* By a "topological algebra" is meant any algebra which contains a "convergence" operator f_L operating only on enumerated sequences, and such that if (1) $f_L(\{x_k^i\})=x_i$ for a sequence of n sequences $\{x_k^i\}$, and (2) $f_i(x_k', \ldots, x_k^n)-y_k$ for fixed i and every positive integer k, then

$$(3) \quad f_L(\{y_k\})=f_i(x_1, \ldots, x_n).$$

This includes van Dantzig's† definitions of topological groups and topological rings, and automatically defines the notion of "topological lattice".

27. *Transfinite joins and meets.* Let A be any algebra, and σ any well-ordered set of subalgebras of A. By $h_1(\sigma)$ denote the set of elements in every subalgebra of σ, and by $h_2(\sigma)$ the meet of the subalgebras which contain every subalgebra

† "Zur topologische Algebra. I. Komplettierungstheorie", *Math. Annalen*, 107 (1933), 587–626.

of σ. It is easily seen† that $h_1(\sigma)$ and $h_2(\sigma)$ are themselves subalgebras of A. Hence the subalgebras of A constitute a "complete" lattice $\bar{L}(A)$ satisfying certain laws resembling L 2–L 4 which have been specified elsewhere‡, and whose study takes us out of algebra into analysis.

28. *Upper and lower limits.* A convergence operator can be defined in $\bar{L}(A)$ by the analogue of an elementary device of real function theory.

Let $a_1, a_2, a_3, \ldots$ be any enumerable sequence of elements of $\bar{L}(A)$, and denote by α_k the subsequence $a_k, a_{k+1}, a_{k+2}, \ldots$. Then we can define

$$\operatorname{Inf}\{a_k\} = h_1[h_2(\alpha_1), h_2(\alpha_2), h_2(\alpha_3), \ldots],$$
$$\operatorname{Sup}\{a_k\} = h_2[h_1(\alpha_1), h_1(\alpha_2), h_1(\alpha_3), \ldots].$$

Regardless of j and k, $h_2(\alpha_j) \subset a_{j+k} \subset h_1(\alpha_k)$; hence we have

THEOREM 28: $\operatorname{Inf}\{a_k\} \subset \operatorname{Sup}\{a_k\}$ *identically.*

DEFINITION 9: $f_L(\{a_k\}) = a$ *if and only if* $\operatorname{Inf}\{a_k\} = a$ *and* $\operatorname{Sup}\{a_k\} = a$.

29. *Topology.* Consider the topology of the abstract convergence space defined by the operator f_L defined in Definition 9. If $c_k = c$ for every k, then clearly $f_L(\{c_k\}) = c$.

Again, $f_L(\{c_k\}) = c$ and $f_L(\{c_k\}) = c'$ imply $c = \operatorname{Inf}\{c_k\} = c'$. And if $f_L(\{c_k\}) = c$ and $k(i) \to \infty$, then

$$c \subset \operatorname{Inf}\{c_k\} \subset \operatorname{Inf}\{c_{k(i)}\} \subset \operatorname{Sup}\{c_{k(i)}\} \subset \operatorname{Sup}\{c_k\} \subset c,$$

and so $f_L(\{c_{k(i)}\}) = c$.

Finally, if $f_L(\{c_k\}) = c$, then no matter what c_0 is given, the augmented sequence $c_0, c_1, c_2, \ldots$ has certainly the same upper and lower limits as before, and hence converges to c. That is, we have

THEOREM 29: *The space defined by the convergence operator* f_L *is a Kneser*§ *"Konvergenzraum" for any complete lattice.*

On the other hand, it need not define the lattice to be a topological lattice. It must in the important case that the lattice is a complete lattice of point-sets. But if the lattice is the complete lattice of closed sets on a line, examples can be given showing that this is no longer the case.

30. *A metric group.* Consider the Boolean algebra $B(\Sigma)$ of the measurable sets in a space Σ having a mass-function|| in the sense of Carathéodory. Let S and T be any two measurable sets of Σ; we shall use the notation $S+T$ for the

† As in "Subalgebras", § 2.
‡ Stated in "Subalgebras", § 3.
§ "Die Deformationssätze der einfach zusammenhangenden Flächen", *Math. Zeits.* 25 (1926), 362.
|| C. Carathéodory, *Vorlesungen über reelle Funktionen* (Berlin, 1927), 2nd ed. p. 238.

sum of S and T, ST for their common part, $\bar{S}$ for the complement of S, and $\mu(S)$ for its measure.

Make a homomorphic image of $B(\Sigma)$ by putting $S=T$ if and only if $\mu(S\bar{T}+\bar{S}T)=0$. Define the "distance" $\rho(S, T)$ from S to T as the smaller of 1 and $\mu(S\bar{T}+\bar{S}T)$. And finally, define the "product" $S . T$ of S and T as $S\bar{T}+\bar{S}T$.

It is easy to show that the equivalence relation is homomorphic, and that $\rho(S, T)$ is metric and makes the image algebra topological in the sense of § 26. Moreover, it is known† that the definition of $S . T$ makes $B(\Sigma)$ into an Abelian group. Since finally

$$\rho(A . C, B . C)=\rho(C . A, C . B)=\rho(A, B)$$

irrespective of A, B, and C, we have

THEOREM 30: *The homomorphic image of the Boolean algebra of the measurable sets in any space having a regular mass-function, formed by disregarding sets of measure zero, is a metric group‡ under a distance-function which makes the algebra topological.*

31. *Unsolved problems.* The preceding material suggests several interesting questions whose answer is unknown.

Some questions concern equivalence lattices. Is any lattice realizable as a lattice of equivalence relations? Is the dual of any equivalence lattice an equivalence lattice? In particular, is the dual of the symmetrical equivalence lattice of degree four (graphed in § 6) an equivalence lattice? More generally, are equivalence lattices a family in the species of algebras of double composition.

Again, it is known that the free distributive lattice generated by n elements is of finite order $D(n)$, but nothing is known about the function $D(n)$ except its first four terms§.

Finally, is any finite modular lattice a sublattice of a direct product of finite projective geometries and Boolean algebras of order two?

† Proved by P. J. Daniell, "The modular difference of classes", *Bull. Amer. Math. Soc.* 23 (1916), 446–50.

‡ In the sense of van Dantzig, *op. cit.*

§ R. Dedekind, *Ges. Werke*, 2, 147, states that $D(1)=1$, $D(2)=4$, $D(3)=18$, $D(4)=166$.

Reprinted from the
BULLETIN OF THE AMERICAN MATHEMATICAL SOCIETY
Vol. 50, No. 10, pp. 764-768
October, 1944

SUBDIRECT UNIONS IN UNIVERSAL ALGEBRA

GARRETT BIRKHOFF

1. Preliminary definitions. By an *algebra*, we shall mean below any collection A of elements, combined by any set of single-valued operations f_α,

$$(1) \qquad y = f_\alpha(x_1, \cdots, x_{n(\alpha)}).$$

The number of distinct operations (that is, the range of the variable α) may be infinite, but for our main result (Theorem 2), we shall require every $n(\alpha)$ to be finite—that is, it will concern *algebras with finitary operations*.

The concepts of *subalgebra*, *congruence relation* on an algebra, *homomorphism* of one algebra A onto (or into) another algebra with the same operations, and of the *direct union* $A_1 \times \cdots \times A_r$ of any finite or infinite class of algebras with the same operations have been developed elsewhere.[1] More or less trivial arguments establish a many-one correspondence between the congruence relations θ_i on an algebra A and the homomorphic images $H_i = \theta_i(A)$ of the algebra (isomorphic images being identified); moreover the congruence relations on A form a lattice (the *structure lattice* of A). In this lattice, the equality relation will be denoted 0; all other congruence relations will be called *proper*.

More or less trivial arguments also show (cf. *Lattice theory*, Theorem 3.20) that the isomorphic representations of any algebra A as a *subdirect union*, or subalgebra $S \leqq H_1 \times \cdots \times H_r$ of a direct union of algebras H_i, correspond essentially one-one to the sets of congruence relations θ_i on A such that $\Lambda\theta_i = 0$. In fact, given such a set of θ_i, the correspondence

$$(2) \qquad \theta: \quad a \to [\theta_1(a), \cdots, \theta_r(a)] = [h_1, \cdots, h_r]$$

exhibits the desired isomorphism of A with a subalgebra of $H_1 \times \cdots \times H_r$, where $H_i = \theta_i(A)$. Incidentally, the number of S_i can

Presented to the Society, April 29, 1944, under the title *Subdirect products in universal algebra*; received by the editors March 10, 1944, and, in revised form, June 5, 1944.

[1] *On the structure of abstract algebras*, Proc. Cambridge Philos. Soc. vol. 31 (1935) pp. 433–454, and in the foreword to the author's *Lattice theory*. The idea of an abstract congruence relation is also developed in chap. VI, §14, of S. MacLane's and the author's *Survey of modern algebra*. Interesting remarks in this connection may be found in J. C. C. McKinsey's and A. Tarski's *The algebra of topology*, Ann. of Math. vol. 45 (1944) esp. pp. 190–191.

be infinite. What is more important, the operations of A need not even be finitary.[2]

Equally trivial arguments extend a well known theorem of Emmy Noether on commutative rings[3] to abstract algebras in general. In order to state this extension, we first define an algebra A to be *subdirectly irreducible* if in any finite or infinite representation (2), some θ_i is itself an isomorphism. This means that the meet θ^* of all proper congruence relations on A is itself a proper congruence relation. In lattice-theoretic language, it means that the structure lattice $L(A)$ of A contains a *point* $\theta^*>0$ such that $\theta>0$ implies $\theta\geqq\theta^*$. Hence if A is subdirectly irreducible, $\theta\cap\theta'=0$ in $L(A)$ implies $\theta=0$ or $\theta'=0$; such an A we shall call *weakly irreducible.* If $L(A)$ satisfies the *descending* chain condition, and A is weakly irreducible, then it is evidently also subdirectly irreducible in the strong sense.

If $L(A)$ satisfies the *ascending* chain condition, then it is evident by induction[3] that there exists a representation of 0 as the meet $0=\theta_1\cap\cdots\cap\theta_r$ of a finite number of irreducible elements. This yields the following easy generalization of Emmy Noether's theorem on commutative rings.

THEOREM 1. *Any algebra A whose structure lattice satisfies the ascending chain condition is isomorphic with a subdirect union of a finite number of weakly irreducible algebras.*

For this result, we still do not need to assume that A has finitary operations.

2. **Main theorem.** Our principal result is the partial extension of Theorem 1 to algebras *without* chain condition. As will be seen in §3, this result will contain as special cases many known theorems and some new theorems.

THEOREM 2. *Any algebra A with finitary operations is isomorphic with a subdirect union of subdirectly irreducible algebras.*

PROOF. For any $a\neq b$ of A, consider the set $S(a, b)$ of all congruence relations θ on A, such that $a\not\equiv b \pmod{\theta}$. If T is any linearly ordered subset of $S(a, b)$, the *union* τ of the $\theta\in T$ is defined by the rule

(3) $$x \equiv y \pmod{\tau} \text{ means } x \equiv y \pmod{\theta} \text{ for some } \theta \in T.$$

It is evident that $a\not\equiv b \pmod{\tau}$, and that *if A has finitary operations,*

[2] This is observed in N. H. McCoy and Deane Montgomery, *A representation of generalized Boolean rings,* Duke Math. J. vol. 3 (1937) p. 46, line 12.

[3] Cf. van der Waerden, *Moderne Algebra,* first ed., vol. 2, p. 36. The unicity theorem on p. 40 does not apply to abstract algebras in general, however.

then τ *is a congruence relation.* Hence, in the structure lattice $L(A)$ of A, the union of any linearly ordered subset of $S(a, b)$ exists and is in $S(a, b)$. But this is the hypothesis of the "first form" of Zorn's Lemma.[4] The conclusion is that $S(a, b)$ contains a *maximal* element, $\theta_{a,b}$. We next consider $H_{a,b}$, the homomorphic image of A, mod $\theta_{a,b}$.

Every proper congruence relation $\theta > 0$ corresponds[5] to a $\theta' > \theta_{a,b}$; and since $\theta_{a,b}$ is maximal in $S(a, b)$, this implies $a \equiv b \pmod{\theta'}$. Hence the *meet* θ^* of the $\theta > 0$ in $H_{a,b}$, defined by

$$(4) \qquad x \equiv y \pmod{\theta^*} \text{ means } x \equiv y \pmod{\theta} \text{ for all } \theta > 0,$$

will satisfy $a \equiv b \pmod{\theta^*}$, and hence $\theta^* > 0$. Hence (cf. §1) $H_{a,b}$ is subdirectly irreducible.

Finally, the meet of *all* $\theta_{a,b}$ is 0, since we have identically $x \not\equiv y \pmod{\theta_{x,y}}$. Hence, by the theorem cited in §1, paragraph 3, A is isomorphic with a subdirect union of the (subdirectly irreducible) $H_{a,b}$, q.e.d.

3. **Applications.** Theorem 2 has importance mainly because subdirectly irreducible algebras may be specifically described in so many cases.

LEMMA 1. *A weakly irreducible distributive lattice or Boolean algebra must consist of* 0 *and* I *alone.*

PROOF FOR DISTRIBUTIVE LATTICES. For any a, the endomorphisms $\theta_a: x \to x \cup a$ and $\theta_a': x \to x \cap a$ have the property[6] that $\theta_a \cap \theta_a' = 0$, and neither defines the equality relation unless $a = 0$ or $a = I$.

PROOF FOR BOOLEAN ALGEBRAS. Let $x \equiv y \pmod{\theta_a}$ mean $|x - y| \leqq a$ (symmetric difference notation); then $\theta_a \cap \theta_{a'} = 0$, and neither defines the equality relation unless $a = 0$ or $a' = 0$ $(a = I)$.

COROLLARY 1. *Any distributive lattice is isomorphic with a ring of sets.*[7]

COROLLARY 2. *Any Boolean algebra is isomorphic with a field of sets.*[7]

---

[4] Cf. J. W. Tukey, *Convergence and uniformity in topology*, Princeton, 1940, p. 7.

[5] We omit discussing the obvious isomorphism between $L(H_{a,b})$ and the sublattice of $\theta' > \theta_{a,b}$ in $L(A)$.

[6] PROOF. If $x \cup a = y \cup a$ and $x \cap a = y \cap a$, then $x = x \cap (x \cup a) = x \cap (y \cup a) = (x \cap y) \cup (x \cap a) = (y \cap x) \cup (y \cap a) = y \cap (x \cup a) = y \cap (y \cup a) = y$—by the distributive laws. θ_a and θ_a' are endomorphisms.

[7] Corollaries 1–2 are theorems of the author and Stone, respectively. Corollary 3 below is due to McCoy and Montgomery, op. cit. footnote 2. Corollary 4 is due to G. Kothe, *Abstrakte Theorie nichtkommutative Ringe*, Math. Ann. vol. 103 (1930) p. 552; N. H. McCoy *Subrings of infinite direct sums*, Duke Math. J. vol. 4 (1938) pp. 486–494.

LEMMA 2. *A subdirectly irreducible commutative ring R without nilpotent elements is a field.*[8]

PROOF. As in §1, R will have a unique minimal ideal (that is, congruence relation) J. But for any $a \neq 0$ in J, since $aa \neq 0$, $aJ > 0$. Moreover since $(aJ)R = a(JR) \leqq aJ$, aJ is an ideal, $0 < aJ \leqq J$. Consequently $aJ = J$—whence J is a *field* (Huntington's postulates) with unit e. The set $0:e$ of all $x \in R$ such that $ex = 0$ is an ideal, and $(0:e) \cap J = 0$ by what we have just shown; hence $0:e = 0$. But for any $x \in R$, $e(x - ex) = 0$; hence $(x - ex) \in 0:e = 0$, and $x = (x - ex) + ex$, $0 = ex \in J$. We conclude that $R = J$ is a field, q.e.d.

One might infer that by Theorem 2 any commutative ring without nilpotent elements was a subdirect product of fields, but this reasoning would be invalid. It is not necessarily true that a homomorphic image of rings without nilpotent elements is itself without nilpotent elements.

On the other hand, any homomorphic image of a *p-ring* (or commutative ring in which $a^p = a$ for some prime p) is itself a p-ring, and evidently without nilpotent elements, since $a^{p^n} = a$ for all n. Furthermore, a field in which $a^p = a$ can contain only p elements, and must be $GF(p)$ (or the "field" 0).

COROLLARY 3. *Any p-ring is a subdirect union of GF(p), or consists of 0 alone.*[7]

Again, any homomorphic image of a *regular* ring in the sense of von Neumann (or ring in which any a has a "relative inverse" u such that $aua = a$) is itself regular, and evidently without nilpotent elements if commutative (since $a^n u^{n-1} = auau \cdots ua = a \neq 0$).

COROLLARY 4. *Any commutative "regular" ring is a subdirect union of fields.*[7]

If one were interested in obtaining corollaries of Theorem 1, one might show that even a *weakly* irreducible p-ring or regular ring was a field. Again, one might show (van der Waerden, op. cit. p. 32) that, in a weakly irreducible commutative ring satisfying the chain condition, every divisor of zero is nilpotent; this would yield E. Noether's theorem that every commutative ring satisfying the chain condition was a subdirect union of a finite number of primary rings.

Similarly, one can show easily that the only weakly irreducible vector space over a field F is the one-dimensional vector space $V(F; 1)$ (or 0). It follows that any vector space is a subdirect union of one-

[8] This lemma was suggested to the author in conversation by N. H. McCoy.

dimensional vector spaces. Actually (due to the existence of bases) a stronger result is well known.

LEMMA 3. *The only weakly irreducible commutative groups G are the "generalized cyclic" groups: the additive subgroups of the rationals, and those of the rationals* mod *one.*

We omit the proof, which follows easily from the fact that a commutative group with two generators is cyclic unless it contains two disjoint subgroups (the latter hypothesis would make G weakly reducible).

COROLLARY 5. *Any commutative group is a subdirect union of generalized cyclic groups.*

The center of any weakly irreducible hypercentral (alias nilpotent) group H is generalized cyclic (the proof is trivial, granted Lemma 3); the converse also holds if H is finite.[9] Hence we have the following corollary.

COROLLARY 6. *Any hypercentral group is a subdirect union of groups with generalized cyclic centers.*

Further, any weakly irreducible commutative l-group (lattice-ordered group) is known[10] to be *simply* ordered. This yields the following corollary.

COROLLARY 7. *Any commutative l-group is a subdirect union of simply ordered* 1-*groups.*

One can easily show (although we omit the proof) that any closed element in a closure algebra (in the sense of McKinsey and Tarski[11]) determines a congruence relation, essentially through relativization with respect to the complementary open set. Then from the definition of well-connectedness one obtains the following corollary.

COROLLARY 8. *Any "closure algebra" is a subdirect union of "well-connected" closure algebras.*

HARVARD UNIVERSITY

---

[9] Theorems of Burnside (cf. H. Zassenhaus, *Gruppentheorie*, Teubner, 1937, p. 107, Satz. 11) and P. Hall, *A contribution to the theory of groups of prime-power orders*, Proc. London Math. Soc. vol. 36 (1933) p. 51, Theorem 2.49.

[10] Cf. the author's *Lattice-ordered groups*, Ann. of Math. vol. 43 (1942) p. 319.

[11] *The algebra of topology*, Ann. of Math. vol. 45 (1944) pp. 141–191. The definition of well-connectedness is on p. 147; the concept of relativization is developed on p. 151.

UNIVERSAL ALGEBRA

Garrett Birkhoff, *Harvard University*

§ 1. **Abstract algebras.** The topic of "universal algebra" should be of interest to the algebraist, as it concisely expresses principles which pervade all branches of algebra. It should be of interest to the mathematical logician, as it is the only field except the foundations of the theory of real functions and axiomatics, in which his proud boast "Mathematics is a branch of logic" is really justified.

Since the development of the algebra of matrices and of the algebra of logic around 1850, it has been increasingly realized that the technique of algebraic manipulation can be fruitfully applied to non-numerical entities. The concept of an abstract system has become more and more all-pervasive in mathematics; thus even in 1898 Whitehead wrote "A treatise on Universal Algebra is to some extent a treatise on certain generalized ideas of space" ([13], p. 32).

However, the correct formulation of universal algebraic concepts has, in my opinion, only been accomplished recently. Thus Whitehead wrote, somewhat vaguely, "Universal algebra is . . . that calculus which symbolizes general operations, defined later, which are called Addition and Multiplication" ([13], p. 18), but developed nothing which can properly be called a theorem of universal algebra.

Emmy Noether and her school actually developed many of the most important ideas of universal algebra, but the most general concept of algebra explicitly mentioned by them is that of a "group with operators." This concept includes groups, rings, vector spaces, and hypercomplex algebras—but it ignores

Boolean algebras and, more generally, lattices.[1] In order to exploit these ideas to the fullest, we develop the idea of a *set with operations.*

For example, we may have *binary* operations such as $f(x, y) = x + y$, or xy, or x/y; we may have *unary* operations such as $f(x) = -x$, $f(x) = \sqrt{2x}$ (in vector algebra); we may have *ternary* operations, such as $f(x, y, z) = xy^{-1}z$ in a group. We shall call unary operations *operators.* Logically, the operation of selecting a *constant,* such as 0 or 1, can be regarded as a *nullary* operation; hence we can speak generally of an *n-ary operation* ($n = 0, 1, 2, \ldots$) on a set A, as a rule f which assigns to certain sequences $x_1, \ldots, x_n$ of elements of A, one or more values[2] $f(x_1, \ldots, x_n)$ in A. If we introduce *convergence* as an *infinitary* operation Lim $\{x_n\}$ on sequences or directed sets, we include topological spaces and even topological algebras in the concept of a set with operations.

In abstract algebra, there also occur binary and other *relations* (such as $a \geqq b$, $a|b$, etc.), but we shall largely ignore these and state simply

Definition 1. An *abstract algebra* is a set with operations.[3] In general, we must also require

(α) The operations are single-valued. (This is for example not required in multigroups.)[4]

(β) The operations are *universally defined*—i.e., $f(x_1, \ldots x_n)$ exists in A for all $x_1, \ldots, x_n \epsilon A$. (This is not true of x/y—

---

[1]Thus it excludes algebras of the "non-numerical genus," in which $a + a = a$ ([13], p. 18; the distinction goes back at least to C. S. Pierce).

[2]The distinction in Bourbaki [5] between "external" and "internal" operators seems entirely superfluous, except as Condition (8) below is involved.

[3]This idea was first developed in [1], [2]; cf. also [10], [5].

[4]Cf. for example W. Prenowitz, "Projective Geometrics as Multigroups," *Am. Jour. of Math.* vol. 65 (1943), pp. 235-256.

though this is not essential, as x/y can be defined in terms of xy. It is essentially not true of Lim $\{x_n\}$.)

(γ) The operations are all *finitary*, i.e., n-ary for finite integer n. (This also is not true of Lim $\{x_n\}$, though the closure operator $X \to \overline{X}$ is unary on the sets of a topological space.) In addition, we may be interested in having also

(δ) The number of distinct operations is finite.

However, this seems to play no essential role, nor need it be true for vector spaces or groups with operators.

§ 2. Subalgebras. By a *subalgebra* of an abstract algebra A, we mean a subset S which is *closed* with respect to the operations of A. (DEFINITION 2.)

This definition includes as special cases the concepts of subgroup, subring, vector subspace, topologically closed subset, etc.

THEOREM 1. Any intersection (set-product) $\wedge S_\sigma$ of subalgebras of A is a subalgebra of A; A is a subalgebra of itself.

COROLLARY. The subalgebras of A form a complete lattice.

Conversely, it has been shown ([1], Thm. 5.1) that any complete lattice is isomorphic with the lattice of all subalgebras of an abstract algebra, even of one satisfying (α) and (β). But (γ) and (δ) cannot be satisfied too, in view of Theorem 3 below.

The intersection $\overline{T} = \wedge S_\alpha$ of all subalgebras S_σ containing a given subset T of A is called the *subalgebra generated by* T. Clearly (i) $T \leqq \overline{T}$, (ii) $\overline{\overline{T}} = \overline{T}$, (iii) If $T \leqq U$, then $\overline{T} \leqq \overline{U}$.

We can also define $\overline{T}$ constructively as the set of all values of *compound operations* with arguments in T, a compound operation of degree n being defined recursively as the result $f(g_1, \ldots, g_k)$ of an operation on compound operations of degree $(n-1)$ and less—and one of degree one as the identical function x_i. For this result condition (γ) is needed.

Finally, one can easily show

THEOREM 2. Any subalgebra T of a subalgebra S of an abstract algebra A, is itself a subalgebra of A.

§ 3. Finiteness conditions. At least two finiteness conditions play an important role in algebra.

(F) Every subalgebra has a finite basis; in symbols, given S, a finite subset F exists with $\overline{F} = \overline{S}$.

Arguments given in van der Waerden ([12], vol. 2, pp. 23-7) for the case of ideals[5] actually belong to universal algebra and show that (F) is equivalent to the "chain condition": every ascending sequence of subalgebras is finite.

Condition (F) only holds exceptionally, whereas the following condition holds in any algebra which satisfies Condition (γ) (i.e., whose operations are all finitary).[6]

THEOREM 3. Condition (γ) implies that, given any subset G and any subalgebra S of A, among the subalgebras T such that $G \wedge T \leqq S$, one M is *maximal.*

This means that if $T > M$ is another subalgebra of A, then it is not true that $G \wedge T \leqq S$. In the case $S = 0$, it reduces to the assertion that, for any G, there is a maximal subalgebra M disjoint from G. If the lattice of subalgebras of A is finitely distributive, it implies the infinite distributive law $X \wedge VY_\alpha = V(X \wedge Y_\alpha)$.

PROOF. The property that $T \wedge G \leqq S$ is "of finite character" in the sense of Tukey,[7] which means that T possesses it if all its finite subsets do. Hence there is a maximal $T = T$ (since $\overline{T} = T$) with this property; $M = T$.

[5] Ideals are subalgebras if we consider addition as a binary operation, and the transformations $x \to ax$ and $x \to xb$ as unary operations.

[6] The discussion of conditions (F) $-$ (γ) is taken from an unpublished manuscript of Mr. Bruce Crabtree. Theorem 3 has been strengthened.

[7] J. W. Tukey, *Convergence and Uniformity in Topology*, Princeton, 1940. Tukey shows that there is a maximal set having any property of finite character (Axiom of Choice).

COROLLARIES. Any ring with unity has a maximal proper ideal and a maximal proper multiplicative ideal (Krull). Any complete normed ring with unity has a maximal proper closed ideal (Gelfand).[8]

Theorem 3 also gives the crux of the extension of the Jordan-Holder Theorem to transfinite series.

THEOREM 3′. Condition (γ) implies that if A has a finite set of generators (i.e., if $A = F$, F finite), then it has a maximal subalgebra.[9]

COROLLARY. A ring with a finite set of generators has a maximal proper ideal.

This sharpens a result of van der Waerden ([12], vol. 2, p. 18).

§ 4. Homomorphisms. Now let A and B be any so-called "similar" algebras ([9]; called algebras of the same species in [2])—i.e., algebras whose operations are identified. Thus A and B might be any two groups, or any two vector spaces over the same field. We suppose also that the operations are *single-valued*—that Condition (α) holds.

DEFINITION 3. By a *homomorphism* of A into B we mean a single-valued correspondence $x \to x\theta$ such that if $f(x_1, \ldots, x_n)$ exists in A, then $f(x_1\theta, \ldots, x_n\theta)$ exists in B and

(1) $$f(x_1\theta, \ldots, x_n\theta) = [f(x_1, \ldots, x_n)]\,\theta.$$

This definition includes as special cases the usual concept of a homomorphism between rings, of a continuous transformation between topological spaces, of a continuous homomorphism between topological groups, etc., etc.

THEOREM 4. The inverse image of a subalgebra under any homomorphism is a subalgebra. (α).

[8] Gelfand's argument involves also the remark that the topological closure of any proper ideal is proper, since $1 - x + x^2 - x^3 + \ldots = (1+x)^{-1}$ *in a neighbourhood* of 1.

[9] In fact, Crabtree has shown that every set of generators is finite.

If Conditions (α) *and* (β) hold (i.e., for homomorphisms between algebras) then the existence statements in Definition 3 are superfluous; a homomorphism is simply a single-valued correspondence satisfying (1). We also note that (1) can be written in another notation as the distributive law

$$(x_1 \circ \ldots \circ x_n)\theta = x_1\theta \circ \ldots \circ x_n\theta,$$

and, for unary operations (operators) ϕ as the commutative law $(x_1\phi)\theta = (x_1\theta)\phi$. Note also

THEOREM 4′. *The image of a subalgebra under any homomorphism is a subalgebra.* (α), (β).

Again, let θ be any homomorphism of A onto B. We define

(2) $\qquad x \sim y \bmod \theta$ in A to mean $x\theta = y\theta$ in B.

The equivalence (i.e., symmetric, reflexive, and transitive) relation (2) enjoys the substitution property

(3) $\qquad x_i \sim x_i' \bmod \theta$ $(i = 1, \ldots, n)$ for all n implies $f(x_1, \ldots, x_n) \sim f(x_1', \ldots, x_n') \bmod \theta$,

if conditions (α), (β) hold. Such equivalence relations are called *congruence relations*. (DEFINITION 4.)

Conversely, given a congruence relation $x \sim y \bmod \theta$ on A, there exists one and (to within isomorphism) only one B and a homomorphism $\theta : A \to B$ such that (2) holds. This has been discussed in detail elsewhere ([4], pp. 159-62); it specializes to the relation between homomorphisms and normal subgroups of a group, ideals of a ring, etc.

This result requires Conditions (α) and (β), and so does not hold for topological spaces.[10] However, under Condition (α) alone, the inverse image of any one-element subalgebra (group identity, ring zero) forms a subalgebra by Theorem 4; hence if all operations are idempotent (e.g., topological spaces, lattices, or groups under $ab^{-1}c$), then the inverse image of any element is a subalgebra.

---

[10] It holds for certain *compact* spaces; it would be interesting to obtain a general condition for this.

In Bourbaki ([5], p. 51), it is remarked that the two isomorphism theorems proved for groups with operators in van der Waerden ([12] vol. 1, p. 136), are really theorems of universal algebra. They follow.

THEOREM 5. If B is the homomorphic image of A determined by the congruence relation θ, then the congruence relations on B correspond one-one to the congruence relations $\theta' \geqq \theta$ on A.

Here $\theta' \geqq \theta$ means that $x \sim y \bmod \theta$ implies $x \sim y \bmod \theta'$.

THEOREM 5'. Any congruence relation on A induces a congruence relation on any subalgebra of A. (α), (β).

Another theorem, which we shall not explain in detail here, is the following ([2], p. 450).

THEOREM 6. The congruence relations on any algebra A form a complete lattice. If Condition (γ) holds, this is a sublattice of the lattice of all partitions of A. (α), (β).

It is not known whether or not, conversely, any complete lattice is the lattice of all congruence relations of a suitable abstract algebra,[11] though one can show by Theorem 8 that (α)–(γ) cannot always be satisfied.

A homomorphism of an algebra into itself is called an *endomorphism*, and it is easy to show that the endomorphisms of any algebra constitute a semi-group of transformations. Whether or not any semi-group is the semi-group of all endomorphisms of a suitable abstract algebra is unknown.

§ 5. Automorphisms. A homomorphism $A \to B$ which is also one-one is called an isomorphism; if $A = B$, it is called an

[11] P. Whitman has proved that every lattice is isomorphic with a sublattice of the lattice of all partitions of a suitable class, Bull. Amer. Math. Soc. 52 (1946), 507-22. I have recently shown that if (γ) holds, the congruence relations on A are a closed sublattice of the lattice of all partitions of A.

automorphism.[12] It is easily shown that

THEOREM 7. The automorphisms of any abstract algebra form a group.

Conversely, any group is the group of automorphisms of a suitable abstract algebra ([2], p. 445), even of one satisfying[13] conditions $(\alpha)-(\delta)$.

If we add to the original operators on an algebra A, either (1) the automorphisms of A, (2) the endomorphisms of A, or (3) the endomorphisms[14] of A onto all of A, we get a revised concept of subalgebra. Those arising from (1) may be called *characteristic*, those from (2), *fully characteristic*, and those from (3) strictly characteristic subalgebras. All these concepts have been defined for groups,[15] and might as well be defined for arbitrary abstract algebras.

Clearly Theorems 1 and 2 apply to such characteristic, fully characteristic, etc., subalgebras. Clearly also any "abstractly defined" subalgebra (centre or commutator-subgroup of group, radical of ring, etc.) will be characteristic; it is always interesting to enquire whether or not it is fully characteristic.

§ 6. Direct union. We can construct the *direct union* $A \times B$ of any two similar algebras, as the set of all couples $[x, y](x\epsilon A, y\epsilon B)$, combined by the rule

(4) $f([x_1, y_1], \ldots, [x_n, y_n]) = [f(x_1, \ldots, x_n), f(y_1, \ldots, y_n)]$

whenever $f(x_1, \ldots, x_n)$ and $f(y_1, \ldots, y_n)$ exist.

---

12 The concepts of isomorphism and automorphism also apply to systems with relations. We write $A \cong B$ to signify that A and B are isomorphic.

13 I have shown that any abstract group is the group of automorphisms of a distributive lattice.

14 In the infinite case, these need not all be automorphisms. We could also take (4) the class of all endomorphisms θ such that $x\theta = y\theta$ implies $x = y$. Note that when endomorphisms are included as operators on A, the concept of endomorphism itself changes!

15 R. Baer, *Bull. Am. Math. Soc.*, vol. 50 (1944), pp. 143-60.

This specializes to the direct product of groups, direct sum of rings, and product of two topological spaces.[16]

Clearly the correspondences

$$\theta : [x, y] \leftrightarrow [y, x], \ \theta' : [x', y'] \leftrightarrow [y', x'],$$

are isomorphisms:

(5) $A \times B \cong B \times A, \quad A' \times B' \cong B' \times A'.$

They are "natural," in the sense that if $a \to a\phi$, $b \to b\psi$ are any homomorphisms $A \to A'$, $B \to B'$, we get the same result by applying first θ and then ϕ, ψ, as by applying first ϕ, ψ and then θ'.

The concept of "natural" mappings, and the associated concepts of "functors" and "categories," have recently been developed as concepts of universal algebra in detail and with numerous applications, by S. Eilenberg and S. MacLane[17] [7].

For groups with operators whose lattice of congruence relations satisfies a finite chain condition, for algebras having only unary operations, and also for lattices, we know[18]

(6) If $A_1 x \ldots x A_m = B_1 x \ldots x B_n$, and no A_i or B_j can be decomposed further, then $m = n$, and the A_i and B_j are isomorphic in pairs.

It is a fascinating conjecture, that this holds for all topological spaces and other "abstract algebras" in the sense of Definition 1. It would be very interesting if even $A^2 \cong B^2$ implied $A \cong B$—or $A^n \cong B^n$ implied $A \cong B$—or even if this were

---

[16]We can also define the direct union for relations R: $[x, y]\ R\ [x', y']$ means xRx' and yRy'.

[17]It is to be observed that many concepts of "metamathematics" ([8], p. 44)—e.g., duality theorems—are special cases of concepts of universal algebra.

[18]The original proof for groups was given by Wedderburn, made rigorous by R. Remak, generalized to groups with operators by W. Krull and O. Schmidt, and a more general proof given by O. Ore, "On the Foundations of Abstract Algebra," *Annals of Math.*, vol. **37**, (**1936**), p. **272**. The proof for lattices was given by the author ("Lattice Theory," p. **23**).

true for finite systems.[19]

One can also construct the direct union of an infinite set of similar algebras.

§ 7. Subdirect union. A subalgebra of a direct union of (similar) algebras A_α, may be called a *subdirect* union of the A_α. An algebra which cannot be represented as a subdirect union of smaller algebras may be called *subdirectly irreducible.* The following general result holds.

THEOREM 8. Any algebra is the subdirect union of subdirectly irreducible algebras, in which in fact the meet of all proper congruence relations is proper.[20] (α), (β), (γ).

This result is trivial in the case of algebras having a finite number of elements. In the infinite case, it yields many theorems for which separate proofs were developed.

§ 8. Identities. In most algebras, a number of *identities* of the form

(7) $p(x_1, \ldots, x_n) = q(x_1, \ldots x_n)$ for all $x_1, \ldots, x_n$,

where p and q are "compound operations" (cf. § 2), are assumed to hold. Typical examples are $x + y = y + x$, $Ox = 0$, $x(y + z) = xy + xz$, etc.

THEOREM 9. Identities valid in A are valid in any homomorphic image of A. (α), (β).

Identities are special cases of *identical implications*, or rules of the form[21]

[19] Important progress on this problem has been made recently by B. Jonsson and A. Tarski, "Direct decompositions of finite algebraic systems," to be published by The Oxford Press.

[20] By a "proper" congruence relation, we mean here one differing from the equality relation $x = y$. Theorem 8, its consequences, and the related literature, are fully discussed in [3].

[21] Tarski and McKinsey ([9], [10]) call these "statements," but this seems to the author too general a word.

(8) If $p_i(x_1, \ldots, x_{n_i}) = q_i(x_1, \ldots, x_{n_i})$ $[i = 1, \ldots, m]$, then $p(x_1, \ldots, x_n) = q(x_1, \ldots, x_n)$.

For example, $ax = ay$ may imply $x = y$, as in groups. However, the so-called "cancellation law"

(9) $ax = ay$ $(a \neq 0)$ implies $x = y$

is not an identical implication.

THEOREM 10. Identical implications valid in A are valid in any subalgebra of A; those valid in any set of algebras are valid in their direct union.[22] (α).

Thus the identical implication $ax = ay$ implies $x = y$, valid in the set J^+ of positive integers, is not valid in J^+ mod n; law (9) valid in the ring J of all integers, is not valid in $J \times J$.

Note also the "calculus of complexes" A^* of any algebra A. This may be defined as the system whose elements are the subsets $X, Y, \ldots$ of A, to which the operations of A are extended by the rule

(10) $f(X_1, \ldots, X_n)$ is the set of $f(x_1, \ldots, x_n)$ in A, for all $x_1 \epsilon X_1, \ldots, x_n \epsilon X_n$.

Not even all identities valid in A are valid in A^*. Thus although a binary operation is commutative or associative in A^* if it is so in A, it need not be idempotent in A^* just because it is idempotent in A.

THEOREM 11. If $p(x_1, \ldots, x_n) = q(x_1, \ldots, x_n)$ is an identity in A, and if no x_i occurs more than once in $p(x_1, \ldots, x_n)$, then $p(X_1, \ldots, X_n) \leqq q(X_1, \ldots, X_n)$ in A^*, set-theoretically.

COROLLARY. If no x_i occurs more than once in p or q, then $p = q$ is an identity in A^*, if it is in A.

The calculus of complexes is also convenient for constructing the homomorphic image defined by a congruence relation on A ([4], pp. 159-62).

---

[22]When Condition (β) is not satisfied, (6) is assumed to mean that $p(x_1, \ldots, x_n)$ is defined for those and only those values of $x_1, \ldots, x_n$ for which $q(x_1, \ldots, x_n)$ is.

Finally, we note that identities with quantifiers, such as "given a, b, $ax = b$ for some x" are preserved under direct unions and homomorphisms, but not necessarily in subalgebras or in calculi of complexes of algebras satisfying them.

§ 9. Free algebras, I. Consider the algebra A^{a^m} of all unctions $\phi_i(x_1, \ldots, x_m)$ from A^m to A; there will be a^{a^m} of them; here a is the cardinal number of elements in A. Thus by definition, if f is any n-ary operator of A,

(11) $f(\phi_1, \ldots, \phi_n)$ on $x_1, \ldots, x_n \epsilon A$ assumes the value

$$f(\phi_1(x_1, \ldots x_n), \ldots, \phi_n(x_1, \ldots, x_n)).$$

In this, consider the *subalgebra* generated by the $o(A)$ *constant* functions $f(x_1, \ldots, x_m) = a$, and the m *identity* functions $f(x_1, \ldots, x_m) = x_i$. In case A is a commutative ring, this subalgebra consists of the ordinary polynomial functions on A (cf. [4], Chap. IV); hence we denote it $P_m(A)$, and call it the *polynomial algebra* in m variables over A. In $P_m(A)$, the subalgebra generated by the identity functions $x_1, \ldots, x_m$ alone will be called the *free algebra* in m variables over A, and denoted $F_m(A)$. Evidently neither $P_m(A)$ nor $F_m(A)$ can have more than r^{r^m} elements, where $r = o(A)$.

It is interesting that this concept of an abstract polynomial function should include the important concept of a *truth-table* invented by Post,[23] as well as ordinary polynomials.

The concept of a free algebra extends to any family of similar algebras A_α. One simply forms the subdirect product of the $F_m(A_\alpha)$, consisting of those vectors p_α with one component in each $F_m(A_\alpha)$, generated by the vectors $x_1, \ldots, x_m$. From Theorem 10 we see

[23] Cf. [11]. Post showed in 1920 that free Boolean algebra was the algebra of "truth-tables" over the two-element Boolean algebra, and constructed corresponding "Post-algebras" over n-element systems.

THEOREM 12. Any identity or identical implication valid in A is valid in $F_m(A)$ and $P_m(A)$; any identity or identical implication valid in all A_α is valid in $F_m(A_\alpha)$. (α), (β).

But the interesting point is rather the converse of Theorem 12:

THEOREM 12′. The identities true in all the A_α are precisely the equalities between functions of the generators $x_1, \ldots, x_m$ of $F_m(A_\alpha)$. (α), (β).

This serves as a descriptive definition of $F_m(A_\alpha)$, but does not make clear why it always exists. From Theorem 12′ we can infer that

(12) $$F_m(F_m(A_\alpha)) \cong F_m(A_\alpha).$$

We also infer that every correspondence $\theta : x_i \to y_i$ from the generators of $F_m(A_\alpha)$ to elements of $F_m(A_\alpha)$ can be extended to an endomorphism of $F_m(A_\alpha)$. This Endomorphism Property is another characterization of free algebras. We note finally the classic characterization: $F_m(A_\alpha)$ is an algebra with m generators satisfying all identities true in every A_α, and homomorphic to every other algebra with m generators satisfying all identities true in every A_α.

Since $F_m(A_\alpha)$ also satisfies all the *identical implications* true in every A_α, we see that *the identities of any algebra or set of algebras imply its identical implications.* The author has, however, been unable to see just what identities imply the cancellation law!

Incidentally, we note that the concept of free algebra can be modified to that of "free product" of similar algebras,[24] and that we can also form free algebras satisfying arbitrary equalities (this is shown in [6]).

---

[24] A. Kurosch, "Uber freie Produkte von Gruppen," *Math. Annalen*, vol. 108 (1933), pp. 26-36. The interesting thing is that the concept also includes that of the direct product of commutative algebras (cf. H. Whitney, "Tensor Products of Abelian Groups," *Duke Math. Jour.*, vol. 4 (1938), pp. 495-528).

§ 10. Free algebras, II. Much of the importance of free algebras stems from the fact that they can also be defined directly from a set Σ of identities of identical implications (i.e., postulates) on compounds of specified n_i-ary operators. Thus let $S = S(\Sigma, m)$ be the set of all algebras with m generators[25] satisfying Σ; $F_m(S)$ will also satisfy Σ, and be in S, by Theorems 12-12′.

Now let $\bar{\Sigma}$ be the set of all identities or identical implications for m variables satisfied in $S(\Sigma, m)$—or equivalently, in $F_m(S)$; it may be thought of as the set of identities, etc., implied by Σ. It was shown by the author ([2], p. 440) that in the case of identities alone, $\bar{\Sigma}$ is the closure of Σ with respect to the two types of inference:

(13) If $p_n = q_n$ $[h = 1, \ldots, n]$ are in $\bar{\Sigma}$, and if f_i is an n-ary operator, then $f_i(p_i, \ldots, p_n) = f_i(q_1, \ldots, q_n)$. (Substitution Property.)

(14) If $p(x_1, \ldots, x_m) = q(x_1, \ldots, x_m)$ is in $\bar{\Sigma}$, then any substitution η of one polynomial $\eta(x_j)$ for all occurrences of each symbol x_j in p or q yields an identity $p(\eta(x_1), \ldots, \eta(x_m)) = q(\eta(x_1), \ldots, \eta(x_m))$ of $\bar{\Sigma}$. (Endomorphism Property.)

Further, in the case of identities alone,

$$F_m(S) = F_m(\bar{\Sigma}) \cong F_m(\Sigma)$$

is the algebra with m generators in which the identities of Σ are taken as equalities.

The author does not know whether or not in the case of identical implications as well, $\bar{\Sigma}$ is the closure of Σ by (1) and (2) alone, or whether other rules of inference must be admitted to take care of identical implications.[26]

---

[25] We would simply say any algebra satisfying Σ (e.g., any group), but the concept of such a class is paradoxical: it could have no cardinal number.

[26] He did not even realize that free algebras could be formed for identical implications, until this was implicitly pointed out by Dilworth [6]. In

We can also consider the relation between algebras (with m generators) and identities on m variables from a more general point of view. If S is any set of similar algebras, let $\Sigma(s)$ denote the set of identities and identical implications, and let $\Sigma_1(S)$ be the set of all identities, satisfied in every $A \epsilon S$. Conversely, if Σ is any set of identities and identical implications, or Σ_1 any set of identities on m variables, let $S(\Sigma)$ and $S(\Sigma_1)$ be the set of all algebras with m generators satisfying Σ and Σ_1, respectively. It is easily seen that

(15) If $\Sigma \geqq \Sigma'$, then $S(\Sigma) \leqq S(\Sigma')$,

(15') If $S \geqq S'$, then $\Sigma(S) \leqq \Sigma(S')$,

(16) $\Sigma(S(\Sigma)) \geqq \Sigma$ and $S(\Sigma(S)) \geqq S$,

and similarly for Σ_1 (identities alone). Hence the correspondences are *polar* in the sense of the author's "Lattice Theory," § 32, and we infer that

THEOREM 13. *The sets S of similar algebras with m generators satisfying $S(\Sigma(S)) = S$ form a complete lattice, dually isomorphic to the complete lattice of sets Σ of identities on m variables satisfying $\Sigma(S(\Sigma)) = S$.*

It is to be noted ([2], § 10) that $\Sigma_1(S(\Sigma_1)) = \Sigma_1$ in the sense of (13)-(14). Also, that $S(\Sigma(S))$ consists of the homomorphic images of subdirect unions of the $A_a \epsilon S$.

The corresponding constructions for $\Sigma(S(\Sigma))$ and $S(\Sigma(S))$ are not known.

§ 11. A new field of research. The preceding remarks suggest research into the logical relation between specific identities (and identical implications) on a single binary operation, for the cases $m = 1, 2, 3$. In particular, the complete lattice defined generally in Theorem 13 should be determined for these three cases.

---

any case, we have the Decision Problem for any Σ—the problem of giving an explicit rule which will determine in a finite number of steps or for any given p, q, whether or not $(p = q) \epsilon \Sigma$.

To get a clearer idea of what is involved, consider the case of a single unary operator ϕ. We have the free algebra x, $x\phi$, $x\phi^2, \ldots$; its elements can be identified with the non-negative integers n, where $n\phi = n + 1$ (just as in the Peano postulates). Any algebra with one generator and one unary operator is a homomorphic image of this; such algebras correspond to setting

(17) $$x\phi^{m+p} = x\phi^m \text{ (period } p\text{, segment } m).$$

Moreover (17) with (m, p) implies (17) with (m', p') if and only if p/p' and $m \geqq m'$; the lattice of Theorem 13 is thus isomorphic to the lattice of positive integers under h.c.f. and l.c.m.

With one unary operator and two generators x, y, we get a more complex structure; with one generator and two unary operators, the free algebra is like the free semi-group with two generators, and so on.

In general, an analogous question can be posed for any class of "similar" algebras.

REFERENCES

[1] G. Birkhoff, On the Combination of Subalgebras, *Proc. Camb. Phil. Soc.*, vol. 29 (1933), pp. 441-64.

[2] G. Birkhoff, On the Structure of Abstract Algebras, *ibid.*, vol. 31 (1935), pp. 433-54.

[3] G. Birkhoff, Subdirect Products in Universal Algebra, *Bull. Amer. Math. Soc.*, (1944).

[4] G. Birkhoff and S. MacLane, *Survey of Modern Algebra*, MacMillan, 1940.

[5] N. Bourbaki, *Éleménts de Mathématique*, Part I, Livre II, Chap. I.

[6] R. P. Dilworth, Lattices with Unique Complements, *Trans. Am. Math. Soc.*, vol. 57 (1945), pp. 123-54.

[7] S. Eilenberg and S. MacLane, General Theory of Natural Equivalence, to appear in *Trans. Am. Math. Soc.*

[8] D. Hilbert and P. Bernays, *Grundlagen der Mathematik*, Berlin, 1944.

[9] J. C. C. McKinsey, The Decision Problem for some Classes of Sentences without Quantifiers, *Jour. Symbolic Logic*, vol. 8 (1943), pp. 61-76.

[10] J. C. C. McKinsey and A. Tarski, The Algebra of Topology, *Annals of Math.*, vol. 45 (1944), pp. 141-91.

[11] E. L. Post, *The Two-Valued Iterative-Systems of Mathematical Logic*, Princeton, 1941.

[12] B. L. van der Waerden, *Moderne Algebra*, 2 vols., Berlin, 1931.

[13] A. N. Whitehead, *Universal Algebra*, Cambridge University Press, 1878.

Reprinted from *Proc. First Canadian Math. Cong.*
Toronto Univ. Press, 1945, pp. 310–326

Reprinted from JOURNAL OF COMBINATORIAL THEORY
All Rights Reserved by Academic Press, New York and London

Vol. 8, No. 1, January 1970
Printed in Belgium

Heterogeneous Algebras*

GARRETT BIRKHOFF AND JOHN D. LIPSON†

Department of Mathematics, Havard University, Cambridge, Massachusetts 02138

Received December 3, 1968

ABSTRACT

Many of the basic theorems about general "algebras" derived in [1, Ch. 6] are extended to a class of *heterogeneous algebras* which includes automata, state machines, and monoids acting on sets. It is shown that some algebras can be fruitfully studied, using different interpretations, both as (homogeneous) algebras and as heterogeneous algebras, and a non-trivial "free machine" is constructed as an application. The extent of the overlap with previous work of Higgins [9] is specified.

1. INTRODUCTION

We generalize in this paper the usual [1, p. 132] notion of an "algebra", so as to include as special cases the notions of a monoid acting on a set, "automaton" (sequential machine) and "state machine" (semi-automaton). We show that most of the general theory of algebraic systems of [1, Ch. 6] applies with undiminished force. Our basic definition is the following; it is essentially equivalent to that of an "algebra with a scheme of operators" (or "$\sum$-algebras") of Higgins [9]; see also [14].

DEFINITION. An *algebra* is a system $A = [\mathscr{S}, F]$ in which:

1. $\mathscr{S} = \{S_i\}$ is a family of non-void sets S_i of different types of elements, each called a *phylum* of the algebra A. The phyla S_i are indexed by some set I; i.e., $S_i \in \mathscr{S}$ for $i \in I$ (or are called by appropriate names).

2. $F = \{f_\alpha\}$ is a set of finitary operations, where each f_α is a mapping

$$f_\alpha : S_{i(1,\alpha)} \times S_{i(2,\alpha)} \times \cdots \times S_{i(n(\alpha),\alpha)} \to S_{r(\alpha)} \tag{1}$$

* Presented at the Yale University Conference on Combinatorial Theory in honor of Professor Oystein Ore (May, 1968).

† This work was partly supported by the Office of Naval Research.

for some non-negative integer $n(\alpha)$, function $i_\alpha : k \to i(k, \alpha)$ from $n(\alpha) = \{1, 2, \ldots, n(\alpha)\}$ to I, and $r(\alpha) \in I$. The operations f_α are indexed by some set Ω; i.e., $f_\alpha \in F$ for $\alpha \in \Omega$ (or are called by appropriate names).

Thus each operation f_α assigns to each $n(\alpha)$-tuple $(x_1, \ldots, x_{n(\alpha)})$, where $x_j \in S_{i(j,\alpha)}$, some value $f_\alpha(x_1, x_2, \ldots, x_{n(\alpha)})$ in $S_{r(\alpha)}$. The operation f_α is said to be $n(\alpha)$-ary: unary when $n(\alpha) = 1$, binary when $n(\alpha) = 2$, ternary when $n(\alpha) = 3$, etc. When $n(\alpha) = 0$ the operation f_α is called "nullary"; it selects a fixed element (distinguished constant) of $S_{r(\alpha)}$.

An algebra which has only one phylum will be called a *homogeneous* algebra; an algebra having more than one phylum, a *heterogeneous algebra*. The discussion of "universal algebra" in [1, Ch. 6] assumes homogeneity, but we shall show below that this assumption is unnecessary.

For concreteness, we first give some familiar examples of heterogeneous algebras.

EXAMPLE 1. A *module* M over a ring R is a heterogeneous algebra $M = [\mathscr{S}, F_1 \sqcup F_2 \sqcup \{\nu\}]$ where[1] $\mathscr{S} = \{V, R\}$ consists a of phylum V of vectors and a phylum R of scalars. The vectors form an Abelian group under the 3 operations of $F_1 = \{+, -, 0\}$. The scalars from the ring R (with unity) under the 5 operations of $F_2 = \{+, -, 0; \cdot, 1\}$. In addition there is a 9th operation $\nu : R \times V \to V$ ("scalar multiplication"). These operations are made to satisfy the familiar module postulates [10, p. 190] $\lambda(a + b) = \lambda a + \lambda b$, $(\lambda\mu)\, a = \lambda(\mu a)$, $(\lambda + \mu)\, a = \lambda a + \mu a$, $1a = a$.

Observe that, when the module M is considered as a *heterogeneous* algebra, the ring R is explicitly defined and enjoys the status of a phylum along with V. Scalar multiplication is defined as a single operation $\nu : R \times V \to V$, and the class of all modules forms a single "family" of algebras, in the following sense.

DEFINITION. Two algebras $A = [\{S_i\}, F]$ and $B = [\{T_i\}, F]$ are said to be *similar*, or to belong to the *same family*, when they have *phyla and operations having the same names* (or index-sets).

Contrast the above definition of a module with the more sophisticated definition of a R-module as a homogeneous algebra $\mathscr{R} = [\{V\}, \{+, -, 0, R\}]$ which is normally invoked in universal algebra [1, p. 132]. In the latter definition, each "element" $\lambda \in R$ is considered as a different unary *operation* $f_\lambda : v \mapsto \lambda v$.

EXAMPLE 2. A monoid M acting on a set S is a heterogeneous algebra $[\{M, S\}, \{*, 1_M; \cdot\}]$, where the operations $* : M \times M \to M$ and 1_M of M

[1] Here and elsewhere, $\sqcup$ denotes *disjoint union.*

and $\cdot : M \times S \to S$ satisfy the identity and associativity laws $1_M \cdot s = s$ and $(m * n) \cdot s = m \cdot (n \cdot s)$, respectively.

In this paper, we shall be especially interested in the following kind of heterogeneous algebra.

EXAMPLE 3. A (*sequential*) *machine* or *automaton* is a heterogeneous algebra $M = [\mathscr{S}, F]$ in which $\mathscr{S} = \{S, A, Z\}$ contains three phyla; a non-void set S of "states," a non-void set A of input symbols (the "input alphabet"), and a finite set Z of output symbols (the "output alphabet"). There are two binary operations in F:

$$\nu : S \times A \to S \qquad (\text{"change of state"}), \tag{2a}$$

$$\zeta : S \times A \to Z \qquad (\text{"output function"}). \tag{2b}$$

A machine may be conveniently specified by a *state diagram* [8, p. 17]. A state diagram is a labeled graph in which the nodes represent states, and the label a/z associated with the arc from node (state) s to t indicates that $\nu(s, a) = t$ and $\zeta(s, a) = z$. For example, the machine M specified by the state diagram of Figure 1 below has $S = \{1, 2, 3\}$, $A = \{a, b, c\}$, and $Z = \{0, 1\}$. The label $a/0$ on the arrow from node 1 to 2 indicates that $\nu(1, a) = 2$ and $\zeta(1, a) = 0$, and similarly for the rest of the state diagram.

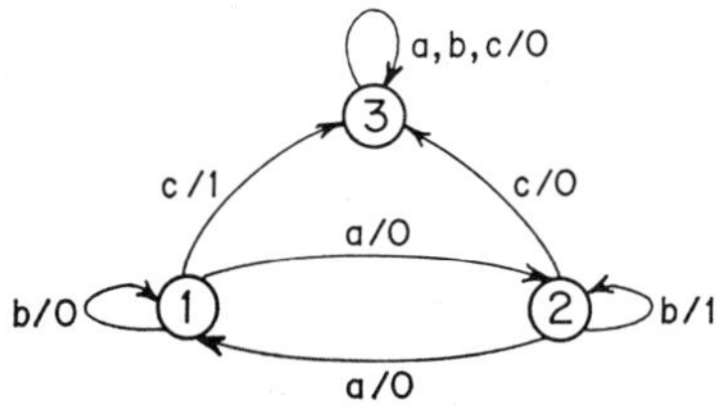

FIGURE 1

EXAMPLE 4. Associated with every machine or automaton is a state machine [8, p.18] or semiautomaton [6, p. 40] obtained by "forgetting" about Z and ζ. Thus a state machine is a heterogeneous algebra $M = [\{S, A\}, \{\nu\}]$. Evidently the class of all state machines constitutes a family of algebras.

A state machine can also be defined as a *homogeneous* algebra $[\{S\}, F]$, where F contains a unary operation $f_a : S \to S$ defined by $s \mapsto \nu(s, a)$ for each letter a of the input alphabet A. The class of all state machines does *not* constitute a family of algebras as homogeneous algebras because the set F of operations depends on the input alphabet A.

2. Subalgebras

Definition. A *subalgebra* $[\{T_i\}, F]$ of an algebra $A = [\{S_i\}, F]$ is a family of subsets $T_i \subset S_i$ $(i \in I)$ closed under the operations of F. More precisely, the condition is that for each $f_\alpha \in F$, if $t_k \in T_{i(k,\alpha)}$ for $k = 1, 2,..., n = n(\alpha)$ then $f_\alpha(t_1, t_2, ..., t_n) \in T_{r(\alpha)}$.

Note that the possibility that some T_i are void is not excluded by the above definition. However, if F contains any nullary operation, say f_α, which selects an element $t \in S_{r(\alpha)}$, then we require every subalgebra $[\{T_i\}, F]$ of A to contain this t. A subalgebra $[\{T_i\}, F]$ with one or more T_i void is said to be *degenerate*.

When applied to machines, the above definition of subalgebra yields a notion of a *submachine* which is equivalent to that in [8, *p*. 19]. Given a machine $M = [\{S, A, Z\}, \{\nu, \zeta\}]$ and subsets $S_1 \subset S$, $A_1 \subset A$, $Z_1 \subset Z$, then $M_1 = [\{S_1, A_1, Z_1\}, \{\nu, \zeta\}]$ is a submachine of M when (i) S_1 contains with each of its states s all those states $\nu(s, a)$ accessible from s via inputs a of A_1, and (ii) for every state s of S_1 and input symbol a of A_1, Z_1 contains the output symbol $\zeta(s, a)$.

Diagrams of three submachines of the machine M of Figure 1, Example 3, are given in Figure 2.

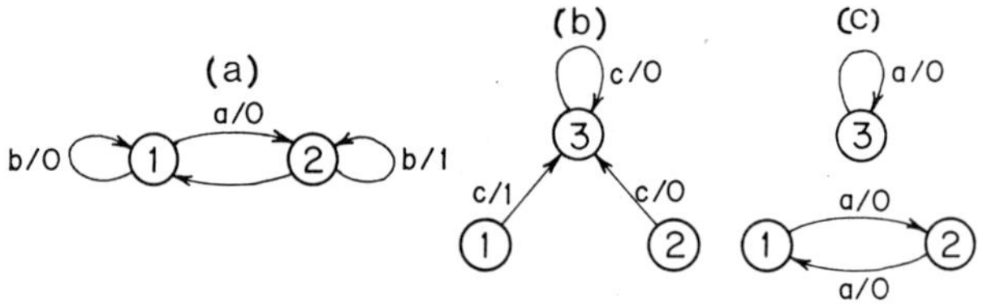

Fig. 2. Sample submachines.

Let $B_\nu = [\{T_{i,\nu}\}, F]$ be a family of subalgebras of $A = [\{S_i\}, F]$. Then the *intersection* $\bigcap_\nu B_\nu$ is the system $[\{\bigcap_\nu T_{i,\nu}\}, F]$, and we have, as in [9, p. 120],

Proposition 1. *Any intersection* $\bigcap_\nu B_\nu$ *of subalgebras* $B_\nu = [\{T_{i,\nu}\}, F]$ *of* A *is a subalgebra.*

Let $A = [\{S_i\}, F]$ be an algebra, and let $\mathcal{T} = \{T_i\}$ be contained in A; i.e., $T_i \subset S_i$ for all $i \in I$. Denote by $\overline{\mathcal{T}} = [\{\overline{T}_i\}, F]$ the intersection of all subalgebras of A containing $\mathcal{T}$. Then $\overline{\mathcal{T}}$ will be called the subalgebra *generated* by $\mathcal{T}$, and $\mathcal{T}$ a "generating family of sets" for $\overline{\mathcal{T}}$.

For families $\mathcal{T} = \{T_i\}$ and $\mathcal{U} = \{U_i\}$ we clearly have: (i) $\mathcal{T} \subset \overline{\mathcal{T}}$, (ii) $\overline{\overline{\mathcal{T}}} = \overline{\mathcal{T}}$, and (iii) if $\mathcal{T} \subset \mathcal{U}$, then $\overline{\mathcal{T}} \subset \overline{\mathcal{U}}$. In other words [1, p. 112], we have

PROPOSITION 2. *The correspondence* $\mathcal{T} \to \bar{\mathcal{T}}$ *is a closure operation* [1, p. 111] *on the set* $\sqcup_{i \in I} S_i$.

As another consequence, we have (cf. [1, p. 111])

PROPOSITION 3. *The subalgebras of an algebra form a complete lattice.*

EXAMPLE 5. Let M be a monoid of functions acting on a set S. Then $U = [\{M, \mathscr{P}(S)\}, F]$ is a heterogeneous algebra, where $F = \{\cdot, 1, \cap, \cup, ', *\}$ contains besides the monoid operations of M and Boolean operations on $\mathscr{P}(S)$, the binary cross-operation $* : M \times B \to B$ which assigns to each $f \in M$ and $T \in \mathscr{P}(S)$ the *image* of T under f.

This example is closely related to the *homogeneous* algebra $V = [\mathscr{P}(S), F]$, where $F = \{\cap, \cup, ', M\}$ consists of Boolean operations and the "actions" of $f \in M$ on the $T \in \mathscr{P}(S)$. Note that U and V have very different subalgebra lattices. The least subalgebra of V consists of the field of sets generated (as a Boolean subalgebra of $[\mathscr{P}(S), \cap, \cup, ']$) by the set

$$\Gamma = \{T \in \mathscr{P}(S) \mid f(T) \subset T \quad \text{all} \quad f \in M\},$$

whereas U has many smaller subalgebras.

3. Morphisms

For similar algebras $A = [\{S_i\}, F]$ and $B = [\{T_i\}, F]$, we have the following

DEFINITION. A *morphism* Φ from A to B is a set of functions

$$\phi_i : S_i \to T_i, \tag{3}$$

one for each $i \in I$, such that for any $f_\alpha \in F$, $n = n(\alpha)$,

$$f_\alpha \circ (\phi_{i(1,\alpha)} \times \cdots \times \phi_{i(n,\alpha)}) = \phi_{r(\alpha)} \circ f_\alpha. \tag{4}$$

As usual, morphisms which are injective (ϕ_i injective for all i), surjective (ϕ_i surjective for all i), or bijective (ϕ_i bijective for all i), are called *mono*morphisms, *epi*morphisms, and *iso*morphisms, respectively.

Thus in Example 1, the above definition makes a morphism of vector spaces $[\{R^m, R\}, F] \to [\{S^m, S\}, F]$, R a field, mean what is usually called a *semilinear* transformation. Again, if $\mathbf{Z}$ and $\mathbf{Z}_n$ have their usual meanings (ring of integers and integers mod n), and we consider the modules $\mathbf{Z}^2$ and $\mathbf{Z}_n{}^2$ as heterogeneous algebras,

$$M = [\{\mathbf{Z} \times \mathbf{Z}, \mathbf{Z}\}, F], \qquad M_n = [\{\mathbf{Z}_n \times \mathbf{Z}_n, \mathbf{Z}_n\}, F],$$

as in Example 1, then the assignments

$$\phi_1 : (a, b) \to ([a]_n, [b]_n), \ \phi_2 : a \mapsto [a]_n$$

define an epimorphism of M onto M_n.

In order to obtain the usual definition of morphism of R-modules [10, p. 193], in which the domain and codomain modules are assumed to have the same ring R of scalars and $\phi_2 : R \to R$ to be the identity morphism on R, one must consider the modules as homogeneous algebras [1, p. 132]. This interpretation has the advantage that the sum of any two linear transformations is itself a linear transformation.

When applied to automata (Example 3), the above definition of morphism specializes to the following definition [8, p. 20]:

Let $M_1 = [\{S_1, A_1, Z_1\}, \{\nu_1, \zeta_1\}]$ and $M_2 = [\{S_2, A_2, Z_2\}, \{\nu_2, \zeta_2\}]$ be machines. Then the set of functions

$$\phi_i : S_1 \to S_2, \quad \phi_2 : A_1 \to A_2, \quad \phi_3 : Z_1 \to Z_2, \tag{5}$$

is a *morphism of machines* when

$$\nu_2(\phi_1(s), \phi_2(a)) = \phi_1(\nu_1(s, a)), \tag{6a}$$

$$\zeta_2(\phi_1(s), \phi_2(a)) = \phi_3(\zeta_1(s, a)) \tag{6b}$$

are identically satisfied.

As an illustration of a morphism of machines, consider the machines M_1 and M_2 specified by the state diagrams of Figure 3. It is readily checked that the mappings

$$\begin{array}{lll} \phi_1 : p \mapsto s & \phi_2 : a \mapsto x & \phi_3 : 1 \mapsto 0 \\ \quad\;\; q \mapsto t & \quad\;\; b \mapsto y & \quad\;\; 0 \mapsto 1 \\ \quad\;\; r \mapsto t & \quad\;\; c \mapsto y & \end{array}$$

constitute a morphism from machine M_1 to machine M_2.

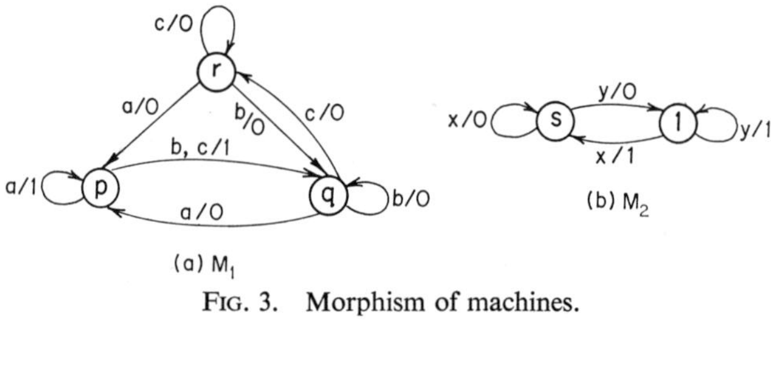

FIG. 3. Morphism of machines.

If $\Phi = \{\phi_i\}$ and $\Psi = \{\psi_i\}$ are morphisms of algebras $A \to B$ and $B \to C$, respectively, their *composite*, denoted $\Phi \circ \Psi$, is the set of mappings $\{\phi_i \circ \psi_i\}$.

PROPOSITION 4. *Any family of similar algebras forms a* concrete *category* [10, p. 64] *with respect to its morphisms.*

COROLLARY. *The endomorphisms of any algebra form a monoid.*

The preceding proposition relates our general algebraic approach to automata to that of Eilenberg and Wright [5]. However, their technical definitions [5, §12] are quite different from ours, being much more general. (Ours correspond much more closely to those usually used.)

It is easily verified that, if $\Phi = \{\phi_i : S_i \to T_i\}$ is an isomorphism from an algebra A to an algebra B, then $\Phi^{-1} = \{\phi_i^{-1} : T_i \to S_i\}$ is an isomorphism from B to A, and from the above corollary we conclude

PROPOSITION 5. *The automorphisms of any algebra A form a group* Aut A.

A generalization of [1, p. 135, Theorem 3] is stated in

PROPOSITION 6. *For any morphism $\Phi = \{\phi_i\} : A \to B$:*

(i) *if $A' = [\{S_i'\}, F]$ is a subalgebra of A then $\Phi(A') = [\{\phi_i(S_i')\}, F]$ is a subalgebra of B;*

(ii) *if $B' = [\{T_i'\}, F]$ is a subalgebra of B then $\Phi^{-1}(B') = [(\phi_i^{-1}(T_i')\}, F]$ is a subalgebra of A.*

PROPOSITION 7. *Let $\Phi = \{\phi_i\}$ be a morphism $A \to B$. If $\mathscr{I} = \{T_i\}$ is contained in $A = [\{S_i\}, F]$ (i.e., $T_i \subset S_i$ for all $i \in I$), then $\Phi(\bar{\mathscr{I}}) = \overline{\Phi(\mathscr{I})}$; in words, the image of the subalgebra of A generated by $\mathscr{I}$ is equal to the subalgebra of B generated by $\Phi(\mathscr{I}) = \{\phi_i(T_i)\}$.*

COROLLARY. *If $\Phi : A \to B$ is an epimorphism with $A = \bar{\mathscr{I}}$, then $B = \overline{\Phi(\mathscr{I})}$; i.e., B is generated by $\Phi(\mathscr{I}) = \{\phi_i(T_i)\}$.*

PROPOSITION 8. *Let $\Phi = \{\phi_i\}$ and $\Psi = \{\psi_i\}$ be morphisms $A \to B$, and suppose that $A = [\{S_i\}, F]$ is generated by $\mathscr{I} = \{T_i\}$; i.e., $A = \bar{\mathscr{I}}$. If $\phi_i(x) = \psi_i(x)$ for all $x \in T_i$ and all $i \in I$ then $\Phi = \Psi$ (i.e., $\phi_i = \psi_i$ for all $i \in I$).*

4. Congruences

A standard theorem on (homogeneous) algebras asserts that the epimorphic images of any algebra. A are all determined, up to isomorphism, by the congruence relations on A. We now generalize this theorem to heterogeneous algebras; since one equivalence relation on each phylum is involved in the generalization, we replace the phrase "congruence relation" by the single word congruence.

Definition. A *congruence* on an algebra $A = [\{S_i\}, F]$ is a family $\mathscr{E} = \{E_i\}$ of equivalence relations, with E_i defined on S_i for each $i \in I$, which for each $f_\alpha \in F$ and $x_j, y_j \in S_{i(j,\alpha)}$ has the following *substitution property:*

$$x_j E_{i(j,\alpha)} y_j \quad (j = 1, 2, \ldots, n(\alpha)) \quad \text{implies}$$

$$f_\alpha(x_1, \ldots, x_{n(\alpha)}) \, E_{r(\alpha)} \, f_\alpha(y_1, \ldots, y_{n(\alpha)}) \tag{7}$$

Proposition 9. *Let $\mathscr{E} = \{E_i\}$ be a congruence on an algebra $A = [\{S_i\}, F]$ and let $x \mapsto P_{E_i}(x)$ be the mapping which carries each $x \in S_i$ into its equivalence class in S_i/E_i. Then the operations f_α on $\{S_i/E_i\}$ given by, for $n = n(\alpha)$,*

$$f_\alpha(P_{E_{i(1,\alpha)}}(x_1), \ldots, P_{E_{i(n,\alpha)}}(x_n)) = P_{E_{r(\alpha)}}(f_\alpha(x_1, \ldots, x_n)) \tag{8}$$

define an algebra $B = [\{S_i/E_i\}, F]$ which is an epimorphic image of A under $\Phi = \{P_{E_i}\}$.

Proof: By the substitution property of the E_i, the operations f_α defined by (8) are single-valued. Also by (8), $\Phi = \{P_{E_i}\}$ is a morphism from A to B; moreover, each ϕ_i is clearly surjective so that Φ is an epimorphism.

The algebra B in the statement of Proposition 9 is called the *quotient algebra* of A relative to the congruence $\mathscr{E}$, and is denoted $A/\mathscr{E}$.

A converse to Proposition 9 is provided by

Proposition 10. *Let $\Phi = \{\phi_i\}$ be an epimorphism $A \to B$. Then a congruence $\mathscr{E} = \{E_i\}$ can be defined in A such that B is isomorphic to $A/\mathscr{E}$.*

As in [9, p.120], we have the following heterogeneous analog of Theorem 6 of [1, p. 137].

Proposition 11 (Morphism Theorem for Heterogeneous Algebras). *The epimorphic images of any algebra A are determined up to isomorphism by the quotient algebras $A/\mathscr{E}$ defined by the congruences $\mathscr{E}$ on A.*

The congruences $\mathscr{E} = \{E_i\}$ on an algebra $A = [\{S_i\}, F]$ are *partially ordered* as follows: for congruences $\mathscr{E} = \{E_i\}$, $\mathscr{F} = \{F_i\}$

$$\mathscr{E} \leqslant \mathscr{F} \text{ when } xE_i\, y \text{ implies } xF_i\, y \text{ for all } i \in I. \tag{9}$$

This poset has universal bounds $\mathscr{L} = \{L_i\}$, $\mathscr{U} = \{U_i\}$ defined by:

$$\left.\begin{aligned} &xL_i\, y, \quad \text{if and only if} \quad x = y, && (10a)\\ &xU_i\, y, \quad \text{for all} \quad x, y \in S_i, && (10b)\end{aligned}\right\} \text{ for all } \; i \in I.$$

As in [9, p. 121], sharpened by the argument of [1, Ch. 6, Theorem 8], we have also

PROPOSITION 12. *The poset $H(A)$ of all congruences on an algebra $A = [\{S_i\}, F]$ forms a complete lattice, which is lattice-monomorphic to the product $\Pi = \Pi(S_1) \times \Pi(S_2) \times \cdots \times \Pi(S_I)$ of the partition lattices $\Pi(S_i)$.*

PROPOSITION 13. *Let $B = A/\mathscr{E}$ be any epimorphic image of the algebra $A = [\{S_i\}, F]$. Then the congruences on B are the partitions of the phyla of B defined by the congruences $\mathscr{F} \geqslant \mathscr{E}$ on A.*

Proposition 13 also has the following immediate corollary.

COROLLARY. *Let $\mathscr{E} = \{E_i\}$ and $\mathscr{F} = \{F_i\}$ be congruences on an algebra $A = [\{S_i\}, F]$ with $\mathscr{E} \leqslant \mathscr{F}$. Then $A/\mathscr{F}$ is an epimorphic image of $A/\mathscr{E}$.*

5. DIRECT PRODUCTS AND POWERS OF ALGEBRAS

Let $A = [\{S_i\}, F]$ and $B = [\{T_i\}, F]$ be any two similar heterogeneous algebras. Then the *direct product* $A \times B$ of A and B is the algebra $[\{S_i \times T_i\}, F], f_\alpha$ defined for $n = n(\alpha)$ by:

$$\begin{aligned} &f_\alpha((x_{i(1,\alpha)}, y_{i(1,\alpha)}), \ldots, (x_{i(n,\alpha)}, y_{i(n,\alpha)}))\\ &\qquad = (f_\alpha(x_{i(1,\alpha)}, \ldots, x_{i(n,\alpha)}), f_\alpha(y_{i(1,\alpha)}, \ldots, y_{i(n,\alpha)})). \end{aligned} \tag{11}$$

Thus, in Example 1 of Section 1, the direct product of two modules $M_1 = [\{V_1, R_1\}, F]$ and $M_2 = [\{V_2, R_2\}, F]$, regarded as heterogeneous algebras, is $M_1 \times M_2 = [\{V_1 \times V_2, R_1 \times R_2\}, F]$ with the scalar multiplication in $M_1 \times M_2$ defined by $(\lambda_1, \lambda_2)(v_1, v_2) = (\lambda_1 v_1, \lambda_2 v_2)$.

Note that when $R = R'$ the direct product of modules as defined above does *not* agree with the (standard) definition of the direct sum of two R-modules as *homogeneous* algebras [10, p. 209]; in the latter case scalar multiplication is defined only when $\lambda_1 = \lambda_2$.

In Example 3 of Section 1, the direct product of machines $M_1 = [\{S_1, A_1, Z_1\}, \{\nu_1, \zeta_1\}]$ and $M_2 = [\{S_2, A_2, Z_2\}, \{\nu_2, \zeta_2\}$, regarded as heterogeneous algebras, is the machine $M_1 \times M_2 = [\{S_1 \times S_2, A_1 \times A_2, Z_1 \times Z_2\}, \{\nu, \zeta\}]$, whose next-state function ν and output function ζ are defined by:

$$\nu((s_1, s_2), (a_1, a_2)) = (\nu_1(s_1, a_1), \nu_2(s_2, a_2)), \tag{12a}$$

$$\zeta((s_1, s_2), (a_1, a_2)) = (\zeta_1(s_1, a_1), \zeta_2(s_2, a_2)). \tag{12b}$$

As usual, the corresponding definition for the direct product of state machines is obtained from the above by forgetting about outputs (Z, ζ, and (12b)).

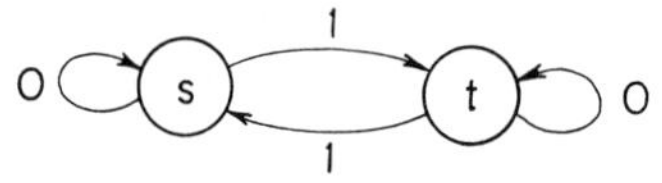

FIG. 4(a). State Machine M

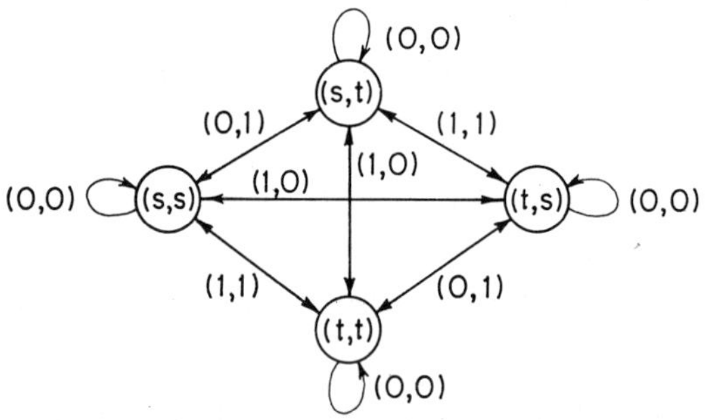

FIG. 4(b). *Heterogeneous* Direct Product $M \times M$

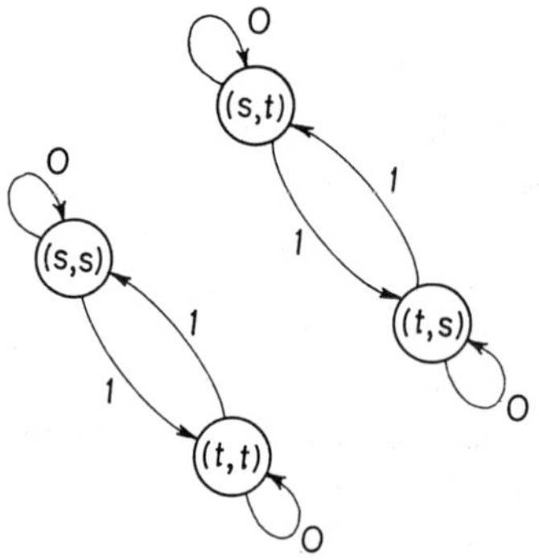

FIG. 4(c). *Homogeneous* Direct Product $M \times M$

A more restrictive definition of direct product for machines is obtained when they are considered as *homogeneous* algebras; this is the definition of Rabin and Scott [11, p. 74]; it is defined only for "similar" machines having fixed alphabets A, Z. Moreover, even in this case, the definitions are not equivalent.

Thus, let M have $A = Z = \{0, 1\}$. If M is considered as a *heterogeneous* algebra, the alphabet of $M \times \cdots \times M = M^r$ consists of all r-bit words. If, on the other hand, M is considered as a homogeneous algebra, the alphabet of M^r still consists of just 0 and 1.

The diagrams of Figure 4 will illustrate the distinction (for the case $r = 2$).

We now generalize the definition of direct product given above.

Let Γ be the index set of a family of similar algebras $A_\gamma = [\{S_{i,\gamma}\}, F]$, and define the (unrestricted) *direct product* $\prod_\Gamma A_\gamma$ as the algebra $[\{\mathfrak{A}_i\}, F]$ where each $\mathfrak{A}_i$ $(i \in I)$ is the set of all functions $a_i : \gamma \to a_i(\gamma) \in S_{i,\gamma}$ with

$$f_\alpha(a_{i(1,\alpha)}, \ldots, a_{i(n,\alpha)}) = a_{r(\alpha)} \in A_{r(\alpha)} ,$$

where

$$a_{r(\alpha)} : \gamma \mapsto f_\alpha(a_{i(1,\alpha)}(\gamma), \ldots, a_{i(n,\alpha)}(\gamma)). \tag{13}$$

As usual, the direct product $\prod_\Gamma A_\gamma$ is independent of the order and order of combination of the factors.

A special case of interest arises when $A_\gamma = A$ for all $\gamma \in \Gamma$. In this case we denote $\prod_\Gamma A_\gamma$ by A^Γ and refer to it as the Γ-th (direct) *power* of A.

Consider again the direct product $\prod_\Gamma A_\gamma = [\{\mathfrak{A}_i\}, F]$ of the algebras $A_\gamma = [\{S_{i,\gamma}\}, F]$. For any $\delta \in \Gamma$ we define the *projection* P_δ as the set of mappings $\{p_{i,\delta}\} (i \in I)$

$$p_{i,\delta} : \mathfrak{A}_i \to S_{i,\delta} : a_i \mapsto a_i(\delta). \tag{14}$$

As in [9, p. 120], where more is stated, we have

PROPOSITION 14. *For any direct product of heterogeneous algebras, P_δ is an epimorphism $\prod_\Gamma A_\gamma \to A_\delta$.*

6. Word Algebras

In this section and the next, the concepts of *word algebra* and *free algebra* will be extended from homogeneous to heterogeneous algebras.

Consider the species of all algebras $A = [\{S_i\}, F]$ having a given set $F = \{f_\alpha\}$ of operations, with index-set I of phyla. For any given family of non-void generator sets $X_i = (x_1{}^i, x_2{}^i, \ldots, x^i_{m_i}\}$, one for each $i \in I$, one can construct a (free) *word algebra* $W_{\mathscr{X}}(F)$, where the symbol $\mathscr{X}$ stands for the set of indexed sets X_i. If **m** stands for the "vector" of non-zero cardinal numbers $m_i = | X_i |$, then $W_{\mathscr{X}}(F)$, is determined up to isomorphism by **m**; hence we can write $W_{\mathbf{m}}(F)$ for the isomorphism-type of the $W_{\mathscr{X}}(F)$ with given **m**.

The construction of the word algebra $W_{\mathbf{m}}(F)$ is as follows [1, p. 141]: Define $W_0(i) = X_i$, and, recursively, $W_\rho(i) = \sqcup_{\alpha \in A_i} f_\alpha(u_1, u_2, \ldots, u_{n(\alpha)})$, where:

(i) A_i is the set of $f_\alpha \in F$ with values in the i-th phylum,

(ii) all $u_j = p_j(x_1{}^1, \ldots, x^1_{m_1}, \ldots, x_1{}^i, \ldots, x^i_{m_i}, \ldots)$ are in $\sqcup_{k<\rho} W_k(i(j, \alpha))$,

and

(iii) some $u_j \in W_{\rho-1}(i(j, \alpha))$.

Then $\sqcup_{\rho \in N} W_\rho(i) = W_i$, and $W_{\mathbf{m}}(F)$ is the algebra $[\{W_i\}, F]$.

The elements of W_i are called W_i-polynomials (words), those of $W_\rho(i)$ are called W_i-polynomials *of rank* ρ. Equality in $W_{\mathbf{m}}(F)$ means formal identity: $x_j{}^i = x_k{}^l$ means $j = k$, $i = l$, and $f_\alpha(u_1, \ldots, u_{n(\alpha)}) = f_\beta(v_1, \ldots, v_{n(\beta)})$ means that $\alpha = \beta$ and $u_k = v_k$ for all $k = 1, 2, \ldots, n(\alpha) = n(\beta)$.

By construction, the sets X_i $(i \in I)$ constitute a generating family of sets for $W_{\mathbf{m}}(F) \cong W_{\mathscr{X}}(F)$, where $\mathscr{X} = \{X_i\}$ and $m_i = | X_i |$.

EXAMPLE 6. We apply the above construction to the species $\mathscr{M}$ of state machines $\mathscr{M} = [\{S_1 = S, S_2 = A\}, \{\nu\}]$ of Example 4 of Section 1, and construct the (free) *word machine* generated by set of states $X_1 = \{s, t\}$ and set of input letters $X_2 = \{x, y, z\}$. In this example $\mathbf{m} = (2, 3)$, and we denote the word machine by $W_{\mathbf{m}}(\mathscr{M})$.

The states of this machine are the set of W_1-polynomials s, t, $\nu(s, x)$, $\nu(s, y)$, $\nu(s, z)$, $\nu(\nu(s, x), x)$, $\nu(\nu(s, x), y)$, etc.

NOTATION. For convenience we denote $\nu(\nu(\cdots(\nu(s, x_1), x_2), \ldots), x_n)$ in abbreviated form by $s \cdot x_1 x_2 \cdots x_n$.

Returning to Example 6, we can now give an explicit description of the states W_1 of $W_{\mathbf{m}}(\mathscr{M})$, namely,

$$W_1 = \{u\alpha \mid u \in X_1, \alpha \in X_2{}^*\},$$

where $X_2{}^*$ is the free monoid generated by $X_2 = \{x, y, z\}$ under concatenation. We define $u \cdot e$, where e is the identity element of $X_2{}^*$ (or "empty tape"), by $u \cdot e = u$. The input symbols of $W_{\mathbf{m}}(\mathscr{M})$ are the W_2-polynomials, namely, x, y, and z.

Note that for any (non-void) X_1 and X_2, W_1 is *never finite*, so that $W_m(\mathcal{M})$ is *never* a *finite* state machine.

PROPOSITION 15. *Let* $A = [\{S_i\}, F]$ *be an arbitrary F-algebra, and* $W_{\mathscr{X}}(F) = [\{W_i\}, F]$ *the word algebra generated by* $\mathscr{X} = \{X_i\}$. *Then any family* $\Phi = \{\varphi_i\}$ *of mappings* $\varphi_i : X_i \rightarrow S_i$ $(i \in I)$ *extends uniquely to a morphism* $\bar{\Phi} : W_{\mathscr{X}}(F) \rightarrow A$.

IDEA OF PROOF: Intuitively speaking, $\bar{\Phi}$ is the family of valuation maps which carries each W_i-polynomial

$$p(x_1{}^1,..., x^1_{m_1},..., x_i{}^i,..., x^i_{m_i},...)$$

into what one gets by replacing the (free) generators $x_j{}^k$ by their values $\phi_k(x_j{}^k) \in S_k$. This results in an element

$$p(\phi_1(x_1{}^1),..., \phi_1(x^1_{m_1}),..., \phi_i(x_1{}^i),..., \phi_i(x^i_{m_i}),...) \qquad (15)$$

of the phylum S_i.

As in [9, p. 122], we also have

PROPOSITION 16. *Any F-algebra* $A = [\{S_i\}, F]$ *generated by* $\mathscr{X} = \{X_i\}$ *is an epimorphic image of the word algebra* $W_{\mathscr{X}}(F)$.

PROOF: By Proposition 15, there is a morphism Φ: $W_{\mathscr{X}}(F) \rightarrow A$ with $\varphi_i(x_j{}^i) = x_j{}^i$ for all $x_j{}^i \in X_i$ and $i \in I$. Its image $\Phi(W_{\mathscr{X}}(F))$ is a subalgebra which contains all X_i and hence A (since $\mathscr{X}$ generates A). Therefore Φ is onto, completing the proof.

7. FREE ALGEBRAS

We now define and construct free *heterogeneous algebras*, proving an existence and uniqueness theorem which generalizes the results of [1, Ch. 6, §7], from homogeneous to general heterogeneous algebras. This generalizes a result of Higgins [9, §5], who considered the special case that Γ was a variety, so that $F_{\mathscr{X}}(\Gamma) \in \Gamma$. In this special case, condition F3 below is redundant, but it is needed to ensure uniqueness in our more general case. See also Grätzer [14].

Let Γ be a class of similar algebras $A = (\{S_i\}, F]$, and let $\mathscr{X} = \{X_i\}$ be a family of sets, each X_i having non-zero cardinality m_i. We then have the following

DEFINITION. An algebra $C = [\{U_i\}, F]$ is said to be the *free* Γ-algebra generated by $\mathscr{X}$, and denoted $C_{\mathscr{X}}(\Gamma)$, when

F1. C is generated by $\mathscr{X}$.

F2. For any algebra $A \in \Gamma$ and set of mappings $\phi_i : X_i \to S_i$ $(i \in I)$, each ϕ_i extends (uniquely) to a mapping $\bar{\phi}_i : U_i \to S_i$ such that $\bar{\Phi} = \{\bar{\phi}_i\}$ is a morphism $C \to A$.

F3. C is *minimal* subject to F1 and F2 in the following sense: if B is any other algebra satisfying F1 and F2, then C is an epimorphic image of B.

REMARK. Since $\mathscr{X}$ generates $C_{\mathscr{X}}(\Gamma)$, the extension $\bar{\Phi}$ postulated in F2 is unique by Proposition 8.

Note that the word algebra $W_{\mathscr{X}}(F)$ always satisfies F1 and F2; F3 is needed to eliminate this and other algebras that are "too large" and fail to satisfy the identities holding in all algebras of Γ. We now show how to construct $C_{\mathbf{m}}(\Gamma)$, beginning with the special case that $\Gamma = \{A\}$ is a single algebra.

We first fix generator sets $X_i = \{x_j^i\}$ of cardinalities $m_i = |X_i|$, and let $\mathscr{X} = \{X_i\}$. We then construct $C_{\mathbf{m}}(A)$, we consider the set Ψ of all phylum-preserving assignments $\Phi : x_j^i \mapsto a_j^i \in S_i$. We can think of Φ as having as "components" arbitrary mappings $\varphi_i : X_i \to S_i$, one for each phylum $i \in I$; this suggests writing $\Phi : \mathscr{X} \to S$. Let $A^{|\Psi|}$ be the direct product ($|\Psi|$-th power of A) of $|\Psi|$ copies of A, and let $\mu : \mathscr{X} \to A^{|\Psi|}$ map each $x_j^i \in X_i$ into the element $\mathbf{a}_j^i \in A^{|\Psi|}$ whose Φ-component is $a_j^i = \varphi_i(x_j^i)$; let $\mathfrak{A} = \{\mathbf{a}_j^i\}$

PROPOSITION 17. *The subalgebra* $\bar{\mathfrak{A}} = [\bar{X}_i, F]$ *of* $A^{|\Psi|}$ *generated by the* $\mathbf{a}_j^i$ *above is the free A-algebra* $C_{\mathbf{m}}(A)$ *with* m_i *generators in the i-th phylum.*

PROOF: By construction, F1 holds. Moreover the proof of F2 is only a little more difficult; the morphism desired is obtained by fixing attention on the appropriate Φ-component of $C_{\mathbf{m}}(A)$. Finally, if B is any other F-algebra which satisfies F1 and F2 for $\Gamma = \{A\}$, then the $|\Psi|$ morphisms $\bar{\Phi} : B \to A$ whose existence is asserted in F1 and F2 define an epimorphism $\bar{\Psi} : B \to C_{\mathbf{m}}(A)$ as constructed above.

REMARK. The fact that $\mathbf{m}$ determined $C_{\mathbf{m}}(A)$ up to isomorphism was evident above. We now show that it follows abstractly from conditions F1-F3. Indeed, let C and $\tilde{C}$ be free F-algebras generated by $\mathscr{X}$ and $\tilde{\mathscr{X}}$ whose corresponding phyla X_i and $\tilde{X}_i$ are bijective for bijections β_i (have the same cardinality, so that $\mathbf{m} = \tilde{\mathbf{m}}$), then the extension of $\{\beta_i\}$ will be an isomorphism $\beta : C \to \tilde{C}$. Thus we may also refer the isomorphism-type of $C_{\mathscr{X}}(\Gamma)$ as *the free* Γ-algebra with m_i generators in its i-th phylum, and denote it by $C_{\mathbf{m}}(\Gamma)$, where $\mathbf{m}$ is the "vector" whose i-th component is the non-zero cardinal number m_i.

By Proposition 16, $\bar{\mathscr{X}}$ is an epimorphism image of the word algebra $W_{\mathscr{X}}(F) = [\{W_i\}, F]$, whence by Proposition 11 $\bar{\mathscr{X}} = W_{\mathscr{X}}(F)/\mathscr{E}$ for some congruence $\mathscr{E}$ of W_i-polynomials defined in Section 6

$$p(x_1{}^1, \ldots, x_{m_i}^1, \ldots, x_1{}^i, \ldots, x_{m_i}^i, \ldots),$$

where the $x_j{}^i \in X_i$ $(j = 1, 2, \ldots, m_i)$ freely generate the i-th phylum. For polynomials p_1, $p_2 \in W_{\mathscr{X}}(F)$, we see from definition of $\bar{\mathscr{X}}$ that p_1 and p_2 are *equal as functions* $\prod_I S_i^{m_i} \to S_i$; i.e., whenever p_1 and p_2 have the same value for *every* family of valuations $\Phi = \{\phi_i : X_i \to S_i\}$ of the generators $x_j{}^i \in X_i$ to the $a_j{}^i \in S_i$. By definition, these equivalences $p_1 \equiv p_2 \pmod{\mathscr{E}}$ are *precisely the identities valid in* A.

Proposition 17 represents $C_{\mathbf{m}}(A)$ as a subalgebra of a power (product of copies) of A, one for each set of valuations $\Phi = \{\phi_i\}$. We thus have the following

Corollary. *If* $A = [\{S_i\}, F]$ *is a* "finite" *algebra (i.e.,* A *has a* "finite" *number of phyla* S_i *each of which is of* "finite" *order* $|S_i|$) *and* $\mathbf{m} = (m_i)$ *is a finite vector of* $m_i \in P$, *then the free* A*-algebra* $C_{\mathbf{m}}(A)$ *is a (finite) subalgebra of the* "finite" *algebra* $A^{[\prod_I |S_i|^{m_i}]}$.

We shall now generalize Proposition 17 to any set Γ of F-algebras $A_\gamma = A(\gamma)$. We first fix generator sets $X_i = \{x_j{}^i\}$ of cardinalities $m_i = |X_i|$, and let $\mathscr{X} = \{X_i\}$ as before. Proposition 17 associates with $\mathscr{X}$ and each $A(\gamma) \in \Gamma$ a free algebra $C_\gamma = C_{\mathscr{X}}(A(\gamma))$ with generator sets X_i, and a monomorphism, $\bar{\Phi}_\gamma$ from C_γ to a power (product of copies) of $A(\gamma)$. We now let γ range over Γ; the result is a mapping Φ from $\mathscr{X}$ to $\prod_\Gamma A(\gamma)^{\mathbf{m}}$. Let $\mathscr{T} = \{T_i\}$ be the *F-subalgebra* generated by $\Phi(\mathscr{X})$ in this product of copies of the $A(\gamma)$; we shall call this $C_{\mathscr{X}}(\Gamma)$, and designate its isomorphism-type by $C_{\mathbf{m}}(\Gamma)$. We then have

Proposition 18. *Let there be given a set* Γ *of F-algebras* $A(\gamma)$, *and indexed generator sets* X_i *of cardinalities* m_i $(i \in \Gamma)$, *one for each phylum. Then there exists an F algebra* $C_{\mathbf{m}}(\Gamma)$ *which satisfies conditions* F1-F3; *it is a subalgebra of products of copies of the* $A(\gamma) \in \Gamma$.

We now ask: given a class Γ of similar algebras, when will the free algebra $C_{\mathbf{m}}(\Gamma)$ be a member of Γ? Proposition 18 establishes $C_{\mathbf{m}}(\Gamma)$ as a subalgebra of a direct product of powers of the $A(\gamma) \in \Gamma$, as in [9, p. 124],

Corollary 1. *A sufficient condition for* $C_{\mathbf{m}}(\Gamma) \in \Gamma$ *is that* Γ *be closed under the taking of subalgebras and direct products.*

Corollary 2. *The identities valid in $C_{\mathbf{m}}(\Gamma)$ are precisely the identities in m_i or fewer symbols for elements from the i-th phylum which are valid in all $A_\gamma \in \Gamma$.*

In the more general context of $\sum$-algebras, Grätzer [14] has proved a much stronger result: if J is any set of identities meaningful for the operations of F, then among all F-algebras satisfying all identities of J and having m_i or fewer generators of the i-th phylum, $C_{\mathbf{m}}(\Gamma)$ is one of which all other are subalgebras of epimorphic images.

8. Free Machines

In this section we use Proposition 17 to construct the *free* (state) *machine* $F_{\mathscr{X}}(M)$ generated by one state letter s, and two input letters x and y (i.e., $\mathscr{X} = \{X_1, X_2\}$ where $X_1 = \{s\}$, and $X_2 = \{x, y\}$), where $M = [\{S, A\}, \{\nu\}]$ is the state machine specified by the state diagram of Figure 5.

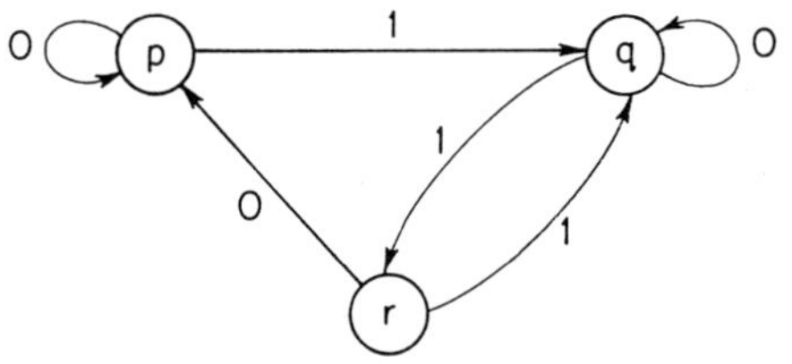

Fig. 5. Another state machine.

By Proposition 17, $F_{\mathscr{X}}(M)$ is a subalgebra of $M^{M^{\mathbf{m}}}$, where the vector $\mathbf{m} = (1, 2)$ for our example. Thus $F_{\mathscr{X}}(M)$ is a subalgebra of the dirct power M^{12}.

We now determine the state and input phyla of $F_{\mathscr{X}}(M)$ by computing a *truth-table* (Table I) which displays the values in M of the polynomials of the word machine generated by $\mathscr{X}$ (Example 6) for all possible assignments (valuations) Φ of the free input symbols x and y to the input symbols $\{0, 1\}$ of M and the free state symbol s to the states $\{p, q, r\}$ of M.

From Table I we see that $F_{\mathscr{X}}(M)$ has 9 states, which we can conveniently designate by s, $s.\,x$, $s.\,y$, $s.\,xx$, $s.\,xy$, $s.\,yx$, $s.\,yy$, $s.\,xyx$, $s.\,xyy$; and two input letters x and y. The state diagram for $F_{\mathscr{X}}(M)$ is given in Figure 6.

From either the truth-table of the state diagram of $F_{\mathscr{X}}(M)$, we can ascertain by inspection all *identities* holding in the given machine M. One such identity is

$$s.\,xxx = s.\,x;$$

TABLE I

TRUTH-TABLE FOR $F_{\mathscr{X}}(M)$

Valuations s	p				q				r			
(x, y)	00	01	10	11	00	01	10	11	00	01	10	11
State Polynomials												
s	p	p	p	p	q	q	q	q	r	r	r	r
$s.x$	p	p	q	q	q	q	r	r	p	p	q	q
$s.y$	p	q	p	q	q	r	q	r	p	q	p	q
$s.xx$	p	p	r	r	q	q	q	q	p	p	r	r
$s.xy$	p	q	q	r	q	r	p	q	p	q	q	r
$s.yx$	p	q	q	r	q	p	r	q	p	q	q	r
$s.yy$	p	r	p	r	q	q	q	q	p	r	p	r
$s.xxx = s.x$	p	p	q	q	q	q	r	r	p	p	q	q
$s.xxy = s.y$	p	q	p	q	q	r	q	r	p	q	p	q
$s.xyx$	p	q	r	r	q	p	q	q	p	q	r	r
$s.xyy$	p	r	q	q	q	q	p	r	p	r	q	q
$s.yxx = s.xyy$	p	r	q	q	q	q	p	r	p	r	q	q
$s.yxy = s.xyy$	p	r	q	q	q	q	p	r	p	r	q	q
$s.yyx = s.x$	p	p	q	q	q	q	r	r	p	p	q	q
$s.yyy = s.y$	p	q	p	q	q	r	q	r	p	q	p	q
$s.xyxx = s.yx$	p	q	q	r	q	p	r	q	p	q	q	r
$s.xyxy = s.yy$	p	r	p	r	q	q	q	q	p	r	p	r
$s.xyyx = s.xx$	p	p	r	r	q	q	q	q	p	p	r	r
$s.xyyy = s.xy$	p	q	q	r	q	r	p	q	p	q	q	r
Input Polynomials												
x	0	0	1	1	0	0	1	1	0	0	1	1
y	0	1	0	1	0	1	0	1	0	1	0	1

this identity states that, no matter what state the machine M is in initially, the application of a tape consisting of 3 repetitions of either one of the input symbols 0, 1 results in the same final state as applying a tape consisting of a single occurrence of that same symbol.

As another example, consider the identity

$$s.\,yyx = s.\,x,$$

which holds in M (and hence in $F_{\mathscr{X}}(M)$). This identity states that, for any initial state, the processing of a tape consisting of any input symbol repeated twice followed by any other input symbol (perhaps the same one) results in the same final output symbol.

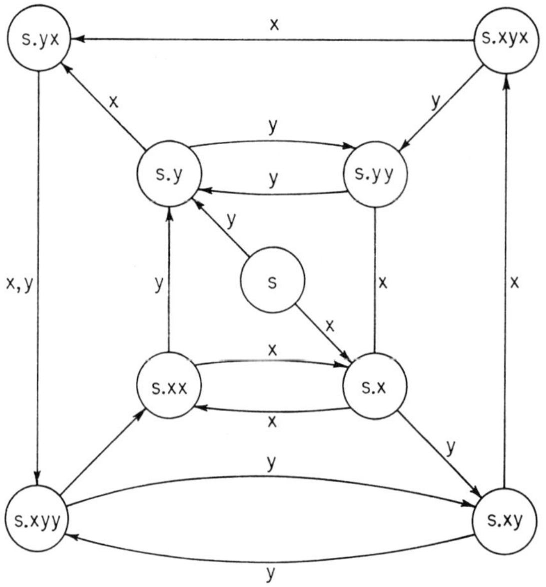

FIG. 6. State diagram of $F_{\mathfrak{X}}(M)$.

In discussing Example 6, we observed that the word machine is never a *finite* state machine. For the case of free machines the situation is quite different. Specifically, from the representation of the free algebra $F_{\mathbf{m}}(\Gamma)$ provided by Proposition 17, we have the following

PROPOSITION 19. *Let Γ be a finite set of finite state machines $M(\gamma) = [\{S(\gamma), A(\gamma)\}, \{\nu, \zeta\}]$. Then the free machine $F_{\mathbf{m}}(\Gamma)$ with m generators of the state phylum, and m' generators of the input phylum (m, m' finite) is a (finite) submachine of the finite state machine*

$$\prod_{\Gamma} A(\gamma)^{|S(\gamma)|^m |A(\gamma)|^{m'}}.$$

REFERENCES

1. G. BIRKHOFF, "Lattice Theory", 3rd ed., American Mathematical Society, Providence, R. I., 1967.
2. G. BIRKHOFF, On the Structure of Abstract Algebras, *Proc. Cambridge Philos. Soc.* **31** (1935), 433–54.
3. G. BIRKHOFF, Universal Algebra, *Proc. First Canad. Math. Congr.* (1945), 310–26.
4. P. M. COHN, "Universal Algebra", Harper & Row, New York, 1965.
5. S. EILENBERG AND J. B. WRIGHT, Automata in General Algebras, *Information and Control* **11** (1967), 452–70.

6. A. Ginzburg, *Algebraic Theory of Automata*, Academic Press, New York, 1968.
7. G. Grätzer, *Universal Algebra*, Van Nostrand Reinhold, New York, 1969.
8. J. Hartmanis and R. E. Stearns, *Algebraic Structure Theory of Sequential Machines*, Prentice-Hall, Englewood Cliffs, N. J., 1966.
9. P. J. Higgins, Algebras with a Scheme of Operators, *Math. Nachr.* **27** (1963), 115–32.
10. G. Birkhoff and S. MacLane, *A Survey of Modern Algebra*, 3rd ed., Macmillan, New York, 1965.
11. E. F. Moore (ed.), *Sequential Machines: Selected Papers*, Addison-Wesley, Reading, Mass., 1964.
12. M. A. Arbib (ed.), *The Algebraic Theory of Machines, Languages, and Semigroups, Academic Press*, New York, 1968.
13. E. R. Caianiello, (ed.), *Automata Theory*, Academic Press, New York, 1966.
14. G. Grätzer, *Trans. Amer. Math. Soc.* **135** (1969), 517–42.

PRINTED IN BRUGES, BELGIUM, BY THE ST. CATHERINE PRESS, LDT.

UNIVERSAL ALGEBRA AND AUTOMATA

GARRETT BIRKHOFF AND JOHN D. LIPSON

1. Introduction. In a previous paper [**4**], we showed that the basic theorems of "universal algebra," as developed for *homogeneous* algebras in [**1**] and [**5**], applied more generally to a class of *heterogeneous* algebras which includes group representations, vector spaces as usually defined in elementary textbooks, and (sequential) machines. The present note applies this theory to machines *with outputs* (as opposed to *state machines*, where outputs are simply ignored). We show that the standard mathematical machine theory [3, Chapter 3] concerning "covering," "equivalence," and "reduced machine" also belongs to universal algebra. Another application of the theory of free *heterogeneous* algebras [**4**, §7] is given in constructing a *free machine* with outputs.

For convenience of reference we give some definitions and examples, taken in large part from [**4**].

A *heterogeneous algebra* is a system $A = [\mathcal{S}, F]$, where $\mathcal{S} = \{S_i\}$ is a family of nonvoid sets S_i $(i \in I)$, the "phyla" of the algebra A; and $F = \{f_\alpha\}$ is a family of finitary operations, where each f_α $(\alpha \in \Omega)$ is a mapping

$$f_\alpha\colon S_{i(1,\alpha)} \times S_{i(2,\alpha)} \times \cdots \times S_{i(n(\alpha),\alpha)} \to S_{r(\alpha)} \tag{1.1}$$

for some nonnegative integer $n(\alpha)$, "value-index" $r(\alpha) \in I$, and function $i_\alpha\colon k \mapsto i(k, \alpha)$ from $\{1, 2, \ldots, n(\alpha)\}$ to I.

Most discussions of universal algebra (e.g., those in [**1**] and [**5**]) assume a single phylum. As in [**4**], here we shall call algebras with just one phylum *homogeneous*.

EXAMPLE 1. A *vector space* is a heterogeneous algebra $[\{A, \Lambda\}, \{+, -, 0, \oplus, \ominus, 0, \times, ^{-1}, 1, \cdot\}]$ with two phyla: vectors and scalars. Here $[A, \{+, -, 0\}]$ is an additive group, $[\Lambda, \{\oplus, \ominus, 0, \times, ^{-1}, 1\}]$ is a field (the field of scalars), and $\cdot : \Lambda \times A \to A$ is scalar multiplication.

EXAMPLE 2. A *group representation* is a heterogeneous algebra $[\{G, A, \Lambda\}, \{\circ, ^{-1}, +, -, \text{etc.}\}]$ with three phyla: the group elements $g, h, \ldots$, vectors, and scalars. The operations are group composition $\circ$ and inverse formation $^{-1}$; the vector space operations for $\{A, \Lambda\}$ of Example 1; and group action $\gamma(g, \mathbf{x}) = g(\mathbf{x}) \in A$ is the effect of $g \in G$ acting on the element $\mathbf{x} \in A$.

For us the most interesting (and relevant) class of heterogeneous algebras is provided by *automata* or *sequential machines*. In this paper, we shall treat *Moore* machines defined as follows.

EXAMPLE 3. A (sequential) *machine* or *automaton* is a heterogeneous algebra $M = [\{S, A, Z\}, \{\nu, \zeta\}]$ with three phyla: a set S of "states," a set A of input symbols (the "input alphabet"), and a set Z of output symbols (the "output alphabet"). There are two operations

(1.2) $\nu: S \times A \to S$ ("change of state"),

(1.2′) $\zeta: S \to Z$ ("output").

The *Mealy* machines treated in [3, Chapter 3], in which ζ is assumed to be a mapping $S \times A \to Z$, can be equally well treated as heterogeneous algebras. Indeed, from any Mealy machine $[\{S, A, Z\}, \{\nu, \zeta\}]$ we can construct an equivalent Moore machine $[\{T, A, Z\}, \{\tilde{\nu}, \tilde{\zeta}\}]$ by setting $T = S \times A, \tilde{\nu}(t, b) = \tilde{\nu}((s, a), b) = \nu(s, b)$ and $\tilde{\zeta}(t) = \zeta(s, a)$ for any $t = (s, a) \in T = S \times A$ and $b \in A$.

A *state machine* or *semi-automaton* is obtained from the above by "forgetting" about the output symbols Z and output function ζ. Thus, a state machine is a *heterogeneous* algebra $M = [\{S, A\}, \{\nu\}]$. Alternatively, a state machine can be defined as a *homogeneous* algebra $M = [\{S\}, \{\nu_a, \nu_b, \ldots\}]$, where for each $a \in A$, ν_a is a unary operation $S \to S$. In this case the input alphabet plays the role of an "underlying" structure, analogous to vector space theory where one fixes the underlying field of scalars. The difference between the homogeneous and heterogeneous definitions of automata has basic algebraic implications, as was illustrated in [2, §10] with special reference to *free* algebras.

Turning to the basic definitions from the theory of heterogeneous algebras, a *subalgebra* $B = [\{T_i\}, F]$ of an algebra $A = [\{S_i\}, F]$ is a collection of subsets $T_i \subset S_i$ $(i \in I)$ closed under the operations of F. If $\tau = \{T_i\}$ is contained in A, i.e., $T_i \subset S_i$ for all $i \in I$, then we denote by $\bar{\tau} = [\{\bar{T}_i\}, F]$ the intersection of all subalgebras of A containing τ. Much as in the homogeneous case, $\bar{\tau}$ is called the subalgebra *generated* by τ, and the T_i "generator sets" for $\bar{\tau}$.

Two algebras $A = [\{S_i\}, F]$ and $B = [\{T_i\}, F]$ are said to be *similar* when their phyla and operations have the same names and attributions $n(\alpha)$, $r(\alpha)$, and $i(k, \alpha)$ in (1.1). (If we regard subscripts as "names" of phyla and operations, then it suffices for A and B to have the same formulas (1.1).)

For similar algebras $A = [\{S_i\}, F]$ and $B = [\{T_i\}, F]$, a *morphism* from A to B is a set $\Phi = \{\phi_i\}$ of functions $\phi_i: S_i \to T_i$, one for each $i \in I$, such that, for any $f_\alpha \in F$,

$$f_\alpha \circ (\phi_{i(1,\alpha)} \times \cdots \times \phi_{i(n(\alpha),\alpha)}) = \phi_{r(\alpha)} \circ f_\alpha. \tag{1.3}$$

As usual, morphisms which are injective (ϕ_i injective for all i), surjective (ϕ_i surjective for all i), or bijective (ϕ_i bijective for all i) are called *mono*morphisms, *epi*morphisms, and *iso*morphisms, respectively.

A *congruence* on an algebra $A = [\{S_i\}, F]$ is a family $\mathscr{E} = \{E_i\}$ of equivalence relations, one for each phylum S_i of A, which for each $f_\alpha \in F$ has the following substitution property:

$$x_j \, E_{i(j,\alpha)} \, y_j \qquad (x_j, y_j \in S_{i(j,\alpha)} \quad \text{for} \quad j = 1, 2, \ldots, n(\alpha))$$

(1.4) $$\text{implies}$$

$$f_\alpha(x_1, \ldots, x_{n(\alpha)}) \, E_{r(\alpha)} \, f_\alpha(y_1, \ldots, y_{n(\alpha)}).$$

We then have the following

MORPHISM THEOREM FOR HETEROGENEOUS ALGEBRAS [**4**, §4]. *Each congruence $\mathscr{E} = \{E_i\}$ on a heterogeneous algebra $A = [\{S_i\}, F]$ determines an epimorphism $\Phi = \{\phi_i\}$ via the natural maps $\phi_i\colon S_i \to S_i/E_i$, and (conversely) all epimorphic images of A are obtained (up to isomorphism) in this way.*

Given any "species" $\mathfrak{A}$ of similar algebras, specified by a family $F = \{f_\alpha\}$ of "operation symbols," one can construct the (free) *word algebra* $W_{\mathbf{m}}(\mathfrak{A})$ of that species for any vector $\mathbf{m} = (m_i)$ $(i \in I)$ of nonnegative integers, as follows ([**4**, §6]; cf. [**1**, p. 141]).

Each phylum has a "generator set"

(1.5) $$W_0(i) = X_i = \{x_1^i, x_2^i, \ldots, x_{m_i}^i\}.$$

Recursively for "rank" $\rho = 1, 2, 3, \ldots$, we define

(1.6) $$W_\rho(i) = \bigcup_{f_\alpha \in A_i} f_\alpha(u_1, u_2, \ldots, u_{n(\alpha)}),$$

where (i) A_i is the set of $f_\alpha \in F$ with values in the ith phylum, (ii) every $u_j = u_j(x_1^1, \ldots, x_j^i, \ldots) \in W_\sigma(i(j, \alpha))$ for some $\sigma \leqq \rho - 1$, and (iii) some u_j is of rank $\rho - 1$. Then $\bigcup_{\rho \in N} W_\rho(i) = W_i$, and $W_{\mathbf{m}}(F)$ is the algebra $[\{W_i\}, F]$ with the operations f_α defined recursively by (1.6).

The elements of W_i are called W_i-polynomials ("words"), those of $W_\rho(i)$ are called W_i-polynomials of rank ρ. Equality in $W_{\mathbf{m}}(F)$ means formal identity. We also denote $W_{\mathbf{m}}(F)$ by $W_{\mathfrak{X}}(F)$, where $\mathfrak{X} = \{X_i\}$ is the family of generating sets.

EXAMPLE 4. Consider the species $\mathscr{G}$ of all groups acting on sets; that is, of all algebras $A = [\{G, S\}, \{*, \cdot\}]$, where $*$ is the group operation and $s \cdot g$ is the point into which $g \in G$ carries $s \in S$. For $\mathbf{m} = (m_1, m_2)$, $W_{\mathbf{m}}(\mathscr{G})$ describes the free group $FG(m_1)$ with m_1 generators acting intransitively on m_2 sets of transitivity, each of which is a "regular" (Cayley) representation of $FG(m_1)$.

EXAMPLE 5. Applying the above construction to the species $\mathscr{M}$ of (Moore) machines $[\{S, A, Z\}, \{\nu, \zeta\}]$, one obtains the *word machine* $W_{\mathbf{m}}(\mathscr{M})$ with m_1 generating states, m_2 generating input letters, and the void set of generating output letters. Thus, for $\mathbf{m} = (2, 3, 0)$, let $X_1 = \{s, t\}$, $X_2 = \{a, b, c\}$, and $X_3 = \varnothing$. Then

$W_{\dot{\mathfrak{m}}}(\mathscr{M}) = W_{\mathfrak{x}}(\mathscr{M})$ will have the states

$$s, t, \nu(s, a), \ldots, \nu(t, c), \nu(\nu(s, a)), \ldots$$

and (cf. Example 6 of [**4**, §3]) the output symbols

$$z, \zeta(s), \zeta(t), \zeta(\nu(s, a)), \ldots, \zeta(\nu(t, c)), \zeta(\nu(\nu(s, a))), \ldots.$$

Again we note that $W_{\mathfrak{x}}(\mathscr{M})$ is *not* a finite state machine, nor is its output phylum finite.

Given any W_k-polynomial $w = w(x_1^1, \ldots, x_j^i, \ldots)$ in $W_{\mathbf{m}}(F)$ and algebra $A = [\{S_i\}, F]$, w determines a function $\prod_I S_i^{m_i} \to S_k$ in a natural way, by simply "evaluating" the polynomial w for arbitrary assignments $x_j^i \mapsto s_j^i \in S_i$. For any family Γ of similar algebras $A_\gamma = [\{S_{i,\gamma}\}, F]$, the free Γ-algebra [**4**, §7] $C_{\mathbf{m}}(\Gamma)$ with m_i generators of the ith phylum is obtained up to isomorphism as a certain epimorphic image of the (free) word algebra $W_{\mathbf{m}}(F)$, specifically

$$C_{\mathbf{m}}(\Gamma) \cong W_{\mathbf{m}}(F)/\mathscr{E}^\Gamma \tag{1.7}$$

where $\mathscr{E}^\Gamma = \{E_i^\Gamma\}$ is the congruence on $W_{\mathbf{m}}(F)$ defined by making $u\ E_i^\Gamma\ v$ mean that u and v are equal *as functions* $\prod_I S_{i,\gamma}^{m_i} \to S_{k,\gamma}$ for *every* algebra $A = [\{S_{i,\gamma}\}, F]$ in Γ. The equivalences $u\ E_i^\Gamma\ v$ are precisely the *identities* in m_i or fewer symbols for elements of the ith phylum which are valid in all $A_\gamma \in \Gamma$.

In [**4**, §8] the concept of a free heterogeneous algebra was applied in constructing a free *state* machine. In §3 of this paper we extend this construction to that of a free machine *with outputs*.

2. *J*-faithful *K*-morphisms. We now generalize the usual [**3**, Chapter 3] concepts of "covering," "equivalence," and "reduced machine" to a new universal algebraic concept: that of a "J-faithful K-morphism."

DEFINITION. Let $A = [\{S_i\}, F]$ and $B = [\{T_i\}, F]$ be two similar algebras. For any set K of phyla (that is, for any $K \subset I$, the index set of phyla), we call a collection $\Phi = \{\phi_i\}$ of functions $\phi_i: S_i \to T_i$ a *K-morphism* when for any W_k-polynomial w over $\{S_i\}$ with $k \in K$ (that is, with value-phylum in K), we have

$$\phi_k(w(\mathbf{s})) = w(\Phi(\mathbf{s})) \tag{2.1}$$

in B. We call Φ *J-faithful* (for given $J \subset I$) when all ϕ_j with $j \in J$ are one-one.

The algebras A and B are called *(J, K)-equivalent* if there is a J-faithful K-morphism from A to B *and* one from B to A.

When $K = I$ and $J \subset I$ is arbitrary, a J-faithful K-morphism is an ordinary morphism of (heterogeneous) algebras; when $J = K = I$, it is an isomorphism.

EXAMPLE 6. Let $[\{G, S\}, \{*, \cdot\}]$ be a group G acting on a set S, where $*$ is the group operation and $g \cdot s$ is the point into which $g \in G$ carries $s \in S$. Let E be any equivalence relation dividing S into "imprimitive subsets," and let $[\{H, S/E\}, \{*, \cdot\}]$ be the induced group of permutations of S/E. Then the natural mapping $\Phi = \{\phi_1, \phi_2\}$ with $\phi_1: G \to H$ and $\phi_2: S \to S/E$ is a $\{G, S\}$-morphism; it is faithful on the group phylum if and only if $g \cdot s \equiv s \pmod{E}$ for all $s \in S$ implies $g = 1$.

EXAMPLE 7. For *machines* (Example 3) with given input alphabet A and output alphabet Z, what is usually called a "covering" is essentially just an $\{A, Z\}$-faithful Z-morphism.

To see this, let $M = [\{S, A, Z\}, \{\nu, \zeta\}]$ and $M' = [\{S', A, Z\}, \{\nu', \zeta'\}]$ be two machines, and let $\Phi = \{\phi, 1_A, 1_Z\}$ be a mapping $M \to M'$. By definition, Φ is trivially $\{A, Z\}$-faithful. It is a Z-morphism precisely when every expression with value in Z, applied to corresponding (initial) states and corresponding (identical) input tapes $\mathbf{a} = a^1 \cdots a^r$, gives rise to the same final output z^r. This is to say that the output expressions

$$w(s, \mathbf{a}) = \zeta(\nu(\ldots(\nu(s, a^1), a^2), \ldots), a^r)$$

and

$$w(\phi(s), \mathbf{a}) = \zeta'(\nu'(\ldots(\nu'(s, a^1), a^2), \ldots), a^r)$$

should yield the same value for all $\mathbf{a}$. Since this is true for all r, the condition is that for any (initial) state $s \in S$ and input tape $\mathbf{a} = a^1a^2 \cdots a^r$, there is a corresponding state $s' \in S'$, specifically $s' = \phi(s)$, from which the same output tape $z = z^1z^2 \cdots z^r$ is produced. This is precisely the condition that machine M *cover* machine M' [**3**, §§3–4]. Moreover, if M' also covers M, then by definition, M and M' are said to be *equivalent* (that is, equivalent in terms of their capabilities of computing output tapes from input tapes). Thus the concept of (J, K)-equivalence of algebras specializes to that of equivalence of machines.

The connection between epimorphisms and congruences established in [**4**, §4] can be partially extended to J-faithful K-morphisms. This extension leads to the new universal algebraic concept of the "(J, K)-reduced image" associated with a given heterogeneous algebra and sets J, K of phyla, which yields as a special case the concept of the *reduced machine* of a given machine.

THEOREM 1. *Let $\Phi = \{\phi_i\}$ be a J-faithful K-morphism $A \to B$. Then the "equivalence kernel" $\mathscr{E}_\Phi = \{E_{\phi_i}\}$ defined on the phyla S_i of A by*

$$s\, E_{\phi_i}\, t \quad \textit{iff}\ \phi_i(x) = \phi_i(y) \tag{2.2}$$

satisfies the following conditions:

(2.3)
(i) *E_{ϕ_j} is the equality relation for $j \in J$;*
(ii) *for any W_k-polynomial w over $\{S_i\}$ with $k \in K$,*

$$s_j^i\, E_{\phi_i}\, t_j^i \qquad (s_j^i, t_j^i \in S_i;\ i \in I)$$

implies

$$w(s_1^1, \ldots, s_j^i, \ldots)\, E_{\phi_k}\, w(t_1^1, \ldots, t_j^i, \ldots).$$

Using a more compact notation, (ii) *becomes*

(ii′) $\mathbf{s}\, \mathscr{E}_\Phi\, \mathbf{t}$ *implies* $w(\mathbf{s})\, E_{\phi_k}\, w(\mathbf{t})$.

We now define the analogue of a congruence for the case of J-faithful K-morphisms as any family $\mathscr{E} = \{E_i\}$ of equivalence relations which satisfy properties (i) and (ii) of the above lemma. Specifically, we have the following:

DEFINITION. A *(J, K)-equivalence* on an algebra $A = [\{S_i\}, F]$ is a family $\mathscr{E} = \{E_i\}$ of equivalence relations, with E_i defined on S_i for each $i \in I$, which satisfy the following conditions:

(2.4)
(i) E_j is the equality relation for $j \in J$,
(ii) for any W_k-polynomial w over $\{S_i\}$ with $k \in K$,

$$\mathbf{s} \mathscr{E} \mathbf{t} \text{ implies } w(\mathbf{s})\, E_k\, w(\mathbf{t}).$$

THEOREM 2. *The (J, K)-equivalences on an algebra A form a closed sublattice of the lattice* [**4**, *Proposition* 12] *of all equivalences $\{E_i\}$ on A.*

A (J, K)-equivalence does not in general give an epimorphic (J-faithful) image of A, because the substitution property (1.4) may not be satisfied for those operations f_α with value-phylum $r(\alpha)$ not in K. However, under appropriate restrictions on J and K, the greatest element of the lattice of (J, K)-equivalences of A, which we denote by $\mathscr{E}^R = \{E_i^R\}$ (R for "reduced"—see below), yields a unique minimal epimorphic image of A, which we call the (J, K)-*reduced* image of A. This is the content of the following result.

THEOREM 3. *Let $K \subset J$, and suppose that*

(*) *there is no operation f_α with value-phylum $r(\alpha) \in J$.*

*Then $A/\mathscr{E}^R$ is a J-faithful epimorphic image of A. Furthermore $A/\mathscr{E}^R$ is a (J, K)-**reduced** image of A in the following (strong) sense: If B is any algebra (J,K)-equivalent to A, then $A/\mathscr{E}^R \cong B/\tilde{\mathscr{E}}^R$ when $\tilde{\mathscr{E}}^R$ is the maximal element of the lattice of (J, K)-equivalences of B.*

PROOF. First we remark that $\mathscr{E}^R$ is the coarsest (J, K)-equivalence on A, meaning that $\mathscr{E}^R$ is characterized by the following properties:

(i) for $j \in J$, E_j^R is the equality relation, and

(ii) for $i \notin J$, $s\, E_i^R\, t$ means that to substitute s for t in any W_k-polynomial leaves the value unchanged (unchanged, because $K \subset J$).

We now show that $\mathscr{E}^R$ is a congruence on A. For any $f_\alpha \in F$, assume $s_j\, E_{i(j,\alpha)}^R\, t_j$ for $j = 1, 2, \ldots, n = n(\alpha)$. By assumption, the value-phylum $r(\alpha)$ of f_α is not in J; thus we need only check property (ii) above: that substituting $f_\alpha(s_1, \ldots, s_n)$ for $f_\alpha(t_1, \ldots, t_n)$ in any W_k-polynomial leaves the value unchanged. For any W_k-polynomial w ($k \in K$) we have

$$\begin{aligned} w(\ldots, f(t_1, \ldots, t_n), \ldots) & \\ &= \tilde{w}(\ldots, t_1, \ldots, t_n, \ldots) \quad \text{for some } W_k\text{-polynomial } \tilde{w}, \\ &= \tilde{w}(\ldots, s_1, \ldots, s_n, \ldots) \quad \text{because } s_j\, E_{i(j,\alpha)}^R\, t_j, \\ &= w(\ldots, f_\alpha(s_1, \ldots, s_n), \ldots), \end{aligned}$$

so that $\mathscr{E}^R$ is a congruence, and $A/\mathscr{E}^R$ is a J-faithful epimorphic image of A, as was to be proved.

The meaning of the (J, K)-*reduced* property of $A/\mathscr{E}^R$ is summarized by the following mapping diagram.

$$
\begin{array}{ccc}
A & \underset{\Psi}{\overset{\Phi}{\rightleftarrows}} & B \\
{\scriptstyle\Pi}\big\downarrow & & \big\downarrow{\scriptstyle\Pi'} \\
A/\mathscr{E}^R & \underset{\Theta}{\longrightarrow} & B/\tilde{\mathscr{E}}^R
\end{array}
$$

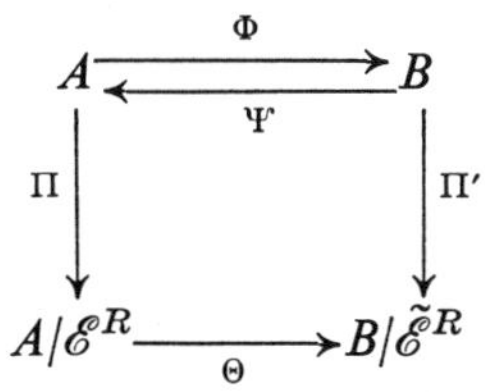

Here $\Phi = \{\phi_i\}$ and $\Psi = \{\psi_i\}$ are given J-faithful K-morphisms (thus making A and B (J, K)-equivalent), and Π, Π' are the natural epimorphisms $A \to A/\mathscr{E}^R$, $B \to B/\tilde{\mathscr{E}}^R$. Then the result is that $A/\mathscr{E}^R \cong B/\tilde{\mathscr{E}}^R$ under the map $\Theta = \{\theta_i\}$ defined by

$$\theta_i\colon [s]_{E_i^R} \mapsto [\phi_i(s)]_{\tilde{E}_i^R},$$

with inverse

$$\theta_i^{-1}\colon [t]_{\tilde{E}_i^R} \mapsto [\psi_i(t)]_{E_i^R}.$$

The verification that $\Theta = \{\theta_i\}$ is an isomorphism as claimed is left to the reader.

The uniqueness of the (J, K)-reduced image is given by the following:

COROLLARY. *If two (J, K)-reduced images are equivalent, then they are isomorphic.*

For machines we have seen in Example 7 that a $J = \{A, Z\}$-faithful $K = \{Z\}$-morphism of machines corresponds to what is called a "covering." The $(\{A, Z\}, \{Z\})$-reduced image corresponds to the *reduced machine* of a given machine, and Theorem 3 yields the important fact from machine theory [6, Theorem 1.1] that corresponding to any machine there is a unique (up to isomorphism) reduced (in terms of number of states) machine with the same input/output properties, which is an epimorphic image of the original machine. In this case, the $\mathscr{E}^R$ of the general theory specializes to what Hartmanis and Stearns [6, §2.5] call the maximal "output-consistent" partition of the set of states. Thus we see that Theorem 3 reveals the essentially *universal algebraic* content of the "reduced machine" result from machine theory.

The procedure [3, §3.6] for constructing the reduced machine generalizes to the following recursive construction of the (J, K)-reduced image of any finite algebra $A = [\{S_i\}, F]$ (for any $K \subset J$, provided no f_α has its value-phylum in J). We define $\mathscr{E}_\rho$ for $\rho = 0, 1, 2, \ldots$ by (i) $E_{\rho,j}$ is equality for any $j \in J$, (ii) for x, y in S_i with $i \notin J$, $x\,E_{\rho,i}\,y$ means that to substitute x for y in any W_k-word w over $\{S_i\}$ of rank ρ or less with value in a phylum of K leaves this value unchanged. Clearly

$$(2.5) \qquad\qquad \mathscr{E}_0 \supset \mathscr{E}_1 \supset \mathscr{E}_2 \supset \mathscr{E}_3 \supset \cdots ;$$

moreover to test $x\,E'_{\rho,i}\,y$, it suffices to test x, y with $x\,E_{\rho-1,i}\,y$. Finally, the results of the following theorem are readily verified.

THEOREM 4. *If A is finite (i.e., S_i finite for all $i \in I$), then there is some positive integer σ such that $\mathscr{E}_\sigma = \mathscr{E}_{\sigma+1}$. Moreover, $\mathscr{E}_\sigma = \mathscr{E}_{\sigma+k}$ for every positive integer k, and $\mathscr{E}_\sigma = \mathscr{E}^R$, the maximal (J, K)-equivalence on A.*

3. Free machines. In [**4**, §8] we gave an example of a free *state* machine (or *semi*-automaton). In this section we focus our attention on machines *with outputs*, and determine the free machine associated with a given machine using the universal algebra construction employed in [**4**] in determining the free *state* machine of [**4**, Figure 5].

EXAMPLE 8. For comparative purposes we derive the free machine $F_{\mathfrak{X}}(M)$ associated with the (Moore) machine M of Figure 1 below, which is the state machine of [**4**, Figure 5] with outputs as indicated. (E.g., the label $p/0$ indicates that whenever the machine makes a transition into state p it emits an output of 0.)

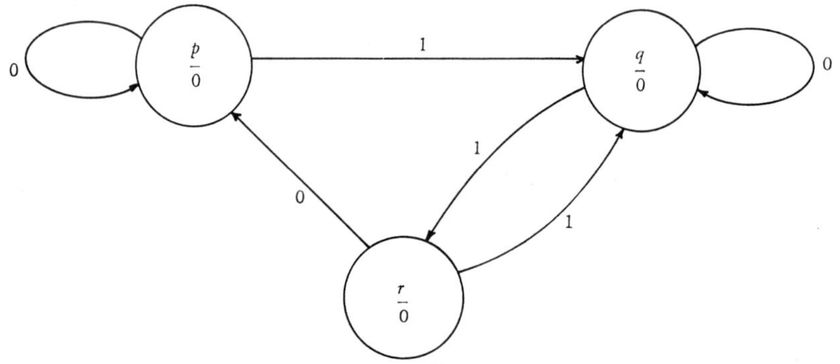

FIGURE 1. Machine M

The generating set $\mathfrak{X}$ of $F_{\mathfrak{X}}(M)$ consists of $X_1 = \{s\}$ where s is the generating state, a set $X_2 = \{x, y\}$ of generating input letters (thus X_1 and X_2 are as in [**4**, §8]), and no generating output letter as in Example 5 (so that $X_3 = \varnothing$).

By [**4**, Proposition 17], $F_{\mathfrak{X}}(M)$ is a subalgebra ("submachine") of $M^{M^{\mathbf{m}}}$, where $\mathbf{m} = (1, 2, 0)$ for our example. Thus $F_{\mathfrak{X}}(M)$ is a subalgebra of the direction power M^{12}.

The construction of $F_{\mathfrak{X}}(M)$ is carried out as in [**4**, §8] except that there are now output polynomials as well as input and state polynomials. We determine the state and input phyla of $F_{\mathfrak{X}}(M)$ by computing a *truth table* (Table 1) which displays the values in M of the polynomials of the word machine generated by $\mathfrak{X}$ (Example 5) for all possible assignments of the free input symbols x and y to the input symbols $\{0, 1\}$ of M and the free state symbol s to the states $\{p, q, r\}$ of M. We denote the state polynomial $\nu(\ldots(\nu(\nu(s, x_1), x_2), \ldots), x_n)$ by $s \cdot x_1x_2 \cdots x_n$, and the output polynomial $\zeta(\nu(\ldots(\nu(\nu(s, x_1), x_2), \ldots), x_n))$ by $s * x_1x_2 \cdots x_n$, $\zeta(s)$ by $s * \lambda$.

From Table 1 we see that $F_{\mathfrak{X}}(M) \subset M^{12}$ has 9 states, which, as in [**4**, §8], we can conveniently designate by s, $s \cdot x$, $s \cdot y$, $s \cdot xx$, $s \cdot xy$, $s \cdot yx$, $s \cdot yy$, $s \cdot xyx$, $s \cdot xyy$;

Table 1
Truth-table for $F_{\mathfrak{X}}(M)$

Valuations												
s	p				q				r			
(x, y)	00	01	10	11	00	01	10	11	00	01	10	11
State Polynomials												
s	p	p	p	p	q	q	q	q	r	r	r	r
$s \cdot x$	p	p	q	q	q	q	r	r	p	p	q	q
$s \cdot y$	p	q	p	q	q	r	q	r	p	q	p	q
$s \cdot xx$	p	p	r	r	q	q	q	q	p	p	r	r
$s \cdot xy$	p	q	q	r	q	r	p	q	p	q	q	r
$s \cdot yx$	p	q	q	r	q	p	r	q	p	q	q	r
$s \cdot yy$	p	r	p	r	q	q	q	q	p	r	p	r
$s \cdot xxx = s \cdot x$	p	p	q	q	q	q	r	r	p	p	q	q
$s \cdot xxy = s \cdot y$	p	q	p	q	q	r	q	r	p	q	p	q
$s \cdot xyx$	p	q	r	r	q	p	q	q	p	q	r	r
$s \cdot xyy$	p	r	q	q	q	q	p	r	p	r	q	q
$s \cdot yxx = s \cdot xyy$	p	r	q	q	q	q	p	r	p	r	q	q
$s \cdot yxy = s \cdot xyy$	p	r	q	q	q	q	p	r	p	r	q	q
$s \cdot yyx = s \cdot x$	p	p	q	q	q	q	r	r	p	p	q	q
$s \cdot yyy = s \cdot y$	p	q	p	q	q	r	q	r	p	q	p	q
$s \cdot xyxx = s \cdot yx$	p	q	q	r	q	p	r	q	p	q	q	r
$s \cdot xyxy = s \cdot yy$	p	r	p	r	q	q	q	q	p	r	p	r
$s \cdot xyyx = s \cdot xx$	p	p	r	r	q	q	q	q	p	p	r	r
$s \cdot xyyy = s \cdot xy$	p	q	q	r	q	r	p	q	p	q	q	r
Input Polynomials												
x	0	0	1	1	0	0	1	1	0	0	1	1
y	0	1	0	1	0	1	0	1	0	1	0	1
Output Polynomials												
$s * \lambda$	0	0	0	0	1	1	1	1	0	0	0	0
$s * x$	0	0	1	1	1	1	0	0	0	0	1	1
$s * y$	0	1	0	1	1	0	1	0	0	1	0	1
$s * xx = s * \lambda$	0	0	0	0	1	1	1	1	0	0	0	0
$s * xy$	0	1	1	0	1	0	0	1	0	1	1	0
$s * yx = s * xy$	0	1	1	0	1	0	0	1	0	1	1	0
$s * yy = s * \lambda$	0	0	0	0	1	1	1	1	0	0	0	0
$s * xyx$	0	1	0	0	1	0	1	1	0	1	0	0
$s * xyy = s * x$	0	0	1	1	1	1	0	0	0	0	1	1

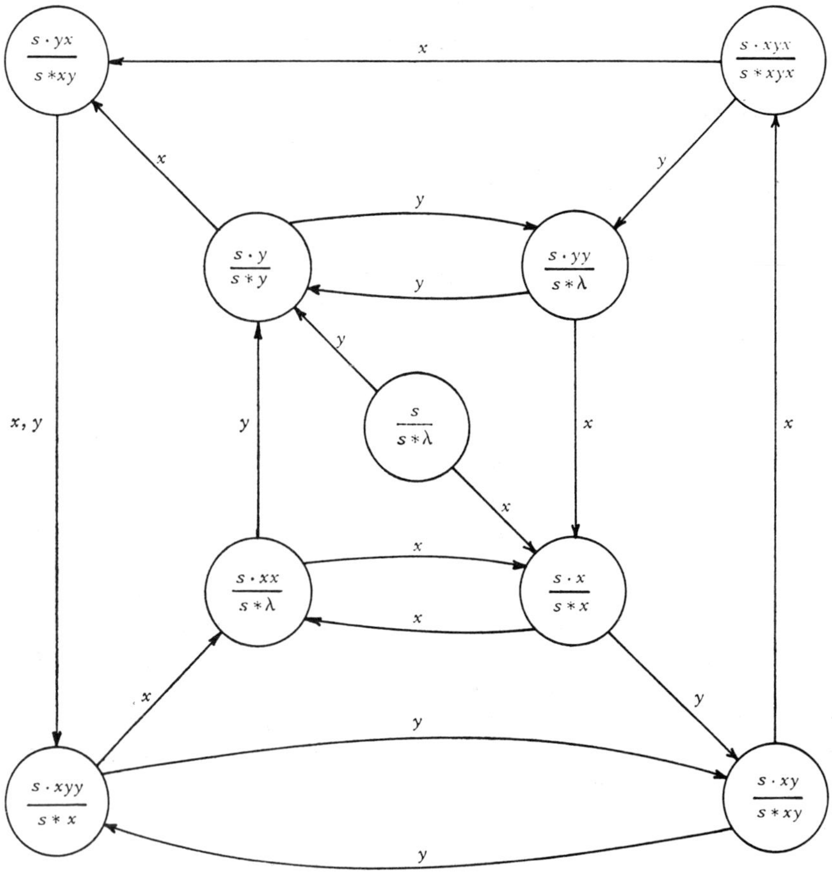

FIGURE 2. Free machine $F_{\mathfrak{X}}(M)$

two input letters x and y; and 5 output letters which we designate by $s * \lambda$, $s * x$, $s * y$, $s * xy$, $s * xyx$. The state diagram for $F_{\mathfrak{X}}(M)$ is given in Figure 2.

In [**4**, §8] we observed that the (state) *identities* holding in machine M can be ascertained by inspection from the associated free machine $F_{\mathfrak{X}}(M)$. E.g., one such identity is $s \cdot xxx = s \cdot x$ which, in machine theory terms, indicates that for any state s of M, the application of an "input tape" consisting of three repetitions of any input symbol (i.e., of either 000 or 111) results in the same final state as applying a tape consisting of a single occurrence of that same symbol.

Similarly, the free (Moore) machine provides additional information concerning the output aspects of the machine M; specifically, the *output identities* holding in M can be ascertained by inspection from $F_{\mathfrak{X}}(M)$. E.g., one such identity is $s * xy = s * yx$. This states that the input symbols enjoy a commutative property—the output tape produced by applying an input tape to M initially in any one of the states p, q, or r is unaffected by permuting the symbols of the input tape.

References

1. G. Birkhoff, *Lattice theory*, 3rd ed., Amer. Math. Soc. Colloq. Publ., vol. 25, Amer. Math Soc., Providence, R.I., 1967. MR **37** #2638.

2. ———, *The role of modern algebra in computing*, SIAM-AMS Proc., vol. 4, Amer. Math. Soc., Providence, R.I., 1971, pp. 1–48.

3. G. Birkhoff and T. C. Bartee, *Modern applied algebra*, McGraw-Hill, New York, 1970.

4. G. Birkhoff and J. D. Lipson, *Heterogeneous algebras*, J. Combinatorial Theory **8** (1970), 115–133. MR **40** #4119.

5. G. Grätzer, *Universal algebra*, Van Nostrand, Princeton, N.J., 1968. MR **40** #1320.

6. J. Hartmanis and R. E. Stearns, *Algebraic structure theory of sequential machines*, Prentice-Hall, Englewood Cliffs, N.J., 1966. MR **34** #4068.

Harvard University

University of Toronto

Reprinted from *Proc. Tarski Symp.*, Leon Henkin et al., eds.
Proc. XXV Symp. Pure Math., Am. Math. Soc., 1974, pp. 41–51.

Note on universal topological algebra

Garrett Birkhoff

We recall [LT3, p. 69] that an element c of a lattice L is called *neutral* if and only if $(c, x, y)\, D$ for all $x, y \in L$ – i.e., if and only if any triple (c, x, y) including c generates a distributive lattice. In a recent letter, M. Janowitz raised the question of proving that the set of all neutral elements in a metric lattice is closed in the metric topology. Actually, von Neumann and the author were surely aware of this result in the 1930's, but to find the simplest and most general proof is an amusing exercise in *universal topological algebra*, a subject which seems to have a very meager literature.

Namely, one can argue as follows. Any metric lattice is a *continuous lattice* in its metric topology, in the sense that

$$x_n \to x \quad \text{and} \quad y_n \to y \quad \text{imply} \quad x_n \wedge y_n \to x \wedge y \quad \text{and} \quad x_n \vee y_n \to x \vee y; \tag{1}$$

see [LT3, p. 233]. Moreover, since any finitely generated distributive lattice is finite [LT3, p. 60], the statement that a is neutral is equivalent to verifying that

$$f(c, x, y) = g(c, x, y) \tag{2}$$

for a finite set J of pairs of lattice words, namely, those giving the multiplication table of the free distributive lattice with three generators.

Now let $\mathfrak{A} = [S, F]$ be any *continuous algebra*, i.e., an algebra with a *univalent* convergence structure on a class of directed sets such that

$$x_\alpha \to u \quad \text{and} \quad x_\alpha \to v \quad \text{imply} \quad u = v, \tag{3}$$

and, for each (finite) n, every n-ary operation f_ν is *continuous* in the sense that

$$x(\alpha, k) \to x_k \quad \text{for} \quad k = 1, \ldots, n \quad \text{implies} \quad f_\nu(x(\alpha, 1), \ldots, x(\alpha, n)) \to f_\nu(x_1, \ldots, x_n). \tag{4}$$

Then the following result is immediate.[1]

LEMMA. *In any continuous algebra, all words are continuous functions of their arguments.*

---

[1] This lemma and the concept of a continuous algebra are taken from Gerald Edgar's Ph.D. Thesis.

Presented by A. Horn. Received December 17, 1974. Accepted for publication in final form February 28, 1975.

This is because words are composites of the operations $f \in F$ of $\mathfrak{A}$, and any composite of continuous functions is continuous. It implies the following result.

THEOREM 1. *Let $\mathfrak{A}$ be any continuous algebra with a univalent convergence structure, and let J be any set of equations*

$$\phi_j(c, x_1, \dots, x_r) = \psi_j(c, x_1, \dots, x_r) \tag{5}$$

between the words of $\mathfrak{A}$. Then the set of $C \in \mathfrak{A}$ satisfying (5) *for all $x_1, \dots, x_r \in \mathfrak{A}$ and all $(\phi_j, \psi_j) \in J$ is closed.*

Proof. If $c_\alpha \to c$, and

$$\phi_j(c_\alpha, x_1, \dots, x_r) = \psi_j(c_\alpha, x_1, \dots, x_r) \tag{5_α}$$

for all $x_1, \dots, x_r \in \mathfrak{A}$ and all $(\phi_j, \psi_j) \in J$, then

$$\phi_j(c, x_1, \dots, x_r) = \lim \phi_j(c_\alpha, x_1, \dots, x_r) = \lim \psi_j(c_\alpha, x_1, \dots, x_r) = \psi_j(c, x_1, \dots, x_r).$$

This completes the proof.

COROLLARY 1. *In any metric lattice, and, more generally, in any continuous lattice* (cf. (1)), *the set of all neutral elements is closed.*

The wide range of applicability of Theorem 1 is illustrated by the following basic, but otherwise unrelated result.

COROLLARY 2. *The center of any continuous group (topological group) is a closed subgroup.*

The preceding simplification of an earlier proof of the author was suggested by Dr. Edgar, who has also noted the following generalization.

THEOREM 2. *Let $\mathfrak{A} = [S, F]$ be a continuous algebra with a Hausdorff topology, and let J be a set of equations between words of $\mathfrak{A}$. Let $B \subset S$ be such that*

$$\phi_j(b_1, \dots, b_q; x_1, \dots, x_r) = \psi_j(b_1, \dots, b_q; x_1, \dots, x_r) \tag{6}$$

for all $b_1, \dots, b_q \in B$ and all $x_1, \dots, x_r \in S$. Then the same is true of all $b_1, \dots, b_q \in \bar{B}$.

It is a corollary that the closure of any abelian subgroup of a (Hausdorff) topological group is abelian, etc.

The preceding results hold essentially because the definitions of a 'neutral element' in a lattice, and of an element being in the 'center' in a group, involve only universal quantifiers and do *not* involve *existential quantifiers*. By contrast, the definition of the 'center' of a lattice (cf. [LT3, p. 69]) does involve an existential quantifier: in a distributive lattice L, the center consists precisely of the 'complemented' elements a, for which there *exists* a $b \in L$ such that $a \wedge b = 0$ and $a \vee b = I$. Now consider the following example.

EXAMPLE 1. Let L be the metric distributive lattice of all open subsets of $I = [0, 1]$ modulo sets of measure zero, metrized by Lebesgue measure. Then L is a topological lattice under metric convergence [LT3, p. 233], whose center [LT3, p. 69] consists of the open sets $S \subset I$ such that $m[S] + m[\mathrm{Int}(S')] = 1$. For each positive integer k, the set S_k of all $x \in I$ such that $|x - m/10^n| < 10^{2n}$ for some positive integers $n \leqq k$ and m is in the center, but the limit $S = \bigcup_{k=1}^{\infty} S_k$ of the S_k is an everywhere dense open set whose complement has positive measure at least 7/9; hence S is not in the center.

Another interesting class of examples is the following. For a given topological space X, the open sets form a continuous distributive lattice $L(X)$ if $S_\alpha \to S$ is defined to mean that, for each $x \in X$ and some β, $x \in S_\alpha$ for all $\alpha \geqq \beta$, i.e., in the *relative* topology of $L(X)$ considered as a sublattice of 2^X. The *center* of $L(X)$ consists by definition of the 'clopen' (closed and open sets) of X, i.e., the sets which *disconnect* X. Alan Waterman has shown (personal communication) that the center of $L(X)$ is then closed if and only if X is a disjoint union of connected open sets.

REFERENCE

[LT3] G. Birkhoff, *Lattice Theory*, 3d ed., Am. Math. Soc., 1967.

Harvard University
Cambridge, Massachusetts
U.S.A.

III

Topology

Part of my undergraduate thesis, published as [2] had called my attention to the basic problem of correlating Fréchet's axioms for (sequential) convergence with the Riesz–Kuratowski closure axioms and Hausdorff's neighborhood axioms for set-theoretic topology. I soon recognized that the "transfinite sequences" (i.e., well-ordered sets) used by Baire in his Thesis, and by my father in his theory of "central motions," are inadequate for treating limits in general topological spaces; the neighborhoods of any point for a *partially* and not a well-ordered set.

Finally, in the fall of 1935,[1] I saw that the problem could be solved by replacing sequences by *directed sets*, or partially ordered sets in which any two elements have a common successor. When I mentioned this idea to my father, he recalled that E. H. Moore had considered convergent directed sets of *numbers* a decade earlier, and had applied them to various problems of his General Analysis.[2]

However, nobody had yet applied directed sets to general topology, and I did this in my paper [24]. There I characterized Hausdorff spaces in terms of axioms on convergent directed sets of points, and defined a topological group G whose manifold was a Hausdorff space to be *complete* when any *"Cauchy" directed set* $\{x_\alpha\}$, such that $\{x_\alpha x_\beta^{-1}\} \to 1$, *has a limit* a (such that $x_\alpha \to a$). By proving that "totally bounded" sets are compact in any "complete" topological linear space, I showed the equivalence of this (natural) definition of "completeness" to a more technical one that had been proposed earlier by von Neumann for topological linear spaces.[3] (In the next paper [25], in the same journal, I discussed the philosophical meaning of completeness.)

Such directed sets of *points* are closely related to the "filters" of *sets* introduced by H. Cartan in 1937.[4] The best exposition of both is contained in J. L. Kelley's *General Topology* (van Nostrand, 1955), which aptly shortened the phrase "directed sets of points" to "nets."

In the 1930s, in connection with the effort to topologize the theory of Lie groups (see Part V), I also became interested in a related problem: that of topologizing the (function) "space" S^S of all (linear and nonlinear) transformations $f\colon S \to S$ of a topological space S into itself. I published two papers concerned with this subject: [5] and [8].

Much of [5] was devoted to tightening up the topological reasoning of the Baer–Hasse Supplement to the "Theorie der algebraische Körper" of Steinitz;[5] its focus was algebraic. The other paper, [8], concentrated on topologizing the group of *homeomorphisms* of S, and is reprinted in this volume. In 1946, Richard Arens (*Annals of Math.* **47**, 480–95, and *Am. J. Math.* **68**, 480–95) gave a definitive solution of this problem, using the "compact-open" topology. Apart from a paper by Dieudonné (*Am. J. Math.* **70** (1948), 659–80), there has been little further progress on this topic since that time.

Generalized Arithmetic

In the 1914 edition of Hausdorff's *Mengenlehre*, the concept of what is now called a "Hausdorff space" was preceded by six chapters on the "transfinite arithmetic" of Cantor, to whom the book was dedicated. Only in the last of these chapters did he introduce the concept of a partially ordered set ["teilweise geordnete Menge", or poset]. The shortened 1927 edition omitted both Hausdorff spaces and posets.

Having studied Hausdorff's 1914 edition as an undergraduate, I had by 1935 come to view posets and lattices as fundamental structures, bridging an unnatural gap between cardinal and ordinal numbers. This view was strengthened at the 1935 International Topological Congress in Moscow, when I realized their close connection with Tucker's "cell spaces."[6] Papers [28], [29], and [42] tried to justify this view, by extending Cantor's transfinite arithmetic to general posets, and giving significant applications.

In particular, papers [28] and [42] defined cardinal *and* ordinal operations of addition, multiplication, and exponentiation on posets. As special cases, one obtains sums, products, and powers of cardinal *and* ordinal numbers.

Characteristic results of [28] included the following (cf. [LT1, p. 14]): (i) the T_0-topologies on a finite set X of points correspond to the partial orderings of X under a natural bijection ($p \geq q$ means that $q \in \bar{p}$), (ii) the ring of open subsets of the T_0-space in (i) is isomorphic to $\mathbf{2}^X$, (iii) all finite distributive lattices are obtained in this way. In [29], it is shown that the free distributive lattice on n generators (with universal bounds 0 and 1 adjoined) is the power $\mathbf{2}^{2^n}$ of the ordinal $\mathbf{2}$. In [42], the ideas of [28] were extended to include *ordinal* sums, products, and powers of general posets. There I also showed that these ordinal operations satisfy many of the laws of ordinary arithmetic (though not the commutative laws of addition and multiplication, which fail already for infinite ordinals).

This "generalized arithmetic" was analyzed in depth by M. M. Day in *Trans. AMS* **58** (1945), 1–43. Day pointed out that two of the six operations on posets discussed in [42] had been defined previously for general "relation numbers" in Vol. II of Whitehead and Russell's *Principia Mathematica.*[7] In 1949, Tarski's *Cardinal Algebras* (Oxford Univ. Press), and in 1956 his *Ordinal Algebras* (North-Holland), with appendices co-authored by Bjarni Jónsson and C. C. Chang, axiomatized much of the "arithmetic of relations." They gave many examples of specific systems satisfying these axioms, and hence having similar properties.

After studying these publications, I gave a carefully revised exposition of my ideas about the arithmetic of relations in [LT3]; see Chap. III, §§1–2 and Chap. VIII, §§10, 15. Very recently, the arithmetic of ordered sets and relations has been reviewed and extended in articles by Jónsson, by Davey and Duffus, and by Rival in *Ordered Sets* (Ivan Rival, editor), Reidel, 1982.

Almost by definition, *infinitary* operations of sup and inf are defined in any complete lattice. Hence so are the associated operations of lim sup and lim inf, and we can define *(o)-convergence* in any complete lattice by letting $x_n \to x$ mean that $\limsup\{x_n\} = \liminf\{x_n\} = x$. Under this definition, any complete (or σ-complete) lattice is a Fréchet limit space, as I observed in [15, p. 452].[8]

In 1936, von Neumann and I utilized an idea of Urysohn (*Enseignement Math.* **25** (1926), 77–83) to construct from this (*o*)-convergence a *star-convergence*, and showed that it is equivalent to *metric* convergence in any "metric lattice" (see [24, p. 56], [LT1, §§5–7], and [LT2, p. 62]). A few years later, in [LT1, §§142–3], I used the same device to construct a "relative uniform star topology" from E. H. Moore's "relative uniform convergence," and showed that relative uniform star-convergence equivalent to *metric convergence* in any Banach lattice.

Without specifying the (intrinsic) topology, Problem 11 of [LT1, p. 146] asked "Is every complete lattice topologically (bi)compact?" Orrin Frink gave a positive answer to this question in 1942, by proving that: (i) every complete lattice is (bi)compact in a new *interval topology*, which he constructed by taking closed intervals $[a_\sigma, b_\sigma]$ as a subbasis of closed sets.

Clearly, the infinitary sup operation makes it possible to construct from any complete lattice L an *infinitary* algebra $\mathfrak{A} = \mathfrak{A}(L)$ whose subalgebra lattice is isomorphic with L([3, Thm. 5.1]), as follows. Let the elements of $\mathfrak{A}$ be the same as those of L, and define (i) a *unary* operation $f_a(x) = a \wedge x$ for each $a \in L$, together with (possibly infinitary) join operations $\bigvee_S x$ for every cardinality with $|S| \leq |L|$. The subalgebras of are then the principal ideals of L, from which it follows that the subalgebra lattice of $\mathfrak{A}$, is isomorphic with L.

By 1945, my studies of universal algebra had made me curious to know which lattices are isomorphic with the lattice of all subalgebras of a *finitary* algebra. Orrin Frink and I solved this problem in 1948, by showing ([58, Thm. 2]) that: "A lattice is isomorphic with the lattice of all subalgebras of a suitable abstract algebra with finitary operations if and only if: (i) L is complete, (ii) L satisfies

$$(*) \qquad x_\alpha \uparrow x \quad \text{and} \quad y_\alpha \uparrow y \quad \text{imply } (x_\alpha \wedge y_\alpha) \uparrow x_\alpha y_{\alpha'}$$

and (iii) every element of L is a join of $\uparrow$-inaccessible elements.

Dilworth [1950, p. 11] renamed $\uparrow$-inaccessible elements *compact*, and called lattices satisfying the last condition "compactly generated." These lattices are now generally called *algebraic* [LT3, p. 187]. To prove this analogous result: that every complete algebraic lattice is isomorphic to the "structure lattice" of all *congruence relations* of some finitary algebra is much more difficult; finally, after 15 years, this was proved by Grätzer and E. T. Schmidt (*Acta Sci. Math. Szeged* **24** (1963), 34–59).

Some 20 years later, while writing [LT3], I discovered that Frink's interval topology failed to give the *natural* topology on $\mathbb{R}^2$, and on other lattices without universal bounds. To correct this defect, I proposed in [118] a modified intrinsic topology which seems to avoid this difficulty, while coinciding with Frink's definition in lattices with universal bounds. For the properties of this "new interval topology," see the papers by Kirby Baker in *Pacific J. Math.* **28** (1969), 275–88; by F. K. Holley in *Fund. Math.* **66** (1970), 329–36; and by R. H. Redfield in *Czech. Math. J.* **26** (1976), 527–40.

Notes

[1] See *Bull. AMS* **42** (1936), 44.
[2] E. H. Moore and H. J. Smith, *Am. J. Math.* **44** (1922), 102–21.
[3] See *Trans. AMS* **37** (1935), 3.
[4] *C. R. Paris* **205** (1937), 595–8 and 777–9.
[5] R. Baer and H. Hasse (eds.), *Steinitz' Algebraische Theorie der Körper.*
[6] See *Annals of Math.* **34** (1933), 191–243, and **37** (1936), 92–100. A "cell space" is just another name for a poset.
[7] He also pointed out that, contrary to a statement in [42], the ordinal power of two posets as defined there need not be a poset.
[8] Note that my paper [18], "On the combination of topologies," was also written in the 1930s.

ANNALS OF MATHEMATICS
Vol. 35, No. 4, October, 1934

THE TOPOLOGY OF TRANSFORMATION-SETS

BY GARRETT BIRKHOFF[1]

(Received November 25, 1933)

1. **Introduction.** Tietze[2] observed that the (1,1) continuous transformations of any space into itself constitute a group, of which the deformations are a normal subgroup. Baer[3] has shown that this group can be assigned continuity relations; as a matter of fact, this can be done in many ways, of which we shall discuss three in the text.

Schreier[4] pointed out that in a continuous group, there should be harmony between group operations and limit operations; Kneser[5] has developed this notion in outline for Tietze's groups. Finally, Fréchet and later writers[6] have shown that the full meaning of continuity is had only by spaces homeomorphic with subsets of Hilbert space.

We shall try to unite these tendencies of thought by showing how the (1,1) continuous transformations of a space $\mathfrak{S}$ into itself can be regarded as a group (i) continuous in the sense of Schreier (ii) topologically equivalent to a subset of Hilbert space.

2. **Outline.** In carrying out the program projected in section one, it has been found essential to proceed with great care. For at every step we have a variety of definitions to choose from, and it is only after a detailed examination that we can judge of their relative fruitfulness.

Accordingly, in §§3–9 we lay the groundwork for the subsequent treatment by putting the properties of finite sets of transformations in the most general possible form. In §§10–15 we turn our attention to infinite sequences of transformations, to see the extent to which various convergence definitions yield the classical convergence properties; the answer to this is seen to hinge on the convergence properties of the spaces transformed.

In §§16–20 the adequacy of three convergence definitions from the point of

[1] Society of Fellows, Harvard University.

[2] "Über die topologische Invarianten mehrdimensionaler Mannigfaltigkeiten," Monatsh. f. Math. u. Phys., **19** (1908), esp. pp. 88–93.

[3] "Beziehungen zwischen den Grundbegriffen der Topologie," Heidel. Sitz. 1929, (13). Cf. also Kneser's article.

[4] "Abstrakte kontinuierliche Gruppen," Hamb. Abh. **4** (1926), 15–32.

[5] "Die Deformationssätze der einfach zusammenhängenden Flächen," Math. Zeits. **25** (1926), 362–79.

[6] Notably Hausdorff, Urysohn, and Tychonoff. For the author's point of view, cf. "Axiomatic definitions of perfectly separable metric spaces," Bull. Am. Math. Soc., **39** (1933), 601–7.

view of Schreier and Kneser is discussed; incidentally we get considerable information about their equivalence. But it is in §§21–23 that we reach the core of the paper—namely, the fact there are important transformation-sets to which we can apply simultaneously the theory of abstract continuous groups, and the theory of topology.

3. **Transformations.** Let S be a class of objects s_k, and T a class of objects t_k. By a "transformation of S into T" is meant a rule σ which assigns to each couple (s_i, t_j) one of the following locutions

(i) σ transforms s_i into t_j.

(ii) σ does not transform s_i into t_j.

By the "inverse" σ^{-1} of σ, is meant that transformation of T into S which transforms a given t_i of T into an arbitrary s_j of S if and only if σ transforms s_j into t_i. This relation is *reciprocal*; that is, $(\sigma^{-1})^{-1} = \sigma$.

σ is called $(1 \to 1)$ or "one-valued" if and only if, given s_i, there is just one t_j such that σ assigns the locution (i) to (s_i, t_j). We write this relation in symbols as $t_j = \sigma(s_i)$, or $\sigma(s_i) = t_j$.

σ is called $(1,1)$ or "one-to-one" if and only if σ and σ^{-1} are both one-valued. If there exists a $(1,1)$ transformation of S into T, then the cardinal number of S equals the cardinal number of T. Because of the reciprocal nature of σ and σ^{-1}, if σ is $(1,1)$, then so is σ^{-1}.

4. **Products.** Let σ be any transformation of the class S into the class T, and τ any transformation of T into the class U. By the "product" $\sigma\tau$ of σ and τ, is meant that transformation of S into U which transforms s_i of S into u_j of U if and only if t_k of T exists, such that σ transforms s_i into t_k, while τ transforms t_k into u_j.

The reader will find it easy to construct proofs, in terms of the above definitions, of the following facts:

THEOREM 1: *$\tau^{-1}\sigma^{-1}$ is the inverse of $\sigma\tau$.*

THEOREM 2: *If σ and τ are both $(1 \to 1)$, then so is $\sigma\tau$.*

COROLLARY: *If σ and τ are both $(1,1)$, then so is $\sigma\tau$.*

THEOREM 3: $(\rho\sigma)\tau = \rho(\sigma\tau)$.

5. **The Identity.** Let S be any class. By $\mathbf{1}$ is meant that $(1,1)$ transformation of S into itself which transforms each s_i of S into itself and into itself alone. Obviously

THEOREM 4: *The identity $\mathbf{1}$ is its own inverse. And if σ is any transformation of S into T, then $\mathbf{1}\sigma = \sigma\mathbf{1} = \sigma$.*

If σ is a transformation of S into T, then $\sigma\sigma^{-1} = \mathbf{1}$ if and only if σ transforms each s_i of S into *some* t_j of T, and no two distinct s_i of S into the same t_j of T. While $\sigma^{-1}\sigma = \mathbf{1}$ if and only if each t_j of T is a transform of *some* s_i of S, and no S_i of S is carried into two distinct t_j of T. Repairing the four conditions just obtained, we see

THEOREM 5: $\sigma\sigma^{-1} = \sigma^{-1}\sigma = \mathbf{1}$ *if and only if σ is* $(1,1)$.

6. **Groups and Groupoids.** By a "continuous group" is meant[7] any system $\mathfrak{G}$ whose elements satisfy the postulates

G1: Every ordered pair (a, b) of elements of $\mathfrak{G}$ has a *product* ab in $\mathfrak{G}$.

G2: $(ab)c = a(bc)$ for any a, b, c in $\mathfrak{G}$.

G3: $\mathfrak{G}$ contains an element $\mathbf{1}$ satisfying $a\mathbf{1} = \mathbf{1}a = a$ for every a in $\mathfrak{G}$.

G4: To every a of $\mathfrak{G}$ corresponds an *inverse* a^{-1} satisfying $aa^{-1} = a^{-1}a = 1$.

L1: Concerning any element a and any enumerable sequence of elements a_n of $\mathfrak{G}$ we can say either (i) $\{a_n\}$ converges to a or (ii) $\{a_n\}$ does not converge to a. (In symbols, $a_n \to a$ or $a_n \nrightarrow a$).

LG1: If $a_n \to a$ and $b_n \to b$, then $a_n b_n \to ab$.

LG2: If $a_n \to a$, then $a_n^{-1} \to a^{-1}$.

A system $\mathfrak{G}$ is called a "group" provided only it satisfies G1–G4; a "continuous groupoid" provided it satisfies G1–G3, L1, and LG1; a "groupoid" provided it satisfies G1–G3. Definitions of subgroupoid and subgroup can be easily supplied by the reader.

We can summarize a number of the facts already stated in the following

THEOREM 6: *The transformations of any class into itself are a groupoid, of which the* $(1 \to 1)$ *transformations are a subgroupoid, and the* $(1,1)$ *transformations a subsubgroupoid and also a group.*

7. **Abstract Space.** Let Γ: $(\mathfrak{C}, K)$ be any abstract space, that is,[8] a class $\mathfrak{C}$ of points, and an operation K which assigns to each set S of points of $\mathfrak{C}$ a "derived" set $K(S)$.

Let $\mathfrak{S}$ be any set of points of Γ. By the "space" of $\mathfrak{S}$, is meant that abstract space Σ: $(\mathfrak{S}, L)$ in which L assigns to each set S of points of $\mathfrak{S}$, the "derived" set $L(S)$ consisting of those points of $K(S)$ in $\mathfrak{S}$.

Disregarding for the moment the operation K, it is obvious that we can speak of the transformations of Γ into itself, of Γ_1 into Γ_2, etc. But this is fruitless unless we tie up these transformations with the operation of derivation.

In doing this, it is convenient[9] to restrict ourselves to $(1 \to 1)$ transformations. As we have seen, a $(1 \to 1)$ transformation of the abstract space Γ_1: $(\mathfrak{C}_1, K_1)$ into the abstract space Γ_2: $(\mathfrak{C}_2, K_2)$ is a rule γ assigning to each point x in $\mathfrak{C}_1$ an "image" $\gamma(x)$ in $\mathfrak{C}_2$. It follows immediately that γ assigns to every set S of points of $\mathfrak{C}_1$, an "image" $\gamma(S)$ in $\mathfrak{C}_2$, namely, the set of the images of the points of S.

γ can also be regarded as a transformation of Γ_1 into the space of $\gamma(\mathfrak{C}_1)$, or into the space of any subset of $\mathfrak{C}_2$ which contains $\gamma(\mathfrak{C}_1)$.

The following result is obvious

THEOREM 7: $\sigma\tau(S) = \tau(\sigma(S))$.

---

[7] Cf. O. Schreier, op. cit.; also an article on "Hausdorff Groupoids" by the author, *Annals of Mathematics*, **35**, pp. 351–360.

[8] M. Fréchet, "Les espaces abstraits," Paris, 1926, p. 167. K is evidently a $(1 \to 1)$ transformation of the class of the S into itself.

[9] But by no means necessary; all the definitions given below can be so worded as to apply to the most general transformation between two abstract spaces.

8. **Continuous** $(1 \to 1)$ **Transformations.** A $(1 \to 1)$ transformation γ of Γ_1 into Γ_2 is said to be *continuous*[10] if and only if $\gamma(K_1(S)) \subset K_2(\gamma(S))$ for any set S of points of $\mathfrak{C}_1$.

THEOREM 8: *If Σ is the space defined by the set $\mathfrak{S}$ of Γ_2, and γ is any continuous $(1 \to 1)$ transformation of Γ_1 into Σ, then γ is a continuous $(1 \to 1)$ transformation of Γ_1 into Γ_2.*

Because, formally, $\gamma(K_1(S)) \subset L(\gamma(S)) \subset K_2(\gamma(S))$ for any subset S of $\mathfrak{C}_1$.

THEOREM 9: *The product of two continuous $(1 \to 1)$ transformations is itself a continuous $(1 \to 1)$ transformation.*

That it is $(1 \to 1)$ follows from Theorem 2. To show that it is continuous, suppose $\gamma_1\colon \Gamma_1 \to \Gamma_2$ and $\gamma_2\colon \Gamma_2 \to \Gamma_3$ to be the given transformations, and let S be any point-set in $\mathfrak{C}_1$. Then

$$\begin{aligned} K_3(\gamma_1\gamma_2(S)) &= K_3(\gamma_2(\gamma_1(S))) \supset \gamma_2(K_2(\gamma_1(S))) \\ &\supset \gamma_2(\gamma_1(K_1(S))) = \gamma_1\gamma_2(K_1(S)) \,. \end{aligned}$$

COROLLARY: *The continuous $(1 \to 1)$ transformations of any abstract space into itself are a groupoid.*

In the case that the K_i are defined by convergent sequences,[11] the criterion for continuity given above amounts to requiring that $\{x_k\} \to x$ imply $\{\tau(x_k)\} \to \tau(x)$.

9. **Bicontinuous** $(1,1)$ **Transformations.** A $(1,1)$ transformation γ is said to be *bicontinuous* if and only if γ and γ^{-1} are both[12] continuous in the sense of §8. Suppose then γ, a bicontinuous $(1,1)$ transformation of Γ_1 into Γ_2. Irrespective of $S \subset \mathfrak{C}_1$, we will have

$$\gamma(K_1(S)) \supset K_2(\gamma(S)) \quad \text{and}$$

$$\begin{aligned} \gamma(K_1(S)) &= \gamma(K_1(\gamma^{-1}(\gamma(S)))) \\ &\supset \gamma(\gamma^{-1}(K_2(\gamma(S)))) = K_2(\gamma(S)) \,. \end{aligned}$$

Whence $\gamma(K_1(S)) = K_2(\gamma(S))$. From this we can further infer

$$\begin{aligned} \gamma^{-1}(K_2(S)) &= \gamma^{-1}(K_2(\gamma(\gamma^{-1}(S)))) \\ &= \gamma^{-1}(\gamma(K_1(\gamma^{-1}(S)))) = K_1(\gamma^{-1}(S)) \,. \end{aligned}$$

Moreover these conditions are obviously sufficient to ensure that γ be bicontinuous, giving us

THEOREM 10: *A necessary and sufficient condition that γ be bicontinuous is that $\gamma(K_1(S)) = K_2(\gamma(S))$ irrespective of S.*

---

[10] Cf., e.g., "Les espaces abstraits," p. 177. We are using throughout the notation Γ_i: $(\mathfrak{C}_i, K_i)$.

[11] That is, that the Γ_i satisfy (L1) of §6, and $K(S) \supset p$ if and only if S contains a sequence converging to p.

[12] Continuity does not imply bicontinuity, even in the most regular spaces, as we could easily show by examples.

In other words, a necessary and sufficient condition that a (1,1) transformation γ of an abstract space into itself be bicontinuous is that γ commute with the operation of derivation.

Because of the reciprocal nature of γ and γ^{-1}, it is at once evident that if γ is bicontinuous, then so is γ^{-1}. Moreover by Theorems 7 and 9, if γ and γ' are bicontinuous, then so is $\gamma\gamma'$. Since finally $\gamma\gamma^{-1} = \gamma^{-1}\gamma = 1$, and $1\gamma = \gamma = \gamma 1$, we have

THEOREM 11: *The* (1,1) *bicontinuous transformations of any abstract space into itself constitute a subgroup of the group of all* (1,1) *transformations of the space into itself.*

A bicontinuous (1,1) transformation amounts by Theorem 10 to a homeomorphic correspondence, which is perhaps the most basic concept in abstract topology. The advantage of our definition is that it correlates the various types of transformations worked with in a single pattern.

Theorem 11 was, as has been remarked, asserted by Tietze, but its explicit content has to the author's knowledge been unexplained hitherto, and least of all in relation to general abstract spaces.

In terms of convergence, a transformation τ is bicontinuous if and only if $p_k \rightarrow p$ implies $\tau(p_k) \rightarrow \tau(p)$, and conversely.

10. **Types of Convergence Space.** By a *convergence space*,[13] will be meant any set of points satisfying postulate L1 of §6. A convergence space will be called an *S-space* if and only if the following four single limit properties hold,

SL1: If $x_k = x$, then $x_k \rightarrow x$.
SL2: If $x_k \rightarrow x$ and $x_k \rightarrow y$, then $x = y$.
SL3: If $k(i) \rightarrow \infty$ $[i = 1, 2, 3, \cdots]$ and $x_k \rightarrow x$, then $x_{k(i)} \rightarrow x$.
SL4: If to any $k(i) \rightarrow \infty$ corresponds an $n(i) \rightarrow \infty$ satisfying $x_{k(n(i))} \rightarrow x$, then $x_k \rightarrow x$.

An S-space will be called a *D-space* if and only if the following two double limit properties hold,

DL1: If $x_j^i \rightarrow x_i$ for every positive integer i, and $x_i \rightarrow x$, then $N(i)$ exists so large that $j(i) > N(i)$ implies $x_{j(i)}^i \rightarrow x$.
DL2: If $x_j^i \rightarrow x_i$ for every positive integer i, and $x_{j(i)}^i \rightarrow x$ for every $j(i)$, then $x_i \rightarrow x$.

The following result is known[14]

THEOREM 12: *A necessary and sufficient condition that a D-space be a perfectly*

---

[13] Not to be confused with H. Kneser's "Konvergenzräume," which are convergence spaces satisfying SL1–SL3, plus a weaker condition than SL4, or with M. Fréchet's "Espaces (*L*)," which were the prototypes of all convergence spaces.

[14] Cf. "Axiomatic Definitions of Perfectly Separable Metric Spaces," by the author, Bull. Am. Math. Soc., **39** (1933), p. 607. Perfectly separable metric spaces, or "*PSM*-spaces" are precisely spaces homeomorphic with a subset of Hilbert space.

separable metric space is that it contain enumerable open sets, of which every open set is the sum of a subclass.

By an S-group (S-groupoid) is meant any continuous group (groupoid) whose elements satisfy SL1–SL4. Similarly, by a D-group (D-groupoid) is meant any S-group (S-groupoid) whose elements satisfy DL1–DL2.

11. **Transformation Convergence.** Let $\mathfrak{S}_1$ and $\mathfrak{S}_2$ be any two convergence spaces, and consider $(1 \rightarrow 1)$ transformations σ, σ_k, etc., of $\mathfrak{S}_1$ into $\mathfrak{S}_2$. The sequence $\{\sigma_k\}$ will be said[15] to *A-converge* to σ (in symbols, $\sigma_k \rightarrow_A \sigma$) if and only if $x \subset \mathfrak{S}_1$ implies $\sigma_k(x) \rightarrow \sigma(x)$ in $\mathfrak{S}_2$.

$\{\sigma_k\}$ will be said to *B-converge* to σ (in symbols, $\sigma_k \rightarrow_B \sigma$) if and only if $x_k \rightarrow x$ in $\mathfrak{S}_1$ implies $\sigma_k(x_k) \rightarrow \sigma(x)$ in $\mathfrak{S}_2$. And $\{\sigma_k\}$ will be said to *C-converge* to σ (in symbols, $\sigma_k \rightarrow_C \sigma$) if and only if $x_k \rightarrow x$ in $\mathfrak{S}_1$ both implies and is implied by $\sigma_k(x_k) \rightarrow \sigma(x)$ in $\mathfrak{S}_2$.

The three definitions of convergence just stated ascribe to any convergence space three (in general, topologically distinct) convergence spaces. The points of all three correspond $(1,1)$ with the elements of the groupoid of the $(1 \rightarrow 1)$ transformations of the space into itself, but the definitions of L1 differ.

12. **Conditions** SL1 **and** SL2. In order that condition SL1 should hold for A-convergence, it is sufficient to restrict our attention to $(1 \rightarrow 1)$ transformations, and demand that SL1 hold in $\mathfrak{S}_2$. Since this condition is also in large measure necessary, it is suggested that the proper domain in which to use A-convergence is the domain of $(1 \rightarrow 1)$ transformations.

If we restrict ourselves to *continuous* $(1 \rightarrow 1)$ transformations, then by definition $\sigma_k = \sigma$ implies $\sigma_k \rightarrow_B \sigma$. If further we restrict ourselves to $(1,1)$ *bicontinuous* transformations, then by definition $\sigma_k = \sigma$ implies $\sigma_k \rightarrow_C \sigma$. Since these conditions are respectively necessary as well, it is suggested that B-convergence has for its proper domain of application, continuous $(1 \rightarrow 1)$ transformations, and C-convergence, bicontinuous $(1,1)$ transformations.

Moreover since A-convergence of $(1 \rightarrow 1)$ transformations of $\mathfrak{S}_1$ into $\mathfrak{S}_2$ means simply A-convergence in the transformations of the individual points of $\mathfrak{S}_1$, we see that if any of the conditions SL1–SL4 or DL2 holds in $\mathfrak{S}_2$, then it also holds in the set of the $(1 \rightarrow 1)$ transformations of $\mathfrak{S}_1$ into $\mathfrak{S}_2$. The only reason why this is not true of DL1 is that a question of uniformity enters.

Finally, if SL1 holds in $\mathfrak{S}_1$, since C-convergence and B-convergence both imply A-convergence, a fortiori[16] SL2 on $\mathfrak{S}_2$ implies that SL2 holds for the set

[15] A-convergence is the definition treated by the author in greater detail in an article "Hausdorff Groupoids," *Annals of Mathematics*, Vol. 35 (1934), pp. 351–360. B-convergence is the definition used by H. Kneser and R. Baer in articles already cited. It is also the definition of *isotopy*, as stated, for instance, in S. Lefschetz's "Topology," New York, 1930, p. 77. I am unaware of previous researches into the properties of C-convergence.

[16] For $\sigma_k \rightarrow_C \sigma$ implies $\sigma_k \rightarrow_B \sigma$ implies $\sigma_k \rightarrow_A \sigma$, and $\sigma_k \rightarrow_C \tau$ implies $\sigma_k \rightarrow_B \tau$ implies $\sigma_k \rightarrow_A \tau$. And from $\sigma_k \rightarrow_A \sigma$ and $\sigma_k \rightarrow_A \tau$ follows $\sigma = \tau$.

of the $(1 \to 1)$ transformations of $\mathfrak{S}_1$ into $\mathfrak{S}_2$, relative both to B- and to C-convergence.

13. SL3 **and** SL4. Suppose $\sigma_k \to_C \sigma$; then obviously $\sigma_k \to_B \sigma$. Further, since $\sigma_k(x) \to \sigma(x)$ implies $x_k \to x$, by defining $y_k = \sigma_k(x_k)$ and $y = \sigma(x)$, we see that if the σ_k and σ are $(1,1)$, then $y_k \to y$ implies $\sigma_k^{-1}(y_k) \to \sigma(y)$, whence $\sigma_k^{-1} \to_B \sigma^{-1}$. Conversely, if $\sigma_k \to_B \sigma$ and $\sigma_k^{-1} \to_B \sigma^{-1}$, and we consider only $(1,1)$ transformations, not only does $x_k \to x$ imply $\sigma_k(x_k) \to \sigma(x)$, but $\sigma_k(x_k) = y_k \to y = \sigma(x)$ implies $x_k = \sigma_k^{-1}(y_k) \to \sigma^{-1}(y) = x$ as well. Or

THEOREM 13: *For $(1,1)$ transformations, $\sigma_k \to_C \sigma$ is equivalent to $\sigma_k \to_B \sigma$ plus $\sigma_k^{-1} \to_B \sigma^{-1}$.*

COROLLARY: *$\sigma_k \to_C \sigma$ implies $\sigma_k^{-1} \to_C \sigma^{-1}$.*

Let us now return to the more general case of $(1 \to 1)$ transformations σ, σ_k, etc., of $\mathfrak{S}_1$ into $\mathfrak{S}_2$.

Suppose $\sigma_k \to_B \sigma$, and $k(i) \to \infty$. If $y_i \to y$, setting $x_{k(i)} = y_i$ and $x_k = y$ for $k \neq k(i)$, we see that if SL1 and SL4 hold in $\mathfrak{S}_1$, then $x_k \to y$, whence $\sigma_k(x_k) \to \sigma(y)$. If in addition SL3 holds in $\mathfrak{S}_2$, then $\sigma_{k(i)}(y_i) \to \sigma(y)$, whence $\sigma_{k(i)} \to_B \sigma$. It follows from Theorem 13 that if SL1, SL3, and SL4 hold in both the $\mathfrak{S}_i$, then $\sigma_k \to_C \sigma$ and $k(i) \to \infty$ imply $\sigma_{k(i)} \to_C \sigma$ for $(1,1)$ transformations.

Again, let σ_k be given, and suppose that to any $k(i) \to \infty$ corresponds $n(i) \to \infty$ satisfying $\sigma_{k(n(i))} \to_B \sigma$. Then if $x_k \to x$ and SL3 holds in $\mathfrak{S}_1$, given $k(i) \to \infty$, since $x_{k(n(i))} \to x$ for any, and $\sigma_{k(n(i))} \to \sigma$ for suitable, $n(i) \to \infty$, we can infer that for suitable $n(i) \to \infty$, $\sigma_{k(n(i))}(x_{k(n(i))}) \to \sigma(x)$. Hence if in addition SL4 holds in $\mathfrak{S}_2$, then $\sigma_k(x_k) \to \sigma(x)$, i.e., $\sigma_k \to_B \sigma$. It follows from Theorem 13 that if SL3 and SL4 hold in both the $\mathfrak{S}_i$, while to every $k(i) \to \infty$ corresponds $n(i) \to \infty$ such that $\sigma_{k(n(i))} \to_C \sigma$, then (again for $(1,1)$ transformations) $\sigma_k \to_C \sigma$.

We can summarize some of the results of §§12–13 in

THEOREM 14: *If $\mathfrak{S}_1$ and $\mathfrak{S}_2$ are S-spaces, then the $(1 \to 1)$ transformations of $\mathfrak{S}_1$ into $\mathfrak{S}_2$ constitute an S-space relative to A-convergence, the $(1 \to 1)$ continuous transformations do relative to A- or B-convergence, and the $(1,1)$ bicontinuous transformations do relative to A-, B-, or C-convergence.*

14. **Condition** DL2. We shall see in Theorem 25 that transformations between D-spaces do not always constitute D-spaces.[17] In spite of this, we can easily prove

THEOREM 15: *If $\mathfrak{S}_1$ satisfies* SL1 *and $\mathfrak{S}_2$ satisfies* DL2, *then the $(1 \to 1)$ transformations of $\mathfrak{S}_1$ into $\mathfrak{S}_2$ satisfy* DL2 *relative to B-convergence.*

For suppose $\tau_j^i \to_B \tau_i$, while $\tau_{j(i)}^i \to_B \tau$. Then, given $x_i \to x$, by SL1 $\tau_j^i(x_i) \to \tau_i(x_i)$, while certainly $\tau_{j(i)}^i(x_i) \to \tau(x)$. Consequently by DL2 $\tau_i(x_i) \to \tau(x)$, and by definition $\tau_i \to_B \tau$.

[17] That is, even the $(1,1)$ bicontinuous transformations of a Hausdorff space into itself are not a T-group in the sense of van Dantzig ("Zur topologische Algebra. I. Komplettierungstheorie," Math. Ann. **107** (1933), 587–626). It is for this reason that Hausdorff's Axioms are not suitable for the study of the topology of sets of transformations.

COROLLARY: *If* $\mathfrak{S}_1$ *and* $\mathfrak{S}_2$ *satisfy* SL1 *and* DL2, *then the* (1,1) *transformations of* $\mathfrak{S}_1$ *into* $\mathfrak{S}_2$ *satisfy* DL2 *relative to C-convergence.*

15. **Transformation S-groups.** Let $\mathfrak{S}_1$, $\mathfrak{S}_2$ and $\mathfrak{S}_3$ be any three convergence spaces, let σ_k, σ denote $(1 \to 1)$ transformations of $\mathfrak{S}_1$ into $\mathfrak{S}_2$, and τ_k, τ, $(1 \to 1)$ transformations of $\mathfrak{S}_2$ into $\mathfrak{S}_3$. Suppose $\sigma_k \to_B \sigma$ and $\tau_k \to_B \tau$.

Given $x_k \to x$ in $\mathfrak{S}_1$, we know by definition of $\sigma_k \to_B \sigma$ that $y_k = \sigma_k(x_k) \to \sigma(x) = y$, in $\mathfrak{S}_2$. Hence, since $\tau_k \to_B \tau$, $\sigma_k\tau_k(x_k) = \tau_k(y_k) \to \tau(y) = \sigma\tau(x)$. That is, $\sigma_k\tau_k \to \sigma\tau$, and, combining with Theorems 10 and 14, we get[18]

Theorem 16: *The* $(1 \to 1)$ *continuous transformations of any S-space into itself constitute an S-groupoid relative to B-convergence.*

And from Theorems 11, 13, 14, and 16 we see

Theorem 17: *The* (1,1) *bicontinuous transformations of any S-space into itself constitute an S-group under C-convergence.*

Theorem 17 is to be regarded as the backbone of the remainder of this paper; that is, our main interest will be in the nature of the S-group of the (1,1) bicontinuous transformations of given S-spaces. But our first concern will be, in §§16–20, to see under what circumstances, if any, the more complicated definition of C-convergence can be replaced by the simpler definitions of A- or B-convergence.

16. **A-convergence Implies C-convergence for Lines.** Let us examine the implications of A-convergence with respect to (1,1) bicontinuous transformations τ, τ_k, etc., of the line segment $\mathfrak{L}$: $0 \leqq x \leqq 1$ of the x-axis into itself—or, as we shall say for brevity, with respect to "shifts" of $\mathfrak{L}$.

Suppose $\tau_k \to_A \tau$. $\tau_k(x)$ is certainly monotonic, and evidently increasing or decreasing according as $\tau(x)$ is, for sufficiently large k. Let us suppose *both* to be increasing.

Given $\epsilon > 0$ and x_0, then for $k > k(x_0, \epsilon)$ and any x satisfying $x_0 - \epsilon < x < x_0 + \epsilon$,

$$\tau(x_0 - \epsilon) - \epsilon < \tau_k(x_0 - \epsilon) < \tau_k(x) < \tau_k(x_0 + \epsilon) < \tau(x_0 + \epsilon) + \epsilon .$$

Hence if $x_k \to x$, $\tau_k(x_k) \to \tau(x)$.

But it will be shown in Theorem 20 that in this case $\tau_k(x_k) \to \tau(x)$ implies $x_k \to x$, proving

THEOREM 18: *Relative to the shifts of a line segment, the definitions of A-, B-, and C-convergence are effectively identical.*

It is pretty obvious that Theorem 18 can be generalized to include the shifts of any finite class of line segments. That it cannot be generalized much further, will be shown in §17.

17. **Inadequacy.** Let POQ be any open angle in the plane, and let PQ, PQ',

[18] This piece of reasoning essentially duplicates Kneser's (op. cit.).

and PQ'' be any three arcs connecting P with Q subject to the conditions (i) no ray through O cuts any of them more than once, and (ii) each lies within the last (fig. 1).

Now let $\overrightarrow{OX}$ be any ray from O lying in the angle POQ. Let R be the intersection of $\overrightarrow{OX}$ and PQ''; S that of $\overrightarrow{OX}$ and PQ', and T that of $\overrightarrow{OX}$ and PQ. By a "focal shift" of the interior of the figure bounded by $\overline{OP}$, PQ, and $\overline{QO}$ is meant the transformation which carries the segment $\overline{OS}$ proportionally into $\overline{OR}$, and $\overline{ST}$ proportionally into $\overline{RT}$. A focal shift evidently leaves the boundary of the figure fixed, while it transforms PQ' into PQ''.

Now for a concrete example[19] restricting the generalization of Theorem 18. Let $\mathfrak{S}$ be any manifold containing a two-dimensional region, which we may represent as the right isosceles triangle $x \leqq 1, x - y \geqq 0, x + y \geqq 0$ in Cartesian

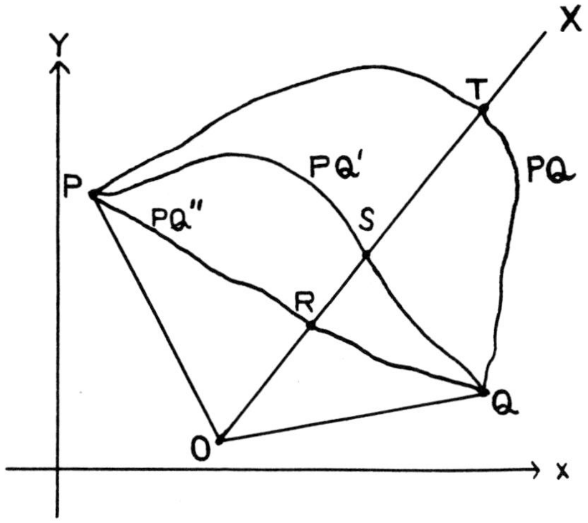

FIG. 1

2-space. Let τ_k leave all points of $\mathfrak{S}$ exterior to the subtriangle W_k bounded by the vertices $(0,0)$, $(1,1/k)$, $(1,1/(k+1))$ fixed. Let it perform a *focal shift* on W_k, in which PQ' is taken as the broken line $(1,1/k)$ to $(\frac{1}{2},1/(2k+1))$ to $(1,1/(k+1))$, and PQ'' as the broken line $(1,1/k)$ to $(\frac{1}{4},1/(4k+2))$ to $(1,1/(k+1))$. Then $\tau_k \to_A 1$.

Again, let σ_k $[k = 2, 3, 4, \cdots]$ be the focal shift with $(1,1)$ as 0, $(0,0)$ as P, $(1,0)$ as Q, the circle-arc with $(\frac{1}{2},k)$ for center as PQ, the broken line $(0,0)$ to $(\frac{1}{2},1/(2k+1))$ to $(1,0)$ as PQ', and the broken line $(0,0)$ to $(\frac{1}{2},2/(2k+1))$ to $(1,0)$ as PQ''. Evidently also $\sigma_k \to_A 1$.

The reader will be able to visualize the transformations if he draws a figure analogous to figure one.

---

[19] This is in its underlying principles the same as the classical construction discriminating between convergence and uniform convergence.

But $\sigma_k \tau_k \nrightarrow_A 1$, because $\sigma_k \tau_k(p) \to p$ for no p: $(x, 0)$ satisfying $\frac{1}{4} < x < \frac{1}{2}$. This shows

THEOREM 19: *If $\mathfrak{S}$ contains a two-dimensional region, then its shifts do not satisfy* LG1 *relative to A-convergence.*

Comparing with Theorems 16 and 17, we get the

COROLLARY: *If $\mathfrak{S}$ contains a two-dimensional region, then A-convergence implies neither B- nor C-convergence.*

Since the construction proving Theorem 19 can be duplicated in its essential features in case $\mathfrak{S}$ contains an n-dimensional region,[20] we see that Theorem 18 cannot have any very important generalizations.

18. ***B*-convergence Often Implies *C*-convergence.** C-convergence always implies B-convergence; we shall see that the two definitions are effectively equivalent for two important types of spaces. For instance, we can prove

THEOREM 20: *B-convergence and C-convergence are effectively equivalent for* $(1,1)$ *bicontinuous transformations between compact S-spaces.*

Suppose (denoting by τ, τ_k, etc., $(1,1)$ bicontinuous transformations of the compact S-space $\mathfrak{S}_1$ into the compact S-space $\mathfrak{S}_2$) $\tau_k \to_B \tau$, while $\tau_k(x_k) \to \tau(x)$. Since $\mathfrak{S}_2$ is compact, to any $k(i) \to \infty$ corresponds $n(i) \to \infty$ such that $x_{k(n(i))} \to y$; hence by Theorem 13 and SL3 $\tau_{k(n(i))}(x_{k(n(i))}) \to \tau(y)$, and by SL2 $\tau(y) = \tau(x)$. Since τ is $(1,1)$, we can infer that $y = x$. Hence, by SL4, $x_k \to x$, and by definition $\tau_k \to_C \tau$.

COROLLARY: *The shifts of any compact S-space constitute an S-group relative to B-convergence.*

We shall digress to point out that there exists a compact "Konvergenzraum"[21] $\mathfrak{S}$, whose shifts do not satisfy LG2 relative to B-convergence (Kneser's convergence definition).

Let the points of $\mathfrak{S}$ be x_k $[k = 1, 2, 3, \cdots]$ and x. Define $x_{k(i)} \to x$ *if* $k(i) \to \infty$, *unless* there are an infinite number of odd integers $(2n + 1)$ such that $k(i) = 2n + 1$ has more than one solution.

Define the sequence $\tau_1, \tau_2, \tau_3, \cdots$ of shifts of $\mathfrak{S}$ as follows,

$$\tau_{2k}\colon x_{2k+1} \to x_{4k},\ x_{2k+1+2i} \to x_{2k-1+2i},\ x_{4k+2i-2} \to x_{4k+2i},$$
$$[i = 1, 2, 3, \cdots];\ \text{the other } x_i \text{ stay fixed.}$$
$$\tau_{2k+1}\colon x_{2k+1} \to x_{4k+2},\ x_{2k+1+2i} \to x_{2k-1+2i},\ x_{4k+2i} \to x_{4k+2i+2},$$
$$[i = 1, 2, 3, \cdots];\ \text{the other } x_i \text{ stay fixed.}$$

Then $\tau_k \to_B 1$, yet since $\tau_k^{-1}(x_{2k}) \nrightarrow x$, $\tau_k^{-1} \nrightarrow_B 1$.

19. **Second Example.** Suppose $\mathfrak{S} = C_1 + C_2 + C_3 + \cdots$, where (i) $C_k \subset C_{k+1}$, (ii) each C_k is a compact connected set, (iii) C_k contains no point or

[20] By "region" we mean of course open subset, and by n-dimensional region, one homeomorphic with a region in Cartesian n-space; such a one will contain a subregion homeomorphic with an n-simplex.

[21] H. Kneser, op. cit., p. 365.

limit point of $\mathfrak{S} - C_{k+1}$, and (iv) $\mathfrak{S}$ is a D-space. Any such space $\mathfrak{S}$ will be called an *O-space.* For instance, any open connected set in Cartesian n-space is an O-space.

THEOREM 21: *For shifts of any O-space* $\mathfrak{S}$, *B-convergence and C-convergence are effectively equivalent.*

Suppose $\tau_k \to_B \tau$, and $\tau_k(x_k) \to \tau(x)$. By SL1 and $\tau_k \to_B \tau$, $\tau_k(x) \to \tau(x)$. Let C_T be the first C_k to contain $\tau(x)$. By (iii), if we omit a finite number of the k, $\tau_k(x_k) \subset C_{T+1}$ and $\tau_k(x) \cdot \subset C_{T+1}$. Hence by (ii) we can join $\tau_k(x)$ and $\tau_k(x_k)$ by a curve Γ_k lying wholly in C_{T+1}.

$\tau^{-1}(C_{T+1})$, being compact, by (iii) lies wholly in some C_J. And unless $\tau_k^{-1}(\Gamma_k) = \Delta_k$ lies wholly in C_{J+1}, we can choose $y_k \subset \Delta_k$ on the boundary of C_{J+1}. Hence if enumerable $\Delta_k \not\subset C_{J+1}$, by (ii) there exists a subsequence of such points $y_{k(i)}$, converging to some limit point y, which will by DL1 be a boundary point of C_{J+1}. But because $\tau_{k(i)}(y_{k(i)}) \subset \Gamma_{k(i)} \subset C_{T+1}$, we know that $\tau_{k(i)}(y_{k(i)}) \to \tau(y) \subset C_{T+1}$, and $y \subset \tau^{-1}(C_{T+1}) \subset C_J$. This contradicts (iii), since y is by hypothesis a limit point of $\mathfrak{S} - C_{J+1}$.

Therefore all but finite $\Delta_k \subset C_{J+1}$. And from here we can proceed (C_{J+1} being compact) as in the proof of Theorem 20.

It is evident that the conclusion of Theorem 21 can be extended to the sum of a finite number of mutually separated O-spaces; it is at least a plausible conjecture that it is true for all homogeneous sets in Cartesian space.

20. **Inadequacy.** Unfortunately, there is an important class of spaces whose shifts do not constitute a continuous group relative to B-convergence. We shall cite a simple example, and leave it to the reader to generalize the construction.

THEOREM 22: *There is a plane set* $\mathfrak{S}$ *whose shifts do not satisfy* LG2 *relative to B-convergence.*

$\mathfrak{S}$ contains $(0,0)$, and in addition the interior of the triangle whose vertices are $(-1,0)$, $(1,1)$, and $(1,0)$—using Cartesian coordinates. τ_k leaves the exterior of the triangle W_k whose vertices are $(-1,0)$, $(1/k, 1/k + 4/3k^2)$, and $(-\frac{1}{2},0)$ fixed, performs a focal shift (cf. §17) on W_k, relative to the broken lines $(-1,0)$ to $(0,1/k)$ to $(-\frac{1}{2},0)$, and $(-1,0)$ to $(-\frac{1}{4},2/3k)$ to $(-\frac{1}{2},0)$, and to the "focus" $(1/k, 1/k + 4/3k^2)$.

The reader will be able to visualize the transformations if he draws a figure analogous to figure one.

Suppose $p_k \to p$. If $p \neq (0,0)$, then the y-coordinate of p is positive, and for k large enough, since $p_k \not\subset W_k$, we have $\tau_k(p_k) = p_k \to p = 1(p)$. While if $p = (0,0)$, then since τ_k *increases* the distance from p of no point by more than $1/k$, it is still true that $\tau_k(p_k) \to p$. Hence by definition $\tau_k \to_B 1$.

Now set $q_k = (0,1/k)$, so that $\tau_k^{-1}(q_k) = (-\frac{1}{4},2/3k)$. Although $q_k \to q = (0,0)$, $\tau_k^{-1}(q_k) \not\to q$; hence $\tau_k^{-1} \not\to_B 1$, and the theorem is proved.[22]

[22] This example contradicts the principle asserted by H. Kneser in footnote 3, p. 366, Math. Zeits., 25 (1926). But our Theorems 20 and 21 confirm the applications he makes of the principle.

21. The Shifts of Compact Metric Spaces. Theorems 17 and 22 show that in general we must regard C-convergence as fundamental, if we wish to incorporate the ideas of Schreier into the theory of the topology of transformation-sets. We shall now show that for important classes of metric spaces, we can include in the same definitions the theory of the topology of Hilbert space.

A metric space is of course one in which to every pair (x, y) of points corresponds a number $\overline{xy}$ called the "distance" between x and y, satisfying

M1: $\overline{xx} = 0$; if $x \neq y$, then $\overline{xy} > 0$.
M2: $\overline{xy} = \overline{yx}$ irrespective of x and y.
M3: $\overline{xy} \leqq \overline{xz} + \overline{zy}$ irrespective of x, y, and z.

THEOREM 23: *If $\mathfrak{S}$ is a compact metric space, then the (continuous) group G of its shifts relative to C-convergence is homeomorphic with a perfectly separable metric space.*

Let σ and τ be any two shifts of $\mathfrak{S}$. By $\overline{\sigma\tau}$ we mean $\overline{\mathrm{Lim}}_{x \subset S}\, \overline{\sigma(x)\tau(x)}$. We shall prove the theorem in three parts: (i) $\sigma_k \to_C \sigma$ if and only if $\overline{\sigma\sigma_k} \to 0$ (ii) the distance function $\overline{\sigma\tau}$ is metric (iii) the space of the shifts is perfectly separable.

$\overline{\sigma(x_k)\sigma_k(x_k)} \leqq \overline{\sigma\sigma_k}$. And since σ is continuous, $\overline{xx_k} \to 0$ implies $\overline{\sigma(x)\sigma(x_k)} \to 0$. Hence if $\overline{\sigma\sigma_k} \to 0$ $\overline{xx_k} \to 0$, then $\overline{\sigma(x)\sigma_k(x_k)} \leqq \overline{\sigma(x)\sigma(x_k)} + \overline{\sigma(x_k)\sigma_k(x_k)} \to 0$, and $\sigma_k \to_B \sigma$. Conversely if $\overline{\sigma\sigma_k} \not\to 0$, we can choose a subsequence $\tau_i = \sigma_{k(i)}$ such that $\overline{\sigma\tau_i} \geqq \epsilon > 0$, and x_i such that $\overline{\sigma(x_i)\tau_i(x_i)} > \frac{3}{4}\epsilon$. Since $\mathfrak{S}$ is compact, there exists a subsequence $y_j = x_{i(j)}$ converging to some point y; setting $\rho_j = \sigma_{i(j)}$ we get $\overline{\sigma(y)\sigma(y_j)} \to 0$ and consequently $\overline{\sigma(y)\rho_j(y_j)} \geqq \overline{\sigma(y_j)\rho_j(y_j)} - \overline{\sigma(y)\sigma(y_j)} > \frac{1}{2}\epsilon$ for sufficiently large j. That is, $\sigma_k \not\to_B \sigma$, whence we see that $\overline{\sigma\sigma_k} \to 0$ and $\sigma_k \to_B \sigma$ are equivalent. Using Theorem 20, we get (i).

Obviously $\overline{\sigma\tau} = 0$ if $\sigma = \tau$; $\overline{\sigma\tau} > 0$ if $\sigma \neq \tau$. Equally obviously $\overline{\sigma\tau} = \overline{\tau\sigma}$. We can also easily prove M3, since for arbitrarily small positive ϵ, $\overline{\sigma(x)\tau(x)} = \overline{\sigma\tau} - \epsilon$, whence $\overline{\sigma\rho} + \overline{\rho\tau} \geqq \overline{\sigma(x)\rho(x)} + \overline{\rho(x)\tau(x)} \geqq \overline{\sigma(x)\tau(x)} \geqq \overline{\sigma\tau} - \epsilon$. This proves (ii).

Let $\epsilon > 0$ and τ be given. Set $\delta(\epsilon, \tau) = \underline{\mathrm{Lim}}_{\overline{\tau(x)\tau(y)} \geqq \epsilon}\, \overline{xy}$. Since $\mathfrak{S}$ is compact, $\delta(\epsilon, \tau) > 0$ identically; otherwise we could find a limit point x and sequences $\{x_k\}$ and $\{y_k\}$ such that $\overline{xx_k} \to 0$ and $\overline{x_k y_k} \to 0$, yet $\overline{\tau(x_k)\tau(y_k)} \geqq \epsilon$. There would ensue $\overline{xy_k} \leqq \overline{xx_k} + \overline{x_k y_k} \to 0$, therefore $\overline{\tau(x)\tau(x_k)} \to 0$ and $\overline{\tau(x)\tau(y_k)} \to 0$, contradicting $\epsilon \leqq \overline{\tau(x_k)\tau(y_k)} \leqq \overline{\tau(x_k)\tau(x)} + \overline{\tau(x)\tau(y_k)}$. Accordingly, if R_k is the domain of the τ for which $\delta(\epsilon, \tau) \geqq 1/k$, then

$$R_1 \subset R_2 \subset R_3 \subset \cdots \quad \text{and} \quad R_1 + R_2 + R_3 + \cdots = G.$$

Let us fix on a particular R_k, and choose in it successively $\tau_1, \tau_2, \tau_3, \cdots$ as long as possible, subject to the condition $i < n + 1$ implies $\overline{\tau_i\tau_{n+1}} \geqq 5\epsilon$. Suppose we got in this way an infinite sequence of τ_i.

For each j, x'_j would exist satisfying $\overline{\tau_1(x'_j)\tau_j(x'_j)} \geqq 4\epsilon$. Moreover $\{x'_j\}$ would have a limit point x_1, to which would correspond an infinite subsequence of $\{x'_j\}$ satisfying $\overline{x_1x'_j} < 1/k$. Consequently

$$\overline{\tau_1(x_1)\tau_j(x_1)} \geqq \overline{\tau_1(x'_j)\tau_j(x'_j)} - \overline{\tau_1(x_1)\tau_1(x'_j)} - \overline{\tau_j(x'_j)\tau_j(x_1)}$$

$$\geqq 4\epsilon - \epsilon - \epsilon = 2\epsilon .$$

Proceeding inductively, we could get $\tau_1, \tau_2, \tau_3, \cdots$ and $x_1, x_2, x_3, \cdots$ such that $i < j$ implied $\overline{\tau_i(x_i)\tau_j(x_i)} \geqq 2\epsilon$. Since $\mathfrak{S}$ is compact, $\{x_i\}$ would have a limit point y, and a subsequence $\{y_k\}$ which converged to y. Restricting to $\overline{yy_k} < 1/2k$, whence $\overline{y_iy_j} < 1/k$, we would have a new infinite subsequence $\{z_k\}$ such that $i < j$ implied $\overline{\tau_i(z_i)\tau_j(z_j)} \geqq \overline{\tau_i(z_i)\tau_j(z_i)} - \overline{\tau_j(z_i)\tau_j(z_j)} = 2\epsilon - \epsilon = \epsilon$. Therefore the $\tau_k(z_k)$ could not have a limit point, contradicting the compactness of $\mathfrak{S}$.

That is, we obtain a finite sequence $\tau_1, \cdots, \tau_n$ such that every τ of R_k satisfies $\overline{\tau\tau_i} < 5\epsilon$ for some i; that is, the τ_i are 5ϵ-dense in R_k. Summing for k, and again for $\epsilon = \frac{1}{2}, \frac{1}{4}, 1/8, \cdots$ we have an enumerable set of τ_i dense in G, giving us[23] (iii).

22. **Generalization.** We can make the following important generalization of Theorem 23, namely

THEOREM 24: *If* $\mathfrak{S} = C_1 + C_2 + C_3 + \cdots$, *and* (i) $C_k \subset C_{k+1}$ (ii) *the* C_k *are compact metric sets* (iii) $x_k \not\subset C_k$ *precludes the convergence of* $\{x_k\}$, *then the group* G *of the shifts of* $\mathfrak{S}$ *is homeomorphic (under* C*-convergence) with a subset of Hilbert space.*

Set $r_n(\sigma, \tau) = \text{Min}\ \{1, \overline{\text{Lim}}_{x \subset c_n}\ (\overline{\sigma(x)\tau(x)} + \overline{\sigma^{-1}(x)\tau^{-1}(x)})\}$. Then define $\overline{\sigma\tau} = \sum_{n=1}^{\infty} (1/n^2) \cdot r_n(\sigma, \tau)$. Evidently $\overline{\sigma\tau} = \overline{\sigma^{-1}\tau^{-1}}$, and we can show as in Theorem 23 that $\overline{\sigma\tau}$ satisfies M1–M3.

Suppose $\overline{\sigma\sigma_k} \to 0$, and let $x_k \to x$ be given. By (iii) and SL3 we can choose N so large that $C_N \supset \{x_k\} + x$. So soon as $\overline{\sigma\sigma_k} < \epsilon/N^2$, and $\overline{\sigma(x)\sigma(x_k)} < \epsilon$, then $\overline{\sigma(x)\sigma_k(x_k)} < 2\epsilon$; similarly $\overline{\sigma^{-1}(x)\sigma_k^{-1}(x_k)} < 2\epsilon$. Therefore $\overline{\sigma\sigma_k} \to 0$ implies $\sigma_k \to_C \sigma$.

Conversely, suppose $\overline{\sigma\sigma_k} \nrightarrow 0$. We can choose a subsequence $\sigma_{k(i)}$ satisfying $\overline{\sigma\sigma_{k(i)}} > 3/L$, and hence, since $\sum_{n=L+1}^{\infty} r_n(\sigma, \tau) \cdot (1/n^2) < 1/L$, $x_i \subset C_L$ satisfying $\overline{\sigma(x_i)\sigma_i(x_i)} > 1/L$ or else $\overline{\sigma^{-1}(x_i)\sigma^{-1}(x_i)} > 1/L$. In any case, by taking a convergent subsequence, we can prove (essentially as in Theorem 23) that $\sigma_k \nrightarrow_C \sigma$. This proves that G is homeomorphic (under C-convergence) with the metric space defined in paragraph one. It remains to show that an everywhere dense enumerable set exists in G.

To show this, observe that, given (i, j), we can prove (again as in Theorem

[23] Cf. for example S. Lefschetz, "Topology," New York, 1930, p. 6.

23) that there are enumerable transformations dense with respect to transformations τ such that $\tau(C_i) \subset C_j$ while $\tau^{-1}(C_i) \subset (C_j)$. But the (enumerable) sum of these is dense in G, as the reader can easily check.

COROLLARY: *In Theorems* 23 *and* 24, *G is a T-group in the sense of van Dantzig.*[24]

In view of the intimate connection between continuous transformations and continuous functions on the one hand, and continuous functions and Hilbert space on the other, we cannot regard Theorems 23 and 24 as very surprising; what is more surprising is that they are not susceptible of more universal generalizations.

23. **Restriction on generality.** In fact, it is not even true that shift-groups of simple metric spaces are in general T-groups in the sense of van Dantzig. We shall illustrate this by an example, which the reader will see is capable of wide generalization.

Let $\mathfrak{S}$ be the sum of the point (0,0) and the rectangle interior $-1 < x < 1$, $0 < y < 2$. Let τ_j^i $[i = 3, 4, 5, \cdots ; j = 1, 2, 3, \cdots]$ leave the exterior of the triangle W_j whose vertices are p_j: $(-1, 1/j + 1/j^2)$, q_j: $(0, 1/j)$, and r_j: $(-1, 1/j - 1/j^2)$ fixed; let it perform a focal shift (§17) on W_j, away from the "focus" q_j, carrying the broken line p_j to $(-1/i, 1/j)$ to r_j into the broken line p_j to $(-\frac{1}{2}, 1/j)$ to r_j.

$\tau_j^i \rightarrow_C 1 = \tau_i$ (as in the proof of Theorem 19), and consequently $\tau_i \rightarrow_C 1$. Nevertheless no matter what $N(i)$ we choose, if we set $j(i)$ greater than i and $N(i)$, then $\tau_{j(i)}^i(-1/i, 1/j(i)) = (-\frac{1}{2}, 1/j(i)) \nrightarrow (0,0)$, in spite of the fact that $(-1/i, 1/j(i)) \rightarrow (0,0)$. This proves

THEOREM 25: *There exists a plane set whose shifts do not satisfy* DL1 *relative to C-convergence.*

Theorem 25 shows why the shifts of a given space are not a Hausdorff space; any Hausdorff space satisfies DL1.

It might be thought, because of the parallelism between Theorems 17–19 and Theorems 23–25, that spaces whose shifts were homeomorphic with a subset of Hilbert space were spaces in which B-convergence was effectively identical with C-convergence. To destroy this conjecture, the plane set of points $(i, 1/j)$ and $(i, 0)$ $[i, j = 1, 2, 3, \cdots]$ is sufficient. Its shifts are homeomorphic (under C-convergence) with a subset of Hilbert space, yet in it B-convergence and C-convergence are not effectively equivalent.

24. **Linear transformations.** Linear transformations deserve a special study because of their central rôle in analysis. Of course in the case of finite dimensions, the set of the linear transformations of one vector-space into any other is homeomorphic with an easily identified subset of ordinary Cartesian space.

Concerning the more complex case of infinite dimensions, we shall prove a few basic and easily demonstrable theorems. We shall deal exclusively with

[24] "Topologische Algebra. I. Komplettierungstheorie," Math. Ann. **107** (1933), 587–626.

"B-spaces" in the sense of Banach[25]—that is, with metrized, topologically complete vector spaces in which distance is invariant under simple translations.

It is known[26] that any $(1 \to 1)$ linear (continuous) transformation τ of a first B-space $\mathfrak{B}_1$ into a second B-space $\mathfrak{B}_2$ has a "norm" $|\tau|$ with the property that $|\tau(x) - \tau(x')| \leqq |\tau| \cdot |x - x'|$ for any x and x' in $\mathfrak{B}_1$. Further, it is known[27] that if $\tau_n \to_A \tau$, then $|\tau_n|$ is bounded, say by τ^*.

In virtue of the simple formula

$$\begin{aligned} |\tau_n(x_n) - \tau(x)| &\leqq |\tau_n(x) - \tau_n(x)| + |\tau_n(x) - \tau(x)| \\ &\leqq \tau^* \cdot |x_n - x| + |\tau_n(x) - \tau(x)| \end{aligned}$$

we can say that if also $|x_n - x| \to 0$, then $|\tau_n(x_n) - \tau(x)| \to 0$. That is, $\tau_n \to_A \tau$ implies $\tau_n \to_B \tau$, and (the converse being obvious)

THEOREM 26: *A-convergence and B-convergence are effectively equivalent for linear transformations of B-spaces.*

COROLLARY: *If a sequence $\{\sigma_n\}$ of linear transformations of the B-space $\mathfrak{B}_1$ into the B-space $\mathfrak{B}_2$ A-converges to the limit σ, while the sequence $\{\tau_n\}$ of linear transformations of $\mathfrak{B}_2$ into $\mathfrak{B}_3$ A-converges to the limit τ, then $\sigma_n \tau_n \to_A \sigma\tau$.*

However, A-convergence does not imply C-convergence, even for $(1,1)$ bicontinuous transformations of the Hilbert space $\mathfrak{H}$ into itself. To see this, let $\xi_1, \xi_2, \xi_3, \cdots$ be a complete set of "orthonormal"[28] points in $\mathfrak{H}$, and let $\tau_n(\xi_k) = \xi_k$ when $k \neq n$, while $\tau_n(\xi_n) = (1/n) \cdot \xi_n$. $\tau_n \to_A 1$, yet since $|\tau_n^{-1}| = n$ is not bounded, $|\tau_n^{-1}| \not\to_A 1$.

THEOREM 27: *Neither the functionals nor the* $(1,1)$ *bicontinuous linear transformations of Hilbert space satisfy* DL1.

To prove the first half of Theorem 27, let $f_j^i(\xi_k) = 0$ if $k \neq 1$ or j; let $f_j^i(\xi_1) = 1$, and $f_j^i(\xi_j) = i$. Then for fixed i, $f_j^i \to_A f$ [where $f(\xi_1) \equiv 1$ and $f(\xi_k) \equiv 0$ if $k \neq 1$]. Yet since $|f_j^i| = i$, $f_{j(i)}^i \not\to_A f$ no matter how we choose $j(i)$.

The second half can be similarly proved by setting $\tau_j^i(\xi_k) = \xi_k$ when $k \neq j$, and $\tau_j^i(\xi_j) = i \cdot \xi_j$.

The effect of a change in the definition of the convergence of transformation sequences on the topology of transformation-sets is strikingly illustrated by the contrast between Theorem 27 and the fact that the linear transformations of a B-space into itself are again a B-space under the obvious definitions of the sum of two transformations and the product of a transformation by a constant, and Banach's definition of the "norm" of a transformation. That is, being metric, they certainly satisfy DL1 if we replace ordinary convergence by uniform convergence.

HARVARD UNIVERSITY.

---

[25] S. Banach, "Théorie des operations linéaires," Warsaw, 1932; cf. p. 53, p. 26. Banach defines convergence as our A-convergence.

[26] Ibid., p. 54, Theorem 1.

[27] Ibid., p. 80, Theorem 5.

[28] Cf. M. H. Stone, "Linear transformations of Hilbert space," New York, 1932, p. 7 (Definition 1.6).

ANNALS OF MATHEMATICS
Vol. 38, No. 1, January, 1937

MOORE-SMITH CONVERGENCE IN GENERAL TOPOLOGY

BY GARRETT BIRKHOFF

(Received April 27, 1936)

1. **Introduction.** In ordinary space, there are three basic topological notions, out of which all others flow. These are the notions of *convergence*, *closure*, and *neighborhood*.

Their interdependence is well-known. The "closure" $\bar{S}$ of any subset S of ordinary space is composed of the limits of the convergent sequences of points of S. A set U is a "neighborhood" of a point x of space if and only if it contains x, and has a closed complement (i.e., a complement $T = U'$ satisfying $T = \bar{T}$). And finally, a sequence $\{x_k\}$ of points of space "converges" to the limit point x (in symbols, $x_k \to x$), if and only if every neighborhood of x contains all but a finite number of the x_k.

Now these definitions of closure in terms of convergence, of neighborhoods in terms of closure, and of convergence in terms of neighborhood are mutually consistent in any metric space, provided one begins by defining $x_k \to x$ to mean $| x_k - x | \to 0$. They are even consistent in any Hausdorff space satisfying the first countability axiom, provided one starts with neighborhoods.

But in many important "spaces" of functions (and of transformations), they are not. One can still pass from closure to neighborhoods and back, relying on the fact that passage from sets to their complements turns open sets into closed sets, and vice-versa. But it is not known how to correlate in a consistent fashion topological properties flowing out of the notions of closure and neighborhood, with those flowing out of the notion of convergence.

The main contribution of this paper is to show how this can be done. To do it, one must speak of the "convergence" of ordered arrays of points in patterns including transfinite sequences as a special case, and amounting with numbers to the generalized notion of limit introduced by E. H. Moore and H. L. Smith [8], and based on an idea of E. H. Moore [7'].

Part I of the paper contains a detailed exposition of the logical equivalence of convergence in this generalized sense, with the notion of closure (and hence of neighborhood). In Part II it is shown how (generalizing a construction introduced by van Dantzig [2]) topological linear spaces can always be "completed" in this sense, without assuming the first countability axiom. In dispensing with this assumption one makes essential use of Moore-Smith convergence.

It is also shown that this completeness is stronger than the definition of completeness (in terms of the compactness of totally bounded sets) introduced by von Neumann [9]. Other applications of Moore-Smith convergence, to the topologization of transformation-sets and general integration, conclude Part II.

Part III contains a brief description of topologies (p-adic, etc.) associated *intrinsically* with various special algebraic systems. By completing the "topological algebras" one gets in this way, one is likely to obtain systems with important and unexpected properties. As a new example, one has the topologized discrete free groups.

Parts II and III are preceded by special prefaces.

BIBLIOGRAPHY

[1] G. Birkhoff, *On the structure of abstract algebras*, Proc. Camb. Phil. Soc. 31 (1935), 433–54.
[2] D. van Dantzig, *Zur topologische Algebra*. I., Math. Annalen 107 (1933), 587–626.
[3] D. van Dantzig, *Zur topologische Algebra*. II., Compositio Math. 2 (1935), 201–23.
[4] M. Fréchet, *Les espaces abstraits*, Paris, 1928.
[5] F. Hausdorff, *Grundzüge der Mengenlehre*, Leipzig, 1914.
[6] C. Kuratowski, *Topologie*, Warsaw, 1934.
[7] E. H. Moore, *On a form of general analysis*, Yale Colloquium Lectures, 1910.
[7′] E. H. Moore, *Definition of limit in general integral analysis*, Proc. Nat. Acad. Sci., vol. 1 (1915), p. 628.
[8] E. H. Moore, and H. L. Smith, *A general theory of limits*, Am. Jour. 44 (1922), 102–21.
[9] J. von Neumann, *On complete topological spaces*, Trans. Am. Math. Soc. 37 (1935), 1–20.
[10] M. H. Stone, *Boolean algebras and their application to topology*, Proc. Nat. Acad. Sci. 20 (1934), 197–202.
[11] L. Vietoris, *Stetige Mengen*, Monats. f. Math. u. Phys., 31 (1921), 173–204.

I. General Topology

2. Generalized convergence in abstract topological spaces. Let $\mathfrak{X}$ be any abstract topological space[1] that is, any aggregate of points whose "open" subsets are a well-defined class including (O1) all sets omitting fewer than two points, (O2) the union of any number of open sets, (O3) the intersection of any two open sets.

Definition 1: By a *directed set* of points x_α of $\mathfrak{X}$ is meant an ordering of points, one to each subscript of a class A, where (D1) given $\alpha \epsilon A$, $\beta \epsilon A$, either α follows β (in symbols, $\alpha > \beta$) or α does not follow β (in symbols, $\alpha \not> \beta$), (D2) if $\alpha > \beta$ and $\beta > \gamma$, then $\alpha > \gamma$, (D3) given $\alpha \epsilon A$, $\beta \epsilon A$, there exists $\gamma \epsilon A$ satisfying $\gamma > \alpha$ and $\gamma > \beta$.

It is immaterial whether or not it is assumed that $\alpha > \beta$ and $\beta > \alpha$ imply $\alpha = \beta$.

It is primarily condition (D3) which was due to Moore and Smith, and which distinguishes directed sets from other "partially ordered sets"[28] (cf. [5], Chap. VI, §1).

Remark: A directed set $\{x_\alpha\}$ is a sequence in the usual sense if and only if A is the class of natural integers; $\{x_\alpha\}$ is a "transfinite sequence" in the usual sense[2] if and only if A is the class of all ordinals less than some limit ordinal.

---

[1] In the sense of [6], p. 15. This includes Hausdorff spaces (cf. [5], p. 213, and [4], p. 186) as special cases.

[2] Cf. C. W. Vickery, *Spaces in which there exist uncountable convergent sequences of points*, Tohoku Math. Jour. 40 (1934).

DEFINITION 2: The directed set $\{x_\alpha\}$ is said to *converge* to the *limit point* x (in symbols, $x_\alpha \to x$) if and only if, given any open set S containing x, there exists an $\alpha_0 = \alpha(S)$ such that $\alpha > \alpha_0$ implies $x_\alpha \epsilon S$.

The full reciprocity between this generalized notion of convergence and openness (and hence closure) is shown by

THEOREM 1: *A subset S of $\mathfrak{X}$ is open if and only if no directed set of points outside of S converges to a point in S.*

PROOF: Suppose S is open. Then any directed set $\{x_\alpha\}$ converging to any $x \epsilon S$ must have every x_α with $\alpha > \alpha(S)$ in S; hence no directed set of points outside of S can converge to a point in S.

Conversely, suppose S is not open. Then by (O2) the union of its open subsets must exclude at lease one $x \epsilon S$, and every open set U_α containing this x must have at least one point x_α outside of S. Now order the indices α by the rule that α follows β means $U_\alpha \subset U_\beta$; then by the algebra of set-inclusion and (O3), the indices will form a directed set. And by definition, $x_\alpha \to x$—to any open set U_α containing x associate α. Hence there exists a directed set of points outside of S converging to a point in S.

3. **Continuity and product-spaces.** The definitions of convergence and open sets (and hence of closed sets!) in terms of each other given above are not only mutually consistent, but they are also consistent with the simplest conceptions of continuity—whether of functions of one or of several variables. This will be shown in the present section.

THEOREM 2: *Let F be any function from a space $\mathfrak{X}$ to a space $\mathfrak{Y}$. The following conditions are equivalent:*

(1) *If $x_\alpha \to x$ in $\mathfrak{X}$, then $F(x_\alpha) \to F(x)$ in $\mathfrak{Y}$.*

(2) *If $x \epsilon \mathfrak{X}$, and U is any open set of $\mathfrak{Y}$ which contains $F(x)$, then the interior of $F^{-1}(U)$ contains x.*

(The conclusion of condition (2) can be restated as the condition that some open set V containing x is carried by F into a subset of U.)

PROOF: Suppose that for some x and U, the interior of $F^{-1}(U)$ does not contain x. Then by Theorem 1 there exists a directed set x_α outside of $F^{-1}(U)$ tending to x, and the $F(x_\alpha)$, which lie outside of U, cannot tend to $F(x)$. Conversely, if $x_\alpha \to x$, and (2) is satisfied, then given any open set U containing $F(x)$, the interior of $F^{-1}(U)$ is an open set containing x. Hence for some α_0, $\alpha > \alpha_0$ implies $x_\alpha \epsilon F^{-1}(U)$, and so $F(x_\alpha) \epsilon U$, whence $x_\alpha \to x$.

REMARK: Condition (2) is the usual definition of continuity for functions between abstract spaces ([6], p. 66). While condition (1) is the usual definition of continuity in terms of convergence.

THEOREM 3: *Let $\mathfrak{X}$ and $\mathfrak{Y}$ be any two topological spaces, and let the open sets of the product-space $\mathfrak{X} \times \mathfrak{Y}$ be the unions of products $U \times V$ of open sets U of $\mathfrak{X}$ and V of $\mathfrak{Y}$. Then $[x_\alpha, y_\alpha] \to [x, y]$ if and only if $x_\alpha \to x$ and $y_\alpha \to y$.*

PROOF: Suppose $x_\alpha \to x$ and $y_\alpha \to y$, and that W is a neighborhood[3] of $[x, y]$. Then by definition, W is the union of those products $U \times V$ of open sets U in $\mathfrak{X}$ and V in $\mathfrak{Y}$ which lie in W, and so at least one such set must contain $[x, y]$. Since $x_\alpha \to x$ and $y_\alpha \to y$, α_1 and α_2 exist such that $\alpha > \alpha_1$ implies $x_\alpha \epsilon U$ and $\alpha > \alpha_2$ implies $y_\alpha \epsilon V$. And one can find $\alpha_0 > \alpha_1$ and α_2, whence by (D2), $\alpha > \alpha_0$ implies $[x_\alpha, y_\alpha] \epsilon U \times V \subset W$. Hence $[x_\alpha, y_\alpha] \to [x, y]$.

Conversely, suppose $[x_\alpha, y_\alpha] \to [x, y]$. Then given any neighborhood U of x, since $U \times \mathfrak{Y}$ is open in $\mathfrak{X} \times \mathfrak{Y}$, for some α_0, $\alpha > \alpha_0$ implies $[x_\alpha, y_\alpha] \epsilon U \times \mathfrak{Y}$—which is to say $x_\alpha \epsilon U$. Hence $x_\alpha \to x$; similarly $y_\alpha \to y$. This completes the proof.

A similar argument clearly leads to a similar theorem on the product of any finite number of topological spaces. By combining this fact with Theorem 2, we see that a function of (for instance) three variables is continuous if and only if $x_\alpha \to x$, $x_\alpha \to y$, and $z_\alpha \to z$ imply $F(x_\alpha, y_\alpha, z_\alpha) \to F(x, y, z)$—or equivalently, if and only if to any neighborhood W of $F(x_0, y_0, z_0)$ correspond neighborhoods U_x of x_0, U_y of y_0, and U_z of z_0 such that $F(x, y, z) \epsilon W$ for any $x \epsilon U_x$, $y \epsilon U_y$, and $z \epsilon U_z$.

4. **Properties of convergence.** It is natural to ask, what formal properties does convergence possess? One would like to know two things about such properties—the way in which they generalize properties of ordinary convergent sequences, and whether they imply conversely the properties of open sets which were assumed at the start.

The latter question is answered in the affirmative below, and the general notion of a directed set plays an essential rôle in giving the answer.

The following definition will be used frequently:

DEFINITION 3: A subset B of the subscripts α of a directed set $\{x_\alpha\}$ is called *cofinal* if and only if, given α, $\beta \epsilon B$ exists satisfying $\beta > \alpha$.

REMARK: Any infinite subset of an ordinary sequence $x_1, x_2, x_3, \cdots$ is cofinal. Moreover, in general, any cofinal subset of a directed set is a directed set.

The reader will find no difficulty in verifying that the following properties of generalized convergence hold in any topological space $\mathfrak{X}$,

(4α) If $x_\alpha = x$ for every α, then $x_\alpha \to x$.

(4β) If $x_\alpha \to x$ and the β are a cofinal subset of the α, then $x_\beta \to x$.

THEOREM 4: *A topological space $\mathfrak{X}$ is a Hausdorff space if and only if*

(4γ) *$x_\alpha \to x$ and $x_\alpha \to y$ imply $x = y$.*

(A topological space is called a *Hausdorff* space if and only if any two distinct points of it have disjoint neighborhoods. Cf. conditions (D) and (D′) of [11], p. 174.)

PROOF: If $\mathfrak{X}$ is a Hausdorff space, if $x \neq y$, and if $x_\alpha \to x$, then choosing disjoint

[3] By a *neighborhood* of a point x of a topological space $\mathfrak{X}$, is meant an open set of $\mathfrak{X}$ containing x.

open sets U containing x and V containing y, we see that for every $\alpha > \alpha_0$, $x_\alpha \epsilon U$, hence no $x_\alpha \epsilon V$, and $x_\alpha \rightarrow y$ is impossible. That is, if $\mathfrak{X}$ is a Hausdorff space, then $x_\alpha \rightarrow x$ and $x_\alpha \rightarrow y$ imply $x = y$. Conversely, if $\mathfrak{X}$ contains distinct points x and y all of whose neighborhoods overlap, then ordering to each pair (U, V) of neighborhoods U of x and V of y a symbol α, setting $\alpha > \alpha'$ if and only if $U \subset U'$ and $V \subset V'$, and assigning to each α any $x_\alpha \epsilon U \cap V$, we have a directed set x_α converging to x and to y. That is, if $\mathfrak{X}$ is not a Hausdorff space, then $x_\alpha \rightarrow x$ and $x_\alpha \rightarrow y$ do not imply $x = y$.

THEOREM 5: *In a topological space $\mathfrak{X}$, it is true that* (4δ) *if $x_\alpha \rightarrow x$ and for fixed α, $x^\alpha_\beta \rightarrow x_\alpha$, then, denoting generically by B functions $\alpha \rightarrow x^\alpha_\beta = x^\alpha_{\beta(\alpha)}$, and saying that (α_2, B_2) follows (α_1, B_1) if and only if α_2 follows α_1 and $B_2(\alpha) > B_1(\alpha)$ for all α, the couples (α, B) form a directed set, and $x^\alpha_{\beta(\alpha)} \rightarrow x$.*

PROOF: That the (α, B) are a directed set is obvious, since given (α_1, B_1) and (α_2, B_2), one can find $\alpha_3 > \alpha_1, \alpha_2$, and for each α, $B_3(\alpha) > B_1(\alpha), B_2(\alpha)$. Now given an open set U containing x, one can so choose α_0 that $\alpha > \alpha_0$ implies $x_\alpha \epsilon U$, and for each $\alpha > \alpha_0$ so choose $B_0(\alpha)$ that $\beta > B_0(\alpha)$ implies $x^\alpha_\beta \epsilon U$; hence $(\alpha, B) > (\alpha_0, B_0)$ implies $x^\alpha_{B(\alpha)} \epsilon U$, whence $x^\alpha_B \rightarrow x$.

THEOREM 6: *In a topological space $\mathfrak{X}$, $x_\alpha \rightarrow x$ if and only if* (4ε) *given an undirected cofinal subset N of subscripts $\alpha(\nu)$, one can find a directed set B of indices β, and a function $\nu(\beta)$ such that $x_{\alpha(\nu(\beta))} \rightarrow x$.*

PROOF: If $x_\alpha \rightarrow x$, then one can set $B = N$, and $\nu(\beta) = \beta$; by (4β) $x_{\alpha(\nu(\beta))} \rightarrow x$. Conversely, if x_α does not tend to x, then for some neighborhood U of x the x_α not in U are a cofinal subset (by Definitions 2 and 3) from which one cannot possibly by elimination and rearrangement extract a directed set converging to x.

THEOREM 7: *If $\mathfrak{X}$ is any system of points, in which it is decided which directed sets converge to which points, then $\mathfrak{X}$ is a topological space under the criterion of Theorem* 1 *provided* (4α) — (4δ) *hold and $x_\alpha \rightarrow x$ is equivalent to* (4ε).

PROOF: We have to show that the open sets satisfy (O1)–(O3) of §2, and that directed sets converge according to Definition 1. But by (4α) and (4γ), if $\{x_\alpha\}$ is outside of a set $\mathfrak{X} - x$ omitting only one point, then $x_\alpha \rightarrow y$ implies that $y = x$; this verifies (O1). Again, if S is the union of open sets, then a directed set outside of S must be outside of every such open set, and hence can converge to no point in any such open set—and hence to no point of S; this verifies (O2). Finally, it is not hard to show[4] that if $\{x_\alpha\}$ is any directed set, and B is any subset of $\{x_\alpha\}$ which is not cofinal, then the indices γ not in B are a cofinal subset. Hence if $S \cap T$ is the common part of two open sets S and T, any directed set $\{x_\alpha\}$ outside of $S \cap T$ must contain a cofinal subset outside of S, or else one outside of T—this cofinal subset can converge to no point of $S \cap T$, hence neither can $\{x_\alpha\}$. This verifies (O3).

It remains to show that $x_\alpha \rightarrow x$ if and only if, given a neighborhood U of x, $\alpha_0 = \alpha(U)$ exists such that $\alpha > \alpha_0$ implies $x_\alpha \epsilon U$. But if $x_\alpha \rightarrow x$, and U is open,

[4] For, given α, take α_0 with no $\beta > \alpha_0$. Then $\alpha_1 > \alpha, \alpha_0$ exists: α_1 is not in B, yet $\alpha_1 > \alpha$.

then by (4β) the points outside of U are non-cofinal, whence by Definition 3 the points in U include every x with $\alpha > \alpha(U)$. Conversely, if x_α does not tend to x, then by (4ϵ) one can find an undirected cofinal subset N of subscripts $\alpha(\nu)$ yielding no $x_{\alpha(\nu(\beta))} \to x$. But this simply says that the limits of convergent directed sets of points of N, which by (4δ) are a closed set,[5] do not include x. Hence the set-complement N' of N is an open set containing x, but containing no point $x_{\alpha(\nu)}$ of a cofinal subset of $\{x_2\}$—whence no $\alpha(N')$ can exist making $\alpha > \alpha(N')$ imply $x_\alpha \epsilon N'$, completing the proof.

(The converse of Theorem 7 has already been proved.)

4a. **Digression on the metrization problem.** In section four we obtained properties of the convergence of directed sets which were necessary and sufficient for a Hausdorff topology. Actually, these properties are extensions of well-known properties of ordinary sequences.

[Thus (4α) – (4γ) simply extend Fréchet's definition of an L-space. (4δ) extends to directed sets the condition that derived sets be closed: that if for all i, $x_j^i \to x_i$, and if $x_i \to x$, then $j(i)$ exists such that $x_{j(i)}^i \to x$. (4ϵ) extends the condition that if every subsequence of a sequence $\{x_i\}$ contains a subsubsequence converging to x, then $x_i \to x$.]

We shall now digress to show how nearly this leaves one in a position to map a convergence-space onto a coördinate space, solely by postulating properties of convergence!

In fact, using a device described elsewhere,[6] one can show

THEOREM 7a: *A Hausdorff space $\mathfrak{X}$ is regular if and only if in it, $x_\beta^\alpha \to x_\alpha$ for every α, and $x_{\beta(\alpha)}^\alpha \to x$ for every $\beta(\alpha)$, imply $x_\alpha \to x$.*

[PROOF: Let X be any closed set of $\mathfrak{X}$, and x any point not in X. If one cannot surround X and x by disjoint open sets, then every neighborhood U_x^α of x has a closure intersecting X in some point x_α. Hence by Theorem 1, one can find a directed set $\{x_\beta^\alpha\} \subset U_x^\alpha$ converging to x_α. Clearly, irrespective of $\beta(\alpha)$, $x_{\beta(\alpha)}^\alpha \to x$; nevertheless, x_α does not converge to x. Conversely if $\mathfrak{X}$ is *regular*, then if $x_\beta^\alpha \to x_\alpha$ and $x_{\beta(\alpha)}^\alpha \to x$ identically, the closure of $\{x_\alpha\}$ contains x—otherwise we could separate $\{x_\alpha\}$ and x by open sets, and find for each α a $\beta(\alpha)$ so large that $x_{\beta(\alpha)}^\alpha$ lay outside the open set containing x. But (since the hypotheses hold for every cofinal subset of the $\{x_\alpha\}$), by (4ϵ), this implies that $x_\alpha \to x$.]

But a Hausdorff space which is *normal* can be mapped topologically onto a coördinate-space by a simple construction due to P. Urysohn.[7] Hence the only gap left to fill is the characterization in terms of convergence, of those regular Hausdorff spaces which are normal. Since this distinction is vacuous for sepa-

[5] (4δ) assumes that if $x_\beta^\alpha \to x$, and $x_\alpha \to x$, then there exists a directed set of the x_β^α converging to x; in more familiar language, that *derived sets are closed*.

[6] Cf. the author's *Axiomatic definitions of perfectly separable metric spaces*, Bull. Am. Math. Soc. 39 (1933), 601–7.

[7] *Zum Metrisationsproblem*, Math. Annalen 94. (1925), 309–15. Cf. also E. W. Chittenden, *On the metrization problem*, Bull. Am. Math. Soc. 33 (1927), 13–34.

rable (by a theorem of Tychonoff) and for bicompact spaces, we see how very little there is left to do.

5. **Convergence of systems of sets.** What will be useful in Part III, and is also interesting for its own sake, is the notion of the convergence of a system of sets, as defined by[8]

DEFINITION 4: A system Σ of sets S_α of a topological space $\mathfrak{X}$ will be called *overlapping* if and only if[9] the common part $S_\alpha \cap S_\beta$ of any two sets of Σ contains some third set S_γ of Σ. Σ will be said to *converge* to the point $x \epsilon \mathfrak{X}$ (in symbols, $\Sigma \to x$) if and only if it is overlapping and every neighborhood U_x of x contains some set S_α of Σ.

This definition is essentially equivalent to the notion of the convergence of a directed set of points, since

THEOREM 8: *Let Σ be any overlapping system of sets S_α. Then the S_α are a directed set if one defines $\alpha > \beta$ to mean S_α is included in S_β. While $\Sigma \to x$ if and only if under this ordering $x_\alpha \epsilon S_\alpha$ implies $x_\alpha \to x$.*

PROOF: The first statement is obvious. To prove the second, note (a) that if $S_\alpha \subset U_x$, then $\beta > \alpha$ implies $S_\beta \subset S_\alpha \subset U_x$, whence $\Sigma \to x$ and $x_\alpha \epsilon S_\alpha$ imply $x_\alpha \to x$, and (b) that if x_α does not tend to x for some $x_\alpha \epsilon S_\alpha$, then the x_α outside of some U_x are a representative subset, whence no $S_\alpha \subset U_x$ (otherwise $\beta > \alpha$ would imply $x_\beta \epsilon S_\beta \subset S_\alpha \subset U_x$), and so Σ would not tend to x.

An example of the meaning of the convergence of a system of sets is furnished by the fact that the neighborhoods of any point x of a topological space converge to x. In fact, a necessary and sufficient condition that a system of neighborhoods of x converge to x, is that they form a "complete" system in the usual sense.

6. **The "type" of a space.** One naturally wants to know when the rather intricate theory given above is needed, and when one can get along with simpler kinds of convergence.

The principle involved is, that in discussing any space $\mathfrak{X}$, one needs to use enough kinds of directed sets to make the *topology* of $\mathfrak{X}$ implicitly described in a statement of which directed sets of these kinds converge to which points. And for this it is sufficient that the closure $\bar{S}$ of any set S be composed of the limits of convergent directed sets *of these kinds* of points of S (cf. Theorem 1).

One can show that the first countability axiom ([5]), p. 263) roughly expresses the conditions under which ordinary sequences are enough (Theorem 9), and that even transfinite sequences of unrestricted ordinal number are inadequate under some circumstances (Theorem 10).

The precise formulation of these ideas leads directly to the concept of the *type* of a topological space.

---

[8] Abstract 41-9-355 of the Bull. Am. Math. Soc.

[9] I.e., if and only if they are a directed set when ordered with respect to set-inclusion.

DEFINITION 5:[10] Let Ω be any collection of abstract directed sets A^ξ of indices. A topological space $\mathfrak{X}$ will be called of *type* $\subseteqq \Omega$ if and only if the closure $\bar{S}$ of any set S in $\mathfrak{X}$ is composed of the limits of the convergent directed sets x_α of points of S, whose indices belong to some $A^\xi \epsilon \Omega$. By A^ϕ [ϕ any ordinal number], will be denoted the directed set of ordinals $< \phi$, one ordinal being said to "follow" another if and only if it is greater than or equal to it. A space $\mathfrak{X}$ will be called *of ordinal type* if and only if it is of the type of the transfinite sequences.

THEOREM 9: *A space is of type A^1, if and only if it is discrete. If it satisfies the first countability axiom, then it is of type A^ω [ω the first infinite ordinal].*

The proofs, which are easy, are omitted. It can even be shown that if the directed sets of Ω are all countable, then any space of type $\subseteqq \Omega$ is of type $\subseteqq A^\omega$. The reader may find it instructive to consider the simplifications made possible by the assumptions that $\mathfrak{X}$ is of type A^1 resp. A^ω.

THEOREM 10: *The space of real functions $x(t)$ defined over the interval $0 \leqq t \leqq 1$ and topologized relative to point-wise convergence,[11] is not of ordinal type.*

PROOF: Let S consist of all characteristic functions of finite sets—that is, of all functions a finite number of whose values are unity, and the rest of which are zero.

Then the closure $\bar{S}$ of S consists of all characteristic functions of sets—that is, of all functions assuming the values zero and unity exclusively. But the set $\tilde{S}$ of the limits of convergent transfinite sequences of points of S contains only characteristic functions of countable sets. To see this, suppose $x_\alpha \to x$, where each x_α is in S. Then consider the sets T_α of points t such that $x_\beta(t) \neq 0$ for every $\beta > \alpha$. T_α increases with α, but is always finite. Now choose $\alpha_1, \alpha_2, \alpha_3, \cdots$ to be minimal subject to the condition that T_{α_k} contains at least k points. Each x_α is followed by some x_{α_k}, unless the T_{α_k} are finite in number—one need only let k exceed the number of non-zero values of $x_\alpha(t)$. Hence $T_{\alpha_1} + T_{\alpha_2} + T_{\alpha_3} + \cdots$ includes every t such that $x_\beta(t) \neq 0$ for every β after some α—and therefore every t such that $x(t) \neq 0$. But T is obviously countable.

It is not even true that $\tilde{\tilde{S}} = \tilde{S}$ above. In fact, under the hypothesis of the continuum, $\tilde{\tilde{S}} = \bar{S}$. This shows that even unlimited use of transfinite sequences leads one to situations inconsistent with our usual topological ideas.

THEOREM 11: *Any space $\mathfrak{X}$ is of limited type.*

PROOF: By Theorem 8, it is sufficient to use directed sets of the types of the neighborhoods of the various points of $\mathfrak{X}$, and these form a limited collection.

Theorem 11 shows the way around logical paradoxes inherent in the fact that

[10] The notion of *type* is closely related to the notion of the *character* of a topological space at a point, suggested by P. Alexandroff (*Bikompakte topologische Raume,* Math. Annalen 92 (1924), p. 268). One distinction is that a character is just a cardinal number, while a *type* is a partially ordered set, and therefore more discriminating.

[11] This is the space Q of [4], p. 162.

the "class" of all directed sets includes the "class" of all ordinals (which is well-known to be a non-constructive notion).

An open problem in general topology, is that of finding the most important *essential* kinds of directed sets. For instance, among sequences, it would seem that only those of types A', A^{ω}, and other types A^{ϕ} whose ordinal is the initial ordinal of given power, are essential.

II. Applications to Topological Algebra

7. **Outline.** Part II of the paper will contain four applications of generalized convergence to topological algebra.

In the first application, some results of van Dantzig on completability are extended. Van Dantzig [2] has shown that in topological groups (satisfying, in the non-commutative case, a certain "completability axiom") and in topological linear spaces, closure is reciprocal with a suitable definition of completeness, *provided the first countability axiom holds.* The irrelevance of this provision is shown in §8.

The second application concerns a definition of the completeness of topological linear spaces proposed by von Neumann [9]. Von Neumann showed that several important function spaces and operator spaces were "complete" in the sense that all their closed totally bounded subsets were compact. In §9, we shall show that this condition is weaker than the (extensionally attainable) property of being closed in every containing linear space.[12]

The third application concerns a fundamental problem in the study of groups of topological transformations. The problem is this. Let $\mathfrak{H}$ be any Hausdorff space, and let $G(\mathfrak{H})$ be the group of homeomorphisms of $\mathfrak{H}$ into itself. When can $G(\mathfrak{H})$ be described properly as a topological group? This problem is considerably clarified in §10 by elimination of the inconsistencies between topologizations of $G(\mathfrak{H})$ in terms of convergence and topologizations in terms of closure and neighborhoods.

The fourth application is to abstract integration. It consists of a simple topologico-algebraic definition of an integral of functions from an abstract domain with a σ-ring of measurable sets, to a convex topological linear space, in a way specializing to the Lebesgue integral (as defined by Fréchet) for real-valued functions. The definition flows directly out of the idea of Moore and Smith [7], that the partitions are a directed set, but does seem to constitute a considerable technical advance over the definitions in the literature.

8. **Completability of certain topological algebras.** Let G be any topological group—that is, any Hausdorff space[13] whose points are the symbols of an ab-

[12] This result was announced in Abstract 41-9-355 of the Bull. Am. Math. Soc. It has since been extended by Graves (cf. infra) and A. Weil, *Recouvrements das espaces topologiques*, Comptes Rendus 202 (1936), p. 1002.

[13] Any topological space $\mathfrak{X}$ satisfying the stated conditions is a regular Hausdorff space, since given a closed set X and a point x not in X, one can find a neighborhood U of l so small that $xUU^{-1}X = 0$, whence $xU \cap XU = 0$.

stract group, in which the functions xy and x^{-1} defining group products and group inverses are *continuous*. By Theorem 1, a subgroup S of G is *closed* if $\{x_\alpha\} \subset S$, $x_\alpha \to x$, and $x \epsilon S$ are incompatible. But $x_\alpha \to x$ is only possible if $x_\alpha x_\beta^{-1} \to l$ as α and β increase.[14]

Therefore if in a topological group S, $x_\alpha x_\beta^{-1} \to l$ implies that $x \epsilon S$ can be found satisfying $x_\alpha \to x$, then S is closed in every over-group, and so is "complete" in the proper sense of the word. This immediately raises the questions: is every topological group S closed in every over-group, "complete" in the sense just described? Is every topological group S a dense subgroup of a "complete" group S^*?

These questions can be partially answered in the affirmative, by a direct extension of the methods of van Dantzig. Namely, if S is not complete in the sense described, we adjoin to $\{x_\alpha\}$ a fictitious limit x, and show that we can extend the group operations to the system so obtained.

We shall omit the details, since the principles involved are elementary, and are mostly stated in [2]. We shall only mention the main results, which are

(8.1) *If we call a directed set $\{x_\alpha\}$ of elements of a topological group G "fundamental" if and only if* (as *α and β increase*) $x_\alpha x_\beta^{-1} \to l$, *if we identify two fundamental sets $\{x_\alpha\}$ and $\{y_\beta\}$ if and only if $x_\alpha y_\beta^{-1} \to l$, and if we define inverses and products through the rules*

$$\{x_\alpha\}^{-1} = \{x_\alpha^{-1}\} \qquad \{x_\alpha\}\cdot\{y_\beta\} = \{x_\alpha \cdot y_\beta\}$$

then the fundamental sets[15] *constitute a group G^* if and only if $y_\beta \to l$ and $\{x_\alpha\}$ fundamental imply $x_\alpha^{-1} y_\beta x_\alpha \to l$. This is always true if G is commutative.*

(8.2) *If G^* exists, it is complete.* $G = G^*$ (*under the correspondence mapping the directed set of one element x onto x*) *if and only if G is complete; in any case, G is mapped onto a dense subset of G^*.*

(8.3) *The above results extend to topological linear spaces, regarded as commutative groups with respect to vector addition—and G^* always exists.*

(8.4) *A topological linear space L is complete if and only if, denoting by U_α the neighborhoods of its origin O, every overlapping system $U_\alpha + f_\alpha$ of translation-images of all the U_α converges to a limit $f \epsilon L$.*

9. **Totally bounded subsets of complete topological linear spaces.** In the present section, it will be shown that any closed "totally bounded" subset S of a "complete" topological linear space L is bicompact—but that Hilbert space is only sequentially complete under the weak topology.[16]

The proof of the first (and principal) statement just made goes as follows. Let S contain $\aleph$ points, and let the neighborhoods U_α of the origin be well-ordered. Then

[14] The $x_\alpha x_\beta^{-1}$ are a directed set, if we define $(\alpha, \beta) > (\alpha_1, \beta_1)$ to mean $\alpha > \alpha_1$ and $\beta > \beta_1$.

[15] The fundamental sets are a limited collection, in virtue of Theorem 11. It would be less elegant, but possible, to give an analogous construction involving only systems of sets.

[16] The author is indebted to J. von Neumann for the proof of the latter fact.

LEMMA: *One can select a translation-image $V_\alpha = f_\alpha + U_\alpha$ of each U_α, such that every finite intersection*

$$V_{\alpha(1)} \cap \cdots \cap V_{\alpha(s)}$$

contains $\aleph$ points of S.

PROOF: By transfinite induction, we need merely prove that if the lemma is true for the U_α with $\beta < \alpha$, then it is true for the U_α with $\beta \leqq \alpha$. This is what we shall do.

By the definition of total boundedness, $g_1, \cdots, g_n$ exist with

$$S \subset [g_1 + U_\alpha] \cup \cdots \cup [g_n + U_\alpha].$$

Hence if the lemma were false, for each $k = 1, \cdots, n$ there would exist finite intersections $W_k \equiv V_{\beta k(1)} \cap \cdots \cap V_{\beta k(s_k)} \cap [g_k + U_\alpha]$ $[\beta_i(j) < \alpha]$, containing fewer than $\aleph$ points of S. And by transfinite arithmetic, the union $W_1 \cup \cdots \cup W_n$ of the W_k would contain fewer than $\aleph$ points of S. Hence, using the distributive law of set-combination,

$$\begin{aligned} X &\equiv \prod_{i,j} V_{\beta i(j)} \cap S \\ &\subset \left\{\prod_{i,j} V_{\beta i(j)}\right\} \cap \left[\sum_{k=1}^{n} g_k + U_\alpha\right] \\ &= \sum_{k=1}^{n} \left\{\prod_{i,j} V_{\beta i(j)} \cap [g_k + U_\alpha]\right\} \\ &\subset W_1 \cup \cdots \cup W_n \end{aligned}$$

would contain fewer than $\aleph$ points of S—whence $\prod_{i,j} V_{\beta i(j)} \cap S$ would contain fewer than $\aleph$ points (of S), contradicting the hypothesis.

THEOREM 12: *In any complete topological linear space, every closed totally bounded set is bicompact.*

PROOF: In the lemma just proved, the V_α are over-lapping, whence by (13.4), $V_\alpha \to x$. It is obvious that under these circumstances every neighborhood of x contains $\aleph$ points of S—whence by definition, S is bicompact.

COROLLARY: *If a topological linear space is sequentially complete, its closed totally bounded subsets are compact, in the sense that all their infinite sequences have convergent subsequences.*

We shall conclude the section by showing that although Hilbert space (denoted by $\mathfrak{H}$) is sequentially complete relative to its weak topology, it is not complete relative to arbitrary fundamental sets. To see this, note first the duality between $\mathfrak{H}$ and the isomorphic space $\mathfrak{F}$ of its bounded linear functionals. Hence it is sufficient to show that $\mathfrak{F}$ is not weakly closed in the space $\mathfrak{L}$ of all linear (but not necessarily continuous) functionals F satisfying $F(\lambda f + \mu g) = \lambda F(f) + \mu F(g)$.

But this can be verified by using a "Hamel basis" $h_1, h_2, h_3, \cdots, h_\alpha, \cdots$ for $\mathfrak{H}$ under which each $f \epsilon \mathfrak{H}$ has a unique expression as a finite linear sum $f =$

$\lambda_1 h_{k(1)} + \cdots + \lambda_r h_{k(r)}$. The neighborhoods of any $F_0 \epsilon \mathfrak{L}$ are the sets of F such that

$$|F(f') - F_0(f')| < \epsilon, \cdots, \qquad |F(f^\nu) - F_0(f^\nu)| < \epsilon$$

for some $\epsilon > 0$ and finite set $f^1, \cdots, f^\nu$. Clearly any such neighborhood contains elements of $\mathfrak{F}$, whence $\bar{\mathfrak{F}} = \mathfrak{L} > \mathfrak{F}$, completing the proof.

10. **The topology of groups of transformations.** It has been shown,[17] that although it is easy to topologize the group $G(\mathfrak{X})$ of the self-homeomorphisms of any topological space $\mathfrak{X}$ in such a way as to make it an L-group in the sense of Schreier, and although for this $\mathfrak{X}$ need itself be only an L-space, one cannot conclude that $G(\mathfrak{X})$ is a topological group under this definition. There is no assurance, that derived sets in $G(\mathfrak{X})$ need be closed.

In view of the example of Theorem 10 above, one might conjecture that this was because of the difference between closure with respect to sequential convergence and closure with respect to neighborhoods. If this were the case, then the modified

DEFINITION 6: Let $\mathfrak{H}$ be any Hausdorff space; $G(\mathfrak{H})$ the group of the self-homeomorphisms of $\mathfrak{H}$. A directed set $\{T_\alpha\}$ of such self-homeomorphisms will be said to *converge* to the limit T if and only if $x_\beta \to x$ implies $T_\alpha(x_\beta) \to T(x)$ and $T_\alpha^{-1}(x_\beta) \to T(x)$ as α, β increase.

would lead to a neighborhood topology. But it does not; the example of [1′] still holds.

However, one does have the salient properties $(4\alpha) - (4\gamma)$. Furthermore, group multiplication and passage to the inverse are continuous. But it is not proposed to go more deeply into these questions; it is only suggested that (4δ) should be replaced by a condition which is preserved in passing from $\mathfrak{H}$ to $G(\mathfrak{H})$, and by the weakest possible such condition.

11. **Application to abstract integration.** In the present section, an integral will be developed for functions $F(p)$ from the points p of a space $\mathfrak{S}$ with a completely additive set-function $\mu(S)$ to the elements of any convex topological linear space $\mathfrak{L}$ (cf. [9]). This integral specializes to the author's integral for functions with values in a Banach space[18] in that case, and so to the Lebesgue integral in the case of the real number system.

It does not seem to have any immediate uses. On the other hand, it is interesting in that it exhibits the immense generality of Moore's conception of integration.[19] Also, it is *purely topologico-algebraic.*

[17] G. Birkhoff, *The topology of transformation-sets*, Annals of Math. 35 (1934), 861–75. This will be referred to as [1′].

[18] Using the strong topology of Banach space. If we use the weak topology, it specializes to the "inner product" integral, whereby $\int F(p)d\mu = J$ if and only if for every linear functional f, $\int f(F(p))d\mu = f(J)$, the left-hand integrals being lebesgue integrals.

[19] Moore-Smith thought of the integral as a generalized sum, and reduced the problem of integration to that of ordering suitable finite sums. This contrasts with the view that an

The definition is this. $F(p)$ will be said to be *integrable* with respect to $\mu(S)$, and to have the *integral* $J(F)$—a relation written $J(F) = \int_{\mathfrak{S}} F(p)d\mu$—if and only if, given any convex neighborhood U of 0 in $\mathfrak{L}$, one can find a partition Δ of $\mathfrak{S}$ into measurable subsets $S_1, S_2, S_3, \cdots$, finite or countable in number, and n so large that for any $n < h_1 < \cdots < h_r$ and $p_k \epsilon S_k$,

$$(11) \qquad \left\{\sum_{k=1}^{r} \mu(S_k)\cdot F(p_k) + \sum_{i=1}^{r} \mu(S_{h_i})\cdot Fp_{h_i})\right\} \epsilon J(F) + U.$$

Then (by [9], Definition (2b), (6)) for each $p_k \epsilon S_k$, $\eta_k > 0$ exists so small that if $0 \leqq \lambda_k \leqq \eta_k$, $\mu(S_k)\cdot F(p_k)$ is in $(1/2n)U$; hence for any $q_k \epsilon S_k$ (since replacing p_k by q_k in (15) changes the sum by at most $2U$), if $\lambda_k < 1/4n$ as well, then $\lambda_k\cdot\mu(S_k)\cdot F(q_k)\epsilon(1/2n)U + (2/4nU \subset (1/n)U$. Therefore, summing, if $\eta > 0$ is chosen smaller than Inf $(1/4n, \eta_1, \cdots, \eta_r)$ then $0 \leqq \lambda_k \leqq \eta$ implies

$$(11\alpha) \qquad \left\{\sum_{k=1}^{n} (1 - \lambda_k)\mu(S_k)\cdot F(p_k) + \sum_{k=1}^{n} \mu(S_{h_i})\cdot F(p_{h_i}) - J\right\} \epsilon\, 2U.$$

The proof of the uniqueness of J under the hypothesis of existence can be sketched as follows.

Given any subpartition Δ^1 of Δ, one can find finite classes of subsets $S_{i,j}$ of each $S_i[i = 1, \cdots, n]$, the sum of whose measures is proportionately within $\frac{1}{2}\eta$ of $\mu(S_i)$. Now using convexity,[20] one sees that (11α) is satisfied if these $S_{i,j}$ are substituted for the S_i and $\frac{1}{2}\eta$ for η (one collects the $S_{i,j}$ having each fixed i, and uses the associativity and commutativity of vector addition). Hence, given any two integrals J and J'', with partitions Δ and Δ'' relative to which they satisfy (11α), comparing each with $\Delta\cdot\Delta''$ one can show that $\{J - J''\}\epsilon 4U$.

If $\mathfrak{L}$ is *complete*, one need not exhibit an integral J in order to prove integrability. One need merely assume that for every U one can find a partition Δ into measurable subsets and $n > 0$ so large that

$$(11\beta) \qquad \begin{cases} \sum_{k=1}^{h} \mu(S_k)\cdot F(p_k) - F(q_k)\ \epsilon\ U & \text{if} \quad p_k, q_k\ \epsilon\ S_k \\ \sum_{i=1}^{r} \mu(S_{h_i})\cdot F(p_{h_i})\ \epsilon\ U & \text{if} \quad n < h_1 < \cdots < h_r \end{cases}$$

---

integral is a *mean*, the view used so effectively by J. von Neumann in his papers on functions defined over groups (Trans. Am. Math. Soc., 1934–5).

[20] Use of convexity and its linear properties shows that (15α) is equivalent to the apparently stronger requirement

$$(15\gamma) \qquad \left\{\sum_{k,j} \mu_{k,j}F(p_{k,j}) - J\right\} \epsilon\, 2u$$

for all finite sums satisfying (a) $p_{k,j} \epsilon S_k$ (b) $\sum_j \mu_{k,j}$ lies between $1 - \eta$ and 1 for $k = 1, \cdots, n$ (c) $\sum_j \mu_{k,j} = \mu(S_k)$ for $k > n$.

REMARK 1: Thus integration practically amounts to taking the limit of the finite sums $\sum \mu(S_k) \cdot F(P_k)$ ordered with respect to (1) the partition Δ, (2) the size of the set-union of the S_k. Unfortunately, this ordering does not define a directed set!

REMARK 2: If $\mathfrak{L}$ is complete, then the integral just defined is "completely additive" in the sense of [9], §15. The proof will be omitted.

III. Algebraic Topologies

12. **Introduction.** The aim of Part III is to correlate the constructions which have been used to topologize isolated algebraic systems by various authors, and to subsume them under two main headings: topologizations by congruences and topologizations by ordering.

Since these constructions are in all cases *intrinsic* (i.e., invariant under automorphisms), it seems legitimate to call the resulting topologies *algebraic* topologies.

The reader will recognize some of the systems discussed—such as the real number system—as absolutely basic. Others—the p-adic numbers, for example —are well-known; one or two are new.

But the main point throughout is the unification which is possible. Also, the principles underlying algebraic topologization as such have never before been brought into the foreground in an explicit and emphatic manner.

13. **Topologies defined by congruences.** In §§13–15, we shall discuss algebraic topologies defined by families of congruences. In doing this, we shall first describe the process of introducing such topologies in general language. We shall then illustrate the process by three specific examples: p-adic numbers, a dual to Stone's topologization of the prime ideals of arbitrary Boolean algebras [10], and a new topologization of discrete free groups. We shall conclude by discussing extensions.

The general process of topologizing by congruences is this. Let A be any *abstract algebra* (in the sense of a formal calculus)—that is, any system of *elements* related by *operations*. It is convenient to denote the elements of A by small Latin letters, and the operations by special symbols (such as $+$, $\circ$, $-$, $\cap$, $\cup$). By a *partition* π of A is meant as usual a division of the elements of A into a number of disjoint subclasses, whose union reconstitutes A. Two elements $x \epsilon A$ and $y \epsilon A$ are called *equivalent* under π (a relation written $x \sim y(\pi)$) if and only if they lie in the same π-subclass. A partition π of A is called *homomorphic* if and only if[21] for any operation $\circ$ of A operating on a sequence $x_1, \cdots, x_r$ of its elements, the assumptions $x_1 \sim y(\pi), \cdots, x_r \sim y(\pi)$ imply

$$x_1 \circ \cdots \circ x_r \sim y_1 \circ \cdots \circ y_r(\pi)$$

—that is, if and onlv if it is a *conaruence*.

[21] All these definitions are to be found in [1], and are immediate abstractions from the usual usage of modern algebra.

Now let $\mathfrak{F}$ be any family of homomorphic partitions θ_α of A, with the property that $x \sim y(\theta_\alpha)$ for all $\theta_\alpha \epsilon \mathfrak{F}$ implies $x = y$. Then if we look on the θ_α-subclasses of A as open subsets—and also on arbitrary unions of finite intersections of θ_α-subclasses of A as open subsets—it is clear that we obtain *a topology relative to which A is a totally disconnected Hausdorff space.* And using a remark of Graves,[22] one can complete the space so obtained topologically, obtaining "ideal" elements[23] to which one can extend the operations of the algebra.

Furthermore, one can show that the operations of A are continuous in this topology—in other words, that it makes A into a *topological algebra.* And finally, the topological algebra formed by completing A is usually *bicompact* if for all α, the θ_α-subclasses are finite in number. The proofs of these facts are omitted.

Example 1: The p-adic numbers of Hensel (first explicitly topologized by Vietoris [11], page 174) and the "b_ν-adic" numbers of van Dantzig [3]. The reader is referred to [3] for a discussion of how in any ring, in which one has a preferred family of ideals—and especially of powers I^n of a single ideal I—one can introduce a topology and then complete the resulting topological ring.

Example 2: Topologized Boolean algebras. Stone [10] proved that if B is any Boolean algebra, and $x \neq y$ are any two distinct elements of B, then B has a homomorphic partition θ into two subclasses, such that $x \nsim y(\theta)$. Hence the family $\mathfrak{F}$ of "prime ideals" of B defines a totally disconnected topology over B, and one can complete B so as to make it *bicompact.*[24]

Example 3: The free discrete groups D_n generated by n symbols. In each such D_n, one has a descending sequence of "commutator-subgroups,"

$$D_n = D_n^1 > D_n^2 > D_n^3 > \cdots ,$$

whose common part is the identity.[25] Hence D_n can be topologized so as to make it a totally disconnected Hausdorff space, and then completed. This example is new.

---

[22] Cf. the following note, *On the completing of a Hausdorff space*, this number of these Annals.

[23] The existence of these elements, without topological connotation, was first asserted by H. Prüfer, *Neue Begründung der algebraischen Zahlentheorie*, Math. Annalen 94 (1925), p. 198, who obtained them directly from what we would call "overlapping" families of θ_α-subclasses. The basic idea comes from L. E. J. Brouwer, *On the structure of perfect sets of points*, Proc. Amst. Acad. 12 (1910), 785-94.

[24] This correspondence is dual to that of Stone. Stone correlated the open and closed subsets of any totally disconnected Hausdorff space with the Boolean algebra which they form under set-inclusions. In the algebra points appear as prime ideals; they constitute *all* prime ideals if any only if the space is bicompact. Conversely, if one regards the prime ideals of a Boolean algebra B as points, and elements of B as open and closed sets "containing" the prime ideals which include them, one gets a totally disconnected bicompact space $\mathfrak{X}(B)$.

[25] Cf. W. Magnus, *Beziehungen zwischen Gruppen und Idealen in einem speziellen Ring*, Math. Annalen III (1935), 259–80, for the facts used in Example 3.

Consider also the "valuation" (Bewertung) which associates with each $x \epsilon D_n$ the absolute value

$$(17\alpha) \qquad | x | \equiv \text{Inf}_{x \epsilon D_n^k} 2^{-k}.$$

One has the formulas (whose similarity with the formulas of ring-valuation is easily recognizable),

$$(17\beta) \qquad | xy | \leqq \text{Max} (| x |, | y |)$$

$$(17\gamma) \qquad | x^{-1}y^{-1}xy | \leqq | x | \cdot | y |$$

The metric distance function $f(x, y) = | xy^{-1} |$ topologizes D_n just like the algebraic topology described above.

14. **Extension to coset topologization.** It is not essential in topologizing a group, to use exclusively *homomorphic* partitions. For if G is a group, and $\mathfrak{F}$ is any family of subgroups of G which contains with any subgroup S_α, all its conjugates $x^{-1}S_\alpha x$, one can regard the right-cosets $xS_\alpha[x \epsilon G, S_\alpha \epsilon \mathfrak{F}]$ as open and closed sets—as defining disjunctions of G into disconnected parts. (It follows that the left-cosets $S_\alpha y = y(y^{-1}S_\alpha y)$ do the same thing; hence the definition is really symmetric.)

As in §13, the (unrestricted) unions of the finite intersections of the S_α topologize G algebraically.

Example 4: Let $G_\aleph$ be the group of all permutations of $\aleph$ symbols ($\aleph$ any number), and let the S_α be the subgroups holding the different individual symbols fixed.

This example has been discussed independently by various authors (Krull, Math. Annalen 100 (1928), p. 689, and R. Baer). Actually, the topological group formed in this way is *complete*, and can be shown (using results of J. Schreier and S. Ulam, Studia Math. IV) to have no closed normal subgroups, and hence to be *simple*, provided $\aleph$ is infinite.

An intriguing but unrelated topologization of abstract groups—namely, of the continuous semi-simple groups—is due to van der Waerden.[26]

15. **Topologization of infinite direct products.** Suppose we have any aggregate $\mathfrak{A}$ of topological algebras A_α of a given kind—say, groups, or sets (which are the degenerate case in which the family of operations is vacuous)—and we wish to form their *direct product* A.

Algebraically, the elements of A are the functions $x(\alpha)$ assigning to each index an element $x_\alpha \epsilon A_\alpha$, and the operations of A are defined—in the case of groups; the principle is the same for all algebraic systems—by letting $x \circ y = z$ mean $x_\alpha \circ y_\alpha = z_\alpha$ for all α. But this does not define the topology of A.

In the case that $\mathfrak{A}$ is a finite aggregate, it seems best to make A the topological

[26] *Stetigkeitssätze für halbeinfache Liesche Gruppen*, Math. Zeits. 36 (1933), 780–87.

product of the A_α (Cartesian product in the sense of [6]). But what if $\mathfrak{A}$ is infinite?

It is not suggested that there is any one "best" answer to this; the whole theory of function-spaces points to the contrary conclusion. But one should always remember the topology under which $x_\beta \to x$ means $x_\beta(\alpha) \to x(\alpha)$ for all α, and recognize it as defined through the *congruences* θ_α—where $x \sim y(\theta_\alpha)$ means $x(\alpha) = y(\alpha)$—in a way specializing to the construction of §13 if the A_α are all discrete.

16. **Topologization by order.** The other main kind of algebraic topologization is through *ordering relations*. In treating this situation, we shall bring together two ideas which are to be found separately in the literature.

The first idea has been developed by various authors,[27] and asserts that in any partially ordered system,[28] one can define successively (1) least upper bounds and greatest lower bounds (2) limits superior and limits inferior (3) limits. Existence of none of these is assumed. The second idea is that one can complete any partially ordered system so as to ensure the existence of at least (1) and (2), in a determinate way. This idea specializes to the "Dedekind cut" axiom for numbers, and has been applied by H. MacNeille[29] to arbitrary partially ordered sets.

Now the first idea can clearly be regarded as a definition of limits and thus of *closure*, and the second as involving *completeness*; this suggests that they are bound up with each other. This is, however, true only to a limited extent. In particular, no system is "closed in every containing system," and so completeness does not depend on closure in the way one would hope. And again, partially ordered sets are not usually topologically "dense" in the complete "lattices" which they define.

The facts are these. To any partially ordered set S corresponds a unique complete lattice[30] S^* formed by adjoining as ideal elements all "Dedekind sections"; the details are described by MacNeille (op. cit.).

In S^* one can introduce an algebraic topology by defining (by analogy with the case of real numbers) $x_\alpha \to x$ ($\{x_\alpha\}$ any directed set) to mean

$$(16\alpha) \qquad \begin{aligned} \text{l.u.b.}_{\alpha} \{\text{gr.l.b.}_{\beta>\alpha} x \cup x_\beta\} &= x \\ \text{gr.l.b.}_{\alpha} \{\text{l.u.b.}_{\beta>\alpha} x \cap x_\beta\} &= x \end{aligned}$$

---

[27] Cf. [5], p. 142; [1], p. 452; O. Ore, *Foundations of abstract algebra*, Annals of Math. 36 (1935), p. 408; H. MacNeille, *Partially ordered sets*, Harvard Doctoral Thesis (1935). Also [11], p. 181, example (11).

[28] By a *partially ordered system* is meant any set S of elements $x, y, z, \ldots$ in which an *inclusion relation* $x \supset y$ is defined satisfying ([5], p. 139): (K1) $x \supset x$, (K2) if $x \supset y$ and $y \supset x$, then $x = y$, (K3) if $x \supset y$ and $y \supset z$, then $x \supset z$.

[29] *Extensions of partially ordered sets*, Proc. Nat. Acad. 22 (1936), 45–9.

[30] By a *lattice* is meant a partially ordered set in which any *two* elements have a join of l.u.b. $z = x \cup y$ (such that $z \supset x$, $z \supset y$, and that $w \supset x$ plus $w \supset y$ imply $w \supset z$), and a dual *meet* or gr.l.b. $z' = x \cap y$ (such that $x \supset z'$, $y \supset z'$, and that $x \supset w$ plus $y \supset w$ imply $z' \supset w$). A lattice is called complete if and only if *unrestricted* sets of elements have a gr.l.b. and a l.u.b.

And one can then introduce in S an algebraic topology by letting $x_\alpha \to x$ in S mean that $x_\alpha \to x$ in S^*; this is in conformity with the principle that if T is *any* topological algebra, and T^* is formed by completing T, then the topology of T is formed from that of T^* by "relativization" ([6]).

Now one can prove that if S is a *lattice*, then S is dense in S^* (cf. Theorem 3 of *The meaning of completeness*, following this article). Proof: Let $\{x_\alpha\}$ consist of the $x_\alpha \epsilon S$ satisfying $x_\alpha \supset x$ [x any element of S^*]. Let $\beta > \alpha$ mean $x_\beta \subset x_\alpha$; since S is a lattice, this defines $\{s_\alpha\}$ as a directed set. And since in S^*, $x =$ gr.l.b. x_α, and $x_\alpha =$ l.u.b.$_{\beta>\alpha} x_\beta$, (16α) is satisfied.

Again, any topologically closed sublattice S of a complete lattice L^* is complete (cf. Theorem 4 of *The meaning of completeness*). Proof: The elements of any subset of S, together with their finite joins (which are also in S), converge as above to their least upper bound.

Example: The rational numbers are a dense subset of the real number system, and in any closed subset of the real number system $-\infty \leqq x \leqq +\infty$, gr.l.b. and l.u.b. always exist.

One may conclude by recalling that the lattice operations are not generally continuous in the topology ([1]). Nevertheless,[31] if one has any lattice with a numerical dimension-function $p(x)$ satisfying

$$(16\beta) \qquad x > y \text{ implies } p(x) > p(y)$$

$$p(x) + p(y) = p(x \cap y) + p(x \cup y)$$

then one has a metric distance function $| x - y | = p(x \cup y) - p(x \cap y)$ relative to which the lattice operations are continuous, and moreover the metric topology is identical with the algebraic topology, as extended by the rule

(16γ) If every cofinal subset $\{x_{\beta\alpha(\beta)}\}$ of a directed set $\{x_\alpha\}$ contains a cofinal subsubset $\{x_{\alpha(\beta(\gamma))}\}$ converging to x in the sense of (16α), then $x_\alpha \to x$.

This suggests that the algebraic topologization by order has concrete significance.

Society of Fellows, Harvard University.

[31] The proofs, which were evolved by J. von Neumann and the author jointly, will be published elsewhere.

Annals of Mathematics
Vol. 38, No. 1, January, 1937

THE MEANING OF COMPLETENESS

By Garrett Birkhoff

(Received June 15, 1936)

1. **Introduction.** It is a philosophical problem with wide mathematical implications, to ascertain the conditions under which it is legitimate to speak of a system as being "complete."

As the corresponding problem has been solved for the notion of closure, and as the two solutions are closely related, it seems best to begin by recalling the characteristic properties of closure. As a matter of fact, it will be shown that completeness is usually associated with a closure property, which determines it uniquely (Theorem 5).

The bibliography of the preceding article (*Moore-Smith convergence in general topology*, to be cited as MC) will be used throughout.

2. **Closure.** The notion of closure is one which concerns the subsets $S, T, U, \cdots$ of a fundamental system A. As was pointed out by E. H. Moore,[1] there are two equivalent ways of defining it.

One may define it operationally, as a rule ascribing to each subset S of A another subset $\bar{S}$ called the "closure" of S, where[2]

C1: $\bar{S} \supset S$ C2: $\bar{\bar{S}} = \bar{S}$
C3: *If* $S \supset T$, *then* $\bar{S} \supset \bar{T}$.

Or one may define it as a dichotomy, which divides the subsets of A into two classes, the "closed" and the "non-closed," with the qualifications

C*1: *The system A itself is closed.*
C*2: *The elements common to any number of closed subsets of A form a closed subset.*

To pass from the postulates (C) to the postulates (C*), one of course defines a subset S of A to be closed if and only if $\bar{S} = S$; conversely, one may pass from the postulates (C*) to the postulates (C) by defining the closure of any subset S of A to be the common part (intersection) of all closed subsets of A which contain S. The proof that under these definitions conditions (C*) resp. conditions (C) are satisfied, can be easily supplied by the reader.

It should be recalled also that any definition of closure in A automatically defines a closure property in every subset B of A. By the closure "in B" of any subset S of B is meant the common part $\bar{S}_B = \bar{S} \cap B$ of the closure of S and B. The reader can easily verify the well-known[3] fact that the operation of closing "in B" satisfies conditions (C).

---

[1] [7], p. 55.
[2] Cf. F. Riesz, Rome Congress (1908), Vol. 2, p 18.
[3] Cf. [6], p. 17. One must prove $\bar{S}_B \supset S$, $(\bar{\bar{S}}_B)_B = \bar{S}_B$, and that $S \supset T$ implies $\bar{S}_B \supset \bar{T}_B$.

3. **Completeness.** It is clear from the last section that by a "*closure property*" of a system, is essentially meant a property *extensionally attainable within a superclass.* By a "*completeness property,*" on the other hand, is meant in a general way a property of systems of a given family of systems which is *extensionally attainable within the family.* Thus closure is a property of subsystems, while completeness is a property of systems by themselves.

This distinction will be made clearer by the following examples, at least some of which should be familiar to the reader.

(3.1) In any topological space, the property of being topologically closed is a closure property.

(3.2) In any abstract algebra (group, ring, etc.), the property of being a subalgebra (subgroup, subring, etc.) is a closure property. It is the property of being closed with respect to a certain class of operations.

On the other hand,

(3.3) In the family of metric spaces, the property that every fundamental sequence should converge to a limit, is a completeness property.

(3.4) In commutative semi-groups,[4] the property of being a group is a completeness property.

(3.5) In rings of integrity,[5] the property of being a field is a completeness property.

(3.6) In topological groups, rings, and vector spaces,[6] the property that every "fundamental sequence" should converge to a limit, is a completeness property.

(3.7) In partially ordered sets, the property that every subset should have a gr.l.b. and an l.u.b. is a completeness property.[7]

(3.8) In (commutative) fields, the property of being "algebraically closed" is a completeness property.[8]

(In arc-connected locally simply connected spaces, the property of being simply connected closely resembles a completeness property.)

4. **Similarity to closure.** The formal similarity between completeness and closure can be clearly brought out by introducing the symbolism (within systems $A, B, \cdots$ of a given family): $A \supset B$ to mean "B can be imbedded in A," or "B is isomorphic (homeomorphic) with a subset of A;" $A \sim B$ to mean "A is isomorphic with B" (it not being assumed that in all cases $A \supset B$ and $B \supset A$ imply $A \sim B$); A^* to mean the complete system generated by a system A. Then it is known[9] that in each of cases (3.3)–(3.7),

[4] By a *commutative semi-group,* is meant a system in which a binary commutative and associative operation $a \circ b$ is defined, such that $a \circ x = a \circ y$ implies $x = y$.

[5] B. L. van der Waerden, *Moderne Algebra,* vol. 1, p. 39. Thus the ring of the positive and negative integers can be completed to form the field of rational numbers.

[6] [2] and [9]; these will be discussed in greater detail in Part II, §8.

[7] Cf. H. MacNeille, *Partially ordered sets,* Harvard Doctoral Thesis, 1935. Also [5], p. 139, and MC, §15.

[8] Cf. B. L. van der Waerden, op. cit., vol. 1, p. 199.

[9] Except in case (3.6). Here the first countability axiom of Hausdorff and (in the case of

E1: $A^* \supset A$ E2: $(A^*)^* \sim A^*$
E3: *If* $A \supset B$, *then* $A^* \supset B^*$.

It will be shown in the next section, that if a suitable explanation is attached, conditions (E) fully characterize completeness.

5. **The full characterization of completeness.** The notion of completeness is, speaking in exact terms, one which concerns a family $\mathfrak{F}$ of systems $A, B, C, \cdots$, in which *isomorphism* is defined, satisfying

I: *Among the one-one correspondences* $a \rightleftarrows b$ *between the elements of two systems* $A \in \mathfrak{F}$ *and* $B \in \mathfrak{F}$, *certain ones are "isomorphic." The correspondence carrying each* $a \in A$ *into itself is isomorphic; the inverse of any one, and the product of any two isomorphic correspondences are isomorphic (reflexive, symmetric and transitive laws of isomorphism).*

We shall also need for our characterization, the usual notion of an *extension* of a correspondence. One can define this notion as follows.

Let ϕ be any one-one (or, for that matter, many-one) correspondence between a system B and a subset of a second system C. Let further β resp. γ be any two one-one correspondences between B and a subset of a third system B_1 resp. C and a subset of a fourth system C_1. Then a correspondence ϕ^* between B_1 and C_1 will be called an *extension* of ϕ if and only if $\phi^*(\beta(b)) = \gamma(\phi(b))$ for every $b \in B$.

One can now give a rigorous definition of completeness, in terms of isomorphic correspondences between different systems of $\mathfrak{F}$. By a *completing correspondence* will be meant a correspondence $A \to A^*$ between the systems of $\mathfrak{F}$, satisfying

E1: $A^* \supset A$. *That is, there is an isomorphism* α *between* A *and a subsystem of* A^*, *which is unique in the sense that any isomorphic correspondence* $A \sim A_1$ *can be* "extended" *to an isomorphism* $A^* \sim (A_1)^*$.
E2: $(A^*)^* \sim A^*$. *That is, if* A^* *is the correspondent of an* $A \in \mathfrak{F}$, *then* α *carries* A^* *into all of* $(A^*)^*$.
E3: *If* $A \supset B$, *then* $A^* \supset B^*$. *That is, any isomorphism* $\omega: b \to \omega(b)$ *between* B *and a subsystem* $\omega(B)$ *of* A *can be extended to an isomorphism* ω^* *between* B^* *and a subsystem* $\omega^*(B^*)$ *of* A^*.

One can strengthen E3 by requiring that E′3: $\omega^*(B^*)$ be unique, or even that E″3: ω^* be unique. E″3 implies E′3, and also the uniqueness condition in E1.

In cases (3.3)–(3.6), E″3 holds; in case (3.8), E′3 holds but E″3 does not; in case (3.7), not even E′3 holds. In all cases, E1–E3 hold.

6. **Exact connection between completeness and closure.** In the present section, we shall show how to associate with every completing correspondence satisfying E′3, a closure property which reciprocally determines it.

---

non-commutative groups) a "completeness axiom" are used in proving completability. The irrelevance of the first countability axiom is shown in MC, §8.

DEFINITION 1: In E′3, by the *closure* $\bar{B}_A$ of B, is meant the common part $B^* \cap A$ of B^* and A. (Unless E′3 holds, $\bar{B}_A$ need not be single-valued.)

THEOREM 1: *Definition 1 defines a closure property within any system* $A \in \mathfrak{F}$.

PROOF: In case $A = A^*$, this is evident since conditions (E) can be rewritten as conditions (C). In the general case, it follows by the principle of "relativization" enunciated in the last paragraph of §2.

THEOREM 2: *Any isomorphic correspondence preserves closure.*

PROOF: This follows from the second half of condition E1 and Definition 1.

Let us now agree to call a system A of $\mathfrak{F}$ *complete* if and only if there exists a B^* isomorphic with A.

THEOREM 3: *A complete system* A^* *is closed in any containing system. Conversely, any closed subsystem* X *of a complete system* B^* *is complete.*

PROOF: The first statement is true by Definition 1 and E3. The second statement is true since $X = X^* \cap (B^*)^*$ by hypothesis, and $(B^*)^* \sim B^*$—whence the isomorphism taking X into X^* takes it into the *whole* of X^*.

THEOREM 4: *Any correspondence* α *completing any* A *of* $\mathfrak{F}$ *maps it onto a "dense" subset of* A^*. *Conversely, any isomorphic correspondence* β *between a* $B \in \mathfrak{F}$ *and a dense subset of any* A^* *is a completing correspondence.*

PROOF: By Definition 1, the closure of $\alpha(A)$ in A^* is $A^* \cap A^* = A^*$; this proves the first statement. Again, by the hypotheses of the second statement, $A^* = A^* \cap B^*$, whence $B^* = A^*$; this proves the second statement.

It is interesting that in examples (3.3)–(3.7), but not in example (3.8), it is true that the only automorphism of each A^* which leaves every element of A (regarded as a subsystem of A^*) fixed, is the identical automorphism.

THEOREM 5: *The closure property associated with any completing correspondence* (*) *uniquely determines* (*).

PROOF: Theorem 3 determines completeness in terms of isomorphic mappings and closure; Theorem 4 determines completing correspondences $A \to A^*$ in terms of isomorphic mappings, closure (as reflected by denseness), and completeness—and hence indirectly in terms of isomorphism and closure.

Finally, it is evident that by paraphrasing conditions (E), one can discover exactly which closure properties are associated with completing correspondences.

SOCIETY OF FELLOWS,
HARVARD UNIVERSITY.

Reprinted from DUKE MATHEMATICAL JOURNAL
Vol. 3, No. 2, June, 1937

AN EXTENDED ARITHMETIC

BY GARRETT BIRKHOFF

1. **Introduction.** In this paper there are defined three combinatorial operations upon partially ordered sets X and Y resulting in partially ordered sets which will be denoted by $X + Y$, XY, and X^Y respectively.

In the case where X and Y are finite unordered sets with cardinal numbers m and n respectively, the operations yield the finite unordered sets of cardinal numbers $m + n$, mn, and m^n in the commonplace sense. In the more general case where the requirement of finiteness is dropped, they yield the usual foundations for the arithmetic of general cardinal numbers.[1]

It will be proved that the formal properties of general cardinal arithmetic[2] persist as laws of composition for our extended arithmetic of general partially ordered sets. On the other hand, no algorithm for well-ordering the class of partially ordered systems is given, and so the theorem of transfinite arithmetic which asserts that the cardinal numbers are well-ordered has no analogue.

It will also be shown that our extended arithmetic is of considerable use in describing algebraic systems. Thus although it differs from Hausdorff's ordinal arithmetic when applied to sequences, it is apparently more consequential than the latter.[3]

2. **The extended arithmetic.** The extended arithmetic which is proposed will be described by defining first the domain of *elements* to which its operations apply, and then defining the resultants of its operations.

The elements are *partially ordered systems* in the usual sense of Hausdorff—that is, systems X, Y, Z, $\cdots$ whose members (denoted by small Latin letters) are related by an inclusion relation $x \leqq x'$ satisfying

P1: $x \leqq x$. (Reflexiveness)
P2: $x \leqq x'$ and $x' \leqq x$ imply $x = x'$. (Anti-symmetry)
P3: $x \leqq x'$ and $x' \leqq x''$ imply $x \leqq x''$. (Transitivity)

Two partially ordered systems X and Y will be called *isomorphic* (written

Received May 22, 1936; in revised form, December 31, 1936.

[1] Cf. F. Hausdorff's *Mengenlehre*, Berlin, 1927, p. 29, p. 62.

[2] The possibility of such relations as $x + 1 = x$, $2x = x$, and $x^2 = x$ distinguishes general from finite cardinal arithmetic.

[3] Although transfinite numbers have numerous uses, the only constructions of sums, products, or powers of transfinite numbers which have been really interesting hitherto have been those of (1) the power of the continuum as $2^{\aleph_0}$ ($\aleph_0$ denotes countable infinity), and (2) transfinite ordinals such as $\omega + 1$, 3ω, or ω^2 by ordinal addition and multiplication, and only the second of these is lost in our extended arithmetic.

$X = Y$ in this article) if and only if there exists a one-one correspondence between their elements which preserves inclusion.

By the *sum* $X + Y$ of two such systems X and Y is meant the system whose members include both the members x of X and the members y of Y, in which $x \leqq x'$ and $y \leqq y'$ keep their meaning, while $x \leqq y$ and $y \leqq x$ are always denied.

By the *product* $X \cdot Y$ of X and Y is meant the system whose members are all couples $[x, y]$ with $x \in X$ and $y \in Y$, and in which $[x, y] \leqq [x', y']$ means that $x \leqq x'$ in X and $y \leqq y'$ in Y.

By the *power* X^Y of one such system X with respect to a second such system Y as exponent is meant the system whose members are the *monotonic functions* $f(y)$ with domain Y and range in X (that is, all functions such that $y \leqq y'$ in Y implies $f(y) \leqq f(y')$ in X), ordered by having $f \leqq g$ mean that $f(y) \leqq g(y)$ for all y.

The reader will have no difficulty in verifying that $X + Y$, $X \cdot Y$ and X^Y are partially ordered systems. Further, if X and Y are *lattices*,[4] then so is $X \cdot Y$. Moreover any laws such as the modular and distributive laws which hold in X and Y hold in $X \cdot Y$. While if X is a lattice and n is the power of Y, then X^Y is a sublattice of X^n, and so X^Y is a modular resp. distributive lattice if X is.

The proofs of these facts will be omitted. Also, we shall not prove that the above definitions yield an extension of the cardinal arithmetic of Hausdorff—this is evident if one looks at Hausdorff's definitions (loc. cit.).

3. **Applications.** It is interesting to consider various arithmetic combinations of especially simple partially ordered systems, which have an independent algebraic importance.

As regards the simple systems, we shall let n denote the unordered aggregate of n elements, C_n the sequence of n elements (n finite), symbols $\aleph_\alpha$ the transfinite cardinals (= unordered aggregates), and adopt the conventional notation for transfinite ordinals. Finally, we shall let $B = C_2$ denote the Boolean algebra of two elements, and P_n the one-dimensional projective geometry with n points on its line. Then

(3.1) The finite Boolean algebras are the B^n.
(3.2) The Boolean algebra of all subsets of any aggregate of power $\aleph$ is $B^\aleph$.
(3.3) The finite distributive lattices are the B^X, where X denotes a variable finite partially ordered set.
(3.4) The "quotient-lattice" associated by Ore[5] with each abstract lattice L is L^B.

[4] By a "lattice" is meant a partially ordered system L in which any two elements x and x' have a g.l.b. $x \cap x'$ such that $x'' \leqq x \cap x'$ means that $x'' \leqq x$ and $x'' \leqq x'$, and a l.u.b. $x \cup x'$ such that $x'' \geqq x \cup x'$ means that $x'' \geqq x$ and $x'' \geqq x'$. By the *modular* law is meant the law that $x \leqq x''$ implies $x \cup (x' \cap x'') = (x \cup x') \cap x''$; the *distributive* law asserts that $(x \cup x') \cap (x' \cup x'') \cap (x'' \cup x) = (x \cap x') \cup (x' \cap x'') \cup (x'' \cap x)$.

[5] *On the foundations of abstract algebra*. I, Annals of Math., vol. 36 (1935), p. 425. Ore calls lattices *structures*.

(3.5) The integers ordered with respect to divisibility (the relation $m \mid n$) are a sublattice of $\omega^{\aleph_0}$.
(3.6) The "free" Boolean algebra generated by n symbols is B^{2^n}.
(3.7) The "free" distributive lattice generated by n symbols and with 0 and I added, is B^{B^n}.
(3.8) The "free" modular lattice generated by three symbols is a sublattice of $B^3 \cdot P_3$.
(3.9) The most general configuration generated in n-space by an r-plane and an s-plane through the origin, after iterated sections, linear sums and taking of orthogonal complements, is $B^4 \cdot P_4$.

The proofs of (3.1)–(3.9) are various. Assertions (3.1), (3.2) and (3.6) are known.[6] Assertions (3.3) and (3.7) are proved in the author's article, *Rings of sets*, which will appear in the next issue of this journal. Inspection of Ore's definition, which is identical with our definition of L^B, yields (3.4). Statement (3.5) is a corollary of the unique representation of any integer as a product of powers of ascending primes. The result (3.8) has been proved by the author (*On the structure of abstract algebras*, Proc. Camb. Phil. Soc., vol. 31 (1935), p. 443, Theorem 14), while (3.9) has been recently proved by J. von Neumann; the proof will be published elsewhere.

4. **Arithmetic identities.** It is obvious that addition and multiplication are commutative—in symbols, that

(4.1) $$X + Y = Y + X \quad \text{and} \quad X \cdot Y = Y \cdot X.$$

They are also associative—that is,

(4.2) $$X + (Y + Z) = (X + Y) + Z \quad \text{and} \quad X \cdot (Y \cdot Z) = (X \cdot Y) \cdot Z.$$

For both $(X + Y) + Z$ and $X + (Y + Z)$ consist of all members of either X, Y, or Z, with the provision that $x \leqq x'$, $y \leqq y'$, and $z \leqq z'$ preserve their meaning, while $x \leqq y$, $x \geqq y$, $y \leqq z$, $y \geqq z$, $z \leqq x$, and $z \geqq x$ are always denied. And both $X \cdot (Y \cdot Z)$ and $(X \cdot Y) \cdot Z$ consist of all triples $[x, y, z]$ with $x \in X$, $y \in Y$ and $z \in Z$, where $[x, y, z] \leqq [x', y', z']$ means that $x \leqq x'$, $y \leqq x'$ and $z \leqq z'$. Again

(4.3) $$X \cdot (Y + Z) = X \cdot Y + X \cdot Z \quad \text{and} \quad (X + Y) \cdot Z = X \cdot Z + Y \cdot Z.$$

(In words, multiplication is distributive with respect to addition.) For $X \cdot (Y + Z)$ and $X \cdot Y + X \cdot Z$ alike consist of all couples $[x, y]$ and $[x, z]$ with $x \in X$, $y \in Y$, and $z \in Z$, where $[x, y] \leqq [x', y']$ means that $x \leqq x'$ and $y \leqq y'$, $[x, z] \leqq [x', z']$ means that $x \leqq x'$ and $z \leqq z'$, while $[x, y] \leqq [x', z]$ and $[x, y] \geqq [x', z]$ are always denied. This proves right-distributivity; left-distributivity follows by commutativity.

[6] For instance (3.1) is proved as Theorem 25.1 of the author's *On the combination of subalgebras*, Proc. Camb. Phil. Soc., vol. 29 (1933), p. 460; (3.6) follows from this and E. Schröder's *Algebra der Logik*; (3.2) is immediately obvious.

Again, although exponentiation is not commutative—in general, $X^Y \neq Y^X$—it satisfies the usual identities

$$(4.4) \qquad X^Y X^Z = X^{Y+Z} \quad \text{and} \quad X^Z Y^Z = (XY)^Z,$$

$$(4.5) \qquad X^1 = X \quad \text{and} \quad (X^Y)^Z = X^{YZ}.$$

The first identity of (4.4) is easy to prove. The system $X^Y X^Z$ consists of all couples $[f, g]$ where f and g have Y resp. Z for domains, and so are equivalent (Y and Z being non-overlapping in $Y + Z$) to a single function h with domain $Y + Z$. Moreover $[f, g] \leqq [f', g']$ means that for all $y \in Y$ and $z \in Z$, $f(y) \leqq f'(y)$ and $g(z) \leqq g'(z)$—that is, that for all $u \in (Y + Z)$, $h(u) \leqq h'(u)$. Hence $X^Y \cdot X^Z = X^{Y+Z}$.

Again, $X^Z Y^Z$ is the set of all function-couples $[f, g]$, where f and g are from Z to X resp. Z to Y, and $[f, g] = [f', g']$ means that $f(z) \leqq f'(z)$ and $g(z) \leqq g'(z)$ for all z. But each such $[f, g]$ can be regarded as a function h carrying each $z \in Z$ into $[f(z), g(z)] \in XY$—and so, since $h \leqq h'$ if and only if $[f, g] \leqq [f', g']$, $X^Z Y^Z = (XY)^Z$.

That $X^1 = X$ is obvious; it is a corollary (using (4.4)) that $X^2 = XX$, $X^3 = XXX, \cdots$, and that $X^m X^n = X^{m+n}$.

Actually, the second half of (4.5) is not simple to prove, and we shall start by analyzing X^{YZ}. By definition, this consists of all monotonic functions f with arguments $[y, z]$ and values x $[x \in X, y \in Y, z \in Z]$. Such functions f associate with each $z \in Z$, a function g_z with arguments $y \in Y$ and values $g_z(y) = f([y, z])$ in X. But for any z, $y \leqq y'$ implies $[y, z] \leqq [y', z]$ in YZ, hence

$$g_z(y) = f([y, z]) \leqq f([y', z]) = g_z(y')$$

and so g_z is in X^Y.

Furthermore, if $z \leqq z'$ and y is fixed, then

$$g_z(y) = f([y, z]) \leqq f([y, z']) = g_{z'}(y),$$

and so the correspondence $f\colon z \rightarrow g_z$ is monotonic, which makes X^{YZ} a subset S of $(X^Y)^Z$. While $f \leqq f'$ if and only if $f([y, z]) \leqq f'([y, z])$ for all $[y, z]$—which means that for all z, $g_z(y) \leqq g'_z(y)$ for all y, which means that for all z, $g_z \leqq g'_z$, and so X^{YZ} is isomorphic with S. But conversely, given $f \in (X^Y)^Z$, if $y \leqq y'$ and $z \leqq z'$, then $g_z(y) \leqq g_{z'}(y) \leqq g_{z'}(y')$, and so $f \in X^{YZ}$, which completes the proof of the fact that X^{YZ} and $(X^Y)^Z$ are isomorphic.

5. **Decomposition theorems.** It is evident that if $X = X_1 + \cdots + X_r = Y_1 + \cdots + Y_s$ is any partially ordered system, written in two ways as the sum of additive components, then by set-theory $X = Z_{11} + \cdots + Z_{rs}$, where $Z_{ij} = X_i \cap Y_j$ denotes the set of elements common to X_i and Y_j, ordered as in X. For if $x \in Z_{ij}$ and $x \leqq x'$, then $x' \in X_i$ and $x' \in Y_j$, whence $x' \in Z_{ij}$.

It follows that if X is finite, it has one and only one representation $X = X_1 + \cdots + X_q$ as the sum of (non-void) partially ordered sets not themselves further reducible. Actually, if we regard the elements of X as vertices of a graph, and join two vertices x and x' when $x < x'$ or $x > x'$ and no element z with $x < z < x'$ or $x > z > x'$ can be interpolated between x and x', then the irreducible additive components of X are the connected components of its graph.

The author has proved elsewhere[7] that any finite *lattice* L has a similar unique representation $L = L_1 \cdots L_q$ as the product of constituents not themselves further reducible. The prime-factor theorem of arithmetic asserts that the same conclusion is valid if L is a totally unordered aggregate.

Can we unite both these results in the single assertion that each finite *partially ordered system* X can be written in one and only one way as a product $X_1 \cdots X_q$ of "prime" (= indecomposable) factors? It is quite possible.

6. **Solution of equations.** One naturally asks if it is true that in the finite case, the rules that

$$X + Y = X + Z \quad \text{implies} \quad Y = Z, \tag{6.1}$$

$$X \cdot Y = X \cdot Z \quad \text{implies} \quad Y = Z, \tag{6.2}$$

which are true for pure cardinals and ordinals, are valid for general partially ordered sets.

It is easy to prove (6.1) by appealing to the result that every finite partially ordered system X has a unique decomposition into a sum of irreducible components. For, making this decomposition, we have

$$X + Y = (X_1 + \cdots + X_q) + (Y_1 + \cdots + Y_r),$$

$$X + Z = (X_1 + \cdots + X_q) + (Z_1 + \cdots + Z_s).$$

One sees that by ordinary subtraction, each kind of component must occur in Y and in Z alike, the number of times it occurs in $X + Y = X + Z$ minus the number of times it occurs in X, whence $Y = Z$.

This argument would prove (6.2) similarly if we knew that the proposition stated at the end of §5 was true; in any event, it holds for lattices, since they have unique decompositions into irreducible multiplicative factors.

If it held in general, would it imply that one could, by introducing negatives and quotients as ideal elements, extend our arithmetic to form an abstract field of elements of the symbolic form $(X - Y)/Z$? This seems highly improbable.

7. **Lexicographic combinations.** Let X be any partially ordered system whose members are themselves (not necessarily distinct) partially ordered systems Y_x.

We shall define $\sum_X Y_x$ (in words, the lexicographic sum of the Y_x relative to the ordering X) as the system whose members are the $y_x \in Y_x$ $[x \in X]$, in which $y_x \leqq y'_x$ preserves its meaning in Y_x, and $y_x \leqq y'_{x'}$ $[x \neq x']$ means that $x < x'$.

[7] *On the lattice theory of ideals*, Bull. Am. Math. Soc., vol. 40 (1934), p. 616, Theorem 2 and its corollaries.

Similarly, we shall define $\prod_X Y_x$ (in words, the lexicographic product of the Y_x relative to the ordering X) as the system whose members are the functions f carrying each $x \in X$ into an $f(x) \in Y_x$, and in which $f \leqq g$ means that for every x_0, either $f(x_0) \leqq g(x_0)$ or there exists an $\bar{x}_0 < x_0$ such that $f(\bar{x}_0) < g(\bar{x}_0)$ and $f(x) \leqq g(x)$ for all $x < \bar{x}_0$.

In case X is totally unordered $\sum_X Y_x$ and $\prod_X Y_x$ are the *cardinal* sums and products of Hausdorff extended as in §3. In case the Y_x are sequences arranged in the sequential order X, $\sum_X Y_x$ and $\prod_X Y_x$ are the *ordinal* sums and products of Hausdorff (loc. cit.).

If all the Y_x are isomorphic—that is, letting them all be a particular partially ordered system Y—we get a new binary operation of exponential type. For although the lexicographic sum $\sum_X Y$ of the occurrences of Y relative to the ordering X is simply the lexicographic product $\prod_{X<Y} X \cdot Y$ of X and Y relative to the ordering $X < Y$, the lexicographic product $\prod_X Y$, which we may denote lex Y^X, is a new system which could not easily be defined otherwise. Its elements are the different "words" f with letters from X, one in each position of Y, and ordered in lexicographic order.

Lexicographic combination is non-commutative, and seems to have no interest aside from the fact that lexicographic combinations of simply ordered (or well-ordered) systems are always themselves simply ordered (resp. well-ordered). This property makes them useful in ordering words in dictionaries.

HARVARD UNIVERSITY.

Reprinted from DUKE MATHEMATICAL JOURNAL
Vol. 3, No. 3, September, 1937

RINGS OF SETS

BY GARRETT BIRKHOFF

1. **Definitions.** Following Hausdorff,[1] a family $\mathfrak{F}$ of subsets of a class I is said to form a "ring" if and only if it contains, with any two sets[2] S and T, their *sum* (or union) $S \cup T$ and their *product* (or intersection) $S \cap T$. Clearly a ring contains, with any finite number of subsets $S_1, \cdots, S_n$, their sum $S_1 \cup \cdots \cup S_n$ and their product $S_1 \cap \cdots \cap S_n$.

The family $\mathfrak{F}$ is said to constitute a "complete ring" if and only if it contains, with any subfamily $\mathfrak{S}$ of sets S_α, their sum $V_{\alpha \in \mathfrak{S}} S_\alpha$ and their product $\Lambda_{\alpha \in \mathfrak{S}} S_\alpha$. The family $\mathfrak{F}$ is also said to be a "σ-ring" if and only if it contains, with any *countable* subfamily $\mathfrak{S}$ of sets S_α, their sum $V_{\alpha \in \mathfrak{S}} S_\alpha$ and their product $\Lambda_{\alpha \in \mathfrak{S}} S_\alpha$.

It is obvious that rings containing only a finite number of sets, and σ-rings containing only a countable number of sets, are necessarily complete rings. These theorems can be improved by using chain conditions; however, the family $\mathfrak{C}$ of all finite sets of integers is a countable ring which is not a σ-ring (and a fortiori not complete), while the family $\mathfrak{D}$ of all countable subsets of the continuum is a σ-ring which is not complete.

2. **The importance of the subject.** Rings of sets are mathematically important for a number of reasons. They are conceptually important because one can define them so simply in terms of two fundamental operations. They are also important because the sets of any class I carried within themselves by any one-valued transformation of I into itself are a complete ring. (The proof of this will be left to the reader.) Also, as is well known, the open and closed subsets of any topological space constitute rings, and the measurable subsets of any Cartesian n-space constitute a σ-ring.

Again, the reader will immediately see that

(2α) The sets common to all the rings (resp. σ-rings or complete rings) of any aggregate of rings of subsets of any class I themselves form a ring (resp. σ-ring or complete ring).

It follows that the closed subsets of any topological space Σ invariant under any group of transformations constitute a ring. The study of these rings is important in dynamics,[3] where, however, the existence of minimal closed and connected constituents introduces special considerations. It follows also that

Received January 16, 1937.

[1] *Mengenlehre*, 1927 (2d ed.), p. 77.

[2] We shall systematically use small Latin letters to denote elements, Latin capitals to denote sets of elements, and German capitals to denote families of sets.

[3] Especially in the theory of so-called "central motions". Cf. G. D. Birkhoff, *Dynamical Systems*, 1927, Chap. VII, §6 ff.

the subsets of any class I carried within themselves under any aggregate A of one-valued transformations τ_α of I into itself form a complete ring.

Moreover, all complete rings of sets belong to at least one aggregate A of transformations in this way. More precisely, any complete ring $\mathfrak{R}$ of sets belongs to the "groupoid"[4] of all one-valued transformations carrying every $S \in \mathfrak{R}$ into itself. This shows that rings of sets play the same rôle in the theory of groupoids of one-valued transformations as is played by transitivity and intransitivity in the theory of groups of permutations (one-one transformations).[5]

3. **Equivalent notions.** If we add the empty set O and the all-set I to any complete ring of subsets of a class I, we still have a complete ring. Hence the theory of rings of sets is contained in that of rings containing O and I.

THEOREM 1. *The complete rings of subsets of I which contain O and I can be identified with the different quasi-orderings of I or with the different completely distributive topologies on I.*

Explanation 1. By a "quasi-ordering" of I is meant a binary relation $x \geqq y$ satisfying

P1: $x \geqq x$ (reflexiveness),

P2: $x \geqq y$ and $y \geqq z$ imply $x \geqq z$ (transitivity).

By a "completely distributive topology" is meant a unary operation $S \to \bar{S}$ (called closure) on the subsets of I which satisfies

C1: $\bar{S} \geqq S$, C2: $\bar{O} = O$, C3: $\bar{\bar{S}} = \bar{S}$;

C4: if $S = \underset{\alpha}{V} S_\alpha$, then $\bar{S} = \underset{\alpha}{V} \bar{S}_\alpha$.

(These are related to well-known axioms of Hausdorff on "partial ordering", and of Riesz-Kuratowski on closure.)

Explanation 2. By an "identification" we mean a one-one correspondence preserved under all permutations of the elements of I. It follows that if we call two families of sets of I resp. two relations on I resp. two operations in I "equivalent" if and only if there exists a permutation of the elements of I carrying one into the other, then the numbers of non-equivalent rings of sets, of non-equivalent quasi-orderings, and of non-equivalent completely distributive

[4] A family G of one-valued transformations of I into itself is termed a "groupoid" if and only if it contains the identity ι: $x \to x$ and the product $\sigma\tau$: $x \to \tau[\sigma(x)]$ of any two of its members σ and τ. The author is preparing an article on groupoids in collaboration with S. Ulam.

[5] The sets invariant (i.e., the sets identical with, and not merely supersets of, their transforms) under any permutation or set of permutations constitute a "complete field"—i.e., a complete ring which contains, with any set, its complement. Moreover, any complete field belongs to the group of all transformations leaving its subsets invariant ("intransitive" on its subsets)—this leads to the usual partial descriptions of groups of permutations through their "transitive systems".

Actually, in the case of *groups* of permutations of I, any subset carried within itself under all their permutations is necessarily invariant.

topologies on I are the same—as well as the numbers of distinct complete rings of sets, of distinct quasi-orderings, and of distinct completely distributive topologies.

Proof of theorem. Let $\mathfrak{R}$ be any complete ring of sets containing O and I. Make the definitions: (1) $x \geqq y$ $(\mathfrak{R})$ means that every $S \in \mathfrak{R}$ containing x contains y, and (2) $\bar{S}$ is the product of all sets $T_\alpha \in \mathfrak{R}$ containing S. That the relation and operation so introduced satisfy P1–P2 and C1–C2 is obvious; it is also obvious that the correspondence between them and $\mathfrak{R}$ is preserved under all permutations of the elements of I.

To prove C3–C4, recall that, since $\mathfrak{R}$ is a complete ring, $\bar{S}$ is the least set in $\mathfrak{R}$ containing S. This proves C3 and

(3α) $S \in \mathfrak{R}$ if and only if $S = \bar{S}$.

Now suppose $S = \underset{\alpha}{V} S_\alpha$. Clearly $\bar{S} \geqq \bar{S}_\alpha$ irrespective of α; hence $\bar{S} \geqq \underset{\alpha}{V}\bar{S}_\alpha$. But conversely $\underset{\alpha}{V}\bar{S}_\alpha \in \mathfrak{R}$, since $\mathfrak{R}$ is a complete ring, and $\underset{\alpha}{V}\bar{S}_\alpha \geqq \underset{\alpha}{V}S_\alpha = S$; hence $\underset{\alpha}{V}\bar{S}_\alpha \geqq \bar{S}$. This proves C4.

It remains to prove that *every* quasi-ordering and *every* completely distributive topology belong to such an $\mathfrak{R}$, and that distinct $\mathfrak{R}$ determine distinct quasi-orderings and distinct topologies—four assertions in all.

By (3α), if $\mathfrak{R} \neq \mathfrak{R}'$, then certainly $\mathfrak{R}$ and $\mathfrak{R}'$ yield distinct topologies. This proves one assertion. We next wish to prove that

(3β) *Every* completely distributive topology is determined by a suitable $\mathfrak{R}$.

Under any such topology, consider the family $\mathfrak{F}$ of "closed" sets $S = \bar{S}$. Clearly $\mathfrak{F}$ contains O, I, and (by C4) $\underset{\alpha}{V}S_\alpha$ if it contains every S_α. But it also contains $\underset{\alpha}{\Lambda}S_\alpha$ under the same hypotheses.

Proof. If $\bar{S}_\alpha = S_\alpha$ for every α, then $\underset{\alpha}{\Lambda}\bar{S}_\alpha = \underset{\alpha}{\Lambda}S_\alpha$, and so $\overline{(\underset{\alpha}{\Lambda}S_\alpha)} \leqq S_\alpha$ for all S_α, whence $\overline{(\underset{\alpha}{\Lambda}S_\alpha)} \leqq \underset{\alpha}{\Lambda}\bar{S}_\alpha = \underset{\alpha}{\Lambda}S_\alpha$, and so by C1 $\underset{\alpha}{\Lambda}S_\alpha$ is closed. Hence $\mathfrak{F}$ is a complete ring of sets with O and I. Moreover, if S is any set, then $\bar{S}$ is the product of the $T_\alpha \in \mathfrak{F}$ containing S—by Cl, $\underset{\alpha}{\Lambda}T_\alpha = \underset{\alpha}{\Lambda}\bar{T}_\alpha \geqq \bar{S}$, and, by C1–C3, $\bar{S}$ is a closed set $T_\alpha \geqq S$. Thus $\mathfrak{F}$ "determines" the given topology. This proves (3β).

Again, if $\mathfrak{R}$ is given, then

(3γ) $S \in \mathfrak{R}$ if and only if $x \in S$ and $x \geqq y$ $(\mathfrak{R})$ imply $y \in S$.

Proof. If $S \in \mathfrak{R}$, by definition the second statement holds. Conversely if the second statement holds, then S contains, with every x, the set $S(x)$ of all $y \leqq x$ $(\mathfrak{R})$—i.e., the product of the $S_\alpha \in \mathfrak{R}$ with $x \in S_\alpha$; obviously $S(x) \in \mathfrak{R}$—and so S is the sum $VS(x)$ of the $S(x)$ of the $x \in S$, and is in $\mathfrak{R}$. By (3γ), if $\mathfrak{R} \neq \mathfrak{R}'$, then $\mathfrak{R}$ and $\mathfrak{R}'$ determine different quasi-orderings.

Finally, every quasi-ordering ρ is determined by some $\mathfrak{R}$. For, given ρ, let $\mathfrak{R}(\rho)$ consist of all S such that $x \in S$ and $x \geqq y$ imply $y \in S$. Clearly $O \in \mathfrak{R}(\rho)$ and $I \in \mathfrak{R}(\rho)$. Also, if a family $\mathfrak{S}$ of S_α is in $\mathfrak{R}(\rho)$, then $(VS_\alpha) \in \mathfrak{R}(\rho)$ and

$(\Lambda S_\alpha) \in \mathfrak{R}(\rho)$. Thus $\mathfrak{R}(\rho)$ is a complete ring of sets containing O and I. Further, if $x \geqq y$, then obviously $x \geqq y$ $(\mathfrak{R}(\rho))$ in the sense that $x \in S \in \mathfrak{R}(\rho)$ and $x \geqq y$ imply $y \in S$. Conversely if $x \geqq y$ $(\mathfrak{R}(\rho))$, then the set $S(x)$ of all $z \leqq x$ (which is in $\mathfrak{R}(\rho)$ by P2 and contains x by P1) contains y—by definition of $x \geqq y$ $(\mathfrak{R}(\rho))$—and so $x \geqq y$. This proves the fourth assertion.

4. **The case of fields of sets.** Which quasi-orderings and which completely distributive topologies correspond to complete fields[6] of sets? And what does this make Theorem 1 reduce to for fields of sets?

THEOREM 2. *In Theorem* 1, *a quasi-ordering corresponds to a (complete) field of sets if and only if it is an equivalence relation; a topology does, if and only if the closures of its points are the subsets of a partition of I.*

Explanation. By an "equivalence relation" is meant a quasi-ordering which satisfies

P3′: $x \geqq y$ implies $y \geqq x$.

By a "partition" of a class I is meant a division of its elements into disjoint subsets, whose sum is I.

Proof. Let $\mathfrak{R}$ be a complete ring of sets, and let $S(x)$ be the product of the sets $S_\alpha \in \mathfrak{R}$ containing x. Then $x \geqq y$ $(\mathfrak{R})$ means $y \in S(x)$. If $\mathfrak{R}$ is a field, and $y \in S(x)$, then the complement $S'(y)$ of $S(y)$ cannot contain x—otherwise $x \in S'(y) \cap S(x) \leqq S(x) - y < S(x)$—and so $y \in S(x)$ implies $x \in S(y)$. This proves P3′. Again, topologically, $S(x)$ is the closure of x. Hence if $\mathfrak{R}$ is a field, unless $S(x)$ and $S(y)$ are disjoint, $S(x) \cap S(y)$ contains some point z, and $x \geqq z$ and $y \geqq z$, whence by P2 and P3′ $x \geqq y$ and $y \geqq x$, and therefore $S(x) = S(y)$.

Conversely, if P3′ holds, and $\mathfrak{R}$ is the family of sets S such that $x \in S$ and $y \leqq x$ imply $y \in S$, then $S \in \mathfrak{R}$ implies that x not in S and $y \leqq x$ imply y not in S (otherwise $y \in S$ and $x \leqq y$ by P3′), whence $S' \in \mathfrak{R}$ and $\mathfrak{R}$ is a field. The fact that the sums of the parts of any partition of I are a complete field of sets is obvious.

COROLLARY.[7] *The complete fields of subsets of I which contain O and I can be identified with the different equivalences on I or with the different partitions of I.*

5. **Rings of sets and distributive lattices.** We shall deal below with rings of sets without assuming completeness.

Suppose we consider rings of sets simply as collections of symbols (forgetting that the symbols denote sets of points) related by inclusion, addition and multiplication. Then any ring of sets appears as a "distributive lattice", or system $\mathfrak{R}$ of elements S, T, U satisfying[8]

[6] A (complete) ring of sets is called a (complete) field if and only if it contains the complement of every one of its members.

[7] Part of this result is proved by H. Hasse, *Höhere Algebra*, vol. I, 1933, p. 15, and B. L. van der Waerden, *Moderne Algebra*, p. 14.

[8] Cf. the author's *On the structure of abstract algebras*, Proc. Camb. Phil. Soc., vol. 31

L1: $S \cap S = S$ and $S \cup S = S$.

L2: $S \cap T = T \cap S$ and $S \cup T = T \cup S$.

L3: $(S \cap T) \cap U = S \cap (T \cap U)$ and $(S \cup T) \cup U = S \cup (T \cup U)$.

L4: $S \cap (S \cup T) = S \cup (S \cap T) = S$.

L6: $S \cup (T \cap U) = (S \cup T) \cap (S \cup U)$ and

$$S \cap (T \cup U) = (S \cap T) \cup (S \cap U).$$

Moreover, two rings of sets seem indistinguishable when and only when they are "isomorphic"—i.e., admit a one-one correspondence preserving inclusion, sums and products.[9]

Conversely, every abstractly given distributive lattice is known to be obtainable from at least one ring of sets.[10]

6. **Representation theory for distributive lattices.** It is generally true in representation theories for abstract algebras that one gets the simplest results by considering homomorphic (many-one) as well as isomorphic (one-one or "true") representations.

A full representation theory for Boolean algebras by fields of sets has been developed by Stone,[11] and it is interesting to see the complications which arise in the more general case of distributive lattices. These show that the assumption that complements exist cannot be eliminated in Stone's theory.

First, let $\mathfrak{R}$ be any distributive lattice, and let θ be any congruence relation[12] on $\mathfrak{R}$. Then the elements congruent to O form an "ideal" $\mathfrak{O}$ in the sense that

I1: $X \in \mathfrak{O}$ and $A \in \mathfrak{R}$ imply $A \cap X \in \mathfrak{O}$.

I2: $X \in \mathfrak{O}$ and $Y \in \mathfrak{O}$ imply $X \cup Y \in \mathfrak{O}$.

In case $\mathfrak{R}$ is a Boolean algebra, $\mathfrak{O}$ determines θ, but this is not generally true in distributive lattices.

Proof. With Boolean algebras, S and T are congruent mod θ if and only if $(S \cap T') \cup (S' \cap T) \in \mathfrak{O}$, whereas O is an ideal in the chain of three elements $I > X > O$, determined by two distinct congruence relations.

(1935), pp. 433–454. O. Ore calls distributive lattices "arithmetic structures". Considerable work has been done by Fritz Klein on the decomposition of distributive lattices important in number theory; M. Ward has also given categorical definitions of such systems.

[9] Actually, any one-one correspondence preserving any one of these three preserves all; this is not true of many-one correspondences.

[10] Cf. the author's *On the combination of subalgebras*, Proc. Camb. Phil. Soc., vol. 29 (1933), pp. 441–464, Theorem 25.2.

[11] M. H. Stone, *The theory of representations of Boolean algebras*, Trans. Amer. Math. Soc., vol. 40 (1936), pp. 37–111. By a "representation" of a distributive lattice L, we mean a homomorphism between L and a ring of sets.

[12] I.e., any partition of the elements of $\mathfrak{R}$ determining an abstract homomorphism. This is a basic notion of general abstract algebra, whose detailed definition we shall omit.

Again, let $\mathfrak{R}$ be any distributive lattice, and A any element of $\mathfrak{R}$. The relation $X \cong Y \bmod A$ meaning $X \cup A = Y \cup A$ is a congruence relation.

Proof. That it is an equivalence relation is obvious. Moreover, by L1–L6,

$$(X \cup Y) \cap A = (X \cup A) \cup (Y \cup A),$$

$$(X \cap Y) \cup A = (X \cup A) \cap (Y \cup A);$$

hence the correspondence $X \rightarrow X \cup A$ defines a homomorphism of $\mathfrak{R}$ onto a subring of itself.

If $\mathfrak{R}$ is a finite Boolean algebra, there are no other congruence relations on $\mathfrak{R}$; this is not true for finite distributive lattices which are not Boolean algebras (proof omitted).

7. **Prime ideals.** Let us now suppose that R is any distributive lattice, and let us attempt to give a full representation theory for R.

Let θ: $R \rightarrow \mathfrak{R}$ be any homomorphism from R to a ring of subsets of a class I. We may classify the points of I into three categories: those contained in every set $X \in \mathfrak{R}$, those contained in no set $X \in \mathfrak{R}$, and the others. The first two categories of points are trivial, and so we can assume that $O \in \mathfrak{R}$ and $I \in \mathfrak{R}$.

Under these circumstances, every $p \in I$ divides the elements of R into two categories: those corresponding to sets including p, and those corresponding to sets excluding p. The second set of elements is an "ideal", while the first is a "dual ideal" D in the sense that

D1: $x \in D$ and $a \in R$ imply $a \cup x \in D$.

D2: $x \in D$ and $y \in D$ imply $x \cap y \in D$.

Hence the representation of R through $\mathfrak{R}$ is characterized to within equivalence[13] by which divisions of R into an ideal and complementary dual ideal occur, and how many times each occurs.

But conversely, by I1–I2 and D1–D2, if one is given any correspondence associating each division π of R into an ideal J and complementary dual ideal D with a cardinal number $n(\pi)$, then this belongs to a representation of R by a ring of sets, and so if we define (with Stone, op. cit.) an ideal to be "prime" if and only if its complement is a dual ideal, we have

THEOREM 3. *The inequivalent representations of a given distributive lattice R as a ring of sets are the different functions whose arguments are the "prime ideals" of R, and whose values are cardinal numbers.*

Remark 1. With Boolean algebras, the number of elements in any prime ideal and its dual are the same. Also, no prime ideal contains any other prime ideal. Neither of these properties is true in distributive lattices not Boolean algebras (e.g., the chain $I > X > O$).

[13] I.e., to within differences between the various points $p \in I$. This is standard terminology.

Remark 2. It is natural to call a representation "irredundant" if and only if no prime ideal appears as a point more than once.

8. **The finite case.** Only exceptionally are the prime ideals of infinite Boolean algebras known. But in each finite Boolean algebra of order 2^n they are known to be n sublattices of order 2^{n-1}.

We shall go further and determine the prime ideals of all finite distributive lattices.

Accordingly, let R be any finite distributive lattice, P any prime ideal in R, and $D = R - P$ the dual of P. Form any connected chain[14] $O < x_1 < x_2 < \cdots < x_r = I$ in R; it is clear that in such a chain there will be exactly one "link" $x_i < x_{i+1}$ such that $x_i \in P$ and $x_{i+1} \in D$, and that $x_k \in P$ for $k \leqq i$, while $x_k \in D$ for $k > i$.

(8α) We have $y \in P$ or $y \in D$ according as $v \equiv x_i \cup (y \cap x_{i+1}) = (x_i \cup y) \cap x_{i+1}$ is x_i or x_{i+1}.

Proof. Since $x_i \leqq x_{i+1}$, $x_i \cup (y \cap x_{i+1}) = (x_i \cup y) \cap x_{i+1}$ (by L6 and contraction). Again, for any y, obviously $x_i \leqq v \leqq x_{i+1}$; hence either $v = x_i$ or $v = x_{i+1}$ (no further interpolation being possible). But if $[x_i \cup (y \cap x_{i+1})] = x_i \in P$, then by I1 $(y \cap x_{i+1}) \in P$, and so by D2 (since $x_{i+1} \in D$), $y \in P$. Similarly, if $x_i \cup (y \cap x_{i+1}) = x_{i+1} \in D$, then by I2 (since $x_i \in P$), $y \cap x_{i+1} \in D$, and so by D1, $y \in D$.

Definition. By a "prime factor" of a distributive lattice is meant any symbol x/y, where $y < x$ and no element can be interpolated between y and x. A prime factor x/y will be called a "cleavage" for a given prime ideal P if and only if $y \in P$ and $x \in (R - P)$.

(8β) Any prime factor a/b is a cleavage for some prime ideal.

Proof. Let $x \in P$ if and only if $(b \cup x) \cap a = b$; this makes $x \in (R - P)$ if and only if $(b \cup x) \cap a = a$, since for all x, $b \leqq (b \cup x) \cap a = b \cup (x \cap a) \leqq a$, and a/b is prime. Clearly $a \in (R - P)$ and $b \in P$ (by L4). It remains to prove I1–I2 and D1–D2. But I1 and D1 are obvious, since $(b \cup x) \cap a$ is decreased resp. increased by substituting $x \cap y$ resp. $x \cup y$ for x. Moreover, under the hypotheses of I2,

$$b = [b \cup (x \cap a)] \cup [b \cup (y \cap a)] = b \cup [(x \cap a) \cup (y \cap a)]$$
$$= b \cup [(x \cup y) \cap (x \cup a) \cap (y \cup a) \cap a] = b \cup [(x \cup y) \cap a].$$

This proves I2. The proof of D2 is dual.

THEOREM 4. *Let R be any finite distributive lattice, and let its prime ideals be $P_1, \cdots, P_r$. Then in every connected chain $O < x_1 < \cdots < x_r = I$, each x_{i+1}/x_i is a cleavage for just one P_i—whence $r = n$.*

Proof. By (8α), if $P_i \neq P_j$, they can have no cleavage in common, and by (8β), every prime factor is a cleavage for some P_i.

We have the Jordan-Dedekind theorem[15] on the constancy of the number of

[14] A chain is called "connected" (or dense by Ore) if no further terms can be interpolated in it.

[15] R. Dedekind, *Werke*, vol. II, p. 254.

links in connected chains as one corollary, and using Theorem 3, we have the further

COROLLARY. *A finite distributive lattice has (to within equivalence) exactly one irredundant isomorphic representation as a ring of sets—and the number of points involved is the number of links in its connected chains.*[16]

9. **The finite case** (continued). Let R denote again any finite distributive lattice, let its prime ideals be $P_1, \cdots, P_n$, and let their duals be $D_1, \cdots, D_n$.

Let further $s_i = s(P_i)$ and $p_i = p(D_i)$ be the sum of the $x \in P_i$ resp. the product of the $x \in D_i$. By I2, $s_i \in P_i$, and by D2, $p_i \in D_i$; hence (cf. I1–D1) $x \in P_i$ means $x \leqq s_i$ and $x \in D_i$ means $x \geqq p_i$.

Now let I denote the partially ordered set[17] of the s_i. Call a subset S of I "closed" if and only if $s_i \in S$ and $s_j \leqq s_i$ imply $s_j \in S$.

(9α) R is isomorphic with the ring of "closed" subsets of I under the correspondence $S \rightleftharpoons \bigwedge_{s_i \in S} s_i$.

Proof. Let S be a "closed" subset of I. Then by I1–I2 and D1–D2, $\bigwedge_{s_i \in S} s_i$ is in the P_i corresponding to these s_i, and no others. But given $x \in R$, the subset of $s_i \geqq x$ is closed, $y = \bigwedge_{s_i \geqq x} s_i$ is in the same P_i as x, and hence $y \cup x$ and $y \cap x$ are, and so by (8β) no prime factor can be inserted between them, and $x = y = \bigwedge_{s_i \geqq x} s_i$. Thus the correspondence $x \rightleftharpoons \bigwedge_{s_i \geqq x} s$ is one-one. But it clearly preserves inclusion, while by Theorem 1 the closed subsets of I are a ring of sets. This completes the proof.

Consequently two finite distributive lattices having isomorphic partially ordered sets of s_i are isomorphic. But the converse is obvious, since the s_i are intrinsically defined. Since, finally, if X is any (abstractly given) partially ordered set, the ring of its closed subsets is a distributive lattice having the "closures" of points of X for s_i, we obtain

THEOREM 5.[18] *There is a one-one correspondence between the partially ordered sets of n elements and the distributive lattices whose connected chains are of length n.*

In the notation of a previous article (this volume of this Journal, p. 311), by (9α) this is the correspondence $X \rightleftharpoons B^X$.

Remark 1. The connected components $X_1, \cdots, X_s$ of X correspond to the indecomposable direct factors of

$$B^X = (B^{X_1}) \times \cdots \times (B^{X_s})$$

in the direct decompositions of B^X.

[16] Cf. *On the combination of subalgebras*, Theorem 17.2.

[17] A set is "partially ordered" (the terminology is Hausdorff's, *Grundzüge der Mengenlehre*, 1914, Chap. VI) by a quasi-ordering satisfying P3: $x \geqq y$ and $y \geqq x$ imply $x = y$. Any subset of a partially ordered set (such as a distributive lattice) is partially ordered by the same relation.

[18] Theorem 5 was announced without proof by the author in a note *Sur les espaces discrets*, Comptes Rendus, vol. 201 (1935), p. 19.

Remark 2. The "Hasse[19] diagram" for X gives an infinitely more compact and intelligible way of writing down a general distributive lattice B^X than the multiplication table used by Dedekind, or than the "Hasse diagram" for B^X itself used by recent authors.

Remark 3. Let $\mathfrak{R}$ be any finite ring of sets, and $L = B^X$ the distributive lattice isomorphic with $\mathfrak{R}$. To find X, take the quasi-ordering determined by $\mathfrak{R}$; identify points x and y satisfying both $x \geqq y$ ($\mathfrak{R}$) and $y \geqq x$ ($\mathfrak{R}$); the partial ordering induced by the quasi-ordering on the sets of "identified" points will yield X.

10. **The indecomposable elements.** Let us again suppose that R is a finite distributive lattice with prime ideals $P_1, \cdots, P_n$ having duals $D_1, \cdots, D_n$.

(10α) Each $s(P_i) = s_i$ is product-indecomposable. Dually, each $p(D_i) = p_i$ is sum-indecomposable.

Explanation. An element a of a lattice R is called "product-indecomposable" when no two elements $x > a$ and $y > a$ exist with $x \cap y = a$; it is called sum-indecomposable when (dually) no two elements $x < a$ and $y < a$ exist with $x \cup y = a$.

Proof. If $x > s_i$ and $y > s_i$, then $x \in D_i$ and $y \in D_i$, whence $(x \cap y) \in D_i$ and $x \cap y \neq s_i$.

(10β) If $x \in R$ is product-indecomposable, it is an s_i. If it is sum-indecomposable, it is a p_i, dually.

Proof. If x is product-indecomposable, then it yields a unique prime factor a/x; let P_i be the corresponding prime ideal. Clearly $x = s(P_i)$, since if $x < s(P_i)$, we would have $y = s(P_i)$, whence $y \in P_i$.

COROLLARY. *The number of sum-indecomposable resp. product-indecomposable elements of a finite distributive lattice is the length of its connected chains.*

10a. **The free distributive lattices.** Consider the "free" distributive lattice generated by n symbols $x_1, \cdots, x_n$; Theorem 1 inclines one to adjoin to it elements O and I such that $O < x_i < I$ for all x_i.

If this is done, then the product-indecomposable elements form a Boolean algebra B^n of 2^n elements. More precisely, they are the elements, O, x_k, $x_i \cup x_j$, $x_i \cup x_j \cup x_k$, $x_h \cup x_i \cup x_j \cup x_k$, $\cdots$, $x_1 \cup \cdots \cup x_{k-1} \cup x_{k+1} \cup \cdots \cup x_n$, $x_1 \cup \cdots \cup x_n$. The corresponding prime factors are

$$x_1 \cap \cdots \cap x_n/0,$$

$$x_k \cup (x_1 \cap \cdots \cap x_{k-1} \cap x_{k+1} \cap \cdots \cap x_n)/x_k,$$

. . . .

$$(x_1 \cup \cdots \cup x_{k-1} \cup x_{k+1} \cup \cdots \cup x_n) \cup x_k \Big/ (x_1 \cup \cdots \cup x_{k-1} \cup x_{k+1} \cup \cdots \cup x_n),$$

$$I/(x_1 \cup \cdots \cup x_n).$$

[19] Cf. H. Hasse, *Höhere Algebra*, vol. II, 1927, p. 103, p. 123.

It is a corollary that the free distributive lattices with O and I adjoined are the B^{B^n}.

The proofs of the above statements are tedious; they depend on the knowledge of canonical expressions for the elements of the free distributive lattice.[20]

11. **A general decomposition theorem.** Let R be any (finite or infinite) distributive lattice, and let

$$x = x_1 \cap \cdots \cap x_r = y_1 \cap \cdots \cap y_s$$

be any two representations of an element $x \in R$ as a product. Then irrespective of i, $x_i = x_i \cup x = x_i \cup (\underset{j}{\Lambda} y_j) = \underset{j}{\Lambda}(x_i \cup y_j)$. Hence if x_i is product-indecomposable, some $x_i \cup y_j = x_i$. This means some $y_j \leqq x_i$. Symmetrically, some $x_k \leqq y_j$. Hence either $x_k = y_j = x_i$, or x_i is *redundant* in the strong sense that some $x_k < x_i$, whence

$$x = x_1 \cap \cdots \cap x_{i-1} \cap x_{i+1} \cap \cdots \cap x_r .$$

Thus if the decompositions are irredundant, the x_i and y_j are equal in pairs, $r = s$, and so

(11α) *In a distributive lattice, no element has more than one irredundant product-decomposition (sum-decomposition) into elements not themselves further decomposable.*

But conversely, any modular lattice which is not distributive is known[21] to contain a sublattice of five elements a, b, x_1, x_2, x_3 satisfying $a < x_i < b$, $x_i \cap x_j \equiv a$, and $x_i \cup x_j \equiv b$ $[i \neq j]$. Now starting with the two product-decompositions $a = x_1 \cap x_2$ and $a = x_2 \cap x_3$ of a, making further decompositions as long as possible, and eliminating redundant components, we see that any factor for the second decomposition which contains x_1 must contain x_2 or x_3 and hence b—whereas the first decomposition and those derived from it must possess at least one factor containing x_1 but *not* b. Hence if the above process is terminating, we will surely get two distinct product-decompositions of a. But in the presence of the chain-condition, the process *is* terminating. This completes the proof of

THEOREM 6.[22] *A modular lattice satisfying the ascending chain condition is distributive if and only if each of its elements has a unique irredundant product-decomposition.*

[20] The latter are given by Th. Skolem, *Über gewisse "Verbände" oder "Lattices"*, Avh. Norske Videnskaps Akademi i Oslo, Mat.-Naturv. Klasse, 1936, no. 7, pp. 7, 8. From them it is immediately obvious that the elements specified above are the *only* product-indecomposable elements—but there are just enough such elements to give the lattice 2^n dimensions; hence they are *all* product-indecomposable.

[21] Cf. Theorem 4 of the author's *On the lattice theory of ideals*, Bull. Amer. Math. Soc., vol. 40 (1934), p. 617.

[22] This result was announced by the author in Abstract 41-1-75 of the Bull. Amer. Math Soc., vol. 41 (1935), p. 32.

This result is especially interesting in the light of recent proofs by Kurosch and Ore that, in any modular lattice, the number of factors in any two irredundant product-decompositions of the same element into indecomposable factors is the same.[23]

12. **Some enumeration problems.** One very impartial test of one's ability to classify finite systems is one's ability to enumerate them. This suggests the problem of determining the following combinatorial functions.

(12.1) The number $F_1(n)$ of different rings of subsets of n elements. (This is the number of sublattices of the Boolean algebra B^n of 2^n elements.)

(12.2) The number $F_2(n)$ of non-equivalent rings of such subsets. (This is the number of such sublattices non-conjugate under the group of automorphisms of B^n.)

(12.3) The number $F_3(n)$ of non-isomorphic rings of such subsets. (This is the number of non-isomorphic distributive lattices of "dimensions" n.)

(12.4) The number $F_4(n)$ of non-isomorphic partial orderings of n elements.

Remark 1. If we replace "ring" by "field" in the above, $F_1(n)$ becomes a known combinatorial function defined by the recurrence

$$H^* (n + 1) = \sum_{h=0}^{n} \binom{n}{h} H^* (n - h).$$

This has been studied by Aitken (Edin. Math. Notes, vol. 28 (1933), pp. xviii–xxiii). Again, $F_2(n)$ becomes the partition function—a celebrated asymptotic formula for which has been given by Hardy and Ramanujan. And lastly, $F_3(n)$ becomes n.

Remark 2. In virtue of Theorems 3 and 5, $F_3(n) = \sum_{k=1}^{n} F_4(n)$. Also, $F_2(n)$ is by Theorem 1 the number of non-equivalent quasi-orderings of n elements, and $F_1(n)$ is the number of *different* quasi-orderings of n elements.

A table for these functions for small n follows.

	1	2	3	4	5	6
$F_1(n)$	1	3	29			
$F_2(n)$	1	3	9	30		
$F_4(n)$	1	2	5	15	51	250

[23] A. Kurosch, *Durchschnittsdarstellungen mit irreduziblen Komponenten in Ringen und in sog. Dualgruppen*, Rec. Math. (Moscow), vol. 42 (1935), pp. 613–16. O. Ore, *On the foundations of abstract algebra*. II, Annals of Math., vol. 37 (1936), p. 270, Theorem 11. The result of Kurosch-Ore contains a decomposition theorem of E. Noether for ideals, and a less well-known result of Remak's on finite groups, as special corollaries.

In calculating these values, assume that $F_2(n)$ is the number of functions from the different partially ordered sets of $k \leqq n$ elements to cardinal numbers whose sum is n. Also $F_1(n)$ can be calculated combinatorially from $F_2(n)$ by summing the occurrences of each type of ring of subsets, over the types existing. To find $F_4(n)$, separate each partially ordered set into its connected components.

It would be very interesting to know more about the $F_k(n)$, numerically or asymptotically. $F_4(n)$ resembles the function describing the number of groups of order 2^n—whose first values are 1, 2, 5, 14, 51, 266, $\cdots$. It appears to increase more rapidly than the function describing the number of non-isomorphic symmetric relations between n objects (or alternatively, the number of non-homomorphic graphs with n vertices), whose first values are 1, 2, 4, 11, 27. But as almost nothing is known about the rate of growth of these functions, these comparisons are not very reliable.

13. **Homomorphic images and sublattices.** Let us try to determine the homomorphisms and sublattices of a given finite distributive lattice, guided by the previous results.

Some authors,[24] inspired by the numerous analogies between lattices and rings, have correlated the congruence relations on lattices with "ideals" and "normal sublattices". But except in the "complemented" case in which each element x possesses a complement x' with $x \cap x' = 0$ and $x \cup x' = I$, this correlation is incomplete.

Actually, in the case of finite distributive lattices, and more generally with arbitrary modular lattices of finite dimensions (the author will publish proofs elsewhere, in an article on modular lattices), congruence relations correspond one-one to subsets of the set of prime factors.

It follows that, if $L = B^X$ is any finite distributive lattice, the congruence relations on it are obtained by setting $x \equiv y(\theta)$ if and only if x and y contain the same P_i. Hence, to obtain the homomorphic images B^Y of B^X, set Y equal to any subset of X having on that subset the same inclusion relation as X.

The determination of the sublattices of B^X is even easier. First, recall that B^X is isomorphic with the ring of subsets of X which are "closed" with respect to the partial ordering of X, by (9α). But a sublattice is clearly just a subring—and by Theorem 1 these subrings are the families of sets "closed" under quasi-orderings ρ of X such that $x \geqq y(\rho)$ whenever $x \geqq y$ in X. Hence, to obtain the sublattices of B^X, strengthen the inclusion relation in X to any quasi-ordering and consider the partially ordered set Y obtained from this after elements x and y such that $x \geqq y$ and $y \geqq x$ have been identified; B^Y will be the general sublattice of B^X.

HARVARD UNIVERSITY.

[24] Cf. for instance Gr. C. Moisil, *Recherches sur l'algèbre de la logique*, Annales Sci. de l'Univ. de Jassy, vol. 22 (1936), pp. 1–118.

Reprinted from DUKE MATHEMATICAL JOURNAL
Vol. 9, No. 2, June, 1942

GENERALIZED ARITHMETIC

BY GARRETT BIRKHOFF

1. **Introduction.** Since the time of Cantor, it has been the fashion to divide all arithmetic at the root into two separate branches: cardinal and ordinal. Each of these branches is supposed to have its peculiar operations of addition, multiplication, and exponentiation. Only as an afterthought are the two branches connected, by a roughly[1] homomorphic correspondence from ordinal arithmetic to cardinal arithmetic, which is ismorphic when restricted to finite ordinals and cardinals.

In the present paper, an entirely different point of view is advanced. Instead of giving finite and transfinite arithmetic a split personality, half ordinal, half cardinal, I believe that one should regard both aspects as fragments of a unified general arithmetic of partially ordered systems.

I should like to stress three arguments in favor of this point of view.

In the first place, what are usually considered as purely cardinal operations extend in a natural way to ordinal numbers and other partially ordered systems, and vice versa. Moreover, when applied to the wider context of general partially ordered systems, the six operations of "generalized arithmetic" are found to have important new applications.[2] The variety and importance of these will stand comparison with the applications of transfinite arithmetic, as that term has been understood heretofore.[3]

In the second place, almost all arithmetical laws which are valid in transfinite arithmetic, as that term is understood now, are equally valid when the operations are applied to the most general partially ordered systems. In fact, the big gap comes between ordinary arithmetic and transfinite arithmetic; much more is lost by admitting infinite numbers as legitimate objects for arithmetic operations than is lost by including partially ordered sets in the middle ground between totally ordered sets (finite ordinals) and totally unordered sets (finite cardinals). Moreover, the slight loss is more than compensated by the availability of *new cross-laws* connecting cardinal with ordinal operations.

Finally, adoption of the broader point of view towards arithmetic developed below fits the traditional transfinite arithmetic into the general framework of

Received October 18, 1941.

[1] Ordinal exponentiation does not quite fit into this statement, and involves special complications. Also, the proof of this connection involves the well-ordering principle (axiom of choice).

[2] Much may be found about the extension of cardinal operations and applications of the extended definitions in [1]. However, the scope of the present program is nowhere suggested in that paper.

[3] The need for the *operations* of transfinite arithmetic was never very great; the need in topology for even transfinite ordinals has now largely disappeared, thanks to the increased use of the more effective and simpler tool of Moore-Smith convergence.

modern algebra. This gives fresh insight into known facts, and suggests new problems and results.

2. **Numbers, subnumbers, and homonumbers.** Let us agree to mean by the word *number* any non-void partially ordered set. That is ([3], Chap. VI, §2, or [2], p. 5), a "number" is a set A of elements $x, y, z, \cdots$, connected by a reflexive, transitive, and anti-symmetric[4] relation $x \geqq y$. Numbers will be denoted by italic capital letters throughout the sequel.

We shall call two numbers A and B *equal* (in symbols, $A = B$) if and only if they represent *isomorphic* partially ordered sets. This relation has the usual reflexive, symmetric, and transitive properties; moreover, it conforms to accepted usage.

The usual meaning of inequality between cardinal numbers and also that between ordinal numbers appear as special cases of the concept of subnumber as now defined.

Definition. A number A will be called a *subnumber* of a number B (in symbols, $A \subset B$) if and only if A is isomorphic to a *subset* of B.

We shall state without proof the evident

Theorem 1. *The relation of being a subnumber is consistent, reflexive and transitive; unity is a subnumber of every number. Formally,*

(1) *if* $B = C$, *then* $A \subset B$ *implies* $A \subset C$ *and* $B \subset D$ *implies* $C \subset D$;

(2) *for all* A, $A \subset A$;

(3) *if* $A \subset B$ *and* $B \subset C$, *then* $A \subset C$;

(4) *for all* A, $1 \subset A$.

The concept of subnumber may be supplemented by the closely related concept of homonumber, suggested by the general ideas of modern algebra. This concept, in the present context, is new.

Definition. A number A will be called a *homonumber* of a number B (in symbols, $A \prec B$), if and only if there is a many-one or one-one correspondence of B onto A which preserves order, so that if a and a' are the images of b and b', respectively, then $b \geqq b'$ in B implies $a \geqq a'$ in A.

Theorem 2. *The relation of being a homonumber is consistent, reflexive and transitive; unity is a homonumber of every number. Formally,*

(5) *if* $B = C$, *then* $A \prec B$ *implies* $A \prec C$ *and* $B \prec D$ *implies* $C \prec D$;

(6) *for all* A, $A \prec A$;

[4] It has been pointed out to the author by J. W. Tukey that most of the results below are independent of this restriction, and indeed the definition of ordinal exponentiation is simplified. However, this further generalization will not be made here since it might be confusing to many.

(7) *if* $A \prec B$ *and* $B \prec C$, *then* $A \prec C$;

(8) *for all* A, $1 \prec A$.

We note that the ordinal ω is not a homonumber of $\omega + 1$, although it is a subnumber of it. For, any homonumber of $\omega + 1$ would have a last element i, whereas ω has none.

We now come face-to-face with the principal properties of cardinal and ordinal numbers, which are lost in the generalized arithmetic developed here. First, the relation $\subset$, which is *anti-symmetric* for cardinals (Bernstein's theorem) and ordinals, is not anti-symmetric[5] in general. Second, it is obviously not true that for all A, B either $A \subset B$ or $B \subset A$, although this is well known to be true for ordinals ([2], Theorem 1.8), and hence (using the well-ordering principle) for cardinals. In summary, the *comparability* property is lost.[6]

3. **Cardinal and ordinal addition.** The usual definitions of addition for cardinal and ordinal numbers generalize in obvious ways to arbitrary partially ordered sets.[7]

DEFINITION. By the *cardinal sum* of A and B (in symbols, $A + B$) is meant the number consisting of all the elements in A or B, where inclusion within A and within B keep their original meaning, while neither $a \geqq b$ nor $a \leqq b$ holds for any $a \in A$, $b \in B$. By the *ordinal sum* $A \oplus B$ of A and B is meant the number consisting of all elements in A and all those in B, where inclusion within A and within B keep their original meaning, while $a > b$ holds for *all* $a \in A$ and $b \in B$.

Thus for finite numbers, we can construct the diagrams [2] of $A + B$ and of $A \oplus B$ as follows. That of $A + B$ is obtained by laying the diagrams of A and B side-by-side, that of $A \oplus B$ by laying that of A above that of B and drawing lines from all minimal elements of A to all maximal elements of B. Thus the graph of a cardinal sum is always disconnected; while if A has a least element o and B a greatest element i, then the graph of $A \oplus B$ has a "node", or line which, if severed, would disconnect the graph. The converses of these also hold.

THEOREM 3. *Cardinal and ordinal addition are both single-valued, isotone, and associative. Cardinal addition is commutative, and homomorphic to ordinal addition. Formally,*

(9) *if* $A = B$ *and* $C = D$, *then* $A + C = B + D$ *and* $A \oplus C = B \oplus D$;

(10) *if* $A \subset B$ *and* $C \subset D$, *then* $A + C \subset B + D$ *and* $A \oplus C \subset B \oplus D$;

(11) *if* $A \prec B$ *and* $C \prec D$, *then* $A + C \prec B + D$ *and* $A \oplus C \prec B \oplus D$;

[5] Let A consist of all fractions $m + 1/(n + 1)$, where m and n are positive integers; let B consist of all those with $m > 1$ or $n = 1$. Then $A \subset B$ and $B \subset A$, yet $A \neq B$.

[6] Slightly more is lost: the fact that the cardinals and ordinals form well-ordered sets under the relation $A \subset B$.

[7] For the usual definitions, cf. [3] or [4]. The generalizations were outlined in [1]; they are obvious enough.

(12) $A + (B + C) = (A + B) + C$ *and* $A \oplus (B \oplus C) = (A \oplus B) \oplus C$;

(13) $A + B = B + A$;

(14) $A \oplus B < A + B$.

Proof. The proofs of (9)–(11) follow by just putting together the correspondences between the summands. Formulas (12)–(13) are obvious; the correspondence giving (14) is just the identical correspondence from A to A and B to B.

Remark. It is known that $\omega = 1 \oplus \omega \neq \omega \oplus 1$: ordinal addition of *infinite* ordinals is not commutative. It is also true that ordinal addition of *finite* cardinals is non-commutative.

Finally, we can state some results connecting inclusion with addition, which are true except for the combination of homomorphic inclusion with ordinal addition. We have

(15) if $A \subset B + C$, then $A = D + E$, where $D \subset B$ and $E \subset C$;

(16) if $A \subset B \oplus C$, then $A = D \oplus E$, where $D \subset B$ and $E \subset C$;

(17) if $B + C < A$, then $A = D + E$, where $B < D$ and $C < E$;

(18) $A \subset A + B$, $B \subset A + B$, $A \subset A \oplus B$, and $B \subset A \oplus B$;

(19) $A < A + B$, and $B < A + B$.

Of these results, (15)–(17) assert the hereditary nature of decomposability, and (15)–(16) are converses of (10)–(11). While (18) would be trivial if one admitted the void set 0 as a number,[8] it would then be a corollary of (10).

4. **Digression: unique decomposition theorems.** It may be shown that decomposition into either cardinal or ordinal summands is essentially unique.

THEOREM 4. *Any two decompositions of a number A into cardinal summands or ordinal summands have a common refinement.*

COROLLARY. *A number has at most one cardinal or ordinal decomposition into indecomposable summands; in the finite case, this always exists.*

Proof. It is easy to show that a partition of a "number" A represents a decomposition of A into cardinal summands if and only if $x \geqq y$ implies that x and y are in the same subdivision of A. But it is easy to show that the product (in the ordinary sense) of any two partitions with this property itself has this property, and is the desired refinement. Similarly, a partition of A represents a decomposition of A into ordinal summands if and only if, given any two pieces A_i and A_j of the partition, either $x > y$ for all $x \in A_i$, $y \in A_j$, or the reverse holds. With a little trouble, one can also show that the product of any two such partitions is also such a partition.

[8] There are two troubles with this. First, 0^0 and ^{00} would then be ambiguously defined (they could be either 0 or 1), and second, (8) would no longer be true.

We note that in the case of ordinal sums, even the order of summation is prescribed. With cardinal sums, the representation as a sum of indecomposable summands is only unique to within rearrangement of the factors.

5. **Cardinal multiplication.** The usual notion of the product of two cardinal numbers also has an obvious and known (cf. [1] or [2]) generalization to arbitrary partially ordered sets or, in our terminology, to arbitrary "numbers".

DEFINITION. By the *cardinal product* of two given numbers A and B (written AB) is meant the set of all couples (a, b) $(a \in A,\ b \in B)$, where $(a, b) \geqq (a', b')$ if and only if $a \geqq a'$ in A and $b \geqq b'$ in B.

THEOREM 5. *Cardinal multiplication is single-valued, isotone, commutative, and associative; it admits* 1 *as an identity, is distributive on cardinal sums, and semi-distributive on ordinal sums. Formally,*

(20) $A = B$ *implies* $AC = BC$ *and* $CA = CB$;

(21) $A \subset B$ *implies* $AC \subset BC$ *and* $CA \subset CB$;

(22) $A < B$ *implies* $AC < BC$ *and* $CA < CB$;

(23) $AB = BA$ *for all* A, B;

(24) $A(BC) = (AB)C$ *for all* A, B, C;

(25) $1A = A1 = A$ *for all* A;

(26) $A(B + C) = AB + AC$ *and* $(A + B)C = AC + BC$;

(27) $A(B \oplus C) > AB \oplus AC$ *and* $(A \oplus B)C > AC \oplus BC$.

The verification of each of these laws individually, except (27), is a straightforward and elementary exercise which involves only substituting in definitions and using obvious correspondences (cf. [1] for (23), (24), (26)). To prove (27), consider the obvious one-one correspondence between $A(B \oplus C)$ and $AB \oplus AC$. Each element of either can be identified with a couple (a, b) or (a, c) $(a \in A,\ b \in B,\ c \in C)$. In both, $(a, b) \geqq (a', b')$ if and only if $a \geqq a'$ and $b \geqq b'$, and similarly for $(a, c) \geqq (a', c')$. In $A(B \oplus C)$, we have $(a, b) \geqq (a', c)$ if and only if $a \geqq a'$; in $AB \oplus AC$, we have $(a, b) \geqq (a', c)$ identically; these give (27).

To show that equality does not hold in (27), note that, in terms of lattice diagrams, we have the situation shown in Fig. 1. As a corollary of (21), (22),

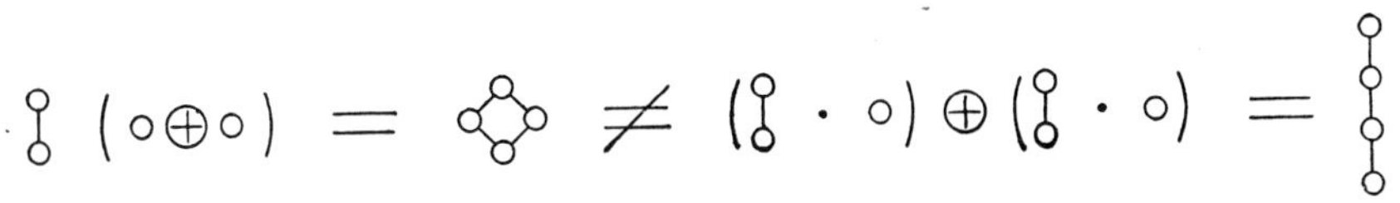

FIG. 1

and (25), we get also

(28) $A = A1 \subset AB$ and $A = A1 \prec AB$, for all B.

This is analogous to (18)–(19) above.

6. **Ordinal or lexicographic multiplication.** The usual definition ([3], p. 78) of the lexicographic product of two ordered sets applies without change to arbitrary "numbers". When so applied, it specializes not only to the usual product of two ordinals, but also (curiously enough) to the product of two cardinals, as usually understood. Nevertheless, we shall not regard it as the correct generalization of ordinary cardinal multiplication, for the reason that it does not, in general, satisfy the identities of cardinal arithmetic.

DEFINITION. By the *ordinal product* of two numbers A and B (in symbols, $A \circ B$) is meant the set of all couples (a, b) $(a \in A, b \in B)$, where $(a, b) \geqq (a', b')$ if and only if $a > a'$ in A *or* $a = a'$ in A and $b \geqq b'$ in B.

In the finite case, we can construct the diagram of $A \circ B$ from the diagrams of A and B as follows. In each circle representing an element a of A, put a replica B_a of B. Then draw segments from all the maximal elements of each B_a and all the minimal elements of each $B_{a'}$ for a' covering[9] a. This rule may be justified by the *covering condition* of

LEMMA 1. *In $A \circ B$, (a, b) covers (a', b') if and only if* (i) *$a = a'$ and b covers b', or* (ii) *b is minimal and b' maximal in B, while a covers a' in A.*

THEOREM 6. *Ordinal multiplication is single-valued, isotone, and associative; it admits* 1 *as an identity, and is semi-distributive on ordinal and cardinal sums alike. Formally,*

(29) $A = B$ *implies* $A \circ C = B \circ C$ *and* $C \circ A = C \circ B$;

(30) $A \subset B$ *implies* $A \circ C \subset B \circ C$ *and* $C \circ A \subset C \circ B$;

(31) $A \prec B$ *implies* $C \circ A \prec C \circ B$;

(32) $A \circ (B \circ C) = (A \circ B) \circ C$ *for all* A, B, C;

(33) $1 \circ A = A \circ 1 = A$ *for all* A;

(34) $(A \oplus B) \circ C = A \circ C \oplus B \circ C$;

(35) $(A + B) \circ C = A \circ C + B \circ C$ *and* $A \circ (B + C) \prec A \circ B + A \circ C$.

Proof. Rules (29)–(31) are immediate if (a, c) is made to correspond to (b, c) if and only if a corresponds to b; the details are easy to check. The proofs of (32)–(33) are also immediate.

In regard to (34)–(35), we use the cardinal one-one correspondence already utilized on proving (26)–(27). First, we have the two equalities. In all cases, the couples (a, c) are ordered as in $A \circ C$ and the couples (b, c) as in $B \circ C$; hence we need merely compare couples (a, c) with couples (b, c'). In (34), it is easy

[9] By the statement a' *covers* a, it is meant that $a' > a$, yet $a' > x > a$ for no x.

to show that always, on both sides, $(a, c) \geqq (b, c')$, while in (35), (a, c) and (b, c') are unrelated in both cases. Then, we have the inequality. In both cases, the couples (a, b) are ordered as in $A \circ B$ and the couples (a, c) as in $A \circ C$; hence we need merely compare (a, c) with (b, c'). But these are never comparable in $A \circ B + A \circ C$; hence the correspondence certainly preserves all inequalities.

Remarks. Ordinal multiplication is thus more closely connected with cardinal than with ordinal addition.

The non-commutativity of ordinal multiplication, known in the infinite case, clearly appears also in the finite case.

One might expect $A \circ (B \oplus C)$ and $A \circ B \oplus A \circ C$ to be related in some way. However, if A, B, and C are finite *and* A is simply ordered, one may show by a little numerical computation that both expressions have the same number of elements *and* of relations; hence, if related by any inequality, they must be isomorphic. Now set A = the ordinal two (or two-element chain), $B = 3$, and $C = 2$. Drawing the appropriate diagrams, we get $A \circ (B \oplus C) \neq A \circ B \oplus A \circ C$.

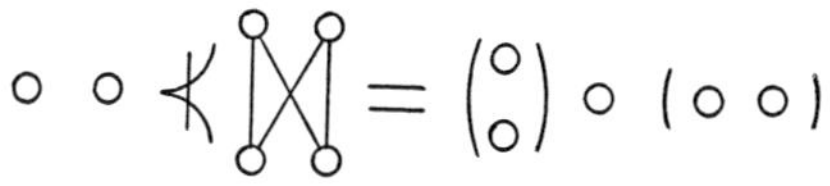

FIG. 2

Surprisingly enough, $A < B$ need *not* imply $A \circ C < B \circ C$; cf. Fig. 2. The same example shows that $A \not< B \circ A$ is possible (for $A = 2$, B the two-element chain as above). On the other hand, it is an immediate corollary of (34)–(35) and the fact that 1 is a subnumber and homonumber of every number, as well as an identity for ordinal multiplication, that

(36) $A \subset A \circ B, B \subset A \circ B, A < A \circ B$, for all A, B.

7. **Cardinal exponentiation.** The usual definition (cf. [3], p. 37) of a cardinal power of a cardinal number is a special case of a general definition, applicable to arbitrary numbers.[10] This general definition is not suggested by any very obvious considerations, but plays an important rôle in lattice theory.

DEFINITION. By the *cardinal power* A^B of the "base" number A raised to the "exponent" B is meant the set of all those functions $f(x)$ with domain B and range in A, which are *isotone* in the sense that $x \geqq y$ in B implies $f(x) \geqq f(y)$ in A. This set is ordered by making $f \geqq g$ in A^B mean that $f(x) \geqq g(x)$ in A for all $x \in B$.

THEOREM 7. *Cardinal exponentiation is single-valued and semi-isotone; it satisfies the usual exponentiation laws with respect to the other cardinal operations and* 1:

[10] This generalization was given in [1]; cf. also [2], p. 13.

(37) $A = B$ *implies* $A^C = B^C$ *and* $C^A = C^B$;

(38) $A \subset B$ *implies* $A^C \subset B^C$;

(39) $A \prec B$ *implies* $C^A \subset C^B$;

$$\left.\begin{array}{ll}(40) & A^{B+C} = A^B A^C, \\ (41) & (AB)^C = A^C B^C, \\ (42) & (A^B)^C = A^{BC},\end{array}\right\} \textit{for all } A, B, C;$$

(43) $A^1 = A$ *and* $1^A = 1$ *for all* A.

Proof. Law (37) is evident from the abstract nature of the definition of cardinal exponentiation. Since each isotone function from C to A is a fortiori one from C to B if $A \subset B$, and the same inclusion relation holds, (38) is also immediate. Regarding (39), let θ be the given correspondence from B to A. With each g in C^A associate $f = g\phi$, defined by the identity $f(b) = g(b\theta)$. By hypothesis, $b \geqq b'$ implies $b\theta \geqq b'\theta$, hence $g(b\theta) \geqq g(b'\theta)$ and so $f(b) \geqq f(b')$: in short, every $f = g\phi$ is isotone. Finally, if $f^* = g^*\phi$, $f(b) \geqq f^*(b)$ for all b if and only if, for all $a = b\theta$, $g(a) = g(b\theta) \geqq g^*(b\theta) = g^*(a)$, completing the proof. This proves (39). Incidentally, if $A = C =$ the ordinal $1 \oplus 1$ and B is the cardinal number 2, then we have an example where $A \prec B$ yet $A^C = 1 \oplus 1 \oplus 1 \not\prec B^C = 2$. The proofs of (40)–(42) are contained in [1]; those of (43) are trivial. This proves Theorem 7.

It is an immediate corollary of (38) and (43) that

(44) $A \subset A^B$ for all A, B.

In fact, the left-hand side consists of all constant functions occurring on the right-hand side.

8. **Ordinal exponentiation: past methods.** It seems to me that the weakest point of classical transfinite arithmetic comes when ordinal exponentiation is defined.

Consider Cantor's original definition ([3], p. 118)

$$\xi^1 = \xi, \qquad \xi^{\eta+1} = \xi^\eta \xi, \qquad \xi^{\sup \eta} = \sup(\xi^\eta).$$

This inductive definition is *essentially* non-constructive. It is not even equivalent to known constructive definitions, unlike the corresponding inductive definitions of ordinal sums and products

$$\xi + 1 = \xi + 1, \qquad \xi + (\eta + 1) = (\xi + \eta) + 1, \qquad \xi + (\sup \eta) = \sup(\xi + \eta),$$

$$\xi 1 = \xi, \qquad \xi(\eta + 1) = \xi\eta + \xi, \qquad \xi(\sup \eta) = \sup(\xi\eta),$$

which are equivalent to the constructive definitions of §§4, 6.

Second, and this is also not the case with ordinal sums and products, it destroys the otherwise perfect homomorphism from ordinal arithmetic to cardinal arithmetic. Thus, in the notation of [3], whereas $2^{\omega} = \omega$ is an equation between ordinals, the corresponding cardinal equation $2^{\aleph_0} = \lambda^{\aleph_0}$ is false.

Again, consider Hausdorff's alternative definition: Y^X is the set of all functions from X to Y, ordered according to the first non-zero difference. This is in close conformity with the corresponding cardinal definition, and sufficiently constructive; thus it avoids the defects of Cantor's definition. But it has a peculiar defect all its own: Y^X, although a chain, is not usually an ordinal;[11] thus 2^{ω} is not an ordinal. To be sure, it gives approximately the order-type of the real continuum (actually, that of the Cantor discontinuum), which is a very pretty result. But $2^{2^{\omega}}$ is not even simply ordered, and if we use *it* as an exponent, we get something indescribable. I think it is fair to say that here Hausdorff gave up and defined a "partially ordered set" as one of those pathological things which he got by his construction.

The definition of ordinal exponentiation given below is equivalent to Hausdorff's for both ordinals and cardinals, is constructive, and has the added advantage that, under it, the family of *chains* (simply ordered sets) will at least be closed.

9. **Ordinal exponentiation: new definition.** The change in Hausdorff's definition of ordinal exponentiation which I propose is the following.

DEFINITION. By the *ordinal power* ${}^XY$ is meant the set of all functions f: $y = f(x)$ from X to Y, where $f \geqq g$ means that to each x with $f(x) \ngeqq g(x)$ corresponds an $x' > x$ with[12] $f(x') > g(x')$.

This evidently coincides with Hausdorff's definition in the case that X is an ordinal. Its greatest defect is that, although the relation $f \geqq g$ is reflexive and transitive, it is not anti-symmetric: ${}^XY$ is often[13] only a *quasi-ordered* set ([2], p. 7). But it is well known (loc. cit., Theorem 1.2) that such a set becomes a partially ordered set, if $f \equiv g$ is defined to mean $f \geqq g$ and $g \geqq f$. Hence the defect is not essential.

THEOREM 8. *Ordinal exponentiation is single-valued, is slightly isotone, satisfies the law of addition of exponents with respect to both cardinal and ordinal addition and an ordinal semi-associative law of exponentiation. Formally,*

(45) $A = B$ *implies* ${}^CA = {}^CB$ *and* ${}^AC = {}^BC$;

(46) $A \subset B$ *implies* ${}^CA \subset {}^CB$;

[11] In a nutshell, ordinals are not closed under Hausdorff's definition, although cardinals, paradoxically, are. If any definition yielded an ordinal (i.e., failed to have this defect) of the correct power and was constructive (i.e., did not have the defects of Cantor's definition either), it would constructively well-order the continuum. The difficulty of doing this is sufficiently well known (cf. K. Gödel, *The Consistency of the Axiom of Choice and of the Generalized Continuum-hypothesis*, Princeton, 1940).

[12] The idea is that any difference in the values of f and g at x' dominates the values at all points coming afterwards.

[13] Technically, this is the case unless X satisfies the ascending chain condition or Y is totally unordered (a cardinal number).

$$\left.\begin{array}{ll}(47) & {}^{B+C}A = {}^{B}A\,{}^{C}A, \\ (48) & {}^{B\oplus C}A = {}^{B}A \circ {}^{C}A, \\ (49) & {}^{A\circ B}C \prec {}^{A}({}^{B}C),\end{array}\right\} \textit{for all } A, B, C;$$

(50) ${}^{1}A = A$ *and* ${}^{A}1 = A$ *for all* A.

Proof. Law (45) is evident from the abstract nature of the definition of ordinal exponentiation. Again, since each function from C to A is a fortiori one from C to B if $A \subset B$, and inclusion is defined in the same way, (46) holds. Next, we are to prove (47) and (48). The functions f from $B + C$ or $B \oplus C$ to A correspond one-one with the pairs of functions (g, h), one from B to A and the other from C to A. In the cardinal case, $f \geqq f'$ if and only if $g \geqq g'$ and $h \geqq h'$; in the ordinal case, since $a > b$ for all $a \in A$, $b \in B$, $f \geqq f'$ if and only if $g > g'$ or $g = g'$ and $h \geqq h'$. Therefore, the correspondence defines the asserted isomorphism in both cases. Law (50) is trivial. While as for (49), the functions from $A \circ B$ to C assign to each couple (a, b) a value $c = f(a, b)$, hence to each fixed a, a function $f_a(b)$ from B to C; this is simply the usual one-one correspondence from ${}^{A\circ B}C$ to ${}^{A}({}^{B}C)$. But in the first case, $f \ngeqq g$ means that, for some (a, b), (i) $f(a', b') > g(a', b')$ for no $a' > a$, regardless of b', (ii) $f(a, b') > g(a, b')$ for no $b' > b$, and (iii) $f(a, b) \ngeqq g(a, b)$. But now condition (i) implies $f_{a'} > g_{a'}$ for no $a' > a$ while conditions (ii) and (iii) assert that $f_a \ngeqq g_a$; combining, $f \ngeqq g$ in ${}^{A\circ B}C$ implies $f \ngeqq g$ in ${}^{A}({}^{B}C)$. Dualizing, $f \geqq g$ in ${}^{A}({}^{B}C)$ implies $f \geqq g$ in ${}^{A\circ B}C$, which was what we wanted to prove. We note that if A and B satisfy the ascending chain condition, then the equality holds in (49).

10. **Dualization.** In addition to the six binary operations which we have just discussed, there is an important unary operation: that of dualization. This is trivial for cardinals and ordinals, but is very important in most other cases.

Definition. By the *dual* of a number X (in symbols, X^*) is meant the number obtained from X by replacing the inclusion relation in X by its converse (cf. [2], p. 8).

Graphically, this amounts to turning the diagram of X upside down, i.e., to *reversing* the order in X.

Theorem 9. *Dualization is single-valued, involutory, and isotone; it is an isomorphism for all cardinal operations, a dual isomorphism for ordinal addition and multiplication, and a semi-isomorphism on ordinal exponentiation. Formally,*

(51) *if* $X = Y$, *then* $X^* = Y^*$, *while* $(X^*)^* = X$;

(52) *if* $X \subset Y$, *then* $X^* \subset Y^*$; *and if* $X \prec Y$, *then* $X^* \prec Y^*$;

(53) $(X + Y)^* = X^* + Y^*$, $(XY)^* = X^*Y^*$, *and* $(X^Y)^* = X^{*Y^*}$;

(54) $(X \oplus Y)^* = Y^* \oplus X^*$ *and* $(X \circ Y)^* = Y^* \circ X^*$;

(55) $({}^{Y}X)^* = {}^{Y}X^*$.

Proof. All of the above results may be obtained by the reader by appealing to the appropriate definitions. The peculiar non-duality of ordinal exponentiation may help to explain the many vagaries of this operation.

11. **Closure properties.** We shall define below various special classes of numbers, with particular reference to their closure under the various arithmetic relations and operations discussed above. For this, it will be convenient to give names to certain types of closure which appear repeatedly.

First, if S is any set with a binary relation ρ, we shall call a subclass P of S *hereditary* under ρ, when P contains with any element a, all x such that $x\rho a$. (For this terminology, cf. C. Kuratowski, *Topologie*, Warsaw, 1933, p. 29.)

Next, if S is a set with a binary operation $\cdot$, we shall call a subclass P of S *closed* under the operation if it contains $a \cdot b$ whenever it contains a and b. This concept extends also to unary, ternary, and other operations.

Finally, the subclass P will be called a *caste* under the given binary operation, provided it contains $a \cdot b$ if *and only if* it contains both a and b. In the language of genetics, the property of belonging to P is *recessive.*

As examples of recessive properties, we have the following familiar cases: (i) *homogeneity*, for polynomials under multiplication, (ii) case of being a *unit* in a commutative ring (divisor of unity), (iii) case of being *primary* under a given prime ideal, under ideal multiplication.

A "caste" thus defines a congruence relation with two equivalence classes, P and $S - P$; and the complement of a caste has the properties of a (multiplicative) *prime ideal.* What is more important, the property of being a caste under a given operation is a "closure property" in the sense of [2] ("extensionally attainable" in the sense of E. H. Moore). In fact, the caste-closure $\bar{P}$ of a set P is its closure with respect to the operations (i) of including with any element, *all* its ancestors, and (ii) of including with any two elements, their product. For instance, if S is a lattice under the binary operation $\cup$, the caste-closure of any subset is just the *ideal* generated by that subset.

12. **Kinds of numbers.** The following special classes of numbers will be considered below: cardinal numbers, ordinal numbers, chains, lattices, complete lattices, striated numbers, and finite numbers.

A *cardinal* number means a number A such that $x \geqq y$ in A implies $x = y$. With any number X may be associated *its* cardinal number $c(X)$; this is composed of the elements of X, but with a new inclusion relation, which is allowed to subsist only between identical elements.

An *ordinal* number is a number A, every non-void subset S of which has a greatest (first) element s, satisfying $s \geqq x$ for all $x \in S$. This is the usual well-ordering condition. A *chain* is a so-called simply ordered system; a number A such that for any $x, y \in A$ either $x \geqq y$ or $y \geqq x$.

Thus any ordinal number is a chain, while the only number which is both an ordinal and a cardinal is 1, the partially ordered system with a single element.

In applications, a special rôle is played by those numbers which are *lattices* in the sense of [2], that is, numbers A in which, given x and y, there exist a smallest element $x \cup y$ containing both and a largest element $x \cap y$ containing both. Numbers such that this is true not only for two-element subsets, but for arbitrary subsets, are called *complete lattices.*

By a *bounded* number will be meant a number having a least element o and a greatest element i, such that $o \leqq x \leqq i$ for all x. By a *striated* number will be meant a number A which satisfies the Jordan-Dedekind chain condition, in the sense of [2]. More precisely, A will be called striated if and only if each $x \in A$ has a numerical dimension $d[x]$ which is a non-negative integer assuming bounded values, and is such that if x covers y, then $d[x] = d[y] + 1$. By the *length* $d[A]$ of a striated number A is meant the maximum length of a chain in A; this is $d[i] - d[o]$ if A is bounded.

Finally, the notion of a *finite* number will be understood in the obvious way; A is finite if and only if its cardinal number $c(A)$ is finite, that is, if and only if there is no one-one correspondence between A and a proper subset of itself.

13. **Closure properties of classes of numbers.** One can represent in concise tabular form most of the closure properties of the classes of numbers just defined, with respect to the relations and operations of generalized arithmetic. The rows of the table represent the different classes of numbers, and the columns the relations and operations of arithmetic. Thus the entry in the i-th row and j-th column describes the closure properties of the i-th class of numbers with respect to the j-th arithmetic operation or relation.

THEOREM 10. *The following table of closure properties is correct.*

	$\subset$	$<$	$+$	$\oplus$	$\cdot$	$\circ$	X^Y	${}^YX$	*
Cardinal....................	H	H	R	O	R	R	BD	BD	C
Ordinal.....................	H	H	O	R	O'	R	O''		
Chain.......................	H	H	O	R	O'	R	O''	R'	C
Lattice.....................			O	C	R		BD	BD	C
Complete lattice..............			O	C	R	R	BD	BD?	C
Bounded.....................		H	O	C	R	R	BD	BD	C
Striated....................			R	R	R	R	BD'	BD'	C
Finite......................	H	H	R	R	R	R	R'	R'	C

Explanation. BD (base dominant) means resultant is in subset if and only if base X is. BD' means resultant is in subset if and only if base is, and exponent is finite. C means subset is closed under operation (if operation is unary *, this is really the same as R). H means property is hereditary (supra). O means resultant of operation never has property; O' means resultant never has property unless one factor is 1; O'' means power never has property unless base is 1 or base is two-element chain and exponent has property. R means property is recessive (subset in question is caste); R' means property is recessive unless base is 1.

Proof. In almost all cases, the truth of the assertions indicated by the entries is well known or easily verified. We shall only sketch proofs in a few exceptional cases.

For instance, consider the assertion that X^Y is a lattice (complete lattice) if and only if X is. The sufficiency follows since the subset X^Y of isotone functions is a (closed) sublattice of $X^{c(Y)}$; the necessity follows since, if X is not a lattice, the constant functions in X^Y corresponding to meetless or joinless sets of elements of X are meetless respectively joinless in X^Y.

Again, consider the closure property of complete lattices under ordinal multiplication. It is easily shown that

$$\sup(a_\alpha, b_\alpha) = (\sup a_\alpha, \sup_{\alpha \in \sigma} b_\alpha),$$

where σ is the (possibly void) set of all α with $a_\alpha = \sup a_\alpha$. From this it follows easily that complete lattices form a caste under ordinal multiplication.

The closure of chains under ordinal exponentiation is easy to prove. For $f \geqq g$ unless for some x, $f(x) \ngeqq g(x)$, which is the same as $f(x) < g(x)$ if X is a chain, while $f(x') = g(x')$ for all $x' > x$. But in this case, if Y is a chain, it is easy to show that $f < g$.

The author has been unable to prove that the property of being a complete lattice is base dominant under ordinal exponentiation without assuming the ascending chain condition for the exponent Y. In this case, we can define $g = \sup f_\alpha$ as follows. For any $y \in Y$, let A_y denote the subset of all α such that $f_\alpha(y') < g(y')$ for some $y' \in Y$; recursively, we define $g(y) = \sup f_\alpha(y)$ for all $\alpha \notin A_y$.

The other non-obvious cases concern striated lattices. The closure properties under addition are obvious, and

$$d[A + B] = \sup(d[A], d[B]); \qquad d[A \oplus B] = d[A] + d[B]. \tag{56}$$

Under multiplication, we have (a, b) covering (a', b') in AB if and only if $a = a'$ while b covers b' or vice versa. Lemma 1 of §6 takes care of the ordinal case. Together, they give the closure properties of striated numbers, and

$$d[AB] = d[A] + d[B] \quad \text{and} \quad d[A \circ B] = d[A]d[B]. \tag{57}$$

Similarly, under exponentiation, one can verify that

$$d[A^B] = d[A]c(B). \tag{58}$$

The case of ordinal exponentiation is much more complicated, and would take up more space than it is worth.

14. **Special closure properties of lattices.** The closure rules for lattices under ordinal multiplication and exponentiation are so curious as to deserve special mention.

THEOREM 11. *The ordinal product $L \circ M$ of two lattices is a lattice if and only if L is simply ordered or M is bounded.*

Proof. Clearly $(x, y) \cup (x', y')$ must be (x, y), (x', y'), $(x, y \cup y')$, or $(x \cup x', o)$, according as $x > x'$, $x < x'$, $x = x'$, or x and x' are incomparable. These conditions can always be fulfilled if and only if M has an o or the fourth case never arises, i.e., if L is a chain. Dualizing, we get the assertion of the theorem.

Since no l-group is bounded except the trivial l-group having a single element, we get the

COROLLARY.[14] *The ordinal product $G \circ H$ of two l-groups is an l-group if and only if G is simply ordered.*

THEOREM 12. *For ${}^XY$ to be a lattice, it is necessary and sufficient that one of the following three conditions hold*: (i) *Y is a lattice and X a cardinal number*, (ii) *Y is a bounded lattice*, (iii) *Y is a chain and X a semi-root.*

Explanation. A "semi-root" is a partially ordered set in which the elements above each fixed element form a chain.

First, Y must be a lattice, or else not even all pairs of constant functions will have joins and meets. If Y is a lattice, then since

(59) if X is a cardinal number, then ${}^XY = Y^X$,

it is sufficient that X be a cardinal number, by Theorem 10. Again, if Y is a bounded lattice, then ${}^XY$ is a lattice. The only problem is in case $f(x)$ and $g(x)$ are incomparable. In this case, call a *critical value* of x one such that $f(x') = g(x')$ for all $x' > x$, whereas $f(x) \neq g(x)$. Set $h(x) = f(x) \cup g(x)$ at all critical values, and $h(t) = o$ at all points less than critical values. Repeating this process on $(h, f) = h_1$, $(h_1, g) = h_2$, $\cdots$, and using transfinite induction (this is a "sweeping-down process" for critical values), we will arrive ultimately at $f \cup g$, which thus exists. Every h_i is contained in all upper bounds to f and g.

There remains the case that Y is not bounded and X is not a cardinal number. In this case, Y must be a chain, or we could choose $x > x'$ with $f(x)$ and $g(x)$ incomparable but $f(t) = g(t)$ for all $t > x$, whence if $h = f \cup g$, we would have $h(x') = o$, and dually, contradicting the assumption that Y was not bounded. Further, unless X is a semi-root, we can find $x' > x$, $x'' > x$, with x', x'' incomparable. Again, since Y is not bounded, $Y \neq 1$; hence we can choose f and g such that $f(t) = g(t)$ for all $t \neq x', x''$, $f(x') > g(x')$, and $f(x'') < g(x'')$. Again, if $h = f \cup g$, clearly $h(x) = o$; forming $f \cap g$ similarly, Y would have to be bounded, contrary to hypothesis. Hence Y is a chain and X is a semi-root. The sufficiency of these conditions is easy. Given f and g, form $h = f \cup g$ by making $h(x) = f(x)$ unless x is below a critical value t at which $f(t) < g(t)$; at such points, set $h(x) = g(x)$.

[14] This result was implicitly conjectured by Mr. J. C. Abbott while doing graduate work at Harvard University in 1938–1939.

For the notion of l-group, cf. the author's *Lattice-ordered groups*, Annals of Mathematics, vol. 43(1942), pp. 298-331.

Just as before, we have the

Corollary. *If Y is an l-group, then ${}^XY$ is an l-group if and only if X is a cardinal number, or X is a semi-root and Y is simply ordered.*

15. **Cardinals and ordinals: special properties.** There are various special properties of ordinal and cardinal numbers which should be mentioned, if only because so many of them hold for more general classes of numbers.

First we note the following more or less trivial properties of the function $c(A)$. We have

(60) $c(A + B) = c(A \oplus B) = c(A) + c(B)$;

(61) $c(AB) = c(A \circ B) = c(A)c(B)$;

(62) $A \prec c(A)$ for all A;

(63) $A^B \subset A^{c(B)}$ and ${}^BA \prec {}^{c(B)}A$.

Then we have the counterpart of (59),

(64) if A is a cardinal, then $A \circ B = AB$.

The most important special properties of ordinal and cardinal are the following *anti-symmetric* and *comparability* laws.

Theorem 13. *If A and B are both cardinals or both ordinals, then*

(65) *$A \subset B$ and $B \subset A$ imply $A = B$;*

(66) *either $A \subset B$ or $B \subset A$.*

These laws are well known. We shall see later that the anti-symmetry law is valid also for finite numbers. We may also note without proof that if A and B are both cardinals or both *finite* ordinals, then

(67) $A \prec B$ if and only if $A \subset B$.

An interesting partial extension of this result is the fact that *if B is a chain*, then

(68) $A \prec B$ implies $A \subset B$.

To see this, suppose we take a single representative $b(a)$ from the antecedents of each $a \in A$; the correspondence $b(a) \to a$ will then be one-one and preserve order; hence it will be an isomorphism.

Another special property of *finite* ordinals is seen in the commutative laws

(69) $A \oplus B = B \oplus A$ and $A \circ B = B \circ A$,

which are valid *for these numbers*. We have further[15]

[15] Cf. S. Sherman, *Some new properties of transfinite ordinals*, Bulletin of the American Mathematical Society, vol. 47(1941), pp. 111–116.

(70) $A \circ (B \oplus C) \subset (A \circ B) \oplus (A \circ C)$, for any ordinals.

Other important special laws for cardinals are the following converses of (18).

THEOREM 14. *If A and B are both cardinals, then*

(71) $A \subset B$ *implies* $A = B$ *or* $A + X = B$ *for some* X;

if A and B are both ordinals, then

(72) $A \subset B$ *implies* $A = B$ *or* $A \oplus X = B$ *for some* X.

In somewhat the same vein, we may note that if $B \supset A$, and A, B are ordinals, then either $B = Q \circ A$ or $B = Q \circ A \oplus R$ $(R < A)$ for some unique Q, R (right division algorithm). This fact enables one to develop a factorization theory for finite and infinite ordinals (cf. [3]).

16. **Finite numbers: special properties.** When we come to finite numbers, we find first that the anti-symmetric laws hold. More precisely, we have

THEOREM 15. *If A and B are finite numbers, then*

(65) $A \subset B$ *and* $B \subset A$ *imply* $A = B$, *and*

(73) $A \prec B$ *and* $B \prec A$ *imply* $A = B$.

Proof. Law (65) is trivial, since $c(A) = c(B)$. As for (73), first note that since $c(A) \leqq c(B)$ and conversely, A and B have equally many elements. Hence the homomorphisms are one-one. A similar argument shows that they must leave the number of ordered couples (x, y) such that $x \geqq y$ invariant. Hence they are isomorphisms.

More interesting is the study of cancellation laws. These are lost in ordinary transfinite cardinal arithmetic, and half lost in transfinite ordinal arithmetic. The results stated below put them in their true setting.

THEOREM 16. *If A is any finite number, then*

(74) $A + X = A + Y$ *implies* $X = Y$.

If A satisfies the ascending chain condition, then

(75) $A \oplus X = A \oplus Y$ *implies* $X = Y$,

and dually, if A satisfies the descending chain condition,

(75′) $X \oplus A = Y \oplus A$ *implies* $X = Y$.

Proof. As for (74), this follows from the unique decomposition theorem for cardinal addition; an explicit proof can also be given. As for (75)–(75′), by duality, we need only prove (75). If (75) is not true, we can assume (by symmetry) that under the given isomorphism θ from $A \oplus X$ to $A \oplus Y$, $a\theta \in Y$ for some $a \in A$. But this means that for $y = a\theta$, $a\theta^{-1} > y\theta^{-1} = a$, since $a > y$ in $A \oplus Y$ and θ^{-1} is an isomorphism. It follows that A would have to possess an infinite ascending chain $a < a\theta^{-1} < (a\theta^{-1})^{-1} < \cdots < a\theta^{-n} < \cdots$, contrary to hypothesis.

COROLLARY. *The cancellation law* (75) *is valid for ordinals.*

The author has not attempted to generalize the one-sided cancellation law for ordinal multiplication to all numbers which satisfy the ascending chain condition, but conjectures that this is possible.

If X is finite, or satisfies the ascending chain condition, then ${}^XY$ can be defined to consist of all functions $y = f(x)$ from X into Y, where $f \gtrneqq g$ means that for some (maximal) $x, f(x) \gtrneqq g(x)$, while for all $x' > x, f(x) = g(x)$. Using this definition, we can prove the associative law of exponentiation:

(76) ${}^{A \circ B}C = {}^A({}^BC)$, if A and B satisfy the ascending chain condition.

Indeed, the usual one-one correspondence subsists between the elements $c = f(a, b)$ of ${}^{A \circ B}C$ and those $c = f_a(b)$ of ${}^A({}^BC)$. In the former, $f \gtrneqq g$ means that, for some a, b, (i) $f(a', b') = g(a', b')$ for all $a' > a$ and (i′) $f(a, b') = g(a, b')$ for all $b' > b$, while (ii) $f(a, b) \gtrneqq g(a, b)$. In the latter, $f \gtrneqq g$ means that, for some a, (i) $f_{a'} = g_{a'}$ for all $a' > a$, while (iii) $f_a \gtrneqq g_a$. But (iii) means in turn that, for some b, (i′) $f_a(b') = g_a(b')$ for all $b' > b$, while (ii) $f_a(b) \gtrneqq g_a(b)$. The isomorphism can now be read off from the equivalence between the two forms of (i), (i′), (ii).

17. **Bounded numbers.** Bounded numbers also have a number of special properties not true of all numbers. In the first place, we can state the following simple results:

$$\left.\begin{array}{ll}(77)\ A \prec A \oplus B, & B \prec A \oplus B\\ (78)\ A \prec B \text{ implies } A \circ C \prec B \circ C\end{array}\right\} \text{for bounded numbers.}$$

The reader should have no trouble in proving (77). To prove (78), let θ map B on A as assumed, and let $S(a)$ denote the set of $b \in B$ such that $b\theta = a$. In each $S(a)$, we can (by finite or transfinite induction) choose a maximal non-void set $T(a)$ of incomparable elements—elements such that $x > y$ for no $x, y \in T(a)$. Relative to $T(a)$, each element b of $S(a)$ will fall into just one of the following categories: (i) $b > b'$ for some $b' \in T(a)$, (ii) $b \in T(a)$, (iii) $b < b'$ for some $b' \in T(a)$. Now map (b, c) on $(b\theta, i)$ of $A \circ C$ in case (i), on $(b\theta, c)$ in case (ii), and on $(b\theta, o)$ in case (iii). It may be checked that if $b > b'$, then the image of (b, c) contains that of any (b', c') whether $b\theta > b'\theta$ *or* $b\theta = b'\theta$; also, that of (b, c) obviously contains that of (b, c') for any $c' \leqq c$.

THEOREM 17. *Any two decompositions of a bounded number into cardinal factors have a common refinement.*[16]

COROLLARY 1. *Any finite bounded number can be factored uniquely into indecomposable ("prime") factors.*

[16] This result is proved in [2], Theorem 2.9.

This implies the following extension of the cancellation law for the multiplication of finite cardinals.

COROLLARY 2. *$AX = AY$ implies $X = Y$ if X, Y, A are finite and bounded.*

This result holds more generally if AX and AY have a finite "center" in the sense of [2]. It suggests the conjectures that if AX and AY are finite, then $AX \subset AY$ may imply $X \subset Y$, and possibly even $AX \prec AY$ may imply $X \prec Y$.

The author knows no example which would prove that the boundedness condition was irredundant in Corollaries 1–2 above. But in (78), if C is the cardinal two, A is one, and B is the ordinal two, we have $A \prec B$ yet $C = A \circ C \not\prec B \circ C$; hence the boundedness condition is not redundant.

Regarding cancellation laws, the author conjectures that the following law is valid for finite numbers: $A^C = B^C$ implies $A = B$ if A, B, C are finite. In the case C is a cardinal number, it follows if a unique factorization theorem is known (e.g., if A, B are bounded). In general, it is not even known whether $A^2 = B^2$ implies $A = B$; this has been conjectured by S. Ulam for general abstract systems. It is certain that $C^A = C^B$ does *not* imply $A = B$; thus if C is a cardinal number, then $C^A = C$ for all lattices, and indeed for all numbers A not representable as cardinal sums.

18. **Special interpretations with lattices.** In the case of lattices, it is natural to replace the relation $A \subset B$ by the stronger relation $A \subset {}^*B$, meaning that A is a *sublattice* of B. Similarly, it is natural to replace the relation $A \prec B$ by the stronger relation $A \prec {}^*B$, meaning that A is a *lattice-homomorphic* image of B. We have the following cross-connection:

(79) $A \prec {}^*B$ implies $A \subset B$ if B is a finite lattice.

For, the correspondence $a \rightarrow \sup_{b\theta = a} b$ is an isomorphism. If B is distributive, we even have $A \subset {}^*B$.

Many of the isotonicity and duality laws (cf. (10), (11), (18), (19), (21), (22), (52), etc.) proved above for the relations $\subset$ and $\prec$ are valid also for the stronger relations $\subset^*$ and $\prec^*$. In particular, we have

(80) $A \subset B$ implies $C^A \prec {}^*C^B$.

At least in case C is the ordinal two, we have (see Garrett Birkhoff, *Rings of sets*, this Journal, vol. 3(1937), p. 454) the curious counterpart that $A \prec B$ implies $C^A \subset {}^*C^B$—and in fact, that all sublattices of C^B may be obtained in this way.

We also have (and in the finite case this follows from laws (79) and (80))

(81) $A \subset B$ implies that $C^A \subset C^B$ if C is complete.

Proof. Given f from A to C, define $g = f\theta$ by

$$g(b) = \sup_{a \leq b} f(a) \qquad \text{for any } b \in B.$$

Clearly g is isotone; and, if f is isotone, makes $g(b) = f(b)$ for all $b \in A$. Hence g is an *extension* of f, and the correspondence $f \to g$ is one-one; it is evidently isotone.

The author has no counterexample to (81) for numbers not complete lattices, but the possibility of extension does not exist in all cases.

19. **Applications.** We now come to the main argument in favor of a broader attitude towards the six arithmetic operations and dualization: the fact that in the wider context of general partially ordered sets, many new applications of these operations are found. Let us study this situation, first as to the cardinal operations, and then as to the ordinal operations.

For the sake of comparison, it should first be stressed that the cardinal operations really have very few applications in traditional transfinite arithmetic.[17] The operations of addition and multiplication are actually trivial, since the sum of any two infinite numbers, like their product, is simply the *larger* of the two summands (multiplicands). The remaining operation, that of exponentiation, is primarily useful in constructing from $\aleph_0$ the only known infinite cardinals, including $c = 2^{\aleph_0}$.

In contrast to this slim array of classical applications, there are known at least nine distinct applications of our extended cardinal arithmetic to questions of lattice theory,[18] especially to the theory of Boolean algebras and distributive lattices. Besides, they may be applied to topology ([2], p. 15). If M and N are any two abstract complexes, then $M + N$ represents their topological sum and MN their topological (or "Cartesian") product. While if M represents any subdivision of a manifold without boundary, then M^* represents the dual of the subdivision.

Again, it is fair to ask, what applications of the *ordinal* operations of traditional transfinite arithmetic are known? Transfinite induction should not be included, as it does not involve addition, multiplication, or exponentiation.[19] The operations of addition and multiplication are primarily useful in that they afford a neat notation for countable ordinals; the same is true of Cantor's inductively defined operation of exponentiation. These ordinals are used in such places as the Baire classification of functions. Also, with Hausdorff's exponentiation operation, 2^{ω} gives the Cantor discontinuum.

Equally important, it seems to me, are the uses of these operations to partially ordered systems which are not well-ordered. In the first place, ordinal multi-

[17] The distinction between $\aleph_0$ and c, although fundamental in modern analysis, is independent of the *operations* of cardinal arithmetic.

[18] These are listed in [1], §3, and will not be repeated here. They mainly concern exponentiation, although the operation of cardinal multiplication (forming the direct product) is also of fundamental importance in lattice theory.

[19] It would be a mistake to minimize the importance of transfinite induction. However, it should be noted that transfinite sequences are being replaced by directed sets in topology (cf. J. W. Tukey's *Convergence and Uniformity in Topology*, Princeton, 1940), and that transfinite induction is being replaced by the Lemma of Zorn in many other connections.

plication is useful in the construction and description of non-Archimedean ordered groups,[20] which are so basic in modern valuation theory. Again, the most general vector lattice with finite basis can be described as ${}^X R$, where R is the real number system and X is the most general "semi-root".[21] Further, the lattice of l-ideals of ${}^X R$ is B^X, where B denotes the ordinal two, thus establishing a curious connection between cardinal and ordinal exponentiation. Finally, the most general vector lattice can be built up from R by repeated cardinal and ordinal multiplication, to form such vector lattices as $(R \circ (RR))\,(R \circ R)$.

Bibliography

1. G. Birkhoff, *An extended arithmetic*, this Journal, vol. 3(1937), pp. 311–316.
2. G. Birkhoff, *Lattice Theory*, New York, 1940.
3. F. Hausdorff, *Grundzüge der Mengenlehre*, first edition, Leipzig, 1914.
4. M. H. Stone, *The Theory of Real Functions*, Ann Arbor, Michigan, 1940.

Harvard University.

[20] Cf., for example, H. Hahn, *Ueber die nichtarchimedische Grössensysteme*, S.-B. Wiener Akad., Math.-Nat. Klasse, Abt. IIa, vol. 116(1907), pp. 601–653.

[21] For the facts stated here, cf. the author's paper *Lattice-ordered groups* and the doctoral thesis of Mr. Murray Mannos.

REPRESENTATIONS OF LATTICES BY SETS

BY

GARRETT BIRKHOFF AND ORRIN FRINK, JR.

This paper deals with the representations of a general lattice L by sets. After a preliminary extension of Tukey's concept of a "property of finite character" to closure properties, necessary and sufficient conditions are given for L to be isomorphic with the lattice of all subalgebras of a suitable abstract algebra. It is shown that in any lattice L satisfying these conditions, every element is a meet of completely meet-irreducible elements, and that this generalizes the main result of Garrett Birkhoff [3](1) on subdirect unions in universal algebra. Komatu's necessary and sufficient conditions are derived for L to be isomorphic with the lattice of all ideals of another lattice A.

Attention is then turned to more general representations of lattices by sets of elements of any kind, and in particular by sets of dual ideals. It is first shown that meet-representations correspond to sets of dual ideals, and that isomorphic representations are furnished by all meet-irreducible, by all completely meet-irreducible, and by all principal dual ideals. In distributive lattices, meet-irreducible and prime dual ideals are the same; the representation by meet-irreducible dual ideals gives the representation theorem of Stone [2]; the representation by completely meet-irreducible dual ideals gives that of Garrett Birkhoff [1; 3]. The latter is perhaps preferable on grounds of economy; but in lattices with the disjunction property of Wallman [1], the still more economical representation by maximal dual ideals is to be preferred.

In any case, the concept of a completely irreducible ideal, which is applicable also to rings, seems worthwhile.

The paper concludes with some instructive counter-examples, and with a description of how, in the case of lattices with the descending chain condition, some of our representation schemes reduce to that introduced by A. D. Campbell [1].

PART I. LATTICES OF SUBALGEBRAS

1. Closure properties of finite character. Let A be any abstract algebra, in the most general sense; let Φ denote the class of all subalgebras of A, or, equivalently, the property of being a subalgebra. It is well known that any intersection of subalgebras is a subalgebra, and since A is a subalgebra of itself, it follows that Φ is a *closure* property on the subsets of A, and is extensionally attainable in the sense of E. H. Moore. We shall now show that if

---

Presented to the Society, December 31, 1947; received by the editors July 18, 1947.

(1) Numbers in brackets refer to the bibliography at the end of the paper.

the operations of A are *finitary*(²) (that is, algebraic, rather than topological), then Φ is also "of finite character"(³), in the following general sense.

DEFINITION. A property Φ of the subsets S of a set I is "of finite character" if and only if, for some set Ψ_0 of finite subsets F of I, and set Ψ_1 of ordered pairs (G, F) such that $G \leqq F$ and $F \in \Psi_0$, it is true that $S \in \Phi$ if and only $(S \cap F, F) \in \Psi_1$ for all $F \in \Psi_0$. If no $F \in \Psi_0$ contains more than n elements, we shall say that Φ is "of character n" or less.

LEMMA 1. *The property of being a subalgebra is of finite character, in any algebra with finitary operations.*

Proof. A set S is in Φ if and only if, for every finite subset $F = \{a_0, a_1, \cdots, a_n\}$ such that $\{a_1, \cdots, a_n\} \leqq S$ and $a_0 = f_\alpha(a_1, \cdots, a_n)$, for some operation f_α of the algebra A we have $a_0 \in S$. Incidentally, we see in this way that an n-ary operation is of character $n+1$.

THEOREM 1. *For a closure property Φ on a set I, the following three conditions are equivalent:*

(i) *For some determination of I as an abstract algebra with finitary operations, $S \in \Phi$ means that S is a subalgebra;*

(ii) *The property Φ is of finite character;*

(iii) *The set-union X of any directed family*(⁴) *of sets $X_\alpha \in \Phi$ itself belongs to Φ.*

Proof. By Lemma 1, (i) implies (ii). Again, let (ii) hold, and let X be the set-union of any directed family of X_α in Φ. If F is any finite subset of I, we can enumerate the elements of $X \cap F$ as $a_1, \cdots, a_n$; for some $\alpha(1), \cdots, \alpha(n)$, clearly $a_i \in X_{\alpha(i)}$. Any common successor X_γ of $X_{\alpha(1)}, \cdots, X_{\alpha(n)}$ will contain $X \cap F$; but $X_\gamma \leqq X$, hence $(X \cap F, F) = (X_\alpha \cap F, F) \in \Psi_1$ by hypothesis. Therefore X is closed, and (ii) implies (iii). Finally, suppose that (iii) is satisfied. For each determination α of a finite F and an a in $\overline{F} - F$, we define an n-ary operation f_α, as follows:

$$(1) \qquad \begin{aligned} f_\alpha(x_1, \cdots, x_n) &= a, && \text{if every } x_i \in F, \\ f_\alpha(x_1, \cdots, x_n) &= x_1, && \text{if some } x_i \notin F. \end{aligned}$$

Here n is the number of elements in F. This definition makes I into an abstract algebra A with finitary operations. By (1) and the definition of subalgebra, X is a subalgebra if and only if for every finite subset F_α of X, we have $\overline{F}_\alpha \leqq X$. But if $X \in \Phi$, clearly $\overline{F}_\alpha \leqq \overline{X} = X$; hence X is a subalgebra. Con-

(²) The terminology is that of Garrett Birkhoff, *Lattice theory*, chap. II, and [3] *in universal algebra.*

(³) The present definition includes that of J. W. Tukey, *Convergence and uniformity in topology*, Princeton, 1940. Tukey's definition is well adapted to independence properties, but not to closure properties.

(⁴) In the sense of Moore-Smith: given X_α and X_β, there exists an X_γ in the family, which contains both X_α and X_β.

versely, suppose X is a subalgebra. The $F_\alpha \leqq X$ form a directed family; hence so do the $\bar{F}_\alpha \leqq X$, also partially ordered by set-inclusion. Hence, by (iii), $\bigcup \bar{F}_\alpha \in \Phi$. But $X = \bigcup F_\alpha \leqq \bigcup \bar{F}_\alpha \leqq X$, so that $X \in \Phi$, completing the identification of Φ with the property of being a subalgebra. Therefore (iii)→(i), completing the proof.

2. **Lattice-theoretic implications.** We now determine the implications of the preceding section for the abstract lattice L of all subalgebras of an abstract algebra A, partially ordered by set-inclusion. It is well known that L is *complete* if and only if, for some class I and closure property Φ on I, L is isomorphic with the lattice of all subsets of I in Φ.

We now ask, what does it mean for L that A has finitary operations—or equivalently, by Theorem 1, that Φ is of finite character? We shall show that this is equivalent to two further restrictions on L.

LEMMA 2. *In the complete lattice L of all subalgebras of any abstract algebra with finitary operations,*

$$(2) \qquad X_\alpha \uparrow X \quad \textit{and} \quad Y_\beta \uparrow Y \quad \textit{imply} \quad (X_\alpha \cap Y_\beta) \uparrow X \cap Y,$$

for any directed sets.

Proof. By (ii) of Theorem 1, X and Y are the set-unions of the X_α and Y_β respectively; moreover $\cap$ means set-intersection, and (2) is known to hold for set-unions and intersections.

Incidentally, (2) follows from the apparently weaker special case:

$$(2') \qquad X_\alpha \uparrow X \quad \text{implies} \quad X_\alpha \cap Y \uparrow X \cap Y.$$

For, assuming (2′), we see that $\bigcup(X_\alpha \cap Y_\beta)$ contains every $X \cap Y_\beta$, hence it contains $\bigcup(X \cap Y_\beta) = X \cap Y$, using (2′) again.

Incidentally also, (2) and (2′) hold for *finite* sequences in *any* lattice. Thus, for two-element sequences, (2′) reduces to

$$(*) \qquad \text{if} \quad x \leqq z, \quad \text{then} \quad (x \cup z) \cap y = (x \cap y) \cup (z \cap y),$$

which formally resembles the modular identity(5). Condition (2) asserts essentially that *meets are continuous in the order topology.*

The second restriction on L is also of a topological nature, and is suggested by a consideration of the *principal subalgebras* $S = \{s\}$ of A, each generated by a single element s. Such subalgebras are seen to be $\uparrow$*-inaccessible* (or inaccessible from below), in the sense that if, for some directed set $\{X_\alpha\}$, we have $X_\alpha \uparrow S$, then some individual X_α equals S. For, since S is the set-union of the X_α, by (iii) some X_α contains s, hence $\bar{s} = S$. But every $X_\alpha \leqq S$; hence this $X_\alpha = S$.

(5) Thus the modular identity is equivalent to the condition that each one of the six conceivable distributive equalities between a triple of elements implies all five others.

Caution: Being $\uparrow$-inaccessible is equivalent to being finitely generated; not every $\uparrow$-inaccessible subalgebra need be principal.

Since every subalgebra is (obviously) the join of the principal subalgebras which it contains, we infer the following lemma.

LEMMA 3. *In the lattice L of Lemma 2, every element is a join of $\uparrow$-inaccessible elements.*

We are now in a position to characterize abstractly those lattices which are isomorphic with the lattice of all subalgebras of some abstract algebra with finitary operations.

THEOREM 2. *An abstract lattice L is isomorphic with the lattice of all subalgebras of a suitable abstract algebra A with finitary operations, if and only if it is complete, satisfies* (2), *and satisfies the condition that every element is a join of $\uparrow$-inaccessible elements.*

Proof. By Lemmas 2 and 3, we need only prove the sufficiency of our conditions. Accordingly, let L be given as described. We let the elements of A be the $\uparrow$-inaccessible elements of L. We call a subset S of A "closed" if and only if $a, b \in S$, $x \in A$ and $x \leqq a \cup b$ in L imply $x \in S$. This is a closure property of character three; hence by Theorem 1, the lattice M of all "closed" subsets is a subalgebra lattice of the desired type. Hence it remains only to show that M and L are isomorphic; this we now do.

Evidently, if $x \in L$, the set $S(x)$ of all $a \leqq x$ is closed. Conversely, let $S \in M$ be any closed subset of A; define $x(S) = \bigcup a_\alpha$ to be the join in L of the $a_\alpha \in S$. Consider the directed set of all joins S_ϕ of *finite* sets ϕ of $a \in S$; in L, $S_\phi \uparrow x(S)$ by construction. Hence, by (2′), $a \leqq x(S)$ implies $a = a \cap x(S) = \bigcup (a \cap S_\phi)$. Hence, a being $\uparrow$-inaccessible, some $a \cap S_\phi = a$, that is, some S_ϕ contains a. In other words, $a \leqq a_1 \cup \cdots \cup a_n$ for some *finite* subset $\phi = \{a_1, \cdots, a_n\}$ of S. Since S is closed, it follows by finite induction that $a \in S$. That is, $a \leqq x(S)$ implies $a \in S$; but the converse is trivial, hence $S(x(S)) = S$. Finally, since every x is (by hypothesis) the join of join-inaccessible elements, $x(S(x)) = x$. Hence our isotone (that is, order preserving) correspondence is one-to-one, and M and L are isomorphic.

It is a corollary that we can strengthen (2) to

$$(2'') \qquad X_\beta^\sigma \uparrow X^\sigma \quad \text{implies} \quad \sup_{\beta(\sigma)} \{\bigcap_\sigma X^\sigma_{\beta(\sigma)}\} = \bigcap X^\sigma.$$

3. **Atomicity; completely irreducible elements.** We now show that the lattices considered in Theorem 2 satisfy also a kind of atomicity condition. Let L satisfy the conditions of Theorem 2, and suppose $x > y$ in L. By hypothesis, we can choose a $\uparrow$-inaccessible element z such that $z > y$ and $z \leqq x$. If C is a maximal chain of elements $z_\tau < z$, than $c = \bigcup z_\tau < z$ by $\uparrow$-inaccessibility. Since C is maximal, however, $c < t < z$ is impossible; hence z covers c.

Thus we have:

LEMMA 4. *If $x>y$ in a lattice satisfying the conditions of Theorem 2, then there exists a pair z, c, such that $x \geqq z > c \geqq y$, and z covers c.*

This is a weak *atomicity* condition (see *Lattice theory*, p. 13). If L is a Boolean algebra, $z \cap c'$ is a *point* contained in x. Hence (*Lattice theory*, p. 95) L is an atomic Boolean algebra. We conclude(6):

THEOREM 3. *If the subalgebras of an abstract algebra with finitary operations form a Boolean algebra B, then B is isomorphic with the atomic Boolean algebra of all subsets of a suitable class.*

More generally, let L be any complete lattice satisfying (2), and let a be any $\uparrow$-inaccessible element of L. Let $C = \{x_\alpha\}$ be any maximal chain such that no $x_\alpha \in C$ contains a; such a C exists by Zorn's lemma. Form $c = \bigcup x_\alpha$; since every $x_\alpha \cap a < a$, we have by (2), $c \cap a = \bigcup (x_\alpha \cap a) < a$, and so it is false that $c \geqq a$. But C is maximal; hence $c \in C$, which proves the following lemma.

LEMMA 5. *Every maximal chain C of elements, none of which contains a, has a largest element c, if a is an $\uparrow$-inaccessible element of a complete lattice.*

Next, suppose $x > c$. Since $c \geqq x_\alpha$ for all $x_\alpha \in C$, we still have a chain if we add x to C. Since C was maximal subject to the condition that $x_\alpha \geqq a$ is false, it follows that $x \geqq a$. Hence $x \geqq c \cup a$. But $c \cup a > a$. We conclude that, among all elements $t > c$, there is a *least* one, namely $c \cup a$.

LEMMA 6. *In any complete lattice L, the set T of elements $t_\alpha > c$ has a least element m, if and only if c is completely meet-irreducible, in the sense that $c = \bigcap y_\beta$ implies that some $y_\beta = c$.*

Proof. If c is completely meet-irreducible, then $\bigcap t_\alpha \neq c$ by hypothesis; but $\bigcap t_\alpha \geqq c$; hence $m = \bigcap t_\alpha > c$ is a least element of T. Conversely, if such a least element m exists, and $c = \bigcap y_\beta$, then all $y_\beta \geqq c$. But not all $y_\beta > c$, or $\bigcap y_\beta \geqq m$; hence some $y_\beta = c$.

REMARK. Complete meet-irreducibility thus implies, but is in general a stronger condition than, the dual of $\uparrow$-inaccessibility.

Combining the preceeding results, we get the following theorem.

THEOREM 4. *Let a be any $\uparrow$-inaccessible element of a complete lattice L satisfying* (2) .*Then every maximal chain C of elements x of L such that $x \geqq a$ is false has a largest element c. Moreover, c is completely meet-irreducible; $a \cup c$ is the smallest element properly containing c.*

(6) A related result was recently communicated to us orally by A. Tarski. The results of §§1–2 were described at the Princeton Bicentennial Conference on Mathematics, in December, 1946.

Conversely, let c be completely meet-irreducible, and let m be the smallest containing element, which exists by Lemma 6. If m is a join of $\uparrow$-inaccessible elements a_α, then there exists an $a_\alpha \leqq m$, such that $a_\alpha \leqq c$ is false. Clearly c is maximal subject to the condition of not containing a_α. We conclude:

THEOREM 5. *A subalgebra of an abstract algebra A with finitary operations is completely meet-irreducible in the lattice of subalgebras of A, if and only if it is maximal subject to failure to contain a* $\uparrow$*-inaccessible subalgebra.*

4. Applications to congruence relations. Similar results hold for the lattice H of all *congruence relations* θ on an abstract algebra A. Each such θ may be described by a subset $S(\theta)$ of the set $A \times A$ of all ordered couples (a, b) of elements a, b in A in the usual way: $(a, b) \in S(\theta)$ means that $a \equiv b \pmod{\theta}$.

Moreover, being a congruence relation is a closure property, since the reflexive, symmetric, transitive, and substitution laws on relations(7) are each extensionally attainable. Further, the conditions that θ be reflexive, symmetric, and transitive are of character three or less; if A has finitary operations, the substitution property is also of finite character. We conclude, by Theorems 1 and 2:

THEOREM 6. *The lattice H of all congruence relations on any abstract algebra with finitary operations satisfies the conditions of Theorem 2, and is isomorphic with the lattice of all subalgebras of some other abstract algebra B.*

We do not know whether the converse is true. The most promising tool to attack this question seems to be Whitman's theorem that any lattice is isomorphic with a sublattice of the lattice of all partitions of a suitable aggregate, combined with the fact that any H as defined above is also such a sublattice.

THEOREM 7. *In any lattice L satisfying the conditions of Theorem 2, every element a is a meet of completely meet-irreducible elements*(8).

Proof. Let $m = \bigcap c_\gamma$ be the meet of the completely meet-irreducible elements $c_\gamma \geqq a$. Unless $m = a$, clearly $m > a$, and some $\uparrow$-inaccessible element b satisfies $b \leqq m$, but not $b \leqq a$. Form a maximal chain D of elements d_δ such that d_δ includes a but not b. Let d be the largest element of D; by Theorem 4, d is completely meet-irreducible, $d \geqq a$ holds, but $d \geqq b$ does not. Hence d is a c_γ. But this implies $d \geqq m \geqq b$, which is a contradiction. Hence $m = a$, which was to be proved.

5. Applications to lattice ideals and dual ideals. In any lattice A, an ideal is a "subalgebra" with respect to the binary operation $\cup$ and the unary

(7) These define congruence relations; see for example Birkhoff and MacLane, *Survey of modern algebra*, chap. VI, §14.

(8) This generalizes the main result of Garrett Birkhoff, *Subdirect unions in universal algebra*, Bull. Amer. Math. Soc. vol. 50 (1944) pp. 764–768.

operations f_a: $f_a(x)=x\cap a$. Hence the conclusions of Theorems 2–5 and 7 apply. Also, by Lemma 6, every maximal ideal M is completely meet-irreducible.

THEOREM 8. *An ideal J of a lattice A is principal if and only if it is an $\uparrow$-inaccessible element of the lattice L of ideals of A.*

Proof. The "only if" is covered by the proof of Lemma 3; the "if" may be proved as follows. The principal ideals $T_\alpha \leqq X$ form a sublattice of L, since $\{t\}\cup\{u\}=\{t\cup u\}$; hence they form a directed set. Moreover clearly $\bigcup T_\alpha = X$. But unless X is principal, every $T_\alpha < X$, and so X is *not* $\uparrow$-inaccessible, completing the proof. Theorem 8 is due to A. Komatu, Proc. Imp. Acad. Tokyo vol. 19 (1943) pp. 119–124.

COROLLARY 1. *An ideal of a lattice A is completely meet-irreducible if and only if it is maximal subject to failure to contain some element of A.*

A second corollary is the fact that the $\uparrow$-inaccessible elements of L form a *sublattice* of L. Conversely, if the $\uparrow$-inaccessible elements of any lattice which satisfies the conditions of Theorem 2 form a sublattice, the construction given in the proof of Theorem 2 makes S "closed" if and only if it is an ideal. We conclude:

THEOREM 9. *An abstract lattice L is isomorphic with the lattice of all ideals of a suitable lattice A if and only if it satisfies the conditions of Theorem 2, and further the condition that the $\uparrow$-inaccessible elements of L form a sublattice.*

The lattice A is, of course, just this sublattice of $\uparrow$-inaccessible elements. Note that if L satisfies the ascending chain condition, all ideals are principal and the lattice A is L itself.

The preceding results apply equally to dual ideals, since a dual ideal of A is simply an ideal in the dual of A. It is *dual* ideals which are important in the general theory of the representation of lattices by sets, to which we now turn our attention.

PART II. REPRESENTATIONS BY SETS OF DUAL IDEALS

6. **Dual ideals and meet-representations.** We first state some definitions concerning lattice ideals and representations of lattices. The notation and terminology are those of G. Birkhoff [2].

A *dual ideal* of a lattice L is a set D of elements of L such that D contains the meet $x\cap y$ of two elements of L if and only if it contains both x and y.

A dual ideal which is not the entire lattice L is said to be *prime* if it contains either x or y whenever it contains the join $x\cup y$.

A dual ideal is said to be *completely prime* if whenever it contains the join $\bigcup x_\alpha$ of an arbitrary set $\{x_\alpha\}$ of elements, it contains at least one element x_α of the set.

A dual ideal D is said to be *meet-irreducible* if it is not the set-intersection of two dual ideals each distinct from D.

The concept of a *completely meet-irreducible* ideal or dual ideal, like that of a completely meet-irreducible element of a lattice, has already been discussed in §§3 and 5 (see Lemma 6, and Corollary 1 to Theorem 8). A dual ideal is completely meet-irreducible if it is not the set-intersection of any number of dual ideals distinct from itself. Meet-irreducible here means intersection-irreducible. If the lattice order relation were to be reversed in the lattice of all dual ideals, as is sometimes done (see Dilworth [1] and Frink [2]), then intersections of dual ideals would correspond to joins rather than meets, and the term *join-irreducible* would be in order.

A *meet-representation* of a lattice L is a correspondence $x \rightarrow R(x)$ between the elements x of L and certain sets $R(x)$, which sends lattice meets into set-intersections; that is, $R(x \cap y)$ is the set-intersection of $R(x)$ and $R(y)$.

It can be seen that a meet-representation preserves also the lattice order relation, in the sense that $x \leqq y$ implies that $R(x)$ is a subset of $R(y)$. If the correspondence defining a meet-representation is one-to-one, it is said to define an *isomorphic meet-representation.* In this case $R(x) = R(y)$ implies that $x = y$, whence $x < y$ implies that $R(x)$ is a *proper* subset of $R(y)$.

In considering meet-representations of a lattice L by sets of objects of some sort, there is no loss of generality if we confine attention to sets of dual ideals. For any "object" A which is an element of a representative set $R(x)$ determines a dual ideal, namely the collection D of all elements x of L such that A is a member of $R(x)$. That D is a dual ideal follows from the definition of dual ideal and from the fact that we have a meet-representation. If two "objects" A and B determine the same dual ideal in this way, then one of them is superfluous.

Conversely, it will now be shown that any collection of dual ideals of a lattice L determines a meet-representation of L.

THEOREM 10. *Any collection K of dual ideals of a lattice L determines a meet-representation of L. The representation is isomorphic if and only if for every pair x, y of distinct elements of L there exists a dual ideal in K containing one element of the pair but not the other.*

Proof. Given the collection K, we assign to each lattice element x the set $R(x)$ consisting of all dual ideals which are in K and which contain the element x. Consider now the representative sets $R(x)$, $R(y)$, and $R(x \cap y)$. We have a meet-representation if $R(x \cap y)$ is always the set-intersection of $R(x)$ and $R(y)$. Now note that a dual ideal D is a member of $R(x)$ if and only if D is a member of K and x is a member of D. Since D is a dual ideal, $x \cap y$ is in D if and only if x and y are in D. Hence if D is in K, then D is in $R(x \cap y)$ if and only if D is in both $R(x)$ and $R(y)$. But this means that $R(x \cap y)$ is the set-intersection of $R(x)$ and $R(y)$, which was to be proved.

The meet-representation just defined is isomorphic provided $R(x)$ and $R(y)$ are distinct whenever x and y are distinct. This clearly requires that the collection K contain at least one dual ideal D containing one of the pair x, y but not the other. This completes the proof.

Theorem 10 immediately provides different representations which are obtainable by special choice of the collection K. The two most obvious choices for K are the collection of *all* dual ideals, and the collection of all *principal* dual ideals. Since distinct elements determine distinct principal ideals, we have the following corollary.

COROLLARY. *Isomorphic meet-representations of any lattice L are obtained by assigning to each element x of L the set of all dual ideals containing x, or the set of all principal dual ideals containing x.*

It will be noted later (Theorem 16) that the representation by principal dual ideals preserves not merely finite meets, but meets of arbitrarily many elements.

7. Representations by irreducible and completely irreducible ideals. It is desirable that the collection K which determines a representation should contain as few elements as possible, being just large enough to discriminate between distinct elements of the lattice. We now show that K may be taken to be the collection of all completely meet-irreducible dual ideals of the lattice.

THEOREM 11. *An isomorphic meet-representation of any lattice L is obtained by assigning to each element x of L the set of all completely meet-irreducible dual ideals of L which contain x.*

Proof. By Theorem 10, it is sufficient to show that if x and y are distinct elements of L, there exists a completely meet-irreducible dual ideal D containing one but not the other as an element. Since x and y are distinct, then either x is not a member of the principal dual ideal $\{y\}$, or y is not a member of the principal dual ideal $\{x\}$. Suppose the latter; then by Zorn's lemma $\{x\}$ can be extended to a dual ideal D which (1) does not contain y, and (2) is maximal with respect to the property of not containing y. Hence by Corollary 1 to Theorem 8, D is completely meet-irreducible. Also, it contains x but not y. Likewise if x is not a member of the principal ideal $\{y\}$, then a completely meet-irreducible dual ideal exists containing y but not x. Hence by Theorem 10 the representation is isomorphic. This completes the proof.

Since any completely meet-irreducible dual ideal is also meet-irreducible, we have the following corollary.

COROLLARY. *An isomorphic meet-representation of any lattice L is obtained by assigning to each element x of L the set of all meet-irreducible dual ideals of L which contain x.*

We now wish to show the connection of the preceding results with other well known results on the representation of particular types of lattice by sets. In the first place, note that while the two preceding representations of Theorem 11 and its corollary are equivalent for finite lattices, they are not equivalent in general. Thus, consider the distributive lattice of all real numbers with the usual order relation. Completely meet-irreducible dual ideals consist of open semi-infinite intervals (x, ∞). The merely meet-irreducible dual ideals include also the closed semi-infinite intervals $[x, \infty)$. The latter are *principal* dual ideals.

8. **Prime ideals and distributive lattices.** Theorem 11 was the result of an attempt to extend to the general lattice, as far as may be possible, the well known results of Garrett Birkhoff [1, 2] and Stone [2] concerning the isomorphic representation of the general distributive lattice as a ring of sets of prime ideals. We now examine the relation between this representation of distributive lattices by sets of prime ideals and the representations of Theorem 11 and its corollary by means of completely meet-irreducible and meet-irreducible dual ideals. It will be shown that in a distributive lattice, prime ideals and irreducible ideals are identical. Hence the representation of a distributive lattice L given by the corollary of Theorem 11 coincides with the Stone representation by prime ideals, while the representation of L by means of completely meet-irreducible dual ideals given by Theorem 11 provides the representation of Birkhoff [1; 3], which is perhaps to be preferred on grounds of economy.

It should be noted that there is a close connection between the notion of a prime dual ideal and the dual notion of a *prime ideal.* In fact, prime ideals and prime dual ideals are complements of each other. Hence any representation by prime dual ideals determines a representation by prime ideals, and conversely.

THEOREM 12. *In any lattice, prime dual ideals are meet-irreducible. In a distributive lattice, a dual ideal is prime if and only if it is meet-irreducible.*

Proof. Suppose the dual ideal D is prime but not meet-irreducible. Then D is the set-intersection of two dual ideals A and B both distinct from D. Therefore A contains an element a not in D, and B contains an element b not in D. The join $a\cup b$ is in both A and B, and hence in D. Since D is prime, either a or b must be in D, which is a contradiction. This proves the first part of the theorem.

Now suppose the lattice L is distributive, and the dual ideal D is meet-irreducible. To prove that D is prime, suppose $a\cup b$ is in D, but neither a nor b is in D. Consider the two dual ideals $D\cup a$ and $D\cup b$, consisting of all elements x such that $x \geqq d\cap a$ and $x \geqq d\cap b$ respectively, where d is any element of D. Then both $D\cup a$ and $D\cup b$ are distinct from D. We shall now show that the set-intersection of $D\cup a$ and $D\cup b$ is D. Clearly every element of D

is in this intersection. Conversely, suppose that x is any element of the intersection. Then $x \geqq d \cap a$ and $x \geqq d' \cap b$, where d and d' are elements of D. Then $x \geqq d \cap d' \cap a$ and $x \geqq d \cap d' \cap b$, whence $x \geqq (d \cap d' \cap a) \cup (d \cap d' \cap b)$. There fore, by the distributive law, $x \geqq (d \cap d') \cap (a \cup b)$. But $(d \cap d') \cap (a \cup b)$ is an element of D, and hence x is an element of D. This shows that D is the set-intersection of $D \cup a$ and $D \cup b$. But this involves a contradiction, since D was assumed to be meet-irreducible. Hence D is prime. This completes the proof.

It follows from Theorem 12 that the representation of distributive lattices by sets of meet-irreducible dual ideals provided by the corollary to Theorem 11 is identical with the Birkhoff-Stone representation by prime ideals (or equivalently, by prime dual ideals) already referred to.

A representation of a lattice by sets is said to be a join-representation if it preserves joins; that is, if $R(x \cup y)$ is the set-union of $R(x)$ and $R(y)$. In the case of a distributive lattice, the representations both by meet-irreducible and by completely meet-irreducible dual ideals are join-representations as well as meet-representations. In fact, any representation of a lattice by means of prime dual ideals is both a meet-representation and a join-representation, as will now be shown.

THEOREM 13. *If K is any collection of prime dual ideals of a lattice L, then the correspondence which assigns to each element x of L the set of all ideals of K which contain x is both a meet-representation and a join-representation of L.*

Proof. By Theorem 10 the representation is a meet-representation. If D is any dual ideal of K, then since D is prime, it follows that x or y is in D whenever $x \cup y$ is in D. Hence D is in either $R(x)$ or $R(y)$ whenever D is in $R(x \cup y)$. Conversely, if D is in either $R(x)$ or $R(y)$, it is in $R(x \cup y)$ by definition of dual ideal. Therefore $R(x \cup y)$ is the set-union of $R(x)$ and $R(y)$, which was to be proved.

It should be noted that, although by Theorem 13 any representation of a lattice L by prime dual ideals is both a meet-representation and a join-representation, it cannot be an isomorphic representation unless the lattice L is distributive, since the "ring of sets" on which L is mapped by the representation is itself necessarily distributive.

9. **Representations by maximal dual ideals.** It was shown by Stone [1] that in Boolean algebras, which are distributive and relatively complemented lattices, prime ideals and maximal ideals are identical. In a merely distributive lattice, or in a lattice which is relatively complemented but not distributive, prime ideals and maximal ideals may not be identical. It has already been noted that distributive lattices may be represented by sets of prime ideals. Likewise, as we shall show, there are general classes of lattices, such as relatively complemented lattices, which may be represented by sets of maximal ideals. Neither kind of ideal, however, will suffice for the isomorphic

representation of all lattices. For, on the one hand, the lattice of all real numbers has no maximal ideals. On the other hand, the lattice of all subspaces of a projective geometry with more than two points has no prime ideals.

For the representation of the general lattice by sets we have seen in Theorem 11 and its corollary that meet-irreducible and completely meet-irreducible dual ideals suffice, and in Theorem 12 that these ideals specialize to prime ideals in distributive lattices. On the other hand, in many lattices which can be represented by sets of maximal ideals, the meet-irreducible and completely meet-irreducible dual ideals specialize to maximal dual ideals. But the situation is not so simple here, and we shall show by an example that there are cases where the representation of a lattice by maximal dual ideals is distinct from the representation of Theorem 11. But first we must consider the question of what lattices may be represented by sets of maximal dual ideals.

It was shown by Frink [2] that every complemented modular lattice may be isomorphically represented, with preservation of meets, by sets of maximal dual ideals. More generally, any relatively complemented lattice, whether modular or not, may be so represented. In fact, it will be shown that any lattice with the *disjunction property* has an isomorphic meet-representation by sets of maximal dual ideals. The proof of this, as well as the definition of the disjunction property, is due essentially to Wallman [1], although Wallman was mainly interested in the case of distributive lattices.

DEFINITIONS. A lattice L with zero and unit elements O and I is said to be complemented if corresponding to every element a of L there exists an element a' of L such that $a \cup a' = I$, and $a \cap a' = O$. The element a' is then said to be a *complement* of a.

A lattice L is said to be *relatively complemented* if $a < b < c$ implies the existence of an element b' such that $b \cap b' = a$, and $b \cup b' = c$. The element b' is then said to be a complement of b relative to the elements a and c.

A lattice L with O element is said to have the disjunction property if whenever $a < b$, there exists an element a' such that $a \cap a' = O$, and $a' \cap b \neq O$.

It is easy to see that a relatively complemented lattice with O element has the disjunction property. A fortiori, a complemented modular lattice, which is of necessity relatively complemented, has the disjunction property. We now show that lattices with the disjunction property may be represented by sets of maximal dual ideals.

THEOREM 14. *If L is a lattice with the disjunction property, then an isomorphic meet-representation of L is obtained by assigning to each element x of L the set of all maximal dual ideals containing x.*

Proof. By Theorem 10 it must be shown that if x is distinct from y, then there exists a maximal dual ideal containing one but not the other of the pair x, y. Since x is distinct from y, then either $x \cap y$ is distinct from x, or it is distinct from y. Suppose the former; then $x \cap y < x$, and by the disjunction property, there exists an element z of L such that $x \cap y \cap z = O$, but $x \cap z \neq O$. By Zorn's lemma, there exists a maximal dual ideal containing $x \cap z$. This maximal dual ideal does not contain y, since then it would have to contain $x \cap y \cap z = O$, whence it would contain every element of L. Hence it contains x but not y. Likewise if $z \cap y$ is distinct from y, there is a maximal dual ideal containing y but not x. Hence by Theorem 10, the representation of L by sets of maximal dual ideals is an isomorphic meet-representation. This completes the proof.

We now wish to examine the relation between the representation of a lattice by sets of completely meet-irreducible dual ideals given in Theorem 11, and the representation by sets of maximal dual ideals just given in Theorem 14. We first note that by Corollary 1 to Theorem 8, a dual ideal is completely meet-irreducible if and only if it is maximal subject to failure to contain some element of the lattice. Since, in a lattice with O element, a maximal dual ideal is maximal subject to failure to contain the zero element O, we see that in such a lattice every maximal ideal is completely meet-irreducible. Conversely, in certain lattices with the disjunction property, such as the lattice of all linear subspaces of a projective geometry, it can be shown that every completely meet-irreducible dual ideal is maximal. Perhaps this is also true in every complete complemented modular lattice, although we have not yet been able to prove this. On the other hand, as we shall now show by an example, in some complemented modular lattices which are not complete, there exist completely meet-irreducible dual ideals which are not maximal. A fortiori, merely meet-irreducible dual ideals need not be maximal in complemented modular lattices, or in lattices with the disjunction property.

10. **An example.** Let S be the projective coordinate space of countably infinite dimension, with coordinates taken to be the integers reduced modulo 2. (A general discussion of projective coordinate spaces will be found in the paper by Frink [2].) The points of S are all infinite sequences $\{x_n\}$ of integers reduced modulo 2 such that $x_n = 0$ except for a positive finite number of values of n. Collinearity and subspaces are defined in the usual way. The collection of all subspaces of S is a complete complemented modular lattice.

Consider now the sublattice L consisting of all subspaces of S which are either of finite dimension, or are complements of subspaces of finite dimension. Note that although L is a complemented modular lattice, it is not a complete lattice. Let P denote the class of all elements of L which are of infinite dimension, and F the class of all elements of finite dimension. Although F is a countable class, P has the power of the continuum, since it contains a hyperplane corresponding to each sequence of integers reduced modulo 2 such as $\{y_n\}$, namely the subspace consisting of all points $\{x_n\}$ of S such that $\sum x_n y_n = 0$.

It is easily seen that P is both a prime dual ideal of L and a maximal dual ideal of L. We now construct a dual ideal of L which is a proper subset of P and which contains at least one complement of every element of F. To do so, select at random one complement of each element of F to form a collection K. Extend K to be a dual ideal D by adjoining to it all superspaces of all finite intersections of elements of K. Since K is a countable set, it can be seen that D is also a countable set. Hence D is a proper subset of P, since P is not countable.

Let A be an element of P which is not in D. Extend D to be a dual ideal M which is maximal relative to failure to contain A. This can be done by Zorn's lemma. Note that M can contain no element of F, since it contains a complement of each element of F. Hence M is a proper subset of P. By Corollary 1 to Theorem 8, M is completely meet-irreducible, but M is not maximal, since it is contained in the larger dual ideal P. We have thus exhibited in the complemented modular lattice L a completely meet-irreducible dual ideal which is not maximal. It follows that the representation of a lattice given by Theorem 11 is in general distinct from that given by Theorem 14. In lattices with the disjunction property, the representation by maximal dual ideals is in general more economical than that involving completely meet-irreducible dual ideals.

Incidentally, the example just constructed answers a question raised in the paper by Frink [2]. If a complemented modular lattice is indecomposable, is the projective space which it determines necessarily irreducible? The answer is in the negative, since the lattice L of the example is indecomposable, but the projective space determined by it is reducible, since lines containing the dual ideal P as a point are degenerate, and consist of just two points.

11. **Preservation of arbitrary meets and joins.** We shall call a dual ideal D of a lattice L a *complete* dual ideal if it contains the meet $\bigcap x_a$ of an arbitrary set $\{x_a\}$ of its elements whenever this meet exists in L. This is related to the notion of a *completely prime* dual ideal, defined in §6. In fact it can be seen that a dual ideal in a lattice L is completely prime if and only if its complement is a complete dual ideal in the lattice dual to L. In terms of these notions it is possible to state conditions that a representation of a lattice by sets of dual ideals shall preserve arbitrary meets or arbitrary joins of elements when these exist.

THEOREM 15. *The meet-representation of a lattice L which assigns to each element x of L the set of all dual ideals of a collection K which contain x preserves arbitrary meets of elements of L if and only if all the dual ideals of K are complete dual ideals, and preserves arbitrary joins if and only if all the ideals of K are completely prime.*

Proof. Suppose $x=\bigcap x_a$, and let $R(x)$ and $R(x_a)$ be the representative sets of x and x_a in the representation. To say that arbitrary meets are preserved is to say that $R(x)$ is the set-intersection of the set $R(x_a)$, that is, that a dual ideal D of K is in $R(x)$ if and only if it is in all the sets $R(x_a)$. Since D is in $R(x_a)$ if and only if x_a is in D, this means that x is in D if and only if each x_a is in D. But this is to say that D is a complete dual ideal.

Now let $x = \bigcup x_a$. To say that the representation preserves arbitrary joins is to say that $R(x)$ is the set-union of the sets $R(x_a)$, which is to say that a dual ideal D is in $R(x)$ if and only if it is in at least one of the sets $R(x_a)$. But this means that x is in D if and only if at least one of the elements x_a is in D, or in other words, if and only if D is completely prime. In either case, therefore, the collection must consist entirely of dual ideals which are complete, or completely prime. This completes the proof.

It is easily seen that every principal ideal is complete. Conversely, in a complete lattice, every complete ideal is principal, since the meet x of *all* elements of D must exist and be a member of D. Hence D must be the principal ideal $\{x\}$. We have, therefore, the following theorem.

THEOREM 16. *Representations of a lattice L by sets of principal dual ideals preserve arbitrary meets of elements of L. Conversely, if L is a complete lattice, then the representations by principal dual ideals are the only representations which preserve arbitrary meets.*

It is more difficult to discover significant isomorphic meet-representations which preserve arbitrary joins. Some rather strong condition must hold in order that enough completely prime dual ideals may exist to give an isomorphic representation.

In a distributive lattice, meet-irreducible dual ideals are prime by Theorem 12. It might be thought that similarly, in a lattice satisfying some infinite distributive law, such as $x \cap \bigcup y_a = \bigcup (x \cap y_a)$, completely irreducible dual ideals are completely prime. If this were so, then the isomorphic representation of Theorem 11, using completely meet-irreducible dual ideals, would preserve arbitrary joins in such a lattice.

But consider the following counter-example. Let L be the lattice of all finite subsets of an infinite set, together with their complements. Then L is a Boolean algebra, and so it obeys all the usual infinite distributive laws. The collection D of all elements of L which are infinite sets is a maximal dual ideal of L, and is hence completely meet-irreducible. But D is not completely prime, since it contains joins of finite sets without containing any finite sets.

The lattice L of this example is not complete, and the question remains open whether, in a complete lattice satisfying some infinite distributive law, completely meet-irreducible dual ideals are completely prime. It can be shown that this conjecture is verified for the case of complete atomic Boolean algebras. Whether it holds in general is an important unsolved problem concerning representations of the type of Theorem 11.

Another important unsolved problem of a similar nature concerns the possibility of isomorphic representations which preserve meets and joins of countably many elements in lattices in which such countable meets and joins exist. For example, the question whether the Boolean algebra M/N of measurable sets modulo null sets has an isomorphic representation by sets which preserves countable meets and joins is of considerable importance in the theory of probability(9). The type of dual ideal that is required for such a representation is easily found by modifying the argument used in the proof of Theorem 15. Instead of complete dual ideals and completely prime dual ideals, it is necessary to use σ-complete and σ-prime dual ideals. The definitions of these differ from the definition of complete and completely prime dual ideals only in that they involve countable meets and joins, instead of arbitrary meets and joins. The principal difficulty is to determine whether enough of these ideals exist in a given lattice to furnish an isomorphic representation.

12. **Representations by sets of lattice elements.** In Theorem 16 and in the corollary to Theorem 10 we have considered meet-representations by sets of principal dual ideals. Since a principal dual ideal $\{x\}$ is completely determined by the element x and conversely, we might just as well have considered meet-representations of a lattice by sets of elements of the lattice, rather than by sets of dual ideals. A. D. Campbell [1] has, in particular, studied meet-representations of lattices by sets of lattice elements of a special kind, namely join-irreducible elements. We now point out the relation of our results to his.

Recall from §3 that an element a of a lattice L is said to be *join-irreducible* if it is not the join of two elements each distinct from a, and is said to be *completely join-irreducible* if it is not the join of any number of elements of L each distinct from a.

THEOREM 17. *A principal dual ideal $\{x\}$ of a lattice is meet-irreducible if and only if the element x is join-irreducible. Likewise $\{x\}$ is completely meet-irreducible if and only if x is completely join-irreducible.*

Proof. Suppose x is not join-irreducible; then $x=y\cup z$, where y and z are each distinct from x. Then the principal dual ideal $\{x\}$ is the set-intersection of the principal dual ideals $\{y\}$ and $\{z\}$. Hence $\{x\}$ is not meet-irreducible. Likewise if $x=\bigcup x_a$, where the elements x_a are all distinct from x, then $\{x\}$ is the set-intersection of the distinct principal dual ideals $\{x_a\}$, whence $\{x\}$ is not completely meet-irreducible.

Conversely, suppose the principal dual ideal $\{x\}$ is the set-intersection of the dual ideals D and E, each distinct from $\{x\}$. Then D and E contain elements d and e not in $\{x\}$. Hence $d\cap x$ is distinct from x, since otherwise $d\geqq x$, and d would be in $\{x\}$. Likewise $e\cap x$ is distinct from x. But it is easily seen that $x=(d\cap x)\cup(e\cap x)$, whence x is not join-irreducible. For, on the one hand, $(d\cap x)\cup(e\cap x)$ is in $\{x\}$, since it is in D and E, and x is the set-inter-

(9) Here the answer is in the negative. See L. H. Loomis, *On the representation of σ-complete Boolean algebras*, Bull. Amer. Math. Soc. vol. 53 (1947) pp. 757–760.

section of D and E; whence $(d\cap x)\cup(e\cap x)\geqq x$. On the other hand $(d\cap x)\cup(e\cap x)\leqq x$ in any lattice. It follows that if x is join-irreducible, then $\{x\}$ is meet-irreducible.

Finally, suppose that $\{x\}$ is the set-intersection of the collection $\{D_a\}$ of dual ideals D_a each distinct from $\{x\}$. Select from each D_a an element d_a such that $d_a<x$. This is seen to be possible, since we may take d_a to be $e_a\cap x$, where e_a is an element of D_a which is not in $\{x\}$. Now consider the join $\bigcup d_a$. This join exists and is the element x. For on the one hand x is an upper bound of the elements d_a. On the other hand, if y is any other upper bound, then y is in each dual ideal D_a and hence in their intersection $\{x\}$. Therefore $y>x$, and consequently x is the least upper bound or join of the elements d_a, which are all distinct from x. It follows that x is not completely join-irreducible. This completes the proof.

Corresponding to the meet-representation of a lattice determined by any collection K of principal dual ideals $\{x\}$, as given by the corollary to Theorem 10, there is an equivalent representation by sets of the corresponding lattice elements x, since principal dual ideals correspond one-to-one with the elements which determine them. Hence we have the following further corollary to Theorem 10:

COROLLARY. *Given any set M of elements of a lattice L, a meet-representation of L is obtained by assigning to each element x of L the set of all elements y of M such that $y\leqq x$. This representation is isomorphic if and only if whenever the elements x and z of L are distinct, there exists an element y of M such that of the two statements $y\leqq x$ and $y\leqq z$, one is true and the other is false.*

It is easily seen that all dual ideals of a lattice are principal if and only if the lattice satisfies the descending chain condition. In such a lattice, all representations by sets of dual ideals are essentially representations by sets of lattice elements. In particular, the representation of Theorem 11 is, by Theorem 17, essentially just the representation by completely join-irreducible elements. For the case of lattices of finite length, this representation has already been discussed by A. D. Campbell [1].

BIBLIOGRAPHY

G. BIRKHOFF

1. *On the combination of subalgebras*, Proc. Cambridge Philos. Soc. vol. 29 (1933) pp. 441–464.
2. *Lattice theory*, Amer. Math. Soc. Colloquium Publications, vol. 25, New York, 1940.
3. *Subdirect unions in universal algebra*, Bull. Amer. Math. Soc. vol. 50 (1944) pp. 764–768.

A. D. CAMPBELL

1. *Set-coordinates for lattices*, Bull. Amer. Math. Soc. vol. 49 (1943) pp. 395–398.

R. P. DILWORTH

1. *Ideals in Birkhoff lattices*, Trans. Amer. Math. Soc. vol. 49 (1941) pp. 325–353.

N. Dunford and M. H. Stone

1. *On the representation theorem for Boolean algebras*, Revista Ciencias Lima vol. 43 (1941) pp. 447–453.

O. Frink

1. *Representations of Boolean algebras*, Bull. Amer. Math. Soc. vol. 47 (1941) pp. 755–756.
2. *Complemented modular lattices and projective spaces of infinite dimension*, Trans. Amer. Math. Soc. vol. 60 (1946) pp. 452–467.

M. H. Stone

1. *The theory of representations for Boolean algebras*, Trans. Amer. Math. Soc. vol. 40 (1936) pp. 37–111.
2. *Topological representations of distributive lattices and Brouwerian logics*, Časopis pro Peštovani Mathematiky a Fysiky vol. 67 (1937) pp. 1–25.

H. Wallman

1. *Lattices and topological spaces*, Ann. of Math. (2) vol. 39 (1938) pp. 112–126.

Harvard University,
Cambridge, Mass.
The Pennsylvania State College,
State College, Pa.

Reprinted from *Trans. Am. Math. Soc.* **64** (1948), 299–316

Reprinted from *Revista Tucumán* **14** (1962), 325–331

A NEW INTERVAL TOPOLOGY FOR DUALLY DIRECTED SETS

by

GARRETT BIRKHOFF *

To my friend Félix Cernuschi

(Recibido el 15 de junio de 1962)

1. — *Frink's interval topology.* Frink [3, p. 569] has defined an interval topology for lattices, which has the valuable property that it makes every complete lattice compact. This topology is constructed by taking as a *subbasis* of closed sets all *intervals* in an extended sense. In lattices whithout universal bounds**, Frink's "intervalls" include, besides *closed intervals* $[a, b]$ in the usual sense [2, p. 1], also *semi-infinite* intervals (of the form $(-\infty, b]$ and $[a, +\infty)$, and the *infinite* interval $(-\infty, +\infty)$ — that is, the whole lattice.

Unfortunately, Frink's interval topology seems unsuitable for vector lattices, and for other lattices without universal bounds. Thus, in the real number system R, it fails to make the set Z of all integers closed: any unbounded set which is closed in Frink's interval topology must contain at least one semi-infinite interval. More generally***, it fails to make any nontrivial vector lattice into a Hausdorff space: in a vector lattice, it makes every nonvoid open set U contain, for any $a \neq 0$ and some $n = n(a, U)$, all x with $|x| > n|a|$.

Also, one of Frink's main results [3, Thm. 4] is incorrect for lattices like R which do not have universal bounds****: Frink's interval to-

* The research described below was initiated under National Science Foundation Grant NSF 14,508.

** In a partly ordered set, the least element $-\infty$ (or 0) and the greatest element $+\infty$ (or I) are called universal bounds.

*** The author is indebted to Hugh Gordon for this observation (personal communication).

**** This fact was called to the author's attention by A. B. Ramsay. Incidentally, [3, Thm. 2] is also incorrect; see [2, p. 146].

pology for $R^2 = R \times R$ is not the product of the topologies for the factor R individually, precisely because the "closed intervals" in Frink's extended sense include intervals which are unbounded.

The present note proposes a new interval topology for lattices, which is equivalent to Frink's on any lattice with universal bounds (see § 3), which gives to R its natural topology, and which has various other desirable properties. Because of these facts, and because it satisfies the theorems stated by Frink, the author proposes that it should be called simply *the* interval topology henceforth.

In particular, it seems more suitable than the *relative topology* obtained by embedding a given lattice in its completion by cuts, and then using Frink's interval topology. For example, suppose one topologizes R^2 in this way. One finds that the completion by cuts of R^2 (obtained by adjoining $-\infty$ and $+\infty$) is not a Hausdorff space in Frink's interval topology, since any two nonvoid neighborhoods of $-\infty$ and $+\infty$, respectively, have a nonvoid intersection. Whereas the new interval topology gives R^2 its natural topology. The author's interpretation of the situation is, that the completion by cuts of R^2 is a pathological lattice·

2. — *The new interval topology.* The proposed new interval topology is defined in terms of closed intervals alone, as follows.

DEFINITION 1. Let D be any dually directed set*, and let $\mathcal{C}$ be the $\bigcap$-ring** of all intersections of finite unions of closed intervals $[a, b]$ of D. Then a subset S of D will be called *closed* in the *interval topology* if and only if $C \varepsilon \mathcal{C}$ implies $S \cap C \varepsilon \mathcal{C}$.

Thus, by definition, the closed intervals of D are a *subbasis* for the family $\mathcal{C}$ of what one might call *bounded closed* subsets of D. The concept of subbasis played a key role in Frink's a work [3], and his ideas (in modified form) will be used extensively below. (We recall that a subset $\mathcal{F}$ of a $\bigcap$-ring $\mathcal{C}$ of sets is called a *subbasis* of $\mathcal{C}$ if and only if

* A dually directed set is a partly ordered set in which any two elements have a common upper bound and a common lower bound. This is equivalent to the condition that every finite subset of D be bounded, and holds in any lattice.

** By definition, a $\bigcap$-ring is a ring of sets closed under arbitrary intersection (and finite union).

$\mathcal{C}$ is the family $\mathcal{C}(\mathfrak{F})$ of all intersections of finite unions of sets $F \varepsilon \mathfrak{F}$, and that this family $\mathcal{C}(\mathfrak{F})$ is always a $\bigcap$-ring of sets).

In addition, we will use extensively the lattice-theoretic concept of the *residual* [2, p. 201] of $\mathcal{C}$, considered in the 1-semigroup (Brouwerian lattice) of all subsets of D, as in [2, p. 204, Thm. 5]. To make the present exposition more self-contained, we define this concept here.

DEFINITION 2. Let $\mathcal{C}$ be any family of subsets of a set Λ. Then the residual $\mathcal{C} : \mathcal{C} = \mathcal{C}^*$ of $\mathcal{C}$ is the family of all subsets T of Λ such that $C \varepsilon \mathcal{C}$ implies $T \cap C \varepsilon \mathcal{C}$.

By definition, then, the family of *all* closed sets in D is the residual $\mathcal{C}^* = \mathcal{C} : \mathcal{C}$ of the family $\mathcal{C}$ of "bounded" closed sets. We next justify the use of the word "bounded" in this connection.

LEMMA 1. A set which is closed in the interval topology is bounded if and only if it belongs to $\mathcal{C}$.

Proof. In any dually directed set, the family of all bounded sets contains all intervals $[a, b]$; it is closed under finite union and arbitrary intersection; hence it contains $\mathcal{C}$. This shows that every set in $\mathcal{C}$ is bounded. Conversely, if $T \varepsilon \mathcal{C}^*$ is bounded, then $T \subset C$ for some interval $C = [a, b] \varepsilon \mathcal{C}$; hence $T = T \cap C \varepsilon \mathcal{C}$, by definition of $\mathcal{C}^*$.

We now come to the first essential result: that any dually directed set D is a T_1-space in the new interval topology. In fact, we will derive this from considerations applicable to residuals of families of "bounded" closed sets generally.

LEMMA 2. If $\mathcal{C}$ contains the empty set ϕ and is a $\bigcap$-ring, then $\mathcal{C}^* = \mathcal{C} : \mathcal{C}$ is a $\bigcap$-ring which contains ϕ and Λ.

Proof. Since $\mathcal{C} \subset \mathcal{C}^*$ trivially and $\phi \varepsilon \mathcal{C}^*$ evidently $\phi \varepsilon \mathcal{C}^*$. Likewise, since $\Lambda \cap C = C \varepsilon \mathcal{C}$ trivially for all $C \varepsilon \mathcal{C}$, $\Lambda \varepsilon \mathcal{C}^*$. Again, if $S \cap C \varepsilon \mathcal{C}$ and $T \cap C \varepsilon \mathcal{C}$ for all $C \varepsilon \mathcal{C}$, then $(S \cup T) \cap C = (S \cap C) \cup (T \cap C) \varepsilon \mathcal{C}$. Finally, if $S_\alpha \cap C \varepsilon \mathcal{C}$ for all α in an index set and all $C \varepsilon \mathcal{C}$, then

$$(\bigcap S_\alpha) \cap C = \bigcap (S_\alpha \cap C) \varepsilon \mathcal{C},$$

since $\mathcal{C}$ is closed under arbitrary intersection.

COROLLARY 1. Le $\mathfrak{F}$ be a family of subsets of a set Λ whose intersections include all points. Then the residual $\mathcal{C} : \mathcal{C}$ of the $\bigcap$-ring

$\mathcal{C} = \mathcal{C}(\mathcal{F})$ of sets having $\mathcal{F}$ for subbasis consists of the *closed* subsets of Λ, under a T_1-topology defined by this construction.

Proof. By Lemma 1, $\mathcal{C}^*$ contains $\mathcal{C}$ and is a $\bigcap$-ring; moreover by hypothesis, it contains all points.

DEFINITION 3. A family $\mathcal{C}$ of closed sets of a T_1-space Λ will be called a *core* of closed sets if and ony if the family $\mathcal{G}$ of all closed sets of Λ is the residual of the $\bigcap$-ring $\mathcal{C}$ generated by $\mathcal{F}$ (i.e., having $\mathcal{F}$ for subbasis).

The preceding corollary shows that any family $\mathcal{F}$ of subsets of a set Λ, whose intersections include all points, can be taken as a core of closed subsets for some T_1-topology.

Definition 1 defines the (new) *interval topology* of a dually directed set D as the particular T_1-topology obtained in the above way by using the *finite intervals* as a *core* of *closed sets.* We have proved

COROLLARY 2. In the (new) interval topology, any dually directed set is a T_1-space.

3. — *Relation to Frink's interval topology.* The (new) interval defined by Definition 1 is related to that defined by Frink as follows.

THEOREM 1. The interval topology defined above coincides with that of Frink, if and only if D has universal bounds.

Proof. If D has universal bounds, then the set of finite intervals $[a, b]$ is the same as the set of all intervals. Hence $\mathcal{C}$ consists precisely of the "closed" subsets in the Frink interval topology of [3, p. 569, foot], which has the set of all intervals as a subbasis. On the other hand, since every set in $\mathcal{C}^*$ is bounded if D has universal bounds, we also have $\mathcal{C} = \mathcal{C}^*$ by Lemma 1; hence $\mathcal{C}$ also consists of the "closed" subsets 'closed" in the new interval topology. This proves the firts half of the theorem.

To prove the other half, suppose that the dually directed set D has no universal upper bound $+\infty$. Then, in Frink's interval topology, any *closed* set which is unbounded above must contain some terminal segment $[a, +\infty)$ — since this is true of his subbasis of closed sets, and the class of all sets bounded above is an ideal (i.e., closed under finite union and under intersection with anything). On the other hand, one can construct in D (using transfinite induction) an unbounded increasing transfinite sequence which is unbounded above, in which for each limit-ordinal $\aleph$, $x_{\aleph}$ is an upper bound to the x_α with $\alpha < \aleph$ if such an upper bound exists, and in which no element is covered by its succesor. This sequence does *not* contains any terminal segment — yet it is closed in the new interval topology. This construction and its dual show that unless D has universal bounds, the new interval topology fails to coincide with that of Frink.

4. — *Connection with k-spaces.* The concept of a core of closed sets, defined in § 2, has an interesting connection with the concept of a *k-space* invented by Hurewicz*. The following statement, for example, simply rephrases the usual definition of a k-space.

DEFINITION 4. A topological space is a *k-space* if and only if the residual of the $\cap$-ring of its *compact* sets is the $\cap$-ring of all its *closed* sets.

COROLLARY. Any subbasis of compact sets is a core for the family of all closed sets in any k-space.

In k-spaces, there are however cores of compact sets which are *not* subbases. For example, in any metric space Λ, the particular compact sets which consist of convergent sequences and their limit points form a core of (compact) closed sets for the metric topology of Λ, which are not a subbase for the $\cap$-ring of all compact sets, since every set in the $\cap$-ring which they generate is countable.

The preceding corollary is related to a general method for constructing k-spaces. This construction depends on the well-known fact that, in the $\cap$-ring of all closed sets of a T_1-space, the property of compactness is characterized by the following condition.

DEFINITION 5. A family $\mathfrak{F}$ of sets has the *compactness property* if and only if, whenever a subfamily $\mathfrak{G} \subset \mathfrak{F}$ of sets has a void intersection, there exists a *finite* subfamily $\mathfrak{G}_f \subset \mathfrak{G}$ whose intersection is void.

---

* According to David Gale, Proc. Am. Math. Soc. 1 (1950), 303-8; the author is indebted to Richard Arens for this reference. Some interesting facts about k-spaces are proved in [4, pp. 230, 240]. See also J. W. Alexander, Proc. Nat. Acad. Sci. 25 (1939), 52-4.

We now recall the Theorem of Alexander [1], proved by Frink as [3, Thm. 8] (see also [4, p. 139]) : If a subbasis $\mathfrak{F}$ of $\mathfrak{C}$ has the compactness property, then so does $\mathfrak{C}$. This theorem can be applied to construct a family of k-space topologies on a given space Λ, as follows.

Let $\mathfrak{F}$ be any family of subsets of Λ which has the compactness property, and whose intersections include all points. Then $\mathfrak{F}$ is a subbasis for a family $\mathfrak{C}$ of compact sets, in a T_1-topology on Λ under which $\mathfrak{C} : \mathfrak{C}$ is the $\bigcap$-ring of all closed sets. Though, as in the preceding example, $\mathfrak{C}$ may not include all compact sets, one can easily prove

LEMMA 3. If $\mathfrak{C}$ has the compacteness property, then every $C \varepsilon \mathfrak{C}$ is compact in the topology defined by the residual $\mathfrak{C} : \mathfrak{C}$.

Proof. It suffices to show that the subsets of any given $T \subset C$ which are members of $\mathfrak{C} : \mathfrak{C}$ have the compactness property. But since $T \varepsilon \mathfrak{C} : \mathfrak{C}$ and $T \subset C$ imply $T = T \cap C \varepsilon \mathfrak{C}$, this is obvious.

Putting the preceding results together, we obtain.

THEOREM 2. Let $\mathfrak{F}$ be any family of subsets of a set Λ, such that $\mathfrak{F}$ has the compactness property, and that every point $p \varepsilon \Lambda$ is an intersection of members of $\mathfrak{F}$. Then is a *core* of closed sets for a T_1-topology under which Λ is a *k-space*.

Proof. As above, $\mathfrak{F}$ is a core of closed sets for the T_1-topology on Λ, with $\mathfrak{C}^* = \mathfrak{C} : \mathfrak{C}$ as the $\bigcap$-ring of closed sets. By Lemma 3, the $\bigcap$-ring $\mathfrak{K}$ of all compact sets in this topology satisfies $\mathfrak{C} \subset \mathfrak{K} \subset \mathfrak{C}^*$. To complete the proof, it suffices by the definition of a k-space to prove

LEMMA 4. In the preceding construction, $\mathfrak{K}^* = \mathfrak{C}^*$.

Proof of Lemma 4. Clearly $C \varepsilon \mathfrak{C}^*$ closed and $K \varepsilon \mathfrak{K}$ compact imply $C \cap K \varepsilon \mathfrak{K} \subset \mathfrak{C}^*$; hence every member of $\mathfrak{C}^*$ is in $\mathfrak{K}^*$. Conversely, suppose $T \varepsilon \mathfrak{K}^*$, so that $T \cap K \varepsilon \mathfrak{K}$ for all $K \varepsilon \mathfrak{K}$. This implies that $T \cap C$ is compact (by Lemma 3) for all $C \varepsilon \mathfrak{C} \subset \mathfrak{K}$, which implies (since $T \cap C \varepsilon \mathfrak{K} \subset \mathfrak{C}^*$ as above) that $(T \cap C) \cap C = T \cap C \varepsilon \mathfrak{C}$. But $T \cap C \varepsilon \mathfrak{C}$ for all $C \varepsilon \mathfrak{C}$ implies $T \varepsilon \mathfrak{C}^*$, and so we have shown that $T \varepsilon \mathfrak{K}$ implies $T \varepsilon \mathfrak{C}^*$, completing the proof of Lemma 4 and hence of Theorem 1.

Very possibly, a more elegant proof of Lemma 4 can be based on a consideration of the closed subsets of Λ as a Brouwerian lattice.

5. — *Conditionally complete lattices.* It was shown at the end of § 2 that any dually directed set D was a T_1-space in the (new) interval topology. We now consider in some detail the case that D is a conditionally complete lattice. In this case, the relative topology on any finite interval $[a, b]$ has the same subbasis of closed sets as that defined by Frink; hence it is equivalent to it. Hence [3, Thm. 9] $[a, b]$ is a *compact* set if D is conditionally complete. From this fact and Theorem 2, there follows

THEOREM 3. Any conditionally complete lattice is a T_1-space which is a k-space in its (new) interval topology, and in which every closed bounded set is compact.

We now prove a converse of Theorem 3.

THEOREM 4. A subset S of a dually directed set D which is *compact* in the interval topology must be *bounded.*

Proof. Suppose S compact but unbounded above; we will reach a contradiction. Then D has no biggest element $+\infty$, but the intervals $[a, +\infty)$ are closed. Hence every intersection $S_a = S \cap [a, +\infty)$ is compact. Moreover any finite family of $S_{a(i)}$ has an intersection which contains $S \cap [a, +\infty)$ for any upper bound b of the $a(i)$ —which exists since D is directed. Since S has no upper bound, $S \cap [b, +\infty)$ is nonvoid; hence the set of *all* S_a has the finite intersection property [4, p. 135]. Since the S_a are compact, it follows that $\bigcap S_a$ is nonvoid. But for any $c \in \bigcap S_a$, we have $c \geqslant a$ for all a, which is impossible.

The supposition that S is unbounded below leads to a similar contradiction, proving the result stated.

COROLLARY. A closed subset of a conditionally complete lattice is compact in the interval topology if and only if it is bounded.

REFERENCES

[1] J. W. ALEXANDER, "Ordered sets, complexes, and the problem of bicompactification", Proc. Nat. Acad. Sci. 25 (1939), 296-8.
[2] G. BIRKHOFF, "Lattice Theory', rev. ed., American Mathematical Society, New York, 1948.
[3] O. FRINK, "Topology in lattices", Trans. Am. Math. Soc. 51 (1942), 569-82.
[4] J. L. KELLY, *"General Topology"*, van Nostrand, Princeton, 1955.

IV

Lie Groups and Lie Algebras

By 1935, my fascination with groups (already mentioned in the Preface) had broadened to include Lie groups and their Lie algebras. These were "hot" subjects of research at the time, partly because rigorous global versions of Lie's three fundamental theorems were being proved for the first time.[1] This led to an intense development of the theory of topological groups, as defined by Schreier's neighborhood axioms for topological groups. My paper [20] helped to clarify these axioms, by showing that a topological group is metrizable if and only if it satisfies the first countability axiom.

A related question concerned the (global) representations of Lie groups and Lie algebras by matrices. My papers [22] and [27] (reprinted in this volume) dealt with this problem. In [22], I exhibited a Lie group which is not isomorphic with any group of matrices, though its covering group is. In [27], I described a method for constructing a universal "enveloping" (linear) associative algebra $E(\mathfrak{A})$ from any Lie algebra $\mathfrak{A}$, into which the Lie algebra may be isomorphically embedded so that $[ab]$ goes into $ab - ba$. The proof was based on a "straightening lemma" inspired by Philip Hall's treatment of commutators in regular p-groups; unfortunately even when $\mathfrak{A}$ is finite-dimensional, $E(\mathfrak{A})$ is infinite-dimensional. Thus, if $\mathfrak{A}$ is the zero algebra of dimension r, $E(\mathfrak{A})$ consists of all (commutative) polynomials $p(a_1, \ldots, a_r)$.

Soon after, E. Witt independently proved this result, which is now called the Birkhoff–Witt theorem,[2] adding a number of important extensions. These results, developed much further by Harish-Chandra and others,[3] have led to a substantial theory with applications to infinite-dimensional group representations. For this theory, see J. Dixmier, *Enveloping Algebras*, North-Holland, 1977.

I also collaborated with Philip Whitman in writing a sequel to [27] after World War II. Our paper ([60]) contains a representation theory for Lie and Jordan algebras, modelled on the representation theory for linear associative algebras in Emmy Noether's famous paper, "Hyperkomplexe Systeme und Darstellungstheorie" (*Math. Zeits* **30** (1929), 641–92).

Analytical groups. My most ambitious paper on Lie groups was [52]. As I previously stated in [26], my aim was to provide a *topologico-algebraic* theory of *local* Lie groups, in the more general *infinite-dimensional* setting of Banach spaces. I hoped, of course, that my paper would contribute to the solution of Hilbert's Fifth Problem, which was then in the limelight because von Neumann and Pontrjagin recently had solved it in the compact and Abelian cases, respectively. Their work inaugurated a sustained 20-year effórt which culminated in an affirmative general solution in 1953.[4] (It is an interesting fact that the analogous proposition for groups of transformations is false.)

However, as the title "Analytical groups" of [32] suggests, my tools were *not* topological. Instead, assuming group multiplication to be uniformly continuously *differentiable*, so that the

Lie algebra A of the group G would consist of bounded linear operators, I exploited the *exponential mapping* $e^a = g$ from A to G. Specifically, I showed that the "SCH-series" defined by the formula $a \circ b = \gamma(a, b) = \ln(e^a e^b)$ defined a *local* analytical group. I summarized my main results as follows:

The paper deals with systems (called "analytical groups") in which an associative multiplication is defined, and which can be so mapped on a Banach prameter-space that if one multiplies all elements by any fixed element near the origin, vector differences are left nearly invariant. (See ref. 6 below).

It is proved that if G is any analytical group (more properly, analytical group nucleus), then

(1) G is a topological group nucleus in the usual sense.
(2) One can introduce canonical parameters into G.
(3) G has an infinitesimal (Lie) algebra $L(G)$.
(4) The analytical subgroups of G correspond biuniquely to the closed subalgebras of $L(G)$, a subgroup being normal if and only if the corresponding subalgebra is invariant.
(5) If G is under canonical parameters, then there exists a formal series of polynomials determined by $L(G)$ which expresses the rule for forming group products.
(6) One can define product integrals for functions with values in $L(G)$, which include the Lebesgue integral (the case G is the additive group of real numbers), and all known product integrals (the case G is a group of matrices).
(7) Quite general functions $x(\lambda)$ with real arguments and values in a Banach space B determine formal series in elements of B and their brackets, which express the product integral $\int x(\lambda)\, d\lambda$ under canonical parameters for *any* analytical group G whose parameter-space contains B and whose "commutation modulus" is sufficiently small.
(8) All the operations defined (e.g., vector addition under canonical parameters, product integration) are *topologico-algebraic*—preserved under topological isomorphisms.

4. Extension to infinite dimensions. Perhaps the main advantage of the above assumptions, is the fact that many *infinite* continuous groups satisfy them. This marks a real advance in the analytical theory of groups.[5]

Statement (6) above refers to my paper [30] on non-commutative product integration, a topic which I have recently reviewed in [199].—My summary of [32] continued:

The infinite-dimensional analytical groups treated in the literature are of two kinds: the infinite continuous groups of analytical transformations

$$x_i' = f_i(x_1, \ldots, x_n) \qquad (i = 1, \ldots, n)$$

of n-dimensional space discussed by Lie [10][6] and Cartan [4], and the groups of linear operators on Hilbert space recently studied by Delsarte [6]. Each of these authors omits to define the meaning of the convergence $T_n \to T$ of a sequence of transformation T_n to a limit T—in other words, to define the topological structure of the corresponding abstract groups.

This omission, and the omission to establish a rigorous correlation between the actual transformations of such groups and so-called "infinitesimal" transformations, are not trivial. In fact, although the present paper supplies a complete theory for a class of groups including those studied by Delsarte, the author does not even know what the facts are in the case of the groups studied by Lie and Cartan. Part of the difficulty is that the group manifolds are not metric-linear; part of it is that canonical parameters do not define even locally a one-one representation of the group manifold.

As of 1984, Banach manifolds are quite well understood (see for example R. S. Palais in *Topology* **5** (1966), 1–16); so are infinite-dimensional Lie algebras of vector fields (see I. M. Singer and

S. Sternberg, *J. d'Analyse Math.* **15** (1965), 1–114). Moreover, Omori has proved many interesting results about "Banach-Lie" groups and their actions on finite-dimensional manifolds.[7] However, there still exists no rigorous global, general theory of the "infinite continuous groups" studied by Lie and Cartan.

Later work. Regarding the Lie–Élie Cartan theory of continuous groups as one of the most inspiring areas of mathematics, I continued to think about it and its applications after 1940. In my wartime research involving fluid dynamics, I had noticed that a large fraction of the "exact" analytic solutions of the nonlinear Euler and Navier-Stokes equations utilized the group-theoretic notion of "dynamic similitude," as did the rational interpretation of model experiments.

Similar applications had already been treated in Sedov's *Similarity and Dimensional Methods in Mechanics* (first ed., 1943), and I made my observations the subject of two chapters of my book on *Hydrodynamics* (see the "Bibliography of Garrett Birkhoff's Books and Papers, 1933–1986" on pages ix–xv). The ideas involved have since been greatly generalized, by Ovsiannikov, Ibragimov, Barenblatt, W. F. Ames, and many others,[8] but they involve questions far outside the scope of this volume.

In a somewhat different direction, I published in 1956 a very simple proof (see [67]) of Lie's classic result, that any n-dimensional manifold M admitting an $n(n + 1)/2$-parameter group of rigid motions is locally isometric either to $\mathbb{R}^n$, or to an n-sphere of suitable radius in $\mathbb{R}^{n+1}$, or to a hyperbolic n-space of suitable constant negative curvature.

Notes

[1] See W. Mayer and T. Y. Thomas, "Foundations of the theory of Lie groups," *Annals of Math.* **36** (1935), 770–882.

[2] *J. für Math.* **177** (1937), 152–60; see also W. Schmid, *Bull. AMS* **6** (1982), 175–89.

[3] Harish-Chandra's papers in vols. 70 and 75–77 of the *Trans. AMS* are especially basic.

[4] D. Montgomery and L. Zippin, *Topological Transformation Groups*, Wiley, 1955; see also the comments of C. T. Yang in F. Browder (ed.), *Mathematical Developments Arising from Hilbert's Problems*, Proc. Symp. Pure Math. XXVIII (1976), pp. 142–6. Hilbert's Fifth Problem was to show that any locally Euclidean topological group can be parameterized so as to make its multiplication operator analytic.

[5] Cf. Abstract 41-3-129 of the Bulletin of the American Mathematical Society (1935); also *Continuous groups and linear spaces*, Matematicheskli Sbornik, vol. 1 (1936), pp. 635–642; an address delivered at the First International Topological Conference, Moscow, September 5, 1935.

[6] See vol. vi, Papers XI, XII, and XVIII of Lie's *Gesammette Mathematische Abhandlungeun*, Teubner, 1927.

[7] See his "Infinite Dimensional Lie Transformation Groups," Springer Lecture Notes in Math. [427], 1947; also Math. Revs. 47-4286 and 58-28320; for the book quoted, see Math. Revs. 55-4263.

[8] See L. V. Ovsiannikov, *Group Analysis of Differential Equations*, Academic Press, 1982; G. I. Barenblatt, *Similarity, Self-Similarity, and Intermediate Asymptotics*, Consultants Bureau, New York, 1979; G. W. Bluman and J. D. Cole, *Similarity Methods for Differential Equations*, Springer-Verlag, 1974; P. Olver, *Applications of Lie Groups to Differential Equations*, Springer-Verlag, 1986; and [186].

Reprinted from the
TRANSACTIONS OF THE AMERICAN MATHEMATICAL SOCIETY
Vol. 39, No. 3, pp. 496-499
May, 1936

PRINTED IN THE U.S.A.

ON THE ORDER OF GROUPS OF AUTOMORPHISMS*

BY
GARRETT BIRKHOFF AND PHILIP HALL

1. **Introduction.** Consider the following problem. Let G be any group of finite order g, and let A denote the group of the automorphisms of G. What can one infer about the order a of A, simply from a knowledge of g: in other words, to what extent is a a numerical function of g?

The main known result relating to this problem is due to Frobenius.† It limits the orders of the individual elements of A in terms of g, and hence tells which primes can be divisors of a.

The present paper is independent of the work of Frobenius, and presupposes only the theorems of Lagrange and Sylow. Its main result is the following

THEOREM 1. *Let G be any group of finite order g. Let $\theta(g)$ denote the order of the group of the automorphisms of the elementary Abelian group of order g, and let r denote the number of distinct prime factors of g. Then the order a of the group A of the automorphisms of G is a divisor of $g^{r-1}\theta(g)$.*

The function $\theta(g)$ is computed numerically from g as follows. Write g as the product $p_1^{n_1}p_2^{n_2}\cdots p_r^{n_r}$ of powers $p_k^{n_k}$ of distinct primes. Then

$$\theta(p_k^{n_k}) = (p_k^{n_k} - 1)(p_k^{n_k} - p)\cdots(p_k^{n_k} - p_k^{n_k-1})$$
$$= p_k^{n_k(n_k-1)/2}\cdot(p_k - 1)(p_k^2 - 1)\cdots(p_k^{n_k} - 1)$$

and

$$\theta(g) = \theta(p_1^{n_1})\theta(p_2^{n_2})\cdots\theta(p_r^{n_r}).$$

For example, $\theta(12) = \theta(3)\theta(4) = 2\cdot(3\cdot 2) = 12$.

One can strengthen Theorem 1 in special cases, by

THEOREM 2. *If G is solvable, then a is a divisor of $g\theta(g)$.*

THEOREM 3. *If G is "hypercentral," that is, the direct product of its Sylow subgroups, then a is a divisor of $\theta(g)$.*

2. **Preliminary lemmas.** The following two statements are immediate corollaries of Lagrange's and Sylow's Theorems, respectively:

* Presented to the Society, December 26, 1933; received by the editors August 20, 1935.

† *Über auflösbare Gruppen*, II, Berliner Sitzungsberichte, 1895, p. 1030. Cf. Burnside's *Theory of Groups*, 1st edition, pp. 250–252.

LEMMA 1. *Let H be any group whose elements induce automorphisms homomorphically (i.e., many-one isomorphically) on a second group G. Then the index in H of the subgroup "centralizing" G (i.e., leaving every element of G invariant) divides the order of the group of the automorphisms of G.*

LEMMA 2. *Let G be any group, and r any positive integer. If the order of every prime-power subgroup of G divides r, then the order of G divides r.*

As a further preliminary step, it is well to verify the somewhat less obvious

LEMMA 3. *Let P be any group of prime-power order p^n, inducing substitutions homomorphically on $r=p^\alpha q$ letters $x_1, \cdots, x_r$ [p^α the highest power of p dividing r]. Then there is a letter x_k such that, if S denotes the subgroup of substitutions of P which omit x_k, the index of S in P divides r.*

Let S_i denote that subgroup of P whose substitutions omit the letter x_i; by Lagrange's Theorem, the index of S_i in P is a power $p^{\beta(i)}$ of p. Hence the transitive system including x_i contains exactly $p^{\beta(i)}$ letters. But the sum of the numbers of letters in the different transitive systems is not a multiple of $p^{\alpha+1}$; hence $\beta(i) \leqq \alpha$ for some $i=i_0$. Setting $S_i=S_{i_0}$, we have Lemma 3.

LEMMA 4.† *Let G be any group of prime-power order p^n. Then the order a of the group A of the automorphisms of G divides $\theta(p^n)=(p^n-1)(p^n-p) \cdots (p^n-p^{n-1})$.*

By Lemma 2, it is sufficient to prove the result for every subgroup Q of A of prime-power order q^m. But given Q, one can define $Q_1>Q_2>Q_3> \cdots >Q_r=1$ and $S_1<S_2<S_3< \cdots <S_r=G$ recursively as follows:

(1) Q_1 is the group Q.

(2) Given Q_k, S_k is the subgroup of the elements of G "centralized" by Q_k (i.e., invariant under every automorphism of Q_k).

(3) Given Q_k and S_k, Q_{k+1} is a proper subgroup of Q_k whose index in Q_k divides the number of elements in $G-S_k$.

The only questionable point in the existence of these subgroups concerns the possibility of (3); this is ensured by Lemma 3.

Moreover multiplying together on one side the indices of the Q_{k+1} in the Q_k, and on the other their multiples, the degrees of the $G-S_k$, one sees that q^m divides the product of those factors (p^n-p^i) corresponding to the orders

† A more delicate result implying this, but presupposing a study of the structure of groups of prime-power order, is given by P. Hall in *A contribution to the theory of groups of prime-power order*, Proceedings of the London Mathematical Society, vol. 36 (1933), p. 37.

of complexes $G-S_k$. Hence a fortiori q^m divides $\theta(p^n)$, and the lemma is proved.

3. **Proof of principal theorem.** We are now in a position to prove Theorem 1.

Accordingly, let G be any group of finite order g, let $g=p_1^{n_1}\cdots p_r^{n_r}$, let $\theta(g)$ denote the order of the group of the automorphisms of the elementary Abelian group of order g, and let A (of order a) denote the group of the automorphisms of G.

By Sylow's Theorem, G contains subgroups S_j^i of orders $p_i^{n_i}$ $[i=1,\cdots,r;$ $j=1,\cdots,s_i]$. By Sylow's Theorem also,† s_i is the index in G of the "normalizer" of any S_j^i (i.e., the set of elements $a\epsilon G$ such that $aS_j^i=S_j^ia$); hence, by Lagrange's Theorem and the fact that S_j^i is contained in its own normalizer, s_i divides $g/p_i^{n_i}$.

Again, the automorphisms of G obviously permute the S_j^i of given order $p_i^{n_i}$ homomorphically. Therefore, by iterated use of Lemma 3, any subgroup Q of A of prime-power order q^m contains a subgroup Q_1 whose index in Q divides the product $\prod_{i=1}^{r}(g/p_i^{n_i})=g^{r-1}$, and which normalizes at least one $S_{j(i)}^i$ of each order $p_i^{n_i}$. But by Lemma 1 and iterated use of Lemma 4, Q_1 has a subgroup Q^* whose index in Q_1 divides $\theta(g)$, and which "centralizes" $S_{j(1)}^i,\cdots,S_{j(r)}^r$ [i.e., leaves every element of these subgroups of G invariant]. But the $S_{j(i)}^i$ generate G; hence Q^* contains only the identity, and q^m divides $g^{r-1}\theta(g)$.

Theorem 1 now follows from Lemma 2 and the fact that Q was permitted to be an arbitrary group of prime-power order.

4. **Special cases of solvable and hypercentral groups.** The proofs of Theorems 2–3 are now immediate.

In fact, Theorem 3 is really a corollary of Lemma 4. For the Sylow subgroups of a hypercentral group are characteristic. Denoting them by $S_1,\cdots,S_r$, one sees immediately that the group of the automorphisms of G is the direct product of the groups of the automorphisms of the S_k, making the theorem obvious.

To prove Theorem 2, suppose that G is solvable, and use the stronger known result,‡ analogous to Sylow's Theorem, that G contains subgroups of every index $p_k^{n_k}$. Now in the proof of Theorem 1 presented in §3, if q does not divide g, it is numerically evident that q^m divides $\theta(g)$. Hence, by Lemma 2, it is sufficient to show that if q divides g, then q^m divides $g\theta(g)$.

---

† More particularly, the part that states that the inner automorphisms of G are transitive on the Sylow subgroups of any fixed order.

‡ Cf. P. Hall, *A note on soluble groups*, Journal of the London Mathematical Society, vol. 3 (1928), p. 99.

But to say that q divides g is evidently to say that $q=p_k$ for suitable k; without loss of generality, we can assume $k=1$. In this case Q normalizes some Sylow subgroup S of G of order $p_1^{n_1}$; this follows from Lemma 3 and the fact that the number of Sylow subgroups of order $p_1^{n_1}$, being a divisor of $p_2^{n_2} \cdots p_r^{n_r}$, is not divisible by q. Moreover Q has a subgroup Q_1 whose index in Q divides q^{n_1} [and hence g] which "normalizes" (i.e., leaves invariant) a subgroup H of order $p_2^{n_2} \cdots p_r^{n_r}$ (and index $p_1^{n_1}$) in G; this follows from Lemma 3 and the fact that by Hall's Theorem cited above, the number of such subgroups H is a divisor of $p_1^{n_1}$.

Finally, by Lemmas 1 and 4, the index in Q_1 of the subgroup Q_2"centralizing" S divides $\theta(q^{n_1})$. And by induction on g, the index in Q_2 of the subgroup Q^* "centralizing" H divides $(p_2^{n_2} \cdots p_r^{n_r})\cdot\theta(p_2^{n_2} \cdots p_r^{n_r})$, or, since it is by Lagrange's Theorem a power of $q=p_1$ and relatively prime to $p_2^{n_2} \cdots p_r^{n_r}$, it divides $\theta(p_2^{n_2} \cdots p_r^{n_r})$. But S and H, if only by Lagrange's Theorem, generate G; hence $Q^*=1$. Combining, one sees that if q divides g, then q^m divides $g\theta(p_1^{n_1})\theta(p_2^{n_2} \cdots p_r^{n_r})$, that is, $g\theta(g)$. But this is just what we wished to prove.

5. **Possible improvement of results.** It is natural to ask what likelihood there is of improving the results expressed in Theorems 1–3.

It is well known that the least upper bound to the possible values of a for fixed g is at least $\theta(g)$; this is shown by the elementary Abelian group of order g. Consequently Theorem 3 is a best possible result. Moreover in general $\theta(g)$ is not a common multiple for the possible values of a, as is shown by the dihedral group of order six and many other groups of similar structure.

On the other hand, there is no known example of a group for which a fails to divide $g\theta(g)$; this suggests the possibility of replacing $g^{r-1}\theta(g)$ in Theorem 1 by $g\theta(g)$, and omitting Theorem 2 altogether.

This leaves the determination of lower bounds and common divisors of a in terms of g unattempted. The cyclic groups of order g should throw considerable light on this more trivial question.

Also, the case in which G is simple would probably repay study.

HARVARD UNIVERSITY,
CAMBRIDGE, MASS.

KING'S COLLEGE,
CAMBRIDGE, ENGLAND.

A Note on Topological Groups

by

Garrett Birkhoff

Cambridge, Mass.

It is natural to define as „Hausdorff groups", those systems which bear the same relation to Hausdorff spaces as the „L-groups" of Schreier [4] bear to L-spaces.

These systems, which are well-known under various names (including „topological groups") can be defined briefly as follows.

A Hausdorff group is any system G (1) which is a Hausdorff space relative to a certain class of neighborhoods (2) which is an abstract group (3) whose group operations are continuous in its topology — that is, in which

HG1: Given any neighborhood U_{ab} of a group product ab, there exist neighborhoods U_a of a and U_b of b such[1]) that $U_a U_b \subset U_{ab}$.

HG2: Given any neighborhoods U_a of any element $a \varepsilon G$, there exists a neighborhood $U_{a^{-1}}$ of the inverse a^{-1} of a such that $(U_{a^{-1}})^{-1} \subset U_a$.

The main result of the present note is the proof that a Hausdorff group is „metrizible" (i.e., homeomorphic with a metric space) if and only if it satisfies Hausdorff's first countability axiom (the axiom that each point a has a complete [2]) system of neighborhoods which is countable).

Before giving the proof, let us for purposes of orientation recall a few known facts about Hausdorff groups.

---

[1]) The notations $U_a U_b$ and $(U_a{}^{-1})$ are those of the calculus of complexes. According to this notation, if S and T are any non-vacuous subsets of G, ST denotes the (non-vacuous) set of products st [$s\varepsilon S$, $t\varepsilon T$], and S^{-1} the set of inverses s^{-1} [$s\varepsilon S$]. $S \cap T$ means the set-theoretic product of S and T.

[2]) A system of neighborhoods of a point is called „complete" if and only if every open set containing the point totally includes a suitable neighborhood of the system.

Any Hausdorff group G is homogeneous — the transformations T^x_y: $T^x_y(g) = xgy$ are a transitive group of homeomorphisms of G with itself. Again, the connected component of G containing the identity is a normal subgroup of G; the other connected components being the group-theoretic cosets of this normal subgroup.

And finally ([2], M. 7 and TG. 14), if G satisfies the second countability axiom of Hausdorff (i.e., the axiom that there exists a countable set of neighborhoods for G, a suitable subset of which forms a complete system for each point), it is known to be metrizible. In fact, if G is Abelian or compact, then the topologizing distance function can be so chosen as to be invariant under the group of transformations T^x_y of the preceding paragraph.

We now come to the proof, which is quite easy.

LEMMA: Let G be any Hausdorff group satisfying the first countability axiom. Then the identity *1* of G has a complete system of neighborhoods V_1, V_2, V_0, . . . with the properties (2) $V_k = V_k^{-1}$, and (2) $V_k^3 \equiv V_k V_k V_k \subset V_{k-1}$ [whence in particular, $V_1 \supset V_2 \supset V_3 \supset \ldots$].

PROOF: Let U_1, U_2, U_3, . . . be any countable complete system of neighborhoods of *1*. By HG2, the U_k^{-1} are open. Therefore the $W_k = U_k \cap U_k^{-1}$ form a system of neighborhoods of *1* which is also complete, having the property (1).

Again, one can define V_1, V_2, V_3, . . . from the rules (α) $V_1 = W_1$, and (β) V_{k+1} is the first W_i such that $W_i^3 \subset V_k \cap W_1 \cap \ldots \cap W_k$. It is obvious that this system exists, is complete, and satisfies both conditions of the Lemma.

THEOREM: A Hausdorff group G is metrizible if and only if it satisfies the first countability axion.

PROOF: That the condition is necessary is obvious. Therefore it is sufficient to prove that if G satisfies the first countability axiom, it is metrizible.

To prove this, add to the neighborhood system of the Lemma, the open set $V_0 = G$. Then define „ecart'' through the equation

$$\varrho(x, y) = \text{Inf}_{xy^{-1} \varepsilon V_k} (\tfrac{1}{2})^k.$$

Obviously $\varrho(x, x) = 0$, and $\varrho(x, y) > 0$ if $x \neq y$. Also obviously, the sets $U_e(a)$ of points x satisfying $\varrho(a, x) < e$ [$e > 0$] are a complete system of neighborhoods for any point a. Moreover since $V_k = V_k^{-1}$, $xy^{-1} \varepsilon V_k$ if and only if $yx^{-1} \varepsilon V_k$, whence $\varrho(x, y) = \varrho(y, x)$. And finally, since $V_h V_i V_j \subset V_k$ if $k > h, i, j$, one sees

(E) If $\varrho(x, y) < e$, $\varrho(y, y') < e$, and $\varrho(y', z) < e$, then $\varrho(x, z) < 2e$.

But Chittenden [1] has shown that it follows from these facts without reference to group properties, that G is metrizible, which completes the proof.

One can also avoid reference to Chittenden's argument by simply defining „distance" through the equation.

$$\varrho^*(x, y) = \operatorname{Inf}_{u_0 = x,\, u_n = y} \sum_{k=1}^{n} \varrho(u_{k-1}, u_k).$$

It is obvious that $\varrho^*(x, y)$ is symmetric and satisfies the triangle inequality. The proof is therefore complete if we can show that $\varrho^*(x, y)$ is topologically equivalent to $\varrho(x, y)$. But this follows from the inequalitites

$$\tfrac{1}{2}\varrho(x, y) \leqq \varrho^*(x, y) \leqq \varrho(x, y).$$

The second inequality is obvious; to prove the first, note that given $u_0 = x, u_1, u_2, \ldots, u_n = y$, if one makes the definition $|U| = \varrho(u_0, u_1) + \ldots + \varrho(u_{n-1}, u_n)$, one can always find h such that

$$\sum_{k=1}^{n} \varrho(u_{k-1}, u_k) \leqq \tfrac{1}{2} |U| \quad \text{and} \quad \sum_{k=h+1}^{n} \varrho(u_{k-1}, u_k) \leqq \tfrac{1}{2} U.$$

But evidently $\varrho(u_h, u_{h+1}) \leqq |U|$, and by induction on k $\varrho(x, u_h) \leqq \leqq |U|$ and $\varrho(u_{h+1}, y) \leqq |U|$. It follows by (E) that $\varrho(x, y) = 2\,|U|$, whence $|U| \geqq \frac{1}{2}\varrho(x, y)$, completing the proof.

Let us now call a homogeneous space „microseparable", when it contains a separable open set. We then have

Corollary 1: If G is microseparable and connected, then it is separable (satisfies Hausdorff's second countability axiom).

Proof: In metrizible spaces, the properties of being separable and of having everywhere dense sets are equivalent. Hence (by homogeneity), some neighborhood of the identity of G has a countable everywhere dense set. But G is connected, and so the (countable) finite products of the elements of this set are everywhere dense in G.

Corollary 2: If G is locally compact and satisfies the first countability axiom, then it satisfies the second.

Proof: A compact metric space is separable.

Corollary 2 permits one to replace the second countability axiom by the first in the assumption of a theorem of Freudenthal (3) on „end-points" of Hausdorff groups.

Society of Fellows, Harvard University.

(Received December 24th, 1935.)

BIBLIOGRAPHY:

[1] E. W. Chittenden, On the equivalence of ecart and voisinage [Trans. A. Math. Soc. **18** (1917), 161—166].

[2] D. van Dantzig, Zur topologischen Algebra, I [Math. Annalen **107** (1932), 587—616].

[3] H. Freudenthal, Über die Enden topologischer Räume und Gruppen [Math. Zeitschr. **33** (1931), 692—713].

[4] O. Schreier, Abstrakte kontinuierliche Gruppen [Abh. Hamb. **4** (1925), 15—32].

Reprinted from *Compositio Math.* **3** (1936), 427–430

LIE GROUPS SIMPLY ISOMORPHIC WITH NO LINEAR GROUP†

BY GARRETT BIRKHOFF

1. *Introduction.* One of the most interesting conjectures concerning finite continuous groups is the conjecture that every Lie group is topologically isomorphic with a group of matrices. The proof of this conjecture, even in the small, would establish the truth of the famous conjecture that every Lie group nucleus (or *germ*) is a piece of a Lie group.‡ This makes it of interest to know that there exist Lie groups in the large, simply isomorphic even in the purely algebraic sense—and a fortiori topologically isomorphic in the large—with no group of matrices. It is to the proof of this fact that the present note is devoted.

2. *The Basic Lemma.* The proof ultimately rests on the following lemma.

LEMMA 1. *Let* Γ *be any group of linear transformations. Suppose* Γ *contains elements* S *and* T *whose commutator* $R=S^{-1}T^{-1}ST$ *is of prime order* p, *and satisfies* $SR=RS$, $TR=RT$. *Then* Γ *is of degree at least* p.

By the *degree* of Γ is meant the *dimensions*—that is, the maximum number of linearly independent elements—of the linear space Σ on which Γ operates. The vector elements of Σ will be written $x, y, z, \cdots$.

PROOF. Since R is of order p, Σ contains a vector x such that $Rx=\alpha x$, where α is a primitive pth root of unity.§ Now let Λ denote the linear subspace of *all* vectors $x\epsilon\Sigma$ satisfying $Rx=\alpha x$. If $x\epsilon\Lambda$, then

$$R(Sx) = S(Rx) = S(\alpha x) = \alpha(Sx).$$

---

† Presented to the Society, September 3, 1936.

‡ For a fuller description of the status of these conjectures, see [3], especially §17. See also [1], p. 24, middle.

Numbers in square brackets refer to the Bibliography at the end of this paper.

§ This follows from [4], Theorem 125.

That is, $Sx \in \Lambda$, showing that S, and likewise T, transforms Λ into itself.

But now observe that *within* Λ, $S^{-1}T^{-1}ST = \alpha I$ (where I denotes the identical matrix), whence $T^{-1}ST = S$. But $T^{-1}ST$ and S have (see [**4**], Theorem 126) the same characteristic roots; hence so do S and αS, as linear transformations of Λ. Moreover since S is non-singular, its characteristic roots are not zero; hence it has at least p characteristic roots

$$\mu_0, \alpha\mu_0, \cdots, \alpha^{p-1}\mu_0, \qquad (\mu_0 \neq 0).$$

It follows that Λ, and therefore Σ, has at least p dimensions.

3. *The Main Theorem*. With the help of this lemma, one can easily exhibit a Lie group† simply isomorphic with no linear group. Let G_3 denote the group of all matrices

$$M(x, y, z) = \begin{pmatrix} 1 & x & z \\ 0 & 1 & y \\ 0 & 0 & 1 \end{pmatrix}.$$

And let N denote the discrete normal subgroup of matrices $M(0, 0, n)$, n any integer. Finally, let $G_3^* = G_3/N$.

THEOREM 1. *G_3^* is a Lie group simply isomorphic with no linear group.*

PROOF. That G_3^* is a Lie group can be verified directly, and also follows from general principles (see [**1**], p. 12). It remains to show that it is simply isomorphic with no linear group. But let p be any prime; then the images S of $M(1, 0, 0)$ and T of $M(0, 1/p, 0)$ both commute with $R = S^{-1}T^{-1}ST$, which is the image of $M(0, 0, 1/p)$ in G_3, while R is of order p. Hence by Lemma 1 any linear group simply isomorphic with G_3^* would have to be of degree at least p, and since p can be *any* prime, this is absurd.

COROLLARY. *No group having G_3^* as a subgroup is simply isomorphic with a linear group.*

REMARK 1. Since G_3 was a linear group, we see that there can

† By a *Lie group* we shall mean a *connected finite continuous group* in the usual sense; *mixed* groups will be excluded. See [**1**], p. 7.

exist no construction yielding, from representations of a given group as a linear group, non-trivial representations of its homomorphic images as linear groups.

REMARK 2. As all the two-parameter Lie groups are known ([**1**], p. 25), and can be realized in the large as linear groups, G_3^* is the simplest example of a group isomorphic in the large with no linear group.

4. *Additional Definitions.* In §§4–6 we shall show how to find whole families of Lie groups simply isomorphic with no linear group. But in order to do this, we shall need to recall some familiar parts of group theory.

By the *central* of a Lie group G is meant the set of all elements of G commuting with all other elements; this is a topologically closed and invariant subgroup of G.

Every Lie group G has a *Lie algebra* A, defined from the set of the infinitesimal generators $U, V, \cdots$ of G by regarding commutation (the taking of Poisson brackets) as a non-associative multiplication. Two Lie groups are locally isomorphic if and only if they have isomorphic Lie algebras ([**2**], [32.2]).

We shall call G *hypercentral* if and only if the associated Lie algebra is *nilpotent*, in the sense that all products of sufficient length r reduce to zero. This terminology is justified since G is hypercentral if and only if, denoting by Z_1 the subgroup of G consisting of the identity 0, and by Z_{k+1}/Z_k inductively the central of G/Z_k, we have $Z_r=G$. (Actually, Z_k contains the invariant sub-algebra A_{r-k} of A consisting of linear combinations of products of lengths $\geqq(r-k)$.)

REMARK. Any Lie group of *triangular* matrices $A=\|a_{ij}\|$ satisfying $a_{ii}=1$ and $a_{ij}=0$ if $i>j$ is hypercentral. All Poisson brackets of length exceeding its degree vanish.

5. *A Theorem of Linear Groups.* We shall now prove a result of some intrinsic interest,† which will be used in the sequel.

THEOREM 2. *Let U, V, W be any three matrices which satisfy $UV-VU=W$, $UW=WU$, $VW=WV$. Then the matrices $M(\lambda, \lambda', \lambda'')=\exp(\lambda U+\lambda' V+\lambda'' W)$ form a group H, topologically isomorphic in the large with G_3.*

† Theorem 2 is especially interesting as U, V, W have the formal properties of the position, momentum, and scalar operators p, q, $qp-pq$ of quantum mechanics.

EXPLANATION. As is customary,† we use the notation

$$\exp X = I + X + \frac{1}{2!} X^2 + \frac{1}{3!} X^3 + \cdots .$$

PROOF. Since for any X, $[\exp X] \circ [\exp(-X)] = I$, and since in H one can prove the special identity

$$(1) \qquad M(\lambda, \lambda', \lambda'') \circ M(\mu, \mu', \mu'') = M(\lambda + \mu, \lambda' + \mu', \lambda'' + \mu'' - \lambda'\mu),$$

clearly H is a group. Further, (1) exhibits a continuous homomorphism‡ of G_3 into H, since (1) expresses the rule for matrix multiplication in G_3.

We shall show that this is a topological isomorphism, in other words, that if $M(\lambda_n, \lambda_n', \lambda_n'') \equiv M_n \to M(\lambda, \lambda', \lambda'')$, then $\lambda_n \to \lambda$, $\lambda_n' \to \lambda'$, and $\lambda_n'' \to \lambda''$. By group-homogeneity, it is sufficient to prove this for the special case $\lambda = \lambda' = \lambda'' = 0$, $M(\lambda, \lambda', \lambda'') = I$. This is what we shall do.

The kernel of the demonstration is a well known theorem of Lie ([**2**], p. 163) which shows that one can so transform the matrices of H that the generating matrices $U = \|u_{ij}\|$ and $V = \|v_{ij}\|$ are *triangular*, that is, satisfy $u_{ij} = v_{ij} = 0$, if $i > j$. But now computing the matrix $W = UV - VU = \|w_{ij}\|$, we see that $w_{ij} = 0$ unless $(j - i) \geqq 1$, while it is easily verified to be a general property of matrix multiplication, that if Y and Z are any two matrices such that $y_{ij} = 0$ unless $(j - i) \geqq \alpha_1$, and $z_{ij} = 0$ unless $(j - i) \geqq \alpha_2$, and $X = YZ$, then $x_{ij} = 0$ unless $(j - i) \geqq \alpha_1 + \alpha_2$. It is a corollary that the non-zero coefficients of W nearest the principal diagonal, that is, minimizing $(j - i)$ subject to $w_{ij} \neq 0$, appear as $\lambda'' w_{ij}$ in $\exp(\lambda'' W)$, and so the subgroup of the $\exp(\lambda'' W)$ is topologically isomorphic in the large with the translation-group $x \to x + t$.

Unless $\lambda_n \to 0$, we can, taking a suitable subsequence, assume without loss of generality that $1/\lambda_n = \bar{\lambda}_n \to \bar{\lambda}$. But irrespective of n,

$$M_n^{-1} \circ \exp(-\bar{\lambda}_n V) \circ M_n \circ \exp(\bar{\lambda}_n V) = \exp W \neq I;$$

† See J. von Neumann, Mathematische Zeitschrift, vol. 30 (1929), pp. 3–42.

‡ For the distinction between continuous homomorphisms and topological isomorphisms see H. Freudenthal, *Einige Sätze über topologische Gruppen*, Annals of Mathematics, vol. 37 (1936), p. 46.

while on the other hand, $M_n \to I$, exp $(\bar\lambda_n V) \to$ exp $(\bar\lambda V)$, and $I^{-1} \circ \exp(-\bar\lambda V) \circ I \circ \exp(\bar\lambda V) = I$. Since group multiplication and passage to the inverse are continuous operations, this is absurd.

This proves $\lambda_n \to 0$; similarly $\lambda_n' \to 0$. Hence it follows that exp $(\lambda_n'' W) \to I$, whence by the preceding paragraph $\lambda_n'' \to 0$, which completes the proof.

Remark. It is a corollary of §5 alone that G_3^* is topologically isomorphic in the large with no linear group. (For its generators satisfy the hypotheses of Theorem 2.)

6. *The Extended Theorem.* Using Theorems 1 and 2, one can exhibit without difficulty a whole class of Lie groups simply isomorphic with no linear group. First we note an almost obvious lemma.

Lemma 2. *Any non-Abelian hypercentral Lie group G has infinitesimal generators U, V, W satisfying $[U, V] = W$ and $[X, W] = 0$ for every X.*

Proof. Since G is not Abelian, U_0 and V_0 exist satisfying $[U_0, V_0] = V_1 \neq 0$. Moreover either $[X, V_1] = 0$ for every X, or $[U_1, V_1] = V_2 \neq 0$ for some infinitesimal generator U_1. But since the Lie algebra of G is nilpotent, the latter alternative cannot recur indefinitely, and so we finally get elements U_q and V_q such that $[U_q, V_q] = V_{q+1}$, while $[X, V_{q+1}] = 0$ for every X.

Lemma 3. *Any non-Abelian hypercentral Lie group G of matrices has a subgroup S_3 whose central lies in the central of G, topologically isomorphic in the large with G_3.*

Proof. By Lemma 1, the U, V, and W of Lemma 2 generate a subgroup S_3 topologically isomorphic in the large with G_3, whose central therefore consists of the exp (λW). But since the exp (λW) commute with all the infinitesimal generators X of G, and G (being connected) is generated by these, the exp (λW) lie in the central of G.

Theorem 3. *Any non-Abelian hypercentral Lie group G of matrices is locally topologically isomorphic with a Lie group G/N which is simply isomorphic with no linear group.*

Proof. Refer to Lemma 3, and let N be the subgroup of the

exp (nW), n any integer. Then N is a discrete subgroup of the central of G, and so (see [1], p. 12) G/N is a Lie group locally topologically isomorphic with G.

But the homomorphism $G \rightarrow G/N$ carries S_3 into S_3/N, which is simply isomorphic with $G_3/N = G_3^*$. This and the corollary to Theorem 1 complete the proof.

E. Cartan [5] has shown that the universal covering group of the group of projective transformations of the line is topologically isomorphic in the large with no linear group.

BIBLIOGRAPHY

[1] E. Cartan, *Théorie des groupes finis et continus et l'analysis situs*, Mémorial des Sciences Mathématiques, no. 42, 1930.

[2] L. P. Eisenhart, *Continuous Groups of Transformations*, 1933.

[3] W. Mayer and T. Y. Thomas, *Foundations of the theory of continuous groups*, Annals of Mathematics, vol. 36 (1935), pp. 770–822.

[4] A. Speiser, *Gruppentheorie*, 2d ed., 1927.

[5] *La Topologie des Groupes de Lie*, Paris, 1936, p. 18.

Society of Fellows, Harvard University

Reprinted from *Bull. Am. Math. Soc.* **42** (1936), 883–888

Continuous groups and linear spaces

Garrett Birkhoff (Cambridge, Mass.)

1. The geometrical classification of continuous groups. Perhaps the best way to introduce the subject of continuous groups, is to say briefly what an abstract continuous group is.

In a general way, by an abstract continuous group is meant a system whose elements are simultaneously the points of a geometrical manifold and the symbols of an abstract group, and whose group operations determine smooth functions of the group manifold to itself.

By letting the geometry of the group manifold suggest the meaning of smoothness, one is led to a purely geometrical basis for classifying continuous groups.

Thus, in groups whose manifolds are L-spaces in the sense of Fréchet[1], it is natural to regard smoothness as meaning

LG1: If $x_k \to x$ and $y_k \to y$, then $x_k y_k \to xy$.

LG2: If $x_k \to x$, then $x^{-1} \to x^{-1}$.

This is, of course, Schreier's definition of the class of L-groups.

Again, in groups whose manifolds are Hausdorff spaces, it is natural to regard smoothness as meaning continuity in the sense that

HG1: If U_{xy} is any neighborhood ot the group product xy, then there exist neighborhoods U_x of x and V_y of y, such that $uv \varepsilon U_{xy}$ for every $u \varepsilon U_x$, $v \varepsilon V_y$.

HG2: If $U_{x^{-1}}$ is any neighborhood of the group inverse x^{-1}, then there exists a neighborhood U_x of x, such that $u \varepsilon U_x$ implies $u^{-1} \varepsilon U_{x^{-1}}$. This is the usual definition of a topological group.

Consider now groups whose manifolds are n-dimensional varieties. It is obvious that „smoothness" has a stronger meaning here than in the preceding cases, and refers to analytical properties such as approximate invariance of vector differences under pre- and past-multiplication by small elements, differentiability, etc. This leads one to the usual definition of Lie groups.

These facts suggest trying to define similar classes of groups, using for the basic class of group manifolds some class of infinite-dimensional linear spaces, such as Hilbert space, or the class of Banach spaces, or still more generally the class of topological linear spaces [including, for example, the space (s) of infinite sequences].

---

[1] That is, spaces in which convergence is defined, and assumed to have certain rudimentary properties of ordinary convergence.

2. Groups whose manifolds are Banach spaces. My attempts to define such more extensive classes of groups have led me to formulate the following principle:

Most properties of Lie groups are equally true of continuous groups whose manifolds are (locally) Banach spaces.

By a „Banach space" is meant, of course, any linear space having a metric distance function which is 1) invariant under all parallel translations, 2) multiplied by $|\lambda|$ when each element is multiplied by the scalar constant λ, 3) metrically complete[1].

The most direct way to show the truth of this principle seems to be to abandon analytical methods, and to rely instead on arguments which involve only formal identities [of which the simplest example is the identity $(xy)^{-1}=y^{-1}x^{-1}$] and passage to the limit. Properties whose existence can be demonstrated by such arguments are clearly invariant under continuous isomorphisms, and it is, therefore, proper to characterize the arguments themselves as topologico-algebraic, since they involve only topology and algebra.

In order to show the lines followed by such arguments in the general case of groups whose manifolds are Banach spaces, I should first like to digress to point out how very easy it is to recast the theory of Lie groups so that it involves only questions of topological algebra.

How far removed this is from the original viewpoint of Lie may be inferred from the fact that for some time it was not thought essential that a group should contain the inverse of its transformations, or believed that passage to the inverse was an intrinsic group operation.

3. Topologico-algebraic theory of Lie groups. The recasting of the theory of Lie groups in topologico-algebraic form depends on rocognizing other operations than the two (group multiplication and passage to the inverse) just mentioned as intrinsic.

The first such operation is raising to a scalar power. It is well-known that, within restricted neighborhoods of the identity 1 of any Lie group G, the equation $x^n = a$ has one and only one solution x for fixed a and non-zero integer n. Hence $x^m = a^{\frac{m}{n}}$ is also uniquely determined. By rational approximation and passage to the limit, one sees that the operation of raising a given element a to a given scalar power a^λ is an operation uniquely determined by the algebra and the topology of G.

Using this fact, it is easy to state the definition

$$x \oplus y = \lim_{\lambda\to 0} (x^\lambda y^\lambda)^{\frac{1}{\lambda}}. \tag{3,1}$$

The existence of $x \oplus y$ (again, for sufficiently small x and y) is also well-known. In fact $x \oplus y$ simply corresponds to the vector sum of x and y under canonical parameters.

Furthermore, if one defines

$$\lambda x = x^\lambda \tag{3,2}$$

then all the usual rules of the vector calculus hold with respect to the newly defined vector sums and scalar products. This is obvious, since canonical parameters map G onto a region about the origin of a vector space.

---

[1] I. e., a Banach space is a „B-space" or „complete normed vector space" in the sense of S. Banach, Théorie des opérations linéaires, Warsaw, 1932.

And finally, one can define the binary operation of „commutation" through the identity

$$[x, y] = \lim_{\lambda \to 0} (x^{\lambda} y^{\lambda} x^{-\lambda} y^{-\lambda})^{\frac{1}{\lambda}}. \tag{3, 3}$$

Now by selecting any basis of linearly independent elements $x_1, \ldots, x_n$ one gets the constants of structure of G from the equations

$$[x_i, x_j] = c_1^{ij} x_1 + \ldots + c_n^{ij} x_n. \tag{3, 4}$$

Since G is determined to within analytical isomorphism by its constants of structure, one concludes that it is indeed true that the characteristic properties of abstract Lie groups are topologico-algebraic.

4. Topologico-algebraic definition of Lie groups. Incidentally, it is a truth not generally realized, that if one admits the operations which have just been defined on the postulational level, then one can very easily define finite continuous groups in purely topologico-algebraic terms. One need merely postulate the existence of group products xy and (locally) of scalar powers $x^{\lambda} = \lambda x$. Then by asserting that $x \oplus y$ as defined in (3,1) exists, and postulating those rules of the vector calculus which cannot be proved from the definition, one clearly has a representation of a group on a vector space V. It is now easy to postulate finite dimensionality and twice differentiability of the „function of composition" $u(x, y) = xy$. This implies that one has a[1] canonically represented Lie group, and completes the definition.

This definition has, of course, no bearing on Hilbert's problem, of determining whether there are L-groups in the sense defined earlier, whose manifolds are homeomorphic with Riemannian varieties, which are not continuously isomorphic with Lie groups. It is known from results of von Neumann and van Kampen, that if such groups exist, they are neither compact nor commutative.

5. Known infinite continuous groups. Now, let us consider some of the known groups which, although not Lie groups, are known to have analytical properties — which is the same as saying that they have been regarded as mapped locally on linear spaces.

One class of such groups consists of the infinite continuous groups of analytical transformations

$$x_i' = f_i(x_1', \ldots, x_n') \quad (i = 1, \ldots, n)$$

of n-dimensional varieties studied by Lie and Cartan[2]. Among such groups may be mentioned: the group of all analytical deformations of n-dimensional space, the subgroups of all conformal respectively volume-preserving analytical deformations, and so on.

Another class consists of the groups of linear operators on Hilbert space more recently studied by Delsarte[3]. Among such groups may be mentioned: the group of

[1] In view of the known theorem that any such group with a twice differentiable function of composition is a Lie group.

[2] S. Lie, Unendliche Transformationsgruppen, „Leipz. Ber.", 1891. É. Cartan. Sur la structure des groupes infinis de transformations, „Ann. Éc. Norm.", **21**, (1904), 153—206, and **22**, (1905), 219—308.

[3] J. Delsarte, Les groupes de transformations linéaires dans l'espace de Hilbert, „Mém. Sci. Math.", Fasc. 57, (1932).

all bounded operators, the group of all unitary operators, and the „Fredholm" group of all transformations T:

$$T[f(x)]=f(x)+\int_0^1 K(x,y)f(y)\,dy,$$

on the space of functions of class L_2, for which

$$\int_0^1\int_0^1 [K(x,y)]^2\,dx\,dy<+\infty.$$

Now it is a plain fact that the manifold of none of these groups has been defined in the literature. No mathematician has hitherto defined even the meaning of the convergence $T_n \to T$ of a sequence of transformations T_n to the limit T — in other words, not even the topology of the group manifolds has been defined.

That this is a serious omission, is evident from the fact that if one adopts the usual definition of continuity, then the corresponding abstract groups are not[1] in general even L-groups! Hence it is fair to say that no adequate definition, let alone theory, of infinite continuous groups exists at the present time. This is doubly true since hitherto no connection has been traced between the symbols for the so-called „infinitesimal transformations" of infinite continuous groups, and actual group elements.

6. Proposed mapping on linear spaces. Nevertheless, it is not difficult to propose ways of mapping the above groups on linear spaces which are highly suggestive — at least yield topological groups — and exhibit those analytical properties which are known.

Thus in the case of groups of analytical transformations of n-dimensional varieties it is appropriate to define continuity as meaning simultaneous continuity in the coefficients of the formal power series expressing the transformations. This is even more obvious with the group S_n of all formal substitutions T of the form

$$[T(x)]_i=\sum_j a_{ij}x_j+\sum_{jk} a_{ijk}x_jx_k+\sum_{jkl} a_{ijkl}x_jx_kx_l+\ldots$$

Again, in the case of the group of all unitary operators — or more generally of all bounded linear operators with inverses — on Hilbert space, one naturally defines the „distance" $[T-U]$ between two operators to be the modulus of their difference. While in the case of the „Fredholm" group, it is natural to define the „distance" between two such transformations as the integral of the squared absolute value of the difference between the corresponding „kernels" $K(x,y)$.

The first two group manifolds are easily recognized as pieces of the so-called[2] space (s) of infinite sequences. The third is a Banach space, but not a Hilbert space; the manifold of the Fredholm group is Hilbert space itself.

7. Regular continuous groups. Since the third and fourth group manifolds are Banach spaces, the general principle which I announced earlier would lead one to expect that the corresponding groups would have most of the properties of Lie groups. This is true, and I should like to state now in somewhat greater detail what can be proved on entirely general grounds.

[1] Cf. my paper „The topology of transformation-sets", „Annals of Math.", **35**, (1934), 870, Theorem 19.

[2] Banach, op. t., p. 10.

The assumptions from which the properties are proved can be stated as follows:

R1: G is an abstract group, a region R about whose identity is also (relative to a suitable coordinate system) regarded as a region about the origin of a Banach space.

R2: Given $\mu > 0$, there exists $\delta > 0$ so small that if $|x| < \delta$ and $|y| < \delta$, then $|(g-h)-(xgy-xhy)| \leq \mu \cdot |g-h|$. Assumption R2 amounts to saying that the translation-group of the group manifold approximately preserves vector differences. I shall for convenience call any group which satisfies R1—R2 a „regular continuous group".

Theorem 1. *Any regular continuous group G is a fortiori a topological continuous group. Moreover, its topology and its group multiplication table uniquely determine the following operations: $\lambda x = x^\lambda$ (called canonical scalar multiplication by λ respectively raising to the power λ), $x \oplus y$ (called canonical addition) and $[x, y]$ (called commutation).*

The definition of these operations is the same as in the case of Lie groups, and has been stated already [cf. (3,1)—(3,3)].

Theorem 2. *There is a unique way of remapping G on its original Banach coordinate-space in such a way that 1) vector differences near the origin are approximately invariant, 2) canonical addition and canonical scalar multiplication become vector addition and scalar multiplication of coordinates. This remapping is uniquely determined by properties 1), 2); it is also uniquely determined by 1) and the formal identity $\lambda x \cdot \mu x = (\lambda + \mu) x$. It will be called the „canonical" mapping of G.*

Theorem 3. *Under canonical mapping, the commutation operator $[x, y]$ is a bounded bilinear operator satisfying $[x, y] = -[y, x]$ and Jacobi's identity*

$$[x, [y, z]] + [y, [z, x]] + [z, [x, y]] = 0.$$

Theorem 4. *Under canonical mapping, the „function of composition" $u(x,y) = xy$ is an analytical function of x and y (regarded as elements of the Banach coordinate space). This function is definable by explicit series whose terms involve only multiple commutators (i. e., expressions like $[x, [[y, x], y]]$) — and so are polynomials.*

Moreover, new and easily remembered algebraic algorithms enable one to calculate such a series at will; if one prefers, one can accomplish the same end by a geometrical process.

It is a corollary of theorem 4 that the operation of commutation determines the group multiplication table locally; this suggests that the usual converse of Lie's third fundamental theorem can be extended to Lie algebras defined in Banach spaces.

8. Constructions used in proof. There is not time enough to give the full proof of these theorems here. Nevertheless, the methods and constructions involved may at least be outlined; actually, the details are not very difficult to supply.

A preliminary simplification results from making a change of scale. By multiplying the norm function by a sufficiently large constant factor, one can assume 1) that R contains the entire sphere S: $|x| < 1$, and 2) that within S

$$|(g-h)-(xgy-xhy)| \leq \frac{1}{100} |g-h|. \tag{8,1}$$

Attention is then confined to the interior of S.

It is a corollary of (8,1) that if in a group product $w_1 w_2 w_3 \ldots w_M$, $v_k = w_k + u_k$ is substituted for each w_k, then the product $v_1 v_2 v_3 \ldots v_M$ is

$$w_1 w_2 w_3 \dots w_M + (u_1 + \dots + u_M) \text{ to within } \frac{1}{100}[|u_1| + \dots + |u_M|].$$

Moreover, by R2 if $\sum_{k=1}^{M} |w_k|$ and $\sum_{k=1}^{M} |u_k|$ are sufficiently small, then

$$|(w_1 \dots w_M) + (u_1 + \dots + u_M) - (v_1 \dots v_M)| \leq \mu [|u_1| + \dots + |u_M|] \quad (8,2)$$

where μ can be made as small as desired.

One can then assign to each subdivision Δ of any path X: $x = x(\lambda)$ $[0 \leq \lambda \leq \Lambda]$ of length less than one-half and issuing from the origin, a relative „value" $v_\Delta(X)$. Namely, if the points of subdivision of X are in order

$$x_0 = x(0), \; x_1 = x(\lambda_1), \dots, \; x_n = x(\Lambda) \quad [0 \leq \lambda_1 \leq \dots \leq \Lambda]$$

then one defines $v_\Delta(x)$ as the group product

$$(x_1 - x_0)(x_2 - x_1)(x_3 - x_2) \dots (x_n - x_{n-1}).$$

It follows from (8,2) that $v_\Delta(X)$ converges to a limit $v(X)$ as the maximum of the $|x_k - x_{k-1}|$ tends to zero. Let us call $v(X)$ the „value" of X, and two paths with the same value „equivalent".

The canonical remapping of G can now be defined as the correspondence mapping each element x of G onto the value of the straight ray drawn from the origin to x.

Lemma. *The canonical remapping approximately preserves vector differences and is one-one.*

Proof. That it approximately preserves vector differences is a corollary of (8,2), as may be seen by setting $w_k = w$, $u_k = u$, and $v_k = v$ irrespective of k; a fortiori, distinct points have distinct images. Moreover, the origin is a fixed point under the remapping; and — using (8,2) — one can order to any two points x and y_n a point y_{n+1} mapped 100 times as near x as y_n. Using successive approximation and completeness, we see that each point is the exact image under the remapping of a suitable antecedent, completing the proof.

With this lemma at our command, it is no trick at all to display the various operations referred to in theorem 1 as topologico-algebraic invariant operations, or to prove theorem 2.

For example, under the canonical remapping, $x^n = nx$ almost by definition; it is a corollary of the approximate preservation of vector differences that $y^n = a$ has a unique solution y in G, and that scalar powers x^λ can be defined by rational approximation as topologico-algebraic invariants.

Again, by use of (8,2) and some purely algebraic identities worked out recently by P. Hall [1] in connection with finite groups, one can show that

$$|(x^m y^n x^{-m} y^{-n}) - mn(xyx^{-1}y^{-1})| \leq \frac{mn}{100} \cdot |x| \cdot |y|.$$

Hall's identities can be interpreted geometrically as the breaking up of a path integral around a parallelogram of sides $m\alpha$ and $n\beta$ into integrals around mn parallelograms of sides α and β (this is analogous to the usual proof of Stokes' theorem). From

[1] „A contribution to the theory of groups of prime-power orders", „Proc. Lond. Math. Soc.", **36**, (1933), 29–95.

this it follows that the commutation operation $[x, y]$ defined in (3,3) exists, and has a modulus at most one hundredth (regarded as a bilinear operator).

Finally, an explicit expansion for the function of composition $u(x, y)$ can be obtained purely algebraically by writing

$$\begin{aligned} xy &= \left(\frac{1}{n}x\right)^n \left(\frac{1}{n}y\right)^n = \\ &= \left[\left(\frac{1}{n}x\right)\left(\frac{1}{n}y\right)\right]^n \cdot R_1 = \\ &= \left[\left(\frac{1}{n}x\right)\left(\frac{1}{n}y\right)\left(x^{\frac{1}{n}}y^{\frac{1}{n}}x^{-\frac{1}{n}}y^{-\frac{1}{n}}\right)^{\frac{n}{2}}\right]^n \cdot R_2 = \\ &= \ldots \end{aligned}$$

where the residues R_k can be made arbitrarily small by selecting n and k both sufficiently large. By letting n tend to infinity, we get an explicit expansion

$$xy = x + y + \frac{1}{2}[x, y] + \ldots$$

for xy. The essential algorithm involved consists in ordering commutators according to their „weight"; using this, Hall has obtained a related expansion for $(xy)^n$ in terms of powers of x, y, and their commutators. I shall not attempt even to indicate the proof of convergence.

9. Alternative definitions of regular continuous groups. One can also give alternative definitions of regular continuous groups, which will perhaps make clearer exactly which systems belong to the class.

In the first place, let G be any abstract group, a region about whose identity is so mapped onto a region about the origin of a Banach space B that the function of composition $u(x, y) = xy$ is continuously differentiable[1]. It follows since $x \cdot 1 = 1 \cdot x = x$ that the total derivatives of $u(x, y)$ at $x = y = 1$ reduce to the identical linear transformation. Hence, the continuity even at $x = y = 1$ of the total derivative of $u(x, y)$ implies R2, and so G is a regular continuous group.

And secondly, one may interpret regular continuous groups as generalized Banach spaces. For this purpose addition must be regarded as a special kind of group multiplication, and scalar multiplication as raising to a power. With this understanding, one can weaken the usual postulates for Banach space in such a way that the class of systems satisfying the weakened postulates is precisely the class of regular continuous groups. I shall not try to state the exact postulates; the main changes consist in replacing the assumption of commutativity of vector addition by approximate commutativity, and the distributivity of scalar multiplication with respect to vector addition by approximate distributivity.

This shows in particular that Banach spaces constitute the class of commutative, simply connected regular continuous groups. In a similar way, Lie groups constitute the class of locally compact regular continuous groups.

10. Groups whose manifolds are spaces (s). I think that what I have said shows conclusively that regular continuous groups — that is, abstract continuous groups whose manifolds are Banach spaces — have most of the properties of Lie groups.

[1] In the sense of M. Fréchet, La notion de différentielles dans l'analyse générale, «Ann. Éc. Norm.», (3), 42, (1925), 293–323.

I should like to conclude by pointing out how the theory ot continuous groups mapped locally on the space (s) of infinite sequences differs from the theory of regular continuous groups.

One important difference is purely geometrical. One cannot integrate distance differentials, even along straight line segments. This means that the manifolds of such groups — unlike the manifolds of groups mapped locally on Banach spaces — cannot even be regarded as generalized Finsler spaces. Hence, one cannot define „rectifiable" curves along which to integrate a group value.

An even more essential difference is that the operation of raising an element x to a fractional power is no longer locally single-valued in such groups.

To see this, let a_θ denote a rigid rotation through a small angle θ, of the circumference of the unit circle, and suppose $a_{\frac{1}{2}\theta}$ were the only solution of the equation $x^2 = a_\theta$. Then $ta_\theta = a_\theta t$ would have to imply $ta_{\frac{1}{2}\theta} = a_{\frac{1}{2}\theta}t$. For under these assumptions,

$$(t^{-1}a_{\frac{1}{2}\theta}t)^2 = t^{-1}(a_{\frac{1}{2}\theta})^2 t = t^{-1}a_\theta t = a_\theta .$$

But this is false, for arbitrarily small t; periodicity of period θ does not imply periodicity of period $\frac{1}{2}\theta$.

Hence one cannot possibly establish canonical parameters in the usual sense, or extend the usual proof that isomorphism between infinitesimal transformations with respect to commutation (i. e., „structure-isomorphism") implies local isomorphism between finite group elements.

It seems fruitless, therefore, to try to extend the theory of Lie groups *directly* to groups such as the group of all substitutions in formal power series. It seems that it may be much more fruitful to study such groups *indirectly*, as *combinations* of regular continuous groups.

I am intending to make such a study, starting with the fact that the group just mentioned, all known topological linear spaces, and many other continuous groups are continuously isomorphic with subgroups of (in other words, can be *embedded* in) finite or infinite direct products of regular continuous groups.

Непрерывные группы и линейные пространства

Гаррет Биркхоф (Кэмбридж, С. Ш. А.)

(Резюме)

Рассматривается полная топологическая группа с элементами $x, y, z, \ldots$ Постулируется для достаточно малой окрестности нуля существование и единственность степеней x^λ при любых действительных λ и существование пределов

$$\lim_{\lambda \to 0} (x^\lambda y^\lambda)^{\frac{1}{\lambda}} = x + y.$$

Допускается, что операции $x + y$ и $\lambda x = x^\lambda$ удовлетворяют аксиомам векторных пространств. В топологических группах такого типа сохраняется значительная часть классической теории Ли.

ANNALS OF MATHEMATICS
Vol. 38, No. 2, April, 1937

REPRESENTABILITY OF LIE ALGEBRAS AND LIE GROUPS BY MATRICES

BY GARRETT BIRKHOFF

(Received September 14, 1936)

1. **Introduction.** Let A be any associative hypercomplex algebra over any commutative field F. If one defines in A *alternants* $[xy]$ by setting

$$[xy] = yx - xy$$

then with respect to the (generally non-associative) "products" $[xy]$, the elements of A form a new hypercomplex algebra $L(A)$ over F. Moreover it is easy to verify the well-known identities of Lie-Jacobi in $L(A)$, namely

$$[xy] + [yx] = 0 \qquad [[xy]z] + [[yz]x] + [[zx]y] = 0.$$

Hypercomplex algebras satisfying these identities are usually called "Lie algebras," and it is clear that every module (= linear subset) in A which contains the alternant of any two of its members, forms a Lie algebra.

The first main result proved below is that (Theorem 1) conversely every Lie algebra can be obtained in this way.

But the result is defective in that, although $L(A)$ is of finite order whenever A is, it is not proved that every Lie algebra L of finite order can be obtained from an associative algebra of finite order. In other words, it is not proved that every such L can be represented isomorphically by finite matrices. This problem is of course by Lie's Third Fundamental Theorem equivalent in the cases that F is the real resp. complex field to the classical question: is every Lie group nucleus G isomorphic locally[1] with a group nucleus of matrices?

The main result bearing on this problem which has been proved hitherto is due to Lie, and states that in case G has a discrete central, it is locally isomorphic with the group of linear transformations which its inner automorphisms induce on its infinitesimal elements (its so-called "adjoint" group). It is known[2] that this corresponds to the statement that any Lie algebra L of finite order which possesses no element a satisfying $[xa] = 0$ for all x can be obtained from an "adjoint" associative algebra of finite order.

The second new result proved below is the fact that (Theorem 4) in the

[1] It is known (cf. infra) that there exist Lie groups not isomorphic in the large with any group of finite matrices. The reader's attention is called to a paper of I. Ado (Russian) in the Bull. physico-math. society of Kazan 6 (1935), which contains the theorem that every Lie algebra over the real or complex field is isomorphic with a Lie algebra of matrices.

[2] N. Jacobson, "Rational methods in the theory of Lie algebras," Annals of Math. 36 (1935), 875–81.

extreme opposite case that L is *nilpotent,* it can be obtained from a nilpotent associative algebra of finite order. And using this it is proved that (Theorem 6) any "hypercentral" Lie group nucleus is locally isomorphic with a simply connected Lie group of matrices—whence the universal covering group of any "hypercentral" Lie group is topologically isomorphic with a Lie group of matrices.

2. **Canonical polynomials and "straightening".** Let L be any Lie algebra, and let us suppose that $e_1, e_2, e_3, \cdots$ constitute a basis of linearly independent elements of L, well-ordered in some fixed way.[3] Further, let the rule for commutation in L be expressed by the equations

$$[e_i e_j] = \sum_k c_k^{ij} e_k.$$

Since we are in the realm of pure algebra, all sums considered are finite.

Now suppose A is any associative algebra containing L and generated by the elements of L. Since A is generated by L, any element of A can be written as a polynomial—that is, linear combination of products $\xi = e_{i(1)} \cdots e_{i(q)}$— in the e_i.

Suppose now we call a "straightening" of any polynomial, a substitution for one of its terms $\xi = e_{i(1)} \cdots e_{i(q)}$ of the *equal* element

$$e_{i(1)} \cdots e_{i(j-1)} e_{i(j+1)} e_{i(j)} e_{i(j+2)} \cdots e_{i(q)} + \sum_k c_k^{i(j+1)\,i(j)} e_{i(1)} \cdots e_{i(j-1)} e_k e_{i(j+2)} \cdots e_{i(q)}$$

in case $i(j + 1) < i(j)$.

It is clear that after at most $\frac{1}{2}q(q - 1)$ straightenings, one can replace any such product ξ by an equal polynomial $\xi^* + \sum_k a_k \xi_k$, where ξ^* is a product of the same degree as ξ and has the "canonical" form

$$e_{h(1)}^{p1} \cdots e_{h(r)}^{p_r} \qquad [h(1) < \cdots < h(r)]$$

and the ξ_k are products of lower degree. Hence, by induction

LEMMA 1: *After being straightened, any element of A can be shown to be equal to a linear combination of canonical power-products of the e_i.*

Observe that one can calculate the canonical polynomial equivalent to a given polynomial of A simply by knowing L; the nature of A is irrelevant. This suggests, given L, reducing symbolic polynomials in its basis-elements to canonical form without introducing A. But as this can be done in various ways, it is essential to know that

LEMMA 2: *The reduction of polynomials in the e_i through straightening to canonical form, is independent of the method of straightening.*

PROOF: Let ξ be any product $e_{i(1)} \cdots e_{i(q)}$, and let $\phi'(\xi)$ and $\phi''(\xi)$ be the results of two different straightenings of ξ. Then if we can find ways of straight-

[3] It follows from the axiom of choice that any module has such a basis: one need merely add to a partial basis successively new linearly independent elements as long as any exist.

ening $\phi'(\xi)$ and $\phi''(\xi)$ respectively into the same polynomial $\phi'''(\xi)$, we have shown by induction on the degree and the number of straightenings still possible of the product of highest degree, that *all* ways of straightening ξ lead to the same canonical polynomial

$$\gamma(\phi'(\xi)) = \gamma(\phi'''(\xi)) = \gamma(\phi''(\xi)).$$

This is what we shall do.

It is clear that there are essentially only two cases, which may be summarized in the two sets of formulas:

$$\text{I.}\ \begin{cases} \xi = \xi_1 e_{i'} e_{j'} \xi_2 e_{i''} e_{j''} \xi_3 \\ \phi'(\xi) = \xi' + \eta' = \xi_1 e_{j'} e_{i'} \xi_2 e_{i''} e_{j''} \xi_3 + \sum_k c_k^{j'i'} \xi_1 e_k \xi_2 e_{i''} e_{j''} \xi_3 \\ \phi''(\xi) = \xi'' + \eta'' = \xi_1 e_{i'} e_{j'} \xi_2 e_{j''} e_{i''} \xi_3 + \sum_k c_k^{j''i''} \xi_1 e_{i'} e_{j'} \xi_2 e_k \xi_3. \end{cases}$$

$$\text{II.}\ \begin{cases} \xi = \xi_1 e_h e_i e_j \xi_2 \\ \phi'(\xi) = \xi' + \eta' = \xi_1 e_i e_h e_j \xi_2 + \sum_k c_k^{ih} \xi_1 e_k e_j \xi_2 \\ \phi''(\xi) = \xi'' + \eta'' = \xi_1 e_h e_j e_i \xi_2 + \sum_k c_k^{ji} \xi_1 e_h e_k \xi_2. \end{cases}$$

In Case I, ξ' and ξ'' can be further straightened, thus

$$\xi' \to \xi''' + \eta_1'' = \xi_1 e_{j'} e_{i'} \xi_2 e_{j''} e_{i''} \xi_3 + \sum_k c_k^{j''i''} \xi_1 e_{j'} e_{i'} \xi_2 e_k \xi_3$$

$$\xi'' \to \xi''' + \eta_1' = \xi_1 e_{j'} e_{i'} \xi_2 e_{j''} e_{i''} \xi_3 + \sum_k c_k^{j'i'} \xi_1 e_k \xi_2 e_{j''} e_{i''} \xi_3.$$

And straightening the $e_{i''} e_{j''}$ resp. $e_{i'} e_{j'}$ terms in η' resp. η'', one finds that $\eta' + \eta_1''$ can be straightened into the same form as $\eta_1' + \eta''$—giving finally

$$\phi'''(\xi) = \mu' + \eta_1' + \eta_1'' + \sum_{k'} \sum_{k''} c_{k'}^{j'i'} c_{k''}^{j''i''} \xi_1 e_{k'} \xi_2 e_{k''} \xi_3.$$

Similarly in case II, evidently $h > i > j$, and so we can straighten further by setting

$$\begin{aligned} \xi' &\to \xi_1 e_i e_j e_h \xi_2 + \sum_k c_k^{jh} \xi_1 e_i e_k \xi_2 \\ &\to \xi_1 e_j e_i e_h \xi_2 + \sum_k c_k^{ji} \xi_1 e_k e_h \xi_2 + \sum_k c_k^{jh} \xi_1 e_i e_k \xi_2 \\ &= \xi''' + \eta_1'' + \eta_1'''. \end{aligned}$$

$$\begin{aligned} \xi'' &\to \xi_1 e_j e_h e_i \xi_2 + \sum_k c_k^{jh} \xi_1 e_k e_i \xi_2 \\ &\quad \xi_1 e_j e_i e_h \xi_2 + \sum_k c_k^{ih} \xi_1 e_j e_k \xi_2 + \sum_k c_k^{jh} \xi_1 e_k e_i \xi_2 \\ &= \xi''' + \eta_1' + \eta_2'''. \end{aligned}$$

Hence it is sufficient to show that $\eta' + \eta_1'' + \eta_2'''$ and $\eta_1' + \eta'' + \eta_2'''$ can be straightened into the same form. But if one transposes $e_k e_j$, $e_k e_i$, $e_k e_h$, $e_j e_k$, and $e_h e_k$ whenever they are in the wrong order, one finds that this assertion comes down precisely to Jacobi's identity, which completes the proof.

3. Corollaries of Lemmas 1-2. From Lemmas 1–2 one can deduce our first main result. For starting with a Lie algebra purely abstractly, taking the canonical polynomials in its basis-elements e_i as elements of a hypercomplex algebra A, multiplying them symbolically and straightening the products to canonical form through Lemma 1, it follows[4] from Lemma 2 that multiplication is associative. Hence since by the first identity of Lie-Jacobi and definition,

$$e_j e_i - e_i e_j = c_k^{ij} e_k .$$

THEOREM 1: *Any Lie algebra L can be imbedded in a linear associative algebra $A_u(L)$.*

COROLLARY: *Any Lie algebra is isomorphic with an algebra of infinite matrices, with respect to the operation of forming alternants $[XY] = YX - XY$.*

For if one adds to the basis of any linear associative algebra A a "principal unit" e satisfying $ex = xe = x$ for all x, then the correspondence between the elements x of A and the linear transformations X: $a \to ax = X(a)$ of A is *isomorphic* (it is in any case homomorphic). This well-known construction goes back to Poincaré.[5]

Now recall that if A is any linear associative algebra in which L is embedded isomorphically and which is generated by L, then the correspondence between polynomials in the basis-elements e_i of L and their values in A preserves all equalities true in $A_u(L)$. Hence

THEOREM 2: *The ways of imbedding a given Lie algebra L in a linear associative algebra A are all obtained by taking the invariant subalgebras S of $A_u(L)$ which place the different linear combinations of the e_i in different residue classes, and then forming the homomorphic images $A_u(L)/S$.*

Thus $A_u(L)$ is a kind of universal linear associative algebra containing L. Finally, we have as a corollary of Theorem 1,

THEOREM 3: *The free Lie algebra with n generators is isomorphic with the free algebra of alternants involving n symbols.*

In other words, the identities of Lie-Jacobi imply all all other identities true of alternants.

The author has been informed that much of §3 was also discovered, but not published, by E. Artin.

---

[4] Given monomials ξ_1, ξ_2 and ξ_3, one writes down $\xi_1 \xi_2 \xi_3$ purely symbolically; straightening first $\xi_1 \xi_2$ one gets $(\xi_1 \xi_2)\xi_3$, and straightening first $\xi_2 \xi_3$ one gets $\xi_1(\xi_2 \xi_3)$.

[5] L. E. Dickson, "Algebras and their arithmetics," Chicago, 1922, pp. 92–98 discusses it more elaborately.

4. The case of nilpotent Lie algebras. A Lie algebra L is called *nilpotent* if and only if all its brackets of sufficient length w vanish,[6] and a matrix $X = \| x_{ij} \|$ is called *triangular* if and only if the elements below the principal diagonal vanish (i.e., $i < j$ implies $x_{ij} = 0$), and *properly triangular* if and only if in addition the principal diagonal consists of zeros.

Suppose L is a nilpotent Lie algebra. Define $L_1 = L$, and L_k $[k = 2, 3, \cdots]$ inductively as the set of all brackets $[xy]$ with $x \in L_i$ and $y \in L_{k-i}$, and $0 < i < k$—that is, define L_k as the set of all complex brackets of length k. Further, let J_h $[h = 1, 2, 3, \cdots]$ denote the set of linear combinations of elements of $L_h, L_{h+1}, L_{h+2}, \cdots$—that is, of polynomials in brackets of length $\geqq h$. Then the J_h are invariant subalgebras of L, and by the hypothesis of nilpotence, for some finite integer w,

$$L = J_1 > J_2 \dot{>} J_3 > \cdots > J_w = 0.$$

Evidently L possesses a basis of linearly independent elements $e_1, \cdots, e_r$ such that

$$\begin{array}{ll} e_1, \cdots, e_{n(1)} & \text{are a basis for } J_{w-1} \\ e_1, \cdots, e_{n(2)} & \text{are a basis for } J_{w-2} \\ \cdots & \cdots \\ e_1, \cdots, e_{n(w-1)} & \text{are a basis for } J_1 = L. \end{array}$$

Moreover obviously $n(1) < n(2) < \cdots < n(w-1) = r$.

Now taking the particular basis $e_1, \cdots, e_r$, let us form $A_u(L)$ as in §3. And to each e_k let us ascribe a numerical "weight" $s = s(e_k)$, so chosen that e_k is in J_s but not in J_{s+1}. Further, to each product let us ascribe as "weight" the sum of the weights of its factors, and to each polynomial, the least of the weights of its monomial terms. Evidently (since if $[e_i e_j] = c_k^{ij} e_k$, then $s(k) < s(i) + s(j)$ implies $c_k^{ij} = 0$ by our choice of basis), straightening preserves lower bounds to the weights of the terms of any polynomial, and multiplying a polynomial by another has the same property.

Hence the polynomials of weight $> w$ constitute an *invariant subalgebra* S of $A_u(L)$.

But $A_u(L)/S$ has the canonical power-products of length $\leqq w$ as a (redundant) basis; hence it has a finite order at most $r + r^2 + \cdots + r^w$. Since finally no linear combination of the e_i is of weight $> w$, we see that the different elements of L lie in different residue classes of S, and so

THEOREM 4: *Any nilpotent Lie algebra of finite order can be imbedded in a (nilpotent) linear associative algebra of finite order.*

If one defines w-nilpotence as meaning that all brackets of length $\geqq w$ vanish, one gets (using Poincaré's construction again) the somewhat more precise

---

[6] By the "length" of any (complex) bracket such as $[[xy]z]$ is meant the number of letters in it, repeated occurrences of the same letter being counted repeatedly.

COROLLARY: *Any w-nilpotent Lie algebra of order r is isomorphic with a Lie algebra of finite matrices of degree at most* $(r^{w+1} - 1)/(r - 1)$, *with coefficients in the same field.*

While if one arranges the basis-elements of $A_u(L)/S$ in order of increasing weight (starting with the adjoined principal unit e_σ of weight zero), one sees—again since multiplying by a monomial increases, and straightening never decreases weight—that

THEOREM 5: *The matrices of the preceding corollary are properly triangular.*

5. **Corollaries of Theorems 4-5.** So far no restriction except commutativity has been placed on the abstract field F underlying the algebras discussed. We shall now specialize to the cases of the real and complex fields, and study the implications of Theorems 4–5 for the theory of finite continuous groups—assuming Lie's Third Fundamental Theorem (but not its converse!).

First let us term a Lie group nucleus "hypercentral" if and only if its infinitesimal algebra is nilpotent.[7]

THEOREM 6: *Every hypercentral Lie group nucleus G is locally isomorphic with a group of matrices whose manifold is homeomorphic in the large with Cartesian r-space.*

PROOF: By definition, the infinitesimal algebra of G is nilpotent—and so by Theorem 5 is isomorphic with an algebra A of properly triangular matrices. It follows by Lie's Third Fundamental Theorem that G is locally isomorphic with the Lie group nucleus generated by these matrices.

But these matrices are properly triangular, and so all logarithmic and exponential series[8] involving them or even polynomials in them (which will also be properly triangular) are actually polynomial—contain only a finite number of non-vanishing terms. Hence by a formal identity of Hausdorff,[9] exponentials of these matrices are a group G^* in the large. Actually, $e^X e^Y = e^{\phi(X,Y)}$ where $\phi(X, Y)$ is a suitable polynomial in X and Y and their alternants. Again, since the logarithmic series is finite, and a fortiori convergent and continuous, the correspondence $X \leftrightarrows e^X - I$ is bicontinuous. Therefore canonical parameters give a one-one representation in the large, and the group G^* has a manifold homeomorphic with the linear r-space of its infinitesimal generators.

COROLLARY 1: *The universal covering group of every hypercentral Lie group is topologically isomorphic in the large with a linear group.*[10]

---

[7] This is equivalent to requiring that its algebraically defined "lower central series" (using the terminology of P. Hall) terminate with the identity.

[8] By e^X we mean $1 + X + (1/2!)X^2 + \cdots$, and by Log $(1 + X)$, the limit of the series $X - \frac{1}{2}X^2 + \frac{1}{3}X^3 - \cdots$, in case it exists. The ideas used are to be found in J. von Neumann, "Gruppen linearen Transformationen," Math. Zeits. 30 (1929), 3–42.

[9] F. Hausdorff, "Die symbolische Exponentialformel in der Gruppentheorie," Leipz. Ber. 58 (1906), Theorem B, p. 29.

[10] By Schreier's well-known theorem that any two simply connected locally isomorphic

Corollary 2: *The converse of Lie's Third Fundamental Theorem is valid in the large for nilpotent Lie algebras (with real or complex coefficients).*

Corollary 2 has been proved without restriction by E. Cartan [Fasc. 42 des Sci. Math. (1930), p. 18, bottom].

6. **Linear groups with nilpotent algebras.**[11] In this section an argument of E. Cartan (communicated by letter) is given, which gives the topology of the most general linear group "of rank zero" (i.e., with nilpotent Lie algebra).

Let L be any nilpotent Lie algebra of finite order r; then L is by §5 the infinitesimal algebra of a simply connected group $\mathfrak{U}$ of strictly triangular matrices—in which the exponential and logarithmic functions are both single-valued. By Schreier's theory of local isomorphisms one concludes that to get the most general Lie group having L for Lie algebra, one should take a general discrete subgroup $\mathfrak{K}$ of the central $\mathfrak{Z}$ of $\mathfrak{U}$, and form $\mathfrak{U}/\mathfrak{K}$.

But since two matrices $X \in \mathfrak{U}$ and $Y \in \mathfrak{U}$ commute if and only if Log Y and Log X commute, $\mathfrak{Z}$ is connected, and even isomorphic with the translation-group of n-space, while $\mathfrak{K}$ is generated by $k \leqq n$ linearly independent matrices $Z_1, \cdots, Z_k$. Taking the Log Z_i, we see that $\mathfrak{K}$ is part of a k-parameter connected normal subgroup $\mathfrak{K}^*$ of $\mathfrak{Z}$, whence $\mathfrak{K}^*/\mathfrak{K}$ is the k-parameter torus group.

Therefore if $\mathfrak{U}/\mathfrak{K}$ is isomorphic with a linear group, $\mathfrak{K}^*/\mathfrak{K}$ corresponds to a group of diagonal matrices whose non-zero terms all have absolute value unity, and which commute with every $X \in (\mathfrak{U}/\mathfrak{K})$. And by a theorem proved elsewhere,[12] the derived subgroup $\mathfrak{U}'$ of $\mathfrak{U}$ generated by Poisson brackets of its infinitesimal generators, can have no elements in common with this.

It follows that by taking suitable generators in $\mathfrak{U}'/\mathfrak{U}$, we can get a subgroup $\mathfrak{G}$ containing $\mathfrak{U}'$, such that $\mathfrak{G} \cap \mathfrak{K}^* = 0$, $\mathfrak{G} \cup \mathfrak{K}^* = L$. But $\mathfrak{K}^*$ being in the central, we see that L must be the *direct* sum of $\mathfrak{G}$ (which is simply connected, by reference to $\mathfrak{U}$) and the toroidal group. This proves

Theorem 7: *Any group of matrices whose Lie algebra is nilpotent is a direct product of a toroidal group of diagonal matrices and of a simply connected Lie group.*

Harvard University.

---

groups are isomorphic in the large. But there exist hypercentral Lie groups simply isomorphic with no linear group even in the purely algebraic sense. Cf. the author's note, Bull. Am. Math. Soc. 42 (1936), 883–888. Also, Cartan has pointed out ("La topologie des groupes de Lie," Hermann, Paris, 1936, p. 18) that the universal covering group of the projective group on one real variable is topologically isomorphic with no linear group —which controverts the conjecture that all simply connected Lie groups are isomorphic in the large with linear groups.

[11] Added March 4, 1937.

[12] "Lie groups isomorphic with no linear group," Bull. Am. Math. Soc. 42 (1936), 882–8. The result used is Theorem 2.

ANALYTICAL GROUPS*

BY
GARRETT BIRKHOFF

Introduction

1. **Abstract groups.** The present paper will deal with *abstract* continuous groups. This means that it will discuss symbols which behave like transformations, without specifying the domain on which the transformations operate. The reader will be assumed to be conversant with abstract groups as algebraic entities.

2. **Questions in the large.** It is well-known that the theory of continuous groups in the large differs essentially from the theory in the small. Some things, such as the one-one correspondence between closed subgroups of a Lie group and subalgebras of the Lie algebra of its infinitesimal generators, are true only locally;† others, such as the introduction by Weyl and Haar of invariant mass, are possible only when one deals with groups in the large.

The present paper is a theory *in the small* exclusively; it neither involves implicitly nor resolves explicitly the difficulties in the large. In this it resembles the original theory of Lie.

3. **Actual contents.** Thus the paper avoids two large classes of questions. What questions does it answer—what are its assumptions, and how can one summarize its conclusions?

The paper deals with systems (called "analytical groups") in which an associative multiplication is defined, and which can be so mapped on a Banach parameter-space that if one multiplies all elements by any fixed element near the origin, vector differences are left nearly invariant.‡

It is proved that if G is any analytical group (more properly, analytical group nucleus), then

(1) G is a topological group nucleus in the usual sense.

(2) One can introduce canonical parameters into G.

(3) G has an infinitesimal (Lie) algebra $L(G)$.

(4) The analytical subgroups of G correspond biuniquely to the closed

* Presented to the Society, December 31, 1936; received by the editors December 17, 1936 and, in revised form, May 3, 1937.

† Again, the group of topological automorphisms of the group of the torus differs radically from that of the group of translations of the plane, in spite of the fact that these two groups are locally isomorphic.

‡ A Banach space is of course simply a system having certain prescribed elementary properties of euclidean space which are shared by various important function spaces. Cf. §8.

subalgebras of $L(G)$, a subgroup being normal if and only if the corresponding subalgebra is invariant.

(5) If G is under canonical parameters, then there exists a formal series of polynomials determined by $L(G)$ which expresses the rule for forming group products.

(6) One can define product integrals for functions with values in $L(G)$, which include the Lebesgue integral (the case G is the additive group of real numbers), and all known product integrals (the case G is a group of matrices).

(7) Quite general functions $x(\lambda)$ with real arguments and values in a Banach space B determine formal series in elements of B and their brackets, which express the product integral $\int x(\lambda)d\lambda$ under canonical parameters for *any* analytical group G whose parameter-space contains B and whose "commutation modulus" is sufficiently small.

(8) All the operations defined (e.g., vector addition under canonical parameters, product integration) are *topologico-algebraic*—preserved under topological isomorphisms.

4. **Extension to infinite dimensions.** Perhaps the main advantage of the above assumptions, is the fact that many *infinite* continuous groups satisfy them. This marks a real advance in the analytical theory of groups.*

The infinite-dimensional analytical groups treated in the literature are of two kinds: the infinite continuous groups of analytical transformations

$$x_i' = f_i(x_1, \cdots, x_n) \qquad (i = 1, \cdots, n)$$

of n-dimensional space discussed by Lie [10]† and Cartan [4], and the groups of linear operators on Hilbert space recently studied by Delsarte [6]. Each of these authors omits to define the meaning of the convergence $T_n \to T$ of a sequence of transformations T_n to a limit T—in other words, to define the topological structure of the corresponding abstract groups.

This omission, and the omission to establish a rigorous correlation between the actual transformations of such groups and so-called "infinitesimal" transformations, are not trivial. In fact, although the present paper supplies a complete theory for a class of groups including those studied by Delsarte, the author does not even know what the facts are in the case of the groups studied by Lie and Cartan. Part of the difficulty is that the group manifolds are not metric-linear; part of it is that canonical parameters do not define even locally a one-one representation of the group manifold.

* Cf. Abstract 41-3-129 of the Bulletin of the American Mathematical Society (1935); also *Continuous groups and linear spaces*, Matematicheskiĭ Sbornik, vol. 1 (1936), pp. 635–642; an address delivered at the First International Topological Conference, Moscow, September 5, 1935.

† Numbers in brackets refer to the bibliography at the end of the paper.

5. **Continuous groups: topological and analytical.** This illustrates the importance of geometrical properties of group manifolds; we shall now see how continuous groups can be classified on a purely geometrical basis.

A "continuous" abstract algebra (whether group, ring, or field) is a system whose elements are simultaneously the points of a geometrical manifold and the symbols of a formal calculus, and whose algebraic operations determine "smooth" functions of the manifold into itself. By letting the geometry of the manifold suggest the proper definition of smoothness, one is led to a purely geometrical classification of continuous abstract algebras.

Thus with groups whose manifolds are general topological spaces, one naturally regards "smoothness" of the group operations as meaning that group multiplication and passage to the inverse are continuous in the topology of the group manifold. Such groups are called *topological.*

Similarly, with groups whose manifolds are n-dimensional analytical varieties, it is natural to assume that the group operations are analytical in the coordinates; this leads to the usual concept of a *Lie* group.

Now it is a remarkable fact, that two analytical systems which are continuous images of each other, are in general analytical images of each other. This seems to hold even in pure geometry: thus dimensionality, originally known to be invariant only under analytical transformations, is now realized to be a topological invariant. We shall extend the domain of validity of this principle below, by proving that *continuous* isomorphisms between Lie groups are necessarily *analytical.**

6. **Groups as topological algebras.** The result just stated, combined with (8), suggests that one can develop a theory for analytical groups in which group multiplication and passage to the limit are the only notions introduced as undefined primitives.†

Indeed, this program is technically feasible: it is shown below that one *can* give topologico-algebraic definitions of analytical groups. But as the argument is really *metric*, it would be misleading to make it pseudo-topological—even though it is less analytical and more topologico-algebraic‡ than any

* Discontinuous (and hence non-analytical) isomorphisms exist; there is one between the group of translations of the line and the group of translations of the plane. To see this, form in each an independent basis with respect to linear combination with rational coefficients. (However, van der Waerden, Mathematische Zeitschrift, vol. 36 (1933), pp. 780–787, has shown that isomorphisms between compact semi-simple Lie groups are always analytical.) Conceivably two Lie groups which are isomorphic and have homeomorphic manifolds are eo ipso analytically isomorphic.

† Especially since O. Schreier [15] has obtained so much information about group manifolds by such a theory.

‡ Thus pure group algebra—especially that of commutation—is shown to yield many results (especially in Chaps. IV–V) which could not be obtained by general analytical methods.

previous reasoning yielding the same results.

All this relates to the well-known problem of determining the weakest analytical assumptions demonstrably equivalent to an assumption of unrestricted analyticity. The weakest assumption in the literature* (cf. [11]) is that the function of group multiplication has continuous *second* derivatives. It is shown below that if one assumes continuous *first* derivatives, then one can deduce the whole theory† of abstract Lie groups.

Chapter I. Technical machinery

7. **A remark on notation.** It will shorten the argument in the sequel to use the following notational conventions: $M(\lambda)$ for any positive function of a real variable λ such that $\lim_{\lambda\to 0} M(\lambda)=0$; $O(\lambda)$ for any such function satisfying $O(\lambda)\leqq K\cdot|\lambda|$ for some $K<+\infty$; $o(\lambda)$ for any such function satisfying $o(\lambda)\leqq|\lambda|\cdot M(\lambda)$ for some $M(\lambda)$. (The relation of the last two definitions to Landau's well-known o-O notation‡ is obvious.)

Thus let $\phi(x_1, \cdots, x_r)$ and $\psi(x_1, \cdots, x_r)$ be any two real-valued functions of the same (not necessarily numerical!) variables $x_1, \cdots, x_r$. By the preceding definition,

$$\phi(x_1, \cdots, x_r) \leqq M(\psi(x_1, \cdots, x_r))$$

means that given $\eta>0$, $\delta>0$ exists so small that $\psi(x_1, \cdots, x_r)<\delta$ implies $\phi(x_1, \cdots, x_r)<\eta$. The inequalities $\phi(x_1, \cdots, x_r)\leqq O(\psi(x_1, \cdots, x_r))$ and $\phi(x_1, \cdots, x_r)\leqq o(\psi(x_1, \cdots, x_r))$ have similar meanings.

It is obvious that in terms of this notation, the following substitutions are legitimate:

$$(7\alpha) \qquad O(\lambda) \quad \text{for} \quad o(\lambda), \qquad \text{and} \quad M(\lambda) \quad \text{for} \quad O(\lambda).$$

$$(7\beta) \qquad M(\lambda) \quad \text{for} \quad M(O(\lambda)), \quad \text{and} \quad O(\lambda) \quad \text{for} \quad O(O(\lambda)).$$

$$(7\gamma) \qquad M(\lambda+\mu) \quad \text{for} \quad M(\lambda)+M(\mu).$$

$$(7\delta) \qquad M(\lambda) \quad \text{for} \quad M(\lambda)/M[1-M(\lambda)].$$

Thus if $\phi(x_1, \cdots, x_r)\leqq M(\psi_1(x_1, \cdots, x_r))+M(\psi_2(x_1, \cdots, x_r))$, then by (7γ), $\phi(x_1, \cdots, x_r)\leqq M(\psi_1(x_1, \cdots, x_r)+\psi_2(x_1, \cdots, x_r))$.

It goes without saying that the M-functions, o-functions and O-functions appearing in the text vary from group to group, and from inequality to inequality—although since only a finite number of such functions are used in

* Except when dealing with compact (von Neumann) and abelian (Pontrjagin) groups, where one need only assume that one has a topological group locally homeomorphic with euclidean space.

† The author announced this result in Abstract 41-5-192 (1935) of the Bulletin of the American Mathematical Society.

‡ Cf. G. H. Hardy, *Pure Mathematics*, 5th edition, Cambridge University Press, 1928, p. 448.

dealing with any one group, there exists a single $M(\lambda)$, $o(\lambda)$, and $O(\lambda)$ which works in all inequalities for that group.

8. **Formal definition of "analytical group."** The properties of "analytical groups" which will be assumed were indicated in §2; they can be stated explicitly as

DEFINITION 1. By an *analytical group* will be meant any region about the origin of a Banach space, in which an associative multiplication is defined for elements near the origin Θ, satisfying

(1) $$x \circ \Theta = \Theta \circ x = x \quad \text{for all} \quad x.$$

(2′) $$|(xa - xb) - (a - b)| \leqq M(|x| + |b| + |a|) \cdot |a - b|.$$

(2″) $$|(ay - by) - (a - b)| \leqq M(|a| + |b| + |y|) \cdot |a - b|.$$

In words, the origin is the group-identity e, and vector differences are nearly invariant under group translations $T_y^x : a \to xay$. (By xy or $x \circ y$ is meant the group product of x and y.)

(By a *Banach space* is meant a B-space in the sense of Banach [1]—that is, a linear space in which an absolute value $|x|$ is defined which (1) is positive for $x \neq \Theta$, (2) satisfies the triangle inequality $|x+y| \leqq |x| + |y|$, (3) is multiplied identically by $|\lambda|$ under any scalar expansion $x \to \lambda x$, and (4) makes the space complete*—such that if $\lim_{m,n\to\infty} |x_m - x_n| = 0$, then x exists such that $\lim_{n\to\infty} |x - x_n| = 0$.)

9. **A topological group nucleus.** Combining (2′)–(2″), we get immediately,

(2) $$|(xay - xby) - (a - b)| = M(|x| + |a| + |b| + |y|) \cdot |a - b|.$$

Again, setting $b = e = \Theta$ in (2′) and $a = e = \Theta$ in (2″), one obtains,

(3′) $$|x \circ y - (x + y)| \leqq M(|x| + |y|) \cdot |y|,$$

(3″) $$|x \circ y - (x + y)| \leqq M(|x| + |y|) \cdot |x|,$$

which can be combined into the single inequality

(3) $$|x \circ a \circ y - (x + a + y)| = M(|x| + |a| + |y|) \cdot (|x| + |y|).$$

In words, near the origin group translations T_y^x differ little from the corresponding linear translations $L_y^x : a \to a + x + y$.

(9α) *Multiplication is continuous near* Θ.

Proof. If $|x|$, $|y|$, $|a|$ and $|b|$ are small, then

$$|(x \circ y) - (a \circ b)| = |\{(x \circ y) - (a \circ y)\} + \{(a \circ y) - (a \circ b)\}|$$
$$= O(|x - a| + |y - b|).$$

* Incidentally, $\{x_n\}$ is metrically "fundamental" if and only if it is "fundamental" in the topologico-algebraic sense (of van Dantzig) that $\lim_{m,n\to\infty} x_m^{-1} \circ x_n = 0$. Cf. (9δ).

(9β) *Every sufficiently small element* x *has a unique inverse* x^{-1} *satisfying* $x\circ x^{-1}=x^{-1}\circ x=\Theta$, *and* $|x^{-1}|\leqq 2\cdot|x|$.

Proof. Suppose $M(5|x|)<\frac{1}{2}$. Define $y_0=\Theta$ and by induction $y_{n+1}=y_n-(xy_n)$. Then

$$|xy_{n+1}| = |(xy_{n+1}-xy_n)-(y_{n+1}-y_n)|, \quad \text{by definition},$$
$$\leqq M(|x|+|y_n|+|y_{n+1}|)\cdot|xy_n|, \quad \text{by } (2'),$$

since $|y_{n+1}-y_n|=|-xy_n|=|xy_n|$. It follows by induction that $|xy_{n+1}|\leqq\frac{1}{2}^{n+1}\cdot|x|$, and $|y_{n+2}|\leqq(2-\frac{1}{2}^{n+1})\cdot|x|$—whence $M(|x|+|y_{n+1}|+|y_{n+2}|)<\frac{1}{2}$. Hence $\lim_{m,n\to\infty}|y_m-y_n|=0$, and so by completeness a y exists satisfying $|y|\leqq 2\cdot|x|$ and $\lim_{n\to\infty}|y-y_n|=0$. Now by (9α), $xy=\Theta$, and so y is a right-inverse of x. Similarly x has a left-inverse z with $zx=\Theta$. Moreover $y=(zx)y=z(xy)=z$; hence $y=z\equiv x^{-1}$ is a full inverse of x; its uniqueness follows since $xx'=\Theta$ implies $x'=(x^{-1}x)x'=x^{-1}(xx')=x^{-1}$, while $x''x=\Theta$ implies $x''=x''(xx^{-1})=(x''x)x^{-1}=x^{-1}$.

(9γ) *Passage to the inverse is continuous near* Θ.

Proof. Let $(x+u)$ be given. Substitute x^{-1} for y_0 and $x+u$ for x in the proof of (9β). By (9α), $(x+u)y\leqq 2\cdot|u|$ in a small enough neighborhood; hence in the construction of $(x+u)^{-1}$ by successive approximation,

$$|(x+u)^{-1}-x^{-1}|\leqq|y-y_0|=4\cdot|u|.$$

We can summarize (9α)–(9γ) in

THEOREM 1. *Every analytical group contains a topological group nucleus in the usual sense.**

A topological space in which an associative multiplication is defined satisfying (9α)–(9γ) everywhere is called a topological group (cf. [15]).

(9δ) $|x^{-1}|\leqq|x|+o(|x|)$; *in fact*, $|x^{-1}+x|=o(|x|)$.

Proof. By (3′), $|x+x^{-1}|\leqq M(|x|+|x^{-1}|)\cdot|x|$; but by (9β), $M(|x|+|x^{-1}|)=M(|x|)$. Hence $x^{-1}=-x+u$, where $|u|=M(|x|)\cdot|x|=o(|x|)$, proving the result.

Digression on axiomatics: Setting $y=\Theta$ resp. $x=\Theta$ in (3′) resp. (3″), we obtain (1). Further, near Θ, (3′), (3″) make $by=a$ imply that $|y|$ is nearly $|b-a|$. Hence if we are dealing with a topological group nucleus, then (2′) and (2″) hold. (Proof: By symmetry, it suffices to prove (2′). But by (3′), writing $b^{-1}a=y$, whence $a=by$,

* Cf. B. L. van der Waerden, *Vorlesungen über kontinuierlichen Gruppen*, Göttingen, 1932. For the analogous notion of a Lie group nucleus (alias "germ," cf. [11]).

$$|(a-b)-y| = |by-b-y| \leqq M(|b|+|y|)\cdot|y|$$
$$|(xa-xb)-y| = |xby-xb-y| = M(|x|+|b|+|y|)\cdot|y|.$$

And so by the triangle law, since by continuity $M(|y|)=M(|a^{-1}b|) \leqq M(|a|+|b|)$ (cf. §7),

$$(2') \qquad |(xa-xb)-(a-b)| \leqq M(|x|+|b|+|a|)\cdot|a-b|\,.)$$

10. **Groups in the large.** Let H be any full topological group. Obviously any one-one bicontinuous map of a neighborhood of the identity of H onto a region of a Banach space which satisfies (1), (2′), (2″)—or alternatively, by the last paragraph, (3′), (3″)—defines that neighborhood as an analytical group. We are unable to prove* that any system satisfying Definition 1 is conversely a piece containing the identity of a full topological group.

Full topological groups which can be mapped locally onto Banach space in such a way as to satisfy Definition 1 will be termed *full* analytical groups; this will distinguish full groups from the analytical group nuclei with which we shall be concerned below and which, for brevity, we have called simply "analytical groups."

11. **Changes of parameters.** It is important to know which transformations of Banach spaces play the role of analytical coordinate transformations in the theory of abstract Lie groups—that is, which when applied to a given analytical group G attached to a parameter space, turn G into another topologically isomorphic analytical group H.

One can specify at once two classes of such transformations associated with an arbitrary Banach space B, namely:

(11a) The group of "distortions" of B—that is, of those transformations

* This has been proved for finite continuous groups by E. Cartan ([5], p. 18). Cartan omits to mention the decisive fact that if L is any Lie algebra, and N is its largest invariant "integrable" subalgebra, then L contains a semi-simple subalgebra S such that $S \cap N=0$ and $S+N=L$ (cf. J. H. C. Whitehead, Proceedings of the Cambridge Philosophical Society, vol. 32 (1936), pp. 229–238). This omission led Mayer-Thomas to question ([11], p. 806) the validity of Cartan's proof. Cartan has since published another equally technical proof (*Sur la Topologie des Groupes de Lie*, Paris, 1936, p. 22).

Neither of these proofs can be extended to the infinite continuous group nuclei treated below; each depends on lemmas which need not be true in infinite dimensions. For instance the fact that not all closed linear subspaces S of Banach spaces B have complements T such that $S \cap T=0$ and $S+T=B$ prevents one from using Cartan's special proof for solvable groups.

On the other hand Mayer-Thomas' argument (due independently to Paul Smith) for the case of group nuclei which can be embedded in a full group generalizes to infinite continuous groups—one takes the subgroup of the full group generated by the nucleus given, and retopologizes this subgroup by redefining distance as geodesic distance along paths in the subgroup.

Esthetically, one would expect to find a simple proof that every analytical group nucleus can be embedded in a full group, since it is easy to define the full group, if one knows that it exists.

T of B into itself which leave Θ fixed and satisfy (*) $|T(a+x)-T(a)-x| \leqq M(|a|+|x|)\cdot|x|$.

(11b) The class of alterations of the norm function $|x|$ of B to a new norm function $\|x\|$ such that the ratios $|x|/\|x\|$ and $\|x\|/|x|$ are uniformly bounded.

Remark. The latter correspond one-one to choices of bounded open convex regions $\|x\|<1$ of B. (Cf. A. Kolmogoroff, op. cit. in §17.)

THEOREM 2. *Any succession of transformations of types* (11a), (11b) *of the parameter-space of an analytical group G, turns G into a topologically isomorphic analytical group.*

Proof. It is obviously sufficient to prove the theorem for single transformations of types (11a) and (11b); again, the main difficulty is to prove analyticity. With (11b), one needs merely write $|x|/R \leqq \|x\| \leqq R\cdot|x|$, and to replace $M(\lambda)$ in (3) by $R^2M(\lambda/R) \leqq M(\lambda)$. (Cf. §7.)

Consider case (11a). Setting $a+x=b$ in (*), we see that (**) $|T(b)-T(a)-(b-a)| \leqq M(|a|+|b|)\cdot|b-a|$—i.e., vector differences, and hence absolute values near Θ are nearly invariant under T. Hence—the proof as in (9β) is by successive approximation—T is one-one and so by (**) bicontinuous near the origin. Therefore it suffices to prove (3′), (3″)—or even, by symmetry, (3′). This we shall do. Note that T^{-1} is of type (11a), and leaves vector differences near Θ almost invariant. Hence

$$|T^{-1}(a+x)-(T^{-1}(a)+T^{-1}(x))| \leqq M(|a|+|x|)\cdot|x|, \text{ by } (*),$$

$$|T^{-1}(a)\circ T^{-1}(x)-(T^{-1}(a)+T^{-1}(x))| \leqq M(|a|+|x|)\cdot|x|, \text{ by } (3').$$

Hence by the triangle inequality,

$$|T^{-1}(a)\circ T^{-1}(x)-T^{-1}(a+x)| \leqq M(|a|+|x|)\cdot|x|$$

and so, by (**),

$$|T(T^{-1}(a)\circ T^{-1}(x))-(a+x)| \leqq M(|a|+|x|)\cdot|x|.$$

But this *is* (3′) in terms of the new parameters, q.e.d.

We shall regard topologically isomorphic groups as essentially identical—as differing merely in their parametric representation.

12. **Rectifiable paths.** Let us recall a few familiar geometrical notions, so as to have a consistent notation and terminology for subsequent use. These notions are proper to abstract metric spaces,† and so apply to Banach spaces.

By a *path* is meant a continuous image P: $p(\lambda)$ of a line interval‡ $[0, \Lambda]$.

† The ideas go back to Fréchet's Thesis; cf., also, K. Menger, *Zur Metrik der Kurven*, Mathematische Annalen, vol. 103 (1930), p. 471, §5.

‡ As is conventional, $[0, \Lambda]$ denotes the set of real numbers λ which satisfy $0 \leqq \lambda \leqq \Lambda$

Two paths P and Q are called "geometrically equivalent" (written $P \approx Q$) if and only if they can be identified by proper choice of parameters—i.e., if and only if one can establish a one-one sense-preserving correspondence between the intervals of which they are images, such that corresponding points have the same image. Clearly the relation of being geometrically equivalent is reflexive, symmetric and transitive.

Again, by a *segment* ΔP of P is meant the image of any subinterval Δ: $[\lambda_1, \lambda_2]$ of $[0, \Lambda]$. By a *partition* π of P is meant a division of $[0, \Lambda]$ into successive subintervals Δ_k: $[\lambda_{k-1}, \lambda_k]$, where $\lambda_0 = 0$, $\lambda_n = \Lambda$, and $k = 1, \cdots, n$. By the "product" of any two partitions π and π' of P is meant the partition $\pi \cdot \pi'$ whose subintervals are the intersections of the subintervals of π with those of π'. And π is called a "subpartition" of π' (in symbols, $\pi \leqq \pi'$) if and only if $\pi = \pi \cdot \pi'$.

By the π-approximate length of P under any partition π is meant $|P|_\pi \equiv \sum_{k=1}^{n} |P(\lambda_k) - P(\lambda_{k-1})|$, and by the "length" of P is meant $|P| = \sup |P|_\pi$. A path P is called "rectifiable" if and only if $|P| < +\infty$. Obviously

(12α) *If* $P \approx Q$, *then* $|P| = |Q|$.

The "diameter" $|\pi|$ of a partition π of a rectifiable path P is defined as $\sup |\Delta P|$. It is not hard to show

(12β) $|P| = \lim_{|\pi| \to 0} |P|_\pi$.

And since $|\pi| \leqq |\pi'|$ provided $\pi \leqq \pi'$, we see

(12γ) $|P| = \lim_{\pi \downarrow} |P|_\pi$ *in the sense of Moore-Smith.*†

13. **More notation.** We shall now introduce some special but natural notation for handling *rectifiable paths issuing from the origin* (=identity) *of an analytical group nucleus.*

If P_k is any path with domain $[0, \Lambda_k]$, then $t(P_k)$ denotes $p_k(\Lambda_k) - p_k(0)$.

By the *path-sum* of r admissible paths $P_1, \cdots, P_r$, will be meant the path $P = P_1 \oplus \cdots \oplus P_r$ formed by adding to $P_1 \oplus \cdots \oplus P_{r-1}$ a segment congruent to P_r under linear translation through $t(P_1 \oplus \cdots \oplus P_{r-1})$. And by the *path-product* of the P_k, will be meant the path $\tilde{P} = P_1 \circ \cdots \circ P_r$ formed by adding to $P_1 \circ \cdots \circ P_{r-1}$ a segment congruent to P_r under group left-translation through $t(P_1 \circ \cdots \circ P_{r-1})$. Thus P and $\tilde{P}$ have $[0, \Lambda_1 + \cdots + \Lambda_r]$ for domain, and for $0 \leqq \lambda \leqq \Lambda_{k+1}$,

$$(13.1) \qquad \begin{cases} p(\Lambda_1 + \cdots + \Lambda_k + \lambda) = t(P_1) + \cdots + t(P_k) + p_{k+1}(\lambda), \\ \tilde{p}(\Lambda_1 + \cdots + \Lambda_k + \lambda) = t(P_1) \circ \cdots \circ t(P_k) \circ p_{k+1}(\lambda). \end{cases}$$

† This means that, given any neighborhood of $|P|$, one can find a π_0 such that $\pi \leqq \pi_0$ implies that $|P|_\pi$ lies in that neighborhood of $|P|$.

Since linear and group translations leave distances invariant resp. nearly invariant, P and $\tilde{P}$ are admissible.

We shall now develop an abstract correspondence between paths which generalizes the correspondence between the sum-integral $\int x(\lambda)d\lambda$ and the product integral $\hat{\int} x(\lambda)d\lambda$ of functions whose values $x(\lambda)$ are matrices. (N.B., $t(\Delta_k P)$ is the analogue of $x(\lambda)\Delta\lambda$.)

Accordingly, let P be any admissible path, and let π be any partition of P into segments $\Delta_1 P, \cdots, \Delta_r P$. Denote by P_k the image of $\Delta_k P$ after linear translation through $-t(P_1 \oplus \cdots \oplus P_{k-1})$, and by Q_k the image of $\Delta_k P$ after left-multiplication by the group-inverse of $t(Q_1 \circ \cdots \circ Q_{k-1})$. Then by construction

$$P = P_1 \oplus \cdots \oplus P_r = Q_1 \circ \cdots \circ Q_r.$$

We shall define the two dualistic paths

$$P_\pi^* = P_1 \circ \cdots \circ P_r \qquad \text{and} \qquad P_\pi \dagger = Q_1 \oplus \cdots \oplus Q_r$$

formed by interchanging the operations of path-addition and path-multiplication. Then we shall prove that the P_π^* and $P_\pi\dagger$ approach fixed limiting positions P^* and $P\dagger$ as $|\pi|$ tends to zero.

14. **Evaluation of paths.** Of course, the meaning of this statement depends on how one defines limits—on how one *topologizes* the "space" of images of a fixed interval.

Let P and Q be any two images of the same interval $[0, \Lambda]$. We shall make the definition

$$|P - Q| = \sup_{0 \leq \lambda \leq \Lambda} p(\lambda) - q(\lambda).$$

It is clear that this definition of distance makes the images of $[0, \Lambda]$ the "points" of an abstract metric space, in the sense defined earlier;‡ this depends only on the fact that the images of $[0, \Lambda]$ are themselves in a metric space.

We now come to some statements involving group properties. In stating and proving them we shall write $\prod_{k=1}^r x_k$ for $(x_1 \circ \cdots \circ x_r)$, and $\sum_{k=1}^r x_k$ for $(x_1 + \cdots + x_r)$.

(14α) $|\prod_{k=1}^r x_k - \sum_{k=1}^r x_k| = o(\sum_{k=1}^r |x_k|)$. *Consequently,* $|\prod_{k=1}^r x_k| \leq O(\sum_{k=1}^r |x_k|)$.

Proof. By the triangle inequality,

$$\left| \prod_{k=1}^{r} x_k - \sum_{k=1}^{r} x_k \right| \leq \left| \left[\left(\prod_{k=1}^{r-1} x_k \right) \circ x_r \right] - \left[\left(\prod_{k=1}^{r-1} x_k \right) + x_r \right] \right|$$

‡ Fréchet, op. cit., p. 36, introduces this very definition of distance, and shows that it is metric.

$$+\left|\prod_{k=1}^{r-1} x_k - \sum_{k=1}^{r-1} x_k\right|$$

$$\leqq |x_r| \cdot M\left(\left|\prod_{k=1}^{r-1} x_k\right|\right) + M\left(\sum_{k=1}^{r-1} |x_k|\right)\cdot\left(\sum_{k=1}^{r-1}|x_k|\right)$$

by (3) and induction on r. Recombining—since, by induction on r, $|\prod_{k=1}^{r-1}x_k| \leqq O(\sum_{k=1}^{r-1}|x_k|)$—we get

$$\left|\prod_{k=1}^{r} x_k - \sum_{k=1}^{r} x_k\right| \leqq M\left(\sum_{k=1}^{r-1}|x_k|\right)\left(\sum_{k=1}^{r-1}|x_k|\right) \leqq o\left(\sum_{k=1}^{r}|x_k|\right).$$

(14β) *We have the inequality*

$$\left|\prod_{k=1}^{r} x_k - \prod_{k=1}^{r} y_k - \sum_{k=1}^{r}(x_k - y_k)\right| \leqq M\left(\sum_{k=1}^{r}|x_k| + \sum_{k=1}^{r}|y_k|\right) \cdot\left(\sum_{k=1}^{r}|x_k - y_k|\right).$$

Hence if $M(\sum_{k=1}^{r}[|x_k| + |y_k|]) < 1$, *then*

$$\left|\prod_{k=1}^{r} x_k - \prod_{k=1}^{r} y_k\right| \leqq 2\left(\sum_{k=1}^{r}|x_k - y_k|\right).$$

Proof. By the triangle inequality iterated,

$$\left|\prod_{k=1}^{r} x_k - \prod_{k=1}^{r} y_k - \sum_{k=1}^{r}(x_k - y_k)\right| \leqq \sum_{k=1}^{r}\left|\left(\prod_{i=1}^{k-1} x_i\right)x_k\left(\prod_{i=k+1}^{r} y_i\right) - \left(\prod_{i=1}^{k-1} x_i\right)y_k\left(\prod_{i=k+1}^{r} y_i\right) - (x_k - y_k)\right|$$

$$\leqq \sum_{k=1}^{r} M\left(\sum_{k=1}^{r}|x_k| + \sum_{k=1}^{r}|y_k|\right)\cdot|x_k - y_k|, \qquad \text{by (2)},$$

since $|\prod_{i=1}^{k-1}x_i| \leqq O(\sum_{i=1}^{r}|x_i|)$ and $|\prod_{i=k+1}y_i| \leqq O(\sum_{i=1}^{r}|y_i|)$ by (14α).

(14γ) *Let* $P_1, \cdots, P_r$ *and* $Q_1, \cdots, Q_r$ *be admissible paths, each* P_k *having the same domain as* Q_k. *Further, let* $|P|$ *denote* $\sum_{k=1}^{r}|P_k|$ *and* $|Q|$ *denote* $\sum_{k=1}^{r}|Q_k|$. *Then*

$$|(P_1 \oplus \cdots \oplus P_r) - (Q_1 \oplus \cdots \oplus Q_r)| \leqq \sum_{k=1}^{r}|P_k - Q_k|.$$

And if $|P| + |Q|$ *is so small that* $M(|P| + |Q|) < 1$, *then*

$$|(P_1 \circ \cdots \circ P_r) - (Q_1 \circ \cdots \circ Q_r)| \leqq 2\sum_{k=1}^{r}|P_k - Q_k|.$$

Proof. The first inequality follows from (13.1) and the triangle inequality. The second follows from (13.1) and (14β).

Thus with paths of sufficiently small total length, both path-sums and path-products are uniformly continuous functions of their arguments in our metric "path-space."

LEMMA. *Let P be any sufficiently short path. Then if $\pi' \leqq \pi$, $|P_\pi^* - P_{\pi'}^*| \leqq M(|\pi|)$ and $|P_\pi\dagger - P_{\pi'}\dagger| \leqq M(|\pi|)$.*

Proof. It is an essential preliminary remark that each segment of any P_π^* or $P_\pi\dagger$ has nearly the same length as the corresponding segment of P, since it is obtained from it by group and linear translation of subsegments through relatively small distances—and such translations by (2) leave distances nearly invariant.

Now write $P_\pi^* = P_1 \circ \cdots \circ P_r$. Clearly $P_{\pi'}^*$ is obtainable from P_π^* by replacing each component $P_k = P_{k,1} \oplus \cdots \oplus P_{k,s}$ by the path $\tilde{P}_k = P_{k,1} \circ \cdots \circ P_{k,s}$. But referring to (14$\alpha$), we see that $|\tilde{P}_k - P_k| \leqq o(|P_k|) \leqq M(|\pi|) \cdot |P_k|$. Hence by (14$\gamma$),

$$|P_\pi^* - P_{\pi'}^* \leqq 2M(|\pi|) \cdot \sum_{k=1}^{r} |P_k| = M(|\pi|) \cdot |P|.$$

Similarly, write $P_\pi\dagger = Q_1 \oplus \cdots \oplus Q_r$. Clearly $P_{\pi'}\dagger$ is obtainable from $P_\pi\dagger$ by replacing each component $\tilde{Q}_k = Q_{k,1} \circ \cdots \circ Q_{k,s}$ by a path $\tilde{Q}_k = Q_{k,1} \oplus \cdots \oplus Q_{k,s}$. By (14$\alpha$) and the preliminary remark, $|\tilde{Q}_k - Q_k| \leqq o(|Q_k|) \leqq M(|\pi|) \cdot |Q_k|$. Hence by (14$\gamma$),

$$|P_\pi\dagger - P_{\pi'}\dagger| \leqq M(|\pi|) \cdot \sum_{k=1}^{r} |Q_k| = M(|\pi|) \cdot |P|.$$

THEOREM 3. *Let P be any sufficiently short path. Then paths P^* and $P\dagger$ exist such that*

$$|P_\pi^* - P^*| \leqq M(|\pi|) \quad \text{and} \quad |P_\pi\dagger - P\dagger| \leqq M(|\pi|).$$

Proof. By the above lemma, the P_π^* and $P_\pi\dagger$ converge in the sense of Cauchy-Fréchet. But this means that for every fixed λ, the $p_\pi^*(\lambda)$ and $p_\pi\dagger(\lambda)$ do, and hence (the space being complete) have limits $p^*(\lambda)$ and $p\dagger(\lambda)$. These limits define P^* and $P\dagger$; the inequalities of Theorem 3 then follow from the corresponding inequalities in the lemma and passage to the limit.

(14δ) $(P^*)\dagger = (P\dagger)^* = P$.

Proof. For every partition π, $(P_\pi^*)_\pi\dagger = (P_\pi\dagger)_\pi^* = P$ by definition. And to replace each segment of P_π^* or $P_\pi\dagger$ by the corresponding segment of P^* resp. $P\dagger$ makes by (14γ) a proportionally small change in $(P_\pi^*)_\pi\dagger$ resp. $(P_\pi\dagger)_\pi^*$. Hence $(P^*)_\pi\dagger \to P$ and $(P\dagger)_\pi^* \to P$ uniformly as $|\pi| \to 0$.

(14ϵ) $|t(P^*)-t(P)| \leqq o(|P|)$ *and* $|t(P\dagger)-t(P)| \leqq o(|P|)$.

Proof. For every π, $t(P_\pi^*)=t(P_1) \circ \cdots \circ t(P_r)$ where $t(P)=t(P_1)\oplus \cdots \oplus t(P)$. Hence the first inequality merely restates (14α). The proof of the second inequality is the same, since (cf. the preliminary remark in the proof of the lemma above) $|P\dagger| \leqq O(|P|)$.

$$(14\zeta)\quad (P_1\oplus \cdots \oplus P_r)^* = P_1^* \circ \cdots \circ P_r^*$$

and

$$(P_1 \circ \cdots \circ P_r)\dagger = P_1\dagger \oplus \cdots \oplus P_r\dagger.$$

Proof. $(P_1\oplus \cdots \oplus P_r)^*$ is in particular the limit as $\sup|P_{k,i}|\to 0$ of $P_{1,1} \circ \cdots \circ P_{r,s(r)}$, where

$$P_{k,1} \oplus \cdots \oplus P_{k,s(k)} = P_k.$$

Thus it is the limit as $\sup|\pi_k|\to 0$ of $(P_1)_{\pi_1}^* \circ \cdots \circ (P_r)_{\pi_r}^*$. By (14$\gamma$), this limit is $P_1^* \circ \cdots \circ P_r^*$. This proves the first identity; the proof of the second is similar.

Conversely (14ϵ)–(14ζ) define the correspondences $P\to P^*$ and $P\to P\dagger$.

(14η) *If Q is any path, and Δ: $[\lambda, \mu]$ is any interval of its domain, then* $q^{-1}(\lambda) \circ q(\mu) = t((\Delta Q\dagger)^*)$.

Remark. By $q^{-1}(\lambda)$ is of course meant $[q(\lambda)]^{-1}$.

Proof. Set $Q\dagger = P$; $p^*(\mu)=p^*(\lambda) \circ t((\Delta P)^*)$ by (14ζ); the result follows by transposing $p^*(\lambda)=q(\lambda)$.

(14θ) *If $P\approx Q$, then $P^*\approx Q^*$ and $P\dagger \approx Q\dagger$.*

Proof. Obvious from the definitions.

Chapter II. Canonical parameters

15. **Scalar powers.** In §§16–17, we shall consider straight rays P_x: $p_x(\lambda)=\lambda x$ $(0\leqq\lambda\leqq 1)$ and their star correspondents P_x^*.

Obviously $|P_x| = |x|$, and so by (14ϵ),

(15α) $|t(P_x^*)-x| \leqq o(|x|)$.

(15β) $|t(P_{x+y}^*)-t(P_x^*)-t(P_y^*)| \leqq M(|x|+|y|)\cdot|y|$.

Proof. Let π denote the partition of $[0, 1]$ into n equal parts. Then setting $x_k=x/n$ and $y_k=(x+y)/n$ in (14β), we get (15β) for $(P_{x+y})_\pi^*$, $(P_x)_\pi^*$ and $(P_y)_\pi^*$. Passing to the limit as $n\to\infty$, we get (15β).

Combining (15β) with (15α), we see that the so-called "canonical transformation" $T: x\leftarrow t(P_x^*)$ satisfies‡ $|T(x+y)-T(x)-y| \leqq M(|x|+|y|)\cdot|y|$—is of type (11a). Hence (cf. Theorem 2) we have

‡ By $T: x\leftarrow t(P_x^*)$ we mean that the position x is imagined to be occupied by the element $t(P_x^*)$.

THEOREM 4. *The canonical transformation carries any analytical group G into a topologically isomorphic analytical group.*

Again, by definition, $P_{(\lambda\mu)x} = P_{\lambda(\mu x)}$. While unless $\lambda\mu < 0$, $P_{(\lambda+\mu)x} \approx P_{\lambda x} \oplus P_{\mu x}$, whence $t(P_{(\lambda+\mu)x}) = t(P_{\lambda x}^*) \circ t(P_{\mu x}^*)$. But

(15γ) *Let* $R_x = P_x \oplus P_{-x}$. *Then* $t(R_x^*) = 0$.

Proof. Let π denote the partition of R_x into $2n$ equal segments, and set $\lambda = 1/n$. Then

$$\begin{aligned} |t((R_x)_\pi^*)| &= |(\lambda x)^{n-1} \circ (\lambda x \circ - \lambda x) \circ (-\lambda x)^{n-1}| \\ &\leqq |(\lambda x)^{n-1} \circ (-\lambda x)^{n-1}| + 2(|\lambda x \circ - \lambda x|) \end{aligned}$$

by (2), substituting $(\lambda x)^{n-1}$ for x, $(-\lambda x)^{n-1}$ for y, $(\lambda x \circ -\lambda x)$ for a and Θ for b, and requiring x to be so small that $M(|x| + |a| + |y|) < 1$, whence

$$|xay| \leqq |xy| + |a| + M(|x| + |a| + |y|) \cdot |a| \leqq |xy| + 2|a|.$$

But by induction on n and (14α), this yields

$$\begin{aligned} |t((R_x)_\pi^*)| &= (n-1) \cdot o(|\lambda x|) + o(|\lambda x|) = n \cdot o(|\lambda x|) \\ &= n \cdot M(|\lambda x|) \cdot |\lambda| \cdot |x| = M(|\lambda x|) \cdot |x|. \end{aligned}$$

To complete the proof, let $n \to \infty$, so that $M(|\lambda x|) \to 0$.

But if $\lambda\mu < 0$, $P_{\lambda x} \oplus P_{\mu x} \approx P_{(\lambda+\mu)x} \oplus P_{-\mu x} \oplus P_{\mu x}$; hence in all cases $t(P_{(\lambda+\mu)x}) = t(P_{\lambda x}^*) \circ t(P_{\mu x}^*)$, and so we have

THEOREM 5. *For fixed* x, *the* $t(P_{\lambda x}^*)$ *are (locally) topologically isomorphic with the additive group of the* λ.

But by Theorem 4 the canonical transformation is one-one; hence the function x^λ defined by making $t(P_y^*) = x$ and $x^\lambda = t(P_{\lambda y}^*)$ is defined and single-valued near the origin.

(15δ) $x^1 = x$ (by definition), $x^\lambda \circ x^\mu = x^{\lambda+\mu}$, *and* (since $P_{(\lambda\mu)x} = P_{\lambda(\mu x)}$) $(x^\lambda)^\mu = x^{\lambda\mu}$.

(15ϵ) x^λ *is a topologico-algebraic function of* x, *in the sense that any topological isomorphism carrying* x *into* y *carries* x^λ *into* y^λ.

Proof. The assertion is true for positive integral $\lambda = n$ since $(x \circ \cdots \circ x) = x^{1+\cdots+1} = x^n$. It is also true for positive rational λ since $y^n = x$ if and only if $y = (y^n)^{1/n} = x^{1/n}$; while since $x \circ y = \Theta$ if (by 15γ)) and only if (by (9β)) $y = x^{-1}$, it is true for all rational $\lambda = m/n$. Finally, since the rationals are dense in the real continuum and x^λ depends continuously on λ, it is true for all λ.

16. **Canonical parameters.** We are now in a position to introduce canonical parameters.

A group will be said to be under "canonical parameters" if and only if the canonical transformation T: $x \leftarrow t(P_x^*)$ is the identical transformation I: $x \rightarrow x$.

(16α) *Any analytical group is transformed into canonical parameters by the canonical transformation—that is, the canonical transformation is idempotent.*

Proof. After T has been performed once, if π denotes the partition of (0, 1) into n equal parts, then by definition and Theorem 5, $t((P_x)_\pi^*) = (x/n)^n = x$, whence, passing to the limit, iteration of T leaves all points fixed.

(16β) *Under canonical parameters,* $x^\lambda = \lambda x$; *hence scalar multiplication under canonical parameters is an intrinsic topologico-algebraic operation.*

Proof. By definition of x^λ resp. canonical parameters, $x^\lambda = t(P_{\lambda x}^*) = \lambda x$.

(16γ) *In any analytical group,* $x + y = \lim_{\lambda \to 0} (\lambda x \circ \lambda y)/\lambda$.

Proof. Referring to the inequality (3), we get for fixed x and y since $\lambda(x+y) = \lambda x + \lambda y$,

$$|(\lambda x \circ \lambda y) - \lambda(x + y)| \leqq M(|\lambda|) \cdot |\lambda|.$$

Hence, dividing through by the scalar λ,

$$|(\lambda x \circ \lambda y)/\lambda - (x + y)| \leqq M(|\lambda|)$$

which completes the proof.

Combining (16γ) with (16β), we get

THEOREM 6. *If G and H are any two analytical groups under canonical parameters, then any topological isomorphism between G and H is linear—it preserves vector sums and scalar products.*

COROLLARY 6.1. *The group of topological automorphisms of any analytical group is spatially isomorphic with a group of linear transformations of its parameter-space.*

COROLLARY 6.2. *If G and H are any two analytical groups, then any continuous isomorphism between G and H can be expressed as the product of three transformations of the parameter-space of G, of types* (11a), (11b), *and* (11a).‡

COROLLARY 6.3. *Admissible paths* (cf. §13) *are carried into admissible paths under topological isomorphisms between analytical groups.*

(16δ) *An analytical group is under canonical parameters if and only if* $x \circ x = x + x$ *for all* x.

‡ One should prove further: *Any topological isomorphism between two groups whose function of composition is analytical, amounts to an analytical transformation of coordinates.* To complete the proof, it would suffice to show that in such groups $t(P_x^*)$ is an analytical function of x—a fact already known (from the theory of differential equations) for Lie groups.

Proof. If $x \circ x = x+x$, then by induction $x^{2^n} = 2^n x$, $x = (2^{-n}x)^{2^n}$, whence $t(P_x^*) = x$, and we have canonical parameters. Conversely, under canonical parameters, $x \circ x = x^2 = 2x = x+x$.

17. **Digression: Topologico-algebraic postulates.** It is a curious fact that, by inverting the remarks of the last few sections, one can obtain *topologico-algebraic postulates defining Lie groups*, involving only *intrinsic* operations (i.e., operations invariant under topological isomorphisms). To show this, one need use only superficial reasoning, arguing from the above properties of canonical parameters.†

One can do this even for infinite continuous groups. The general procedure is: 1°: characterize Banach spaces topologico-algebraically (as those complete topological linear spaces possessing a convex open "bounded" set‡); 2°: define linear transformations and thence Fréchet total derivatives (cf. §18) topologico-algebraically;§ 3°: postulate that the group is a Banach space relative to addition under canonical parameters ("canonical addition") and raising to scalar powers; 4°: postulate that an associative operation of multiplication satisfying $x \circ x = x+x$ and continuously differentiable on the Banach space, be defined.

Because of the preceding results and Corollary 2 of Theorem 15, these postulates are satisfied by all analytical groups under canonical parameters. Conversely, by Theorem 8 any system satisfying these postulates is an analytical group, which is by (16δ) under canonical parameters.

In the special case of Lie groups—the case that the parameter space has a finite basis (or equivalently,‖ is locally compact)—one can simplify these postulates to the requirements (i) elements $a_1, \cdots, a_r$ exist such that any element near the identity can be represented uniquely as a product $a_1^{\lambda_1} \circ \cdots \circ a_r^{\lambda_r}$ of small powers $a_k^{\lambda_k}$ of the a_k, and (ii) the function of composition is continuously differentiable¶ in $(\lambda_1, \cdots, \lambda_r)$-space.

18. **Digression: metric postulates.** The present section will be devoted to sketching a proof of

---

† These ideas were announced in Abstract 41-5-192 of the Bulletin of the American Mathematical Society (1935).

‡ For the terminology cf. J. von Neumann, *On complete topological spaces*, these Transactions, vol. 37 (1935), pp. 1–20. For the characterization cf. A. Kolmogoroff, *Zur Normierbarkeit eines allgemeinen topologisches lineares Raumes*, Studia Mathematica, vol. 5 (1935), pp. 29–33.

§ Replace the usual epsilon-delta definitions by "for every given neighborhood there exists a neighborhood so small · · · ."

‖ Cf. [1], p. 84, Theorem 8.

¶ This can be phrased topologico-algebraically. For instance, $x \circ y = f(x, y)$ has continuous first derivatives if and only if $\partial f/\partial x(a, b) = \lim_{\lambda \to 0}((a+\lambda x) \circ b)/\lambda$ and $\partial f/\partial y(a, b) = \lim_{\lambda \to 0}(a \circ (b+\lambda y))/\lambda$ exist and are continuous functions of a and b.

THEOREM 7. *One can redefine the class of analytical groups under canonical parameters by weakening the postulates for Banach spaces.*

This result will not be used elsewhere.

Sketch of proof. Substitute "group products" $x \circ y$ for vector sums $x+y$, and "scalar powers" x^λ for scalar products λx, continue to use an (extrinsic) norm function $|x|$, and make the following alterations in the usual postulates (cf. [1]) for Banach space (after first confining their validity to a small region about the identity): (1) replace the two conditions $x+y=y+x$ and $\lambda(x+y)=\lambda x+\lambda y$ by the single weaker condition $|x^\lambda \circ y^\lambda \circ (x \circ y)^{-\lambda}| \leqq |\lambda| \cdot |x| \cdot |y|$, and (2) replace the condition $|x+y| \leqq |x|+|y|$ by the weaker condition $|x \circ y| \leqq |x|+|y|+|x| \cdot |y|$.

The reader should have no difficulty in proving that the altered postulates hold in any analytical group under canonical parameters and under a suitable norm function (cf. Theorems 1 and 5 for the algebraic identities, and (27β)—where it is shown that essentially $|(x \circ y)-(x+y)| \leqq |x| \cdot |y|$—for the strong metric inequalities).

But conversely, if one defines $x+y=\lim_{\lambda \to 0}(x^\lambda \circ y^\lambda)^{1/\lambda}$ and $\lambda x=x^\lambda$ in any system G satisfying the new postulates, then the space becomes a neighborhood of the origin of a Banach space B, and the map of G on B satisfies (1), (2′), (2″) and $x \circ x=x+x$—completing the outline of the proof.

19. **Digression: differentiability postulates.** We now come to the connection between Definition 1 and differentiability conditions, namely

THEOREM 8. *Let G be any topological group nucleus, some neighborhood of whose identity e is mapped onto a region of a Banach space B, in such a way that $x \circ y=f(x, y)$ has first total derivatives everywhere, which are continuous at e. Then G is an analytical group under the map.*

Proof. Theorem 8 is clearly meaningless until continuous total derivatives have been defined; actually, it refers to the usual definitions due to Fréchet.† Fréchet says that $f(x, y)$ has a total derivative A with respect to x at $x=a$, $y=b$ if and only if there exists a linear transformation A such that

$$(18') \qquad |f(a+x, b)-f(a, b)-Ax| \leqq o(|x|),$$

where Ax denotes the transform of x by A. One similarly defines total derivatives with respect to y. Further, Fréchet calls the two total derivatives $A(x, y)=\partial f/\partial x(x, y)$ and $B(x, y)=\partial f/\partial y(x, y)$ *continuous at* $x=a$, $y=b$ if and only if

† M. Fréchet, *La notion de différentielles dans l'analyse générale*, Annales de l'École Normale Supérieure, (3), vol. 42 (1925), pp. 293–323. For a similar concept of an infinite continuous group, cf. A. D. Michal and V. Elconin, *Abstract transformation groups*, American Journal of Mathematics, vol. 59 (1937), pp. 129–144.

$$(18'') \quad \begin{cases} |A(a+u, b+v)x - A(a,b)x| \leqq M(|u|+|v|)\cdot|x|, \\ |B(a+u, b+v)y - B(a,b)y| \leqq M(|u|+|v|)\cdot|y|. \end{cases}$$

Clearly $A(e, e)=B(e, e)=I$, the identical linear transformation—since irrespective of u, $u \circ e = e \circ u = u$.

Once these definitions and this fact have been stated, the proof of Theorem 8 follows familiar lines. Assuming the existence everywhere and continuity at $x=y=e$ of $A(x, y)$ and $B(x, y)$, one constructs the real functions

$$\phi(\lambda) = |(\lambda x \circ a) - (\lambda x + a)|,$$
$$\psi(\mu) = |(x \circ a \circ \mu y) - (x + a + \mu y)|.$$

Clearly (18′) implies that the upper right-derivatives of $\phi(\lambda)$ and $\psi(\mu)$ are bounded by $|A(\lambda x, a)-I|\cdot|x|$ and $|B(x \circ a, \lambda y)-I|\cdot|y|$, respectively. Hence by the theory of real functions,

$$(3) \quad |(x \circ a \circ y) - (x + a + y)| \leqq K(|a|+|x|+|y|)\cdot(|x|+|y|),$$

where $K(|a|+|x|+|y|)$ is small as long as $|A(\lambda x, a)-I|$ and $|B(x \circ a, \mu y) - I|$ are small identically on $0 \leqq \lambda, \mu \leqq 1$—and so by the continuity of these is an M-function, q.e.d.

Remark. Fréchet's definition obviously specializes to the usual definition of continuous total differentiability when B is finite-dimensional—and is satisfied in this case provided continuous first partial derivatives with respect to all coordinates exist.† (This remark has immediate application to the theory of Lie groups—it shows that if the function $x \circ y = f(x, y)$ has continuous first partial derivatives, then one is dealing with an "analytical group.")

In summary, §§17–19 have contained three alternative definitions of analytical groups, equivalent to Definition 1. One can view these from two angles. They may be regarded from a conceptual angle as giving a better picture of what an analytical group is. Or they may be regarded as giving content to Definition 1 itself—that is, as furnishing examples of analytical groups from other contexts.

Chapter III. Linear groups

20. **Axiomatization.** It is a simple fact, that *one can axiomatize algebras of linear operators‡ on Banach spaces.*

To see this, one must first recall that the operators on *any* linear space B which are defined everywhere, and carry vector sums into vector sums and scalar multiples into scalar multiples, constitute a hypercomplex algebra with

† C. J. de la Vallée-Poussin, *Cours d'Analyse Infinitésimale*, Louvain, 1914, p. 141.

‡ By a "linear operator," we mean ([1], p. 23) any continuous additive, everywhere defined function. This conflicts with the usage for Hilbert spaces, where such operators are called *bounded.*

a principal unit I. (We shall use the notation O for the transformation carrying every $x \epsilon B$ into Θ; I for the identity $x \rightarrow x$; $S, T, U, \cdots$ for other operators.)

One must next observe that if B is a Banach space, then relative to vector sums $T+U$, products λT with scalars, and the "modulus" $\|T\| = \sup_{x \neq \Theta} |Tx|/|x|$ (cf. [1], p. 54), the linear operators on B constitute another Banach space. The proof of this will be left to the reader.†

Finally, $\|T \circ U\| \leqq \|T\| \cdot \|U\|$.

More generally, *any* algebra of linear operators on a Banach space B which contains I and is topologically closed (under the "uniform" topology defined by the metric $\|T-U\|$) has all of the properties just described.

But conversely, let $\mathfrak{H}$ be any system having these properties—i.e., any "metric hypercomplex algebra."‡ Then (applying a classical construction) each element $T \epsilon \mathfrak{H}$ induces a linear transformation θ_T: $X \rightarrow XT$ on the elements $X \epsilon \mathfrak{H}$. Moreover since $\|IT\| = \|I\| \cdot \|T\|$ and $\|XT\| \leqq \|X\| \cdot \|T\|$, the "modulus" of θ_T is precisely $\|T\|$. Thus $\mathfrak{H}$ can be realized as a closed algebra of linear operators on itself, including the identity θ_I: $X \rightarrow XI = X$.

21. **Linear operators with inverses.** Linear operators do not constitute a group under multiplication. But the linear operators S with inverses S^{-1} satisfying $SS^{-1} = S^{-1}S = I$ do. And one can easily prove

THEOREM 9. *Let $\mathfrak{H}$ be any metric hypercomplex algebra. Then the map $(I+T) \rightarrow T$ of the elements $(I+T) \epsilon \mathfrak{H}$ with $\|T\| < \frac{1}{2}$ onto the linear space defined by $\mathfrak{H}$, exhibits these elements as an analytical group $\mathfrak{G}$ under multiplication.*

Proof. Refer to Definition 1. The only properties in any doubt are (2′)–(2″). But

$$\begin{aligned} \Xi &\equiv \| [(I + X) \circ (I + Y) - (I + X) \circ (I + Z)] - [Y - Z] \| \\ &= \| [X \circ Y - X \circ Z] \| = \| X \circ (Y - Z) \|, \quad \text{by algebra}, \\ &\leqq \|X\| \cdot \|Y - Z\|, \quad \text{by hypothesis}, \end{aligned}$$

proving (2′). One obtains (2″) similarly.

THEOREM 10. *The canonical transformation of $\mathfrak{G}$ is given explicitly by the convergent power series*

$$T \leftarrow \exp (T) - I \equiv T + \frac{1}{2!} T^2 + \frac{1}{3!} T^3 + \cdots = t(P_T^*).$$

† For instance, if $\{T_n\}$ is a fundamental sequence of linear operators, then for any x, $\{T_n x\}$ is a fundamental sequence in B, whose limit we shall define as Tx. By continuity, $T(x+y) = Tx + Ty$ and $|Tx - Ty| \leqq \lim_{n \to \infty} \|T_n\| \cdot |x - y|$.

‡ More properly, any metric *associative* hypercomplex algebra. Omitting the associative law, we get a more general definition (cf. §30), which however yields no realization theorem.

Proof. The questions of convergence are settled by the inequalities $\|T^n\| \leqq \|T\|^n$ and $\|T+U\| \leqq \|T\|+\|U\|$, and the assumption $\|T\| < \frac{1}{2}$. But now dividing P_T into n equal parts, we get by the binomial expansion

$$t(P_T)_\pi^* = \left(I + \frac{1}{n} T\right)^n - I = T + \frac{1}{n^2} C_{n,2}T^2 + \frac{1}{n^3} C_{n,3}T^3 + \cdots$$

which converges (cf. supra) to $\exp(T) - I$.

The inverse of the canonical transformation is of course given by the power series

$$T \leftarrow \log (I + T) = T - \tfrac{1}{2}T^2 + \tfrac{1}{3}T^3 - \cdots ,$$

but we shall not use this fact.†

22. **Generalization of Theorem** 9. A metric algebra $\mathfrak{X}$ need not possess a unit I nor satisfy $\|I\| = 1$ in order that the symbolic elements $I+X$ with $X \epsilon \mathfrak{X}$ and $\|X\| < \frac{1}{2}$ should form an analytical group nucleus when multiplied according to the rule

$$(I + X) \circ (I + Y) = I + (X + Y + X \circ Y). \tag{22.1}$$

The arguments of §21 do not involve these assumptions.

An important example of such an algebra is due to Delsarte [6], and is also cited by Yosida (op. cit.). It is the algebra $\mathfrak{A}$ of all infinite matrices $A = \|a_{ij}\|$ for which $\sum_{i,j} |a_{ij}|^2 < +\infty$. If we set $\|A\|^2 = \sum_{i,j} |a_{ij}|^2$, we have a Banach space, in which products $C = A \circ B = \|c_{ij}\|$ can be defined by the usual rule $c_{ij} = a_{ik}b_{kj}$ —the series being convergent by Schwarz' inequality, and satisfying, besides, $\|C\| \leqq \|A\| \cdot \|B\|$.

The algebra $\mathfrak{A}$ corresponds of course to the algebra of Schmidt kernels in the theory of integral equations, and is isometric with Hilbert space.

23. **Function of composition.** The formulas of the preceding section lead directly to explicit expressions for the function $X \circ Y$ of composition.

Under the original parameters, $X \circ Y = F(X, Y)$ is analytic since (by the distributivity of multiplication) it is *linear in both variables*—and among the functions between linear spaces, next to constant functions, linear functions

† Remark: The above treatment was suggested by that of J. von Neumann [12]. The main changes are: explicit discussion of transformations as abstract elements, and use (following Banach) of the "modulus" $\|X\|$ for norm.

The concept of a metric hypercomplex algebra ("complete normed vector ring") was announced by the author in Abstract 41-3-104 of the Bulletin of the American Mathematical Society (1935); a similar definition is given by K. Yosida (*On the group embedded in the metrically complete ring*, Japanese Journal of Mathematics, vol. 13 (1936), pp. 7–26). Yosida does not require $\|I\| = 1$; cf. §22.

Another example, discussed at length by M. H. Stone, consists of the linear operators T_a: $f(x) \rightarrow f(x)a(x)$ on the space of bounded functions on an abstract class. This is a closed subalgebra of the algebra of §20.

are the most purely analytic. Thus the second partial derivatives of $F(X, Y)$ are constant and so the higher derivatives all vanish identically.

Moreover by Theorem 10, if we denote by X^m as usual $X \circ \cdots \circ X$, then we have the following explicit expression for $X \circ Y = G(X, Y)$ *under canonical parameters*,

$$\begin{aligned} G(X, Y) &= \log (I + F(\exp X - I, \exp Y - I)) \\ &= \log\left(I + \sum_{m=1}^{\infty}\sum_{n=1}^{\infty} \frac{1}{m!n!} F(X^m, Y^n)\right) \\ &= \sum_{k=1}^{\infty} (-1)^{k-1}/k \left\{\sum_{m=1}^{\infty}\sum_{n=1}^{\infty} \frac{1}{m!n!} F(X^m, Y^n)\right\}^k \end{aligned}$$

whose first terms can be found easily, and are monomials.

It has been shown by J. E. Campbell [3] and F. Hausdorff [8] that this series can also be developed in terms of X, Y, and iterations of the bilinear function $[X, Y] = XY - YX$. The resulting "SCH-series" will be proved in Chapter V to be valid also for non-linear analytical groups.

24. **Digression: polynomials and analyticity.** The *algebraic* significance of the SCH-series will be discussed in Chapter V; what about its *analytical* significance?

It exhibits $G(X, Y)$ as analytical in the strong sense that (1) it is the limit of an absolutely convergent series of polynomials of increasing degrees,† (2) its derivatives all exist and can be found through term-by-term differentiation of the series, (3) hence the Taylor's series for $G(X, Y)$ converges absolutely to $G(X, Y)$—all within a sphere of positive radius.

Although it is not entirely clear when a function between Banach spaces is "analytical"—there may be various generalizations of the established notion for functions between euclidean spaces—it seems undeniable that at least any function with properties (1)–(3) should be called analytical.

25. **Adjoint of an analytical group.** In the present section, we shall show that the notion of the *adjoint* of a Lie group can be extended without real modification to the case of analytical groups. We state this more precisely in the following theorem:

† For polynomial functions between Banach spaces, cf. S. Mazur and W. Orlicz, *Grundlegende Eigenschaften der polynomische Operatoren*, Studia Mathematica, vol. 5 (1935), pp. 50–68 and pp. 179–189. One can define polynomials through continuity + the identical vanishing of $(n+1)$st differences, through the identical vanishing of $(n+1)$st derivatives, or as sums of multilinear functions in a variable repeated $0, \cdots, n$ times; and these definitions are equivalent.

Unlike these authors, we are concerned with functions of two variables. N.B.: A polynomial function on r variables which is homogeneous of degree k in each, is homogeneous of degree kr (and not of degree k) on the product-space of the variables.

THEOREM 11. *Let G be any analytical group under canonical parameters. Then each element $g \epsilon G$ determines a linear transformation θ_g: $x \to g^{-1}xg$ on the parameter-space of G, and the correspondence $g \to \theta_g$ is continuously homomorphic.*

Proof. Since G is a topological group θ_g is a topological automorphism. Hence by Corollary 6.1 it is a linear transformation on G. Moreover by the well-known identity $(gh)^{-1}x(gh) = h^{-1}(g^{-1}xg)h$, the correspondence $g \to \theta_g$ is homomorphic. It remains only to show that it is continuous under the *uniform* topology. But

$$
\begin{aligned}
| h^{-1}xh - g^{-1}xg | &= O(| h^{-1}x^{-1}hg^{-1}xg |), \quad \text{by (3)}, \\
&= O(| g^{-1}[(hg^{-1})^{-1}x^{-1}(hg^{-1})x]g) \\
&= O(| (hg^{-1})^{-1}x^{-1}(hg^{-1})x) \\
&\qquad\qquad (\text{since } \|\theta_g\| = O(| g |), \quad \text{by } (14\beta)) \\
&= O(| g - h |) \cdot | x |, \quad \text{by } (27\beta),
\end{aligned}
$$

whence $\|\theta_g - \theta_h\| = O(|g-h|)$, completing the proof.

The validity of the proof of course depends on proving (27β) without the aid of Theorem 11. We shall do this in §27.

The correspondence $g \to \theta_g$ does not always carry open sets into open sets: it need not be "gebietstreu" in the sense of Freudenthal.

CHAPTER IV. COMMUTATION

26. **Outline.** The present chapter will be devoted to showing how every analytical group G possesses a bilinear "commutation function" $[x, y]$. In Chapter V, it will be shown that $[x, y]$ determines G to within local isomorphism.

The commutation function $[x, y]$ belonging to a given group G is most easily defined as the bilinear asymptote at $x = y = 0$ to the purely algebraic commutator function

$$(x, y) = K(x, y) \equiv x^{-1}y^{-1}xy.$$

The fact that (x, y) *has* a bilinear asymptote is proved below (in §28) from the relations (deduced in §27)

$$
(27\alpha) \qquad \begin{cases} | (u \circ x, y) - (x, y) - (u, y) | \leqq M(| x | + | y |) \cdot | (u, y) |, \\ | (x, v \circ y) - (x, y) - (x, v) | = M(| x | + | y |) \cdot | (x, v) |, \end{cases}
$$

$$
(27\beta) \qquad | (x, y) | = O(| x | \cdot | y |),
$$

while the fact that $[x, y]$ is a topologico-algebraic invariant associated with G is almost obvious (cf. §29).

Moreover one can deduce the familiar identities

$$(30\alpha)\qquad \begin{cases}[x, y] + [y, x] = 0,\\ [[x, y], z] + [[y, z], x] + [[z, x], y] = 0\end{cases}$$

as corollaries of formal identities on group products. These results can be summarized in the statement that G possesses a *metric Lie algebra* $L(G)$. Chapter IV concludes with various applications of $L(G)$, to the case that G is under canonical parameters.

In the proofs of Chapter IV, group algebra plays a novel and essential role.

27. **The approximate bilinearity of** $K(x, y)$. The present section will be devoted to showing that $(x, y) = K(x, y)$ is approximately bilinear at $x = y = 0$, in the sense that (27α)–(27β) are true.

The proof of (27α) is almost immediate. One has the formal identity

$$(27\gamma)\qquad \begin{aligned}(u \circ x, y) &= x^{-1}u^{-1}y^{-1}uxy\\ &= (u, y)_x \circ (x, y)\end{aligned}$$

under the convention that g_x denotes $x^{-1}gx$. But by the fundamental inequality (2) of §8,

$$(27\delta)\qquad |(u, y)_x - (u, y)| \leqq M(|x|)\cdot|(u, y)|,$$

whence $|(u, y)_x| = O(|(u, y)|)$. Hence

$$\begin{aligned}\Xi &\equiv |(u \circ x, y) - (x, y) - (u, y)|\\ &\leqq |(u \circ x, y) - (x, y) - (u, y)_x| + |(u, y)_x - (u, y)|\\ &\leqq M(|(x, y)|)\cdot|(u, y)_x| + M(|x|)\cdot|(u, y)|\\ &\qquad\qquad \text{(by (27}\gamma\text{) and (3) of §9, and (27}\delta\text{))}\\ &\leqq M(|x| + |y|)\cdot|(u, y)|,\end{aligned}$$

since $|(u, y)_x| = O(|(u, y)|)$. But this is the first half of (27α); the second half follows from the symmetry between left- and right-multiplication.

As a special instance of (27α), we have

$$|(x^m, y) - (x^{m-1}, y) - (x, y)| \leqq M(|x^m| + |y|)\cdot|(x, y)|.$$

Hence, since $|x^m| = O(|mx|) = O(m|x|)$, by induction

$$|(x^m, y) - m(x, y)| \leqq M(m|x| + |y|)\cdot m\cdot|(x, y)|.$$

Combining with the symmetric formula in (x, y^n), we get

$$(27\epsilon)\qquad |(x^m, y^n) - mn(x, y)| = M(m|x| + n|y|)\cdot mn|(x, y)|.$$

Consequently, within some small radius ρ of the origin,

$$(27\zeta) \qquad |(x, y)| \leqq O(|(x^m, y^n)|/mn).$$

But clearly within this sphere, given $x \neq 0$ and $y \neq 0$, one can so choose m and n that $\frac{1}{2}\rho < |x^m|, |y^n| < \rho$—whence, $|(mx, ny)|$ being bounded within this sphere, we get $|(x^m, y^n)| \leqq O(|mx| \cdot |ny|)$, and so by (27ζ),

$$(27\beta) \qquad |(x, y)| \leqq O(|x| \cdot |y|).$$

It is a corollary, since $y \circ x \circ K(x, y) = x \circ y$, and likewise $(y \circ x) + (x \circ y - y \circ x) = x \circ y$, that (by (3))

$$(27\beta') \qquad |xy - yx| \leqq O(|x| \cdot |y|).$$

28. **The asymptote** $[x, y]$. Substituting from (27β) in (27α), and recalling that $x + w = u \circ x$ implies† $|w| \sim |u|$, we get

$$(28\alpha) \qquad \begin{cases} |(x + w, y) - (x, y) - (w, y)| \leqq M(|x| + |y|) \cdot |w| \cdot |y|, \\ |(x, y + w) - (x, y) - (x, w)| = M(|x| + |y|) \cdot |x| \cdot |w|, \end{cases}$$

from which there follows

$$(28\alpha') \qquad |(x + u, y + v) - (x, y)| \leqq O(|u| + |v|).$$

Now start anew with (28α)–$(28\alpha')$, and use the same algebraic analysis used in proving (27ϵ). By (28α),

$$|(mx, y) - ((m - 1)x, y) - (x, y)| \leqq M(m|x| + |y|) \cdot |x| \cdot |y|.$$

Hence by induction on m, we get

$$|(mx, y) - m(x, y)| \leqq M(m|x| + |y|) \cdot m|x| \cdot |y|.$$

Combining with the symmetric formula in (x, ny), we have

$$(28\beta) \qquad |(mx, ny) - mn(x, y)| \leqq M(m|x| + n|y|) \cdot mn \cdot |x| \cdot |y|.$$

By double use of (28β), we get for $0 < h/m, k/n < 1$,

$$\left|\left(\frac{h}{m} x, \frac{k}{n} y\right) - \frac{hk}{mn}(x, y)\right| \leqq M(|x| + |y|) \cdot \frac{hk}{mn} \cdot |x| \cdot |y|,$$

whence, by rational approximation and passage to the limit, using $(28\alpha')$ to establish continuity, we have

$$(28\gamma) \qquad \left|\frac{1}{\lambda\mu}(\lambda x, \mu y) - (x, y)\right| \leqq M(|x| + |y|) \cdot |x| \cdot |y|$$

for $0 < \lambda, \mu < 1$. Therefore if $\lambda + \mu + \lambda' + \mu' < \epsilon$, then

† By $|w| \sim |u|$ we mean that $||w| - |u|| \leqq M(|x| + |u| + |w|) \cdot |u|$; this relation is evidently reflexive, symmetric, and transitive.

$$\left|\frac{1}{\lambda\mu}(\lambda x, \mu y) - \frac{1}{\lambda'\mu'}(\lambda' x, \mu' y)\right| = M(\epsilon)\cdot |x|\cdot|y|$$

and so, by the completeness of the parameter-space

$$[x, y] \equiv \lim_{\lambda,\mu\downarrow 0} \frac{1}{\lambda\mu} K(\lambda x, \mu y) \tag{28δ}$$

exists. Furthermore, by (28γ),

$$|\,[x, y] - (x, y)\,| \leqq M(|x| + |y|)\cdot|x|\cdot|y|. \tag{28ϵ}$$

Finally, since $(-x+x, y)=(0, y)=0$, by (28α)

$$|(-x, y) - [-(x, y)]| \leqq M(|x| + |y|)\cdot|x|\cdot|y|.$$

whence we see that

$$[x, y] = \lim_{\lambda,\mu\to 0} \frac{1}{\lambda\mu}(\lambda x, \mu y) \tag{28ζ}$$

exists.

29. **The bilinearity of** $[x, y]$, **etc.** In this section, we shall prove the bilinearity and topologico-algebraic invariance of $[x, y]$.

The invariance of $[x, y]$ under continuous isomorphisms between groups under canonical parameters follows from the definition and Theorem 6. And by (28α), "distortions" of type (11a) change $(\lambda x, \mu y)$ by $o(|\lambda|\cdot|\mu|)$, from which invariance under general continuous isomorphisms follows by Corollary 6.2.

As for the bilinearity of $[x, y]$, by (28α)

$$\Xi_1 \equiv \left|\frac{1}{\lambda\mu}(\lambda[x+u], \mu y) - \frac{1}{\lambda\mu}(\lambda x, \mu y) - \frac{1}{\lambda\mu}(\lambda u, \mu y)\right|$$

$$= M(|\lambda x| + |\mu y|)\cdot\frac{1}{\lambda\mu}\cdot|\lambda u|\cdot|\mu y|$$

whence, passing to the limit, $[x+u, y]-[x, y]-[u, y]=0$. Hence $[x+u, y] = [x, y]+[u, y]$; and $[x, y+v]=[x, y]+[x, v]$ by symmetry. Also, by (27β) and (28ϵ), $[x, y]=O(|x|\cdot|y|)$, and so is bounded. Hence it is bilinear.

In summary of the above results,

THEOREM 12. *(x, y) has a bilinear asymptote $[x, y]$ which is a topologico-algebraic invariant of G.*

Remark. In a linear group, algebra based on the expansion $(I+\lambda X)^{-1} = I-\lambda X+\lambda^2X^2-\lambda^3X^3+\cdots$ shows

$$\frac{1}{\lambda^2}(\lambda X, \lambda Y) = (XY - YX) + \text{terms of higher order}$$

whence, passing to the limit, $[X, Y] = XY - YX$.

30. **Metric Lie algebras.** One can now deduce relations (30α) from algebraic identities on group products.

In the first place, since $(y, x) = (x, y)^{-1}$, and $u^{-1} + u$ is nearly zero, clearly $[x, y] + [y, x] = 0$. That is, $[x, y]$ is skew-symmetric.

The proof that $[x, y]$ satisfies Jacobi's identity,

$$[[x, y], z] + [[y, z], x] + [[z, x], y] = 0$$

is less simple. It depends very essentially on realizing that by (27β) and (28ϵ),

$$\begin{aligned} \Xi_2 &\equiv |((x, y), z) - [[x, y], z]| \\ &\leqq |((x, y), z) - ([x, y], z)| + |([x, y], z) - [[x, y], z]| \qquad (30\beta) \\ &\leqq M(|x| + |y| + |z|) \cdot |x| \cdot |y| \cdot |z| \end{aligned}$$

and, besides, on remarking that since $v \circ u = u \circ v \circ (v, u)$, to permute two commutators in a group product changes the value by an amount which is by (27β) small to the fourth order.

But direct computation based on cancellation proves†

$$(x, y)((x, y), z)(z, y)(z, x)((z, x), y)(y, x)(y, z)((y, z), x)(x, z) = \Theta.$$

Therefore, permuting terms, and cancelling

$$(x, y)(y, x) = (z, y)(y, z) = (z, x)(x, z) = \Theta,$$

we get by the preceding remark, the inequality

$$|((x, y), z)((y, z), x)((x, z), y)| \leqq O(|x| + |y| + |z|) \cdot |x| \cdot |y| \cdot |z|.$$

Hence by (30β) and the fundamental relation (3),

$$|[[x, y], z] + [[y, z], x] + [[z, x], y]| = M(|x| + |y| + |z|) \cdot |x| \cdot |y| \cdot |z|.$$

Replacing x, y, z by $\lambda x, \lambda y, \lambda z$ where λ is small, and using linearity, we get Jacobi's Identity in the limit.

Summarizing, we may say (in the language of Chapter III),

THEOREM 13. *Relative to sums $x+y$, scalar products λx, and "brackets" $[x, y]$, the parameter-space of any analytical group nucleus G is a metric Lie algebra $L(G)$.*

Remark 1. In §§26–30 we have nowhere assumed that G was under canonical parameters.

† This formula was suggested to the author by identities in §2.3 of [7].

Remark 2. Since $|[x, y]| \leqq O(|x| \cdot |y|)$, after changing the scale (i.e., multiplying the norm by a suitable constant) we can assume simply $|[x, y]| \leqq |x| \cdot |y|$.

Remark 3. Brackets $[x, y]$ are defined for all x, y in the Banach space B, unlike $x \circ y$ which is defined only locally.

We shall show (Corollary 15.1) that G is determined to within local isomorphism by $L(G)$, and that conversely any metric Lie algebra belongs to an analytical group nucleus. This shows that the problem of enumerating the analytical group nuclei with a given parameter-space is equivalent to that of enumerating the different metric Lie algebras on the same linear space.

31. **Subgroups and normal subgroups.** The results of §§31–32 will refer to analytical groups G under canonical parameters. A subset S of elements of G will be called an *analytical subgroup nucleus* if and only if, relative to the topology and group multiplication table of G, S is itself an analytical group nucleus. An analytical subgroup nucleus S will be called *normal* (or invariant) if and only if for every $g \epsilon G$, $g^{-1}Sg$ contains some neighborhood of the identity of S.

If S is an analytical subgroup nucleus, then each $x \epsilon S$ must lie on a one-parameter subgroup x^λ in S, and hence (by Theorem 6) a segment λx in G must lie in S. Again, the length of this segment must exceed some fixed positive constant; otherwise we could find $\{x_n\}$ such that $\lambda_n x_n \epsilon S$ implies $\lambda_n x_n \to 0$, and this is impossible in an analytical group nucleus.

Therefore S must contain with x and y, $k(\lambda x, \lambda y)/\lambda^2$ for some fixed $k > 0$ and all λ on $[0, 1]$; hence it must contain with x and y, $k[x, y]$ (since, being *complete*, it is *closed* in G). Similarly, it must contain with x and y, $x + y = \lim_{\lambda \to 0}(\lambda x \circ \lambda y)/\lambda$. And finally, if two such subgroup nuclei contain elements on the same class of segments $\lambda x \epsilon G$, then they clearly generate (in case G is a group) the same subgroup of G, and so may be identified.

These facts may be summarized in

(31α) *Let G be any analytical group nucleus under canonical parameters. The analytical subgroup nuclei S of G are pieces of closed subalgebras of the metric Lie algebra $L(G)$, two subgroups being identical if and only if the subalgebras are.*

If S is "normal" (i.e., invariant under all inner automorphisms), then $x \epsilon S$ and $g \epsilon G$ imply that for some $k > 0$, $k[g, x] = \lim_{\lambda \to 0}(k\{\lambda x \circ \lambda g_{\lambda x}\}/\lambda^2) \epsilon S$. Furthermore,

$$g + x = \lim_{n \to \infty} \left[\left(\frac{1}{n} g \right) \circ \left(\frac{1}{n} x \right) \right]^n$$

$$= g \circ \prod_{k=1}^{n} \left\{ \left(\frac{1}{n} g\right)^{k-n} \circ \left(\frac{1}{n} x\right) \circ \left(\frac{1}{n} g\right)^{n-k} \right\},$$

$$\epsilon g S = Sg.$$

Hence $g+S=Sg$, and

(31β) *If S is normal, then the associated subalgebra of $L(G)$ is invariant*† *and the cosets of S are the hyperplanes parallel to the manifold of S.*

We shall prove converses to (31α)–(31β) in (32β) and corollary 15.5.

32. **The adjoint group.** Using the commutation function, one can easily deduce an explicit series for the adjoint group of §25.

Define T: $u \to T(u) = (y/n)^{-1} \circ u \circ (y/n)$. Then T is a linear transformation, and

$$\left| T(u) - \left(u + \left[u, \frac{1}{n} y\right]\right) \right| \leqq \left| u \circ \left(u, \frac{1}{n} y\right) - u - \left(u, \frac{1}{n} y\right) \right|$$
$$+ \left| \left(u, \frac{1}{n} y\right) - \left[u, \frac{1}{n} y\right] \right|$$
$$\leqq \frac{1}{n} \cdot M\left(|u| + \frac{1}{n} |y| \right) |u| \cdot |y|$$

(by (3), (27β) and (28ϵ)).

Hence by n-fold iteration and the binomial expansion,

$$\left| T^n(u) - \left\{ u + [u, y] + C_{n,2} \cdot \frac{1}{n^2} [[u, y], y] + \cdots \right\} \right|$$
$$\leqq M\left(|u| + \frac{1}{n} |y| \right) |u| |y|.$$

Whence, since $T^n(u) = y^{-1} \circ u \circ y$, passing to the limit, we have

$$| w(u, y) | \equiv \left| \{ y^{-1} \circ u \circ y \} - \left\{ u + [u, y] + \frac{1}{2!} [[u, y], y] + \cdots \right\} \right|$$
$$= o(|u|) \cdot |y|.$$

But since the terms are all linear in u, clearly

$$| w(u, y) | = n \left| w\left(\frac{1}{n} u, y\right) \right| = n \cdot o(1/n) \cdot |u| \cdot |y|.$$

That is, letting $n \uparrow \infty$, $|w(u, y)| = 0$, and so

† In the usual sense, that $x \epsilon S$ and $g \epsilon L(G)$ imply $[g, x] \epsilon S$.

$$(32\alpha)\quad y^{-1}xy = x + [x, y] + \frac{1}{2!}[[x, y], y] + \frac{1}{3!}[[[x, y], y], y] + \cdots .$$

From (32α) we deduce as a corollary,

(32β) *If the subalgebra associated with a given subgroup S of an analytical group G is invariant, then S is a normal subgroup.* (Converse of (31β).)

Chapter V. Function of composition

33. **Introduction.** The main purpose of this chapter is to show in §§34–36 how the function $x \circ y = f(x, y)$ of composition of any analytical group under canonical parameters, can be written as the sum of an infinite series of polynomials determined by the commutation† function $[x, y]$—and to deduce in §37 various corollaries from this fact.

F. Schur [16] first showed that this series was valid in all groups under canonical parameters. Campbell [3] and Hausdorff [8] have since obtained it by other methods,‡ and so we shall call it the "*SCH*-series."

The present exposition is preferable on three grounds to those cited. It applies to infinite-dimensional groups. It paraphrases identities on pure group products [§§38–40], and does not require Taylor's series or manipulations with matrix polynomials (which are unnatural in non-linear groups). And most important, it generalizes easily to yield similar series expressing the definite (product) integrals over fixed time intervals of variable linear combinations of infinitesimal transformations, in a form which (like the *SCH*-series§) is independent of the group which they generate.

In §§38–40, the paraphrases in terms of identities on group products, of the *SCH*-series and other identities in the theory of continuous groups, are developed. They are not a part of the technical argument—unlike the paraphrases of the identities of Lie-Jacobi, which are actually used in proving the latter. They have been included because they correlate the theories of discrete groups and continuous groups in a way essential to the full understanding of either.

---

† Expressions (x, y) or $[x, y]$ will be called "simple" commutators and brackets, respectively; the commutator (ϕ, ψ) of any two commutators ϕ and ψ of "lengths" $w(\phi)$ and $w(\psi)$—where for uniformity individual letters are regarded as commutators of length one—will be called a "complex" commutator of "length" $w(\phi)+w(\psi)$. Similarly with complex brackets $[\phi, \psi]$ of "length" $w(\phi)+w(\psi)$.

‡ Schur starts with the obvious identity $f(x, (\lambda+\delta)y) = f(x, \lambda y) \circ \delta y$, determines $d/d\lambda\{f(x, \lambda y)\}$ from this, and integrates the resulting differential equation. Campbell and Hausdorff develop the series by setting $e^x e^y = e^{f(x,y)}$, and use the algebra of matrices to solve for $f(x, y) = \log[1 + (e^x e^y - 1)]$—thus introducing an extraneous operation of addition.

§ The *SCH*-series is the case where x operates first for a unit of time, followed by y operating for a unit of time.

34. **Product-equivalence of paths.** Let G be any analytical group under canonical parameters. Then

(34α) *The problem of determining* $x \circ y = f(x, y)$ *is equivalent to that of determining, given two short paths* P *and* Q, *whether or not* $t(P^*) = t(Q^*)$.

(We shall express the relation $t(P^*) = t(Q^*)$ by writing $P \sim Q$, and saying P is *product-equivalent* to Q. By (14θ), $P \approx Q$ implies $P \sim Q$.)

Proof. Since $x \circ y = t((P_x \oplus P_y)^*)$ under canonical parameters, we have found the $z = f(x, y)$ when‡ we have found the $P_z \sim P_x \oplus P_y$. While conversely, $t(Q^*)$ is approximated arbitrarily closely and hence determined by the $t(Q_\pi^*) = t(Q_1) \circ \cdots \circ t(Q_r)$ for the different partitions π of Q—and the $t(Q_1) \circ \cdots \circ t(Q_r)$ are determined by Q and the function of composition.

From (34α) and the known existence of an *SCH*-series expressing $f(x, y)$ in terms of the commutation function, we certainly can infer that $t(Q^*)$ is determined by Q and the commutation function in a way valid in all groups G under canonical parameters. But it by no means gives us explicit series for Q^* (except when $Q = P_x \oplus P_y$)—and it is such series that we shall finally obtain, getting the *SCH*-series as a special case (cf. §36).

Our first step will be to determine, given Q, all the $P \sim Q$. To this end we prove

(34β) *Let* P *and* Q *be any admissible paths with domain* $[0, \Lambda]$. *Then* $P \sim Q$ *if and only if some* U: $u(\lambda)$ *exists, such that* $u(0) = u(\Lambda) = 0$ *and*

$$| \delta p - [u^{-1}(\lambda) \circ \delta q \circ u(\lambda) + \delta u\dagger] | \leqq o(| \Delta Q | + | \Delta U |).$$

Proof. Suppose $P \sim Q$, and write $p^*(\lambda) = q^*(\lambda) \circ u(\lambda)$. Since $p^*(0) = 0 = q^*(0)$ and $p^*(\Lambda) = t(P^*) = t(Q^*) = q^*(\Lambda)$, $u(0) = u(\Lambda) = 0$. Define $R = P^*$, so that $P = R\dagger$. Clearly if Δ: $[\lambda, \mu]$ is any interval, then by (14η)

$$\begin{aligned} t((\Delta P)^*) &= t((\Delta R\dagger)^*) = r^{-1}(\lambda) \circ r(\mu) \\ &= \{u^{-1}(\lambda) \circ [q^{*-1}(\lambda) \circ q^*(\mu)] \circ u(\lambda)\} \circ \{u^{-1}(\lambda) \circ u(\mu)\} \\ &= \{u^{-1}(\lambda) \circ t((\Delta Q)^*) \circ u(\lambda)\} \circ t((\Delta U\dagger)^*). \end{aligned}$$

But $|\Delta P| = O(|\Delta R|) \leqq O(|\Delta Q^*| + |\Delta U|) \leqq O(|\Delta Q| + |\Delta U|)$; besides $|t((\Delta P)^*) - t(\Delta P)| \leqq o(|\Delta P|)$, and similarly with ΔQ and ΔU (by (14e)) even after the inner automorphism induced by $u(\lambda)$. Moreover by (3) $|x \circ y - (x+y)| = o(|x| + |y|)$; consequently if we write $\delta p = t(\Delta P)$, $\delta q = t(\Delta Q)$ and $\delta u = t(\Delta U)$, we get

$$| \delta p - [u^{-1}(\lambda) \circ \delta q \circ u(\lambda) + \delta u\dagger] | = o(| \Delta Q | + | \Delta U |).$$

---

‡ We recall the notation P_x for the path $p_x(\lambda) = \lambda x$ defined on $[0, 1]$, and $P_x \oplus P_y$ for the broken line R: $r(\lambda) = \lambda x$ on $[0, 1]$, and $r(\lambda) = x + (\lambda - 1)y$ on $[1, 2]$.

Conversely, suppose that this inequality is satisfied for some $u(\lambda)$ (of bounded variation‡) with $u(0)=u(\Lambda)=0$. Then, when we write $r(\lambda)=q^*(\lambda) \circ u(\lambda)$, obviously $t((R\dagger)^*)=t(R)=t(Q^*)$. Moreover by the argument above, $r\dagger(\lambda)$ satisfies the given inequality. Therefore by the triangle inequality,

$$|\delta p - \delta r\dagger| \leqq M(|\Delta Q| + |\Delta U|)\cdot(|\Delta Q| + |\Delta U|).$$

Hence if π is any partition of $[0, \lambda]$, writing $\|\pi\|$ for sup $(|\Delta Q|+|\Delta U|)$, and summing inequalities, we get

$$\begin{aligned}|p(\lambda) - r\dagger(\lambda)| &= |[p(\lambda) - p(0)] - [r\dagger(\lambda) - r\dagger(0)]| \\ &\leqq M(\|\pi\|)\cdot(|Q| + |U|),\end{aligned}$$

whence in the limit $p(\lambda)\equiv r\dagger(\lambda)$.

We can rewrite (34β) perhaps more suggestively in the notation of differentials, as

$$(34\gamma) \qquad dp = u^{-1}(\lambda) \circ dq \circ u(\lambda) + du\dagger.$$

35. **Devices for calculation.** Consider the terms of this formula. By (32α), $u^{-1} \circ dq \circ u$ can be calculated explicitly from U, Q and the commutation function.

Again, although we have not shown how to calculate $U\dagger$ from U explicitly§ by using the commutation function, we can now do so in case U is *unidimensional.*

(A path U: $u(\lambda)$ will be called "unidimensional" if and only if it is confined to a straight line—i.e., if and only if for some u_0, $u(\lambda)=\alpha(\lambda)u_0$. If U is unidimensional, then by Theorem 5, $U_\pi^*=U_\pi\dagger=U$ identically, whence in the limit $U^*=U\dagger=U$. By a "unidimensional alteration" of any path Q with domain $[0, \Lambda]$, will be meant any path $P=R\dagger$ determined from an R: $r(\lambda)=q^*(\lambda) \circ [\alpha(\lambda)u_0]$ for which $\alpha(0)=\alpha(\Lambda)=0$. In this case, clearly $P\sim Q$ and furthermore by (34γ),

$$(35\alpha) \qquad dp = u^{-1}(\lambda) \circ dq \circ u(\lambda) + du.$$

And so P is determined by Q, $u(\lambda)$ and the commutation function.)

Since (32α) gives an infinite series in any case, the fact that only unidimensional alterations can be computed explicitly suggests the following procedure: decomposing a given Q into undimensional constituents, altering these one at a time, and justifying the computations by proving general properties of paths represented by infinite series. This we shall do, first proving

‡ I.e., such that the curve U: $u(\lambda)$ is rectifiable.

§ N.B.: $U\dagger$ differs from U by $M(|U|)$—and hence one can deform a given Q little by little into any desired shape (e.g., a straight ray), whose final position will be *determined* by Q and the commutation function. But its *calculation* involves integrating a (highly involved) differential equation.

(35β) *Let* $u_1(\lambda)$, $u_2(\lambda)$, $u_3(\lambda)$, $\cdots$ *be any twice differentiable functions with domain* $[0, \Lambda]$ *and values in a Banach space. Suppose that the* $\sup |u_k| \equiv \sup_{0 \leq \lambda \leq \Lambda} |u_k(\lambda)|$, *the* $\sup |u_k'|$, *and the* $\sup |u_k''|$ *all form convergent series. If* $[\lambda, \lambda + d\lambda]$ *is any subinterval of* $[0, \Lambda]$, $u(\lambda)$ *denotes* $\sum_{k=1}^{\infty} u_k(\lambda)$, *and* δu_k *denotes* $u_k(\lambda + d\lambda) - u_k(\lambda)$, *then*

$$\left| \delta u - d\lambda \left[\sum_{k=1}^{\infty} u_k'(\lambda) \right] \right| \leq O(|d\lambda|^2) \leq o(|d\lambda|).$$

Remark. It is a corollary that u is differentiable and has $\sum_{k=1}^{\infty} u_k'(\lambda)$ for derivative.

Proof. Since by the comparison test, all the series involved converge absolutely (and uniformly!), and the terms of absolutely convergent series can be permuted, clearly $\delta u = \sum_{k=1}^{\infty} \delta u_k$. Moreover for every k,

$$|\delta u_k - u_k'(\lambda) d\lambda| \leq \tfrac{1}{2}[\sup |u_k''|] \cdot d\lambda^2.$$

Summing, we get by the triangle law

$$\left| \delta u - d\lambda \left[\sum_{k=1}^{n} u_k'(\lambda) \right] \right| \leq d\lambda \sum_{n+1}^{\infty} \sup |u_k'(\lambda)| + d\lambda^2 \cdot \sum_{k=1}^{n} \sup |u_k''|.$$

When we pass to the limit, this becomes

$$\left| \delta u - d\lambda \left[\sum_{k=1}^{\infty} u_k'(\lambda) \right] \right| \leq d\lambda^2 \cdot \sum_{k=1}^{\infty} \sup |u_k''| \leq O(|d\lambda|^2).$$

It will be convenient to signify that the hypotheses of (35β) are satisfied by writing

$$U = U_1 + U_2 + U_3 + \cdots = \sum_{k=1}^{\infty} U_k.$$

We shall now get a path $R\dagger \sim P_x \oplus P_y$, from which we shall be able to calculate $f(x, y)$ by using an algorithm applicable to all analytical combinations of unidimensional paths. (The analyticity of $P_x \oplus P_y$ is concealed.)

THEOREM 14. *Let* R: $r(\lambda) = \lambda x \circ \lambda y$ *be defined on* $[0, 1]$. *Then* $P_x \oplus P_y \sim R\dagger$. *And (assuming* $|[x, y]| \leq |x| \cdot |y|$ *by* §30) *if* $|x| + |y| < 1/10$, *then*

$$r\dagger(\lambda) = \lambda y + \lambda x + \frac{\lambda^2}{2!}[x, y] + \frac{\lambda^3}{3!}[[x, y], y] + \cdots \equiv s(\lambda).$$

Proof. It is obvious from identities established in §14 that

$$t((P_x \oplus P_y)^*) = t(P_x) \circ t(P_y) = x \circ y = t(R) = t((R\dagger)^*).$$

The proof is complete if we can show that $|\delta r\dagger - \delta s| \leqq o(|d\lambda|)$. For if this is so, then the upper right-derivative of $|r\dagger(\lambda) - s(\lambda)|$ is zero everywhere, and so $r\dagger(\lambda) = s(\lambda)$. But by (35β), δs differs from $d\lambda\{y + x + \lambda[x, y] + \cdots\}$ by $o(|d\lambda|)$—and this is by (32α) $d\lambda\{y + y^{-\lambda} \circ x \circ y^{\lambda}\}$. Again, by (3) $d\lambda\{y + y^{-\lambda} \circ x \circ y^{\lambda}\}$ differs from

$$t((\delta R\dagger)^*) = (x^{\lambda} \circ y^{\lambda})^{-1} \circ (x^{\lambda+d\lambda} \circ y^{\lambda+d\lambda})$$
$$= (y^{-\lambda} \circ x^{d\lambda} \circ y^{\lambda}) \circ y^{d\lambda}$$

by $M(|d\lambda| \cdot |x|) \cdot |d\lambda| \cdot |y| \leqq o(|d\lambda|)$. And by (14ε) we have $|t((\delta R\dagger)^*) - \delta r\dagger| \leqq o(|d\lambda|)$—completing the chain of links of length $o(|d\lambda|)$ between δs and δr, and hence the proof.

36. **Evaluation of regular paths.** We can now find $f(x, y) = t(R) = t((R\dagger)^*)$ by a process which enables one to find series expressing $t(P^*)$ for *any* short path P which is "regular" in a sense defined below.

Accordingly, let G be any analytical group under canonical parameters, in which a scale of length has been so chosen that $[x, y] \leqq |x| \cdot |y|$. Let P be any path in G which can be written

$$P = P_1 + P_2 + P_3 + \cdots \qquad \text{(in the sense of (35}\beta)),$$

$$P_i\colon\ p_i(\lambda) = \rho_i(\lambda) \cdot b_i \qquad (0 \leqq \lambda \leqq 1),$$

where (1) the $\rho_i(\lambda)$ are analytical scalar functions with $\sum_{i=1}^{\infty} \int |d\rho_i| < 1/10$, (2) the b_i are brackets in elements $x_1, \cdots, x_r$ arranged in order of increasing length, and containing with any b_i and b_j, also $[b_i, b_j] = b_{f(i,j)}$. Such a path will be called *regular.*

Remark 1. By inserting dummy terms $0 \cdot b_i$, one can make *any* sum of scalar multiples of brackets in $x_1, \cdots, x_r$ satisfy (2) simply because the number of different brackets of any preassigned length w in $x_1, \cdots, x_r$, is finite.

Remark 2. If $|x| + |y|$ is small enough, then the $r\dagger(\lambda)$ of Theorem 14 is regular.

Remark 3. Since $|[x, y]| \leqq |x| \cdot |y|$, $|b_i| \leqq 1$ identically if $|x_1| \leqq 1, \cdots, |x_r| \leqq 1$.

THEOREM 15. *Let P be any regular path. Then $t(P^*)$ is $\sum_{i=1}^{\infty} \gamma_i b_i$, where each γ_i can be calculated from $\rho_1(\lambda), \cdots, \rho_i(\lambda)$ in a finite number of rational operations, integrations, and differentiations. The calculations are independent of G.*

Outline of proof. We shall construct paths $P'' \sim P' = P$, $P''' \sim P''$, $P^{\text{iv}} \sim P'''$, $\cdots$ by successive unidimensional alterations. Each $P^{\nu+1}$ will be "regular" in the same sense that P is, except that 1/10 may be replaced by some other constant $< 1/5$. Moreover the $\rho_i^{\nu+1}(\lambda)$ for $i \leqq \nu$ will be of the form $\lambda\gamma_i$—where γ_i is independent of ν—and the $\rho_i^{\nu+1}(\lambda)$ for $i>\nu$ will be increasingly negligible—whence $t(P^*)=\sum_{i=1}^{\infty}\gamma_i\cdot b_i$.

Definition of $P^{\nu+1}$ by induction. If one sets

$$u_\nu(\lambda) = [\lambda\rho_\nu^\nu(1) - \rho_\nu^\nu(\lambda)]\cdot b_\nu \equiv \beta_\nu(\lambda)\cdot b_\nu$$

and can obtain a $P^{\nu+1}=\sum_{i=1}^{\infty}\rho_i^{\nu+1}(\lambda)\cdot b_i$ from P^ν through unidimensional alteration by $u_\nu(\lambda)$, then assuming the term-by-term differentiability of all series, by (32α) and (35α), we obtain heuristically

$$(*) \qquad dp^{\nu+1} = dp^{\nu} + d\beta_\nu(\lambda)b_\nu + \sum_{j,k=1}^{\infty} d\rho_j^{\nu}\cdot[\beta_\nu(\lambda)]^k\cdot b_{i(j,k)}\cdot\frac{1}{k!},$$

where $b_{i(j,1)}\equiv[b_j, b_\nu]$ and $b_{i(j,k)}\equiv[b_{i(j,k-1)}, b_\nu]$. But clearly $i(j, k)=i$ has in no case an infinity of solutions (j, k). Hence we can certainly *define*

$$\rho_i^{\nu+1}(\lambda) = \rho_i^{\nu}(\lambda) + \sum_{i(j,k)=i}\int\frac{1}{k!}[\beta_\nu(\lambda)]^k\cdot d\rho_j^{\nu}$$

with the assurance of obtaining analytical $\rho_i^{\nu+1}(\lambda)$—and using only rational operations, integration, and differentiation.

Actual proof. Let us do this. Then—since the length of no $b_{i(j,k)}$ exceeds that of b_ν—certainly by construction $\rho_\nu^{\nu+1}(\lambda)=\lambda\rho_\nu^\nu(1)=\lambda\gamma_\nu$, and for $i<\nu$, $\rho_i^{\nu+1}(\lambda)=\rho_i^\nu(\lambda)=\lambda\gamma_i$ by induction. Furthermore

(36α) *The series* (*) *converge in the sense of* (35β). *Consequently* (*collecting terms*) $P^{\nu+1}=\sum_{i=1}^{\infty}P_i^{\nu+1}$ *in the same sense. Moreover* $\sum_{i=1}^{\infty}\int|d\rho_i^{\nu+1}|<1/5$.

Remark. They even converge absolutely if we replace each bracket by the product of the absolute values of its entries.

Proof. If $\sigma(\lambda)$, $\beta(\lambda)$ and $\rho(\lambda)$ are *any* real analytical functions, then certainly

$$\begin{cases} \sup|\sigma| \leqq \int|d\sigma| = \int|\beta|^k\cdot|d\rho| \\ \qquad\qquad \leq \left[\int|d\beta|\right]^k\cdot\left[\int|d\rho|\right], \\ \sup|\sigma'| \leqq \left[\int|d\beta|\right]^k\cdot\sup|\rho'|, \\ \sup|\sigma''| \leqq k\cdot\left[\int|d\beta|\right]^{k-1}\cdot\sup|\rho'| + \left[\int|d\beta|\right]^k\cdot\sup|\rho''| \end{cases}$$

(differentiation is indicated by superscribing primes). Hence by induction on ν,—since $\sum_{k=1}^{\infty}\lambda^k=\lambda/(1-\lambda)$ and $\sum_{k=1}^{\infty}k\lambda^k<+\infty$ if $|\lambda|<1$—the series (*) converges in the sense of (35β). Moreover (since grouping terms never increases sums of absolute values) for the same reasons $\sum_{i=1}^{\infty}\int|d\rho_i^{\nu+1}|$ (which bounds $\sum_{i=1}^{\infty}\sup|\rho_i^{\nu+1}|$) does not exceed the corresponding sum for P^ν by a proportion of more than $\int|d\rho_\nu^\nu|/(1-\int|d\rho_\nu^\nu|)$. And by induction this is at most $5\int|d\rho_\nu^\nu|/4$. Consequently

$$\sum_{i=\nu+1}^{\infty}\int|d\rho_i^{\nu+1}| \leqq \sum_{i=\nu}^{\infty}\int|d\rho_i^{\nu}| - \int|d\rho_\nu^{\nu}| + \frac{1}{5}\left(\frac{5}{4}\int|d\rho_\nu^{\nu}|\right)$$

$$\leqq \sum_{i=\nu}^{\infty}\int|d\rho_i^{\nu}| - \frac{3}{4}\int|d\rho_\nu^{\nu}|$$

and

$$\sum_{i=1}^{\nu}\int|d\rho_i^{\nu+1}| \leqq \sum_{i=1}^{\nu-1}\int|d\rho_i^{\nu}| + \int|d\rho_\nu^{\nu}|.$$

But four-thirds of the first sum, plus the second sum, is non-increasing as $\nu\uparrow\infty$—whence the second sum is always bounded by $\frac{4}{3}\cdot\frac{1}{10}<\frac{1}{5}$, and the first tends to zero.

This proves (36α). Hence (regrouping the terms of (*) through (32α)), by (32α) and (35α), $P^{\nu+1}\sim P^\nu\sim P$. And since by inequalities just proved, $|t((P^{\nu+1})^*)-\sum_{i=1}^{\nu}\gamma_i b_i|$ tends to zero as ν increases, $t(P^*)\equiv t((P^\nu)^*)=\sum_{i=1}^{\infty}\gamma_i\cdot b_i$.

This completes the proof of Theorem 15.

37. **Corollaries of Theorem** 15. Theorem 15 has several immediate corollaries of primary theoretical importance. We shall list some of these now.

COROLLARY 15.1. *One can write $f(x, y)$ as the sum of an infinite series of scalar multiples of brackets of x and y arranged in order of increasing weight; each coefficient can be computed after a finite number of rational operations, and are rational numbers.*

Proof. In Theorem 14, $r\dagger(\lambda)$ is (cf. Remark 2 above) a regular path whose $\rho_i(\lambda)$ are polynomials (of degree at most the length $w(b_i)$ of b_i) with rational numbers as coefficients. These properties are preserved under the rational operations, differentiations, and integrations performed above—any polynomial can be differentiated or integrated by rational operations on its coefficients.

(The reader will find it instructive to compute the terms of degrees two and three.)

Caution. Because of the linear interdependence (due to the identities of Lie-Jacobi) between the brackets of length w, the series of Theorem 15 is not unique; its computation depends on the arrangement of the brackets of each length w.

COROLLARY 15.2. *The function $x \circ y = f(x, y)$ of composition of any analytical group G under canonical parameters is analytical.*

Proof. By §24, brackets are polynomial functions.

COROLLARY 15.3. *If the Lie albebra of G is "w-nilpotent" (that is, if all brackets of length w vanish), then $f(x, y)$ is a polynomial of degree at most r.*

COROLLARY 15.4. *Two analytical groups having topologically isomorphic Lie algebras are locally topologically isomorphic (and so analytically isomorphic).*

Proof. Within some neighborhood of the identity, and under canonical parameters, they have the same function of composition.

COROLLARY 15.5. *Let L be the Lie algebra of any analytical group G, and let S be any closed subalgebra of L. Then the elements in S near the origin are an analytical subgroup nucleus.*

Proof. They are a subgroup (by Corollary 15.1), satisfy (1), (2), (2′), and are a complete linear subspace of L.

From Corollary 5 and (31α), we get

COROLLARY 15.6. *The analytical subgroup nuclei of any analytical group G under canonical parameters, are the closed subalgebras of its metric Lie algebra.*

COROLLARY 15.7. *A locally compact analytical group is a Lie group in the usual sense.*

Proof. Any locally compact Banach space is finite-dimensional by [1], p. 84, and the function of composition is by Corollary 2 analytical under canonical parameters.

COROLLARY 15.8. *A commutative analytical group nucleus under canonical parameters is a neighborhood of the origin in a Banach space.*

38. **Digression: paths and group-products.** Since to assert $x_1 \circ \cdots \circ x_n = y_1 \circ \cdots \circ y_n$ is to assert

$$P_{x_1} \oplus \cdots \oplus P_{x_n} \sim P_{y_1} \oplus \cdots \oplus P_{y_n},$$

and since every admissible path can be approximated arbitrarily closely by broken lines, one would expect product-equivalences‡ $P \sim Q$ between images of an interval $[0, \Lambda]$ to correspond to algebraic identities between group products. We shall sketch in §38 some crude examples of such correspondences.

The identity $xy = yx(x, y)$ shows that if Q is any broken line, one can replace any two segments of Q by the opposite sides of the parallelogram which

‡ We recall the notation $P \sim Q$ meaning $t(P^*) = t(Q^*)$.

they determine, without altering $t(Q^*)$, provided a small deviation (x, y) is inserted.

The graphical principle (essential in the classical proofs of Green's and Stokes' Theorems) that any path-deformation can be split up into elementary deformations across parallelograms, is analogous to the algebraic principle that any permutation of terms in a sequence is the product of transpositions.

The derivation in §34, given a path Q, of paths $P\sim Q$ by choosing $v^*(0)=v^*(\Lambda)=0$ and setting

$$dp = v^{*-1}(\lambda) \circ dq \circ v^*(\lambda) + dv$$

corresponds to taking a product $x_1 \circ \cdots \circ x_n$ and a second product $u_1 \circ \cdots \circ u_n = e$, defining $v_k^* = u_1 \circ \cdots \circ u_k$ and proving by induction $\prod_{i=1}^k [(v_{i-1}^{*-1} \circ x_i \circ v_{i-1}^*) \circ u_i] = x_1 \circ \cdots \circ x_k \circ v_k^*$, and thus concluding that

$$(38\alpha) \qquad \prod_{k=1}^{n} x_k = \prod_{k=1}^{n} [(\overset{*-1}{v_{k-1}} \circ x_k \circ \overset{*}{v_{k-1}}) \circ u_k].$$

39. **Digression: the Rearrangeability Principle.** In correlating the argument of §§34–36 with formal identities on group products, let us begin by recalling a recent result of P. Hall ([7], Theorem 3.1), namely

$$(39\alpha) \qquad (xy)^n \equiv x^n y^n z_1^{\phi_1(n)} \cdots z_t^{\phi_t(n)} \pmod{H_w},$$

where the z_k are complex commutators in x and y of lengths $<w$ arranged in order of increasing length, the exponents ϕ_k are polynomials of degree $w(z_k)$, and H_w is the normal subgroup whose elements are the products of commutators of lengths $\geqq w$.

That there exist (not necessarily polynomial) *functions* $\phi_k(n)$ such that (39α) is satisfied, is very easy to show. For since $uv = vu(u, v)$, one can transpose any two adjacent terms in any product involving x, y, and their commutators, by inserting commutators of lengths greater than the length of either transposed term. Hence one can first shift all the occurrences of x in such a product to the extreme left, then all the occurrences of y to positions just to the right of these, and similarly with $z_1, \cdots, z_t$.

This method, combined with the rule that any permutation can be accomplished by successive transpositions, obviously yields a general

Rearrangeability Principle. If one is given *any* product ψ involving elements $x_1, \cdots, x_n$ and their commutators, *any* integer w, and *any* ordering ρ of the x_k and their commutators of weights $<w$, then ψ is congruent modulo commutators of weights $\geqq w$ to a product of powers of the x_k and their commutators arranged in the sequence ρ.

More than this, one can *distribute* their occurrences according to any preassigned distribution function.

These principles are the key to the algebraic situation. Using them, one can show for instance that if $m=n^w$, then

$$x^m y^m \equiv \prod_{k=1}^{n} v_k \pmod{H_w}, \tag{39β}$$

where each v_k is of the form $x^{m/n}y^{m/n}z_1^{\zeta_1(m;k)} \cdots z_t^{\zeta_t(m;k)}$ and $|\zeta_h(m;i)-\zeta_h(m;j)| \leq 1$, which means that the v_k are all nearly equal.

Proof. Write $x^m y^m = (x^{m/n})(x^{m/n}) \cdots (x^{m/n})(x^{m/n}y^m)$. Then transpose the occurrences of y (inserting commutators, of course) until you obtain the identity

$$x^m y^m = (x^{m/n}y^{m/n}u_1)(x^{m/n}y^{m/n}u_2) \cdots (x^{m/n}y^{m/n}u_3),$$

where the u_k are congruent (mod H_w) to products of the commutators z_k of lengths $<w$. Proceed by induction, dividing the occurrences of each z_h $(h=1, \cdots, t)$ into n nearly equal lots, and you will get (39β).

Now suppose x and y are elements of a continuous group under canonical parameters. Write $x^m=\bar{x}$ and $y^m=\bar{y}$; since the v_k are nearly equal, if we know by (27β) that the elements of H_w are relatively small, we see that $|f(\bar{x}, \bar{y})-nv_1|$ is small, where for n large v_1 is nearly determined by x, y, and the commutation function $[x, y]$.

40. **Digression (cont.): analyticity and other remarks.** We do not have to go far beyond the same principles to see from an algebraic standpoint even why an SCH-series exists, in the way that it does.

To see this, observe that for fixed $x^m=\bar{x}$, $y^m=\bar{y}$ and very large n, since x and y are correspondingly small, (1) products are nearly sums, and (2) commutators are nearly equal to the corresponding brackets. Hence if b_h denotes the bracket in $\bar{x}$ and $\bar{y}$ corresponding to the commutator in x and y denoted by z_h, and $\lambda_h = n\zeta_h(m; 1)/n^{w(z_h)}$, then the smallness of $|f(\bar{x}, \bar{y})-nv_1|$ implies the smallness of $|f(\bar{x}, \bar{y})-\{\bar{x}+\bar{y}+\sum_{h=1}^{t}\lambda_h b_h\}|$. This gives one the first $(t+2)$ terms of an SCH-series, approximately.

Actually, the λ_h are polynomials whose dominating terms are independent of m, although the reasons for this are number-theoretical and not at all trivial, and the calculation of the dominating terms is not even impossibly laborious.

Similar reasoning yields an algebraic paraphrase of Theorem 15. Take any path X: $x(\lambda)=\sum_{i=1}^{r}\rho_i(\lambda)\cdot x_i$. Divide X into $m=n^w$ equal parts, set

$\mu_i{}^k = \rho_i(k,n) - \rho_i([k-1]/n)$ and $x = y^m$, and obtain through the Rearrangeability Principle (as with (39β)), an identity‡

$$(40\alpha) \qquad \prod_{k=1}^{n}\left(\prod_{i=1}^{r} y_i^{[m\mu_i{}^k]}\right) \equiv \prod_{k=1}^{n} v_k \pmod{H_w},$$

where the v_k are products $\prod_{h=1}^{t} z_h{}^{\xi_h(m;k)}$ of nearly equal powers of commutators z_h in the y_i. But replacing each commutator z_h of length w_h in the y_i by $(m^{-w_h})\cdot b_h$, where b_h denotes the bracket in the x_i corresponding to z_h—the substitution is nearly one of equals for equals—and setting $\gamma_h(m) = nm^{-w_h}\zeta_h(m;1)$, (40α) becomes

$$(40\alpha) \qquad t(X^*) \text{ is nearly } \sum_{h=1}^{t} \gamma_h(m)\cdot b_h,$$

the calculation of $\gamma_h(m)$ being the same for all groups.

41. **Every metric Lie algebra belongs to a group.** We can now prove by considerations of convergence, that

THEOREM 16. *Every metric Lie algebra L is the Lie algebra of an analytical group nucleus.*

Proof. Define group products $x \circ y = f(x, y)$ in L through the *SCH*-series. There are three points to establish: the convergence of the series, the validity of the inequalities (2′)–(2″), and the associative law $f(f(x, y), z) = f(x, f(y, z))$.

By Remark 2 of §30, we can assume $|[x, y]| \leqq |x|\cdot|y|$. Then by the proof of Theorem 15 (cf. the remark after (36α)), if we substitute for each bracket in the *SCH*-series, the product of the absolute values of its entries, and if these are $<1/10$, then the sum of the absolute values of the resulting series is bounded by $2(|x|+|y|)$. The *convergence* of $f(x, y)$ provided $|x|+|y| < 1/10$ is a weak corollary of this.

Again, expanding $[f(x, a) - f(x, b)] - (a - b)$ in *SCH*-series, we have by Theorem 14 after cancellation and pairing off of corresponding terms, scalar multiples of differences such as

$$\begin{aligned}\Phi &= [x, [a, x], a] - [x, [b, x], b] \\ &= [x, [a-b, x], a] + [x, [b, x], a-b]\end{aligned}$$

whose magnitude is bounded by $|x|\cdot|a-b|$ times the number n_i of entries in the bracket, times what we would get if we replaced every bracket by the product of the absolute values of all but one of its entries. But the sum

‡ $[m\mu_i{}^k]$ denotes conventionally the integral part of $m\mu_i{}^k$.

of the products of these last two factors still converges absolutely provided $|a|+|b|+|x|<1/20$, so that $n_i(1/20)^{n_i-1}<10(1/10)^{n_i}$. Hence

$$|(xa-xb)|-|(a-b)|\leqq K\cdot|x|\cdot|a-b|$$

within this region. This implies (2′); (2″) follows by symmetry. It remains to prove the associative law.

Here we do the obvious thing: substitute the *SCH*-series for u in the *SCH*-series for $f(u, z)$, and likewise the *SCH*-series for $f(y, z)$ for v in the *SCH*-series for $f(x, v)$, and expand in both cases by the distributive law. We will get two series of monomial brackets in x, y, z, with possible repetitions. If they are absolutely convergent, then by the continuity implied in (2′)–(2″) they will converge to $f((x, y), z)$ and $f(x, f(y, z))$ respectively. We shall next prove that they are absolutely convergent.

If $|x|+|y|+|z|<1/80$, and we replace each bracket in the series for $f(f(x, y), z)$ by the product of the absolute values of its entries, then the sum of the absolute values of what we get is by the distributive law (on scalars) what we *would* get if we replaced brackets by products in the *SCH*-series for $f(u, z)$, replaced z by $|z|$, and u by the sum of the absolute values of the terms in the *SCH*-series for $f(x, y)$. And since both of these are $<1/40$, the series for $f(f(x, y), z)$ is absolutely convergent. The absolute convergence of the series for $f(x, f(y, z))$ follows by symmetry.

Hence to prove that $f(f(x, y), z)=f(x, f(y, z))$ we need only show that irrespective of n, the sum of the terms of length $\leqq n$ is the same for the two series. The demonstration of this essentially algebraic fact completes the proof.

Demonstration. Form the multiplicative group of all non-commutative polynomials $I+U=I+\lambda_1X+\lambda_2Y+\lambda_3Z+\cdots$ in X, Y, Z, ignoring terms of degree $>n$. This is a (4^n-1)-parameter Lie group, in which $(I+U)^{-1}=I-U+U^2-\cdots+(-1)^nU^n$. Since the group is analytical, the functions $f(f(X, Y), Z)$ and $f(X, f(Y, Z))$ are identically equal near $X=Y=Z=0$, and hence formally equal. Moreover as in all linear groups, $[U, V]=VU-UV$. But by Theorem 3 of the author's *Representability of Lie algebras and Lie groups by matrices*, Annals of Mathematics, vol. 38 (1937), pp. 526–532, any identity between alternants $VU-UV$ follows formally from the identities of Lie-Jacobi. Hence the equality between the sums of the terms of degree $\leqq n$ in the two series follows formally from the identities of Lie-Jacobi (which we assumed at the beginning).

Bibliography

1. S. Banach, *Théorie des Opérations Linéaires*, Warsaw, 1932.

2. G. Birkhoff, *Integration of functions with values in a Banach space*, these Transactions, vol. 38 (1935), pp. 357–378.

3. J. E. Campbell, *On a law of combination of operators*, Proceedings of the London Mathematical Society, vol. 28 (1897), pp. 381–390.

4. E. Cartan, *Notice sur les Travaux Scientifiques de M. Élie Cartan*, Chap. VIII, Paris, 1931.

5. E. Cartan, *Les groupes continus et l'analysis situs*, Mémorials des Sciences Mathématique, Fasc. 42, Paris, 1930.

6. J. Delsarte, *Les groupes de transformations linéaires dans l'espace de Hilbert*, Mémorials des Sciences Mathématiques, Fasc. 57, Paris, 1932.

7. P. Hall, *A contribution to the theory of groups of prime-power orders*, Proceedings of the London Mathematical Society, vol. 36 (1933), pp. 29–95.

8. F. Hausdorff, *Die symbolische Exponentialformel in der Gruppentheorie*, Leipzig Berichte, vol. 58 (1906), pp. 19–48.

9. S. Lie, *Transformationsgruppen*, Leipzig, 1888.

10. S. Lie, *Unendlich continuirliche Gruppen*, Abhandlungen, Sachsische Gesellschaft der Wissenschaften, vol. 21 (1895), pp. 43–150.

11. W. Mayer and T. Y. Thomas, *Foundations of the theory of continuous groups*, Annals of Mathematics, vol. 36 (1935), pp. 770–782.

12. J. von Neumann, *Gruppen linearen Transformationen*, Mathematische Zeitschrift, vol. 30 (1929), pp. 3–42.

13. S. Saks, *Théorie de l'Intégrale*, Warsaw, 1933.

14. L. Schlesinger, *Neue Grundlagen für eine Infinitesimalkalkul der Matrizen*, Mathematische Zeitschrift, vol. 33 (1931), pp. 33–61.

15. O. Schreier, *Abstrakte kontinuierliche Gruppen*, Hamburger Abhandlungen, vol. 4 (1926), pp. 15–32.

16. F. Schur, *Neue Begründung der Theorie der endlichen Transformations gruppen*, Mathematische Annalen, vol. 35 (1889), pp. 161–197.

17. V. Volterra, *Sulle equazione differenziali lineari*, Rendiconti dei Lincei, vol. 3 (1887). pp 391–396.

Harvard University,
Cambridge, Mass.

Reprinted from *Trans. Am. Math. Soc.* **43** (1938), 61–101

REPRESENTATION OF JORDAN AND LIE ALGEBRAS

BY

GARRETT BIRKHOFF AND PHILIP M. WHITMAN(1)

1. **Introduction.** In a linear associative algebra A one can introduce a new product $\theta(x, y)$ in terms of the given operations by setting

$$\theta(x, y) = \alpha xy + \beta yx, \tag{1}$$

where α and β are scalars independent of x and y, α and β not both zero. Albert [3] observes(2) that if a linear subset S of A is closed under θ (in particular, if S is A itself) then S is of one of three types: S is an associative algebra, closed under the given multiplication xy; or S is a Lie algebra with product obtained by setting $\alpha=1$ and $\beta=-1$ in (1):

$$[x, y] = yx - xy; \tag{2}$$

or S is a Jordan algebra with product obtained by setting $\alpha=\beta=1/2$ in (1):

$$x \cdot y = (xy + yx)/2. \tag{3}$$

We propose to study various generalizations, properties, and representations of Lie and Jordan algebras.

2. **Definitions and problems.** We begin with a generalization of the idea of equation (1) of the previous section.

Let $\mathfrak{A}$ be any set of abstract algebras(3) closed under given n_i-ary basic operations f_i, and let Θ be any set of operations $\theta_1, \cdots, \theta_n$ obtained by compounding the f_i. If $A \in \mathfrak{A}$, then the elements of A together with the operations $\theta_1, \cdots, \theta_n$ form an algebra $\Theta(A)$. All algebras which can be obtained in this manner for fixed Θ [and hence fixed $\mathfrak{A}$] are called θ-algebras. Clearly the definition of $\Theta(A)$ is also applicable to the case where A is closed under the θ_i but not under the f_i; we consider examples of this in Theorems 8–10

Presented to the Society, August 23, 1946, under the title *Representation theory for certain non-associative algebras*; received by the editors December 8, 1947.

(1) This paper was presented in part to the Algebra Conference, University of Chicago, July, 1946. The junior author wishes to express his appreciation of a Frederick Gardner Cottrell Grant by the Research Corporation which assisted this research.

(2) In describing earlier work on the subject, it must be remembered that A is usually given as an algebra of matrices or of linear transformations. We shall assume familiarity with the correspondence between associative algebras and algebras of matrices. Any algebra of matrices is associative under ordinary matrix multiplication, while (essentially through its "regular representation") every linear associative algebra is isomorphic to an algebra of matrices. The general theory is due to E. Noether [21]. Numbers in brackets refer to the references cited at the end of the paper.

(3) For the general theory of algebras, see G. Birkhoff [5], [8]; McKinsey and Tarski [18], [19], [22].

below. However, for the present we require closure under the f_i as well.

By a *Lie algebra* we mean an algebra L such that $L=\Theta(A)$ for some associative algebra A when $\Theta=\{\theta_1, \theta_2\}$ where

$$\theta_1(x, y) = x + y, \qquad \theta_2(x, y) = yx - xy; \tag{4}$$

cf. (2).

By a *special*(4) *Jordan algebra* we mean an algebra J such that $J=\Theta(A)$ for some associative algebra A when $\Theta=\{\theta_1, \theta_2\}$ where

$$\theta_1(x, y) = x + y, \qquad \theta_2(x, y) = (xy + yx)/2; \tag{5}$$

cf. (3). The field of scalars of course must not be of characteristic 2.

In these two cases respectively, $\Theta(A)$ may be denoted $L(A)$ and $J(A)$.

Conversely, if X is a given algebra (not necessarily associative) closed under its operations which are called $\theta_1, \theta_2, \cdots, \theta_n$ then we may seek to find an algebra A consisting of the same elements as X but with operations f_i, such that $X=\Theta(A)$. We may then say that we have exhibited X as a θ-algebra. In general, given an arbitrary X and Θ, it is not possible(5) to find an A by means of which we may exhibit X in the above sense. Hence, as usual in representation theory, we find it convenient to consider homomorphisms as well as isomorphisms, and to extend the meaning of our terms accordingly.

DEFINITION. Let X be a particular algebra with elements x_i and operations $\theta_1, \cdots, \theta_n$, let $\mathfrak{A}$ be a set of algebras, and let $\bar\theta_1, \cdots, \bar\theta_n$ be specified as compound operations on the elements of the algebras of $\mathfrak{A}$. Then a *θ-embedding*, or θ-representation, of X is a correspondence, $\alpha: x\rightarrow\alpha(x)$, from X into $A\in\mathfrak{A}$, such that

$$\alpha(\theta_i(x_1, \cdots, x_m)) = \bar\theta_i(\alpha(x_1), \cdots, \alpha(x_m)) \tag{6}$$

for all i and all $x_1, \cdots, x_m\in X$. We shall restrict ourselves to the case where A is generated by the $\alpha(x_i)$.

The algebra A is then called a *θ-envelope* of X.

The θ-embedding is called an *iso-θ-embedding* if the correspondence $x\rightarrow\alpha(x)$ is one-to-one, and then A is an iso-θ-envelope of X.

If $\alpha_1, \alpha_2, \cdots$ are θ-embeddings of X, in θ-envelopes $\{A_1, A_2, \cdots\}\in\mathfrak{A}$ then

$$x \rightarrow \alpha(x) \equiv (\alpha_1(x), \alpha_2(x), \cdots) \tag{7}$$

is a θ-embedding of X in a subalgebra $A_u(X)$ of the direct union $A_1\otimes A_2\otimes \cdots$, namely, the subalgebra generated by the set of all $(\alpha_1(x_i), \alpha_2(x_i), \cdots)$. But α_n

(4) The word *special* (sometimes *concrete*) is used to distinguish these algebras from those defined by identities without reference to an associative algebra; cf. Albert [4], Kalisch [16]. The question remains open whether special Jordan algebras can be defined by identities.

(5) For example, if Θ is the set of operations (5), it is known that the identity $a^2(ba) = (a^2b)a$ must be satisfied in X; cf. [15]. This does not, however, exclude the possibility of a comparable representation if other operations than the given f_i are taken as basic.

is a homomorphic image of α, in the sense that if $\alpha(x_i)=\alpha(x_j)$, then $\alpha_n(x_i)=\alpha_n(x_j)$, while by (6) and (7), both α and α_n are homomorphisms with respect to the θ_i. Hence we have the following theorem.

THEOREM 1. *If $\mathfrak{A}$ is closed under the operations of taking direct unions and subalgebras then there exists $A_u(X)\in\mathfrak{A}$ such that there is a θ-embedding θ_u of X in $A_u(X)$ and any other θ-embedding of X in an algebra of $\mathfrak{A}$ is a homomorphic image of θ_u.*

DEFINITION. θ_u is called the *universal* θ-embedding of X in $\mathfrak{A}$, and $A_u(X)$ is called the free θ-envelope of X [with reference to $\mathfrak{A}$] or universal θ-algebra of X. In the particular cases of equations (4) and (5) we shall speak respectively of Lie embeddings and envelopes and Jordan embeddings and envelopes.

Evidently $A_u(X)$ is the free algebra of $\mathfrak{A}$ in the sense that every $A_i\in\mathfrak{A}$ is a homomorphic image of $A_u(X)$, since the correspondence

$$[(a_1, a_2, \cdots, a_{i-1}, a_i, a_{i+1}, \cdots) \in A_u(X)] \to [a_i \in A_i]$$

is obviously such a homomorphism.

Then by applying the same homomorphism to the compound expressions in the operations of $\mathfrak{A}$ which define the θ_i, we see that $\Theta(A_i)$ is a homomorphic image of $\Theta(A_u)$. Hence $\Theta(A_u)$ is a free algebra for $\Theta(A)$, $A\in\mathfrak{A}$.

If some θ-embedding of X is one-to-one, X is called a *θ-algebra*. In this case we may identify the elements of X with their images in A.

If X is a θ-algebra, then θ_u must be one-to-one, for if it were many-to-one, so would be each other embedding (the latter being a homomorphic image of θ_u) contrary to hypothesis.

Among the problems which may be stated are these: When is X a θ-algebra? What identities are satisfied by θ-algebras for a given Θ, in particular by special Jordan algebras? Is the set of all θ-algebras, for given Θ, closed under the operations of taking subalgebras, direct unions, and homomorphic images?

As far as concerns subalgebras, it is obvious that the answer is yes: if Y is a subalgebra of X, and $X=\Theta(A)$, then we need only take the subalgebra B of A generated by the images of elements of Y, and $Y=\Theta(B)$.

Likewise, suppose X_1, X_2, $\cdots$ are given to be θ-algebras: $X_i=\Theta(A_i)$, $A_i\in\mathfrak{A}$. Then $X_1\otimes X_2\otimes\cdots$ can be put into one-to-one correspondence with the subset of $A_1\otimes A_2\otimes\cdots$ consisting of the $(\alpha_1(x_i), \alpha_2(x_j), \cdots)$, and the latter generates $A_1\otimes A_2\otimes\cdots$. Then

$$\Theta(A_1 \otimes A_2 \otimes \cdots) = \Theta(A_1) \otimes \Theta(A_2) \otimes \cdots = X_1 \otimes X_2 \otimes \cdots.$$

Thus this set of θ-algebras is closed under subalgebras and direct unions. Closure under the taking of homomorphic images remains undecided.

It is known [8, p. 324] that the set $\mathfrak{A}$ is definable by identities if and only if it is closed under the operations of taking subalgebras, direct unions, and homomorphic images.

Consider the congruence relation ϕ_i on $A_u(X)$ which identifies elements $(b_1, b_2, \cdots)$ and $(c_1, c_2, \cdots)$ of $A_u(X)$ if and only if $b_i = c_i$ for fixed i. As before, the algebra obtained by this identification is precisely A_i. In the case of linear algebras (including Lie, Jordan, and associative algebras) any congruence relation ϕ_i on $A_u(X)$ is determined by the set K_i of elements which are congruent to 0. Clearly K_i is a (two-sided) ideal; hence we may write $A_i = A_u(X)/K_i$.

It is natural to ask: for what K is $A_u(X)/K$ an iso-θ-envelope of X? Also we may seek to determine $A_u(X)$ for various X; in particular we would like to know how to solve the decision problem for X.

3. **A general property related to θ-embeddings.** We consider a canonical form for polynomials in a linear (not necessarily associative) algebra.

THEOREM 2. *In a linear algebra, any polynomial in elements e_i can be expressed as a linear combination of monomials $e_{i(1)}^{p(1)} e_{i(2)}^{p(2)} \cdots e_{i(r)}^{p(r)}$ with $i(1) < i(2) < \cdots < i(r)$, provided*

$$e_j e_i = \lambda_{ij} e_i e_j + \sum_k c_k^{ij} e_k,$$

where the λ_{ij} and c_k^{ij} are scalars.

Proof. Just as in the corresponding proof in [6], we can systematically shift the e_i with small subscripts to the left by introducing terms of lower degree and using induction. It is not guaranteed that the result of this procedure is unique.

This shows that the usual theory for noncommutative polynomials in one variable (Jacobson [14]) can be applied also to noncommutative polynomials in several variables. The scalars λ_{ij} and c_k^{ij} do not have to be permutable with the e_i; we can have $e_i\lambda = \phi_i(\lambda)e_i$.

4. **Determination of Lie envelopes.** We seek solutions, for Lie algebras, of some of the problems already mentioned.

Let X be any linear algebra satisfying

$$[x, y] + [y, x] = 0. \tag{8}$$

Then X has a basis (finite or infinite) of elements $e_1, e_2, \cdots$. Hence, for given x and y, $[x, y]$ is some finite linear combination of the e_i. In particular, this applies if x and y are basis elements; say

$$[e_i, e_j] = \sum_k c_k^{ij} e_k,$$

where only a finite number of e_n enter into the sum (though the basis may be infinite), and the c_k^{ij} are scalars ("structure constants"). From (2), we have in any Lie-envelope of X,

$$e_j' e_i' = e_i' e_j' + \sum_k c_k^{ij} e_k'$$

where e_k' is the image of e_k: $e_k' = \alpha(e_k)$.

Then Theorem 2 can be applied. It was shown in [6] and [24] that if

$$[[x, y], z] + [[y, z], x] + [[z, x], y] = 0 \tag{9}$$

also holds (so that X is a Lie algebra) then this construction produces a linear associative algebra $L_u(X)$ with infinite basis, and that X is the Lie algebra obtained from $L_u(X)$ by (2). Moreover, it is apparent from the construction that elements have been identified in $L_u(X)$ only when required by the hypothesis; hence, any other Lie-embedding of X is a homomorphic image of $L_u(X)$. Hence, in the previous notation, $L_u(X)$ is $A_u(X)$.

Thus every linear algebra satisfying (8) and (9) has an iso-Lie-embedding in a linear associative algebra. In fact [6, Theorem 2] all Lie-embeddings have been determined by rational methods. Conversely, starting with a linear associative algebra and using $[x, y] = yx - xy$ we get an algebra in which these laws hold. Thus the embedding problem for Lie algebras has been solved.

However, we do not obtain in the abstract case the theorem of I. Ado [1] and E. Cartan [10] that every linear algebra with *finite* basis over the real or complex field satisfying (8)–(9) has an isomorphic Lie-embedding with a finite basis and conversely.

Let us consider an example of Lie-embedding.

THEOREM 3. *Let G be the regular representation of a Lie group, and let $X^1, \cdots, X^r$ be the differential operators defining its Lie algebra L. Then the free Lie-envelope of L is isomorphic to the (associative) operator algebra generated by the X^i.*

Proof. Define G locally by canonical parameters; then the X^i are analytic and (see for instance Campbell [9, p. 332])

$$X^i = \partial/\partial x_i + \sum_k X_k^i \partial/\partial x_k, \qquad X_k^i(0) = 0.$$

Hence for any monomial in the X^i,

$$(X^1)^{n(1)} \cdots (X^r)^{n(r)} = \partial^{n(1)+\cdots+n(r)}/\partial x_1^{n(1)} \cdots \partial x_r^{n(r)} + \cdots,$$

where the last dots represent terms in which the differential operators are either of order less than $n(1) + \cdots + n(r)$ or else have coefficients which vanish at the group identity 0. Thus any monomial in the X^i is a linear combination of monomials of equal or lower degree, and the associative algebra is isomorphic to the free Lie-envelope.

We consider next a generalization of Hilbert's Basis Theorem.

THEOREM 4. *Let R be the ring of formal polynomials in $e_1, \cdots, e_n$ (n finite), with scalars in the field F, subject to the law*

$$e_j e_i = e_i e_j + \sum_k c_k^{ij} e_k. \tag{10}$$

Let J be a left ideal of R. Then J has a finite ideal basis.

Proof. Let $H_n(J)$ be the set of those homogeneous polynomial forms q of degree n such that $q+r\in J$ for some r of degree less than n (that is, let $H_n(J)$ be the set of "leading constituents" of degree n of the polynomials in J). We observe that each H_n, with 0 adjoined, is a linear subspace, since the sum or difference of two homogeneous polynomials of degree n either is again such a polynomial or is 0, and likewise for the product of such a polynomial by a scalar, while if q_1+r_1 and q_2+r_2 are in J, so are $(q_1\pm q_2)+(r_1\pm r_2)$ and $c(q_i+r_i)=cq_i+cr_i$, since J is an ideal.

Let $H(J)$ be the set of polynomial forms comprising the linear subspace generated by the $H_n(J)$ ($n=0, 1, 2, \cdots$). We assert that the elements of $H(J)$, taken as polynomial forms in either the ring R or the ring K of commutative polynomials generated by $e_1, \cdots, e_n$, are an ideal. For if h_1, $h_2\in H(J)$, so do ch_1 and h_1+h_2 since $H(J)$ is a linear space, while if $h\in H(J)$ and $q\in R$ or K, then write q and h as sums of homogeneous polynomials

$$q = q_1 + \cdots + q_s,\ h = h_1 + \cdots + h_t,\ h_i \in H_{f(i)}(J),\ d(q_i) = d_i$$

where $d(p)$ is the degree of p. Then $qh=\sum_{i,j}q_ih_j$. But q_ih_j is homogeneous of degree $d_i+f(j)$. Also $h_j\in H_{f(j)}$ implies $h_j+r\in J$ for some r of degree less than $f(j)$. Then q_ir is of degree less than $d_i+f(j)$, and $q_ih_j+q_ir=q_i(h_j+r)\in J$ since J is an ideal. Thus by construction $q_ih_j\in H_{d_i+f(j)}(J)$. Hence, $qh\in H(J)$ since $H(J)$ is a linear space. Thus $H(J)$ is an ideal. In this regard the only difference between $H(J)$ as a subspace of R and as a subspace of K is that different polynomials are identified in the two cases.

Let H^* denote the elements of the ideal $H(J)$, taken as polynomials in the ring K of commutative polynomials in $e_1, \cdots, e_n$. By Hilbert's Basis Theorem(6), H^* has a finite ideal-basis $p_1^*, \cdots, p_m^*$. Since $H(J)$ and H^* contain the same polynomial forms, we may consider $p_1^*, \cdots, p_m^*$ as belonging also to $H(J)$, in which case we shall denote them $p_1, \cdots, p_m$.

Thus $p_i\in H(J)$; by construction of H, p_i is a linear combination of elements of various $H_j(J)$:

$$p_i = \sum_j b_j^i q_j; \qquad q_j \in H_j(J); \qquad b_j^i \in F.$$

(6) See, for instance, van der Waerden [23].

But by construction of H_j, given $q_j \in H_j(J)$ then there exists r_j of degree less than j such that $q_j + r_j \in J$. Set

$$t_i \equiv \sum_j b_j^i (q_j + r_j).$$

Then $t_i \in J$. Let U be the ideal of R generated by the t_i. Then $U \subset J$.

Hence, $H_n(U) \subset H_n(J)$ for all n. But suppose $h \in H_n(J)$. Then $h^* \in H^*$, where h^* is the same polynomial form as h. Hence, $h^* = \sum_j y_j^* p_j^*$, $y_j^* \in H^*$. Let y_j be the polynomial form in H which becomes y_j^* in H^*. Then by (10), $\sum_j y_j p_j$ has the same leading constituent as h^*, and hence as h.

But by construction the t_i have the same leading constituents as the p_i, hence $\sum_j y_j t_i$ has the same leading constituent as the given h. Thus $H_n(J) \subset H_n(U)$ so $H_n(J) = H_n(U)$ for all n.

The proof is then completed by the following lemma.

Lemma. *Let S be a subspace of a subspace J of R. If $H_n(S) = H_n(J)$ for all n, then $S = J$.*

Proof. Suppose $S < J$. Then there would exist a polynomial p of lowest degree n ($n > 0$ since S includes 0) which is in J but not in S.

But $H_n(S) = H_n(J)$ contains all leading constituents of elements of J. Let q be the leading constituent of p. Then $q \in H_n(J)$. But $H_n(S) = H_n(J)$, so $q \in H_n(S)$ also. Hence there exists r, of lower degree than q, such that $q + r \in S$. Then $p - (q + r)$ is of lower degree than p, since p and $q + r$ have the same leading constituent. Hence $p - (q + r) \in S$ by hypothesis on p. But $q + r \in S$, $p = p - (q + r) + (q + r) \in S$, contrary to assumption that $p \notin S$. Thus the proof is completed.

5. **Determination of Jordans envelopes.** Having discussed the free Lie-envelopes of various algebras, we turn now to free Jordan envelopes. In this case let us denote $A_u(X)$ by $J_u(X)$. In all work with Jordan algebras, we require the base field to be of characteristic not 2, in view of (3).

Theorem 5. *If X has a finite basis, so does $J_u(X)$.*

Proof. Let X have the finite basis $e_1, \cdots, e_n$. Then $J_u(X)$ is generated by the monomials in $e_1, \cdots, e_n$ by Theorem 2. Moreover,

$$\sum_k c_k^{ii} e_k = e_i \cdot e_i = (e_i e_i + e_i e_i)/2 = e_i e_i$$

so square-free monomials generate $J_u(X)$. Since n is finite, $J_u(X)$ has a basis of not more than $2^n - 1$ elements.

No general solution of the decision problem for $J_u(X)$ is known, but in special cases a solution can be found. It is readily verified that a zero, idempotent, or unit in A has the same property in $J_u(X)$ and conversely. We consider several examples of Jordan envelopes, mostly of "irreducible r-number algebras" [15, p. 63].

As one example, let X be the free zero-algebra with basis $e_1, \cdots, e_n$. By (3), $e_ie_j+e_je_i=2e_i\cdot e_j=0$ for all i, j. In particular, let $i=j$. Then $e_i^2=0$. Hence, the free Jordan envelope of the free zero-algebra is an ideal of order 2^n-1, excluding the unit element, in the extensive algebra of Grassmann(7).

Again, let X be the algebra with basis $e_0, e_1, \cdots, e_n$, with

$$e_0\cdot e_i = e_i\cdot e_0 = e_i \qquad (i = 0, \cdots, n),$$

$$e_i\cdot e_j = 0 \qquad (i \neq j;\ i, j = 1, \cdots, n),$$

$$e_i\cdot e_i = -e_0 \qquad (i \neq 0).$$

Then the free Jordan envelope is the Clifford numbers(8).

Theorem 6. *If X is the (special) Jordan algebra of all n by n matrices ($n \geqq 2$) then $J_u(X)$ is the direct sum $M \oplus M$, where M is the ordinary associative algebra of all n by n matrices.*

Proof. Let e_{ij} be the matrix with a single 1, in the ith row and jth column, and zeros elsewhere. In X, the multiplication table is, by (3),

$$e_{ij}\cdot e_{kl} = (\delta_{jk}e_{il} + \delta_{il}e_{kj})/2. \tag{11}$$

Set

$$a_{ij} \equiv e_{ij}e_{ji}\ (i \neq j);\quad a_{ii} \equiv a_{ij}e_{ji} \equiv e_{ij}e_{ji}e_{ji}\ (i \neq j);\quad b_{ij} \equiv e_{ji} - a_{ji}; \tag{12}$$

a_{ii} will be shown in (17) to be independent of j. We seek to obtain the multiplication table for $J_u(X)$.

$$e_{ij}e_{kk} = 0 \qquad (k \neq i, j), \tag{13}$$

for, since e_{kk} is idempotent,

$$e_{ij}e_{kk} = e_{ij}e_{kk}e_{kk} = \{2(e_{ij}\cdot e_{kk}) - e_{kk}e_{ij}\}e_{kk} = (0 - e_{kk}e_{ij})e_{kk}$$
$$= -e_{kk}(e_{ij}e_{kk}) = -e_{kk}(0 - e_{kk}e_{ij}) = e_{kk}e_{kk}e_{ij} = e_{kk}e_{ij};$$

but also $e_{ij}e_{kk}=0-e_{kk}e_{ij}$; adding, $e_{ij}e_{kk}=0$. Likewise,

$$e_{kk}e_{ij} = 0 \qquad (k \neq i, j). \tag{14}$$

$$e_{ij}e_{ij} = 0 \qquad (i \neq j), \tag{15}$$

for $e_{ij}e_{ij}=0-e_{ij}e_{ij}$ by (11).

$$e_{ij}e_{jk} = e_{ii}e_{ik} \qquad (i, j, k \text{ all distinct}), \tag{16a}$$

for by (14),

(7) See, for instance, Chevalley [11, p. 145].
(8) See, for instance, Chevalley [11, p. 61].

$$
\begin{aligned}
0 = e_{ij}(e_{ii}e_{jk}) &= (e_{ij}e_{ii})e_{jk} = (e_{ij} - e_{ii}e_{ij})e_{jk} \\
&= e_{ij}e_{jk} - e_{ii}e_{ij}e_{jk} = e_{ij}e_{jk} - e_{ii}(e_{ik} - e_{jk}e_{ij}) \\
&= e_{ij}e_{jk} - e_{ii}e_{ik} + e_{ii}e_{jk}e_{ij} = e_{ij}e_{jk} - e_{ii}e_{ik}.
\end{aligned}
$$

(16b) $$e_{ij}e_{jj} = e_{ii}e_{ij} \qquad (i \neq j),$$

for $I = \sum e_{kk}$ and by (14),

$$
\begin{aligned}
e_{ij}e_{jj} = Ie_{ij}e_{jj} &= (e_{ii} + e_{jj})e_{ij}e_{jj} = e_{ii}(e_{ij}e_{jj}) + (e_{jj}e_{ij})e_{jj} \\
&= e_{ii}(e_{ij} - e_{jj}e_{ij}) + (e_{ij} - e_{ij}e_{jj})e_{jj} \\
&= e_{ii}e_{ij} - 0 + e_{ij}e_{jj} - e_{ij}e_{jj} = e_{ii}e_{ij}.
\end{aligned}
$$

Combining (16a), (16b), and (12), we get

(16) $$a_{il} = e_{ij}e_{jl} = e_{ik}e_{kl} \qquad \text{for all } j \text{ and } k \text{ if } i \neq l.$$

(17) $$e_{ij}e_{jk}e_{ki} = e_{il}e_{lm}e_{mi} = e_{im}e_{mi}e_{ii} = a_{ii} \qquad (i \neq j, k, l, m),$$

for by (16), $e_{ij}e_{jk}e_{ki} = e_{ij}e_{jm}e_{mi} = e_{il}e_{lm}e_{mi}$. In particular, this shows that the definition of a_{ii} is independent of j.

For $k \neq i, j, l$, $e_{ij}a_{kl} = e_{ij}e_{kk}e_{kl} = 0$.

For $k \neq i, j$, $e_{ij}a_{kk} \equiv e_{ij}a_{kj}e_{jk} = 0\, e_{jk} = 0$.

For $i \neq j, k$, $e_{ij}a_{ik} \equiv e_{ij}e_{ij}e_{jk} = 0$ by (16) and (15).

For $i \neq j$, $e_{ij}a_{ii} \equiv e_{ij}a_{ij}e_{ji} = 0\, e_{ji} = 0$.

For $j \neq k$, $e_{ij}a_{jk} \equiv e_{ij}e_{jk}e_{kk} = a_{ik}$ by (16) or (17).

For $i \neq j$,

$$
\begin{aligned}
e_{ij}a_{jj} &\equiv e_{ij}e_{ji}e_{ii}e_{ij} = e_{ij}e_{ji}e_{ij}e_{jj} \\
&= e_{ij}(e_{ii} + e_{jj} - e_{ij}e_{ji})e_{jj} = 0 + e_{ij}e_{jj} - 0 \equiv a_{ij}.
\end{aligned}
$$

For $i \neq j$, $e_{ii}a_{ij} = e_{ii}e_{ii}e_{ij} = e_{ii}e_{ij} = a_{ij}$.

Hence, $e_{ii}a_{ii} = e_{ii}e_{ij}a_{ji} = e_{ij}e_{jj}a_{ji} = e_{ij}a_{ji} = a_{ii}$. Similar formulas hold for $a_{ij}e_{kl}$, by (16) and symmetry. Summarizing,

(18) $$e_{ij}a_{kl} = \delta_{jk}a_{il} = a_{ij}e_{kl} \qquad (\text{all } i, j, k, l).$$

For $j \neq i, k$, $a_{ij}a_{kl} \equiv e_{ij}e_{jj}a_{kl} = 0$.

For $i \neq j$, $a_{ii}a_{jk} \equiv e_{ij}e_{jj}e_{ji}a_{jk} = e_{ij}e_{ji}e_{ii}a_{jk} = 0$.

For $i \neq j$, $a_{ij}a_{jk} \equiv e_{ij}e_{jj}a_{jk} = e_{ij}a_{jk} = a_{ik}$.

Hence, for $i \neq j$, $a_{ii}a_{ij} \equiv a_{ij}e_{ji}a_{ij} = a_{ij}a_{jj} = a_{ij}$.

Likewise, $a_{ii}a_{ii} \equiv e_{ij}a_{ji}a_{ii} = e_{ij}a_{ji} = a_{ii}$. Summarizing,

(19) $$a_{ij}a_{kl} = \delta_{jk}a_{il} \qquad (\text{all } i, j, k, l).$$

For $i \neq k$, $b_{ij}a_{kl} \equiv (e_{ji} - a_{ji})a_{kl} = e_{ji}a_{kl} - a_{ji}a_{kl} = 0$.

For all i, j, $b_{ij}a_{ik} \equiv (e_{ji} - a_{ji})a_{ik} = a_{jk} - a_{jl} = 0$. By symmetry,

(20) $$b_{ij}a_{kl} = 0 = a_{ij}b_{kl} \qquad (\text{all } i, j, k, l).$$

For $i \neq j$, $b_{ij} \equiv e_{ji} - a_{ji} = e_{ji}I - a_{ji} = e_{ji}e_{ii} + e_{ji}e_{jj} - e_{ji}e_{ii} = e_{ji}e_{jj}$.
Hence if $j \neq i, k, l$, $b_{ij}b_{kl} = e_{ji}e_{jj}(e_{lk} - a_{lk}) = 0$.
For $j \neq k, i$, $b_{ij}b_{kj} = e_{ji}e_{jj}e_{jk}e_{jj} = e_{ji}e_{jk}e_{kk}e_{jj} = 0$.
For $i \neq k$, $b_{ij}b_{jk} \equiv (e_{ji} - a_{ji})(e_{kj} - a_{kj}) = e_{ji}e_{kj} = e_{ki} - e_{kj}e_{ji} = b_{ik}$.
For $i \neq j$,

$$\begin{aligned} b_{ij}b_{ji} &= e_{ji}e_{jj}e_{ij}e_{ii} = e_{ji}(e_{ij} - e_{ij}e_{jj})e_{ii} = e_{ji}e_{ij}e_{ii} \\ &= (e_{ii} + e_{jj} - e_{ij}e_{ji})e_{ii} = e_{ii} + 0 - a_{ii} \equiv b_{ii}. \end{aligned}$$

For all i,

$$\begin{aligned} b_{ii}b_{ii} &= (e_{ii} - a_{ii})(e_{ii} - a_{ii}) \\ &= e_{ii} - 2a_{ii} + a_{ii} = b_{ii}. \end{aligned}$$

For $k \neq i, j$, $b_{ij}b_{kk} = (e_{ji} - a_{ji})(e_{kk} - a_{kk}) = 0$. By symmetry, $b_{ii}b_{jk} = 0$ for $i \neq j, k$. Summarizing,

$$b_{ij}b_{kl} = \delta_{jk}b_{il} \qquad \text{(all } i, j, k, l). \tag{21}$$

Thus by (19)–(21), the a_{ij} multiply among themselves like matrix units, as do the b_{ij}, while $a_{ij}b_{kl} = 0 = b_{ij}a_{kl}$. Hence the subalgebra of $J_u(X)$ generated by the a_{ij} and b_{kl} is $M \oplus M$. But this subalgebra contains $a_{ij} + b_{ji} = e_{ij}$, for all i and j, so the subalgebra is the whole of $J_u(X)$, proving the theorem. In obtaining the products we have allowed for the possibility that all the subscripts are distinct. But nowhere have we assumed the existence of subscripts which do not appear explicitly in the factors, except that if only a single subscript appeared, then we assumed the existence of a second. Hence the theorem holds for $n = 2, 3, \cdots$.

THEOREM 7([9]). *If X_S is the special Jordan algebra of all symmetric n by n matrices ($n \geqq 2$), then $J_u(X_S)$ is isomorphic to the n by n total matrix algebra over the same field.*

Proof. Let E_{ij} be the matrix with 1 in the ith row and jth column, and also in the ith column and jth row, and 0 elsewhere. In the notation of the proof of Theorem 6, $E_{ii} \equiv e_{ii}$, $E_{ij} \equiv E_{ji} = e_{ij} + e_{ji}$ $(i \neq j)$. In X_S, the multiplication table is, by (3),

$$\begin{aligned} E_{ij} \cdot E_{kl} &= 0 && \text{if } i \neq k, l, \text{ and } j \neq k, l; \\ E_{ij} \cdot E_{jl} &= E_{il}/2 && \text{if } i \neq l; \\ E_{ij} \cdot E_{ij} &= E_{ii} + E_{jj} && \text{if } i \neq j; \\ E_{ii} \cdot E_{ii} &= E_{ii}. \end{aligned} \tag{22}$$

Set

$$A_{ii} \equiv E_{ii}; \qquad A_{ij} \equiv E_{ij}E_{jj} \qquad (i \neq j). \tag{23}$$

([9]) This example was first studied by F. D. Jacobson and N. Jacobson; cf. [13].

We seek the multiplication table for $J_u(X_S)$.

$$E_{ij}E_{kk} = 0 \qquad (k \neq i, j), \tag{24}$$

for, since E_{kk} is idempotent,

$$\begin{aligned} E_{ij}E_{kk} &= E_{ij}E_{kk}E_{kk} = \{2(E_{ij}\cdot E_{kk}) - E_{kk}E_{ij}\}E_{kk} \\ &= (0 - E_{kk}E_{ij})E_{kk} = -E_{kk}(0 - E_{kk}E_{ij}) = E_{kk}E_{kk}E_{ij} = E_{kk}E_{ij}; \end{aligned}$$

but also $E_{ij}E_{kk} = 0 - E_{kk}E_{ij}$; adding, we get (24). Likewise,

$$E_{kk}E_{ij} = 0 \qquad (k \neq i, j). \tag{25}$$

Hence $A_{ii}A_{jj} = \delta_{ij}A_{ii}$.

$$E_{ij}E_{jk} = E_{ii}E_{ik} \qquad (i \neq k), \tag{26}$$

for we may suppose $i \neq j$ and then by (24) and (22),

$$\begin{aligned} 0 &= E_{ij}(E_{ii}E_{jk}) = (E_{ij}E_{ii})E_{jk} = (E_{ij} - E_{ii}E_{ij})E_{jk} \\ &= E_{ij}E_{jk} - E_{ii}(E_{ij}E_{jk}) = E_{ij}E_{jk} - E_{ii}(E_{ik} - E_{jk}E_{ij}) \\ &= E_{ij}E_{jk} - E_{ii}E_{ik} + (E_{ii}E_{jk})E_{ij} = E_{ij}E_{jk} - E_{ii}E_{ik} + 0, \end{aligned}$$

and transposition gives (26).

$$E_{ij}E_{ij} = E_{ii} + E_{jj} \qquad (i \neq j), \tag{27}$$

for $2E_{ij}E_{ij} = E_{ij}E_{ij} + E_{ij}E_{ij} = 2(E_{ij}\cdot E_{ij}) = 2(E_{ii} + E_{jj})$.

For $j \neq i, k$, $A_{ii}A_{jk} \equiv E_{ii}E_{jk}E_{kk} = E_{ii}E_{jj}E_{jk} = 0$.

For $i \neq j$, $A_{ii}A_{ij} = E_{ii}E_{ii}E_{ij} = E_{ii}E_{ij} = A_{ij}$. Similarly, for $i \neq k$, $A_{ij}A_{kk} = \delta_{jk}A_{ik}$.

For $j \neq i, k$, $A_{ij}A_{kl} \equiv E_{ij}A_{jj}A_{kl} = 0$.

For i, j, k distinct, by (23) and (26),

$$\begin{aligned} A_{ij}A_{jk} &\equiv E_{ij}A_{jj}A_{jk} = E_{ij}A_{jk} = E_{ij}E_{jk}E_{kk} = E_{ik}E_{kk}E_{kk} \\ &= E_{ik}E_{kk} \equiv A_{ik}. \end{aligned}$$

By (27), for $i \neq j$,

$$\begin{aligned} A_{ij}A_{ji} &= E_{ij}E_{jj}E_{jj}E_{ji} = E_{ij}E_{jj}E_{ij} = E_{ii}E_{ij}E_{ij} \\ &= E_{ii}(E_{ii} + E_{jj}) = A_{ii}. \end{aligned}$$

Summarizing,

$$A_{ij}A_{kl} = \delta_{jk}A_{il} \qquad (\text{all } i, j, k, l). \tag{28}$$

Hence the subalgebra of $J_u(X_S)$ generated by the A_{ij} is a total matrix algebra. But this subalgebra contains

$$A_{ij} + A_{ji} = E_{ij}E_{jj} + E_{ji}E_{ii} = E_{ij}(E_{ii} + E_{jj}) = E_{ij}I = E_{ij}$$

and is therefore the whole of $J_u(X_S)$ and the theorem holds.

THEOREM 8. *If X_H is the special Jordan algebra of all Hermitian n by n matrices ($n \geqq 2$) over the complex numbers, then $J_u(X_H)$ is isomorphic to the n by n total matrix algebra over the complex numbers.*

Proof. Using the previous notation and $(-1)^{1/2} = i$, let

$$B_{ij} \equiv -B_{ji} \equiv i(e_{ij} - e_{ji}) \qquad \text{for } i \neq j.$$

In X_H, the multiplication table is, by (3), given by (22), commutativity, and

$$\begin{aligned} E_{ij}\cdot B_{kl} &= 0 && \text{if } k \neq i, j, l \text{ and } l \neq i, j, k;\\ E_{ij}\cdot B_{ij} &= 0 && \text{where } i \neq j;\\ E_{ij}\cdot B_{jk} &= B_{ik}/2 && \text{where } j \neq k;\\ B_{ij}\cdot B_{kl} &= 0 && \text{if } i, j, k, l \text{ are all distinct};\\ B_{ij}\cdot B_{ij} &= E_{ii} + E_{jj} && \text{where } i \neq j;\\ B_{ij}\cdot B_{jk} &= -E_{ik}/2 && \text{if } i, j, k \text{ are distinct.}\end{aligned} \tag{29}$$

In addition to (23), set (for $i \neq j$)

$$P_{ij} \equiv E_{ii}B_{ij}, \qquad P_{ii} \equiv E_{ji}P_{ji} \equiv E_{ij}E_{jj}B_{ji}; \tag{30}$$

P_{ii} will be shown in (34) to be independent of j.

$$E_{ii}B_{jk} = 0 \qquad (i, j, k \text{ distinct}), \tag{31}$$

for by (29),

$$\begin{aligned} E_{ii}B_{jk} &= E_{ii}E_{ii}B_{jk} = E_{ii}(0 - B_{jk}E_{ii}) = -(E_{ii}B_{jk})E_{ii}\\ &= -(0 - B_{jk}E_{ii})E_{ii} = B_{jk}E_{ii},\end{aligned}$$

while $E_{ii}B_{jk} = 0 - B_{jk}E_{ii}$; addition yields (31). Similarly,

$$B_{ij}E_{kk} = 0 \qquad (i, j, k \text{ distinct}). \tag{32}$$

$$E_{ij}B_{jk} = E_{ii}B_{ik} \equiv P_{ik} \qquad (k \neq i, j), \tag{33}$$

for we may suppose $i \neq j$, and then

$$\begin{aligned} E_{ij}B_{jk} &= IE_{ij}B_{jk} = (E_{ii} + E_{jj})E_{ij}B_{jk} = E_{ii}E_{ij}B_{jk} + E_{jj}E_{ji}B_{jk}\\ &= E_{ii}(B_{ik} - B_{jk}E_{ij}) + E_{ji}E_{ii}B_{jk} = E_{ii}B_{ik} - 0 + 0.\end{aligned}$$

$$E_{ij}E_{jj}B_{ji} = E_{ik}E_{kk}B_{ki} \qquad (i \neq j, k) \tag{34}$$

(and hence P_{ii} is independent of j), for

$$E_{ij}E_{jj}B_{ji} = E_{ij}E_{jk}B_{ki} = E_{ik}E_{kk}B_{ki}.$$

$$B_{ij}B_{ij} = E_{ii} + E_{jj} \qquad (i \neq j), \tag{35}$$

for $2B_{ij}B_{ij} = B_{ij}B_{ij} + B_{ij}B_{ij} = 2(B_{ij}\cdot B_{ij}) = 2(E_{ii} + E_{jj})$.

For $k\neq i, j, l$, $E_{ij}P_{kl}\equiv E_{ij}E_{kk}B_{kl}=0$.
For $k\neq i, j$, $E_{ij}P_{jk}\equiv E_{ij}E_{jj}B_{jk}=E_{ii}E_{ij}B_{jk}=E_{ii}E_{ii}B_{ik}=E_{ii}B_{ik}\equiv P_{ik}$.
For i, j, k distinct, $E_{ij}P_{kk}\equiv E_{ij}E_{jk}P_{jk}=E_{ii}E_{ik}P_{jk}=0$.
For $i\neq k$, $E_{ii}P_{kk}\equiv E_{ii}E_{ik}P_{ik}=E_{ik}E_{kk}P_{ik}=0$.
For $i\neq j$, $E_{ij}P_{jj}\equiv E_{ij}E_{ij}E_{ii}B_{ij}=(E_{ii}+E_{jj})E_{ii}B_{ij}=E_{ii}B_{ij}\equiv P_{ij}$.
For all j, $E_{jj}P_{jj}\equiv E_{jj}E_{ji}E_{ii}B_{ij}=E_{ji}E_{ii}E_{ii}B_{ij}=E_{ji}E_{ii}B_{ij}\equiv P_{jj}$.
Thus $E_{ij}P_{kl}=\delta_{jk}P_{il}+\delta_{ik}P_{jl}$ if $i\neq j$, and $A_{ii}P_{jk}\equiv E_{ii}P_{jk}=\delta_{ij}P_{ik}$.

Hence, for $i\neq j$, $A_{ij}P_{kl}\equiv E_{ij}E_{jj}P_{kl}=\delta_{jk}E_{ij}P_{jl}=\delta_{jk}P_{il}$. But in spite of the unsymmetric appearance of (30), P_{ij} can be written in a similar form with the E's after the B's:

$$P_{ij} \equiv E_{ii}B_{ij} = B_{ij} - B_{ij}E_{ii} = B_{ij}(E_{ii} + E_{jj}) - B_{ij}E_{ii} = B_{ij}E_{jj};$$

$$\text{(36)}\quad P_{ii} \equiv E_{ij}P_{ji} = E_{ij}B_{ji}E_{ii} = (0 - B_{ji}E_{ij})E_{ii} = B_{ij}E_{ji}E_{ii}$$
$$= B_{ij}E_{jj}E_{ji} = P_{ij}E_{ij}.$$

Summarizing previous formulas, and those symmetric to them in view of (36),

$$\text{(37)}\qquad A_{ij}P_{kl} = \delta_{jk}P_{il} = P_{ij}A_{kl} \qquad \text{(all } i, j, k, l).$$

For $j\neq i, k$, $P_{ij}P_{kl}=B_{ij}E_{jj}P_{kl}=B_{ij}0=0$.
For i, j, k distinct,

$$P_{ij}P_{jk} = B_{ij}E_{jj}E_{jj}B_{jk} = B_{ij}E_{jj}B_{jk} = P_{ij}B_{jk}$$
$$= E_{ii}B_{ij}B_{jk} = E_{ii}(- E_{ik} - B_{jk}B_{ij}) = - A_{ik}.$$

Similarly, if $i\neq j$, $P_{ij}P_{ji}=E_{ii}B_{ij}B_{ji}=E_{ii}(-E_{ii}-E_{jj})=-A_{ii}$.
For $i\neq j$, $P_{ii}P_{jk}\equiv E_{ji}P_{ji}P_{jk}=E_{ji}0=0$.
For $i\neq j$, $P_{ii}P_{ij}\equiv E_{ji}P_{ji}P_{ij}=E_{ji}(-E_{jj})=-E_{ij}E_{jj}\equiv -A_{ij}$. Similarly, for $i\neq j$, $P_{ij}P_{jj}=-A_{ij}$.
For $i\neq j$, $P_{ii}P_{jj}=E_{ji}P_{ji}P_{jj}=E_{ji}0=0$.
For all i, $P_{ii}P_{ii}=E_{ji}P_{ji}P_{ii}=E_{ji}(-A_{ji})=-E_{ji}E_{ji}E_{ii}=-(E_{ii}+E_{jj})E_{jj}=-A_{jj}$. Summarizing,

$$\text{(38)}\qquad P_{ij}P_{kl} = - \delta_{jk}A_{il} \qquad \text{(all } i, j, k, l).$$

By (28), (37), and (38), the subalgebra of $J_u(X_H)$ generated by the A_{ij} and P_{ij} is isomorphic to the n by n total matrix algebra over the complex numbers, under the correspondence $A_{ij}\leftrightarrow e_{ij}$, $P_{ij}\leftrightarrow ie_{ij}$. But this subalgebra contains the E_{ij} as in the proof of Theorem 7, and also contains

$$P_{ij} - P_{ji} = E_{ii}B_{ij} - E_{jj}B_{ji} = E_{ii}B_{ij} + E_{jj}B_{ij} = (E_{ii} + E_{jj})B_{ij} = IB_{ij} = B_{ij}$$

and hence is the whole of $J_u(X_H)$. Thus the theorem holds.

THEOREM 9. *If X_Q is the special Jordan algebra of all Hermitian n by n matrices ($n\geqq 3$) over the quaternions, then $J_u(X_Q)$ is isomorphic to the n by n total matrix algebra over the quaternions.*

Proof. Using the previous notation and denoting the quaternion units by *i*, *j*, *k*, set in addition

$$C_{ij} \equiv j(e_{ij} - e_{ji}) \equiv - C_{ji}; \qquad D_{ij} \equiv k(e_{ij} - e_{ji}) \equiv - D_{ji} \qquad (i \neq j).$$

In X_Q, (29) holds, as do similar formulas with B replaced by C and by D; also

$$
\begin{aligned}
&B_{ij}\cdot C_{kl} = 0,\ C_{ij}\cdot D_{kl} = 0,\ D_{ij}\cdot B_{kl} = 0 && (i, j, k, l \text{ distinct});\\
(39)\quad &B_{ij}\cdot C_{jk} = D_{ik}/2,\ C_{ij}\cdot D_{jk} = B_{ik}/2,\ D_{ij}\cdot B_{jk} = C_{ik}/2 && (i, j, k \text{ distinct});\\
&B_{ij}\cdot C_{ij} = 0,\ C_{ij}\cdot D_{ij} = 0,\ D_{ij}\cdot B_{ij} = 0 && (i \neq j).
\end{aligned}
$$

In addition to (23) and (30), set (for $i \neq j$)

$$
(40)\qquad
\begin{aligned}
Q_{ij} &\equiv E_{ii}C_{ij}, & Q_{ii} &\equiv E_{ji}Q_{ji} \equiv E_{ij}E_{ji}C_{ji},\\
R_{ij} &\equiv E_{ii}D_{ij}, & R_{ii} &\equiv E_{ji}R_{ji} \equiv E_{ij}E_{ji}D_{ji}.
\end{aligned}
$$

Just as for (30), Q_{ii} and R_{ii} are independent of j. Likewise, formulas (31)–(38) hold with P replaced by Q and by R; it remains only to determine such products as $P_{ij}Q_{kl}$ and $Q_{ij}P_{kl}$.

$$(41)\qquad B_{ij}C_{jk} = R_{ik} \qquad (i, j, k \text{ distinct}),$$

for, by the analogues of (31)–(32),

$$
\begin{aligned}
B_{ij}C_{jk} &= B_{ij}IC_{jk} = B_{ij}E_{ji}C_{jk} = (- B_{ji}E_{jj})C_{jk}\\
&= - (B_{ji} - E_{jj}B_{ji})C_{jk} = B_{ij}C_{jk} - E_{jj}B_{ij}C_{jk}\\
&= (E_{ii} + E_{jj})B_{ij}C_{jk} - E_{jj}B_{ij}C_{jk} = E_{ii}B_{ij}C_{jk}\\
&= E_{ii}(D_{ik} - C_{jk}B_{ij}) = E_{ii}D_{ik} \equiv R_{ik}.
\end{aligned}
$$

$$(42)\qquad B_{ij}C_{ji} \equiv - B_{ij}C_{ij} = R_{ii} + R_{jj} \qquad (i \neq j),$$

since by (41) we have, for 3 by 3 matrices or larger,

$$
\begin{aligned}
B_{ij}C_{ji} &= IB_{ij}C_{ji} = (E_{ii} + E_{jj})B_{ij}C_{ji} = E_{ii}B_{ij}C_{ji} + E_{jj}B_{ji}C_{ij}\\
&= E_{ik}B_{kj}C_{ji} + E_{jk}B_{ki}C_{ij} = E_{ik}R_{ki} + E_{jk}R_{kj} = R_{ii} + R_{jj}.
\end{aligned}
$$

For $j \neq k$, $P_{ij}Q_{kl} = (P_{ij}I)Q_{kl} = P_{ij}E_{jj}Q_{kl} = 0$.
For i, j, k distinct, $P_{ij}Q_{jk} = E_{ii}B_{ij}C_{jk}E_{kk} = E_{ii}R_{ik}E_{kk} = R_{ik}E_{kk} = R_{ik}$.
Similarly, for $j \neq i$, $P_{ij}Q_{ji} = E_{ii}(R_{ii} + R_{jj})E_{ii} = R_{ii}$.
For $i \neq j$, $P_{ii}Q_{ij} \equiv E_{ij}P_{ji}Q_{ij} = E_{ij}R_{jj} = R_{ij}$.
For $i \neq j$, $P_{ij}Q_{jj} \equiv P_{ij}Q_{ji}E_{ji} = R_{ii}E_{ij} = R_{ij}$.
For all i, $P_{ii}Q_{ii} \equiv E_{ij}P_{ji}Q_{ii} = E_{ij}R_{ji} = R_{ii}$.

Thus $P_{ij}Q_{kl} = \delta_{jk}R_{il}$. Similarly, $Q_{ij}P_{kl} = -\delta_{jk}R_{il}$. Similar formulas hold for $Q_{ij}R_{kl}$, $R_{ij}Q_{kl}$, $R_{ij}P_{kl}$, $P_{ij}R_{kl}$. Thus the A_{ij}, P_{ij}, Q_{ij}, and R_{ij} multiply in a manner isomorphic to the total matrix algebra over the quaternions, under the correspondence $A_{ij} \leftrightarrow e_{ij}$, $P_{ij} \leftrightarrow ie_{ij}$, $Q_{ij} \leftrightarrow je_{ij}$, $R_{ij} \leftrightarrow ke_{ij}$. The theorem follows as before. Unlike the previous proofs, the proof of (42) assumes the existence of three different subscripts. Indeed, we show next that Theorem 9 is false for $n=2$; $J_u(X_Q)$ has order $4n^2$ if $n>2$, but order $8n^2$ if $n=2$.

THEOREM 10[10]. *If X_2 is the special Jordan algebra of all Hermitian 2 by 2 matrices over the quaternions, then $J_u(X_2)$ is the direct sum $M_Q \oplus M_Q$ where M_Q is the associative algebra of all 2 by 2 matrices over the quaternions.*

Proof. Let $I=e_{11}+e_{22}$, $E=e_{12}+e_{21}$, $F=e_{11}$, $B=\boldsymbol{i}(e_{12}-e_{21})$, $C=\boldsymbol{j}(e_{12}-e_{21})$, $D=\boldsymbol{k}(e_{12}-e_{21})$. Then in $J_u(X_2)$, I is a unit and, by (39),

$$\begin{aligned} &EE = BB = CC = DD = I, \qquad FF = F, \\ &BC = -CB, \qquad DB = -BD, \qquad DC = -CD, \\ &BE = -EB, \qquad CE = -EC, \qquad DE = -ED, \\ &BF = B - FB, \qquad CF = C - FC, \qquad DF = D - FD. \end{aligned} \tag{43}$$

Hence every element in $J_u(X_2)$ can be written as a linear combination of products, in a specified order, of some or all or none of the symbols E, F, B, C, D (with I inserted if none of the other symbols appears in the term), no symbol appearing more than once in a term. Hence the order of $J_u(X_2)$ is at most $2^5=32$. We shall not assume (though it is true) that this form of an element is unique.

Set $U\equiv(I-BCDE)/2$, $V\equiv(I+BCDE)/2$. By (43), U and V are orthogonal idempotents which commute with F, and $EU=VE$, $EV=UE$, and similarly for E replaced by B, by C, and by D. Set $Y\equiv V+(U-V)F$, $Z\equiv U+(V-U)F$. Then $Y+Z=U+V=I$, so $Z=I-Y$. By calculation, Y and Z are orthogonal idempotents in the center of $J_u(X_2)$. Since $Y+Z=I$, $J_u(X_2)$ is the direct sum $YJ_u(X_2)\oplus ZJ_u(X_2)$, where $YJ_u(X_2)$ contains $YV=V-VF$, $YVE=VEF$, $YU=UF$, $YUE=UFE$. These four elements generate a subalgebra M of $YJ_u(X_2)$. By calculation using (43), one sees that M is a 2 by 2 total matrix algebra with basis UF, UFE, VEF, $V-VF$; the unit element of M is $UF+V-VF=Y$. Let $T\equiv UFE-VEF$; then by computation Y, TB, TC, TD are a basis of a subalgebra Q of $YJ_u(X_2)$ isomorphic to the quaternions, under the correspondence $Y\leftrightarrow 1$, $TB\leftrightarrow \boldsymbol{i}$, $TC\leftrightarrow \boldsymbol{j}$, $TD\leftrightarrow \boldsymbol{k}$, and these elements commute with those of M. Hence $YJ_u(X_2)$ contains the direct product $M\otimes Q$ of order 16. Similarly $ZJ_u(X_2)$ contains $M\otimes Q$. But as we noted earlier, the order of $J_u(X_2)$ is at most 32. Hence $M\otimes Q=YJ_u(X_2)=ZJ_u(X_2)$ and the theorem holds.

6. **Jordan algebras and convex power families.** We shall now show that special Jordan algebras have much the same relation to convex families of (real) matrices that Lie algebras have to Lie groups of (real) matrices. In both cases, the relation is valid only locally.

First consider the concept of a k-parameter family ("Schar") $\mathfrak{S}$ of matrices $X=(x_{ij})$, in the sense of Lie. By this is meant a set of matrices, depending differentiably on k "essential" parameters in a neighborhood of the identity matrix I. Clearly $\mathfrak{S}$ is always locally compact, in the topology defined by the norm $|X|=(\sum_{i,j} x_{ij}^2)^{1/2}$. Furthermore, if $X=I+A$ with

[10] This form of the theorem and proof was suggested by the referee.

$|A|<1$, we may(11) define $\ln X=A-A^2/2+A^3/3-\cdots$; the series is absolutely convergent. We may further define

$$X^t = \exp(t \ln X) = I + Y + Y^2/2! + Y^3/3! + \cdots,$$

where $Y=t \ln X$. The X^t form a one-parameter Lie group, with $X^1=X$.

Now it is well known that if $\mathfrak{S}$ is a local Lie group, then for some $\delta>0$, $X\in S$ and $|\ln X|<\delta$ and $|t \ln X|<\delta$ imply $X^t\in\mathfrak{S}$; this is a corollary of the existence of canonical parameters. Hence the concept of a local Lie group is a special case of the following concept of a "local power family"; and the usual concepts of infinitesimal generator and equality may be generalized to local power families as follows.

DEFINITION. A *local power family* is a set $\mathfrak{S}$ of matrices which is locally compact, and such that for some $\delta_1>0$, $X\in\mathfrak{S}$ and $|\ln X|\leqq\delta_1$ and $|t\ln X|\leqq\delta_1$ together imply $X^t\in\mathfrak{S}$. The *infinitesimal matrices* of $\mathfrak{S}$ are the set $J(\mathfrak{S})$ of matrices Y such that $\exp(tY)\in\mathfrak{S}$ for all sufficiently small t. Two local power families are *locally equal* if and only if they coincide in some neighborhood U_δ: $|X-I|<\delta$ of I.

LEMMA 6.1. *If $\mathfrak{S}$ is a local power family, and $X\in\mathfrak{S}$ and $|\ln X|<\delta_1$, then* $\ln X\in J(\mathfrak{S})$.

Proof. $X^t=\exp(\ln X^t)=\exp(t \ln X)$. By definition of a local power family, $X^t\in\mathfrak{S}$ for t sufficiently small. Hence by definition of $J(\mathfrak{S})$, $\ln X\in J(\mathfrak{S})$.

We note also that from the definitions, $J(\mathfrak{S})$ is closed under scalar multiplication. Now, given δ such that $\delta<1$ and $\delta<\delta_1$, set $J_\delta(\mathfrak{S})\equiv J(\mathfrak{S})\cap\overline{U}_\delta$, where $\overline{U}_\delta$ is the set of X with $|X-I|\leqq\delta$. But from the closure of $J(\mathfrak{S})$ under scalar multiplication, $J_\delta(\mathfrak{S})$ is closed under scalar multiplication out to radius δ. Further, since $\ln X$ and $\exp Y$ are continuous and mutually inverse, and $\mathfrak{S}$ is by hypothesis locally compact, $J_\delta(\mathfrak{S})$ is locally compact. But in view of the closure of $J(\mathfrak{S})$ under scalar multiplication, $Y\in J(\mathfrak{S})$ is equivalent to $tY\in J_\delta(\mathfrak{S})$ for sufficiently small t; hence $J(\mathfrak{S})$ consists of the scalar multiples of the elements of $J_\delta(\mathfrak{S})$, and bounded subsets of $J(\mathfrak{S})$ are compact; in particular, $J(\mathfrak{S})$ is closed. It is further easily shown that two local power families are locally equal if and only if they have the same set $\mathfrak{J}$ of infinitesimal matrices—which implies that some neighborhood of each consists of the $\exp Y[Y\in\mathfrak{J},\ |Y|<\delta]$.

THEOREM 11. *Let $\mathfrak{S}$ be any local power family of matrices. Then the infinitesimal matrices of $\mathfrak{S}$ form a Jordan algebra if and only if $\mathfrak{S}$ is "locally convex," in the sense that for some $\delta>0$, the set $\mathfrak{S}_\delta\equiv\mathfrak{S}\cap U_\delta$ is convex. (Here U_δ denotes the convex "sphere" of all X with $|X-I|<\delta$.)*

Proof. Suppose $J(\mathfrak{S})$ is a Jordan algebra. Take $\delta<\delta_1$. If $X\in\mathfrak{S}_\delta$ then $|X-I|<\delta$ and $Y=\ln X\in J(\mathfrak{S})$ and $X=\exp Y=I+Y+Y^2/2+\cdots$. Since $J(\mathfrak{S})$ is a Jordan algebra, it is closed under sums and powers, while we have

(11) See von Neumann [20].

already seen that it is closed under limits. Hence $Y+Y^2/2!+\cdots\in J(\mathfrak{S})$. Thus $X=I+A$ with $A\in J(\mathfrak{S})$ and $|A|<\delta$. Conversely, if $A\in J(\mathfrak{S})$ and $|A|<\delta<1$, then $J(\mathfrak{S})$ contains $Y=\ln(I+A)=A-A^2/2+A^3/3+\cdots$, being closed under sums, powers, and limits. If also δ is sufficiently small, then $|Y|<\delta_1$. By definition of $J(\mathfrak{S})$, $Z=\exp(uY)\in\mathfrak{S}$ for sufficiently small u. Taking $|u|<1$ and $t=1/u$, $|\ln Z|=|uY|<\delta_1$ and $|t\ln Z|=|Y|<\delta_1$, so by definition of a local power family, $\mathfrak{S}$ contains $Z^t=(\exp Y)^{ut}=I+A$. We conclude that if $J(\mathfrak{S})$ is a Jordan algebra then locally $\mathfrak{S}$ consists of $U_\delta\cap[I+J(\mathfrak{S})]$, where $I+J(\mathfrak{S})$ denotes the set of all $I+A$ for $A\in J(\mathfrak{S})$. But U_δ is convex by construction, while $I+J(\mathfrak{S})$ is convex since $J(\mathfrak{S})$ is by hypothesis an algebra. Hence $\mathfrak{S}$ is locally convex.

Conversely, suppose that $\mathfrak{S}$ is convex; we wish to show that $J(\mathfrak{S})$ is a Jordan algebra. Since $J(\mathfrak{S})$ is always closed under multiplication by scalars, we must show that $A\in J(\mathfrak{S})$ and $B\in J(\mathfrak{S})$ imply $A+B\in J(\mathfrak{S})$ and $(AB+BA)/2\in J(\mathfrak{S})$; this we now do.

If $A\in J(\mathfrak{S})$ then by definition $\exp(At)\in\mathfrak{S}$ for sufficiently small t. Since $\mathfrak{S}$ is convex, it contains

$$C\equiv[\exp(At)+\exp(Bt)]/2=I+(A+B)t/2+(A^2+B^2)t^2/4+\cdots.$$

Then

$$\begin{aligned}\ln C&=[(A+B)t/2+(A^2+B^2)t^2/4+\cdots]\\&\quad-[(A+B)^2t^2/4+\cdots]/2+\cdots;\\ D&\equiv\ln C^{2u/t}=(2u/t)\ln C\\&=u\{(A+B)+[(A^2+B^2)/2-(A+B)^2/4]t+\cdots\}.\end{aligned}$$

Obviously, for t and u sufficiently small (and u independent of t), $|\ln C|<\delta_1$ and $|(2u/t)\ln C|=|D|<\delta_1$. By definition of a local power family, $C^{2u/t}\in\mathfrak{S}$. Then $\exp(Eu)\in\mathfrak{S}$ for sufficiently small u, where

$$E\equiv\ln C^{2/t}=(A+B)+[(A^2+B^2)/2-(A+B)^2/4]t+\cdots. \tag{44}$$

Hence, by definition, $E\in J(\mathfrak{S})$. Hence, since $J(\mathfrak{S})$ is closed, it contains $\lim_{t\to 0}E=A+B$. Thus $J(\mathfrak{S})$ is closed under scalar multiplication and addition, so, by (44), it contains

$$\begin{aligned}4[E-(A+B)]/t&=4[(A^2+B^2)/2-(A+B)^2/4]+\cdots\\&=[A^2+B^2-AB-BA]+\cdots\end{aligned}$$

for all sufficiently small t, where the dots indicate terms containing t as a factor. Since $J(\mathfrak{S})$ is closed, it must therefore contain

$$H\equiv\lim_{t\to 0}4[E-(A+B)]/t=A^2+B^2-AB-BA.$$

In particular, let $B=0$, noting that $0\in J(\mathfrak{S})$ by closure under scalar multiplication. This gives $A^2 \in J(\mathfrak{S})$; likewise $B^2 \in J(\mathfrak{S})$. Hence $A^2+B^2-H \in J(\mathfrak{S})$; that is, $AB+BA \in J(\mathfrak{S})$. Hence $(AB+BA)/2 \in J(\mathfrak{S})$, and $J(\mathfrak{S})$ is a Jordan algebra, proving the theorem.

The first half of the proof essentially applies if $\mathfrak{J}$ is any Jordan algebra of matrices which is closed under limits, even if $\mathfrak{S}$ is not given. For suppose $\mathfrak{J}$ is such an algebra. Denote by $S(\mathfrak{J})$ the set of all $I+A$ $[A \in \mathfrak{J}]$. We call $S(\mathfrak{J})$ a *power family*. Suppose $X \in S(\mathfrak{J})$ and $|X-I|<1$. By definition of $S(\mathfrak{J})$, $X=I+A$ for some $A \in \mathfrak{J}$. Then

$$(I + A)^t = I + tA + t(t - 1)A^2/2! + \cdots .$$

Then $B \equiv tA+t(t-1)A^2/2!+ \cdots \in \mathfrak{J}$ by closure, so $(I+A)^t=I+B \in S(\mathfrak{J})$. Obviously, $S(\mathfrak{J})$ is convex.

This may be regarded as the convex power family generated by $\mathfrak{J}$, and is the analog of the concept of a global Lie group. We thus establish a one-to-one correspondence between Jordan algebras of matrices and global convex power families.

The above discussion applies to matrices with complex coefficients, without essential change.

7. Postulates for binary mean. In connection with Jordan multiplication (3), where we take the mean of XY and YX, it seems of interest to consider certain properties of means([12]).

We postulate a binary operation m on abstract elements $A, B, \cdots,$ with the properties

$$AmA = A; \tag{45}$$

$$AmB = BmA; \tag{46}$$

$$(AmB)m(CmD) = (AmC)m(BmD). \tag{47}$$

From (46) and (47) it follows immediately that

$$(AmB)m(CmD) = (AmD)m(CmB). \tag{48}$$

Let $\mathfrak{S}$ be a system each of whose elements is an unordered set of 2^n letters (not necessarily distinct), where n is a non-negative integer depending on the element. If $A \in \mathfrak{S}$, denote by $l(A)$ the value which n has for the particular element A. Define equality in $\mathfrak{S}$ thus: if A and B are in $\mathfrak{S}$, with $l(A)=k$ and $l(B)=n$, then $A=B$ if and only if either $k \leqq n$ and each distinct letter appears in the set B exactly 2^{n-k} times as often as in A, or $n \leqq k$ and each distinct letter appears in A exactly 2^{k-n} times as often as in B. AmB is defined to be the unordered set consisting of each letter of A repeated 2^n times and each letter of B repeated 2^k times.

THEOREM 12. *The system $\mathfrak{S}$ just defined is the free*([13]) *algebra on a countable number of elements satisfying* (45)–(47).

([12]) For a study of means of ordinary numbers, see Huntington [12].

([13]) For the general concept of free algebras, see for instance Birkhoff [8].

Proof. First we verify that $\mathfrak{S}$ satisfies (45)–(47). AmA consists, by the above definition, of each letter of A 2^k times, and then again each letter of A 2^k times—in other words, of each letter of A 2^{k+1} times. Then by definition of equality, $AmA=A$.

It is evident from the definitions that $AmB=BmA$.

As for (47), we observe that since the elements in $\mathfrak{S}$ are unordered sets, it is only a question of the multiplicities of the letters. Let $l(A)=k$, $l(B)=n$, $l(C)=p$, $l(D)=q$. If the set A consists of the distinct letters a_i with multiplicities α_i, we may write $A=\{\alpha_i a_i\}$, $B=\{\beta_i b_i\}$, $C=\{\gamma_i c_i\}$, $D=\{\delta_i d_i\}$. Then by construction of $\mathfrak{S}$,

$$AmB = \{2^n\alpha_i a_i,\ 2^k\beta_i b_i\}, \qquad l(AmB) = 2^{k+n+1};$$

$$CmD = \{2^q\gamma_i c_i,\ 2^p\delta_i d_i\}, \qquad l(CmD) = 2^{p+q+1}.$$

Hence

$$(AmB)m(CmD) = \{2^{n+p+q+1}\alpha_i a_i,\ 2^{k+p+q+1}\beta_i b_i,\ 2^{k+n+q+1}\gamma_i c_i,\ 2^{k+n+p+1}\delta_i d_i\},$$

a result whose symmetry shows that it is independent of the order in which A, B, C, D are taken, so that (47) holds. Thus $\mathfrak{S}$ satisfies (45)–(47).

Secondly we wish to show that any finite or countable system $\mathfrak{R}$ satisfying (45)–(47) is a homomorphic image of $\mathfrak{S}$. By (45), in $\mathfrak{R}$ we have $AmA=A$; thus by inserting repetitions of the given elements we can write any given element in $\mathfrak{R}$ as a mean of 2^n elements. Likewise any mean A of 2^k elements of $\mathfrak{R}$ can be written as a mean of 2^n elements, if $k\leqq n$, simply by increasing the multiplicity of each element in A by the factor 2^{n-k}, by (45).

We desire $\mathfrak{R}$ to be a homomorphic image of $\mathfrak{S}$; since the letters in the sets in $\mathfrak{S}$ are unordered, we shall need that repeated means in $\mathfrak{R}$ are independent of the order in which the elements are taken. For a mean of two elements of $\mathfrak{R}$, this condition is precisely (46). For a mean of four or more elements, (47) and (48) give the result in special cases, but we must prove it in general. We proceed by induction.

Suppose it is true for $n<k$ $(k\geqq 2)$ that the mean of 2^n elements of $\mathfrak{R}$ is independent of their order, and that there is given a mean M of 2^k elements. Let Q_1 stand for the first one-fourth of the places in the given repeated mean, Q_2 for the second fourth of the places therein, and so on, while the first half of the places is called H_1 and the second half H_2. Then the mean of the elements of Q_1 is some element of $\mathfrak{R}$, the mean of those of Q_2 is another, and so on, so that we have for the given mean

$$M = (Q_1mQ_2)m(Q_3mQ_4).$$

Suppose it is desired to arrange the elements involved in the mean in the order $a, b, c, \cdots$. If $a\in H_1$, then by induction we may move a to the desired position in H_1, and so in M, without altering the mean. If $a\in H_2$, then by (46), we may interchange the elements of H_1 with the elements of H_2, so now $a \in H_1$ and as before a can be put in the desired place. It is desired that b follow a. If $b \in H_1$, the previous change having already been made, this can be achieved by induction. If $b \in H_2$, then by (46) applied to $Q_3 m Q_4$, we can put b in Q_3; then by (47) we can move it to Q_2, so $b \in H_1$ and can be handled by induction as before.

If there are only four elements in M, then a and b complete the desired order for H_1; the other elements must be in H_2 and by induction H_2 can be rearranged as desired.

If there are more than four elements in M, then a and b are both in Q_1 and c is desired as the next letter. If $c \in H_1$, rearrange H_1 by induction. Otherwise, $c \in H_2$, and we can move it to H_1 (and if Q_1 is not filled, to Q_1) just as was done with b above. By continuing in a similar manner, we can fill Q_1 with the letters which it is desired should be there, and by induction arrange them in the desired order. Then each other letter is in Q_2 or in H_2. Say g is desired as the first letter of Q_2. If g is in Q_2, we can move it to Q_3 by (47) without affecting Q_1 which is already arranged. If g is in Q_4 we can move it to Q_3 by induction which permits rearrangement of H_2, likewise without affecting Q_1. Hence in any case we can put g in Q_3. Suppose it is desired that h follow g. If h is in Q_2, we can move it to Q_4 by (48), without disturbing either Q_1 which is arranged, or Q_3, which contains g. By induction, we can rearrange H_2 so as to get g and h in Q_3. By repeating this process we can fill Q_3 with the elements which it is desired shall ultimately be in Q_2. Then by (47) we can put these elements in Q_2, and by induction we can rearrange Q_2 in the desired order. Thus H_1 is put in order; all remaining elements must be in H_2 which can then be arranged by induction.

Thus we have shown that any mean in $\mathfrak{R}$ can be represented as a mean of 2^k elements for some k, and that these elements can be rearranged in any desired order—that is, that they are essentially unordered. If $\mathfrak{R}$ is given, let the elements of $\mathfrak{R}$ constitute the letters of $\mathfrak{S}$ and let each set $A \in \mathfrak{S}$ correspond to the (essentially unordered) mean of these elements in $\mathfrak{R}$. If $A = B$ in $\mathfrak{S}$, then the corresponding means A' and B' in $\mathfrak{R}$ will be equal, for if $A = B$ in $\mathfrak{S}$ then by definition of equality in $\mathfrak{S}$ each letter in the shorter (say in A) appears with a uniformly greater multiplicity in the other; in $\mathfrak{R}$, by (45), these two means are equal so $A' = B'$. Likewise, if A corresponds to A' and B corresponds to B' then by the construction of the correspondence AmB corresponds to $A'mB'$. Thus $\mathfrak{R}$ is a homomorphic image of $\mathfrak{S}$ as desired and the theorem is proved.

But now it is clear that if $A_1, \cdots, A_n$ are any n linearly independent matrices (or other vectors), and if AmB is interpreted as $(A+B)/2$, then distinct elements of $\mathfrak{S}$ (as defined above) represent different matrices. Hence (45)–(47) are a *complete set of postulates for binary means.*

It would be interesting to find similar postulates for ternary and n-ary means, but these are less relevant to Jordan algebras.

References

1. I. Ado, Bull. Soc. Phys.-Math. Kazan vol. 7 (1935) pp. 3–43.

2. A. A. Albert, *On a certain algebra of quantum mechanics*, Ann. of Math. vol. 35 (1934) pp. 65–73.

3. ———, *On Jordan algebras of linear transformations*, Trans. Amer. Math. Soc. vol. 59 (1946) pp. 524–555.

4. ———, *A structure theory for Jordan algebras*, Ann. of Math. vol. 48 (1947) pp. 546–567.

5. Garrett Birkhoff, *On the structure of abstract algebras*, Proc. Cambridge Philos. Soc. vol. 31 (1935) pp. 433–454.

6. ———, *Representability of Lie algebras and Lie groups by matrices*, Ann. of Math. vol. 38 (1937) pp. 526–532.

7. ———, *Analytical groups*, Trans. Amer. Math. Soc. vol. 43 (1938) pp. 61–101.

8. ———, *Universal algebra*, Proceedings of the Canadian Mathematical Congress, Montreal, 1946, pp. 310–326.

9. J. E. Campbell, *Introductory treatise on Lie's theory of finite continuous transformation groups*, Oxford, 1903.

10. E. Cartan, *Les représentations linéaires des groupes de Lie*, J. Math. Pures Appl. vol. 17 (1938) pp. 1–12.

11. C. Chevalley, *Theory of Lie groups*, Princeton, 1946.

12. E. V. Huntington, *Sets of independent postulates for the arithmetic mean, the geometric mean, the harmonic mean, and the root-mean-square*, Trans. Amer. Math. Soc. vol. 29 (1927) pp. 1–22.

13. F. D. Jacobson and N. Jacobson, *Classification and representation of semi-simple Jordan algebras*, to be published in Trans. Amer. Math. Soc.

14. N. Jacobson, *Non-commutative polynomials and cyclic algebras*, Ann. of Math. vol. 35 (1934) pp. 197–208.

15. P. Jordan, J. v. Neumann, and E. Wigner, *On an algebraic generalization of the quantum mechanical formalism*, Ann. of Math. vol. 35 (1934) pp. 29–64.

16. G. K. Kalisch, *On special Jordan algebras*, Trans. Amer. Math. Soc. vol. 61 (1947) pp. 482–494.

17. G. Kowalewski, *Einführung in die Theorie der kontinuierlichen Gruppen*, Leipzig, 1931.

18. J. C. C. McKinsey and A. Tarski, *The algebra of topology*, Ann. of Math. vol. 45 (1944) pp. 141–191.

19. ———, *On closed elements in closure algebras*, Ann. of Math. vol. 47 (1946) pp. 122–162.

20. J. v. Neumann, *Über die analytischen Eigenschaften von Gruppen linearer Transformationen und ihrer Darstellungen*, Math. Zeit. vol. 30 (1929) pp. 3–42.

21. E. Noether, *Hyperkomplexe Grossen und Darstellungstheorie*, Math. Zeit. vol. 30 (1929) pp. 641–692.

22. A. Tarski, *A remark on functionally free algebras*, Ann. of Math. vol. 47 (1946) pp. 163–165.

23. B. L. van der Waerden, *Moderne Algebra*, 2d. ed., vol. 2, Berlin, 1940.

24. E. Witt, *Treue Darstellung Liescher Ringe*, J. Reine Angew. Math. vol. 177 (1937) pp. 152–160.

Harvard University,
Cambridge, Mass.
Tufts College,
Medford, Mass.

Reprinted from *Trans. Am. Math. Soc.* **65** (1949), 116–136

V

Lattice-Ordered Algebraic Structures

Vector Lattices[1]

The theory of vector lattices stems from a seminal 1928 paper of F. Riesz. The approach he suggested there was carried much further in 1936–7 by H. Freudenthal and L. Kantorovich. I first became aware of the concept when reviewing the paper "Lineare halbgeordnete Räume" by Kantorovich for the *Zentralblatt* in 1937. Shortly before, Stan Ulam had interested me in stochastic processes, and I conceived the idea of extending the ergodic theorem to such non-deterministic processes. The most natural such extension is to a class of Banach lattices resembling the spaces $L_1(\mathbb{R}^n)$, which I named abstract (L)-spaces.

I was able to prove a mean ergodic theorem (see [33]) by adapting my father's combinatorial approach to such spaces. My result was strengthened by Kakutani and Yosida (*Proc. Imp. Acad. Japan* **15** (1939), 165–8), and was the starting point of Kakutani's theory of (L)-spaces and (M)-spaces (*Annals of Math.* **42** (1941), 523–37 and 994–1024), as well as the axiomatic characterization of L_p-spaces by Bohnenblust (*Duke Math. J.* **6** (1940), 627–40).

Most important, this new approach stimulated Riesz to revise and extend a paper he had published in Hungarian in 1936 into a now classic article (*Annals of Math.* **41** (1940), 174–206) containing his theory of so-called *Riesz spaces.* In these spaces, the lattice assumption of the existence of $f \wedge g$ and $f \vee g$ is replaced by the weaker assumption that, in the positive cone, given $f_1 + f_2 = g_1 + g_2$, four elements f_{ij} can be found such that $f_1 = f_{11} + f_{12}, f_2 = f_{21} + f_{22}$, and $g_1 = f_{11} + f_{21}$, $g_2 = f_{12} + f_{22}$. He showed that in any such "Riesz space," the order-bounded linear *functionals* form a vector lattice.

This paper was a major stimulus for Chapter IX on vector lattices in [LT1], which contained the following new results: the identity $|x \wedge z - y \wedge z| + |x \vee z - y \vee z| = |x - y|$; the classification of finite-dimensional vector lattices; the equivalence of relative uniform star-convergence with metric convergence in Banach lattices; the concept of a Banach lattice; and the concept of the "conjugate" of a vector lattice.

The preceding ideas and results have provided a firm foundation for much later work in this field, including the books *Functional Analysis in Partially Ordered Linear Spaces* by Kantorovich, Vulikh, and Pinsker; H. Nakano's *Semi-Ordered Linear Spaces*; H. H. Schaefer's *Banach Lattices and Positive Operators*; W. A. J. Luxemburg and A. C. Zaanen's *Riesz Spaces*; A. Peressini's *Ordered Topological Vector Spaces*; and *Locally Solid Riesz Spaces*, by C. D. Aliprantis and O. Burkinshaw.

Positive Linear Operators

The stochastic operators studied in [33] are *positive* linear operators, that is, linear operators P with the property that $f > 0$ implies $Pf > 0$. In the case of a finite-dimensional vector lattice $\mathbb{R}^n$, matrices which correspond to positive operators are nonnegative; such matrices were studied around 1910 by Perron and Frobenius.[2] Soon after, Jentzsch extended their results to positive linear integral operators on $C[a, b]$. He showed that these, too, have a dominant *positive eigenvector* ϕ_0, with positive eigenvalue λ, such that the interated transforms $P^n f = f_n$ of any positive f under that action of P approach $\lambda^n c\phi_0$ for some $c(f) > 0$.

In 1948, Krein and Rutman (*Uspehi Mat. Nauk* **9**, 3–95) proved that a positive linear operator on a partially ordered vector space has a unique positive eigenvector with dominant positive eigenvalue, under a wide variety of compactness hypotheses.

In a series of papers published from 1955 on, H. H. Schaefer greatly extended the spectral theory of positive linear operators. His results are included in his comprehensive book *Banach Lattices and Positive Operators*, cited three paragraphs above; see also G.-C. Rota (*Bull. AMS* **67** (1961), 556–8).

Beginning in 1955 (with [93]), I applied a new tool to the study of positive linear operators: a "projective quasi-metric" analogous to one used by Hilbert in geometry. Positive linear operators are *contractions* in this quasi-metric, giving proofs of the existence of dominant positive eigenvectors that are more constructive than compactness arguments. Even more advantageous, the contraction property implies asympotic uniqueness theorems for *one-parameter families* of positive linear operators $P_{s,t}$ $(s \leq t)$ having the Chapman–Kolmogoroff property that $P_{r,s}P_{s,t} = P_{r,t}$. Namely, for any fixed s, the images $P_{s,t}(C)$ of the positive cone approach asymptotically a positive time-dependent *ray* $\{c(t)\}$. See [131] for details; the final theory is presented in [LT3, Chap. XVI].

Such families of operators arise in population theory, in nuclear reactor theory, and elsewhere. In nuclear reactor theory the existence and uniqueness of the critical flux distribution is explained by this theory, in both multigroup diffusion models ([99], [106]) and transport theory models ([100], [119]). The function space consists of the rays issuing from the origin and interior to the "positive cone"; the metric on this space is given by the logarithm of the cross-ratio.

Averaging operators. Positive linear operators also arise in the theory of turbulence, as *Reynolds operators R* acting on function rings (abstractly, on "f-rings"; see "Lattice-Ordered Algebraic Structures" below). These are positive linear operators safisfying the "Reynolds identity":

$$(*) \qquad R(fg) = Rf \cdot Rg = R[(f\text{-}Rf)(g\text{-}Rg)].$$

The Reynolds operator of turbulence is in addition a projection (i.e., $R(Rf) = Rf$) and therefore satisfies the stronger "averaging identity":

$$(**) \qquad R(fRg) = Rf \cdot Rg.$$

An operation satisfying the averaging identity $R1 = 1$ is called an averaging operator. The late J. Kampé de Fériet showed that $(*)$ and $(**)$ are equivalent for positive linear operators in finite-dimensional algebras.

In [68], I generalized the preceding results to f-rings with *1*. More interesting, I showed that on the f-ring $C(X)$, X any compact Hausdorff space, every averaging operator is the subdirect product of *scalar* averaging operators. Many further results were obtained by Mme. Dubreil and J. L. Kelley. I reviewed the subject in [107, Part II] and (very summarily) in [LT3, pp. 407–10].

Note. The definitive work on this subject is a paper by G.-C. Rota, where a necessary and sufficient condition is found to guarantee that a Reynolds operator is an averaging operator and where a complete classification is given of all Reynolds operators.[3]

I have applied positive linear operators to systems of ordinary differential and differential-delay equations, in a series of papers co-authored by Leon Kotin: [127], [132], [135], [141], [143], [148], [156], and [180]. For example, in [141], we used positivity considerations to motivate the usual (natural) basis of solutions of the modified Bessel, Hermite, confluent hypergeometric, Airy, Legendre, and Laguerre DEs.

Doubly Stochastic Matrices[4]

Arithmetic Means of Permutations. An arithmetic mean of permutations is, by definition, a (square) matrix which can be written in the form

$$A = \sum_{k=1}^{s} \lambda_k P_k \qquad [\lambda_k \geq 0 \quad \lambda_1 + \cdots + \lambda_s = 1], \tag{1}$$

the P_k being $n \times n$ permutation matrices. Evidently, every matrix of the form (1) is nonnegative and satisfies

$$\sum_{i=1}^{n} a_{ij} = \sum_{j=1}^{n} a_{ij} = 1 \quad \text{for all } i, j = 1, \ldots, n. \tag{1'}$$

Such *doubly stochastic* matrices arise naturally in probability theory; note also that $n \times n$ *magic squares* are multiples of such matrices by $n(n^2 + 1)/2$.

The converse is also true. We have the following theorem.

Theorem. *Any $n \times n$ doubly stochastic matrix is an arithmetic mean of permutation matrices.*

There are two noteworthy corollaries:

1) The extreme points of the convex set of all $n \times n$ doubly stochastic matrices are the $n \times n$ permutation matrices.
2) The convex hull of the set of all $n \times n$ permutation matrices is the set of $n \times n$ doubly stochastic matrices.

The proof is simple. A theorem of Philip Hall [1] states that every $n \times n$ matrix whose entries are all 0 or 1 contains either a permutation submatrix, or an $(i + 1) \times (n - i)$ submatrix of zeros. It follows that any nonnegative matrix C which does not contain an $(i + 1) \times (n - i)$ submatrix of zeros must contain a positive scalar multiple cP of some permutation matrix P. If $c = \max\{c_{ij} | p_{ij} = 1\}$, then clearly $C - cP$ is nonnegative, yet it has one more zero entry than C.

Other Lattice-Ordered Algebraic Structures

Simply ordered groups, rings, and fields were intensively studied around the turn of the century in connection with axiomatizations of the real field; in particular, the work of Hilbert, Hölder, and Hahn should be cited.

The success of the theory of vector lattices inspired similar studies of more general partially ordered and lattice-ordered algebraic structures in the 1940s. First came my paper [42] on *lattice-ordered groups*, commutative or not. In that paper, the Riesz interpolation property (see Vector Lattices) was analyzed in this more general group context in [28]. Then, in 1945, in a paper ([48]) reprinted here, I studied the special properties of Lie l-groups and lattice-ordered Lie algebras. The result that any complete l-group is commutative was proved around that time by Iwasawa.

In [LT2], written in 1947, Chapter XIII extended the theory of "residuated lattices" due to Ward and Dilworth (1939), to include *noncommutative* lattice-ordered monoids and semigroups. The algebra of binary relations, which had been axiomatized around 1940 by McKinsey and Tarski, is an important special case, having the auxiliary unary operation of conversion. A few years later, definitive axioms for the algebra of relations (conforming to the general principles of universal algebra) were worked out by Tarski, Jónsson, and Chin. For later developments based on these axioms, see B. Jónsson, *Alg. Universalis* **15** (1982), pp. 273–98. Somewhat different axioms were given in [LT3, p. 344]; in the early printings of [LT3], the hypothesis of completeness was inadvertently omitted.

From around 1950 on, the theory of "lattice-ordered algebraic structures" (aptly so named by L. Fuchs)[5] has flourished. Investigations have been made into the properties of *partially* ordered as well as lattice-ordered groups, semigroups, monoids, etc., and their classification. My paper with R. S. Pierce ([91]), written in 1955 and reproduced in the present volume, filled a conspicuous gap by developing a theory of *lattice-ordered rings.* It derived many new results, including the theorem that all Archimedean f-rings are commutative. It has stimulated later research workers in the field, such as M. Henriksen, B. de Pagter, and C. B. Huijmans, and has led to the theory of f-algebras, of which rings of continuous functions are important examples.

Notes

[1] Several portions of this introduction, especially including the last paragraph, were condensed from a review kindly supplied by Profs. C. D. Aliprantis and W. A. J. Luxemburg.

[2] Cf. [99], co-authored by Richard Varga. For more recent expositions, see E. Seneta, *Nonnegative Matrices and Markov Chains*, 2d ed., Springer-Verlag, 1981.

[3] For Rota's work, see *Proc. Symp. Applied Math.* **XVI**, Am. Math. Soc., 1964, 70–83.

[4] This is an edited partial translation of [53] from the original Spanish into English.

[5] L. Fuchs, *Partially Ordered Algebraic Systems*, Pergamon Press, 1963.

Reprinted from the Proceedings of the NATIONAL ACADEMY OF SCIENCES,
Vol. 24, No. 3, pp. 154–159. March, 1938.

DEPENDENT PROBABILITIES AND SPACES (L)

BY GARRETT BIRKHOFF

HARVARD UNIVERSITY

Communicated February 1, 1938

1. *Introduction.*—The purpose of the present paper is to express the theory of dependent probabilities in new terms.

These terms are: (*a*) the general theory of linear operators on Banach space, and (*b*) the relation $f < g$. The abstract theory of partially ordered Banach spaces has already been formulated by Kantorovitch;[1] it involves such notions as: upper bound, lower bound, least upper bound or sup, greatest lower bound or inf, lim sup, lim inf, positive part, negative part, absolute value and disjointness.

Firstly, the fundamental definitions are stated in a form which includes all known cases; this has never been done before. Secondly, Markoff's fundamental theorem on "probabilities in chain" is proved in a form including all known cases. And lastly, a new theorem, which specializes in the *deterministic* case to von Neumann's well-known Mean Ergodic Theorem,[2] is proved with added generality in the *stochastic case.*

The present paper merely sketches the proofs, which will be given in full elsewhere.

2. *Postulates.*—The model with which we shall work is described in the following:

DEFINITION 1: *By a space* (L), *we mean any space* Σ *which satisfies the following six postulates.*

P0: Σ is a linear space with real scalars, and a relation $f > 0$ (to be read, f is positive), is defined on Σ.

P1: If $f > 0$ and $g > 0$, then $f + g > 0$.

P2: If $f > 0$ and λ is a scalar, then $\lambda > 0$ implies $\lambda f > 0$ and conversely.

P3: Relative to the definition, $f > g$ (read, f is greater than g) means $f - g > 0$, Σ is a *lattice.*[3]

P4: A "norm" $\eta(f)$ is defined on Σ, relative to which Σ is a Banach space.[4]

P5: Norm is additive on positive elements; $f > 0$ and $g > 0$ imply $\eta(f+g) = \eta(f) + \eta(g)$.

Example: Let B denote the Boolean algebra of all subsets X of a class I_n of n points, or of Borel subsets of an interval I (or of any region!) modulo sets of measure zero. Then the additive, continuous functions defined on B satisfy (P0)–(P5), if by $f > 0$ we mean $f(X) \geqq 0$ for all X and $f(I) > 0$, and by $\eta(f)$ we mean $f(I)$ when $f > 0$ and sup $|f(X)| + |f(X')|$ in general Thus the space (L) and its finite-dimensional analogues are "spaces (L)."

Consequences of (P0)–(P2): Define $f > g$ to mean $f - g > 0$. Then (1) Σ is a partially ordered set in the sense of Hausdorff, (2) translations $x \to x + a$ preserve order, (3) homothetic expansions $x \to \lambda x$ preserve or invert order according as $\lambda > 0$ or $\lambda < 0$. We note that by (1)–(2), (P3) follows from (P0)–(P2) and the assumption that any element f has a "positive part" $f^+ = f \smile 0$, such that $x \geqq f^+$ implies $x \geqq 0$ and $x \geqq f$ and conversely.

Consequences of (P0)–(P3): If we set $f^+ = f \smile 0$, $f^- = f \frown 0$, and $|f| = f^+ - f^-$, then (4) the "Jordan decomposition" $f = f^+ + f^-$ holds, whence $f + g = (f \smile g) + (f \frown g)$ by (2), (5) $f^+ \frown (-f^-) = 0$—in words, f^+ and $-f^-$ are *disjoint,* (6) the dual distributive laws $f \smile (g \frown h) = (f \smile g) \frown (f \smile h)$ and $f \frown (g \smile h) = (f \frown g) \smile (f \frown h)$ are valid, (7) the triangle law on absolute values holds: $|f - g| + |g - h| \geqq |f - h|$, (8) the functions $f \smile g$ and $f \frown g$ are *monotone* in both variables, and *uniformly continuous* in that $|(f \smile g) - (f^* \smile g)| \leqq |f - f^*|$ and $|(f \frown g) - (f^* \frown g)| \leqq |f - f^*|$.

Consequences of (P0)–(P5): (9) The functions $f \smile g$ and $f \frown g$ are metrically continuous, in virtue of (8), (10) the functional $\lambda(f) = \eta(f^+) - \eta(f^-)$ is *linear*, and $\eta(f) = \lambda(|f|)$, (11) every set of elements of Σ having an upper bound has a least upper bound (and dually).

These results can be found in Kantorovitch, op. cit.

3. *Normal Subspaces and Decompositions.*—In proving our Mean Ergodic Theorem (Theorem 3), but not elsewhere, we shall want two further definitions, which seem to be new.

DEFINITION 2: *A subspace of a linear space satisfying* (P0)–(P3) *is called "normal" if and only if it contains* (a) *with any* f, *also* $|\mathrm{f}|$, *and* (b) *with any positive* f, *all "parts"* x *of* f (*i.e., all positive* x *with* x < f).

DEFINITION 3: *By a "direct decomposition" of* Σ, *is meant a choice of complementary normal subspaces—that is, of subspaces* S *and* T *such that* $\mathrm{S} \frown \mathrm{T} = 0, \mathrm{S} + \mathrm{T} = \Sigma$.

Remarks: (1) The normal subspaces of Σ correspond to its homomorphisms in just the same way that the normal subgroups of a group correspond to *its* homomorphisms, and (2) the decompositions of Σ correspond one–one to its representations as a direct union.

4. *Connections with Dependent Probabilities.*—Spaces (*L*) are connected with the theory of dependent probabilities by three fundamental definitions.

DEFINITION 4: *By a "distribution" is meant a positive element of* Σ *with norm one.*

DEFINITION 5: *By a "transition operator" on* Σ *is meant an additive operator which carries distributions into distributions.*

DEFINITION 6: *A transition operator* T *describing the dependence of the state of a system at time* t′ *on its state at a previous instant* t, *is called "independent" of an operator* U *relating the instants* t″ *and* t′ [t″ > t′], *if and only if the instants* t″ *and* t *are related by the transition operator* TU: f → (fT)U.

As authorities for these definitions, we can cite the usual formulations of Bayes' Theorem, of the theory of Markoff chains, of Kolmogoroff's more general theory of "stochastic processes." Also, Fourier's theory of heat flow is expressed by transition operators: the invariance of $\lambda(f)$ is the gist of the first, and that of the set of $p \geq 0$ of the second, law of thermodynamics. Finally, the flows of phase-space envisaged by Poincaré in his version of classical mechanics, induce automorphisms on the space (*L*)—and hence are transition operators in our sense, as well as "unitary operators on Hilbert space."

Conclusions: (1) The set Δ of all distribution functions is a closed convex subset of Σ, of diameter sup $|(p - q)| \leqq 2$, (2) the distance $\eta(|p - q|)$ is the "stochastic distance" recently defined by Mazurkiewicz—it is *not* equivalent to the traditional notion of "convergence in probability," (3)

$|fT| \leqq |f|$, whence $\eta(fT) \leqq \eta(f)$ (T is of "modulus" unity, and a "contraction," and so uniformly continuous!).

5. *Hypothesis of Markoff.*—Now let Σ be any space (L), and T a fixed transition operator on Σ.

DEFINITION 7: *An* f *in* Σ *is called a "fixpoint" if and only if* $fT = f$. *A distribution which is a fixpoint is called "stable."*

Results: (1) The fixpoints are a closed linear subspace of Σ. Hence the stable distributions are a closed convex subset of Δ, and their number is either zero, or one (the "metrically transitive" case[5]), or infinity. All three cases are possible, but the second is the most interesting.

Hypothesis of Markoff (weakened): For some n, $d = \inf_{p \in \Delta} pT^n > 0$.

THEOREM 1: *If* T *satisfies Markoff's hypothesis, then there is a unique stable distribution* p_0. *Moreover the* pT^k *tend to* p_0 *uniformly, with the rapidity that the terms of a convergent geometrical progression tend to zero.*

Proof: First, $\eta(pT^n - qT^n) \leqq (1 - |d|)\eta(p - q)$ for any $p, q \in \Delta$. The conclusion now follows by a generalization to complete metric spaces (like Δ) of a simple argument due to Carl Neumann and often exploited by Picard, which is purely geometrical.

COROLLARY 1: $\operatorname{Sup} pT^n \leqq p + \sum_{k=0}^{\infty} (pT^{k+1} - pT^k)$ *is finite, for any fixed* p. (Cf. §2, conclusion (11)).

COROLLARY 2: *Let* $T_1, \ldots, T_n$ *be any sequence of transition operators, and let* d_i *denote* $\operatorname{Inf}_{p \in \Delta} pT_i$. *Then for all* p, q *in* Δ, $\eta(pT_1 \ldots T_n - qT_1 \ldots T_n) \leqq 2\prod_{i=1}^{n}(1 - |d_i|)$.

6. *Ergodic Hypothesis.*—Unless the conclusion of Corollary 1 holds, the means of the pT^k at best tend to 0. Hence we shall fix p, and make the

ERGODIC HYPOTHESIS: The pT^k have an upper bound. This is fulfilled if p is the integral of a bounded density-function, and T leaves measure invariant: the integral of the upper bound to the density function is an upper bound to the pT^k.

THEOREM 2: *The Ergodic Hypothesis implies the existence of at least one stable distribution.*

Proof: Form $h = \operatorname{Lim} \sup_{k \to \infty} pT^k = \operatorname{Inf}_n \sup_{k \geqq n} pT^k$; evidently $hT = T$, $|h| \geqq 1$, and so $h > 0$. Hence $h/|h|$ is a stable distribution.

THEOREM 3 (mean ergodic theorem): *The Ergodic Hypothesis implies that the means* $\frac{1}{n}\sum_{k=0}^{n-1} pT^k$ *converge* weakly, *in the sense that if* $\lambda(f)$ *is any linear functional, then the numerical means* $\phi_n(p) = \lambda\left(\frac{1}{n}\sum_{k=0}^{n-1} pT^k\right)$ *converge in the ordinary sense.*

Proof: By a generalization of a Lemma of Hahn (cf. §7), λ is the sum of its positive and negative parts. Again, by a simple Lemma of Banach (op. cit., p. 54) each part is a constant multiple of a functional satisfying $0 \leqq \lambda(f) \leqq \eta(f)$ for all $f > 0$. Hence we need only consider this case. Again, if k is large, then $h = \lim\sup_{k\to\infty} pT^k$ contains an arbitrarily large part of pT^k, together with all transforms of this part; hence we can assume $p \leqq h$, where $hT = h$.

We shall make these assumptions, and in the proof, shall treat all "parts" f of h on the same footing. First, define $\bar{\phi}(f) = \lim\sup_{n\to\infty}\phi_n(f)$, $\underline{\phi}(f) = \lim\inf_{n\to\infty}\phi_n(f)$. Clearly $0 \leqq \underline{\phi}(f) \leqq \bar{\phi}(f) \leqq \eta(f)$; clearly also $\underline{\phi}(fT) = \underline{\phi}(f)$ and $\bar{\phi}(fT) = \bar{\phi}(f)$. The functionals $\underline{\phi}$ and $\bar{\phi}$ are monotone; they need *not* be linear, but $\underline{\phi}$ is convex while $\bar{\phi}$ is concave. Hence the functionals (we use a construction of F. Riesz)

$$(\bar{\alpha}f) = \sup \sum_i \bar{\phi}(f_i) \qquad \underline{\alpha}(f) = \inf \sum_i \underline{\phi}(f_i)$$

where the summations are with respect to all decompositions of f into (finite or countable; it makes no difference) parts f_i, are, respectively, the least linear functional $\geqq \bar{\phi}$, and the greatest linear functional $\leqq \underline{\phi}$. Moreover $\bar{\alpha}(fT) = \bar{\alpha}(f)$ and $\underline{\alpha}(fT) = \underline{\alpha}(f)$; the functionals are invariant.

Now since $0 \leqq \underline{\alpha} \leqq \underline{\phi} \leqq \bar{\phi} \leqq \bar{\alpha} \leqq \eta$, and $h \geqq f$, in order to conclude $\underline{\phi}(f) = \bar{\phi}(f) = \mathrm{Lim}_{n\to\infty}\phi(f)$, we need only show that $\underline{\alpha}(f) = \bar{\alpha}(f)$, whence, since $\bar{\alpha} - \underline{\alpha}$ is non-negative and linear, we need only show $\bar{\alpha}(h) \leqq \lambda(h) \leqq \underline{\alpha}(h)$. By duality, we need only show $\bar{\alpha}(h) \leqq \lambda(h)$. This is just what we shall prove.

7. *Extension of a Lemma of Hahn.*—For it, we shall need an extension of a Lemma of Hahn.[6] Let $\lambda(x)$ be any linear functional on Σ, let Λ^+ denote the set of $u > 0$ such that $0 < x \leqq u$ implies $\lambda(x) > 0$, and define Λ^- dually. Further, let Λ^0 denote the set of $u > 0$ such that $0 < x \leqq u$ implies $\lambda(x) = 0$.

LEMMA: *Σ is decomposed into three components: a component Λ^+ on which* $x > 0$ *implies* $\lambda(x) > 0$, *a component Λ^0 on which* $\lambda(x) = 0$, *and a component Λ^- on which* $x > 0$ *implies* $\lambda(x) < 0$

COROLLARY 1: *Any linear functional can be resolved into its positive part and its negative part.*

8. *Completion of Proof.*—Choose $\epsilon > 0$, and denote by g_n the component of h (cf. §7) on which $\phi_n(x) - \bar{\alpha}(x) + \epsilon\eta(x)$ is non-negative. Then irrespective of ϵ,

LEMMA: *The join* u *of the* g_n *is* h.

Proof: Consider $r = h - u$. evidently for all n, $r \leqq h - g_n$. Hence $\bar{\phi}(x) \leqq \sup \phi_n(x) \leqq \bar{\alpha}(x) - \epsilon\eta(x)$ for all $x \leqq r$, and so $\bar{\alpha}(r) = \sup \Sigma\bar{\phi}(x_i) \leqq \bar{\alpha}(r) - \epsilon\eta(r)$, whence $\eta(r) = 0$ and $r = 0$.

Now let h_n denote the part of g_n not in $g_1 \smile \ldots \smile g_{n-1}$; the h_n are the components of a direct decomposition of h. Choose M so large that if h^* denotes $h - \sum_{k=1}^{m} h_k$, then $|h^*| < \epsilon$. We shall show that for all $N > M$,

$$\text{(E)} \quad N\lambda(h) \geqq N\bar{\alpha}(h) - N\epsilon\eta(h) - N\epsilon - M\bar{\alpha}(h)$$

from which, dividing through by N, and letting $N \to \infty$, we will get $\lambda(h) \geqq \bar{\alpha}(h) - \epsilon\eta(h) - \epsilon$. Now letting $\epsilon \to 0$, the proof is complete.

The proof of (E) reproduces the combinatorial essence of G. D. Birkhoff's proof of the Strong Ergodic Theorem.[2] We rely on the fact that the "components" of h form a Boolean algebra, and may be treated like sets.

[1] L. Kantorovitch, "Lineare halbgeordnete Raume," *Math. Sbornik*, **2**, 121–68 (1937). Cf. also H. Freudenthal, "Teilweise geordnete Moduln," *Proc. Akad. Wet. Amsterdam*, **39**, 641–51 (1936).

[2] J. von Neumann, "Proof of the Quasi-Ergodic Hypothesis," these PROCEEDINGS, **18**, 70–82 (1932). Our method is that used by G. D. Birkhoff for his stronger result; cf. "Proof of a Recurrence Theorem for Strongly Transitive Systems, and Proof of the Ergodic Theorem," these PROCEEDINGS, **17**, 650–60 (1931).

[3] In the sense of the author's "On the combination of subalgebras," *Proc. Camb. Phil. Soc.*, **29**, 441–64 (1933). Synonyms are "Verband" (Fr. Klein) and "structure" (O. Ore). We shall use the notation $f \cup g$ for sup (f, g) and $f \cap g$ for inf (f, g).

[4] S. Banach, "Théorie des opérations linéaires," Warsaw, 1933. By general consent, the "B-spaces" of Banach, op. cit., are called Banach spaces; they are complete, metric, linear spaces.

[5] In the sense of G. D. Birkhoff and Paul Smith, "Structure Analysis of Surface Transformation," *Jour. Math.*, **7**, 365 (1928).

[6] The author is much indebted to J. von Neumann for suggesting that this lemma could be generalized. He is also indebted to S. Ulam for many conversations on the whole subject.

ANNALS OF MATHEMATICS
Vol. 43, No. 2, April, 1942

LATTICE-ORDERED GROUPS

BY GARRETT BIRKHOFF

(Received December 10, 1941)

1. Introduction

We shall be concerned below with lattice-ordered groups, or *l-groups*,[1] in the sense of the following definition.

DEFINITION. *An l-group is*

(I) a group, *on which is defined a binary inclusion relation which is* "homogeneous" *in the sense that*

$$\text{(II)} \qquad x \geqq y \quad \textit{implies} \quad a + x + b \geqq a + y + b \quad \textit{for all } a, b,$$

and relative to which

(III) *the group is a* lattice.

This defines l-groups as abstract algebras; as such, we can (and shall) apply to them such general algebraic concepts as l-subgroup (subalgebra), isomorphism, homomorphism, and so on.

Three important topics will be included as special cases under the single heading of l-groups: the additive and multiplicative groups of ordered fields, which have long been studied by Hahn, Artin, and others, and are now extensively used in valuation theory; the study of abstract number and ideal theory initiated by Dedekind, and recently amplified by Krull, Ward, Lorenzen, Clifford, Dilworth and others; and the semi-ordered function spaces studied very recently by Riesz, Freudenthal, Kantorovitch, the author, Bohnenblust, Stone, Kakutani, and others.

It should be stressed, however, that up to the present time only l-groups which are commutative *or* simply ordered have been studied; and it came as a considerable surprise to the author that the non-commutative case involved so few new difficulties.

The material below breaks up rather naturally into several parts. First (§§2–8) Postulates (I)–(III) are discussed, and various other equivalent systems of postulates (together with numerous examples) are derived. Then, after brief preliminaries on algebraic formalism, the general structure and decomposition theory of l-groups is treated (§§9–13). After this, a complete classification of *commutative* l-groups whose structure lattice has finite length is given (§§14–20). After this, in §§21–26, special properties of *complete* l-groups are discussed. Fifth, two important generalizations are taken up (§§27–28). The paper then concludes with a list of sixteen unsolved problems (§§30–31), some of which are fundamental.

---

[1] We are adopting the convenient terminology of M. H. Stone, "A general theory of spectra. II.," Proc. Nat. Acad. Sci. 27 (1941), pp. 83–87.

2. Explanation of (I)

The reader will be assumed to be familiar with the definitions of a group and of a commutative group, and with the algebraic manipulation of the elements of such groups under the additive notation. Thus 0 will denote the group identity, $-a$ the group inverse of a, $a + b$ the result of combining a with b, and na (n any integer) will denote the nth "power" of a in the cyclic subgroup generated by a.

In the commutative case, the rules of manipulation may be summarized in the statement that the group behaves like a vector space over the domain of integers. As it may be shown that every element of an l-group is of infinite order—that $na = 0$ implies $n = 0$ or $a = 0$,—even the cancellation laws hold. In addition,[2] an equation of the form $nx = ma$ ($n \neq 0$) has at most one solution. If such a solution exists, it may be denoted $(m/n)a$, and regarded as a rational scalar multiple of a. In particular (*op. cit.*, §1) the correspondence $(m/n)a \to (m/n)$ is, for any fixed a, and *isomorphism* of the set of rational multiples of a and a subgroup (which always contains all integers) of the additive group of all rational numbers. Thus the set of all rational scalar multiples of a may be thought of as a generalized cyclic subgroup.

3. Explanation of (II)

The concept of homogeneity applies to any binary relation on a group.

DEFINITION. *A binary relation* $\geqq$ *on a group* G *is called* left-homogeneous *if and only if* $x \geqq y$ *implies, for all* $a \in G$, *that* $a + x \geqq a + y$ *and* right-homogeneous *if and only if it implies* $x + a \geqq y + a$. *A relation which is both left- and right-homogeneous is called* homogeneous.

THEOREM 1. *Homogeneity is equivalent to the assertion that* (II′) *every group translation* $x \to a + x + b$ *is a lattice-automorphism.* (I)[3]

PROOF. The condition (II′) is clearly sufficient. To prove its necessity, recall first that all group translations are one-one. Second, not only does $x \geqq y$ imply $a + x + b \geqq a + y + b$, but conversely $a + x + b \geqq a + y + b$ implies

$$(-a) + a + x + b + (-b) \geqq (-a) + a + y + b + (-b)$$

or $x \geqq y$. That is, (II) implies that any group translation is an automorphism with respect to the relation $\geqq$, as asserted.

THEOREM 2. *Homogeneity is equivalent to the assertion that every transformation of the form*[4] $x \to a - x + b$ *is a dual automorphism.* (I)

[2] For the special properties of such groups, cf. Reinhold Baer, "Abelian groups without elements of finite order," Duke Jour. 3 (1937), pp. 68–122.

[3] The postulate numbers in parentheses after the statement of a theorem refer to the postulates which are needed to prove the theorem in question. Many of the theorems below have a generality which far transcends the theory of l-groups.

[4] Especially interesting are the "inversions" $x \to a - x + a$, which are of period two and have a for fixpoint.

(This means that the correspondence replaces the given homogeneous relation by its converse.)

PROOF. Assuming (II), $x \geqq y$ is equivalent to

$$a + (-x) + x + (-y) + b \geqq a + (-x) + y + (-y) + b$$

by Theorem 1. But this is $a - y + b \geqq a - x + b$, and so the condition is necessary. It is sufficient since it implies that $x \to 0 - ((-b) + x + (-a)) + 0 = a - x + b$ is the product of two dual automorphisms, hence an automorphism.

DEFINITION. *An element a of an l-group G is called* positive *if $a \geqq 0$. The set of all positive elements of G will be denoted G^+.*

THEOREM 3. *Homogeneity is equivalent to the assertion that, for some set of "positive" elements invariant under all inner automorphisms $x \to -a + x + a$, $x \geqq y$ if and only if $x - y$ is positive.* (I)

PROOF. Assuming (II), clearly $x \geqq y$ if and only if $x - y \geqq y - y = 0$; moreover $t \geqq 0$ implies $-a + t + a \geqq -a + 0 + a = 0$ for all a. Conversely, for any set S invariant under all inner automorphisms, the relation $(x - y) \in S$ is homogeneous since $(a + x + b) - (a + y + b) = -(-a) + (x - y) + (-a)$ is, for all $a, b \in G$, the transform of $x - y$ under an inner automorphism.

COROLLARY. *If G is commutative, homogeneity is equivalent to the assertion that, for some set of positive elements, $x \geqq y$ if and only if $x - y$ is positive.*

4. Explanation of (III)

Postulate III asserts that the inclusion relation $x \geqq y$ satisfies the usual conditions,

P_1. *For all x, $x \geqq x$,*

P_2. *If $x \geqq y$ and $y \geqq x$, then $x = y$,*

P_3. *If $x \geqq y$ and $y \geqq z$, then $x \geqq z$,*

L′. *Any two elements x and y have a* l.u.b. $x \smile y$,

L″. *Any two elements x and y have a* g.l.b. $x \frown y$.

We recall that in any lattice,[5] the three relations $x \geqq y$, $x \frown y = y$, and $x \smile y = x$ are mutually equivalent; indeed, this is even true in any "partially ordered system" satisfying P_1–P_3. It follows that an automorphism with respect to one of the relation or operations $\geqq$, $\smile$, $\frown$ is necessarily an automorphism with respect to all three. Hence we get as a corollary of Theorem 1,

THEOREM 4. *Left-homogeneity is equivalent to either of the dual left-distributive laws*[6]

$$a + (x \smile y) = (a + x) \smile (a + y), \tag{1}$$

$$a + (x \frown y) = (a + x) \frown (a + y). \tag{1'}$$

right-homogeneity to either right-distributive law (I, P_1–P_3).

[5] The terminology and notation are identical with that of the author's book "Lattice theory," New York, 1940, although scant use will be made of the theorems proved there.

[6] Discovered by Dedekind and independently Freudenthal; see footnote 13.

(In case L′–L″ do not hold, the existence of the join (meet) on one side of an equation is intended to be equivalent to the existence of that on the other.)

We can prove from the left- and right-distributive laws just stated, and finite induction, also the following more general finite distributive laws

$$a + \vee y_j = \vee (a + y_j) \quad \text{and} \quad \vee x_i + a = \vee (x_i + a),$$
$$\vee x_i + \vee y_j = \vee (x_i + y_j),$$
$$\sum_i (\vee_j x_{i,j}) = \vee_{j(i)} (\sum_i x_{i,j(i)}),$$

and their lattice duals.

THEOREM 5. *Homogeneity is equivalent to the "monotonicity law":*

(2) $x \geqq x'$ *and* $y \geqq y'$ *imply* $x + y \geqq x' + y'$. (I, P_1, P_3)

PROOF. Applying homogeneity twice, we get

$$x + y \geqq x + y' \geqq x' + y',$$

whence (2) follows by P_3. Conversely, assuming P_1, we get as special cases of (2), $x + y \geqq x + y'$ and $x + y \geqq x' + y$, implying homogeneity.

Again, a permutation of the elements of a partially ordered system is a dual automorphism if and only if it interchanges the operations $\smile$ and $\frown$. Hence, from Theorem 2, we get

THEOREM 6. *Homogeneity is equivalent to the laws*

(3) $a - (x \frown y) + b = (a - x + b) \smile (a - y + b),$

(3′) $a - (x \smile y) + b = (a - x + b) \frown (a - y + b)$. (I, P_1–P_3)

We note as a special case

(4) $x \frown y = -(-x \smile -y)$ and dually.

From this we see that *the lattice postulate* L″ *is redundant*, in the sense that it is implied by I, II, P_1–P_3, and L′.

5. Stone's postulates

But now P_1–P_3 and L′ are equivalent by pure lattice theory to the assertion that our system admits an idempotent, commutative and associative operation $x \smile y$, in which $x \geqq y$ means $x \smile y = x$. Hence splitting (1) in two parts (right- and left-translations), we get as a corollary of Theorem 4 and the redundance of L″,

THEOREM 7 (Stone[7]). *An l-group may be defined as a group, with a second*

[7] Stone assumed the group to be commutative, in which case one of the distributive laws (1″) can be omitted (*cf.* Stone, *op. cit.*).

binary operation $\smile$ *which is idempotent, commutative, and associative, and satisfies the distributive laws*

$$(1'') \qquad a + (x \smile y) = (a + x) \smile (a + y)$$
$$(x \smile y) + b = (x + b) \smile (y + b).$$

It is a curious fact that, in virtue of the duality principle, substitution of $\frown$ for $\smile$ in the above system of postulates should also define an l-group!

Not only can we delete L″ from our list of postulates, but we can even weaken L′.

Definition. *By the* positive part a^+ *of an element* a *of an l-group, is meant* $a \smile 0$; $a^- = a \frown 0$ *is dually called the* negative part *of* a.

Using right-homogeneity, we get

$$(5) \qquad a \smile b = (b - a)^+ + a = (a - b)^+ + b.$$

Combining (5) with the dualization law (3), we get

$$(6) \qquad a \frown b = -(-a + (a - b)^+) = -(a - b)^+ + a.$$

There follows immediately

Theorem 8. *The lattice hypotheses* L′–L″ *can be replaced by the condition that, for all* a, $a \smile 0$ *should exist.* (I, II, P_1–P_3)

Also, a subgroup of an l-group is an *l-subgroup* if and only if it contains the positive part of each of its members. Substituting in Theorem 7, we get a further corollary.

Theorem 9. *An l-group may be defined as a group with a unary operation* $a \to a^*$ *which satisfies*

$$(7) \quad 0^* = 0, \qquad\qquad (8) \quad c = c^* - (-c)^*,$$

(9) *the operation* $(a - b)^* + b$ *is associative.*

A worth-while problem would be to find a less clumsy form of (9). In this connection, $(a^*)^* = a^*$ might be a useful partial substitute. One might also try setting the middle letter of the associative law equal to 0.

6. Examples

In the next two sections, we shall be using Theorem 3 as our main tool.

First, we note that in order to describe an l-group G up to isomorphism, it is sufficient by Theorem 3 to describe the set G^+ of "positive" elements; indeed, this principle is independent of Postulate III. We shall now describe some important examples of l-groups in this way.

Example 1. G is the additive group of real numbers; G^+ consists of all those which are non-negative.

Example 2. G is the additive group of the integers; G^+ is defined as in Example 1.

Example 3. G is the group of all positive rational numbers under multiplication (the integer one is the group identity); G^+ is the set of all positive integers.

EXAMPLE 4. G is the group of all vectors $x = (x', x'')$ with two real components; G^+ contains x if and only if $x' > 0$, or $x' = 0$ and $x'' \geqq 0$.

EXAMPLE 5. G is the additive group of all real functions defined on the interval $0 \leqq x \leqq 1$; G^+ consists of all those which are non-negative (satisfy $f(x) \geqq 0$ for all x).

EXAMPLE 6. G is the additive group of functions of bounded variation on $0 \leqq x \leqq 1$ with $f(0) = 0$; G^+ defined as in Example 5.

EXAMPLE 7. G as in Example 6; G^+ consists of all "increasing" functions (functions for which $x \geqq y$ implies $f(x) \geqq f(y)$).

We shall now list some examples of non-commutative l-groups. The simplest example consists of the two-parameter non-Abelian Lie group, lexicographically ordered as follows.

EXAMPLE 8. G consists of all couples (x, y) of real numbers, where addition is defined by the formula

$$(x, y) + (x', y') = (x + x', e^{x'}y + y');$$

G^+ consists of all those couples with $x > 0$ or $x = 0$, $y \geqq 0$.

EXAMPLE 9. G has three generators of infinite order, and defining relations $a + b = b + a$, $a + c = c + b$, $b + c = c + a$; G^+ contains $ma + m'b + nc$ if and only if $n > 0$, or $n = 0$ while $m \geqq 0$ and $m' \geqq 0$.

EXAMPLE 10. G consists of the $x > 0$ of any ordered field or skew-field[7a] (division ring) under multiplication; G^+ consists of all $x \geqq 1$.

For purposes of comparison, we shall also list various other examples which satisfy Postulates I–II and part, but not all, of Postulate III.

EXAMPLE 11. G is any group; G^+ consists of the identity 0 alone.

EXAMPLE 12. G is the multiplicative group of all non-zero elements of any algebraic number field; G^+ is the subset of all (algebraic) integers in G.

EXAMPLE 13. G is the group of all elements of any integral domain of characteristic infinity under addition; G^+ is the subset of all sums of squares.

7. Postulates of order reinterpreted

It is trivial that the systems described in Examples 1–13 satisfy Postulates I–II if $a \geqq b$ is defined to mean $(a - b) \in G^+$ (cf. Theorem 3). We shall now give simple tests for the validity of parts P_1–P_3 of Postulate III.

LEMMA 1. *The reflexive law* P_1 *is equivalent to* (9). *The group identity is positive.* (I, II)

For $(a - a) \in G^+$ is equivalent to $0 \in G^+$ by group theory. This condition is evidently satisfied in Examples 1–12 above.

LEMMA 2. *The transitive law* P_3, *the monotonicity law* (2) *of Theorem* 5, *and the condition that*

(10) *Any sum of positive elements is positive, are mutually equivalent.* (I, II, P_1)

PROOF. By Theorem 5, P_3 implies (5) modulo I, II, P_1. Again (5) implies

[7a] Cf. K. Reidemeister, "Grundlagen der Geometrie", p. 40.

the closure of G^+ as the special case $a \geqq 0$ and $b \geqq 0$ imply $a + b \geqq 0 + 0 + 0$. Finally, since $(a - b) + (b - c) = (a - c)$, the closure of G^+ implies P_3 as in Theorem 3.

COROLLARY. *The positive elements of any l-group form a semigroup.*[8]

It is also a corollary that P_3 holds in Examples 1–13 above.

LEMMA 3. *The antisymmetric law* P_2 *is equivalent to asserting that* (11) *a and* $-a$ *are both positive only if* $a = 0$. (I, II)

PROOF. If $(x - y) \in G^+$ and $(y - x) \in G^+$ imply $(x - y) = 0$, then P_2 holds. Conversely, if P_2 holds, $z \geqq 0$ and $-z \geqq 0$ imply $z = 0$.

It may now be checked easily that P_2 holds in Examples 1–11 above, although not in Examples 12–13.

A similar lemma, irrelevant here, is that the symmetric law ($a \geqq b$ implies $b \geqq a$) is equivalent to asserting that $a \in G^+$ implies $-a \in G^+$. From this and Lemmas 1–2 it follows that G^+ defines an *equivalence* relation if and only if it is a *subgroup* of G. (I, II)

Finally, we can read off from Lemmas 1–2 and Theorem 8, the following not very satisfactory result.

LEMMA 4. *The lattice hypotheses* L′–L″ *are equivalent to the following condition:* (12) *Given a, there exists* a^+ *such that u and* $(u - a)$ *are both positive if and only if* $(u - a^+)$ *is.* (I, II, P_1, P_3)

From Theorem 3 and Lemmas 1–4, we conclude as the final theoretical result of this section,

THEOREM 10. *An l-group may be defined as a group G with a subset* G^+ *of "positive" elements which satisfies conditions* (9)–(12).

We also conclude that Examples 1–10 above are l-groups. In Examples 1, 2, 4, 8, 10 this is true because the ordering is simple: for all a, either a or $-a$ is in G; and so a^+ is a or 0 accordingly. In Example 3, $(m/n)^+$ is the numerator of m/n when written in lowest terms; in Examples 5–6, f^+ is the "positive part" of f as usually defined (equal, for all x, to the larger of $f(x)$ or 0); in Example 7, f^+ is the "positive variation" of f. In Example 9, $(ma + m'b + nc)^+$ is 0 if $n < 0$, $(ma + m'b + nc)$ if $n > 0$, and $m^+a + m'^+b$ if $n = 0$.

8. Fifth set of postulates

We have characterized l-groups by four sets of postulates. Our definition was in terms of the group operation and a binary relation; Theorem 7 in terms of the group operation and a binary operation; Theorem 9 in terms of the group operation and a unary operation; Theorem 10 in terms of the group operation and a unary relation or set. We shall now give a fifth set of postulates for l-groups which, oddly enough, is in terms of the group operation alone!

Evidently any l-group or other lattice has the following "Moore-Smith" property:

---

[8] By a *semigroup*, we mean a system closed under an associative binary operation and having an identity element, in which the laws of concellation hold ($a + x = a + y$ implies $x = y$ and so does $x + a = y + a$).

(13) *Given* a, b, *there exists* c *with* $c \geqq a$ *and* $c \geqq b$.

LEMMA 1 (Clifford[9]). *The Moore-Smith property is equivalent to the assertion that*

(14) *Every element is a difference of positive elements.* (I, II, P_1, P_3)

PROOF. Assuming (13) with $b = 0$, we get $a = c - (-a + c)$, where $c \geqq 0$ and $-a + c = -a + (c - a) + a \geqq -a + 0 + a = 0$. Conversely, if $a = a' - a''$ and $b = b' + b''$, where a', a'', b', b'' are positive, then $c = a' + b'$ exceeds both a and b.

Now let A be any group with a relation $\geqq$ satisfying II, P_1, P_3 and (14). We shall show that A is determined to within isomorphism by the semigroup A^+ of its positive elements. The proof is related to the general theory of the extension of semigroups to groups.

THEOREM 11. *In the notation of the calculus of complexes,* $a + A^+ = A^+ + a$, *for all* $a \in A$.

PROOF. Both sets consist of the elements containing a.

COROLLARY. *Given* a *and* x *in* A^+, *there exist a unique* $y \in A^+$ *such that* $a + x = y + a$ *and* z *in* A^+ *such that* $x + a = a + z$.

The existence follows from Lemma 1; the uniqueness from the cancellation postulate defining semigroups.

Now observe that A consists by (14) of the differences $b - c$ of elements of A, equated and combined by the rules

(15) $b - c = b' - c'$ *if and only if* t, u *exist in* A^+ *such that* $b + t = b' + u$ *and* $c + t = c' + u$,

(16) $(b - c) + (b' - c') = (b + b') - (c' + c'')$, *where* c'' *is the unique solution of* $b' + c'' = c + b'$.

The sufficiency of (15) is clear; as regards the necessity, if we choose $s \geqq b, b'$, $t = -b + s$, $u = -b' + s$, then $b + t = s = b' + u$, while if $b - c = b' - c'$, then $b + t - t - c = b' + u - u - c'$, whence $-t - c = -u - c'$ and $c' + u = c + t$.

Clearly equations (15)–(16) describe the group structure of A in terms of that of A. Moreover since

(17) $(b - c) \in A^+$ *if and only if* $b = c + t$ *for some* $t \in A^+$,

the *lattice* structure of A can also be described in terms of the *group* structure of A^+. In fact, $b - c \geqq b' - c'$ if and only if t, u exist such that $b + t \geqq b' + u$ and $c + t \leqq c' + u$.

Conversely, suppose S is any semigroup in which, for all a, $a + S = S + a$ (in multiplicative language, such that the left-multiples of any element are all right-multiples, and conversely). Then equations (15)–(16) may be shown to define a group.[10] We shall omit the details; one shows that (15) defines an

---

[9] A. H. Clifford, "Partially ordered Abelian groups," Annals of Math. 41 (1940), pp. 465–473, esp. p. 467. From the equation $a = 1/4((a + 1)^2 - (a - 1)^2)$, we see that (14) holds in Example 13.

[10] R. Baer has proved, in conversation, that a group can be constructed whenever, given a and b, x and y can be found such that $a + x = b + y$.

equivalence relation, which is a congruence relation with respect to the addition defined by (16), and relative to which the latter is associative, and gives any element $b - c$ an inverse $c - b$. Furthermore, under (17), the set of positive elements forms a subset of A isomorphic with S.

It follows, by Theorem 10, that we get an l-group provided (11)–(12) hold. But now (11) is clearly equivalent to

(17′) *If* $a + b = 0$ *in* S, *then* $a = b = 0$.

Finally, if any two elements of S have a l.u.b. with respect to the definition

(17″) $b \geqq c$ *if and only if* $b = c + t$ *for some* $t \in S$,

then for any $a = a' - a''$ of $A(a', a'' \in S)$ there exists $a^+ = (a' \smile a'') - a''$, which proves that condition (12) holds. There follows

THEOREM 12 (von Neumann[11]). *An l-group may be defined as the extension to a group of a (multiplicative) semigroup* S, *in which* (i) $ab = 1$ *implies* $a = b = 1$, (ii) $aS = Sa$ *for all* a, (iii) *any two elements have a least common multiple. In this group* S *consists of the positive elements.*

COROLLARY[12]. *A commutative l-group may be defined as the extension to a group of a commutative semigroup* S, *in which* (i) *and* (iii) *hold.*

In fact, (i) is not really essential, if we are willing to introduce an equivalence relation.

9. Distributive law; disjoint elements

The following material belongs logically directly after §3, and is independent of the results of §§4–8 above.

THEOREM 13. *In any l-group, we have for all* a, b,

$$a - (a \frown b) + b = b \smile a. \tag{18}$$

PROOF. Substituting a for x and b for y in formula (3), Theorem 6, we get (18) explicitly.

COROLLARY 1 (Dedekind[13]). *In any commutative l-group,*

$$a + b = (a \frown b) + (a \smile b) \quad \textit{for all } a, b. \tag{19}$$

In Example 3, the *modular law* (19) specializes to the celebrated identity $ab = (a, b)\,[a, b]$ of number theory. It also specializes, setting $b = 0$, to

COROLLARY 2. *For any* a, $a = a^+ + a^-$.

In words, each element a is the sum of its positive part and its negative part (so-called *Jordan decomposition*).

THEOREM 14. *Any l-group is a distributive lattice*[14].

---

[11] This result was communicted orally to the author.

[12] This result seems to have been known for ideals, but not in abstracto. The author has been unable to find a precise reference; cf. Krull's "Idealtheorie."

[13] Discovered in 1897; cf. Ges. Werke, Brunswick, 1931, vol. II, p. 133, formula (13); rediscovered by H. Freudenthal, "Teilweise geordnete Moduln," Amsterdam Proc. 39 (1936), p. 642.

[14] In the commutative case, discovered by Dedekind, *op. cit.*, p. 135, formulas (18)–(19); rediscovered by Freudenthal, *op. cit.* p. 642, formulas (3.2).

PROOF. Bergmann has shown ("Lattice Theory", p. 75) that a lattice is distributive if and only if $a \frown x = a \frown y$ and $a \smile x = a \smile y$ imply $x = y$. But they imply by (18),

$$x = (a \frown x) - a + (x \smile a) = (a \frown y) - a + (y \smile a) = y.$$

THEOREM 15. *In any l-group*[15], *we have*

$$(20') \qquad a \frown b = 0 \quad \textit{and} \quad a \frown c = 0 \quad \textit{imply} \quad a \frown (b + c) = 0,$$

$$(20'') \qquad a \smile b = 0 \quad \textit{and} \quad a \smile c = 0 \quad \textit{imply} \quad a \smile (b + c) = 0.$$

FIRST PROOF. By hypothesis and formula (1′), $c = (a \frown b) + c = (a + c) \frown (b + c)$. Substituting,

$$0 = a \frown c = a \frown (a + c) \frown (b + c) = a \frown (b + c),$$

since $a \leqq a + c$. The second conclusion follows by duality.

SECOND PROOF. Since a, b, c are positive, clearly $a \frown (b + c) \geqq 0$. But by the distributive law (1′),

$$0 = 0 + 0 = (a \frown b) + (a \frown c)$$
$$= a + a \frown a + c \frown b + a \frown b + c \geqq a \frown (b + c),$$

proving (20′). Formula (20″) follows dually.

We can reword Theorem 15 in terms of the important concept of disjointness.

DEFINITION. *Two positive elements a and b will be called disjoint—in symbols,* $a \perp b$,*—if and only if* $a \frown b = 0$.

In Example 3, this specializes to the concept of relative primeness. Theorem 15 asserts that the set of positive elements disjoint to any a is closed under addition. Furthermore, if in Theorem 13 we assume $a \frown b = 0$ and apply the commutative law to $b \smile a$, we get the

LEMMA 1. *Disjoint (positive) elements are permutable,*

$$(21) \qquad \textit{If } a \frown b = 0, \textit{ then } a + b = b + a.$$

LEMMA 2. *If* $b \frown c = 0$, *then* $(b - c)^+ = b$ *and* $(b - c)^- = -c$.

PROOF. By our preceding formulas, $(b - c) \smile 0 = (b \smile c) - c = b - (b \frown c) + c - c = b$, and dually.

LEMMA 3. *If* $na \geqq 0$, *then* $a \geqq 0$.

PROOF. Expanding by the distributive law (1′), $n(a \frown 0) = na \frown (n - 1)a \frown (n - 2)a \frown \cdots \frown a \frown 0$. But if $na \frown 0 = 0$, this equals $(n - 1)a \frown (n - 2)a \frown \cdots \frown a \frown 0 = (n - 1)(a \frown 0)$. Now cancelling, we get $a \frown 0 = 0$, as desired.

---

[15] In the commutative case, observed by Dedekind, *op. cit.*, p. 132; Proof 1 is Dedekind's, Proof 2 is von Neumann's. Observe that in the proof, no restriction need be put on the group operation (*e.g.*, associativity); only distributivity is needed. Theorem 15 can be generalized (§§27, 28).

Combining Lemma 3 with its dual, we get

THEOREM 16. *In an l-group, every element is of infinite order except the identity.*

Another corollary is the fact that, in any *commutative* l-group, $na \geqq nb$ implies $n(a - b) \geqq 0$, and so $a \geqq b$. The author has been unable to prove the plausible conjecture that this remains true in any l-group.

LEMMA 4. *The positive and negative parts of any element are disjoint; in symbols,*

(22) *For any* a, $(a \smile 0) \frown (-a \smile 0) = a^+ \frown (-a^-) = 0$.

PROOF. Clearly $-(a \frown 0) = (-a \smile 0)$; hence the two left-hand terms are equal. But now by the distributive law, $(a \smile 0) \frown (-a \smile 0) = (a \frown -a) \smile 0$, so we need only show that $-(a \frown -a) = -a \smile a \geqq 0$. But clearly $a \smile -a \geqq a \frown -a$; hence, subtracting, $(a \smile -a) - (a \frown -a) = (a \smile -a) - (-(a \smile -a)) \geqq 0$, or $2(a \smile -a) \geqq 0$. Now use Lemma 3 with $n = 2$.

10. Free l-groups; absolute

Now let a be any element of any l-group, and set $b = a \smile 0$, $c = -a \smile 0$, so that b and c are positive and disjoint, and $a = b - c$ (*cf.* Cor. 2 of Thm. 13 and Lemma 4 above). Further, by Theorem 15 and induction, $b \perp nc$ and $mb \perp nc$ for all positive integers m and n. Further, by Lemma 1, b and c are permutable, and so generate a commutative group, in which, for all integers m and n,

$$(mb + nc) \pm (m'b + n'c) = (m \pm m')b + (n \pm n')c.$$

Finally, $(mb + nc)^+$ is $mb + nc$ unless m or n is negative, is 0 if m and n are negative, is (by Lemma 2 above and the disjointness of positive integral multiples of b and c) mb if n is negative but m is not, and is nc if m is negative but n is not.

It follows that the $mb + nc$ form an l-subgroup, which is closed under lattice and group operations (Theorem 8), and is homomorphic with the l-group of all couples (m, n) of integers, in which $(m, n) \geqq 0$ means that $m \geqq 0$ and $n \geqq 0$. We shall (cf. §16) refer to this as the *square* of the l-group of the integers under addition.

THEOREM 17. *The free l-group with one generator is isomorphic with the square of the l-group of integers under addition.*

In this group, a appears as the element $(1, -1)$, a^+ as $(1. 0)$, and a^- as $(0, -1)$. We can read off various corollaries from this representation.

THEOREM 18. *In any commutative l-group* A, *the correspondence* $a \to na$ *is, for any positive integer* n, *an isomorphism of* A *onto an l-subgroup of itself.*

PROOF. By pure group theory, it is a group homomorphism; by Theorem 16, it is a group isomorphism; by Theorem 17, we get $(na)^+ = (n, -n)^+ = (n, 0) = na^+$, and so it is isomorphic with respect to the unary operation of taking the positive part; by formulas (4)–(5), it is therefore a lattice isomorphism.

DEFINITION. *By the absolute* $|a|$ *of an element* a *of an l-group, is meant* $a \smile -a$.

THEOREM 19. *In any l-group, we have identically:*

(23) *If* $a \neq 0$, *then* $|a| > 0$, *while* $|0| = 0$

(24) $|na| = |n| \cdot |a|$ *for any integer* n,

(25) $|a| = a^+ - a^-$,

(26) $|a - b| = (a \smile b) - (a \frown b)$,

(27) $|(a \smile b) - (a^* \smile b)| \leqq |a - a^*|$ *and dually.*

PROOF. Formulas (23)–(25) are special cases of the representation of Theorem 17. Again, using (25),

$$|a - b| = ((a - b) \smile 0) - ((a - b) \frown 0) = ((a \smile b) - b) - ((a \frown b) - b)$$

from which (26) follows by group algebra. Finally, to prove (27), expand the left-hand side by (26) to get $a \smile b \smile a^* - (a \smile b) \frown (a^* \smile b)$, whence by the distributive law, $|(a \smile b) - (a^* \smile b)| = (a \smile a^*) \smile b - (a \frown a^*) \smile b$. This reduces (27) to the case $a \geqq a^*$, or $a = a^* + t$ $(t \geqq 0)$. But $((a^* + t) \smile b) = a^* \smile (b - t) + t \leqq (a^* \smile b) + t$, which takes care of this special case.

REMARK. In a *commutative* l-group, we can also prove the triangle inequality $|a + b| \leqq |a| + |b|$, but this does not seem to hold in general; also, the author has been unable to generalize Theorem 7.8 of "Lattice Theory" to l-groups which are not commutative.

Concerning the free l-group with two or more generators, much less can be said. As an Abelian group, one can show that it has an infinite number of disjoint independent elements. On the other hand, using the three distributive laws (1), (1′), and that of Theorem 14, one can represent every element as a finite *meet* of finite *joins* of finite *sums*

$$\bigwedge_i \bigvee_j \sum n_k^{i,j} a_k$$

of the given generators a_k and their inverses.[16]

11. l-ideals

It is well-known that the different homomorphic images of a given abstract algebra can all be found by enumerating its different congruence relations.[17] Also, with any group, the congruence relations correspond one-one with normal subgroups: to each normal subgroup N of a group G corresponds the congruence relation dividing G into the cosets of N. Therefore, the congruence relations

[16] The construction is identical with that used to prove Theorem 5.13 of "Lattice Theory."

[17] By a "congruence relation" on an abstract algebra with binary operations is meant an equivalence relation (i.e., reflexive, symmetric and transitive relation) denoted $\equiv$ which has, if $\circ$ is any binary operation, the "substitution property": (S) $a \equiv a'$ implies $a \circ b \equiv a' \circ b$ and $b \circ a \equiv b \circ a'$.

on an *l-group* are those decompositions into cosets of normal subgroups which have the substitution property (S) for the two lattice operations—or equivalently, by (4)–(5), make $a \equiv b$ imply $a^+ \equiv b^+$. But these are easy to describe.

DEFINITION. *By an* l-ideal *of an l-group G, is meant a normal subgroup of G which contains with any a, also all*[18] *x with* $|x| \leqq |a|$.

Clearly G and 0 are l-ideals of G; they are called *improper* l-ideals; all other l-ideals of G are called *proper* l-ideals.

It is a corollary that any l-ideal is a *convex* l-subgroup in the sense of containing with any a and b, also $-a$, $a + b$, $a \frown b$, $a \smile b$, and every x between $a \frown b$ and $a \smile b$. Indeed, if $a \frown b \leqq x \leqq a \smile b$, then

$$|x| = x \smile -x \leqq (a \smile b) \smile -(a \frown b)$$
$$= a \smile b \smile -b \smile -a = |a| \smile |b| \leqq |a| + |b|.$$

THEOREM 20. *The congruence relations on any l-group A are the partitions of A into the cosets of its different l-ideals.*

PROOF. If N is the set of elements congruent to 0 under a congruence relation, then $a \in N$ and $|x| \leqq |a|$ imply $a \frown -a \leqq x \leqq a \smile -a$; hence $0 \frown 0 \leqq x \leqq 0 \smile 0 \bmod N$, and so $x \in N$. Conversely, if N is an l-ideal, then $x \equiv x' \bmod N$ implies $|(x \smile y) - (x' \smile y)| \leqq |x - x'|$ by (27), and therefore $x \smile y \equiv x' \smile y \bmod N$. Using left-right symmetry and duality, we see that N defines a congruence relation with respect to both lattice operations, completing the proof.

LEMMA 1. *If* $x \leqq a + b$, *where x, a, b, are positive, then* $x = s + t$, *where* $0 \leqq s \leqq a$, $0 \leqq t \leqq b$.

PROOF. Set $t = x \frown b$; then $x = s + t$, where $0 \leqq s \leqq x - (x \frown b) = x \smile b) - b \leqq (a + b) - b = a$ and $0 \leqq t \leqq b$, as desired.

THEOREM 21. *The l-ideals and any l-group form a complete distributive sublattice of the (modular) lattice of all its normal subgroups.*

PROOF. Clearly, any intersection of l-ideals is itself an l-ideal. To prove that the sum $S + T$ of any two[19] l-ideals S and T is an l-ideal, suppose that $s \in S$, $t \in T$, and $|x| \leqq s + t$. Then for some $s' \in S$, $t' \in T$, $-(s + t) = s' + t'$, and so

$$|s + t| = (s + t) \smile (s' + t') \leqq (0 \smile s \smile s') + (0 \smile t \smile t').$$

Hence $x^+ \leqq |x| \leqq |s + t| \leqq s'' + t''$ ($s'' \in S$, $t'' \in T$). Using Lemma 1, we can show now that $S + T$ contains x^+, likewise $-x^-$, and so $x = x^+ + x^-$. Therefore $S + T$ is an l-ideal.

---

[18] The terminology is that of Stone (*op. cit.*); the concept is due to the author, who called l-ideals "normal subspaces"; F. Riesz, "Sur la théorie générale des opérations linéaires", Annals of Math. 41 (1940), pp. 174–206, called them "Familles presque complètes." Another good term would be "absolute (normal) subgroup." Kakutani uses l-ideals in a slightly different sense.

[19] From this it follows that the sum of any number of l-ideals is an l-ideal—by the general logical principle that for any "closure" involving only finite operations, the closure of any family of "closed" sets is the set-union of joins of finite subfamilies of "closed" sets.

It remains to prove that if S, T, and U are l-ideals, then $S \frown (T + U) = (S \frown T) + (S \frown U)$. But since, in any case, $S \frown (T + U) \geqq (S \frown T) + (S \frown U)$ by the lattice-theoretic semi-distributive law, and $x = x^+ - (-x^-)$, it suffices to show that every positive x in $S \frown (T + U)$ is in $(S \frown T) + (S \frown U)$. But $x \epsilon S \frown (T + U)$ means that $x \epsilon S$ and $x = t + u$ $(t \epsilon T, u \epsilon U)$. Hence, as above, $x = | t + u | \leqq t'' + u''$, where $t'' \epsilon T$, $u'' \epsilon U$ are *positive*. Therefore, by Lemma 1, $x = t' + u'$, where $t' = x \frown t''$ is in $S \frown T$ and $u' \leqq x \frown u''$ is in $S \frown U$. This proves $x \epsilon (S \frown T) + (S \frown U)$, as desired.

Corollary. *The congruence relations on any l-group form a complete distributive lattice.*[20]

Remark. If A is any *commutative* l-group, and T is any l-ideal of an l-ideal S of A, then T is itself an l-ideal of A: the property of being an l-ideal is thus *hereditary*. This follows because any subgroup of a subgroup is itself a subgroup, and by the transitivity of inclusion. However, as Example 9 illustrates, the same law does not hold for all non-commutative l-groups—essentially because a normal subgroup of a normal subgroup of a group G need not be normal in G.

12. Disjoint l-ideals

The following sections, through §20, will deal with non-commutative l-groups only incidentally. In the main, they will be devoted to obtaining a more complete picture of the structure of commutative l-groups, including a determination of all possible structure lattices of finite length, and of all those "simple" commutative l-groups which have no proper l-ideals.

Definition. *Two elements a and b of an l-group G are called* disjoint *if and only if* $| a | \frown | b | = 0$.

Theorem 22. *The set $\{a\}^*$ of all elements disjoint from any fixed element a is a subgroup which contains with any b, all x satisfying $| x | \leqq | b |$.*

Proof. By (23), $\{a\}^*$ contains 0; by Theorem 15, it is closed under addition; since $| -b | = | b |$, it contains with any element its group inverse; hence it is a subgroup. The second assertion follows by the monotonicity law.

Corollary. *In a* commutative *l-group, the set of all elements disjoint from any fixed element is an l-ideal.*

Example 9 shows that, in the non-commutative case, the set need not be a normal subgroup.

We note also, since $\{a\}^*$ cannot contain a unless $a = 0$, either $a = 0$, $\{a\}^* = 0$, or $\{a\}^*$ is a *proper* l-ideal. This suggests the concept of a weak unit.

Definition. *An element a of an l-group is called a* weak unit[21] *if the only element disjoint to it is* 0.

---

20 This is the "structure lattice" of the l-group in the sense of the author, "On the structure of abstract algebras," Proc. Camb. Phil. Soc. 31 (1935), p. 450. It describes the structure (in the usual sense) of the l-group. Theorems 20–21 are due to the author.

21 The concept is due to Freudenthal, op. cit.; the useful terms "weak unit" and "strong unit" (infra) to Bohnenblust. We note that any separable Banach lattice has a weak unit.

13. Simply ordered groups

A partially ordered set is called "simply ordered" when, of any two elements, one includes the other, so that

P_4. *Given x, y, either* $x \geqq y$ *or* $y \geqq x$.

This automatically implies L′–L″.

DEFINITION. *A simply ordered group*[22] *is an l-group in which* P_4 *holds.*

We note without proof the following trivial results. An l-group is simply ordered if and only if, for any a, either a or its inverse $-a$ is positive. An l-group is simply ordered if and only if every subgroup is an l-subgroup. The structure lattice of any simply ordered l-group is itself simply ordered (a chain).[23]

DEFINITION. *Two l-ideals of an l-group are called* disjoint *if and only if their intersection is* 0.

It is easy to show that this is the case if and only if every element of the first ideal is disjoint from every element of the second.

THEOREM 23. *A* commutative *l-group has two disjoint proper l-ideals unless it is simply ordered.*

PROOF. Unless the l-group is simply ordered, it has an element a which is neither positive nor negative, so that neither a^+ nor a^- is 0. Hence $S = \{a^+\}^*$ will be a proper l-ideal containing a^- but not a^+. Moreover the set S^* of all elements disjoint from all elements of S will contain a^+ but not a^-. Furthermore, being an intersection of l-ideals, it will be an l-ideal. Finally, every element of S is disjoint from every element of S^*.

COROLLARY. *The structure lattice of a* commutative *l-group A is simply ordered if and only if A is simply ordered.*

Example 9 shows that the hypothesis of commutativity is essential in the preceding results.

DIGRESSION. We have seen (Theorem 16) that in an l-group, every element is of infinite order. We shall now show that, in the *commutative* case, this is the only group-theoretic restriction implied by being an l-group.

THEOREM 24 (F. Levi[24]). *Any abstract commutative group whose elements are all of infinite order, is the additive group of a simply ordered l-group.*

PROOF. Let A be any Abelian group without any element of finite order except the identity. By a well-ordered *rational basis* for A, we mean a well-

---

In fact, if $\{x_i\}$ is any everywhere dense countable set of positive elements, and $\lambda_i = 1/2^n \, || \, x_i \, ||$ for all i, then $e = \Sigma \, \lambda_i x_i$ is a weak unit.

[22] Often called an "ordered group"; this is consistent with the terminology "semi-ordered group" for what we have called a "partially ordered group."

[23] For if the l-ideal S contains an element not in the l-ideal T, then the absolute of this element must exceed (not being included in) the absolute of every element of T, so that $T \leqq S$.

[24] "Arithmethische Gesetze im Gebiete diskreter Gruppen," Rendic. Palermo 35 (1913), pp. 225–236.

ordered (finite or infinite) subset of elements a_α of A such that every non-zero element of A is a finite rational combination $n_1a_{\alpha(1)} + \cdots + n_ra_{\alpha(r)}$ $(\alpha(1) < \cdots < \alpha(r))$ of the a_α, while $\sum n_ia_{\alpha(i)} = 0$ implies every $n_i = 0$—or equivalently, $\sum (m_i/n_i)a_{\alpha(i)} = 0$ implies that every $(m_i/n_i) = 0$. The existence of a well-ordered rational basis can be proved directly by transfinite induction, just as in the case of vector spaces.

Moreover relative to such a basis, any element of A not the identity may be called positive or negative according as its first non-zero coefficient is positive or negative. This "lexicographic" ordering of A clearly defines from it a simply ordered group (commutative l-group).

Corollary. *A commutative group is the additive group of an l-group if and only if it is without elements of finite order except the identity.*

14. Archimedean l-groups

A gross way of comparing the magnitude of elements of l-groups is given by the following

Definition. *An element a of an l-group is called* incomparably smaller *than a second element b (in symbols, $a \ll b$) if and only if $na < b$ for any integer n.*

Otherwise stated, $a \ll b$ means that b is an upper bound for the entire cyclic subgroup generated by a. Thus in Example 4, $(0, 1) \ll (1, 0)$. It is easily verified that the relation $\ll$ is antisymmetric and transitive; it is closely related to the concept of an Archimedean l-group.

Definition. *An l-group is called* Archimedean *if and only if $a \ll b$ implies $a = 0$.* (I, II, P_1–P_3)

The independence of the Archimedean property just stated from the lattice property L′–L″ is illustrated by the easily proved fact that *any subgroup of an Archimedean l-group is itself Archimedean* with respect to the same order relation, whether it is an l-subgroup or not.

The Archimedean property can be formulated in other ways. It amounts to asserting that the l-group has no bounded subgroups except 0. It is equivalent to requiring that if the set of all positive multiples of a has an upper bound, then $a \leqq 0$ (Clifford). In the case of l-groups, using Cor. 2 of Thm. 13, it is equivalent to the apparently weaker requirement that if $a > 0$, then the sequence $a, 2a, 3a, \cdots$ has no upper bound.

In a simply ordered group, the Archimedean property is thus equivalent to the traditional condition that for any $e > 0$ and any b, $ne > b$ for all sufficiently large positive integers n. This means that if we let U denote the set of all rational numbers m/n such that $nb \geqq me$, and L the set of those such that $nb \leqq me$ (n positive), we get non-void sets. Moreover L and U together include all elements (by P_4), and have at most one element in common. Hence they are the two halves of a *Dedekind cut*. Again, no two distinct elements b and b' can determine the same cut, or we would have $(b - b') \ll e$. Finally, by the monotonicity law (2), addition of elements is isomorphic to the addition of cuts. We conclude

THEOREM 25. *Any simply ordered Archimedean l-group is isomorphic to a subgroup of the additive group of all real numbers, and so is commutative.*[25]

THEOREM 26. *An Archimedean l-group may have a non-Archimedean homomorphic image.*

PROOF. Consider the l-quotient-group of the l-group of all functions on the interval $0 \leqq x < +\infty$, modulo the l-ideal of bounded functions. In this, $x^2 > 0$, yet $x^2 \ll x^4$.

DIGRESSION. We have seen that in any l-group, for any element a, the equation $nx = ma$ $(n \neq 0)$ has at most one solution, which we can denote $(m/n)a$ if it exists. It is worth remarking now that in any *Archimedean* l-group, we can define uniquely scalar products λa of a by *any* real number λ. To see this, suppose a positive; there is at most one x such that $(m/n)a < x$ for all $m/n < \lambda$ and $(m/n)a > x$ for all $m/n > \lambda$. (If two, x and x', then $x - x' \ll a$.) This x we may denote λa, and prove that, whenever all terms exist, the usual laws of the vector calculus hold.

15. Strong units: principal l-ideals

We have just seen that in any Archimedean simply ordered l-group, to any $e > 0$ and b corresponds a positive integer n such that $ne > b$. This may be generalized.

DEFINITION. *By a* strong unit *of an l-group A, is meant*[26] *an element $e \in A$ such that for any $b \in A$, $ne > b$ for some positive integer n.*

Thus a strong unit must be positive. Many l-groups do not have any strong unit. For example, the l-group of all continuous real functions on the domain $0 \leqq x < +\infty$ has the weak unit $f(x) = 1$ but no strong unit; this is a weak corollary of the Theorem of du Bois-Reymond.[27] On the other hand, in the l-group of all bounded real functions on any domain, the function $f(x) = 1$ is a strong unit. We also note

LEMMA 1. *Any strong unit is a weak unit.*

PROOF. For any e, $e \frown a = 0$ implies $ne \frown a = 0$ for all e (Thm. 22). But if e is a strong unit, $ne > a$ for some n and so $e \frown a = 0$ implies $a = ne \frown a = 0$, whence e is a weak unit.

Even in l-groups without strong units, l-ideals may have strong units. In fact, in any commutative l-group, every positive element is a strong unit for an appropriate l-ideal.

THEOREM 27. (F. Riesz.[28]) *In a* commutative *l-group, for any $a > 0$, the set $J(a)$ of all b such that $|b| \leqq na$ for some positive integer n forms an l-ideal having a as strong unit. Moreover $J(a)$ is the smallest l-ideal which contains a.*

---

[25] This result is due to H. Cartan, "Un théorème sur les groupes ordonnes," Bull. Sci. Math. 63 (1939), 201–205.

[26] The concept goes back to Archimedes; the term to Bohnenblust.

[27] *Cf.* for instance, G. H. Hardy, "Orders of Infinity," Cambridge Tracts, 2d ed., 1924, p. 8. In this example, our relation $a \ll b$ is practically the usual relation $f = o(g)$.

[28] F. Riesz, *op. cit.*, p. 188.

Proof. If $|b| \leqq ma$ and $|c| \leqq na$, then clearly $|b \pm c| \leqq (m + n)a$; while if $|b| \leqq ma$ and $|x| \leqq |b|$, then $|x| \leqq ma$; hence $J(a)$ is an l-ideal. Obviously, a is a strong unit of $J(a)$. Finally, any l-ideal containing a must contain every na and so all b with $|b| \leqq na$.

Corollary. *Any commutative non-Archimedean l-group has a proper l-ideal.*

For if $a \ll b$ for some $a \neq 0$, then $J(|a|)$ is an l-ideal which fails to contain b, yet contains $a \neq 0$, and so is proper.

Definition. *An l-ideal of an l-group will be called* principal *if and only if it has a strong unit.*

Theorem 28. *If the structure lattice of a* commutative *l-group has finite length r, every l-ideal is principal.*

Proof. Let J be an l-ideal of such an l-group A. The case $J = 0$ is trivial. If $J > 0$, choose any $a_1 \neq 0$ in J and form $J(|a_1|)$. If $J > J(|a_1|)$, choose any a_2 in J but not in $J(|a_1|)$ and form $J(|a_1| + |a_2|)$. After repeating this process at most r times, we will get a principal l-ideal equal to J.

Theorem 29. *In any* commutative *l-group A, the principal l-ideals form a topologically dense sublattice of the structure lattice of A.*

Proof. It can be proved easily that

$$J(a \frown b) = J(a) \frown J(b) \quad \text{and} \quad J(a + b) = J(a) + J(b),$$

hence they form a sublattice. This sublattice is dense in the structure lattice of A, since any l-ideal J is the supremum (in fact, set-union) of the finite joins $\bigvee_{i \in \sigma} J(a_i)$ of the principal l-ideals contained in J, and these form an ascending directed set of principal l-ideals which thus converges to its supremum in the sense of Moore-Smith.

16. Extension problem

It is natural to say that an l-group is *simple* if and only if it has no proper l-ideals—or, equivalently, no proper congruence relations. Analogy with pure group theory then suggests the program[29] of first determining all simple l-groups, and then showing how the most general l-group whose "structure lattice" is of finite length can be built up from its simple quotient-l-groups.

The first problem has been solved in the commutative case. Indeed, a simple commutative l-group must be simply ordered (by Theorem 23) and Archimedean (by the Cor. of Thm. 28). Hence (by Theorem 26) we have

Theorem 30. *The only* commutative *simple l-groups are the subgroups of the additive group of real numbers.*

The second problem involves in particular the specific task of enumerating all the l-groups having a given l-ideal J and l-quotient-group A/J ("Extension Problem"). While not attempting a complete solution of this, some fragmentary results may be stated.

[29] The logical outline is the same, but the technique is very different. Cf. O. Schreier, "Über die Erweiterungen der Gruppen," Monats. Math. u. Phys. 34 (1926), p. 165, and Hamb. Abh. 4 (1927), pp. 321–346.

Given two l-groups S and T, one can form the l-group ST of all couples (s, t) $(s \in S,\ t \in T)$, where both the group operation and the lattice operations are performed on the S-components and T-components independently, so that

$$(s, t)\circ(s', t') = (s\circ s', t\circ t')$$

where $\circ$ is $+$, $\frown$, or $\smile$. This is the direct union of S and T in the sense of universal algebra; we shall call it the *cardinal product* ST of S and T. The elements $(0, t)$ form an l-ideal of $ST = A$ isomorphic with T, and the l-quotient-group A/T is isomorphic with S. Hence *the extension problem always has at least one solution.*

One can also form the lexicographic or *ordinal product*[30] $S\circ T$ of any two l-groups. This consists of the couples (s, t) $(s \in S,\ t \in T)$ just as before. But the set of positive elements consists of those couples (s, t) with $s > 0$ or $s = 0$ and $t \geqq 0$, instead of those with $s \geqq 0$ and $t \geqq 0$ as in the case of cardinal products. In any case, $S\circ T$ is a partially ordered group. If S is *simply* ordered, it is an l-group, in which the elements $(0, t)$ form as before an l-ideal isomorphic with T, whose l-quotient-group is isomorphic with S. Hence if S is simply ordered, the extension problem has at least two solutions.

17. Direct decompositions

In the cardinal product $ST = A$, both S and T correspond to l-ideals. Moreover they correspond to *complementary* l-ideals, in the usual sense that $S \frown T = 0$ and $S + T = A$. Just as in the case of pure group theory, the converse also holds.

THEOREM 31. *An l-group A is isomorphic to the cardinal product ST if and only if it contains complementary l-ideals isomorphic with S and T respectively.*

PROOF OF CONVERSE.[31] Suppose A has l-ideals S and T. Then by group theory, each element $a \in A$ has a unique representation $a = s + t$ $(s \in S, t \in T)$, while group operations are performed on the S- and T-components independently. As regards order, $s + t \leqq s' + t'$ if and only if

$$(-s' + s) \leqq (t' - t) \leqq |\, t' - t \,|,$$

whence $(-s' + s) \leqq |\, t' - t \,| \frown |\, -s + s' \,| \in T \frown S = 0$, and likewise $t - t' \leqq 0$. This means $s \leqq s'$ and $t \leqq t'$, q.e.d.

From the preceding result, Theorem 21, and the general theory of distributive lattices, we obtain just as in "Lattice Theory," Theorem 5.15, the following corollaries.

THEOREM 32. *Any two representations of an l-group as a cardinal product have a common refinement.*

---

[30] For the general significance of cardinal and ordinal products, cf. the author's article "Generalized arithmetic," to appear in the Duke Journal of Mathematics. It is shown there that the ordinal product of two lattices is itself a lattice if and only if the left-factor is simply ordered, or the right-factor has universal bounds.

[31] For a brief proof, relying more heavily on principles of universal algebra, *cf.* also "Lattice Theory," p. 110, below Theorem 7.11.

COROLLARY. *If the structure lattice of an l-group A has finite length, then A has a unique representation as the cardinal product of indecomposable factors.*

18. Main structure theorem

In the present section, we shall show that the structure of a commutative l-group is of a very special kind. Indeed, by Theorem 23, any commutative l-group in which the l-ideal 0 is meet-irreducible (or "prime"), is simply ordered. From this (cf. footnote 23) we conclude

LEMMA 1. *The structure lattice of a commutative l-group in which the l-ideal* 0 *is meet-irreducible, is a chain.*

But now if J is any l-ideal of an l-group A, the l-ideals of A which contain J form a lattice isomorphic with the structure lattice of A/J; indeed, this is a principle of universal algebra, holding for all congruence relations. Combining this result with Lemma 1, we get

LEMMA 2. *The elements of the structure lattice of any commutative l-group which contain any meet-irreducible element, form a chain (simply ordered set).*

If we apply Lemma 2 to the general representation theory of finite distributive lattices ("Lattice Theory," Theorem 5.3), we get a conclusive result.

Any distributive lattice L of finite length may be described in terms of the partially ordered set X of its meet-irreducible elements a_i. Every element $c \in L$ is the meet $\wedge a_i$ of the set S_c of the meet-irreducible elements which contain c. Moreover, as in "Lattice Theory," Theorem 5.3, the correspondence $c \to S_c$ is a dual isomorphism between L and the "J-closed" subsets of X—i.e., the subsets of X which contain with any a_i all $a_j \geqq a_i$.

This clearly applies to the structure lattice of any l-group, provided it has finite length. Moreover if the l-group is commutative, Lemma 2 restricts X greatly.

DEFINITION. *A partially ordered system X is called a* semitree *if, for any element $a \in X$, the set of all $x \leqq a$ is a chain; it is a* tree *if it has a least element* 0. *The dual of a tree (semitree) is called a* root (semiroot).[32]

We have shown that the *meet-irreducible* ("prime") *l-ideals of any l-group form a semiroot.* But now it is easy to show that any finite semiroot is the sum of the subsets contained in its different maximal elements: the elements underneath its different maximal elements form components having no connection with each other (no common subelements or superelements).

Consequently, either the structure lattice contains complemented elements (namely, the meets of the sets of elements under the different maximal meet-irreducible elements), or the set X of meet-irreducible elements has a I. In the first case, the l-group is directly decomposable, by Theorem 31. In the second case, the J-closed subset consisting of I alone is a least non-void J-closed subset,

[32] The Hasse diagram of any "tree" looks like a tree, and that of a "root" like a root (tree upside down). Further, the graph of a "tree" (or root!) is a tree in the technical sense of the theory of graphs. G. Kurepa has studied roots extensively, under the name of "tableaux ramifies."

which thus corresponds under our dual isomorphism to a *greatest* proper l-ideal. We can state our result as follows.

THEOREM 33. *A commutative l-group whose structure lattice has finite length, either* (i) *is a cardinal product, or* (ii) *has a unique maximal proper l-ideal.*

19. Solution of extension problem

We shall now show that a commutative l-group A with a unique maximal proper l-ideal J is a kind of mixed ordinal product of A/J and J. This will give us a method for constructing, by successive extensions, all commutative l-groups having finite structure lattices.

First, an element a of A not in J must be either positive or negative. For consider the sum of the l-ideals generated by a^+ and a^-; it contains a, hence is not contained in J, hence it is A. But this expresses A as a sum of disjoint l-ideals; by hypothesis, A is join-irreducible; hence one of the l-ideals is A and the other (being disjoint) is 0, and a^+ or a^- is 0, as desired.

Second, a is positive or negative in A according as it is positive or negative in A/J, since a homomorphism carries positive elements into positive elements and dually. Hence A is determined to within isomorphism by its group structure, the order structure of J, and the order structure of A/J. The positive elements of A are those which have their (A/J)-component greater than zero, *or* have their (A/J)-component equal to zero and their J-component positive.

This definition gives, conversely, from any abstract Abelian group A which has a lattice-ordered subgroup J and simply ordered quotient-group A/J, an l-group which may be called a *mixed ordinal product* of J and A/J. Clearly the mixed ordinal products of J and A/J correspond one-one to the solution of the group-theoretic extension problem of finding all Abelian groups A with a subgroup isomorphic with J and a quotient-group isomorphic with A/J. In case A is the direct union of J and A/J, we get the pure ordinal product; otherwise, we get something different.

Now by Theorem 33, and induction (*cf.* the last Remark of §11) on the length of the structure lattice, we get

THEOREM 34. *Any commutative l-group whose structure lattice has finite length can be built up from simple l-groups by forming successive cardinal products and mixed ordinal products.*

This result can be applied directly to vector lattices. It is known[33] that the additive group of real numbers is the only simple vector lattice. Moreover it can be shown that for finite-dimensional vector lattices, the only group-theoretic solution of the extension problem is given by the direct union. We conclude

COROLLARY 1. *Any vector lattice of finite dimension can be built up from the group of real numbers under addition by repeated formation of cardinal and ordinal products.*

[33] Mr. Murray Mannos, a graduate student at Harvard University, is writing a dissertation on vector lattices of finite dimension which includes this and many other results.

We can state this somewhat cabalistically, using the generalized arithmetic notation of the author, as

COROLLARY 2. *The most general vector lattice of finite dimension is* ${}^{Y}R^{\#}$, *where* $R^{\#}$ *denotes the additive group of real numbers, and* Y *denotes the most general semiroot.*[34]

Incidentally, the structure lattice of ${}^{Y}R^{\#}$ is $B^{Y'}$, where Y' denotes the semitree dual to Y, ordinal exponentiation is replaced by cardinal exponentiation, and B is the chain of two elements.

Going back to Lemma 2 of §18, the discussion of distributive lattices following it, and using Corollary 2 for the converse, we get a final result.

THEOREM 35. *A lattice of finite length is the structure lattice of a* commutative *l-group, if and only if it can be written* B^{Y}, *where* Y *is the most general semitree.*

20. Subdirect decompositions

We shall now consider the representations of commutative l-groups as l-subgroups of cardinal products of smaller l-groups—or, as we shall say for short, as *subdirect* products.

Just as in the case of groups (cf. "Lattice Theory," p. 52) it may be shown that the representations of an l-group as a subdirect product correspond one-one to choices of sets of l-ideals having 0 for meet. In the case of structure lattices of finite length, we can thus show that commutative l-groups are subdirect products of l-groups in which 0 is meet-irreducible, and hence (§18, Lemma 1) of simply ordered l-groups. We shall now show that the restriction to the case of structure lattices of finite length is unnecessary.

LEMMA 1. *Let* a *be any non-zero element of a commutative l-group* A. *There exists an l-ideal* J *in* A *such that* $a \notin J$ *yet* J/J *is meet-irreducible in* A/J.

PROOF. By transfinite induction, we can construct a maximal l-ideal J which does not[35] contain a. It follows that any l-ideal of A which properly contains J will contain $J(a)$; hence J is meet-irreducible. We infer that the meet of all meet-irreducible l-ideals of A is 0 in any case; hence that A is a subdirect product of l-quotient-groups A/J in which 0 is meet-irreducible, and so which are simply ordered.

THEOREM 36. *Any commutative l-group is isomorphic with an l-subgroup of a cardinal product of simply ordered l-groups.*[36]

---

[34] It has been pointed out to the author by A. H. Clifford and I. Kaplansky that Theorem 34 and its corollaries may be looked on as generalizing to the lattice-ordered case, the basic results of H. Hahn ("Über die nichtarchimedischen Grossensysteme," S.-B. Wiener Akad. Math.-Nat. Klasse Abt. IIa, 116 (1907), pp. 601–653) on the classification of simply ordered groups.

[35] The construction is identical with that used by Stone in constructing prime ideals in Boolean rings; it has been used so often that it will not be repeated here. Since an l-ideal J is meet-irreducible if and only if $|a| \frown |b| \in J$ implies $|a| \in J$ or $|b| \in J$, there is justification for calling the meet-irreducible l-ideals *prime* l-ideals.

[36] This is closely related to Satz 14 of P. Lorenzen, "Abstrakte Begrundung der multiplikativen Idealtheorie," Math. Zeits. 45 (1939), pp. 533–553.

A special problem is that of trying to make the simply ordered l-groups *Archimedean*, so as to get a representation by means of real functions. For this to be possible, the original l-group must certainly be Archimedean; this condition would also be sufficient if it were not for Theorem 26. Much work has been done in attacking special cases of the problem.[37]

21. Effect of chain condition

We shall now turn our attention to l-groups in which all bounded sets have l.u.b. and g.l.b. A special case is furnished by l-groups which satisfy the chain condition.

DEFINITION. *An l-group will be said to satisfy the* chain condition[38] *if and only if*

(C) *every non-void set of positive elements includes a* minimal *member.*

Any element which covers 0 *will be called a* prime.

LEMMA 1. *Any two primes are permutable.*

This is a corollary of Lemma 1 of §9. It is a corollary that the primes generate an Abelian subgroup, consisting of all elements which can be expressed as sums $n_1p_1 + \cdots + n_sp_s$ of a finite number of distinct primes.

Now let $a > 0$ be given, and consider all those differences $a - \sum n_ip_i$ which are positive. By the chain condition, one of these must be minimal, and so cannot contain any prime q (otherwise $a - (\sum n_ip_i + q)$ would be smaller). Again by the chain condition, every positive element b except 0 contains a prime, namely, some minimal x such that $0 < x \leqq b$. Hence our minimal difference must be 0, so that $a = \sum n_ip_i$.

But every element can be expressed as a difference of positive elements: $c = c^+ - (-c)^+$ for all c; hence

LEMMA 2. *Any element not* 0 *can be expressed as a sum of integral multiples of a finite number of distinct primes, as* $a = n_1p_1 + \cdots + n_sp_s$.

Putting Lemmas 1–2 together, we infer that our l-group is commutative. Now if we distinguish positive and negative coefficients, we get an expression for any $a \neq 0$ as

$$a = m_1p_1 + \cdots + m_rp_r - n_1q_1 - \cdots - n_sq_s. \quad (m_i, n_j > 0)$$

Clearly a cannot be positive unless $q_j \leqq m_1p_1 + \cdots + m_rp_r$ for all j. But since distinct primes are disjoint, by Theorem 15 q_j is disjoint from $\sum m_ip_i$; hence a cannot be positive unless no negative coefficients occur.

LEMMA 3. *In Lemma* 2, *a is positive if and only if every* n_i *is positive.*

---

[37] Cf. F. Bohnenblust, *op. cit.*; S. Kakutani, "Weak topology, bicompact set, and the principle of duality," Proc. Imp. Acad. Tokyo 16 (1940), pp. 63–67, Thm. 6; Stone, *op. cit.*; M. and S. Krein, Doklady 27 (1940), pp. 427–430; and K. Yosida, "On vector lattice with a unit," Proc. Imp. Acad. Tokyo 17 (1941), pp. 121–124.

[38] Ore uses the word "Archimedean" to mean the same thing, but our terminology is more common. In the simply ordered case, (C) implies that every non-void set of positive elements has a least member (well-ordering condition), so that the integers form the only simply ordered l-group satisfying the chain condition.

It is a corollary that a is zero (positive and negative) if and only if every n_i is positive and negative, which is absurd. It is a corollary that the representation of Lemma 1 is unique; for if a had two different representations, their formal difference would give a representation of 0. We can summarize.

THEOREM 37. *Let A be any l-group which satisfies the chain condition. Then A is commutative, and each non-zero element of A can be expressed uniquely as a sum of integral multiples of distinct primes.*[39] *Such a sum is positive if and only if no coefficient is negative.*

It is a corollary that A is determined to within isomorphism by the cardinal number of the set of its primes.

22. Application to ideal theory

This suggests an approach to the so-called "fundamental theorem of ideal theory" quite different from the modern approach,[40] and much nearer to the classical one. Let F be any field, and let H be any subring of "integers" of F which contains unity. By an *ideal* in F, we mean a subset which contains with any two elements their sum and difference, and with any element all its integral multiples. Multiplication of ideals is according to the usual definition.

It is clear that the non-zero ideals form a lattice with respect to set-inclusion, which in many important cases can be proved by extremely general arguments to satisfy the chain condition.[41]

It is also clear that multiplication of ideals is commutative and associative, and that ideal multiplication is distributive on addition (the lattice-join). Therefore we have all of the postulates of Theorem 7 satisfied except the existence of inverses.

It follows that, in the most important cases, in order to establish the unique factorization of ideals into primes, we need only supplement general arguments by proving that *every ideal has an ideal inverse*—or equivalently, that the product of every ideal by a suitable ideal gives a principal ideal.

23. Completeness

Many important l-groups are complete, in the sense of the following

DEFINITION. *An l-group A is called* complete *(σ-complete) if and only if every non-void (resp. countable) bounded set has a* g.l.b. *and a* l.u.b.

REMARK 1. By Theorem 2, the existence of g.l.b. implies that of l.u.b.; and

---

[39] In the commutative case, this result is essentially well-known. *Cf.* for example M. Ward, "Residuated distributive lattices," Duke Jour. 6 (1940), pp. 641–651; also A. Clifford, "Arithmetic and ideal theory of abstract multiplication," Bull. Am. Math. Soc. 40 (1934), p. 329, Thm. 2.

[40] For the modern treatment of E. Noether, *cf.* van der Waerden's "Moderne Algebra," 1st ed., vol. Z, pp. 98–102. For the classical treatment *cf.* D. Hilbert, "Théorie des corps de nombres algébriques," Paris, 1913. Remarks much like ours are made on p. 13 of Krull's "Idealtheorie."

[41] *Cf.* van der Waerden, *op. cit.*, §80. By a "positive" ideal, we mean one which contains H, which is an identity for multiplication. The "negative" ideals are thus the ideals which are *integral*, in the usual terminology.

using Theorem 1, one can even show that it is enough to require that every non-void set of *positive* elements have a g.l.b.

REMARK 2. The chain condition implies completeness. For if S is a non-void set of positive elements s_α, then the *finite* meets $\bigvee s_{\alpha(i)}$ include a minimal member a by the chain condition. But every $s_\alpha \frown a$, being itself a finite meet and so not properly contained in a, will be a. Thus a is a lower bound for S; it obviously contains every lower bound.

Next, let x be any element of any l-group A. If s is any upper bound for the set $\{nx\}$, then by Theorem 1 so are $s + x$ and $s - x$. It follows that $\{nx\}$ cannot have a *least* upper bound unless $x \geqq 0$ and $x \leqq 0$.

LEMMA 1. *The set of all integral multiples of a non-zero element cannot have a* l.u.b. (I, II, P_2)

COROLLARY. *Unless* $A = 0$, *any l-group* A *contains a countable set without a least upper bound.*

It also follows that, if A is σ-complete, the set nx cannot have an upper bound (or it would have a l.u.b.). In other words,

THEOREM 38. *Any σ-complete l-group is Archimedean.*

COROLLARY. *If an l-group can be embedded group- and order-isomorphically in a complete l-group, then it is Archimedean.*

Conversely, Clifford (*op. cit.*) has proved that any commutative Archimedean l-group[42] can be completed by cuts in the sense of Dedekind-MacNeille, to give a complete commutative l-group. Combining, we have

THEOREM 39 (Clifford). *A commutative l-group can be embedded in a complete l-group if and only if it is Archimedean.* (I, II, P_1–P_3, (14))

24. Infinite distributivity

It was proved (Theorem 1) that in an l-group, any group translation is a lattice automorphism. Consequently, it carries infinite joins and meets into infinite joins and meets, respectively. The formulas expressing this fact appear as the infinite distributive laws

$$(28)\qquad \begin{array}{ll} a + \bigvee x_\alpha = \bigwedge (a + x_\alpha) & a + \bigwedge x_\alpha = \bigwedge (a + x_\alpha) \\ \bigvee x_\alpha + b = \bigwedge (x_\alpha + b) & \bigwedge x_\alpha + b = \bigwedge (x_\alpha + b) \end{array}$$

Similarly, since every correspondence of the form $x \to a - x$ is a dual automorphism, we have the formal laws

$$(29)\qquad a - \bigvee x_\alpha = \bigwedge (a - x_\alpha) \quad \text{and dually.}$$

Now let $v = \bigvee x_\alpha$. Then, for all a and α,

$$0 \leqq (a \frown v) - (a \frown x_\alpha) \leqq v - x_\alpha \quad \text{by (27).}$$

---

[42] Actually, L′–L″ may be replaced for this purpose by the far weaker condition (14) (Moore-Smith property). In the present case, the cuts appear as so-called v-ideals; *cf.* Krull's v-Gruppensatz, "Idealtheorie," p. 120.

But $\wedge(v - x_\alpha) = v - \vee x_\alpha = v - v = 0$ by (29); and by what we have just seen, $0 \leqq \wedge[(a \frown v) - (a \frown x_\alpha)] \leqq \wedge(v - x_\alpha)$; hence

$$0 = \wedge[(a \frown v) - (a \frown x_\alpha)] = (a \frown v) - \vee(a \frown x_\alpha).$$

Transposing, we get the first of the further infinite distributive laws

$$(30) \qquad a \frown \vee x_\alpha = \vee(a \frown x_\alpha) \quad \text{and} \quad a \smile \wedge x_\alpha = \wedge(a \smile x_\alpha);$$

the second follows by duality. Summarizing, we have

THEOREM 40 (Kantorovitch[43]). *The infinite distributive laws* (28)–(30) *hold in any complete l-group.*

25. Closed l-ideals

In a complete *commutative* l-group, the complemented l-ideals may also be characterized in terms of closure properties. To see this, let us define for any set S of elements of an l-group G, the polar[44] S^* of S as the set of all elements disjoint from every element of S.

If S is a complemented l-ideal with complement T, then $y \in T$ implies, for all $x \in S$, that

$$||x| \frown |y|| = |x| \frown |y| \leqq |x| \text{ and } |y|.$$

Hence $|x| \frown |y| \in S \frown T = 0$, and $x \perp y$, proving $y \in S^*$. Conversely, if $z = x + y$ $(x \in S, y \in T)$ is in S^*, then

$$0 = |z| \frown |x| = (|x| + |y|) \frown |x| = |x|,$$

whence $z = y$ is in T. This shows $T = S^*$; by symmetry, $S = T^* = (S^*)^*$.

But now for any subset T, the set T^* is an l-ideal by Theorem 22, provided G is commutative. Further, by (30), if G is complete, then T^* is a *closed* l-ideal in the sense of the following definition.

DEFINITION. *An l-ideal J of a complete l-group G is called* closed[45] *if and only if J contains with any bounded subset $\{x_\alpha\}$, also $\vee x_\alpha$.*

REMARK. Since the correspondence $x \to -x$ leaves J setwise invariant and inverts order, it follows that J also contains $\wedge x_\alpha$. Further, since any l-ideal is convex (§11), closure in the sense of the preceding definiton is equivalent to topological closure in the intrinsic topology.[46]

---

[43] "Lineare halbgeordnete Räume," Math. Sbornik, 2 (44) (1937), pp. 121–168, esp. Theorems 10–21. Kantorovitch assumed commutativity, but this does not play an essential role.

[44] It follows from the general theory of relations (*cf.* "Lattice Theory", §32), since the relation of disjointness is symmetric and anti-reflexive, that (i) if we denote $(S^*)^*$ by $\bar{S}$, then the operation $S \to \bar{S}$ is a closure operation, (ii) if we call S "closed" when $S = \bar{S}$, then any intersection of "closed" sets is itself closed, (iii) 0 is closed, (iv) the correspondence $S \to S^*$ is a dual automorphism of the lattice of "closed" sets.

[45] Closed l-ideals are the "familles completes" of F. Riesz, *op. cit.*, Riesz proved Theorem 42 for principal l-ideals. Condition (ii) below shows the concept also specializes to that of a "v-ideal" (Krull).

[46] As defined on p. 32 of the author's "Lattice Theory."

We have seen that any complemented l-ideal is the polar of its complement, and that the polar of any subset of a complete commutative l-group is a closed l-ideal; we shall now complete the circle of reasoning by showing that any closed l-ideal is complemented, yielding

THEOREM 41 (Riesz). *For any l-ideal J of a complete* commutative *l-group, the following assertions are equivalent*: (i) *J is complemented*, (ii) $J = (J^*)^*$, (iii) *J is closed. If* (i) *holds, then J^* is the complement of J.*

COMPLETION OF PROOF. If J is a closed l-ideal of any complete l-group G, then for any positive $a \in G$ we can form the J-component a_J of a, as

$$a_J = \bigvee_{x \in J} x \frown a = \bigvee_{x \in J, x \geqq 0} x \frown a.$$

Since G is complete, and $0 \leqq x \frown a \leqq a$ for all $x \geqq 0$, a_J exists. Moreover since J is closed and every $x \frown a$ is in J, a_J is in J. Hence for all positive $z \in J$, since $(z + a_J)$ is positive and in J,

$$a_J \leqq (z + a_J) \frown a \leqq \bigvee_{x \in J, x \geqq 0} x \frown a = a_J .$$

But now by the distributive law (1),

$$(z + a_J) \frown a = z \frown (a - a_J) + a_J ,$$

whence, cancelling, $z \frown (a - a_J) = 0$. Thus $a - a_J$ is in J^*. It follows that $J + J^*$ includes all positive elements $a = a_J + (a - a_J)$ of G—and hence all elements of G by Cor. 2 of Thm. 13, so that $J + J^* = G$. But evidently $J \frown J^* = 0$, which shows that J is complemented with complement J^*, as asserted in the Theorem.

COROLLARY. *Any intersection of complemented l-ideals of a complete* commutative *l-group is itself complemented.*

26. Weak units and direct decompositions

Since any intersection of closed l-ideals is itself closed, it is natural to try to describe explicitly the intersection of all closed l-ideals which contain a fixed positive element a—in other words, the closed l-ideal *generated* by a.

We can answer this question (in complete commutative l-groups) by direct appeal to Theorem 41. Using condition (ii), we see that $(a^*)^*$ is the smallest closed l-ideal which contains a; further, it is the largest closed l-ideal having a for weak unit. We can also describe $(a^*)^*$ in another way, using Theorem 27. Clearly any closed l-ideal which contains a will contain all x such that $x = \bigvee na \frown x = \bigwedge na \smile x$; but conversely, the set of all such x is a closed l-ideal containing a. It is of course the topological closure of the principal l-ideal generated by a.

Now let A be any l-group with weak unit e. If A can be represented as the cardinal product $A_1 \cdots A_n$ of smaller l-groups, then the components of e in the different A_i are disjoint elements whose sum is e.

DEFINITION. *By a* decomposition *of a positive element e of an l-group A, is* *meant a set of disjoint elements* e_i *whose sum is* e. *By a* component *of* e *is meant an element* e' *such that*[47] $e' \frown (e - e') = 0$.

THEOREM 42. *The components of any positive element of any l-group form a Boolean algebra.*

PROOF. They are the elements x of the distributive lattice of all elements $0 \leqq x \leqq e$ which have complements, by definition and Theorem 13. These form a Boolean algebra, by Theorem 6.2 of the author's "Lattice Theory."

THEOREM 43. *Let* A *be any complete commutative l-group with weak unit* e. *Then the direct decompositions of* A *correspond one-one with the decompositions of* e.

PROOF. We have already seen that the components of e under any direct decomposition of A create a decomposition of e. But conversely, let $e = e_1 + \cdots + e_n$ be any decomposition of e, and let A_i denote the closed l-ideal generated by e_i. Since the e_i are disjoint, we will have $e_i^* \supset A_j$ if $i \neq j$, and so $A_i \perp A_j$—or, what comes to the same thing, $A_i \frown A_j = 0$. But the sum of the A_i contains $e_i + \cdots + e_n$, and is a closed l-ideal; hence it contains $A = 0^* = (e^*)^*$.

This completes the proof; we note in passing that the example of the ordinal product of the additive group of the integers, with the cardinal product of the additive group of the integers with itself (in symbols, $J \circ (JJ)$), shows that the hypothesis of completeness is not redundant.

27. Residuated lattices

The concept of l-group can be generalized in two ways: one can weaken either the group or the lattice postulates. The least essential group postulate seems to be the one requiring the existence of inverses. If this is dropped,we arrive at something very close to the usual concept of a *residuated lattice.*[48]

DEFINITION. *Let* G *be any (additively written)* groupoid, *or associative system with identity* 0. *If* G *is also a lattice, and satisfies*

$$(28) \qquad a + \vee x_\alpha = \vee (a + x_\alpha) \quad \textit{and} \quad \vee x_\alpha + b = \vee (x_\alpha + b),$$

it will be called an l-groupoid. *In any l-groupoid, the* left-residual $a{:}b$ *of* b *by* a *is defined as the join of all* x *such that* $xb \leqq a$. *The* right-residual $a{::}b$ *of* b *by* a *is defined as the join of all* y *such that* $by \leqq a$.

Clearly every l-group is an l-groupoid, in which $a{:}b$ is $a - b$ and $a{::}b$ is $-b + a$. Also, by (28), $(a{:}b) + b \leqq a$ and $b + (a{::}b) \leqq a$. The concept of l-groupoid is not self-dual; in any l-groupoid we have the monotonicity law (2), but not the dual of (28), even for finite meets.

Much of the importance of l-groupoids stems from

---

[47] The concepts just defined, together with Theorems 42–43, are due essentially to Freudenthal, *op. cit.*

[48] This concept, and (implicitly) that of l-groupoid, are due to M. Ward and R. P. Dilworth ("Residuated lattices," Trans. Am. Math. Soc. 45 (1939), pp. 335–354, and "Noncommutative residuated lattices," *ibid.* 46 (1939), pp. 426–444). The main contribution of the present section is to show that the concept applies to important systems other than ideals.

THEOREM 44 (Ward). *The ideals of any ring form an l-groupoid if inclusion is taken to mean set-inclusion and if ideal multiplication is taken as the group operation.*

We shall omit the proof, which is immediate. A special further property of ideals is $x + y \leqq x \frown y$; this is not a consequence of the postulates for an l-groupoid, and implies $x \leqq 0 \frown x$, or $0 \geqq x$ for all x, as a special case. Conversely, if every $x \leqq 0$, then $x + y \leqq 0 + y = y$ and similarly $x + y \leqq x$, whence $x + y \leqq x \frown y$, for all x, y.

DEFINITION. *A* residuated lattice *is an l-groupoid in which $x + y \leqq x \frown y$ for all x, y,—or equivalently, in which every element is negative.*

No l-group is a residuated lattice. However, we have

THEOREM 45. *Let G be any l-group, and S any set of negative elements of G which contains 0 and is closed under $+$ and $\vee$. Then S is a residuated lattice.*

COROLLARY. *The set of all negative elements of any l-group or l-groupoid is a residuated lattice.*

For instance, by Theorem 45, the non-positive non-increasing real functions on any interval, the non-positive convex functions on any interval, and the non-positive subharmonic functions on any plane region, form residuated lattices.[49]

THEOREM 46. *An abstract lattice L is residuated when $\frown$ is taken as the group operation, if and only if the dual of L is a Brouwerian logic. In this case, the residuation operation : specializes to the implication operation $\rightarrow$.*

PROOF: Compare the definitions given above with Theorem 8.4 of "Lattice Theory."

THEOREM 47 (J. W. Duthie[50]). *The binary relations on any set form an l-groupoid, if the relative product is taken as the group operation, while the lattice operations are given their usual significance.*

We note also that the $\vee$-ideals of any commutative groupoid form a residuated lattice.

PROOF. The different postulates defining an l-groupoid are proved in Schroder's "Algebra der Logik," vol. III, esp. formula (29), p. 100, and formula (6), p. 79. The proof can be supplied by anyone familiar with the definitions.

The relations form a Boolean algebra under inclusion; and it has been proved by Ward-Dilworth (*op. cit.*, Thm. 7.4) that the only way to make a Boolean algebra residuated is to take lattice-meet as the group operation; hence we know in advance that relations cannot form a residuated lattice.

We note that in every l-groupoid, all left-residuals $a{:}a$ of elements with them-

---

[49] These and other function-theoretic examples of the same type were signalized in §133 of "Lattice Theory," where however the connection with residuated lattices was not remarked.

[50] Communicated to the author orally; this result was not mentioned by O. Ore in his Colloquium Lectures on relations. For the definitions of relative product, join, and meet, for binary relations, *cf.* A. Tarski, "Introduction to Logic," New York, 1941, pp. 90–93, or E. Schroder, "Algebra der Logik." It is interesting that the conversion operator $a \rightarrow \breve{a}$ should act as an *involution* on the algebra of relations.

selves are idempotent; $a{:}a + a{:}a = a{:}a$. For by the definition of left-residual, we have

$$(a{:}a) + (a{:}a) + a \leqq (a{:}a) + a \leqq a,$$

whence $(a{:}a) + (a{:}a) \leqq a{:}a$. Conversely, $a + 0 = a$, whence $0 \leqq a{:}a$, and so $(a{:}a) = (a{:}a) + 0 \leqq (a{:}a) + (a{:}a)$, completing the proof.—In residuated lattices, $a{:}a = 0$, and the result just proved is trivial.

Finally (cf. Dilworth, *op. cit*), we can prove

$$(20'') \qquad a \smile b = a \smile c = 0 \quad \text{implies} \quad a \smile (b + c) = 0$$

in any l-groupoid; in fact, the proof of Theorem 15 applies as it stands!

28. Riesz' Interpolation Property[51]

The most basic of the lattice postulates (see §4) seem to be the reflexive law P_1 and the transitive law P_3; in general, a system with a reflexive and transitive relation is called a quasi-ordered set.

DEFINITION. *A* quasi-ordered group *is a group G with a homogeneous reflexive and transitive relation. If the relation is also anti-symmetric (satisfies* P_3*), then G is called a* partially ordered group (*or semiordered group*).

It is well-known ("Lattice Theory", Thm. 1.2) that in any quasi-ordered set, if $a \smile b$ is defined to mean that $a \geqq b$ and $a \leqq b$, we get an equivalence relation, and that we can consistently identify "equivalent" elements to get a partially ordered set. It is easily shown that in a quasi-ordered group, the $x \sim 0$ form a *normal subgroup* N, while the other equivalence classes form the *cosets* of N. This gives

THEOREM 48. *The algorithm of identifying a and b whenever* $a \geqq b$ *and* $a \leqq b$, *yields from any quasi-ordered group a partially ordered group.*

Existence postulates such as the Interpolation Properties to be discussed below and the lattice postulates L′–L″ apply to quasi-ordered groups just as well as to partially ordered groups; only uniqueness properties are lost. However, by Theorem 48, no real generality is lost if we restrict ourselves to partially ordered groups.[52]

DEFINITION. *Let m, n be any cardinal numbers. A partially ordered set will be said to have the* (m, n) *Interpolation Property if and only if, given* $x_1, \cdots, x_m$ *and* $y_1, \cdots, y_n$, *such that* $x_i \leqq y_j$ *for all i, j, we can find a z such that* $x_i \leqq z \leqq y_j$ *for all i, j.*

SPECIAL CASES. The reflexive law makes the $(m, 1)$ and $(1, n)$ Interpolation Properties trivial. The $(0, 2)$ Interpolation Property is the Moore-Smith property discussed in §8; it implies the $(0, n)$ Interpolation Property for all finite n.

---

[51] The author is greatly indebted to conversations with George Mackey and John von Neumann for material of the present section; the basic ideas go back to F. Riesz, *op. cit.*

[52] Partially ordered groups can be bizarre enough. For instance, consider the additive group of reai numbers, and let the "positive" elements be those which exceed unity; $na > 0$ need not imply $a > 0$.

The $(0, \beta)$ Interpolation Property for all β is equivalent to the existence of a universal element I, and can hold in no partially ordered group except 0 (§22, Lemma 1, Cor.). Again, the (α, β) Interpolation Property for all non-zero cardinals is equivalent to *conditional completeness*: the condition that every non-void set bounded above have a least upper bound, and dually. To see this, given any bounded set of elements x_i, form the non-void set y_j of upper bounds to the x_i; then $x_i \leqq y_j$ identically, so that z will exist with $x_i \leqq y_j$ for all i, j; by definition, $z = \bigvee x_i$. Similarly, the (α, β) Interpolation Property for all cardinals, zero included, is equivalent to completeness.

But, algebraically speaking, the most interesting case is the (2, 2) *Riesz Interpolation Property*. By induction, this implies every (m, n) Interpolation Property with m, n finite and not zero. It is clearly weaker than the lattice property, since if $x_i \leqq y_j$ for all i, j, then $x_i \leqq \bigvee x_i \leqq \bigwedge y_j \leqq y_j$ for all i, j.

For example (F. Riesz, *op. cit.*), the polynomials, and also the rational functions with non-vanishing denominator, on any bounded closed region, form partially ordered groups which have the Riesz Interpolation Property but are not lattices.

THEOREM 49. *The following conditions on any partially ordered group G are equivalent*:

(i) *The Riesz Interpolation Property,*

(ii) *The condition of Lemma* 1, §11.

If G is commutative, they are both equivalent to

(iii) *The condition that if* $a_1 + a_2 = b_1 + b_2$, *and* a_1, a_2, b_1, b_2 *are positive, then there exist positive elements* $c_{11}, c_{12}, c_{21}, c_{22}$, *such that* $\sum_{j=1}^{2} c_{ij} = a_i$ *and* $\sum_{i=1}^{2} c_{ij} = b_j$. (*Riesz Refinement Postulate*)

PROOF. First, (i) implies (ii). For if $0 \leqq x, a, b \leqq a + b$ then $0 \leqq x, a$ and $x - b \leqq x, a$ (transposing); hence if (i) holds, there exists s with $0 \leqq s \leqq a$, $s \leqq x$ whence $x = s + t$ $(t \geqq 0)$, and $x - b \leqq s$ whence $s + t \leqq x \leqq s + b$ and so $t \leqq b$. Conversely, (ii) implies (i). By right-homogeneity, it suffices to prove that if $0, x \leqq y, x + b$ then there exists s with $0, x \leqq s \leqq y, x + b$. But indeed, $0 \leqq x + b \leqq y + b$ since $x \leqq y$; hence $x + b = s + t$ $(0 \leqq s \leqq y$, $0 \leqq t \leqq b)$, whence $x \leqq x + t \leqq x + b = s + t$ and $s \geqq x$, $s \leqq x + b$.

Finally, if G is commutative, then (ii) and (iii) are equivalent. For $0 \leqq x \leqq a + b$ $(a \geqq 0, b \geqq 0)$ is equivalent to $a + b = x + (a + b - x)$, where all four summands are positive. To say that under these circumstances $x = s + t$ $(0 \leqq s \leqq a, 0 \leqq t \leqq b)$ is equivalent to saying that $(a + b - x) = (a - s) + (b - t) = s' + t'$, where $b \geqq s' \geqq 0$, $a \geqq t' \geqq 0$—whence s, s', t, t' behave as c_{ij} for (iii).

THEOREM 50. *In any partially ordered group which has the Riesz Interpolation Property, we know*

$$(20') \qquad a \frown b = 0 \quad \textit{and} \quad a \frown c = 0 \quad \textit{imply} \quad a \frown (b + c) = 0.$$

PROOF. Suppose $x \leqq a, b + c$. Then a and b are upper bounds to 0 and $x - c$, since $x - c \leqq x \leqq a$ and $b - (x - c) = (b + c) - x \geqq 0$. Hence an element can be inserted between $0, x - c$ and a, b. But since $a \frown b = 0$, this element must be 0. Hence $x - c \leqq 0$, $x \leqq c$ as well as $x \leqq a$, and $x = 0$.

By duality (20″) holds also; for the further study of commutative partially ordered groups with the Riesz Interpolation Property, with especial emphasis on the linear functionals on such groups, see F. Riesz, *op. cit.*

29. Unsolved problems, general case

We shall conclude this paper with a list of problems of varying degrees of interest and difficulty. For the purpose of classification, these will be divided into those which involve general l-groups, and those which relate primarily to commutative l-groups.

PROBLEM 1. Show that $na > nb$ for one positive n implies $a > b$.

SUGGESTIONS. This is easy in the simply ordered case, or if a and b are permutable (see §9, Lemma 3).

PROBLEM 2. Show that if $a > 0$ and $b > 0$, then

$$-a - b + a + b \ll a + b.$$

In words, the commutator of a and b is incomparably smaller than $a + b$.

SUGGESTION. If the commutator is in the center, then

$$n(a + b) \geqq -na - nb + n(a + b) = \binom{n}{2}(-a - b + a + b).$$

Hence if the conjecture of Problem 2 can be proved, we have $(a + b) \geqq 1/2n(-a - b + a + b)$ for every even integer n, giving the desired result. This method, with the aid of finite induction, might be successfully applied at least to hypercentral l-groups.

PROBLEM 3. Prove that every Archimedean l-group is commutative.

This result would be a corollary of the result conjectured in Problem 2. Using Theorem 38, we would infer as a second corollary that every *complete l-group was commutative*. Hence to disprove the conjectures of Problems 3–4, it would be enough to find a complete non-commutative l-group, or an Archimedean non-commutative l-group.

PROBLEM 4. Prove that a complete l-group either satisfies the chain condition or has at least the cardinal number of the continuum.

PROBLEM 5. Find an l-group without proper l-ideals which is non-commutative.

SUGGESTIONS. By Theorem 30, it would suffice to find a simple l-group which was non-Archimedean or not simply ordered. By Theorem 25, this is also necessary, so that if the author's conjecture is correct, either a non-Archimedean or a non-simply ordered simple l-group must exist. The author conjectures that the former is certainly the case.

PROBLEM 6. Find all l-group orderings (homogeneous lattice orderings) of the free group with two generators. Is the commutator-subgroup necessarily an l-ideal?

SUGGESTION. See Problem 2.

PROBLEM 7. Find a necessary and sufficient condition that an abstract group be isomorphic with the additive group of an l-group.

SUGGESTION. By Theorem 16, it is necessary that every element be of infinite order; by Theorem 24, this is sufficient in the commutative case; the author conjectures that it is also sufficient in the hypercentral case.

PROBLEM 8. Suppose that in an l-groupoid $0:(0:x) = x$ and $0::(0::x) = x$ for all x. What can be inferred?

SUGGESTIONS. The correspondence $x \to 0:x$ will then be a lattice involution, so that the dual of (28) also holds. What about the commutative case? Will $0:(x + y) = 0:x + 0:y$?

30. Unsolved problems, commutative case

Any commutative group without elements of finite order whose cardinal number is at most that of the continuum, is isomorphic with an additive subgroup of the ordered group of real numbers under addition—proof by rational bases,—and so is isomorphic with an Archimedean l-group.

PROBLEM 9. Is *every* commutative group without elements of finite order isomorphic with the additive group of an *Archimedean* l-group?

PROBLEM 10. Find a necessary and sufficient condition that a commutative partially order group be group- and order-isomorphic with an additive subgroup of a cardinal product of simply ordered *Archimedean* l-groups—or equivalently, by real functions.[53]

PROBLEM 11. Given l-groups B and C, reduce the problem of finding all l-groups A having an l-ideal J isomorphic with C and l-quotient-group A/J isomorphic with B to a problem in pure group extension, in the commutative case.

This problem was implicitly solved in special cases in §19; the special cases B simple and C simple might well be attacked first.

PROBLEM 12. Find all Lie l-algebras: Lie algebras over the real field which are vector lattices relative to a set of positive elements which is invariant under all inner automorphisms.

SUGGESTIONS. Use the known classification of vector lattices with finite basis (Cors. 1–2 of Theorem 35). The author conjectures that a Lie algebra can be made into a Lie l-algebra only if it is *solvable* (or "integrable").

PROBLEM 13. Find all Lie l-groups in the large.

The problem in the small is contained in Problem 12; the fact that all elements have infinite order should simplify it.

PROBLEM 14. Construct a theory of l-rings.

---

[53] The work of von Neumann (unpublished), Stone (*cf.* footnote 35) et al. shows that any such Archimedean group is isomorphic with a homomorphic image of such a cardinal product.

The only postulates known (Stone, *op. cit.*) cover only a very special case: subrings of cardinal unions of simply ordered l-rings, corresponding to rings of functions. Cf. also A. A. Albert, "On ordered algebras", Bull. Am. Math. Soc. 46 (1940), pp. 521–522.

PROBLEM 15. Find a more direct substitute for condition (8) in Theorem 9: i.e., a simple condition or set of simple conditions on the operation $a \to a^+$ necessary and sufficient to make the operation $(a - b)^+ + b$ associative.

HARVARD UNIVERSITY

Lattice-ordered Lie groups

By GARRETT BIRKHOFF, Cambridge (Mass.)

Fundamental definitions.

§ 1. By a *lattice-ordered Lie group*, or *Lie l-group*, I shall mean a system which is (I) a Lie group[1]), (II) a lattice, in which (III) the group translations $x \to axb$ are lattice automorphisms. If (IV) the lattice operations *join* $a \cup b$ and *meet* $a \cap b$ are continuous in the topology[2]), the Lie l-group will be called a *topological* Lie l-group, or *Lie tl-group*. A group satisfying (II)—(III) is called an l-group; one which satisfies (II)—(IV) will be called a *topological l-group*, or *tl*-group.

By a *Lie l-algebra*, we shall mean a Lie algebra L over the real field, which is an l-group under vector addition and a lattice-ordering, in which for any scalar $\lambda \geqq 0$ and vector $X \geqq 0$ the product[3]) $\lambda X \geqq 0$, and in which the inner automorphisms are lattice-automorphisms. This means that, if A denotes the linear operator $X \to [X, A]$ in L, then

$$X \to X (\exp A) = X(\sum_{k=0}^{\infty} A^k/k!) = X + XA + XA^2/2! + XA^3/3! + \cdots \tag{1}$$

leaves the set of positive elements $X > 0$ setwise invariant. We shall discuss elsewhere the extension of the concept of Lie l-algebra to Lie algebras over other ordered fields.

Finally, we shall discuss two conditions which may or may not be satisfied by a Lie l-group, G, with identity E.

Scalar Homogeneity Condition. If $\exp A \geqq E$, then for all $\lambda \geqq 0$, $\exp \lambda A \geqq E$.

Vector Homogeneity Condition. The relations $\exp(A - B) \geqq E$ and $\exp A \geqq \exp B$ are equivalent to each other.

---

1) For the concept of group, cf. *A. Speiser*, „Gruppentheorie", 2nd edition, 1927; on this occasion, it is a particular pleasure to recall the great stimulus which this book has given to me. — For the concept of Lie group, cf. *W. Mayer* and *T. Y. Thomas*, "Foundations of the theory of continuous groups", Annals of Math. 36 (1935), 770—822. The concept of lattice-ordered group, or l-group, was developed in additive notation by the author in the Annals of Math., vol. 43 (1942), pp. 298—331, to be referred to below as [*LOG*]. Below we use the multiplicative notation.

2) We recall that a *lattice* is a system in which the operations $\cup$, $\cap$ are idempotent, commutative, associative, and satisfy the law of contraction $a \cap (a \cup b) = a \cup (a \cap b) = a$. Cf. the author's "Lattice Theory", New York, 1940, referred to as [*LT*].

3) This is implied by the requirement that L be a tl-group under vector addition and lattice-ordering, and is equivalent to it if L has a finite basis.

To see the significance of these two conditions, let us suppose G represented locally by canonical parameters. This maps G on its Lie algebra L through the correspondence

$$T \rightleftharpoons X \quad (T \varepsilon G,\ X \varepsilon L) \quad \text{means} \quad T = \exp X\,; \tag{2}$$

moreover the correspondence is bicontinuous and differentiable near the identity E of G (which corresponds to the origin 0 of L). We *define* $X \geqq Y$ in L to mean $\exp X \geqq \exp Y$ in G; this defines an order-isomorphism between L and a subset of G, which is bicontinuous, and even differentiable near $E = 0$. Hence it partially orders L; defines on L a reflexive, anti-symmetric, and transitive relation ([LT], Thm. 1. 1).

The Vector Homogeneity Condition clearly asserts that $X \geqq Y$ in L if and only if $X - Y \geqq 0$ in L; This means that L is a partially ordered group under its ordering and vector addition. Furthermore, the Scalar Homogeneity Condition asserts that $X \geqq 0$ in L implies $\lambda X \geqq 0$ in L for all $\lambda \geqq 0$ — that the non-negative elements form a *cone*, and (by definition) that L is a partially ordered vector space[1]). Hence the non-negative elements form a *convex* cone (since $X \geqq 0$ and $Y \geqq 0$ imply $\lambda X + \mu Y \geqq 0$ for all $\lambda, \mu \geqq 0$). Furthermore, since the inner automorphisms of G are lattice automorphisms, we get

Theorem 1. *The Lie algebra L of any Lie l-group G which satisfies the Scalar and Vector Homogeneity conditions, is a partially ordered Lie group.*

Theorem 2. *The Lie algebra L of a Lie l-group G which satisfies the Scalar and Vector Homogeneity Conditions, is a Lie l-algebra provided that all joins and meets of elements in some neighborhood of E are powers of infinitesimal elements.*

A corresponding theorem holds for partially ordered Lie groups, without the extra hypothesis.

Discussion of simple examples.

§ 2. It is clear that the real number system R is a Lie tl-group under its usual ordering, or under the reverse, and under no other ordering. On the other hand, under any Hamel basis (or basis over the rational subfield of scalars), it has 2^c (c = power of continuum) orderings making it into a Lie l-group. None of these satisfies the Scalar Homogeneity

[1]) If a vector space is a partially ordered group, and $X \geqq 0$ and $\lambda \geqq 0$ imply $\lambda X \geqq 0$, then H is called a „partially ordered vector space".

2

condition, except the two making R into a tl-group. Other examples of Lie tl-groups can be easily constructed as follows.

Theorem 3. *Let G and H be any two Lie l-groups. Let $G \times H$ denote the system whose elements are the couples (g, h) $[g \varepsilon G, h \varepsilon H]$, and in which*

$$(g, h) \circ (g', h') = (g \circ g', h \circ h') \tag{3}$$

whether $\circ$ stands for group multiplication, join, or meet. Then the direct union $G \times H$ is a Lie l-group. If G and H are tl-groups then so is $G \times H$. If G and H satisfy the Homogeneity Conditions, so does $G \times H$, and $L(G \times H)$ (the partially ordered Lie algebra of $G \times H$) is the direct sum of $L(G)$ and $L(H)$.

We omit the proof, which is trivial (cf. [*LT*], pp. 3, 13). It may be asked why nothing is said of differentiable Lie l-groups; the reason is that $A \cup E = A^+$ is not a differentiable operation, even in R.

Corollary. For every positive integer n, $R^n = R \times \cdots \times R$ is a tl-group.

A less superficial construction is the following.

Theorem 4. *Let G and H be any Lie l-groups, and let $\theta : g \to \alpha_g$ be any continuous[1]) homomorphism from G into the group of topological group — and lattice — automorphisms of H. Let $G \circ H$ consist of the couples (g, h) $[g \varepsilon G, h \varepsilon H]$, where*

$$(g, h)\,(g', h') = (gg', \alpha_{g'}(h)h') \text{ group-theoretically} \tag{4}$$

$$(g, h) \geqq 0 \text{ if and only if } g > 0, \text{ or } g = 0 \text{ and } h \geqq 0. \tag{5}$$

Then $G \circ H$ is a Lie l-group if G is simply ordered[1]).

Proof. It is well-known that $G \circ H$ is a Lie group, and (cf. [LOG], p. 316) a lattice; condition (III) above follows from the easily proved fact that the set of positive elements of $G \circ H$ is invariant under all inner automorphism (cf. [LOG], Thm. 3). However $G \circ H$ is *not* a tl-group.

Corollary 1. Let G be any simply connected (solvable) r-parameter Lie group, containing a chief series

$$E = G_0 < G_1 < \quad < G_r = G \tag{6}$$

of normal Lie subgroups, where G_i/G_{i-1} is cyclic for all i. Then G can be made into a simply ordered Lie i-group in 2^r ways.

[1]) Cf. *L. Pontrjagin*, „Topological Groups", Princeton, 1939. — A partially ordered group is called *simply* ordered if every X is either positive $(X > E)$, zero $(X = E)$ or negative $(X < E)$.

§ 3. The construction of the *lexicographic union* $G \circ H$, described for Lie l-groups in Theorem 5, applies also to Lie l-algebras.

Definition. Let L and M be any two Lie l-algebras, and let $\theta : a \to A$ be any homomorphic mapping of L into the Lie algebra of *derivations*[1]) of M. By the *lexicographic union* $L \circ M$ of L and M (relative to θ), is meant the linear algebra of couples (a, b) $[a \varepsilon L, b \varepsilon M)$, where $(a, b) + (a', b') = (a + a', b + b')$, $\lambda(a, b) = (\lambda a, \lambda b)$,

$$[(a, b), (a', b')] = [a, a'] + [b, b'] + Ab' - A'b, \tag{7}$$

and $(a, b) \geqq 0$ means $a > 0$ or $a = 0$ and $b \geqq 0$.

Theorem 5. *If L is a simply ordered Lie l-algebra and M is a Lie l-algebra, then $L \circ M$ is a Lie l-algebra.*

Sketch of proof. The Lie algebra part is really a corollary of Theorem 5 and Lie's Third Fundamental Theorem. However, it is interesting that a purely algebraic proof for Lie algebras over arbitrary fields is also possible. The vector lattice part is a corollary of [LOG], p. 316.

Corollary 1. Let L be any Lie algebra of dimension r, which contains a chief series of invariant subalgebras

$$0 < L_1 < L_2 < \cdots < L_r = L \qquad (L_k \text{ of dimension } k)\,. \tag{8}$$

Then L can be made into a simply ordered Lie l-algebra in at least 2^r ways.

The remarkable fact is that the converse is also true.

Theorem 6. *A real Lie algebra L of finite dimension r can be made into a Lie l-algebra if and only if it has a chief series* (8) *with zero quotient-algebras L_i / L_{i-1}.*

Proof. By Theorem 33 of [LOG], if we consider a Lie l-algebra L of finite dimension purely as a vector lattice, either $L = M_1 \times \cdots \times M_h$, where $M_1, \ldots, M_h$ are the unique ([LOG], Theorem 32) directly indecomposable constituents of L, or $L = R \circ N$, where R is the one-dimensional zero-algebra (Lie algebra of a cyclic group), and N is the unique $(r - 1)$-dimensional l-ideal of L. In the first case, any lattice automorphism of L must permute the M_i; hence any infinitesimal inner

[1]) We use the word „derivation" in the sense of *N. Jacobson*, „Abstract derivation and Lie algebras", Trans. Am. Math. Soc. 42 (1937), 206—24, to mean $A([b, b']) = [Ab, b'] + [b, Ab']$. Then θ is required to satisfy $A''b = A'(ab) - A(A'b)$, if $A'' = \bar{\theta}([a, a'])$.

4

automorphism must leave them invariant individually, and so L is the *direct union* of the M_i as Lie algebras. But any direct union of Lie algebras having chief series of the type described also has one; hence, by induction on r, L does. — In the other case, N is invariant under all lattice-automorphisms, and hence is also invariant under the adjoint group. By induction, N has a chief series of the type described, whose terms are invariant under all lattice-automorphisms of N, and hence under all inner automorphisms of L. Hence $L = M_1 \times \cdots \times M_h$ or $L = R \circ N$ also as a Lie l-algebra, and in either case L has a chief series of the type described. — The converse is Corollary 1 of Theorem 5.

Corollary 1. Any Lie l-algebra of finite dimension is isomorphic as a Lie algebra with a simply ordered Lie algebra.

Corollary 2. Any Lie l-algebra is solvable.

These remarks essentially answer the questions raised in Problem 12 of [LOG]. However, in view of the side conditions required to form a Lie l-algebra from a Lie l-group, they do not solve Problems 2 and 13. — The author is not aware of any insolvable Lie group without elements of finite order. If it could be shown that no such insolvable (i. e., "non-integrable") Lie group existed, one could conclude that every Lie l-group was solvable. The author has not studied this question carefully.

Commutativity of topologically lattice-ordered Lie groups.

§ 4. We now turn our attention to Lie tl-groups, and begin by proving a very elementary result.

Theorem 7. *A simply ordered topological l-group G must be topologically one-dimensional.*

Proof. Since any topological group is homogeneous, it suffices to show that G is one-dimensional at E. Every interval $A^{-1} < X < A$ $(A > 0)$ is a neighborhood of E with 0-dimensional boundary A^{-1}, A; hence under the interval topology, G is onedimensional. Every set closed under the interval topology is, by definition, closed under any topology making G a tl-group; hence[1]) G is one-dimensional under any topology making G a tl-group.

Corollary. The only simply ordered Lie tl-group is the group R of real numbers under addition.

---

[1]) Cf. *W. Hurewicz* and *H. Wallman*, „Dimension Theory", Princeton, 1941, p. 91, Theorem VI 7.

Lemma 1. Any Lie *tl*-group satisfies the Scalar Homogeneity Condition: $e^X \geqq E$ implies $e^{\lambda X} \geqq E$ for all $\lambda \geqq 0$.

Proof. By [LOG], § 9, Lemma 3, $e^{(m/n)X} \geqq E$ for all positive integers m, n. Hence, by continuity, $e^{\lambda X} \geqq E$ for all non-negative $\lambda = \text{Lim}\,(m_k/n_k)$.

Lemma 2. Any Lie *tl*-group satisfies half of the Vector Homogeneity Condition: $e^{X-Y} \geqq E$ implies $e^X \geqq e^Y$.

Proof. By definition, $e^x \geqq e^y$ is equivalent to $e^x e^{-y} \geqq E$. But it is not hard to show that

$$e^X e^{-Y} = \lim_{n \to \infty} \{\prod_{k=1}^{n} (V^{k/n} W^{1/n} V^{-k/n}) \prod_{k=1}^{n} (V^{(n-k)/n} W^{1/n} V^{(k-n)/n})\}, \tag{9}$$

where $V \equiv e^{(X+Y)/2}$ and $W \equiv e^{(X-Y)/2}$. By hypothesis, $W \geqq E$; hence for all k, n, $W^{1/n}$ and its conjugates $V^{k/n} W^{1/n} (V^{k/n})^{-1}$ are non-negative. Hence for all n, the product in curly brackets of $2n$ terms is non-negative; by continuity, so is the limit $e^X e^{-Y}$, q. e. d.

Remark. It would be easy to prove the entire Vector Homogeneity Condition was satisfied in a Lie *tl*-group, if we could assume that $W^2 \geqq T^2$ implied $W \geqq T$. For then $e^x \geqq e^y$ would imply, for all $m = 2^n$, $e^{x/m} e^{-y/m} \geqq E$; hence $e^{x-y} = \lim_{n \to \infty} (e^{x/m} e^{-y/m})^m \geqq E$. But, though this was conjectured as Problem 1 in [LOG], Example 9 of that paper provides an easy counterexample: $a + 2b - c \ngeqq a$, yet $2(a + 2b - c) = 2a + b + c \geqq 2a$. (More interesting counterexamples to Problem 1 and Problem 2 have been found, but not yet published, by *C. J. Everett* and *S. Ulam.*)

Lemma 3. In a Lie *tl*-group under canonical parameters, the non-negative elements form a closed convex cone C.

Proof. By the Scalar Homogeneity Condition, they form a cone with apex at $E = e^0$. This is closed near E, by continuity; hence being a cone it is closed everywhere. It is convex since, if $e^X \geqq E$ and $e^Y \geqq E$, then

$$e^{X+Y} = \lim_{\lambda \to 0} (e^{\lambda X} e^{\lambda Y})^{1/\lambda} \geqq E\,. \tag{10}$$

We shall now have to introduce some purely geometrical considerations about closed convex cones in r-dimensional Euclidean space. It is clear that any such cone either contains an r-dimensional interior, or is contained in an $(r-1)$-dimensional subspace[1]). Under the second hypothesis, the set of TU^{-1}, where $T, U \geqq E$ are restricted to a small neighborhood of the origin, will lie in a small dihedral sector since, in a Lie group,

[1]) Cf. *T. Bonnesen* and *W. Fenchel*, „Konvexe Körper", Berlin, 1934.

multiplication is differentiable. But this contradicts the identity $V = (V \frown E)(V \smile E)$ valid for all V in any l-group, and the fact that in a tl-group, $\operatorname{Lim}_{V \to E} V \frown E = \operatorname{Lim}_{V \to E} V \smile E = E$. Hence the first hypothesis must be correct.

Lemma 4. The convex cone C of Lemma 3 contains an r-dimensional interior.

Now let T be any element interior to C. By the differentiability of group multiplication, for sufficiently small positive λ, the set of $V \leqq T^{\lambda}$ — i. e., the set of $T^{\lambda}U^{-1}(U \varepsilon C)$ — includes E in its interior. So does the set of $W \geqq T^{-\lambda}$ dually; moreover the sets consist of two conoidal regions in nearly antipodal directions. By considering projections on a perpendicular to any "plane of support" (Stützebene)[1]) exterior to C, we see that the intersection of the sets can be made arbitrarily small by choosing λ small enough. Denoting by A any T^{λ} small enough so that the set of X satisfying $T^{-\lambda} \leqq X \leqq T^{\lambda}$ is bounded and lies in the region where canonical parameters are one-one, we see

Lemma 5. In any Lie tl-group, there exists a positive A such that the interval $\mathfrak{U}$ of U satisfying $A^{-1} \leqq U \leqq A$ (i. e., satisfying $|U| \leqq A$) is compact and contains E in its interior.

Unfortunately, we do not yet know that, for all n, the set of U such that $A^{-n} \leqq U \leqq A^{n}$ is $\mathfrak{U}^{n}$; hence we cannot yet conclude that all lattice intervals are compact. But we can say, since it contains $\mathfrak{U}^{n}$, that A is a *strong unit* in the sense of [LOG], and that, since every compact set is contained in some $\mathfrak{U}^{n}$, *every compact set is lattice-theoretically bounded.*

Lemma 6. In any tl-group, every compact interval is σ-complete.

For let $U_1 \geqq U_2 \geqq U_3 \geqq \cdots$ be any decreasing sequence of elements of the given interval. Then by compactness there exists a subsequence $\{U_{k(i)}\}$ converging to some V, which must also lie in the interval. Moreover for all n, $U_n \smile V = \operatorname{Lim}_{i \to \infty} U_n \smile U_{k(i)} = U_n$; hence V is a lower bound. Finally, if W is any lower bound of $\{U_k\}$, then

$$W \smile V = \operatorname{Lim}_{i \to \infty} W \smile U_{k(i)} = \operatorname{Lim}_{i \to \infty} U_{k(i)} = V ;$$

hence V is a greatest lower bound.

Corollary. For every $T \geqq 0$ and every non-negative $U \varepsilon \mathfrak{U}$ of Lemma 5, $U' = \operatorname{Lim}_{n \to \infty} U \frown T^{n}$ exists.

For the sequence of $U'_n = U \frown T^{n}$ lies in $\mathfrak{U}$ and is non-decreasing. — We shall now apply the corollary just proved to obtain a fundamental

---

[1]) The existence of such a plane for a closed convex cone not overlapping its antipodal cone $-C$ is easy to establish; cf. the reference of footnote 1, p. 214.

7

decomposition of G into the elements such that $U = U'$ and those such that $U \frown U' = E$. The basic idea is due to *F. Riesz* (cf. [LOG], § 25); we have however to proceed without assuming commutativity.

Lemma 7. If we define $U'' = U'^{-1}U$ (Lemma 6, Corollary), then $U'' \frown T = E$.

Proof. Let U'_n denote $U \frown T^n$, and $U''_n = U'^{-1}_n U$. Then we will have by construction, for all n,

$$U'_{n+1} = U \frown T^{n+1} = (U'_n U''_n) \frown (T^n T)$$
$$\geqq (U'_n U''_n) \frown (U'_n T) = U'_n (U''_n \frown T) \geqq U'_n (U'' \frown T) .$$

Hence, by induction, $U'_n \geqq (U'' \frown T)^n$ for all n; therefore the set of $(U'' \frown T)^n$ is bounded above by U'. Since $U'' \frown T \geqq E$, this implies (cf. [LOG], p. 322) $U'' \frown T = E$.

Theorem 8. *Any Lie tl-group G is a direct union of the closed l-subgroup (actually, l-ideal) generated by any* $T \geqq 0$, *and the closed l-subgroup disjoint from* T.

Proof. First, it is clear that the two subsets just defined are closed subgroups in any *tl*-group. For if

$$U = U' = \mathrm{Lim}_{n\to\infty} U \frown T^n \quad \text{and} \quad V = \mathrm{Lim}_{n\to\infty} V \frown T^n, \quad \text{then}$$
$$UV \geqq \mathrm{Lim}_{n\to\infty} UV \frown T^n \geqq \mathrm{Lim}_{n\to\infty} (U \frown T^n)\,(V \frown T^n) = UV$$

by continuity, and dually for $U = \mathrm{Lim}_{n\to\infty} U \smile T^{-n}$. The elements disjoint from T form a subgroup by [LOG], Thm. 22; the subgroup is closed, by continuity.

In a *Lie tl*-group, the two subgroups generate the whole group. Near the identity, this follows from Lemma 6, Corollary, and Lemma 7. But the whole group is generated by any neighborhood of the identity. Finally, since disjoint elements are permutable ([LOG], p. 307), we see that every element of one subgroup is permutable with every element of the other. Hence[1]) G is group-theoretically the direct product of the two subgroups. Since the subgroups are elementwise disjoint, meaning $U' \frown V'' = E$, this is also true lattice-theoretically.

Incidentally, the entire proof would go through in any σ-complete *tl*-group; the construction can be made directly in the large. It also goes through in any *tl*-group in which intervals are compact.

---

[1]) Cf. *A. Speiser*, „Gruppentheorie", 2nd ed., p. 28.

8

Corollary. The additive group R of real numbers under its usual ordering is the only directly indecomposable Lie *tl*-group. Moreover R and the additive group J of integers are the only directly indecomposable σ-complete *tl*-groups.

For unless a Lie or σ-complete *tl*-group is simply ordered, it contains an element T such that $T \cup E$ and $T^{-1} \cup E$ are both positive and disjoint; hence, as in Theorem 8, they define a proper direct decomposition. The conclusion is now obvious (cf. Thm. 7 for Lie *tl*-groups; [LOG], Thms. 25, 38 for σ-complete *tl*-groups).

A simple induction on dimension (using a T near E to decompose) now gives, in the case of Lie *tl*-groups,

Theorem 9. *The only Lie tl-groups are the powers* R^n *of the additive group of real numbers. Hence they are all commutative, Archimedean, and (conditionally) complete.*

It would seem as if a similar argument should enable one to show at least that every σ-complete *tl*-group was commutative[1]) (cf. a stronger conjecture in [LOG], p. 329).

---

[1]) We must prove $TU = UT$. We can easily reduce the problem to the l-ideal for which T is a weak unit. Then, following Freudenthal, but modifying the argument so as to avoid assuming commutativity, we should be able to express U as an integral of $\lambda dT(\lambda)$, and prove commutativity. — Incidentally, any σ-complete l-group is a *tl*-group under its intrinsic topology. (Cf. [*LOG*], § 24).

(Received the 9 march 1945.)

Separatdruck aus der

FESTSCHRIFT zum 60. Geburtstag von Prof. Dr. ANDREAS SPEISER

Zürich 1945, Orell Füßli Verlag

Lattice-ordered Rings

Garrett Birkhoff and R. S. Pierce *)

Harvard University, Cambridge, Massachussetts, U.S.A.

(Presented by L. Nachbin; received February 4, 1956)

1. PARTLY ORDERED RINGS.

This paper is devoted to the systematic foundation of a theory of lattice-ordered rings. Although there is an extensive literature concerning (simply) ordered rings and fields **), we know of only a few fragmentary results about lattice-ordered rings. These will be referred to in appropriate places below. The underlying concept is that of a partly ordered ring, defined as follows.

Definition. A partly ordered ring, or *po-ring*, is an (associative) ring which is partly ordered, and whose elements satisfy

(1) $a \geqq 0$ and $x \geqq y$ imply $a + x \geqq a + y$,

(2) $a \geqq 0$ and $b \geqq 0$ imply $ab \geqq 0$.

Remark 1. Although multiplication need not be commutative, addition is. Hence, any po-ring is a *commutative po-group* in the usual sense (G. Birkhoff, 1949, p. 214). Therefore, one can apply the known theory of such po-groups (G. Birkhoff, 1949, Ch. XIV) to such po-rings, to derive theorems not involving multiplication. Also, one can define an *l-ring, ordered ring,* or an *Archimedean po-ring* to be a po-ring which, regarded as a (commutative) po-group, is an *l-group,* ordered group, or Archimedean po-group, as the case may be.

Remark 2. Using (1), the reader will easily verify that condition (2) is equivalent to

(2′) $a \geqq 0$ and $x \geqq y$ imply $ax \geqq ay$

Example 1. Any ring can be made into a po-ring trivially, by defining $x \geqq y$ if and only if $x = y$.

*) Jewett fellow of the Bell Telephone Laboratories.

**) P. Dubreil, *Algèbre,* Ch. VC; N. Bourbaki, 1952, Livre II, Ch. VI; G. Birkhoff, 1949, pp. 227-228 and references given there.

EXAMPLE 2. Any po-group can be made into a po-ring by defining ab = 0 for all a and b. The resulting ring is a zero ring, which is an *l-ring* if the original po-group is an *l-group*.

Corresponding to the extreme generality of the preceding examples, and the meagerness of the general theories of rings and of po-groups, one finds that the general theory of po-rings is very slight. The following result *) is worth stating.

THEOREM 1. The set R^+ of all positive elements of a po-ring satisfies

(I) $0 \varepsilon R^+$, (II) $a \varepsilon R^+$ and $-a \varepsilon R^+$ imply $a = 0$,

(III) $a \varepsilon R^+$ and $b \varepsilon R^+$ imply $a + b \varepsilon R^+$ and $ab \varepsilon R^+$,

(IV) $a \geqq b$ if and only if $(a - b) \varepsilon R^+$.

Conversely, if R^+ is any subset of a ring R satisfying (I) — (III), then the relation $\geqq$ defined by (IV) makes R into a po-ring.

EXAMPLE 3. Let G be a commutative po-group satisfying the Moore-Smith condition, so that (G. BIRKHOFF, 1949, p. 217) $G = G^+ - G^+$. Let E(G) denote the ring of all endomorphisms of G; let $E(G)^+$ consist of those endomorphisms θ such that $G^+ \theta \leqq G^+$.

LEMMA 1. E(G) is a po-ring.

Proof. Conditions (I) and (III) of Theorem 1 are obvious. To prove (II), suppose $\theta \varepsilon E(G)^+$ and $-\theta \varepsilon E(G)^+$. Then for all $g \varepsilon G^+$, $g\theta = -(g(-\theta))$ is in G^+ and in $-G^+$; hence, $g\theta = 0$ for all $g \varepsilon G^+$. Since $G = G^+ - G^+$, it follows that $G\theta = G^+\theta - G^+\theta = 0$. Thus, $\theta = 0$.

EXAMPLE 4. Any ordered ring is a po-ring.

By definition, an ordered ring is just a po-ring in which, for any a, either $a > 0$, $a = 0$, or $-a > 0$ (trichotomy condition). We recall that, in an ordered ring, any sum of non-zero squares is positive (by (2)). As is well known, this property uniquely determines the order in the fields of real and rational numbers.

Though the property that all squares are positive does not hold for all l-rings (even in the commutative case; see Remark 3, § 4), it does define an interesting class of po-rings.

EXAMPLE 5. Let R be a commutative ring in which no sum of non-zero squares is zero. Then relative to the set R^+ of sum of squares, R is a partly ordered ring.

For conditions (I) and (III) of Theorem 1 are obvious, and (II) is assumed.

*) N. BOURBAKI, 1952, Livre II, Ch. VI, p. 32. The proof is like that of G. BIRKHOFF, 1949, Ch. XVI, theorem 1. The analog of theorem 2, *loc. cit.*, is also evident.

This example plays a basic role in the theory of formally real fields *), that is, fields in which no sum of non-zero squares is zero. It is known that any formally real field can be made into an ordered field.

2. LATTICE ORDERED RINGS.

We have already defined lattice-ordered rings, or l-rings, to be rings which are also lattice ordered groups (l-groups), and which satisfy (2). There are many kinds of l-rings besides the zero l-rings of Example 2 and the ordered rings of Example 4. We mention two.

EXAMPLE 6. Let R be a linear (associative) algebra over an ordered field K, with basis $\{e_i\}$, and multiplication defined by

(3) $$e_i\, e_j = \Sigma_k\, \gamma_{ij}^k\, e_k, \text{ with all } \gamma_{ij}^k \geqq 0.$$

Define R^+ as the set of $\Sigma\alpha_i\, e_i$ with all $\alpha_i \geqq 0$. Then R is an l-ring.

In particullar, every full matrix algebra $M_n(K)$ is an l-ring under this ordering, since $e_{ij}\, e_{kl} = 0$ if $j \neq k$, and $e_{ik}\, e_{kl} = e_{il}$. In $M_n(K)$, there are zero sums of non-zero squares:

$$\begin{pmatrix} 0 & 1 \\ -1 & 0 \end{pmatrix}^2 + \begin{pmatrix} -1 & 0 \\ 0 & -1 \end{pmatrix}^2 = \begin{pmatrix} 0 & 0 \\ 0 & 0 \end{pmatrix}$$

EXAMPLE 7. Let C(X) be the (commutative) ring of all continuous real-valued functions f(x) on a topological space X. Then C(X) is an l-ring under the usual definitions of $f + g$, fg, and of $C(X)^+$ as the set of all f with $f(x) \geqq 0$ for all $x \in X$.

Not every ring can be made into an l-ring; the rational complex numbers form a case in point (§ 5, Example 9g).

LEMMA 2. If G is a complete l-group, then the set $E^*(G)$ of bounded endomorphisms of G forms an l-ring.

Proof. In view of Lemma 1, one has only to show that $E^*(G)$ is a lattice. But this is known: (G. BIRKHOFF, 1949, p. 245).

By Remark 1 of § 1, we can apply to l-rings the usual notations of the theory of l-groups (G. BIRKHOFF, 1949, Ch. XIV), such as $a^+ = a \cup 0$, $a^- = a \cap 0$, $|a| = a^+ - a^-$. Besides the relations involving these operations which are valid in l-groups, there are others valid in l-rings.

THEOREM 2. In any l-ring R,

(4) $a \geqq 0$ implies $a(b \cup c) \geqq ab \cup ac$, $a(b \cap c) \leqq ab \cap ac$,
$(a \cup b)c \geqq ac \cup bc$, and $(a \cap b)c \leqq ac \cap bc$,

(5) $|ab| \leqq |a||b|$.

*) E. ARTIN AND SCHREIER, 1926, *Abh. Math. Sem. Hamburg* 5; B. L. VAN DER WAERDEN, 1930-1931, section 67; T. SZELE, 1952, *Proc. Amer. Math. Soc.* 3, 410-413; R. E. JOHNSON, *ibid.*, 414-416.

Proof. The inequalities (4) are clear, since $a(b \cup c) \geqq ab$ and $a(b \cup c) \geqq ac$ by (2′), etc. Also N. BOURBAKI, 1952, p. 150,

$$-|a||b| = -a^+b^+ + a^+b^- + a^-b^+ - a^-b^- \leqq a^+b^+ + a^+b^- + a^-b^+ + a^-b^- = ab \leqq a^+b^+ - a^+b^- - a^-b^+ + a^-b^- = |a||b|,$$

which proves (5).

We now come to a basic metamathematical theorem, which legitimizes the application of certain techniques of *universal algebra* *). A class of abstract algebras which can be characterized by identities involving finitary (e.g., binary) operations defined for *all* pairs of elements, is called *equationally definable*. It is known that commutative l-groups and rings are equationally definable. But an l-ring is just a ring which is also an l-group, satisfying (2). Since (2) is equivalent, in such a system, to the identity

(2″) $[(a \cup 0)(b \cup 0)] \cap 0 = 0,$

we obtain the following result.

THEOREM 3. The class of l-rings is equationally definable; so is the class of commutative l-rings.

COROLLARY 1. The class of l-rings is closed under the formation of subalgebras, direct unions and homomorphic images.

COROLLARY 2. The homomorphic images of any l-ring R are determined up to isomorphism by the congruence relations on R.

(Note that no corresponding result is true for po-rings. See § 3 for further results.)

COROLLARY 3. Every l-ring is a subdirect union of subdirectly irreducible l-rings (G. BIRKHOFF, 1949, p. 92).

For any cardinal number n, one can also speak of the free l-ring with n generators, but we shall not apply this concept here.

3. L-IDEALS AND L-RADICAL.

The theory of congruence relations on an l-ring is very simple.

DEFINITION. A subset I of an l-ring R is an l-ideal if $a \in I$, $b \in I$, $c \in R$ imply $a \pm b \in I$, $ac \in I$ and $ca \in I$, and if $a \in I$ and $|x| \leqq |a|$, then $x \in I$.

That is, the l-ideals of R are just the ring ideals which are also l-ideals in the sense of (G. BIRKHOFF, 1949, Ch. XIV). To avoid confusion, we will define an *l-module* of R to be a subset which is an *l-ideal* of R in

*) G. BIRKHOFF, 1949, Foreward on algebra; G. BIRKHOFF, Proc. First Canadian Math. Congress, 1945, 310-326. The suggestive phrase *equationally definable* seems to be due to TARSKI.

the sense of (G. BIRKHOFF, 1949, Ch. XIV), i.e., such that $a \varepsilon I$, $b \varepsilon I$ imply $a \pm b \varepsilon I$, and $a \varepsilon I$ and $|x| \leqq |a|$ in R imply $x \varepsilon I$.

THEOREM 4. The congruence relations on any l-ring R are the partitions of R into the cosets of its different l-ideals.

This theorem follows directly from the corresponding results in the theories of rings and l-groups, since a congruence relation on R, regarded as an l-ring, is simply one for R as an l-group and as a ring. We denote the quotient-ring of R modulo an l-ideal I, by R/I.

The l-ideals of an l-ring form a sublattice of the complete distributive lattice (G. BIRKHOFF, 1949, p. 222) of all l-modules of R. Clearly, any intersection of l-ideals is an l-ideal; so is the sum of any two l-ideals; hence we get

COROLLARY 1. The l-ideals of any l-ring R form a complete sublattice of the distributive lattice of all l-modules of R.

COROLLARY 2. If the lattice of all l-ideals of an l-ring R satisfies either chain condition, then R has a unique representation as a direct union of a finite number of indecomposable factors (see G. BIRKHOFF, 1949, p. 143).

The calculus of l-ideals in an l-ring is analogous to the calculus of ordinary ideals in an associative ring. The *sum* (or join) $I + J$ of two l-ideals I and J is defined as usual; the *l-product* $I \cdot J$ of I and J may be defined by

(6) $I \cdot J$ is the set of c with $|c| \leqq \Sigma a_i b_i$ for suitable $a_i \varepsilon I$, $b_i \varepsilon J$.

(This is equivalent to the set of c with $|c| \leqq ab$ for some $a \varepsilon I$, $b \varepsilon J$, since $\Sigma a_i b_i \leqq (\Sigma |a_i|) \Sigma |b_i|)$). We will write $I^2 = I \cdot I$, $I^3 = I \cdot I^2$, etc. It is easy to show that, if I, J, and K are all l-ideals of R, then $I \cdot (J + K) = (I \cdot J) + (I \cdot K)$. One can also define left and right l-ideals, but more interesting seems to be the concept of l-radical. Here, for the first time, the *associativity* of R is important.

DEFINITION. The l-radical of an l-ring is the set N of all $a \varepsilon R$ such that, for some positive integer $n = n(a)$,

(7) $x_0|a|x_1|a|x_2 \ldots x_{n-1}|a|x_n = 0$

for all $x_0, \ldots, x_n \varepsilon R$.

THEOREM 5. The l-radical of R is an l-ideal, which is the union of the nilpotent l-ideals of R. Every element of N is nilpotent.

Proof. If I is a nilpotent l-ideal with $I^n = 0$, then evidently (7) holds for all $a \varepsilon I$. Conversely, if $a \varepsilon N$ satisfies (7), then $(|a|R)^{n+1} = (R|a|)^{n+1} = (R|a|R)^n = (|a| + |a|R + R|a| + R|a|R)^{2n+1} = 0$; hence a is contained in a nilpotent l-ideal. Finally, (7) clearly implies $|a^{2n+1}| = 0$; every $a \varepsilon R$ is nilpotent.

COROLLARY 1. The l-radical of a commutative l-ring is the set of all elements $x \varepsilon R$ such that $|x|$ is nilpotent.

Proof. For any such s, the l-ideal J(x) of u ε R such that $|u| \leqq$ $\leqq n|x| + a|x|$ for some integer n and some a ε R, is nilpotent.

COROLLARY 2. If R is an l-ring which satisfies the ascending chain condition on l-ideals, then the radical of R is nilpotent.

Proof. If R satisfies the ascending chain condition, then it contains a maximal nilpotent l-ideal M, with $M^m = 0$, for some positive integer m. If $I^n = 0$, then $(I + M)^{m+n} = 0$, by the usual argument (N. JACOBSEN, 1943, p. 63). Hence, I + M, which obviously contains M, is nilpotent; since M is maximal, I + M > M is impossible. Therefore I + M = M, and $I \leqq M$. By theorem 5, M is the radical of R.

COROLLARY 3. If R is an l-ring which satisfies the descending chain condition on l-ideals, then the l-radical of R is nilpotent.

Proof. The proof is a slight modification of one, due to R. Brauer (N. JACOBSEN, 1943, p. 64), for the analogous theorem in associative rings. Let N be the l-radical of R. By the descending chain condition, for some integer y, $N^k = N^{k+1}$. Let $M = N^k$. Then $M^2 = M$. Assume $M \neq 0$. Let K be an l-ideal which is minimal with the properties: $K \leqq M$ and $M K M \neq 0$. This exists, since $M^3 = M \neq 0$. Then a ε K exists with $a \geqq 0$ and $M a M \neq 0$. Let $J = \{c \in R \,|\, |c| \leqq \Sigma m_i\, a\, m_i',\ m_i \text{ and } m_i' \text{ in } M\}$. Then J is an l-ideal with $0 \neq J \leqq K$ and $M J M \neq 0$. Hence, J = K by minimality. Thus $a \leqq m_1\, a\, m_1' + \ldots + m_r\, a\, m_r' \leqq m\, a\, m'$ where $m = |m_1| + \ldots + |m_r| \in M \cap R^+$ and $m' = |m_1'| + \ldots + |m_r'| \in M \cap R^+$. Then $a \leqq m\, a\, m' \leqq m^2\, a\, m'^2 \leqq \ldots \leqq m^n\, a\, m'^n = 0$ for suitably large n, because, by theorem 5, m and m' are nilpotent. This contradicts $M a M \neq 0$. Thus $M = 0$.

COROLLARY 4. If R is commutative, or if R satisfies either chain condition for l-ideals, then the l-radical of R/N is 0.

EXAMPLE 8. Let R_0 be the l-ring of all two-by-two real matrices, ordered as in Example 6. Define R_1 to be the subring of R_0 consisting of all real multiples of $E = \begin{pmatrix} 0 & 1 \\ 0 & 0 \end{pmatrix}$.

Now let R be the set of all infinite matrices (X_{ij}), i, j = 1, 2, ..., such that (1) $X_{ij} \in R_0$, (2) $X_{ij} = 0$ if $i \geqq j$, (3) each row contains only finitely many non-zero terms, and (4) $X_{ij} = \alpha_{ij} E \in R_1$ for all but a finite number of (i, j). Because of (3), R forms a ring with the usual mulltiplication. Moreover, if we define $R^+ = \{(X_{ij}) | X_{ij} \geqq 0 \text{ all } i, j\}$, then R becomes an l-ring.

Let N be the radical of R. By (2), it is clear that every (X_{ij}) with $X_{ij} = 0$ for all but a finite number of (i, j) is in N. In fact, it is not hard to show that N is precisely the set of such (X_{ij}) and in particular, $N \neq R$. On the other hand, it folllows from (4) and the fact that $E^2 = 0$, that the product of any two elements of R is zero except at a finite number of (i, j) and hence lies in N. Thus, R/N is a zero ring and in particular has non-zero radical. This shows that the conclusion of Corollary 4 is not true for all l-rings.

4. LATTICE ORDERED ALGEBRAS.

We shall now discuss a special class of l-rings which includes those defined in Example 6.

DEFINITION. By a lattice-orderea algebra, or *l-algebra,* is meant an l-ring which, regarded as an l-group, is a *vector lattice* (G. BIRKHOFF, 1949, Ch. XV) over an ordered field K.

Results analogous to these of §§ 2 — 3 hold also for l-algebras. In particular, the class of all l-algebras is equationally definable. Invariant l-subalgebras can be defined as l-ideals which are also subspaces over K; these correspond one-to-one to congruence relations. It is easy to show that the l-radical, defined by (7), is an invariant l-subalgebra; we omit the details.

Any finite-dimensional l-algebra A satisfies the ascending and descending chain conditions on invariant l-subalgebras. Hence, by Corollary 2 of Theorem 4, A can be uniquely represented as a direct product of directly indecomposable factors. Also, the radical N of A is nilpotent, so that the radical of A/N is zero.

More interesting is the enumeration of all two-dimensional l-algebras over the real field, because this shows how *pathological* l-algebras can be. (One dimensional l-algebras are either zero-algebras, or isomorphic with K: hence trivial.)

This enumeration is not difficult, if one uses the known classifications of two-dimensional real vector lattices and of two dimensional real linear associative algebras. It is known *) that there are seven non-isomorphic two-dimensional real linear associative algebras with basis e_1, e_2, all others being reducible to these by changes of basis. These are listed below. For each such algebra, there are generally many possible l-orderings. But, as a vector lattice, each real two-dimensional l-algebra A is isomorphic (G. BIRKHOFF, 1949, p. 240 either to R^2 (Archimedean case) or to $R \circ R$ (simply ordered, non-Archimedean case). Correspondingly, the sector A^+ of positive elements a satisfies either

a. (Archimedean) A^+: $\alpha \leqq \operatorname{Arg} a \leqq \beta$, $0 < \beta - \alpha < \pi$, or

b. (non-Archimedean) A^+: $\alpha < \operatorname{Arg} a \leqq \alpha + \pi$, or $\alpha \leqq \operatorname{Arg} a < \alpha + \pi$.

The condition (2), which specifies when A is an l-algebra, imposes restrictions on α, β in each case; we list these restrictions.

*) BIRKHOFF AND S. MACLANE, *Survey of Modern Algebra,* rev. ed., p. 242, exercices 12-14.

EXAMPLE 9a. Zero algebra: $ab = 0$. No restrictions on α, β other than those imposed above.

EXAMPLE 9b. Nilpotent algebra: $e_1^2 = e_2$, $e_1e_2 = e_2e_1 = e_2^2 = 0$. In the Archimedan and non-Archimedean cases alike, A^+ must contain e_2 (i.e., the y-axis).

In Examples 9c — 9e, the correspondence $e_1 \to e_1$, $e_2 \to -e_2$ is a ring-automorphism. After performing this automorphism if necessary, we can reduce to one of the cases described below.

EXAMPLE 9c. $e_1^2 = e_1$, $e_1e_2 = e_2e_1 = e_2^2 = 0$. In the Archimedean case, A^+ must contain e_1 (the x-axis), and be contained in the right half plane, $-\pi/2 \leqq \theta \leqq \pi/2$. In the non-Archimedean case, A^+ can be taken as the right half plane, $-\pi/2 < \theta \leqq \pi/2$.

EXAMPLE 9d. $e_1^2 = e_1$, $e_1e_2 = e_2$, $e_2e_1 = e_2^2 = 0$. In the Archimedean case, A^+ must lie in the right half plane. In the non-Archimedean case, A^+ is the same as in Example 9c.

EXAMPLE 9e. Dual numbers: $e_1^2 = e_1$, $e_1e_2 = e_2e_1 = e_2$, $e_2^2 = 0$. In the Archimedean case, $0 \leqq \alpha < \beta < \pi/2$. The non-Archimedean case is the same as in Example 9c.

EXAMPLE 9f. Direct sum: $e_1^2 = e_1$, $e_2^2 = e_2$, $e_1e_2 = e_2e_1 = 0$. In the Archimedean case, there are two possibilities:

(I) A^+ is the first quadrant, $\alpha = 0$ and $\beta = \pi/2$, or

(II) $-\pi/4 \leqq \alpha \leqq 0$, $\arctan(\tan^2 \alpha) \leqq \beta \leqq \pi/4$.

There are no non-Archimedean l-orderings.

EXAMPLE 9g. Complex numbers: $e_1^2 = e_1$, $e_1e_2 = e_2e_1 = e_2$, $e_2^2 = -e_1$. There are no l-orderings.

We give a detailed proof for Example 9g. Since $0 = e_1^2 + e_2^2$, the algebra cannot be simply ordered (discussion of Example 4). In the Archimedean case, the positive sector A^+ will subtend some angle $\gamma > 0$. By (2), $(A^+)^2 \leqq A^+$, but $(A^+)^2$ will subtend an angle 2γ. This leads to a contradiction.

The same argument shows that the rational complex numbers cannot be l-ordered so as to form an l-ring, since such an l-ordering would induce the usual order in the rationals (G. BIRKHOFF, 1949, p. 220, Lemma 3).

REMARK 3. Note that in Example 9e, if $\alpha > 0$, we get a commutative l-ring whose unity e_1 is not positive (though a square).

REMARK 4. In most cases, the l-ordering condition imposes no *natural* order.

REMARK 5. In Example 9f(II), the l-radical is 0, yet the commutative l-algebra is not the direct union of *simplle* l-algebras, since it has just one l-ideal, spanned by e_1.

EXAMPLE 10. Let $A = A(G)$ be the real group algebra of the finite group G. Lattice order A by defining $\Sigma\, \alpha_i\, g_i \geqq 0 (g_i \varepsilon G)$ if and only if all $\alpha_i \geqq 0$, as in Example 6. Since $g_i\, g_j = g_{(i,j)}$, A is an l-algebra.

REMARK 6. A(G) has no proper l-ideals. For if $J > 0$ is an l-ideal, it contains some positive $\Sigma\, \alpha_i\, g_i$. Hence, it contains some $\alpha_i\, g_i$ $(\alpha_i > 0)$, with $|\alpha_i\, g_i| \leqq |\Sigma\, \alpha_i\, g_i|$. Thus J contains the group identity $1 = (\alpha_i\, g_i)(\alpha_i^{-1}\, g_i^{-1})$, which is the ring unity of A(G). Consequently, being a ring ideal, $J = A(G)$. Hence, A(G) is a simple l-algebra, but not a full matrix algebra.

Remarks 5 and 6 show that the structure theory of l-algebras with zero l-radical does not parallel the Wedderburn theory of ordinary algebras with zero radical. In general, l-algebras can be quite *pathological*.

5. UNITS; ARCHIMEDEAN L-ALGEBRAS.

The concepts of strong unit and weak unit (G. BIRKHOFF, 1949, p. 223) apply to l-rings *qua* l-groups; we repeat the definition.

DEFINITION. A positive element e in an l-ring R is called a *weak* unit if

$$e \cap a = 0 \quad \text{implies} \quad a = 0 \text{ in } R,$$

and a *strong* unit if, for every $a \varepsilon R$, a positive integer n can be found such that $-n \cdot e \leqq a \leqq n \cdot e$.

In general l-rings with *ring-unity* 1 (such that $1 \cdot x = x \cdot 1 = x$ for all $x \varepsilon R$), the ring-unity need not be a weak unit (cf. the full matrix algebra of Example 6), or even positive (cf. Example 9e). However, in Example 7, it is always a weak unit, and a strong unit if X is compact. We shall develop the significance of this distinction further in § 8.

We shall now introduce, for vector lattices over an ordered field K, a concept of *strong unit over K*, which is equivalent to the preceding concept if K is Archimedean (e.g., real).

DEFINITION. Let V be a vector lattice over an ordered field K. An element $a \varepsilon V$ will be called a *strong unit* of V over K, if every $x \varepsilon V$ satisfies $x \leqq \alpha\, a$ for some $\alpha = \alpha(x) \varepsilon K$.

LEMMA 1. Each finite-dimensional vector lattice has a strong order unit.

Proof. Let $e_1, \ldots, e_n$ be any basis for V. Then $a = |e_1| + \ldots + |e_n|$ is strong order unit of V over K. For, if $x = \lambda_1\, e_1 + \ldots + \lambda_n\, e_n$, and $\alpha = |\lambda_1| + \ldots + |\lambda_n|$, then $\alpha\, a \geqq |\lambda_1||e_1| + \ldots + |\lambda_n||e_n| \geqq \lambda_1\, e_1 + \ldots + \lambda_n\, e_n = x$.

DEFINITION. Let V be a vector lattice with strong unit over K. The *i-radical* of V is the set i(V) of all $x \varepsilon V$ satisfying $\alpha\, |x| \leqq u$ for every strong unit u of V and every $\alpha \varepsilon K^+$.

REMARK 7. The preceding condition is also equivalent to $|x| \leqq u$ for every strong unit u in V. For if u is a strong unit over K, then so is α^{-1} u. Here and below, $\alpha > 0$ is assumed.

LEMMA 2. If A is an l-algebra with a strong unit over K, then i(A) is an invariant l-subalgebra of A which contains no strong unit over K. Every $x \varepsilon A$ satisfying $\alpha |x| \leqq v$ for one strong unit v of A and all $\alpha \varepsilon K^+$ is contained in i(A). Finally, $i(A/i(A)) = 0$.

Proof. Since $2u \nleqq u$, it is clear that i(A) contains no strong unit. Again, $\alpha|x| \leqq u$ and $\alpha|y| \leqq u$ imply $\alpha|x \pm y| \leqq \alpha|x| + \alpha|y| \leqq 2u$ for all $\alpha \varepsilon K^+$, whence $2\beta |x \pm y| \leqq 2u$ for all $\beta \varepsilon K^+$; so i(A) is a module. Also, $\alpha|x| \leqq u$ implies $\beta|\gamma x| \leqq u$ for all $\beta \varepsilon K$; hence i(A) is a subspace; it is an l-subspace since $|y| \leqq |x|$, $x \varepsilon i(A)$ imply $\alpha|y| \leqq \alpha|x| \leqq u$ for all $\alpha \varepsilon K^+$.

Again, suppose $x \varepsilon i(A)$ and $a \varepsilon A$. For any strong unit u, $|a|u \leqq \beta u$ for some $\beta \varepsilon K^+$. Hence, for any $\alpha \varepsilon K^+$, $\alpha|ax| \leqq \alpha|a||x| \leqq |a|u \leqq \beta u$; thus $(\beta^{-1}\alpha)|ax| \leqq u$ for all $(\beta^{-1}\alpha) \varepsilon K^+$, and $ax \varepsilon i(A)$. Similarly, $xa \varepsilon i(A)$, whence i(A) is an l-ideal.

If $\alpha|x| \leqq v$ for one strong unit v of A, and all $\alpha \varepsilon K^+$, and u is any other strong unit, then $\beta u \geqq v \geqq \alpha|x|$ for some $\beta \varepsilon K^+$ and all $\alpha \varepsilon K^+$, whence $(\beta^{-1}\alpha)|x| \leqq u$ for all $(\beta^{-1}\alpha) \varepsilon K^+$.

To prove the last assertion, let $x \to \bar{x}$ be the natural homomorphism of A onto A/i(A). If u is a strong unit of A over K, then $\bar{u}$ is a strong unit of A/i(A) over K. Suppose $\bar{x} \varepsilon i(A/i(A))$, that is, $\alpha|\bar{x}| \leqq \bar{u}$ for all $\alpha \varepsilon K^+$. Then $\alpha|x| \leqq u + y_\alpha$ where $y_\alpha \varepsilon i(A)$. But $y_\alpha \leqq u$, so $\alpha|x| \leqq 2u$. Hence, $x \varepsilon i(A)$ and $\bar{x} = 0$.

DEFINITION. Let V be a vector lattice over the ordered field K. Then V will be called *Archimedean* over K if, for any u, $v \varepsilon K^+$, $\alpha u \leqq v$ for all $\alpha \varepsilon K^+$ implies $u = 0$.

Thus, in Example 6, R is Archimedean over K. Conversely, it is known (G. BIRKHOFF, 1949, p. 240) that the only Archimedean vector lattices over the real field are those involved in Example 6.

COROLLARY. Every real, Archimedean l-algebra is isomorphic to an l-algebra of the type defined in Example 6.

LEMMA 3. If a vector lattice V has a strong unit u, then $i(V) = 0$ if and only if V is Archimedean.

Proof. If V is Archimedean over K, then $x \varepsilon i(V)$ implies $x = 0$ by definition; hence $i(V) = 0$. Conversely, if V is not Archimedean, then some $x > 0$ satisfies $\alpha x \leqq y$ for all $\alpha \varepsilon K^+$; hence, $\alpha x \leqq y < \beta u$ for some strong unit βu; thus $x \varepsilon i(V)$, and $i(V) > 0$.

THEOREM 6. If A is a finite-dimensional l-algebra over K, then $I = i(A)$ is contained in the l-radical of A.

Proof. By Theorem 5, it suffices to show that $I^n = 0$ for some n. Since A is finite-dimensional and each I^n is an invariant l-subalgebra, it is sufficient to prove that $I^{k+1} < I^k$ unless $I^k = 0$. This we now do.

By Lemma 1, I^k will have a strong unit u_k. Let u be a strong unit of A. Every $a \varepsilon I^{k+1}$ satisfies an inequality of the form $|a| \leqq \Sigma x_i y_i$, where $x_i \varepsilon I$ and $y_i \varepsilon I^k$. But for some $\beta, \gamma \varepsilon K^+$, $|x_i| \leqq \beta u_l$ and $|y_i| \leqq \gamma u_k$; hence, $|x_i y_i| \leqq \beta \gamma u_l u_k$. Also, since I^k is an l-ideal with strong unit u_k, the is a $\delta \varepsilon K^+$ such that $u u_k \leqq \delta u_k$. Hence, $\alpha|x_i y_i| \leqq \alpha\beta\gamma u_l u_k \leqq \beta\gamma u u_k \leqq \beta\gamma\delta u_k$, for all $\alpha \varepsilon K^+$, and fixed β, γ, δ. It follows that $x_i y_i \varepsilon i(I^k)$, whence $I^{k+1} \leqq i(I^k) < I$ (by Lemma 2, completing the proof.

COROLLARY 1. Let A be a finite dimensional l-algebra over K. If the l-radical N of A is 0, then A is Archimedean over K.

Proof. By Theorem 6, $i(A) \leqq N = 0$; hence, by Lemma 3, A is Archimedean.

COROLLARY 2. Let A be a finite-dimensional real l-algebra with zero l-radical. Then A is isomorphic to one of the algebras defined in Example 6.

Again, by (G. BIRKHOFF, 1949, p. 240), if V is an ordered, real vector lattice, then $V/i(V)$ is one-dimensional. This implies

COROLLARY 3. If A is an ordered, finite-dimensional, real l-algebra, then $A/i(A)$ is one-dimensional and A/N is at most one-dimensional.

6. REPRESENTATION THEORY.

In Example 3 and Lemma 1 of § 1, we have discussed po-rings of endomorphisms of commutative po-groups; actually, any po-ring can be represented in this way.

DEFINITION. By a *p-representation* of a po-ring R, is meant a ring homomorphism $r \to \theta_r$ of R into a po-ring E(G) of endomorphisms of a po-group G, such that $r \varepsilon R^+$ implies $g\,\theta_r \varepsilon G^+$ for all $g \varepsilon G^+$ (i.e., such that $r \varepsilon R^+$ implies $\theta_r \varepsilon E(G)^+$). A p-representation is called *faithful* if $r \to \theta_r$ is one-to-one and $r \varepsilon R^+$ if and only if $\theta_r \varepsilon E(G)^+$.

THEOREM 7. Let R be an associative po-ring with a positive ring-unity 1 satisfying $x1 = 1x = x$ identically. Then the correspondence

(8) $r \to \theta_r$: $x\,\theta_r = xr$,

defines a faithful p-representation of R, provided R satisfies the Moore-Smith condition $R = R^+ - R^+$.

Proof. By Lemma 1, § 1, E(R) is a po-ring. The correspondence $r \to \theta_r$ is a ring isomorphism (N. JACOBSON, 1943, p. 16) which defines the usual *regular* representation of R as a ring. By (2), $r \varepsilon R^+$ implies

$x\ \theta_r = xr \ \varepsilon\ R^+$ for all $x\ \varepsilon\ R^+$; hence $\theta_r\ \varepsilon\ E(R)^+$. Conversely, $\theta_r\ \varepsilon\ E(R)^+$ implies $r = lr = 1\ \theta_r\ \varepsilon\ R^+$.

More generally, if R is *any* associative po-ring, we can adjoin a positive ring-unity 1, forming R*, and faithfully p-represent R in E(R*).

In general, E(G) is not an l-ring. In fact, if G is a finite dimensional vector lattice over the real field, then E(G) is an l-ring if and only if G is Archimedean. (This fact is easily proved using (G. BIRKHOFF, 1949 p. 240), Lemma 2, 2, Theorem 5 and Theorem 6.) Thus if G is the lexicographic union of two replicas of the real field, then E(G) does not even satisfy the Moore-Smith condition. Nevertheless, all of the non-Archimedean algebras of Examples 9a-9e have natural representations in E(G).

DEFINITION. A p-representation will be called an *l-representation* if R is an l-ring, G an l-group, and

(9a) $\theta_{a \cup b} = \theta_a \cup \theta_b$ and (9b) $\theta_{a \cap b} = \theta_a \cap \theta_b$

LEMMA 1. Let Φ: $g \to g\ \Phi = h$ be any group-homomorphism from an l-group G into an l-group H. Then each of the following conditions is necessary and sufficient for Φ to be an l-group-homomorphism:

(10a) $(g \cup g')\Phi = g\Phi \cup g'\Phi$, (10b) $(g \cap g')\Phi = g\Phi \cap g'\Phi$,

(10c) $|g|\ \Phi = |g\ \Phi|$, (10d) $g^+\ \Phi = (g\ \Phi)^+$,

(10e) $g \cap g' = 0$ implies $g\ \Phi \cap g'\ \Phi = 0$.

Proof. Clearly (10a)-(10b) are jointly necessary and sufficient; hence we need only show that each of conditions (10a) — (10e) implies all the others. First, (10a) implies $(g \cap g')\Phi = -[(-g) \cup (-g')]\Phi = -[(-g)\Phi \cup (-g')\Phi]$ by (10a) $= -[(-g\Phi) \cup (-g'\Phi)] = g\Phi \cap g\Phi$, or (10b). Dually, (10b) implies (10a). Again, (10a) implies (10c), setting $g' = -g$; (10a) implies (10d), setting $g' = 0$. Conversely, since $g \cup g' = (g - g')^+ + g$, (10d) implies (10a); since $g + |g| = 2g^+$, (10c) and (10d) are equivalent. This proves the equivalence of (10a) — (10d). Finally, (10b) trivially implies (10e). Conversely, if (10e) is satisfied and g and g' are any elements of G, $[g - (g \cap g')] \cap [g' - (g \cap g')] = 0$, so $g\Phi \cap g'\Phi - (g \cap g')\Phi = [g - (g \cap g')]\Phi \cap [g' - (g \cap g')]\Phi = 0$. Thus (10b) is satisfied.

COROLLARY. For a p-representation to be an l-representation, each of the following conditions is necessary and sufficient:

(9a) $\theta_{a \cup b} = \theta_a \cup \theta_b$, (9b) $\theta_{a \cap b} = \theta_a \cap \theta_b$,

(9c) $\theta_{|a|} = |\theta_a|$, (9d) $\theta_{a+} = (\theta_a)^+$,

(9e) $a \cap b = 0$ implies $\theta_a \cap \theta_b = 0$.

COROLLARY 2. An l-representation is faithful if and only if it is one-to-one.

Proof. If $a \to \theta_a$ is a one-to-one l-representation, then $\theta_a \geqq 0$ implies $\theta_{a-(a \cup 0)} = \theta_a - \theta_{a \cup 0} = \theta_a - \theta_a \cup 0 = \theta_a - \theta_a = 0$; thus $a = a \cup 0$ and $a \geqq 0$.

If A is an l-algebra over an ordered field K, then we can define a *K-invariant* l-representation of A to be an l-representation $a \to \theta_a$ of A in E(V), where V is a vector lattice over K, such that $\alpha(x\theta_a) = x\theta_{\alpha a}$ where $\alpha \in K$, $x \in V$ and $a \in A$. If a has a positive ring-unity 1 and if $a \to \theta_a$ is an l-representation of A in E(G) such that θ_1 is the identity endomorphism of G, then G can be considered as a vector lattice over K by definin $\alpha g = g\,\theta_{\alpha 1}$ and with this definition, θ is a K-invariant l-representation.

LEMMA 2. Let V be a vector lattice over the ordered field K. Suppose V has a *canonical basis* $\{e_1, e_2, \ldots, e_n\}$, such that $\Sigma\alpha_i e_i \geqq 0$ if and only if all $\alpha_i \geqq 0$. Let A be an l-algebra over K and suppose θ is a p-representation of A in E(V) which is K-invariant. Then θ is an l-representation if and only if

(11) $a \cap b = 0$ implies $e_i\,\theta_a \cap e_i\,\theta_b = 0$ for $i = 1, 2, \ldots, n$.

Proof. Suppose θ is an l-representation. Then $a \cap b = 0$ implies $\theta_a \cap \theta_b = 0$. Define $e_i\,\Phi = e_i\,\theta_a \cap e_i\,\theta_b$ for all i and extend Φ linearly to an endomorphism of V. Clearly, $0 \leqq \Phi \leqq \theta_a, \theta_b$. Thus $\Phi = 0$ and (11) follows. Reversing the argument shows that if (11) is satisfied, then $a \cap b = 0$ implies $\theta_a \cap \theta_b = 0$. Thus, by Corollary 1 of Lemma 1, Φ is an l-representation.

There is a very simple theory of the *reducibility* of l-rings Θ of endomorphisms of commutative l-groups G. We may say that an l-module J of G half-reduces Θ, if and only if (12) $x \in J$ and $\theta \in \Theta$ imply $x\,\theta \in J$. It is easy to show that, under these circumstances, Θ is also ring homomorphic to a subring of E(G/J). Moreover, if G is a vector lattice over an ordered field K and if G has a canonical basis as in Lemma 2, and finally if J is a K-module, then Θ has a natural K-invariant l-representation in E(G/J): $\theta \to \theta$, where $(x + J)\theta = x\theta + J$. This follows from Lemma 2. Whether or not every l-module of an arbitrary l-group G which half reduces Θ defines an l-representation of Θ, we do not know.

LEMMA 3. The l-modules of G which half-reduce Θ are a sublattice of the distributive lattice of all l-modules of G.

We omit the proof, which is trivial .It follows (G. BIRKHOFF, 1949, p. 157, Theorem 2) that the l-modules which fully reduce Θ form a Boolean algebra. Much as in (G. BIRKHOFF, 1949, p. 143), this gives a strongly unique canonical reduction of l-algebras of matrices, regarded as algebras of linear transformations of the n-dimensional Archimedean vector lattice R^n.

EXAMPLE 11. Let A be a real, Archimedean l-algebra with the canonical basis $\{e_1, e_2\}$, with $e_1e_2 = e_2e_1 = e_1$, $e_2^2 = e_2$, $e_1^2 = \delta\, e_1 + (1 + \delta)\, e_2$, δ being a real number satisfying $0 < \delta < 1$ (see Example 9f). Thus e_2 is the ring-unity of A.

We will show that A has no l-representation by finite dimensional matrices such that e_2 is represented by the unit matrix. This is equivalent, by Lemma 2, § 6, to showing that there exists no finite matrix $T = (t_{ij})$ such that $t_{ij} \geqq 0$, $t_{ii} = 0$ for all i, j, and which satisfies $T^2 = \delta T + (1 + \delta) I$.

Suppose T were such a matrix. Then

(a) $\Sigma_k t_{ik} t_{kj} \delta t_{ij}$ if $i \neq j$ and

(b) $\Sigma_k t_{ik} t_{ki} = 1 + \delta$ for all i.

First we observe that $t_{ij} t_{ij} \leqq \delta^2$. This is clear if $t_{ij}t_{ji} = 0$; otherwise, since $\delta t_{ij} = \Sigma_k t_{ik} t_{kj}$, there exists $k \neq i, j$ such that $t_{ik} > 0$. By (a), $t_{ji}t_{ik} \leqq \delta t_{jk}$, so $t_{jk} > 0$ and $t_{ij}t_{jk} \leqq \delta t_{ik}$. Multiplying gives $t_{ij} t_{ji} t_{ik} t_{jk} \leqq \delta^2 t_{ik} t_{jk}$ and hence $t_{ij}t_{ji} \leqq \delta^2 < 1$. In particular, $(t_{ij}t_{ji})^2 \leqq t_{ij}t_{ji}$.

Now let $i \neq k$. Then by (a), $\delta^2 t_{ik}t_{ki} = (\Sigma_j t_{ij} t_{jk})(\Sigma_m t_{km} t_{mi}) \geqq \Sigma_j (t_{ij}t_{ji})(t_{jk}t_{kj})$. Summing both sides over all k ($\neq$ i) and using (b) gives $\delta^2(1 + \delta) \geqq \Sigma_j(t_{ij}t_{ji})(1 + \delta - t_{ji}t_{ij}) = (1 + \delta)^2 - \Sigma_j(t_{ij}t_{ji})^2 \geqq (1 + \delta)^2 - \Sigma_j(t_{ij}t_{ji}) = (1 + \delta)^2 - (1 + \delta)$. Cancelling gives $\delta^2 \geqq \delta$, which is impossible if $0 < \delta < 1$.

7. REGULAR L-RINGS.

We have seen above (Examples 9a — 9g, 11, Remarks 3 — 6) that l-rings can be quite pathological. This suggests looking for special classes of l-rings having a deeper theory. Such a class seems to be that of *regular* l-rings, in the sense which we will now define.

DEFINITION. An l-ring is *regular* if and only if its regular representation is an l-representation.

From Theorem 7, and the Corollary of Lemma 1, we deduce immediately

THEOREM 8. For an l-ring to be regular, it is necessary and sufficient that $a \cap b = 0$ imply $\theta_a \cap \theta_b = 0$, where θ is the regular representation of R.

EXAMPLE 12. Let A be an l-algebra over an ordered field K, which admits a *canonical basis* E with the property that $\alpha_1 e_1 + \ldots + \alpha_n e_n \geqq 0$ ($e_i \in E$) if and only if all $\alpha_i \in K^+$.

COROLLARY 1. In example 12, E(A) is an l-algebra. A is regular if and only if $r \neq s$ implies $e_i e_r \cap e_i e_s = 0$ for all i.

This corollary is a special case of Lemma 2, § 6.

COROLLARY 2. Every group algebra is regular (Example 10).

COROLLARY 3. Every full matrix algebra is regular (Example 6).

It is obvious that any zero l-ring is regular. So is any direct union of regular l-rings. It is also obvious that the ring unity (if any) of any regular l-ring is positive. Further, we have.

THEOREM 9. Let A be an (Archimedan) l-algebra over K, having a canonical basis $e_1, \ldots, e_n$. If A is regular and J is an l-invariant subalgebra, then A/J is regular.

Proof. As an l-module, J is spanned by a finite subset of the canonical basis; hence, A/J can be constructed from A by suppressing this subset. In view of Corollary 1 of Theorem 8, the regularity of A/J is now obvious.

COROLLARY. Any homomorphic image of a real, finite-dimensional, regular, Archimedean l-algebra is regular.

However, the l-subalgebras of a regular l-algebra need not be regular. Thus, let $A = A(G)$ be the regular group algebra (Example 10) of a non-commutative group G, and let Z be the center of A. Then Z is a subalgebra and sublattice, since (B. L. VAN DER WAERDEN, 1930-1931, vol. 2, p. 164) it consists of the $\Sigma\alpha_i\, c_i$, where the $c_i = \Sigma x^{-1}\, g_i\, x$ are (disjoint) sums of complete classes of conjugate elements. Hence the c_i are a canonical basis for the l-subalgebra Z. To show that Z is not regular, we need only exhibit distinct c_j, c_k with $c_ic_j \cap c_ic_k = 0$ for some i, by the Corollary 1 of Theorem 8. Now $c_ic_j > 0$ and if $c_ic_j \cap c_ic_k = 0$ for all $j \neq k$, then it follows that $c_ic_j = \alpha_{ij}\, c_{k(i,\, j)}$ where $\alpha_{ij} > 0$.

Consequently, the mapping $g_i \rightarrow c_i = \Sigma^{-1} g_i x$ is a homomorphism of G with kernel 1, that is an isomorphism, which is possible only if G is commutative. In particular, if G is the symmetric group on three letters, $c_1 = e$, c_2 is the sum of two-cycles, and c_3 of three-cycles, then $c_2c_1 \cap c_2c_3 = c_2 \cap 2c_2 = c_2$.

8. FUNCTION RINGS.

We shall now turn our attention to a still more special class of l-rings, which we shall call *function rings*, or *f-rings*, because they typically consist of functions with values in an ordered ring (or field). We shall define this class of l-rings abstractly.

DEFINITION. An *f-ring* is an l-ring in which

(13) $a \cap b = 0$ and $c \geqq 0$ imply $ca \cap b = ac \cap b = 0$.

An *f-algebra* is an l-algebra over an ordered field K, which satisfies (13) i.e., is an f-ring.

EXAMPLE 13. Any ordered ring is an f-ring. Any direct union of ordered rings is an f-ring. Any sub-ring of an f-ring is an f-ring. Hence, any sub-direct union of ordered rings is an f-ring.

EXAMPLE 14. Any zero l-ring is an f-ring. (See § 1.)

EXAMPLE 15. Let R be any l-ring; let S be the subset of *splitting elements* $s \in R$ such that $|s|b \cap c = b|s| \cap c = 0$, if $b \cap 0$.

Then S is an l-module and l-subring of R which is an f-ring. It contains the ring unity of R, if this is positive.

THEOREM 10. *Let R be an l-ring with ring-unity 1. If 1 is a strong unit, then R is an f-ring. Conversely, if R is an f-ring, then 1 is a weak unit.*

Proof. (cf. G. BIRKHOFF, 1949, p. 150, (33)). Let $a \cap b = 0$ and $c \geqq 0$. If 1 is a strong unit, then $0 \leqq c \leqq n\ 1$ for some integer n. Hence, by the theory of l-groups (G. BIRKHOFF, 1949, p. 219), $0 \leqq ca \cap b \leqq \leqq n\, a \cap b = 0$. Similary, $ac \cap b = 0$. Conversely, in an f-ring, $a \cap 1 = 0$ implies $a = a \cap a = a \cap (1\ a) = 0$.

COROLLARY. *A finite-dimensional Archimedean l-algebra with unity is an f-algebra, if and only if its unity is a weak unit.*

For, in this case, a weak unit is necessarily a strong unit.

LEMMA 1. *An l-ring is an f-ring if and only if its elements satisfy the following identities:*

(14) $(a \cup 0) \cap (-a \cup 0)(c \cup 0) = 0,$

(14′) $(a \cup 0) \cap (c \cup 0)(-a \cup 0) = 0.$

Proof. In an l-group, the set of pairs a, b with $a \cap b = 0$ is the set of pairs $(a \cup 0), (-a \cup 0) = b$ by G. BIRKHOFF, 1949, p. 220, lemma 2, and the set of $c \geqq 0$ is the set of $c \cup 0$. The result is now obvious.

THEOREM 11. *The class of l-rings is an equationally definable class of abstract algebras.*

COROLLARY. *Any f-ring is a subdirect union of subdirectly irreducible f-rings.*

(The proof is immediate by G. BIRKHOFF, 1949, 92, Theorem 10).

LEMMA 2. *In any f-ring R, the set K(a) of alll $x \varepsilon R$ disjoint from a (i.e., such that $|a| \cap |x| = 0$) is an l-ideal. The set J(a) of all $y \varepsilon R$ with $|y| \leqq n|a| + b_1|a| + |a|b_2 + c_1|a|c_2$ for some positive integer n and elements b_1, b_2, c_1, c_2 of R^+ is an l-ideal. Moreover, $J(a) \cap K(a) = 0$.*

Proof. In any l-group, K(a) is an l-module (G. BIRKHOFF, 1949, p. 219, 232); by (13), it is an l-ideal in an f-ring. K(a) is clearly an l-ideal in any l-ring. In an f-ring, if $|x| \cap |a| = 0$, then $|x| \cap (n|a| + b_1|a| + |a|b_2 + + c_1|a|c_2) = 0$ by (13) and G. BIRKHOFF, 1949, p. 219, Theorem 6, so $x \varepsilon J(a) \cap K(a)$ implies $x = 0$.

LEMMA 3. *Any subdirectly irreducible f-ring is simply ordered.*

Proof. If R is not simply ordered, then it contains incomparable elements x and y. Hence, $a = (x - y)^+$ and $b = (y - x)^+$ are disjoint positive elements in R. Hence, the l-ideals J(a) and K(a) respectively contain a and b and $J(a) \cap K(a) = 0$. Thus R is subdirectly reducible.

Conversely, any ordered ring is a sub-directly irreducible f-ring, since its l-ideals form a chain (G. BIRKHOFF, 1949, p. 226, Example 1).

COROLLARY. Any f-field is simly ordered.

Proof. Any field is simple, hence subdirectly irreducible. In fact, any l-simple f-ring is simply ordered for the same reason.

Combining Theorem 11 and Lemma 3, and comparing with Example 13, we get

THEOREM 12. An l-ring is an f-ring, if and only if it is a subdirect union of ordered rings.

REMARK 10. By using l-invariant subalgebras, the preceding proof can be modified to show that any f-algebra over an ordered field K is a subdirect union of ordered f-algebras over K.

COROLLARY 1. In any f-ring R, the following identities are satisfied (N. JACOBSON, 1943, p. 150)

(15) if $a \geqq 0$, then $a(b \cup c) = ab \cup ac$, $a(b \cap c) = ab \cap ac$,
$(b \cup c)a = ba \cup ca$, and $(b \cap c)a = ba \cap ca$;

(16) $|ab| = |a| \cdot |b|$;

(17) if $a \cap b = 0$, then $ab = 0$;

(18) $a^2 \geqq 0$ for all $a \in R$; in particular, if R has a ring unity 1, then $1 \geqq 0$;

(19) $(a, b, c)d = (ad, bd, cd)$ and $a(b, c, d) = (ab, ac, ad)$

(In (19), (a, b, c) denotes the median operation.)

Proof. Equations (15) — (19) are obvious in an ordered ring, and they are preserved under subdirect union.

COROLLARY 2. Let A be a finite-dimensional Archimedean f-algebra over the real field. Then A has the form of example 6, with $e_ie_j = 0$ if $i \neq j$, and $e_i^2 = e_i$ or 0.

Proof. By (17), and the Corollary of Lemma 2, § 5.

COROLLARY 3. Any f-ring is regular.

COROLLARY 4. Any f-ring without zero divisors is simply ordered.

Proof. By (17), $a^+ \cdot a^- = 0$ in any f-ring. Hence, if R is without zero-divisors, $a^+ = 0$, or $a^- = 0$, so that $a \geqq 0$, or $a \leqq 0$.

LEMMA 4. In any f-ring, if $a \geqq 0$, $b \geqq 0$, and is any positive integer, then

(20) $n\,|ab - ba| \leqq a^2 + b^2$.

Proof. It suffices to prove (20) for ordered rings, by Theorem 12. In an ordered ring, we can suppose $a \geqq b$. Then for some integer k, $nb = ka + r$, where $0 \leqq r < a$. Hence,
$n|ab - ba| = |ka^2 + ar - ka^2 - ra| = |ar - ra| \leqq a^2 \leqq a^2 + b^2$.

THEOREM 13. Any Archimedean f-ring is commutative.

This is a corollary of Lemma 4.

REMARK. All the properties of f-rings which we have proved in § 8 remain valid if associativity is not assumed. (The definition of J(a) in Lemma 2 has to be modified slightly, but otherwise the proofs are valid as given.) Using an argument like the proof of Lemma 4, it is possible to show, without associativity, that if $a \geqq 0$, $b \geqq 0$, $c \geqq 0$ and n is any integer, then

$$n|(ab)c - a(bc)| \leqq (ab)(a+b+ab) + a(a+a^2+ba) + (cb)(c+b+cb) + \\ + c(c+c^2+bc);$$

hence, *any Archimedean f-ring is associative*.

9. PARTIAL CHARACTERIZATIONS OF F-RINGS.

The preceding results give a partial characterization of f-rings. In particular, the *distributive* laws (15) are quite characteristic for f-rings; so are (16) and (19). In fact, we have

LEMMA 1. In any l-ring (ont assumed to be associative), each of the three identities (15), (16), (19) implies the other two.

Proof. (16) implies (15) by Lemma 1, § 6. Also, (19) implies (15), since if $c \geqq a, b$, then $(a, b, c) = a \cup b$ and if $d \geqq 0$, then $cd \geqq ad, bd$, so $(ad, bd, cd) = ad \cup bd$. Thus, by (19), $(a \cup b)d = (a, b, c)d = (ad, bd, cd) = ad \cup bd$. Similarly, $d(a \cap b) = da \cap db$, and dually.

Conversely, suppose (15) is satisfied. We will show that (16) and (19) also hold. It is convenient to note two identities from the theory of commutative l-groups:

(i) $|a| \cap |b| = 0$ implies $|a| + |b| = |a + b|$,

(ii) if a_1, b_1, c_1 are each disjoint from all of a_2, b_2, c_2, then
$$(a_1, b_1, c_1) - (a_2, b_2, c_2) = (a_1 - a_2, b_1 - b_2, c_1 - c_2).$$

Both (i) and (ii) are obvious in an ordered, commutative group and hence are valid by G. BIRKHOFF, 1949, p. 224, Theorem 13 in any commutative l-group.

Now, by Lemma 1, § 6, (16) is a consequence of (15) whenever $b \geqq 0$. Thus $|ab^+| = |a|b^+$ and $|ab^-| = -|a|b^-$. Hence, using (i),

$$|a||b| = |a|b^+ - |a|b^- = |ab^+| + |ab^-| = |ab^+ + ab^-| = |ab|,$$

since $|ab^+| \cap |ab^-| \leqq |a||b^+| \cap |a||b^-| = |a|(|b^+| \cap |b^-|) = 0$.

Also, it is clear that (15) implies (19) if $d \geqq 0$. Thus, using (ii),

$$(a,b,c)d = (a,b,c)d^+ + (a,b,c)d^- = (ad^+, bd^+, cd^+) - (-ad^-, -bd^-, -cd^-) \\ = (ad^+ + ad^-, bd^+ + bd^-, cd^+ + cd^-) = (ad, bd, cd),$$

since each of ad^+, bd^+, cd^+ is disjoint from all of $-ad^-$, $-bd^-$, $-cd^-$. For instance,

$$0 \leqq |ad^+| \cap |bd^-| \leqq |a||d^+| \cap |b||d^-| \leqq (|a| \cup |b|)|d^+| \cap (|a| \cup |b|)|d^-|$$
$$= (|a| \cup |b|)(|d^+| \cap d^-|) = 0.$$

Example 9b, with $\alpha = 0$ and $\beta = \pi/2$, is an instance of an l-ring satisfying (15), (16) and (19), which is not an f-ring. That (15) is *almost* equivalent to the defining condition (13), is however shown by the following result.

THEOREM 14. Let R be an l-ring which satisfies (15), and

(i) $ac = 0$ for all $c \in R$ implies $a = 0$, and

(i′) $ca = 0$ for all $c \in R$ implies $a = 0$.

Then R is an f-ring.

Proof. If $a \cap b = 0$, $c \geqq 0$, and $d \geqq 0$, then by (15)

$$0 \leqq d(ca \cap b) = dca \cap db \leqq (dc \cup d), a \cap (dc \cup d)b =$$
$$= (dc \cup d)\ (a \cap b) = 0.$$

It follows that $d(ca \cap b) = 0$ for all $d \in R$. Hence, by (i), $ca \cap b = 0$. Similarly, $ac \cap b = 0$, q.e.d.

COROLLARY 1. If R is an l-ring with a ring-unity, or zero l-radical, then (15) is equivalent to (13).

COROLLARY 2. Any lattice-ordered field F, in which every square is positive, is simply ordered.

Proof. If $c \geqq 0$, then $c^{-1} = c(c^{-1})^2 \geqq 0$. Hence, $a \rightarrow ac$ has the order preserving inverse $a \rightarrow ac^{-1}$, and is a lattice-automorphism. By Corollary 1, F is therefore an f-ring. It then follows from Corollary 4 of Theorem 12 that F is simply ordered.

It should be observed that a field may be an l-ring without being simply ordered. For example, the field obtained by adjoining the square root of two to the rational numbers can be lattice-ordered by definind $\alpha + \beta\sqrt{2} \geqq 0$ if and only if $\alpha \geqq 0$ and $\beta \geqq 0$. Clearly, this is not a simple ordering.

LEMMA 2. In an l-ring R, the condition

(17) if $a \cap b = 0$, then $ab = 0$,

implies that all squares in R are positive.

Proof. If (17) is satisfied, then for any $c \in R$, $c^+c^- = c^-c^+ = 0$. Thus, $c^2 = (c^+)^2 + (c^-)^2 \geqq 0$.

The converse of Lemma 2 is false. In Example 9b with $\alpha = \pi/4$, $\beta = 3\pi/4$, every square is positive, but (17) fails.

The Example 9d with $\alpha = 0$, $\beta = \pi/2$ shows that condition (15) alone does not imply (17). Of course, if the conditions (i) and (i′) of Theorem 14 are satisfied, then (15) implies (13) and consequently (17). Moreover

LEMMA 3. If R is an l-ring satisfying (15) which is either commutative or has the property that all squares are positive, then R satisfies (17).

Proof. Suppose first that R is commutative. Then if $a \cap b = 0$, $0 = (a \cup b)(a \cap b) = (a^2 \cup ba) \cap (ab \cup b^2) \geqq ba \cap ab = ab \geqq 0$.

Now suppose that R has the property that all squares are positive. Then if a, b are positive, $ab \leqq ab + ba = a^2 + b^2 - (a - b)^2 \leqq a^2 + b^2$; thus $a \cap b = 0$ implies

$0 \leqq ab = ab \cap (a^2 + b^2) \leqq (ab \cap a^2) + (ab \cap b^2) = a(a \cap b) + (a \cap b)b = 0$, or $ab = 0$.

LEMMA 4. If R is an l-ring which contains no non-zero, positive, nilpotent elements, then R satisfies (17) if and only if R is an f-ring.

Proof. If $a \cap b = 0$ and $c \geqq 0$, then $ab = ba = 0$ by (17). Hence, $0 \leqq (ac \cap b)^2 \leqq b(ac) = (ba)c = 0$. Thus, $ac \cap b = 0$. Similarly, $ca \cap b = 0$.

COROLLARY. A commutative l-ring with zero l-radical satisfies (17) if and only if it is an f-ring.

If R is an l-ring in which (17) is satisfied, and if R has a ring-unity 1, then $1 \geqq 0$ (by Lemma 2) and 1 is a weak order unit. For if $a \cap 1 = 0$, then $a = a \cdot 1 = 0$. It is remarkable that the converse of this observation is true.

THEOREM 15. Let R be an l-ring with a positive ring unity 1. Then R satisfies

(17) $a \cap b = 0$ implies $ab = 0$

if and only if 1 if a weak order unit.

For the proof, we need a lemma which is of independent interest.

LEMMA 5. Let R be an l-ring with a positive unity 1 which is a weak order unit. If $a \in R^+$ is such that $a \cap 1$ is nilpotent, then $a \leqq 1$. Thus, if a is a positive, nilpotent element in R, then $a \leqq 1$.

Proof. First, we show that $a \cap 2 \leqq 1$. Let B(R) be the set of all *bounded* elements of R: $B(R) = \{x \in R \mid |x| \leqq n$ for some integer multiple n of $1\}$. Clearly, B(R) is an l-module and a subring of R. By Theorem 10, B(R) is an f-ring. New $a \cap 2 \in B(R)$. If $a \cap 2 \leqq 1$, then by Theorem 12, there is a homomorphism $b \to \bar{b}$ of B(R) onto an ordered ring such that $\bar{a} \cap \bar{2} > \bar{1}$ Thus, $\overline{a \cap 1} = \bar{a} \cap \bar{2} \cap \bar{1} = \bar{1}$, so $\overline{a \cap 1}$

is not nilpotent. But this is impossible if $a \cap 1$ is nilpotent. Consequently, $a \cap 2 \leqq 1$.

It follows from $a \cap 2 \leqq 1$ that $(a - 1) \cap 1 \leqq 0$, or $((a - 1) \cup 0) \cap 1 = 0$. Since 1 is a weak unit, this implies $(a - 1) \cup 0 = 0$, or $a - 1 \leqq 0$. Hence, $a \leqq 1$.

Proof of Theorem 15. Case I: $a \cap b = 0$, $a \leqq 1$ and $b \leqq 1$. Multiplying the inequality $a \leqq 1$ by b gives $ab \leqq b$. Similarly, $ab \leqq a$. Hence $0 \leqq a \leqq a \cap b = 0$, so $ab = 0$.

Case II: $a \cap b = 0$ and $b \leqq 1$. We will show that $ab = 0$; the same proof, with terms appropriately commuted at each step, shows that $ba = 0$.

Put $a' = a - a \cap 1$, $c = 1 - a \cap 1$. The proof is in eight steps.

a) $a' \cap c = (a - a \cap 1) \cap (1 - a \cap 1) = (a \cap 1) - (a \cap 1) = 0$.

b) $cb = (1 - a \cap 1)b = b - (a \cap 1)b = b$, since $(a \cap 1) \cap b = 0$ and hence $(a \cap 1)b = 0$ by case I.

c) $a'c \leqq a'$, because $c \leqq 1$ and $a' \geqq 0$ (see (2')).

d) $c(a'c \cap 1) = 0$. For $0 \leqq c \cap (a'c \cap 1) \leqq c \cap a' = 0$, by a), so $c(a'c \cap 1) = 0$ by case I.

e) $(a'c \cap 1)^2 = 0$, since $0 \leqq (a'c \cap 1)^2 \leqq (a'c)(a'c \cap 1) = a'(c(a'c \cap 1)) = 0$, by d).

f) $a'c \leqq 1$, by d) and lemma 5.

g) $a'b = 0$, because $0 \leqq a'c \cap b \leqq a' \cap b \leqq a \cap b = 0$ by c), and hence $a'b = a'(cb) = (a'c)b = 0$ by b), f) and case I.

h) $ab = (a' + a \cap 1)b = a'b + (a \cap 1)b = 0$, by g) and case I.

Case III: $a \cap b = 0$. Put $a' = a - a \cap 1$. By a) of case II, $a' \cap (1 - a \cap 1) = 0$. Thus, by case II, $a' - a'(a \cap 1) = a'(1 - a \cap 1) = 0$, that is, $a' = a'(a \cap 1)$. Consequently,

$ab = (a' + a \cap 1)b = a'b + (a \cap 1)b = a'(a \cap 1)b + (a \cap 1)b = 0$, by case II, since $(a \cap 1) \cap b = 0$.

Corollary 1. An l-ring with a positive ring-unity 1 and no non-zero, positive, nilpotent elements is an f-ring if and only if 1 is a weak order unit.

Proof. By Theorem 15 and Lemma 4.

Corollary 2. A commutative l-ring with zero l-radical and a positive ring-unity 1 is an f-ring if and only if 1 is a weak order unit.

Corollary 3. An Archimedean l-ring with positive ring-unity 1 is an f-ring if and only if 1 is a weak order unit.

Proof. Suppose 1 is a weak order unit. By Corollary 1, it will be sufficient to show that R has no non-zero, positive, nilpotent elements. Suppose $a \geqq 0$ and a is nilpotent. Then na is nilpotent for every integer n. Thus, by Lemma 5, $na \leqq 1$. But since R is Archimedean, this implies $a = 0$.

COROLLARY 4. The class of l-rings with a positive ring-unity which is a weak order unit is equationally definable. In particular, the homomorphic image of such an l-ring has a positive ring-unity which is a weak order unit.

Proof. The class of l-rings with positive ring-unity which is a weak order unit is identical with the class of l-rings with positive ring-unity which satisfy (17). But (see the proof of Lemma 1, § 8), (17) is equivalent to

(17′) $(a \cup 0)(a \cap 0) = 0$ for all $a \in R$.

The Corollary is now obvious.

COROLLARY 5. Let A be a finite-dimensional, real l-algebra with a ring-unity 1 which is a weak order unit. Then A is an f-algebra and 1 is a strong order unit.

Proof. Let N be the l-radical of A. Let $a \to \bar{a}$ be the homomorphism of A onto A/N. Then A/N is Archimedean (by Corollary 1 of Theorem 6 and Corollary 4 of Theorem 5) and by Corollary 4, $\bar{1}$ is a weak order unit of A/N. But this implies $\bar{1}$ is a strong order unit in A/N. Then by Lemma 5, 1 is a strong order unit in A. Hence, by Theorem 10, A is an f-algebra.

We will now give an example of an l-ring which is not an f-ring, but which has a positive ring-unity which is a weak order unit.

EXAMPLE 16. Let R be the ordered ring of real numbers. Let P be the ring of all real polynomials $a_1x + a_2x^2 + \dots + a_nx^n$ with no constant term. Order P lexicographically by defining:

$$a_1x + a_2x^2 + \dots + a_nx^n > 0 \text{ if } a_n > 0.$$

Let A be the set of all quadruples

$$(p, \alpha, q_1, q_2), \quad p, q_1, q_2 \in P, \quad \alpha \in R.$$

Define

$$(p, \alpha, q_1, q_2) + (p', \alpha', q_1', q_2') = (p+p', \alpha+\alpha', q_1+q_1', q_2+q_2')$$
$$(p, \alpha, q_1, q_2)(p', \alpha', q_1', q_2') =$$
$$(2pp'+\alpha p'+\alpha' p, \alpha\alpha', p'(q_1+q_2)+p(q_1'+q_2')+\alpha' q_1+\alpha q_1', p'(q_1+q_2) +p(q_1'+q_2')+\alpha' q_2+\alpha q_2'),$$

$(p, \alpha, q_1, q_2) \geqq 0$ if and only if $p > 0$, or $p = 0$ and $\alpha > 0$, or $p = 0$ and $\alpha = 0$ and $q_1 \geqq 0$ and $q_2 \geqq 0$.

It can be verified by direct computation that R is a commutative and associative l-ring. (Considered as a partly ordered set, $A = P \circ (R \circ (P \oplus P))$ and therefore A is a lattice. See G. BIRKHOFF, 1949, p. 25, Theorem 6 and Exercise 2. The ring-unity of A, (0, 1, 0, 0), is positive and is a weak order unit. However, A is not an f-ring, since $(0, 0, q_1, 0) \cap (0, 0, 0, q_2) = 0$ and $(p, 0, 0, 0)(0, 0, q_1, 0) \cap (0, 0, 0, q_2) = (0, 0, 0, pq_1 \cap q_2) > 0$ if $p > 0$, $q_1 > 0$ and $q_2 > 0$.

10. IDEALS IN F-RINGS.

In f-rings, the l-ideals have many special properties. For instance

THEOREM 16. In any f-ring R, the set Z_n of all elements satisfying $a^n = 0$ is an l-ideal. The l-radical N of R is the set $\vee Z_n$ of all nilpotent elements of R.

Proof. By definition, we must prove that

(21) $a_n = 0$ and $b_n = 0$ implies $(a + b)^n = 0$,

(22) $a^n = 0$ and $|x| \leqq |a|$ implies $x^n = 0$,

(23) $a^n = 0$ implies $(xa)_n = (ax)^n = 0$ for all $x \varepsilon R$.

By Theorem 12, it suffices to prove these implications in each simly ordered, subdirectly indecomposable component of R; this we do. In each such component, either $a \leqq b$, in which case, $(a + b)^n \leqq (2b)^n = 2^n b^n = 0$, or $a \geqq b$, in which case $(a + b)^n \leqq (2a)^n = 0$, proving (21). Similarly, $|a| = \pm a$, so $a^n = 0$ and $|x| \leqq |a|$ implies $0 \leqq |x^n| = |x|^n \leqq |a|^n = (\pm)^n a^n = 0$, proving (22). Finally, if $a^n = 0$ and $0 \leqq ax \leqq xa$, then

$0 \leqq (ax)^n \leqq (xa)^n = x(ax)^{n-1}a \leqq x(xa)^{n-1}a \leqq \ldots \leqq x^n a^n = 0$,
whence $(ax)^n = 0$. If $0 \leqq xa \leqq ax$, the argument is dual.

To prove the last statement, observe, by Theorem 5, that every element of N is nilpotent, hence lies in some Z_n, and conversely, every $Z_n \leqq N$.

COROLLARY 1. The quotient-ring of any f-ring modulo its l-radical has zero l-radical.

COROLLARY 2. In an f-ring with zero l-radical, $ab = 0$ implies $|a| \cap |b| = 0$.

Proof. $0 \leqq (|a| \cap |b|)^2 \leqq |ab| = 0$, so $|a| \cap |b| \varepsilon N$ and $|a| \cap |b| = 0$.

COROLLARY 3. Any Archimedean f-ring with a ring-unity has zero l-radical.

Proof. By Theorem 10, the ring-unity is a weak order unit. Hence, by the argument used to prove Corollary 3 of Theorem 15, the ring has no positive nilpotent elements. By Theorem 16, the l-radical is zero.

One of us will show elsewhere that an f-ring R has zero l-radical if and only if R is isomorphic to a subdirect union of ordered rings having no divisors of zero. In the presence of the descending chain condition on l-ideals, a sharper analogue of one Wedderburn's classic structure theorems holds.

Define an f-ring to be l-simple if it contains no proper l-ideals. Thus, for instance, any ordered field is l-simple. So is the ordered ring of integers.

LEMMA 1. Any ordered ring R, whose l-radical is zero and which satisfies the descending chain condition on l-ideals, is l-simple.

Proof. Assume that R is not l-simple. Let I be the minimal l-ideal satisfying $0 < I < R$. Then $b, c \in I$, $b > 0$ and $c > 0$ imply $bc < \min\{b, c\}$. For if $x \in R - I$ and $x > 0$, then $cx < x$. Thus, by Corollary 2 of Theorem 16, $bcx < bx$ and $(b - bc)x > 0$. Since R is ordered, this implies $bc < b$. Similarly, $bc < c$, so $bc < \min\{b, c\}$.

Now let $a > 0$ in I. Then $J = \{d \in R \mid |d| \leqq bac,\ b, c \in I\}$ is an l-ideal, and, since a is not nilpotent, $0 < J \leqq I$. By minimality, $I = J$. Thus, $a \leqq bac$, for some $b, c \in I$. But $bac < ba < a$, which is a contradiction.

THEOREM 17. Any f-ring R, whose l-radical is 0 and which satisfies the descending chain condition on l-ideals, is isomorphic to a direct union of l-simple ordered rings.

Proof. By Theorem 12 and the descending chain condition on l-ideals, there exist l-ideals $I_1, \ldots, I_n$ in R such that $\Lambda I_i = 0$ and R/I_i is an ordered ring. Let $J_j = \{a \in R \mid a^m \in I_j, \text{ some integer } m\} \supseteq I_j$. Then J_j is an l-ideal and R/J_j is an ordered ring with zero radical. By Lemma 1, R/J_j is l-simple, that is, J_i is a maximal proper l-ideal of R. We can suppose that the J_j are all distinct, so that if $i \neq j$, $J_i \cup J_j = R$. Then, using the distributivity of the lattice of l-ideals, it follows that $(J_1 \cap \ldots \cap J_{i-1}) \cup J_i = R$ for all i. If $a \in J_j$ for all j, then $a^{m(j)} \in I_j$ for all j and if $m = \max_j m(j)$, then $a^n \in \Lambda I_j = 0$. Thus $a^n = 0$ since R has zero radical, this implies $a = 0$. Thus $\Lambda I_j = 0$. Consequently, by G. BIRKHOFF, 1949, p. 87, Theorem 4, R is isomorphic to the direct union of the simple rings R/J_j.

THEOREM 18. The l-ideals of any f-ring R form a complete, relatively pseudo-complemented, distributive lattice.

Proof. Let I be any l-ideal of R; define I^* as the set of $x \in R$ which are disjoint from every element of I (G. BIRKHOFF, 1949, p. 232). By Lemma 2, § 8, I^* is an l-ideal. Obviously I^* contains every ideal J with $I \cap J = 0$; hence, I^* is a pseudo-complement of I (G. BIRKHOFF, 1949, p. 147). Since any quotient-ring of an f-ring is an f-ring, and the l-ideals of R/K are just the L/K, where L is an l-ideal of R, the same result holds for relative pseudo-complements.

12. COMPLETE L-RINGS.

The theory of complete and σ-complete l-rings is important because of its applications to operator theory, and also because the real numbers can be defined as the only complete, ordered field. We have already essentially proved

THEOREM 19. Any σ-complete l-ring R with a positive ring-unity which is a weak order unit is a commutative f-ring with zero l-radical.

Proof. Being σ-complete, R is Archimedean (G. BIRKHOFF, 1949, p. 229). By Corollary 3 of Theorem 15, it is an f-ring; by Theorem 13, it is therefore commutative. Hence, by Corollary 3 of Theorem 16, it has zero l-radical.

Combining Theorem 10 with Theorem 19, we have the

COROLLARY. A σ-complete l-ring with a positive ring-unity 1 is an f-ring if and only if 1 is a weak order unit.

Since any σ-complete ordered field is isomorphic to the real field, it follows that every σ-complete l-algebra with a ring unity is an algebra over the real field. Therefore, there is little loss in generality if we always consider σ-complete l-algebras over the real field. By the Corollary of Lemma 2, § 5, such an algebra, if finite dimensional, is of the type defined in Example 6 — and conversely.

In the infinite-dimensional case, one can construct other σ-complete l-algebras.

EXAMPLE 17. Let A be a bounded, self-adjoint, linear operator on a Hilbert space $\mathcal{H}$ Let $\mathcal{A}$ be the closure in the weak topology of operators of the set of all operators of the form

$$\alpha_0 I + \alpha_1 A + \alpha_2 A^2 + \dots + \alpha_n A^n,$$

where I is the identity transformation of $\mathcal{H}$ and the α_i are real numbers. For B ε $\mathcal{A}$, define $B \geqq 0$ if $(x, Bx) \geqq 0$ for all x ε $\mathcal{H}$ With this partial ordering, $\mathcal{A}$ is a σ-complete l-ring with the ring unity I a strong order unit. (See M. H. STONE, 1940, or B. Sz. Nagy, *Spektraldarstellung linearer Transformationen des Hilbertschen Raumes*).

Much work has been done (see Remark 2 below) on representation theories for σ-complete l-algebras with a ring unity which is a strong order unit. When applied to Example 17, the representation of the l-algebra can be used to deduce the spectral representation theorem for bounded, self-adjoint, linear operators on a Hilbert space. Using Theorem 19, we can obtain the representation theorems for a σ-complete l-algebras with a ring unity which is a strong order unit. When applied to Example 17, the representation of the l-algebra can be used to deduce the spectral representation theorem for bounded, self-adjoint, linear operators on a Hilbert space. Using Theorem 19, we can obtain the representation theorems for a σ-complete l-algebra with a unity which is respectively a strong and a weak order unit, either from Theorem 12, or more directly by studying the *decompositions of the unity,* as in G. BIRKHOFF, 1949, p. 251.

LEMMA 1. Let A be a σ-complete f-algebra with ring unity 1. Then the components of 1 form a σ-complete Boolean algebra.

Proof. By a *component of 1* in any vector lattice is meant an element e such that $e \cap (1 - e) = 0$. In the interval (distributive) sublattice of elements x, $0 \leqq x \leqq 1$, these components are the relatively complemented elements, since $e \cup (1 - e) = e + (1 - e) - e \cap (1 - e) = 1$. Hence G. BIRKHOFF, 1949, p. 152, they form a Boolean algebra. If A is complete (σ-complete), so is this Boolean algebra. Since A is an f-ring, $e(1 - e) = e - e^2 = 0$ by (17), so that these components are idempotent. More generally, if e_1 and e_2 are any two components of 1, $e_1e_2 = e_1 \cap e_2$.

Combining Theorem 19 and Lemma 1 with the arguments of G. BIRKHOFF, 1949, pp. 251-252, one can prove

THEOREM 20. Let A be a complete (σ-complete) l-algebra (not assumed to be commutative or associative) with ring-unity 1 which is a strong order unit. Then A is isomorphic with the f-algebra C(X) of ALL continuous functions on the Boolean space X associated with the complete (resp. σ-complete) Boolean algebra of all components of 1.

Using similar techniques, one can prove the corresponding result for complete and σ-complete l-rings.

THEOREM 20′. Let R be a σ-complete l-ring with ring-unity 1 which is a strong order unit. Let X be the Boolean space associated with the Boolean algebra of components of 1. Then for some unique closed subspace X′ of S, R is isomorphic to the f-ring C(X, X′) of all continuous, real-valued functions on X which are integer valued in X′. If R is complete, then X′ is open and closed.

If R is only σ-complete, then X′ need not be open and closed. However, X′, as a closed subspace of the Boolean space X, corresponds to a σ-complete ideal of the Boolean algebra of components of 1. Topologically, this means that if Y is any open F_σ in X which is disjoint from X′, then the closure of Y is also disjoint from X′.

REMARK 1. In Theorem 20, it is not necessary to assume that A is σ-complete, but only *monotone σ-complete,* that is, to assume that every decreasing sequence of positive elements has a g.l.b. From this, and the other hypotheses on A, σ-completeness can be deduced (see M. H. STONE, 1940).

REMARK 2. The Theorem 20 is due essentially to M. H. STONE (see M. H. STONE, 1940 and M. H. STONE, *Can. Jour. of Math.,* vol. 1, p. 176). STONE made the unnecessary assumptions of commutativity, associativity and the positivity of squares. The redundancy of these assumptions has been pointed out by various authors (see YOSIDA AND NAKAYAMA, Proc. *Imp. Acad. Tokyo,* 18 (1942), p. 550 and R. V. KADISON, 1951. Credit is also due to H. NAKANO (see H. NAKANO, 1950, and references there), who extensively developed the theory of σ-complete and complete l-algebras, and to F. RIESZ, whose work on the spectral representation of operators on Hilbert space presaged the abstract representation theorem for σ-complete l-algebras (see F. RIESZ, 1940, *Ann. of Math.,* vol. 41 (1940), p. 174).

The Theorem 20′ seems to be new, although J. VON NEUMANN developed in unpublished 1940 lectures a similar representation theorem for σ-complete l-groups.

We turn now to the representation theorem for σ-complete l-algebras whose ring unity is a weak order unit. It is known (G. BIRKHOFF, 1949, p. 252) that any σ-complete vector lattice with a weak order unit can be represented as a vector lattice of Baire functions on a Boolean space modulo functions which vanish except on a nowhere dense subset. It is possible to show that this representation preserves multiplication in an l-algebra. We can also obtain the representation directly from Theorem 20 by passing from the subalgebra of *bounded* elements to the full algebra by means of a limiting process.

THEOREM 21. Let A be a complete (σ-complete) l-algebra with ring-unity which is a weak order unit. Let X be the Boolean space of the complete (σ-complete) Boolean algebra of components of the unity of A. Let D(X) denote the set of all real-valued functions which are continuous on an open, dense F_σ in X, with functions which are equal on a dense subset identified. Then D(X) is a complete (resp. σ-complete) f-algebra and A is l-isomorphic to a closed (in the order topology) subalgebra of D(X). This subalgebra contains all continuous functions on X.

A similar result (analogous to Theorem 20′) can be proved for l-rings.

REMARK. Theorem 21 does not seem to appear in the literature. However, M. H. STONE (see M. H. STONE, *Proc. Nat. Acad. Sci.,* 27 (1941), p. 83) has indicated a similar extension of the strong unit vector lattice representation theorem to the weak unit case. (See also G. BIRKHOFF, 1949, p. 252).

COROLLARY. In any σ-complete l-algebra A with a ring unity 1 which is a weak order unit, if $a \geqq 0$ and if we define $x = \vee(\alpha \cdot a \cap \alpha^{-1} \cdot 1)$, where the join is over all strictly positive rational numbers, then $x^2 = a$.

Proof. This is easily verified when a is a non-negative real number. Hence, it is true in D(X) and A.

THEOREM 22. Let A_1 and A_2 be σ-complete l-algebras with unity elements which are weak order units. Then any ring isomorphism between

A_1 and A_2 is also a lattice isomorphism and any l-group isomorphism between A_1 and A_2 is also a ring isomorphism.

Proof. By Corollary 1, Theorem 12 and the Corollary of Theorem 21, a $\geqq 0$ if and only if a has a square root. Thus, the first statement follows. The second statement is an immediate consequence *) of the Corollary of Theorem 21.

13. UNSOLVED PROBLEMS.

Our study of l-rings led us to formulate a large number of questions, which we did not answer ourselves. Some of these are listed below.

Let R be a commutative ring, partly ordered by letting R^+ consist of the finite sums of squares (Example 5). When can one strengthen the order, so as to make R into an ordered ring?

Can the real numbers be made into an l-ring by some ordering other than the usual one? Can the complex numbers be made into an l-ring?

Solve the word problem for the free, commutative, real l-algebra (l-group) with n generators. (We conjecture that it is isomorphic with the l-group of real functions which are continuous and piecewise polynomial of degree at most n over a finite number of pieces.) Same problem for free (commutative) l-rings, for free f-rings. (The former is probably very difficult.)

Develop a special theory of commutative l-rings. Is there a *natural* (e.g., regular) commutative l-ring, whose l-radical is properly contained in its ring radical?

Develop a calculus of l-ideals (see G. BIRKHOFF, 1949, Chapters XIII and XIV). Is every l-irreducible representation of a (regular) l-ring (finite-dimensional l-algebra) contained in the regular representation? Does the reduction theory of § 6 extend to representations by bounded endomorphisms of a complete vector lattice? Does every finite-dimensional, real, Archimedean l-algebra admit some (ont necessarily regular) l-representation in E(V), where V is a finite-dimensional real vector lattice? (See Example 11.)

Is every quotient-ring of a regular l-ring regular? What can one say about regular l-rings having a positive ring unity? What about *doubly regular* l-rings having a positive ring unity, i.e., regular l-rings whose anti-isomorphs are also regular?

Is every l-ring with zero l-radical, having a ring unity which is a weak order unit an f-ring?

We hope that others will find it interesting to work on these probles.

*) The idea of this proof is due to F. RIESZ, *Acta Szeged,* **10** (1941).

BIBLIOGRAPHY

BIRKHOFF, G., 1942, *Lattice ordered groups, Annals of Math.* **43**, 298-331.

BIRKHOFF, G. 1949, *Lattice Theory*, rev. ed., *Amer. Math. Soc. Colloquium Publications*, vol. **25**.

BIRKHOFF, G., 1949, *Moyennes des fonctions bornées, Coll. internat. du C. N. R. S., Algèbre et théorie des nombres*.

BOURBAKI, N., 1952, *Eléments de Mathématique*, Livre II, Algèbre, Ch. VI, Paris.

JACOBSON, N., 1943, *The Theory of Rings, Amer. Math. Soc. Mathematical Survey* **2**.

KADISON, R. V., 1951, *A representation theory for commutative topological algebra, Memoirs of the Amer. Math. Soc.*, **7**.

NAKANO, H., 1950, *Modern Spectral Theory*, Tokyo.

STONE, M. H., 1940, *A generall theory of spectra* I, *Proc. Nat. Acad. Sci.*, **26**, 280-283.

VAN DER WAERDEN, B. L., 1930-1931, *Moderne Algebra*, Berlin.

VI

History of Algebra

My first essay on the history of algebra, [31], was written as a companion piece to accompany a biographical sketch of Galois by George Sarton, the famous historian of science.[1] At the age of 24, I felt honored by Sarton's invitation to assess Galois' contributions to mathematics and took it as a challenge.

At the time (1935), Galois was being romanticized as the founder of group theory, whose manuscripts should have excited instant and universal admiration, "who instead spent a considerable portion of his five or six productive years in a hopeless fight against the stupidities and malicious jealousy of teachers and the smug indifference of academicians."[2]

My assessment, independent of these opinions, was based on a careful study of Galois' works, which were instead published only some fifteen years after his death. I was impressed above all by the obscure and in places bombastic statements in Galois' drafts; I realized that a great many ideas had been lifted from Lagrange's "Résolution algébrique des équations", published 60 years earlier. My conclusions at the time were as follows ([31], p. 262):

> Lagrange proved that any polynomial $p(x_1, \ldots, x_n)$ in the roots x_k of (I), assumed in general a number $n(p)$ of values equal to the quotient of $(n!)$ by the number $O(p)$ of permutations of the x_k leaving it invariant. He urged that $n(p)$ was the intrinsic degree of an equation satisfied by $p(x)$; we may point out that $O(p)$ is in a sense a measure of its symmetry.
>
> Lagrange made the further very essential remark, that the symmetries of any polynomial formed a set of permutations including with any two, their "product" (i.e., the result of performing them successively), and thus are a group in the modern technical sense.
>
> An Italian named Ruffini seized this hint, and in his book *Teoria generale delle equazioni* (1799), gave all the possible groups of permutations of five letters, proved that in particular none of these contained exactly forty or exactly thirty elements, and then concluded (with inadequate reasons) that Lagrange was right.
>
> Ruffini's work was useful, even to Abel, and his book drew attention to the importance of the internal structure (e.g., the subgroups) of the "symmetric" group of all permutations of n letters, for the theory of equations.
>
> As was stated above, Abel proved conclusively the truth of Lagrange's conjecture, and it must have seemed to some that with this result the theory of equations ended.
>
> It is not too much to say that Galois out-moded the whole of the previous theories of Lagrange, Vandermonde, Gauss, and Abel, as well as showing what kernel of truth was in Ruffini. He showed that a simpler proof of Abel's result could be found along purely group-theoretic lines, and that by extending the arguments used in this new proof in a wholly natural manner, one obtained necessary and sufficient conditions for equations of all degrees to be algebraically solvable. Moreover by continuing in this vein of ideas, one could get a flock of precise and altogether surprising results.
>
> The main reason why Galois could succeed in developing a complete theory of equations on the basis of group-theoretic considerations, where Ruffini could not, was that Galois had an additional technical idea: that of a normal subgroup.

My first attempt to assess twentieth century mathematics a brief tribute to von Neumann's brilliant contributions to lattice theory [61], reprinted in this volume. My reminiscences (in [155]) on the early history of lattice theory, however, were too long to be included. Today, they should be regarded as a supplement to H. Mehrten's definitive *Die Entstehung der Verbandstheorie*.

The other papers reprinted ([160], [169]) describe new trends in algebra stimulated by the advent of the computer. I wrote these papers shortly after publishing my book *Modern Applied Algebra* with T. C. Bartee (the seventh book in the "Bibliography of Garrett Birkhoff's Books and Papers, 1933–1986" on pages ix–xv in this volume). They were meant to show that the applications of algebra to computer science suggested are mainly concerned with the topics totally ignored in the classic treatises of van der Waerden and Bourbaki. These applications suggest a whole series of deep and fascinating new mathematical questions.

In two other articles ([182]) on the origins of axiomatic algebra, written on the occasion of the Bicentennial of the American Declaration of Independence, I have tried to balance E. T. Bell's exaggerated statement that "the newer abstract algebra ... is practically all German."[3] I recalled in these articles substantial British and American contributions, later so thoroughly reworked, first by the school of Emmy Noether, and later by Bourbaki, that the Anglo-American flavor ran the danger of being lost.

Notes

[1] *Osiris* **3** (1937), 241–59. Sarton had founded the journals *Isis* and *Osiris*. His booklet *The Study of the History of Mathematics* can be consulted with profit by would-be historians of mathematics today.

[2] Quoted from E. T. Bell's *Development of Mathematics*, p. 227. Bell's chapter on Galois in his *Men of Mathematics* is entitled "Genius and Stupidity". Tom Rothman's article in *Am. Math. Monthly* **89** (1982), 84–106, provides a brilliant antidote to the popular romanticization of Galois. For a balanced account of Galois' contributions, see Morris Kline's *Mathematical Thought from Ancient to Modern Times*, Secs. 31-4 and 31-6.

[3] Am. Math. Soc. *Semicentennial Publications*, vol. 2 1938.

Reprinted from the AMERICAN MATHEMATICAL MONTHLY
Vol. 80, No. 7, August–September, 1973,
pp. 760–782

CURRENT TRENDS IN ALGEBRA

GARRETT BIRKHOFF, Harvard University

1. Introduction. Symbolic algebra is much older than many mathematicians suppose; it can be traced back at least to Diophantus of Alexandria (ca. 250 A.D.) and Brahmagupta (ca. 598–665 A.D.). For this early work, see Cajori [**7**, Arts. 101–5] and Ball [**1**, pp. 154–6]. Even so-called "modern" algebra is over a century old!

Garrett Birkhoff is the Putnam Professor of Pure and Applied Mathematics at Harvard, where he did his undergraduate and graduate work, was a Junior Fellow in the Society of Fellows, and has served on the faculty since. He has been a Visiting Lecturer at the University of Washington, University of Cincinnati, and the National University of Mexico, and held a Guggenheim Fellowship. He has served as President of SIAM, Vice-President of the AMS, the MAA, and the American Academy of Arts and Sciences, and Chairman of the CBMS. He is a member of the American Philosophical Society and the National Academy of Sciences, and has received honorary degrees from the National University of Mexico, the University of Lille, France, and the Case Institute of Technology.

His extensive publications in modern algebra, fluid mechanics, numerical analysis, and nuclear reactor theory include the books *Hydrodynamics* (Princeton University Press, 1950); *Lattice Theory* (American Mathematical Society Colloquium Publications, 1940, Third Edition 1967); *Survey of Modern Algebra* (with S. Mac Lane, Macmillan, 1941, 1953, 1965); *Jets, Wakes, and Cavities* (with E. H. Zarantonello, Academic Press, 1957); *Ordinary Differential Equations* (Ginn, 1962); *Algebra* (with S. MacLane, Macmillan, 1967); *Modern Applied Algebra* (with T. C. Bartee, McGraw-Hill, 1970). *Editor.*

When you realize this, you should not find it too hard to believe that the availability of high-speed computers is giving rise to new trends in algebra. My ultimate aim is to sketch for you, in §§8–10, what I think these trends are. But I wish to lead up to this theme by a brief résumé of the development of algebra as we know it today, over the past several centuries.

2. Classical algebra. The name *modern algebra* was originally intended (in 1930) to signify a contrast with *classical algebra*, which was generally understood to mean the *theory of equations*. This may be defined as the art of solving *numerical problems* by *manipulating symbols*, and seems to have originated with Al-Khwarizmi and other Islamic mathematicians during the period 800–1000 A.D. As we know, its most essential idea consists in replacing each verbal statement about *numerical* quantities by a symbolic *equation*, whose terms can be rearranged and combined by well-established general laws to give a sequence of equivalent but, hopefully, simpler equations. The original equation can be considered as "solved" when the unknown quantity has been isolated on one side of the equality symbol =, on the other side of which is some expression involving only known quantities.

Though the word "root" (of an equation) can be traced back to the Sanskrit,[1,2] and the word "power" (of a number) appears in al-Khwarizmi's *Algebra* ("al-jabr"), development of classical algebra in its present form was very gradual. The "al-jabr" of the Arabs did not become widely used in Western Europe, and the symbols + and − did not achieve their present significance, until nearly 1500. A major advance followed shortly thereafter, the solution of cubic and quartic equations by radicals being already contained in Cardan's *Ars Magna* (1545).

For the next two centuries, progress in algebra was mainly[3] in connection with its applications: to (analytic) geometry, which gave a vivid meaning to negative numbers, and to the calculus through the use of infinite series. Until after 1750, the significance of imaginary roots and complex numbers remained quite obscure, and even discussions of simultaneous linear equations and determinants were unsystematic and fragmentary.

But from 1750 to 1830, thanks especially to the work of Euler, Lagrange, and Gauss, classical algebra developed rapidly into approximately its present form. Thus the exponential function e^z became defined for all complex z as a power series, and as a result $a^z = e^{z \ln a}$ became well-defined for all positive a and complex z. The "Lagrange resolvent" was also invented by Euler [**13**, p. 27].

Above all, the Fundamental Theorem of Algebra was recognized as such, clearly stated, and proved. Euler considered its *real* forms, whose equivalence is easily shown. Two of these are:

(a) Every real polynomial of degree $n > 2$ has proper factors.

(b) Every real polynomial can be (uniquely) factored into real linear and quadratic factors.

1. All notes are collected together at the end of the paper.

Condition (a) follows for $n < 5$ from Cardan, and for $n = 5$ because every real polynomial of odd degree has real roots. Euler satisfied himself that it was true for all n, but his proof is obscure.

Conditions (a) and (b) are easily shown to be equivalent also to the usual statement of the Fundamental Theorem of Algebra:

(c) Every complex polynomial can be factored into linear factors.

Gauss gave many relatively rigorous proofs of (c) from about 1800 on, and made it clear that all polynomial equations had solutions in terms of complex numbers $x + yi$, $i = \sqrt{-1}$, while the geometrical interpretation of complex numbers as points in the (x, y)-plane gave them a more than symbolic meaning.

Gauss also developed systematic iterative as well as elimination techniques for solving systems of simultaneous linear equations, and the laws of determinants also became generally known—all by 1825 or so.

A few years later, Galois and Abel showed that it was impossible to solve a general equation of the fifth degree by radicals[4], and after this mathematicians gradually began to turn their attention from the theory of equations to *non*-numerical applications of symbolic algebra (e.g., to groups, vectors and matrices).

MODERN ALGEBRA TO WORLD WAR I

3. "Modern" algebra to 1860. As a result, although real and complex algebra dominated the textbook literature for a full century after 1830, "modern" algebra had already achieved some notable successes by 1860.

Actually, already by 1770, Lagrange was interested in the "symmetric group" of all permutations of n letters and its subgroups, whose relevance to the solution by radicals of the general polynomial equation

$$x^n + a_1x^{n-1} + \cdots + a_n = (x - x_1)(x - x_2)\cdots(x - x_n) = 0, \tag{1}$$

he clearly recognized. A by-product of this interest was the Lagrange Theorem, that the order of any subgroup of a group G divides the order of G.

Ruffini, Galois, and Cauchy made further contributions to the development of group theory before 1845 [**13**, pp. 45–53]; Galois also made (in 1830) a fundamental contribution to the theory of fields, by constructing a *finite field* of each prime-power order p^r. (For formal definitions of groups and fields, see §3.)

Somewhat earlier Legendre and Gauss (1801) had initiated the study of *commutative rings*, by constructing the ring Z_n of the integers "modulo" n (i.e., in which integral multiples of n are set equal to zero) and the ring $Z[i]$ of all "Gaussian integers" $m + ni$, where $m, n \in Z$ are ordinary integers[5] and again $i = \sqrt{-1}$. Moreover Gauss, had proved that factorization into primes was *unique* in $Z[i]$.

By 1850, *noncommutative rings* were also being studied. Thus Hamilton introduced his *quaternions* in 1843; since they contain the complex numbers as a special case, they may be called *hypercomplex numbers*. And in the first edition of his book *Ausdehnungslehre* (1844) H. Grassmann discussed both *vector algebra* (a fairly natural generalization of Descartes' symbolic method for treating geometry) and, somewhat vaguely, hypercomplex numbers in general. These concepts were made much more precise (and their connections with n-dimensional geometry clarified) by Cayley; by Hamilton in the Preface to his book on *Quaternions* (1859); and by Grassmann in the second edition of his book (1878). Moreover, Cayley showed in 1858 [**13**, p. 84] that the theory of determinants of Vandermonde and Laplace was only one aspect of a much more powerful *matrix algebra*. Matrix algebra is much like ordinary algebra, except that for general matrices A and B, $AB \neq BA$: the multiplication of matrices, like that of quaternions, is *non*-commutative. Indispensable for all pure and applied mathematicians today, matrices were first introduced formally by Cayley in 1858, and gradually revolutionized linear algebra.[6]

Shortly before, two other novel areas of modern algebra had been opened up. In 1854, Boole had published his *Introduction to the Laws of Thought*, in which he showed that a substantial part of Aristotelian logic was described by an analog of ordinary algebra now called "Boolean algebra." This novel "algebra of logic" satisfied not only most of the laws of ordinary algebra, but also the curious identities

$$a^2 = a + a = a \text{ (which today would be written } a \wedge a = a \vee a = a),$$

$$(a + b)a = a, \text{ and } (a + b)(a + c) = a + bc.$$

4. The axiomatic approach. We have just seen that many of the major branches of so-called "modern algebra" (rechristened "the new math" by the popular press in the post-Sputnik era) were already known to mathematicians by 1860. However, the axiomatic approach to the foundations of algebra did not come until later. Lagrange derived the Lagrange theorem for groups and Galois constructed Galois fields without ever thinking of groups or fields as defined by postulates at all; their assumptions were entirely intuitive! Even the names "commutative" and "distributive" for the corresponding laws of manipulation were not introduced (by Servois) until 1814,[7] nor the term "associative" (by Hamilton) until 1835.

The emancipation of algebra from exclusive concern with the real and complex fields owes much to the philosophical speculations about algebra of Peacock, Woodhouse,[8] Hamilton, de Morgan, Boole, and Cayley, but E. T. Bell's claim [**3**, pp. 180–1] that it was Peacock who: "first perceived common algebra as an abstract hypothetico-deductive science of the Euclidean pattern" goes too far. Though Peacock anticipated Hankel in announcing the "principle of permanence of equivalent forms," his "Symbolical Algebra" is mainly concerned with geometrical applications, and does not even mention axioms or postulates. In these qualities it resembles H. Grassmann's *Ausdehnungslehre* (1844).[9]

The role of axioms emerges much more clearly from the *Formenlehre* of R. Grassmann (1872); the *Operationskreis der Logikkalkul* of E. Schröder (1877); the axiomatic treatments of groups, fields, modules, and ideals by Cayley (1878), Frobenius and Stickelberger (1879), Dedekind,[10] Weber (1882, 1893), and E. H. Moore; and the independent contemporary work of Benjamin Peirce and his son, C. S. Peirce, at Harvard (1870–1881).[11]

Influenced by these writings, Peano[12] initiated in 1888 his axiomatic approach to arithmetic, about which I shall say much more later. A decade later, in his *Grundlagen der Geometrie* [**9**], Hilbert tried to improve on Euclid. He succeeded from the standpoint of rigor, but not from that of pedagogy! Perhaps his most fundamental contribution to axiomatics was his clear formulation of the notions of independence, consistency and completeness for axiom systems.

In 1902, E. H. Moore showed that Hilbert's own axioms were not independent, and during the next ten years E. V. Huntington, L. E. Dickson, and O. Veblen made other painstaking analyses of the independence of postulate systems for groups, fields in general, the real and complex fields in particular, the algebra of logic, and the foundations of geometry. One can get an excellent picture of this work by reading the papers by Moore and Huntington;[13] for a more colorful if less reliable survey, see [**2**, Ch. 3].

Partly as a result of such papers, the postulational approach to algebra finally became standard. Mathematicians found that amazingly few and simple postulates, many fewer than those of Euclidean geometry,[14] could provide a sufficient basis for very extensive algebraic theories. For example, all of group theory can be derived from general principles of logic and the following postulates, due to E. V. Huntington (1906).

DEFINITION. A *group* G is a set of elements (to be denoted by small Latin letters), any two of which, say x and y, have a *product* xy which satisfies the following conditions:

G1. Multiplication is *associative*: $x(yz) = (xy)z$ for all $x, y, z \in G$.

G2. For any two elements $a, b \in G$, there exist $x, y \in G$ such that $xa = b$ and $ay = b$.

(We have used Peano's notation $x \in G$ above; it signifies that "the element x is a member of (belongs to) the set G.")

Ingenious arguments can be used to deduce from these postulates various other simple conditions, for example, that: (i) any group G contains a unique "idempotent" element e satisfying $ee = e$, (ii) this element satisfies $ex = xe = x$ for all $x \in G$ (acts as an "identity" for G), (iii) the elements x and y in G2 are uniquely determined by a and b, and so on.

Similarly, the entire theory of fields can be deduced from the following set of postulates, also due to Huntington.

DEFINITION. A *field* is a set F of elements, any two of which have a *sum* $x + y$ and a *product* xy which satisfy the following conditions:

F1. Addition and multiplication are *commutative*:

$$x + y = y + x \text{ and } xy = yx \text{ for all } x, y \in F.$$

F2. Addition and multiplication are *associative*:

$$x + (y + z) = (x + y) + z \text{ and } x(yz) = (xy)z, \text{ all } x, y, z \in F.$$

F3. Multiplication is *distributive* on sums:

$$x(y + z) = xy + xz \text{ for all } x, y, z \in F.$$

F4. For any $a, b \in F$, there exists some $x \in F$ such that $a + x = b$.
F5. If $a + a \neq a$, then there exists some $y \in F$ such that $ay = b$. (Actually, Huntington weakened F5 by adding the condition $b + b \neq b$ to its hypothesis.)
(Of course, the hypothesis $a + a \neq a$ is just an indirect way of assuming that $a \neq 0$, necessary here because Huntington wanted to avoid assuming the existence of a "zero" 0 in F.)

The postulational approach to algebra, combined with an awareness of the relevance of all kinds of algebraic systems, stimulated an interest in enumerating *all possible algebraic systems* satisfying specified conditions: all finite fields (Galois had found them all), all groups of given order n, and so on. In this enumeration, one must of course identify all groups (or fields) which are *isomorphic*, that is, whose elements are related by a *bijection which preserves group multiplication* (in fields, which preserves addition *and* multiplication). Such a bijection is called an *isomorphism*.

5. Morphisms and subalgebras. More generally, it is helpful to know when two algebraic systems A and B are related by a (homo)*morphism*, or mapping θ: $A \to B$ which preserves all their defining operations. Finally, it is helpful to recognize the *subalgebras* of A, i.e., the subsets S of A which satisfy all postulates; under these circumstances, A is conversely called an *extension* of S. (Thus the complex field is an extension of the real field.) To test for being a subalgebra, it is usually sufficient to test for *closure* with respect to suitable operations. In a group, for example, a subgroup must contain: (i) the identity, (ii) with any x also x^{-1}; and (iii) with x and y also xy. In fields, one must require closure under addition, subtraction, multiplication, and division.

The preceding concepts apply to all of the usual kinds of algebraic systems; I shall come back to them in my next lecture.

6. Some deeper developments: 1860–1914. During the same decades that its foundations were being clarified by the postulational method, the scope and depth of algebra grew enormously. I can only indicate very sketchily a few especially remarkable results here.

First, Galois theory became clarified as follows; I shall stick to extensions of the rational field Q to fix ideas, but the results generalize to extensions of any field. Let $F = Q[x_1, \cdots, x_n]$ be the field generated by the roots of a polynomial

$$p(x) = (x - x_1)(x - x_2) \cdots (x - x_n) = x^n + a_1 x^{n-1} + \cdots + a_n = 0$$

with coefficients $a_k \in Q$. Define the *Galois group* $F(f: Q)$ of F (and of $p(x)$) over Q to be the group of all automorphisms α of F such that $\alpha(x) = x$ for all $x \in Q$. Then the theorem of Galois states that the equation $p(x) = 0$ is solvable by *radicals* in terms of the coefficients (i.e., over Q) if and only if the Galois group $G(F: Q)$ is "solvable" in the following sense.

DEFINITION. Define a *composition series* of a finite group G to be a chain of subgroups of G,

$$1 < S_1 < S_2 < \cdots < S_r = G,$$

each of which is a maximal normal subgroup of the one following. Form the associated quotient-groups S_k / S_{k-1}. Then G is called *solvable* when these quotient-groups are all *Abelian* (it is equivalent that they all be of prime order).

Second, pure group theory acquired depth. Among the many remarkable theorems about finite groups proved in the half-century 1860–1914, I shall mention only a few. First, it was shown that the set of S_k/S_{k-1} is the same (up to isomorphism and rearrangement) for all composition series (Jordan-Hölder Theorem). Again, it was shown that any group of prime-power order p^n is solvable. Finally, it was shown that if p^n divides the order of a group G, then G has a subgroup of order p^n (Sylow theorem).

Third, in the area of algebraic number theory, Dedekind developed ideal theory, and applied it to generalize the pioneer result of Gauss on the unique factorization of Gaussian integers, to a sweeping unique factorization theorem for any algebraic number field (i.e., any subfield of the complex field C having finite linear dimension over the rational subfield Q). Namely, he showed that factorization into prime ideals is unique.[15]

Dedekind's deep interest in ideal theory and in unique factorization into primes also led him to consider the operations of greatest common divisor (g.c.d.) and least common multiple (l.c.m.) from a postulational standpoint. Recognizing their analogy with "and" and "or" in Boolean algebra, he was led to develop and apply the elementary theory of *lattices* ("*Dualgruppen*"), *modular lattices, distributive lattices*, and *vector lattices* in two pioneer papers (1897, 1901), thus founding a major new branch of algebra which contained Boolean algebra as a special case.

7. Linear associative algebras. In 1870, at about the same time that Dedekind was developing ideal theory into a powerful tool, Benjamin Peirce of Harvard made a pioneer study of the systems of "hypercomplex numbers" vaguely adumbrated by Grassmann, Hamilton and Cayley. Peirce began by defining a "linear algebra" over a field F as a set A whose elements are arbitrary linear combinations

(2) $$\mathbf{a} = (a_1, \cdots, a_r) = a_1 \mathbf{i}_1 + \cdots + a_r \mathbf{i}_r$$

of r basis elements $\mathbf{i}_l$, multiplied by some rule of the form

$$(2') \qquad \mathbf{a}\cdot\mathbf{b} = (\Sigma a_l b_m)\mathbf{i}_l\cdot\mathbf{i}_m = \Sigma a_l b_m \gamma_{lmn}\mathbf{i}_n;$$

the constants γ_{lmn} can be any scalars (elements of F). He called a linear algebra *associative* when the multiplication defined by (2′) is associative.

A very notable linear associative algebra is provided by Hamilton's quaternions, which have four basic elements $\mathbf{1}, \mathbf{i}, \mathbf{j}, \mathbf{k}$ and hence 64 constants (mostly zero) defined by the rules

$$(3) \qquad \mathbf{1}\cdot\mathbf{a} = \mathbf{a}\cdot\mathbf{1} = \mathbf{a} \text{ for all } \mathbf{a}, \qquad \mathbf{i}^2 = \mathbf{j}^2 = \mathbf{k}^2 = -\mathbf{1},$$

$$(3') \qquad \mathbf{i}\cdot\mathbf{j} = -\mathbf{j}\cdot\mathbf{i} = \mathbf{k}, \quad \mathbf{j}\cdot\mathbf{k} = -\mathbf{k}\cdot\mathbf{j} = \mathbf{i}, \quad \mathbf{k}\cdot\mathbf{i} = -\mathbf{i}\cdot\mathbf{k} = \mathbf{j}.$$

The identities of (3′) are clearly those for vector products. The quaternion algebra $R[\mathbf{i},\mathbf{j},\mathbf{k}]$ over the real field is also a *division algebra*: any nonzero quaternion $\mathbf{a} = a_0 + a_1\mathbf{i} + a_2\mathbf{j} + a_3\mathbf{k} \neq \mathbf{0}$ has an inverse, given by

$$(3'') \qquad \mathbf{a}^{-1} = (a_0 - a_1\mathbf{i} - a_2\mathbf{j} - \mathbf{a}_3\mathbf{k})/(a_0^2 + a_1^2 + a_2^2 + a_3^2).$$

Peirce[16] showed that the complex numbers and the quaternions formed the *only* hypercomplex division algebras over the real field.

Even more important is the *full matrix algebra* $M_n(F)$ of all n^2-matrices $A = \| a_{lm} \| = \Sigma a_{lm} e_{lm}$. The basis elements e_{lm} of $M_n(F)$ are multiplied by the rules that

$$(4) \qquad e_{lm}e_{l'm'} = \begin{cases} e_{lm'} & \text{if } m = l' \\ 0 & \text{otherwise.} \end{cases}$$

Hence, the constants are given (in a slightly changed notation) by

$$(4') \qquad \gamma_{lm,l'm',l''m''} = \begin{cases} 1 & \text{if } l' = m, l'' = l, m'' = m' \\ 0 & \text{otherwise.} \end{cases}$$

From 1870 on, many mathematicians tried to classify linear associative algebras over the real and complex field, using the Fundamental Theorem of Algebra as a tool where convenient. Papers by Frobenius (1878, 1903), Molien (1893), and Cartan (1898) were especially noteworthy.[17]

In a remarkable paper published in 1907, Wedderburn showed that most of the structure theorems of Cartan and Frobenius could be proved for linear associative algebras over an arbitrary field! In particular, he proved the following basic results, whose precise meaning will be explained below. For further details, see [**3**, Ch. 11]. Wedderburn himself stated that "Most of the results contained in the present paper have already been given, chiefly by Cartan and Frobenius, for algebras over the rational field."

(i) Any linear associative algebra is the direct sum (in the vector space sense) of a "semisimple" subalgebra and a unique "nilpotent" invariant subalgebra;

(ii) The semi-simple summand in (i) is the direct sum of "simple" linear associative algebras, in a unique way;

(iii) Each *simple* summand in (ii) is, for some n, the "full matrix algebra" $M_n(D)$ of all $n \times n$ matrices $A = \| a_{ij} \|$ with entries a_{ij} in a suitable "division algebra" D over F, the field of scalars of the original linear associative algebra.

To explain (i), we recall that a linear algebra is called "nilpotent" when, for some finite integer n, all products $a_1 a_2 \cdots a_n$ of n factors vanish. A "subalgebra" of an algebra is a subset closed under addition and multiplication (as well as linear combination over the field of scalars); such a subalgebra K is called "invariant" when $k \in K$ implies $ak \in K$, and $ka \in K$ for any element a, even if not in K; this is the condition that K be an *ideal* in the sense of ring theory.

Not all linear algebras are associative. The most important family of non-associative algebras is the family of *Lie algebras*. In these, the associative law is replaced by the following three identities:

$$[aa] = 0, \ [ab] + [ba] = 0, \ [[ab]c] + [[bc]a] + [[ca]b) = 0,$$

true for all a, b, c. In the 1870's, Lie had shown that real and complex Lie algebras provided the key to the understanding of *continuous groups* based on a finite number of parameters. It was therefore most remarkable that Killing (1888–1890) and Élie Cartan (1894), were able to prove that Lie algebras satisfied structure theorems somewhat analogous to those for associative algebras stated above—and to determine all "simple" Lie algebras over C. This work of Killing and Cartan on the structure of Lie algebras came *before* the analogous work of Molien and Cartan on linear associative algebras[17a].

One can, perhaps, summarize the preceding developments in the statement that more was known about "modern algebra" by research algebraists in 1914 than most Ph.D's know today. However, algebra was still regarded as subordinate to classical analysis, and the complex field reigned supreme. Thus, of the two advanced texts on algebra (as distinguished from number theory) most widely used in 1900, Weber's began with a chapter on algebraic functions and Serret's with one on continued fractions!

8. Symbolic logic to Gödel. In retrospect, it seems not too surprising that the dramatic successes of 19th century algebraists and logicians should have encouraged some imaginative mathematicians to develop a *symbolic logic* which would reduce all theorem-proving to mechanical symbol manipulations according to prescribed rules or "axioms." Actually, this idea goes back at least to Leibniz, who envisioned around 1700 symbolic methods capable of "increasing the power of reason far more than any optical instrument has ever aided the power of vision." To his fertile mind, the powerful symbolic algebra of the differential and integral calculus (much of which he invented) must have seemed a direct confirmation of the potentialities of symbolic methods.

The symbolic approach was developed tremendously by Peano from 1889 on. His main contributions to it may be found in his *Formulario Matematico* (5th ed.,

1908), whose preface states that: "All progress in mathematics is in response to the introduction of symbols (ideographic signs). ... Among two symbolic systems, the one with fewer symbols is, in general, preferable. But the fundamental use of [symbolic methods] is to facilitate calculation." The preface continues with a review of the origin of various symbols, including $+$, $\times$, D (derivative), $\int$, and those for vector and Boolean algebra. It then proposes for general adoption the symbols $\in$ (for membership) and $\exists$ (there exists). Peano claims that with these, and a handful of other symbols and symbolic conventions, all mathematics can be presented in symbolic form.[18]

Actually, Peano was not the first mathematician to conceive of a purely symbolic mathematics. In 1634, Hérigone had written in the Preface of his *Cursus Mathematicus*: "I have invented a new method of making demonstrations, brief and intelligible, without the use of any language," and his symbolic style was adhered to by Wallis (1656) and Barrow (1655, 1660).[19]

Peano then substantiates his claim by 386 pages of text containing symbolic synopses of: (1) Mathematical Logic, (2) Arithmetic, (3) Algebra, (4) Vectors ("Geometry"), (5) Limits, (6) Derivatives, (7) Integrals. Most successful are Parts (1) and (2); the latter contains Peano's celebrated construction[20] of the nonnegative integers by his "successor function": $1 = 0+$, $2 = 1+$, $3 = 2+, \cdots$, and his derivation of the laws of arithmetic from it is superb. In 70 additional pages, Peano extends his purely symbolic treatment to plane curves, differential equations, and various other topics.

However, Peano's *Formulaire* must be viewed as primarily a thought-provoking *tour de force*, in spite of its wealth of ideas and insights. Nowhere does he list the rules of symbol-manipulation for passing from one formula to the next; he fails to provide a system of axioms for logic. His proofs, like Euclid's in geometry, can only be verified by attributing *meanings* to words.

This major gap was filled by Whitehead and Russell in their three volume masterpiece *Principia Mathematica* [**18**]. Here they specified carefully the symbol-manipulations ("rules of inference") which can be used infallibly in passing from hypotheses to conclusions in symbolic logic (mathematical reasoning).

Using their specified rules of inference as "axioms" for symbolic logic, Whitehead and Russell showed that one can paraphrase symbolically at least the construction of the real field R from the positive integers, as well as much of set theory and arithmetic. These major achievements were presented as empirical evidence supporting the thesis that *all mathematical theorem-proving can be reduced to mechanical symbol-manipulations* (i.e., to pure symbolic logic).[21]

Nobody disputes the claims of Whitehead and Russell, that their rules of inference for "Peanese" (the symbolic language of Peano), are (i) infallible subject to restrictions stated in English in their text, and (ii) sufficient for much of elementary mathematics. However, the actual mathematical coverage of *Principia* (in nearly

2000 pages!) is far less than Peano's, and it cannot be said that their symbolic methods used "increase the power of reason;" I think they *decrease* it, probably for psychological reasons.[22]

9. Hilbert and Gödel, 1918–31. Because of its capability of replacing special axioms for the different branches of mathematics by theorems (cf. *Principia Mathematica*, Preface, first paragraph), Hilbert said in 1918 that "Russell's Axiomatization of Logic is the crowning achievement of axiomatics."[23] And Hilbert spoke with authority, as the man who had rigorized the axioms of Euclid in his famous *Grundlagen der Geometrie* only 20 years before. I quote from the introduction to this book:

"Geometry—like number theory—requires for its deductive *(folgerichtige)* construction only a few basic theorems *(Grundsätze)*. These theorems are called *axioms*,[24] and their connected development has had numerous treatments since Euclid.... The following book is a new attempt to develop the simplest possible complete axiom system for geometry ... so as to clarify the significance of the different groups of axioms and the consequences of the individual axioms."

In much the same spirit of *axiomatic analysis*, Hilbert and his collaborators, especially his co-authors W. Ackermann and P. Bernays,[25] made after 1918 major efforts to prove *deductively* (by metamathematical arguments) the adequacy of the axioms of Whitehead and Russell (the evidence of *Principia Mathematica* was empirical). They focused attention on two main questions:

(i) Are these axioms *contradiction-free*, i.e., using them, is it impossible to prove both p and its contradiction $\sim p$?

(ii) Can one test the truth or falsity of any given proposition (e.g., of arithmetic) in a finite number of steps?

Hilbert may have been attracted to these questions partly because he had established an analog of the first in his *Grundlagen der Geometrie*, by using Cartesian geometry as a model for Euclidean plane geometry, and of the second for polynomial ideal bases by general transfinite arguments using the "ascending chain condition."

Question (i) was given a positive answer by Ackermann (who had earlier proved the redundancy of one of the Whitehead-Russell axioms) and von Neumann in 1927, *under suitable restrictions*. These restrictions, which are quite technical,[26] seemed quite harmless at first sight, and led to a feeling of optimism about Hilbert's program in the years 1927–1930.

Question (ii), the *Entscheidungsproblem* or Decidability problem, was however given a negative answer, even for arithmetic propositions, by Gödel in 1931. By an ingenious use of metamathematical reasoning, ultimately based on Cantor's diagonal construction, he inferred from this undecidability the *incompleteness* of the Whitehead-Russell-Hilbert system in the following sense. Assuming as true the additional *consistency axiom*, that "false formulas are unprovable," one can prove a number-theoretic formula which would not be provable without it. It is a corollary that one cannot prove that Hilbert's axioms are contradiction-free, so that in particular Question (i) is undecidable.

Thus Gödel's paper shattered Hilbert's high hopes. To quote Hermann Weyl[27]: "Gödel enumerated the symbols, formulas, and sequences of formulas in Hilbert's formalism in a certain way, and thus transformed the assertion of consistency into an arithmetic proposition. He could show that this proposition can neither be proved nor disproved within the formalism. This can mean only two things: either the reasoning by which a proof of consistency is given must contain some argument that has no formal counterpart within the system, i.e., we have not succedeed in completely formalizing the procedure of mathematical induction; or hope for a strictly 'finitistic' proof of consistency must be given up altogether. When Gentzen (1936) finally succeeded in proving the consistency of arithmetic he trespassed those limits indeed by claiming as evident a type of reasoning that penetrates into Cantor's 'second class of ordinal numbers'."

Gödel's result ended abruptly a half-century of optimism about symbolic logic, at least as formalized by Peano, Whitehead, and Russell. It showed that their formalizations were incapable of resolving the paradoxes and ambiguities of Cantor's theory of infinite sets.[28]

THE REIGN OF MODERN ALGEBRA, 1930–1970.

10. The rise of "modern" algebra. Just before Gödel shattered the high hopes of symbolic logicians for formalizing all mathematics in terms of "Peanese", van der Waerden's *Moderne Algebra* (1930–31) precipitated a new revolution. The goal of this brilliantly written book is clearly stated in its preface.

"The 'abstract', 'formal' or 'axiomatic' direction, which has given to algebra renewed momentum,[29] has above all led to a series of new concepts in *group* theory, *field* theory, *valuation* theory, and the theory of *hypercomplex numbers*, to insight into new connections and to far-reaching results. The main aim of this book is to introduce the reader into this new world of concepts."

As I have indicated, both the axiomatic approach and much of the content of "modern" algebra dates back to before 1914. However, even in 1929, its concepts and methods were still considered to have marginal interest as compared with those of analysis in most universities, including Harvard. By exhibiting their mathematical and philosophical unity, and by showing their power as developed by Emmy Noether and her other students (most notably E. Artin, R. Brauer, and H. Hasse), van der Waerden made "modern algebra" suddenly seem central in mathematics. It is not too much to say that the freshness and enthusiasm of his exposition electrified the mathematical world—especially mathematicians under 30 like myself.

In particular, it made classical *real and complex algebra* seem passé, or at least a part of analysis and not of "algebra" in the true sense. This view is exemplified in

Moderne Algebra, where the real and complex fields are not even *defined* until after Galois theory has been presented, and the existence and uniqueness of a smallest algebraically closed extension of *any* field (Steinitz, 1910) are proved purely algebraically (by transfinite induction). What a contrast with the texts of Weber, Serret, and Perron!

11. Lattice theory. This new attitude was a major stimulus in the rebirth of lattice theory, which had lain dormant since the pioneer papers of Dedekind. In 1933, I wrote that lattice theory provided "a point of vantage from which to attack combinatorial problems in ··· abstract algebra."[30] And by 1938, enough progress had been made in applying it to logic, algebra, geometry, probability, measure and integration theory, and functional analysis to cause the American Mathematical Society to hold a symposium on the then very fresh subject.[31]

12. College algebra. The displacement of classical algebra by modern algebra took time. Thus it was not until after World War II that modern algebra became popular at the college level in our country—a popularity due partly to the *Survey of Modern Algebra* which Mac Lane and I had published in 1941. Actually, our approach seems quite conservative today! Thus, unlike van der Waerden, we presented the essentials of the theory of equations before defining groups, and the theory of real and complex matrices (including the Principal Axis Theorem for symmetric and Hermitian matrices) with geometric applications before Galois theory. We also included Boolean algebra, thinking it essential for students to understand the algebra of sets and logic; I shall return to this later.

13. Bourbaki's influence. Abstract mathematics, as reformulated by N. Bourbaki[32] in his *Éléments de Mathématique*, was popularized in French universities not long after. This many-volume treatise, mostly written in the decade 1945–55, attempts to develop all of (pure) mathematics systematically from the notions of *set* and *function*: it presents the content of mathematics as concerned with abstractly conceived relational *structures over sets* and mappings (especially *morphisms*) between them; cf. Book 1, Ch. 4.

Algebraic structures are treated in this spirit in Book 2, as defined by sets of *elements* with (internal or external) finitary *operations*. The reader is then led authoritatively and surely through a carefully polished and systematic sequence of definitions, examples, and theorems about groups, rings, fields, and most of the other kinds of systems I have mentioned. Other branches of mathematics are treated in much the same style in later books. The net effect is to make mathematics appear as a *polished monolith, built purely deductively from the notions of set and function.*

14. The flowering of abstract algebra. The enthusiasm generated by van der Waerden's book, reinforced in the ways that I have described, has given rise to an unprecedented flowering of all aspects of abstract algebra over the past 40 years. In particular, the theories of *groups*, *rings* and *fields* (to which the bulk of *Moderne Algebra* was devoted) have achieved new levels of depth and sophistication, of which perhaps the most dramatic example is the result that *every finite group of odd order is solvable.* This result, proved by Thompson and Feit in over 200 pages of very technical reasoning, had long been conjectured — but to prove it would have seemed hopeless to most mathematicians in 1930.

The last 40 years have also seen the theories of Lie, Jordan, and multilinear algebras mature to a point that makes what was known in 1930 seem amateurish if not naive. The same is true of lattice theory, semigroup and quasigroup theory, category theory, and homological and combinatorial algebra, all of which were either unknown or nearly so in 1930. Finally, algebraic geometry has become rigorized as a new branch of axiomatic algebra, based securely on deep results about commutative rings and their ideals and valuations.[33]

15. Wider repercussions. The tidal wave generated by enthusiasm about abstract algebra had wider repercussions. Thus to young men in 1930, like myself, van der Waerden's book made *classical analysis* stemming from the calculus (''*analyse infinitésimale*''), which had dominated mathematics for over two centuries, suddenly seem old and tired. Indeed, the abstract approach adopted by van der Waerden for algebra soon became fashionable in functional analysis and topology. The idea that all mathematics could be viewed as topological algebra gained a strong impetus from the solution of Hilbert's Fifth Problem, which showed that the hypothesis of differentiability could be replaced by mere continuity in the theory of Lie groups: any locally Euclidean continuous group is isomorphic to an analytic Lie group [**22**, p. 184]. Even research on partial differential equations, the traditional stronghold of the applied mathematician, has increasingly centered around the quest for new abstract concepts permitting one to prove extremely general existence and uniqueness theorems.

Partly because of such shifts in emphasis, by 1960 most younger mathematicians had come to believe that all mathematics should be developed axiomatically from the notions of set and function, and this approach had come to seem no longer modern but classical! By 1959, van der Waerden had changed his title from ''*Moderne Algebra*'' to ''*Algebra.*'' And in the 1960's, Mac Lane and I wrote another ''Algebra'' which went further in the direction of abstraction, by organizing much of pure algebra around the central concepts of morphism, category, and ''universality.'' The ''universal'' approach to algebra, which I had initiated in the 1930's and 1940's stressing the role of lattices, was developed much further in two important books by Cohn and Grätzer. In a parallel development, Lawvere (1965) proposed ''The category of categories as a foundation for mathematics,'' beginning with the statement[34]:

> In the mathematical development of recent decades one sees clearly the rise of the conviction that the relevant properties of mathematical objects are those which can be stated in terms of their abstract structure rather than in terms of the elements which the objects were thought to be made of. The question thus naturally arises whether one can give a foundation for mathematics

which expresses wholeheartedly this conviction concerning what mathematics is about, and in particular, in which classes and membership in classes do not play any role. Here by "foundation" we mean a single system of first-order axioms in which all usual mathematical objects can be defined and all their usual properties proved. A foundation of the sort we have in mind would seemingly be much more natural and readily-usable than the classical one when developing such subjects as algebraic topology, functional analysis, model theory of general algebraic systems, etc.

16. The "new mathematics" of 1960. In the post-Sputnik era of the early and middle 1960's, enthusiasm went even further. Especially in the United States, a vogue developed for exposing school children to formal concepts of set, function and axiom often only half-appreciated by their teachers! Its proponents encouraged the spread of the myth that these constituted a "New Mathematics," unknown fifty years earlier. One ostensible aim of this vogue was to indoctrinate young people so that they could fill a supposed shortage of mathematical teachers and research workers. This seemed highly desirable at a time when our postwar "baby bulge" and prosperity was quadrupling of the demand for college teachers of mathematics, while an unquestioning faith in the value of basic science was increasing the support for research in pure mathematics at a rate of 10–15 per cent annually. But as of 1972, it all seems strangely out-of-date!

To summarize, algebra developed harmoniously during the years 1930–60, with its main stream flowing smoothly, swiftly, and finally triumphantly in the channels I have described. Some measure of its triumph may be found in the fact that, whereas three of the first four Fields medals were awarded in Analysis (in 1936 and 1950), three of the four awarded in 1970 were in Algebra.

However, in the last 5–10 years, powerful new currents have become apparent. Some of these have arisen as countercurrents to extremism; thus René Thom has recently written a thought-provoking article entitled *'Modern' Mathematics: An Educational and Philosophical Error*,[35] in which he urges that geometry should replace algebra because "any question in algebra is either trivial or impossible to solve. By contrast, the classic problems of geometry present a wide variety of challenges."

However, I do not wish to dwell on the exaggerations of a decade which most of us recall with nostalgia. Extreme abstraction in research circles, attempts to inculcate premature sophistication in children, and uncritical expansionism in basic physical science have provoked reactions which by now threaten to go too far in the opposite direction.

Instead, I wish to describe four *positive* current trends in algebra which, in my opinion, hold great promise for the future.

FOUR COMPUTER-INFLUENCED CURRENT TRENDS

17. The new numerical algebra. Already in the 1940's a new revolution was brewing, whose ultimate implications for mathematics are unpredictable. Namely the construction of efficient *high-speed digital computers* was making it feasible to solve mathematical problems whose effective solution would have previously been prohibitively costly and time-consuming. To many mathematicians, including myself, it had become evident by 1950 that the resulting *revolution in applied mathematics* would open up challenging new areas for basic research. In particular, since digital computers can only represent real numbers to a *finite* number of significant digits, and can only represent values of real functions at a *finite* number of points (approximate "nodal values" at "mesh-points"), their use in solving differential equations (e.g., from physics or engineering) requires a very careful *numerical analysis* of *roundoff* and *truncation* errors.[36]

Thus, to actually *solve* a system of differential equations (to a desired approximation), one usually first replaces it by an approximating system of *algebraic equations* (obtained perhaps by finite difference or finite element methods), whose unknowns typically represent nodal values at mesh-points, which is then solved (also approximately) on a digital computer. I shall say nothing about this first step of *discretization* here, because the theorems in numerical analysis and approximation theory required to justify it belong to classical analysis and not to algebra. Suffice it to say that it often leads to very large matrices and associated systems of simultaneous linear equations, which may involve 50,000 or more unknowns! The main problem is to solve these efficiently.

These matrices typically have many special properties, which must be exploited to achieve efficiency. They are usually very *sparse* (have mostly zero entries), and often symmetric, or symmetrizable by permutations or linear transformations. Their diagonal elements may be "dominant" (i.e., at least as great as the sum of the absolute values of the other entries), and they may have positive diagonal and negative off-diagonal entries. Matrices having all of the above properties are essentially what are called *Stieltjes matrices*; they arise naturally in *network flow problems.*

One usually wants to either: (i) *solve* the linear system (written symbolically $Ax = b$), or (ii) determine *eigenvalues* of A (the former are of course the roots of $|A - \lambda I| = 0$). As regards (i), most mathematicians imagined in 1940 that large linear systems should be solved (if at all!) by *Gaussian elimination*, and that the rest was sheer drudgery. A few eminent analysts (including Gauss, Jacobi, and von Mises) had appreciated the value of *iterative* methods (also used by Gauss) and had studied their rates of convergence, but these methods were (and still are!) totally ignored in textbooks on "linear algebra." Similar remarks apply to eigenvalue problems, where the experience of most mathematicians was limited to 3×3 (if not to 2×2) matrices $A = \| a_{ij} \|$, whose eigenvalues they might have found using textbook formulas to solve the cubic characteristic equation

$$\lambda^3 - (a_{11} + a_{22} + a_{33})\lambda^2 + \beta\lambda - A = 0,$$

where

$$\beta = a_{22}a_{33} + a_{33}a_{11} + a_{11}a_{22} - a_{23}a_{32} - a_{31}a_{13} - a_{12}a_{21}.$$

In practice, such textbook methods are extremely inaccurate and inefficient for most large matrices[37], and they were replaced in the 1950's by new algorithms, whose invention and analysis created a major new area of "classical" algebra: the *new numerical algebra.* Excellent surveys of what is now known about this area are contained in authoritative books by Varga [**17**], Wilkinson [**19**], and Young [**20**]; every forward-looking young algebraist should at least be cognizant of their contents!

18. Sparse matrices. The past five years have also seen substantial improvements (over Gauss) in *elimination* techniques for solving large systems with sparse coefficient-matrices. In particular, these have drawn on graph theory for ideas; see [**15**] for a cross-section of current work.

There are many other interesting new areas of research in (real and complex) numerical algebra. I shall just mention three of the most important; references to activity in them may be found in many review journals:

(a) Finding the roots of polynomial equations of degrees up to 100.
(b) "Unconstrained" minimization of functions of many variables.
(c) Linear programming and other techniques for finding minima of functions subjected to "constraints" by equations and inequalities.

Actually these "new" areas also originated in the 1940's, if not earlier. Thus by 1947, linear programming was defined, and the "simplex method" of solving its problems invented by George Dantzig; see p. 20 of G. Hadley's *Linear Programming* (Addison-Wesley, 1962). Moreover, its fundamental techniques were made accessible at the college freshman level by Kemeny, Snell, and Thompson 10 years later, in their popular *Introduction to Finite Mathematics* (Prentice-Hall, 1957).

19. Integer arithmetic. In programming languages for computers, a basic distinction is made between *exact* "integer arithmetic" and *approximate* "real arithmetic." I have omitted the problems of "integer programming" and of solving Diophantine equations on computer in the above discussion, because they involve integer and not real and complex numerical algebra. Nevertheless, activity in these fields represents another strong trend in contemporary numerical algebra.

20. Theory of automata. Although many mathematicians think of high-speed computers as simply "number-crunchers" or supersliderules whose primary mathematical role is to carry out elaborate numerical computations, and although "arithmetic units" may be the most highly organized special pieces of computer "hardware," computers are actually much more versatile. Large general purpose computers are designed to be *universal* instruments, capable of expediting all kinds of "mental" tasks. Much as the Industrial Revolution was made possible by machines which could perform all kinds of "physical" tasks more cheaply and efficiently than human beings, the Computer Revolution is aimed at doing the same with mental tasks. This prospect makes the study of computers especially fascinating. From a mathematical standpoint, partly because general purpose computers are *digital* assemblies of a finite set of components, their study is based on a new, *purely algebraic* concept which I shall now define axiomatically.

DEFINITION. A *finite state machine* (or "automaton") M consists of a collectiom A of "input symbols," a collection S of "states," and a collection Z of "output symbols," related by two operations $\nu: A \times S \to S$ and $\zeta: S \times Z \to Z$. The operation ν assigns to each "input symbol" $a \in A$ and "prior state" $s \in S$ a "new state" $\nu(a, s) \in S$; the operation ζ assigns to a and s a "printout" $\zeta(a, s) \in Z$. More concretely, such a finite state machine M can be thought of as evolving from a specified *starting state* s_0, *recursively* by $s_k = \nu(s_{k-1}, a_k)$, and as *printing out* $z_k = \zeta(s_{k-1}, a_k)$ for $k = 1, \cdots, n$ in succession. In this way, it converts strings of input symbols or *programs* $a_1, a_2, \cdots, a_n$ into printouts $z_1, z_2, \cdots, z_n$.

Abstractly, a finite state machine is clearly just a new kind of algebraic system $M = [A, S, Z; \nu, \zeta]$. If one simplifies M by ignoring Z and ζ (this is called a "forgetful functor" in category theory), the simplified M just describes the *action of a free semigroup* (the set A^* of all possible input "programs") *on a set* (the set S of states). The resulting theory of state machines without output fits nicely into axiomatic (or "modern") algebra and, as has recently been shown,[39] so-called "universal algebra" can be applied to it.

21. Turing machines. Quite similar to finite state machines, but a little more complicated, are the "Turing machines" invented by the logician Turing in 1936, before high-speed general purpose digital computers existed. Turing proved that they could indeed carry out most processes of mathematical "thought." Thus they are capable of printing out the binary or decimal expansion of any "definable" (alias "computable") real number, such as e, π, or the kth zero of the Bessel function $J_n(x)$, and they can "deduce all the provable formulas of the *restricted* Hilbert functiona calculus," giving all true theorems and no false ones.

Some two decades after Turing showed that his machines could, *in principle*, carry out the kind of mechanical theorem-proving dreamed of by Leibniz, Whitehead and Russell, and Hilbert, Hao Wang did this *in practice*. Namely, he wrote a special program which produced "proofs" in minutes for all the 350 theorems in the predicate calculus with equality that were actually stated in Whitehead and Russell's *Principia Mathematica*![40]

22. Computational complexity; optimization. A third and very strong trend in algebra, and indeed in mathematics generally, is a concern with *computational complexity* and with *optimization*. In all *applications* of algebra, of course, the efficiency of symbol-manipulation is a prime consideration, but for many years it was taboo to discuss it in research journals devoted to pure mathematics.

This snobbish taboo against discussing efficiency obscured some very important basic facts. Thus, in the area of mathematical logic, the scholarly books by Whitehead and Russell and the Hilbert school did *not* seriously try to improve the efficiency of formal deductive schemes, whereas Leibniz and Peano were really trying to (and did; especially Leibniz!) develop symbolic techniques for making mathematical reasoning more efficient and, therefore, more powerful. This difference becomes painfully obvious if one compares the number of symbols required by Whitehead and Russell to derive the basic formal properties of sets and relations, with the number of words needed by mathematicians to get equally far. So far, it is only in the area of the propositional calculus of logic itself, and by using a powerful computer, that mechanical theorem-proving has been realized on a substantial scale (by Hao Wang, see §21).

Having finally recognized the importance of efficiency, mathematical logicians have begun to analyze the "computational complexity" of applying general definitions to particular cases. Their analysis has already borne fruit in the development of shorter procedures for multiplying numbers and matrices.

Concern with computational complexity in algebra has as its ultimate goal, of course, the *optimization* of symbolic methods. In turn, the question of optimization has already suggested a number of basic problems whose solution should be a continuing challenge, stimulating coming generations of *pure* algebraists. Two of these are, respectively: (i) the "shortest form" problem of Boolean algebra, and (ii) the "most efficient coding" problem of information theory.

Other fascinating optimization problems, concerning which surprising discoveries have recently been made, are: (iii) what is the least number of operations on digits required to multiply two n-digit integers? (iv) what is the smallest number of arithmetic operations required to multiply together two $n \times n$ matrices? (v) how can one solve n simultaneous linear equations in n unknowns with the fewest additions, subtractions, multiplications and divisions? I regret that I do not have time to discuss these problems here, and must refer you to the literature ([**21**] and [**11**, vol. 2, pp. 258–78]).

23. Combinatorial algebra. A fourth current trend in algebra is towards emphasis on *combinatorial* ideas,[41] and especially on those involving *graphs* or *networks*. This trend is surely due to an intuitive recognition of the fact that digital computers and the deductive procedures of mathematics have a structure whose analysis requires combinatorial methods. As Hermann Weyl wrote in 1949: "The network of nerves joining the brain with the sense organs is a subject that by its very nature invites combinatorial investigation. Modern computing machines translate our insight into the combinatorial structure of mathematics into practice by mechanical and electronic devices."[42]

From burgeoning elementary courses in "Discrete Mathematics" which are intended to *precede* courses in axiomatic algebra,[43] probability and statistics, to the ambitious 7-volume treatise [**11**] on *The Art of Computer Programming* being written by Donald Knuth, the new emphasis is the same: permutations, combinations partitions, generating functions, trees, sorting, searching, recurrences, and difference equations, block designs, and so on. Even a casual reading of the books I have cited makes it very clear that the 200 year reign of the Calculus and Analysis has ended— and that they will continue to be displaced in our colleges by courses in Algebra in the broadest sense of discrete mathematics and the *science* (no longer just art!) of symbol manipulation.

In a sense, this trend continues the revolution begun by van der Waerden, but there has been a major change. No longer do axioms and deductive systems, patterned after Euclid's *Elements*, seem so fundamental. Neither do groups or rings, with their subgroups, subrings and morphisms. Their place is taken by various *relational structures* (including partial orderings and "complexes" in the sense of combinatorial topology) which are far less amenable to the general algebraic techniques which played such a central role in the "modern algebra" of 1930–1960.

Instead, the kinds of algebraic structures (as contrasted with "relational" structures) which are most relevant to digital computers and combinatorics are loops, monoids and lattices (or groupoids, semigroups and semilattices), which were largely ignored by most algebraists in 1930–1960. Loosely speaking, much as *groups* are related to *symmetries*, so *loops* are related to *designs* (or "patterns"), *monoids* to *actions* (e.g., of input instructions on the states of an automaton), and *lattices* to *structure*.

In particular, Rota[44] and his associates have shown that lattice theory provides a point of vantage from which to attack combinatorial problems in general, and not just those of algebra as I had stated in 1933 (see §7). Going even further, N. S. Mendelsohn has very recently applied concepts of universal algebra to generate combinatorial designs and vice-versa [**23**, pp. 123–32].

One naturally wonders where all these new trends will lead to. I am myself sure of only one thing: that they will *not* make the classical "modern algebra" expounded in van der Waerden obsolete, any more than this made real and complex algebra or the calculus obsolete. As Knuth emphasizes ([**11**, vol. 1, p. 1]; see also [**1**]) the word *algorithm* (or "algorism") which is so central to the mathematics of computation is just a corruption of the name Al-Khwarizmi, the originator of the word "algebra."

Indeed, the four current trends in algebra which I have been describing were merely *stimulated* by the consideration of digital computers, in much the same way that the calculus and analysis were stimulated by thinking about geometry, mechanics and mathematical physics. They are simply opening up new areas of mathematics for future generations to study, with an ever increasing variety and richness of interrelations and applications, in which old and new ideas will mingle and be reshaped. Within a few decades, new concepts and trends may well emerge from this mingling and reshaping. Certainly, this kind of continuing evolution is the only thing that can keep algebra perennially a fresh and exciting subject!

Notes

[1] See footnote on page 761.

[2] For this and other facts, I am indebted to Professor David Pingree of Brown University; Thomas Hawkins, Gian-Carlo Rota, Gerald Sachs, and John Tate made other very helpful comments.

[3] A notable exception is provided by the binomial theorem, discovered by Pascal in 1653. For readable accounts of the facts summarized in this section, see Rouse Ball [**1**] and E. T. Bell [**3**].

[4] Their expositions were very obscure; see G. Birkhoff, *Isis* 3 (1973), 260–7. That of Galois was clarified by Betti in 1852.

[5] We here follow the usual custom of letting Z (for the German "*Zahl*" meaning integer) stand for the set $\{0, \pm 1, \pm 2, \cdots\}$. Gauss attributed the consideration of integers mod n ("modular numbers") to Legendre.

[6] For penetrating historical surveys of linear and non-commutative algebra, see N. Bourbaki, [**6**, pp. 78–91 and 120–28]. For a readable summary of Cayley's contribution, see pp. 102–15 of E. T. Bell [**2**].

[7] Gergonne's Annales 5 (1814–15), p. 93; for Hamilton's ideas, see his *Mathematical Papers*, vol. III, Cambridge Univ. Press, 1967. Leibniz and Cramer had very fragmentary ideas about determinants; see [**1**, p. 375] and D. J. Struik, *A Source Book in Mathematics*, Harvard University Press, 1969, p. 180.

[8] R. Woodhouse, Phil. Trans. 91 (1801), 89–119; G. Peacock, Reps. Brit. Assn. Adv. Sci. 3 (1834), 185–32 and *Algebra*, 2 vols., 1845; A. de Morgan, Trans. Camb. Phil. Soc., 7 (1839) 173–87 and 287–300; G. Boole, Cambridge and Dublin Math. J., 3 (1848) 183–98.

[9] F. Klein, *Entwicklung der Mathematik im* 19*ten Jahrhundert*, vol. 1, p. 175, characterized this as "almost unreadable."

[10] In his supplements to Dirichlet's *Vorlesungen über Zahlentheorie*, 1863, 1871.

[11] Benjamin Peirce, *Linear Associative Algebra*, Boston, 1870; see also Amer. J. Math., 3 (1880) 15–57, and 4 (1881) 97–229 (reprinted from Proc. Am. Acad. Boston, 1875).

[12] See his *Collected Papers*. vol. 2, Cremonese, Rome, 1958, p. 134. In the Amer. Math. Society *Semicentennial Addresses*, vol. 2, p. 15, Bell attributed the postulational approach to Peano! Peano was also the first to *number* his theorems.

[13] Volumes 3–6 of the Transactions of the (then young) American Mathematical Society (1902–5) contain a dozen articles on postulate systems by the men named above.

[14] Eulcid's *Elements*, which included "axioms" for magnitudes (algebra) as well as "postulates" for geometry, were written in Alexandria, Egypt, around 300 B. C.; see Ball [**1**].

[15] For a historical discussion of ideal theory and Dedekind's work on algebraic numbers, see [**3**, Ch. 10].

[16] Op. cit. supra, pp. 216–29. The same result was proved independently by Frobenius, op. cit. infra.

[17] G. Frobenius, Crelle, 84 (1878) 1–63, and Berlin Sitzb. (1903) 504–37 and 634–5. Wedderburn's *Lectures on Matrices*, Amer. Math. Soc., 1934, contains a complete bibliography to 1933.

[17a] See Thomas Hawkins, Archive for History of Exact Sciences, 8 (1972) 243–87.

[18] A related symbolic style of writing was used by E. H. Moore in his *Introduction to a Form of General Analysis*, New Haven Colloquium, Yale Univ. Press, 1910.

[19] See F. Cajori, "Past struggles between symbolists and rhetoricians. . .", Proc. Int. Math. Congress Toronto (1924), vol. 2, pp. 937–41.

[20] First published in 1889 (*Arithmetices principia nova methodo exposita*).

[21] The fact that this was so had been airily asserted a decade earlier by Russell in his witty *Principles of Mathematics*, of which *Principia Mathematica* was originally intended to be comprised in a second volume!

[22] See G. Birkhoff, "Mathematics and Psychology," SIAM Review, 11 (1969) 429–69.

[23] *Werke*, vol. 3, p. 153; Math. Annalen 78, 405–15.

[24] Hilbert is here slurring over Euclid's distinction between "axioms" (for magnitudes in general) and "postulates" (for geometrical entities).

[25] Of the books [**10**] and *Grundlagen der Mathematik* (2 vols., 1939), respectively.

[26] See S. C. Kleene, *Introduction to Metamathematics*, Van Nostrand, 1932, pp. 204–5.

[27] This MONTHLY, 53 (1946) 1–18. Gödel's original paper was published in the Monats. Math. Phys., 38 (1931) 173–98.

[28] Careful historical reviews of the question touched on here may be found in N. Bourbaki, [**6**, Ch. 1], and (by P. Bernays) in Hilbert's *Werke*, vol. 3, pp.. 196–217; this volume also contains Hilbert's papers on logic.

[29] In German, "der die Algebra ihren erneuten Aufschwung verdankt."

[30] Proc. Camb. Phil. Soc., 29 (1933) 441.

[31] Bull. Amer. Math. Soc., 44 (1938) 793–827.

[32] A pen-name assumed in 1937 by a group of then young French mathematicians, who wished to overthrow the domination of French mathematics by classical analysts. See this MONTHLY, 57 (1950) 221–32 for authentic statement of Bourbaki's opinions, including the view that the axiomatic method is "a *standardization* of mathematical technique," and that the principal mathematical structures are those of a group, of order, and of a topological space.

[33] For example, anyone doing serious research on algebraic "geometry" today is expected to consider the two-volume treatise on *Commutative Rings* by O. Zariski and P. Samuel as standard *preliminary* material, but not to know Newton's classification of real cubic curves!

[34] F. William Lawvere, "The category of categories as a foundation for mathematics," *Proc. Conf. Categorical Algebra*, La Jolla, 1965 (S. Eilenberg *et al*, eds.), Springer, 1966.

[35] *American Scientist*, Nov. – Dec., 1971.

[36] Mathematicians habituated to exclusively deductive reasoning should realize that, in practice, error analysis relies very heavily on empirical evidence as well as on theoretical principles.

[37] Though not as nearly inefficient as Cramer's Rule, which is still often the only prescription given to students!

[38] See Marvin Minsky, *Computation: Finite and Infinite Machines*, Prentice-Hall, 1967.

[39] G. Birkhoff and J. D. Lipson, "Heterogeneous Algebras," J. Comb. Analysis, 2 (1969).

[40] H. Wang, IBM J. Res. Develop., 4 (1960) 2–22. For the general question of the computer as a "brain," see the reference of note 22.

[41] Wallis, Tchirnhaus, and Leibniz all recognized before 1700 that combinatorics belonged to algebra. See [**13**, p. 14] and [**21**, p. 2].

[42] E. F. Beckenbach (editor), *Applied Combinatorial Mathematics*, Wiley, 1964, p. 537.

[43] As currently recommended by the CUPM Panel on the Impact of Computing on Mathematics Courses. On an intermediate level, see C. L. Liu, *Introduction to Combinatorial Mathematics*, McGraw-Hill, 1968; on a more advanced level, see M. Hall, *Combinatorial Theory*, Ginn, 1967.

[44] "On the foundations of combinatorial theory," J. für Wahrsch., 2 (1966) 340–68; *Combinatorial geometries* (preliminary edition), M.I.T. Press, 1970; and refs. given there.

References

1. W. W. Rouse Ball, A Short History of Mathematics, 3rd ed., Macmillan, New York, 1901.

2. Eric T. Bell, Mathematics: Queen and Servant of Sciences, McGraw-Hill, New York, 1951.

3. ———, The Development of Mathematics, McGraw-Hill, New York, 1940.

4. Garrett Birkhoff and Thomas C. Bartee, Modern Applied Algebra, McGraw-Hill, New York, 1970.

5. Garrett Birkhoff and Saunders Mac Lane, A Survey of Modern Algebra, Macmillan, New York, 1941.

6. Nicolas Bourbaki, Éléments d'Histoire des Mathématiques, Hermann, Paris, 1960.

7. Florian Cajori, A History of Mathematical Notations, 2 vols., Open Court, Chicago, 1928–9.

8. George Grätzer, Universal Algebra, Van Nostrand, Princeton, N. J., 1968.

9. David Hilbert, Grundlagen der Geometrie, 1899; 2nd. ed., 1901. Authorized translation by E. J. Townsend, Open Court, Chicago, 1902, 1910.

10. David Hilbert and W. Ackermann, Grundzüge der theoretische Logik, 4th ed., 1949.

11. Donald Knuth, Algorithms, 7 projected volumes, Addison-Wesley, Reading, Mass., 1969.

12. S. Mac Lane and G. Birkhoff, Algebra, Macmillan, New York, 1967.

13. Uta Merzbach, "... Development of Modern Algebraic Structures from Leibniz to Dedekind," Ph. D. Thesis, Harvard, 1965.

14. Giuseppe Peano, Formulario Matematico, 4th ed., Torino, 1908.

15. Donald Rose and Ralph Willoughby (eds.), Sparse Matrices and their Applications, Plenum Press, New York, 1971.

16. B. L. van der Waerden, Moderne Algebra, 2 vols., Springer, New York, 1930–31.

17. Richard S. Varga, Matrix Iterative Analysis, Prentice-Hall, Englewood Cliffs, N.J., 1962.

18. Alfred N. Whitehead and Bertrand Russell, Principia Mathematica, 3 vols., Cambridge Univ. Press, 1911.

19. James Wilkinson, The Algebraic Eigenvalue Problem, Clarendon Press, Oxford, 1966.

20. David M. Young, Iterative Solution of Large Linear Systems, Academic Press, New York, 1971.

21. Garrett Birkhoff and Marshall Hall (eds.), Computers in Algebra and Number Theory, SIAM-AMS Proceedings, vol. IV, Amer. Math. Society, 1971.

22. Deane Montgomery and Leo Zippin, Topological Transformation Groups, Wiley-Interscience, New York, 1955.

23. W. Tutte (ed.), Recent Progress in Combinatorics, Academic Press, New York, 1969.

The Role of Modern Algebra in Computing[1]

Garrett Birkhoff

1. **Introduction.** This Symposium has as its main theme the applications of digital computers to algebra and number theory; its primary concern is with how such computers can serve "pure" mathematicians. My primary concern will be with the complementary role played by algebra in the science of digital computing, hence with services which mathematicians can render (and have rendered) to computing.

Here by *algebra* I mean the use of *symbol manipulation* in the widest sense, as this seems to describe most accurately its meaning.[2] When the symbols being manipulated stand for real and complex numbers, we have *real and complex algebra*, or algebra in the *classical* sense. When the symbols represent statements, we have the *propositional calculus* (including Boolean algebra), which is the oldest part of symbolic logic. Other interpretations of the symbols lead to group, ring, module, and field theory, and to other parts of *modern algebra* familiar to contemporary "pure" algebraists.

Both classical and modern algebra are important for computing: classical algebra for the highly developed science of *numerical* computation, and modern algebra for the developing science of *nonnumerical* computation (alias "symbol manipulation"). However, the applications of classical algebra to numerical computation involve many ideas from analysis; the resulting science of "numerical algebra" might aptly be called modern applied arithmetic.

Hence I shall say little about real or complex algebra here, but shall concentrate on those modern algebraic ideas and techniques which are most relevant to computing.

Modern algebra. Surprisingly, the aspects of symbolic algebra which are most important for computing are *not* those which received the most

---

AMS 1969 *subject classifications.* Primary 9430; Secondary 0830.

[1]Report prepared with support from the Office of Naval Research under Contract NR-04-188.

[2][**27**, §1.1]; [**12**, Chapter XXVI]; W. W. Rouse Ball, "A Short History of Mathematics," 3rd edition, Macmillan, 1901, p. 189; see also §4 below.

attention in van der Waerden's "Moderne Algebra": Boolean algebras and lattices, binary relations and graphs, and combinatorial algebra play a much greater role in computing than the theory of infinite commutative rings and fields, to which the bulk of van der Waerden's book is dedicated. This inclusion of combinatorics in algebra is in agreement with Tchirnhaus, who claimed already before 1700 that "the combinatorial art stems from algebra," if not with Leibniz, who claimed that combinatorics, as the art of synthesis, included algebra [**16**a, pp. 287, 297].

To survey the applications of modern algebra to computing in a half-hour requires great oversimplification and superficiality, which I hope you will excuse. To compensate for this superficiality, I shall try to present known facts in a fresh light and mention some unpublished technical results. Throughout, I shall emphasize work done at Harvard ([7]–[**10**] and [**T1**]–[**T6**]), an emphasis which I hope you will also excuse.

Optimization. Not only has algebra influenced computing, but the problems of computing are influencing algebra. This is especially true of various problems of *optimization* including those of *finding algorithms of minimum "computational complexity"*, say for multiplying together two $n \times n$ matrices or testing a polynomial with integral coefficients for irreducibility over $\mathbf{Z}$; see the papers by Winograd and Zassenhaus in this volume.

The influence on algebra of the concepts of optimization and computational complexity (and computability) can perhaps be best appreciated by analogy. The ancient Greeks took great interest in rationalizing geometry through constructions with ruler and compass (as analog computers), and in correlating the results with numbers. By considering such constructions and their optimization in depth, they were led to the existence of irrational numbers, and to the problems of constructing regular polygons, trisecting angles, duplicating cubes, and squaring circles. These problems, though of minor technological significance, profoundly influenced the development of number theory.

I think that our understanding of the potentialities and limitations of algebraic symbol manipulation will be similarly deepened by attempts to solve problems of optimization and computational complexity arising from digital computing.

A. Binary Algebra; Lattices; Semigroups

2. **Boolean algebra.** Since most digital computers are constructed from bistable or *binary elements*, it is natural that the algebra of 0 and 1, which I shall refer to as *binary algebra*, should be important for computing. In particular, because human logic is also binary, binary algebra is central to logic design for computers, regardless of whether these are built using relays, vacuum tubes, or semiconductors.

The simplest kind of binary algebra is the *Boolean algebra* of elementary set theory and logic, and especially important is the *free Boolean algebra* with n generators. Already before 1850, Boole showed that this was (in modern notation) $\mathbf{2}^{2^n}$. More concretely, it is the Boolean algebra of all functions $f: \mathbf{2}^n \to \mathbf{2}$, where $\mathbf{2} = \{0, 1\}$ is the two-element Boolean algebra. If the elements of $\mathbf{2}^n$ are represented as n-vectors $\mathbf{x} = (x_1, \ldots, x_n)$ ("n-bit words"), the generators can be taken as the n functions δ_i: $(x_1, \ldots, x_n) \to x_i$. And in 1913, Skolem[3] showed that the (distributive) sublattice of $\mathbf{2}^{2^n}$, generated by the "evaluation maps" δ_i was $\mathbf{2}^{2^n}$, the set of all isotone functions f: $\mathbf{2}^n \to \mathbf{2}$ (and the free distributive lattice with n generators).

On the other hand, each function $\mathbf{2}^n \to \mathbf{2}$ can be regarded as a *switching function* which assigns to each "state" of n binary "input" elements a "state" of a specified output element. Hence theorems about Boolean algebras can be reinterpreted as statements about switching circuits. Boole's results make possible the *systematic* design of logic processors for computers from AND-gates, OR-gates, and inverters. Likewise, Skolem's Theorem can be paraphrased as the assertion that precisely the isotone switching functions can be realized by series-parallel networks (using AND-gates and OR-gates, but not inverters).

However, the most important and challenging questions of switching theory concern the most economical or *optimal* logic design for a network which will realize a given Boolean function f: $\mathbf{2}^n \to \mathbf{2}$. Like most questions of optimal design, this question is ambiguous because "cost" assignments are variable; one natural interpretation consists in asking for the *shortest* (fewest-symbol) symbolic expression based on the operations $\wedge$, $\vee$, $'$ which will realize a given f. Although ingenious techniques for shortening Boolean polynomials have been devised by Quine and others, nobody has yet discovered a systematic algorithm for reducing a general Boolean polynomial in 20 variables (say) to *shortest* form, without comparing an impossibly large number of short forms. Therefore, if we define *switching theory* as the branch of modern (i.e., non-numerical) algebra concerned with optimizing logic design, we must admit that the main theoretical problem of switching theory has not yet been solved.[4]

3. **Binary groups.** Also because digital computers are made up of binary elements, codes used with them often make use of properties of elementary Abelian groups of order 2^n, which may properly be called "binary groups." One application of such codes is to synthesize reliable message-transmitting "organisms" (including computers) from unreliable components.[5] The simplest way to accomplish this is by "multiplexing," but modern algebra is needed to achieve optimal or even economical designs.

Specifically, to minimize the probability of error in message transmission

---

[3]Third Scand. Math. Congress (1913), 149–163. For other properties of $\mathbf{2}^{2^n}$, see [**LT3**, Chapter III, §4] and H. N. Shapiro, Comm. Pure Appl. Math. **23** (1970), 299–312. (Here and below, **LT***n*] refers to the *n*th edition of [**7**].)

[4]For switching theory, see [**9**, Chapter 6]; also [**26**, Chapter 4], especially §§1 and 6. For various theoretical difficulties, see J. P. Roth, Trans. Amer. Math. Soc. **88** (1958), 301–326.

[5]See [**38**a, vol. V, pp. 329–378, especially pp. 353–368].

at given cost, encoding-decoding procedures called binary (m, n) *group codes* are often used. In group codes, each m-bit block of the message or "message word" is encoded as a longer n-bit "code word" $(n > m)$. Such n-bit words can be visualized as the vertices of a unit n-cube. The *distance* between two vertices is defined to be the length of the shortest path joining them along edges of the cube (its graph), or, equivalently, the square of the Euclidean distance between them in n-space. In other words, for $\mathbf{x} = (x_1, \ldots, x_n)$ and $\mathbf{y} = (y_1, \ldots, y_n)$:

$$(1) \qquad d(\mathbf{x},\mathbf{y}) = \sum (x_i - y_i)^2, \quad \text{each } x_i, y_i = 0 \text{ or } 1.$$

Also, $d(x,y)$ is the number of coordinates i with $x_i \neq y_i$.

Suppose that a sequence of m-bit message words is to be sent through a *binary symmetric channel* in which, by definition, each bit has a probability p of being correctly received $(0 < p < 1)$. The relevant optimization problem is to *maximize the code rate* $R = m/n$ for a given (very small) probability Q of error when the message has been *decoded*, for fixed p. Shannon proved very early that, for any $\epsilon > 0$, one can make $Q < \epsilon$ and $R > p - \epsilon$ (thus achieving arbitrarily large efficiency), provided long enough code blocks are used. This is a very satisfactory *existence theorem*, but Shannon's construction would require very complicated and costly capital equipment to implement. Algebraic coding theory[6] aims at constructing simpler optimal or near-optimal codes.

Most algebraic codes are binary group codes, in which the code words form a *subgroup* of the elementary Abelian group of order 2^n. Though it is not clear that optimal codes must be group codes, I know of no (m, n) code not a group code which is superior to every (m, n) group code. Moreover systematic decoding is certainly helped by having the group structure built into the code.

Obviously, the chance of confusing two n-bit code words is negligible when the "distance" between them is large. Hence to *optimize* coding, one wishes to know for any n and $l < n$ the maximum number $F(n, l)$ of vertices on an n-cube, such that any two are a distance at least l apart—i.e., such that $\mathbf{x} \neq \mathbf{y}$ implies $d(\mathbf{x},\mathbf{y}) \geqq l$.

For odd $l = 2k+1$, $F(n, 2k+1)$ is the maximum number of disjoint spheres of radius k which can be "packed" in $\mathbf{2}^n$. If one takes the centers of these spheres for *code words*, then one can systematically correct any set of k or fewer errors in transmitting an n-bit message block, by assigning to every received n-bit block which is in one of these spheres the m-bit message block corresponding to the code word at its center.

For this reason, when the hypercube $\mathbf{2}^n$ can be exactly covered by disjoint spheres of radius k, one speaks of a *perfect* packing (or code). This is the case that the obvious inequality

$$(2) \qquad F(n, 2k+1) \leqq \mathbf{2}^n \Big/ \left[1 + \binom{n}{1} + \cdots + \binom{n}{k}\right]$$

[6]See [9] for an elementary exposition, and Berlekamp's article in W. T. Tutte (editor), "Recent Progress in Combinatorics," Academic Press, 1969.

reduces to an equality. As Dr. van List has said, the only known perfect error-correcting codes are the binary Hamming codes [**9**, p. 252] and the two Golay codes [**5**]; there probably are no others. However, the Hamming codes correct only one error ($k = 1$, $l = 3$ above); the problem of *binary code optimization* is *unsolved* for $k > 1$ [**1**, vol. X, pp. 291–297].

The most powerful known systematic[7] error-correcting codes are the Bose-Chaudhuri-Hocquenghem or BCH-codes [**9**, Chapter 12]. The construction of these uses the properties of finite (Galois) fields of order 2^n, which one may call *binary fields*. A $(2^n - 1 - (2k+1)n, 2^n - 1)$ BCH-code can be designed to correct k errors [**9**, p. 355]; thus a (215,255) BCH-code can correct up to 5 errors with 40 check digits. This is fairly efficient; but each sphere of radius 5 in the hypercube $\mathbf{2}^{255}$ contains only about 8 billion (2^{33}) vertices; hence the "packing" leaves over 99% of all vertices not "covered." Thus, it is far from "perfect"; moreover, $k \ll n$. (Other "good" codes with $k \ll n$ can be based on the Chinese Remainder Theorem.[8])

Finally, for $n = 2^r$ and $l = 2^{r-1}$, I believe that $F(n, l) = F(2^r, 2^{r-1}) = 2r$. Specifically, the r generators δ_i and their r (antipodal in the hypercube $\mathbf{2}^{2^r}$) complements δ_i' are separated by a distance $l = 2^{r-1}$ or (if antipodal) $2l = 2^r$; hence $F(2^r, 2^{r-1}) \geqq 2r$. My conjecture is that equality holds.

Concluding remark. The two unsolved problems in binary algebra which I have described illustrate the fact that *genuine applications can suggest simple and natural but extremely difficult problems*, which are overlooked by pure theorists. Thus, while working for 30 years (1935–1965) on generalizing Boolean algebra to lattice theory, I regarded finite Boolean algebras as trivial because they could all be described up to isomorphism, and completely ignored the basic "shortest form" and "optimal packing" problems described above.

4. **Binary relations and graphs.** The *binary relations* between two sets S and T form a Boolean algebra $\mathbf{2}^{S \times T}$ in an obvious way. If S and T are finite, with elements listed as $s_1, \ldots, s_m$ and $t_1, \ldots, t_n$, then the set of binary relations from S to T is bijective with the set of $m \times n$ matrices $R = \|r_{ij}\|$ with entries 0 and 1: $r_{ij} = 1$ means that s_i and t_j are in the relation R. This illustrates how the binary relations from S to T form a binary algebra under Boolean operations performed componentwise.

When $S = T$, the algebra of binary relations has a richer structure, because the set $\mathbf{2}^{S \times S}$ of all binary relations on a set S also forms a *monoid* under composition. The analysis of the properties of the resulting algebraic system $[\mathbf{2}^{S \times S}; \wedge, \vee, ', \circ]$ forms an important part of the algebra of logic as developed

[7]Especially from the standpoint of efficient implementation (including decoding). The optimal codes to be defined in Part C, like those of negligible redundancy whose existence was established by Shannon, are hard to implement electronically.

[8]See [**1**, loc. cit.]. Also, John Lipson and Erwin Bareiss have important unpublished manuscripts giving other applications of this theorem.

by Boole, Schröder, and Whitehead and Russell. Only since 1940 have the involved algebraic properties of this system been disentangled, and the system identified as a *lattice-ordered monoid* [**7**, pp. 343–345].

Because of the rich algebraic structure of relation algebra and its basic role in logic, I would expect the algebra of binary relations to be useful for computing and computer logic (cf. §10), it is also useful for specifying the zero elements of matrices (cf. Part D). However, I know of no programming language which utilizes this richer structure. Neither do I know of any computer having a "logic unit" (analogous to the "arithmetic unit" implementing approximate addition and multiplication electronically), which utilizes the rich algebraic structure of the algebra of relations.

Graphs. The binary relations on a set S can also be represented symbolically as *directed graphs*, whose vertices designate the elements of S, with an arrow going from vertex i to vertex j if and only if $r_{ij} = 1$. Such directed graphs are omnipresent in computer science. Graphs appear in flow charts for programs, and in state diagrams for gating (logic) networks.

I maintain that graphs and directed graphs constitute part of algebra in the sense of providing techniques of symbol manipulation, as well as of being connected by a cryptomorphism with the algebra of relations. In support of this view I quote [**24**, pp. 49–50]: "To express . . . system structure symbolically, there has emerged . . . various kinds of flowgraphs . . . evolving into a new kind of notation . . . flowgraphs can be manipulated and "solved" just as . . . conventional algebraic and functional symbols . . . may be manipulated and solved."

Actually, the strictly one-dimensional or *sequential* alphanumeric symbolism of linguistic theory (also preferred by typesetters) is not strictly adhered to even in algebra. Thus one often prefers to manipulate two-dimensional algebraic displays such as matrices or the following:

$$\frac{x^{n+1} - y^{n+1}}{x - y} = \sum_{k=0}^{n} x^{n-k} y^k.$$

Moreover, labelled directed graphs are also used in pure algebra, as diagrams for finite posets [**9**, p. 38], and for (very small) categories of mappings. Finally, we shall see in Part D the utility for Gauss elimination of the concepts of the graph and directed graph of a matrix.

Graphs and configurations. By a *configuration* is meant a system consisting of a set S_0 of "points," a set S_1 of "lines," and an *incidence* relation stating which points are on which lines. It is required that at least two points $p, q \in S_0$ be on each line $L \in S_1$; when there exist exactly two such points, the configuration is called a loop-free *graph.* When no two distinct lines have the same two (incident) points, the graph is called *simple.*[9]

Given any enumeration of the points and lines of a finite graph or other

[9]See [**9**, p. 56] and [**15**, p. 18].

configuration Γ, the incidence matrix of Γ is the relation matrix of its incidence relation as defined above. One can also define a simple loop-free graph, relative to any enumeration of its points, by the *adjacency matrix*. $A(\Gamma) = \|\alpha_{ij}\|$, where $\alpha_{ij} = 1$ if $p_i p_j$ is an edge of the graph and $\alpha_{ij} = 0$ otherwise.

As defined by its adjacency relation, a graph is thus a (homogeneous) "relational system," which brings it within the scope of universal algebra [**20**, p. 224]; as defined by its incidence relation, it is a heterogeneous relational system.

5. **Lattices.** Although "binary algebras" (i.e., Boolean algebras and binary groups and fields) have a special importance for digital computers, their role is by no means exclusive. Thus, an important role is also played by *lattices*: posets (i.e., partially ordered sets) L, any two of whose elements have least upper bounds and greatest lower bounds in L. Lattices include Boolean algebras as a special case: the case of complemented distributive lattices.

Non-Boolean lattices are important for computer science because not only the subsets but also the *partitions* of the elements of any system (e.g., of the components or states of a machine) form a lattice [**23**, §2.1]. Moreover, those subsets which are "closed" under specified sets of operations, and those partitions which have some desirable property such as the substitution property for specified operations [**23**, p. 68], also typically form lattices. In particular, the "state splittings" of a machine are embedded in such a lattice [**23**, Chapter 5], and this fact makes some aspects of automaton theory (see §§9–10) more understandable.

Closure and dependence. Lattices also arise from closure operations of many kinds; see [**LT3**, Chapter 5]. Lattices arising from the following three closure operations on vectors are especially important for computing.

DEFINITION. Let $V = V_n(F)$ be any vector space, and let S be the set of *all* vectors of V. By the *linear span* $\lambda(A)$ of a set of vectors $\alpha_1, \ldots, \alpha_r$ of S is meant the set of all linear combinations $\xi = c_1\alpha_1 + \cdots + c_r\alpha_r$ of the α_i. When $\Sigma\, c_i = 1$, ξ is said to belong to the *affine span* $\beta(A)$ of A. When the scalars belong to an ordered field and all $c_i \geqq 0$, as well as $\Sigma\, c_i = 1$, $\gamma = \Sigma\, c_i\alpha_i$ is said to belong to the *convex span* (or hull $\gamma(A)$) of A.

Each of the operations λ, β, γ is a *closure operation* c on the subsets of S, in the sense that [**7**, Chapter V] $c(X) \supset X$ for all X, $c(c(X)) = c(X)$ for all $X \subset S$, and $X \supset Y$ implies $c(x) \supset c(Y)$. Hence the "closed" subsets (i.e., linear subspaces, affine subspaces, and convex subsets in the three cases of interest here) form a *lattice*, and hence a (homogeneous) algebra in a very precise sense to be discussed in §8.

Given a closure operation c on $\mathbf{2}^S$, one says that $y \in S$ is *dependent* on a set $X \subset S$ when $y \in c(X)$. The dependence relations so defined from the closure operations λ, β above have a special *exchange property* due to Steinitz and Mac Lane.

SM. If neither p nor q is dependent on X, but q is dependent on $p \cup X$, then p is dependent on $q \cup X$.

It follows that the nonvoid linear subspaces and the affine subspaces of any vector space form geometric lattices: the so-called *projective geometry* $P_{n-1}(F)$ and *affine geometry* $A_n(F)$, of lengths $n-1$ and n, respectively; see [**7**, Chapter IV].

More generally, let S be *any* set of vectors in $V_n(F)$; one can define closure operators λ_S, β_S, and γ_S, consisting of all linear, affine, or affine combinations ξ as above which are in S. This defines (for λ_S and β_S) very large classes of geometric lattices, which may be considered as *subgeometries* of the geometries $P_{n-1}(F)$ and $A_n(F)$ just defined.

Given a *finite* set S of vectors in $V_n(F)$, where F is an ordered field, the convex closures of the subsets of S define what is called a *convex polytope* [**20**a, p. 31]. The lattice defined in this way satisfies the Jordan-Dedekind Chain Condition, but does not in general have the exchange property. (Instead, it has a weaker "Radon property.")

Three fascinating unsolved problems of lattice theory concern the characterization of those (finite) lattices which arise from the preceding construction, and the ways of *representing* (geometric) lattices as subgeometries of $P_{n-1}(F)$ and $A_n(F)$. In addition, these characterization problems lead to many difficult combinatorial questions.[10]

6. **Combinatorial complexes.** I now recall a far-reaching generalization of the notion of a graph, essentially due to Poincaré: that of a combinatorial complex [**3**].

Definition. An unoriented n-dimensional *combinatorial complex* is a collection of nonvoid sets S_k of *k-cells* ($k = 0, 1, \ldots, n$), together with associated *incidence matrices* specifying for each $k = 1, \ldots, n$ which $(k-1)$-cells are incident on which k-cells.

It is usually intended that each n-cell above be a convex polytope in the algebraic sense specified in §5. Since a one-dimensional convex polytope is necessarily just a finite line-segment, a graph is just a one-dimensional complex. It is usually also required that two cells meet on at most one face (subcell) of each; this condition holds in "simple" graphs. In applications to the topology of manifolds, moreover, at most two n-cells are allowed to meet on any $(n-1)$-cell or "facet", but the terminology has never become standardized.[11]

A very simple family of two dimensional complexes, that of *rectangular polygons* subdivided by parallels to their sides, is discussed in Appendix A.

[10] See for example V. Klee and D. W. Walkup, Acta. Math. **117** (1967), 53–77.

[11] For other definitions of combinatorial complexes, see S. Lefschetz, "Algebraic Topology", Amer. Math. Soc. 1942, p. 89, and the references given there. The definition given here seems closest to that of M. H. A. Newman. The basic reference is E. Steinitz, "Polyeder und Raumeinteilungen," Enz. Math. Wiss. 3AB 12 (1922), 1–139.

Another family of complexes is that of simplical complexes (in two dimensions, these consist of triangles).

The notion of a combinatorial complex has recently become important for computing, because the *finite element methods* used to solve on computers typical problems of solid mechanics begin by decomposing plates and shells into polygonal "elements." The resulting configuration is an unoriented 2-dimensional combinatorial complex. I shall explain in Part E the importance for computations using "finite element" methods of specifying such complexes carefully. In Appendix A, I shall describe some preliminary ideas for identifying rectangular polygons (up to isomorphism) and assigning addresses to their cells.

In any combinatorial complex whose n-cells are convex polytopes, the k-cells are just the elements of height k, and the incidence relation of the resulting complex (which has one r-cell, the dimension (height) of the span of S) is just the covering relation of the lattice.

Complexes as semilattices. By letting its incidence relation be the covering relation, any unoriented n-dimensional complex can be regarded as a poset P in which (i) all maximal chains have the same length n (implying the Jordan-Dedekind Chain Condition, and (ii) for any maximal element γ, if Γ consists of all elements $x \leqq \gamma$, there is an isomorphism θ from $[\Gamma, \leqq]$ to the set of all "faces" of an n-dimensional convex polytope Π under which $x \leqq y$ holds if and only if $\theta(x) \subset \theta(y)$ in Π).

Conversely, any poset P of finite length is defined up to isomorphism by its *incidence matrix*, the relation matrix of its covering relation. When P is a topological complex, and one enumerates first all its 0-cells, then all its 1-cells, then all its 2-cells,..., one obtains this strictly triangular incidence matrix as the direct sum $\bigoplus \Gamma_k = \Gamma(P)$ of incidence matrices generalizing those for graphs: Γ_k is the relation matrix of covering ("incidence") between k-cells and $(k-1)$-cells. (One has a further direct decomposition of $\Gamma(P)$ into the $\Gamma(P_l)$, where the P_l are the connected components of P.)

In the locally Euclidean case, each $(n-1)$-cell of an n-dimensional complex Γ is incident on at most two n-cells. (Any locally Euclidean graph is a sum of disjoint simple paths and simple cycles.) If one defines the boundary ∂C of a k-dimensional subcomplex C of Γ as the set of $(k-1)$-cells incident on only *one* k-cell, then more generally $\partial(\partial C) = 0$. However relatively "little is known concerning the geometric embeddability of specifically finite-dimensional simplical complexes in . . . Euclidean spaces,"[12] or even about which geometric lattices are convex polytopes over the real field, let alone about the embeddability of complexes in general.

Figures 1a-1b depict the diagrams of posets corresponding to a triangle

[12]See R. A. Duke, Amer. Math. Monthly **78** (1970), 597–603, and references given there. For still other applications of lattices to combinatorial problems see G.-C. Rota and L. H. Harper, Advances in Probability **1** (1971), 171–215.

(2-simplex) and a quadrangle, respectively, when the void set $\emptyset$ is included as a "(-1)-cell." Note that they are both lattices (the first is a Boolean algebra). This is a special case of the following result, which applies in particular to simple graphs.[13]

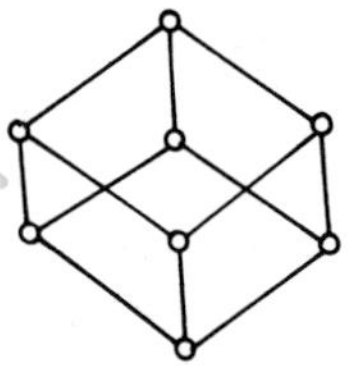

FIGURE 1a

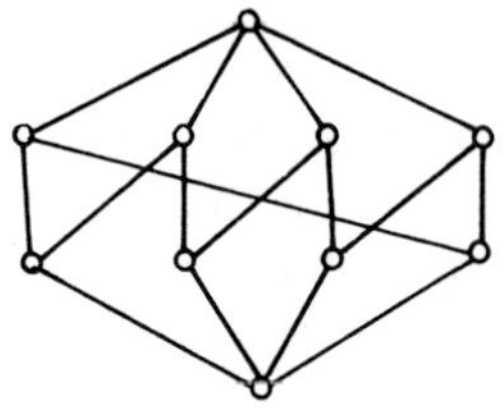

FIGURE 1b

THEOREM 1. *The closed cells of any combinatorial complex form with the void set $\emptyset$ a* semilattice *of finite length under intersection.*

This semilattice satisfies the Jordan-Dedekind Chain Condition, but is not usually semimodular [**7**, p. 40]. Its length is the dimension of the complex, plus one.

COROLLARY. *The points and closed edges of any simple (symmetric) graph form with $\emptyset$ a semilattice of length* 2.

By known properties of semilattices [**7**, p.22], Theorem 1 has a dual.

THEOREM 1′. *The closed cells of any combinatorial complex form, with an all-element I, a semilattice under join.*

One can also add both the void set $\emptyset$ and an all-element I to any complex, getting a lattice. When this is done to graphs, the notion of sublattice gives the usual concept of a "selection subgraph." (We recall that the sublattice concept is also useful when one considers projective geometries as lattices.)

Unfortunately, when graphs are considered as semilattices, the notions of direct product, morphism, and free algebra seem not to be very natural or useful. It seems more natural to consider graphs as "heterogeneous" algebras, and more fruitful to consider them as posets (or "partial lattices"; see §11).

Other applications of (geometric) lattices and posets to computing will be described in §15 and Part E.

7. **Semigroups.** I do not wish to exaggerate the importance for computer science of lattices (including Boolean algebras), or of binary groups and fields. All of these have a quite special structure. A much more general class of algebraic systems is provided by semigroups, which are indeed basic for a great part of algebra. They may be defined as follows.

[13] See [**LT1**, §18], [**LT2**, §10], and [**LT3**, Chapter IV, §11], where a slightly different poset interpretation is given.

DEFINITION. A *semigroup* is an algebra $H = [X, c]$ which consists of a set X of elements combined by a single binary composition operation $c: X^2 \to X$, which is *associative* in the sense that

$$(3) \qquad c(c, x(y, z)) = c(c(x, y), z) \quad \text{for all } x, y, z \in X.$$

Here $c(x, y)$ is commonly written $x \circ y$ or just xy.

Semigroups differ trivially from *monoids*, since every monoid is a semigroup and one can make any semigroup not a monoid into a monoid by adding an identity 1. *Groups* are just monoids in which every element x has an inverse x^{-1}, with $f(x, x^{-1}) = f(x^{-1}, x) = 1$.

Likewise, a semilattice is just a commutative semigroup in which every element is an idempotent. And finite lattices differ trivially from finite semilattices: one need only adjoin an I, or a 0, as the case may be.

Finally, *rings* are just algebras with two binary operations, + and $\cdot$, which are commutative groups under + and semigroups (or monoids according to taste) under $\cdot$, and in which the usual distributive laws are satisfied:

$$x(y+z) = xy+xz \quad \text{and} \quad (x+y)z = xz+yz, \quad \text{all } x, y, z.$$

Semigroups acting on sets. Semigroups arise in computing in many contexts; as we shall see, an especially direct application is to the theory of state machines (see §9) through the following intermediate concept.

DEFINITION. A *left-semigroup acting on a set* S is a triple $\mathscr{L} = \{H, S, \psi\}$, where $H = [X, c]$ is a semigroup, S is a set, and ψ is a mapping $\psi: X \times S \to S$ with the property that

$$(4) \qquad \psi(c(g, h), s) = \psi(g, \psi(h, s)), \qquad \text{all } g, h \in X \quad \text{and} \quad s \in S.$$

A *right-semigroup* $\mathscr{R} = \{H, S, \varphi\}$ is defined similarly, but with $\varphi: S \times X \to S$ and (4) replaced by

$$(4') \qquad \varphi(s, c(g, h)) = \varphi(\varphi(s, g), h).$$

B. AUTOMATA AND UNIVERSAL ALGEBRA

8. **Algebras.** The concept of semigroup provides an excellent introduction to the study of abstract algebra because of its simplicity, generality, and relative concreteness. Moreover it relates to computing through the notion of a "state machine"; see §9. However, it does not include nonassociative loops or quasi-groups; neither does it include most Lie or Jordan algebras.

A much more general class of algebraic systems, which includes Lie and Jordan algebras as well as semigroups, groups, lattices, rings and fields is provided by the following notion of an "algebra." I proposed it around 1935, and it has since gained wide acceptance.

DEFINITION. An *algebra* is a system $A = [S, F]$, where S is a set of *elements* and F is a set of *finitary operations*:

$$(5) \qquad f_i: S^{n(i)} \to S, \qquad n(i) \in N.$$

Universal algebra. In spite of the enormous variety of the systems to which the preceding definition applies, all of them have a substantial number of nontrivial properties in common. Many of these properties concern subalgebras, (homo)morphisms, congruence relations, direct products, etc. Some of them follow fairly directly from the ideas of the Emmy Noether school, but many others involve Dedekind's concept of a *lattice* which was ignored by this school. These common properties also include some less obvious results about free algebras, identities, and "varieties" of algebras. Moreover, they include still other theorems, trivial for finite algebras, which assert that the complete lattices of subalgebras and congruence relations of any algebra are "algebraic." Finally, an increasing set of recent theorems about general "algebras" invoke the concept of a category (see Example 9 below).

The subject of *universal algebra*[14] is concerned with such theorems about "algebras" in general; it provides the most general context in which a wide range of nontrivial algebraic theorems has so far been proved. By unifying and clarifying the foundations of algebra, in somewhat the same way that symbolic logic has helped to systematize the foundation of mathematics and automaton theory provides a general foundation for the theory of digital computer, universal algebra may be regarded as a further significant step towards fulfilling Leibniz' old dream (see §12) of automating the symbolic method. However, it must be confessed that "universal algebra" has contributed more to the clarification and unification of the foundations of algebra than to the development of powerful new techniques (except for some existence proofs).

Furthermore, to prove general theorems about the existence of free algebras, etc., one must assume that one is dealing with families of algebras defined by axioms stated as "sentences" of rather special logical forms which avoid existential quantifiers and negations. The "universal" proofs do not apply directly even to groups, when defined as monoids in which every element has a left- and a right-inverse, or when defined as semigroups in which any equation of the form $ax = b$ or $ya = b$ has a solution.

To apply the "universal" proofs, one must consider groups as having not only a binary (multiplication) operation, but also a 0-ary operation ("select 1") and a unary operation ("take the inverse a^{-1} of a"), as well as a binary operation. This is because: (i) the notion of "subalgebra" becomes ambiguous with existential quantifiers, (ii) only "positive" sentences are necessarily preserved under epimorphisms, and (iii) only sentences equivalent to "universal Horn sentences" are preserved under direct products.[15]

Cryptomorphisms. We have seen that graphs can be defined in several formally different ways. This is true of many kinds of algebraic systems. Trivial

[14]See [**2**, Part IV]; [**7**, Chapter VI]; [**16**]; and P. M. Cohn, "Universal Algebra," Harper and Row, 1965. The name was borrowed from the title of [**32**]; the technical content was not.

[15]Much of "universal algebra" does not apply to the class of fields, in which division is only a "partial" operation; see §11. For the other statements above, see [**20**, pp. 226, 281, 285].

examples are provided by the correspondences $\wedge$, $\rightleftharpoons$, $\vee$ in any lattice and $xy \rightleftharpoons yx$ in semigroups. Less trivially, one can convert any Boolean algebra into a Boolean ring by a "compile" transformation which translates I into 1, a' into $\gamma(a') = a+1$, and $a \vee b$ into $\gamma(a \vee b) = a+b+ab$. Conversely, one can convert any Boolean ring into a Boolean algebra by replacing 1 by I and $a+b$ by $\beta(a+b) = ab' \vee a'b$.

I have proposed [7, p. 154] the word *cryptomorphism* to describe such "compile" methods for translating from one mode of symbolic representation to another.[16] The above example, and the ways of representing graphs as algebraic systems (e.g., by incidence or adjacency matrices, or by circles and arcs), show that two algebraic systems can be "crypto-isomorphic" in very subtle ways.

Note that γ and β are unfortunately not true inverses: neither $\beta(\gamma(E)) = E$ nor $\gamma(\beta(F)) = F$ holds for general expressions. Thus, for example,

$$\gamma(\beta(a+b)) = ab' + a'b + ab'a'b \tag{6}$$

is not formally the same as $a+b$. One can however obtain inverse "compile" transformations if one introduces also operators δ and δ^* for reducing elements to canonical form in Boolean algebras and Boolean rings respectively. Then the composite operators $\delta^*\gamma$ and $\delta\beta$ are inverse "compilers" for canonical forms.

As a less trivial example, the mapping $xy - yx \mapsto [x, y]$ is a cryptomorphism from any linear associative algebra to a Lie algebra. The right-inverse cryptomorphisms $[x, y] \mapsto xy - yx$ from any Lie algebra L to linear associative algebras determine the representations of L by matrices; and it is known that every Lie algebra is cryptomonomorphic to some linear associative algebra. The cryptomorphisms $[xy + yx]/2 \mapsto \langle x, y \rangle$ share this property, and can even (by definition) be crypto-isomorphisms in the important case of "special" Jordan algebras.

9. **State machines.**[17] Universal algebra applies to computer science through the theory of state machines and (see §10) automata. This is evident from the following definition.

DEFINITION. A *state machine* is an algebra $A = [S, F]$, where S is a set of elements called "states," and F is a set of unary operators acting on S designated by an (input) *alphabet* of "input symbols" $a, b, c, \ldots$. (Typically, $F = \{0,1\}$ is binary.)

In the theory of automata, the action (effect) of an input symbol $a \in F$ on the state s is usually [9, §3.3] designated by $\nu(a, s)$ instead of $a(s)$. As an application of universal algebra, it is routine to construct the free (homogeneous) state machine $F_X(M)$ generated from the particular state machine of Figure 2a and

[16] Cryptomorphisms are closely related to the "algebraic functors" of category theory; cf. F. W. Lawvere, Ph.D. Thesis, Columbia, 1964, where one can also find the remarks about Lie and Jordan algebras made below.

[17] §§9–10 represent joint work with Dr. John D. Lipson, who also collaborated in drafting §17.

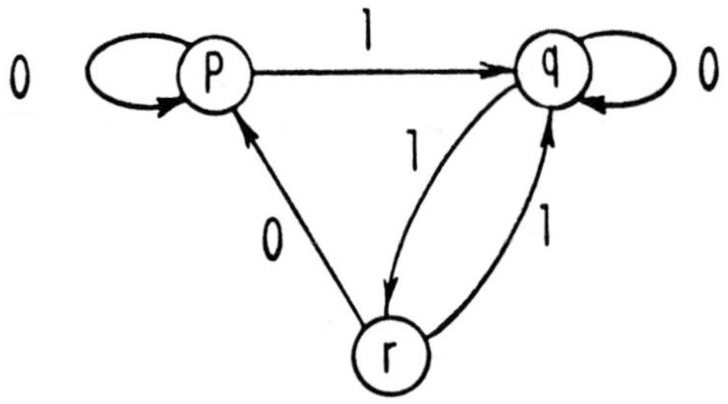

FIGURE 2a. Machine M.

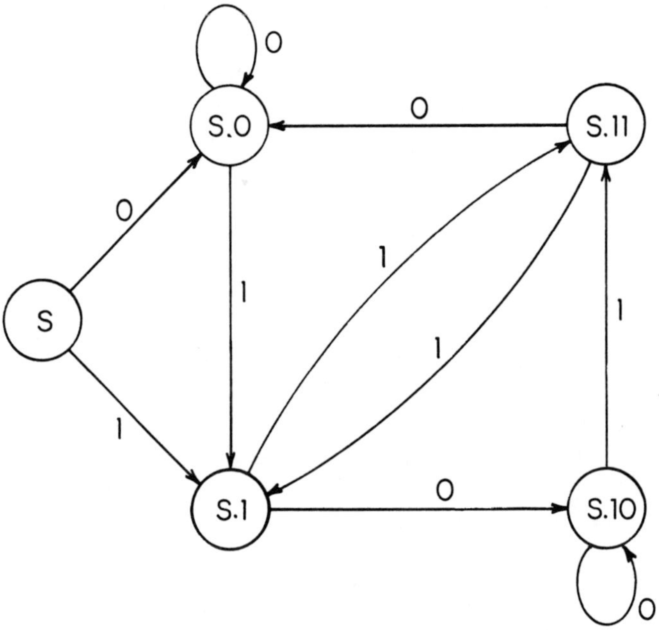

FIGURE 2b. Free *Homogeneous* Machine $F_X(M)$.

the fixed input alphabet $\{0, 1\}$; the diagram of $F_X(M)$ is shown in Figure 2b.

Although the theory of automata is still too fragmentary and too general to be very useful to machine designers, it has already developed significantly from a purely theoretical standpoint. Thus, the Krohn-Rhodes Theorem [**T1**][18] represents an ingenious analog of the Jordan-Hölder Theorem. Also, one can define and prove by universal algebra the existence of a unique (up to isomorphism) *free* automaton with n generators associated with a given machine [**10**]. Finally, one can show that the usual construction [**9**, Chapter 3] of the

[18]Also Trans. Amer. Math. Soc. **116** (1965), 540–564. See also [**5**, Chapter 5], [**25**, Chapter 9], [**23**], and A. Meyer and C. Thompson, Math. Systems Theory **3** (1969), 110–118, which corrects [**23**].

minimal state machine equivalent to a given (completely specified) finite-state machine applies to *any* ("universal") algebra with only unary operations.

The preceding remarks about state machines have analogs for the automata to be discussed in §10 (these are just state machines with outputs). Whether or not the theory of automata belongs to "applied" mathematics or "pure" computer science, the concept is philosophically exciting because, as the name suggests, it is plausible that a sufficiently fast automaton having enough storage could, *if properly programmed*, simulate many activities of the human brain. Thus, it would fulfill Leibniz' dream of "a new kind of instrument, increasing the power of reason far more than any optical instrument has ever aided the power of reason."[19]

10. **Heterogeneous algebras.** Very recently, John Lipson and I [**10**] have substantially generalized the class of algebras for which the theorem of "universal algebra" can be proved. Our basic definition is the following:

DEFINITION. A *heterogeneous algebra* $\mathfrak{A} = [\mathfrak{S}; F]$ is a family $\mathfrak{S}$ of non-overlapping sets S_k called phyla, together with a set F of $n(i)$-ary operations, or functions

$$f_i\colon S_{k(i,1)} \times \cdots \times S_{k(i,n(i))} \to S_{k(i,0)}. \tag{7}$$

Algebras having the same phylum indices i and the same functions $n(i)$ and $k(i,j)$ are said to be of the same *type*.

The class of heterogeneous algebras includes the following important and familiar varieties.

EXAMPLE 1. As in [**10**, Example 1], a *vector space* is a heterogeneous algebra $[A, \Lambda; +, -, \oplus, \ominus, \times, \cdot]$ with two phyla: vectors and scalars. Here $[A; +, -]$ is an additive group with two operations $+\colon A^2 \to A$ and $-\colon A \to A$; $[\Lambda; \oplus, \ominus, \times]$ is a field; and $\cdot : \Lambda \times A \to A$ is a scalar multiplication.

EXAMPLE 2. A *group representation* is a heterogeneous algebra $[G, A, \Lambda;$ $\circ, {}^{-1}, +, -,$ etc.], with three phyla: the group elements $g, h, \ldots$; vectors; and scalars. The operations are group composition $\circ$ and inverse formation ${}^{-1}$; the vector space operations for $\{A, \Lambda\}$ of Example 1; and group action γ. Here $\gamma(g, \mathbf{x}) = g(\mathbf{x}) \in A$ is the effect of $g \in G$ acting on the element $\mathbf{x} \in A$.

The class of heterogeneous algebras also includes *directed graphs*, which may be defined (cryptomorphically) in two ways as follows.

EXAMPLE 3. A directed graph can be interpreted as a heterogeneous algebra $[N, A; \partial^+, \partial^-]$ in the above sense. It has two sets or "phyla" of elements: a set N of *nodes* and a set A of *arcs*; and it has two unary operations $\partial^+\colon A \to N$ and $\partial^-\colon A \to N$.

EXAMPLE 3′. One can also regard a simple directed graph as a (nonverbal) symbolic representation of a *binary relation* on the set N of its nodes,

[19] Those interested in the "artificial intelligence" aspects of automaton theory should consult [**31**], [**8**], and the references given there.

and consider it as a heterogeneous algebra $[N, \mathbf{2}; f]$, where $\mathbf{2}$ is the Boolean set of truth-values 0,1, and $f: N \times N \to \mathbf{2}$ is a binary operation on N to $\mathbf{2}$.

The second definition identifies the directed graph with its *relation matrix*; thus the algebra of relations (§4) is applicable to (the adjacency relation) in directed graphs. For algebraic topology, still a third (cryptomorphic) definition is relevant, namely, the following.

EXAMPLE 3″. A directed graph is a heterogeneous algebra $[A, N, \mathbf{Z}_2; f]$, in which $f: A \times N \to \mathbf{Z}_2$ is defined by:

$$(8) \qquad \begin{aligned} f(a,n) &= 1 \quad \text{if } n \text{ is the final node of } a, \\ &= -1 \quad \text{if } n \text{ is the initial node of } a, \\ &= 0 \quad \text{otherwise.} \end{aligned}$$

Given a chain $C = \Sigma x_i a_i$ $(x_i \in \mathbf{Z}_2)$ in $\mathbf{Z}_2{}^A$, one can then define $\partial C = \Sigma\, x_i f(a_i, n_j) n_j \in \mathbf{Z}_2{}^N$.

Analogs of this definition for higher-dimensional complexes make $\partial(\partial C) = 0$.

Automata. As was observed in [**10**], state machines can be defined not only as ("homogeneous") algebras with one phylum as in §8, but also (and more naturally) as heterogeneous algebras. Moreover, automata with output alphabets can also be defined in a natural way as heterogeneous algebras.

EXAMPLE 4. A (sequential) machine or *automaton* is a *heterogeneous* algebra $M = [\mathscr{S}, F]$ in which $\mathscr{S} = \{S, A, Z\}$ contains three phyla: a nonvoid set S of "states," a nonvoid set A of input symbols (the "input alphabet") and a finite set Z of output symbols (the "output alphabet"). There are two binary operations in F:

$$(9a) \qquad \nu\colon\ S \times A \to S \qquad (\text{"change of state"}),$$
$$(9b) \qquad \zeta\colon\ S \times A \to Z \qquad (\text{"output functions"}).$$

A *state machine* or *semi-automaton* is obtained as a two-phylum heterogeneous algebra from the above by "forgetting" about the output symbols of Z and the output function ζ. This "forgetful functor" defines a state machine as a heterogeneous algebra $M = [\{S, A\}, \{\nu\}]$.

Both the "heterogeneous" and the "homogeneous" definitions of state machines are in the literature: the heterogeneous in [**19**] and the homogeneous in [**9**] and in Minsky [**31**]. Moreover, the difference between the heterogeneous and homogeneous definitions has basic algebraic consequences (e.g., in [**10**, §5] compare the two kinds of direct products of state machines). We now discuss these differences, with special reference to *free algebras*.

As in §9, a state machine is also definable as a homogeneous algebra by $M = [S, \{f_a\}]$, where for each letter a of the input alphabet F contains a unary operation $f_a: S \to S$

$$(10) \qquad f_a\colon s \mapsto \nu(s, a).$$

In the homogeneous case this input alphabet is *fixed* and plays the role of an

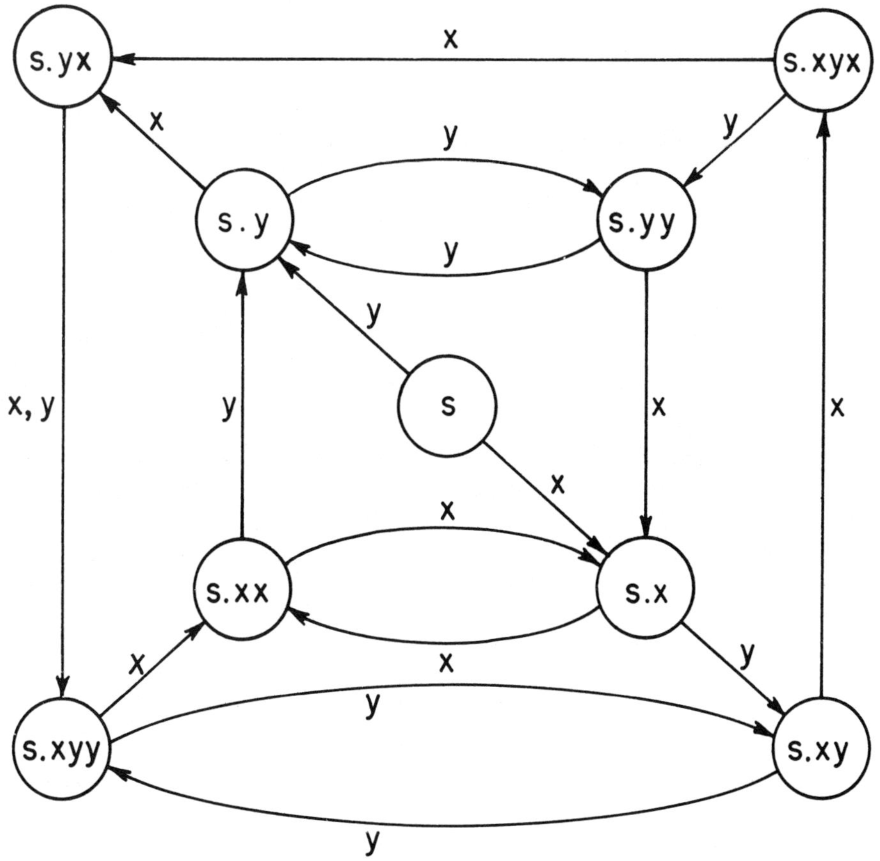

FIGURE 3. Free *Heterogeneous* Machine $F_{\mathfrak{X}}(M)$.

"underlying" structure, analogous to vector space theory where one fixes the underlying field of scalars. To illustrate the contrast, we have displayed in Figure 3 the free *heterogeneous* state machine $F_{\mathfrak{X}}(M)$ generated by one (starting) state letter s and two input letters 0, 1 (i.e., $\mathfrak{X}$ contains $X_1 = \{s\}$ and $X_2 = \{0, 1\}$ as in [**8**, §8]), from the state machine M of Figure 2a. Contrast Figures 2b and 3.

We conclude this section by observing that the proof of Theorem 22 of [7, p. 153] holds with only minor modifications for *heterogeneous* algebras. Consider the class of *all* the algebras $\mathfrak{A} = [\mathfrak{S}; F]$ having given nonvoid phylum-indices k (which we can interpret as the "names" of the phyla), operation-indices i (which we can interpret as the "names" of the operations), and the same *finite* $k(i,j)$ and $n(i)$ in (7). Then for any set of cardinal numbers $r(k)$, one for each phylum, we can define the *free word algebra* $\mathscr{W}_{\mathbf{r}}(F) = [\mathfrak{S}; F]$ of all formal expressions involving the $f_i \in F$ and x_{kl} $(l = 1, \ldots, r(k))$ with $r(k)$ generators in the kth phylum, as in [**10**, §6] and [7, pp. 141–142].

Given $p, q \in \mathscr{W}_r(F)$, define the *polarity*

$$(p = q)\rho\mathfrak{A} \quad \text{means that} \quad p = q \quad \text{in } \mathfrak{A}, \tag{11}$$

that is, no matter what element from the kth phylum of $\mathfrak{A}$ is substituted for each symbol x_{kl}, the equation $p = q$ holds. Then the following is true.

THEOREM 1. *Under the polarity* (11), *the "closed" sets of algebra* $\mathfrak{A}$ *(in the given class) are those closed under the formation of subalgebra, direct product, and epimorphic image; the "closed" sets of identities are the sets* Δ *closed under the following rules of inference:*

(i) *If* $p_h = q_h$ *is in* Δ *for* $h = 1, \ldots, n(i)$, *then* $f_i(p_1, \ldots, p_{n(i)}) = f_i(q_1, \ldots, q_{n(i)})$ *is in* Δ.

(ii) *If* $p = q$ *is in* Δ, *then any substitution of a polynomial* $n(x)$ *for all occurrences of the primitive symbol* x_j *in* p *and* q *is in* Δ.

11. **Partial algebras.**[20] Not only does all of "universal algebra" apply with minor modifications to any heterogeneous algebra, but some fragments of it apply to any partial algebra, defined as follows ([**16**], [**T3**]).

DEFINITION. A *partial algebra* $A = [S, F]$ is a set S of elements, related by a set F of finitary (partial) "operations," each of which is a partial function $f_i: S^{n(i)} \to S$.

EXAMPLE 5. Let $M = [S; 1, \cdot]$ be any *monoid* in which

$$ax = 1 \quad \text{holds if and only if} \quad xa = 1. \tag{12}$$

Then M is crypto-isomorphic to a unique partial algebra $[S; 1, \cdot, ^{-1}]$ (a "partial group") in which the three conditions $ax = 1$, $xa = 1$, and $x = a^{-1}$ are equivalent.

EXAMPLE 6. Similarly, one can define a *field* as a partial algebra which is a commutative group under addition, a commutative monoid under multiplication, which satisfies the distributive laws, and in which for all $a = 0$, a^{-1} is defined and satisfies $aa^{-1} = a^{-1}a = 1$.

In [**T3**], Vern Poythress has defined *free* partial algebras with the same set F of (partial) operations. A *p-morphism* is a partial function $\varphi: S \to T$ defined on a set X of generators of A such that, for any (n-ary, partial) operation $f \in F$, if $f(b_1, \ldots, b_n)$ is defined in B and $b_i = \varphi_{a_i}$ for $i = 1, \ldots, n$, then we have $f(a_1, \ldots, a_n)$ is defined in A and

$$\varphi f(a_1, \ldots, a_n) = f(\varphi_{a_1}, \ldots, \varphi_{a_n}) = f(b_1, \ldots, b_n). \tag{13}$$

For A, B fields, a p-morphism is what is called a specialization. Poythress has also shown that the field $Q(x_1, \ldots, x_n)$ of all rational functions over Q in n indeterminates x_i is the *free field* with n generators in the sense of the following definition (taking $\mathscr{C}$ to be the class of all fields).

[20] Vern Poythress helped to write this section; for the notion of "specialization," see O. Zariski and P. Samuel, "Commutative Rings," Van Nostrand, 1960, vol. II, p. 1.

DEFINITION. Let C be a class of partial algebras with a fixed set F of (partial) operations. An algebra $A = [S, F]$ is *C-free* over a subset $X \subset S$ when: (i) X generates A, and (ii) given $B = [T, G] \in C$, any (partial) function $\alpha: X \to T$ extends to a p-morphism $\varphi: A \to B$.

EXAMPLE 7. A *poset* can be considered as a *partial join-semilattice* $P = [S; \vee]$. The binary operation is idempotent, commutative in the strong sense that $y \vee x$ exists and equals $x \vee y$ whenever the latter exists, is associative in the weak sense that $x \vee (y \vee z) = (x \vee y) \vee z$ whenever both exist, and has the property that $x \vee (x \vee y)$ is defined whenever $x \vee y$ is.

Dually, a poset can be defined as a partial meet-semilattice. Or, it can be defined as a *partial lattice* (which is both a join- and a meet-semilattice, in which moreover $y = x \vee y$ if and only if $x = x \vee y$).

It follows that the cells of any topological *complex* can be considered as a partial lattice (excluding φ and the whole manifold). With this interpretation, the *direct product* of any two complexes corresponds to the product subdivision of the Cartesian product complex, as stated in [**LT1**]. In particular, *graphs* (whose importance for computing we have noted) appear as partial lattices of rank two.

EXAMPLE 8. Graphs have a (cryptomorphic) interpretation as *heterogeneous partial* algebras with two phyla: points and lines; and two partial operations $\vee: A_0 \times A_0 \to A_1$ and $\wedge: A_1 \times A_1 \to A_0$; the idea is to write $p \vee q = L$ when the edge L has vertices p and q.

Finally, I want to call your attention to another example (partly because Eilenberg has tried to develop from it new foundations for the theory of automata), and to make a final remark.

EXAMPLE 9. A *small category* $[\mathscr{P}, \mathscr{M}; \partial^-, \partial^+, \circ]$ can be defined as a heterogeneous partial algebra with two phyla: a set $\mathscr{P}$ of *objects* $S, T, U, \ldots$, and a set $\mathscr{M}$ of *morphisms* $f, g, \ldots$. Each $f \in \mathscr{M}$ has a *domain* $\partial^- f \in \mathscr{P}$ and a *codomain* $\partial^+ f \in \mathscr{P}$; thus as with directed graphs, $\partial^-: \mathscr{M} \to \mathscr{P}$ and $\partial^+: \mathscr{M} \to \mathscr{P}$ are regarded as unary operations. For given $S, T \in \mathscr{P}$, the set of *all* $f \in \mathscr{M}$ with $\partial^- f = S$ and $\partial^+ f \in T$ is denoted hom(S, T).[21] The *composition* operation is a *partial* binary operation $\circ$: $\mathscr{M} \times \mathscr{M} \to \mathscr{M}$; $g \circ f$ of which is defined precisely when $\partial^+ f = \partial^- g$. In addition, one postulates the associative law $h \circ (g \circ f) = (h \circ g) \circ f$ and the existence for every $S \subset \mathscr{P}$ of a special $1_S \in \mathscr{M}$ with appropriate properties.

REMARK. One can also interpret many systems as *multi-algebras*, whose operations are *multiple*-valued functions. For example, a directed graph **G** can be considered as a multi-algebra with a single unary operation, which with each node $n \in V$ the set $f(n) \subset V$ of all nodes which are the tips of arrows originating in n. From this definition one can reconstruct **G**: its edges are just the pairs $(n, n') \in V \times V$ with $n' \in f(n)$.

---

[21]This definition differs slightly from Mac Lane-Birkhoff, p. 508 ff. where hom is considered as a *multiple*-valued operation $(S, T) \mapsto \text{hom}(S, t)$ with multiple values in $\mathscr{M}$—i.e., as a heterogeneous partial *multi*-algebra; cf. the following remark.

12. **Mathematical logic.** Although the notion of a (heterogeneous) algebra includes graphs and automata, and has a highly nontrivial theory, it does not cover all applications of the symbolic method to computers. Not even the more general notion of a relational system [**20**, p. 224] seems to be sufficiently general.

Already before 1700, Leibniz had conceived of a much more general "logical calculus," modeled after the then new symbolic algebra of Viète, which would greatly facilitate all reasoning.[22] His starting point was the idea that simple concepts could be designated by letters, complex concepts by algebraic expressions, and assertions by equations, inequalities, and other relational formulas. This idea was stated in his *Fundamenta calculi ratiocinatoris*. In a later version, he proposed assigning to each basic word a "characteristic number," which would detach the word from its meaning.

Around 1880, Frege initiated a new era in symbolic logic, considered as "a language that need not be supplemented by any intuitive reasoning,"[23] It is interesting to note that Frege's symbolic logic made essential use of labelled trees (graphs), and little use of the binary, etc., operations which are so central to my version of "universal algebra."

Symbolic (i.e., algebraic) mathematical logic[24] was developed much further by Peano in his "Formulaire des Mathématiques" (1895–1903). The successes of Boole, Peano, and other mathematicians in developing symbolic treatments of substantial fragments of logic and arithmetic induced Whitehead and Russell to attempt a much more ambitious task in their "Principia Mathematica" (1910–1913). Their goal was to derive all mathematics mechanically from a purely formal *symbolic logic* consisting of: (i) small sets of "primitive propositions" (postulates) intended to characterize various groups of related mathematical concepts, and (ii) well-defined "rules of inference" for manipulating symbolic statements. Although this purely symbolic approach to theorem-proving and mechanical proof-checking is not very efficient for most of mathematics,[25] and Gödel has established the inadequacy of existing systems of symbolic logic (especially for handling quantifiers),—nevertheless symbolic logic has thrown valuable light on the foundations of mathematics.

I think it would be illuminating and most appropriate to formalize "universal algebra" in terms of a revised system of symbolic logic, using techniques like those of Whitehead and Russell, Hilbert-Ackermann, etc. Among other things, this formalization should include the all-pervasive notions of subalgebra and

[22]See [**16a**] and G. H. R. Parkinson, "Leibniz: Logical Papers," Oxford, 1966.

[23]See van Heijenoort, "From Frege to Gödel," Harvard University Press, 1967, pp. 2–4. One could mention also E. H. Moore's "General Analysis," which was also written in a Peano-like symbolic notation.

[24]For an excellent modern exposition of symbolic logic see S. C. Kleene, "Introduction to Metamathematics," Van Nostrand, 1952.

[25]More emphasis on efficiency is needed (and less on existence); see L. Wos et al., J. ACM **14** (1967), 698–709.

morphism. Conversely, "universal algebra" should be extended to cover quantifiers.[26] Such a formalization of universal algebra would be appropriate because symbolic logic aims to reduce *all* theorem-proving to a branch of algebra, and because the "automaton" algebras of §§9–10 are simplified versions of the Turing machines invented to mechanize the procedures of "Principia Mathematica." (I have not yet found a satisfactory way to define Turing machines as "algebras," without including **Z** pretty obviously.)

13. **Mathematical linguistics.** Directly related to the theory of automata is another offshoot of symbolic logic: *mathematical linguistics*. This treats printed *statements* as *strings of symbols* from a finite "alphabet," combined by concatenation—which gives a semigroup when done freely, and a monoid if the empty set (a vacuous statement) is allowed. Thus the notion of a programming language is included in the following extremely general definition.

EXAMPLE 10. A "language" is a subset of A^*, the free monoid generated (under a concatenation) by the symbols of some alphabet A. Hence it is a *partial monoid.*

Unfortunately, the concepts of universal algebra (as defined in §8) do not seem to be very fruitful for "languages." Thus, the role of a "sublanguage" is not played by the simple notion of a submonoid or subsemigroup, but rather by the notion of the set of statements generated by so-called *production rules* (given in Backus normal form). These production rules are auxiliary *unary* operations which typically refer to *specified symbols* (letters). Thus, rules like $a \mapsto ab$ or $b \mapsto cbd$ can be considered as production rules, analogous to rules of *grammar* (for which they are intended to substitute), producing grammatical or "acceptable" symbolic "sentences." They do not resemble anything else in the branches of modern algebra most familiar to mathematicians, nor in universal algebra as currently treated.

The original idea of such production rules was similar to that of rules of inference in symbolic logic: they were intended to generate all grammatical and no ungrammatical "sentences," just as the rules of inference in symbolic logic were intended to generate all true and no false mathematical theorems, thus reducing all mathematical theorem-proving to algebraic manipulations according to the specified rules of inference.

Indeed, modern programming languages for computers resemble symbolic logic in their format; and their logical and arithmetic capabilities are reminiscent of these of the formalisms of Boole and Peano. Moreover Newell, Hao Wang, and others have written successful computer programs for mechanical theorem-proving in logic itself.[27] There is no doubt of the close connection between mathematical linguistics and mathematical logic.

There is some interaction between modern algebra and both theorem-

[26] So far as the first-order predicate calculus is concerned, this has been done by Tarski and Grätzer [**20**, Chapter 6].

[27] For references to and comments on these achievements, see [**8**, §6.5].

proving and mathematical linguistics; see for example J. ACM **12** (1965), 23–41. Using related ideas, John C. Reynolds has proved that atomic formulas constitute a complete nonmodular lattice.[28] As another application, R. M. Burstall and P. J. Landin[29] use universal algebra based on Cohn's *Universal Algebra* to "prove the correctness of a compiler for evaluating expressions using a stack machine." But on the whole, these connections are exceedingly fragmentary.

Indeed, perhaps the most conspicuous common feature of universal algebra, the theory of automata, symbolic logic, and mathematical linguistics is their extreme generality. Thus, the subject of *mathematical linguistics* is intended to apply to both symbolic logic and to programming languages, and to human ("natural") languages as well. But much as universal algebra by itself seems inadequate for deriving deep results about (say) finite groups, so mathematical linguistics by itself seems to be ineffectual for obtaining deeper results about symbolic logic, programming languages, *or* human languages.

To obtain deeper results, one should probably begin by being less general; it is not clear how much the language of symbolic logic should have in common with programming languages. Thus, most statements of symbolic logic are *declarative* whereas those of programming languages are *imperative*: they are "commands" intended to make an automaton perform certain operations; the appropriate algebraic concept is (as in representation theory) that of a programming language *acting* on an automaton. More specifically, machine languages act on *computers* (whose "outputs" may be arrays of numbers with identifying labels), while higher-level programming languages act on *compilers* (whose "outputs" consist of other computer programs which may be in machine or assembler language).

Indeed, I think the time is ripe for a systematic study of more realistic models of computers than are provided by automata in general. Thus, I think one might well define a *computer* as a special kind of automaton possessing: (i) capabilities for storing addresses, (ii) an integer *arithmetic* unit, (iii) Boolean *logic* capabilities, (iv) a standard *word-length* ("byte") to aid in parsing, and (v) alphanumeric *output* capabilities. One could then consider the matched capabilities of "programming languages" (and compilers!) for *acting* on such a computer, in somewhat the same spirit that one now considers the capabilities of groups for "acting" on given sets (as permutations) or vector spaces (as linear transformations).

If it is any comfort, universal algebra should be applicable to such more complex systems. Thus, likewise, the idea of a programming language for a computing machine can be interpreted as a *heterogeneous partial algebra*, whose "programs" form one phylum (as in Example 10), each member of which consists of a sequence of instructions to be carried out by the automaton of

[28] Machine Intelligence **5** (1969), 135–152.

[29] Machine Intelligence **4** (1968), 17–43; see also Landin in ibid. **5** (1969), 99–120.

Example 4 or the state machine of §9 (containing another phylum of "states," including perhaps a "starting state").

C. Combinatorial Algebra

14. **Relevance to computing.** Many algorithms for digital computers are obviously *combinatorial* in nature. Their description involves labelled directed graphs called "flow charts," which may be designed to handle "stack-like," "tree-like," or "ring-like" (perhaps associative) data structures [**27**, Chapter 2]. To analyze their efficiency, one often needs to solve *enumeration* problems, also of a combinatorial nature.

Moreover such an analysis, when made from the standpoint of optimization, may lead to unexpected improvements in efficiency. For example, such improvements have recently been made by Stephen Cook and S. Winograd, for the problems of multiplying together two n-digit numbers and two $n \times n$ matrices, respectively.[30]

As a result, attempts to optimize computer algorithms lead to an incredible variety of combinatorial problems (cf. [**27**]), for which few general techniques of solution are known. During the past decade, Rota and others (cf. [**17**], [**30**], [**34**], etc.) have made increasingly clear the basically algebraic nature of some general techniques. In Part C, I shall try to illustrate these by a few simple examples, taken largely from the work of Rota and some of his students and associates. A characteristic feature of this work is its emphasis on partial orderings and *lattices*.

These notions arise very naturally in enumeration by recursion. This is because in counting complex combinatorial structures, one can often proceed by recursion over a *partial ordering* not a linear ordering, which is often a lattice (e.g., of subsets or partitions).

In Parts D and E, I shall discuss other applications of combinatorial algebra to computing which concern *linear dependence*. As was shown in 1935 by Hassler Whitney [**41**] and myself, the general theory of linear dependence can be most naturally formulated in terms of the cryptomorphic notions of a combinatorial geometry and a geometric lattice.[31] As has been mentioned in §5, these notions also apply to the theory of affine dependence.

Although typical examples of geometric lattices are furnished by the subspaces spanned by the subsets of a finite set of points in projective space, examples also arise in other combinatorial contexts, apparently unrelated to projective geometry. Thus in [**41**], Whitney used this algebraic formalism to describe the dependence of circuits in graphs. Again, consider a bipartite

---

[30] See [**T0**]; also S. A. Cook and S. O. Aanderaa, Trans. Amer. Math. Soc. **142** (1969), 291–314; S. Winograd, J. ACM **14** (1967), 793–802; [**27**, pp. 258–279]. For inner products and matrix multiplication, see V. Strassen, Numer. Math. **13** (1969), 354–356; S. Winograd, IEEE Trans. **C-17** (1968), 693–694.

[31] Formerly called a "matroid" and a "matroid lattice," respectively. See [**41**], [**LT1**] and [**LT2**].

graph representing a relation $R \subset A \times B$. Say that $K \subset A$ is independent when there is a one-to-one subrelation of R (or matching) which is everywhere defined on K. Then the family of all such sets K defines a combinatorial geometry on the set A.

Thus one can apply the properties of linear dependence to disparate combinatorial situations.

15. **Incidence algebras and Moebius functions.** Associated with every poset $P = [X, \leqq]$ are its *incidence* function n: $P \times P \to \mathbf{Z}$ and its *zeta* function ζ: $P \times P \to \mathbf{Z}$, defined respectively by:

$$(14) \qquad \begin{aligned} n(x, y) &= 1 \quad \text{if } x < y, \\ &= 0 \quad \text{otherwise,} \end{aligned} \qquad \begin{aligned} \zeta(x, y) &= 1 \quad \text{if } x \leqq y, \\ &= 0 \quad \text{otherwise.} \end{aligned}$$

Relative to any listing (enumeration) of its elements, these functions define the incidence matrix and zeta matrix of P. Figures 4a–4b depict the matrices $N = \|n_{ij}\|$ and $\Xi = \|\zeta_{ij}\|$ for $X = \mathbf{4}$ in its usual ordering; they are strictly triangular and triangular.

$$N = \begin{bmatrix} 0 & 1 & 1 & 1 \\ 0 & 0 & 1 & 1 \\ 0 & 0 & 0 & 1 \\ 0 & 0 & 0 & 0 \end{bmatrix}, \qquad \Xi = \begin{bmatrix} 1 & 1 & 1 & 1 \\ 0 & 1 & 1 & 1 \\ 0 & 0 & 1 & 1 \\ 0 & 0 & 0 & 1 \end{bmatrix}, \qquad \Gamma = \begin{bmatrix} 0 & 1 & 0 & 0 \\ 0 & 0 & 1 & 0 \\ 0 & 0 & 0 & 1 \\ 0 & 0 & 0 & 0 \end{bmatrix}.$$

FIGURE 4a FIGURE 4b FIGURE 4c

Evidently, N and $\Xi = I + N$ are just the *relation matrices* of the binary relations of strict inclusion and inclusion, respectively. Similarly, one can define the *covering* function $\gamma(x, y)$ and *covering relation* $\Gamma = \|\gamma_{ij}\|$ associated with the covering relation on P. But whereas the values (0 or 1) of these matrices were regarded as *Boolean* in §4, they are here regarded as in $\mathbf{Z}$. (For $P = [X, \leqq]$ the poset of a complex, Γ is its incidence relation matrix.)

More generally, we can regard them as in any integral domain D, and refer to the *incidence algebra* and *zeta algebra* of P (over D), meaning by this the *D-module* of all functions having zero values wherever $n(x, y)$ resp. $\zeta(x, y)$ have zero values. Here multiplication is given by the usual rule for multiplying matrices:

$$(15) \qquad C = AB \quad \text{means} \quad c(x, z) = \sum_y a(x, y) b(y, z),$$

which is "convolution" for P the semigroup $\mathbf{N}$.

The preceding modules provide useful descriptions of various interesting combinatorial functions. For example, consider the generating function

$$(16) \qquad 1/(I - t\Gamma) = I + t\Gamma + t^2\Gamma^2 + t^3\Gamma^3 + \cdots + t^n\Gamma^n + \cdots;$$

the coefficient $\Gamma^n = \|\gamma_n(x,y)\|$ represents the number of *simple paths* of length n from x to y in the directed graph ("Hasse diagram") of the poset P.

As in [7, p. 102], the Moebius function of P is defined from the incidence function of P by

$$\|\mu(x,y)\| = \|I+N\|^{-1} = I-N+N^2-N^3+\cdots. \tag{17}$$

Note that when $P = \mathbf{P}$, the ordered set of positive integers, we obtain the classic Riemann zeta function by setting

$$1/\zeta(s) = \sum_{k=1}^{\infty} \mu(k)/k^s, \qquad \mu(k) = \mu(1,k). \tag{17'}$$

Many enumeration problems can be solved by "Moebius inversion" using an appropriate Moebius function;[32] we here give a simple example. First, let $P = \Pi(S)$ be the partition lattice of a set S of n elements [7 p. 95]. Then, if x is a refinement of the partition y (i.e., if $x \leqq y$), and $k(i)$ is the number of blocks of the partition y which are split into i blocks by x, it has been shown by Rota and others that

$$\begin{aligned} \mu(x,y) &= (-1)^l \prod_{r=2}^{n} (r!)^{k(n)} \quad \text{if } x < y \\ &= 0 \quad \text{otherwise}, \end{aligned} \tag{18}$$

where $l = n - \Sigma\, k(i)$.

We now use this Moebius function to compute the number of sets E of edges which can be drawn joining the nodes (vertices) of a given set V of n nodes, so as to obtain a simple connected graph. In all, there are $2^{n(n-1)/2}$ ways of drawing in nodes so as to get a graph over V. Every graph on the set of vertices S induces a partition of the set S into connected components. Let $g(y)$ be the number of graphs whose partition is some refinement of the partition y. Then clearly

$$g(y) = \sum_{x \leqq y} f(x), \tag{19}$$

where $f(x)$ is the number of graphs whose partition is precisely the partition x. By applying the Moebius inversion formula we obtain immediately

$$f(y) = \sum_{x \leqq y} \mu(x,y) g(x); \qquad g(x) = 2^{k(1)C_{n,1} + k(2)C_{n,2} + \cdots}, \tag{20}$$

which gives the number of graphs having partition y in terms of the quantity $g(x)$, which is easily computed as above, and the Moebius function. Letting y be the trivial partition with one block, one obtains the desired number of connected simple graphs.

The Moebius function of a partially ordered set (poset) is useful in other contexts, of which we shall only mention one. If one takes a convex poly-

---

[32]See [34]; the example given here was kindly provided by Professor Rota, who also made many other valuable contributions to and criticisms of this paper. In (20), $C_{n,k}$ is simply the number of (connected) blocks of k nodes in the partition x.

hedron in n-dimensional space, one can associate with it an *incidence lattice*, which is obtained by ordering the cells (faces, etc.) of the polyhedron by inclusion. It is an open problem to characterize which lattices are incidence lattices of convex polyhedra. For dimension three this problem was solved by Rademacher and Steinitz. It was recently shown by Rota that a necessary condition for a lattice to be the incidence lattice of a convex polyhedron is that the Moebius function of the incidence lattice take alternatingly the values $+1$ and -1 at successive levels. This result extends the classical Euler identity for the cells of a convex polyhedron. In fact, it implies not only the Euler identity but also the classical Dehn-Sommerville equations [**20**a, Chapter 9].[33]

Tutte-Grothendieck function. Many other algebraic invariants can be defined on posets, somewhat analogous to those defined from combinatorial complexes in algebraic topology. In this spirit, T. Brylawski[34] has recently imitated the techniques used by Grothendieck in defining the so-called Grothendieck group of an Abelian category. Brylawski succeeded in associating a ring to every hereditary class of combinatorial geometries. A hereditary class of geometric lattices consists of a class of geometric lattices which is closed under the operation of taking subsets on the set in which the geometry is defined, as well as contractions, that is, taking segments of the associated geometric lattice. It was shown by Brylawski that the computation of the characteristic polynomial (21) below, as well as the computation of several other invariant quantities of geometries, such as the numbers of bases, independent sets, spanning sets, etc., could be reduced to simple computations in what he called the Tutte-Grothendieck ring. Among graphs in particular, he has characterized series-parallel networks (cf. §2) by their Tutte-Grothendieck functions.

16. **Critical problems; symmetry.** Moebius inversion also provides an interesting reformulation of the problem of code optimization; generalizing §2, we consider linear group codes over $F = GF(q)$. To be *optimal* among such codes with code word length n correcting l errors, the *subspace of code words must have maximum dimension* among those which are *disjoint* from the subset S of all words (vectors) having fewer than $2l+1 = d$ nonzero coordinates.

It turns out that the determination of this maximum dimension is connected with Moebius inversion on the combinatorial geometry (geometric lattice) $L = L(n, d)$ of all flats (closed subspaces) of L spanned by points with d nonzero coordinates. Specifically, consider the *characteristic polynomial*

$$\sum_x \mu(0, x)\, \lambda^{n-\dim(x)} = p(\lambda), \tag{21}$$

---

[33]See G.-C. Rota, "Möbius function and Euler characteristic," in the Rado Festschrift, Academic Press, 1970, where the result is extended to affine polyhedra.

[34]T. Brylawski, Ph.D. Thesis, Dartmouth, 1970. See also D. A. Smith, Duke Math. J. **34** (1967), 617–633, and **36** (1969), 15–30 and 353–367.

where μ is the Moebius function of L. The required maximal dimension is the first positive integer λ for which $p(\lambda)$ is positive.

The characteristic polynomial defined above can be defined in any geometric lattice, and the problem of finding the first positive integer λ for which $p(\lambda)$ is positive is called by Crapo and Rota the *critical problem*. Clearly, this reformulation of the optimal coding problem as a "critical problem" does not solve it. However, the fact that a host of combinatorial problems are equivalent to critical problems gives some hope of developing general methods for solving them. At least, it should suggest themes for generalizing ingenious special methods successful for individual problems so as to solve groups of related problems.

Symmetry. Many computational problems involve geometrical or other *symmetries*. Typically, these symmetries constitute a *group G acting on a set S* of variables (often unknowns). In order to recognize 0's (see Part D) and to avoid ambiguities and unnecessary duplication of computational effort, it is important that computer programs for treating such problems take account of such symmetries. In enumeration problems, this is done by Pólya's Theorem [**5a**, pp. 144–184].

In many numerical problems, one must recognize "equivalence under the group G" of all such symmetries, when these are applied to polynomial expressions and power series (e.g., generating functions) in the variables of S. Here one has an important *Galois connection* between the lattice of subgroups $H, K, \ldots$ of G and the lattice of partitions $\pi, \pi', \ldots$ of S, defined by the *imprimitivity polarity* ρ:

$$(22) \qquad H\rho\pi \quad \text{iff} \quad x\pi y \quad \text{and} \quad \theta \in H \quad \text{imply} \quad \theta(x)\pi\theta(y).$$

The *intransitivity polarity* σ

$$(23) \qquad H\rho S \quad \text{iff} \quad \theta \in H \quad \text{and} \quad x \in S \quad \text{imply} \quad \theta(x) \in S$$

is even more important.[35] Moreover a special role is played by the *invariant* polynomials $p(x_1, \ldots, x_n)$ such that $p(x_1, \ldots, x_n) = p(x_1\gamma, \ldots, x_n\gamma)$ for any permutation γ of G; *invariant theory* is concerned with the calculation of a *basis* of such invariant polynomials; I shall consider problems of this type in Part E.

An extremely difficult problem concerns the enumeration of isomorphism-types (i.e., the number of equivalence classes, such as the number of nonisomorphic graphs or groups of a given order). I know of no effective general algebraic or combinatorial techniques for solving this problem. A related and equally difficult problem is that of testing two given graphs or groups for isomorphism.

---

[35]See G.-C. Rota, Bull. Amer. Math. Soc. **75** (1969), 330–334. For other interplays between Galois connections and Moebius functions, see [**34**, Theorem 1] and H. H. Crapo, Archiv Math. (Basel) **19** (1968), 595–607.

In my opinion, the most effective way to attack these problems is through *man-computer symbiosis* [**8**, §22.1], in which theoretical ideas are combined with machine computations analogous to those which have been described by other speakers at this symposium.[36]

17. **Flowgraphs.** Instead of discussing general ideas further, I shall conclude Part C by describing briefly a new kind of heterogeneous algebra, which can be realized by very simple finite-state machines and has been programmed for standard computers, so as to *compute* answers to various combinatorial problems. This will show again how "universal algebra" gives a unified viewpoint which applies to automata, graphs, and other combinatorial structures as well as to the groups, rings, and fields studied in traditional courses on "modern algebra."

This new kind of heterogeneous algebra is the class of flowgraphs. The relevant concept was originated over 15 years ago and applied to circuit design problems by S. J. Mason (see [**20**, Chapter 2]). Its formal definition as a heterogeneous algebra is as follows [**T2**, §2.2][37]; note that, like an automaton, a flowgraph is a *labelled directed graph.*

DEFINITION. A *flowgraph* in n indeterminates $x_1, \ldots, x_n$ over an integral domain D is a heterogeneous algebra $\mathfrak{F} = [N, A, D; \Phi, \psi]$, where $[N, A; \Phi]$ is a directed graph (Example 3), and $\psi: A \to D[x]$ is a function which assigns to each arc $(i, j) \in A$ a "label" or "weight" $\psi(i, j) \in D[\mathbf{x}] = D[x_1, \ldots, x_n]$. The *transmission matrix* of the flowgraph $\mathfrak{F}$ above is $T = \|t_{ij}\|$, where

$$(24) \qquad \begin{aligned} t_{ij} &= \psi(i,j) && \text{if } (i,j) \in A, \\ &= 0 && \text{otherwise.} \end{aligned}$$

The *generating function matrix* of $\mathfrak{F}$ is $\Gamma = \|\gamma_{ij}\| = (I - T)^{-1}$.

When there is a preferred starting node s and final node f (as is usually the case), then we call $g = \gamma_{sf}$ the flowgraph *generating function.*

To illustrate the preceding concepts and their applications to combinatorial problems, we solve a specific problem from [**18**, p. 79].

PROBLEM. Find the number of n-digit binary sequences in which an occurrence of the pattern 010 is (eventually) followed by an occurrence of the pattern 110.

SOLUTION. *Step* 1. Construct an automaton $\mathscr{A}$ which recognizes precisely the sequence (of arbitrary length) to be enumerated.

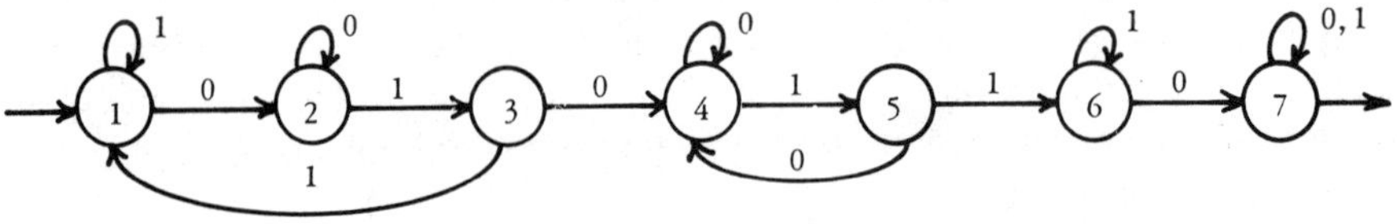

FIGURE 5a. Automaton $\mathscr{A}$.

[36]For a theoretical reduction of the problem described above to one of Möbius inversion, see Rota (op. cit. supra). A machine algorithm for testing graphs for isomorphism is described by D. G. Corneil and C. C. Gottlieb, J. ACM **17** (1970), 51–64.

[37]The rest of this section was kindly adapted by John Lipson from his Thesis [**T2**].

Step 2. Transform $\mathscr{A}$ into a flowgraph $\mathfrak{F}$ for enumerating paths from the starting state to the final or "accepting" state of $\mathscr{A}$.

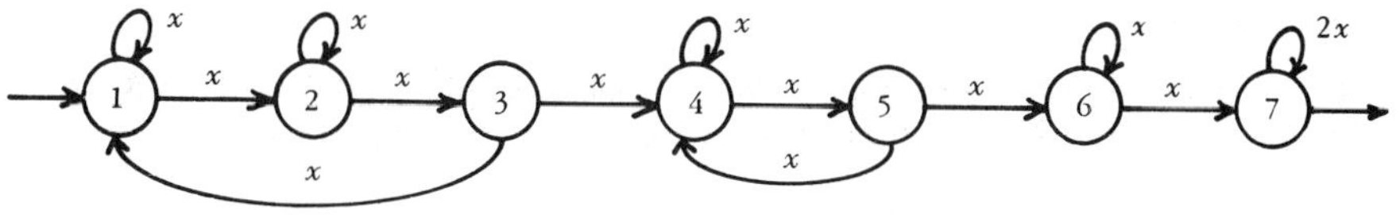

FIGURE 5b. Flowgraph $\mathfrak{F}$.

Step 3. Compute the generating function $g = g(x)$:

$$g = [(1-T)^{-1}]_{sf} \tag{25}$$

where s is the starting node, f is the final node and $T = \|t_{ij}\|$ is the flowgraph "transmission" matrix. For the above flowgraph $\mathfrak{F}$,

$$\begin{aligned} g &= x^6/(1-6x+13x^2-12x^3+4x^4+x^5-3x^6+2x^7) \\ &= x^6+6x^7+13x^8+72x^9+201x^{10}+521x^{11}+1282x^{12}+\cdots. \end{aligned} \tag{26}$$

The coefficient of x^n in the above power series gives the number of sequences (or "strings") of length n having the property specified; thus there are 1282 of them having length twelve.

In the above example the denominator of $g(x)$ can be factored as $(1-x)(1-2x)(1-3x+2x^2+x^5)$; its smallest root is $x = 1/2$, and so (for large n) the number of acceptable strings of length $n+1$ is asymptotically twice the number having length n, hence of the order of 2^n.

The transmission matrix of the above flowgraph admits a factorization $T = xA$; such flowgraphs are called unit-delay flowgraphs and have useful special properties. For such flowgraphs:

$$g(x) = [(I-xA)^{-1}]_{sf} = C_{fs}/|I-xA| = h(x)/d(x), \tag{27}$$

where $d(x)$ is the reciprocal of the characteristic polynomial $c(x) = |xI-A|$, so that $d(x) = x^n c(1/x)$. Writing $g(x) = \Sigma\, g_n x^n$, we have the linear recurrence relation

$$g_{n+1} = 6g_n - 13g_{n-1} + 12g_{n-2} - 4g_{n-3} - g_{n-4} + 3g_{n-5} - 2g_{n-6},$$

from which $g_{13}, g_{14}, g_{15}, \ldots$ are easily computed. In other examples, Bareiss' two-step integer-preserving Gaussian elimination scheme[38] can be used to advantage.

To compute the integral coefficients of the rational generating functions arising in such problems, Dr. Lipson has found modular arithmetic most effective. Thus he showed (using Hadamard's bound on the determinant of a matrix) that on the IBM 360/50 computer (32 bit word length), correct coefficients could be computed by modular arithmetic for any binary input automaton having 20 or fewer states.

[38] E. H. Bareiss, Math. of Comp. **22** (1968), 565–578.

An interesting extension of the above method for computing flowgraph generating functions can be based on the following theorem about principal ideal domains.[39]

THEOREM. *If the elements $m_1, m_2, \ldots, m_k$ are pairwise relatively prime in a principal ideal domain D, then there is an isomorphism φ of rings*

$$D\Big/\left(\prod_{i=1}^{k} m_i\right) \approx \prod_{i=1}^{k} D\Big/(m_i), \tag{28}$$

where φ: $(\Pi_{i=1}^{k} m_i)+r \to (m_i)+r, \ldots, (m_k)+r$.

The inverse function φ^{-1} is important from a computational viewpoint. For D the principal ideal domain **Z**, the computation of φ^{-1} is tantamount to the *Chinese Remainder Algorithm*, an important number theoretic result; while for D the principal ideal domain $F[x]$, the computation of φ^{-1} is tantamount to polynomial interpolation. Both the cases **Z** and $F[x]$ are important for symbolic computation: **Z** for computing with (large) integers, and $F[x]$ for computing with (large degree) polynomials. Furthermore, both of these situations arise in applications of flowgraphs.

D. LINEAR SYSTEMS

18. **General remarks.** The rest of my talk will concern the role of *nonnumerical* algebra in optimizing the *numerical* solution of systems of N simultaneous linear equations in N unknowns:

$$\sum_{j=1}^{N} a_{ij}x_j = k_i \quad (i,j = 1, \ldots, N), \qquad \text{or} \qquad AX = K. \tag{29}$$

Nonnumerical algorithms are basic to real algebra because the *real arithmetic of digital computers is only approximate*. Thus one cannot test real (or complex) numbers for equality or real vectors for linear dependence, or real matrices for rank on digital computers; moreover the "real numbers" of digital computers do *not* satisfy such identities as $a+(b+c)=(a+b)+c$, $aa^{-1}=1$, or $a(b+c)=ab+ac$ [**27**, vol. 2, pp. 196–204]. Therefore, one must devise *nonnumerical* algorithms to recognize and utilize such exact algebraic identities and relations of linear dependence.

It turns out that many of the deepest questions involved in devising optimal algorithms are basically *combinatorial* (hence purely algebraic); they do not concern roundoff, stability, or the condition number. Only the relation matrix $R(A)$ and directed graph $\mathbf{G}(A)$ of the coefficient-matrix A of (29) are relevant; these are defined as follows:

DEFINITION. The *relation matrix* $R = \|r_{ij}\| = R(A)$ of $A = \|a_{ij}\|$ is defined by

$$\begin{aligned} r_{ij} &= 1 \quad \text{if } a_{ij} \neq 0, \\ &= 0 \quad \text{otherwise.} \end{aligned} \tag{30}$$

[39] S. Mac Lane and G. Birkhoff, "Algebra," Macmillan, 1967.

The *directed graph* G(A) of A has for nodes the integers $1, \ldots, n$, and $R(A)$ for its adjacency matrix.

My discussion will refer especially to the linear systems (29) about which I know most: large systems ($N = 100$–$50{,}000$) which arise from elliptic boundary value problems such as the "source" problem described by the DE

$$-\nabla \cdot [p(x,y)\nabla u] = s(x,y), \qquad p(x,y) > 0. \tag{31}$$

Matrices A arising from such DE's are special: they are highly *sparse, positive definite, symmetric matrices.*

Today, a variety of competing methods are used to obtain approximate solutions to elliptic problems.[40] These fall broadly into three categories

(i) Difference approximations (usually 5-point for (31)) solved by *elimination*, perhaps in double precision arithmetic.

(ii) Difference approximations (usually 5-point) solved by *iterative* methods (variants of SOR and ADI) going back to the 1950's.

(iii) Finite element methods approximations utilizing *variational* principles, leading to systems (29) with somewhat less sparse matrices, usually solved by elimination.

The $64 question is, of course, *which method is best*, and when? Unfortunately, this optimization problem can rarely be solved and is even hard to formulate rigorously. However, it leads to a number of interesting theoretical questions, and these will be the main concern of the rest of my talk.

In Part D, I shall describe the important role played by graph theory in all three of the above kinds of methods. (In this connection, it is a curious historical fact that Frobenius failed to recognize the relevance of graph theory to linear algebra.[41]) In Part E, I shall indicate the special importance of geometric lattices for understanding finite element methods, thus giving additional coherence to my message.

19. **Successive overrelaxation.** I shall begin by pointing out that the graph concept plays an important role even in *iterative* methods for solving large-scale linear systems arising from source problems, and that already Gauss[42] had considered solving real and complex linear systems not only by elimination, but alternatively by *iterative* methods [**38**]. Indeed, it seems appropriate to mention at this Symposium that Gauss was a truly *pure and applied* mathematician who gladly assumed responsibility for massive astronomical and geodetic calculations, and took a special interest in *numerical methods.* Modern computing owes much to him and to other mathematicians like

---

[40]For a detailed technical discussion of (i)–(iii) from the standpoint of solving elliptic boundary value problems, see my NSF Regional Conference monograph, "Numerical Solution of Elliptic Problems," SIAM Publications, 1971.

[41]See [**28**, pp. 240–241], for complaints by D. König about the cavalier attitude of Frobenius towards graph theory.

[42]See [**38**] and G. Forsythe, MTAC **5** (1951), 255–258.

Jacobi, Cauchy (who introduced the gradient method), L. Seidel, Runge, L. F. Richardson, and other pioneering spirits.[43] Many of their ideas (including perhaps "diakoptik elimination," see §20) are still being explored by research workers today.

I shall now discuss a few algebraic and combinatorial considerations which lead one to solve large linear systems by iterative methods. I shall consider specifically the linear system (29) obtained from the source problem (30) by the usual 5-point difference approximation, using an $n \times n$ array of interior mesh-points. This gives $N = n^2$ equations in n^2 unknowns, whose coefficient-matrix A is *sparse* with about $5n^2$ nonzero entries.

If textbook Gauss elimination is applied blindly to this system, about $n^6/3$ multiplications will be performed, mostly by zero. If multiplications by zero are omitted, and the matrix is given minimal bandwidth (which is nearly achieved if the mesh-points are run through in their natural order by successive rows), the number of multiplications is reduced to about $2n^4$.

If the nondiagonal entries of A are transposed, giving $DX = BX + K$, we can solve *approximately* by the *iterative* Jacobi method:

$$(32) \qquad DX^{(r+1)} = BX^{(r)} + K, \qquad \text{or} \qquad X^{(r+1)} + D^{-1}BX^{(r)} + K_1,$$

where $K_1 = D^{-1}K$. Note that the graph of the nonnegative matrix B, defined to have for nodes the indices $1, \ldots, N$ and edges (i, j) precisely when $b_{ij} \neq 0$, looks just like the graph of mesh-points and mesh-lines. It is bipartite, which is another way of saying that the matrix B is 2-cyclic (has Young's Property A).

This is important for the Successive Overrelaxation (SOR) method, whose properties were first established by David Young in [**T6**]. With this iterative method, the number of multiplications required to solve (29) to given accuracy can be reduced to $O(n^3)$.

I shall not try to describe the method here, but I do want to emphasize the many ingenious algebraic ideas which its theory utilizes. These include the properties of Stieltjes matrices, the Perron-Frobenius theory of nonnegative matrices, as well as the graph-theoretic ideas mentioned already. If we call the symmetric adjacency matrix of the graph $G(B)$ of B above its *relation matrix*, $R(B)$, then [**LT3**, pp. 385–386] the mapping $B \mapsto R(B)$ is an *l-epimorphism* from the l-semigroup of nonnegative matrices onto the l-semigroup of relation matrices, which carries matrix addition into relation join.

For the preceding source problem, the graph $G(B)$ suggests a physical analogy with a *linear network problem*: the 5-point difference approximation corresponds to a fixed resistivity in each edge or link, i.e., to a potential drop which is a linear function of the flux. Such linear network problems were already studied by Kirchhoff and J. C. Maxwell.[44] Maxwell knew that the

---

[43]Cf. R. von Mises and H. Pollaczek-Geiringer, ZaMM **9** (1929), 58–77 and 152–164.

[44]See G. Birkhoff and J. L. Diaz, Quar. Appl. Math. **13** (1956), 431–443, and G. J. Minty, J. Math. Mech. **15** (1966), 485–520.

equilibrium flow in such a network *minimizes a suitable quadratic function*:

(33) $$q(X) = \tfrac{1}{2}X^TAX + K^TX + c, \qquad X = (x_1, \ldots, x_N).$$

Here A is a real *Stieltjes matrix* [**38**, p. 85], that is, a real symmetric positive definite matrix with negative off-diagonal entries, while K and X are real column vectors. Physically, $q(X)$ represents the rate of dissipation of energy. Mathematically, the minimum of $q(X)$ occurs where $\nabla q = \mathbf{0}$, which is where (29) holds.

This observation makes possible the use of variational ideas which motivate overrelaxation, and which becomes most effective when combined with the techniques which I shall discuss in Part E.

20. **Gauss elimination.** For source problems (31) in a square subdivided by an $n \times n$ mesh, iterative methods become definitely more efficient than Gauss-Choleski elimination with minimum bandwidth $2n+1$, for the reasons outlined in §19, when n is sufficiently large. Indeed, careful recent experiments[45] indicate that SOR becomes more efficient than elimination for $n > 40$, and hence for $N = n^2 > 1600$.

However, it is not clear that the preceding elimination scheme is *optimal*: though the relevant coefficient-matrix A has only 5 nonzero entries per row, due to the *fill-in* of zero entries by nonzero entries during "elimination," as much arithmetic is done as if there were initially $2n+1$ nonzero entries per row. Moreover elimination methods have the great attraction (especially for algebraists) of being formally exact and valid over *any field*, including finite fields to which iterative methods are inapplicable. For this and other reasons, there is a great current interest in the problem of *optimizing Gauss elimination* for linear systems (29) having *sparse coefficient-matrices*.[46]

To formulate this problem, it is convenient to rewrite (29) as

(34) $$\sum_{S(\sigma)} a_{\sigma\tau}x_\tau = k_\sigma, \qquad \tau \in S(\sigma) \subset S, \quad \sigma \in S.$$

Here the subscripts σ, τ refer to *addresses* in the computer where numbers are stored (perhaps in "arrays"). To convert (34) to (29), one needs ordering bijections φ and ψ: from S to $\{1, \ldots, N\}$ specifying substitutions $i = \varphi(\sigma)$ and $j = \psi(\tau)$ for σ and τ; the "fill-in" of zero entries by nonzero entries depends on ψ. The optimization problem is to choose ψ so as to minimize the resulting number of arithmetic operations.

This fact leads to the basic question of *optimal ordering*: how can one list the equations in an order which will minimize the number of arithmetic operations which must be performed in Gauss elimination if (off-diagonal) 0's are omitted?

[45] G. J. Fix and K. E. Larsen, unpublished manuscript.

[46] The discussion of optimizing elimination in §§20–22 was written in collaboration with Donald J. Rose, and concerns questions discussed in [**T4**].

Minimum bandwidth. For optimal ordering, an often useful[47] and widely advocated [**43**] prescription is to so order the rows and columns as to achieve (i) minimum bandwidth—or, alternatively, (ii) minimum bandwidth below the main diagonal, as in a Hessenberg matrix [**26**, p. 379]. However, as will be shown in §21 by an example taken from [**T4**], the criterion of minimum bandwidth does not always yield minimum fill-in; moreover the criterion of minimum fill-in is cleanest. Furthermore, potential users should be warned that the problem of finding permutation matrices P and Q such that PAQ has minimum bandwidth is highly nontrivial. Steward [**36**], and also Harary and Dulmage and Mendelson[48] have solved problem (ii), in the sense of describing an algorithm for finding P and Q such that PAQ is block upper triangular with diagonal blocks of least size. However, no general computer program exists which solves the *optimization problem* of finding a P and Q which *minimize* the bandwidth of PAQ with a *minimum* order of computational complexity. The same is true of minimizing the bandwidth of PAP^T for symmetric A (with least order of computational complexity).

Criteria for optimality. Though I shall concentrate on algorithms for *optimal orderings* of variables for Gaussian elimination here, I want to emphasize that optimal elimination has minimum fill-in as one aspect but, as so often, *any of several different criteria for optimality may be appropriate, depending on the circumstances.*

For example, the optimal algorithm for solving a given linear system $AX = B$ with fewest multiplications need not be the same as that for solving $AX = B_i$ with fixed A and a large number of right-hand sides B_i (see [**42**, p. 221]).

In general, the solution of linear systems (29) consists in two distinct processes: "triangularization" by a sequence of premultiplications by nonsingular quasi-elementary matrices to get

$$UX = E_rE_{r-1} \cdots E_1AX = E_rE_{r-1} \cdots E_1B = UB, \tag{35}$$

with U upper triangular, and "back-substitution"

$$LUX = F_sF_{s-1} \cdots F_1(UX) = LUB \tag{35'}$$

with the F_i also quasi-elementary. Note that the multiplication-count and storage-count proceed somewhat differently for (35′) than (35).

Real and complex fields. In terminating this part of my discussion, I want to emphasize again that it ignores the major problem of *roundoff.* As Wilkinson [**42**] and Forsythe and Moler [**19**] explain, in solving large-scale linear systems (29) on a computer, one must control the *condition number* $\|A\|\cdot\|A^{-1}\|$ (which is the ratio $\lambda_{\max}(A)/\lambda_{\min}(A)$ of the maximum to the minimum eigenvalue of A if A is positive definite symmetric and the Euclidean norm is

[47]E. Cuthill and J. McKee, Proc. ACM 23rd Nat. Conf. (1969).

[48]F. Harary, J. Math. and Phys. **38** (1959), 104–111; also "Graph Theory and Theoretical Physics," Academic Press. 1967, p. 167 ff.

used), to limit the amplification of roundoff. One may also want to scale and/or pivot equations (although this is unnecessary if A is positive definite and symmetric).

In practice, a *mixed strategy* which combines elimination and iteration (e.g., by decomposing A into block tridiagonal or block 2-cyclic form) may be more effective than either pure elimination or pure iteration. Furthermore, questions about programming and machine characteristics may also be relevant [**39**, p. 19]. Moreover, the entries a_{ij} of the matrix $A = \|a_{ij}\|$ in (29) may be specified by a few *formulas* over large sub-arrays, and not stored as *numbers*.

However, the preceding questions relate to numerical analysis and computer science, and not to classical *or* modern algebra; therefore I shall ignore them here.

21. **Symmetric Gauss elimination.** Many matrices A which arise in physical contexts are symmetric. For such matrices, "symmetric Gauss elimination" and the closely related Cholesky method are distinctly preferable to ordinary Gauss elimination and its variants.[49]

Symmetric Gauss elimination and the Cholesky method are usually presented in the context of *real* linear algebra. I shall now show that symmetric Gauss elimination can be applied to "definite" symmetric matrices over *any* field (even one of characteristic two), defined as follows.

DEFINITION. A matrix A over a field F will be called *definite symmetric* when it is symmetric and $XAX^T = 0$ implies $X = 0$.

Note that, over the real field, a symmetric matrix is "definite" in the preceding sense if and only if it is positive definite or negative definite in the usual sense. Hence no diagonal entry a_{ii} of a definite symmetric matrix over any field can be zero, because $a_{ii} = E_i A E_i^T$, where E_i is the ith unit (row) vector, and so the process of symmetric Gauss elimination described below can always be carried out.

Therefore, we can write

$$A = \begin{bmatrix} a & C^T \\ C & M \end{bmatrix},$$

where $a \neq 0$, and apply Gaussian row elimination to the first column and then apply column elimination to the first row. This replaces A at the first step by

$$\begin{bmatrix} a & 0 \\ 0 & M_1 \end{bmatrix},$$

where $M_1 = M - C^T C/a$ remains definite (see Westlake [**39**, p.21]. Continuing recursively, A is replaced after n such steps by a definite diagonal matrix D,

[49]See D. Hartree, "Numerical Analysis," Oxford, 1952, §8, 4; rounding errors amplify less [**42**].

where

(36) $$A = LDL^T \qquad (L \text{ unit lower triangular}).$$

It is moreover easy to compute L in the process, after which one can solve other equations of the same form with variable B by

(37) $$X = BA^{-1} = BL^{T-1}D^{-1}L^{-1}.$$

The Cholesky method for real matrices differs from symmetric Gauss elimination as defined above only in that a factor $a^{1/2}$ is applied twice so as to make $D = 1$ and $A = GG^T$. Both Cholesky and symmetric Gauss elimination involve only stable decomposition for positive definite symmetric *real* matrices; see Wilkinson [**42**], p. 231–232, Equation (44.13).

REMARK. It is evident that symmetric Gauss elimination can be generalized to apply to equations of the form $B\mathbf{x} = \mathbf{h}$, for any "diagonally symmetrizable" matrix B of the form $B = DA\tilde{D}$ with $D, \tilde{D}$ diagonal and A symmetric. Furthermore, such diagonally symmetrizable matrices are easily recognized by the property that

$$a_{ij}a_{ik}a_{kl} = a_{lk}a_{kj}a_{ji} \quad \text{for all } i, j, k, l.$$

The proof generalizes an argument of Seymour Parter and J. W. T. Youngs (J. Math. Anal. Appl. **4** (1962), 102–110), and will be omitted.

Symmetric reordering. For any permutation matrix P, it is evident that $X \mapsto XP$ carries any definite symmetric matrix A into PAP^T and $q(X) = XAX^T$ into $q_P(X) = (XP)A(XP)^T$: symmetry and definiteness are preserved. So is the *set* of diagonal entries and (for *real* matrices) so are the properties of being diagonally dominant and/or a Stieltjes matrix. Hence it seems appropriate to call such a transformation a *symmetric reordering* (or "pivoting") of the rows and columns of A.

This is different from "pivoting" in the usual sense ([**42**, p. 206], [**26**, p. 2–24]), which can be any transformation $A \mapsto PAQ$, with P,Q arbitrary permutation matrices. Unless $Q = P^T$, such more general pivoting destroys the properties of the preceding paragraph. Hence such general pivoting is not appropriate for symmetric matrices—any more than ordinary Gauss elimination is, relying as it does exclusively on elementary *row* transformations of A.

For the (positive definite real symmetric) *Stieltjes matrices* [**38**] arising from linear *network* problems, including systems (29) or (34) arising from the standard 5-point approximation to source problems (30), it seems especially appropriate to use only symmetric reorderings. For, in this case, the ith equation and the ith variable both refer physically to the (potential and current equilibrium at the) ith node of the network. Hence, for network problems, the group of "symmetric pivotings" $A \mapsto PAP^T$ of the matrix A can be interpreted as induced by *reordering nodes*.

22. **Optimal ordering.** In [**T4**], Donald Rose has analyzed carefully the *optimal orderings* of the rows (equations) and columns (unknowns) of a *sym-*

metric matrix; i.e., those "symmetric" orderings (with $\psi = \varphi$ below (34)) which *minimize fill-in* for symmetric Gauss elimination. I shall try to summarize his findings.

Parter[50] has defined the (symmetric) *graph* $G(A)$ of the coefficient-matrix A of the linear system (11) to have nodes $i = 1, \ldots, n$, and edges (i, j) for all i, j with a_{ij} *or* a_{ji} nonzero. He showed that if A was a Stieltjes or other strictly *diagonally dominant* matrix and $G(A)$ was a *tree* (or forest[51]), fill-in could be entirely avoided by proper "monotone orderings" of the equations.

The basic *degree one algorithm* consists in working from peripheral (or "pendant") nodes inwards. Specifically, call a node "peripheral" when its degree is 0 or 1. Any tree or forest has at least one peripheral node; let x_i correspond to such a peripheral node of $G(A)$. Then the ith equation has the form $a_{ii}x_i + a_{ij}x_j = b_i$; therefore one can eliminate x_i by simply storing the equation

$$x_i = a_{ii}^{-1}b_i - a_{ii}^{-1}a_{ij}x_j = A_i + B_i x_j, \tag{38}$$

and substituting from (38) into the jth equation which, by definition of $G(A)$, is the only other equation into which x_i enters.

This results in $N-1$ equations in the $N-1$ remaining variables, whose graph is a subgraph of $G(A)$. Since any subgraph of a tree or forest is itself a tree or forest, the algorithm can be repeated $N-1$ times to solve for some x_k. Back-substitution into equations like (38) completes the process, with minimum fill-in (except fortuitously).

Parter's algorithm has been generalized in the *minimum degree algorithm* due to Tinney and others.[52] This eliminates at each step a variable σ (graph node) of minimum (remaining) degree *and* all the adjacent edges. When $G(A)$ is a tree, it gives Parter's algorithm. For systems (29) whose graph is the "snowflake graph" of Figure 6, it is better than the minimum bandwidth algorithm. In this example, the minimum remaining degree never exceeds two, and we can apply the following algorithm.

Degree two elimination algorithm. If i is a node of degree two in $G(A)$, then the ith equation of (29) will be of the form

$$d_i x_i = a_i x_{\varphi(i)} + b_i x_{\psi(i)} + c_i. \tag{39}$$

The algorithm consists in adding $d_i^{-1}a_{i,\varphi(i)}$ times the ith equation to the $\varphi(i)$th equation, and $d_i^{-1}a_{i,\psi(i)}$ times the ith equation to the $\psi(i)$th equation. This will *eliminate* x_i from the other equations, *without increasing* $\deg \varphi(i)$ or $\deg \psi(i)$.

Triangulated graphs. Parter's ideas have also been significantly extended by Donald Rose in his Thesis [**T4**], where he has also related them to the concept of a triangulated graph introduced by Berge for other purposes. Namely,

[50] See [**32**]; also A. Jennings, Computer J. **9** (1967), 281–284.

[51] A "forest" is a disjoint sum of trees.

[52] N. Sato and W. F. Tinney, IEEE, PAS (1963), 944–950; W. F. Tinney and J. W. Walker, Proc. IEEE **55** (1967), 1801–1809. For computer experiments, see [**43**, pp. 25, 35].

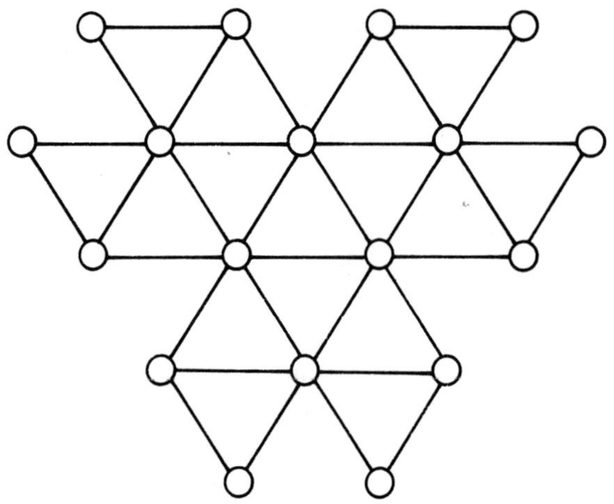

FIGURE 6. Snowflake Graph.

call a graph G *triangulated* when for every cycle γ of length $l > 3$ there is an edge of G joining two nonconsecutive nodes of γ. For example, the "snowflake graph" of Figure 6 is triangulated. Rose has proved the following basic result [**T4**, p. 3.4].

THEOREM. *Let A be a positive definite symmetric matrix, and let $G = G(A)$ be its graph. Then the following conditions are equivalent:* (i) *G is triangulated,* (ii) *every minimal a, b separator is a clique,* (iii) *there exists an ordering which makes G monotone transitive,* (iv) *with this ordering, symmetric Gaussian elimination minimizes fill-in (is a perfect elimination process).*

Tearing and patching. A dual approach to the problem of optimizing elimination can be based on the idea of "tearing and patching" networks, whose utility was emphasized by Gabriel Kron[53] in his "diakoptiks." This method depends on finding small *cut-sets S* of the graph $G = G(A)$ of a system (29) or (34). By this is meant [**15**, p. 17] a set of edges which *separates* $G - S$ into two or more nonvoid components T and U joined by no edge of G.

A computer program for "diakoptik elimination" might proceed by first decomposing G into its connected components [**9**, Chapter 2], then determining all one-node cut-sets, then all two-node cut-sets, and so on.

E. PIECEWISE POLYNOMIAL INTERPOLATION

23. **G. D. Birkhoff's problem.** Almost every mathematician is aware of the importance of polynomial and rational functions for numerical computing. Most basic is Lagrange's theorem that, given $n+1$ distinct points $x_0, x_1, \ldots, x_n$

[53]See Steward, Tewarson, and Tinney [**43**, pp. 25–44 and 65–74]; also [**36**] and [**37**]; H. H. Happ, "Diakoptiks and Networks," Academic Press, 1970. Greechie has used similar "tearing and patching" methods to synthesize and decompose orthomodular lattices from their diagrams.

and $n+1$ values $y_0, y_1, \ldots, y_n$, there exists one and only one set of polynomial coefficients $a_0, a_1, \ldots, a_n$ such that, for $i = 0, 1, \ldots, n$:

$$a_0 + a_1 x_i + a_2 x_i^2 + \cdots + a_n x_i^n = f(x_i) = y_i. \tag{40}$$

Though commonly stated for the real field, the theorem is true over *any field*, because of the formula for the *Vandermonde determinant*.[54]

$$|x_i^{j-1}| = \prod_{i>j} (x_i - x_j). \tag{41}$$

Clearly, this product is nonzero for distinct x_i; hence the transformation X: $\Sigma_{j=0}^{n} a_j x_i^j \rightarrow y_i$ is nonsingular. (In the case $x_i = x_0 + ih$ of equal spaced interpolation, $|x_i^{j-1}| = \Pi_{k=1}^{n-1} k^{n-k} h^{n(n-1)/2}$.)

In the limiting case of "coalescent" x_i, Lagrange's Theorem yields *Hermite interpolation*.[55]

$$f^{(k)}(x_i) = \sum_{j=k}^{\nu-k} [j(j-1)\cdots(j-k+1) a_j x_i^{j-k}] = y_i^{(k)}, \tag{42}$$

for $i = 0, 1, \ldots, n$, $k = 0, \ldots, K(i)$ and $\nu = \Sigma_{i=0}^{n}[K(i)+1]$. The resulting system of ν equations in ν unknowns is also *nonsingular*, over any field whose characteristic $\chi > \operatorname{Max} K(i)$.

When only twenty years old, my father [**11**] proposed the following algebraic *generalized Hermite interpolation* problem. For which *sets* of pairs (i, k) of nonnegative integers is defined by (42) always (algebraically) possible? This is G. D. Birkhoff's interpolation problem.

The two-point G. D. Birkhoff interpolation problem was given the following solution by Pólya [**33**].

PÓLYA'S THEOREM. *Let m_k be the number of conditions on the kth derivative (for $i = 0, 1$) and let $J_j = \Sigma_{k=0}^{j} m_j$. Then the ν equations* (42) *are always nonsingular if and only if $M_j \leqq j+1$ for $0 \leqq j \leqq \nu - 2$.*

Ferguson [**18**] has extended Pólya's results as follows. A set of interpolation conditions is said to satisfy the *strong Pólya conditions* when M_j, the total number of interpolation conditions $f^{(k)}(x_i) = y_i^k$ with $k \leqq j$, satisfies $M_j \leqq j+2$ for $j = 0, \ldots, n-2$. He has proved that G. D. Birkhoff's interpolation problem is well-set for a fixed set of (i, k) and *all complex x_i* if and only if it is a Hermite system or a (two-point) Pólya system.

For further results on this challenging problem I refer you to the literature.[56]

Clearly, G. D. Birkhoff's problem involves both algebraic and combinatorial ideas; and his own interest in it was stimulated by the idea that polynomial *interpolation* was a fruitful source of good *approximation* formulas,

---

[54] Birkhoff-Mac Lane, "Survey of Modern Algebra," 3rd ed., p. 284.

[55] Philip Davis, "Interpolation and Approximation," Ginn, 1963, p. 52.

[56] See I. J. Schoenberg, J. Math. Anal. Appl. **16** (1966), 538–543; A. Sharma and J. Prasad, SIAM J. Numer. Anal. **5** (1968), 864–881; I. M. Sheffer, Amer. J. Math. **57** (1935), 587–614. G. G. Lorentz and K. L. Zeller, SIAM J. Numer. Anal. **8** (1971), 43–48.

useful for computation and for theoretical analysis. Thus, his ultimate goal was to derive mean value theorems for the interpolation *error* (alias "remainder"): to show that very general schemes of polynomial interpolation were not only *algebraically* well-set[57] but also *convergent* (*analytically* well-set)(over the real field), as the mesh-length tended to zero for *fixed* ν.

However, G. D. Birkhoff's problem seems more a fascinating purely mathematical question suggested by computing ("mechanical quadrature") than one which will influence actual computing practice significantly.

24. **Piecewise polynomial interpolation.** Much more important for actual computation is interpolation by *piecewise polynomial* functions, such as cubic and bicubic polynomial splines. In *finite element methods* especially, one commonly deals with such functions, defined by a different polynomial formula in each (polyhedral) cell of a suitable combinatorial *complex* (see §6). *Compatibility* conditions (e.g., of continuous differentiability) across the interfaces between cells lead to many problems concerning *linear dependence* of a kind already hinted at in §6 and §14.

In some cases (e.g., of piecewise linear functions defined on the triangles of a "simplicial" subdivision), these problems have trivial solutions, because strictly *local* interpolation formulas are adequate. More challenging theoretically are the linear dependence problems arising from *global* methods in which the interpolating function of each cell depends on *all* given values.

Univariate splines. The simplest and most widely used global interpolation scheme is provided by *cubic spline* interpolation to values y_i at $n+1$ points x_i with $x_0 < x_1 < \cdots < x_n$, and given end slopes y'_0, y'_n. The best way to handle this consists in taking the slopes $y'_1, \ldots, y'_{n-1}$ at interior meshpoints as unknowns which, if known, would reduce the problem to one of (local) cubic *Hermite* interpolation of a cubic polynomial in each interval or "cell" $[x_{i-1}, x_i]$ to the four numbers $y_{i-1}, y_i, y'_{i-1}, y'_i$. The y'_i can be determined from the given data by the condition of *continuous curvature*, a condition which is equivalent at $x = x_i$ to (for $\Delta x_i = x_i - x_{i-1}$):

$$\begin{aligned} \Delta x_i y'_{i-1} + 2(\Delta_{i-1} + \Delta x_i) y'_i + \Delta x_{i-1} y'_{i+1} \\ = 3[(\Delta x_i \Delta y_{i-1}/\Delta x_{i-1}) + (\Delta x_{i-1} \Delta y_i/\Delta x_i)]. \end{aligned} \tag{43}$$

The coefficient-matrix of the system (43) is always nonsingular over the real field (for distinct x_i).

However, even over the complex field with $n = 3$, the choice $\Delta x_1 = 1$, $\Delta x_2 = i$, $\Delta x_3 = (i+7)/25$ yields a *singular* coefficient-matrix. Therefore, although some interesting work has been done with complex splines,[58] I believe that most of the algebraic theory of "spline" and other global piecewise poly-

[57] In the terminology of Birkhoff and de Boor (cf. H. L. Garabedian, editor, "Approximation of Functions," Elsevier, 1965, pp. 169–170).

[58] J. H. Ahlberg, E. N. Nilson, and J. L. Walsh, Trans. Amer. Math. Soc. **129** (1967), 391–413; [**35**, pp. 1–27].

nomial interpolation schemes is essentially limited to the real field and other ordered fields. One can generalize the notions of "polyhedron" and complex to (perhaps convex) domains in F^n, if F is any such ordered field.

For (univariate) cubic splines, the complex in question is the simple *linear graph* sketched below.

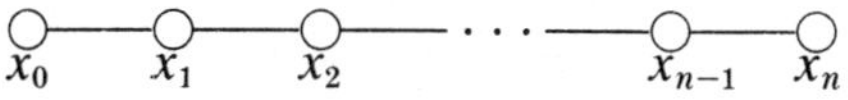

One is interested in the values of $y_i = y_i^0$, $y_i' = y_i^1$, and $y_i'' = y_i^2$ at the $n+1$ mesh-points x_i, giving $3n+3$ numbers in all. By elementary formulas for Hermite interpolation on $[x_{i-1}, x_i]$, we have n (homogeneous linear) dependence relations of each of the forms:

$$(44) \qquad 2y_{i-1}^2 + y_i^1 + 2y_{i-1}^1 \Delta x_i = 3(y_i^0 - y_{i-1}^0),$$

$$(44') \qquad 2y_i^2 + y_{i-1}^1 - 2y_i^1 \Delta x_i = 3(y_{i-1}^0 - y_i^0),$$

where $\Delta x_i = x_i - x_{i-1}$ and $i = 1, \ldots, n$.

From the preceding $2n$ dependence relations, we can obtain the $(n-1)$ "smoothness" conditions (43) by eliminating the $n+1$ y_j^2. Indeed, since the cubic "spline subspace" is $(n+3)$-dimensional and the $2n$ equations (44)-(44′) are linearly independent, *every* true equation between the $3n+3$ variables y_i^k $(k = 0, 1, 2)$ is a linear combination of these $2n$ equation.—Analogous results hold for splines of any odd degree $2m+1$.

Dependence matrix. The $2n$ homogeneous linear compatibility equations $\Sigma\, a_{ki}^j y_i^k = 0$ of (44)-(44′) in the $3n+3$ *interpolation* variables y_i^k can be specified by a $2n \times (3n+3)$ *dependence matrix* $A = \|a_{ki}^j\| = \|a_\lambda^j\|$ $(j = 1, \ldots, 2n)$. Their significance consists in the fact that the $y_i^k = y_\lambda$ cannot be assigned arbitrarily: having specified any subset S of the set $\Lambda = \{y_\lambda\}$ of all interpolation variables y_λ, we have automatically specified all variables which are linearly *dependent* on the y_λ $(\lambda \in S)$.

The mapping $S \mapsto \bar{S}$ from S to the set of variables dependent on the y_λ $(\lambda \in S)$ is a closure operation, and the closed subsets of interpolation variables form a finite *geometric lattice*, the *dependence lattice* of the matrix A above. In (44)-(44′), by Pólya's Theorem with $\nu - 2 = 2$, any four of the six variables y_{i-1}^k, y_i^k except for $\{y_{i-1}^1, y_i^1, y_{i-1}^2, y_i^2\}$ are linearly independent.

25. **Bivariate splines.** Given a subdivided *rectangular polygon* $(\mathscr{R}, \pi \times \pi')$ as in Appendix A, it is interesting to consider the *bivariate spline functions* of degree $2m-1$ in each variable and of class $C^{2m-2}(\mathscr{R})$, as specified by the functionals

$$(45) \qquad \varphi_{ij}^{kl} = \frac{\partial^{k+l} u}{\partial x^k \partial y^l}(x_i, y_j), \qquad k, l = 0, 1, \ldots, m.$$

A complete determination of the linear dependence relations among the φ_{ij}^{kl} is, in general, a formidable task.

Tensor products. In the special case that $\mathscr{R}$ is a rectangle, the resulting dependence lattice is the *direct product* of the lattices of dependence relations of univariate spline functions of degree $2m-1$ on $(\mathscr{L}, \pi)$ and $(\mathscr{L}', \pi')$, respectively. This is due to the underlying *tensor product* construction of bicubic splines. (Likewise, there are important cases, corresponding loosely to cases of "separable variables," in which solution by elimination is greatly facilitated by using the concept of a "tensor product" to solve

$$(B \otimes C)u \otimes v = k \otimes l. \tag{46}$$

However, I shall not discuss this technique, which is relevant to Part D, in the present paper.)

Some results concerning the dependence lattice of bivariate spline functions on subdivided rectangular polygons are presented in Appendices B and C of my paper in [**35**]. In particular, results of Carlson and Hall[59] give bases both of spline functions and for the dependence among the φ_{ij}^{kl} of (45).

Dependence lattice. Letting λ designate a multi-index for (i, j, k, l) in (45), the results of Carlson and Hall therefore give a *dependence matrix* $A = \|a_\lambda^\mu\|$ such that the equations

$$\sum a_\lambda^\mu \varphi_\lambda = 0, \qquad \mu = 1, \ldots, M,$$

span *all* true dependence relations among the φ_{ij}^{kl}. Moreover, if the x_i, y_j are rational numbers, then the a_λ^μ are rational too.

To determine the *geometric lattice* $L(A)$ of all (linearly) closed subsets $\bar{S}$ of φ_λ from this matrix is an interesting exercise in rational arithmetic. I conjecture that (for given L), this $L(A)$ is determined up to isomorphism by the *complex* corresponding to $(\mathscr{R}, n)$.

26. **Lattice structures involved.** For general multivariate interpolation by piecewise polynomial functions in *polyhedral complexes*, at least *three* lattice structures are involved. First is that of the polyhedral complex itself, which I have already discussed from an algebraic standpoint in §6. Even more central are the *paired geometric lattices of functions and linear functionals* to which an index or other identification (e.g., storage address) is assigned in a given computer program. These constitute *paired geometric lattices* in the sense of the following definition.

Definition. Let V be a finite-dimensional vector space of functions f, and W the dual space of linear functionals φ on V. Let $F \subset V$ and $\Phi \subset W$ be *finite* sets of functions f_i and functionals φ_j which span V and W, respectively. Let L and M be the *geometric lattices* of all subsets $S \subset W$ resp. $T \subset \Phi$ which are *closed* under linear combination (in V resp. W). Let $N \subset \Phi \times F$ consist of the pairs (φ_j, f_i) such that $\varphi_j(f_i) = 0$.

Consider the *polarity* defined by the biorthogonality relation $\varphi_j(f_i) = 0$; clearly $T \subset S^*$ implies $\bar{T} \subset S^*$ and $S \subset T\dagger$ implies $\bar{S} \subset T\dagger$. Hence the

[59] R. E. Carlson and C. A. Hall, J. Approx. Theory **4** (1971), 37–53.

subsets closed with respect to the polarity defined by N are also elements in M and L. We can therefore consider biorthogonality as a *polarity* between the geometric lattices L and M.

We will call L and M *biorthogonally paired* when the polarity just defined is a *dual isomorphism* between L and M, which are then necessarily complemented *modular* lattices. (A common case occurs when they are both Boolean algebras, because the f_i and φ_j are linearly independent.) It is interesting to know when the polarity is *onto* in even one direction.

An interesting case arises when we have *patch bases*. In general, given a subset K of the *polyhedral complex* G on which the functions of V are defined, we have an interesting subset of functions with *support* in K. Many $\varphi \in \Phi$ refer, moreover, to individual *cells* of K, and thus annihilate all functions whose support excludes K.

It would be interesting to determine (up to isomorphism) some of the lattices defined by piecewise polynomial functions of given degree with respect to specified sets of functions. We do not completely know these lattices even for the univariate cubic splines of §23.

APPENDIX A. SUBDIVIDED RECTANGULAR POLYGONS

1. **Classification of rectangular polygons.** One of the simplest families of combinatorial complexes in $n > 1$ dimensions is the family of (rectangularly) *subdivided rectangular polygons*. These are moreover especially amenable to the use of bicubic splines and other bivariate piecewise polynomial functions. I shall here discuss some ideas for treating simply connected subdivided rectangular polygons in computer programs (cf. [**35**, pp. 212–213]).

It is evident (since the sum of the turning angles is 360°) that any simply connected rectangular polygon with J reentrant corners or *notches* must have $J+4$ protruding corners. When $J=0$, we have a *rectangle*; when $J=1$, we have an *L-shaped region.*

When $J=2$, we may have a U-shaped region, a T-shaped region, a doubly notched rectangle, or a 3-step staircase, as shown in Figures 7a–7d.

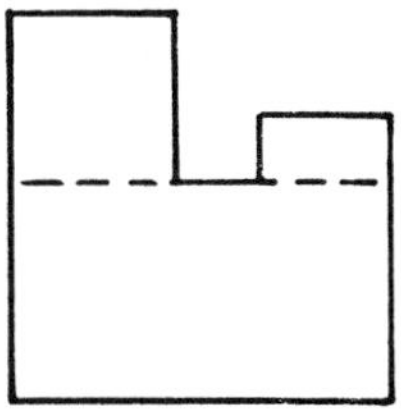
FIGURE 7a

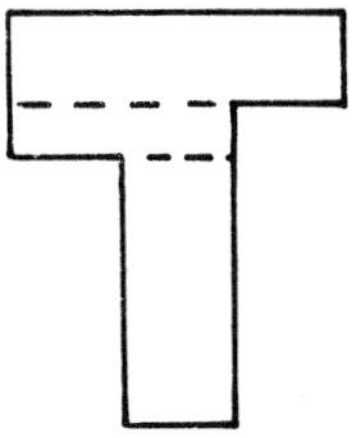
FIGURE 7b

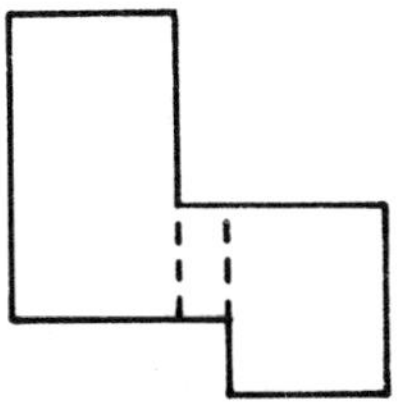
FIGURE 7c

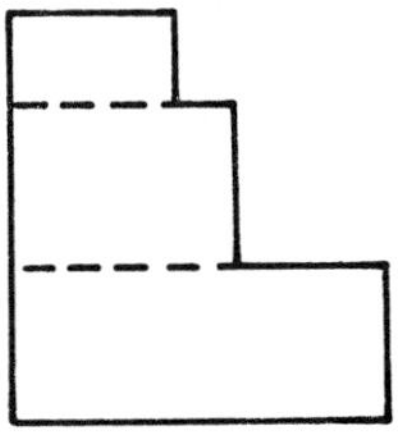
FIGURE 7d

These correspond to the four *cyclic partitions* of the number $J+4=6$ into *two* summands, specifying the numbers of protruding corners between successive notches:

$$6+0, \quad 5+1, \quad 4+2, \quad 3+3.$$

For $J=3$, there are *eight* configurations (inequivalent under the dihedral-symmetric group of all cyclic permutations and reflections) of the sequence of *three* summands in partitions of $J+4=7$. These correspond to the partitions

$$7+0+0,\quad 6+1+0,\quad 5+2+0,\quad 5+1+1,$$
$$4+3+0,\quad 4+2+1,\quad 3+2+2,\quad 3+3+1.$$

For $J=4$, the dihedral group is not the symmetric group, and there are many possible configurations (inequivalent partitions of $J+4=8$); the most symmetric are *crosses* corresponding to the partition $2+2+2+2$. It is an interesting combinatorial problem to determine for general J the number of different kinds of rectangular polygons with J notches, in the above sense.

2. **Cell addresses.** A *subdivided rectangle* (the case $J=0$) is easily specified as an *array* of $m\times n=mn$ subrectangles; one can apply to it the tensor product techniques mentioned in §25.

A subdivided L-shaped region can be specified as the sum of the 3 subrectangles into which it is subdivided by extending the edges incident on reentrant corners (notches) until they meet an (opposite) side. Thus, it can be specified as an $m\times n$ subrectangle with abutting $m'\times n$ and $m\times n'$ subrectangles; see Figure 8a. Two such *rectangular L-complexes* specified by integer sequences $(m, m'; n, n')$ and $(\tilde m, \tilde m'; \tilde n, \tilde n')$ are *isomorphic* if and only if $m=\tilde m$, $m'=\tilde m'$, $n=\tilde n$, $n'=\tilde n'$, or $m=\tilde n$, $m'=\tilde n'$, $n=m$, $n'=\tilde m'$.

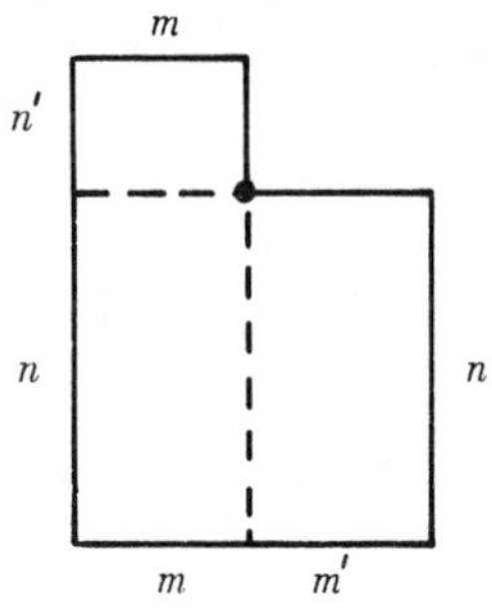

FIGURE 8a

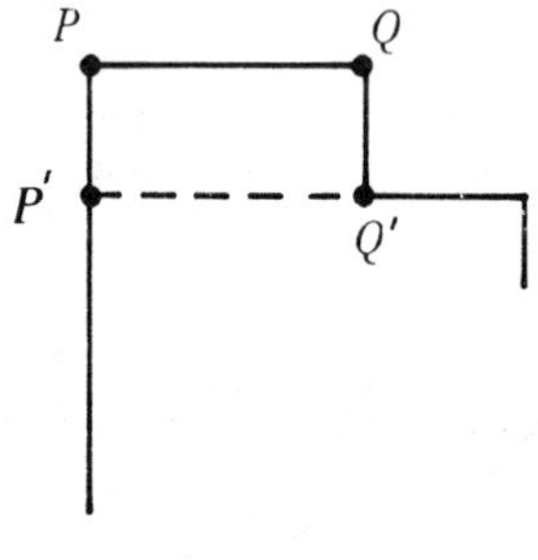

FIGURE 8b

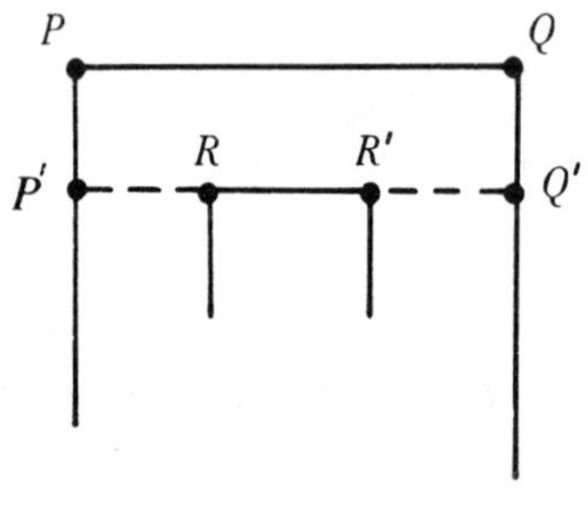

FIGURE 8c

Alternatively, the L-complex of Figure 8a can be described as the sum of an $(m+m')\times n$ rectangle and an abutting $m\times n'$ rectangle, or as the sum of an $m\times(n+n')$ rectangle and an abutting $m'\times n$ rectangle.

Similar constructions are possible for general J. By extending *all* edges in Figures 7a–7d (the cases $J=2$), we get decompositions into 5, 6, 5–7 (depending on the dimensions), and 6 subrectangles; the dashed lines decompose *all* regions into three subrectangles. In general, we have:

THEOREM 1. *Any connected rectangular polygon with J notches can be decomposed into $J+1$ or fewer subrectangles.*

PROOF. The rectangular $(2J+4)$-gon will have at least $J+1$ pairs of consecutive protruding corners; take the edge PQ joining any such consecutive corners. Translate it inwardly until either: (i) one end P' or Q' of the translated edge coincides with another corner, as in Figure 8b, or (ii) the translated $P'Q'$ falls on another edge, as in Figure 8c. In Case (i), the given $(2J+4)$-gon is decomposed into a subrectangle and a rectangular $(2J+2)$-gon (i.e., a $(2(J-1)+4)$-gon) with one less notch and one less protruding corner. In Case (ii), the given $(2J+4)$-gon is decomposed into a subrectangle and *two* rectangular polygons, having in all *two* fewer notches but two more protruding corners. By induction on J, the resulting $(2K+4)$-gon and $(2L+4)$-gon with $2(K+L)+8=2J+4$ can be decomposed into $K+L+2$ subrectangles, where $2(K+L+2)+4=2J+4$; hence the original rectangular $(2J+4)$-gon can be decomposed into $K+L+3$ subrectangles where $2(K+L+3)+2=2J+4$, which proves that $K+L+3=J+1$, as claimed.

Consequently, one can specify the cells of any rectangularly subdivided rectangular $(2J+4)$-gon (in Backus normal form) by listing $J+1$ rectangular *arrays*, and cross-addressing *boundary* 0-cells and 1-cells which occur in *two* arrays. If, as in Figure 9, one makes a decomposition into more than $J+1$ subrectangles, reentrant corner 0-cells may lie in *three* subrectangles, hence one may have to cross-address three addresses.

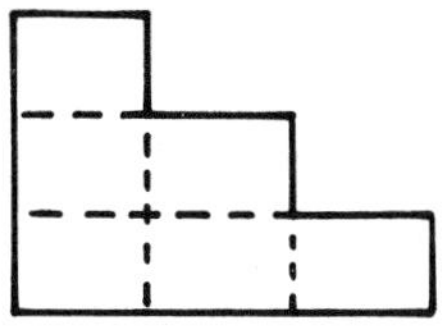

FIGURE 9

REFERENCES

1. Proceedings symposia on applied mathematics, Vols. I-XIX, Amer. Math. Soc., Providence, R. I., 1949–1967.

2. J. C. Abbott (editor), *Trends in lattice theory*, Van Nostrand, Princeton, N.J., 1970.

3. P. S. Aleksandrov, *Combinatorial topology*, OGIZ, Moscow, 1947; English transl., Graylock Press, Albany, New York, 1956. MR **10**, 55; MR **22** # 4056; MR **28** # 3415. See also: D. G. Bourgin, *Modern algebraic topology*, Macmillan, New York, 1963.

4. M. A. Arbib (editor), *The algebraic theory of machines, languages, and semigroups*, Academic Press, New York, 1968. MR **38** #1198.

5. ———, *Theories of abstract automata*, Prentice-Hall, Englewood Cliffs, N.J., 1969.

5a. E. F. Beckenbach (editor), *Applied combinatorial mathematics*, Wiley, New York, 1964. MR **30** #4687.

6. E. R. Berlekamp, *Algebraic coding theory*, McGraw-Hill, New York, 1968. MR **38** #6873.

7. G. Birkhoff, *Lattice theory*, 3rd ed., Amer. Math. Soc. Colloq. Publ., vol. 25, Amer. Math. Soc., Providence, R. I., 1967. MR **37** #2638.

8. ———, *Mathematics and psychology*, SIAM Rev. **11** (1969), 429–469.

9. G. Birkhoff and T. C. Bartee, *Modern applied algebra*, McGraw-Hill, New York, 1970.

10. G. Birkhoff and J. D. Lipson, *Heterogeneous algebras*, J. Combinatorial Theory **8** (1970), 115–133. MR **40** #4119.

11. G. D. Birkhoff, *General mean value theorems with applications to mechanical differentiation and quadrature*, Trans. Amer. Math. Soc. **7** (1906), 107–136.

12. Carl Boyer, *A history of mathematics*, Wiley, New York, 1968. MR **38** #3105.

13. F. H. Branin, *The relation between Kron's method and . . . network analysis*, IRE WESCON Conv. Rec., part 2, 1959, pp. 3–28.

13a. P. Braffort and D. Hirschberg (editors), *Studies in logic and the foundations of mathematics*, North-Holland, Amsterdam, 1967.

14. R. K. Brayton, F. G. Gustavson and R. A. Willoughby, *Some results on sparse matrices*, Math. Comp. **24** (1970), 937–954.

15. R. G. Busacker and T. L. Saaty, *Finite graphs and networks. An introduction with applications*, McGraw-Hill, New York, 1965. MR **35** #79.

16. B. A. Carré, *The partitioning of network equations for block iteration*, Comput. J. **9** (1966), 84–97. MR **33** #3445.

16a. L. Couturat, *La logique de Leibniz*, Paris, 1901.

17. H. Crapo and G.-C. Rota, *Combinatorial geometries*, M.I.T., Cambridge, Mass., 1968. (lithoprinted report).

17a. Irwin Engeler, *Semantics of algorithmic languages*, Springer, New York and Berlin, 1971.

18. D. Ferguson, *The question of uniqueness for G. D. Birkhoff interpolation problems*, J. Approximation Theory **2** (1969), 1–28. MR **40** #599.

19. G. Forsythe and C. B. Moler, *Computer solution of linear algebraic systems*, Prentice-Hall, Englewood Cliffs, N.J., 1967. MR **36** #2306.

19a. L. Fox (editor), *Advances in programming and non-numerical computation*, Pergamon Press, New York, 1966. MR **32** #8540.

20. George Grätzer, *Universal algebra*, Van Nostrand, Princeton, N.J., 1968. MR **40** # 1320.

20a. Branko Grünbaum, *Convex polytopes*, Pure and Appl. Math., vol. 16, Wiley, New York, 1967. MR **37** # 2085. See also *Polytopes, graphs, and complexes*, Bull. Amer. Math. Soc. **76** (1970), 1130–1201.

21. Frank Harary, *Graph theory and theoretical physics*, Academic Press, New York, 1967. MR **37** #6208.

22. ———, *Graphs and matrices*, SIAM Rev. **9** (1967), 83–90. MR **35** # 1501.

23. J. Hartmanis and R. E. Stearns, *Algebraic structure theory of sequential machines*, Prentice-Hall, Englewood Cliffs, N.J., 1966. MR **34** # 4068.

24. W. H. Huggins and Doris R. Entwisle, *Introductory systems and design*, Ginn-Blaisdell, New York, 1968.

25. R. E. Kalman, P. Falb and M. A. Arbib, *Topics in mathematical systems theory*, McGraw-Hill, New York, 1969. MR **40** # 8465.

26. M. Klerer and G. A. Korn (editors), *Digital user's handbook*, McGraw-Hill, New York, 1968.

27. D. E. Knuth, *The art of computer programming*, Addison-Wesley, Reading, Mass., 1968. (7 volumes projected.)

28. D. König, *Theorie der Graphen*, Akademische Verlag, Berlin, 1936; reprint, Chelsea, New York, 1950.

29. N. Levinson, *Coding theory: counterexample to G. H. Hardy's conception of applied mathematics*, Amer. Math. Monthly **77** (1970), 249–258. MR **40** # 8491.

30. C. I. Liu, *Introduction to combinatorial mathematics*, McGraw-Hill, New York, 1968. MR **38** #3154.

31. M. Minsky, *Computations: Finite and infinite machines*, Prentice-Hall, Englewood Cliffs, N.J., 1967.

32. S. Parter, *The use of linear graphs in Gauss elimination*, SIAM Rev. **3** (1961), 119–130. MR **26** #908.

32a. W. W. Peterson, *Error-correcting codes*, M.I.T. Press, Cambridge, Mass.; Wiley, New York, 1961. MR **22** #12003.

33. G. Pólya, *Bemerkangen zur Interpolation und zur Näherungstheorie der Balkenbiegung*, Z. Angew. Math. Mech. **11** (1931), 445–449.

34. G.-C. Rota, *On the foundations of combinatorial theory*. I. *Theory of Möbius functions*, Z. Wahrscheinlichkeitstheorie und Verw. Gebiete **2** (1964), 340–368. MR **30** #4688.

34a. H. A. Schmidt, K. Schütte and H. J. Thiele, *Contributions to mathematical logic*, North-Holland, Amsterdam, 1968.

35. I. F. Schoenberg (editor), *Approximations with special emphasis on spline functions*, Publ. no. 23, Math. Res. Center, U.S. Army, University of Wisconsin, Academic Press, New York, 1969. MR **40** #4638.

36. D. V. Steward, *Partitioning and tearing systems of equations*, J. Soc. Indust. Appl. Math. **2** (1965), 345–365. MR **36** #2307.

37. R. P. Tewarson, *Solution of a system of simultaneous linear equations with a sparse coefficient matrix by elimination methods*, Nordisk Tidskr. Informations-Behandling (BIT) **7** (1967), 226–239. MR **36** #2308.

38. R. S. Varga, *Matrix iterative analysis*, Prentice-Hall, Englewood Cliffs, N.J., 1962. MR **28** #1725.

38a. J. von Neumann, *Collected works*. Vol. V. *Design of computers, theory of automata and numerical analysis*, Macmillan, New York, 1963. MR **28** #1104.

39. J. R. Westlake, *A handbook of numerical matrix inversion and solution of linear equations*, Wiley, New York, 1968. MR **36** #4794.

40. A. N. Whitehead, *Universal algebra*, Cambridge Univ. Press, New York, 1898.

41. H. Whitney, *The abstract properties of linear dependence*, Amer. J. Math. **57** (1935), 509–533; See also: G. Birkhoff, ibid. 801–804.

42. J. H. Wilkinson, *The algebraic eigenvalue problem*, Clarendon Press, Oxford, 1965. MR **32** #1894.

43. R. A. Willoughby (editor), *IBM sparse matrix proceedings*, IBM Report RAI #11707, 1969.

44. A. D. Wyner, *On coding and information theory*, SIAM Rev. **11** (1969), 317–346.

HARVARD DOCTORAL THESES

T0. Stephen A. Cook, *On the minimum computation time of functions*, Trans. Amer. Math. Soc. **142** (1969), 291–314. MR **40** # 2459.

T1. K. B. Krohn, *Algebraic theory of machines*, 1962.

T2. John D. Lipson, *Flow graphs and generating functions*, 1969.

T3. Vern Poythress, *Partial algebras*, 1970.

T4. Donald Rose, *Symmetric elimination . . . and the potential flow network problem*, 1970.

T5. Gary I. Wakoff, *Piecewise polynomial spaces . . .*, 1970.

T6. David M. Young, *Iterative methods for solving differential equations of elliptic type*, 1950.

HARVARD UNIVERSITY

Reprinted from Computers in Algebra and Number Theory, G. Birkhoff and M. Hall, eds.
Am. Math. Soc., 1971, 1–47.

THE RISE OF MODERN ALGEBRA TO 1936

GARRETT BIRKHOFF

Abstract, or "modern" algebra as it has been called for over four decades, has profoundly influenced the thinking of four academic generations of American mathematicians. It strongly influenced my own generation, the generation of Ph.D.'s produced just after World War II, the lucky mathematicians educated in the expansive 1950's and early 1960's, and the annual flood of 1500 Ph.D.'s produced recently from the "baby bulge" following World War II. Initially sweeping over the mathematical world like a tidal wave, and later christened the "new" mathematics by our journalists, all signs point to its now having been absorbed into the mainstream of mathematics (Bell, 1938). Therefore, it seems timely to review its rise — though premature to try to review its accomplishments.

This tidal wave was generated in Germany and assumed a coherent shape in Göttingen during the 1920's under the leadership of Emmy Noether (1882-1935). This, in his careful review of *Fifty Years of Algebra in America, 1888-1938 (1938:32),* E. T. Bell wrote: "this latest phase of algebra is . . . practically all German, if the ideas of Galois be excluded as too remote historically. Its roots are in Dedekind's work . . ., Steinitz' paper of 1910 on fields, and Emmy Noether's abstract school, trained by her either personally or through her writings from about 1922 to her death in 1935."

Its most essential feature is its reliance on the axiomatic approach. Thus, van der Waerden's now classic *Moderne Algebra* (1930), the book that gave "modern" algebra its name and won for it worldwide recognition, describes the goal of the book as follows. "The *abstract, formal* or *axiomatic* direction, to which Algebra owes its renewed upswing in recent years, has above all led to a series of novel concepts giving new connections and far-reaching results in field theory, *ideal* theory, *group* theory, and the theory of *hypercomplex numbers*." Likewise Hermann Weyl, no great admirer of axiomatics, stated: "In her (Emmy Noether's) hands, the axiomatic method had opened new, concrete, profound problems and pointed the way to their solution."

A second essential feature is its emancipation of algebra from primary concern with the real and complex number systems, and of proofs that depend on analysis, for example, of the classical "fundamental theorem of algebra." Thus is treats algebra as a self-contained discipline "whose formulations and methods are diametrically opposite" to those of analysis.[1] It tries to replace analytical methods by rational and set-theoretic methods, including finite chain conditions and transfinite induction.

In particular, it considers the fundamental theorem of algebra as providing just one example of an algebraically complete (or closed) field, and pretty much ignores partial fractions, continued fractions, Sturn sequences, and the like. This

1. H. Hasse, 1930, Die moderne algebraische Methoden, Jahresb. der Deutsche Math. Ver., 39:23-34.

is because its primary emphasis is on wide classes of structures, whose elements can be numbers but are more likely to be transformations, sets, or just symbols.

Among the pioneer abstract algebraists of the Emmy Noether school, perhaps most outstanding were Emil Artin (1892-1962), Richard Brauer, Helmut Hasse, and van der Waerden. Deuring, Fitting, Krull, and E. Witt were her students, whereas Saunders Mac Lane and Oystein Ore (1899-1968) studied at Göttingen. In retrospect, it is easy to recognize the enormous importance of Emmy Noether's work and influence.

This influence was so great that it is easy to overlook the equally fundamental influence of English and French-speaking mathematicians on the development of "modern" algebra. I shall try to make clear this influence, emphasizing especially (partly for sentimental reasons) the contributions of American mathematicians.

Roughly speaking, the rise of modern algebra divides into two main periods: 1921 to 1935, ending with the death of Emmy Noether, when it was centered in Germany; and 1936 to 1950, when it found a new home in our country and was expanded by Bourbaki into a new global view of mathematics. By 1950, its rise had been completed. I shall discuss these two periods in succession.

Emmy Noether

In reviewing the rise of modern algebra, it seems fitting to begin with a glimpse into the background and contributions of Emmy Noether. I shall not try to be systematic; more extensive accounts were given shortly after her death by van der Waerden and Hermann Weyl.[2] I have drawn freely from these sources and from Kimberling (1972) and Constance Reid (1970), whose index will guide you to many fascinating anecdotes.

The daughter of the notable algebraist Max Noether, she wrote her thesis on invariant theory under Gordan, and was his only Ph.D. student. It was only gradually that she fell under the spell of Hilbert's methods and formulation of problems. According to van der Waerden, the essence of her scientific credo became contained in the following maxim: "All relations between numbers, functions and operations first become perspicuous, capable of generalization, and truly fruitful after being detached from specific examples (besonderen Objekten), and traced back to general conceptual connections."

Emmy Noether developed slowly. One wonders what her academic status would have become without the male vacuum created by World War I. Even so, it was only Hilbert's support and influence that got her a position in Göttingen, over the opposition of his colleagues (Reid, 1970: 143, 168). And she never became an "ordentliche Professor."

She was 39 before she published her first major paper, in 1921. It dealt with ideal theory, and its announced purpose was "to generalize the factorization theorems for natural integers and algebraic number fields to arbitrary integral domains and rings." Five years later, she published a second paper (1926),

2. H. Weyl, 1935, Emmy Noether, Scripta Math., 201-220; B. L. van der Waerden, 1935, Nachruf auf Emmy Noether, Math. Annalen, 111:469-476.

giving "an abstract characterization of all (commutative) rings whose ideal theory coincides with that of all integers of an algebraic number field.[3] The best known examples of these rings are provided by the ring of all integers in an algebraic function field in one indeterminate — or more generally, in several indeterminates, provided that one considers, with Kronecker, only ideals of maximum dimension, thus having suitable quotient rings."

The main thrust of these two papers is clear: to develop an axiomatic factorization theory that is valid in any commutative ring with unity having no zero divisors. She shows that, in an integral domain J,[4] it is sufficient to assume two chain conditions and one axiom of "integral closure," namely:

I. *Chain condition on divisors*. Every nested sequence $A_1 \leqslant A_2 \leqslant A_3 \leqslant \ldots$ of ideals A_j has only a finite number of distinct terms.

II. *Chain condition on multiples*. Given a proper ideal A in J, R/A has the property that every descending chain of ideals A_j/A has only a finite number of distinct terms.[5]

V. *Integral closure*. The field $Q(R)$ of quotients of R is *integrally closed:* in $Q(R)$, every element "integral" over R belongs to R.

The "ascending chain condition" of Axiom I above is abstractly equivalent to Hilbert's Basis Theorem (van der Waerden, 1931), originally proved for polynomial ideals by Hilbert. Hilbert himself seems not to have attached very great importance to the result; his proof of it was so abstract that Gordan said of it: "This is no proof, this is theology." Emmy used the "theology" described by her mentor so effectively that rings satisfying it have come to be known as "noetherian" rings.

Emmy Noether used this condition also in her theory of hypercomplex number systems, alias "linear associative algebras." In another major paper (1929), she showed that the theory of group representations developed by Frobenius, I. Schur, and A. Young could be derived as a corollary of the general theory of semisimple algebras.[6] (Note also her important work on "crossed algebras" with Brauer and Hasse, published in Crelle 167(1932:399-404.)

Other Germanic Antecedents

Emmy Noether was the greatest single source of inspiration for van der Waerden's *Moderne Algebra*. However, Artin's influence was almost as great; actually, volume 1 was based largely on Artin's lectures, and some of its brilliance surely reflects Artin's supreme mathematical artistry.

However, van der Waerden also drew on many other contemporary sources, which he has kindly summarized in a long, thoughtful letter (to appear in *Historia Mathematica)*. One notes that his sources are almost exclusively Germanic. Three reasons can be given for this.

3. Emmy Noether obviously had Dedekind's theory in mind. On p. 29, she alludes to the relevance of E. Prüfer, Neue Begründung der algebraischen Zahlentheorie, Math. Annalen, 94(1924):198-243.

4. In an integral domain, E. Noether's Axioms III and IV hold automatically.

5. In van der Waerden (1931, vol. 2), this is replaced by the condition that proper prime ideals are divisorless.

6. This idea stems from Molien's thesis, 1891.

First and most important, *Moderne Algebra* was intended to be a self-contained exposition of recent research; familiarity with classical algebra was tacitly assumed. And most of the recent algebraic research done in the style of Emmy Noether had been done in Germany. Moreover it stemmed from earlier ideas about number theory and algebra also originating in largely German-speaking areas (Germany, the former Austria-Hungary, German Switzerland, and the like).

Thus, much of Artin's work was concerned with the class field theory and the theory of Abelian field extensions created by Hilbert in his 1897 *Zahlbericht*. The Artin-Schreier theory of "formally real" fields was also invented to solve one of Hilbert's famous problems and prove that every real polynomial or rational function whose values are all positive is a sum of squares. (The converse is, of course, obvious.)

From an abstract standpoint, this beautiful theorem can be summarized as follows. Using transfinite induction freely, Steinitz (1910) has proved that every field K has a unique algebraically complete extension Ω. Artin and Schreier showed that if K is "formally real," in the sense that $\sum x_k^2 = 0$ implies that every $x_k = 0$, then there is a *maximal* field P between K and Ω such that $\Omega = P(i)$ (van der Waerden, 1930-31, §68).

Second, Emmy Noether herself attributed her inspiration mainly to Germanic sources. "Alles steht schon bei Dedekind" was one of her favorite statements; and in particular, his celebrated unique factorization theorem for integral ideals in an arbitrary number field inspired her work on ideals. Her axiomatic approach had been used by Dedekind in his later work on lattices in 1897 and 1907[7], by Hilbert (1899) to rigorize the foundations of geometry and (less successfully) physics, and by Steinitz (1910) to develop a general theory of fields. She was inspired not only by Hilbert's Basis Theorem, but also intrigued by the general concept of a (commutative) ring; Kronecker, Molien, and Frobenius were other obvious sources of inspiration for her and her colleagues. Moreover Germany was largely cut off from the allied countries during 1914 to 1928, German mathematicians not having been invited to the International Congresses of 1920 or (primarily because of French objections) 1924.[8]

Finally, German mathematicians in the 1920's believed strongly that Hilbert was the world's greatest mathematician and Göttingen the center of world mathematics — a belief strongly reinforced by the birth of quantum mechanics there.

In view of these facts, it is not surprising that, as of 1930, the Emmy Noether school attributed "modern" algebra most exclusively to Germanic sources. However, the subject was destined to change in character and to move elsewhere very soon. Its next phase of development would owe much more to the influence of British and American ideas. There already existed equally able algebraists in the United States. To quote Hermann Weyl's notice on Emmy Noether:

7. See Emmy Noether's commentary in Dedekind's Ges. Math. Werke, 2:147.

8. It was for this reason that American mathematicians did not want to participate in an International Mathematical Union, under the auspices of the League of Nations, in the 1920's.

"Her methods need not, however, be considered the only means of salvation. In addition to Artin and Hasse, who in some respects are akin to her, there are algebraists of a still more different stamp, such as I. Schur in Germany, Dickson and Wedderburn in America, whose achievements are certainly not behind hers in depth and significance. Perhaps her followers, with pardonable enthusiasm, have not always recognized this fact."[9]

Moreover, the importance of modern algebra was not recognized widely in Germany at the time. Constance Reid wrote (1970:166-167): "She and her work were not . . . much admired in her native land. She was never even elected to the Göttingen Scientific Society . . . her classes usually numbered no more than five or ten."

Algebraic Geometry To 1935

In the introduction to his *Moderne Algebra,* van der Waerden said he omitted "algebraic functions and continuous groups, because transcendental methods are needed to treat them properly." Actually, he and Artin already had begun to free algebraic geometry from the need for transcendental methods (that is, "modernize" it). In the rest of this section, I shall try to give you some idea of what was involved, and how much progress had been made by 1935.

Ever since the publication in 1637 of Descartes' "La Géometrie," as an appendix to his *"Discours sur la Méthode,"* algebra and geometry have been inextricably intertwined. At first, attention was confined largely to real, affine algebraic curves, or loci defined to consist of the points in the real (x, y)-plane satisfying some polynomial equation $p(x, y) = 0$, that is, as the graph of a real algebraic function. For p quadratic, there are three nondegenerate cases: the ellipse, hyperbola, and parabola studied by Apollonius of Perga in the third century BC. For p cubic, Newton found in 1673 that there are 72 kinds.

The classification of algebraic curves becomes much simpler if one replaces the real field by the complex field C, and the affine plane by the *projective* plane. Thus there are only three projective distinct complex cubic curves, that is, sets of projective points $\lambda z = (\lambda z_0, \lambda z_1, \lambda z_2)$ satisfying an equation of the form $p(z_0, z_1, z_2) = 0$, p a homogeneous cubic polynomial. The group of birational transformations introduces still more uniformity.

The situation in higher dimensions is similar. Over any field F, one can define an affine algebraic variety as the locus of points satisfying some finite set of polynomial equations

$$p_1(x_1, \ldots, x_n) = p_2(x_1, \ldots, x_n) = \ldots = p_r(x_1, \ldots, x_n) = 0,$$

and a projective algebraic variety as the set of all projective points λx satisfying $p_j(x_0, x_1, \ldots, x_n)$ for $j = 1, \ldots, r$. Ordinarily, this variety will be an $(n-r)$-dimensional manifold with exceptional singularities.

Associated with each complex algebraic "curve," defined by $p(z,w) = 0$, is an algebraic function $w = f(z)$. In 1850, Puiseux sharpened parts of Newton's analysis of the singularities of algebraic functions by considering them in the

9. See footnote 2.

complex domain.[10] From 1951 on, Riemann showed how the behavior of complex algebraic functions could be understood much more clearly if one considered them as single-valued on a suitable "Riemann surface." This led to the notion of genus and to the all-important Riemann-Roch theorem (1857, 1864). Special interest was taken also, during the nineteenth century, in integrals of algebraic functions (so-called Abelian integrals), including hyperelliptic integrals of the form $\int dz/\sqrt{Q(z)}$, Q a polynomial (quartic Q giving, of course, elliptic integrals).

The above ideas, along with the invariant theory of Cayley and Sylvester, were developed extensively in Germany by Clebsch, Gordan, Brill, and M. Noether (1844-1921), whose daughter Emmy was trained in this tradition. Contemporary with it was the nonrigorous "Schubert calculus," for calculating intersection numbers of pairs of curves on an algebraic surface, among other things.[11] This theory was partially straightened out for surfaces by F. Severi, in a famous paper written in 1912.

Over the complex field, Lefschetz[12] gave in 1921 to 1924 a rigorous topological definition of the intersection multiplicity for two "surfaces," considering them as four-dimensional cycles in the complex projective space P^4, an eight-dimensional orientable manifold. In 1930, van der Waerden had shown how to justify Schubert's calculus in this case, on the basis of Lefschetz' definition.[13] Two years earlier, he had generalized Bézout's theorem to an arbitrary ground field. Thus by 1930, van der Waerden had made substantial progress toward the two main goals of "modern" algebraic geometers: 1) making the theory rigorous, and 2) giving a unified theory over an arbitrary ground field. Moreover he knew that the tools he wanted were available in the general theories of fields, ideals, and elimination developed by Dedekind, Kronecker, Hilbert, Steinitz, and their followers.

Zariski's influential monograph *Algebraic Surfaces,* written in 1934, was influenced much more by Lefschetz than by "modern" algebraic ideas. It refers exclusively to complex projective algebraic varieties (which Zariski calls "algebraic varieties" for brevity). Its stated aim is to emphasize the "interrelations between algebro-geometric, topological, and transcendental [aspects]." Though he refers to ideals in his first section, he never mentions them because, as he has told me, "he still had to learn modern algebra."

The fact that "higher congruences" in number theory could be interpreted as polynomial equations over finite fields, and hence as "algebraic varieties" in a generalized sense, had been noticed by Artin in his Thesis written in 1923. This led Artin to define the zeta function of any finite extension K of the field $F_q(x)$, F_q

10. See J. L. Coolidge, 1940, A history of geometrical methods, Clarendon Press, Oxford, 196-197.

11. Coolidge, Chap. 4; B. L. van der Waerden, 1971, Archive for history of exact sciences, 7:171-180.

12. S. Lefschetz, 1971, Selected papers, Chelsea, 41-198, 283-442; Bull. AMS, 29(1923):242-258. Lefschetz wrote (*ibid.*, 13) that his lot was "to plant the harpoon of algebraic topology into the body of the whale of algebraic geometry."

13. B. L. van der Waerden, 1930, Topologische Begründung des Kalküls der abzählenden Geometrie, Math Annalen, 102:337-362; *op. cit.*, 176.

a Galois field. Artin's definition was simplified by F. K. Schmidt, who also observed that the functional equation

$$z(1/qu) = q^{1-g}u^{2-2g}z(u)$$

simply expressed the Riemann-Roch theorem.[14]

From 1928 on, A. Weil also studied connections between algebraic geometry and number theory. In 1935, he even wrote a monograph on the subject.[15] In particular, he was very interested in Hasse's proof (1934) of the "Riemann hypothesis for curves over finite fields," when $g = 1$, and in applications by Skolem of the technique of p-adic completion to diophantine equations. So one can say that the germs of the takeover of algebraic geometry by the abstract algebraic approach were already in existence in 1935.

British Sources

Although technically extremely deep and skillful, German algebraists of the 1920's had a somewhat limited view of algebra, being primarily concerned with problems arising in algebraic number theory and algebraic geometry. Whereas their axiomatic and set-theoretic style was modern, their problems were classical, often traceable to Gauss, through Hilbert, Dedekind, and Dirichlet.

A much broader concept of algebra was held by British algebraists of the mid-nineteenth century (and, indeed, by Leibniz before 1700). Thus Boole (1854) wrote before 1854: "It is not the essence of mathematics to be concerned with the idea of number and quantity." Likewise, the ultimate forms and processes (of Logic) are mathematical."[16] It was with this philosophy in mind that Boole developed Boolean algebra as the appropriate algebra for logic; it is now considered even more appropriate for sets.

In much the same spirit, Cayley introduced the concept of an abstract group around 1850. Somewhat later, he introduced the algebra of matrices, as distinguished from determinants. This and Hamilton's quaternions led to vector analysis, a subject that owes as much to Green, Stokes, and Maxwell as to Gauss and Grassmann.

Likewise, Cayley "first proposed in [Cambridge Math. J., 4(1845):193-209] the general problem on invariants (that is, functions of the coefficients invariant [under] linear transformation of the facients)."[17] Moreover, he and Sylvester had developed this theory quite far before Clebsch and Gordan proved their first major theorem on the subject in 1868. Emmy Noether (like Hilbert 22 years earlier) wrote her doctoral thesis on invariant theory in 1907, and continued to work on this subject until 1919; the whole story is told ably in (Kimberling, 1972:927-932).

14. See J. Dieudonné, 1972, The historical development of algebraic geometry, Amer. Math. Monthly, 79:851-853.

15. A. Weil, 1935, Arithmetique et geometrie sur les varietes algebriques, Act. Sci. et Ind. #206, Hermann, Paris. For Hasse's work, see Crelle, 172(1935):37-54, and, with H. Davenport as coauthor, 151-182.

16. In Boole's own copy, he added in ink: mathematical "in form." Leibnez had also taken a general view of the symbolic method, and recognized the relevance of some Boolean formulas.

17. Artin, 1965:584. Cayley says he was stimulated by an even earlier paper of Boole, 3(1843):1-20.

These remarks are not intended to belittle the enormous influence on the development of modern algebra of Hilbert's Basis Theorem and other German contributions to invariant theory, but only to show that British contributions were fundamental, too. Even in the limited areas of algebra with which they were primarily concerned, Emmy Noether and her students owed more to British algebraists than they recognized.

And, except for problems arising ultimately from algebraic number theory, algebraic topology, and algebraic geometry, the techniques developed by the Emmy Noether school have not exerted a decisive influence. Thus, current activity in pure group theory has been influenced more by Burnside's (1897) meandering classic on the subject and the deep researches of Philip Hall (which were nearly contemporary with the publication of *Moderne Algebra),* than by anything produced in Germany in the 1920's (for example, by the theory of group extensions). This is not to denigrate the beautiful book of Speiser (1922), of which I shall say more later.

Some difference between British and German ideas about algebra can be seen by looking at Whitehead's *Universal Algebra* (1898). Consider the Table of Contents of the first two "Books":

Book I. *Principles of Algebraic Symbolism*
On the Nature of a Calculus. Manifold. Principles of Universal Algebra.
Book II. *The Algebra of Symbolic Logic.*
Algebra of Symbolic Logic. Existential Expressions. Applications to Logic. Propositional Interpretation.

Whitehead's treatise continues with a discussion of different kinds of algebraic systems, including Boolean algebras. However, it has almost no overlap with the work of the Emmy Noether school. Thus, the relation between the contents of Whitehead (1898) and van der Waerden (1930-31) is expressed most simply through the equation

$$\text{A. N. Whitehead} \cap \text{Emmy Noether} = \emptyset$$

or, (van der Waerden, 1930-31) $\cap$ (Whitehead, 1898) $= \emptyset$.

Formal Logic and Foundations

Generally speaking mid-nineteenth century British algebraists were philosophically inclined, like Leibniz and Grassmann, whereas the most important contributions of the Emmy Noether school were technical and intended for fellow-specialists.

This broader philosophical view of algebra also was shared by Bourbaki (1951), who wrote: "To do algebra is essentially to calculate, that is, to perform algebraic operations on elements of a set . . . the best known example is furnished by [the four operations and rules of] elementary arithmetic." The same idea is expressed by computer scientists when they describe algebra as symbol manipulation, very rightly I think.

This description also brings out the substance of modern algebra as we know it today, as distinguished from classical algebra. In substance, it is concerned with all kinds of systems to which the symbolic method is applicable, whereas classical algebra was primarily concerned with the real and complex fields and polynomials over them. Modern algebra also differs from classical algebra in its axiomatic style, as exemplified by van der Waerden's book, but it is primarily to the substance of modern algebra that British mathematicians have contributed.

Perhaps the most ambitious such contribution was Whitehead and Russell's *Principia Mathematica* (1908-12). This treatise attempts to axiomatize (rather discursively, not at all in the style of van der Waerden) and develop all of mathematics from an extended "algebra of logic" invented largely by Peano and Frege. This book in turn exercised an indirect influence on the work of the Göttingen school through Hilbert's interest in formalizing logic. Thus, Hilbert wrote in 1918:[18] "Russell's Axiomatization of Logic is the crowning achievement of axiomatics."

Indeed, all through the 1920's, Hilbert's main concern was to formalize all mathematics.[19] Thus, he refused to take seriously the paradoxes associated with Cantor's set theory ("From the Paradise made for us by Cantor, no one shall cast us forth"); the brilliant successes of the Emmy Noether school may have contributed to his faith in formalization.

Van der Waerden wrote his book before Hilbert's optimism (and that of Whitehead and Russell) had been shattered by Gödel. After Gödel's work came out, van der Waerden deleted his Chapter VII on the well-ordering theorem. Although his ostensible reason was for expository simplicity, he may also have been influenced subconsciously by his earlier training in Brouwer's intuitionism (see the sources for van der Waerden's *Moderne Algebra*).

In general, the influence on modern algebra of the ideas about logic of Whitehead, Russell, and Hilbert seems to have been limited to encouraging emphasis on the axiomatic approach. (The main thrust of Whitehead and Russell's three volumes was to construct an axiomatic model for formal logic that was adequate for discussing the real field **R**, and to demonstrate its adequacy.)

In contrast, van der Waerden (1930-31) simply reviewed in six pages (his §64) the construction of R from the rational field Q; after two pages on p-adic numbers in his §66, he proved the solvability of quadratic equations and of polynomial equations of odd degree $C = R(i)$, incidentally presenting the theory of Sturm sequences as an application of Euclid's algorithm, and freely using Zermelo's theorem (van der Waerden, 1930-31:231) to derive the Artin-Schreier theory of formally real fields. From this, in turn, he derived the classical Fundamental Theorem of Algebra as a Corollary (van der Waerden, 1930-31:228, Satz 3a). No need for classical analysis or for "visualizing" the complex plane is evident anywhere.

By maintaining a consistently axiomatic approach and avoiding classical analyses, van der Waerden gave to his book great integrity and unity. It carried on the tradition of Dirichlet (1880), Dedekind, and Steinitz (1910). But of course

18. Hilbert, 1932:153; Math. Annalen, 78(1918):405-415.

19. See his address at the Bolongna International Congress, 1(1928):135-142; the skepticism expressed by Lusin on pp. 295-300 of the same volume presents an interesting contrast.

it also ignored analytic number theory, and one may wonder today whether the more eclectic approach of Hardy and Wright (1938) may not be more stimulating to students.

AMERICAN TRADITIONS

Although seldom mentioned in the publications of the Emmy Noether school in the 1920's, American mathematicians already had a strong tradition in several areas relating to "modern" algebra, and especially in hypercomplex algebra, postulate theory, and Boolean algebra. Thus, Wedderburn (1907) was the first to present the theory of linear associative algebras over an arbitrary field (its "modern" form), avoiding its previous restriction (by Molien, Cartan, and others) to algebras over the real and complex fields; see (Birkhoff, 1973). He may have been inspired to develop this abstract viewpoint by E. H. Moore in Chicago, where Wedderburn went as Carnegie Fellow in 1905. And in 1923, Dickson had sharpened and extended Wedderburn's arguments in his *Algebras and Their Arithmetics* (Dickson, 1923), several years before Emmy Noether wrote (1929) her "Hypercomplexe Grössen . . . ."

The pre-1920 "modernity" of American thinking about hypercomplex numbers has been epitomized by Artin[20] as follows:

> From the very beginning the abstract point of view is dominant in American publications, whereas for European mathematicians a system of hypercomplex numbers was by nature an extension of either the real or the complex field. While the Europeans obtained very advanced results in the classification of their special cases with methods that were not well adapted to generalization, the Americans achieved an abstract forumlation of the problem, developed a very suitable terminology, and discovered the germs of the modern methods.
>
> On the American side, one has first of all to consider the very early paper by B. Peirce, "Linear associative algebras" (1870). In it he states explicitly that mathematics should be an abstract logical scheme, the absence of a special interpretation of its symbols making it more useful in that the same logical scheme will in general reflect many diverse physical situations.

One wonders why Emmy Noether made so little of the important and relevant work of Peirce, Wedderburn, and Dickson in her papers. In retrospect, her extensions of Wedderburns's structure theorems to "rings with double chain condition" seems of minor importance, and are not even mentioned in Wedderburn's *Lectures on Matrices* (1934). It is, of course quite otherwise with her applications of these structure theorems to obtain representation theorems for groups and rings. These representation theorems do indeed stem primarily from Molien (1892), Frobenius (1896-1910). amd Schur (1905-1911), although A. Young and Burnside made important contributions independently (Speiser, 1922:143-144).

Like many other of our most eminent mathematicians, Wedderburn was born and trained in Europe. He made other notable contributions to algebra, being the first to prove that every finite division ring is a field, and to argue (nonrigorously, I fear) that the unique factorization theorem was true for finite groups.

20. E. Artin, 1950, The influence of J. H. M. Wedderburn on the development of modern algebra, Bull. AMS, 65-72; Artin, 1965:526-533.

Another distinguished British import was J. J. Sylvester, who taught at Johns Hopkins from 1876 to 1883. However, I think that E. T. Bell (1938) was correct in saying that, although Sylvester's own contributions (1904-12) to algebra, especially invariant theory, were brilliant and varied, he did not exercise a lasting influence on his students.

Far more influential on American mathematics than Wedderburn or Sylvester was E. H. Moore. To quote E. T. Bell:

> In the late 1890's and early 1900's the history of mathematics in this country is largely an echo of Moore's success and enthusiasm at the University of Chicago. Directly through his own work and indirectly through that of the men he trained, Moore put new life in the theory of groups and the foundations of [21] and of mathematics in general, finite algebra and certain branches of analysis as they were cultivated in America. All this work had one feature in common: he strove unceasingly towards the utmost abstractness and generality available.

In other words, the modern spirit was in E. H. Moore's work around 1900.

Among Moore's many students, L. E. Dickson did the most for algebra and number theory. He and his student Adrian Albert secured for Chicago the leading position in the study of hypercomplex number systems, which it held until Albert's untimely death. The leadership has now passed to Yale with Nathan Jacobson, who studied with Wedderburn and Albert.

Bell has reviewed Dickson's publications (Bell, 1938:28-32) so thoroughly and well that I shall not try to supplement Bell's review in any way.

POSTULATE THEORY

Contributions to postulate theory by E. H. Moore, E. V. Huntington, and other American mathematicians were especially relevant to modern algebra since, as van der Waerden pointed out in his Introduction (see Introductory Remarks), the axiomatic approach is the essence of modern algebra's style.

There had been considerably earlier European work on postulate theory, for which I refer you to Birkhoff (1973). After giving an amusing survey of this earlier European work (Bell, 1938:15-16), E. T. Bell gives a detailed account (1938:17-19) of the more important American contributions. Hence, I shall just touch on a few highlights. The earliest American contribution to postulate theory was Huntington's definition of a group in 1902, in which Hilbert's concepts of an independent and of a categorical set of postulates were applied to algebra, apparently for the first time. Related contributions were published in the *Transactions* during the next few years by E. H. Moore, Dickson, and Veblen, whereas Huntington continued his elegant and basic studies of postulate systems for all kinds of "algebras" for at least three more decades.

These studies of postulate systems were strongly influenced by Hilbert's celebrated *Grundlagen der Geometrie* (1899), which systematically avoided both Peano's use of symbolic logic and Euclid's reliance on visual demonstrations. I mention the first of these features because E. H. Moore's *Introduction to a Form of General Analysis* represented an ambitious and creative attempt to

21. E. T. Bell had a genius for overstatement!

develop analysis in the symbolic style of Peano, which failed to gain wide adoption.[22] And I mention the second because it contributed so much to the modern "algebraization of geometry" (compare the section on Lattice Theory and Algebraic Geometry in my second paper).

In particular, E. V. Huntington wrote several papers on postulate systems for Boolean algebra. Boolean algebra is a subject untouched by the Emmy Noether school, but used extensively by mathematical logicians such as A. N. Whitehead, who came from "the other Cambridge" to Harvard around 1920. The most definitive papers on the foundations of Boolean algebra are those of Marshall Stone,[23] who clarified for the first time the precise relation between Boolean algebra and rings, demonstrated conclusively that Boolean algebra was precisely the algebra of sets, and established its connections with general topology.

Group Theory

Bell (1938:8) observed: "The intensive activity of American algebraists in the theory of groups during [1888-1938] was due to a few active men who induced numerous proselytes to contribute at least one paper apiece relating to groups," and added "without the inspiration of the work of C. Jordan in France, G. Fronbenius and O. Hölder in Germany, and W. Burnside in England, . . . the history of the theory of groups in American would be much shorter."

Perhaps the first American group theorists of any note was Frank Nelson Cole, for whom the Cole Prize in algebra was named. He inspired the early work of G. A. Miller, who lived at Cole's home in Ann Arbor during 1893-95 (Bell, 1938:9). About the same time, E. H. Moore lectured and did research on groups and fields, inspiring Dickson to think about groups in the process.

Other active group theorists were Blichfeldt, who emigrated here from Denmark, and H. B. Manning, whose daughter married the algebraist Malcolm Smiley. But the most active was G. A. Miller, who published a prodigious number of short papers. In particular, Miller collaborated with Blichfeldt and Dickson in a three-part book *Finite Groups,* published in 1916.

Miller was remarkable in another respect: he amassed a fortune of $2,000,000, which he gave to the University of Illinois. As a by-product of this philanthropy, his own collected papers were published; I think it fair to say that the publication was not in response to irresistible public demand.

American Philanthropy

Miller's unexpected bequest was but one of many great contributions made to the support of scholars by American philanthropists. Much earlier Carnegie had set up a pension to help prevent professors from ending their years in poverty. I

22. Whitehead and Russell, (1908-12) were (temporarily) somewhat more successful in getting others to adopt their Peanesque symbolism.

23. See Stone, 1936, and Applications of the theory of Boolean rings to general topology, Trans. Amer. Math. Soc., 41(1937):375-481. Stone made preliminary announcements of his ideas in 1934-35.

believe that the current TIAA and CREF pension plans, on which many of us rely for reasonable comfort during retirement years, stem from Carnegie's gift.

Before World War I, the United States was a debtor nation, and Europe — especially Western Europe — was the great center of wealth and culture. But World War I changed all that. I remember having the comfortable feeling in the 1920's that all our friends were getting more affluent. This affluence, and the philanthropy that was based on it, led not only to a great expansion of our university system, but also to some notable gifts to European mathematical centers. Especially, as head of the Rockefeller Foundation, Max Mason provided Rockefeller money to set up both the Institut Henri Poincaré in Paris and the Mathematical Institut in Göttingen. In Constance Reid's book (1970), Hilbert is quoted as attributing the second gift to Courant's "matchless administrative skill." She may be right: Warren Weaver later donated $2,000,000 of Sloan money to the Courant Institute at N.Y.U.

However I think that Max Mason's appreciation, and the generosity of the Rockefeller family and Sloan, who made his money in our much maligned automobile industry, deserve much more of the credit. In this connection, I recall also the munificence of the Ford Foundation, large gifts from which raised many academic salaries appreciably in the early 1950's.

Harvard: 1928 to 1932

The support given to Göttingen by the Rockefeller Foundation foreshadowed a much greater dependence of science on American institutions in the next two decades. When van der Waerden's book was published, German algebraists could have had no idea of the changes "modern" algebra was to undergo in that time, nor of the influence on it of mathematicians having very different ideas and backgrounds.

Marshall Stone has given you an idea of his training; I will now give you some glimpses of mine. I hope that, in due course, Saunders Mac Lane, Andrè Weil, and other *dramatis personae* will give you authentic views of theirs. My account will be personal, and will center around my own experiences.

It will begin with the International Mathematical Congress at Bologna in 1928. This took place just two years after my father's first trip to Europe, and was the first International Congress since 1912 that included Germans or Austrians. Of the 16 general addresses, six were given by Italian speakers and only two by Americans, Veblen and my father. My father's was especially dramatic; it was entitled "Mathematical Elements in Art," and was opened by heralds with trumpets in the beautiful Palazzo Vecchio in Florence.

Indeed, most of the general addresses were philosophical, historical, or applied in nature: Hilbert on foundations, Hadamard on the development and scientific role of functional analysis, Puppini on public works in Italy, Borel on probability and the exact sciences. Veblen and Castelnuovo gave survey talks on geometry, W. H. Young talked on the mathematical method and its limitations, Volterra on hereditary phenomena, Tonelli on Italian contributions to real variable theory, Amoroso on mathematical economics, von Kármán on mathematical problems of modern aerodynamics, Fréchet and Lusin on set theory and general topology, Marcolongo on Leonardo da Vinci, and my father on mathematics and art. The only really technical talk was by Hermann Weyl on continuous groups and their representations. What a contrast with recent International Congresses.

At 17, I attended only Hilbert's and my father's talks, and felt that Hilbert's objectives were obscure and unconvincing. (I had learned some calculus that summer and German within the year.)

A month later I entered Harvard; it may be interesting to compare my undergraduate education there with Marshall Stone's graduate education of 5 to 10 years earlier. I can confirm his statement that we were taught analysis and mechanics almost exclusively. I took complex variable as a sophomore with Walsh, and I learned my rigor from him; it was a great experience. Those who do not know Walsh should know about his technique, which I recommend. Some people raise their voice when they get to important things; Walsh did the opposite. When he was coming to a point of exceptional importance, his voice got lower and lower, so that to catch what he was saying one really had to hold his breath. He almost whispered when he reached the crucial point. I got a great sense of the nature and importance of rigor in analysis from Walsh. I had the calculus of variations and analysis situs with Morse, and he taught me about integral bases in Minkowski's lattices. Although I had Heinrich Brinkmann as a tutor, I learned less from him; it was my fault.

I wrote a thesis on one-dimensional measure in n-space, which I took terribly seriously and worked very hard at. I submitted it hopefully (all 80 typewritten pages) to the *Transactions* and was quite hurt when Tamarkin wrote me in a very kindly personal letter that, although it showed promise, I mustn't think that things like this got published. But a tiny piece of it, on topological axioms for metrizable spaces, was published a year later in the *Bulletin,* nevertheless.

My frequent and stimulating talks with Morse were made natural by Harvard's new tutorial system and House Plan. The latter was made possible by the munificence of Harkness; it gave students a good social environment.

As a Harvard undergraduate, I had less contact with my father, although I took a most interesting half-course on ordinary differential equations from him. However, I didn't believe everything he said — including his assertion that a general linear second order differential equation couldn't be integrated by quadratures. I had no concept of things such as Galois theory, let alone Picard-Vessiot theory, and spent some time trying to discover an ingenious construction that would show that he was wrong. Needless to say, I did not succeed.

Indeed, I would not have even heard of groups had not casual browsing in our departmental library made me aware of Miller, Blichfeldt, and Dickson's *Finite Groups*. After skimming through the first two or three chapters, I decided it would be interesting to enumerate all possible finite groups (up to isomorphism, then a new concept to me). At the time, I had not studied algebra since I was 14, except for a few days spent thinking about Fermat's problem ($x^4 + y^4 = z^4$ and all that) and about solving cubic equations by radicals, both at my father's suggestion, and a little reading about determinants in connection with analytic geometry. Had I not browsed in finite groups by accident, I doubt if I would have ever become an algebraist.

In spite of this immaturity and lack of mathematical sophistication, I got a string of A's and a Henry Fellowship to Cambridge University. My intention was to become a mathematical physicist, having taken basic courses in a lot of analysis and a lot of physics, including thermodynamics, electromagnetism, and quantum mechanics. Fowler was to be my adviser, and I was to attend Dirac's lectures. Thus I imagined myself as on the road to a career that I thought my family would approve of. My father's parting advice was to read Stone's book on *Linear Transformations of Hilbert Space,* and Wiener's papers on generalized harmonic analysis. With this advice still ringing in my ears, then, I left for a year in Europe.

My Year Abroad

The year began with a month in Munich, where I pursued in lonely solitude the group theory that I had discovered in Miller, Blichfeldt, and Dickson. I loved the axioms for a group; I thought that I had never seen anything so perfect. So in the Munich library that summer, I conjectured and patiently proved by myself Kronecker's fundamental theorem on Abelian groups, thus achieving the first step towards my goal of determining all finite groups.

However, I luckily called on my father's friend, Constantin Carathéodory, who was very kind to me. I was impressed by his library, which was utterly beyond anything that I had ever seen. His bookcases filled it (not just its walls); they must have contained most of the best mathematical books written since 1900. He said: "You know, people around here talk quite a bit about Speiser's book on group theory; and if you would like to go on to algebra in general, here are two volumes by van der Waerden which many people say are worth reading." Thus, in 1932, as a Harvard undergraduate, I had never heard of van der Waerden, or Emmy Noether, or Artin or Hasse, the apostles of the faith I was soon to espouse.

So when I got to Cambridge, I bought and studied both books, but did not neglect Stone or Wiener. In the meantime, I attended the International Mathematical Congress in Zurich, with the ambition of understanding at least the general addresses. This time, they were technical enough for anyone. One of them was by Emmy Noether on "Hypercomplex Systems in Relation to Commutative Algebra and Number Theory." It begins: "The theory of hypercomplex systems, of Algebras, has had a strong upswing in recent years, but only very lately has its significance for commutative questions become clear." Reading it today, one sees clearly how completely German algebraists had taken over: no reference to Wedderburn, passing references to Dickson and Chevalley, and the rest is Germanic![24] On the other hand, one also sees no thought of the impact of "modern algebra" on elementary courses; this was to come later.

24. Three years earlier, she was more generous (Noether, 1929).

When I arrived that September in Trinity College, Cambridge, I immediately called on G. H. Hardy. He greeted me and asked "What's your father doing these days? How about that esthetic measure of his?" I replied that my father's book[25] was out. He said "Good; now he can get back to real mathematics."

I was naturally shocked by Hardy's offhand dismissal of years of patient effort devoted to extending the range of applicability of mathematics. In retrospect, I think it shows Hardy's limitation: he had zero appreciation for anything that was not sharp and difficult as *pure* mathematics. Nevertheless, he was a brilliant lecturer, who deepened my knowledge of analysis and gave me a good introduction to number theory.[26] Moreover he gave Marshall Hall and me a friendly welcome and stimulated us intellectually.

In particular, he invited us to a dinner in honor of Hobson, whose "Functions of a Real Variable" made the Lebesgue integral known in England. As an after dinner speaker, he observed that Hobson had done his best work after 50 and expressed the hope that he, Hardy, would have the same fate. He didn't.

Abstract Algebra

Neither Steinitz nor van der Waerden had any visible influence on Hardy. His lectures on algebraic numbers never referred to rings or fields as such, let alone groups. The only person in Cambridge who took any interest in abstract algebra was Philip Hall, who opened my eyes to the deeper problems of group theory.

However, my interest in groups was more wide-ranging and less deep than his, and I soon decided that I could make a more fundamental contribution to a different class of algebraic systems, which I christened lattices, than to groups. Hence, during my twenty-second year, I concentrated my attention on these, still laboring as a self-taught "gifted amateur" in virtual solitude.

Among the mathematicians near Cambridge was A. Young, who had invented group representation theory 30 years previously,[27] independently of Frobenius and Schur. He was a shy cleric, who still came to Cambridge once a week to give a seminar on group representation theory. Marshall Hall and I both went to his first lecture. I discreetly avoided the second; Marshall Hall was there (one of two). Being a Yale man, he was too courteous to abandon the nice old man to an empty room, so he continued to attend for the rest of the term.

By my twenty-second birthday, I had virtually given up on mathematical physics. I was totally unprepared for Dirac's lectures on quantum mechanics. Whereas I expected him to consider the Schroedinger equation as a partial differential equation, I think in retrospect that he must have been explaining his ideas about elementary particles. I had not heard of these at Harvard, and first learned of them when Anderson lectured on the positron in the spring of 1933 at Cambridge, England.

Although I found Stone's book and Wiener's "Generalized Harmonic Analysis" most interesting and challenging, I was also well aware that I had not

25. George David Birkhoff, 1932, Aesthetic Measure, Harvard University Press, 3-225.
26. His lectures were later published in his classic "Theory of Numbers" (Hardy and Wright, 1938).
27. The "Young tableaux" in particular were his creation.

really mastered either in any sense. Hence, by June 1933, I had essentially given up on my mission as conceived when I left Harvard. Instead of becoming any kind of mathematical physicist or even analyst, I turned my back on all that I had learned in my Harvard courses and became an abstract algebraist.

Because I have published elsewhere (Abbott, 1970:1-40) an anecdotal and personal account of my early work on lattices, I shall not go into it here. Suffice to say that I was convinced from the beginning of their intrinsic importance, and indeed devoted nearly half of my research efforts during the eight-year period 1933 to 1941 to their study.

While I was becoming an abstract (or "modern") algebraist in England, adopting the style if not the content of van der Waerden, the world at large was racked by the Great Depression of 1930 to 1935, and Hitler seized power in Germany. I remember vividly the acute recognition by the (London) *Times* of the significance of his coup d'état, and the bovine placidity with which it seemed to be accepted by the American press at the time.

Harvard's Society of Fellows

I have benefited personally many times from American private philanthropy. The Harvard House plan, endowed by Edward Harkness, came into being my junior year; I was one of the first four Henry Fellows to go to England, thanks to an endowment by Lady Julia Henry; Abbott Lawrence Lowell established the Society of Fellows at Harvard with his personal fortune just in time for me to be part of it in 1933 to 1936.

This was a matchless opportunity: to be a full-time researcher at age 22. Other, slightly later, Junior Fellows included Nobel Prize winners Bardeen (twice), Bloembergen, Samuelson, and Woodward. We were encouraged to carry through ambitious independent projects on our own, freed from normal Ph.D. requirements. We dined weekly by candlelight with Lowell, Whitehead, and five other deep and brilliant thinkers and conversationalists,[28] all eager and ambitous to see us make our mark.

During these years I concentrated on developing lattice theory to a subject with stature. I had dreamed up lattices while in England the year before, plucking them out of semithin air as a generalization of the Boolean algebra, which I knew Huntington wrote about. They were not mentioned in van der Waerden; moreover while Philip Hall knew only of Fritz Klein's essentially postulational studies (Klein called them "Verbände"), and was not aware of Dedekind's deeper earlier work, I did not know of Marshall Stone's very deep results on Boolean algebras, which were announced nearly a year after I completed my first paper on lattices.[29] And so I came home, having written a paper on the subject that had been accepted by the Cambridge Philosophical Society for publication in its *Proceedings*. On my return, my father asked me pointedly what one could

28. These were the Senior Fellows; we were the Junior Fellows; the generation gap was bridged in a most congenial and inspiring way.

29. M. H. Stone, 1934, Boolean algebras and their application to topology, Proc. Nat. Acad. Sci., 20:197-202, and 21(1935):103-105. My paper had been submitted on 15 May 1933.

do with lattices that couldn't be done without them. Although I thought that this was not really a very polite question, it honestly compelled me to admit that he was fundamentally right. My admiration for abstract algebra has been moderated by his question ever since.

Ore also informed me through my father about Dedekind's earlier work on lattices (which Dedekind called "Dualgruppen"); Ore had helped Emmy Noether edit Dedekind's *Werke*. It came as a mild shock to learn that many of "my" theorems were just rediscoveries of results published decades earlier by Dedekind. One such result was the fact that the free modular lattice with three generators had just 28 elements.

But in retrospect, I think that I was lucky not to have known about Dedekind's results when I first began thinking about lattices; it would have been discouraging to find nothing new for months. As it was, by the time I learned about Dedekind's work, I had advanced beyond him in several respects (semimodular lattices and the intrinsic topology in lattices, to name two), and this encouraged me to persevere.

I used the free modular lattice with three generators to attract von Neumann's interest. At a mathematics meeting (everybody who could, went to all the mathematics meetings in those days; there weren't nearly so many), I saw him standing alone. I introduced myself to him and said: "I understand you're interested in Hilbert space," and he agreed. So I continued: "Well, suppose you take three subspaces of Hilbert space and form repeated intersections and linear spans, do you know how many you'll get?" He said he didn't, and I said: "You'll get 28." That impressed him, and I think it was what stimulated him to study the lattice of invariant subspaces of Hilbert space (under a given operator). This led to his continuous geometries.

During 1934 to 1940 I talked and corresponded with him frequently, especially about lattices but also about mathematics and mathematicians, often staying at his house. He was a major influence on my scientific thinking and philosophy, second only to my father. In the spring of 1940, we gave a joint seminar on lattices at the Institute for Advanced Study.

Ore also decided that lattices provided a powerful tool for studying the structure of "groups with operators." He demonstrated this in his great 1935 paper on the strucutre of algebras, in which he emphasized that groups with operators were the unifying theme of van der Waerden's book, and that lattices (or "structures," as he called them) were applicable much more generally.

In a less scholarly way, I had formulated the same idea, in a much more general context: that of *universal algebra*. I had borrowed the name from Whitehead's book (1898), trying to reformulate the basic ideas of *Moderne Algebra* rigorously in this more general philosophical context, giving simple examples, such as the (geometric) lattice of all equivalence relations on a finite set and proving a few fairly deep and extremely general theorems.[30] I had emphasized that every algebraic system had associated with it two lattices: the lattice of its subalgebras and the "structure" lattice of its congruence relations.

30. G. Birkhoff, 1935, On the structure of abstract algebras, Proc. Camb. Phil. Soc., 31(1935):433-454.

Topological Groups

During the 1930's, the theory of topological groups began to come into its own, strongly reinforcing the trend away from classical analysis towards more abstract and general concepts. At first, this theory was limited to rather obvious combinations of general group and set-theoretic concepts; the early papers of O. Schreier and D. van Dantzig,[31] which influenced my own thinking considerably, were prime examples. One of Schreier's most impressive achievements was to prove that the covering group of any connected, locally Euclidean, topological group was Abelian.

However, underlying these gropings for sound basic principles were much deeper ideas. Some of these stemmed from theories of "insolvability." Not only the insolvability of the quintic by radicals (classical Galois theory), but the analogous Picard-Drach-Vessiot theory of the insolvability of a general second-order linear homogeneous differential equation by quadratures,[32] as well as that of "monodromy" groups, had shown the power and depth of group-theoretic concepts. A recognition of the relevant groups is also important for geometry, as had been made abundantly clear by Felix Klein in his celebrated Erlanger-Programm, and in physics where the crystallographic groups are important, and where relativistic mechanics differs from classical mechanics most essentially in being governed by the Lorentz group of electromagnetic theory rather than the Galilei-Newton group. In quantum mechanics, which dominated physical research in the 1930's, the theory of group representations had been shown by Weyl and Wigner to play an important role likewise.

An even greater stimulus for research into the theory of topological groups was provided by Hilbert's Fifth Problem: to determine whether or not every locally Euclidean topological group is a Lie group, that is, a group whose "function of composition" is an analytic function relative to suitable coordinates. A great deal was known about Lie groups. Thus, sharpening earlier ideas of Killing (1888), Élie Cartan had in his Thesis written in 1898 determined all simple and even semisimple real and complex Lie groups by very difficult arguments.

However, as of 1935, many basic facts about Lie groups were still unknown. Thus, Lie's own theory was strictly *local,* and it had not yet been proved that every local "Lie group nucleus" could be extended to a *global* Lie group. Neither was it known whether or not every Lie group was locally *or* globally isomorphic with a *linear* group (group of matrices).

Research workers in the 1930's, including myself, were attracted greatly to all these fundamental problems of pure mathematics, whose main thrust combined with that of "modern" algebra to push classical analysis and the theory of

31. O. Schreier, Abstrachte kontinuierliche Gruppen, 1925, Abh. aus dem Math., 15-22, 5(1926):233-244; D. van Dantzig, Zur topologischen Algebra, Math. Annalen, 107(1933):608-626 and later volumes; G. Birkhoff, A note on topological groups, Compositio Math., 3(1936):427-430; Deane Montgomery, What is a topological group?, Amer, Math. Monthly, 52(1945):302-307; R. Arens, A topology for spaces of transformations, Annals of Math., 47(1946):480-495.

32. The "modern" algebraic theory is due to Ritt and Kolchin. See E. R. Kolchin, On certain concepts in the theory of Algebraic Matric Group, Annals of Math., 49(1948):1-42, where some classical references can be found; others are in G. H. Hardy, "The integration of functions . . . ," Cambridge Tracts in Math. and Math. Phys., 1928 No. 2, 2nd ed. For Kolchin's final, very abstract exposition, see his Differential algebra and algebraic groups, Academic Press, 1973.

differential equations (both of which stemmed from the calculus of Newton, Leibniz, and Euler) off center stage.

A major impulse supporting this trend was provided by Haar's 1933 paper,[33] proving that every locally compact topological group could support an essentially unique "right-invariant" Borel measure, invariant under right-translations. Von Neumann applied this result to show that every compact, connected locally Euclidean topological group was isomorphic to a Lie group.

A year later, Pontrjagin wrote a notable paper on the duality between any locally compact Abelian group G and the dual group G^* of its "characters." In particular, he showed that the dual of any compact group was discrete, and conversely. An easy corollary of his results was the fact that any Abelian connected, locally Euclidean topological group was necessarily a Lie group.

From E. Cartan's Thesis written in 1897, on the other hand, it followed that every real or complex Lie algebra was the semidirect sum of a semisimple Lie algebra and a (quasi-Abelian) solvable "radical." Mathematicians therefore began to hope in the latter 1930's that, by combining such structural theorems with the results of Haar, von Neumann, and Pontrjagin, it might be possible to give a general affirmative solution to Hilbert's Fifth Problem; in any case, many of the hitherto unresolved questions concerning Lie groups were resolved quickly by Élie Cartan (now nearly 75) and others. Even I made some modest contributions to their solution.

Moscow, 1935

Toward the end of my term as a Junior Fellow, I attended three memorable meetings: a Topological Congress in Moscow in 1935, the International Mathematical Congress in Oslo in July 1936, and Harvard's Tercentenary in August-September 1936. I shall conclude by relating a few impressions of them.

Because of my father, I was welcomed by Harald Bohr in Copenhagen and Rolf Nevanlinna in Helsinki on my way to Moscow. As in the case of Carathéodory and of Erhard Schmidt, on whom I called during my return, I had the impression of keen, worldly, deeply cultured minds and most gracious manners. (My personal impressions of Emmy Noether and Hilbert were very different.)

With Marshall Stone and David Widder, I also met L. V. Kantorovich in Leningrad. This was two years before he published his pioneer paper on semi-ordered linear spaces, although only a year before he published his classic book with Krylov on the numerical solution of partial differential equations.[34] I reviewed his paper when it came out, and immediately became excited; it and a paper by Freudenthal (whom I met in Moscow) led me to the study of vector lattices and their applications to functional analysis and ergodic theory. But it was not until the 1960's that I became interested in a later edition of his book.

33. A Haar, 1933, Der Massbegriff in der Theorie der kontinuierlichen Gruppen, Annals of Math., 34:147-169; J. von Neumann, 170-190.

34. L. V. Kantorovich, 1937, Lineare halbgeordnete Raüme, Mat. Sbornik, 44:121-128; L. V. Kantorovich and V. I. Krylov, Approximate Methods of Higher Analysis, translated from 1941 edition by Curtis D. Benster, Interscience Noordhoff, 1958.

The Topological Congress in Moscow was a small gathering of many of the most notable topologists of the world; needless to say, it thrilled me, at age 24, to meet them all personally. The Moscow contingent included P. Alexandroff, Pontrjagin, Kolmogoroff, Kurosh, and Gelfand. Gelfand impressed me as a very young man with enormous drive. Others present included Kuratowski, Jakob Nielsen of free group fame (he brought trousers for Alexandroff; Russia was exceedingly poor at the time), and Freudenthal. There was also a strong American contingent (Lefschetz, Alexander, von Neumann, and Stone) of men whom I knew already. The connections of topology with the rest of mathematics were emphasized strongly; moreover, Dirac passed through, which gave the Congress an even broader flavor.

We chatted informally in small groups between lectures, eating bread mounded with fresh caviar and drinking tea. The faith of some younger attendees in the abstract ''modern'' approach was apparent. Thus Kurosh assured me several times with great emphasis that ''Die Strukturn sind sehr wichtig, nicht Wahr?''

On the return trip, I met Saks, Ulam, Eilenberg, and many others in Warsaw. Saks rowed with me in a ''double'' shell on the Vistula, and assured me that he had American cold cereals for breakfast every morning. (G. H. Hardy was a devotee of American apple pie and coffee — as well as of baseball, though he preferred cricket.)

I returned via Berlin and Hamburg. In Berlin, I met Richard and Alfred Brauer, and J. Schröder; we all walked silently past the anti-semitic racial institute at the University of Berlin, run by the famous complex analyst Bieberbach. In Hamburg, I met Emil Artin, and it was clear that the morale of the German scientific community already had been destroyed by Hitler's persecution of those having Jewish grandparent ancestry.

The Oslo Congress

The following year, I attended the last International Mathematical Congress to take place before World War II. On the way there, I again saw Artin in Hamburg and visited Copenhagen. Artin was now most anxious to leave Germany, as he told me while military planes droned ceaselessly overhead and German youth marched, marched, marched. By this time, Springer had transferred the headquarters of the new *Zentralblatt für Mathematik* to Copenhagen, where Neugebauer was running it with superb charm and efficiency. In Copenhagen, Harald Bohr also showed me around the new Matematisk Institute, with a couch in every study; his brother Niels lived in the mansion of the founder of the Tuborg brewery filled with beautiful sculptures by a famous Danish sculptor.

In spite of the destruction by Hitler of German academic morale, the Oslo Congress itself was a gay and brilliant occasion. World War II was still three years off, and the fall of France nearly four. I think most mathematicians whose lives were not personally affected by Nazi persecution hoped that things would get straightened out somehow.

In any case, a wide panorama of mathematical ideas was presented to nearly 500 participants. My father's lecture on the foundation of quantum mechanics was attended by the Crown Prince, and we all met King Haakon. Størmer, Oseen, and Bjerknes gave other invited addresses on various aspects of mathematical physics. Neugebauer spoke on the relation of Greek mathematics to its precursors, and classical analysis was represented by Fueter, Wiener, and Ahlfors. The first two Fields Medals went to Ahlfors and Jesse Douglas, for work in classical analysis.

In this connection, I recall my father being accosted by Archibald in a trolley the afternoon before these Medals were awarded; who asked what he thought of the choice of Fields medallists? My father replied: "The choice is still confidential!" "Nonsense," said Archibald, "Everyone knows that they will be Douglas and Ahlfors."

There were many invited addresses on algebra and number theory. Thus C. L. Siegel lectured on quadratic forms, Hasse on the Riemann Hypothesis in function fields, and Hecke related the theory of elliptic modular functions to Dirichlet L-series, which relate to the Weil conjecture recently proved by de Ligne. Likewise, van der Corput spoke on Diophantine approximation, Mordell on the geometry of numbers, and Élie Cartan about the role of Lie groups in the evolution of "modern" (primarily differential) geometry.

The only invited address concerned with axiomatic or "modern" algebra was by Ore. He described the then very new applications of lattices (which he still called "structures") to the decomposition theorems of algebra.

However, there were also two addresses on functional analysis that were sympathetic to the "modern" abstract viewpoint. Banach discussed the antecedents of the theory of operators on function spaces in the work of Volterra, Hadamard, Hilbert, and Fréchet, and the (G. D.) Birkhoff-Kellogg-Schauder-Leray fixpoint theorem and its applications. Fréchet's talk on abstract spaces was more meandering; while paying homage to some of the great names of the past, he stressed the great activity of many younger mathematicians (including myself) in generalizing old ideas.

The Harvard Tercentenary

Later that summer, Harvard celebrated its three hundredth birthday. It was another gala occasion in which Franklin Delano Roosevelt, Harvard's most famous alumnus, participated. Hardy, Élie Cartan, Levi-Civita, Dickson, and the statistician R. A. Fisher were among the honored foreign invitees; the American Mathematical Society held its summer meeting in conjunction with this celebration in late August.

In his after-dinner speech at the Society banquet in the Copley Plaza Hotel, Hardy stated that the United States had become number one in mathematics, ahead of Germany, France, or England. I think everyone present was thrilled by his statement; only 30 years before, most aspiring American mathematicians had felt the need to study in Europe to acquire the requisite sophistication and depth to do research.

Actually, our country's preeminence, which was to continue for the next quarter-century, was due in large part to political and economic factors. But whatever the reason, it caused modern algebra to enter into a very new and different phase during 1936 to 1960. It is this phase that will be the main concern of my second lecture.

Reprinted from
MEN AND INSTITUTIONS IN AMERICAN MATHEMATICS
Graduate Studies, Texas Tech University, No. 13, 1976

THE RISE OF MODERN ALGEBRA, 1936 TO 1950

GARRETT BIRKHOFF

By 1936, the ideas of the Emmy Noether school of "modern" algebraists had permeated the thinking of quite a few of the most active younger mathematicians in the United States, France, and Russia. In each of these countries, these ideas had been influenced and modified by national traditions. Meanwhile, Emmy Noether had died; Hitler's persecutions had demoralized German universities; and increasing numbers of continental mathematicians were seeking asylum in the British Empire and the United States. For all these reasons, "modern" algebra had become international. But what happened between 1936 and 1950 involved much more than a mere dissemination of German ideas; in the hands of American and French mathematicians, these ideas became transformed into a *new approach to mathematics*. In this paper I shall try to describe some aspects of this transformation of modern algebra that I saw at close range, *as I saw them*. This will give to my account a somewhat personal flavor; I hope you will enjoy it.

You must remember that in 1936, I was only 25 years old; that after four years of undergraduate study of classical analysis and mathematical physics, I had spent four more doing research (mostly on lattices and groups); and that I had not yet done any teaching. In 1936, I fondly expected to continue to do research and to teach "pure" mathematics, hopefully at Harvard, for another 40 years or so. I had met personally, or at least listened to over half of the leading mathematicians of the time, and I was well aware of my good fortune in being attached to a relatively affluent university in a politically stable country. I was firmly resolved to do my best to help both to achieve as high a level of mathematical proficiency as possible.

At the same time, I realized that I was a neophyte, and that I could accomplish little alone. Therefore, I was most grateful for the presence at Harvard of Marshall Stone, of Hassler Whitney, and (from 1934 to 1936 and from 1938 on) of Saunders Mac Lane. Together, I felt, we could make modern algebra, topology, and functional analysis vital components of mathematics at Harvard, alongside of the classical analysis and geometry that I had studied there as an undergraduate.

But I did not realize that within four years political events would change the situation dramatically. The mathematical career that I had imagined as lasting 40 more years in fact lasted only four. After 1940, my own dedication to modern algebra was to become much more diluted and qualified. I became increasingly absorbed in war work (during the years 1940 to 1945) and applied mathematics (from 1945 on). Hopefully, this broader range of interests has given me a better perspective on modern algebra. In any case, I shall try to explain how I view today its evolution from 1936 on, with special emphasis on the years from 1936 to 1940 when I knew it best.

The AMS Semicentennial

The publications of the Semicentennial Anniversary of the founding of the American Mathematical Society in 1938 provide excellent documentation for the transition in mathematical leadership, which was about to sweep the world. In the first place, they described the somewhat provincial (if very original) nature of American mathematics prior to that time. Thus, as I emphasized in my first paper, most mathematicians still regarded modern algebra as a primarily Germanic creation.

A broader view of American mathematics was presented by my father in his lecture "Fifty Years of American Mathematics." My father expressed in this talk some concern at the inundation of our shores by research-oriented European refugees, who might demote young native mathematicians to mere "hewers of wood and drawers of water." And indeed, at the University of Pennsylvania a few years later, German refugees held research professorships, while young American Ph.D.'s had to teach 20 or more hours a week.

The issues involved were very complex. The Institute for Advanced Study, run by Abraham Flexner, became the chief advocate of the preeminence of continental European mathematics and mathematicians. This position was strongly supported, quite naturally, by Oswald Veblen.

My father and many other American mathematicians, on the other hand, were not anxious to see rapid takeover of the best American jobs by European mathematicians, however eminent. As a very junior person, I was not involved in any decision making. However, it was my conviction that the American college and university system, in which there were few "high priests" and research was considered more as a privilege than an obligation, was socially if not intellectually preferable to the continental European system. In particular, I felt that persecutions of college teachers such as occurred under Hitler would have aroused a storm of protest in our country, because our colleges were more human and personal. Conditions are, of course, very different today, and our educational system has become far more dominated by federal and state tax support.

In any case, the natural conflict of interest between young American mathematicians and European refugees never led to much jealousy or hostility that I could see, presumably because a sense of fair play and mutual sympathy dominated most decisions. Another overriding consideration was the well-founded conviction that the United States offered the best place in the world to do scientific work — a state of affairs that was to last for a quarter century at least, but which was altogether unprecedented then. So who could complain?

I shall conclude my comparative discussion of the social milieu for scientific work in Europe and the United States by a few personal reminiscences that may be relevant. I had spent two years as Senior Tutor at Lowell House, in daily contact with undergraduates with whom I usually dined. Another resident there was Heinrich Bruening, the exiled former Chancellor of Germany, with whom I became good friends. A much closer friend was Stanislas Ulam, who lived in

Adams House as a Junior fellow. The Master of Lowell House was Julian Lowell Coolidge, the well-known geometer.

That June I married, going to Europe on a two-month wedding trip. My parents joined us for a week in Ireland; we were invited to lunch by Eamon de Valera, Prime Minister of Ireland, a friend of the mathematician E. T. Whittaker and a former high school teacher of mathematics. Aesthetic measure was discussed at lunch.

My wife and I timed a visit to Cambridge University to coincide with a mathematical meeting at which Fréchet was an invited speaker; he spoke about "structures" (lattices). We visited King's College as the guests of Philip Hall, with whom I also had some stimulating if superficial conversations about algebra.

Although we spent 10 days in Paris, I did not call on any mathematicians there; unfortunately, I did not yet know Henri Cartan, Chevalley, Dieudonné, or André Weil. Neither did we think it safe to take advantage of Stanislas Ulam's invitation to visit a castle in the Carpathians belonging to his uncle. This was the summer of the Czechoslovakian crisis and Munich ("peace in our time"); England was feverishly building airplane factories near the Bristol Channel, as far as possible from German bomber bases.

The summer's most poignant moment was a visit to our hotel one evening by Heinrich Bruening, who brought with him a bunch of carnations for my wife. He had just returned from Holland, where he had gone to the border of Hanover for a secret (and dangerous) rendezvous with his sister, whom he had not seen for many years. The personal tragedy of this kind, world-famous German leader made a deep impression on both of us.

When we returned to the AMS Semicentennial Celebration in New York, where we sat at the head table, it was with a great sense of returning to the security of home and friends. My wife sat next to Lefschetz, in whose coffee (he had clumsy artificial arms) she deposited four lumps of sugar. Dunham Jackson was one of the featured speakers. As Jackson rose to speak, Lefschetz turned to my wife and said: "He's going to tell four funny stories and sit down," which is exactly what Jackson did.

MATHEMATICS 6

Between the Harvard Tercentenary in 1936 and the AMS Semicentennial in 1938, my teaching career had begun in earnest.

The first year was pure apprenticeship. I taught a section of first year calculus and an advanced half course ambitiously entitled "Foundations of Abstract Algebra and Topology." The first was very conventional and moderately successful; it convinced a number of freshmen to concentrate in mathematics. The second was taken by three luckless graduate students, who were exposed to a breathless survey of a great variety of topics, from metric spaces to Lie groups of transformations. Hassler Whitney and I had given an informal seminar on continuous groups the year before, and the subject fascinated me. I had also given a seminar on finite groups as a Junior Fellow, but it was not until 1937-38 that I first taught modern algebra to undergraduates as a full year course numbered Mathematics 6.

This was a major undertaking, intended from the start to change the Harvard curriculum permanently, and to serve as an example to other American colleges. It seemed to me unfortunate that Harvard students, after three years of algebra and geometry in high school, should be faced with three solid years of the calculus in college (Math. 1, 2, 5), the only variety being geometry (Math. 3), mechanics (Math. 4) or possibly probability (Math. 9), before being exposed to modern ideas about algebra.

On the other hand, it was obvious that anything along the lines of van der Waerden would be totally inappropriate for unsophisticated Harvard juniors, let alone even less sophisticated undergraduates elsewhere. Therefore, I carefully prepared about 150 pages of mimeographed notes, which began with sets, combinatorics, and Boolean algebra, and ended with finite groups. I was even so uncivilized as to work on these notes during several half-days in the summer of 1937, while visiting my future wife, not yet even a fiancée, at her family's camp in northern Maine!

The next year Saunders Mac Lane returned to Harvard from Cornell, and taught a quite different Math. 6 in 1938-39. Being an independent and strong-minded character, he began with groups, ended with Boolean algebra, and issued his own notes. I thought it essential to reach some agreement on a stable course content, and we both agreed that it would be desirable to write a joint text that could be used by others, thereby freeing us from the necessity of teaching the course in alternate years in perpetuity. Since the resulting book (1967) has been widely used in many countries and differs essentially from van der Waerden's book, I thought it might be interesting to comment on its basic design and organization as we conceived it at the time.

The first five chapters attempted, in the main, to cover the material in Dickson's *First Course in the Theory of Equations,* but in axiomatic form and modern terminology. Fine's *College Algebra* had been an earlier, also popular text covering much the same material. After studying these chapters, students became reasonably familiar with integral domains and fields in general, and with the real and complex fields, the modular fields Z_p, and polynomial domains in particular. Most important, they became familiar with the technique and style of formal proofs of unique factorization theorems and the like, a side of mathematics almost completely ignored in calculus courses.

We next introduced students to the group concept, bringing out the idea that algebra was *not* exclusively concerned with "numbers"; the axiomatic approach and symbolic method were universal. We continued by showing the power of the axiomatic approach for treating "vector spaces" over arbitrary fields, including an elegant deductive treatment of linear independence and dimension due in part to Hassler Whitney.

There followed three very substantial chapters on matrices with their eigenvectors, canonical forms, determinants, and characteristic polynomials, giving in detail the applications of real symmetric matrices to n-dimensional geometry.

These chapters were drafted primarily by Saunders Mac Lane and polished by me; we both agreed to keep them basis-free (''intrinsic'') and determinant-free as long as possible.

These were succeeded by two rather skimpy chapters, drafted by me and polished by Saunders, on Boolean algebra and transfinite numbers. They were intended to introduce the student to Cantorian set theory, including the all-important distinction between countable and uncountable sets.

With these chapters behind us, it was easy to prove (following Cantor) that almost all real numbers were transcendental, and to acquaint students with some of the beauties of algebraic number theory, including ideal theory and Steinitz' theory of fields. The book concluded with a chapter on Galois theory, in which we proved that the method for solving quartic equations by radicals presented in our fifth chapter had no analog for quintics, because the group of permutations on five letters was ''insolvable.''

I have reviewed the design of Birkhoff-Mac Lane in detail, partly to emphasize how completely it deviated from van der Waerden in spirit and content. Its axiomatic approach was similar,[35] and its discussion of Galois theory comparable. But it was diametrically opposite in its emphasis on the primacy of the real and complex fields, on geometric applications, and in its inclusion of Boolean algebra.

The somewhat earlier *Modern Higher Algebra* by A. A. Albert, which I had reviewed, and Mac Duffee's *Introduction to Abstract Algebra* were equally indigenous. Transplanted onto American soil, ''modern'' algebra had taken on a quite different character.

Lattice Theory

During the years 1937 to 1941 that an Americanized ''modern algebra'' was becoming part of the standard undergraduate curriculum at Harvard, and the first edition of ''Birkhoff-Mac Lane'' was being written and published, many other developments were taking place. One of these was the acceptance in our country of lattice theory as a significant new branch of this same ''modern algebra.''

I have already described my initial efforts (1933 to 1935) to establish and popularize the lattice concept; the extent to which many of my ideas had been anticipated by Dedekind around 1900; and my success in stimulating work by von Neumann and Ore in the subject and its applications. Although van der Waerden's book ignored lattices, it was clear to me that it should not have, because associated with every algebraic system or ''algebra'' were *two* lattices: its subalgebra lattice and the ''structure lattice'' of its congruence relations.

Although Ore and I communicated only rarely, von Neumann and I talked and corresponded extensively, even writing a joint paper in 1936-37 *On the Logic of Quantum Mechanics,* which related complemented modular lattices to physics. This paper was related to von Neumann's ingenious and difficult papers on continuous-dimensional projective geometries published during 1936 to 1938,

35. Even this was based as much on the work of our colleague E. V. Huntington as on any other source.

and to his papers with F. J. Murray on operator theory. In these papers he showed how the (often modular and orthocomplemented) lattice of subspaces of a Hilbert space H that were invariant under a given linear operator $T: H \to H$ helped to classify the "type" of T.

Quite independently, Marshall Stone had become interested in 1933 in Boolean algebras (which are essentially just complemented distributive lattices) and their applications to topology. He had shown in a long paper published in 1937 that Boolean algebras also can be regarded as a special class of "Boolean" rings having an idempotent multiplication — which implies commutativity. He showed in a second long paper that they can be regarded as defining zero-dimensional compact spaces — a very novel and original viewpoint giving great insight into the difficult theory of infinite Boolean algebras.

Independently also, Karl Menger had considered affine and projective geometries from a lattice-theoretic standpoint already in 1927, although not using the word "lattice" or any synonym for it. He published a long paper developing these ideas further in 1937; in the meantime, I had proved (knowing of Veblen's but not of Menger's related work) the crucial result that every complemented modular lattice was a direct product of projective geometries and a Boolean algebra.

The American Mathematical Society took cognizance of all this work and recognized its common thrust by holding a symposium on lattice theory in conjunction with the spring 1938 meeting in Charlottesville, Virginia. The participants were Ore, Stone, von Neumann, Baer, Menger, and myself.[36]

But by this time, my own ambitions for lattice theory had developed much further, and I had begun writing the first edition of *Lattice Theory,* a Colloquium volume that was published in 1940. In it, I gave considerable prominence to the concept of a *vector lattice,* which I defined as a vector space that was also a lattice under an order relation invariant under (additive) group translation. This concept, implicit in writings of Friedrich Riesz, had been axiomatized in 1936-37 by H. Freudenthal and L. Kantorovich, the latter of whom had shown various interesting interconnections with properties of Banach spaces and other topological vector spaces. I showed the relevance of E. H. Moore's basic concept of "relative uniform convergence" to this complex of ideas, which I fitted into the general framework of lattice theory.

Von Neumann and Stone also were interested in this development, and in the spring of 1940, von Neumann and I gave a seminar on lattices and their applications at the Institute for Advanced Study. That same year, Friedrich Riesz published in the *Annals of Mathematics* a French translation of a very original paper on vector lattices (still often called Riesz spaces, to honor his work), first published in Hungarian in 1939. This stimulated me to develop an even more general theory of "lattice-ordered groups," which was published in 1942.

But I am getting well beyond the period 1936 to 1940, to which this part of my paper was intended to be devoted.

36. See Bull. Amer. Math. Soc., 44(1938):793-827. Note that four of the six participants were European emigrés.

Algebraic Geometry, 1936 to 1950

''Modern'' algebraic geometry utilizes the theories of (commutative) rings, fields, valuations, and ideals, to give it rigorous foundations over a general ground field, independent of analysis, that is, of the theories of real and complex functions. In the preceding paper, I recalled that van der Waerden had already begun the task of modernizing algebraic geometry by 1925, but that he had decided to omit it from his *Moderne Algebra*. However in 1933, he resumed his campaign of freeing algebraic geometry from geometric intuition and analytical arguments, in a series of papers published in the *Mathematische Annalen*. Finally, in 1938, he succeeded in rigorizing Severi's 1912 interpretation of Schubert calculus, which dealt with generalizations to higher dimensions of Bézout's theorem on the *intersection multiplicitis* of plane curves. If one remembers that Schubert proposed his calculus in 1879, and that to rigorize it was one of Hilbert's famous unsolved problems, one will appreciate the magnitude of van der Waerden's achievement.

Van der Waerden's final success depended on precise definitions (over an arbitrary field) of the concepts of ''specialization'' and ''algebraic family'' of cycles that he and Chow had developed in 1937. Moreover, in 1938 Krull invented the concept of a ''local ring,''[37] which was also to become essential for ''modern'' algebraic geometry. Thus as late as 1938, German algebraists were still leaders in ''modernizing'' algebraic geometry.

But by this time, Zariski had mastered modern algebra with a vengeance, and was beginning[38] to generalize to varieties over general fields most of the major theorem of classical algebraic geometry, including especially those on the resolution of singularities by birational transformation and on local uniformization. He also developed the important notion of a ''normal'' algebraic variety, that is, one having only a finite number of singular points.

After 1940, our country became the greatest center of activity. This was partly because Weil and Chevalley were here from 1940 to 1946, joining Zariski (and getting moral support from Lefschetz) in a development that was virtually uninterrupted by the war.

During these years, Weil sharpened further the notions of ''generic point'' and ''intersection multiplicity,'' obtaining rigorous *local* definitions over general fields. Since he had number-theoretic applications in mind, he needed to cover the case of inseparable extensions. This work, published in book form in 1946, extended further the rigorization of Severi's 1912 ideas in the context of arbitrary ground fields, thus making them technically independent of classical analysis. (See André Weil, 1946, *Foundations of Algebraic Geometry,* Am. Math. Soc.)

Weil also continued to develop connections between algebraic geometry and number theory, taking full advantage of observations of Hasse and F. K.

37. W. Krull, 1938, Dimensions theorie in Stellenringen, J. Reiene Ange W. Math., 179:204-226.

38. His first publication along these lines was: Some results in the arithmetic theory of algebraic functions of several variables, Proc. Nat. Acad. Sci., 23(1937):410-441; in the preceding five years, he had been mainly using topological methods, following Lefschetz.

Schmidt about the relevance of the generalized Riemann hypothesis and zeta function.

One gets a vivid impression of the completeness of the conquest of algebraic geometry by "modern" algebra in the period 1936 to 1950 by reading the review of Weil's 1946 book by O. F. G. Schilling (another refugee from Europe), and I. S. Cohen's review of J. G. Semple and L. Roth's 1949 *Introduction to Algebraic Geometry* in Math. Revs. 9(1948):303, and 11(1950):535. For more thorough surveys, one can consult the invited hour addresses by Zariski and Weil at the International Congress of 1950, which are published in 2:77-89, 90-103 of its Proceedings. One should also read the addresses by W. V. D. Hodge and B. Segre 1:182-192, 490-493; Hodge still uses complex projective space in his. For a broad historical overview, see the authoritative accounts by Dieudonné (1972) and van der Waerden (1971).

Algebraic Topology

Under the influence of Emmy Noether, by 1928 Heinz Hopf already was using group-theoretic ideas in topology (see Gött. Nachr., Math.-Phys. Kl., 1928). However, if one reads his treatise with Paul Alexandroff on *Topologie* (1935), one sees how small the influence of modern algebra on combinatorial topology was before 1936. Its preface pays tribute to Emmy Noether's influence, but even more to that of the Princeton topologists Veblen, Alexander, and especially Lefschetz. It claims the distinction of being the first book to contain a unified treatment of general ("point-set") topology and combinatorial topology ("analysis situs").

Its most relevant chapter (chapter 5, pp. 205-239) is on "Betti groups." On pages 168-170, it defines chains over any polyhedral complex with coefficients α_i in any Abelian group A or ring R with unity. It uses the latter to define an algebraic complex. After stating that the book would only use as coefficient domains the rings Z and Z_n, the field Q, and the additive group $[Q;-]/(1)$ of rational numbers mod 1, it states that the authors postulate general coefficient domains, because "the most recent [work] shows that other coefficient-domains are also important."

Using the classic formula $\partial\partial E = 0$, it defines (p. 180) r-dimensional *cycles* as chains $\sum \alpha_j c_j^r$ with boundary $\partial(\sum \alpha_j c_j^r) = 0$. It defines the r-th Betti *homology* group as the (Abelian) group of r-cycles modulo the *subgroup* of cycles that are themselves *bounding* cycles $\sum \alpha_j c_j^r = \partial \sum \beta_k c_k^{r+1}$), boundaries of chains of one higher dimension. However, its approach is far from abstract.

At the Topological Conference in Moscow in 1935, A. W. Tucker described a generalized homology theory over arbitrary *partially ordered sets*, which he renamed "cell spaces."[39] I was impressed by the fact that he was led to Hausdorff's postulates for a "Tielweise geordnete Menge" by a totally different route. I have been unable to relate this early work of Tucker to recent developments of homology theory over lattices due to Rota, Mather, and others.

39. See A. W. Tucker, Cell spaces, Annals of Math., 37(1936):92-100; An abstract approach to manifolds, 34(1933):191-243; also Birkhoff, 1948, 14-15.

Although I have always been attracted by this generalization, the main thrust of generalization of homology theory has been in the quite different direction of homological algebra. An excellent analysis of the origins of this new branch of algebra has been given by P. J. Hilton and U. Stammbach on pages 184-186 of *A Course in Homological Algebra* (1970). It stemmed from attempts to define the homology groups of a connected ''aspherical'' space from its fundamental group.

Its basic ideas were initiated by H. Hopf, Eilenberg, and Mac Lane in the years 1945 to 1947. In particular, Eilenberg, Mac Lane, and Chevalley developed cohomology theories for group extensions and for Lie groups and algebras; a vivid idea of contemporary thinking can be gleaned from the Proceedings of the 1950 Congress (2:8-24, 344-362). An important by-product was the abstract theory of *categories*, or classes of ''objects'' and ''morphisms'' having the general properties of algebraic systems $A, B, C, \cdots$ and homomorphisms $f: A > B$, and so forth between them under composition.

World War II

My own dedication to lattices, groups (both finite and continuous), ''general'' topology, and ''general'' analysis (to use E. H. Moore's apt terminology), and indeed to abstract mathematics generally, was rudely interrupted by World War II. During 1936 to 1938 and even during the ''phoney'' war that preceded the fall of France, I had hoped that the European powers could keep Hitler in check. But by the spring of 1940, it became clear that this would not be the case and indeed, that Hitler might soon rule the world.

At the same time, I also saw with devastating clarity how useless were the beautiful abstractions with which I had become enamored for defeating Hitler; the classical analysis and mathematical physics that I had studied as an undergraduate could be far more helpful. Accordingly, I began to reorient my scientific perspectives, spending some time browsing in applied mathematics, including exterior ballistics and hydrodynamics.

Hitler's invasion of Russia in July 1941 began to make the lineup for the final struggle clear, whereas Pearl Harbor brought an immediate sense of urgency and dedication five months later. From then on, I concentrated increasingly on teaching the calculus, mechanics, potential theory, and hydrodynamics; I also began looking seriously for solutions to mathematical problems that might contribute to the war effort.

At first, it was difficult to find such problems. Our National Defense Research Council (NDRC) had taken no official cognizance of mathematics as such; President Conant and his associates could not see how it would contribute to victory. But within a year, Warren Weaver had obtained sponsorship for a committee including Marston Morse, John von Neumann, and me to analyze the quantitative improvement in the effectiveness of antiaircraft shells that was likely to be achieved by installing in them the then secret ''proximity'' fuses, activated by radar, that had been developed by Merle Tuve.

Not long after, I collaborated with my father in a study sponsored by the Bureau of Ordnance of the Navy, of the impact on water of bombs and torpedoes released by airplanes. After another year, the scope of the study was enlarged to include Norman Levinson and Lynn Loomis. This began an association with the Navy on problems of naval research that has continued ever since.

My closest contact with wartime military research was as a consultant to the Ballistics Research Laboratory at the Aberdeen proving ground in Maryland. Here I had the privilege of occupying a desk in the office of Robert H. Kent, chief scientist and a very remarkable person. I think it fair to say that he was our most outstanding ordinance scientist in World War II. My first assignment concerned the evaluation of controlled fragmentation characteristics of antiaircraft shells; it was similar to the work I had done for Warren Weaver's committee, and very pedestrian.

My most useful contribution was to help explain the effectiveness of ''shaped charge'' conical liners in penetrating tank armor when placed in high explosive shells launched even at low speeds (for example, by bazookas). The instant I saw X-ray shadowgraphs of exploding shaped charges with conical liners being shown to ''Bob'' Kent by ''Jack'' (John C.) Clark, who had just taken them, I had a sense of *dêjá vu*. I had been discussing very similar schematic drawing of ''impinging jet'' phenomena with my class in hydrodynamics a few months before, and had observed that the most important relationships could be deduced by high school algebra and trigonometry from the laws of conservation of mass, momentum, and energy. (I was then teaching three terms a year, and could only come to Aberdeen during Harvard's reading periods, examination periods, and brief between-semester interludes.)

The same observation had been made by G. I. Taylor in England shortly before, and we published a joint paper on the subject several years later (G. Birkhoff, D. P. MacDougall, E. M. Pugh, and G. I. Taylor, J. Appl. Phys., 19(1948):563-582).

My desk in ''Bob'' Kent's office made me privy to other fascinating interchanges. One of these occurred toward the end of the war in Germany. Von Neumann by this time had begun making pioneer numerical experiments on the leading digital computers of the time. He had observed that the kinetic theory of gases predicts essentially the same statistical behavior of a gas from a wide variety of force laws, and was trying to simulate plane shock wave propagation with a ''gas'' consisting of about 100 molecules in this spirit. He was presenting informally his ideas and results to a small but select group, which included Kent and von Kármán, the famous aeronautical engineer.

When von Neumann had finished his talk, with its dizzying prospects of glamorous future developments, von Kármán said with a mischievous smile: ''Of course you realize that Lagrange used just the same model in his *Mécanique Analytique*, nearly two centuries ago.'' I imagine that von Neumann must have felt somewhat deflated at that moment.

Postwar Reconstruction

With the surrender of Germany in the spring of 1945, wartime tensions began to relax, and I accepted a summer professorship at the University of Mexico. Although it was a wonderfully refreshing change in many respects (I lectured on lattice theory in a totally new and very friendly environment), it was also sad because my father had died the year before, and many of the leading people were working on his theory of gravitation and other problems he had proposed.

By the time I returned to Cambridge with my family, the first atomic bomb had burst over Hiroshima, Japan had surrendered, and the era of postwar reconstruction had begun. Its mathematical aspects were quite different in various countries.

Great Britain, which had staunchly borne the brunt of the war the longest (after Germany) and had been preparing for it since 1937 at least, seemed devitalized except in areas (such as fluid mechanics) where strenuous wartime efforts had been called for. In such areas, she was preeminent.

Russia, which had suffered the greatest human and material losses, nevertheless retained enormous mathematical vitality. Somehow, her scientists had been kept busy at their profession when circumstances permitted it.

German science was badly fragmented, and those mathematicians who had stayed in Germany must have felt the opprobrium with which Germany, as of 1945, was generally regarded. Any remaining vestiges of arrogance quickly disappeared below the surface. The stark reality of an East Germany ruthlessly dominated by Moscow and the devastations of Hitler's last years made almost everyone want a return to normalcy. This normalcy included, incidentally, generous salaries and pensions for a number of exiled mathematicians who had been unjustly dismissed.

The United States

In our country, the period of postwar reconstruction initiated a quarter-century of incredible scientific expansion and affluence, with a sustained "growth rate" of over ten per cent yearly. This period was inaugurated by a great expansion in higher education: thanks to the G. I. Bill of Rights, great numbers of veterans returned to our colleges and universities. Those of us equipped to supervise Ph.D. theses had many able students who were especially interested in areas of mathematics that had been active during the preceding two decades. This resulted in an enormous increase in activity in modern algebra, topology, and functional analysis at the expense of more traditional fields. In particular, the sales of "Birkhoff-Mac Lane" skyrocketed from about 800 to about 2500 copies per year, and classical analysis became dethroned from its position of primacy, even at Harvard.

Indeed, I had an uneasy feeling that with the death of my father, Kellogg, and others, the Harvard Mathematics Department had perhaps become too modern: the revolution that Stone, Whitney, Mac Lane, and I had been striving for in the prewar years might have been too successful. Therefore, after the war, I regularly taught ordinary differential equations and often other courses in applied analysis and mechanics.

Partly for this reason, unlike my colleagues Mac Lane and Whitney, I never resumed full-time activity in the abstract mathematics that had dominated my thinking during 1933 to 1940. But the main reason was my judgment that the "ivory tower" of prewar academe was not likely to return for many years, if ever during my lifetime, and that therefore I should try to contribute to both pure and applied mathematics, and to use ideas from each to stimulate the other — in much the same spirit that this had been done by Poincaré, my father, and H. Weyl. I realized that this was an ambitious plan, and that it would be easy to achieve nothing significant in either area by trying to achieve too much.

I picked fluid mechanics, with which much of my wartime "applied" research had been concerned, as a worthy and challenging area of application. And I made arrangements to spend the spring terms of 1947 and 1948 at the California Institute of Technology and Cambridge University, respectively, two of the world's greatest centers for research in fluid mechanics. The fact the Caltech was a leading center of lattice theory was an added attraction, and I incidentally gave the Walker-Ames lectures at the University of Washington on lattice theory that same spring. I used the opportunity to polish a second edition of my book *Lattice Theory*, which was duly published by the American Mathematical Society in 1948.

I also gave lectures on "universal algebra," concerning which my ideas had developed and matured considerably since 1935, both at the First Canadian Mathematical Congress in Montreal in 1945 and at the Princeton Bicentennial in 1946. The first of these turned out to be anticlimactic for a very peculiar reason. I had prepared what I thought was a fascinating talk, but I unfortunately followed von Neumann. Von Neumann gave a brilliantly optimistic sketch of the potentialities of high-speed, large-scale digital computers, both as substitutes for expensive physical experiments (for example in wind tunnels or shock tubes), and as means for solving nonlinear partial differential equations with which classical analysis could not begin to cope. When he sat down there was a thunderous ovation; one of the audience rose to say that this was the most fascinating talk he had ever heard in his whole life. After this, any topic from pure algebra would have seemed like an anticlimax. The recollection of von Neumann's deflation by von Kármán gave only meager consolation.

Groups and "Hydrodynamics"

As has often been the case with me, my postwar activities were influenced considerably by a surprise invitation to give the Taft lectures at the University of Cincinnati, and to publish them in book form. I decided to give them on hydrodynamics, basing them in part on wartime impressions of the superficiality of many academic rationalizations and partly on some connections with the group-theoretic notion of "dynamic similarity" with which my studies of model experiments had made me familiar. I used my visit to Caltech in 1947 and my Guggenheim Fellowship in 1948 to deepen my knowledge; by the time I completed my manuscript, I had visited a large fraction of the greatest hydraulic and aeronautical laboratories of the Western world.

The last three chapters of the book, which dealt with dimensional analysis, the notion of a self-similar solution and other applications of symmetry (that is, group) concepts, and connected virtual mass (Kelvin and Kirchhoff) with the geometry of the Euclidean group manifold (suitably metrized), represented a sustained attempt to demonstrate the relevance of abstract mathematics for natural philosophy. These chapters attempted to do for fluid mechanics, in some small way, what Felix Klein had done for geometry in his Erlanger Programm, and Weyl and Wigner had done for quantum mechanics.

Actually, I found that the notion of "self-similar" solution had been anticipated by the Russian mathematicians L. I. Sedov (Doklady URSS, 47(1945):91-93, 52(1946):17-20), and K. P. Staniukovich (Doklady URSS, 48(1945):310-312). For their ideas, see their books, which have been translated into English: L. I. Sedov, 1959, *Similarity and Dimensional Methods in Mechanics;* K. P. Staniukovich, 1959, *Unsteady Motion of Continuous Media*. Notable further extensions of these ideas have since been made by L. V. Ovsjannikov, who has published a brief synopsis of the new results of his book, *Group Properties of Differential Equations*, in the *Atti del Convegno Lagrangians* (1964).

In the United States, although my book as a whole was popular, only recently have pure or applied research mathematicians begun to develop further the ideas presented in these chapters.

In 1949, stimulated by J. Kampé de Fériet, I made a second valiant attempt to relate modern algebra to hydrodynamics by applying algebraic concepts to an identity $T(f\mathrm{T}g) = (\mathrm{T}f)\,(\mathrm{T}g)$ on "averaging" operators first postulated by Osborne Reynolds in his classical studies of turbulence. Its implications were studied further by Mme. Dubreil-Jacotin, Gian-Carlo Rota, and others.

Bourbaki

No story of the rise of modern algebra would be complete which ignored the role of Bourbaki. As everyone knows, this was a pseudonym adopted in the 1930's by a brilliant group of young French mathematicians that initially included Henri Cartan, Claude Chevalley, Jean Dieudonné, and Andre Weil. Although I knew of Bourbaki, of course, he seemed quite remote until after the fall of France.

By this time, he had already begun publishing his celebrated treatise on mathematics, which began with three books on set theory, algebra, and general topology. Its "abstract and axiomatic" style of exposition was very like that of van der Waerden. However, its announced aim was much more comprehensive: "to give a solid foundation . . . to all of modern mathematics," based firmly on a rigorous treatment of "the fundamental structures of analysis." Curiously, the definition of 'structure,' promised in 1939, seems not to have been forthcoming until 1957 (Act. Sci. Ind. #1258, Book 1, ch. 4).

Though Bourbaki has never written his autobiography, rumor has it that under his banner a revolt was instigated in the 1930's against the firm control by aging mathematicians, born in 1870 or before of French mathematical journals, professorships, and the French Academy. This feeling that a revolution was needed must have been exacerbated by mossback refereeing that, rumor also had it, had forced Chevalley to publish his famous 1935 paper on idèles in Japan.

Bourbaki published the first four chapters of Book 3 in 1940 to 1942; characteristically, the description of it of the real field was deferred until after the reader had been taught H. Cartan's theory of "filters," A. Weil's theory of "uniform spaces," and the elementary theory of topological groups!

After the fall of France, Chevalley and André Weil came to this country as refugees. I even had the honor of going bond for Chevalley, guaranteeing to our government that he would not become a public charge. Weil taught at Lehigh, but without much liking for our American system of education. With difficulty, J. R. Kline (Secretary of AMS) persuaded Weil not to thank the Guggenheim Foundation in the preface of his Colloquium volume on algebraic geometry for rescuing him "from the indignity of teaching the American undergraduate."

Among major European countries, only France emerged from World War II with renewed mathematical vitality. Perhaps this was because after the German half-occupation and the establishment of the Vichy government, her able younger mathematicians had not much they could do except to think about their favorite subject. Whatever the reason, Bourbaki's admirable treatise underwent great expansion during the wartime and postwar years.

Whereas Mac Lane and I had tried to temper the purism of van der Waerden's "modern" algebra in our book, Bourbaki was ultramodern. For instance, his book on *Linear Algebra* discusses vector spaces after modules, tensor products, and projective and inductive limits of modules. And his first theorem about vector spaces states: "Every vector space (over a field K) is a free K-module." Matrices come much later.

Bourbaki's abstractionist philosophy, when originally presented in articles by J. Dieudonné, Revue Sci., 77(1939):224-232, and H. Cartan, Revue Sci., 81(1943):3-11, had evoked little enthusiasm — probably because everyone was worrying about Hitler. In essence, it was that mathematics is the study of axiomatically defined structures, among which a few "mother structures" such as groups are especially fertile. However, the thesis seemed perfect to many pure mathematicians in America in the complacent postwar years. He and André Weil were invited to write feature articles for the *American Mathematical Monthly* in 1950.

Bourbaki reiterated his philosophy. His peroration was the clearly elitist statement: "If he [the mathematician] be reproached with the haughtiness of his attitude, if he be summoned to do his part, if he be asked why he perches on the high glaciers whither no one but his own kind can follow him, he will answer, with Jacobi: For the honor of the human spirit."

In the next issue, in a similar vein of condescension, Weil mentioned van der Pol's equation (really Rayleigh's)[40] as "one of the few interesting problems which contemporary physics has suggested to mathematicians; for the study of

40. See G. Birkhoff and G. C. Rota, 1962, Ordinary differential equations, 2d ed. Ginn, Boston, 143.

nature, which was formerly one of the main sources of great mathematical problems, seems in recent years to have borrowed from us more than it has given us.''

Bourbaki's lofty philosophy captured the imagination of a large fraction of the younger mathematicians of those times. And it foreshadowed the axiomatic purism of the ''New Mathematics'' that swept our country in the 1960's. If mere *users* of mathematics object to the logical order of exposition and great generality, let them realize their intellectual inferiority and bow down.

Weil's article ends with a sharp criticism of American mass production in education. One wonders what he would have written had he known that, by 1972, the United States would be ''producing'' 1500 mathematical Ph.D.'s annually, all supposedly dedicated to research.

The International Congress of 1950

The most definitive landmark of postwar reconstruction in mathematics was the International Mathematical Congress that took place in Cambridge in September 1950.[41] This was the first really large-scale international gathering of mathematicians since 1936. It had originally been planned for 1940, with my father as President and David Widder as Chairman of the Organizing Committee. Funds had been raised, a number of loyal Harvard alumni making individual gifts of $1000.

After my father's death, Veblen was named to take his place, and Widder asked me to take his. I realized that much work would be involved, but decided to be a good sport and accept anyway, partly impelled by curiosity. In fact, the work took about an hour a day for two to three years, but I have no regrets. The cooperation of Ted Martin from M.I.T. made the job much less onerous than it would have been otherwise.

One of the major tasks was to secure additional money, especially for travel grants for distinguished mathematicians who otherwise could not come. I only worked on one part of this, getting substantial funds from UNESCO. There was no official channel for doing this; the logical channel would have been an International Mathematical Union (IMU), but none had been formed in the 1920's because the major mathematical countries had disagreed on including the defeated Central Powers.

Upon reflection, I decided that $25,000 was a fair contribution, in view of the importance of mathematics, the fact that it would receive no other funds from UNESCO, and that it was the most promising occasion for forming an IMU to round out ICSU, UNESCO's International Council of Scientific Unions. ''Bill'' (now Sir William) Hodge, the most active British mathematician on such matters, agreed completely.

We called on the two British UNESCO representatives at that time (1948). The first was the distinguished Chinese scholar Joseph Needham, who told us that UNESCO was very poor, but that it might scrape up $6000 to $8000 from the

41. See Proc. Int. Math. Congress, 1950, Am. Math. Soc., 1(1952):6.

bottom of the barrel. We proceeded through other channels. Fortunately we did get $25,000.

However, this had to be divided with Marshall Stone, who was playing a major role in planning the IMU. After a brief discussion, we agreed to split it fifty-fifty.

Part of the negotiations with UNESCO took place in Paris; my wife and I were staying at the same hotel as J. M. Burgers, the distinguished applied mathematician and fluid dynamicist. He said he was greatly relieved that the IMU would not get organized until 1950. He feared that otherwise it would continue to include theoretical mechanics as mathematics had done in the past.[42] As it was, he would have time to organize IUTAM (the International Union of Theoretical and Applied Mechanics) as a separate adherent to ICSU, which he did.

Foreign Participation

Securing broad foreign participation in the Congress was a major concern. The cold war had begun, and Poland and Yugoslavia were the only Iron Curtain countries to send delegates.

For the same reason, it was hard to get visas for known communists, even Trotskyites like Laurent Schwartz. We thought that if Schwartz did not get a visa, the French would probably boycott the Congress, and under nascent McCarthyism, it seemed doubtful if he could. However J. R. Kline, devoted AMS secretary, found out that a certain Washington legal firm with connections in our State Department (under Truman) could get one or two visas through for us *sub rosa,* at a cost of $1000 each. We paid for two visas.

Italy was also feeling touchy, perhaps because Zariski and Weil rather than an Italian had been invited to give hour addresses on algebraic geometry. To placate the Italians, I agreed that we would pay first-class fare for Severi to come to the Congress — nobody else got more than tourist fare, and most only half (the other half being supplied by their own country).

Lighter Moments

The Congress had its lighter side. Bourbaki tried to register, and I strongly favored including and listing him as a dues-paying member, but I was overruled by J. R. Kline.

Again, the Rumanian financier Metaxas, who had earlier founded a prize won by Leray and Schauder, half-offered to set up a $50,000 prize in mathematics, along the lines of the Nobel prizes. However, his reputation was unsavory (he had been denied an American visa), and he did not really put any money "on the line." Partly to avoid the danger of fishing in muddy waters, and partly because Veblen expressed himself as unenthusiastic about prizes, the matter was dropped.

42. Prandtl first introduced "boundary layer theory" at the International Mathematical Congress in Heidelberg in 1904.

Invited Addresses

An analysis of the subjects of the 20 invited addresses (leaving out history and philosophy) will show how much the abstract point of view had come to dominate mathematics since 1936. Gödel spoke on "rotating universes in general relativity theory," but he was surely invited as a logician. Of the remaining 19 papers, five were on algebra and number theory (Albert, Davenport, Ritt on differential algebra; Weil and Zariski on modern algebraic geometry). Hodge spoke on algebraic geometry, in the tradition of Lefschetz.

There were three addresses on topology as such (S. S. Chern, H. Hopf, W. Hurewicz), two on global analysis (H. Cartan, M. Morse), and two on functional analysis (L. Schwartz, S. Kakutani). Moreover H. Whitney talked on "r-dimensional integration in n-space, "developing ideas first presented under the title "algebraic topology and integration theory" — and incidentally ignoring the earlier work of Carathéodory, Hausdorff, and Besicovich on the subject. Thus about 75 per cent of the 20 "core" talks were centered on ideas from algebra and topology.

Of the remaining five talks, two were on probability and statistics (A. Wald, N. Wiener); von Neumann's was on shock intersections (thus, five years after his talk in Montreal; he should have been asked to talk on computing). Thus only two invited addresses were on classical analysis; moreover Beurling never provided a manuscript (a weakness of his). Thus Solomon Bochner, whose paper is included in our symposium, gave the only published invited address dealing with classical analysis.

THE NASCENT INFLUENCE OF COMPUTERS

If Emmy Noether could have been at the 1950 Congress, she would have felt very proud. Her concept of algebra had become central in contemporary mathematics. And it has continued to inspire algebraists ever since.

However, a new revolution in algebra already was brewing then. Much as the axiomatic approach revolutionized *pure* algebra in the period 1890 to 1930 rose to supremacy in 1930 to 1950 and has dominated it the 25 years since then, the digital computer has revolutionized *applied* algebra in the years 1945 to 1975, and it may well reign supreme over all algebra by 2000 — although this remains to be seen. I thought it might be interesting to conclude by describing, at least sketchily, how this revolution already had begun by 1950.

Today, so-called computer science deals in depth with at least three areas of algebra: the theory of automata, algebraic coding theory, and numerical linear algebra. The origins of all three can be traced to before 1950. Although very few pure algebraists are cognizant of these areas yet, the first two build on ideas of modern algebra, and so it is especially appropriate to discuss them here.

These areas are in addition to the use of Boolean algebra to design the *logic networks* of computers. Such uses of Boolean algebra were foreshadowed in a 1938 paper by Claude Shannon on switching circuits for relay networks; the relevance for logic networks of Boolean algebra, which used to be called the "algebra of logic," is hardly surprising.

The *theory of automata* had its origins in a famous 1936 paper by the logician and mathematician Turing. This paper reformulated the notion of "definability" in terms of computability by a class of automata now called *Turing machines*. Remarkably, theoretical models of (sequential) digital computers still resemble Turing machines in outline.

Algebraic coding theory is another fascinating new area of applied algebra. It is a by-product of the "information theory" initiated by Shannon in 1948 (see Bell System Tech. J., 47(1948):379-423). Shannon proved a number of basic existence theorems describing the maximum rate at which information could be reliably transmitted through unreliable channels. These solved theoretically the problem of "synthesizing reliable organisms from unreliable components," a problem that strongly influenced von Neumann's work on computer design. (For this, see vol. 5 of von Neumann's *Collected Works.*)

Unfortunately, Shannon's proofs do not lend themselves to simple electronic implementation, and good coding and decoding schemes are essential for transmitting information efficiently and reliably through imperfect channels. The best such schemes known today are based on properties of (binary) finite groups and fields, hence on modern algebra in the sense of van der Waerden.

Besides inspiring new areas in modern algebra, high-speed computers have revolutionized linear algebra. I cannot resist smiling at the following passage from Artin's review[43] of Bourbaki's book on *Algèbre Linéaire:* "the computational aspect is not neglected: §60 is a complete discussion of matrices." This was not true even in 1950; Bourbaki ignored many ideas familiar to Gauss.[44]

Actually, if solving simultaneous linear equations were as easy as Bourbaki makes it sound, solving most linear partial differential equations would be trivial. For example, a fairly good approximation to the Laplace equation is obtained by constructing a fine square mesh, and making the value at each point the arithmetic mean of the four neighboring values. In principle, this reduces solving the Dirichlet problem, to any desired accuracy, to solving a (very large) system of simultaneous linear equations.

It was precisely this problem that I proposed to David Young in 1948, having in mind solution by computer. In 1950, after two years of patient work and thought, David Young finally had discovered and rationalized his automatic "Successive Overrelaxation" (point SOR) algorithm, which converges an order of magnitude more rapidly than the methods of Gauss. The essence of the Dirichlet problem is contained in the repeated use of the "residual"

$$\sigma_{i,j}^{(r)} = u_{i,j}^{(r)} - \frac{1}{4}\left[u_{i-1,j}^{(r+1)} + u_{i,j-1}^{(r+1)} + u_{i+1,j}^{(r)} + u_{i,j+1}^{(r)}\right]$$

43. E. Artin, Book review of Eléments de mathématique by N. Bourbaki, 1953, Bull. Amer. Math. Soc., 59:474-479. The parts reviewed had appeared in 1942, 1948, 1959, and 1952.

44. For what Gauss knew, see A. M. Ostrowski, Determinanten mit überwiegender Hauptdiogonale und die absolute Konvergenz von linearen Interationsprozessen, Comm. Math. Helv., 30(1956):175-210.

and a well-chosen "overrelaxation factor" ω, to define a new approximate value

$$u_{i,j}^{(r+1)} = u_{i,j}^{(r)} - \omega\sigma_{i,j}^{(r)}$$

Using modifications of this "point SOR" algorithm, one can solve 10,000 equations in as many unknowns in minutes on a high-speed computer.

In work published before 1950, von Neumann and Goldstine[45] had posed a much more general basic problem: given a *random* nonsingular $n \times n$ matrix A, and a computer in which real numbers are stored with r significant digits, when and how can the vector equation $Ax = b$ be solved with s-digit accuracy? This problem has many variants: given s and r, how large can s be made? Given r and s, how large can n be made? The answers, naturally, depend on the matrix A considered.

In this generality, the problem posed by von Neumann and Goldstine remains unresolved to this day. However, they introduced and resurrected a wealth of algebraic concepts: the notion of a random matrix A and the probable error of solving $Ax = b$; the "condition number" of a matrix; the importance of preserving symmetry (destroyed by Gaussian elimination) in computations relating to symmetric matrices; and the fact that "iterative" methods may be more efficient than "direct" methods.

Like successive overrelaxation, these ideas play a central role in "modern" linear algebra. They initiated a revolution that began around 1945, stimulated by new vistas in computing. For more adequate descriptions of how ideas have changed, I refer you to two great classics on modern matrix computation: R. S. Varga, 1962, *Matrix Iterative Analysis,* Prentice-Hall; and J. H. Wilkinson, 1965, *The Algebraic Eigenvalue Problem,* Clarendon Press, Oxford, These books, many ideas of which were known before 1950, describe the revolution in linear algebra that has occurred in the last 25 years; they are unrelated to anything in van der Waerden or Bourbaki.

Together with the new vistas in abstract algebra opened up by the theories of automata, algebraic coding, and other computer-oriented ideas, they made axiomatic algebra cease to be truly "modern" around 1950, primarily because of the advent of high-speed computers.[46]

Bibliography

ABBOTT, J. C., ED. 1970. Trends in lattice theory. Van Nostrand, New York, ix+215 pp.

ARTIN, E. 1965. Collected papers, edited by Serge Lang and John T. Tate. Addison-Wesley, Reading, Massachusetts, 560 pp.

BELL, E. T. 1938. Fifty years of algebra in America, 1888-1938. Amer. Math. Soc. Semicentennial Publ., 2:1-34.

BIRKHOFF, G., AND S. MAC LANE. 1941. Survey of modern algebra. Macmillan, New York, 1948; 3rd ed., 1967.]

______. 1973. Current trends in algebra. Amer. Math. Monthly, 80:760-781.

______. 1973. Algebraic structures, survey article. Encyclopaedia Britannica.

45. See J. von Neumann, 1963, Collected works, vol. 5, Pergamon Press, 411-610; Numerical inverting of matrices of high order, with H. H. Goldstein, Bull. Amer. Math. Soc., 53(1947):1021-1099.

46. In this connection, see also Birkhoff, 1973; Proc. IV, SIAM-AMS Symp. Appl. Math., Computers in algebra and number theory, 1972:1-48, where I have presented my views in more detail.

BIRKHOFF, G., AND S. MAC LANE. 1941. Survey of modern algebra. Macmillan, New York, xix+598 pp. [2nd ed., 1952; 3rd ed., 1965.]

BIRKHOFF, G., P. M. COHN, M. HALL, JR., P. J. HILTON, AND P. SAMUEL. 1974. Algebraic structures in Encyclopaedia Britannica, 15th ed., Encyclopaedia Britannica, Inc., Chicago.

BÔCHER, M. 1907. Introduction to higher algebra. Macmillan, New York, xi+321 pp.

BOOLE, G. 1854. An investigation of the laws of thought. Macmillan, Cambridge, England, xvi+448 pp.

BOURBAKI, N. *ca*. 1951. Éléments de mathématique, Livre II, Algébre. Hermann, Paris.

BURNSIDE, W. 1897. Theory of groups of finite order. Cambridge Univ. Press. London, xvi+512 pp. [2nd ed., 1911.]

CARTAN, É. 1952-55. Oeuvres complètes, 6 vols. Gauthier-Villars, Paris.

CAYLEY, A. 1889-98. Collected mathematical papers. Cambridge Univ. Press, London.

DEDEKIND, R. 1930-32. Gesammelte mathematische Werke, 3 vols. Vieweg, Braunschweig.

______. 1964. Über die Theorie der ganzen algebraische Zahlen. Vieweg, Braunschweig.

DICKSON, L. E. 1923. Algebras and their arithmetics. Univ. Chicago Press, Chicago, xii+241 pp. [1927. Algebren und ihren Zahlentheorie. Zurich. German edition.]

DIEUDONNÉ, J. 1972. The historical development of algebraic geometry. Amer. Math. Monthly, 79:827-866.

DIRICHLET, P. G. L. 1880. Vorlesungen über Zahlentheorie, 3rd ed. Vieweg, Braunschweig, 657 pp.

HARDY, G. H., AND E. M. WRIGHT. 1938. An introduction to the theory of numbers, 2nd ed. Clarendon Press, Oxford, xvi+403 pp.

HAWKINS, T. 1972. Hypercomplex numbers, Lie groups, and the creation of group representation theory. Arch. History Exact Sci., 8:243-287.

HILBERT, D. 1899. Grundlagen der Geometrie. Teubner, Leipzig, 258 pp. [7th ed., 1930.]

______. 1932. Gesammelte Abhandlungen, 3 vols. Springer, Berlin.

KILLING, W. Die Zusammensetzung der stetigen endlichen Transformationsgruppen I, II, III, IV. Math. Ann., 31(1888):252-290, 33(1889):1-4, 34(1889):57-122, 36(1890):161-189.

KIMBERLING, C. H. 1972. Emmy Noether. Amer. Math. Monthly. 79:136-145.

KLINE, M. 1972. Mathematical thought from ancient to modern times. Oxford Univ. Press, New York, 1338 pp.

KRONECKER, L. 1895-1931. Werke, edited by K. Hensel. Teubner, Leipzig.

MACAULEY, F. S. 1916. Algebraic theory of modular systems. Cambridge Tracts No. 19, Cambridge Univ. Press, London.

MAC LANE, S., AND G. BIRKHOFF. 1967. Algebra. Macmillan, New York, xix + 598 pp.

MUIR, T. 1883. A treatise on the theory of determinants, revised and enlarged by W. H. Metzler. Longmans, Green, London, xxiii+408 pp. [2nd ed., 1933; Dover reprint, 1960.]

NOETHER, E. 1926. Abstrakter Aufbau der Idealtheorie. Math. Annalen, 96:36-61, 83(1921):23-67.

______. 1929. Hyperkomplexe Grössen und Darstellungstheorie. Mathematische Zeitschrift, 30:649-692.

NOVY, L. 1973. Origins of modern algebra. Academia, Praha, 252 pp.

PEIRCE, B. 1881. On the uses and transformations of linear algebra. Amer. J. Math., 4:216-221. [Originally published in 1875 by Amer. Acad. Boston.]

PEIRCE, C. S. 1880. On the algebra of logic. Amer. J. Math., 3:15-57, 7(1884):180-202.

REID, C. 1970. Hilbert. Springer, Berlin, 290 pp.

SPEISER, A. 1922. Gruppentheorie. Springer, Berlin, x+262 pp. [2nd ed., 1927; 3rd ed., 1937.]

STEINITZ, E. 1910. Algebraische Theorie der Körper. J. für die reine und angewandte Mathematik, 137:167-309. [Republished with Appendix by R. Baer and H. Hasse, de Gruyter, 1930; Chelsea, 1951.]

STONE, M. H. 1936. The theory of representations for Boolean algebras. Trans. Amer. Math. Soc., 40:37-111.

SYLVESTER, J. J. 1904-12. Collected mathematical papers, edited by H. F. Baker, 4 vols. Cambridge Univ. Press, Cambridge.

VAN DER WAERDEN, B. L. 1930-31. Moderne Algebra, 2 vols. Springer, Berlin. [2nd ed., 1940; 3rd ed., 1950; 4th ed., 1955.]

______. 1971. The foundations of algebraic geometry from Severi to André Weil. Archive Hist. Exact Sci., 7:171-180.

______. Die Galois Theorie von Henrich Weber bis Emil Artin. Archive Hist. Sci., in press.

______. The sources for van der Waerden's "Moderne Algebra." Historia Mathematica, in press.

WEDDERBURN, J. H. M. 1907. On hypercomplex numbers. Proc. London Math. Soc., 6:77-118.

WHITEHEAD, A. N. 1898. Universal algebra. Cambridge Univ. Press, Cambridge.

WHITEHEAD, A. N., AND B. RUSSELL. 1908-12. Principia mathematica, 3 vols. Cambridge Univ. Press, Cambridge.

WUSSING, H. 1969. Die Genesis des abstrakten Gruppen-Begriffes, VEB. Deutscher Verlag Wiss., Berlin.

ZASSENHAUS, H., 1964, Emil Artin, his life and his work. Notre Dame J. Formal Logic, 5:2-9.

Reprinted from
MEN AND INSTITUTIONS IN AMERICAN MATHEMATICS
Graduate Studies, Texas Tech University, No. 13, 1976

Permissions

Birkhäuser Boston thanks the original publishers of the papers of Garrett Birkhoff for granting permission to reprint specific papers in this collection.

I Lattices

[3] Reprinted from *Proc. Camb. Phil. Soc.* **29**, © 1933 by Cambridge University Press.
[4] Reprinted from *Proc. Camb. Phil. Soc.* **30**, © 1934 by Cambridge University Press.
[6] Reprinted from *Bull. AMS* **40**, © 1934 by American Mathematical Society.
[12] Reprinted from *Annals of Math.* **36**, © 1935 by Princeton University.
[16] Reprinted from *Am. J. Math.* **57**, © 1935 by The Johns Hopkins University Press.
[21] Reprinted from *Annals of Math.* **37**, © 1936 by Princeton University.
[36] Reprinted from *Annals of Math.* **40**, © 1939 by Princeton University.
[40] Reprinted from *Bull. AMS* **46**, © 1940 by American Mathematical Society.
[51] Reprinted from *Trans. AMS* **60**, © 1946 by American Mathematical Society.
[54] Reprinted from *Bull. AMS* **53**, © 1947 by American Mathematical Society.

II Universal Algebra

[15] Reprinted from *Proc. Camb. Phil. Soc.* **31**, © 1935 by Cambridge University Press.
[47] Reprinted from *Bull. AMS* **50**, © 1944 by American Mathematical Society.
[49] Reprinted from Toronto Press, © 1945 by University of Toronto Press.
[154] Reprinted from *J. Combinatorial Theory* **8**, © 1970 by Academic Press.
[174] Reprinted from AMS, *Proc. XXV Symp. Pure Math.*, © 1974 by American Mathematical Society.
[179] Reprinted from *Algebra Universalis* **6**, © 1986 by Birkhäuser Verlag.

III Topology

[8] Reprinted from *Annals of Math.* **35**, © 1934 by Princeton University.
[24] Reprinted from *Annals of Math.* **38**, © 1937 by Princeton University.
[25] Reprinted from *Annals of Math.* **38**, © 1937 by Princeton University.
[28] Reprinted from *Duke Math. J.* **3**, © 1937 by Duke University Press.
[29] Reprinted from *Duke Math. J.* **3**, © 1937 by Duke University Press.
[43] Reprinted from *Duke Math. J.* **9**, © 1942 by Duke University Press.
[58] Reprinted from *Trans. AMS* **64**, © 1948 by American Mathematical Society.
[118] Reprinted from *Revista Tucuman* **14**, © 1962 by Revista de Mat. y Fis. Teorica.

IV Lie Groups and Lie Algebras

[19] Reprinted from *Trans. AMS* **39**, © 1936 by American Mathematical Society.
[20] Reprinted from *Compositio Math.* **3**, © 1936 by Martinus Nijhoff Publishers B.V.
[22] Reprinted from *Bull. AMS* **40**, © 1934 by American Mathematical Society.
[27] Reprinted from *Annals of Math.* **38**, © 1937 by Princeton University.
[32] Reprinted from *Trans. AMS* **43**, © 1938 by American Mathematical Society.
[60] Reprinted from *Trans. AMS* **65**, © 1949 by American Mathematical Society.

V Lattice-Ordered Algebraic Structures

VI History of Algebra

Contemporary Mathematicians

Gabor Szego: Collected Papers
Edited by *Richard Askey*
0-8176-3063-5 (complete set)
0-8176-3056-2 (Volume 1: 1915–1927)
0-8176-3060-0 (Volume 2: 1927–1943)
0-8176-3061-9 (Volume 3: 1943–1972)

Lars Valerian Ahlfors: Collected Papers
0-8176-3077-5 (complete set)
0-8176-3075-9 (Volume 1: 1929–1955)
0-8176-3076-7 (Volume 2: 1955–1979)

The Selected Papers of Theodore S. Motzkin
Edited by *D. Cantor, et al.*
0-8176-3087-2

Fritz John: Collected Papers
Edited by *Jurgen Moser*
0-8176-3265-4 (complete set)
0-8176-3266-2 (Volume 1)
0-8176-3267-0 (Volume 2)

Kurt Otto Friedrichs: Collected Mathematical Papers
Edited by *Cathleen Morawetz*
0-8176-3270-0 (complete set)
0-8176-3268-9 (Volume 1)
0-8176-3269-7 (Volume 2)

Jakob Nielsen: Collected Papers
Edited by *Vagn Lundsgaard Hansen*
0-8176-3152-6 (complete set)
0-8176-3140-2 (Volume 1)
0-8176-3151-8 (Volume 2)

Selected Papers on Algebra and Topology
by Garrett Birkhoff
Edited by *Gian-Carlo Rota* and *Joseph Oliveira*
0-8176-3114-3

Shizuo Kakutani: Selected Papers
Edited by *Robert Kallman*
0-8176-3279-4 (complete set)
0-8176-3277-8 (Volume 1)
0-8176-3278-6 (Volume 2)

Alfred Tarski: Collected Papers
Edited by *Steven R. Givant* and *Ralph McKenzie*
0-8176-3284-0 (complete set)
0-8176-3280-8 (Volume 1)
0-8176-3281-6 (Volume 2)
0-8176-3282-4 (Volume 3)
0-8176-3283-2 (Volume 4)